AN INTRODUCTION TO INTERNATIONAL CRIMINAL LAW AND PROCEDURE

Fifth Edition

Building on the success of previous editions, this popular textbook is now expanded and updated in a 5th edition featuring two new co-authors, Elies van Sliedregt and Valerie Oosterveld. A market leader and one of the most globally trusted textbooks on international criminal law, it is known for its accessible and engaging tone and for an even-handed approach that is both critical and constructive. Comprehensively updated and rewritten, this new edition introduces readers to the main concepts of international criminal law and procedure, as well as the domestic and international institutions that enforce it, and addresses the latest challenges and controversies surrounding the International Criminal Court. Written by a team of international criminal lawyers who have extensive academic and practical experience in the field, the book engages with critical questions, political and moral challenges, and alternatives to international justice. It contains helpful references to other literature, making it a valuable research resource.

DARRYL ROBINSON is a Professor at Queen's University Faculty of Law (Canada). As a Legal Officer at Foreign Affairs Canada (1997–2004), he advised on international criminal law and helped negotiate the Statute of the International Criminal Court. He was also an adviser at the International Criminal Court (2004–6). He received the Antonio Cassese Prize for International Criminal Law Studies in 2013 for his innovative contributions to the field. His writings on international criminal law focus on criminal law theory, crimes against humanity, command responsibility, and ecocide.

SERGEY VASILIEV is Professor of International Law at the Faculty of Law, Open University (Netherlands). Previously, he was an Associate Professor at the Faculty of Law, University of Amsterdam, where he taught international, transnational, European, and comparative criminal law and the rule-of-law aspects of criminal justice across several master's degree programs, and an assistant professor of public international law at the Law Faculty, Leiden University. He also served as the founding Director of the Amsterdam Center for Criminal Justice and the Director of the LLM International Criminal Law (including the joint program with Columbia Law School, New York). His recent scholarship has focused on the institutional and governance aspects of international justice.

ELIES VAN SLIEDREGT is Professor of Criminal Law at Tilburg University. She was the 2015 Holding Redlich fellow at the Castan Centre for Human Rights at Monash University, Melbourne and, in 2018, appointed as Fellow of McLaughlin College, York University, Toronto. She is a member of the Royal Netherlands Academy for Arts and Sciences (KNAW), sits on the Advisory Committee on Public International Law (CAVV), and is a trustee of the British Institute of International and Comparative Law (BIICL). She has published extensively in the field of international, European, and comparative criminal law.

VALERIE OOSTERVELD is the Western Research Chair in International Criminal Justice and a full professor at the University of Western Ontario's Faculty of Law. She has published widely on the interpretation of sexual and gender-based crimes by international criminal tribunals. She is the co-editor of the award-winning *Gender and International Criminal Law* (Oxford University Press, 2022). She was awarded the 2023 Canadian Association of Law Teachers Academic Excellence Award and the 2022 Royal Society of Canada Ursula Franklin Award in Gender Studies. She is a member of the Canadian Partnership for International Justice, which won the 2023 Governor-General's Innovation Award and the 2022 SSHRC Impact Partnership Award. A former lawyer with Global Affairs Canada's Legal Bureau, she served on the Canadian delegation to various International Criminal Court-related negotiations.

'This book remains the very best introduction to international criminal law on the market – written clearly enough for laypeople to understand, yet possessing the intellectual rigour and sophistication that academics require.'

Kevin Jon Heller, Professor of International Law and Security,
University of Copenhagen

'It is a challenge, especially in these restless times, to keep pace with all disturbing violent events and integrate them meaningfully in a textbook on international criminal law. This new edition – again – lives up to the high expectations. It combines a well-organized presentation of all the main topics with incisive analysis. Only one point of criticism: the title – "Introduction" – is too modest.'

Harmen van der Wilt, University of Amsterdam

AN INTRODUCTION TO INTERNATIONAL CRIMINAL LAW AND PROCEDURE

FIFTH EDITION

DARRYL ROBINSON

Queen's University

SERGEY VASILIEV

Open University of the Netherlands

ELIES VAN SLIEDREGT

Tilburg University

VALERIE OOSTERVELD

University of Western Ontario

CAMBRIDGE UNIVERSITY PRESS

CAMBRIDGE
UNIVERSITY PRESS

Shaftesbury Road, Cambridge CB2 8EA, United Kingdom

One Liberty Plaza, 20th Floor, New York, NY 10006, USA

477 Williamstown Road, Port Melbourne, VIC 3207, Australia

314–321, 3rd Floor, Plot 3, Splendor Forum, Jasola District Centre,
New Delhi – 110025, India

103 Penang Road, #05–06/07, Visioncrest Commercial, Singapore 238467

Cambridge University Press is part of Cambridge University Press & Assessment,
a department of the University of Cambridge.

We share the University's mission to contribute to society through the pursuit of
education, learning and research at the highest international levels of excellence.

www.cambridge.org
Information on this title: www.cambridge.org/highereducation/isbn/9781009466615

DOI: 10.1017/9781009466660

When citing this work, please include a reference to the DOI 10.1017/9781009466660

First published 2007
Second edition 2010
Third edition 2014
Fourth edition 2019 (version 6, May 2023)
Fifth edition 2024

Printed in the United Kingdom by TJ Books Limited, Padstow Cornwall

A catalogue record for this publication is available from the British Library

A Cataloging-in-Publication data record for this book is available from the Library of Congress

ISBN 978-1-009-46661-5 Hardback
ISBN 978-1-009-46663-9 Paperback

In Memoriam

Robert Cryer (1974–2021)

Brief Contents

Contents

Preface to the Fifth Edition

We grieve the loss of our very dear friend and co-author, Robert Cryer. Rob was a beloved figure and a highly prolific scholar in the international criminal law field. He was a voracious reader with an unparalleled command of both the black letter doctrine and the myriad theoretical perspectives. In addition to his remarkable influence on the field, he has also left a permanent imprimatur on this book, bringing a style that is both accessible and nuanced. Rob was a kind, generous, humble, and enthusiastic colleague. He cared deeply about international criminal justice: he was a clear-eyed observer of its faults and problems but he remained always an optimist about its potential and promise. We miss Rob's warm personality and his unfailing sense of humour. We dedicate this volume to him, with the greatest sorrow for our collective loss.

On a happier note, we are delighted to welcome two new members to our team: Professors Valerie Oosterveld and Elies van Sliedregt. Both are highly respected leaders in the field of international criminal law, with specializations that are perfectly attuned to the needs of this volume. We are thrilled that these wonderful colleagues have agreed to join us, and they have made invaluable contributions in revising and updating the present fifth edition.

Our intention for this book remains to provide an accessible yet stimulating explanation and critical appraisal of international criminal law and procedure for students, academics, and practitioners. We focus on the crimes which are within the jurisdiction of international courts or tribunals – genocide, crimes against humanity, war crimes, and crimes of aggression – and the means of prosecuting them. We also touch on terrorist offences, torture, and ecocide, as they relate to international criminal justice in the broader sense. With each new edition, we have made a concerted effort to keep the book short and readable, by pruning dated material even as we add the most important contemporary developments.

This book provides an overview of principles, defences, and the aims of and alternatives to international criminal justice. We introduce the international and hybrid institutions that enforce and develop international criminal law. We examine international criminal procedures and matters relating to cooperation with courts. We also look at the system of international criminal justice more generally, including national proceedings, which are meant to be the primary locus of international criminal justice.

International criminal law is a vast and rapidly evolving subject. This book is intended as a manageable and stimulating introduction to the field, and therefore does not attempt to be comprehensive or highly detailed on every topic. We hope that we explain the issues clearly, and at a level that inspires further thought and research. We encourage readers to follow up the footnotes and suggestions for further reading. We continue to welcome suggestions for improvement in future editions. The text takes into account key developments in law and jurisprudence up to September 2023.

The book is a collegial endeavour. We have attempted to produce a book which reads as a coherent whole, rather than as a collection of separate papers from different writers. We have all had an input into each chapter, but remain individually responsible for the views expressed in each of our own chapters. The responsibility for Chapters 1, 2, 3, 15, and 16 lies with Elies; for Chapters 4, 5, 9, 17, 18, 19, and 20 with Sergey; for Chapters 6, 7, 10, 13, 14, and 22 with Valerie; and for Chapters 8, 11, 12, and 21 with Darryl. Darryl took on a coordinating role, for which co-authors are grateful to him.

We owe a great deal of thanks to the students and researchers who made this work possible. Our thanks go to: Saskia Hohmann, Emma Goossens, Alexandrine Vergne, Ana de la Cruz Cubeiro, Anna Hansson, Maxime Neuhaus, and David Stumpf of the University of Amsterdam; Alexandra (Lexi) Lewis, Jordan Rivera, and Jessica Weinberg of Queen's University; Patricia Florea of Tilburg University; and Nicole Dotson and Allison Hardy of the University of Western Ontario. We also thank reviewers for their helpful suggestions on chapters to shorten or expand. Our colleagues at Cambridge University Press have, as ever, been exceptionally helpful and encouraging.

Table of International Cases

European Court of Human Rights

European Court of Justice

Extraordinary African Chambers

Human Rights Committee

Inter-American Commission on Human Rights

Inter-American Court of Human Rights

International Criminal Court

International Court of Justice

International Criminal Tribunal for Rwanda (and the International Residual Mechanism)

International Military Tribunals

Residual Special Court for Sierra Leone

Special Court for Sierra Leone

Special Criminal Court for Central African Republic

Special Panels for Serious Crimes (East Timor)

Special Tribunal for Lebanon

Table of National Cases

Argentina

Erich Priebke, Case No. 16.063/94, Supreme Court, Judgment on extradition request, 2.11.1995 82

Simón, Case No. 17.768, Decision 14.6.2005 519

Australia

Nulyarimma v. Thompson [1999] FCA 1192; 165 ALR 62 78, 79

Polyukhovich v. Australia [1991] HCA 32; 172 CLR 501 71, 79, 216

Austria

Duško Cvetković, Beschluss des Oberstern Gerichtshofs Os 99/94–6, 13.7.1994 65

Belgium

Sharon, Cour de Cassation, (2003) 127 ILR 110 494

Bosnia and Herzegovina

Boudellaa et al. v. Bosnia and Herzegovina et al., 11.10.2002, reprinted in (2002) *Human Rights Law Journal* 406 98

Cambodia

People's Revolutionary Court, Judgment, UN Doc. A/34/491, 20.9.1979 71

Canada

Chile

Denmark

Finland

France

Germany

Iraq

Israel

Italy

Netherlands

Bouterse (2000) 51 Nederlandse Jurisprudentie 302 494
Gerbsch, XIII LRTWC 131 366
Guus Kouwenhoven, Hof 's-Hertogenbosch, 20–001906–10, 21.4.2017 73
Menten, 75 ILR 362 222
Rohrig, Brunner and Heintze, (1950) 17 ILR 393 55

Norway

Klinge, III LRTWC 1 21

Peru

Decision 01271–2008-PHC/TC, Constitutional Court, 8.8.2008 64
Judgment, Exp. N° 19–2001-09A.V., Primera Sala Penal Transitoria, Corte Suprema de
    Justicia de la República, 30 December 2009 336

South Africa

Azanian People's Organization (AZAPO) and others v. President of the Republic of
    South Africa, 1996 (4) SA 562 (CC) 513, 524
Mohamed and Dalvie v. President of the Republic of South Africa and Six Others, 2001
    (1) SA 893 (CC); 2001 (7) BCLR 685 (CC) 100
State v. Ebrahim, 1991 (2) SA 553; 1 South African Criminal Law Reports 307 51

Spain

Castro (1999) 32 ILM 596 497
Guatemalan Generals, Tribunal Supremo, Sala de lo Penal, Sentencia 327/2003,
    25.2.2003 62
Pinochet, National Court, Criminal Division (Plenary Session) Case 19/97, 4.11.1998;
    Case 1/98, 5.11.1998 198

Sweden

Extradition of S. A. to the Republic of Rwanda Supreme Court, Case Ö1082-09; NJA
    2009:30 99

Public Prosecutor v. Mbanenande, Stockholm District Court, Case No. B-18271–11,
    20.6.2013 66, 87

Switzerland

Gabrez, Military Tribunal, Division I, Lausanne, 18.4.1997 65

United Kingdom

AC 221 95

Al-Adsani v. Government of Kuwait, Court of Appeal (1996) 107 ILR 536 488

Brown and others v. Government of Rwanda and Secretary of State for the Home
    Department [2009] EWCA 770 99

Chusaburo, III LRTWC 76 367

DPP v. Doot [1973] AC 807 53

Government of Rwanda v. Nteziryayo and others and the Secretary of State for the Home
    Department, High Court of Justice Queen's Bench Division Administrative Court,
    28.7.2017 [2017] EWHC 1912 (Admin) 99

Heyer (Erich) (Essen Lynching), I LRTWC 88 326

Jones v. Kingdom of Saudi Arabia [2006] UKHL 26; [2006] 2 WLR 1424 487, 488, 493

Khurts Bat v. Investigating Judge of the German Federal Court [2011] EWHK 2029
    (Admin); [2012] 3 WLR 180; 147 ILR 633 (Queen's Bench Division) 490

Mofaz, reprinted in (2004) 53 *ICLQ* 769 497

Peleus, 13 ILR 248 378

R v. Bow Street Metropolitan Stipendiary Magistrate, ex parte Pinochet Ugarte (No. 1)
    [1998] 4 All ER 897 492

R v. Bow Street Metropolitan Stipendiary Magistrate, ex parte Pinochet Ugarte (No. 2)
    [1999] 1 All ER 577 492

R v. Bow Street Metropolitan Stipendiary Magistrate, ex parte Pinochet Ugarte (No. 3)
    [2000] 1 AC 147; [1999] 2 All ER 97; [1999] 2 WLR 827 60, 79, 489, 492

R v. Dudley and Stevens (1884–5) LR 14 QBD 273 373

R v. Gul [2012] EWCA Crim. 280, 22.2.2012 315

R v. Horseferry Road Magistrates, ex parte Bennett [1993] 2 All ER 318 51

R v. Jones [2006] UKHL 16 79

R v. Sawoniuk [2000] 2 Crim. App. Rep. 220 65, 70

Sandrock (Otto) (Almelo), I LRTWC 35 326

Tesch and others (Zyklon B), I LRTWC 93 58, 263, 336

Tessmann (Willi), XV LRTWC 177 369, 371

Treacy v. DPP [1971] AC 537; [1971] 2 WLR 112; [1971] 1 All ER 110 84

Velpke Baby Home, VII LRTWC 76 56

United States

Abbreviations

AC	Appeals Chamber
ACHPR	African Charter on Human and Peoples' Rights
ACHR	American Convention on Human Rights
AFRC	Armed Forces Revolutionary Council
AHRLR	African Human Rights Law Reports
AJIL	American Journal of International Law
All ER	All England Law Reports
AP	Additional Protocol (to the Geneva Conventions of 1949)
APM	anti-personnel mine
ASEAN	Association of Southeast Asian Nations
ASIL	American Society of International Law
ASP	Assembly of States Parties (to the Rome Statute)
AU	African Union
BFSP	British and Foreign State Papers
CAR	Central African Republic
CARICOM	Caribbean Community
CAT	UN Convention Against Torture and Other Cruel, Inhuman and Degrading Treatment
CDF	Civil Defence Force
CIS	Commonwealth of Independent States
CJEU	Court of Justice of the European Union
CLR	common legal representative
CLR	Commonwealth Law Reports
CMR	Court Martial Reports
DCC	document containing the charges
DLR	Dominion Law Reports
DRC	Democratic Republic of the Congo
EAC	Extraordinary African Chambers
ECCAS	Economic Community of Central African States
ECCC	Extraordinary Chambers in the Courts of Cambodia
ECHR	European Convention on Human Rights

ECJ	European Court of Justice
ECOSOC	UN Economic and Social Council
ECOWAS	Economic Community of West African States
ECtHR	European Court of Human Rights
EJIL	European Journal of International Law
ETS	European Treaty Series
EU	European Union
EULEX	EU Rule of Law Mission (Kosovo)
FRY	Federal Republic of Yugoslavia
GA	UN General Assembly
GAOR	UN General Assembly Official Records
Hague Recueil	Recueil des cours de l'Academie de droit international
HL	House of Lords (UK)
HRC	UN Human Rights Committee
IACHR	Inter-American Human Rights Commission
IACtHR	Inter-American Court of Human Rights
ICC	International Criminal Court
ICCPR	International Covenant on Civil and Political Rights
ICJ	International Court of Justice
ICL	international criminal law
ICLQ	International and Comparative Law Quarterly
ICLR	International Criminal Law Review
ICRC	International Committee of the Red Cross and Red Crescent
ICTR	International Criminal Tribunal for Rwanda
ICTY	International Criminal Tribunal for the former Yugoslavia
IFOR	Implementation Force (NATO)
IGAD	Intergovernmental Authority on Development (Eastern Africa)
IHL	international humanitarian law
IHT	Iraqi High Tribunal
ILA	International Law Association
ILC	International Law Commission
ILM	International Legal Materials
ILR	International Law Reports
IMT	International Military Tribunal
IMTFE	International Military Tribunal for the Far East
IR	Internal Rules
JCE	joint criminal enterprise
JICJ	Journal of International Criminal Justice
KFOR	Kosovo Force (NATO)
KLA	Kosovan Liberation Army
KSC	Kosovo Specialist Chambers
KWECC	Kosovo War and Ethnic Crimes Court

LJIL	Leiden Journal of International Law
LNTS	League of Nations Treaty Series
LRA	Lord's Resistance Army
LRTWC	Law Reports, Trials of War Criminals
LRV	Legal Representative for Victims
MICT	Residual Mechanism (Mechanism for International Criminal Tribunals)
MINUSCA	UN Stabilization Mission in the Central African Republic
MINUSMA	UN Multidimensional Integrated Stabilization Mission in Mali
MONUC	UN Organization Mission in the Democratic Republic of the Congo
MONUSCO	UN Organization Stabilization Mission in the Democratic Republic of the Congo
NGO	non-governmental organization
OAS	Organization of American States
OAU	Organization of African Unity
OCIJ	Office of the Co-Investigative Judges (ECCC)
OHR	Office of the High Representative (Dayton Peace Agreement)
OIC	Organization of the Islamic Conference
OJ	Official Journal of the European Communities
OPCV	Office of Public Counsel for Victims
OSCE	Organization for Security and Co-operation in Europe
OTP	Office of the Prosecutor
PAUTS	Pan-American Union Treaty Series
PCIJ	Permanent Court of International Justice
PTC	Pre-Trial Chamber
PTJ	Pre-Trial Judge
RPE	Rules of Procedure and Evidence
RSCSL	Residual Special Court for Sierra Leone
RUF	Revolutionary United Front
SAARC	South Asian Association for Regional Cooperation
SADC	Southern African Development Community
SC	UN Security Council
SCC	Special Criminal Court (CAR)
SCR	Supreme Court Reports
SCSL	Special Court for Sierra Leone
SCtC	Supreme Court Chamber (ECCC)
SFOR	Stability Force (NATO-led force, Bosnia)
SITF	Special Investigative Task Force
SOFA	Status of Forces Agreement
SPO	Special Prosecutor's Office (Kosovo)
SPSC	Special Panels for Serious Crimes (East Timor)
STL	Special Tribunal for Lebanon

TC	Trial Chamber
TFV	Trust Fund for Victims (ICC)
TIAS	Treaties and Other International Acts Series
TRCP	Transitional Rules of Criminal Procedure (UNTAET)
TWAIL	Third World Approaches to International Law
TWC	Trials of War Criminals
UKTS	United Kingdom Treaty Series
UNAMID	African Union/UN Hybrid Operation in Darfur
UNICRI	UN Interregional Crime and Justice Research Institute
UNIIC	UN International Independent Commission
UNMIK	UN Mission in Kosovo
UNMISET	UN Mission of Support in East Timor
UNODC	UN Office on Drugs and Crime
UNTAET	UN Transitional Administration in East Timor
UNTS	United Nations Treaty Series
WCC	War Crimes Chamber (Bosnia and Herzegovina)
WCD	War Crimes Department (Serbia)
WLR	Weekly Law Reports

Abbreviations of Book Titles

The following abbreviated titles of books are used in the notes and in the 'Further Reading' sections at the end of each chapter.

Ambos, *Commentary*	Kai Ambos (ed.), *The Rome Statute of the International Criminal Court: Article-by-Article Commentary*, 4th ed. (Munich, 2022)
Ambos, *Treatise*	Kai Ambos, *Treatise on International Criminal Law, Vol. I: Foundations and General Part* (Oxford, 2013) vol. I
Boas, *Practitioner Library III*	Gideon Boas, James L. Bischoff, Natalie L. Reid and B. Don Taylor III, *International Criminal Law Practitioner Library* (Cambridge, 2011) vol. III
Brown, *Research Handbook*	Bartram S. Brown (ed.), *Research Handbook on International Criminal Law* (Cheltenham, 2011)
Cassese et al., *Commentary*	Antonio Cassese, Paolo Gaeta and John R. W. D. Jones (eds.), *The Rome Statute of the International Criminal Court: A Commentary* (Oxford, 2002)
Doria et al., *Legal Regime*	José Doria, Hans-Peter Gasser and M. Cherif Bassiouni (eds.), *The Legal Regime of the International Criminal Court: Essays in Honour of Professor Igor Blishchenko* (Leiden, 2009)
Fischer et al., *International and National Prosecution*	Horst Fischer, Claus Kreß and Sasha Rolf Lüder (eds.), *International and National Prosecution of Crimes under International Law* (Berlin, 2001)

Henckaerts and Doswald-Beck, *ICRC Customary Law*	Jean-Marie Henckaerts and Louise Doswald-Beck, *Customary International Humanitarian Law* (Cambridge, 2000) vol. I
Lee, *Elements and Rules*	Roy Lee et al. (eds.), *The International Criminal Court: Elements of Crimes and Rules of Procedure and Evidence* (New York, 2001)
Lee, *The Making of the Rome Statute*	Roy Lee (ed.), *The International Criminal Court: The Making of the Rome Statute: Issues, Negotiations, Results* (The Hague, 1999)
McDonald and Goldman, *Substantive and Procedural Aspects*	Gabrielle Kirk McDonald and Olivia Swaak Goldman (eds.), *Substantive and Procedural Aspects of International Criminal Law: The Experience of International and National Courts* (Kluwer, 2000)
McGoldrick et al., *The Permanent ICC*	Dominic McGoldrick, Peter Rowe and Eric Donnelly (eds.), *The Permanent International Criminal Court: Legal and Policy Issues* (Oxford, 2004)
Schabas and Bernaz, *Routledge Handbook*	William A. Schabas and Nadia Bernaz (eds.), *Routledge Handbook of International Criminal Law* (London, 2011)
Schabas et al., *Ashgate Research Companion*	William A. Schabas, Yvonne McDermott and Niamh Hayes (eds.), *The Ashgate Research Companion to International Criminal Law: Critical Perspectives* (Farnham, 2013)
Sluiter and Vasiliev, *International Criminal Procedure*	Göran Sluiter and Sergey Vasiliev (eds.), *International Criminal Procedure: Towards a Coherent Body of Law* (London, 2009)
Sluiter et al., *International Criminal Procedure*	Göran Sluiter, Håkan Friman, Suzannah Linton, Sergey Vasiliev and Salvatore Zappalà (eds.), *International Criminal Procedure: Principles and Rules* (Oxford, 2013)

Stahn, *The Law and Practice of the ICC*	Carsten Stahn (ed.), *The Law and Practice of the International Criminal Court* (Oxford, 2015)
Stahn and Sluiter, *Emerging Practice*	Carsten Stahn and Göran Sluiter (eds.), *The Emerging Practice of the International Criminal Court* (Leiden, 2009)

Part I

Introduction

1

Introduction: What Is International Criminal Law?

1.1 MEANING OF INTERNATIONAL CRIMINAL LAW

International law typically governs the rights and obligations of states.[1] Criminal law, conversely, is paradigmatically concerned with prohibitions addressed to individuals, violations of which are subject to penal sanction by a state.[2] The two aspects are sometimes in tension. The development of a body of international criminal law which imposes responsibilities directly on individuals and punishes violations through international judicial mechanisms is also relatively recent. Although there are historical precursors and precedents of and in international criminal law,[3] it was not until the 1990s, with the establishment of the ad hoc Tribunals for the former Yugoslavia and Rwanda, that it could be said that an international criminal law regime had evolved.

International criminal law developed from various sources. War crimes originate from the 'laws and customs of war', which accord certain protections to individuals in armed conflicts. Genocide and crimes against humanity evolved to protect persons from what are now often termed gross human rights abuses, including those committed by their own governments. With the exception of the crime of aggression with its focus on inter-state conflict, the concern of international criminal law is now with individuals and with their protection from wide-scale atrocities. As was said by the Appeals Chamber in the *Tadić* case in the International Criminal Tribunal for the former Yugoslavia (ICTY):

A State-sovereignty-oriented approach has been gradually supplanted by a human-being-oriented approach ... international law, while of course duly safeguarding the legitimate interests of States, must gradually turn to the protection of human beings.[4]

The meaning of the phrase 'international criminal law' depends on its use, but there is a plethora of definitions, not all of which are consistent.[5] In 1950, the most dedicated chronicler of the uses of 'international criminal law', Georg Schwarzenberger, described

---

[1] See e.g. Robert Jennings and Arthur Watts (eds.), *Oppenheim's International Law*, 9th ed. (London, 1994) 5–7.

[2] Glanville Williams, 'The Definition of Crime' (1955) 8 *Current Legal Problems* 107.

[3] See Chapter 6 and e.g. Timothy L. H. McCormack, 'From Sun Tzu to the Sixth Committee, the Evolution of an International Criminal Law Regime' in Timothy L. H. McCormack and Gerry J. Simpson (eds.), *The Law of War Crimes: National and International Approaches* (The Hague, 1997) 31.

[4] *Tadić*, ICTY AC, 2 October 1995, para. 97.

[5] See Claus Kreβ, 'International Criminal Law' in Rüdiger Wolfrum (ed.), *V Max Planck Encyclopaedia of Public International Law* (Oxford, 2012) 717–21.

six different meanings that have been attributed to that term.[6] All of those meanings related to international law, criminal law, and their interrelationship, but none referred to any existing body of international law which directly created criminal prohibitions addressed to individuals. Schwarzenberger believed that no such law existed at the time. 'An international crime', he said in reference to the question of the status of aggression, 'presupposes the existence of an international criminal law. Such a branch of international law does not exist'.[7]

On the other hand, Cherif Bassiouni, writing almost half a century later,[8] listed twenty-five categories of international crimes, being crimes which affect a significant international interest or consist of egregious conduct offending commonly shared values. Such crimes involve more than one state because of differences of nationality of victims or perpetrators or the means employed, or concern a lesser protected interest which cannot be defended without international criminalization. His categories include, as well as the more familiar ones, trafficking in obscene materials, falsification and counterfeiting, damage to submarine cables, and unlawful interference with mail.

Different meanings of international criminal law have their own utility for their different purposes and there is no necessary reason to decide upon one meaning as the 'right' one. Nevertheless, it is advisable from the outset to be clear about the sense in which the term is used in any particular situation. In this chapter we will attempt to elaborate the meaning which we give to the term for the purposes of this book and compare it with other definitions.

The approach taken in this book is to use 'international crime' to refer to those offences over which international courts or tribunals have been given jurisdiction under general international law. They comprise the so-called 'core' crimes of genocide, crimes against humanity, war crimes, and the crime of aggression (sometimes known as the crime against peace). Our use thus does not include piracy, slavery, torture, terrorism, drug trafficking, and many crimes which states parties to various treaties are under an obligation to criminalize in their domestic law. But because a number of the practical issues surrounding the repression of these crimes are similar to those relating to international crimes (in the way we use the term), they are discussed in this book, although only terrorist offences and torture will be discussed in any detail. Some of them (terrorist offences, drug trafficking, and individual acts of torture) have been suggested as suitable for inclusion within the jurisdiction of the International Criminal Court (ICC)[9] and may therefore constitute international crimes within our meaning at some time in the future. Terrorism has been included in the jurisdiction of one 'internationalized' tribunal, the Special Tribunal for Lebanon, but this Tribunal is intended to apply Lebanese domestic law on point, although its practice has been more equivocal (and controversial).[10]

[6] Georg Schwarzenberger, 'The Problem of an International Criminal Law' (1950) 3 *Current Legal Problems* 263.
[7] Georg Schwarzenberger, 'The Judgment of Nuremberg' (1947) 21 *Tulane Law Review* 329, 349.
[8] M. Cherif Bassiouni, 'International Crimes: The Ratione Materiae of International Criminal Law' in M. Cherif Bassiouni (ed.), *International Criminal Law*, 3rd ed. (Leiden, 2008) vol. I, 129, 134–5.
[9] See Final Act of the Rome Conference, A/CONF.183/10, Res. E.   [10] See further Chapters 9 and 14.

Our approach does not differentiate the core crimes from others as a matter of principle, but only pragmatically, by reason of the fact that no other crimes are currently within the jurisdiction of international courts. However, it is clear that, since these crimes have a basis in international law, they are also regarded by the international community as violating or threatening values protected by general international law, as the Preamble to the Rome Statute of the International Criminal Court makes clear.[11]

'International criminal law', as used in this book, encompasses not only the law concerning genocide, crimes against humanity, war crimes, and the crime of aggression, but also the principles and procedures governing the international investigation, prosecution, and adjudication of these crimes. As we shall see, in practice the greater part of the enforcement of international criminal law is undertaken by domestic authorities. National courts both are, and are intended to be, an integral and essential part of the enforcement of international criminal law.[12] In this book, therefore, we shall cover not only the international prosecution of international crimes, but also various international aspects of their domestic investigation and prosecution. However, as mentioned above, this is only one way of conceiving of international criminal law; below we evaluate some of the other approaches to defining the subject.

1.2 OTHER CONCEPTS OF INTERNATIONAL CRIMINAL LAW

1.2.1 Transnational Criminal Law

Until the establishment of international criminal courts and tribunals in the 1990s, the concept of international criminal law tended to be used to refer to those parts of a state's domestic criminal law which deal with transnational crimes, that is, crimes with actual or potential transborder effects. This body of law is now more appropriately termed 'transnational criminal law'.[13] This aligns with the distinction between 'international criminal law' (criminal aspects of international law) and 'transnational criminal law' (international aspects of national criminal law), which can be found in other languages, such as German (*'Völkerstrafrecht'* compared with *'Internationales Strafrecht'*),[14] French (*'droit international pénal'* and *'droit pénal international'*) and Spanish (*'derecho internacional penal'* and *'derecho penal internacional'*).

Transnational criminal law includes the rules of national jurisdiction under which a state may enact and enforce its own criminal law where there is some cross-border aspect of a crime. It also covers methods of cooperation among states to deal with domestic offences and offenders where there is a foreign element and the treaties which

---

[11] See, in particular, preambular paragraphs 3–4, which affirm that such crimes threaten the 'peace, security and well-being of the world', and as such, must be prosecuted.

[12] See ICC Statute, Arts. 17 and 18. As to the situation generally, Judges Higgins, Kooijmans, and Buergenthal have stated: 'the international consensus that the perpetrators of international crimes should not go unpunished is being advanced by a flexible strategy, in which newly established international criminal tribunals, treaty obligations and national courts all have their part to play'. *Case concerning the Arrest Warrant of 11 April 2000 (Democratic Republic of Congo* v. *Belgium)*, Judgment of 14 February 2002, Separate Opinion, para. 51.

[13] See Neil Boister, *An Introduction to Transnational Criminal Law*, 2nd ed. (Oxford, 2018).

[14] Kai Ambos, *Internationales Strafrecht*, 4th ed. (Berlin, 2014).

have been concluded to establish and encourage this inter-state cooperation. These treaties provide for mutual legal assistance and extradition between states in respect of crimes with a foreign element. Other treaties require states to criminalize certain types of conduct by creating offences in their domestic law, and to bring offenders to justice who are found on their territory, or to extradite them to states that will prosecute. While international law is the source of a part of this set of rules, the source of criminal prohibitions addressed to individuals is national law.[15]

1.2.2 International Criminal Law As a Set of Rules to Protect the Values of the International Order

Another, and more substantive, approach to determining the scope of 'international criminal law' is to look at the values which are protected by international law's prohibitions.[16] Under this approach, international crimes are considered to be those which are of concern to the international community as a whole (a description which is not very precise), or acts which violate a fundamental interest protected by international law. Early examples include the suppression of the slave trade.[17] The ICC Statute uses the term 'the most serious crimes of concern to the international community as a whole' almost as a definition of the core crimes,[18] and recognizes that such crimes 'threaten the peace, security and well-being of the world'.[19]

It is true that those crimes which are regulated or created by international law are of concern to the international community; they are usually ones which threaten international interests or fundamental values.[20] But there can be a risk in defining international criminal law in this manner, as it implies a level of coherence in the international criminalization process which may not exist.[21] The behaviour which is directly or indirectly subject to international law is not easily reducible to abstract formulae. Even if it were, it is not clear that these concepts would be sufficiently determinate to provide a useful guide for the future development of law, although arguments from coherence with respect to the ambit of international criminal law can have an impact on the development of the law (as has occurred, *inter alia*, in relation to the law of war crimes

---

[15] See generally Neil Boister, 'Transnational Criminal Law?' (2003) 14 *EJIL* 953, 967–77.

[16] For discussion in relation to the core crimes, see Bruce Broomhall, *International Justice and the International Criminal Court: Between State Sovereignty and the Rule of Law* (Oxford, 2003) 44–51.

[17] This is not included as a crime in the Rome Statute; see Patricia Viseur Sellers and Jocelyn Getgen Kestenbaum, 'Missing in Action: The International Crime of the Slave Trade' (2020) 18 *JICJ* 517–42.

[18] ICC Statute, Arts. 1 and 5. The International Law Commission framed its investigation into international criminal law in the broad sense as being one into the 'Crimes against the Peace and Security of Mankind': 'Draft Code of Crimes Against the Peace and Security of Mankind' in *Report of the International Law Commission on the Work of its Forty-Eighth Session*, UN Doc. A/51/10 (1996). See also Lyal Sunga, *The Emerging System of International Criminal Law* (The Hague, 1997).

[19] ICC Statute, Preamble, para. 3.

[20] M. Cherif Bassiouni, 'The Sources and Content of International Criminal Law' in M. Cherif Bassiouni (ed.), *International Criminal Law*, 2nd ed. (New York, 1999) 3, 98.

[21] See Robert Cryer, 'The Doctrinal Foundations of the International Criminalization Process' in M. Cherif Bassiouni (ed.), *International Criminal Law*, 2nd ed. (New York, 1999) 107. For an example, see Barbara Yarnold, 'Doctrinal Basis for the International Criminalisation Process' (1994) 4 *Temple International and Comparative Law Journal* 85.

in non-international armed conflict, which were developed with reference to the law applicable to international armed conflicts).[22]

1.2.3 Involvement of a State

Another approach to defining 'international crimes' relies upon state involvement in their commission.[23] There is some sense in this. For example, the crime of aggression is necessarily underpinned by an act of aggression committed by the state, which is enabled by high-level state agents.[24] War crimes, genocide, and crimes against humanity often, or even typically, have some element of state or state-like agency. But the subject-matter of international criminal law, as we use it, deals with the liability of individuals, mostly irrespective of whether or not they are agents of a state. In the definition of the crimes which we take as being constitutive of substantive international criminal law, the official status of the perpetrator is almost always irrelevant, with the main exception of the crime of aggression.[25]

1.2.4 Crimes Created by International Law

An international crime may also be defined as an offence which is created by international law itself, without requiring the intervention of domestic law. In the case of such crimes, international law imposes criminal responsibility directly on individuals. The classic statement of this form of international criminal law comes from the Nuremberg International Military Tribunal:

crimes against international law are committed by men, not abstract entities, and only by punishing individuals who commit such crimes can the provisions of international law be enforced . . . individuals have international duties which transcend the national obligations of obedience imposed by the individual state.[26]

The definition of an international crime as one created by international law is now in frequent use.[27] But this criterion may lead to unhelpful debate as to what is and what is not 'created' by international law.[28] The more pragmatic meaning used in this book excludes

---

[22] On such developments, see Chapter 12.

[23] See e.g. M. Cherif Bassiouni, *Crimes Against Humanity in International Criminal Law*, 2nd ed. (The Hague, 1999) 243–6, 256.

[24] See Chapter 13.

[25] The reference in ICC Statute, Art. 8(2)(b)(viii) to the transfer of population 'by the Occupying Power' would also seem to require that the perpetrator is a state agent.

[26] 'Nuremberg IMT: Judgment and Sentences' (1947) 41 *AJIL* 172, 221.

[27] Broomhall, *International Justice and the International Criminal Court* (n. 16) 9–10; Robert Cryer, *Prosecuting International Crimes: Selectivity in the International Criminal Law Regime* (Cambridge, 2005) 1; Hans-Heinrich Jescheck, *Die Verantwortlichkeit der Staatsorgane nach Völkerstrafrecht* (Bonn, 1951) 9; Otto Triffterer, *Dogmatische Untersuchungen zur Entwicklung des materiellen Völkerstrafrechts seit Nürnberg* (Freiburg im Breisgau, 1966) 34; Gerhard Werle and Florian Jeßberger, *Principles of International Criminal Law*, 3rd ed. (Oxford, 2014) 31–3, 45–9.

[28] A slightly different criterion of an international offence, one with a 'definition as a punishable offence in international (and usually conventional) law', leads to the inclusion of a much wider category of crimes, including hijacking, injury to submarine cables, and drugs offences (Yoram Dinstein, 'International Criminal Law' (1975) 5 *Israel Yearbook of Human Rights* 55, 67). Many of these would fall, under our taxonomy, to be considered under the rubric of transnational criminal law.

from detailed discussion certain conduct which has been suggested to be subject to direct liability in international criminal law but which others dispute, such as piracy and slavery,[29] a general offence of terrorism,[30] and individual acts of torture.[31] In other words, in this book, international crimes are defined as those that are undisputedly regarded as international crimes, crimes over which the ICC has jurisdiction: genocide, war crimes, crimes against humanity, and the crime of aggression.

Occasionally the *sui generis* penal system of the international criminal tribunals and courts is described as developing 'supranational criminal law'.[32] This term, to the extent that it has a determinate meaning, is somewhat misleading since it is normally reserved for law imposed by supranational institutions (like the European Union) and not treaty-based or customary international law.[33]

1.3 SOURCES OF INTERNATIONAL CRIMINAL LAW

As international criminal law is a subset of international law, its sources are those of international law enumerated in Article 38(1)(a)–(d) of the Statute of the International Court of Justice; in other words, treaty law, customary law, general principles of law, and, as a subsidiary means for the determination of the law, judicial decisions, and the writings of the most qualified publicists.[34] As will be seen, all of these have been used by the ad hoc Tribunals. They are available for use by national courts insofar as the relevant national system concerned will allow. The ICC Statute contains its own set of sources for the ICC to apply, which are analogous, although by no means identical, to those in the ICJ Statute.[35]

1.3.1 Treaties

Treaty-based sources of international criminal law, either directly or as an aid to interpretation, include the 1907 Hague Regulations, the 1949 Geneva Conventions (and their Additional Protocols), and the 1948 Genocide Convention. They form the basis for many of the crimes within the jurisdiction of the ad hoc Tribunals and the ICC. The Statute of the ICC, which sets out the definitions of crimes within the jurisdiction of the ICC, is, of course, itself a treaty. Security Council Resolutions 827(1993) and 955(1994), which set up the ICTY and International Criminal Tribunal for Rwanda (ICTR), respectively, were adopted

---

[29] See e.g. Broomhall, *International Justice and the International Criminal Court* (n. 16) 23–4; Jean Allain (ed.), *The Legal Understanding of Slavery* (Oxford, 2012); Robin Geiß and Anna Petrig, *Piracy and Armed Robbery at Sea* (Oxford, 2011).

[30] See e.g. Antonio Cassese et al., *Cassese's International Criminal Law*, 3rd ed. (Oxford, 2013) ch. 8.

[31] *Ibid.* 132–5. For a counterpoint see Paola Gaeta, 'International Criminalization of Prohibited Conduct' in Antonio Cassese et al. (eds.), *The Oxford Companion to International Criminal Justice* (Oxford, 2009) 63, 68–9.

[32] E.g. Roelof Haveman, Olga Kavran, and Julian Nicholls (eds.), *Supranational Criminal Law: A System Sui Generis* (Antwerp, 2003).

[33] See e.g. Werle and Jeßberger, *Principles of International Criminal Law* (n. 27) 49–50.

[34] See generally Dapo Akande, 'Sources of International Criminal Law' in Antonio Cassese et al. (eds.), *The Oxford Companion to International Criminal Justice* (Oxford, 2009) 41.

[35] ICC Statute, Art. 21. See Leena Grover, *Interpreting Crimes in the Rome Statute of the International Criminal Court* (Cambridge, 2014); Robert Cryer, 'Royalism and The King: Article 21 of the Rome Statute and the Politics of Sources' (2009) 12 *New Criminal Law Review* 390.

by the Security Council pursuant to its powers under Chapter VII of the UN Charter, and thus find their binding force in Article 25 of the Charter. The source of their binding nature is therefore a treaty. The Statutes of the Tribunals have had an important effect on the substance of international criminal law both directly, as applied by the Tribunals, and indirectly as a source of inspiration for other international criminal law instruments.[36]

It has been suggested that treaties might not suffice to directly create liability of individuals.[37] Such arguments are misplaced. As the Permanent Court of International Justice noted over ninety years ago, treaties can impose obligations directly on individuals, if that is the intent of the drafters.[38]

It is only those treaties or provisions of a treaty which are intended to apply directly to an individual that can give rise to criminal responsibility. The 'suppression conventions', for example, which require states to criminalize conduct such as drug trafficking, hijacking, and terror bombing,[39] are not generally regarded as creating individual criminal responsibility of themselves; the conduct covered by those treaties will be incorporated in national law by whatever constitutional method is used by the state concerned.[40] Further, if a court is to apply the terms of a treaty directly to an individual, it will be necessary to show that the prohibited conduct has taken place in the territory of a state party to the treaty or is otherwise subject to the law of such a Party.[41] The practice of the ICTY has been, with occasional deviations,[42] to accept that treaties may suffice to found criminal liability. This began with the *Tadić* decision of 1995 and the position was reasserted in the *Kordić and Čerkez* appeal.[43] In the *Galić* case, the ICTY Appeals Chamber noted that treaties suffice for criminal responsibility, although 'in practice the International Tribunal always ascertains that the relevant provision is also declaratory of custom'.[44] This is to adopt a 'belt and braces' approach rather than to require a customary basis for war crimes.[45] The proposition that treaties may found international criminal liability is inherent in the ICTR Statute, which criminalizes violations of Additional Protocol II (not all of which were at the time considered customary),[46] and is the most likely basis for aspects of the ICC's jurisdiction.[47]

---

[36] See Theodor Meron, 'War Crimes in Yugoslavia and the Development of International Law' (1994) 88 *AJIL* 78.

[37] Guénaël Mettraux, *International Crimes and the Ad Hoc Tribunals* (Oxford, 2005) 7–9.

[38] *Jurisdiction of the Courts in Danzig* Case 1928 PCIJ Series B. No. 15, 17. See Kate Parlett, *The Individual in the International Legal System: Continuity and Change in International Law* (Cambridge, 2011) 17–26. For a sceptical reading see Roland Portmann, *Legal Personality in International Law* (Cambridge, 2010) 68–73.

[39] See Chapter 14.

[40] The two concepts are not hermetically sealed though, see e.g. International Convention for the Protection of All Persons from Enforced Disappearance, 2006, GA Res. 61/177, Arts. 4–5.

[41] This problem will no longer arise with regard to crimes derived from the four Geneva Conventions which now have universal state participation.

[42] *Galić*, ICTY TC I, 5 December 2003, Separate and Partially Dissenting Opinion of Judge Nieto-Navia, paras. 109–12; *Milutinović et al.*, ICTY AC, 21 May 2003, paras. 10ff. See further Héctor Olásolo, 'A Note on the Principle of Legality in International Criminal Law' (2007) 19 *Criminal Law Forum* 301.

[43] *Kordić and Čerkez*, ICTY AC, 17 December 2004, paras. 41–6, clarifying *Tadić*, ICTY AC, 2 October 1995, para. 143.

[44] *Galić*, ICTY AC, 30 January 2006, para. 85.

[45] Although at least two ICTY Appeals Chamber judges have taken the view that the ICTY only has jurisdiction over customary offences, Mohamed Shahabuddeen, *International Criminal Justice at the Yugoslav Tribunal: A Judge's Recollection* (Oxford, 2012) 61–70; *Galić*, ICTY AC, 30 November 2006, Partially Dissenting Opinion of Judge Schomburg, para. 21.

[46] ICTR Statute, Art. 4; *Report of the Secretary-General Pursuant to Paragraph 5 of Security Council Resolution 955*, S/1995/134 (1994) para. 12.

[47] Marko Milanović, 'Is the Rome Statute Binding on Individuals (and Why We Should Care)' (2011) 9 *JICJ* 25; Marko Milanović, 'Aggression and Legality' (2012) 10 *JICJ* 165.

1.3.2 Customary International Law

The ICTY has accepted that when its Statute does not regulate a matter, one may turn to customary international law (and general principles – see Section 1.3.3).[48] Customary international law, that body of law which derives from the practice of states accompanied by *opinio juris* (the belief that what is done is required by law), has the disadvantage of all unwritten law in that it may be difficult to ascertain its content. This is not always the case, however, when the customary law originates with a treaty or other written instrument, for example a General Assembly resolution which is accepted as reflecting custom, or has been recognized by a court as such.[49] Nevertheless the use of customary international law in international criminal law has sometimes been criticized on the basis that it may be too vague to found criminal liability,[50] or even that no law that is unwritten should suffice to found criminal liability. These claims will be discussed below at Section 1.5.1 in relation to the principle of *nullum crimen sine lege*. Suffice it to say that this was not the position of the Nuremberg or Tokyo International Military Tribunals (IMTs), nor was it that of the ad hoc Tribunals.[51] Indeed the President of the ICTY, Theodor Meron, has argued that 'customary international law now comes up in almost every international court and tribunal . . . [but] . . . it is in the international criminal tribunals . . . that the jurisprudence on customary law has been most rich'.[52] There is little question that the ICTY in particular used customary law in an innovative fashion, to develop international criminal law in areas where its application was unclear or uncertain, and perhaps unforeseen.[53]

1.3.3 General Principles of Law and Subsidiary Means of Determining the Law

The ICTY resorted to general principles of law to assist it in its search for applicable rules of international law.[54] Indeed the Secretary-General's report that accompanied the creation of the ICTY expressly foresaw such a reliance, at least in the context of applicable defences.[55] Still, owing to the differences between international and national trials, the ICTY was wary of uncritical reliance on general principles taken from domestic legal systems and

---

[48] *Kupreškić et al.*, ICTY TC II, 14 January 2000, para. 591. See generally Noora Arajärvi, *The Changing Nature of Customary International Law: Methods of Interpreting the Concept of Custom in International Criminal Tribunals* (London, 2014).

[49] E.g. para. 3(g) of the Definition on Aggression in GA Res. 3314(XXIX), 14 December 1974. See Section 13.2.3 and Mendelson, 'The Formation of Customary Law' ch. 5.

[50] Vladimir Djuro-Degan, 'On the Sources of International Criminal Law' (2005) 4 *Chinese Journal of International Law* 45, 67. See also Olásolo, 'A Note' (n. 42) 301.

[51] For comments on custom before the ICTY, see Mary Fan, 'Custom and General Principles and the Great Architect Cassese' (2012) 10 *JICJ* 1063; Robert Cryer, 'International Criminal Tribunals and the Sources of International Law: Antonio Cassese's Contribution to the Canon' (2012) 10 *JICJ* 1045.

[52] Theodor Meron, *The Making of International Criminal Justice: A View from the Bench* (Oxford, 2011) 29.

[53] See generally Shane Darcy and Joseph Powderly (eds.), *Judicial Creativity at the International Criminal Tribunals* (Oxford, 2010); Beth van Schaack, '*Crimen Sine Lege*: Judicial Lawmaking at the Intersection of Law and Morals' (2008) 97 *Georgetown Law Journal* 119; William Schabas, 'Customary Law or "Judge Made" Law: Judicial Creativity at the UN Criminal Tribunals' in Doria et al., *Legal Regime*, 77.

[54] See Fabián Raimondo, *General Principles of Law in the Decisions of International Criminal Courts and Tribunals* (The Hague, 2008).

[55] *Report of the Secretary-General Pursuant to Paragraph 2 of Security Council Resolution 808* (3 May 1993) para. 58. See Shahabuddeen, *International Criminal Justice* (n. 45) 54–5.

acontextual application of them to international trials.[56] That said, the ICTY and ICTR both resorted to national laws to assist them in determining the relevant international law through this source. According to the *Furundžija* decision, however, care must be taken when using such legislation, not to look simply to one of the major legal systems of the world, as 'international courts must draw upon the general concepts and legal institutions common to all the major legal systems of the world'.[57] In relation to criminal law, general principles of law are not ideal. After all they are, by their nature, general, and thus tend to be a last resort. Also, as the *Erdemović* case showed – with regard to the defence of duress – at times there simply is no general principle to apply.[58] The International Criminal Court (ICC) is to apply, where the first two categories of law do not provide an answer:

general principles of law derived by the Court from national laws of legal systems of the world including, as appropriate, the national laws of States that would normally exercise jurisdiction over the crime, provided that those principles are not inconsistent with [the] Statute and with international law and internationally recognized norms and standards.[59]

The ICC may also apply 'principles and rules of law as interpreted in its previous decisions'.[60] The ICC is not, however, bound by its previous decisions; it has no equivalent to the common law principle of *stare decisis.* That said, the ICTY frequently had recourse to judicial decisions for determining issues of law,[61] and constructed a system of precedents for dealing with its own jurisprudence.[62] The ICC often relies on ad hoc Tribunals' case law to interpret its Statute, but when there are differences in standards/concepts (e.g. on *mens rea* or common purpose liability), the Statute and Elements of Crime take precedence.[63]

The ICTY and ICTR had reference to domestic, as well as international, case law.[64] Domestic case law is a major material source of evidence about international criminal law. However, the assertions of international law in domestic cases can be affected by local idiosyncrasies. These can arise from the domestic statutes that are being evaluated or applied, or from a court seeing international criminal law through a distinctly national lens.[65]

---

[56] *Erdemović*, ICTY AC, 7 October 1997, Separate and Dissenting Opinion of Judge Cassese, para. 5.

[57] *Furundžija*, ICTY TC II, 10 December 1998, para. 178.

[58] *Erdemović*, ICTY AC, 7 October 1997, Joint Separate Opinion of Judges McDonald and Vohrah, paras. 56–72.

[59] ICC Statute, Art. 21(1)(c). This and all other sources of law available to the ICC are qualified by Art. 21(3) which requires application and interpretation of the law to be consistent with internationally recognized human rights, and without adverse discrimination.

[60] *Ibid*. Art. 21(2). William Schabas, *The International Criminal Court: A Commentary on the Rome Statute*, 2nd ed. (Oxford, 2016) 511; Margaret M. deGuzman, 'Article 21' in Ambos, *Commentary*, 932.

[61] See Shane Darcy, *Judges, Law, and War: The Judicial Development of International Humanitarian Law* (Cambridge, 2014); Paolo Lobba and Triestino Mariniello (eds.), *Judicial Dialogue on Human Rights: The Practice of International Criminal Tribunals* (Leiden, 2017).

[62] *Aleksovski*, ICTY AC, 24 March 2000, paras. 89–115. See Robert Cryer, 'Neither Here nor There? The Status of International Criminal Jurisprudence in the International and UK Legal Orders' in Michael Bohlander and Kaiyan Kaikobad (eds.), *Law, Perspectives on Legal Order and Justice, Essays in Honour of Colin Warbrick* (Leiden, 2010) 155.

[63] Gilbert Bitti, 'Article 21 of the Statute of the International Criminal Court and the Treatment of Sources of Law in the Jurisprudence of the ICC' in Stahn and Sluiter, *Emerging Practice*; Volker Nerlich, 'The Status of ICTY and ICTR Precedent in Proceedings Before the ICC' in *ibid*. 305. On the issues that may arise with respect to the application of different forms of international criminal law, see Elies van Sliedregt and Sergey Vasiliev (eds.), *Pluralism in International Criminal Law* (Oxford, 2014).

[64] See e.g. *Tadić*, ICTY AC, 15 July 1999, paras. 255–70.

[65] See Leila Sadat Wexler, 'The Interpretation of the Nuremberg Principles by the French Court of Cassation: From Touvier to Barbie and Back Again' (1994) 32 *Columbia Journal of International Law* 289; Sharon Weill, *The Role of National Courts in Applying International Humanitarian Law* (Oxford, 2014).

Finally, although the writings of scholars are not, in themselves, sources of international criminal law, it is possible to have recourse to the views of scholars, which at times have been highly influential.[66] Care must always be taken to ensure that the statements relied on are accurate statements of the law as it stands, rather than a statement of how the author would like the law to be; this is important, not least because of the *nullum crimen sine lege* principle.[67] Also, selection of scholars from only one, or a limited set of, legal tradition(s) can lead to a skewed view, which is incompatible with an inclusive approach to international criminal law.

1.4 INTERNATIONAL CRIMINAL LAW AND OTHER AREAS OF LAW

The three areas of international law related to international criminal law for which an understanding is the most important are human rights law, international humanitarian law, and the law of state responsibility.

1.4.1 International Criminal Law and Human Rights Law

The development of crimes against humanity and the law of human rights was partially inspired by a wish to ensure that the atrocities that characterized Nazi Germany were not repeated. Thus, the modern law of human rights, including economic and social rights, as well as civil and political rights,[68] has a considerable common base with international criminal law.[69] More recent developments in the enforcement of international criminal law, in particular the creation of the two ad hoc Tribunals, were introduced in response to mass abuses of human rights by states against their own citizens or others within their territory. Hence, parts of international criminal law have developed in this context to respond to egregious violations of human rights in the absence of effective alternative mechanisms for enforcing the most basic of humanitarian standards. International human rights bodies have taken a greater interest in international criminal law and its enforcement under their mandates;[70] such developments raise issues of coordination of their roles.[71]

Human rights obligations are imposed primarily on states, and it is frequently state agents who are the transgressors. Where states are not implementing their human rights

---

[66] E.g. *Krstić*, ICTY AC, 19 April 2004, para. 10; *Stakić*, ICTY TC II, 31 July 2003, para. 519; *Katanga and Ngudjolo*, ICC PTC I, 30 September 2008 (ICC-01/04–01/07–717) paras. 482, 485, 501. More generally see Sandesh Sivakumaran, 'The Influence of Teaching of Publicists on the Development of International Law' (2017) 66 *ICLQ* 1.

[67] See Section 1.5.1.

[68] On the former, see Evelyne Schmid, *Taking Economic, Social and Cultural Rights Seriously in International Criminal Law* (Cambridge, 2015).

[69] See e.g. William A. Schabas, 'Criminal Responsibility for Violations of Human Rights' in Janusz Symonides (ed.), *Human Rights, International Protection, Monitoring, Enforcement* (Aldershot, 2003) 281; Robert Cryer, 'International Criminal Law' in Daniel Moeckli, Sangeeta Shah, and Sandesh Sivakumaran (eds.), *International Human Rights Law*, 3rd ed. (Oxford, 2018) 521.

[70] See Alexandra Huneeus, 'International Criminal Law by Other Means: The Quasi-Criminal Jurisdiction of the Human Rights Courts' (2013) 107 *AJIL* 1; William Schabas, 'Synergy or Fragmentation? International Criminal Law and the European Convention on Human Rights' (2011) 9 *JICJ* 609.

[71] Emmanuel Decaux, 'The Place of Human Rights Courts and International Criminal Courts in the International System' (2011) 9 *JICJ* 597.

obligations, the principles of international criminal law are a useful and necessary alternative to state responsibility. The similarities in the objectives of both bodies of law are clear; both seek to provide a minimum standard of humane treatment. Both, unlike most other branches of international law, have a direct impact on individuals, albeit in somewhat different ways.

The Nuremberg IMT had an influence on the drafting of early human rights instruments.[72] Returning the compliment, the international instruments on human rights played an obvious part in the drafting of the Statutes of the two ad hoc Tribunals and of the ICC Statute.[73] The ad hoc Tribunals also used human rights law, and decisions of international bodies applying that law, to assist them in their interpretation of substantive international criminal law and in developing procedural rules. For example, the ICTY in *Kunarac* explained its past practice thus:

[b]ecause of the paucity of precedent in the field of international humanitarian law, the Tribunal has, on many occasions, had recourse to instruments and practices developed in the field of human rights law. Because of their resemblance, in terms of goals, values and terminology, such recourse is generally a welcome and needed assistance to determine the content of customary international law in the field of humanitarian law.[74]

The ICTR (particularly at trial level) used human rights jurisprudence on hate speech and freedom of expression to assist it in drawing the boundaries of the offences of direct and public incitement of genocide and the crime against humanity of persecution in the cases of the Rwandan Radio Station RTLM,[75] and the musician Simon Bikindi.[76] The crime against humanity of persecution has fairly clear overlaps with human rights law, in that it can involve serious violations of fundamental rights under international law, which do not have to be international crimes in and of themselves. These can include severe violations of socio-economic, as well as civil and political rights.[77]

In international criminal procedure and, in particular, as regards the right to a fair trial, the Tribunals have been especially ready to draw from human rights law.[78] In *Dokmanović*, for example, the ICTY affirmed that an arrest must be made 'in accordance with procedures prescribed by law', as indicated in Article 5(1) of the European Convention for the Protection of Human Rights and Fundamental Freedoms (ECHR) and Article 9(1) of the International Covenant on Civil and Political Rights (ICCPR).[79] In *Tadić*, the Appeals Chamber recognized that a general principle of law may have its source in human rights instruments, in that case the principle that the Tribunal had to be 'established by law'.[80]

---

[72] Schabas, 'Synergy or Fragmentation?' (n. 70) 609–11.

[73] See e.g. the provisions on the rights of the accused in ICTY Statute, Art. 21 and ICTR Statute, Art. 20, largely reproducing Art. 14(1)–(3) and (5) of the International Covenant on Civil and Political Rights (ICCPR); the procedures in the ICC Statute are very heavily influenced by human rights instruments, but see in particular Arts. 55 and 67.

[74] *Kunarac et al.*, ICTY TC II, 22 February 2001, para. 467. See Robert Cryer, 'The Interplay of Human Rights and Humanitarian Law: The Approach of the ICTY' (2009) 14 *Journal of Conflict and Security Law* 511.

[75] *Nahimana et al.*, ICTR TC I, 3 December 2003, paras. 983–1010. [76] *Bikindi*, ICTR TC III, 2 December 2008, paras. 378–97.

[77] *Kupreškić et al.*, ICTY TC II, 14 January 2000, paras. 608–15. [78] See further Chapter 17.

[79] See *Mrkšić, et al.*, ICTY TC II, 22 October 1997, paras. 59–60. [80] *Tadić*, ICTY AC, 2 October 1995, paras. 42–7.

Nonetheless, although there are overlaps between human rights law and international criminal law, they are not synonymous, and there are dangers in treating them as being so. Almost every international crime would be a violation of human rights law, but the converse does not apply. As the ICTY said in the context of persecutions, 'although the realm of human rights is dynamic and expansive, not every denial of a human right may constitute a crime against humanity'.[81] The use of human rights standards by the Trial Chamber in the case of the Rwandan Radio Station RTLM with respect to direct and public incitement to genocide was upheld by the Appeals Chamber, but on the basis that the Trial Chamber was careful to distinguish hate speech, that may be a matter for human rights bodies, and that offence.[82] International criminal courts and tribunals do not exist to prosecute violations of the whole panoply of human rights. Further, human rights obligations are primarily imposed upon states, not individuals, and it is for states to decide how they will enforce them on their own agents; except in the case of the most serious abuses, this will not necessarily be by criminalizing the activity concerned. Finally, whereas human rights norms may be given a broad and liberal interpretation in order to achieve their objects and purposes, in international criminal law there are countervailing rights of suspects that are protected through principles requiring that the law be strictly construed and that ambiguity be resolved in favour of the accused.[83] As has been said elsewhere:

The assumptions of human rights and humanitarian lawyers can also distort ICL reasoning through substantive and structural conflation. Many of the prohibitions of ICL are drawn from, and similar to, prohibitions in human rights and humanitarian law. Faced with familiar-looking provisions, ICL practitioners often assume that the ICL norms are coextensive with their human rights or humanitarian law counterparts, and uncritically transplant concepts and jurisprudence from other domains to flesh out their content. Such assumptions overlook the fact that these bodies of law have different purposes and consequences and thus entail different philosophical commitments.[84]

As the case law of the two Tribunals and the ICC has grown, there is less of a need for these courts to have recourse to human rights jurisprudence to supplement the sources of international criminal law. Such a development ought not to be taken to be evidence of the fragmentation of international law, as it may also be evidence of appropriate contextual interpretation of both areas of law, which operate in harmony, rather than being unified in their roles. Furthermore, the influence of human rights law on international criminal law cannot be ignored or denied.[85] Article 21(3) of the Rome Statute requires that 'the application and interpretation of law pursuant to this article must be consistent with

---

[81] *Kupreškić et al.*, ICTY TC II, 14 January 2000, para. 618; see section 11.3.9.
[82] *Nahimana et al.*, ICTR AC, 28 November 2007, paras. 692–6, 972–88 (although they were more circumspect on crimes against humanity of persecution). See also Partially Dissenting Opinion of Judge Shahabuddeen, paras. 18ff. Cf. Partially Dissenting Opinion of Judge Meron, paras. 3–20 in relation to crimes against humanity of persecution.
[83] See e.g. Darryl Robinson, 'The Identity Crisis of International Criminal Law' (2008) 21 *LJIL* 925; Allison Marston Danner and Jenny Martinez, 'Guilty Associations: Joint Criminal Enterprise, Command Responsibility and the Development of International Criminal Law' (2005) 93 *California Law Review* 75. *Nahimana et al.*, ICTR AC, 28 November 2007, Partially Dissenting Opinion of Judge Meron, para. 8.
[84] Robinson, 'Identity Crisis' (n. 83) 946; cf. Hans-Peter Gasser, 'The Changing Relationship Between International Criminal Law, Human Rights Law and Humanitarian Law' in Doria et al., *Legal Regime*, 1111, 1117.
[85] See e.g. Olivier de Frouville, 'The Influence of the European Court of Human Rights' Case Law on International Criminal Law of Torture and Inhuman or Degrading Treatment' (2011) 9 *JICJ* 633.

internationally recognized human rights', which means that this role is unlikely to end. At the ICC, human rights law plays an important role in the law on reparations and victim participation.[86]

1.4.2 International Criminal Law and International Humanitarian Law

International criminal law also shares common roots with international humanitarian law, the body of law designed to protect victims of armed conflict. Violations of a large number of rules of international humanitarian law are now criminalized as war crimes.[87] Thus, international humanitarian law serves as a point of reference in understanding and interpreting the corresponding war crimes provisions. As with human rights norms, care must be taken before transposing humanitarian law standards directly into international criminal law; the latter has distinct principles of interpretation.[88] There is a synergistic relationship between humanitarian law and international criminal law, especially the law of war crimes.[89] Developments in humanitarian law are reflected in the law of war crimes but, especially when it comes to the customary law of armed conflict, decisions of international criminal tribunals also sometimes feed back into humanitarian law.[90] The 'humanization' of humanitarian law[91] has been assisted, if not driven, through the work of the ICTY in particular.[92]

1.4.3 International Criminal Law and State Responsibility

International criminal law in the sense in which we use it concerns the criminal responsibility of individuals, not states.[93] The responsibility of a state under international law is a matter for a separate branch of international law, and is not dependent upon the legal responsibility of an individual.[94] If an agent of a state is convicted of an international crime, the act in question may, depending upon the circumstances, be attributable to the state, in

---

[86] According to some at the expense of defence rights: Haydee Dijkstal, 'Destruction of Cultural Heritage before the ICC: The Influence of Human Rights Proceedings for Victims and the Accused' (2019) 17 *JICJ* 391–412.

[87] See Paula Gaeta, 'War Crimes and other "Core" International Crimes' in Andrew Clapham and Paula Gaeta (eds.), *The Oxford Handbook of International Law in Armed Conflict* (Oxford, 2014) 737.

[88] See Rogier Bartels, 'Discrepancies Between International Humanitarian Law on the Battlefield and in the Courtroom: The Challenges of Applying International Humanitarian Law in International Criminal Trials' in Mariëlle Mathee, Brigit Toebes, and Marcel Brus (eds.), *Armed Conflict and International Law: Looking for the Human Face, Lieber Amicorum in Memory of Avril McDonald* (The Hague, 2013) 339.

[89] See further Chapter 12.

[90] See e.g. Robert Cryer, 'Of Custom, Treaties, Scholars and the Gavel: The Impact of the International Criminal Tribunals on the ICRC Customary Study' (2006) 11 *Journal of Conflict and Security Law* 239.

[91] Theodor Meron, 'The Humanization of Humanitarian Law' (2000) 94 *AJIL* 239.

[92] Tamás Hoffmann, 'The Gentle Humanizer of Humanitarian Law: Antonio Cassese and the Creation of the Customary Law of Non-International Armed Conflicts' in Carsten Stahn and Larissa van den Herik (eds.), *Future Perspectives on International Criminal Justice* (The Hague, 2010) 58.

[93] See generally André Nollkaemper, 'Concurrence Between Individual Responsibility and State Responsibility in International Law' (2003) 52 *ICLQ* 615; Andrea Bianchi, 'State Responsibility and Criminal Liability of Individuals' in Antonio Cassese et al. (eds.), *The Oxford Companion to International Criminal Justice* (Oxford, 2009) 16; Beatrice Bonafè, *The Relationship Between State and Individual Responsibility for International Crimes* (Leiden, 2009).

[94] James Crawford, 'The System of International Responsibility' in James Crawford, Alain Pellet, and Simon Olleson (eds.), *The Law of International Responsibility* (Oxford, 2010) 17.

which case that state may also be internationally responsible.[95] The same act therefore can give rise to both individual criminal responsibility and state responsibility.[96] The important question is one of attributability of the conduct of the individual to the state. For the crime of aggression, this link is provided for in the definition of the crime. The crime of aggression is committed by persons who are 'in a position effectively to exercise control over or to direct political or military action of a State'.

The question of state responsibility for international crimes was dealt with directly in the *Bosnian Genocide* case where, having determined that genocide had occurred in Srebrenica, the International Court of Justice (ICJ) decided that Serbia was not responsible for the perpetrators of that crime. Controversially, it rejected the standard for attributability of conduct to a state used by the ICTY, asserting that the relevant test may not always be the same between international criminal law and general international law.[97] However, given the state's relationship with the perpetrators, the ICJ determined that Serbia was separately responsible under Article I of the Genocide Convention for its own failures to prevent and punish that crime.[98] More recently, the Genocide Convention has triggered parallel proceedings with regard to the Rohingya in Myanmar[99] and the conflict in Ukraine.[100] In the Myanmar case, the ICJ and the ICC are dealing concurrently with the same set of events. The case at the ICJ filed by Ukraine against Russia is limited to the false claim of genocide used by Russia to justify its 2022 invasion of Ukraine, while the ICC's investigation covers a broader range of events.[101]

The question of whether state conduct can be categorized under international law as *criminal* acts is one which has caused controversy. The final version of the Draft Articles on State Responsibility of the International Law Commission (ILC) no longer uses the concept of state crime, but characterizes the relevant acts as 'serious breaches of obligations under peremptory norms of general international law'.[102]

---

[95] *Case concerning the Application of the Convention on the Prevention and Punishment of the Crime of Genocide (Bosnia and Herzegovina v. Serbia and Montenegro)* ('*Bosnian Genocide* case'), Judgment of 26 February 2007, ICJ, paras. 377–415. See generally Marko Milanović, 'State Responsibility for Genocide: A Follow-Up' (2007) 18 *EJIL* 669. For a critique see Paola Gaeta, 'On What Conditions Can a State be Held Responsible for Genocide?' (2007) 18 *EJIL* 631; Antonio Cassese, 'On the Use of Criminal Law Notions in Determining State Responsibility' (2007) 5 *JICJ* 875; Paola Gaeta, *The UN Genocide Convention: A Commentary* (Oxford, 2009) Part V.

[96] E.g. *Furundžija*, ICTY TC II, 10 December 1998, para. 142.

[97] *Bosnian Genocide* case (n. 95) para. 405. See e.g. Antonio Cassese, 'The *Nicaragua* and *Tadić* Tests Revisited in the Light of the ICJ Judgment on Genocide in Bosnia' (2007) 18 *EJIL* 649; Marina Spinedi, 'On the Non-Attribution of the Bosnian Serbs' Conduct to Serbia' (2007) 5 *JICJ* 829.

[98] *Bosnian Genocide* case (n. 95) paras. 425–50.

[99] This case marks the first time that a non-injured state – The Gambia – brought an action at the ICJ under the Genocide Convention. See *Application of Convention on the Prevention and Punishment of the Crime of Genocide (The Gambia v. Myanmar)*, Judgment of 22 July 2022 (Preliminary Objections, ICJ, where the Court decided it has jurisdiction on basis of Article IX of the Genocide Convention. *Situation in Bangladesh/ Myanmar*, ICC PTC III, 14 November 2019 (ICC-01/19).

[100] *Allegations of Genocide Under the Convention on the Prevention and Punishment of the Crime of Genocide (Ukraine v. Russian Federation)*, Application Instituting Proceedings, 26 February 2022. On 2 March 2022 the ICC opened an investigation. *Situation in Ukraine*, ICC Presidency, 2 March 2022 (ICC-01/22–1).

[101] It has the potential to go beyond, according to Iryna Marchuk and Aloka Wanigasurya, 'Beyond the False Claim of Genocide: Preliminary Reflections on Ukraine's Prospects in Its Pursuit of Justice at the ICJ' (2022) 24 *Journal of Genocide Research* 1, 12.

[102] Articles on Responsibility of States for Internationally Wrongful Acts, A/CN.4/L.602/Rev.1, Arts. 40 and 41. See James Crawford, *State Responsibility* (Cambridge, 2013) 390–4.

1.5 A BODY OF CRIMINAL LAW

The two bodies of law that make up international criminal law (international law and criminal law) are compatible, although the relationship between the two can be fractious. International criminal law should be appraised from the standpoints of both bodies of law. Its sources are those of international law, but its consequences are penal.[103] As a body of international law, it requires an understanding of the sources and interpretation of international law. But it is also criminal law, and as such needs substantive provisions that are clear and exact rather than the often more imprecise formulations of international law.[104] Further, the relevant international courts and tribunals require methods and procedures proper to a criminal court, with due regard to the rights of the accused at all stages of the investigation and proceedings. At a more abstract level, fundamental constraints on the ambit of criminal liability ought to be borne in mind whenever international crimes or their principles of liability are being appraised.[105]

Certain fundamental principles of national criminal law systems have now become entrenched in international law, and more particularly, in human rights law. As we have seen in Section 1.4.1, international criminal law has been influenced strongly by human rights law. One aspect of human rights law with a close analogue in criminal law theory is the prohibition of retroactive criminal prohibitions and penalties (sometimes referred to together as the principle of legality or *nullum crimen, nulla poena sine lege*).[106] This principle is important both in the application of the law and in the drafting of the instruments of the international courts and tribunals.

1.5.1 *Nullum Crimen Sine Lege*

This principle has two aspects: non-retroactivity and clarity of the law, both of which seek to ensure that the law is reasonably publicized, that is, accessible, so people can know whether their planned course of action is acceptable or not.[107] It is a fundamental principle of criminal law that criminal responsibility can only be based on a pre-existing prohibition of conduct that is understood to have criminal consequences.[108] Article 15 of the International Covenant on Civil and Political Rights (ICCPR) states that:

---

[103] See e.g. Cassese et al., *Cassese's International Criminal Law* (n. 30) 7–9. On the nature of criminal law, see Williams, 'The Definition of Crime' (n. 2).

[104] For a discussion of this, and a critique of the lack of attention paid by international criminal lawyers to this aspect of international criminal law, see George P. Fletcher, *The Grammar of Criminal Law: American, Comparative and International*, vol. I: *Foundations* (Oxford, 2007).

[105] For useful examples, see e.g. Mirjan Damaška, 'The Shadow Side of Command Responsibility' (2001) 49 *American Journal of Comparative Law* 455; Claus Kreß, 'The Crime of Genocide Under International Law' (2006) 6 *ICLR* 461. See further Section 1.6.2 and Kai Ambos, *Treatise on International Criminal Law, Vol. I: Foundations and General part* (Oxford, 2013) vol. I, 55. On the principle of fair labelling, which requires that conduct be accurately described in criminal convictions, see Hilmi M. Zawati, *Fair Labelling and the Dilemma of Prosecuting Gender-based Crimes at the International Criminal Tribunals* (Oxford, 2014).

[106] See generally A. P. Simester et al., *Simester and Sullivan's Criminal Law: Theory and Doctrine*, 6th ed. (Oxford, 2018) ch. 1.

[107] See generally Kenneth Gallant, *The Principle of Legality in International and Comparative Law* (Cambridge, 2009); Claus Kreß, 'Nulla Poena Nullum Crimen Sine Lege' in Rüdiger Wolfrum (ed.), *VII Max Planck Encyclopaedia of Public International Law* (Oxford, 2012) 889; Cassese et al., *Cassese's International Criminal Law* (n. 30) ch. 2.

[108] Talita de Souza Dias proposes to apply the foreseeability/accessibility test beyond crime definitions, looking also at mens rea, modes of liability, and defences: Talita de Souza Dias, *Beyond Imperfect Justice. Legality and Fair Labeling in International Criminal Law* (Leiden, 2022).

No one shall be held guilty on account of any act or omission which did not constitute a criminal offence, under national or international law, at the time when it was committed ... Nothing in this article shall prejudice the trial of any person for any act or omission which, at the time it was committed, was criminal according to the general principles of law recognised by the community of nations.[109]

Claims that prosecutions for international crimes violated this principle predate the ICCPR. The Nuremberg and Tokyo IMTs both faced claims that prosecution of crimes against peace involved violations of the *nullum crimen* principle. The Nuremberg IMT, with which the Tokyo IMT agreed, responded by asserting that crimes against peace were already criminalized in international law[110] and that, anyway:

The maxim *nullum crimen sine lege* is not a limitation of sovereignty, but is in general a principle of justice. To assert that it is unjust to punish those who in defiance of treaties and assurances have attacked neighbouring States without warning is obviously untrue, for in such circumstances the attacker must know that he is doing wrong, and so far from it being unjust to punish him, it would be unjust if his wrong was allowed to go unpunished.[111]

At the time, which was before the modern law of human rights, the Nuremberg IMT may have been correct about the law on point.[112] On the other hand, it is possible that the prohibition of retroactive criminal laws was a general principle of law by then,[113] and the *ex post facto* nature of liability for crimes against peace has been used to criticize the Nuremberg and Tokyo IMTs.[114]

Suggestions that customary international law does not suffice to found criminal liability[115] are based on a strict construction of the *nullum crimen* principle (*nullum crimen sine lege scripta*, or 'no crime without written law'), which, whilst applicable in some domestic legal orders, is not the principle applicable in international law.[116] There is no reason in principle why customary international law cannot be used to form the relevant criminal law,[117] and the ICTY has consistently taken this view.[118]

The general practice of the ICTY was to adopt a fairly relaxed standard of the *nullum crimen* principle.[119] However, looking at the aspect of the principle that requires criminal laws to be sufficiently clear, a Trial Chamber asserted in the *Vasiljević case* that:

[f]rom the perspective of the *nullum crimen sine lege* principle, it would be wholly unacceptable for a Trial Chamber to convict an accused person on the basis of a prohibition which, taking into account the specificity of customary international law and allowing for the gradual clarification of the rules of

---

[109] ICCPR, Art. 15. [110] See Section 13.1.2. [111] Nuremberg IMT Judgment (1947) 41 *AJIL* 172, 217.

[112] Although the versions of the Nuremberg judgment in different languages are not consistent on what precisely was meant here, see Guido Acquaviva, 'At the Origins of Crimes Against Humanity: Clues to a Proper Understanding of the *Nullum Crimen* Principle in the Nuremberg Judgment' (2011) 9 *JICJ* 881.

[113] See Gordon Ireland, 'Ex Post Facto From Rome to Tokyo' (1946) 21 *Temple Law Quarterly* 27; *contra* Susan Lamb, 'Nullum Crimen, Nulla Poena Sine Lege in International Criminal Law' in Cassese et al., *Commentary*, 740.

[114] See Sections 6.3.2 and 6.4.2.

[115] Djuro-Degan, 'On the Sources of International Criminal Law' (n. 50) 67; Olásolo, 'A Note' (n. 42) 301.

[116] Alain Pellet, 'Applicable Law' in Cassese et al., *Commentary*, 1057–8. [117] *Ibid.*

[118] See e.g. *Tadić*, ICTY AC, 2 October 1995, para. 94.

[119] William Schabas, *The UN International Criminal Tribunals: The Former Yugoslavia, Rwanda and Sierra Leone* (Cambridge, 2006) 63–7.

criminal law is either insufficiently precise to determine conduct and distinguish the criminal from the permissible, or was not sufficiently accessible at the relevant time. A criminal conviction should indeed never be based upon a norm which an accused could not reasonably have been aware of at the time of his acts, and this norm must make it sufficiently clear what act or omission could engage his criminal responsibility.[120]

Owing to their view that customary law did not provide a sufficiently clear definition of the offence of 'violence to life and person', the judges declined to convict the defendant of that charge.[121] It is true that excessively vague offences can violate the *nullum crimen* principle, but it is questionable whether the Tribunal was correct in this particular finding that the international law on the subject was excessively vague.[122] Clarification of the ambit of offences through case law does not inherently fall foul of the *nullum crimen* principle.[123] Judicial creation of crimes, which some have claimed the ICTY has done,[124] would. However, when addressing the question of international crimes and the *nullum crimen* principle, human rights courts have generally been generous when appraising states' prosecutions of international crimes.[125] For example, in the *Jorgić* case,[126] the European Court of Human Rights (ECtHR) was willing to accept convictions in Germany for genocide on a broader interpretation of that crime than was later adopted by the international criminal tribunals, on the basis that it was at least arguable at the time of the conviction that the German courts' interpretation was correct.

The *nullum crimen* principle played an important role in the drafting of the ICC Statute. The ILC draft Statute with which the negotiations began[127] did not contain definitions of the crimes within the jurisdiction of the ICC, the ILC maintaining that the Statute should be 'primarily an adjectival and procedural instrument'.[128] There was soon, however, a move to define the crimes in the Statute with the clarity and precision needed for criminal law and it was pursuant to that objective that the definitions of crimes and, later, the elements of crimes were set out. The wish of the negotiating states to ensure that they knew exactly what they were signing up to may have been at least as strong a motivating factor as the principle of *nullum crimen* in this regard.

The Statute itself contains a strong restatement of the *nullum crimen* principle. Article 22 reads in part:

1. A person shall not be criminally responsible under this Statute unless the conduct in question constitutes, at the time it takes place, a crime within the jurisdiction of the Court.

---

[120] *Vasiljević*, ICTY TC I, 29 November 2002, para. 193.   [121] *Ibid.* paras. 203–4.

[122] See Antonio Cassese, 'Black Letter Lawyering vs Constructive Interpretation: The Vasiljević Case' (2004) 2 *JICJ* 265.

[123] See Mohamed Shahabuddeen, 'Does the Principle of Legality Stand in the Way of Progressive Development of the Law?' (2004) 2 *JICJ* 1007; Ben Emmerson and Andrew Ashworth, *Human Rights and Criminal Justice* (London, 2001) 281–92.

[124] Mettraux, *International Crimes* (n. 37) 13–18. The line between clarification and creation can be a fine one, see Joseph Powderly, 'Distinguishing Creativity from Activism: International Criminal Law and the "Legitimacy" of Judicial Development of the Law' in Schabas et al., *Ashgate Research Companion*, 223.

[125] For a (legally flawed) exception, see *Habré* v. *Republique de Senegal*, ECOWAS Court of Justice, Judgment of 18 November 2010; for critique see Valentina Spiga, 'Non-Retroactivity of Criminal Law: A New Chapter in the Hissène Habré Saga' (2011) 9 *JICJ* 5.

[126] *Jorgić* v. *Germany*, ECtHR, Judgment of 12 July 2007, paras. 89–116.   [127] See Section 8.2.

[128] *Report of the International Law Commission on the work of its forty-sixth session, UNGAOR 49th Session*, Suppl. No. 10, A/ 49/10 (1994) 71.

2. The definition of a crime shall be strictly construed and shall not be extended by analogy. In the case of ambiguity, the definition shall be interpreted in favour of the person being investigated, prosecuted or convicted.[129]

The first sentence of the second paragraph was intended, rightly or wrongly, to prevent the ICC from engaging in expansions of criminal liability not mandated by the states parties.

In the case of Sudanese national Abd-Al-Rahman, originating from the situation referred to the ICC by the United Nations Security Council (UNSC), the question arose whether the *nullum crimen* principle encapsulated in Article 22 applies to nationals of non-state parties, with regard to offences that were (allegedly) committed before the referral to the ICC. The defence in this case asserted that Abd-Al-Rahman could only be prosecuted for crimes defined under Sudanese law, international law in force in Sudan, or customary international law.[130] None of these sources of law, they argued, defined the crimes stated in the warrants of arrest. The Pre-Trial Chamber found there was no violation of the principle of legality since the prohibited conduct was detailed in the Statute and in force at the time of the events underlying the charges.[131] The Appeals Chamber corrected this ruling, affirming that Article 22 is mainly for 'internal use':

'[i]n interpreting article 22(1) of the Statute in a manner consistent with human rights law, a chamber must look beyond the Statute to the criminal laws applicable to the suspect or accused at the time the conduct took place and satisfy itself that a reasonable person could have expected, at that moment in time, to find him or herself faced with the crimes charged.[132]

The Appeals Chamber eventually held that the conduct *was* foreseeable and that the ICC has jurisdiction.[133] A UNSC referral to the ICC is simply a conferral of powers on the ICC.[134] The customary law status of the ICC Statute is not a given; with regard to nationals of non-state parties it needs to be established separately.

1.5.2 *Nulla Poena Sine Lege*

This component of the legality principle requires that there are defined penalties attached to criminal prohibitions.[135] In customary international law, the punishment for international

---

[129] On which see Bruce Broomhall, 'Article 22' in Ambos, *Commentary*, 713.
[130] *Abd-Al-Rahman*, ICC Defence, 15 March 2021 (ICC-02/05–01/20–302) paras. 54–114.
[131] *Abd-Al-Rahman*, ICC PTC II, 17 May 2021 (ICC-02/05–01/20–391) para. 40. This (introspective) reading of Art. 22(1) expresses the strict legality aspiration of the Rome Statute's drafters; it ignores the reality that the Statute was not applicable law in Sudan at the relevant time.
[132] *Abd-Al-Rahman*, ICC AC, 1 November 2021 (ICC-02/05–01/20–503) para. 86. *Abd-Al-Rahman*, ICC PTC II, 17 May 2021 (ICC-02/05–01/20–391) paras. 86, 92.
[133] *Abd-Al-Rahman*, ICC AC, 1 November 2021 (ICC-02/05–01/20–503), paras. 88–9. See Alexandre Galand, 'The ICC Appeals Judgment on Abd-Al-Rahman Jurisdictional Challenge: A Foreseeable Turn to Substantive Justice?', *EJIL Talk!* (21 November 2021), www.ejiltalk.org/. Galand is critical of the reasoning of the Appeals Chamber that since the Statute was intended to be generally representative of customary international law, there was a presumption of foreseeability.
[134] See Gabriel Lentner, 'UN Security Council Referrals to the ICC and the Principle of Legality', *EJIL Talk!* (12 November 2021).
[135] See Chapter 19 and Kai Ambos, '*Nulla Poena Sine Lege* in International Criminal Law' in Roelof Haveman and Olaoluwa Olusanya (eds.), *Sentencing and Sanctioning in International Criminal Law* (Antwerp, 2006) 17.

crimes may include the death penalty,[136] although many states have undertaken international obligations not to impose such a penalty, or may not permit that sentence in their domestic law.

It appears that concerns about the *nulla poena* principle also caused the Secretary-General, when drafting the ICTY Statute, to require the Tribunal to 'have recourse to the general practice regarding prison sentences in the Courts of the former Yugoslavia'.[137] The ICTR Statute has a similar provision, but with reference to Rwandan sentencing practices.[138] The fact that both states provided for the death penalty at the time of the offences, but the Tribunals could not impose that sentence, made this difficult to apply. The Rome Statute also contains Article 23 entitled '*nulla poena sine lege*' which states, uncontroversially: 'A person convicted by the Court may be punished only in accordance with this Statute'.[139] More generally, the principle in human rights law is more relaxed than the strict interpretation adopted by many civil law states, which require that specific provisions on sentencing are provided for all offences.[140]

1.6 INTERNATIONAL CRIMINAL LAW AND LEGAL THEORY

As a testament to its maturity as a scholarly discipline, international criminal law is now an area of law that has become increasingly theorized.[141] Work has come from theoreticians of international law, criminal law, as well as philosophers more generally.[142] Express theorization of international criminal law began, for the most part, in the era of the Nuremberg IMT. Two of the intellectual architects of that Tribunal, Quincy Wright and Sir Hersch Lauterpacht, both relied, to a greater or lesser extent, on natural law to justify the innovations in law that the Nuremberg IMT's Statute and judgment embodied.[143] Critics of the Tribunal tended to focus on arguments based on legal positivism to query the judgment, or the more general idea that international law could deal with individuals.[144] These critics tended, however, not to make their jurisprudential leanings clear. In the Tokyo IMT, the prosecution, defence, and some of the judges relied expressly on philosophy, be it naturalistic or positivistic, in the formulation of their arguments and opinions, and the criticisms that each made of the other often fell upon these lines.[145] The practice of the more recent criminal tribunals can also be read through the lenses of disagreements along natural law and positivist approaches to international criminal law.[146]

---

[136] *Klinge* III in *Law Reports of Trials of War Criminals I* at 3. See Section 19.1.
[137] ICTY Statute, Art. 24; Lamb, '*Nullum Crimen*' (n. 113) 758–9. [138] ICTR Statute, Art. 23.
[139] See William Schabas, 'Article 23' in Ambos, *Commentary*. [140] Kreβ, '*Nullum Poena*' (n. 107) 898.
[141] For an overview, see Robert Cryer, 'The Philosophy of International Criminal Law' in Alexander Orakhelashvili (ed.), *Research Handbook on the History and Philosophy of International Law* (Cheltenham, 2012) 232. See also Larry May and Zachary Hoskins, *International Criminal Law and Philosophy* (Cambridge, 2010).
[142] It is beyond the remit of this work to explain the intellectual backdrops to the various theories of law. For a primer, see Brian Bix, *Jurisprudence: Theory and Context*, 6th ed. (London, 2012).
[143] Quincy Wright, 'Legal Positivism and the Nuremberg Judgment' (1948) 42 *AJIL* 405; Hersch Lauterpacht, 'The Law of Nations and the Punishment of War Crimes' (1944) 21 *BYBIL* 58. See also Robert Wright, 'War Crimes Under International Law' (1946) 62 *Law Quarterly Review* 40.
[144] Hans Ehard, 'The Nuremberg Trial Against the Major War Criminals and International Law' (1947) 41 *AJIL* 37.
[145] See Neil Boister and Robert Cryer, *The Tokyo International Military Tribunal: A Reappraisal* (Oxford, 2008) ch. 9.
[146] See Cryer, 'The Philosophy of International Criminal Law' (n. 141) 233–58 and Cryer, 'International Criminal Tribunals' (n. 51).

Since the revival of international criminal law as an important area of international law from the early 1990s, philosophers of law have contributed considerably to the debates that have arisen. The philosophical approaches to international criminal law can be broadly separated into three 'fuzzy sets'. There are those that come from theories of international law; those that come from criminal law; and those that specifically relate to creating a philosophy of international criminal law. Many scholars would bristle at being 'pigeon-holed' in such a manner, and there are considerable overlaps between the approaches covered here.

1.6.1 International Criminal Law and the International Legal Theory

International legal theorists have reflected upon international criminal law from various perspectives,[147] particularly from external perspectives, such as critical legal studies, feminism, and Third World Approaches to International Law (TWAIL). Critical scholars have queried the idea that there are clear rules of international criminal law, and investigated the extent to which the creation, application, and interpretation of international criminal law, in all its phases, reflects subjective premises, rather than coherent intellectual premises.[148] Others writing in this tradition have queried the extent to which international criminal law can balance its liberal ideals and the desire to engage in show trials.[149] Such critics tend not, however, to advocate for the abolition of international criminal law, but for self-reflection on the part of its participants, and a questioning of faith in its inherently 'progressive' nature.[150]

Turning to positions that relate to critical legal studies, feminist scholars have focused in particular on how sexual and gender-based crimes have not received sufficient attention or have been misunderstood,[151] and how male privilege remains entrenched in international criminal law.[152] Work on gender in international criminal law has recently been expanded and nuanced in an effort to enhance accountability.[153] Other work from a gender perspective has shown how stereotypes and myths about masculinity, sexual orientation, and gender identity have affected prosecution of sexual offences against men and the targeting

---

[147] The *American Journal of International Law* chose an issue of international criminal law (liability for war crimes in noninternational armed conflict) for their influential Symposium on Method in International Law: see (1999) 93 *AJIL* 291.

[148] See e.g. Gerry Simpson, 'War Crimes: A Critical Introduction' in Timothy L. H. McCormack and Gerry J. Simpson (eds.), *The Law of War Crimes: National and International Approaches* (The Hague, 1997) 1; Christine E. J. Schwöbel (ed.), *Critical Approaches to International Criminal Law: An Introduction* (Abingdon, 2014).

[149] Martti Koskenniemi, 'Between Impunity and Show Trials' (2002) 6 *Max Planck Yearbook of United Nations Law* 1.

[150] Tor Kraver, 'International Law: An Ideology Critique' (2013) 26 *LJIL* 701; Immi Tallgren, 'The Sensibility and Sense of International Criminal Law' (2002) 13 *EJIL* 561.

[151] Christine Chinkin, 'Rape and Sexual Abuse of Women in International Law' (1994) 4 *EJIL* 329; Kelly Dawn Askin, *War Crimes Against Women: Prosecution in International Tribunals* (The Hague, 1997); Patricia Viseur Sellers, '(Re)Considering Gender Jurisprudence' in Fionnuala Ní Aoláin et al. (eds.), *The Oxford Handbook of Gender and Conflict* (Oxford, 2018) 211; Valerie Oosterveld, 'Crimes of Sexual and Gender-Based Violence and the Legacy of the Tribunals' in Michael Scharf and Milena Sterio (eds.), *The Legacy of the Ad Hoc Tribunals in International Criminal Law* (Cambridge, 2019) 197.

[152] Angela Mudukuti, 'Gender Imbalance at the ICC', in Florian Jeßberger, Leonie Steinl, and Kalika Mehta (eds.), *International Criminal Law: A Counter-Hegemonic Project?* (Münster, 2023) 266–78.

[153] See Indira Rosenthal, Valerie Oosterveld, and Susana SáCouto (eds.), *Gender and International Criminal Law* (Oxford, 2022); Rosemary Grey, *Prosecuting Sexual and Gender-Based Crimes at the International Criminal Court: Practice, Progress and Potential* (Cambridge, 2019).

of LGBTQI+ individuals.[154] TWAIL, as an approach to international criminal law, has something of a pedigree, being traceable at least as far back as Judge Pal's famous dissent in the Tokyo IMT.[155] Work based in TWAIL has spoken of the hegemonic nature of international criminal law and its sources.[156] Much scholarly work has gone into uncovering economic, political, and cultural biases and in plotting an inclusive way forward.[157] Critiques of the ICC and its practice in Africa have come from TWAIL perspectives,[158] although scholars have also drawn from other approaches to question international criminal law's sensitivity to local cultures and ideas,[159] and to situate, and critique, international criminal law in a pluralistic world.[160]

Looking towards interdisciplinary work, international relations scholars, particularly those working in the constructivist tradition, have focused on the nature and functioning of international criminal courts and tribunals, and their place in the international order.[161] Others have looked at the question from the 'Grotian' or English School of international relations theory, which considers the interplay of realism and idealism in the international order,[162] the former tending to be more sceptical of international criminal law than the latter. Scholars working in the law and economics tradition have looked at the incentives that exist to obey or disobey international criminal law, to look at such issues as whether international criminal law can deter,[163] and, controversially, what the substance of international criminal law ought to be.[164]

1.6.2 International Criminal Law and the Theory of Criminal Law

Much work has been based around explaining, justifying, and critiquing international criminal law from the point of view of perspectives that draw on liberal approaches to criminal law. For example, Larry May has sought to show how genocide and crimes against humanity are legitimately criminalized at the international level owing to an international 'harm

---

[154] Sandesh Sivakumaran, 'Sexual Violence Against Men in Armed Conflict' (2007) 18 *EJIL* 253; Sandesh Sivakumaran, 'Lost in Translation: UN Responses to Sexual Violence Against Men and Boys in Armed Conflict' (2010) 92 *International Review of the Red Cross* 259; Nicholas Leddy, 'Investigative and Charging Considerations for International Crimes Targeting Individuals on the Basis of Sexual Orientation and Gender Identity' (2022) 20 *JICJ* 911.

[155] See Chapter 6. On Justice Pal, and his links to post-colonial thought, see Barry Hill, *Peacemongers* (Queensland, 2014) ch. 6.

[156] Anthony Anghie and B. S. Chimni, 'Third World Approaches to International Law and Responsibility for Atrocities in International Armed Conflict' (2003) 2 *Chinese Journal of International Law* 77. See generally 'Symposium: Third World Approaches to International Criminal Law' (2016) 14 *JICJ* 915.

[157] See Florian Jeßberger, Leonie Steinl, and Kalika Mehta (eds.), *International Criminal Law: A Counter-Hegemonic Project?* (Münster 2023); Julie Fraser and Brianne McGonigle (eds.), *On the Intersections of Culture at the International Criminal Court* (Cheltenham, 2020).

[158] Kamari Maxine Clarke, *Fictions of Justice: The International Criminal Court and the Challenge of Legal Pluralism in Sub-Saharan Africa* (Cambridge, 2009).

[159] José E. Alvarez, 'Crimes of States/Crimes of Hate: Lessons from Rwanda' (1999) 24 *Yale Journal of International Law* 365.

[160] Brad R. Roth, 'Coming to Terms with Ruthlessness: Sovereign Equality, Global Pluralism and the Limits of International Criminal Law' (2010) 8 *Santa Clara Journal of International Law* 231.

[161] Stephen C. Roach (ed.), *Governance, Order and the International Criminal Court: Between Realpolitik and a Cosmopolitan Court* (Oxford, 2009).

[162] An excellent example is Jason Ralph, *Defending the Society of States: Why America Opposes the International Criminal Court and its Vision of World Society* (Oxford, 2009).

[163] Julian Ku and Jide Nzelibe, 'Do International Criminal Tribunals Deter or Exacerbate Humanitarian Atrocities' (2006) 84 *Washington University Law Review* 777.

[164] Mark Osiel, *Making Sense of Mass Atrocity* (Cambridge, 2009) 10–15, 214–20.

principle', which would be familiar to those working on criminalization at the domestic level.[165] Others have sought to use analogous principles, such as 'fair labelling' which requires crimes to appropriately reflect the specific harms and wrongs that it proscribes.[166] There have also been critiques on the basis that international criminal law does not respect the principle of individual culpability, which again draw from the theory of criminal law.[167]

Theorists of criminal law influenced by civil law approaches to the theory of criminal law, in particular the *Dogmatik* approaches associated with German influenced systems of criminal law, have also contributed considerably to the theory of international criminal law.[168] Such approaches seek to provide taxonomical clarity for parts of criminal law, and deduce substantive results, and critique, from the application of fundamental principles of criminal law.[169] These approaches can be exceptionally sophisticated, and have been influential in international criminal law. However, they can also be unreflexive in their method, insisting on theoretical purity over practical utility. In addition, as with all approaches 'read up' from national systems to the international sphere, there is a risk of applying ideas acontextually, even where, as has been the case, at the domestic level such theories have been developed with international crimes in mind.[170] As such, there have been calls for international criminal law to develop its own *Dogmatik*.[171]

1.6.3 A Separate (?) Theory of International Criminal Law

Owing to the criticisms about the utility and limitations of transferring domestic criminal law theories to international criminal law, and the converse problem of applying international law theories to a penal system, there have been calls for international criminal law to develop its own theories.[172] These, it is said, ought to reflect the collective nature of international crimes, which do not map on easily to theories of criminal law developed domestically.[173] Such suggestions can overstate the differences, and approaches developed

---

[165] Larry May, *Crimes Against Humanity: A Normative Account* (Cambridge, 2005) ch. 5; Larry May, *Genocide: A Normative Account* (Cambridge, 2010) chs. 4–5. See also Larry May, *War Crimes and Just War* (Cambridge, 2007); Larry May, *Aggression and Crimes Against Peace* (Cambridge, 2008).
[166] See e.g. Robert Cryer, 'General Principles of Liability in International Criminal Law' in McGoldrick et al., *The Permanent ICC*, 233. Ashworth was the first to coin 'fair labelling' as a principle: Andrew Ashworth, 'The Elasticity of *Mens Rea*' in Colin Tapper (ed.), *Crime, Proof, and Punishment: Essays in Memory of Sir Rupert Cross* (London, 1981) and developed it in later work: Andrew Ashworth, *Principles of Criminal Law*, 6th ed. (Oxford, 2009) 78. Because of the expressivist function of international trials, 'fair labelling' has become an important principle in international criminal law (see further Chapter 2).
[167] Allison Danner and Jenny Martinez, 'Guilty Associations: Joint Criminal Enterprise, Command Responsibility, and the Development of International Criminal Law' (2005) 93 *California Law Review* 75; Darryl Robinson, 'How Command Responsibility Got So Complicated: A Culpability Contradiction, its Obfuscation and a Simple Solution' (2012) 13 *Melbourne Journal of International Law* 1.
[168] In this context, the term does not have the pejorative implication it may have in the English-speaking world. Roughly speaking, it means a systematic and coherent theory. See George P. Fletcher, 'The Theory of Criminal Liability and International Criminal Law' (2012) 10 *JICJ* 1029.
[169] For a recent example, see Ambos, *Treatise on International Criminal Law* (n. 105).
[170] Claus Roxin, 'Crimes as a Part of an Organized Power Structure' (2011) 9 *JICJ* 19; Thomas Weigend, 'Perpetration Through an Organization: The Unexpected Career of a German Legal Concept' (2011) 9 *JICJ* 91.
[171] Fletcher, 'The Theory of Criminal Law' (n. 168).
[172] See e.g. *ibid.*; Darryl Robinson, *Justice in Extreme Cases: International Criminal Law Meets Criminal Law Theory* (Cambridge, 2020).
[173] See e.g. Mark Drumbl, 'A Hard Look at the Soft Theory of International Criminal Law' in Leila N. Sadat and Michael P. Scharf (eds.), *The Theory and Practice of International Criminal Law, Essays in Honor of M. Cherif Bassiouni* (Leiden, 2010) 1.

at the domestic level have the advantage of centuries of thought, which can, with sensitivity to context, inform the theory and practice of international criminal law.[174] Beyond that, however, significant work at the philosophical level on explaining why the international crimes that exist ought to be criminalized at that level, rather than simply domestically, has been undertaken.[175] Furthermore, similar work has been done to explain and justify why, and when, international courts, or the courts of states that are not directly affected third parties, have a right to punish such offences, and how this relates to the authority of a community beyond the state to define and punish crimes.[176]

Such considerations frequently implicate questions of the aims and objectives of international criminal justice, which the next chapter will discuss. This is indicative of a more general issue. Although theory in international criminal law has, in the past, tended to follow from practice, it now informs it. It would not be possible to elaborate all of the issues that arise in the abstract, but we have sought to integrate some of them throughout this book. This also underlines the fact that law, legal theory, and practice exist in a synergistic fashion in modern international criminal law. Therefore, theoretical approaches ought to be seen as part and parcel of international criminal law rather than a distraction from its study.

Further Reading

Dapo Akande, 'Sources of International Criminal Law' in Antonio Cassese et al. (eds.), *The Oxford Companion to International Criminal Justice* (Oxford, 2009) 41

Kai Ambos, *Treatise on International Criminal Law*, vol. I: *Foundations and General Part* (Oxford, 2013) ch. II

M. Cherif Bassiouni (ed.), *International Criminal Law*, 3rd ed. (Leiden, 2008) vol. I

Machteld Boot, *Genocide, Crimes Against Humanity, War Crimes: Nullum Crimen Sine Lege and the Subject Matter Jurisdiction of the International Criminal Court* (Antwerp, 2002) 127–87

Bruce Broomhall, *International Justice and the International Criminal Court: Between State Sovereignty and the Rule of Law* (Oxford, 2003) ch. 1

Antonio Cassese, 'The Influence of the European Court of Human Rights on International Criminal Tribunals: Some Methodological Remarks' in Morten Bergsmo (ed.), *Human Rights and Criminal Justice for the Downtrodden* (The Hague, 2003) ch. II

Robert Cryer, 'The Philosophy of International Criminal Law' in Alexander Orakhelashvili (ed.), *Research Handbook on the History and Philosophy of International Law* (Cheltenham, 2012) 232

Vladimir Djuro-Degan, 'On the Sources of International Criminal Law' (2005) 4 *Chinese Journal of International Law* 45

---

[174] See e.g. David Luban, 'The Legacies of Nuremberg' (1987) 54 *Social Research* 779.
[175] See e.g. Ambos, *Treatise on International Criminal Law* (n. 105) 57–60.
[176] Florian Jeßberger and Julia Geneuss (eds.), *Why Punish Perpetrators of Mass Atrocities? Purposes of Punishment in International Criminal Law* (Cambridge, 2020); Alejandro Chehtman, *The Philosophical Foundations of Extraterritorial Punishment* (Oxford, 2010); Antony Duff, 'Can We Punish the Perpetrators of Atrocities' in Thomas Brudghom and Thomas Cushman (eds.), *The Religious in Reponses to Mass Atrocity* (Cambridge, 2009) 79.

George P. Fletcher, *The Grammar of Criminal Law: American, Comparative and International*, vol. I, *Foundations* (Oxford, 2007)

Kenneth Gallant, *The Principle of Legality in International and Comparative Law* (Cambridge, 2009)

Leena Grover, *Interpreting Crimes in the Rome Statute of the International Criminal Court* (Cambridge, 2014)

Kevin Jon Heller, 'What is an International Crime? A Revisionist History' (2017) 58 *Harvard International Law Journal* 353

Florian Jeßberger and Julia Geneuss (eds.), *Why Punish Perpetrators of Mass Atrocities? Purposes of Punishment in International Criminal Law* (Cambridge, 2020)

Florian Jeßberger, Leonie Steinl, and Kalika Mehta (eds.), *International Criminal Law: A Counter-Hegemonic Project?* (Münster, 2023)

Nina H. B. Jørgensen, *The Responsibility of States for International Crimes* (Oxford, 2000)

Claus Kreß, 'International Criminal Law' in Rüdiger Wolfrum (ed.), *V Max Planck Encyclopaedia of Public International Law* (Oxford, 2012) 717

Timothy L. H. McCormack, 'From Sun Tzu to the Sixth Committee, the Evolution of an International Criminal Law Regime' in Timothy L. H. McCormack and Gerry J. Simpson (eds.), *The Law of War Crimes: National and International Approaches* (The Hague, 1997) 31

Alain Pellet, 'Applicable Law' in Antonio Cassese, Paola Gaeta and John R. W. D. Jones (eds.), *The Rome Statute: A Commentary* (Oxford, 2002) 1051

Darryl Robinson, *Justice in Extreme Cases: International Criminal Law Meets Criminal Law Theory* (Cambridge, 2020)

Indira Rosenthal, Valerie Oosterveld, and Susana SáCouto (eds.), *Gender and International Criminal Law* (Oxford, 2022)

Alfred P. Rubin, *Ethics and Authority in International Law* (Cambridge, 1997)

Helmut Satzger, *International and European Criminal Law*, 2nd ed. (Oxford, 2018)

Christine Schwöbel (ed.), *Critical Approaches to International Criminal Law: An Introduction* (Abingdon, 2014)

Georg Schwarzenberger, 'The Problem of an International Criminal Law' (1950) 3 *Current Legal Problems* 26

2

The Aims, Objectives, and Justifications
of International Criminal Law

2.1 INTRODUCTION

The assertion of criminal jurisdiction over a person is amongst the most coercive activities any society can undertake. Punishing a person involves depriving them of their liberty or another deliberate setting-back of their interests.[1] Such deprivations require justification.[2] Arguably, criminal law is not, in itself, a good or a bad thing; it is a tool, to be employed to achieve certain goals. Some of those goals may be better pursued by means other than prosecutions.

This chapter introduces some of the justifications for punishment and the purposes it seeks to achieve.[3] It will also consider the wider goals which are claimed for international criminal law, alongside some of the challenges to international criminal law that have arisen. It should be noted at the outset, though, that different aspects of international criminal law enforcement may have different aims and objectives.[4] For example, the broad purpose of international criminal procedure may be to ensure the rule of law and fair trials,[5] whereas the actual implementation of sentences may rely more on rehabilitative ideals than the general justifications of international criminal justice.[6] Here, we are looking at those general aims and justifications.

On a preliminary point, it has been suggested by some that the justifications for punishment may differ, or at least be differently interpreted, between international and domestic criminal law.[7] It is true that the general situations in which international criminal law is invoked are those of mass criminality, which are not the norm in domestic criminal law.[8] In

---

[1] Indeed, in certain cases, unlawful imprisonment is, itself, an international crime. See e.g. ICC Statute, Arts. 7(1)(e) and 8(2)(a)(vii).
[2] See generally Lucia Zedner, *Criminal Justice* (Oxford, 2004) 84–111.
[3] For more general surveys of the justification of punishment, see e.g. David Garland and Anthony Duff, *A Reader on Punishment* (Oxford, 1994); David Garland, *Punishment and Modern Society* (Oxford, 1990).
[4] Jens David Ohlin, 'Goals of International Criminal Justice and International Criminal Procedure' in Sluiter et al., *International Criminal Procedure*, 55.
[5] Jens David Ohlin, 'A Meta-Theory of International Criminal Procedure: Vindicating the Rule of Law' (2009) 14 *UCLA Journal of International Law and Foreign Affairs* 77.
[6] Róisín Mulgrew, *Towards the Development of the International Penal System* (Cambridge, 2013) 207–9. See also Chapter 19.
[7] Elies van Sliedregt, 'Punishment and the Domestic Analogy: Why it Can and Cannot Work' in Florian Jeßberger and Julia Geneuss (eds.), *Why Punish Perpetrators of Mass Atrocities? Purposes of Punishment in International Criminal Law* (Cambridge, 2020), 81–102.
[8] Although not all instances where international criminal law is relevant occur against this background: isolated, or relatively isolated, war crimes remain international crimes.

addition, certain additional aims for international criminal law tend to be grafted onto those which are suggested for domestic systems of criminal law. These include the telling of the history of a conflict, distinguishing individual from group responsibility, reconciling societies, and capacity-building in domestic judicial systems.[9] It is true that international society is not the same as domestic society. Nonetheless, much of the implementation of international criminal law is intended to be at the domestic level; therefore it is questionable whether the objectives of punishment ought to differ significantly between international and municipal criminal law.[10]

It has been suggested that the justifications for punishment at the international level are inconsistent, and at times incoherent.[11] Even if this were the case (and it may well be), it would not necessarily undermine international criminal law. It is true, however, that high expectations have been set for what international criminal law can do. This may lead to 'disenchantment and depression ... when these goals are not being met'.[12]

It must also be remembered, at the outset, that the turn to criminal justice has not occurred in a vacuum. It has occurred in part as a response to dissatisfaction with the other methods of dealing with international criminals, which were either extra-judicial executions, or de facto impunity. The first of these is clearly unlawful now.[13] The second, which was said by Robert Jackson to 'mock the dead and make cynics of the living',[14] is one which is rarely lawful.[15]

2.2 WHAT INTERNATIONAL CRIMINAL JUSTICE IS FOR

Broadly speaking, there are two approaches to justifying punishment: forward-looking (teleological, or consequentialist), which focus on the consequences of punishment; and backward-looking (deontological), which focus on the crime itself.[16] In practice, most criminal justice systems tend to be defended on the basis of a mixture of the two.[17] There are a number of different aims that have been postulated for punishment in international criminal justice. The primary place in which the international courts and tribunals have discussed their aims of punishment is in relation to their imposition of sentences.[18]

---

[9] Antonio Cassese, 'Reflections on International Criminal Justice' (1998) 61 *Modern Law Review* 1, 6–7.

[10] See Robert Sloane, 'The Expressive Capacity of International Punishment: The Limits of the National Law Analogy and the Potential of International Criminal Law' (2007) 42 *Stanford Journal of International Law* 39.

[11] See e.g. Immi Tallgren, 'The Sense and Sensibility of International Criminal Law' (2002) 13 *EJIL* 561; Mirjan Damaška, 'What Is the Point of International Criminal Justice' (2008) 83 *Chicago–Kent Law Review* 329, 331–5 but see Paul Roberts and Nesam McMillan, 'For Criminology in International Criminal Justice' (2003) 1 *JICJ* 315. See also Patrick Keenan, 'The Problem of Purpose in International Criminal Law' (2016) 37 *Michigan Journal of International Law* 421.

[12] Iain Cameron, 'Individual Responsibility under National and International Law for the Conduct of Armed Conflict' in Ola Engdahl and Pål Wrange (eds.), *Law at War: The Law as It Was and the Law as It Should Be: Liber Amicorum Ove Bring* (Leiden, 2008) 58; Damaška, 'What Is the Point' (n. 11).

[13] Additional Protocol I, Art. 75, which represents customary international law. See *Hamdan* v. *Rumsfeld*, 126 S Ct 2749, 2997 (2006); Geneva Conventions 1949, Common Art. 3; International Covenant on Civil and Political Rights (ICCPR), Art. 6; *Suarez de Guerrero* v. *Colombia* (Human Rights Committee 45/79); European Convention on Human Rights (ECHR), Art. 2.

[14] Robert Jackson, 'Report to the President' (1945) 39 *AJIL* 178, 182. [15] See Section 4.3.

[16] For a useful introduction at the domestic level, see Stanley Cohen, 'An Introduction to the Theory, Justifications and Modern Manifestations of Criminal Punishment' (1981–2) 27 *McGill Law Journal* 73.

[17] Regarding this as acceptable: see Herbert L. A. Hart, *Punishment and Responsibility* (Oxford, 1968) ch. 1.

[18] See William Schabas, *The UN International Criminal Tribunals: The Former Yugoslavia, Rwanda and Sierra Leone* (Cambridge, 2006) 554–61. For the ICC: e.g. *Lubanga*, ICC TC, 10 July 2012 (ICC-01/04–01/06–2901) para. 16

The two main aims that they have asserted for their practice are retribution and deterrence.[19] The courts and tribunals have also at times asserted the relevance of rehabilitation of offenders.[20] It is fair to say that the precise relationship between the aims they set out and the specific sentences given is unclear at best.[21]

2.2.1 Retribution

Retributive theories have a long history in criminal law, and are often associated with the philosophy of Immanuel Kant.[22] Retributive approaches focus on the necessity of punishing those who have violated societal norms, on the basis that the offenders deserve punishment for what they have done, irrespective of the possible future benefits of prosecution. Retribution has been considered by some to be particularly important in international criminal law, as other rationales for punishment asserted at the domestic level are less relevant at the international level.[23] Others, though, take the view that the nature of international crimes, in particular their complex character and the diverse intuitions held by stakeholders in international criminal justice, render retributive justifications less convincing.[24] To a pure retributivist though, the consequential utility of prosecutions is irrelevant, since the justification for punishment is deontological, that is, based on ethical considerations. Modern retributive theorists are careful to distinguish their position from that of simple vengeance. It is clear that the international criminal tribunals, when dealing with retributive justifications for punishment, have tried to avoid conflating retributive justifications of punishment with *lex talionis* ('an eye for an eye'). For example, the International Criminal Court (ICC) has asserted, like many International Criminal Tribunal for the former Yugoslavia (ICTY) Chambers before it, that retribution is one of its core aims, alongside deterrence.[25] However:

[w]ith regard to retribution … it is not to be understood as fulfilling a desire for revenge, but as an expression of the international community's condemnation of the crimes, which, by way of

---

(referring to the retributive and deterrent functions identified in the Preamble to the Rome Statute). For further analysis Sections 19.2 and 19.3.

[19] See e.g. *Al Mahdi*, ICC TC VIII, 27 September 2016 (ICC-01/12–01/15–171) para. 66; *Katanga*, ICC TC II, 23 May 2014 (ICC-01/04–01/07–3484) paras. 37–8. *Bemba*, ICC TC III, 21 June 2016 (ICC-01/05–01/08–3399); *Aleksovski*, ICTY AC, 24 March 2000, para. 185.

[20] *Momir Nikolić*, ICTY TC I, 2 December 2003, para. 85.

[21] Silvia D'Ascoli, 'Reconciliation and Sentencing in the Practice of the Ad Hoc Tribunals' in Schabas et al., *Ashgate Research Companion*, 307, 311–14. Vasiliev observes there is no real engagement with punishment objectives in the act of punishment (he calls it 'deliberate performativity'): Sergey Vasiliev, 'Punishment Rationales in International Criminal Jurisprudence: Two Readings of a Non-question' in Florian Jeßberger and Julia Geneuss (eds.), *Why Punish Perpetrators of Mass Atrocities? Purposes of Punishment in International Criminal Law* (Cambridge, 2020) 45–80.

[22] See generally R. A. Duff and David Garland, 'Thinking About Punishment' in R. A. Duff and David Garland (eds.), *A Reader on Punishment* (Oxford, 1994) 1, 2–3.

[23] Jens David Ohlin, 'Towards a Unique Theory of International Criminal Sentencing' in Sluiter and Vasiliev, *International Criminal Procedure*, 373. See also Mordechai Kremnitzer, 'An Argument for Retributivism in International Criminal Law' in Florian Jeßberger and Julia Geneuss (eds.), *Why Punish Perpetrators of Mass Atrocities? Purposes of Punishment in International Criminal Law* (Cambridge, 2020) 161–76.

[24] Andrew K. Woods, 'Moral Judgments and International Crimes: The Disutility of Desert' (2012) 52 *Virginia Journal of International Law* 632.

[25] *Al Mahdi*, ICC TC VIII, 27 September 2016 (ICC-01/12–01/15–171) para. 66.

imposition of a proportionate sentence, also acknowledges the harm to the victims and promotes the restoration of peace and reconciliation.[26]

The ICTY has said similar things.[27] In a passage that appears to place a heavy emphasis on retribution, the ICTY stated that:

In light of the purposes of the Tribunal and international humanitarian law generally, retribution is better understood as the expression of condemnation and outrage of the international community at such grave violations of, and disregard for, fundamental human rights at a time that people may be at their most vulnerable, namely during armed conflict. It is also recognition of the harm and suffering caused to the victims. Furthermore, within the context of international criminal justice, retribution is understood as a clear statement by the international community that crimes will be punished and impunity will not prevail.[28]

One positive aspect of retributivism was pointed out by the Trial Chamber in the *Todorović* case:

It must be understood as reflecting a fair and balanced approach to the exaction of punishment for wrongdoing. This means that the penalty imposed must be proportionate to the wrongdoing, in other words, that the punishment be made to fit the crime.[29]

One difficulty with this is that it is questionable whether punishments for international crimes can be proportionate to what can be enormous levels of wrongdoing and culpability.[30] A strong counter-argument to such assertions is given by Mark Osiel, arguing that there is a sense in which this argument is true, but trivial, 'after all, many ordinary offenders commit multiple offences for which they cannot "repay" ... in fitting measure, within their remaining lifespan'.[31]

More specifically, though, a distinction between *cardinal* and *ordinal* proportionality ought to be recognized.[32] Cardinal proportionality sets out the basic level of severity of response, such as minimum and maximum punishments that a system can give for any crimes. Ordinal proportionality sets where a crime sits on the level of severity within that system. It may simply be that international criminal law and domestic criminal law have different cardinal points, and retributive theory is as much about ordinal as cardinal proportionality, which differs between states as well as between such systems and international criminal tribunals. That is not to say that it cannot throw up oddities, particularly between national jurisdictions and between national and international courts, but again that problem is not one which is unique to international criminal law. Different states, who may have concurrent jurisdiction over criminal offences, generally have different sentencing practices.

---

[26] *Ibid.* para. 67.   [27] *Aleksovski*, ICTY AC, 24 March 2000, para. 185.
[28] *Momir Nikolić*, ICTY TC I, 2 December 2003, paras. 86–7.
[29] *Todorović*, ICTY TC I, 31 July 2001, para. 29. See also *Plavšić*, ICTY TC III, 27 February 2003, para. 23.
[30] Frederik Harhoff, 'Sense and Sensibility in Sentencing: Taking Stock of International Criminal Punishment' in Ola Engdahl and Pål Wrange (eds.), *Law at War: The Law as It Was and the Law as It Should Be, Liber Amicorum Ove Bring* (Leiden, 2008) 125.
[31] Mark Osiel, 'Why Prosecute? Critics of Punishment for Mass Atrocity' (2000) 22 *Human Rights Quarterly* 118, 129.
[32] Andrew von Hirsch, 'Proportionality in the Philosophy of Punishment' (1992) 21 *Crime and Justice* 55, 57.

Still, there are problems with a purely retributive approach. Some claim that it is important, for example, to move beyond a culture of blame.[33] Critics of retributivism may also argue that, as it appears to demand punishment without regard to cost, it sets impossibly high standards, particularly in relation to disadvantaged societies, and requires punishment even where it is pointless. There may be merit in this position, although a Kantian could respond that it misses the point; the important question is not what is practicable, but what is morally necessary. There is a risk of moral absolutism and insensitivity to context in such a position.

2.2.2 Deterrence

Deterrence is perhaps the best known of the justifications of punishment. Such theories were championed in particular by utilitarian political theorists such as Jeremy Bentham, who, in contrast to retributivists, focus on the future-related benefits of prosecution. Punishment is imposed to prevent both the offender and the population more generally from engaging in prohibited conduct. Equally, there are risks involved in using deterrence as a rationale for punishment. The first is that there is nothing inherent in utilitarianism that prevents exceedingly heavy punishment, and indeed punishment of the innocent, to achieve its goals. There are two other critiques of deterrence-based theories in international criminal law. The first is a philosophical one. Deterrence theories can be seen to treat people as merely a means to an end (sending a general deterrent message), which fails to recognize individuals' moral worth as human beings. The second is that deterrence-based approaches treat people as rational calculators, who carefully weigh up the costs and benefits of their actions, and this does not reflect the reality of the type of decision-making that often precedes decisions to commit crimes.[34] Klabbers is critical of deterrence as a justification of punishment in international criminal law. Fighting for a 'higher good', or bigotry, is more likely to be the determinative factor in the minds of those who commit international crimes.[35] This may be true in some situations, but the point probably underestimates the calculating nature of many high-ranking leaders.[36]

Whatever their merits, such critiques have not stopped international tribunals from accepting general and specific deterrence as a justification for punishment, within limits.[37] For example, in the *Tadić* sentencing appeal, the Appeals Chamber, when referring to deterrence, said that 'it is a consideration that may legitimately be considered in sentencing . . . Equally, the Appeals Chamber accepts that this factor must not be accorded

---

[33] See e.g. Desmond Tutu, *No Future Without Forgiveness* (London, 1999).

[34] David Wippman, 'Atrocities, Deterrence and the Limits of International Justice' (1999) *Fordham International Law Journal* 473; Mark Drumbl, 'Collective Violence and Individual Punishment' (2005) 99 *Northwestern University Law Review* 539, 590–1.

[35] E.g. Jan Klabbers, 'Just Revenge? The Deterrence Argument in International Criminal Law' (2001) 12 *Finnish Yearbook of International Law* 249.

[36] Stephen Roach, 'Justice of the Peace? Future Challenges and Prospects for a Cosmopolitan Court' in Stephen Roach (ed.), *Governance, Order and the International Criminal Court* (Oxford, 2009) 225, 226–9; Jakob von Holderstein Holtermann, 'A Slice of Cheese: A Deterrence Argument in Favour of the International Criminal Court' (2010) 11 *Human Rights Review* 289, 306.

[37] E.g. *Al Mahdi*, ICC TC VIII, 27 September 2016 (ICC-01/12–01/15–171) para. 67.

undue prominence in the overall assessment of the sentences to be imposed on persons convicted by the International Tribunal'.[38]

Furthermore, the Appeals Chamber in the *Nikolić* case attempted to deal with some of the critiques of unmodified deterrence theories, asserting that:

> During times of armed conflict, all persons must now be more aware of the obligations upon them in relation to fellow combatants and protected persons, particularly civilians. Thus, it is hoped that the Tribunal and other international courts are bringing about the development of a culture of *respect* for the rule of law and not simply the *fear* of the consequences of breaking the law, and thereby deterring the commission of crimes. One may ask whether the individuals who are called before this Tribunal as accused are simply an instrument to achieving the goal of the establishment of the rule of law. The answer is no. Indeed, the Appeals Chamber has held that deterrence should not be given undue prominence in the overall assessment of a sentence.[39]

Although the reasoning it contains is not a complete answer to the critiques above, as this quote implies, more sophisticated deterrence-based theories work on a more subtle level than some of their critics acknowledge. Deterrence does not necessarily work at the level of rational calculation, but at a preliminary stage, where people are (consciously or otherwise) reviewing available options. Where people simply think that certain options are not open to them, they do not enter the second calculation of their costs and benefits. This is linked to the expressivist and didactic function of punishment, which will be discussed in Section 2.2.5.[40]

Like many criminal theorists, the ICC Statute accepts that there is some role for deterrence in international criminal law.[41] Preambular paragraph 5 of the ICC Statute asserts that the parties are '[d]etermined to put an end to impunity for the perpetrators of these crimes and thus to contribute to the prevention of such crimes'.[42]

Some scholars claim that prosecutions of international crimes can be seen to have a fairly direct deterrent function,[43] although others doubt their methodology.[44] It ought to be noted that there is a significant body of sceptical opinion about deterrence in international criminal law.[45] That said, there is an increasing amount of evidence of deterrence operating in relation to the international criminal tribunals and the ICC. The mere possibility of an

---

[38] *Tadić*, ICTY AC, 26 January 2000, para. 48. The ICC has been less willing to state such limits, see *Al Mahdi*, TC VIII, 27 September 2016 (ICC-01/12–01/15–171) para. 67.

[39] *Momir Nikolić*, ICTY TC I, 2 December 2003, paras. 89–90.

[40] See also Mark Drumbl, *Atrocity, Punishment and International Law* (Cambridge, 2007) 174.

[41] See also, more generally, Payam Akhavan, 'Can International Criminal Justice Prevent Future Atrocities?' (2001) 85 *AJIL* 7; Robert Cryer, 'The Role of Criminal Prosecutions in Increasing Compliance with International Humanitarian Law in Contemporary African Conflicts' in Heike Krieger (ed.), *Inducing Compliance with International Humanitarian Law: Lessons from the African Great Lakes Region* (Cambridge, 2015) 188, 209–14.

[42] See generally Héctor Olásolo, *The Role of the International Criminal Court in Preventing Atrocity through Timely Intervention* (The Hague, 2011).

[43] Hunjoon Kim and Katherine Sikkink, 'Explaining the Deterrence Effect of Human Rights Prosecutions for Transitional Countries' (2010) 54 *International Studies Quarterly* 939.

[44] Pádraig McAuliffe, 'Suspended Disbelief? The Curious Endurance of the Deterrence Rationale in International Criminal Law' (2012) 10 *New Zealand Journal of Public and International Law* 227, 230, 254–6, 260–1.

[45] For a symposium on deterrence and the ICC, see Shai Dotan, 'Who Is Afraid of the International Criminal Court? Deterrence in International Criminal Justice. Foreword?' (2021) 19 *JICJ* 855 with excellent contributions, pro and contra deterrence. For a criminological view, see Braithwaite who argues that when combined with other justice mechanisms – truth commissions, indigenous justice – the ICC can have deterrent effect: John Braithwaite, 'Many Doors to International Criminal Justice' (2020) 23 *New Criminal Law Review* 1–26.

arrest warrant may caution heads of states and government leaders not to travel to/through certain countries, in particular ICC state parties. The ICC, when it issued arrest warrants for Russian President Vladimir Putin and his Commissioner for Children's Rights Maria Lvova-Belova, expressed the hope that this measure would have a deterrent effect on 'the further commission of crimes'.[46]

In the past, the absence of enforcement of international criminal law, and the small number of offenders that international criminal tribunals have prosecuted, undermined the goal of deterrence, as people did not think that they might be punished.[47] Those doubting the possibility of deterrence in international criminal law have pointed to the fact that the creation of the ICTY did not stop crimes being committed in the former Yugoslavia between 1993 and 1995, and many other examples since the revival of international criminal justice where the possibility of prosecution has not prevented atrocities.[48] In relation to Yugoslavia, it might be noted that the Tribunal was at the time a fledgling institution, with very few people in custody. Moreover, it was often thought that the Tribunal would likely be bargained away in a peace deal. Nowadays, the ICTY is looked at rather positively, in terms of its legacy and impact on the development of an international criminal justice system.[49] Moreover, the establishment of the ICC has led to an increase of domestic prosecution of international crimes, just as its drafters had intended.[50] Indeed, if a culture of accountability is created, and domestic courts play their part, then the 'absence of enforcement' critique may become blunted over time. Overall, the evidence is mixed, and interpreting it involves the factoring in of a large number of variables, of which the threat of criminal prosecution is only one.[51]

2.2.3   Incapacitation

Incapacitation is another utilitarian justification of punishment. It has links to individual deterrence, in that it seeks to prevent crimes by keeping the relevant person in detention.[52] This has not had a great influence on international criminal law,[53] although Judge Röling, in his dissenting opinion at the Tokyo International Military Tribunal (IMT), asserted that the justification for prosecuting aggression, in spite of the fact that it was not previously criminal, was that the defendants were dangerous and their influence on Japan had to be excluded by their imprisonment.[54] Some of the arguments against amnesty, which rely on

---

[46] ICC press release, 'Situation in Ukraine: ICC judges issue arrest warrants against Vladimir Vladimirovich Putin and Maria Alekseyevna Lvova-Belova', 23 March 2023.

[47] See Tom Farer, 'Restraining the Barbarians: Can International Law Help?' (2000) 22 *Human Rights Quarterly* 90, 92–3.

[48] McAuliffe, 'Deterrence' (n. 44) 234–7; Carsten Stahn, 'Between "Faith" and "Facts": By What Standard Should We Assess International Criminal Justice?' (2012) 25 *LJIL* 251, 265.

[49] Paul Williams and Michael Scharf, *Peace with Justice: War Crimes and Accountability in the Former Yugoslavia* (Oxford, 2003) 21–2; Margaret M. deGuzman, 'Punishing for Humanity: The Sentencing Legacy of the International Criminal Tribunal for Former Yugoslavia' in Carsten Stahn et al. (eds.) *Legacies of the International Criminal Tribunal for the Former Yugoslavia: A Multidisciplinary Account* (Oxford, 2020).

[50] See further Chapter 4.

[51] James F. Alexander, 'The International Criminal Court and the Prevention of Atrocities: Predicting the Court's Impact' (2009) 54 *Villanova Law Review* 1, 42; Tallgren, 'The Sense and Sensibility' (n. 11) 569.

[52] See e.g. Zedner, *Criminal Justice* (n. 2) 98–101.   [53] Drumbl, 'Collective Violence and Individual Punishment' (n. 34) 589.

[54] Dissenting Opinion of the Member from the Netherlands, 10–51; see Neil Boister and Robert Cryer, *Documents on the Tokyo International Tribunal* (Oxford, 2008) 684–703.

the idea that those who seek amnesties will not quietly retire,[55] are linked to this justification of punishment. Incapacitative theories of punishment are controversial, as they rely on the imprecise science of determining who will reoffend and who will not. They do not focus on what has been done but, in effect, punish people for what they might do in the future.[56]

2.2.4 Rehabilitation

Rehabilitation is a theory of punishment which traces its history back to the eighteenth century,[57] and is based on the idea that the point of criminal sanctions is reformation of the offender. It is a theory of punishment that has many advocates in the human rights community at the domestic level, in particular those who are supporters of restorative justice.[58] It has not made a large impact in international criminal law, in part because many believe that the main perpetrators of international crimes are not the appropriate beneficiaries of rehabilitation. The ICC has stated that:

> the extent to which the sentence reflects the culpability of the convicted person addresses the desire to ease that person's reintegration into society, although, in particular in the case of international criminal law, this goal cannot be considered to be primordial and should therefore not be given any undue weight.[59]

Nonetheless, this is not a universal view, in particular when it comes to the implementation of sentences.[60] Most notable in this regard is the decision of the Trial Chamber in the *Erdemović* case. Erdemović was a young Bosnian Croat who took part in the Srebrenica massacre under duress. In sentencing him to a relatively short five-year period of imprisonment, the ICTY noted his 'corrigible personality' and that he was 'reformable and should be given a second chance to start his life afresh upon release, whilst still young enough to do so'.[61] Reconciliation as a theory of punishment features most prominently in the context of early release decisions.[62]

2.2.5 Expressivist and Didactic Function

One of the more modern theories designed to justify punishment, and one which has considerable support, is that of expressivism and education.[63] Some of the most

---

[55] Some evidence of which may be gleaned from the actions of Charles Taylor after his exile in Nigeria.

[56] Zedner, *Criminal Justice* (n. 2) 100.

[57] *Ibid*. 95–8. See also Andrew von Hirsch and Andrew Ashworth, *Principled Sentencing* (Oxford, 1998) ch. 3.

[58] Interestingly, many such advocates at the domestic level are often far more retributivist when it comes to international crimes.

[59] *Al Mahdi*, ICC TC VIII, 27 September 2016 (ICC-01/12–01/15–171) para. 67; see also *Katanga*, ICC TC II, 23 May 2014 (ICC-01/04–01/07–3484) para. 38. See further Chapter 19.

[60] Mulgrew, *Towards the Development of the International Penal System* (n. 6).

[61] *Erdemović*, ICTY TC, 5 March 1998, para. 16.

[62] Jessica Kelder, Barbora Holá and Joris van Wijk, 'Rehabilitation and Early Release of Perpetrators of International Crimes: Case Study of the ICTY and ICTR' (2014) 14 *ICLR* 1177–203. See also Edith Riegler, 'Rehabilitating Enemies of Mankind: An Exploration of the Concept of Rehabilitation as a Sentencing Aim at the ICTY and the ICC' (2020) 20 *ICLR* 701.

[63] Carsten Stahn, *Justice as a Message. Expressivist Foundations of International Criminal Justice* (Oxford, 2020). It builds on communicative theories of punishment: Antony Duff, *Punishment, Communication and Community* (Oxford, 2001); Andrew von Hirsch, *Censure and Sanctions* (Oxford, 1993) ch. 2; William Wilson, *Central Issues in Criminal Theory* (Oxford, 2002) 61–5; Keenan, 'The Problem of Purpose' (n. 11) 461–6.

sophisticated defences of international criminal law adopt this justification of punishment for international crimes.[64] Expressivist and educational approaches view criminal procedures and punishment as 'an opportunity for communicating with the offender, the victim and wider society the nature of the wrong done'.[65] This is designed to engage offenders, and attempt to make them understand what was wrong with what they have done,[66] whilst also reaffirming the norm in the community and educating society about the unacceptable nature of their conduct. Others add that it reaffirms faith in the rule of law.[67]

Some doubt this approach to punishment, criticizing the idea that international criminals are part of a relevant normative community with whom punishment is meant to communicate.[68] This contention is similarly applicable to domestic crimes, and a strong argument can be made that in international crimes the relevant normative community to which a person has to belong is humanity, rather than any thicker conception of community, and that the possibility of rejection of the message does not mean that it should not be attempted to be inculcated.[69] Also, those accused of international crimes are not the only audience for the message. For international criminal law to perform its expressivist and didactic function, it needs to be aimed at the wider community. There have, however, been suggestions that there are difficulties relating to what the moral message is when broad principles of liability which stretch individual culpability, such as joint criminal enterprise, are used.[70]

The ICC has suggested that part of retribution is 'an expression of the international community's condemnation of the crimes'.[71] The ICTY has also asserted the relevance of the didactic/educational function in the *Kordić and Čerkez* case, referring to:

the educational function ... [which] aims at conveying the message that rules of international humanitarian law have to be obeyed under all circumstances. In doing so, the sentence seeks to internalise these rules and the moral demands they are based on in the minds of the public.[72]

In some circumstances, where specific international crimes reflect a relatively recent moral consensus on point, the didactic function of international criminal law may play a considerable role. Where people are unaware of prohibitions, they are less likely to live up to them. The prohibition of recruitment and use of child soldiers may be an example of this.[73]

At a more nuanced level, the fact that there are lively debates over whether the term genocide may be applied to certain events implies that the expressivist function of punishment and labelling is important in international criminal law.[74] The relevance of the

---

[64] E.g. Damaška, 'What Is the Point' (n. 11) 343; Antony Duff, 'Can We Punish the Perpetrators of Atrocities?' in Thomas Brudholm and Thomas Cushman (eds.), *The Religious in Responses to Mass Atrocity: Interdisciplinary Perspectives* (Cambridge, 2008) 79.

[65] Zedner, *Criminal Justice* (n. 2) 109.

[66] See Wilson, *Central Issues* (n. 63) 62–3; Klaus Günter, 'The Criminal Law of "Guilt" as a Subject of a Politics of Remembrance in Democracies' in Emilios Christodoulidis and Scott Veitch (eds.), *Lethe's Law: Justice, Law and Ethics in Reconciliation* (Oxford, 2001) 3.

[67] Drumbl, *Atrocity* (n. 40) 173. [68] Van Sliedregt, 'Punishment and the Domestic Analogy' (n. 7) 96–7.

[69] Duff, 'Can We Punish' (n. 64) 85–100. [70] Damaška, 'What Is the Point' (n. 11) 350–6.

[71] *Al Mahdi*, ICC TC VIII, 27 September 2016 (ICC-01/12–01/15–171) para. 67.

[72] *Kordić and Čerkez*, ICTY AC, 17 December 2004, paras. 1080–1.

[73] See Cryer, 'The Role of Criminal Prosecutions' (n. 41) 210–13.

[74] Diane Marie Amann, 'Group Mentality, Expressivism and Genocide' (2002) 2 *ICLR* 93; see also Sloane, 'The Expressive Capacity of International Punishment' (n. 10). See generally about 'expressive punishment': Carsten Stahn, *Justice as a Message: Expressivist Foundations of International Criminal Justice* (Oxford, 2020) 323–90.

expressivist function of punishment was seemingly accepted by the ICTY Appeals Chamber in the *Krstić* appeal when it said that:

Among the grievous crimes this Tribunal has the duty to punish, the crime of genocide is singled out for special condemnation and opprobrium. The gravity of genocide is reflected in the stringent requirements which must be satisfied before this conviction is imposed. These requirements – the demanding proof of specific intent and the showing that the group was targeted for destruction in its entirety or in substantial part – guard against a danger that convictions for this crime will be imposed lightly. Where these requirements are satisfied, however, the law must not shy away from referring to the crime committed by its proper name.[75]

Strongly related to the didactic function, it has been suggested that the role of international criminal justice is to highlight that despite their extraordinary scale and nature, international crimes are still crimes. On this basis, the best way forward for international criminal law is to ensure that its utilization is considered normal, rather than needing separate justification from criminal law in general.[76] This may not yet have come to pass, but progress has been achieved. The aims of international criminal justice warrant a long-term view.

2.3 OTHER GOALS

2.3.1 Vindicating the Rights of Victims

There are certain other broader justifications which have been suggested for international criminal law, all of which have a utilitarian focus, and relate in some ways to the future of the societies in which international crimes are committed. The first of these is that prosecutions may engender a sense of justice having been done, or 'closure' for victims,[77] either on the basis that seeing their persecutors prosecuted will have that result, or that the process of testifying will do so. Such a role in relation to victims was noted by the ICC in the *Al Mahdi* case, where the Trial Chamber said that the 'imposition of a proportionate sentence, also acknowledges the harm to the victims'.[78] The ICTY in the *Nikolić* case asserted that 'punishment must therefore reflect . . . the calls for justice from the persons who have – directly or indirectly – been victims of the crimes'.[79]

It can be questioned whether criminal trials and punishment of offenders have the cathartic effects for victims.[80] Given the focus in international criminal tribunals on higher-level offenders, it is doubtful that victims will have an opportunity to see the people who committed offences against them in court (national courts have a large role here). Evidence that the experience of testifying is helpful, is mixed, with some victim–witnesses reporting

---

[75] *Krstić*, ICTY AC, 19 April 2004, paras. 36–7.
[76] David Luban, 'After the Honeymoon: Reflections on the Current State of International Criminal Justice' (2013) 11 *JICJ* 505.
[77] On victims and their participation in international criminal tribunals, see Chapter 18. See also Keenan, 'The Problem of Purpose' (n. 11) 426–7.
[78] *Al Mahdi*, ICC TC VIII, 27 September 2016 (ICC-01/12–01/15–171) para. 67.
[79] *Momir Nikolić*, ICTY TC I, 2 December 2003, para. 86.
[80] Jamie O'Connell, 'Gambling with the Psyche: Does Prosecuting Human Rights Violators Console their Victims?' (2005) 46 *Harvard International Law Journal* 295.

that they were glad they had testified, whilst others did not.[81] The extent to which victims may be helped by prosecutions depends, *inter alia*, on the role they are permitted to play in the proceedings, and, particularly in common-law jurisdictions, this is often minimal, and limited to the utilitarian goal of using them as witnesses. The ICTY and International Criminal Tribunal for Rwanda (ICTR) were therefore not exemplary in their treatment of victim–witnesses. Nonetheless, the ICC Statute has various provisions providing for victim participation in proceedings and for reparations.[82]

2.3.2 Recording History

The claim is that the process of subjecting evidence to forensic scrutiny will promote truth-telling and set down a permanent record of the crimes that will stand the test of time.[83] Some go further to suggest that trials should be structured to create a narrative which will be useful to the relevant post-conflict society.[84] The judgments of international criminal tribunals have often engaged in detailed discussion of the background of the conflicts which have led to the crimes, and have been criticized for doing so.[85] In the *Krstić* judgment, the intention of the tribunal to counter denial and create a record of the Srebrenica massacre was clear, and similar things can be said about the ICTR's characterization of the Rwandan genocide as being rightly labelled as such.[86]

The practice of the ad hoc Tribunals is not entirely consistent; sometimes the Chambers of the Tribunals have disavowed an intention to write history. In the *Karadžić* case, the defendant sought to persuade the ICTY to find, if not for the purposes of legal evaluation then for the purposes of history, that he had been promised immunity from prosecution if he left politics. The Trial Chamber gave short shrift to such a suggestion, stating that '[t]he Trial Chamber rejects the Accused's submission that not having an evidentiary hearing at this stage would be a disservice to history. The Chamber's purpose is not to serve the academic study of history'.[87]

The idea that criminal trials ought to serve truth-telling functions has been criticized. Some think that criminal trials are not always the best place to seek to write history.[88] There are various aspects to this claim. In relation to the Nuremberg and Tokyo IMTs, the claim, made by one of the judges of the Tokyo IMT, was that 'distortions of history did take place' in those Tribunals, at times for political reasons.[89] For the most part, such comments relate to the findings on conspiracy and aggression, rather than war crimes and crimes against humanity.

---

[81] Eric Stover, 'Witnesses and the Promise of the Hague' in Eric Stover and Harvey Weinstein (eds.), *My Neighbour, My Enemy: Justice and Community in the Aftermath of Mass Atrocity* (Cambridge, 2004) 104.

[82] See Chapter 18.

[83] See e.g. Cassese, 'Reflections on International Criminal Justice' (n. 9) 6. See generally Richard Wilson, *Writing History in International Criminal Trials* (Cambridge, 2011); Keenan, 'The Problem of Purpose' (n. 11) 466–72; Lawrence Douglas, *The Memory of Judgment: Making Law and History in Trials of the Holocaust* (New Haven, CT, 2001).

[84] Mark Osiel, *Mass Atrocity, Collective Memory and the Law* (New Brunswick, NJ, 1997).

[85] José Alvarez, 'Rush to Closure: Lessons of the Tadić Judgment' (1998) 96 *Michigan Law Review* 2061; José Alvarez, 'Lessons from the Akayesu Judgment' (1998–9) 5 *International Law Students' Association Journal of International and Comparative Law* 359.

[86] Drumbl, *Atrocity* (n. 40) 175. [87] *Karadžić*, ICTY TC III, 8 July 2009, para. 46.

[88] Martha Minow, *Between Vengeance and Forgiveness* (Boston, 1998) 46–7.

[89] Bert V. A. Röling, 'The Nuremberg and Tokyo Trials in Retrospect' in M. Cherif Bassiouni and Ved Nanda (eds.), *A Treatise on International Criminal Law* (Springfield, IL, 1973) 590, 600. See Donald Bloxham, *Genocide on Trial: War Crimes Trials and*

It is also difficult to write the whole history of a period without straying beyond the bounds of the criminal trial, which is to try a specific person for specific conduct.[90] This gives rise to the concern that the trial may devolve into a political debate about the validity of the different historical accounts that are being told.[91] It is perhaps strange that, in long-running conflicts which are the context to the commission of many atrocities, a criminal court should be seen as the arbitrator between competing historical accounts.[92] Such events are not easily cognizable or interpretable through the medium of criminal law.[93] The rule-bound nature of criminal trials is not one designed to ensure a full discussion of history, and structures the evidence that can be brought before the tribunal.[94] To go beyond this, as Judge Röling put it, there is a difference between the 'real truth' and the 'trial truth'.[95] In addition, as the criminal standard of proof is required for a conviction before an international criminal tribunal, in instances where there have been acquittals before such tribunals, this has been taken as exoneration of both the defendants and the 'side' on whose behalf they acted.[96] This may involve ignoring the nuances of a (frequently lengthy and carefully framed) judgment.

Nevertheless, the contextual elements of international crimes, in particular of crimes against humanity and genocide,[97] require that the larger context in which a person's actions must be placed becomes an issue at trial about which the defence is entitled to introduce evidence as well. Furthermore, the nature of a fair trial process is that it gives those responsible for international crimes the opportunity to raise political messages and to attempt to delegitimize the prosecution.[98] This may be a necessary aspect of such trials, since the alternative, that of silencing the defence, is unacceptable, but balancing the competing interests here is difficult.[99]

The temporal, geographical, and subject-matter jurisdiction of international criminal tribunals means that the story they can tell is by no means the full one,[100] even though some of the international criminal tribunals have used evidence of events outside their jurisdictional reach.[101] The issue of witness tampering may affect the extent to which a true

---

the Formation of Holocaust History and Memory (Oxford, 2001); Richard Minear, *Victors' Justice* (Princeton, NJ, 1971); but see also Yasuaki Onuma, 'Beyond Victors' Justice' (1984) 9 *Japan Echo* 63, 66.

[90] Osiel, *Mass Atrocity* (n. 84) ch. 3; however, see Ruti Teitel, *Transitional Justice* (Oxford, 2000) 74–5.

[91] Indeed, there is historical narrative pluralism, in and outside the courtroom: Barrie Sander, *Doing Justice to History: Confronting the Past in International Criminal Courts* (Oxford, 2021) 276–303.

[92] See Martti Koskenniemi, 'Between Impunity and Show Trials' (2002) 6 *Max Planck Yearbook of United Nations Law* I. Of course, sometimes a court itself is split over the history, as was the case, for example, in the Tokyo IMT. See Gerry Simpson, 'War Crimes: A Critical Introduction' in Timothy McCormack and Gerry Simpson (eds.), *The Law of War Crimes: National and International Approaches* (The Hague, 1997) 1, 26–8.

[93] Koskenniemi, 'Between Impunity' (n. 92) 12–13.

[94] See Douglas, *The Memory of Judgment* (n. 83); Wilson, *Writing History* (n. 83).

[95] Bert V. A. Röling and Antonio Cassese, *The Tokyo Trial and Beyond* (Cambridge, 1992) 50. Many would (rightly) query whether there is one form of 'real truth'.

[96] See Chapter 7.

[97] Both in customary law and in the ICC Statute and its concomitant Elements of Crimes: see Chapters 10 and 11.

[98] See generally Gerry Simpson, 'Politics, Sovereignty, Remembrance' in McGoldrick et al., *The Permanent ICC*, 49.

[99] See generally Koskenniemi, 'Between Impunity' (n. 92).

[100] José E. Alvarez, 'Crimes of Hate/Crimes of State: Lessons from Rwanda' (1999) 23 *Yale Journal of International Law* 365, 375.

[101] *Nahimana et al.*, ICTR TC, 3 December 2003, paras. 100–4.

record may be created. This problem has afflicted both the ad hoc Tribunals[102] and the ICC.[103] Non-cooperation with international trials also affects their ability to issue a comprehensive history.

While such critiques do not undermine the work done by the tribunals in collecting and making public primary evidence such as documents and witness testimony, they do cast aspersions on the role of courts as presenters or interpreters of history. The evidence brought before some tribunals can, however, be very useful in combating later denial of such crimes (as has occurred in relation to the practice of the Nuremberg IMT and the ICTR). The practice of 'plea bargaining' in the Tribunals has been said by some Trial Chambers of the ICTY to assist in the process of truth telling,[104] but other Chambers have doubted that the full story can be told without full trials.[105] When it comes to writing the history of situations in which international crimes have been committed, truth commissions are better placed to write some aspects of that history, although they are not themselves a panacea.[106]

2.3.3 Post-Conflict Reconciliation

Linked both to the satisfaction of victims and to the telling of truths about international crimes, providing a sense of justice through prosecutions for international crimes can possibly facilitate societal reconciliation and provide the preconditions for a durable peace.[107] This is often expressed in the aphorism 'no peace without justice'.[108] Evidence from Latin America, where policies of amnesty were rife in the 1970s but where prosecutions have continuously been sought and are now beginning to occur, provides some support for that position.[109] There is, however, no clear empirical proof of this, and other societies have, for better or for worse, managed without trials[110] (although some would say that those societies are not reconciled).[111] Reconciliation requires forgiveness, a matter that is far from a simple notion.[112] The ICC, though, has claimed that proportionate sentencing promotes 'the restoration of peace and reconciliation'.[113]

---

[102] Robert Cryer, 'Witness Tampering in International Criminal Tribunals' (2014) 27(1) *LJIL* 191.

[103] See e.g. *Bemba*, ICC TC III, 21 March 2016 (ICC-01/05–01/08–3343); *Bemba*, ICC AC, 8 June 2018 (ICC-01/05–01/08–3636-Red); Statement of the ICC Prosecutor, 13 June 2018; Statement of the ICC President, 14 June 2018. The collapse of the cases related to Kenya were attributed by the Prosecutor to witness tampering, see Statement of the ICC Prosecutor, 10 September 2015.

[104] *Jokić*, ICTY TC I, 18 March 2004, para. 77. See Mark Harmon, 'Plea Bargaining: The Uninvited Guest at the ICTY' in Doria et al., *Legal Regime*, 163, 177–9.

[105] *Dragan Nikolić*, ICTY TC II, 18 December 2003, para. 122. See also Schabas, *The UN International Criminal Tribunals* 427–8; Drumbl, *Atrocity* (n. 40) 181–2.

[106] For discussion, see Alison Bissett, *Truth Commissions and Criminal Trials* (Cambridge, 2012) ch. 1 and ch. 22.3.

[107] See e.g. Cassese, 'Reflections on International Criminal Justice' (n. 9) 6.

[108] Indeed, this is the name of one well-known non-governmental organization (NGO) working in the area of international criminal law.

[109] The politics of impunity, on the other hand, are often thought to inspire later crimes, even decades later: see e.g. Harmon, 'Plea Bargaining' (n. 104) 179–82; Jens Ohlin, 'Peace, Security and Prosecutorial Discretion' in Stahn and Sluiter, *Emerging Practice*, 185, 203–5.

[110] See e.g. Priscilla Hayner, *Unspeakable Truths: Transitional Justice and the Challenge of Truth Commissions*, 2nd ed. (London, 2011) ch. 12.

[111] See Richard Wilson, *The Politics of Truth and Reconciliation: Legitimizing the Post-Apartheid State* (Cambridge, 2001). See on the ICTY: Diane Orentlicher, *Some Kind of Justice: The ICTY's Impact in Bosnia and Serbia* (Oxford, 2018).

[112] Martha Nussbaum, *Anger and Forgiveness: Resentment, Generosity, Justice* (New York, NY, 2016).

[113] *Al Mahdi*, TC VIII, 27 September 2016 (ICC-01/12–01/15–171) para. 67.

The UN Security Council provided significant support for the interconnection of peace and justice when it determined that, in the situations in the former Yugoslavia and Rwanda, prosecutions would assist in reconciliation and a return to peace in the area.[114] It is interesting that, in the *Tadić* jurisdictional appeal, the Appeals Chamber of the ICTY simply said that such a decision was within the competence of the Council to make, rather than entering into any discussion of the substantive merits of the point.[115] Later, in the *Nikolić* case, the ICTY gave the idea more direct support:

> In confessing his guilt and admitting all factual details contained in the Third Amended Indictment in open court on 4 September 2003 Dragan Nikolić has helped further a process of reconciliation. He has guided the international community closer to the truth in an area not yet subject of any judgement rendered by this Tribunal, truth being one prerequisite for peace.[116]

Perhaps the high-tide mark of support for the link between criminal justice and peace in the ICTY came in the *Plavšić* case. Biljana Plavšić was co-President of the Republika Srpska during 1992. She surrendered to the Tribunal and pleaded guilty to crimes against humanity, expressing her remorse and stating that in doing so she wished to 'offer some consolation to the innocent victims – Muslim, Croat and Serb – of the war in Bosnia and Herzegovina'.[117] In sentencing Plavšić to eleven years' imprisonment, the Tribunal noted 'that acknowledgement and full disclosure of serious crimes are very important when establishing the truth in relation to such crimes. This, together with acceptance of responsibility for the committed wrongs, will promote reconciliation'.[118] It has been questioned whether this was accurate in the individual case, but the general point remains.

The ambivalent relationship between international criminal justice and peace is perhaps shown by the fact that the Security Council, using its powers to restore and maintain international peace and security under Chapter VII of the UN Charter, may not only refer a situation to the ICC, but also defer the activity of the Court in certain circumstances.[119]

Post-conflict reconciliation via criminal justice may not be possible when communities are divided too deeply to entertain a common narrative or morality. With regard to the ICTY, it has been argued that the Tribunal will never be able to achieve reconciliation in the former Yugoslavia because of a lack of shared perception and consciousness that it acts in the name and for the sake of the entire ex-Yugoslav community.[120] International prosecutions can only be a substitute for domestic processes if the aim of the international court to achieve justice is shared with the local community. Transformation from a conflict, to post-conflict, and then to

---

[114] Such a determination was necessary to invoke Chapter VII of the UN Charter to create the ICTY and ICTR. Some of the most serious doubts that have been expressed about international criminal law relate to the claim that it promotes peace and reconciliation. Anthony D'Amato, 'Peace v. Accountability in Bosnia' (1994) 88 *AJIL* 500; Ian Ward, *Justice, Humanity and the New World Order* (Aldershot, 2004) 131; Anonymous, 'Human Rights in Peace Negotiations' (1996) 18 *Human Rights Quarterly* 249.

[115] See Section 7.2.4. [116] *Dragan Nikolić*, ICTY TC II, 12 December 2003, para. 3.

[117] *Plavšić*, ICTY TC III, 27 February 2003, para. 80. [118] *Ibid*.

[119] ICC Statute, Arts. 13 and 16; see further Sections 8.6 and 8.8.

[120] Milena Tripković, 'Not in Our Name! Visions of Community in International Criminal Justice' in Marina Aksenova, Elies van Sliedregt, and Stephan Parmentier (eds.), *Breaking the Cycle of Mass Atrocities Criminological and Socio-Legal Approaches in International Criminal Law* (Oxford, 2019) 165–80.

a stable society may take many years or decades, if it occurs at all, and many factors contribute to the process. Criminal prosecutions are only one.[121]

2.3.4 Other Asserted Benefits of International Trials

Certain other benefits have also been postulated, not of international criminal law in general, but of international trials. One of the most powerful of these is that international tribunals, with international judges, operating at a distance from the events themselves, are not as open to political manipulation or influence from actors in those societies, or unconscious bias on the part of the judges.[122] Nonetheless, there have been a number of claims before all of the courts and tribunals that judges are biased.[123] Also, it is an often-made critique that the international tribunals are too distant from their primary audience, the victimized community.[124]

It is sometimes claimed that international judges are the best judges of international crimes.[125] There are two possible bases for these claims, the first being that international judges and tribunals are representative of the relevant community affected by international crimes, which is the community of all humanity. But this raises the uneasy question of who defines what that is and what it wants.

The second basis is more prosaic: that international judges are more familiar with the relevant law. It is true that domestic judges are less likely to be fully aware of the intricacies of international criminal law than some of their international counterparts. Indeed, some eminent and experienced international lawyers have sat on the international criminal tribunals. However, not all judges who have sat on international criminal tribunals claim expertise in international criminal law; an in-depth knowledge of the workings of a criminal trial can be as useful for an international criminal judge.

It has also been suggested that international tribunals are better able to investigate and prosecute offences which occur across state borders than domestic courts.[126] This may be the case, but the extent to which it is true depends on the extent of the tribunal's jurisdiction and investigatory powers, which differ between the various courts. Finally, it has been suggested that an international criminal court would provide for uniformity in the process and law for punishing international crimes.[127] There is some truth in this, although there have been a number of different international criminal tribunals, with different procedures and different substantive law, the ICC Statute has promoted harmonization of the law at the domestic level. Still, the value of uniformity is strongly linked to the merits of the law which becomes the standard.[128]

---

[121] See Janine N. Clark, 'Peace, Justice and the International Criminal Court: Limitations and Possibilities' (2011) 9 *JICJ* 521.
[122] Cassese, 'Reflections on International Criminal Justice' (n. 9) 4, 7. [123] See Section 17.3.2. [124] See Section 2.4.
[125] Cassese, 'Reflections on International Criminal Justice' (n. 9) 7.
[126] Cassese, 'Reflections on International Criminal Justice' (n. 9) 8. [127] *Ibid.*
[128] Robert Cryer, *Prosecuting International Crimes: Selectivity and the International Criminal Law Regime* (Cambridge, 2005) 167–84.

2.4 OTHER CRITIQUES OF CRIMINAL ACCOUNTABILITY

Despite the functions which prosecutions may serve and the advantages they offer, there are also many critiques of criminal accountability, and international courts and tribunals in particular. International courts are expensive. But the real question is whether they are worth the money, and the budgetary control over international criminal trials exercised by their funders is an important issue.[129]

International courts and tribunals are also (unlike most hybrid courts) located far away from the places where the crimes occurred.[130] This means that they are inaccessible to many of the victims and seen as responding more to an international audience than the purported beneficiaries. This gives succour to critics who argue that the creation of the Tribunals was more a sop to the conscience of those who failed to prevent or bring an end to the crimes now being punished.[131] The further from the *locus delicti* that trials are held, the more likely it is that they will encounter domestic resistance there, in part because of misrepresentation of their work and allegations of bias.[132] In situations of large-scale commission of crimes, however, it is difficult to imagine any criminal justice system that could fulfil the task of ensuring that all international criminals were punished.[133]

More generally, it has been questioned whether criminal law is an adequate mechanism to comprehend events involving international crimes, particularly large-scale international crimes like genocide. The critique was perhaps most strongly made by Hannah Arendt,[134] but others have also made similar points. Martti Koskenniemi, for example, has said that 'sometimes a tragedy may be so great, a series of events of such political or even metaphysical significance, that punishing an individual does not come close to measuring up to it'.[135]

It could be queried whether trials are any worse than the other methods that have been suggested for dealing with such events, and Arendt was not against the prosecution of international crimes as such, although she was critical of aspects of some proceedings.[136] Still, it is true that most international crimes occur against the background of 'system criminality', where individual and collective responsibility is mixed. As such, individual liability can only be part of the answer.[137] The difficulty is finding ways that adequately express both the individual and collective contributions to international crimes.[138] International trials and international criminal law ought not to serve as an excuse to the

---

[129] See e.g. Sara Kendall, 'Donor's Justice: Recasting International Criminal Accountability' (2011) 24 (3) *LJIL* 585.

[130] Alvarez, 'Crimes of Hate' (n. 100). See further Chapter 9.

[131] See Gary John Bass, *Stay the Hand of Vengeance: The Politics of War Crimes Tribunals* (Princeton, NJ, 2000) ch. 6.

[132] Patrice McMahon and David Forsythe, 'The ICTY's Impact on Serbia: Judicial Romanticism Meets Network Politics' (2008) 30 *Human Rights Quarterly* 412.

[133] William Schabas, 'The Rwanda Case: Sometimes It's Impossible' in M. Cherif Bassiouni (ed.), *Post-Conflict Justice* (New York, 2002) 499.

[134] Lotte Kohler and Hans Saner (eds.), *Hannah Arendt/Karl Jaspers: Correspondence* (New York, 1992) 54, cited in Osiel, 'Why Prosecute?' (n. 31) 128.

[135] Koskenniemi, 'Between Impunity' (n. 92) 2.

[136] Hannah Arendt, *Eichmann in Jerusalem: A Report on the Banality of Evil* (Harmondsworth, 1994) Epilogue.

[137] See André Nollkaemper and Harmen van der Wilt, 'Introduction' in André Nollkaemper and Harmen van der Wilt (eds.), *System Criminality in International Law* (Cambridge, 2009) 1, 4.

[138] Andrea Gattini, 'A Historical Perspective: From Collective to Individual Responsibility and Back' in *ibid.* 126.

international community for not dealing with other difficult and deep-seated problems. For example, the creation of the ICTY and ICTR may have allowed powerful states to cover their unwillingness to take more decisive action.[139] Prosecutions can also be used by states and successor governments to attempt to make the point that they are morally different from those on trial, even where there are international crimes that can be laid at their door too.[140] In addition, substantive international criminal law fails to deal with some conduct very worthy of censure, thus ironically providing some form of perceived legitimacy for it.[141]

International criminal justice, and international courts and tribunals, reflect inequalities in the selection of cases. Selective justice is a problem from the point of view of the rule of law, and it can undermine many of the justifications of punishment.[142] For example, deterrence is unlikely to be possible if potential offenders take the view that they may be able to obtain exemption from prosecution. Retribution is not served well by selective punishment, and it causes the lessons that may be taught by international criminal law to be confused and equivocal.[143]

Some would go further than this, to argue that international criminal law is in some ways a Western construct, and that it is imposed on other societies.[144] With respect to the norms themselves – that is, of genocide, crimes against humanity, crime of aggression, and war crimes – this is almost certainly overstated, in that the core crimes are considered contrary to universal norms. As has been said, 'modern writers on the subject correctly point to Chinese, Islamic, and Hindu traditions that underscore the universal values enshrined in the prohibition of crimes that shock the conscience of mankind'.[145] The treaties establishing the core of war crimes, the Geneva Conventions, have been ratified by the predominant majority of states in the world, and the General Assembly has repeatedly and unanimously condemned genocide, crimes against humanity, and war crimes.[146] Yet, there is value in the argument that, by using custom rather than treaties, the ad hoc Tribunals have preferred the interests of powerful states, which may have more weight in the creation of custom.[147]

When it comes to enforcement, selectivity arguments have taken on a post-colonial aspect, that is, that 'international prosecutions are instituted mainly against citizens of states that are weak actors in the international arena or fail to enjoy the support of powerful nations'.[148] It has also been claimed that decisions about what to do about international crimes are better left to national authorities.[149] The issues involved are not simple, but it

---

[139] See Section 7.2. [140] Simpson, 'War Crimes: A Critical Introduction' (n. 92) 19–26.

[141] Simpson, 'Politics, Sovereignty, Remembrance' (n. 98) 56.

[142] Drumbl, 'Collective Violence and Individual Punishment' (n. 34) 593.

[143] See e.g. Damaška, 'What Is the Point' (n. 11) 361; See also Elies van Sliedregt, 'One Rule for Them – Selectivity in International Criminal Law' (2021) 34(2) *LJIL* 283.

[144] Steven Ratner, Jason Abrams, and James Bischoff, *Accountability for Human Rights Atrocities in International Law: Beyond the Nuremberg Paradigm*, 3rd ed. (Oxford, 2009) 26.

[145] Leila Sadat, 'The Effect of Amnesties Before Domestic and International Tribunals: Law, Morality, Politics' in Edel Hughes, William Schabas and Ramesh Thakur (eds.), *Atrocities and International Accountability* (Tokyo, 2007) 229.

[146] E.g. GA Res. 47/131, 7 April 1993 and GA Res. 63/303, 23 July 2009.

[147] Anthony Anghie and B. S. Chimni, 'Third World Approaches to International Law and Individual Responsibility in Internal Armed Conflict' (2003) 2 *Chinese Journal of International Law* 77, 92–5.

[148] Damaška, 'What Is the Point' (n. 11) 361; Charles Chernor Jalloh, 'Regionalizing International Criminal Law?' (2009) 9 *ICLR* 445.

[149] Anghie and Chimni, 'Third World Approaches' (n. 148) 91–2.

might be noted that a number of post-colonial states (such as Rwanda, Uganda, and the Democratic Republic of the Congo) have asked for international prosecutions of international crimes. Again, a synergistic relationship between national and international approaches to international crimes is probably the most helpful way forward.[150] The answer to such critiques is not to abandon punishment altogether, but to work towards non-selective application of the law. Even some enforcement is probably better than none, and powerful states are finding it more difficult to resist claims for criminal accountability of those who commit international crimes as their officials or on their behalf.[151]

Further Reading

Two symposia/special issues are relevant: (2021) 19 *JICJ* on deterrence in international criminal justice and (2023) 21 *JICJ* on life after conviction which discusses sentencing aims and rehabilitation.

Payam Akhavan, 'The Rise, and Fall, and Rise, of International Criminal Justice' (2013) 11 *JICJ* 527

José E. Alvarez, 'Crimes of Hate/Crimes of State: Lessons from Rwanda' (1999) 23 *Yale Journal of International Law* 365

Kai Ambos, *Treatise on International Criminal Law*, vol. I, *Foundations and General Part* 2nd ed. (Oxford, 2021)

Anthony Anghie and B. S. Chimni, 'Third World Approaches to International Law and Individual Responsibility in Internal Armed Conflict' (2003) 2 *Chinese Journal of International Law* 77

Antonio Cassese, 'On the Current Trend Towards Criminal Prosecution and Punishment of Breaches of International Humanitarian Law' (1998) 9 *EJIL* 2

Mirjan Damaška, 'What Is the Point of International Criminal Justice' (2008) 83 *Chicago–Kent Law Review* 329

Florian Jeßberger and Julia Geneuss (eds.), *Why Punish Perpetrators of Mass Atrocities? Purposes of Punishment in International Criminal Law* (Cambridge, 2020)

Mark Drumbl, *Atrocity, Punishment and International Law* (Cambridge, 2007)

Frederik Harhoff, 'Sense and Sensibility in Sentencing: Taking Stock of International Criminal Punishment' in Ola Engdahl and Pål Wrange (eds.), *Law at War: The Law as It Was and the Law as It Should Be, Liber Amicorum Ove Bring* (Leiden, 2008) 121

Martti Koskenniemi, 'Between Impunity and Show Trials' (2002) 6 *Max Planck Yearbook of United Nations Law* 1

David Luban, 'After the Honeymoon: Reflections on the Current State of International Criminal Justice' (2013) 11 *JICJ* 505

Jens Ohlin, 'Peace, Security and Prosecutorial Discretion' in Stahn and Sluiter, *Emerging Practice*

---

[150] See Ratner et al., *Accountability* (n. 145) 26. Alternatives to criminal prosecutions are evaluated in Chapter 22.
[151] Damaška, 'What Is the Point' (n. 11) 363.

Paul Roberts, 'Restoration and Retribution in International Criminal Justice' in Andrew von Hirsch et al. (eds.), *Restorative Justice and Criminal Justice: Competing or Reconcilable Paradigms?* (Oxford, 2004) 115

Barrie Sander, *Doing Justice to History: Confronting the Past in International Criminal Courts* (Oxford, 2021)

Robert Sloane, 'The Expressive Capacity of International Punishment' (2007) 43 *Stanford Journal of International Law* 39

Carsten Stahn, *Justice as a Message. Expressivist Foundations of International Criminal Justice* (Oxford, 2020)

Immi Tallgren, 'The Sense and Sensibility of International Criminal Law' (2002) 13 *EJIL* 561

Part II

Prosecutions in National Courts

3

Jurisdiction

3.1 INTRODUCTION

Jurisdiction is the power of the state to regulate affairs pursuant to its laws. Exercising jurisdiction involves asserting a form of sovereignty. This fact causes difficulties when jurisdiction is exercised extra-territorially. Where extra-territorial jurisdiction is asserted, sovereignties overlap, and general international law has not yet developed a hierarchy of lawful jurisdictional claims.[1] This chapter discusses the principles of jurisdiction as they relate to international crimes. International law tends to allow jurisdiction over international crimes on broader bases than it offers over other crimes. Therefore, this chapter must be read with the caveat that it is not intended to be a general discussion of the international law of jurisdiction.

3.2 FORMS OF JURISDICTION

There are three categories of jurisdiction: legislative (or prescriptive), adjudicative, and executive (or enforcement) jurisdiction. They will be considered in turn, although, as a matter of international law, in criminal cases 'jurisdiction to prescribe and jurisdiction to adjudicate in criminal matters are generally congruent in scope'.[2]

3.2.1 Legislative Jurisdiction

This is the right of a state to pass laws that have a bearing on conduct. Some states take the view domestically that they are entitled to pass legislation covering matters which take place throughout the globe: hence the cliché that the UK Parliament could pass a statute making it a crime for a French person to smoke on the streets of Paris. However, enforcement of such a statute would be difficult from a practical point of view, as well as problematic in international law, owing to the principle of non-intervention. States are entitled to protest assertions of legislative jurisdiction which are unwarranted under

---

[1] See Section 3.5.4.
[2] Claus Kreß, 'Universal Jurisdiction over International Crimes and the Institut de Droit International' (2006) 4 *JICJ* 561, 564.

international law, and there is an increasing trend towards them doing so. However, other states do not always consider their rights to be heavily affected by those claims until a specific case arises in which they are relied on.

3.2.2 Adjudicative Jurisdiction

This form of jurisdiction is the extent to which domestic courts can apply their state's laws and pass judgment on matters before them. This seems an abstract (legislative) claim that may not directly affect other states; it only crystallizes when a court actually asserts adjudicative jurisdiction over specific conduct. By passing judgment over offences committed abroad, it is possible that courts, hence states, are intervening in the domestic affairs of the state in which the offences were committed. Some African states were critical of the exercise of jurisdiction by French and Spanish courts in cases where Rwandans were suspected of committing crimes against Rwandans.[3]

3.2.3 Executive Jurisdiction

Executive jurisdiction is the most intrusive of jurisdictional claims. It is the right to effect legal process coercively, such as to arrest someone, or undertake searches and seizures. The *Lotus* case,[4] which is generally accepted to reflect the international law on executive jurisdiction accurately, stated that:

The first and foremost restriction imposed by international law upon a State is that – failing the existence of a permissive rule to the contrary – it may not exercise its power in any form in the territory of another state. In this sense jurisdiction is certainly territorial; it cannot be exercised by a state outside its territory.[5]

In the *Eichmann* case, it was accepted by Israel that, irrespective of the morality of its actions in abducting Adolf Eichmann from Argentina and taking him to Israel for trial, doing so without the consent of Argentina violated its sovereignty.[6] Care must be taken, however, to distinguish the exercise of executive jurisdiction over a person and the later exercise of adjudicative jurisdiction over them. That an arrest is illegal does not necessarily bar a court from exercising jurisdiction. The position is often referred to by the Latin aphorism *male captus bene detentus* (wrongly captured, properly detained). In a case where the accused was abducted and handed over to the prosecutor of the International Criminal Tribunal for the former Yugoslavia (ICTY), the Tribunal has

---

[3] This was called an abuse of universal jurisdiction by the African Union: AU Assembly Decision on the Report of the Commission on the Abuse of the Principle of Universal Jurisdiction, AU Doc. Decision Assembly/AU/Dec. i 99 (XI), 1 July 2008. See Roger O'Keefe, 'Domestic Courts as Agents of Development of the International Law of Jurisdiction' (2013) 26 *LJIL* 541, 555–6.
[4] *SS Lotus* (*France* v. *Turkey*), 1927 PCIJ Series A No. 10. [5] *Ibid*. 18.
[6] *Attorney-General of Israel* v. *Eichmann* (1968) 36 ILR 5, paras. 40–50 (District Court). For comment, see e.g. Helen Silving, 'In re Eichmann: A Dilemma of Law and Morality' (1961) 55 *AJIL* 307.

come close to adopting this approach, by claiming that, in relation to its own jurisdiction:

Apart from such exceptional circumstances [egregious human rights violations, not abduction *simpliciter*] however, the remedy of setting aside jurisdiction will ... usually be disproportionate. The correct balance must therefore be maintained between the fundamental rights of the accused and the essential interests of the international community in the prosecution of persons charged with serious violations of international humanitarian law.[7]

As the quotation shows, though, the ICTY left itself some elbow room in extreme cases to refuse jurisdiction. Some national courts have adopted a similar position, that they ought to decline jurisdiction in such situations, as it would compound an illegality.[8] It is not clear that there is an established principle of international law requiring them to do so.[9]

3.3 CONCEPTUAL MATTERS

3.3.1 Question of Proof

It is often said that states are entitled to exercise jurisdiction unless there is a specific rule of international law that prevents them from doing so. This comes from the *Lotus* case's pronouncement that,

[f]ar from laying down a general prohibition to the effect that States may not extend the application of their laws, and the jurisdiction of their courts to persons, property and acts outside their territory, [international law] leaves them in this respect a wide measure of discretion which is only limited in certain cases by prohibitive rules.[10]

However, even if that was the position in 1927 (which is doubtful),[11] it does not reflect state practice, which is to assert a positive ground for the exercise of jurisdiction, rather than to rely on the absence of a prohibition.[12] When the separate opinions in the first ICJ case on jurisdiction in which the '*Lotus* presumption' was relevant (the *Yerodia* case) came to deal with it, the judges disagreed on its continued relevance.[13]

---

[7] *Dragan Nikolić*, ICTY AC, 5 June 2003, para. 30. See also *Barayagwiza*, ICTR AC, 19 November 1999; *Barayagwiza*, ICTR AC, 31 March 2000. See further Section 17.6.2.

[8] See e.g. *R* v. *Horseferry Road Magistrates, ex parte Bennett* [1993] 2 All ER 318 (UK); *State* v. *Ebrahim* [1991] 1 South African Criminal Law Reports 307.

[9] See e.g. the decision of the Bundesverfassungsgericht (1986) *Neue Juristische Wochenschrift* 3021, denying the existence of an 'established principle of international law'; the arguments to the contrary are in Stephan Wilske, *Die völkerrechtswidrige Entführung und ihre Rechtsfolgen* (Berlin, 2000) 338–40.

[10] *SS Lotus* (n. 4) 19.

[11] It may also be a misunderstanding of the case, see Douglas Guilfoyle, 'SS Lotus (*France v Turkey*) (1927)' in Eirik Bjorge and Cameron Miles (eds.), *Landmark Cases in International Law* (Oxford, 2017) 89.

[12] See Michael Akehurst, 'Jurisdiction in International Law' (1972–3) 46 *British Yearbook of International Law* 145, 167; Christopher Staker, 'Jurisdiction' in Malcolm Evans (ed.), *International Law*, 5th ed. (Oxford, 2018) 309, 315. See generally Paola Gaeta, 'The Need Reasonably to Expand National Jurisdiction over International Crimes' in Antonio Cassese (ed.), *Realizing Utopia: The Future of International Law* (Oxford, 2012) 596, 598–601.

[13] *Case concerning the Arrest Warrant of 11 April 2000 (Democratic Republic of the Congo v. Belgium)*, ICJ, Judgment of 14 February 2002 ('*Yerodia*'); see Separate Opinion of President Guillaume, paras. 13–14; Joint Separate Opinion of Judges Higgins, Kooijmans, and Buergenthal, paras. 49–51; Dissenting Opinion of Judge ad hoc Van den Wyngaert, paras. 48–51. See also Jean d'Aspremont, 'Multilateral versus Unilateral Exercises of Universal Jurisdiction' (2010) 43 *Israel Law Review* 301, 311–15.

3.3.2 Treaties and Jurisdiction

It is important to note that states are entitled to pass jurisdiction to one another. The treaty-based transnational crimes are usually examples of where states have agreed between themselves that they may exercise jurisdiction on each other's behalf.[14] An example of this is Article 5(1) and (2) of the 1979 International Convention Against the Taking of Hostages.[15] Such treaties include obligations on (or permissions to) states parties to criminalize certain conduct on quite broad jurisdictional bases, and either to extradite or prosecute suspects. These treaties are often seen, albeit somewhat inaccurately, as creating universal jurisdiction.[16] Strictly speaking, it is 'conferred' jurisdiction. States parties to the treaty/convention agree that other states parties may exercise jurisdiction on their behalf.[17] There is nothing unlawful about this. States are entitled to pass jurisdiction to one another.[18] However, if a state were to assert a right to prosecute someone without a treaty basis that allows for a concession of one of the accepted forms of jurisdiction, it would violate international law, unless the convention can be regarded as reflective of custom.[19] Such claims of customary status are easier to make than prove. In the following sections, this chapter will concentrate on the jurisdiction states have pursuant to customary international law.

3.4 TRADITIONAL HEADS OF JURISDICTION

3.4.1 Territoriality Principle

The territoriality principle is the least controversial basis of jurisdiction. Under this principle, states have the right to exercise jurisdiction over all events on their territory. This includes their airspace and territorial waters, and also includes ships and aeroplanes which are registered in those countries as being what has been described as 'quasi-territorial' jurisdiction.[20] This is the position that the ICC Statute adopts too.[21] States also have quasi-territorial jurisdiction over areas which they are leasing (in accordance with the terms of that lease), or belligerently occupying.[22] The question of when and where a crime has been committed involves complex determinations of statehood and territorial

---

[14] See Section 14.1.2. A very useful discussion of this issue is included in Neil Boister, *An Introduction to Transnational Criminal Law*, 2nd ed. (Oxford, 2018) ch. 16.

[15] International Convention Against the Taking of Hostages, New York, 17 December 1979, entered into force on 3 June 1983, 1316 UNTS 205.

[16] The ICJ is not immune from this trend: see *Questions relating to the Obligation to Prosecute or Extradite (Belgium v. Senegal)*, ICJ, Judgment of 20 July 2012, para. 72.

[17] Boister, *Transnational Criminal Law* (n. 14) 250–64.

[18] Some doubt this: see e.g. Madeline Morris, 'High Crimes and Misconceptions: The ICC and Non-Party States' (2000) 64 *Law and Contemporary Problems* 131. But there is considerable practice to support its legality: see e.g. Dapo Akande, 'The Jurisdiction of the International Criminal Court over Nationals of Non-Parties: Legal Basis and Limits' (2003) 1 *JICJ* 618, 620–34.

[19] Anthony Colangelo, 'The Legal Limits of Universal Jurisdiction' (2006–7) 47 *Virginia Journal of International Law* 149, 166–9.

[20] Boister, *An Introduction to Transnational Criminal Law* (n. 14) 252–3. [21] ICC Statute, Art. 12(2)(a).

[22] Bernard H. Oxman, 'Jurisdiction of States' in Rüdiger Wolfrum (ed.), *Max Planck Encyclopedia of Public International Law* (Oxford, 2012) vol. VI, 547, 548.

holdings.[23] Confronted with a request by the ICC prosecutor for an investigation into the situation in Palestine, Pre-Trial Chamber I found that the Court's territorial jurisdiction extends to the territories occupied by Israel since 1967, namely Gaza and the West Bank, including East Jerusalem.[24]

A state normally has jurisdiction over a crime when the crime originates abroad or is completed elsewhere, so long as at least one of the elements of the offence occurs in its territory. The ICC held that it has territorial jurisdiction over the deportation of Rohingya from Myanmar, a non-state party, to Bangladesh, a state party to the ICC.[25] While most of the events are on the territory of Myanmar, an essential element of 'deportation' is the crossing of a border, and hence the crime is only completed in Bangladesh, thereby falling within the jurisdiction of the ICC.

Some would go further and classify the 'ubiquity' principle as an aspect of territorial jurisdiction. This principle is to the effect that, wherever a part of a crime (including complicity) occurs, there is territorial jurisdiction (as we saw with deportation from Myanmar to Bangladesh).[26] This theory departs from the premise that more than one state has jurisdiction. UK practice is even broader, as it asserts jurisdiction over (inchoate) conspiracies to commit crimes in the United Kingdom, even though all of the conduct occurs abroad, on the basis that the intended offence was to occur in the United Kingdom.[27]

While the exercise of territorial jurisdiction is the normal state of affairs, and *extra*territorial jurisdiction the exception, states have found many ways to extend territorial jurisdiction. Global governance has come with a need to 'territorialize extraterritorial activity'.[28] This makes the line between territorial and extraterritorial elusive. As some have argued, territorial jurisdiction has become an 'illusion'.[29] Against the background of the eroded distinction between territorial and extraterritorial jurisdiction, the ICC's Bangladesh/Myanmar ruling may not be as radical and contrived as some have claimed.[30]

3.4.2 Nationality Principle

The second generally accepted title of jurisdiction is nationality (sometimes known as 'active nationality').[31] States are entitled under international law to legislate with respect to the conduct of their nationals abroad. Article 12(2) of the Bosnia and Herzegovina Criminal Code, for example, states that '[t]he criminal legislation of Bosnia and Herzegovina shall be

[23] Michail Vagias, *The Territorial Jurisdiction of the International Criminal Court* (Cambridge, 2014).
[24] Situation in Palestine, ICC PTC I, 5 February 2021 (ICC-01/18–143).
[25] *Decision on the Prosecutor's Request for a Ruling on Jurisdiction under Article 19(3) of the Statute*, ICC PTC I, 6 September 2018 (ICC-RoC46(3)-01/18–37).
[26] Boister, *An Introduction to Transnational Criminal Law* (n. 14) 253–7.   [27] *DPP* v. *Doot* [1973] AC 807.
[28] Austen Parrish and Cedric Ryngaert, 'Introduction' in Austen Parrish and Cedric Ryngaert (eds.), *The Research Handbook on Extraterritorial Jurisdiction* (Cheltenham, 2023) 1.
[29] Peter Szigeti, 'The Illusion of Territorial Jurisdiction' (2017) 52 *Texas International Law Journal* 369.
[30] See Payam Akhavan, 'The Radically Routine *Rohingya* Case: Territorial Jurisdiction and the Crime of Deportation under the ICC Statute' (2019) 17 *JICJ* 325–45.
[31] For some of the benefits of nationality jurisdiction, see Paul Arnell, 'The Case for Nationality Based Jurisdiction' (2001) 50 *ICLQ* 955.

applied to a citizen of Bosnia and Herzegovina who, outside the territory of Bosnia and Herzegovina, perpetrates a criminal offence'.

Nationality is an important basis of jurisdiction in international criminal law, in particular in relation to armed forces (including peacekeepers) stationed overseas who, in the legislation of most states, 'carry the flag' abroad with them.[32] The principle, nonetheless, applies beyond the armed forces, and also covers civilians. An example of this is section 9 of the UK Offences Against the Person Act 1861, which, as an exception to the usual preference of common law countries for territorial jurisdiction, also asserts jurisdiction over murders committed by British nationals irrespective of the place of commission.

Nationality jurisdiction relies on the link between a national and the state to which they owe allegiance. For the most part, the question of who is a national is relatively uncontroversial and dealt with by the legislation of the state granting nationality. Equally, the extent to which other states are required to accept that nationality (and thus any jurisdiction based on it) is limited by international law.[33] One test for nationality in international law was given in the *Nottebohm* case: that the person with the purported nationality must have a 'genuine connection' with the state of which they are an alleged national.[34]

Some doubt that the *Nottebohm* test is the appropriate test for nationality jurisdiction. They do so on the basis that the *Nottebohm* case was dealing not with a jurisdictional matter, but with the extent to which a state could rely on its own grant of nationality to exercise diplomatic protection with respect to a person who had sought that nationality.[35] These are strong reasons, although it must be noted that others are happy to draw the analogy.[36] Where jurisdiction is being asserted on the basis of the nationality of the offender, the *locus delicti* is being required to accept the jurisdiction of a foreign state over events on its territory, so there are some parallels that may legitimately be drawn. Nonetheless, the broad jurisdiction accepted by international law in relation to international crimes (when compared to ordinary domestic crimes) means that this will rarely be an issue, unless a person who denies nationality is being prosecuted under legislation that does not lawfully adopt broader jurisdictional claims.

For nationality jurisdiction, it is often required that the person over whom that jurisdiction is being asserted was a national at the time of the offence rather than after. Otherwise, it has been claimed, a violation of the *nullum crimen sine lege* principle could occur.[37] Nevertheless, some states provide for jurisdiction in the situation where suspects later acquire their nationality.[38] Those states tend to view such an exercise of the jurisdiction as being a vicarious use of the authority of the state on whose territory the crime was committed (*locus delicti*).[39] As a result, the lawfulness of any such use depends on whether

---

[32] This is important as often, under Status of Forces agreements, territorial states agree to waive their jurisdiction over foreign forces in their territory. See generally Rain Liivoja, *An Axiom of Military Law: Applicability of National Criminal Law to Military Personnel and Associated Civilians Abroad* (Helsinki, 2011).

[33] Staker, 'Jurisdiction' (n. 12) 318–21. [34] *Nottebohm Case (Liechtenstein v. Guatemala)*, ICJ, Judgment of 6 April 1955, 4.

[35] Staker, 'Jurisdiction' (n. 12) 320. More generally, see Chittharanjan Amerasinghe, *Diplomatic Protection* (Oxford, 2008) 92–6, 113–16.

[36] Bruno Simma and Andreas Th. Müller, 'Exercise and Limits of Jurisdiction' in James Crawford and Martti Koskenniemi (eds.), *The Cambridge Companion to International Law* (Cambridge, 2012) 134, 142.

[37] See Roger O'Keefe, 'Universal Jurisdiction: Clarifying the Basic Concept' (2004) 2 *JICJ* 735, 742–3.

[38] See e.g. Swedish Penal Code, ch. 2, s. 2 and Dutch International Crimes Act, Art. 2(2).

[39] This is justified on the basis that many states adopting such a position refuse to extradite their nationals.

the conduct for which the suspect is prosecuted was criminal in the *locus delicti* (or in international law) at the time of its commission. This is also referred to as the requirement of dual criminality.[40]

Some states assert jurisdiction over the activities of their permanent residents (over and above their nationals) when they are abroad. This is an expanded form of nationality jurisdiction,[41] but one which is acceptable under international law, as those who have chosen to reside permanently in a state are clearly understood to be analogous to its nationals. A similar consideration applies to non-nationals who serve in a state's armed forces.

One of the most well-known uses of nationality jurisdiction was the US prosecution of Lieutenant William Calley for his role in the My Lai massacre in Vietnam.[42] This case also provides an example of one of the criticisms often laid at the door of nationality jurisdiction, that prosecutions by states of their own nationals for war crimes tend to be overly lenient.[43]

3.4.3 Passive Personality Principle

Passive personality jurisdiction is jurisdiction exercised by a state over crimes committed against its nationals whilst they are abroad. In most instances, the assertion of such jurisdiction is controversial. All of the judges who expressed an opinion on the matter in the *Lotus* case took the view that customary international law does not accept such a principle.[44] There has been an increase in the use of passive personality jurisdiction, particularly by the United States, in relation to terrorist offences,[45] and there is increasing support for it.[46] However, considerable disagreement remains surrounding the lawfulness of its application.[47] There are fears that passive personality jurisdiction favours powerful states. Concerns have also been raised that passive personality jurisdiction could lead to people being subjected simultaneously to the laws of many different states, which would include prohibitions of which they were understandably unaware.[48]

The latter problem only arises where the law differs between states. This may be less relevant for international crimes, as its prohibitions apply across states rather than reflecting national oddities. One of the few areas in which passive personality jurisdiction has traditionally been accepted is in relation to war crimes.[49] Thus, states have the right to prosecute war crimes committed against their nationals. One of many examples is the *Almelo* case,[50] in which a German national was prosecuted by a British military court for

---

[40] See Harmen van der Wilt, *The Law and Practice of Extradition* (Abingdon, 2022) ch. 3.
[41] See further James Crawford, *Brownlie's Principles of Public International Law*, 8th ed. (Oxford, 2012) 459–60.
[42] *United States* v. *Calley* (1969) 41 CMR 96; (1973) 46 CMR 1131; (1973) 48 CMR 19.
[43] See Timothy L. H. McCormack, 'Their Atrocities and Our Misdemeanours: The Reticence of States to Try Their "Own Nationals" for International Crimes' in Philippe Sands and Mark Lattimer (eds.), *Justice for Crimes against Humanity* (Oxford, 2003) 107. See further Chapter 4.
[44] See e.g. David J. Harris, *Cases and Materials on International Law*, 6th ed. (London, 2005) 281; the judgment itself, however, does not contain a ruling on the matter.
[45] One example is *United States* v. *Yunis* (1991) 30 ILM 403.
[46] Simma and Müller, 'Exercise and Limits' (n. 36) 142–3. China, South Korea, and Japan provide for broad prescriptions of passive nationality jurisdiction: Danielle Ireland-Piper, *Extraterritoriality in East Asia: Extraterritorial Criminal Jurisdiction in China, Japan, and South Korea* (Cheltenham, 2021).
[47] See Staker, 'Jurisdiction' (n. 12). [48] James L. Brierly, 'The "Lotus Case"' (1928) 44 *Law Quarterly Review* 154, 161.
[49] E.g. *Rohrig, Brunner and Heinze* (1950) 17 ILR 393. [50] I LRTWC 35.

killing a UK national in the Netherlands. International law goes beyond this, however, to permit prosecution of offences committed against the nationals of co-belligerent states. For example, in the *Velpke Baby Home* case, the United Kingdom prosecuted German nationals for neglect and mistreatment of Polish children which took place in Germany.[51]

Where passive personality jurisdiction is asserted over international crimes, the same questions arise in relation to determining nationality as for active personality jurisdiction. The relevant time for determining nationality is generally considered to be the time of the offence. Consequently, the fact that a person later gains the nationality of a state that wishes to prosecute offences against them does not grant that state passive personality jurisdiction. As with nationality jurisdiction, however, the broader jurisdiction applicable to inter-national crimes means that this will not normally be a problem. For example, Israel sought to assert passive personality jurisdiction in the *Eichmann* case on behalf of Eichmann's Jewish victims. Its claims on this basis, in relation to the victims who were not Israeli nationals at the time of Eichmann's offences, have been criticized.[52] However, Israel's right to try Eichmann because of the universality principle was generally accepted.

3.4.4 Protective Principle

A state is entitled to assert protective jurisdiction over extra-territorial activities that threaten state security, such as the selling of a state's secrets, spying, or the counterfeiting of its currency or official seal. Although this jurisdictional title could be used to justify the assertion of jurisdiction over aggression, and was asserted by Israel as one of the bases of jurisdiction over Adolf Eichmann,[53] practically all its imaginable uses in relation to international criminal law overlap with territorial, nationality, or passive personality juris-diction. The assertion of the protective principle in *Eichmann* was criticized on the basis that the state of Israel did not exist at the time of the commission of the offences, but under international law, universal jurisdiction existed anyway.[54]

3.5 UNIVERSAL JURISDICTION

3.5.1 Introduction

Universal jurisdiction is the most controversial title of jurisdiction in international criminal law. It is certainly the most talked about.[55] The term 'universal jurisdiction' refers to jurisdiction established over a crime without reference to the place of perpetration, the nationality of the suspect or the victim, or any other recognized linking point between the crime and the prosecuting state. It is the type of jurisdiction limited to specific crimes. There

---

[51] George Brand, *Trial of Heinrich Gerike* (London, 1950). Lauterpacht ('Foreword', *ibid*. xv) went further, to assert that the trial was based on universality, but see George Brand, 'Introduction', *ibid*. xxix.

[52] James E. S. Fawcett, 'The Eichmann Case' (1962) 38 *British Yearbook of International Law* 181, 190–2.

[53] *Attorney-General of Israel* v. *Eichmann* (1968) 36 ILR 18, 54–7, 304.

[54] David Lasok, 'The Eichmann Trial' (1962) 11 *ICLQ* 355, 364.

[55] For a useful overview of the voluminous literature on the subject at the turn of the millennium, see A. Hays Butler, 'The Doctrine of Universal Jurisdiction: A Review of the Literature' (2000) 11 *Criminal Law Forum* 353.

are those who deny that universal jurisdiction exists at all.[56] However, the view more consistent with current practice is that, other than piracy, which is subject to universal jurisdiction owing to its occurring, by definition, on the high seas,[57] states are entitled to assert universal jurisdiction over war crimes, crimes against humanity, genocide, and torture,[58] as those crimes are defined in customary law.[59] There is only a small number of states (about eighteen) with universal jurisdiction over aggression,[60] yet there are no examples of universal jurisdiction prosecutions for aggression.[61] The conflict in Ukraine has led to prosecution of aggression/crimes against peace by domestic courts in Ukraine, that is, on the basis of territorial and not universal jurisdiction.[62]

Jurisdiction tends to inhere in states for the purpose of protecting their own interests. The purpose of universal jurisdiction, on the other hand, is linked to the idea that international crimes affect the international legal order as a whole.[63] Owing to the recognition that such offences affect all states and peoples, and awareness that territorial and nationality states do not always respond fairly and effectively to allegations of international crimes, international law grants all states the right to prosecute them. The precise conditions under which a state may do so, however, are controversial. The discussion below relates to whether states are entitled to assert universal jurisdiction. There is no real evidence that, outside treaty obligations, states are *obliged* to do so.[64]

3.5.2 Approaches to Universal Jurisdiction

Universal jurisdiction has often, at least since the International Court of Justice (ICJ)'s decision in the *Yerodia* case,[65] been separated into two subcategories. These are often termed 'absolute' or 'pure' universal jurisdiction (also known as 'universal jurisdiction *in absentia*') and 'conditional' or 'qualified' universal jurisdiction (sometimes known as 'universal jurisdiction with presence'). Pure universal jurisdiction is when a state seeks to assert jurisdiction over an international crime (usually by investigating it and/or requesting extradition of the suspect) even when the suspect is not present in the territory of the

---

[56] See e.g. Alfred Rubin, 'Actio Popularis, Jus Cogens and Offences Erga Omnes' (2001) 35 *New England Law Review* 265; Marc Henzelin, *Le Principe de l'Universalité en Droit Pénal Internationale* (Brussels, 2000).

[57] Some question whether piracy is an appropriate analogy for modern assertions of universal jurisdiction: see Eugene Kontorovich, 'The Piracy Analogy: Modern Universal Jurisdiction's Hollow Foundation' (2004) 45 *Harvard International Law Journal* 183. Even if this is the case, however, it does not undermine state practice in the area.

[58] See Institut de Droit International, Seventeenth Commission, Universal Jurisdiction over Genocide, Crimes against Humanity and War Crimes (Krakow, 2005) 2. See Kreß, 'Universal Jurisdiction' (n. 2). On torture, see *Furundžija*, ICTY TC II, 10 December 1998, para. 156.

[59] Colangelo, 'The Legal Limits' (n. 19).

[60] Carrie McDougall, 'Prosecuting Putin for his Crime of Aggression: Part Two', *Oxford Human Rights Hub*, 8 March 2022, https://ohrh.law.ox.ac.uk/prosecuting-putin-for-his-crime-of-aggression-against-ukraine-part-two/.

[61] Attempts to persuade German prosecutors to take on the question of aggression with respect to Iraq have failed: see e.g. Claus Kreß, 'The German Chief Federal Prosecutor's Decision Not to Investigate the Alleged Crime of Preparing Aggression against Iraq' (2003) 2 *JICJ* 245. See also Section 4.2.

[62] See Section 4.2.

[63] Rosalyn Higgins, *Problems and Process: International Law and How We Use It* (Oxford, 1994) 56–63; Andreas Zimmermann, 'Violations of Fundamental Norms of International Law and the Exercise of Universal Jurisdiction in Criminal Matters' in Christian Tomuschat and Jean-Marc Thouvenin (eds.), *The Fundamental Rules of the International Legal Order* (Leiden, 2006) 335; Simma and Müller, 'Exercise' (n. 36) 144; Alejandro Chehtman, *The Philosophical Foundations of Extraterritorial Punishment* (Oxford, 2010).

[64] See Boister, *An Introduction to Transnational Criminal Law* (n. 14) 264–8. [65] *Yerodia* (n. 13).

investigating state. Conditional universal jurisdiction is exercised when the suspect is already in the state asserting jurisdiction.

The distinction has gathered considerable acceptance in academic literature.[66] Although the matter is not entirely beyond controversy, the better view is that the distinction is non-existent at a conceptual level.[67] That said, many states limit their use of universal jurisdiction to where a person is present on their territory.[68] This can, at least in part, be explained on the basis that adopting pure universal jurisdiction 'may show a lack of international courtesy'.[69] Where states have adopted such a limit, it appears that some of them have done so as a matter of practical prudence rather than as a matter of law.[70]

3.5.3 Rise of Universal Jurisdiction

The possibility of universal jurisdiction being exercised over war crimes was mooted during the Second World War.[71] A number of cases prosecuted after the Second World War could be justified or explained on the basis of universal jurisdiction.[72] The United Nations War Crimes Commission[73] took the view that 'the right to punish war crimes ... is possessed by any independent State whatsoever'.[74] Equally those cases could be justified on the basis of the expanded passive personality jurisdiction international law accepts for war crimes.

In 1949, the Geneva Conventions provided a treaty-based analogue to universal jurisdiction in relation to their grave breaches provisions. Article 49 of Geneva Convention I (to which the other three Conventions have similar provisions) reads:

Each High Contracting Party shall be under the obligation to search for persons alleged to have committed, or to have ordered to be committed, such grave breaches and shall bring such persons, regardless of their nationality, before its own courts [or hand them over to another High Contracting Party].

The grave breaches regime is often considered a paradigmatic case of universal jurisdiction. Given that (other than Common Article 3) the Conventions only apply to conflicts between High Contracting Parties,[75] by their own terms the grave breaches provisions only have *inter partes* effect as a matter of treaty law. Still, these provisions clearly reflect customary

---

[66] See e.g. Antonio Cassese, 'Is the Bell Tolling for Universality? A Plea for a Sensible Notion of Universal Jurisdiction' (2003) 1 *JICJ* 589, 592–3; Georges Abi-Saab, 'The Proper Role of Universal Jurisdiction' (2003) 1 *JICJ* 596, 601.
[67] O'Keefe, 'Universal Jurisdiction' (n. 37), is a particularly powerful argument to this effect. See also Thomas Weigend, 'Grund und Grenzen universaler Gerichtsbarkeit' in Jörg Arnold et al. (eds.), *Festschrift für Albin Eser* (Munich, 2005) 955; Kreß, 'Universal Jurisdiction' (n. 58) 576–8; Crawford, *Brownlie's Principles* (n. 41) 469.
[68] Fannie Lafontaine, 'Universal Jurisdiction: The Realistic Utopia' (2012) 10 *JICJ* 1277, 1280–3.
[69] *Yerodia* (n. 13), Separate Opinion of Judge ad hoc Van den Wyngaert, para. 3.
[70] See Resolution of the Institut de Droit International, 'Universal criminal jurisdiction with regard to the crime of genocide, crimes against humanity and war crimes' (2005) para. 3(b), treading a middle path between the different approaches: '[e]xercise of universal jurisdiction requires presence of the alleged perpetrator in the territory of the prosecuting State'.
[71] Willard Cowles, 'Universality of Jurisdiction over War Crimes' (1945) 33 *California Law Review* 177.
[72] E.g. *Tesch and others* ('the Zyklon B case') (1947) I LRTWC 93.
[73] The Commission was an inter-Allied body, rather than the (practically) universal international organization.
[74] (1949) XV LRTWC 26 (Commentary). [75] Geneva Conventions, Common Art. 2.

law and the fact that essentially every state in the world has ratified the Conventions makes this a distinction of form rather than substance.[76]

Probably the most famous exercise of universal jurisdiction was the Israeli prosecution of Adolf Eichmann. Eichmann was abducted from Argentina in 1960 by the Israeli security service, Mossad, and flown to Jerusalem to be tried.[77] The District Court in Jerusalem, in affirming Israel's right to prosecute him, stated that:

The abhorrent crimes defined under this Law are not crimes under Israeli law alone. These crimes, which struck at the whole of mankind and shocked the conscience of nations, are grave offences against the law of nations itself (*delicta juris gentium*). Therefore, so far from international law negating or limiting the jurisdiction of countries with respect to such crimes, international law is, in the absence of an international court, in need of the judicial and legislative organs of every country to give effect to its criminal interdictions and to bring the criminals to trial. The jurisdiction to try crimes under international law is universal.[78]

It might be noted that, in spite of its comments about an international criminal court which, in light of the principle of complementarity, now seem anachronistic, the District Court's opinion is a strong affirmation of a right (and perhaps even a duty) to establish universal jurisdiction over international crimes. Israel did rely on other bases of jurisdiction, but its primary jurisdictional claim was universality, as the Israeli Supreme Court explained:

if in our judgment we have concentrated on the international and universal character of the crimes . . . one of the reasons for our so doing is that some of them were directed against non-Jewish groups.[79]

After *Eichmann*, there was little evidence of any political will to engage in universal jurisdiction prosecutions until 1985, when Israel requested the extradition of John Demjanjuk from the United States. Demjanjuk was suspected of being a notorious camp guard in Treblinka known as 'Ivan the Terrible'. The United States agreed to extradite Demjanjuk,[80] who stood trial in Israel, but was acquitted on the basis that, although he was a guard at Sobibor and Trawniki camps, he was not that particular person.[81]

Other examples of assertions of universal jurisdiction around this time were legislative acts such as the UK War Crimes Act 1991[82] and Australia's War Crimes Amendment Act 1988,[83] both of which dealt with offences committed in the Second World War by those acting on

---

[76] The situation with respect to grave breaches of Additional Protocol I is a little more complex, as it is less (although still broadly) ratified. Most, if not all, of the grave breaches provisions of Additional Protocol I, however, reflect customary law.

[77] Israel originally claimed that the 'rendition' (in modern terminology) was undertaken by public-spirited private Israeli citizens, but its assertion was not widely believed. See also Sections 3.2.3 and 4.2.

[78] (1968) 36 ILR 5, para. 12 (District Court).   [79] (1968) 36 ILR 277, para. 12 (Supreme Court).

[80] *Demjanjuk* v. *Petrovsky*, 776 F 2d 571 (USCA 6th Cir. 1985); cert. den. 475 US 1016 (1986); 628 F Supp 1370 (1986); 784 F 2d 1254 (1986).

[81] See Jonathan M. Weinig, 'Enforcing the Lessons of History: Israel Judges the Holocaust' in Timothy L. H. McCormack and Gerry J. Simpson (eds.), *The Law of War Crimes: National and International Approaches* (The Hague, 1997) 103, 115–18. Demjanjuk was finally convicted by a Munich court in 2011 for crimes committed as a guard in Sobibor in 1943. He was sentenced to five years' imprisonment but set free pending an appeal. He died on 17 March 2012 before the appeal judgment could be delivered.

[82] War Crimes Act 1991, s. 1(a). On the Act, see Christopher Greenwood, 'The War Crimes Act 1991' in Hazel Fox and Michael A. Meyer (eds.), *Armed Conflict and the New Law: Effecting Compliance* (London, 1993) 215.

[83] War Crimes Amendment Act 1988, s. 5. See generally Gillian Triggs, 'Australia's War Crimes Trials: A Moral Necessity or Legal Minefield?' (1987) 16 *Melbourne University Law Review* 382.

behalf of the Axis but who later became residents of those two countries. As jurisdiction crystallizes at the time of the offence, these Acts, and the (limited) prosecutions under them, are best seen as based on universal jurisdiction.[84] This is because later residence per se is not a head of jurisdiction, and the basis of jurisdiction is not territoriality or nationality.[85]

The conflicts in Yugoslavia and Rwanda (which notably gave rise to the ICTY and International Criminal Tribunal for Rwanda (ICTR)) led to a number of prosecutions, in particular of people who had come to countries such as Germany and Switzerland as refugees.[86] A number of prosecutions were undertaken in Belgium, pursuant to its Law of 16 June 1993 relating to the Repression of Grave Breaches of the Geneva Conventions of 12 August 1949 and their Protocols I and II of 8 June 1977, which criminalized certain violations of those treaties without regard to the place of their commission.[87]

By 1999, it appeared that universal jurisdiction was gaining considerable momentum. The *Pinochet* litigation throughout Europe,[88] for example, was thought by commentators to represent 'the globalization of human rights law through the affirmation that the consequences of, and jurisdiction over, gross violations are not limited to the state in which they (mostly) occur, or of that of the nationality of the majority of the victims'.[89] In the same year, Belgium revised its 1993 legislation on grave breaches to add to it jurisdiction over genocide and crimes against humanity 'irrespective of where such breaches have been committed'.[90] The presence of the suspect in Belgium was not required for the initiation of proceedings, which could be brought by private parties. The 1999 law also declared that immunities were inapplicable in proceedings relating to the Act.[91]

3.5.4 Retrenchment of Universal Jurisdiction?

Although Belgium's 1993 statute gave rise to a number of proceedings relating to Rwanda, which did not upset the Rwandan government,[92] that law proved to be politically controversial. Proceedings were brought against a number of foreign leaders, among which Ariel Sharon, Yasser Arafat, Fidel Castro, and Hashemi Rafsanjani.[93] These proceedings all led to political embarrassment for Belgium. The case against Abduldaye Yerodia Ndombasi led to a challenge to the Belgian law in the ICJ.

---

[84] See Chapter 4.
[85] It would be possible to argue that jurisdiction could be co-belligerent (or passive personal jurisdiction), but the Acts do not limit themselves to victims who were nationals of the Allied powers.
[86] Andreas Ziegler, 'International Decisions: In re G' (1998) 82 *AJIL* 78; Luc Reydams, *Universal Jurisdiction: International and Municipal Legal Perspectives* (Oxford, 2003) 196–200.
[87] See Reydams, *Universal Jurisdiction* (n. 86) 109–16. [88] See the comments on the various cases in (1999) 93 *AJIL* 690.
[89] Christine Chinkin, 'R v. Bow Street Stipendiary Magistrate, Ex Parte Pinochet (No. 3) [1999] 2 WLR 827' (1999) 93 *AJIL* 703, 711. The precise bases of jurisdiction were made more complex by the fact that jurisdiction under general international law was supplemented in a number of states with arguments based on the Torture Convention.
[90] (1999) ILM 921, Art. 7. For an overview, see Damien Vandermeersch, 'Prosecuting International Crimes in Belgium' (2005) 3 *JICJ* 400.
[91] (1999) ILM 921, Art. 5(3).
[92] See Luc Reydams, 'Belgium's First Application of Universal Jurisdiction: The Butare Four Case' (2003) 1 *JICJ* 428.
[93] See Steven R. Ratner, 'Belgium's War Crimes Statute: A Postmortem' (2003) 97 *AJIL* 888, 890.

The Yerodia *Case*

Abdoulaye Yerodia Ndombasi, at that point foreign minister of the Democratic Republic of the Congo (DRC), was the subject of an international arrest warrant issued by Damien Vandermeersch, a Belgian investigating judge, on 11 April 2000. Six months later, the DRC brought a suit against Belgium in the ICJ, alleging that Belgium had acted unlawfully by asserting universal jurisdiction over Yerodia and ignoring his immunity as a foreign minister.[94] Late in the proceedings, the DRC dropped the claim relating to universal jurisdiction, and concentrated on the issue of immunities, on which the ICJ eventually found in its favour.[95]

Owing to the DRC's litigation strategy, the majority decided that the ICJ did not need to determine the lawfulness of Belgium's assertion of universal jurisdiction. The majority was criticized for this by a number of the judges, including the President of the Court, Gilbert Guillaume,[96] Judges Higgins, Kooijmans, and Buergenthal,[97] and the Belgian ad hoc judge, Christine Van den Wyngaert.[98] Their critiques are telling: logically the question of jurisdiction precedes that of immunity (as there must be immunity from something).[99] Also, the arguments about immunity may have been affected by the arguments about universal jurisdiction (in particular those relating to *ius cogens*).

Unlike the majority decision, a number of the separate and dissenting opinions dealt with universal jurisdiction in detail. They revealed a deeply divided court. Four judges (President Guillaume, Judges Ranjeva, Rezek, and Judge ad hoc Bula-Bula) were opposed to the assertion of jurisdiction, whereas six judges (Judge Koroma, Judges Higgins, Buergenthal, and Kooijmans in their joint opinion, as well as Judge al-Khasawneh and Judge ad hoc Van den Wyngaert) supported it (Judge al-Khasawneh at least implicitly took that view).[100] Although many saw this case as a blow to universal jurisdiction, it must be noted that the majority of judges who expressed a view on the matter upheld it and only one of the judges (Guillaume) questioned the use of universal jurisdiction where the person is found in the territory of the state asserting jurisdiction. Three of the four judges who criticized universal jurisdiction appear only to be referring to such jurisdiction being asserted *in absentia*. Only President Guillaume appeared hostile to any sort of universal jurisdiction outside of piracy and treaty regimes.[101]

Limiting Universality

Belgium's political problems with its law did not end with the *Yerodia* case. Following attempts to indict ex-President George H. W. Bush, Vice-President Dick Cheney, and Colin Powell for war crimes alleged to have been committed by them in the Gulf War in 1991, Belgium came under heavy pressure from the United States to alter its legislation.[102] In

---

[94] See Neil Boister, 'The ICJ in the Belgian Arrest Warrant Case: Arresting the Development of International Criminal Law' (2002) 7 *Journal of Conflict and Security Law* 293; O'Keefe, 'Universal Jurisdiction' (n. 37).
[95] See Chapter 21.   [96] *Yerodia* (n. 13), Separate Opinion of the President, para. 1.
[97] *Yerodia* (n. 13), Joint Separate Opinion of Judges Higgins, Kooijmans, and Buergenthal, paras. 3–5.
[98] *Yerodia* (n. 13), Dissenting Opinion of Judge ad hoc Van den Wyngaert, para. 41.   [99] *Yerodia* (n. 13) para. 46.
[100] Judge Oda also seemed sympathetic: *ibid*. Dissenting Opinion of Judge Oda, para. 12.
[101] *Ibid*., Separate Opinion of President Guillaume, para. 16.   [102] Ratner, 'Belgium's War Crimes Statute' (n. 93).

response, Belgium altered its legislation twice in 2003 to limit its jurisdiction and reintro-duce immunities.[103] Some saw the Belgian action as signalling the demise of broad notions of universality.[104] The Belgian law is no longer as wide, but it retains some universal jurisdiction elements. For example, jurisdiction may be exercised if a perpetrator later becomes a Belgian resident.[105] It is also clear that the Belgian position is not that universal jurisdiction *in absentia* is unlawful. Its stated reason for repealing the Act was that it had been abused. After 2003, Belgium sought the extradition of Hissène Habré, the ex-dictator of Chad, pursuant to a complaint made before the Act was amended, on the basis of absolute universality. This implies that its view is that universal jurisdiction remains available in international law.[106]

The other state whose use of universal jurisdiction appeared to have been reined in somewhat is Spain. Spain was the first state to ask the United Kingdom to extradite General Pinochet.[107] It has, since 1999, also indicted and convicted a number of ex-members of military juntas from Latin America. Although the *Pinochet* case failed to lead to an extradition owing to the UK Home Secretary's determination that the defendant's ill-health prevented it, Spain has used universal jurisdiction successfully in other cases. It has, *inter alia*, obtained the extradition of Ricardo Cavallo, accused of torture in Argentina, and convicted Adolfo Scilingo for crimes against humanity for his role in torture and killings in Argentina after he went to Spain to testify about his actions in another case.[108]

A number of cases since 2000 did, however, place a fairly restrictive interpretation on universal jurisdiction, requiring that Spanish universal jurisdiction be 'subsidiary' to the jurisdiction of the territorial state, with Spain only having jurisdiction if there is no effort to prosecute by that state. This may be a sensible practical limit, but is not required by inter-national law.[109] The Spanish cases also appeared to require the presence of the suspect in Spain, although presence pursuant to extradition, as in the *Cavallo* case, seemed sufficient.[110] A firm reaffirmation of universal jurisdiction, without any of the limitations suggested in the previous cases, came from the Spanish Constitutional Tribunal in the *Guatemala Genocide* case, which expressly repudiated the earlier, more limited, jurisprudence.[111] However, after a number of

---

[103] See *ibid.*; Luc Reydams, 'Belgium Reneges on Universality: The 5 August 2003 Act on Grave Breaches of International Humanitarian Law' (2003) 1 *JICJ* 679.

[104] Cassese, 'Is the Bell Tolling?' (n. 66).   [105] Criminal Procedure Code, Art. 6.1°*bis*.

[106] In that particular case, the extradition request was refused and Senegal agreed to try Habré itself. The proceedings moved very slowly, and in 2012 the ICJ determined that these delays meant that Senegal was violating its duty to prosecute under the Torture Convention: *Questions relating to the Obligation to Prosecute or Extradite* (*Belgium* v. *Senegal*), ICJ, Judgment of 20 July 2012. In May 2016, Habré was convicted by the Extraordinary African Chambers in Senegal and sentenced to life imprisonment. See further Section 9.2.4.

[107] Some, but not all, of the victims of the conduct for which Spain sought to extradite Pinochet were Spanish.

[108] See Christian Tomuschat, 'Issues of Universal Jurisdiction in the Scilingo Case' (2005) 3 *JICJ* 1074; Alicia Gil Gil, 'The Flaws of the Scilingo Judgment' (2005) 3 *JICJ* 1082; Giulia Pinzauti, 'An Instance of Reasonable Universality' (2005) 3 *JICJ* 1092.

[109] *Guatemalan Generals* case, Tribunal Supremo, Sala de lo Penal, Sentencia 327/2003, 25 February 2003. See Hervé Ascensio, 'Are Spanish Courts Backing Down on Universality? The Supreme Tribunal's Decision in Guatemalan Generals' (2003) 1 *JICJ* 690, 695–7. For a (persuasive) argument that this has not become customary, even though as a matter of policy it is very sensible, see Cedric Ryngaert, 'Applying the Rome Statutes Complementarity Principle: Drawing Lessons from the Prosecution of Core Crimes by States Acting under the Universality Principle' (2008) 19 *Criminal Law Forum* 153, 173–7; see also Lafontaine, 'Universal Jurisdiction' (n. 68) 1286–302; however, see also Kreß, 'Universal Jurisdiction' (n. 58) 579–81.

[110] Cassese, 'Is the Bell Tolling?' (n. 66) 590.

[111] Naomi Roht-Arriaza, 'Guatemala Genocide Case' (2006) 100 *AJIL* 207; Hervé Ascenscio, 'The Spanish Constitutional Tribunal's Decision in Guatemalan Generals' (2006) 4 *JICJ* 586.

controversial attempts to prosecute, *inter alia*, American officials, similar pressures to those that were brought to bear on Belgium led the Spanish Parliament to include subsidiarity-based limitations on Spanish exercises of universal jurisdiction.[112]

The Expansion of Universal Jurisdiction

The Belgian and Spanish experiences do not represent universal jurisdiction trends.[113] Research has shown that universal jurisdiction has been quietly expanding, often under the radar because it related to low-level offenders with no efforts to publicize these trials.[114] Some states, having become parties to the Statute of the International Criminal Court, have introduced international crimes into their domestic law and adopted universal jurisdiction over them. Quite a number have created specialized international crimes units, and the EU has established a network of cooperation via contact points in member states, the Genocide Network, hosted by Eurojust.[115]

Germany provides for absolute universal jurisdiction[116] but the prosecutor has discretion to dismiss the case if there is no link to Germany or it is being investigated by a more closely related state or an international criminal court.[117] The United Kingdom and Canada have both included jurisdiction over offences committed by non-nationals who later become linked to them in specified ways. It suffices for Canada's War Crimes and Crimes Against Humanity Act that the person is later present in Canada (section 8). For prosecution in the United Kingdom, the relevant legislation only requires that the person later becomes a resident.[118] Owing to the fact that the ICC Statute does not require states to adopt universal jurisdiction (or even mention it), this acceptance must be based on the position in customary international law.[119] Other states which have adopted universal jurisdiction legislation include Trinidad and Tobago,[120] the Netherlands,[121] Sweden,[122] France,[123]

---

[112] Ley Organcia del Poder Judicial, 4 November 2009. See generally Enrique Carnero Rojo, 'National Legislation Providing for the Prosecution and Punishment of International Crimes in Spain' (2011) 9 *JICJ* 699.

[113] See e.g. Luc Reydams, 'The Rise and Fall of Universal Jurisdiction' in Schabas and Bernaz, *Routledge Handbook*, 337.

[114] Maximo Langer and Mackenzie Eason, 'The Quiet Expansion of Universal Jurisdiction' (2019) 30 *European Journal of International Law* 779; Máximo Langer, 'The Diplomacy of Universal Jurisdiction: The Political Branches and the Transnational Prosecution of International Crimes' (2011) 105 *AJIL* 1; Joseph Rikhof, 'Fewer Places to Hide? The Impact of Domestic War Crimes Prosecutions on International Impunity' (2009) 20 *Criminal Law Forum* 1.

[115] See Eurojust, 'Genocide Network', www.eurojust.europa.eu/judicial-cooperation/practitioner-networks/genocide-network.

[116] Völkerstrafgesetzbuch (Code of Crimes Against International Law), Art. 1.

[117] Art. 153f Strafprozeßordnung (Code of Criminal Procedure). On practice relating to this, see Kai Ambos, 'International Core Crimes, Universal Jurisdiction and § 153F of the German Criminal Procedure Code' (2007) 18 *Criminal Law Forum* 43; Thomas Beck and Christian Ritscher, 'Do Criminal Complaints Make Sense in (German) International Criminal Law? A Prosecutor's Perspective' (2015) 13 *JICJ* 229.

[118] International Criminal Court Act 2001, s. 68(1). On the definition of 'resident' as amended by the Coroners and Justice Act 2009, see Robert Cryer and Paul David Mora, 'The Coroners and Justice Act 2009 and International Criminal Law: Backing into the Future?' (2010) 59 *ICLQ* 803, 810–13.

[119] Although in its comments on universal jurisdiction to the Sixth Committee of the General Assembly, the United Kingdom was equivocal on universal jurisdiction over crimes against humanity and genocide: *The Scope and Application of the Principle of Universal Jurisdiction, Report of the Secretary-General*, UN Doc. A/66/93 (20 June 2011) 10.

[120] International Criminal Court Act 2006, s. 8.

[121] International Crimes Act 2003, s. 2. See Erwin van der Borght, 'Prosecution of International Crimes in the Netherlands: An Analysis of Recent Case Law' (2007) 28 *Criminal Law Forum* 87.

[122] Sweden has universal jurisdiction over any crime with a minimum sentence of four years under a separate provision in the Swedish Criminal Code (SCC). Universal jurisdiction over international crimes is provided for in the (SCC) and the Swedish Act on Criminal Responsibility for Genocide, Crimes Against Humanity and War Crimes (art. 1–11).

[123] Art. 689 of the Code de Procédure Pénale provides for universal jurisdiction (art. 689–11 for ICC crimes). On 23 May 2023, the Cour de Cassation revised its – controversial – decision that universal jurisdiction requires dual criminality verification. See

Peru,[124] Argentina,[125] and Senegal.[126] Oddly enough, Italy, the birthplace of the Rome Statute, still has no ICC implementing legislation and no universal jurisdiction over international crimes. The United States, no frequent friend of universal jurisdiction on the basis of customary law,[127] has adopted 'expanded jurisdiction' with regard to war crimes related to child soldiers.[128] US courts have jurisdiction over persons in US territory, regardless of nationality, who recruit, enlist, or conscript child soldiers. This has been expanded with the Justice for Victims of War Crimes Act,[129] which gives the United States jurisdiction over war crimes beyond the use, recruitment, and enlistment of child soldiers.[130]

A particularly notable example of state practice is the declaration of the African Union of 2008. In this, the Assembly of Heads of State and Government, in spite of condemning the abuse of universal jurisdiction,[131]

recognis[ed] that universal jurisdiction is a principle of international law whose purpose is to ensure that individuals who commit grave offences such as war crimes and crimes against humanity do not do so with impunity and are brought to justice, which is in line with ... the Constitutive Act of the African Union.[132]

This is a significant official statement by fifty-three states, a number of which have had officials investigated on the basis of universal jurisdiction, which recognizes the lawfulness of such jurisdiction. The concern was with the abuse, not the existence, of the universal jurisdiction.

Nonetheless, the African Union has been very critical of some uses of universal jurisdiction. Its expressions of concern about universal jurisdiction have engendered considerable debate,[133] but a careful reading of its practice reveals that the primary concern is immunities, rather than the existence of universal jurisdiction, and that 'contrary to appearances ... universal jurisdiction is unobjectionable to this bloc'.[134] Indeed, the African Union has adopted a draft model law on universal jurisdiction that, in addition to war crimes, suggests that African states should adopt universal jurisdiction over crimes against humanity and genocide, as well as piracy, drug trafficking, and terrorism.[135] In part in response to African Union concerns, the Sixth Committee of the UN General Assembly has been studying the

---

Juliette Rémond Tiedrez, 'France's Highest Court Confirms Universal Jurisidction', EJILTalk!, 1 June 2023, www.ejiltalk.org/france-is-back-on-the-universal-jurisdiction-track/.
[124] Decision 01271–2008-PHC/TC, 8 August 2008, para. 6. [125] Law 26, 200/06, Art. 5.
[126] Loi No. 2007–05 (12 February 2007), art. 2; Penal Code, art. 431; Constitution of Senegal, art. 9.
[127] See John Bellinger and William Haynes, 'A US Government Response to the ICRC Study, Customary International Humanitarian Law' (2007) 85 *International Review of the Red Cross* 443.
[128] Child Soldiers Accountability Act 2007, s. 2135. [129] United States Code, s. 2241.
[130] Adam Pearlman, 'The Justice for Victims of War Crimes Act (U.S.)' (2023) xx *ILM* 1–5.
[131] In particular, the indictment of high-level Rwandan officials by France.
[132] Decision on the Report of the Commission on the Abuse of Universal Jurisdiction (Assembly/AU/14/(XI)) (2008), annexed to Letter from the AU Permanent Observer to the President of the Security Council, UN Doc. S/2008/465.
[133] For detailed reviews, see Harmen van der Wilt, 'Universal Jurisdiction under Attack: An Assessment of African Misgivings towards International Criminal Justice as Administered by Western States' (2011) 9 *JICJ* 1043; Charles Chernor Jalloh, 'Universal Jurisdiction: Universal Prescription? A Preliminary Assessment of the African Union Perspective on Universal Jurisdiction' (2010) 21 *Criminal Law Forum* 1.
[134] O'Keefe, 'Domestic Courts as Agents of Development' (n. 3) 555–6. [135] EXP/MIN/Legal/VI, Arts. 4, 9–14.

question since 2009, and, although states have reaffirmed the validity of the principle, controversies remain.[136]

Turning to the views of the international (and internationalized) criminal tribunals, both the ICTY and ICTR have asserted that states may exercise universal jurisdiction,[137] as has the Special Court for Sierra Leone.[138] Outside this context, the European Court of Human Rights has also accepted that universal jurisdiction exists, at least for genocide,[139] whilst the Inter-American Commission on Human Rights considers such jurisdiction to exist over crimes against international law.[140]

3.5.5 Universal Jurisdiction's Practical Problems

One of the major problems with undertaking prosecutions on the basis of universal jurisdiction is that the existence of jurisdiction per se does not give rise to any obligations on behalf of the territorial or nationality state to assist in any investigation, provide evidence, or extradite suspects.[141] The matter of cooperation falls to treaty obligations or comity.[142] It is perhaps unsurprising that some of the most successful prosecutions on the basis of universal jurisdiction, the Belgian prosecution of the 'Butare Four', the *Niyontenze* case in Switzerland, and the UK prosecution of the Afghan warlord, Faryadi Zardad,[143] occurred with the (sometimes quiet) concurrence of the relevant territorial states. Those states permitted investigations and on-site visits, as well as allowed witnesses to testify in the forum state. Although, in some prosecutions on the basis of universal jurisdiction, witnesses are found in the forum state among the refugee community,[144] the availability of evidence, both human and physical, cannot be presumed. A number of cases based on universal jurisdiction have failed to achieve the standard of proof for a criminal conviction.[145]

Even where witnesses are available, problems of inter-cultural understanding can arise. Translation difficulties, as well as difficulties of appraising the credibility of witnesses testifying through interpreters and from different cultural backgrounds, make the appraisal of witness evidence very difficult.[146] In some cases (the *Sawoniuk* case being

---

[136] See *The Scope and Application of the Principle of Universal Jurisdiction: Report of the Secretary-General*, UN Doc. A/74/192 (9 July 2020).

[137] *Tadić*, ICTY AC, 2 October 1995, para. 62; *Ntuyuhaga*, ICTR TC I, 18 March 1999 (in relation to genocide).

[138] *Kallon and Kamara*, SCSL AC, 13 March 2004, paras. 67–71. [139] *Jorgić v. Germany*, ECtHR, 12 July 2007, paras. 67–70.

[140] Res. 1/03, 24 October 2003.

[141] See Bruce Broomhall, *International Justice and the International Criminal Court: Between Sovereignty and the Rule of Law* (Oxford, 2003) 119–23.

[142] See Chapter 5.

[143] See Robert Cryer, 'Zardad' in A. Cassese et al. (eds.), *The Oxford Companion to International Criminal Justice* (Oxford, 2009) 978–9.

[144] The Syrian diaspora, many of whom have found refuge in Germany, have been instrumental in triggering prosecution of war crimes and crimes against humanity in Germany. On 'diaspora mobilization' see: Huma Haider, 'Transnational Transitional Justice and Reconciliation: The Participation of Conflict-Generated Diasporas in Addressing the Legacies of Mass Violence' (2014) 27 *Journal of Refugee Studies* 207.

[145] E.g. the Duško Cvetković prosecution in Austria and *In re Gabrez* in Switzerland.

[146] See Larissa van den Herik, 'The Difficulties of Exercising Extraterritorial Criminal Jurisdiction: The Acquittal of a Dutch Businessman for Crimes Committed in Liberia' (2009) 9 *ICLR* 211.

an example),[147] this problem is mitigated by on-site visits by the fact-finders, who can thereby achieve a better understanding of the witnesses' cultural and material context.

There is also the possible problem of 'forum shopping', in which victims or NGOs may seek to initiate prosecutions in multiple forums, to maximize the possibility of a conviction.[148] This can raise the important issue of the rights of defendants, who could be prosecuted repeatedly in relation to the same facts, something which, if done in one state, would violate the *ne bis in idem* principle.[149] The absence of such a principle operating between states makes this a possibility, albeit one which is not unique to universal jurisdiction.[150] *Ne bis in idem* did not protect Germain Katanga against subsequent prosecution in the Democratic Republic of Congo after a conviction by the ICC.[151]

3.5.6 Policy-Based and Political Criticisms of Universal Jurisdiction

There have been a number of policy arguments brought against universal jurisdiction, which are of varying persuasiveness. The first of these is that prosecutions based on universal jurisdiction may impact upon foreign policy.[152]

Such concerns have led the executive in a number of states to impose additional hurdles, such as consent of a government lawyer prior to issuing proceedings on this basis.[153] Universal jurisdiction prosecutions may also upset the balance struck between prosecution and amnesty in an emerging democracy, where amnesties have been used.[154] This critique has more purchase when applied to processes such as South Africa's than when compared to General Pinochet's self-granted immunity.[155] On the other hand, international crimes are not simply the concern of one state alone. Crimes against humanity, genocide, and (probably most) war crimes violate *erga omnes* obligations; therefore, all states have an interest

---

[147] Other examples of this include two genocide trials, where Scandinavian courts conducted part of their proceedings in Rwanda: *Public Prosecutor* v. *Bazarama*, District Court of Porvoo Ita-Uusimaa (Finland), Case No. R 09/04, Judgment of 11 June 2010 (see Minna Kimpimäki, 'Genocide in Rwanda: Is It Really Finland's Concern?' (2011) 11 *ICLR* 1550); and *Public Prosecutor* v. *Mbanenande*, Stockholm District Court (Sweden), Case No. B-18271–11, Judgment of 20 June 2013.

[148] NGOs play a key role in bringing the large number of cases that rely on universal jurisdiction. See 'Symposium: Strategic Litigation: The Role of NGOs in International Criminal Justice' (2015) 13 *JICJ* 205, especially Harmen van der Wilt, '"Sadder but Wiser"? NGOs and Universal Jurisdiction for International Crimes', *ibid.* 237.

[149] George Fletcher, 'Against Universal Jurisdiction' (2003) I *JICJ* 580.

[150] See Albin Eser, 'For Universal Jurisdiction: Against Fletcher's Antagonism' (2003–4) 39 *Tulsa Law Review* 955, 957–8, 963–71; Ryngaert, 'Applying the Rome Statute' (n. 109) 155–6.

[151] *Katanga*, ICC Presidency, 7 April 2016 (ICC-01/04–01/07–3693). For critique, see Patryk Labuda, 'Complementarity Compromised? The ICC Gives Congo the Green Light to Re-Try Katanga', *Opinio Juris*, 11 April 2016, http://opiniojuris.org/2016/04/11/complementarity-compromised-the-icc-gives-congo-the-green-light-to-re-try-katanga/. For possible solutions: Keilin Anderson and Adaena Sinclair-Blakemore, '*Ne bis in idem, nulla poena sine lege* and Domestic Prosecutions of International Crimes in the Aftermath of a Trial at the International Criminal Court' (2021) 21(1) *ICLR* 35. See further section 4.8.1 ICC (ICC-01/04–01/07–3679).

[152] Domestic courts may be viewed as engaged in global governance, producing new sites of authority available for forum-shopping and legal conflict: Filiz Kahraman, Nikhil Kalyanpur, and Abraham Newman, 'Domestic Courts, Transnational Law, and International Order' (2020) 26(1) *European Journal of International Relations* 184, 186.

[153] Langer, 'Diplomacy' (n. 114) 1–7. In the United Kingdom, this has led to legislative reform on the question of arrest warrants being sought by private parties: see Police Reform and Social Responsibility Act 2011, s. 153, on which, see Sarah Williams, 'Arresting Developments? Restricting the Enforcement of the UK's Universal Jurisdiction Provisions' (2012) 75 *Modern Law Review* 368.

[154] Henry Kissinger, 'The Pitfalls of Universal Jurisdiction' (2001) 80 *Foreign Affairs* 86, 90–1; Eugene Kontorovich, 'The Inefficiencies of Universal Jurisdiction' (2008) *University of Illinois Law Review* 389.

[155] Kenneth Roth, 'The Case for Universal Jurisdiction' (2001) 80 *Foreign Affairs* 150, 153.

in the response to such offences.[156] From a purely legal point of view, domestic amnesty legislation does not bind any other state, and the problem is, again, not one unique to universal jurisdiction.[157]

The practical ability of more powerful nations both to assert jurisdiction beyond their borders and to pressure other countries into leaving their nationals alone has led to claims that universal jurisdiction can be selective in its application. President Guillaume argued in *Yerodia* that to support universal jurisdiction would be to 'encourage the arbitrary for the purposes of the powerful, purportedly acting for an ill-defined "international community"'.[158]

This argument frequently takes on a neocolonial twist, as per Judge Rezek in the same case, who noted the question of 'how certain European countries would react if a judge from the Congo had indicted their officials for crimes supposedly committed on their orders in Africa'.[159] Judge ad hoc Bula-Bula, however, made the criticism directly on the basis that the exercise of universal jurisdiction was a form of neocolonial intervention by Belgium in the DRC.[160]

There is no evidence that universal jurisdiction prosecutions are directed by states for nefarious political reasons (or at least no more than on other heads of jurisdiction).[161] Indeed, some of the attempted prosecutions have caused political difficulties for states in which indictments have been sought;[162] and states tend to (re)assert executive control over judges and prosecutors to rein in such applications.[163] Even so, where non-governmental actors have sought to bring proceedings, they normally have to bring sufficient evidence to persuade a court or a prosecutor to take the matter on.[164] Actual prosecutions on the basis of universal jurisdiction to date have centred on those who have not been proceeded against in their territorial or nationality states.[165] In such cases, there is a high degree of agreement in principle on the appropriateness of the prosecution of such offenders.[166]

Other offenders who have faced proceedings have tended to be those who are not considered to be representatives of, or protected by, powerful states.[167] This, when added to increased executive control over who is prosecuted on the basis of universal jurisdiction, does give rise to rule of law issues.[168] Selective enforcement, nonetheless, remains a problem in relation to international crimes, whatever the principle of jurisdiction is

---

[156] *Furundžija*, ICTY TC II, 10 December 1998, para. 156; *Legality of the Threat or Use of Nuclear Weapons*, Advisory Opinion [1996] ICJ Reports 226, para. 79; *Kupreškić et al.*, ICTY TC II, 14 January 2000, para. 520 (although this case goes a little far in asserting that all norms of humanitarian law have this status).

[157] See further Chapter 22. [158] *Yerodia* (n. 13), Separate Opinion of President Guillaume, para. 15.

[159] *Ibid*. Separate Opinion of Judge Rezek, para. 9 (translation in Reydams, *Universal Jurisdiction* (n. 86) 229).

[160] *Yerodia* (n. 13), Separate Opinion of Judge Bula-Bula.

[161] 'Final Report on the Exercise of Universal Jurisdiction in Relation to Gross Human Rights Abuses' in ILA, Report of the Sixty-Ninth Conference, Held in London (London, 2000) 403, 422; Ryngaert, 'Applying the Rome Statute' (n. 109) 155–6.

[162] E.g. Christine Bakker, 'Universal Jurisdiction of Spanish Courts over Genocide in Tibet: Can It Work?' (2006) 4 *JICJ* 595, 599–601; Jonny Paul, 'Peres Slams UK Law Jeopardizing IDF Officers', *Jerusalem Post*, 23 November 2008.

[163] Langer, 'Diplomacy' (n. 114) 1–7. As Langer has also noted, it may be that the movement in Western states is more to a 'no safe haven' approach rather than a 'global enforcer' approach: Maximo Langer, 'Universal Jurisdiction is Not Disappearing. The Shift from 'Global Enforcer' to 'No Safe Haven' Universal Jurisdiction' (2015) 13 *JICJ* 245–56.

[164] Prosecutors frequently have discretion in this regard, even in states where this is not a norm: see e.g. Salvatore Zappalà, 'The German Federal Prosecutor's Decision Not to Prosecute a Former Uzbek Minister: Missed Opportunity or Prosecutorial Wisdom?' (2006) 4 *JICJ* 602.

[165] See van der Wilt, 'Universal Jurisdiction' (n. 133) 1064–6. [166] Langer, 'Diplomacy' (n. 114) 9.

[167] *Ibid*. See also Elies van Sliedregt, 'One Rule for Them – Selectivity in International Criminal Law' (2021) 34(2) *LJIL* 283.

[168] Langer, 'Diplomacy' (n. 114) 47–9.

invoked. Some of these problems could be mitigated by the adoption of an international agreement on the exercise of universal jurisdiction.[169] There are no official proposals for such a treaty at present, and, without universal ratification, such a treaty might further muddy the waters of this form of jurisdiction, and call into question the existing customary law on point.[170]

Further Reading

Michael Akehurst, 'Jurisdiction in International Law' (1972–3) 46 *British Yearbook of International Law* 145

Alejandro Chehtman, *The Philosophical Foundations of Extraterritorial Punishment* (Oxford, 2010)

Anthony Colangelo, 'The Legal Limits of Universal Jurisdiction' (2006–7) 47 *Virginia Journal of International Law* 149

Edwin D. Dickinson (Reporter), 'Harvard Draft Convention on Jurisdiction with Commentary' (1935) 29 *AJIL* 439

Menno T. Kamminga, 'Lessons Learned from the Exercise of Universal Jurisdiction over Gross Human Rights Abuses' (2001) 23 *Human Rights Quarterly* 940

Henry Kissinger, 'The Pitfalls of Universal Jurisdiction' (2001) 80 *Foreign Affairs* 86

Claus Kreß, 'Universal Jurisdiction over International Crimes and the Institut de Droit International' (2006) 4 *JICJ* 561

Máximo Langer, 'The Diplomacy of Universal Jurisdiction: The Political Branches and the Transnational Prosecution of International Crimes' (2011) 105 *AJIL* 1

Steven Macedo (ed.), *Universal Jurisdiction: National Courts and the Prosecution of Serious Crimes under International Law* (Philadelphia, PA, 2003)

Roger O'Keefe, 'Universal Jurisdiction: Clarifying the Basic Concept' (2004) 2 *JICJ* 735

Luc Reydams, *Universal Jurisdiction: International and Municipal Legal Perspectives* (Oxford, 2003)

Cedric Ryngaert, *Jurisdiction in International Law* (Oxford, 2008)

Christopher Staker, 'Jurisdiction' in Malcolm Evans (ed.), *International Law*, 5th ed. (Oxford, 2018) 309

---

[169] Such a course of action is suggested in Cassese, 'Is the Bell Tolling?' (n. 66) 595.

[170] Cf. d'Aspremont, 'Multilateral versus Unilateral' (n. 13) 309 et seq., who considers any non-treaty-based assertion of universal jurisdiction to have legitimacy problems.

4

National Prosecutions of International Crimes

4.1 INTRODUCTION

International crimes are primarily intended to be prosecuted at the domestic level. The 1948 Genocide Convention enjoined the trials of persons accused of this crime before competent tribunals of the territorial state or an 'international penal tribunal' provided that Contracting Parties have accepted its jurisdiction.[1] Under the International Criminal Court (ICC) complementarity regime, national courts operate as the courts of first resort.[2] In this 'indirect enforcement system', national jurisdictions play a primary role in enforcing international criminal law.[3] As the main vehicle for international criminal enforcement, national prosecutions are also considered a preferable option – in political, sociological, practical, and legitimacy terms – to their international counterparts.[4] The world vowed after the Second World War never again to allow mass atrocities to occur. However, international crimes continue to be committed in many countries without always resulting in (effective) domestic prosecutions. Indeed, the international criminal justice system has developed to counter the impunity that often persists at the domestic level due to states' unwillingness or inability to hold perpetrators accountable. Despite international obligations in this regard, some legal, political, and practical hurdles complicate national prosecutions. Legal issues such as inadequate legislation, *ne bis in idem* (double jeopardy), and statutory limitations are discussed in this chapter. Amnesties are dealt with in Chapter 22, state cooperation in Chapter 5, and immunities in Chapter 21.

4.2 OVERVIEW OF PRACTICE

War crimes have been regulated in domestic law the longest and have been prosecuted most often.[5] Early examples are prosecutions with respect to the American Civil War in the 1860s and the Anglo-Boer Wars (1880–1 and 1899–1902). The reluctant prosecutions of

---

[1] Genocide Convention, Art. 6. See also 1973 Apartheid Convention, Art. 5. [2] See Chapter 8.
[3] See e.g. M. Cherif Bassiouni, *Introduction to International Criminal Law*, 2nd ed. (Leiden, 2013) 487.
[4] See Chapters 2 and 7.
[5] For national case law, see the ICRC webpage, www.icrc.org/ihl-nat, and the International Crimes Database, https://internationalcrimesdatabase.org/Cases/ByName.

war crimes in Germany and Turkey after the First World War – the Leipzig trials and the Istanbul (Constantinople) trials in the 1920s – were conducted under domestic laws.[6]

No conflict has generated as many national prosecutions as the Second World War, sometimes for international crimes, but in many instances for 'ordinary' crimes. Thousands of cases concerning Nazi crimes have been brought in Germany, with some proceedings against nonagenarian defendants conducted in recent years.[7] Allied States have organized trials in the Pacific sphere, and many other European states have instituted their own prosecutions.[8] The well-known prosecutions include the French cases against Klaus Barbie (head of the Gestapo in Lyon), Paul Touvier (a pro-Nazi militiaman), and Maurice Papon (a high-ranking official of the French Vichy regime), who were convicted for crimes against humanity in 1987, 1994, and 1998, respectively, after very long proceedings plagued with difficulties.[9] Prosecutions have also taken place in Italy (for example, the *Hass and Priebke* case),[10] Austria, the Netherlands, and former Eastern Bloc countries.[11] In the United Kingdom, after the many prosecutions directly after the Second World War, only one related war crimes case, *R* v. *Sawoniuk*, has resulted in a conviction in the recent past.[12]

One of the most famous post-Second World War cases is the *Eichmann* case adjudicated in Israel in the early 1960s. It addressed the novel issues of jurisdiction,[13] including the exercise of jurisdiction upon abduction of the accused from another state.[14] The District Court of Jerusalem and the Supreme Court of Israel also considered defences (superior orders and the 'act of state' doctrine) and the principle of non-retroactivity of criminal law.[15] Adolf Eichmann, a high-ranking SS officer in charge of the logistics of the Holocaust, was captured in Argentina and brought to Israel in 1960 to stand trial for 'crimes against the Jewish people', crimes against humanity, war crimes, and membership of criminal organizations. He was found guilty, sentenced to death, and executed in 1962.[16]

---

[6] See Section 6.2; see also Gerd Hankel, *The Leipzig Trials: German War Crimes and Their Legal Consequences after World War* (Westport, 2014); Joseph Rikhof, 'The Istanbul and Leipzig Trials: Myth or Reality?' in Morten Bergsmo, Cheah Wui Ling, and Yi Ping (eds.), *Historical Origins of International Criminal Law* (Brussels, 2014) vol. I, 259–98.

[7] See Christiaan Rüter and Dick de Mildt (eds.), *Justiz und NS-Verbrechen: Sammlung (west-)deutscher Strafurteile wegen nationalsozialistischer Tötungsverbrechen 1945–2012* (Amsterdam and Munich, 1968–2012), and *DDR-Justiz und NS-Verbrechen: Sammlung (ost-)deutscher Strafurteile wegen nationalsozialistischer Tötungsverbrechen 1945–1998* (Amsterdam and Munich, 2002–9). In July 2015, the 95-year-old Oskar Gröning, the former SS guard and 'bookkeeper of Auschwitz', was convicted for being accessory to at least 300,000 murders and sentenced to four years by the Lüneburg court. Although his appeal and request for pardon failed, he died in March 2018 and did not serve his sentence. In December 2022, the Itzehoe court convicted the 97-year-old former Stutthof camp secretary Irmgard Furchner of complicity in the murders of over 10,000 inmates and handed down a two-year suspended sentence.

[8] See Section 6.5 and generally Axel Marschik, 'The Politics of Prosecution: European National Approaches to War Crimes' in Timothy McCormack and Gerry Simpson (eds.), *The Law of War Crimes: National and International Approaches* (The Hague, 1997) 65–101; Suzannah Linton (ed.), *Hong Kong's War Crimes Trials* (Oxford, 2013).

[9] See Leila Nadya Sadat, 'The French Experience' in M. Cherif Bassiouni (ed.), *International Criminal Law*, 3rd ed. (Leiden, 2008) vol. III, 329.

[10] *Karl Hass and Erich Priebke*, Rome Military Tribunal, 22 July 1997; Military Court of Appeal, 7 March 1998; and Supreme Court of Cassation, 16 November 1998. See Paola Gaeta, 'War Crimes Trials before Italian Criminal Courts: New Trends' in Fischer et al. (eds.), *International and National Prosecution*, 751–68. On other Italian trials, see Pier Paolo Rivello, 'The Prosecution of War Crimes Committed by Nazi Forces in Italy' (2005) 3 *JICJ* 422.

[11] See e.g. Veronika Bílková, 'Post-Second World War Trials in Central and Eastern Europe' in Morten Bergsmo, Cheah Wui Ling, and Yi Ping (eds.), *Historical Origins of International Criminal Law* (Brussels, 2014) vol. II, ch. 41.

[12] [2000] 2 Crim. App. Rep. 220.   [13] See Chapter 3.   [14] See Section 5.4.7.

[15] *Attorney-General of Israel* v. *Eichmann* (1968) 36 ILR 5 (District Court) and *Attorney-General of Israel* v. *Eichmann* (1968) 36 ILR 277 (Supreme Court).

[16] See further Hannah Arendt, *Eichmann in Jerusalem: A Report on the Banality of Evil* (New York, 1963).

US courts also considered jurisdictional issues when deciding to extradite John Demjanjuk to Israel to stand trial for war crimes and crimes against humanity.[17] Israeli courts finally acquitted Demjanjuk because of doubts in respect of his identity as the camp guard 'Ivan the Terrible' of Treblinka.[18] In 2009, though, Demjanjuk was deported from the US to Germany to face trial for his wartime activities. He was convicted in May 2011 for being an accessory to the murder of 27,900 Jews and sentenced to five years in prison. But his conviction did not stand because he died (aged ninety-one) before his appeal could be heard.

Other important cases are the Canadian *Finta* case, where the court introduced very strict mental and material requirements for crimes against humanity and war crimes,[19] and the Australian *Polyukhovich* case, where the constitutional validity of war crimes legislation was challenged with respect to jurisdiction and retroactivity.[20] Both cases ended in acquittals on evidentiary grounds, in part owing to the length of time between the events and the trials.

Conflicts after the Second World War did not produce as many national criminal proceedings. A few examples are the US courts-martial concerning the My Lai massacre during the Vietnam War, although the charges concerned domestic rather than international crimes.[21] There were also cases in Romania and Ethiopia where reference was made to 'genocide',[22] a show trial of Pol Pot and Ieng Sary conducted *in absentia* by the People's Revolutionary Tribunal in Cambodia in August 1979,[23] and controversial prosecutions of crimes committed during the 1971 Pakistan–Bangladesh war.[24]

In the 1990s, international criminal justice experienced a revival after decades of dormancy, with the establishment of the ad hoc Tribunals. The frequency of national prosecutions also increased, particularly in Rwanda and the states of the former Yugoslavia. Rwanda introduced new legislation on the organization of prosecutions for genocide and crimes against humanity in 1996, dividing alleged perpetrators into four categories based on the gravity of the crime and the role played therein, carrying different penalties, and started a large number of prosecutions.[25] But with over 120,000 detainees awaiting trial, the regular court system had to be complemented by semi-formal *gacaca*

---

[17] *Demjanjuk*, US District Court (ND Ohio), 15 April 1985; *Demjanjuk* v. *Petrovsky et al.*, US Court of Appeals (Sixth Circuit), 31 October 1985. See Lawrence Douglas, *The Right Wrong Man: John Demjanjuk and the Last Great Nazi War Crimes Trial* (Princeton, NJ, 2016) chs. 2–3. See also Section 5.4.7.

[18] *Demjanjuk* v. *Israel*, Crim. App. No. 347/88, Supreme Court of Israel, Judgment of 29 July 1993.

[19] *R* v. *Finta* [1994] 1 SCR 701, Supreme Court of Canada, Judgment of 24 March 1994.

[20] *Polyukhovich* v. *Commonwealth of Australia and another* [1991] HCA 32; (1991) 172 CLR 501 FC 91/026, High Court of Australia, Judgment of 14 August 1991.

[21] *United States* v. *First Lieutenant William L. Calley, Jr.*, conviction on the instructions from the military judge to court members, Fort Benning, Georgia, 29 March 1971 (sentence dated 31 March 1971) *United States* v. *Calley*, 48 CMR 19 (1973) (US Court of Military Appeals, 21 December 1973). However, Lieutenant Calley's commander, Captain Medina, was acquitted by court-martial on 22 September 1971.

[22] See William Schabas, 'National Courts Finally Begin to Prosecute Genocide, the Crime of Crimes' (2003) 1 *JICJ* 39; Firew Kebede Tiba, 'The Mengistu Genocide Trial in Ethiopia' (2007) 5 *JICJ* 513, 518.

[23] People's Revolutionary Court, Judgment of 19 August 1979, UN Doc. A/34/491 (20 September 1979) (entering convictions for genocide and sentencing both to death). See Frank Selbmann, 'The 1979 Trial of the People's Revolutionary Tribunal and Implications for the ECCC' in Simon Meisenberg and Ignaz Stegmiller (eds.), *The Extraordinary Chambers in the Courts of Cambodia: Assessing Their Contribution to International Criminal Law* (The Hague, 2016) ch. 4.

[24] See M. Cherif Bassiouni, *Crimes Against Humanity in International Law*, 2nd ed. (The Hague, 1999) 549–51.

[25] Organic Law No. 08/1996 of 30 August 1996.

courts in 2001–12.[26] In spite of the high numbers of cases processed and their contribution to national reconciliation, the standards of justice they meted out caused serious concern.[27]

In the former Yugoslavia, the International Criminal Tribunal for the former Yugoslavia (ICTY) had primary concurrent jurisdiction over international crimes. The relationships between the ICTY and national authorities improved over time and the ICTY referred case files regarding suspects for whom it had issued no indictments to courts in Croatia and Serbia. With respect to Bosnia and Herzegovina, a special scheme ('Rules of the Road') applied until October 2004. The ICTY Prosecutor in effect vetted national cases before a domestic arrest warrant for war crimes was issued, which was a way to avoid unfounded charges.[28] Moreover, as part of the completion strategies of the ICTY and the International Criminal Tribunal for Rwanda (ICTR), a number of cases where the Tribunals had issued an indictment were referred to national jurisdictions under Rule 11*bis*.[29] The Residual Mechanism for International Criminal Tribunals (MICT) holds an analogous referral power and monitors cases referred to national courts.[30]

In addition, prosecutions of crimes committed in Rwanda and the former Yugoslavia have taken place in third states, such as Austria, Belgium, Denmark, Finland, Germany, Norway, Sweden, and Switzerland. The ICTY's first *Tadić* case originated as a domestic case in Germany but was taken over by the ICTY. The 'Butare Four' case in Belgium proceeded after the ICTR had declined to exercise jurisdiction.[31] The trend of prosecutions of core crimes under universal jurisdiction has since extended to other conflict situations. Numerous criminal cases, often based on victim complaints, are now regularly brought to domestic courts, particularly in Europe and Latin America.[32] In 2021–2 the court in Koblenz, Germany convicted two former Syrian security apparatus officials of crimes against humanity.[33] Marked by evidentiary difficulties, universal jurisdiction prosecutions

---

[26] *Gacaca* means 'grass' in Kinyarwanda. See Organic Law No. 40/2000 of 26 January 2001 modified by Organic Law No. 33/2001 of 22 June 2001, as amended by Organic Law No. 16/2004 of 19 June 2004. See further Paul Bornkamm, *Rwanda's Gacaca Courts: Between Retribution and Reparation* (Oxford, 2012); Phil Clark, *The Gacaca Courts, Post-Genocide Justice and Reconciliation in Rwanda: Justice Without Lawyers* (Cambridge, 2011).

[27] E.g. Gerald Gahima, *Transitional Justice in Rwanda* (London, 2013) ch. 6; Human Rights Watch, *Justice Compromised: The Legacy of Rwanda's Community-Based Gacaca Courts* (May 2011). Cf. Nicola Palmer, *Courts in Conflict: Interpreting the Layers of Justice in Post-Conflict Rwanda* (Oxford, 2015) ch. 4 (discussing the different priorities and objectives in the work of *gacaca* courts).

[28] The ICTY Office of the Prosecutor (OTP) reviewed evidence involving nearly 5,000 suspects and approved prosecutions of 848 persons in total: see ICTY, 'Working with the Region', www.icty.org/en/about/office-of-the-prosecutor/working-with-the-region. See Yaël Ronen, 'The Impact of the ICTY on Atrocity-Related Prosecutions in the Courts of Bosnia and Herzegovina' (2014) 3(1) *Penn State Journal of Law and International Affairs* 113.

[29] On completions strategies and Rule 11*bis* referrals, see Sections 7.2.4, 7.3.4, and 9.3.2.

[30] MICT Statute, Art. 6 and MICT Rules of Procedure and Evidence (RPE), Rule 14.

[31] See Luc Reydams, 'Belgium's First Application of Universal Jurisdiction: The Butare Four Case' (2003) 1 *JICJ* 428; Damien Vandermeersch, 'Prosecuting International Crimes in Belgium' (2005) 3 *JICJ* 400.

[32] For recent surveys covering developments in 2022, see Trial International, *Universal Jurisdiction Annual Review 2023* and Civitas Maxima, *2022 Annual Report.*

[33] On 24 February 2021 the Koblenz Higher Regional Court convicted Eyad al-Gharib of aiding and abetting thirty instances of torture, sentencing him to four-and-a-half years of imprisonment. On 13 January 2022, the same court convicted his superior Anwar Raslan, former head of the investigations section of Syria's general intelligence directorate, of killing, torture, serious deprivation of liberty, and sexual violence, and sentenced him to life. See ECCHR, 'First criminal trial worldwide on torture in Syria before a German court', www.ecchr.eu/en/case/first-criminal-trial-worldwide-on-torture-in-syria-before-a-german-court/#case_case.

do not always succeed. One example is the 2022 acquittal in Finland of a former Sierra Leonean militiaman for international crimes he allegedly committed in Liberia.[34]

In the United States and Canada, denaturalization and deportation under the citizenship and immigration legislation have mostly been preferred over criminal prosecution.[35] For example, several recent cases in the United States concerned individuals who had concealed facts of their involvement in international crimes elsewhere and were therefore convicted of immigration fraud and perjury.[36] But in 2009, the first successful Canadian prosecution for genocide, crimes against humanity, and war crimes in Rwanda led to a conviction in the *Munyaneza* case.[37]

In another important trend, the number of domestic prosecutions of business actors as aiders and abettors has been on the rise. Noteworthy examples are cases in the Netherlands, France, and Sweden, all of which involve companies, their executives, and businessmen charged with complicity in extra-territorial international crimes.[38]

The armed conflict in Ukraine following Russia's 2022 all-out invasion has been marked by a large-scale commission of core crimes and has mobilized justice efforts across the board.[39] Several Russian prisoners of war stood trial for war crimes and were convicted by Ukrainian courts, and some cases where the accused were identified, yet not captured, have been conducted *in absentia*.[40] Moreover, several other countries have started investigations into the core crimes committed in Ukraine, which may give an impulse to an array of universal jurisdiction cases before foreign courts in the years to come.[41]

---

[34] On 29 April 2022, the Tampere district court cleared Gibril Massaquoi, the former lieutenant-colonel and spokesman of the Revolutionary United Front, of all charges of war crimes and crimes against humanity due to a reasonable doubt he had committed them. The prosecution appealed the acquittal. See Civitas Maxima, 'Gibril Massaquoi', https://civitas-maxima.org/legal-work/our-cases/gibril-massaquoi/.

[35] See e.g. Irwin Cotler, 'R v. Finta' (1996) 90 *AJIL* 460; Matthew Lippman, 'The Pursuit of Nazi War Criminals in the United States and Other Anglo-American Legal Systems' (1998) 29 *California Western International Law Journal* 1.

[36] Convicted by a Philadelphia court of fraud in immigration documents and perjury, Mohammed Jabbateh (aka Jungle Jabbah) received a maximum sentence of thirty years' imprisonment on 18 April 2018. Jucontee Thomas Woewiyu, a former defence minister and spokesman of the National Patriotic Front of Liberia, was convicted on 3 July 2018 but died pending sentencing. Another conviction in the United States concerns Jean Leonard Teganya, who lied about his involvement in the Rwandan genocide when applying for asylum and was sentenced to 97 months in prison on 1 July 2019. See Civitas Maxima webpage, www.civitas-maxima.org/en/trials; Nicola Palmer, 'Immigration Trials and International Crimes: Expressing Justice and Performing Race' (2021) 25(3) *Theoretical Criminology* 423.

[37] See Robert Currie and Ion Stancu, 'R v. Munyaneza: Pondering Canada's First Core Crimes Conviction' (2010) 10 *ICLR* 829. The second such case (*Mungwarere*) ended in an acquittal in July 2013.

[38] On the Dutch *Van Anraat* and *Kouwenhoven* cases, see Wim Huisman and Elies van Sliedregt, 'Rogue Traders: Dutch Businessmen, International Crimes and Corporate Complicity' (2010) 8 *JICJ* 803. On 21 April 2017, the Dutch Court of Appeal convicted Guus Kouwenhoven, who as the head of two timber companies had provided arms to Charles Taylor's regime in Liberia, for aiding and abetting war crimes and crimes against humanity in Liberia and Guinea (2000–2), sentencing him to 19 years' imprisonment: Hof's-Hertogenbosch, 20–001906-10, 21 April 2017. In France, the cement company Lafarge and its executives have been investigated for complicity in war crimes and crimes against humanity, as a result of the activities of its subsidiary in Syria (2013–14); the Paris appeals court rejected Lafarge's request to dismiss the charges in 2022. In 2023 the trial against the Lundin Energy chairman and a former CEO, charged with complicity in war crimes in 1999–2003 in Sudan, commenced in Stockholm.

[39] As of March 2024, the Ukrainian law-enforcement registered over 123,680 incidents of 'violations of laws and customs of war' (Art. 438 Criminal Code of Ukraine) and over 170 incidents of 'planning, preparation, unleashing or waging of aggressive war and 'propaganda of aggressive war' (respectively Arts. 437 and 436); there is no provision on crimes against humanity in the Code. See the Ukrainian Prosecutor-General's Office webpage, www.gp.gov.ua/en.

[40] See Iryna Marchuk, 'Domestic Accountability Efforts in Response to the Russia–Ukraine War: An Appraisal of the First War Crimes Trials in Ukraine' (2022) 20 *JICJ* 787–803.

[41] See e.g. Sergey Vasiliev, 'The Future of Justice for Ukraine is Domestic', *JusticeInfo.Net*, 29 March 2022, www.justiceinfo.net/en/89434-future-justice-for-ukraine-domestic.html.

4.3 STATE OBLIGATIONS TO PROSECUTE OR EXTRADITE

4.3.1 Treaty Obligations

Some treaties addressing international or transnational crimes oblige states parties to investigate and prosecute the offence in question, or to extradite suspects to another state willing to do so. This is known as the *aut dedere aut judicare* ('to extradite or prosecute') principle.[42] Examples can be found in the four 1949 Geneva Conventions and the 1977 Additional Protocol I.[43] Their 'grave breaches' provisions are phrased in the imperative:

Each High Contracting Party shall be under the obligation to search for persons alleged to have committed, or to have ordered to be committed, such grave breaches and shall bring such persons, regardless of their nationality, before its own courts ... [or] hand such persons over for trial to another High Contracting Party concerned, provided such High Contracting Party has made out a prima facie case.

For other serious violations of the Geneva Conventions, which are not 'grave breaches', the principle does not apply under the treaty scheme, but states still have a right, although not a duty, to prosecute such violations.[44] The principle exists, *inter alia*, in the 1984 Torture Convention,[45] the Convention on Enforced Disappearances,[46] and many terrorism-related treaties.[47] Such treaty clauses are often considered as allowing states to exercise universal jurisdiction,[48] and are normally phrased in mandatory terms.[49] Newer provisions require states to 'submit' cases of alleged violations to 'its competent authorities for the purpose of prosecution'.[50] This is also the case of the draft articles on crimes against humanity prepared by the International Law Commission (ILC).[51] This wording takes into account fair trial rights, such as the presumption of innocence, but should not be understood to lessen the duty to prosecute if the evidence is there.[52] Some civil law jurisdictions provide for compulsory prosecution of crimes when the relevant evidentiary threshold is met. However, the equivalent international law obligation is only applicable between the parties to the respective treaty.

The nature and extent of the obligations contained in the Torture Convention were the subject of the 2012 *Habré* case in the International Court of Justice (ICJ).[53] It concerned the continued delays in the Senegalese prosecution of the ex-head of Chad, Hissène Habré,

---

[42] This maxim was originally devised by Hugo Grotius in *De Jure Belli ac Pacis* (1624) as '*aut dedere aut punire*' ('to extradite or punish'). Hugo Grotius, *De Jure Belli ac Pacis* (Oxford, 1925) Book II, ch. XXI, section IV, 527. See M. Cherif Bassiouni and Edward Wise, *Aut Dedere, Aut Judicare: A Duty to Extradite or Prosecute in International Law* (Dordrecht, 1995).

[43] Geneva Convention I, Arts. 49–50; Geneva Convention II, Arts. 50–51; Geneva Convention III, Arts. 129–130; Geneva Convention IV, Arts. 146–147; Additional Protocol I, Arts. 11, 85–86 and 88.

[44] See Theodor Meron, 'Is International Law Moving Towards Criminalization?' (1998) 9 *EJIL* 18, 23.

[45] Convention Against Torture and Other Cruel, Inhuman or Degrading Treatment or Punishment, 10 December 1984, entered into force 26 June 1987, 1465 UNTS 85, Arts. 5 and 7.

[46] International Convention for the Protection of All Persons from Enforced Disappearances, GA Res. 61/177 Annex, Arts. 9, 11.

[47] Chapter 14.   [48] Section 3.5.

[49] Except for 1973 Apartheid Convention, Art. 5, and 1982 Law of the Sea Convention, Art. 105 (piracy on the high seas), where the exercise of jurisdiction is instead phrased in permissive terms ('may').

[50] See e.g. Torture Convention, Art. 7(1); UN Convention on Transnational Organized Crime, GA Res. 55/25, 15 November 2000, entered into force on 29 September 2003, 2225 UNTS 209, Art. 16(8).

[51] ILC Report, 'Draft articles on Prevention and Punishment of Crimes Against Humanity' (2019) II(2) Yearbook of the International Law Commission, Art. 10.

[52] See e.g. *ibid*. Art. 11.

[53] *Questions relating to the Obligation to Extradite or Prosecute (Belgium v. Senegal)*, ICJ, Judgment of 20 July 2012.

against the backdrop of a Belgian request for his extradition to face charges, *inter alia*, of torture. The ICJ held that parties to the Torture Convention are obliged to criminalize and prosecute torture, including on the basis of universal jurisdiction.[54] The ICJ determined that, by failing to exercise jurisdiction over torture until 2007 (seven years after complaints had been made against Habré in Senegal), Senegal had breached its obligations to conduct a timely preliminary investigation and submit the matter to its competent authorities.

The Court also took the view that the duty to conduct a preliminary inquiry arises as soon as the state has reason to suspect that a person in its territory is responsible for torture and at the latest when a complaint is submitted to the authorities.[55] The duties to conduct a preliminary inquiry and to submit the matter to the competent authorities are not contingent on the receipt of a request for extradition.[56] The obligation is not necessarily to prosecute, but rather to submit the matter to its competent authorities, who should determine whether or not a prosecution should go ahead in the same manner as in the case of any ordinary offence of a similar nature.[57] The primary duty on the state is to submit the matter for prosecution; extradition is an option given to the state which would relieve it of its primary obligation.[58] The *Habré* case, alongside the ILC's final report on the principle,[59] has provided welcome clarity in the area. Although the ICJ's comments are limited to the Torture Convention, they are helpful in interpreting similarly worded provisions in other treaties.[60]

The 1948 Genocide Convention, unlike the Torture Convention, restricts the jurisdictional scope of the duty to prevent and punish the crime to the courts of 'the State in the territory of which the act was committed',[61] and there is no *aut dedere aut judicare* provision.[62] Some argue that the Convention may be read to include such an obligation.[63] However, in the *Bosnian Genocide* case, the ICJ found the obligation to prosecute to be limited to instituting and exercising *territorial* criminal jurisdiction, although states are not precluded from asserting jurisdiction on the basis of the nationality of the accused or other grounds compatible with international law.[64]

4.3.2 Human Rights Law Obligations

Since states have a duty to respect and to ensure the rights granted in the various human rights conventions,[65] it can be argued that this implies a duty to prosecute certain serious violations of human rights which underlie genocide, crimes against humanity, as well as

---

[54] *Ibid*. paras. 74–5. [55] *Ibid*. paras. 86 and 88. [56] *Ibid*. paras. 94–5. [57] *Ibid*. paras. 90, 94. [58] *Ibid*. para. 95.

[59] See e.g. ILC, 'Final Report: The Obligation to Extradite or Prosecute (Aut Dedere Aut Judicare)' (2014) II(2) Yearbook of the International Law Commission.

[60] *Ibid*. para. 15. [61] Genocide Convention, Art. 6; see also *ibid*. Arts. 1, 4 and 5.

[62] The states parties do agree, however, to grant extradition and not consider genocide a 'political crime': *ibid*. Art. 7 (see section 5.4.3).

[63] See e.g. Eric David, *Principes de droit des conflits armés*, 2nd ed. (Brussels, 1999) 667–8 (a modern interpretation of the Convention in light of Art. 1); and Lee A. Steven, 'Genocide and the Duty to Extradite or Prosecute: Why the United States Is in Breach of its International Obligations' (1999) 39 *Virginia Journal of International Law* 425, 460–1 (interpretation of Arts. 1 and 4–7).

[64] *Case concerning Application of the Convention on the Prevention and Punishment of the Crime of Genocide (Bosnia and Herzegovina v. Serbia and Montenegro)*, ICJ, Judgment of 26 February 2007, para. 442.

[65] E.g. International Covenant on Civil and Political Rights (ICCPR), Art. 2(1). See also ECHR, Art. 1; American Convention on Human Rights (ACHR), Art. 1.

most war crimes. This may be supported by case law from the Inter-American Court of Human Rights (IACtHR), in particular the *Velasquez-Rodriguez* v. *Honduras* case,[66] and the *Barrios Altos* case, which takes a very dim view of amnesties.[67] It is difficult to say, however, that these cases on positive duties under human rights treaties can be read as creating an absolute duty to prosecute all international crimes in all circumstances.[68] Cases from the Inter-American system are ahead of the jurisprudence of the European Court of Human Rights (ECtHR) and the UN Human Rights Committee.[69] The IACtHR's interpretive approach and reasoning cannot necessarily be extrapolated to other regional contexts.[70] That said, the gap between the regional regimes of human rights protection may be narrowing. The ECtHR has increasingly recognized that a thorough and effective criminal investigation is part of the right to an effective remedy.[71]

4.3.3 Customary Law Obligations?

Genocide, crimes against humanity, and, at least in part, war crimes are criminalized not only by treaties but also in customary international law.[72] However, state practice, along with the accompanying *opinio juris*, arguably still falls short of supporting the position that states have a general duty to prosecute international crimes. If a duty to prosecute or extradite nevertheless existed in customary international law, it would bind states regardless of whether they are parties to the relevant treaty. The claim is sometimes made by reference to a particular crime, but sometimes by reference to all international crimes.

There are expressions in support of a customary duty, although the evidence of its existence is inconclusive. The 1996 ILC Draft Code of Crimes Against the Peace and Security of Mankind, for example, provided for a duty to prosecute or extradite individuals accused of genocide, crimes against humanity, and war crimes, as defined in the Code, and to prohibit such crimes regardless of where or by whom they were committed.[73] The ICTY Appeals Chamber in *Blaškić* stated that there is a customary obligation to prosecute or extradite those who have allegedly committed grave breaches of international humanitarian law, but without developing the argument further.[74] Moreover, the Preamble to the ICC Statute 'recall[s] the duty of every State to exercise its criminal jurisdiction over those responsible for international crimes', although the jurisdictional scope of this 'duty' is not

---

[66] *Velasquez-Rodriguez v. Honduras*, Inter-American Court of Human Rights (IACtHR), Judgment of 29 July 1988. The classic statement of the argument is Diane Orentlicher, 'Settling Accounts: The Duty to Prosecute Violations of a Prior Regime' (1991) 100 *Yale Law Journal* 2537.

[67] Barrios Altos case (*Chumbipuma Aguierre et al.* v. *Peru*), IACtHR, Judgment of 14 March 2001. See e.g. Lisa J. Laplante, 'Outlawing Amnesty: The Return of Criminal Justice in Transitional Schemes' (2009) 49 *Virginia Journal of International Law* 915. See further Chapter 22.

[68] E.g. Michael Scharf, 'The Letter of the Law: The Scope of the International Legal Obligation to Prosecute Human Rights Crimes' (1996) 59 *Law and Contemporary Problems* 1; Bruce Broomhall, *International Justice and the International Criminal Court* (Oxford, 2003) 98–100; Robert Cryer, *Prosecuting International Crimes: Selectivity in the International Criminal Law Regime* (Cambridge, 2005) 103–5.

[69] See Anja Siebert-Fohr, *Prosecuting Serious Human Rights Violations* (Oxford, 2009).

[70] *Ibid.* 109. See further Section 22.2.1.

[71] ECHR, Art. 13. See *Abu Zubaydah v. Lithuania*, ECtHR, Judgment of 31 May 2018, paras. 672–5.

[72] See further Chapters 10–12.

[73] ILC Draft Code of Crimes Against the Peace and Security of Mankind, Arts. 8–9. See also the 1996 ILC Report, at 42–50.

[74] *Blaškić*, ICTY AC, 29 October 1997, para. 29.

clarified. In making the case for a customary status of this duty, reference has also been made to certain General Assembly resolutions as an expression of *opinio juris*.[75] But close scrutiny of the wording and voting record gives rise to doubts about their authority, and the majority of state practice, particularly on amnesties, speaks against an existing customary duty to prosecute international crimes.[76]

The proponents assert that a customary duty exists even though there is no consistent state practice or *opinio juris* in support of this view. Unsurprisingly, others question this conclusion and its underlying assumptions.[77] A good case can be made, however, that such a duty is emerging concerning prosecutions based on territorial, and perhaps nationality, jurisdiction.[78] The ILC clarified in its final report that its findings should not be construed to the effect that 'the obligation to extradite or prosecute has not become or is not yet crystallising into a rule of customary international law, be it a general or regional one'.[79] The reticence of the ICJ to discuss the matter in *Habré*, and the lack of actual practice, rather indicate the current lack of a customary obligation.

International crimes are subject to permissive universal jurisdiction: states have the right to exercise it if they wish.[80] Accepting the argument of mandatory universal jurisdiction (due to the *jus cogens* status of the crimes or otherwise) would in fact result in most states being in constant breach of the obligation. This begs the question whether any customary obligation to prosecute or extradite includes exercising universal jurisdiction.

4.4 DOMESTIC CRIMINAL LAW AND JURISDICTION

4.4.1 Domestic Legislation

National prosecutions presuppose that there is applicable domestic criminal law and criminal jurisdiction. The Genocide Convention and the 1949 Geneva Conventions explicitly require that the states parties enact necessary legislation.[81] Some states adopt implementing legislation, while others rely in part upon direct application of international law in the domestic system.[82] While not all states need domestic legislation to meet all of their treaty obligations, many of them have enacted amendments or special penal laws on international crimes, to be applied either in a regular or military penal system or both.

Prior to the ICC Statute, there was no convention on crimes against humanity as such, and thus these crimes were only rarely provided for as distinct crimes in domestic law.[83]

---

[75] GA Res. 2840(XXVI), 18 December 1971 and 3074(XXVIII), 3 December 1973; see Jordan Paust, *International Law as Law of the United States* (Durham, NC, 1996) 405.

[76] See Cryer, *Prosecuting International Crimes* (n. 68) 105–10.

[77] *Ibid*. 110–17; cf. Payam Akhavan, 'Whither National Courts? The Rome Statute's Missing Half, Towards an Express and Enforceable Obligation for the Domestic Repression of International Crimes' (2010) 8 *JICJ* 1245, 1259–62. For arguments for and against, see Bassiouni and Wise, *Aut Dedere, Aut Judicare* (n. 42).

[78] See e.g. Darryl Robinson, 'Serving the Interests of Justice: Amnesties, Truth Commissions and the International Criminal Court' (2003) 14 *EJIL* 481; Siebert-Fohr, *Prosecuting Serious Human Rights Violations* (n. 69) ch. 7.

[79] ILC, 'Final Report: The Obligation to Extradite or Prosecute' (n. 59) para. 53.   [80] See Chapter 3.

[81] Genocide Convention, Art. V; Geneva Convention I, Art. 49; Geneva Convention II, Art. 50; Geneva Convention III, Art. 129; and Geneva Convention IV, Art. 146.

[82] See further Ward Ferdinandusse, *Direct Application of International Criminal Law in National Courts* (The Hague, 2006).

[83] The draft convention on crimes against humanity is still in the making at the ILC: see Section 11.1.2.

The crime of aggression is criminalized in a minority of states.[84] While at present forty-five states have ratified the Kampala amendments to the ICC Statute,[85] the majority are yet to enact implementing legislation.

Most of the underlying offences that can constitute genocide or crimes against humanity have long been penalized under domestic law, but as ordinary crimes and not in the qualified form of international crimes. This posed an obstacle to prosecutions in France until the Court of Cassation in *Barbie* established that crimes against humanity, as embodied in the Nuremberg Charter, were directly applicable in France.[86] This ruling paved the way for further prosecutions of Second World War crimes and for subsequent French legislation on genocide and other '*crimes contre l'humanité*'.

Reliance upon provisions concerning ordinary crimes (murder, assault, or rape as self-standing offences) may fall short of the required standard of criminalization under international law and breach the state's duty to enact the legislation necessary considering the seriousness of international crimes.[87] In Australia, the approach of relying on ordinary crimes in meeting the obligations under the Genocide Convention led a domestic court to the conclusion that genocide was not recognized domestically and could not be prosecuted in Australian courts.[88]

In some cases, the special legislation introduced at the domestic level may be unsatisfactory. Even if the crime definitions correspond to those under international law, other aspects, such as the modes of liability set forth in the Genocide Convention, are sometimes inadequately addressed by the application of ordinary domestic criminal law principles.[89] Customary international law norms are not always incorporated.[90] This may hinder prosecution of crimes that are based on customary international law alone.[91] Some states (for example, Germany) do not accept non-codified criminal law, due to a strict interpretation of the legality principle. Others, in particular common law jurisdictions like the United Kingdom where judicial decisions are regarded as a formal source of law, do accept unwritten law (for example, the so-called 'common law crimes'). They also accept the idea of direct application of customary international law by national courts, but not that

---

[84] See Annegret Hartig, *Making Aggression a Crime under Domestic Law: On the Legislative Implementation of Article 8bis of the ICC Statute* (The Hague, 2023) 481–506 (listing provisions criminalizing aggression for thirty-one national jurisdictions, including eight states not party to the ICC Statute).

[85] United National Treaty Collection, Amendments on the crime of aggression to the Rome Statute of the International Criminal Court, https://treaties.un.org/doc/Publication/MTDSG/Volume%20II/Chapter%20XVIII/XVIII-10-b.en.pdf. See further Chapter 13.

[86] Court of Cassation, 26 January 1984, rejecting an earlier ruling by the same court in *Touvier*, 30 June 1976, where crimes against humanity were considered 'ordinary crimes'; see Sadat, 'The French Experience' (n. 9) 293–4.

[87] This approach hindered referral of cases from the Tribunals under Rule 11*bis*: see e.g. *Bagaragaza*, ICTR AC, 30 August 2006. Cf. *Hadžihasanović et al.*, ICTY TC II, 15 March 2006, paras. 253–60 (no duty under conventional or customary law to prosecute war crimes as international crimes nor as ordinary crimes).

[88] *Nulyarimma v. Thompson* [1999] FCA 1192.

[89] See Genocide Convention, Art. III; see also William A. Schabas, *Genocide in International Law*, 2nd ed. (Cambridge, 2009) 350–2.

[90] But see the Canadian Crimes Against Humanity and War Crimes Act 2000, s. 4(4), which reflects custom; and the German Code of Crimes Against International Law 2002, which incorporates rules of customary international law into the definitions of certain crimes.

[91] See Helmut Kreicker, 'National Prosecution of Genocide from a Comparative Perspective' (2005) 5 *ICLR* 313, 319–20. Note, however, that French courts in *Barbie* and other cases accepted criminal responsibility grounded on customary international law.

customary international law is capable of creating offences in domestic law.[92] The power to create new crimes should be reserved for elected assemblies.[93]

Moreover, national legislation has sometimes been carefully designed or interpreted to have a selective application. Perhaps the most criticized feature of the *Barbie* case was the imposition by the French Court of Cassation of the additional requirement that crimes against humanity be committed 'in the name of a State practising a hegemonic political ideology'.[94] This requirement, which also affected subsequent French trials, excluded the application of the definition to crimes during France's decolonization conflicts in Indochina and Algeria. Likewise, earlier Australian law on war crimes, as interpreted in the *Polyukhovich* case, excluded crimes in East Timor.[95] In Israel, the Nazis and Nazi Collaborators (Punishment) Act of 1950, providing for crimes against humanity, war crimes, and 'crimes against the Jewish people', is solely retroactive.[96] Yet another example is the 1991 War Crimes Act in the United Kingdom which was restricted to violations of the laws of war when committed on German or German-occupied territory between 1939 and 1945, an Act that the House of Lords rejected twice with reference to retroactivity and selectivity before it was passed.[97]

As a result, the use of domestic law offences can sometimes lead to standards being applied that are narrower than those set by international law.[98] They might not fully capture the gravity of the offences and the degree of blameworthiness of the defendant.

4.4.2 ICC As a Catalyst for Domestic Legislation

The complementarity principle entails that the ICC is to assume jurisdiction only when states fail to investigate and prosecute the crimes genuinely themselves. This provides a strong incentive for states to adopt the definitions of crimes laid down in the ICC Statute and assert jurisdiction over them to stave off the ICC's intervention.[99] Although not a legal obligation under the Statute, it is generally presumed that states will want to meet the 'complementarity test'.[100] It is also a way for them to express their commitment to combating impunity for international crimes. Many states have passed new penal legislation, and the process is underway in others.[101] This has generated criminal investigations

---

[92] See e.g. R v. *Bow Street Metropolitan Stipendiary Magistrate, ex parte Pinochet Ugarte (No. 3)* [2000] 1 AC 147; and *Nulyarimma* v. *Thompson* [1999] FCA 1192.
[93] The UK House of Lords has held that customary international law can no longer create crimes in the UK legal order; R v. *Jones* [2006] UKHL 16.
[94] Court of Cassation, 20 December 1985. See also Caroline Fournet, *Genocide and Crimes Against Humanity: Confusions and Misconceptions in French Law and Practice* (Oxford, 2013).
[95] *Polyukhovich* (n. 20).
[96] See further Jonathan Wenig, 'Enforcing the Lessons of History: Israel Judges the Holocaust' in Timothy McCormack and Gerry Simpson (eds.), *The Law of War Crimes: National and International Approaches* (The Hague, 1997) 102–22.
[97] See e.g. A. T. Richardson, 'War Crimes Act 1991' (1992) 55 *Modern Law Review* 73, 77; Marschik, 'The Politics of Prosecution' (n. 8) 87–9.
[98] See e.g. Nathan Rasiah, 'The Court-Martial of Corporal Payne and Others and the Future Landscape of International Criminal Justice' (2009) 7 *JICJ* 177.
[99] See Section 8.6. See Jann Kleffner, *Complementarity in the Rome Statute and National Criminal Jurisdictions* (Oxford, 2008); Darryl Robinson, 'The Rome Statute and its Impact on National Law' in Cassese et al., *Commentary*, 1849–69; Julio Bachio Terracino, 'National Implementation of the ICC Crimes: Impact on National Jurisdictions and the ICC' (2007) 5 *JICJ* 421.
[100] E.g. Akhavan, 'Whither National Courts?' (n. 77). But see Section 8.6.2 for cases of uncontested admissibility.
[101] See Olympia Bekou, 'Crimes at Crossroads: Incorporating International Crimes at the National Level' (2012) 10 *JICJ* 677; Olympia Bekou, 'National Implementation of the ICC Statute to Prosecute International Crimes in Africa' in Charles

and prosecutions in, for example, the Democratic Republic of the Congo, Uganda, and the Central African Republic.[102]

The introduction of implementing laws is a complex task. To prevent the ICC from intervening in future situations, many states adopt the offences as defined in the ICC Statute. This is the approach taken by, *inter alia*, Argentina, Australia, Canada, New Zealand, South Africa, and the United Kingdom.[103] Another possibility is to transform the offences into the standard terminology of the national system, as has been done, for example, in Germany.[104] The German approach has been to also include customary international law offences, although there is a risk of going further than other states would accept.[105] Yet another approach is to ensure that 'ordinary' offences already existing in domestic law cover all conduct that falls within the crimes under the Statute. Neither the 'complementarity test' nor the related *ne bis in idem* provisions (see Section 4.7) require that the state mirror the ICC's legal characterization of the underlying conduct, that is, that national law includes core crimes as specific offences and relevant conduct is prosecuted as such. In the implementation process, states must also consider what scope of jurisdiction to assert and the applicable principles of criminal law and penalties, given that the creation of a distinct regime for international crimes might result in fragmentation. States are free to choose solutions other than those provided for in the ICC Statute, although it could affect their capacity to meet the 'complementarity test' and any other international obligations.

4.4.3 Impact of Domestic and International Case Law

National courts consider foreign case law to a greater or lesser extent. While it is natural in common law jurisdictions to pay attention to decisions from other (common law) jurisdictions, civil law jurisdictions often are more reluctant to do so, not least because judicial decisions in those systems are not regarded as sources of law in a formal sense. But the persuasive effect of court decisions, particularly those of higher courts, is similar across the board. In some countries, universal jurisdiction trials contribute to improved translation and interpretation services, public access to the written record and judicial rulings, and more effective communication by law-enforcement with the respective victim communities.[106] In turn, these changes enhance the broader significance and implications of those proceedings. As the practice of the ICTY and ICTR shows, domestic jurisprudence may also be

---

Chernor Jalloh and Ilias Bentekas (eds.), *The International Criminal Court and Africa* (Oxford, 2017) ch. 11. See also a useful National Implementing Legislation Database, https://demo.hrlc.net/en/.

[102] See e.g. Patryk Labuda, *International Criminal Tribunals and Domestic Accountability: In the Court's Shadow* (Oxford, 2023).

[103] See David Turns, 'Aspects of National Implementation of the Rome Statute: The United Kingdom and Selected Other States' in McGoldrick et al., *The Permanent ICC*, 337–87; on Latin America, see Elizabeth S. Vargas (genocide), Ramiro G. Falconí (crimes against humanity), and Salvador H. Carrasco (war crimes) in (2010) 10 *ICLR* 441–73.

[104] See e.g. Helmut Satzger, 'German Criminal Law and the Rome Statute: A Critical Analysis of the New German Code of Crimes Against International Law' (2002) 2 *ICLR* 261.

[105] Robinson, 'The Rome Statute' (n. 99) 1861–2.

[106] On the (mixed) experience in Germany, see Susann Aboueldahab and Fin-Jasper Langmack, 'Universal Jurisdiction Cases in Germany: A Closer Look at the Poster Child of International Criminal Justice' (2022) 31 *Minnesota Journal of International Law* 1.

used by international criminal courts to interpret international law.[107] In particular, such decisions have served as tools for the interpretation of treaties, identification of customary rules or general principles of law, and even as independent authorities.

Decisions of international courts are a recognized, but formally a subsidiary, means for determining the rules of international law. In practice, these decisions, from the Nuremberg and Tokyo International Military Tribunals (IMTs) to the ICC to the hybrid courts, have made important contributions to the development of international criminal law, also at the domestic level. The ICTY and ICTR have made a lasting impact by operating for many years and providing important clarifications of various issues. Some domestic legislation, for example in the United Kingdom, explicitly requires that national courts take into account decisions and judgments of the ICC and any other relevant international jurisprudence.[108] In other states that have incorporated international crimes into domestic law, courts will normally be under an obligation to interpret the domestic provisions in accordance with the interpretation of equivalent international provisions, including that made by international criminal tribunals.[109]

4.5 STATUTORY LIMITATIONS

Most domestic systems envisage statutory limitations, or prescriptions (i.e. time limitations on prosecution). While most civil law jurisdictions provide for general time bars, most common law jurisdictions exclude murder and other serious crimes. Neither the post-Second World War trials, nor the 1949 Geneva Conventions or the Genocide Convention address this issue, but there has been much debate regarding the application of statutory limitations to genocide, crimes against humanity, and war crimes. Statutory limitations aim to prevent unjust delays between the commission of the offence and prosecution (or punishment), but could, if applicable, lead to impunity for the most heinous crimes. In order to close this possible 'technical' escape from liability, treaties on the non-applicability of statutory limitations to genocide, crimes against humanity, and war crimes were adopted under the auspices of the United Nations and the Council of Europe.[110] Some states have passed laws which make statutory limitations inapplicable to such crimes, but these laws vary in scope.[111] There is also municipal and international case law to the effect that statutory limitations shall not apply to international crimes, for example the ICTY ruling regarding torture in *Furundžija* and the relevant human rights

---

[107] See André Nollkaemper, 'Decisions of National Courts as Sources of International Law: An Analysis of the Practice of the ICTY' in William Schabas and Gideon Boas (eds.), *International Criminal Law Developments in the Case Law of the ICTY* (Leiden, 2003) 277–96.

[108] International Criminal Court Act 2001, s. 66(4) (UK). See generally Robert Cryer, 'Neither Here Nor There? The Status of International Criminal Jurisprudence in the International and UK Legal Orders' in Kaiyan Kaikobad and Michael Bohlander (eds.), *International Law and Power: Perspectives on Legal Order and Justice, Essays in Honour of Colin Warbrick* (The Hague, 2010) 183.

[109] See e.g. the *Jorgić* case, German Federal Constitutional Court, 12 December 2000.

[110] Convention on the Non-Applicability of Statutory Limitations to War Crimes and Crimes Against Humanity of 26 November 1968; European Convention on the Non-Applicability of Statutory Limitations to Crimes Against Humanity and War Crimes of 25 January 1974.

[111] For an overview, see Ruth Kok, *Statutory Limitations in International Criminal Law* (The Hague, 2007) ch. 3.

jurisprudence.[112] The ICC Statute explicitly provides that statutory limitations do not apply before it.[113] The Enforced Disappearances Convention, although stopping short of prohibiting statutes of limitation for individual disappearances, provides that any limitation shall take into account the exceptional seriousness of disappearances and shall only run from the end of the offence, given its continuing nature.[114]

Statutes of limitations have hindered some national prosecutions.[115] In the *Barbie* case, for example, the French law on non-application of such limitations was strictly interpreted to apply only to crimes against humanity, thus barring prosecution for war crimes.[116] Similarly, in the Italian *Hass and Priebke* case concerning the massacre of hundreds of civilians during the Second World War, the prescription concerning war crimes punishable with a lesser sentence than life imprisonment initially led the Rome military court to release the defendant.[117] Before that, the lower Argentine courts at first had declined to extradite Priebke to Italy given the statute of limitation, although he was eventually extradited.[118] Similarly, in 1976, Swiss authorities refused extradition to the Netherlands of suspected war criminal Pieter Menten due to statutory limitations and were also prevented from prosecuting the case.[119] Statutory limitations have also been an issue in Spanish prosecutions of Franco-era crimes, although the concept of 'continuing crimes' has provided a way of circumventing national limitations on prosecution.[120]

It has been claimed that the non-applicability of statutory limitations to war crimes has developed into a norm of customary international law,[121] although sometimes the putative customary rule is limited to genocide, crimes against humanity, and torture. While there is clearly a move towards the non-applicability of statutory limitations, the fact remains that many states still apply such limitations to international crimes in their domestic legal orders. Moreover, the UN and European conventions on non-applicability of statutory limitations referenced above have a modest number of states parties.[122] For example, both German and Dutch law retain statutory limitations for the least serious war crimes, even against the general non-applicability of such limitations in the ICC Statute.[123]

---

[112] *Furundžija*, ICTY TC II, 10 December 1998, para. 157. See also *Barrios Altos* (n. 67) para. 41; *Herzog* v. *Brazil*, IACtHR, 15 March 2018, paras. 216–19, 261–9 and *Kononov* v. *Latvia*, ECtHR, Judgment of 17 May 2010, paras. 231–3. An example of a domestic decision is *Sandoval*, Supreme Court of Chile, Judgment of 17 November 2004 (on enforced disappearances).

[113] ICC Statute, Art. 29. [114] Enforced Disappearances Convention, Arts. 5 and 8(1)(b).

[115] See further Christine Van den Wyngaert, 'War Crimes, Genocide and Crimes Against Humanity: Are States Taking National Prosecutions Seriously?' in M. Cherif Bassiouni (ed.), *International Criminal Law*, 2nd ed. (New York, 1999) vol. III, 233–5.

[116] French Court of Cassation, 26 January 1984.

[117] War crimes carrying life imprisonment under Italian law were exempt from statutory limitations, and in its second decision (*Hass and Priebke*, 22 July 1997 (n. 10) the court held the defendants' crimes to be punishable *in abstracto* with an indefinite term and thus imprescriptible. Their convictions and life sentences were upheld by the Supreme Court of Cassation (*Hass and Priebke*, 16 November 1998 (n. 10). See Kok (n. 111) ch.5 s.6.

[118] *Erich Priebke*, Judgment on Extradition Request, no. 16.063/94, Supreme Court of Argentina, 2 November 1995.

[119] See Andreas Ziegler, 'Domestic Prosecution and International Cooperation with Regard to Violations of International Humanitarian Law: The Case of Switzerland' (1997) 7 *Schweizerische Zeitschrift für internationales und europäisches Recht* 561, 570–1.

[120] Samantha Salsench i Linares, 'Francoism Facing Justice: Enforced Disappearances Before Spanish Courts' (2013) 11 *JICJ* 463.

[121] Henckaerts and Doswald-Beck, *ICRC Customary Law*, 614–18.

[122] As of March 2024, the UN Convention had fifty-six states parties and nine signatories and the European Convention had eight Parties and one signatory.

[123] *Wet internationale misdrijven*, BWBR0015252, 19 June 2003, art. 13; Harry Verweij and Martijn Groenleer, 'The Netherlands' Legislative Measures to Implement the ICC Statute' in R. S. Lee, *States' Responses to Issues Arising from the*

The assertion of a customary norm prohibiting statutory limitations for all core crimes may thus be premature. However, domestic legislation does not affect liability under international law, and there is no positive rule of international law providing for the prescription of liability for international crimes.[124]

4.6 NON-RETROACTIVITY

Related to statutory limitations is the principle of non-retroactivity of criminal law, which in turn forms part of the legality principle.[125] The question of compatibility with the non-retroactivity principle arises when a limitation period is extended or set aside retroactively or when extra-territorial jurisdiction is introduced retrospectively. National courts have accepted retroactive criminality with respect to Second World War crimes, insofar as the crimes were considered to be covered by conventional or customary international law at the time the offence was committed. Both the Supreme Court of Canada in *Finta* and the High Court of Australia in *Polyukhovich* accepted this regarding crimes committed abroad. The French Court of Cassation in *Barbie* resolved the issue by considering the prohibition of crimes against humanity as directly applicable international law. States will consider statutory limitations as either substantive or procedural rules, and the principle of legality is only applicable to the former, but there must in any case be grounds for concluding that the crime existed at the time of its commission.[126] Human rights treaties hold that the principle of legality does not preclude trial and punishment for conduct which, at the time of its commission, was criminal under general principles of law recognized by the community of nations.[127] The Grand Chamber of the ECtHR has accepted that a conviction in 2004 for war crimes committed in 1944 did not violate Article 7 of the ECHR.[128]

Some ICC implementing legislation addresses the question of retroactivity. For example, according to the Canadian Crimes Against Humanity and War Crimes Act 2000, crimes committed outside Canada may be prosecuted retrospectively, but prosecution of crimes committed before the adoption of the ICC Statute (on 17 July 1998) is allowed only insofar as the crimes correspond to the state of customary law at the time of their commission.[129] The Act also clarifies that the crimes defined in the ICC Statute are deemed to reflect customary law at the latest when the Statute was adopted, possibly earlier, and that crimes against humanity were criminal according to customary international law or general principles of law recognized by civilized nations prior to the Nuremberg and the Tokyo IMT Charters.[130] The New Zealand International Crimes and International Criminal Courts Act 2000 establishes start dates for jurisdiction over genocide and crimes against

---

ICC Statute: Constitutional, Sovereignty, Judicial Cooperation and Criminal Law (New York, 2005) 97; and Satzger, 'German Criminal Law and the Rome Statute' (n. 104) 272–3. Cf. Sweden, which as of 1 July 2010 repealed the statutory limitations, *inter alia*, for international crimes (see Swedish Penal Code, ch. 35, s. 2).
[124] *Kononov* v. *Latvia* (n. 112), paras. 228–33. [125] See Section 1.5.1.
[126] See Van den Wyngaert, 'War Crimes, Genocide and Crimes Against Humanity' (n. 115) 235–7.
[127] ECHR, Art. 7(2); ICCPR, Art. 15(2). [128] *Kononov* v. *Latvia* (n. 112), paras. 205–27.
[129] Crimes Against Humanity and War Crimes Act 2000, s. 6.
[130] *Ibid*. The Charters were adopted on 8 August 1945 and 19 January 1946, respectively.

humanity,[131] which reflect the date when New Zealand ratified the Genocide Convention (for genocide) and the date when the jurisdiction of the ICTY commenced (for crimes against humanity). Similar provisions exist in the United Kingdom, which retrospectively gave UK courts jurisdiction over certain customary international crimes that have occurred since 1 January 1991.[132]

4.7 *NE BIS IN IDEM* OR DOUBLE JEOPARDY

4.7.1 Application between States

The principle that no one shall be tried or punished more than once for the same offence, expressed as *ne bis in idem* or double jeopardy, is reflected in the major human rights treaties.[133] It is an aspect of the broader principle of finality and the binding effect of judgments (the doctrine of *res judicata*).[134] The principle ensures fairness to defendants and the interest of thorough investigation and preparation of cases by the prosecutorial authorities. It also applies in the context of international cooperation in criminal matters.[135]

But these provisions relate only to proceedings in one and the same state.[136] Hence, it is lawful for a state to prosecute a person for an offence for which they have been prosecuted, and even punished, elsewhere. This is a matter of sovereign equality: one state's courts cannot bind another. Different states view the effects of a foreign criminal judgment differently. In many common law jurisdictions, the plea of *autrefois acquit, autrefois convict* is not restricted to a previous acquittal or conviction in the same domestic jurisdiction.[137] In other states, the practice ranges from almost complete recognition of foreign judgments to no recognition at all, while most states recognize foreign judgments to a limited extent. When retrials are allowed, municipal law sometimes demands that a penalty imposed and served abroad is taken into account in sentencing.

Basic differences in the common law and civil law traditions, on issues such as the finality of a judgment, appeals against acquittals, and determination of the same act or 'object of the trial' (*idem*), influence the application of the principle.[138] While some states apply a narrow interpretation of *idem*, covering only the conduct as labelled in law ('the offence'), other states give it a broader meaning whereby the conduct both in law and in fact

---

[131] International Crimes and International Criminal Court Act 2000, s. 8(4).

[132] Coroners and Justice Act 2009. Section 70 provides for jurisdiction over genocide, war crimes, and crimes against humanity committed since 1991. See Robert Cryer and Paul David Mora, 'The Coroners and Justice Act 2009 and International Criminal Law: Backing into the Future?' (2010) 58 *ICLQ* 803.

[133] E.g. ICCPR, Art. 14(7); and Protocol No. 7 to the ECHR, Art. 4

[134] See José Luis de la Cuesta, 'Concurrent National and International Criminal Jurisdiction and the Principle of "Ne Bis in Idem": General Report' (2002) 73 *International Review of Penal Law* 707. See also Gerard Coffey, 'Resolving Conflicts of Jurisdiction in Criminal Proceedings: Interpreting Ne Bis in Idem in Conjunction with the Principle of Complementarity' (2013) 4 *New Journal of European Criminal Law* 59.

[135] See Section 5.3.3.

[136] See e.g. Christine Van den Wyngaert and Guy Stessens, 'The International Non Bis in Idem Principle: Resolving Some of the Unanswered Questions' (1999) 48 *ICLQ* 779. However, some argue that this is a serious lacuna in the protection of individual human rights, e.g. Alexander Poels, 'A Need for Transnational Non Bis in Idem Protection in International Human Rights Law' (2005) 23 *Netherlands Quarterly of Human Rights* 329.

[137] See e.g. Treacy v. *DPP* [1971] AC 537.

[138] Christine Van den Wyngaert and Tom Ongena, 'Ne Bis in Idem Principle, Including the Issue of Amnesty' in Cassese et al., *Commentary*, 710–15.

is covered. The authoritative interpretation by the ECtHR is that of the broader 'same conduct', or *idem factum*.[139] The Court of Justice of the European Union (CJEU) has also accepted that '*idem*' in Article 54 of the 1990 Convention Implementing the Schengen Agreement refers to the 'identity of material acts', that is, the same facts.[140] There is no full clarity or consensus as to what decisions (*bis*), apart from convictions and acquittals, may bar new proceedings.[141]

Thus, although the principle applies internally in almost all domestic systems, its cross-border application remains controversial.[142] It is not recognized as a customary rule or a general principle of law.[143] But arguably, a customary rule concerning cross-border application of the principle is evolving, at least with regard to international crimes. Rather than complex *ne bis in idem* provisions, which provide a 'first come first served' solution, the EU has adopted a mechanism for avoiding parallel proceedings.[144] In support of the evolving general norm, the ICTY, ICTR, and ICC Statutes all establish that the principle shall apply both ways in the relationship between the international and national courts.

4.7.2 Application vis-à-vis International Criminal Jurisdictions

The establishment of international criminal jurisdictions added another dimension to the *ne bis in idem* principle.[145] In line with the ICTY and ICTR's primary jurisdiction vis-à-vis states,[146] their Statutes provide that no one may be tried for the same conduct after they have been prosecuted at the Tribunal, but the Tribunals are not hindered by domestic proceedings in certain circumstances.[147] The criteria relate both to the quality of the national proceedings and to the interest of underlining the seriousness of international crimes. Only finalized national proceedings can bar prosecution before the Tribunal.[148] Deduction of sentence applies in the event that the Tribunal retries the person.

The ICC also recognizes *ne bis in idem*.[149] This means that the ICC is barred from trying a person for the same conduct (*idem factum*), subject to some exceptions such as where the

---

[139] Zolotukhin v. *Russia*, ECtHR, Judgment of 10 February 2009, paras. 70–84. On Art. 4 of Protocol No. 7 to the ECHR, see e.g. Gradinger v. *Austria*, ECtHR, Judgment of 23 October 1995; and Fischer v. *Austria*, ECtHR, Judgment of 29 August 2001 (broad interpretations of *idem*); Oliveira v. *Switzerland*, ECtHR, Judgment of 30 July 1998 (more narrow interpretation).

[140] See e.g. *Van Esbroeck*, CJEU, Judgment of 9 March 2006, paras. 25–42.

[141] Candidates are other decisions which prevent further proceedings, based on abuse of process, 'extinction' of the right to prosecute, certain out-of-court settlements and, more controversially, plea-bargaining agreements and decisions not to prosecute. The CJEU has adopted a quite far-reaching approach: see e.g. *Gözütok and Brügge*, CJEU, Judgment of 11 February 2003, paras. 31–3. Cf. ACHR, Art. 8(4), which only applies to acquittals.

[142] For one example, see the *Boere* case (Regional Court Aachen, 23 March 2010); Sabine Swoboda, 'Paying the Debts: Late Nazi Trials Before German Courts: The Case of Heinrich Boere' (2011) 9 *JICJ* 243, 261–9.

[143] See e.g. Gerard Conway, 'Ne Bis in Idem in International Law' (2003) 3 *ICLR* 217. Cf. *Karemera et al.*, ICTR TC III, 16 July 2008, para. 4.

[144] Council Framework Decision 2009/948/JHA on prevention and settlement of conflicts of exercise of jurisdiction in criminal proceedings of 30 November 2009 [2009] OJ L328/42, 15 December 2009.

[145] See e.g. Diane Bernard, 'Ne Bis in Idem: Protector of Defendants' Rights or Jurisdictional Pointman' (2011) 9 *JICJ* 863; Håkan Friman et al., 'Charges' in Sluiter et al., *International Criminal Procedure*, 436–46 and 452–4.

[146] See Chapter 7.

[147] ICTY Statute, Art. 10; ICTR Statute, Art. 9. The same applies between the Special Court for Sierra Leone (SCSL) and Sierra Leone: see SCSL Statute, Arts. 8–9.

[148] *Tadić*, ICTY TC II, 14 November 1995; *Musema*, ICTR TC I, 12 March 1996, para. 12. [149] ICC Statute, Art. 20.

national trial was a sham.[150] There is, however, no exception for cases where the national court has dealt with the matter as an 'ordinary crime'; it is the underlying conduct, not the legal characterization, that is decisive. Conversely, convictions and acquittals by the ICC preclude the person from being tried by a national (or another international) court 'for a crime referred to in Article 5' that was subject to the conviction or acquittal.

4.8 POLITICAL AND PRACTICAL OBSTACLES

National prosecutions of international crimes are notoriously selective. This is in part explained by the reluctance of states to prosecute their own nationals, in particular members of the government and the ruling elites. Prosecutorial selectivity within one and the same conflict projects the message that the non-prosecuted parties acted in an irreproachable way, contributing to their political legitimization. Illiberal regimes can wield selective prosecutions against political opponents as a tool to consolidate their own grip on power.

The post-Second World War prosecutions of nationals in West and East Germany and the prosecutions in Rwanda and the former Yugoslavia concerned defendants associated with the previous regimes no longer in power.[151] Notable – yet few – exceptions concern courts-martial in the United States and the United Kingdom of several soldiers for abusing (and in one case killing) detainees in Iraq,[152] and cases against business actors in some European states.[153] The political willingness to pursue national prosecutions and to commit resources to these complex and often highly sensitive cases is decisive.[154] Serious questions of legality also present themselves, such as lack of legislation, vagueness of the law, retro-activity, and long time periods between crime and prosecution.

A case regarding crimes committed in the prosecuting state may well end up putting top officials and hence the state itself on trial. The *Barbie* trial led to embarrassing questions about the French state's collaboration with the Nazis and the commission of international crimes in the conflict in Algeria.[155] The wish to avoid such questions and other political considerations tend to either prevent national prosecutions or make them narrow and selective.[156] Such controversies surrounded the June 2017 shut-down of the Iraq Historical Allegations Team, an inquiry set up by the UK Ministry of Defence in

---

[150] This is subject to exceptions as provided in the ICC Statute, for example revision of conviction or sentence (Art. 84) and appeals against an acquittal (Art. 81).

[151] See Section 9.3.2 (Bosnia and Herzegovina) and Section 9.4.2 (Serbia). See also Ivo Josipović, 'Responsibility for War Crimes Before National Courts in Croatia' (2006) 88(861) *International Review of the Red Cross* 145.

[152] In the United States, see Roberta Arnold, 'The Abu-Ghraib Misdeeds: Will There be Justice in the Name of the Geneva Conventions?' (2004) 2 *JICJ* 999. In the United Kingdom, see Rasiah, 'The Court-Martial of Corporal Payne and Others' (n. 98).

[153] See Section 4.2.

[154] Marschik, 'The Politics of Prosecution' (n. 9) 100; Peter Burbidge, 'Waking the Dead of the Spanish Civil War: Judge Baltasar Garzón and the Spanish Law of Historical Memory' (2011) 9 *JICJ* 753.

[155] See Guyora Binder, 'Representing Nazism: Advocacy and Identity in the Trial of Klaus Barbie' (1989) 98 *Yale Law Journal* 1321; Alain Finkielkraut, *Remembering in Vain: The Klaus Barbie Trial and Crimes Against Humanity* (New York, 1992). On the *Touvier* trial, see Leila Sadat Wexler, 'Reflections on the Trial of Vichy Collaborator Paul Touvier for Crimes Against Humanity in France' (1995) 20(1) *Law and Social Inquiry* 191.

[156] See Neil J. Mitchell, *Democracy's Blameless Leaders: From Dresden to Abu Ghraib: How Leaders Evade Accountability for Abuse, Atrocity and Killing* (New York, 2012).

March 2010 to investigate alleged crimes during the conflict in Iraq.[157] The 2020 Brereton report found credible evidence of war crimes in Afghanistan committed by the Australian Defence Forces and recommended referring several servicemen for criminal investigation; the investigation by the Office of the Special Investigator is yet to yield prosecutions.[158]

Where political will exists to pursue international crimes cases, the costs involved and other criminal justice priorities may impede domestic prosecutions. Another problem is that national courts sometimes show uneasiness and insecurity when dealing with international crimes on account of limited international legal expertise and experience in such cases. They may be subject to contradictory imperatives, seeking to apply both national and international law.[159] Even when they interpret international law in good faith, there is a chance that judges not well versed in it may misunderstand what it requires.[160] Accordingly, the legal reasoning in some judgments can be criticized as inaccurate or superficial, at least when compared with international judgments.[161]

Where states prosecute crimes committed abroad, there are special demands relating to security, logistics, and international cooperation. Some countries have established specialized police and prosecution units to deal with crimes of this kind, for example Australia, Canada, Denmark, the Netherlands, Norway, Sweden, and the United Kingdom. As a way to coordinate its member states' efforts, the EU has set up the Genocide Network which facilitates cooperation in investigating and prosecuting international crimes both between their national authorities and with third states, the ICC, other tribunals, and civil society.[162]

International cooperation may also give rise to problems. In many cases, proceedings have been delayed due to difficulty arresting the suspects.[163] Eichmann was abducted in Argentina, Barbie was 'expelled' (but not extradited) from Bolivia, Touvier was, for a long time, in hiding in France, and many others have escaped justice because of the impossibility to locate them. Documentary and physical evidence is normally difficult to secure and witness evidence is therefore crucial, although it poses problems of its own. The investigation, and sometimes parts of the trials, must in some cases be conducted in the country where the crime was committed.[164]

National prosecutions have regularly taken place long after the event. This may make live evidence impossible to obtain or less reliable. Key witnesses may have forgotten

---

[157] See ICC OTP, *Report on Preliminary Examinations Activities* (2017) paras. 181–203 (concluding that there is a 'reasonable basis to believe' that the UK military committed war crimes against persons in their custody).

[158] See Australian Government, 'Afghanistan Inquiry', www.defence.gov.au/about/reviews-inquiries/afghanistan-inquiry; and Douglas Guilfoyle, Joanna Kyriakakis, and Melanie O'Brien, 'Command Responsibility, Australian War Crimes in Afghanistan, and the Brereton Report' (2022) 91 *International Law Studies* 220–83.

[159] Yaël Ronen, '*Silent Enim Leges Inter Arma* – But Beware the Background Noise: Domestic Courts as Agents of Development of the Law on the Conduct of Hostilities' (2013) 26 *LJIL* 599; Roger O'Keefe, 'Domestic Courts as Agents of Development of the International Law of Jurisdiction' (2013) 26 *LJIL* 541.

[160] See e.g. *Italy* v. *Lozano*, Rome Court of Assize, 25 October 2007, and Court of Cassation, 24 July 2008; and Antonio Cassese, 'The Italian Court of Cassation Misapprehends the Notion of War Crimes: The Lozano Case' (2008) 6 *JICJ* 1077.

[161] Schabas, 'National Courts' (n. 22) 63.

[162] EU Council Decision 2002/494/JHA of 13 June 2002 setting up a European Network of contact points in respect of persons responsible for genocide, crimes against humanity and war crimes; EU Council Decision 2003/335/JHA of 8 May 2003 on the investigation and prosecution of genocide, crimes against humanity and war crimes.

[163] See Chapter 5.

[164] See the Finnish *Bazaramba* case (District Court of Itä-Uusimaa/Porvoo, 11 June 2010, upheld on appeal) and the Swedish *Mbanenande* case (Stockholm District Court, 20 June 2013; upheld yet modified on appeal).

critical events and misidentified the accused, as in the *Polyukhovich* and *Demjanjuk* cases, or their recollections of events may have been contaminated by interactions with other witnesses and victims or with law-enforcement officers, reporters, and NGO representatives in the intervening years. The difficulty of obtaining evidence affects fair trial rights, and some national courts have applied evidentiary rules more liberally to the defence as a protection against unjust convictions. Examples include the *Finta* case in Canada and the *Demjanjuk* case in Israel.[165] Furthermore, old defendants may no longer be fit to stand trial or to serve a prison sentence; examples include the *Papon* case and the abandoned UK trial against Szyman Serafinowicz.[166]

Regardless of these inherent difficulties, domestic prosecutions remain the backbone of international criminal law enforcement because international tribunals cannot undertake prosecution of even a minority of international crimes. Hence, the task of closing the impunity gap lies primarily with municipal courts, and encouraging prosecutions and trials at the domestic level is one of the most important effects that a well-functioning and effective international criminal justice system can produce.

Further Reading

Horst Fischer et al., *International and National Prosecution under International Law* (Berlin, 2001)

Gerd Hankel, *The Leipzig Trials: German War Crimes and Their Legal Consequences after World War* (Westport, 2014)

Annegret Hartig, *Making Aggression a Crime under Domestic Law: On the Legislative Implementation of Article 8bis of the ICC Statute* (The Hague, 2023)

Patryk Labuda, *International Criminal Tribunals and Domestic Accountability: In the Court's Shadow* (Oxford, 2023)

Roy S. Lee (ed.), *States' Responses to Issues Arising from the ICC Statute: Constitutional, Sovereignty, Judicial Cooperation and Criminal Law* (New York, 2005)

Nicola Palmer, *Courts in Conflict: Interpreting the Layers of Justice in Post-Conflict Rwanda* (Oxford, 2015)

Christine Van den Wyngaert and Tom Ongena, 'Ne Bis in Idem Principle, Including the Issue of Amnesty' in Antonio Cassese, Paolo Gaeta and John R. W. D. Jones (eds.), *The Rome Statute of the International Criminal Court: A Commentary* (Oxford, 2002) 705–29

---

[165] Richard May, 'The Collection and Admissibility of Evidence and the Rights of the Accused' in Mark Lattimer and Philippe Sands (eds.), *Justice for Crimes Against Humanity* (Oxford, 2003) 167–9.

[166] See Jane Garwood-Cutler, 'The British Experience' in M. Cherif Bassiouni (ed.), *International Criminal Law*, 3rd ed. (Leiden, 2008) 325–6. See also Susanne Beck, 'Does Age Prevent Punishment? The Struggles of the German Judicial System with Alleged Nazi Criminals: Commentary on the Criminal Proceedings against John Demjanjuk and Heinrich Boere' (2010) 11 *German Law Journal* 347.

5

State Cooperation with Respect to National Proceedings

5.1 INTRODUCTION

Criminal law enforcement is at the heart of state sovereignty. Cooperation in criminal matters is a voluntary undertaking unless a state has taken on commitments by treaty. Over time, states increasingly accepted the need for international legal cooperation, especially for serious crimes with a cross-border dimension. This by definition applies to international crimes, which are of concern to all states. Cooperation is particularly important when the state is exercising jurisdiction over crimes committed abroad, but may also be necessary when it is investigating and prosecuting crimes committed on its own territory.

For a long time, no special regime for state-to-state cooperation concerning genocide, crimes against humanity, and war crimes existed in international law.[1] The Geneva Conventions and Additional Protocol I only refer to cooperation in accordance with domestic legislation.[2] However, this legal gap has recently been bridged. In May 2023, states adopted the landmark Ljubljana–The Hague Convention on International Cooperation in the Investigation and Prosecution of the Crime of Genocide, Crimes Against Humanity and War Crimes (2023 MLA Convention).[3] Enjoying the initial support of eighty states, this treaty sets out obligations regarding cooperation specifically regarding the three core crimes defined in the original version of the ICC Statute. Moreover, states can accept the application of the Convention for any of the additional eight 'annex' international crimes, such as war crime amendments to the ICC Statute, torture and enforced disappearances as self-standing offences, and the crime of aggression.[4] Traditional forms of inter-state cooperation are: extradition, mutual legal assistance, transfer of criminal proceedings, and enforcement of foreign penalties. In addition, there is an ever-increasing cooperation, at various levels of formality, between police and other law-enforcement authorities in different states. There are

---

[1] But see GA Res. 3074(XXVIII), 3 December 1973, which establishes a special regime which does not reflect custom and is not binding on states.

[2] Geneva Convention I, Art. 49; Geneva Convention II, Art. 50; Geneva Convention III, Art. 129; Geneva Convention IV, Art. 146; and Additional Protocol I, Art. 88.

[3] Ljubljana–The Hague Convention on International Cooperation in the Investigation and Prosecution of the Crime of Genocide, Crimes Against Humanity and War Crimes, adopted at the MLA Diplomatic Conference in Ljubljana, 26 May 2023, and signed by 34 states on 14 February 2024 in The Hague ('2023 MLA Convention'). See Alison Bisset, 'The Mutual Legal Assistance Treaty for Core Crimes' (2023) 92 *Nordic Journal of International Law* 229.

[4] 2023 MLA Convention, Arts. 1–2, 5 and Annexes A–H. States may also agree to apply the Convention to cooperation requests on an *ad hoc* basis provided that the conduct concerned constitutes one of the relevant crimes under both international and the requesting state party's domestic law and is an extraditable offence of the requested state party: *ibid.* Art. 6.

also some variations in terminology used by type of jurisdiction: civil law countries typically prefer the term 'international judicial assistance', which reflects the judicial involvement in criminal investigations, while common law jurisdictions rather refer to 'international or mutual legal assistance'. Cooperation of states with international criminal jurisdictions is governed by distinct legal regimes and raises issues of its own (see Chapter 20). Likewise, the present chapter does not discuss in detail the cooperation modalities within the EU.[5]

5.2 INTERNATIONAL AGREEMENTS AND OTHER BASES OF COOPERATION

Originally informal, extradition was the first form of criminal law cooperation to be regulated by international (bilateral and later multilateral) agreements. Other forms of cooperation were subsequently added, first as auxiliary measures to extradition and only later as independent forms of assistance. In the 1960s, further steps were taken, especially within the Council of Europe, to extend cooperation to transfer of criminal proceedings (delegation of prosecution) and post-conviction measures.

Most states require a bilateral or multilateral agreement (and thus, reciprocity) as a condition for providing cooperation, but states can also grant assistance unilaterally. Some states have concluded a great number of bilateral agreements. Some of the countries that previously did not do so, like China, now increasingly seek agreements.[6] Some regions have advanced multilateral regimes. In Europe, both the Council of Europe and the European Union have been active in this field. Extradition treaties have also been adopted in the context of other regional and subregional organizations,[7] as well as within the Commonwealth. But there is no global extradition or mutual legal assistance treaty of general application. Many states rely on international and national regimes that are rudimentary, outdated, or restricted to specific crimes. The new Ljubljana–The Hague Convention is an example of a crime type-specific treaty.

The primary function of most multilateral treaties on international or transnational crimes is to oblige the states parties to criminalize certain acts and provide for jurisdiction and cooperation modalities. The older treaties address cooperation only in very general terms. The contracting parties to the 1948 Genocide Convention 'pledge themselves to grant extradition in accordance with their laws and treaties'.[8] The 1977 Additional Protocol

---

[5] See André Klip, *European Criminal Law: An Integrative Approach*, 4th ed. (Antwerp, 2021) chs. 6–9; Valsamis Mitsilegas, *European Criminal Law*, 2nd ed. (Oxford, 2022) ch. 4.

[6] For example, Treaty on Extradition between Australia and The People's Republic of China, Sydney, 6 September 2007 (not yet ratified by Australia). But see Chien-Huei Wu, Howard Jyun-Syun Li, Mao-Wei Lo, and Wen-Chin Wu, 'Long Arm of the Regime: Who Signs Extradition Agreements with China?' (2024) 24 *International Relations of the Asia-Pacific* 101; Matthew Bloom, 'A Comparative Analysis of United States's Response to Extradition Requests from China' (2008) 33 *Yale Journal of International Law* 177.

[7] E.g. the Organization of American States (OAS), the League of Arab States, the Commonwealth of Independent States (CIS), the Southern African Development Community (SADC), the Economic Community of Central African States (ECCAS), and the East African Intergovernmental Authority on Development (IGAD).

[8] Genocide Convention, Art. 7. See also Geneva Convention I, Art. 49; Geneva Convention II, Art. 50; Geneva Convention III, Art. 129; and Geneva Convention IV, Art. 146.

I to the Geneva Conventions, as well as the 1984 Torture Convention, require the parties to afford each other 'the greatest measure of assistance'.[9] More recent treaties, however, elaborate further on legal cooperation in criminal matters and detail regimes for extradition, mutual legal assistance, and other forms of legal cooperation. Examples of multilateral UN treaties are the 1988 Drug Trafficking Convention,[10] the 2000 Transnational Organized Crime Convention (the 'Palermo Convention'),[11] and the 2003 Corruption Convention.[12] The Ljubljana–The Hague Convention regulates extradition, mutual legal assistance, and transfer of sentenced persons in considerable detail.[13] Specialized organizations have been important actors in this area. Best known is the International Criminal Police Organization (Interpol), established in 1923 and with 196 member countries. It provides a police communications system, databases of criminals, stolen property, firearms, fingerprints and DNA profiles, and operational police support services.[14]

5.3 BASIC FEATURES

Both in law and in practice, cooperation in criminal matters is characterized by a tension between state sovereignty and a common interest and solidarity among states in combating crimes, which in turn requires a degree of trust in other legal systems. State-to-state cooperation is horizontal in nature in accordance with sovereign equality. This is manifested by reciprocity requirements and extensive grounds to refuse cooperation requests. There is an evident link between international cooperation and the exercise of extra-territorial criminal jurisdiction.[15] The more far-reaching the extra-territorial jurisdiction that a state seeks to assert, the more controversial it will likely be due to competing jurisdiction of other states. This in turn may hamper cooperation.

5.3.1 Traditional Assistance and 'Mutual Recognition'

Traditionally, the requesting state asks for assistance with a certain measure and the requested state, if it grants the request, executes the measure, for instance taking a DNA swab, in accordance with its domestic law. Strict formalities and lengthy procedures often plague cooperation. Furthermore, the results are often not useful in the requesting state, particularly if the laws of the two states are very different regarding, for example, the admissibility of evidence. Efforts have therefore been made to improve this traditional format, *inter alia*, by allowing the requesting state to prescribe procedural requirements and

---

[9] Additional Protocol I, Art. 88; Torture Convention, Art. 9.

[10] UN Convention Against Illicit Traffic in Narcotic Drugs and Psychotropic Substances, Vienna, 20 September 1988, entered into force 11 November 1990, 1582 UNTS 95 ('1988 Narcotic Drugs Convention'), Arts. 6–11.

[11] UN Convention on Transnational Organized Crime, GA Res. 55/25, 15 November 2000, entered into force on 29 September 2003, 2225 UNTS 209, Arts. 13–14, 16–21.

[12] UN Convention Against Corruption, GA Res. 58/4, 31 October 2003, entered into force on 14 December 2005, 2349 UNTS 41, Arts. 43–50. In addition, the Convention entails an advanced scheme for cooperation concerning asset recovery: Arts. 51–59.

[13] 2023 MLA Convention, Parts III–V. [14] See further the Interpol webpage www.interpol.int/INTERPOL-expertise/Databases.

[15] See e.g. Christopher Blakesley and Otto Lagodny, 'Finding Harmony Amidst Disagreement over Extradition, the Role of Human Rights, and Issues of Extraterritoriality under International Criminal Law' (1991) 24 *Vanderbilt Journal of Transnational Law* 1. See Chapter 3.

to participate when measures are taken on its behalf.[16] There is also a move away from the traditional, and often inefficient, diplomatic channel for cooperation requests in favour of specialized central authorities in the states, often located within the Ministry of Justice or Home Office,[17] or even direct communications between the judicial authorities in the different states.

Within the EU, a further, and more radical, step has been taken with the introduction of a principle of 'mutual recognition' of foreign judicial decisions as the cornerstone for legal cooperation among the member states.[18] This regime entails an almost automatic execution of other member states' judicial orders with minimum formality. The European Arrest Warrant (EAW) is the most widely used and successful mutual recognition instrument in the EU.[19]

5.3.2 Double Criminality, Rule of Speciality, and Statutory Limitations

States retain broad powers to refuse requests from other states. The principle of 'double criminality' (or 'dual criminality') requires that the underlying act or omission is criminal in both the requesting and the requested state. The principle stems from the principle of legality (*nullum crimen sine lege*), but is also closely linked to state sovereignty and reciprocity.[20] Although the double criminality requirement may hinder effective cooperation, it also serves to protect human rights. In the application of the double criminality rule, some states require identical crimes, while others are satisfied if the underlying facts constitute any crime (of sufficient gravity, if required) in both legal systems.

With respect to core crimes, many of the ICC state parties will have codified the crimes in their (implementing) legislation, and thus double criminality requirement is less likely to be an obstacle even where the principle is retained.[21] Double criminality does not constitute a ground for refusing extradition or mutual legal assistance under the 2023 MLA Convention.[22]

The rule of speciality, which is common in extradition treaties,[23] requires the requesting state to bring proceedings only with respect to the crimes for which the suspect was extradited. Without this rule, the double criminality principle and other conditions for extradition, such as the political offence exception, would be undermined. Where the

---

[16] See e.g. 2000 Palermo Convention, Art. 18 and 2001 Additional Protocol II to the 1959 European Convention on Mutual Assistance in Criminal Matters, Arts. 2 and 8. Cf. 2023 MLA Convention, Art. 32(1) ('to the extent not contrary to the domestic law of the requested state Party') and (3) ('if the requested State Party consents').

[17] E.g. 2023 MLA Convention, Arts. 20–21. A state may opt for transmitting requests and related communication through diplomatic channels and/or through the Interpol: *ibid.* Art. 21(2).

[18] See André Klip, *European Criminal Law*, 4th ed. (Antwerp, 2021) 473–525.

[19] Council Framework Decision of 13 June 2002 on the European Arrest Warrant and the surrender procedures between Member States [2002] OJ L190/1–20, 18 July 2002, as amended by Council Framework Decision 2009/299/JHA of 26 February 2009 ('EAW Framework Decision'). See Section 5.4.1.

[20] See Harmen van der Wilt, *The Law and Practice of Extradition* (Abingdon, 2022) ch. 3. [21] See Section 4.4.2.

[22] 2023 MLA Convention, Arts. 30 and 51.

[23] E.g. 1957 European Extradition Convention, Paris, 13 December 1957, entered into force 18 April 1960, ETS No. 024, as amended by the 2012 Fourth Additional Protocol to the Convention (Art. 3), Arts. 14–15; and 2003 UK–US Extradition Treaty, Art. 18(1) and (2). See also 2023 MLA Convention, Art. 52.

requested state consents, however, the speciality rule will not preclude prosecution of other offences in the requesting state.

Another potential obstacle is statutory limitations, or time limits on prosecution, which in some domestic systems apply generally and may bar cooperation.[24] The 1957 European Extradition Convention allows statutory limitations as a discretionary ground for refusal.[25] The Ljubljana–The Hague Convention, however, excludes the application of any statute of limitations contrary to international law for the crimes it covers.[26] In some systems, like the United Kingdom, serious offences are not subject to such limitations, but extradition may still be refused as 'unjust and oppressive' because of the passage of time (a *habeas corpus* ground).[27] However, the tendency is towards abandoning statutory limitations in the requested state as a ground, at least a mandatory one, to refuse extradition.[28]

5.3.3 *Ne Bis in Idem* or Double Jeopardy

The principle of *ne bis in idem*, precluding a person from being tried or punished repeatedly for the same offence, is a general principle in most national systems, but one that is normally confined to application within the same system.[29] Traditionally, international extradition agreements acknowledge the principle with regard to the requested state, by prohibiting extradition if that state has already passed a final judgment against the fugitive.[30] This is also a ground to refuse other forms of cooperation.[31] While some treaties aim at preventing double punishment only,[32] others seek to prevent double prosecutions too.[33]

There is no general rule of international law preventing extradition because of a judgment in a third state. The lack of common standards for the application of the *ne bis in idem* principle complicates cooperation.[34]

5.3.4 Human Rights and Legal Cooperation

In international cooperation in criminal matters there is often a tension between the fundamental human rights afforded to individuals and the state interest in efficient law-enforcement

---

[24] On statutory limitations, see Section 4.5. [25] 1957 European Extradition Convention, Art. 10.
[26] 2023 MLA Convention, Arts. 52(2)(i) and 11. [27] Extradition Act 2003, ss. 11, 14, 79 and 82 (UK).
[28] E.g. the 1990 Convention Implementing the Schengen Agreement of 14 June 1985 [2000] OJ L239, 22 September 2000, Art. 62; 1996 EU Extradition Convention, Art. 8; and the 2012 Fourth Additional Protocol to the 1957 European Extradition Convention, Art. 1. See also the Revised Manual to the UN Model Treaty on Extradition.
[29] On *ne bis in idem*, see Section 4.7.
[30] 1957 European Extradition Convention and the Additional Protocol, 15 October 1975, entered into force, ETS No. 86, 20 August 1979 ('1975 Additional Protocol') Art. 9; EAW Framework Decision, Art. 3(2); 2023 MLA Convention, Art. 51(2)(c).
[31] 2023 MLA Convention, Art. 30(1)(c).
[32] See e.g. European Convention on Transfer of Proceedings in Criminal Matters, 15 May 1972, entered into force 30 March 1978, ETS No. 073, Arts. 35–37 (mandatory ground for refusal) and Convention on Laundering, Search, Seizure and Confiscation of the Proceeds from Crime, 8 November 1990, entered into force on 1 September 1993, ETS No. 141, Art. 18(1)(e) (optional ground for refusal).
[33] See e.g. 1990 Convention Implementing the Schengen Agreement, Arts. 54–58 (albeit with certain exceptions).
[34] Section 4.7.

and prosecution. In common law jurisdictions, the 'rule of non-inquiry' has often discouraged the courts from inquiring into the fairness of the proceedings of the requesting state.[35] One argument for this rule, and for limiting the grounds for refusing cooperation, is that it promotes cooperation.[36] But human rights considerations point in the opposite direction: cooperation, particularly extradition, should not be granted if the fundamental human rights of the person concerned would be at risk.

An early expression of the human rights concerns is the *non-refoulement* principle from international refugee law, which provides that a refugee should not be returned to a country where they are likely to be persecuted.[37] However, the 1951 Refugee Convention does not apply to those in respect of whom there are serious reasons for considering that they may have committed a 'crime against peace, a war crime, or a crime against humanity' or 'a serious non-political crime'.[38] Persons excluded from refugee status under Article 1(F) would still benefit from other general human rights protections.

The notion that domestic human rights protection, constitutional or otherwise, is applicable also to legal cooperation is self-evident and established by courts in many states. It was long unclear, however, whether international human rights obligations would apply to, and even trump, international cooperation obligations. But in the groundbreaking *Soering* decision of 1989, the European Court of Human Rights (ECtHR) established that states party to the European Convention on Human Rights (ECHR) have certain obligations to protect individuals against a serious breach of their human rights in another state: 'knowingly to surrender a fugitive to another state where there were substantial grounds for believing that he would be in danger of being subjected to torture', or to inhuman or degrading treatment, would be a violation of the ECHR.[39] Also, 'a flagrant denial of a fair trial' in the requesting country may hinder extradition.[40] The UN Human Rights Committee (HRC) has followed suit when interpreting the International Covenant on Civil and Political Rights (ICCPR).[41]

Many treaties contain a 'discrimination clause': an extradition or other cooperation request may be rejected if made 'for the purpose of prosecuting or punishing a person on account of that person's race, religion, nationality, ethnic origin or political opinion or . . . [if] compliance with the request would cause prejudice to that person's position for any of these reasons'.[42] Under the 2023 MLA Convention, a discriminatory motive behind an extradition request constitutes a mandatory ground for refusal and is a discretionary ground to refuse mutual legal assistance.[43]

---

[35] E.g. the United States takes a strict approach to the rule of non-inquiry. See John T. Parry, 'International Extradition, the Rule of Non-Inquiry, and the Problem of Sovereignty' (2010) 90 *Boston University Law Review* 1973, 1975.

[36] For a sceptical view, see William Magnuson, 'The Domestic Politics of International Extradition' (2012) 52 *Virginia Journal of International Law* 839, 888.

[37] Convention relating to the Status of Refugees, 28 July 1951, entered into force 22 April 1954, 189 UNTS 149, Arts. 1(A)(2) and 33.

[38] *Ibid.* Art. 1(F).   [39] *Soering* v. *United Kingdom*, ECtHR, Judgment of 7 July 1989, para. 88.

[40] *Ibid.* para. 113. See Section 5.4.5.   [41] See e.g. *Ng* v. *Canada*, HRC, 5 November 1993.

[42] E.g. 1997 Terrorist Bombings Convention, Art. 12 and 1999 Terrorism Financing Convention, Art. 15; 1957 European Extradition Convention, Art. 3(2). On terrorism, see further Chapter 14.

[43] 2023 MLA Convention, Arts. 30(1)(a) and 51(1)(a).

Human rights standards play a role not only in extradition but also in criminal proceedings. Material obtained abroad through mutual legal assistance and affected by violations, for example torture,[44] may be found inadmissible in the requesting state. Other obstacles relate to data protection concerning transferred information and third-party rights in case of the seizure or freezing of property.

5.4 EXTRADITION

Extradition is the surrender of a person by one state to another, the person being either accused of an (extraditable) crime in the requesting state or unlawfully at large after conviction. This is a considerable intrusion into the liberty of the person concerned, but one which is justified by the common interest of states in combating crimes and expunging safe havens for fugitives. The terms 'surrender' or 'transfer' are typically used to refer to the delivery of persons by states to international tribunals or between members of a regional organisation such as the EU, which is not subject to traditional grounds for refusal associated with extradition.

Extradition is one option to meet the obligation of *aut dedere aut judicare*.[45] It has been argued that the obligation has obtained customary status in relation to international offences.[46] The issue is whether states have an obligation to extradite the offender of an international crime under customary international law (assuming the state does not prosecute the fugitive instead). The final report of the International Law Commission (ILC) on the topic remained inconclusive.[47] State practice does not yet support the view that the duty to extradite in such cases is rooted in customary international law, which should thus rather be seen as *de lege ferenda* (desirable law for the future). While the state facing the option to prosecute or extradite has discretion to choose, it has been suggested that extradition to a more interested state should be given priority when that is possible.[48]

Extradition is normally subject to strict requirements. The already mentioned principle of double criminality and the rule of speciality apply, and the offences must also be of a certain gravity to be extraditable. The requested state may deny extradition with reference to *ne bis in idem*, which sometimes also covers a pardon or an amnesty in that state or a third state.[49]

5.4.1 Extradition Agreements and the European Arrest Warrant

Many states insist on reciprocity and require an international agreement for extradition. Apart from numerous bilateral agreements, the basic multilateral treaty in Europe is the

---

[44] See e.g. *A (FC)* v. *Secretary of State for the Home Department (No. 2)* [2005] UKHL 71; [2006] 2 AC 221; and *El Haski* v. *Belgium*, ECtHR, Judgment of 25 September 2012.

[45] Chapter 4. See e.g. 2023 MLA Convention, Art. 14(1) ('if it does not extradite or surrender the person to another State ... [State Party in whose territory a person is found, shall] submit the case to its competent authorities for the purposes of prosecution').

[46] Raphaël van Steenberghe, 'The Obligation to Extradite or Prosecute: Clarifying Its Nature' (2011) 9 *JICJ* 1092.

[47] ILC, 'Final Report: The Obligation to Extradite or Prosecute (Aut Dedere Aut Judicare)' (2014) II(2) *Yearbook of the International Law Commission*, para. 53.

[48] E.g. Steenberghe, 'The Obligation to Extradite or Prosecute' (n. 46) 1110–15.

[49] The 1975 Additional Protocol (ch. II.2) and the 1978 Second Additional Protocol (ch. IV.4) to the 1957 European Extradition Convention; 2023 MLA Convention, Arts. 51(1)(c) and (2)(c) (without mentioning amnesty or pardon).

1957 European Extradition Convention and its Additional Protocols, adopted by the Council of Europe, which represent a traditional scheme. The EU has followed suit and adopted two Conventions in 1995 and 1996, which provide for simplified proceedings and reduced grounds for refusal, but they are not widely ratified.[50] The 2023 MLA Convention is the first traditional multilateral agreement regulating extradition specifically for international crimes.[51]

Among the EU member states, the EAW has replaced the traditional extradition scheme since 1 January 2004. A warrant in one member state shall be recognized and enforced in all other member states, with many traditional grounds for refusal being inapplicable. Despite the advantages of this scheme from an enforcement perspective, the virtual impossibility for member states to refuse execution has proven problematic for the protection of the rights of the persons subject to an EAW.

5.4.2 Extradition Procedures

The extradition procedures follow the law and practice of the requested state and applicable extradition agreements. Traditionally, the requesting state seeks the arrest and extradition of the accused or convicted person, or the provisional arrest to be followed within a certain timeframe by a surrender request. The requested state institutes proceedings to execute the request. In most states, both the executive and the judiciary have a role to play in the proceedings: a court considers whether the request satisfies the formal requirements and the actual surrender is an executive decision.

In common law countries, the *habeas corpus* principle extends also to extradition and offers an additional ground to challenge a foreign request.[52] These countries also require supporting evidence satisfying a *prima facie* test. Moreover, courts in many common law jurisdictions have long applied a rule of non-inquiry regarding the good faith and motive behind the extradition request or the standards of criminal justice of the requesting state.[53] It would conflict with the principle of comity if courts were to 'assume the responsibility for supervising the integrity of the judicial system of another sovereign nation'.[54] Instead, such considerations of justice and international relations form part of the executive decision whether to extradite. In civil law jurisdictions as well, the presumption is that the extradition request is made in good faith, but the courts often accept challenges by the fugitive regarding human rights violations.

---

[50] 1995 EU Convention on Simplified Extradition Procedures, 10 March 1995 [1995] OJ C78/2, 30 March 1995, and the 1996 EU Extradition Convention.

[51] 2023 MLA Convention, Arts. 49–65.

[52] On the UK law, see e.g. Chris Nicholls et al., *Nicholls, Montgomery and Knowles on The Law of Extradition and Mutual Assistance*, 3rd ed. (Oxford, 2013) 164–9.

[53] For jurisprudence, see John Dugard and Christine Van den Wyngaert, 'Reconciling Extradition with Human Rights' (1998) 92 *AJIL* 189–91; and M. Cherif Bassiouni, *International Extradition: United States Law and Practice*, 6th ed. (New York, 2014) 632–62.

[54] *Jhirad* v. *Ferrandina*, US Court of Appeals (2d Cir.), 12 April 1976, para. 22. See also e.g. *Hoxha* v. *Levi*, US Court of Appeals (3d Cir.), 3 October 2006.

5.4.3 Extraditable and Non-Extraditable Offences

Extradition is normally restricted to serious offences, often by reference to a minimum level of punishment.[55] In practice, most international and transnational crimes are sufficiently serious for extradition.

In addition, certain classes of offences are typically excluded from extradition. Most agreements provide that offences of a political nature are non-extraditable.[56] The requested state avoids getting involved in conflicts abroad and preserves its right to grant political asylum. However, what will be considered a 'political offence' is not clearly defined in international law, which leaves room for considerable discretion.[57] Its scope of application has been reduced in some jurisdictions by distinguishing between 'absolute' and 'relative' political offences, where only the former will always prevent extradition.

Today, a number of terrorism treaties explicitly provide that the crimes in question shall not be regarded as political offences for the purpose of extradition. The 1948 Genocide Convention also has such a clause, and the Ljubljana–The Hague Convention features a similarly worded provision.[58] Another, often excluded, group of offences is military offences.[59] These are offences according to military law, not ordinary criminal law, and should not hinder extradition for international crimes such as war crimes. Fiscal offences are also traditionally exempt from extradition unless states specifically agree otherwise.[60]

5.4.4 Non-Extradition of Nationals

Many states, primarily civil law jurisdictions, prohibit the extradition of their own nationals. The principle is based on a historical duty of the state to protect its citizens, sovereignty, and distrust in foreign legal systems. This principle is often constitutionally protected.[61] As a counterweight, many of these states provide for extensive criminal jurisdiction over offences committed by their nationals (and permanent residents) abroad. The Ljubljana–The Hague Convention recognizes the fugitive's nationality of the requested state as a discretionary ground to refuse extradition, but a refusal on such a ground triggers the duty to prosecute.[62]

---

[55] See e.g. 2023 MLA Convention, Art. 49(2). Some countries, e.g. the United Kingdom and the United States, have traditionally referred to a list of offences, with the drawback of repeatedly requiring amendments, but this approach is giving way to the minimum penalty and double criminality requirements.

[56] E.g. extradition from the United States to the United Kingdom was denied in a number of cases involving members of the Irish Republican Army; see Bassiouni, *International Extradition* (n. 53) 693–707.

[57] See e.g. Bert Swart, 'Human Rights and the Abolition of Traditional Principles' in A. Eser and O. Lagodny (eds.), *Principles and Procedures for a New Transnational Criminal Law* (Freiburg, 1992) 505–34. See generally Van der Wilt, *The Law and Practice of Extradition* (n. 20) ch. 5; Christine van den Wyngaert, *The Political Offence Exception to Extradition: The Delicate Problem of Balancing the Rights of the Individual and the International Public Order* (The Hague, 1980).

[58] Genocide Convention, Art. 7; 2023 MLA Convention, Art. 5(6). [59] E.g. 1957 European Extradition Convention, Art. 4.

[60] *Ibid.* Art. 5.

[61] See e.g. Michael Plachta, '(Non-)Extradition of Nationals: A Never-Ending Story?' (1999) 13 *Emory International Law Review* 77; Van der Wilt, *The Law and Practice of Extradition* (n. 20) ch. 2.

[62] 2023 MLA Convention, Arts. 54(1) and 14.

5.4.5 Death Penalty, Life Imprisonment, and Other Human Rights Grounds

Many states prohibit extradition when the fugitive may face the death penalty unless the requesting state undertakes not to impose this penalty in the case at hand or at least not to enforce it.[63] This is in keeping with commitments made in certain human rights treaties and the *Soering* principle that a state is bound by its human rights obligations with respect to extradition. Some international treaties also enshrine this extradition condition.[64] The death penalty as such is not banned under customary international law, and the *Soering* case addressed the matter as a part of the prohibition of torture or inhumane or degrading treatment or punishment.[65]

The 1984 Torture Convention also provides that extradition is not allowed to a country where the person concerned would be in danger of torture.[66] Inhumane and degrading treatment or punishment is a less clear concept. While the *Soering* case found that 'the death row phenomenon' falls under this prohibition, the UN Human Rights Committee instead attacked the methods of execution.[67] Corporal punishment, poor prison conditions, lack of appropriate medical care, and harsh interrogation methods may also meet the criteria for refusal.[68] However, the fact that the fugitive will potentially face very high penalties and detention in solitary confinement in a maximum-security facility is not necessarily sufficient for refusing extradition.[69] The Ljubljana–The Hague Convention frames the respective mandatory ground for refusal in broad terms. Besides torture or other cruel, inhuman or degrading treatment or punishment, it mentions 'substantial grounds to believe' that the person, if extradited, would be subjected to 'a flagrant violation of the right to a fair trial' or other fundamental human rights in the requesting state party in accordance with the requested state's law.[70]

Life imprisonment is also rejected in some states, and there are treaties precluding extradition given a risk of life imprisonment.[71] The European Court of Human Rights has held that the extradition of a terrorist suspect to the United States where they would face a life sentence without a prospect of release, amounted to inhuman treatment in violation of Article 3 of the ECHR.[72] The Court has also established that a grossly disproportionate sentence amounts to a human rights violation (ill-treatment), and thus prevents extradition, which applies also to life sentences.[73]

---

[63] See William Schabas, 'Indirect Abolition: Capital Punishment's Role in Extradition Law and Practice' (2003) 25 *Loyola of Los Angeles International and Comparative Law Review* 581.

[64] E.g. 1957 European Extradition Convention, Art. 11; 2023 MLA Convention, Art. 51(1)(b).

[65] ECHR, Art. 3. See also *Öcalan* v. *Turkey*, ECtHR, Judgment of 12 May 2005, paras. 162–75.

[66] 1984 Torture Convention, Art. 3(1).

[67] See *Ng* v. *Canada*, HRC, 5 November 1993; and *Kindler* v. *Canada*, HRC, 11 November 1993.

[68] See e.g. *Tyrer* v. *United Kingdom*, ECtHR, Judgment of 25 April 1978; *Ireland* v. *United Kingdom*, ECtHR, Judgment of 18 January 1978; *Musial* v. *Poland*, ECtHR, Judgment of 20 January 2009; *Grzywaczewski* v. *Poland*, ECtHR, Judgment of 31 May 2012; *Torreggiani and others* v. *Italy*, ECtHR, Judgment of 8 January 2013; and *Boudellaa et al.* v. *Bosnia and Herzegovina et al.*, Human Rights Chamber for Bosnia and Herzegovina, Judgment of 11 October 2002.

[69] *Babar Ahmad and others* v. *United Kingdom*, ECtHR, Judgment of 10 April 2012, paras. 200–24, 235–44; and *Aswat* v. *United Kingdom*, ECtHR, Judgment of 16 April 2013, paras. 57–8 (but the fugitive's severe mental illness meant that extradition would violate the prohibition).

[70] 2023 MLA Convention, Art. 51(1)(d).

[71] E.g. Inter-American Extradition Convention, Caracas, 25 February 1981, entered into force on 28 March 1992, OAS Treaty Series No. 60, Art. 9; 2023 MLA Convention, Art. 51(2)(a).

[72] *Trabelsi* v. *Belgium*, ECtHR, Judgment of 4 September 2014, paras. 138–9.

[73] *Harkins and Edwards* v. *United Kingdom*, ECtHR, Judgment of 17 January 2012, paras. 132–8.

As noted in Section 5.3.4, a common clause in international agreements, inspired by the *non-refoulement* principle, prevents extradition when there are substantial grounds for believing that there is a discriminatory purpose behind the prosecution or punishment in the requesting state.[74] The 2023 MLA Convention includes both a 'discrimination clause' and a prospect of flagrant fair trial and other human rights breaches as obligatory grounds for refusal.[75]

In practice, diplomatic assurances by the requesting state relating, for example, to non-application or non-enforcement of the death penalty, guarantees against torture, and the right to a new trial, often make extradition possible despite human rights concerns.[76] But such assurances are difficult to follow up on, and there are no sanctions or remedies in case they are breached. In a spate of cases, extradition of genocide suspects to Rwanda was declined by a number of states (Finland, France, Germany, Switzerland, and the United Kingdom),[77] with reference to decisions by the ICTR refusing the referral of proceedings to Rwanda under ICTR Rule 11*bis*.[78] Likely violations of fair trial rights were raised, such as difficulties in securing the attendance of defence witnesses. However, the standard applied by the ICTR is different from that under the ECHR and Rwanda reformed its system in order to make ICTR referrals and extradition possible. Hence, in July 2009, Sweden granted extradition to Rwanda in a genocide case.[79] After the ECtHR agreed that the extradition to Rwanda would not violate the ECHR,[80] other states have followed suit, although practice has not been uniform.[81]

5.4.6 Re-Extradition

In order to observe all the conditions for extradition, and often as part of the rule of speciality, the requesting state is generally not allowed to re-extradite the fugitive to a third state without the consent of the requested state. This is provided, for example, in the 1957 European Extradition Convention concerning re-extradition for offences committed before the surrender to the requesting state,[82] in the 2023 MLA Convention,[83] and in many bilateral treaties. There are examples, however, where the requirements for re-extradition have, in effect, been circumvented by instead deporting the fugitive under immigration laws (see the next section).[84]

---

[74] E.g. 1957 European Extradition Convention, Art. 11; International Convention Against the Taking of Hostages, New York, 17 December 1979, entered into force 3 June 1983, 1316 UNTS 205, Art. 9; 1981 Inter-American Extradition Convention; and the 1990 Commonwealth Scheme for the Rendition of Fugitive Offenders, Art. 4(5).

[75] 2023 MLA Convention, Art. 51(1)(a) and (d).

[76] E.g. *Nivette* v. *France*, ECtHR, Judgment of 14 December 2000; *Harkins and Edwards* v. *United Kingdom*, ECtHR, Judgment of 17 January 2012.

[77] E.g. *Brown (aka Banyani) and others* v. *Government of Rwanda* [2009] EWCA 770. [78] See Section 7.3.4.

[79] Decision by the Government of Sweden concerning extradition to Rwanda, 9 July 2009; see also the Decision by the Swedish Supreme Court of 26 May 2009 (Case Ö1082–09).

[80] *Ahorugeze* v. *Sweden*, ECtHR, Judgment of 27 October 2011. However, the suspect had already been released by the Swedish Supreme Court and left the country when the ECtHR handed down its decision, preventing the actual extradition.

[81] States which have granted extradition to Rwanda include: Canada (*Seyoboka*), Denmark (*Mbarushimana* and *Twagirayezu*), Germany (*Twagiramungu*), and Norway (*Bandora* and *Nkuranyabahizi*). However, the High Court of Justice in the UK and the Dutch Supreme Courts have denied extradition of genocide suspects: *Government of Rwanda* v. *Nteziryayo and others* [2017] EWHC 1912 (Admin), 28 July 2017; *Karangwa*, Supreme Court of the Netherlands, ECLI:NL:HR:2023:864, 6 June 2023.

[82] 1957 European Extradition Convention, Art. 15. [83] 2023 MLA Convention, Art. 53.

[84] See e.g. *Bozano* v. *France*, ECtHR, Judgment of 18 December 1986.

5.4.7 Abduction, Rendition, or Expulsion

When there are no extradition arrangements, or these are inapplicable (for example, due to the political offence exception) or seen as ineffective, some states will resort to other measures in order to apprehend the fugitive – abduction or 'irregular rendition'.[85] This may be conducted in a particular case, such as the *Eichmann* case,[86] or even as a state policy for certain cases, such as the United States' anti-terrorist rendition programme. Such activities often violate international law with respect to the territorial sovereignty of another state and the human rights of the individual concerned.[87] However, less dramatic actions, such as luring the fugitive out of his home country, are less likely to violate international law.[88]

In accordance with the maxim *male captus, bene detentus*, national courts have long been prepared to try accused persons regardless of how they came under the jurisdiction of the court, even if the arrest and surrender of the person were unlawful under national or international law. In the *Eichmann* case, the District Court of Jerusalem saw no obstacle to trying the accused even though he had been abducted from Argentina, without that state's consent, by Israeli agents. While this principle still applies in some states, notably the United States, it is being replaced in other states by the so-called abuse of process doctrine.[89]

Originally established by the UK House of Lords, 'abuse of process' has been applied by courts, *inter alia*, in the United Kingdom, New Zealand, Australia, South Africa, and Zimbabwe, refusing to exercise jurisdiction due to irregularities when the fugitive was apprehended and transferred. But the case law is inconsistent and different factors have had an impact on the decision whether to decline jurisdiction: involvement by officials of the forum state; the nationality of the accused; protests by the injured state; the possibility of seeking extradition; the treatment of the accused; and the gravity of the crimes.[90] In addition, an 'Eichmann exception' has been argued concerning 'universally condemned offences'.[91]

State authorities sometimes choose to deport a fugitive under immigration laws instead of dealing with the matter as extradition.[92] This is usually much faster and the surrender is then unconditional. But, as the South African Constitutional Court has stated,[93] deportation and extradition serve different purposes; the former method must not be used unlawfully

---

[85] See Van der Wilt, *The Law and Practice of Extradition* (n. 20) ch. 8; Silvia Borelli, 'Extraordinary Rendition' in Ben Saul (ed.), *Research Handbook on International Law and Terrorism* (Cheltenham, 2013) ch. 19.

[86] See Chapters 3 and 4.

[87] See Venice Commission, *Opinion on the International Legal Obligations of Council of Europe Member States in Respect of Secret Detention Facilities and Inter-State Transport of Prisoners* (17 March 2006), www.venice.coe.int/webforms/documents/default.aspx?pdffile=CDL-AD(2006)009-e; and *El-Masri* v. *Former Yugoslav Republic of Macedonia*, EctHR, Judgment of 13 December 2012.

[88] This conclusion was made by the German Constitutional Court: see Matthias Hartwig, 'The German Federal Constitutional Court and the Extradition of Alleged Terrorists to the United States' (2004) 5 *German Law Journal* 185.

[89] For a survey of national case law, see *Dragan Nikolić*, ICTY TC II, 9 October 2002, paras. 79–93. See also Silvia Borelli, 'Terrorism and Human Rights: Treatment of Terrorist Suspects and Limits on International Cooperation' (2003) 16(4) *LJIL* 803, 808–10; Robert Currie, 'Abducted Criminals Before the International Criminal Court: Problems and Prospects' (2007) 18 *Criminal Law Forum* 349.

[90] *Dragan Nikolić*, ICTY TC II, 9 October 2002, para. 95. [91] See Section 17.7.3.

[92] Quite apart from such practice in individual cases, some states have opted, as a matter of policy, to deal with war criminals through deportation and denaturalization rather than criminal prosecution and extradition. See Section 4.2.

[93] *Mohamed and Dalvie* v. *President of the Republic of South Africa and six others* Constitutional Court, 2001(1) SA 893.

and with the effect that no undertaking was obtained regarding the non-imposition of the death penalty. The *Soering* principle also applies to deportation and other forms of expulsion, which, as disguised forms of extradition, may amount to a human rights violation.[94]

5.5 MUTUAL LEGAL ASSISTANCE

Mutual legal assistance developed from the so-called 'letters rogatory'.[95] This stands for a comity-based system of requests for assistance with collecting evidence. Today, it is mainly treaty-based and covers a wide range of measures.[96] These may relate to a criminal investigation, prosecution, or trial, and include taking witness statements, search and seizure, serving documents, and tracing persons and information.

The usefulness of such assistance in the requesting state depends in part upon the nature of its criminal procedures. The more adversarial the proceedings, the greater the importance normally attached to witnesses appearing in the courtroom and being subject to cross-examination. Evidence obtained abroad by foreign authorities thus becomes less attractive. In inquisitorial systems, where written evidence is regularly relied upon, this is less of a problem, although there might be concerns that the evidence was not obtained in a required manner. Thus, while common law jurisdictions were traditionally more hesitant than civil law jurisdictions to make use of mutual legal assistance, cooperation is now generally seen as an important tool for combating crimes.

Many states require an agreement and only a few dispense with this condition. In addition to bilateral or multilateral agreements, the assistance may also be based upon an ad hoc agreement for the case at hand. States party to the 2023 MLA Convention must afford one another 'the widest measure of mutual legal assistance' for the investigations, prosecutions, and judicial proceedings relating to international crimes, and the treaty provides a (non-exhaustive) list of as many as twelve forms of cooperation.[97]

Regional conventions on mutual legal assistance also exist among states in the Americas (OAS), the Caribbean (CARICOM), Western Africa (ECOWAS), Central Africa (ECCAS), Eastern Africa (IGAD), Southern Africa (SADC), the Commonwealth of Independent States (CIS), Southeast Asia (ASEAN), and South Asia (SAARC).[98] Hence, there is an extensive network of treaties, operating within regions but not between them. Some regional treaties are open to non-members. Thus, Brazil, Chile, Israel, South Korea, and

---

[94] *Chahal* v. *United Kingdom*, EctHR, Judgment of 15 November 1996; *Bolzano* v. *France*, EctHR, Judgment of 18 December 1986, para. 60.

[95] Among some states, the practice of sending delegations to another state to conduct its own investigation ('Commission Rogatory') also existed.

[96] For a comprehensive survey of multilateral treaties in Europe, see David McClean, *International Co-operation in Civil and Criminal Matters*, 3rd ed. (Oxford, 2012).

[97] 2023 MLA Convention, Arts. 23–24.

[98] Inter-American Convention on Mutual Legal Assistance in Criminal Matters, 23 May 1992; Caribbean Mutual Legal Assistance Treaty in Serious Criminal Matters, 6 July 2005; Economic Community of West African States Convention on Mutual Assistance in Criminal Matters, 29 July 1992; ECCAS Mutual Assistance Pact, 24 February 2002; IGAD Mutual Legal Assistance Convention, 8 December 2009; Minsk Convention on Legal Assistance and Legal Relations in Civil, Family and Criminal Matters, 22 January 1993; Kishinev (Chisinau) Convention, 7 October 2002; SADC Protocol on Mutual Legal Assistance in Criminal Matters, 3 October 2002; ASEAN Treaty on Mutual Assistance in Criminal Matters, 29 November 2004; SAARC Convention on Mutual Legal Assistance in Criminal Matters, 3 August 2008.

South Africa have adhered to the 1959 European Convention on Mutual Legal Assistance. The Commonwealth Scheme on Mutual Assistance (the 'Harare Scheme')[99] is an example of an arrangement that is not confined to a geographic region.

Globally, advanced schemes for mutual legal assistance are provided in more recent treaties on transnational crimes, for example the 1998 Drug Trafficking Convention, the 2000 Palermo Convention, the 2003 Corruption Convention, and the 2001 Cyber Crime Convention.[100] The Ljubljana–The Hague Convention provides a comprehensive regime for mutual legal assistance in relation to international crimes.

Mutual legal assistance is circumscribed by conditions, or grounds for refusal, which are similar to those applicable to extradition, but are often phrased in facultative rather than mandatory terms.[101] There is an evident trend to do away with, or at least restrict, the various grounds for refusal.[102]

In spite of improvements such as allowing the requesting state to prescribe procedures to be followed, nuances of procedure in different countries still pose obstacles. Apart from procedural incompatibility, questions arise as to whether fair trial rights are sufficiently safeguarded in the requesting state. Another shortcoming is that the accused cannot independently seek assistance from a foreign state; it has to be done between public authorities or courts in the different states.[103] Claims of immunity may also hamper cooperation.[104] But the major obstacle is that the process is slow, cumbersome, and fraught by practical problems, often due to ineffective implementation, indirect communications, and language barriers.

5.6 TRANSFER OF PROCEEDINGS

Criminal proceedings may be transferred from one state to another when both have jurisdiction over the offence. A double criminality requirement always applies and is often far-reaching. One important multilateral convention is that adopted by the Council of Europe.[105] This measure is infrequently used since states insist on reciprocity while not many of them have ratified it.[106]

The rationale for transfer of proceedings is generally that the accused has ties to the requesting state or that proceedings there would be more convenient. Numerous grounds

---

[99] Scheme Relating to Mutual Assistance in Criminal Matters within the Commonwealth ('Harare Scheme'), 28 July–1 August 1986, reproduced in (1986) 12 *Commonwealth Law Bulletin* 1118 (later amended in April 1990, November 2002, and October 2005).

[100] Convention on Cybercrime, 23 November 2001, entered into force on 1 July 2004, ETS 185.

[101] See e.g. the 1959 European Convention on Mutual Assistance in Criminal Matters; 2023 MLA Convention, Art. 30(1).

[102] See e.g. the 2000 EU Convention on Mutual Assistance in Criminal Matters and its 2001 Additional Protocol; and the 2000 Palermo Convention; 2023 MLA Convention, Art. 30(3)–(5).

[103] The refusal to seek measures abroad at the request of the accused may, however, affect the fairness of the subsequent trial, see e.g. *Papageorgiou* v. *Greece*, ECtHR, Judgment of 9 May 2003.

[104] See e.g. *Case concerning Certain Questions of Mutual Legal Assistance in Criminal Matters* (*Djibouti* v. *France*), ICJ, Judgment of 4 June 2008. On immunities, see further Chapter 21.

[105] European Convention on the Transfer of Proceedings in Criminal Matters, 15 May 1972, entered into force 30 March 1978, ETS 73. See also the 1990 UN Model Treaty on Transfer of Proceedings in Criminal Matters. Transfer of criminal proceedings is also referred to in other multilateral treaties: e.g. Art. 8 of the 1988 Narcotic Drugs Convention.

[106] For example, the 1972 European Convention on the Transfer of Proceedings in Criminal Matters has twenty-five states parties and ten signatories.

for refusal apply and a transfer of proceedings can be difficult in practice; for example, prosecutorial and judicial decisions taken in the transferring state have little effect, if any, and evidence collected may be inadmissible in the requesting state.

5.7 ENFORCEMENT OF PENALTIES

While states have historically been reluctant to recognize foreign criminal judgments formally, cooperation does exist regarding the enforcement of foreign prison sentences and other penalties. Apart from humanitarian aspects, this possibility sometimes facilitates extradition: an otherwise reluctant state may accept extradition provided that the fugitive is returned to serve any sentence imposed.[107]

Both bilateral and multilateral agreements on the point have been concluded. In Europe, the Council of Europe took the lead with the 1970 European Convention on the International Validity of Criminal Judgments and the 1983 Convention on the Transfer of Sentenced Persons (and its 1997 Additional Protocol). A mandatory double criminality requirement applies, as do numerous conditions and grounds for refusal. Transfer of sentenced persons is also one of the forms of cooperation under the Ljubljana–The Hague Convention.[108] The penalty will either be converted into a new penalty in the administering state, after which it is enforced there, or continued enforcement of the sentence, in terms of its legal nature and duration, will take place in that state.[109]

Further Reading

M. Cherif Bassiouni (ed.), *International Criminal Law*, vol. II: *Multilateral and Bilateral Enforcement Mechanisms*, 3rd ed. (Leiden, 2008)

M. Cherif Bassiouni (ed.), *International Extradition: United States Law and Practice*, 6th ed. (New York, 2014)

John Dugard and Christine Van den Wyngaert, 'Reconciling Extradition with Human Rights' (1998) 92 *AJIL* 187

David McClean, *International Co-operation in Civil and Criminal Matters*, 3rd ed. (Oxford, 2012)

Clive Nicholls, Claire Montgomery, Julian Knowles, Anand Doobay and Mark Summers, *The Law of Extradition and Mutual Assistance*, 3rd ed. (Oxford, 2013)

United Nations Office on Drugs and Crime (UNODC), *Manual on Mutual Legal Assistance and Extradition* (New York, 2012), www.unodc.org/documents/organized-crime/ Publications/Mutual_Legal_Assistance_Ebook_E.pdf

Harmen van der Wilt, *The Law and Practice of Extradition* (Abingdon, 2022)

---

[107] See generally Michael Plachta, *Transfer of Prisoners under International Instruments and Domestic Legislation: A Comparative Study* (Freiburg, 1993).
[108] 2023 MLA Convention, Part V. [109] *Ibid.* Arts. 75–76.

Part III
International Prosecution

6

The History of International Criminal Prosecutions: Nuremberg and Tokyo

6.1 INTRODUCTION

International criminal law, or something similar to it, has a very long history.[1] For example, in Europe, its closest precursor was the chivalric system of laws of war, which applied in the medieval era.[2] The most notable of the trials that were related to this system was that of Peter von Hagenbach in Breisach in 1474.[3] Although its status as a legal precedent is highly limited, the issues involved at that trial – superior orders, sexual offences, cooperation in evidence gathering, and pleas as to the jurisdiction of the court – have clear present-day relevance.[4] The purpose of this chapter, however, is to introduce the modern history of international criminal prosecutions rather than provide a comprehensive overview of the entire history of the subject. Therefore, we start in the early part of the twentieth century, at the end of the First World War.

6.2 1919 COMMISSION ON THE RESPONSIBILITY OF THE AUTHORS OF THE WAR

After the First World War, the Allies set up a fifteen-member commission to investigate the responsibility for the start of the war, violations of the laws of war and what tribunal would be appropriate for trials.[5] It reported in March 1919, determining that the central powers were responsible for starting the war[6] and that there were violations of the laws of war and humanity.[7] It recommended that high officials, including Kaiser Wilhelm Hohenzollern, be tried for ordering such crimes and on the basis of command responsibility.[8]

---

[1] See Morten Bergsmo et al. (eds.), *The Historical Origins of International Criminal Law* (Brussels, 2014–17) vols. I–V; Kevin Heller and Gerry Simpson (eds.), *The Hidden Histories of War Crimes Trials* (Oxford, 2013); Timothy L. H. McCormack, 'From Sun Tzu to the Sixth Committee, The Evolution of an International Criminal Law Regime' in Timothy L. H. McCormack and Gerry J. Simpson (eds.), *The Law of War Crimes: National and International Approaches* (The Hague, 1997) 31.

[2] See e.g. Maurice H. Keen, *The Laws of War in the Late Middle Ages* (London, 1965); Theodor Meron, *Bloody Constraint: Crimes and Accountability in Shakespeare* (New York, 1998).

[3] See Georg Schwarzenberger, *International Law as Applied by International Courts and Tribunals* (London, 1968) vol. II, ch. 39.

[4] See e.g. Robert Cryer, *Prosecuting International Crimes: Selectivity and the International Criminal Law Regime* (Cambridge, 2005) 17–21.

[5] Report of the Commission to the Preliminary Peace Conference, reprinted in (1920) 14 *AJIL* 95. On the report, see Gerry Simpson, 'International Criminal Law and the Past' in Gideon Boas, William Schabas and Michael Scharf (eds.), *International Criminal Justice: Legitimacy and Coherence* (Cheltenham, 2012) 123, 123–4, 132–5.

[6] *Ibid.* 107. [7] *Ibid.* 114–15. [8] *Ibid.* 116–17, 121.

Further to this, the commission suggested the setting up of an Allied 'High Tribunal' with members from all of the Allied countries to try violations of the laws and customs of war and the laws of humanity.[9] This aspect was criticized by the commission's US and Japanese members. The US members said that they knew 'of no international statute or convention making violation of the laws and customs of war – not to speak of the laws or principles of humanity – an international crime'.[10] The Japanese representatives questioned 'whether international law recognises a penal law applicable to those who are guilty'.[11] The majority, however, clearly considered there to be a body of international criminal law, albeit one which did not include aggression as a crime.[12]

As a result, the Treaty of Versailles provided, in Article 227, that the Kaiser was to be 'publicly arraigned' for 'a supreme offence against international morality and the sanctity of treaties' before an international tribunal. It was never implemented, as the Netherlands refused to hand the Kaiser over to the Allies on the basis that the offence was a political one.[13] Articles 228 and 229 of the Treaty of Versailles also provided for prosecutions of German nationals for war crimes before Allied courts, including mixed commissions where the victims came from more than one state. These provisions, however, were never put into practice. Some prosecutions, but far fewer than the Allies wanted, were undertaken by Germany itself in Leipzig between 1921 and 1923. The proceedings were characterized by bias towards the defendants, questionable acquittals, and lenient sentences.[14] However, two of these cases later formed important precedents in international criminal law.[15] The report of the commission accurately presaged many of the difficulties modern international criminal law has faced.

6.3 NUREMBERG INTERNATIONAL MILITARY TRIBUNAL

6.3.1 Creation of the Tribunal

In 1937, a treaty to create an international criminal court to try terrorist offences was negotiated,[16] but this was not supported by states and never came into force. The real leap forward in international criminal law came at the end of the Second World War. The Allies initially issued a declaration in Moscow in 1943, which promised punishment for Axis war criminals, but stated that this was 'without prejudice to the case of the major criminals whose offences have no particular geographical location and who will be punished by a joint declaration of the governments of the Allies'.[17]

---

[9] *Ibid.* 122. [10] *Ibid.* 144–6. [11] *Ibid.* 152.

[12] *Ibid.* 118. See Kirsten Sellars, *'Crimes Against Peace' and International Law* (Cambridge, 2013) 2–11.

[13] See M. Cherif Bassiouni, 'World War I: "The War to End All Wars" and the Birth of a Handicapped International Criminal Justice System' (2002) 30 *Denver Journal of International Law and Policy* 244, 269–73.

[14] Claus Kreß, 'Versailles – Nuremberg – The Hague: Germany and International Criminal Law' (2006) 40 *International Lawyer* 15, 16–20.

[15] *The Dover Castle* (1922) 16 *AJIL* 704; *The Llandovery Castle* (1922) 16 *AJIL* 708. See Kreß, 'Versailles – Nuremberg – The Hague' (n. 14) 16–18.

[16] 1937 Convention for the Creation of an International Criminal Court. See Manley O. Hudson, 'The Proposed International Criminal Court' (1938) 32 *AJIL* 549.

[17] Declaration of Moscow, 1 November 1943.

After considerable discussion amongst the Allies during the war, Churchill was persuaded by the United States and the Soviet Union that a trial of such persons was preferable
to their summary execution.[18] As a result, France, the United Kingdom, the United States,
and the Soviet Union met in London to draft the charter of an international tribunal. The
negotiations leading to the London Charter, which formed the basis of the Nuremberg
International Military Tribunal (IMT), were tense, particularly because the US and Soviet
representatives clashed over a number of important issues. The representatives of the Soviet
Union thought that the purpose of the tribunal was simply to determine the punishment to be
meted out to the defendants, who they thought were to be presumed guilty. This was
unacceptable to the United States. Differences between the civil law states (France and
the Soviet Union) and their common law counterparts (the United Kingdom and the United
States) on the appropriate procedures for the trial also caused considerable difficulties.[19]
Nonetheless, on 8 August 1945, the four Allies signed the London Agreement, which
created the Tribunal.[20] After this, nineteen other states also adhered to the Charter, albeit
without rights to participate in the trial itself.

6.3.2 The Tribunal and the Trial

The Tribunal had eight judges: four principal judges, one for each of the major Allies
(France, the Soviet Union, the United Kingdom, and the United States), and four alternates
(understudies drawn from the same states). The President of the Tribunal was Lord Justice
Geoffrey Lawrence from the United Kingdom, who exercised a firm, but largely fair, hand
over the proceedings. Each of the main Allies was entitled to appoint a chief prosecutor. The
defence was undertaken by a number of German lawyers, the leading lights of whom were
Hermann Jahreiss, an international lawyer from Cologne, and Otto Kranzbühler, a talented
naval judge-advocate.

The indictment was received by the Tribunal on 10 October 1945, at its official seat in
Berlin. It contained four main charges, all of which were based on Article 6 of the IMT's
Charter. Count one was the overall conspiracy, which was handled by the US prosecution
team. Count two concerned crimes against peace. This count was dealt with by the UK
prosecutors. Count three charged war crimes and count four concerned crimes against
humanity. The prosecution of these two offences was split between the French and Soviet
prosecutors, the French dealing with the western zone of conflict, the Soviet with the
eastern European sphere. Twenty-four defendants were arraigned before the tribunal.[21]

[18] See Arieh Kochavi, *Prelude to Nuremberg: Allied War Crimes Policy and the Question of Punishment* (Durham, NC, 1998).
[19] Robert Jackson, *Report to the President of Robert H. Jackson, US Delegate to the International Conference on Military Trials*
        (London, 1945); Sellars, '*Crimes Against Peace*' (n. 12) ch. 3.
[20] 1945 London Agreement for the IMT, 82 UNTS 279.
[21] Karl Dönitz, Hans Frank, Wilhelm Frick, Hans Fritzsche, Walter Funk, Hermann Göring, Rudolf Hess, Alfred Jodl, Ernst
        Kaltenbrunner, Wilhelm Keitel, Konstantin von Neurath, Franz von Papen, Willem Raeder, Joachim von Ribbentrop, Alfred
        Rosenberg, Fritz Saukel, Hjalmar Schacht, Baldur von Schirach, Arthur Seyss-Inquart, Albert Speer, and Julius Streicher.
        Martin Bormann was tried *in absentia* (it was subsequently established that he was already dead by the time of the trial); Gustav
        Krupp was declared mentally incapable of standing trial; and Robert Ley committed suicide in custody prior to the trial.

There were also prosecutions of six criminal organizations.[22] Having received the indictment, the Tribunal moved to the city it is now associated with, Nuremberg.[23]

In the opening session, the US Chief Prosecutor, Justice Robert Jackson (who had represented the United States at the London negotiations),[24] began the prosecution case with a stirring speech, embodying many of the ideas that have later been adopted into the ideals of international criminal law. Jackson described the Tribunal as 'the greatest tribute ever paid by power to reason', and sought to deflect concerns about the fairness of the trial and the non-prosecution of Allied nationals by saying that, 'while this law is first applied against German aggressors, the law includes, and if it is to serve a useful purpose it must condemn, aggression by any other nations, including those which sit here now in judgment'.[25]

The trial took place over ten months and 403 open sessions. In the end, three of the defendants (Schacht, Fritzsche, and von Papen) were acquitted, as were three of the six indicted organizations (the SA, the High Command, and the Reich Cabinet).[26] Of the remaining defendants, twelve were sentenced to death and seven to periods of imprisonment ranging from ten years to life. The Soviet judge, Major-General Nikitchenko, dissented from all the acquittals and the life sentence for Rudolf Hess. He would have declared all the defendants and organizations guilty, and sentenced Hess to death.[27]

The judgment of the Tribunal, in addition to its findings on the facts,[28] represented a considerable contribution to international law. The judgment dealt at some length with the defence contention that the prosecution of crimes against peace was contrary to the *nullum crimen sine lege* principle.[29] In spite of the fact that the judgment took the view that the Tribunal's Charter was binding as to what law the Tribunal ought to apply, the judgment engaged in a detailed, if in the final analysis unconvincing, review of pre-war developments, in particular the 1928 Kellogg–Briand Pact.[30] It used that treaty (which was not intended to create criminal liability) and a number of non-binding sources to create a case that aggressive war was criminalized by customary international law.[31] The Tribunal may have been on more solid ground in relation to positive international law when it asserted that the *nullum crimen* principle was not established as an absolute principle in international

---

[22] See Telford Taylor, *The Anatomy of the Nuremberg Trial* (London, 1993) 501–33.

[23] See generally Guénaël Mettraux (ed.), *Perspectives on the Nuremberg Trial* (Oxford, 2008).

[24] The Russian judge (Nikitchenko) had also represented his country at the negotiations.

[25] 1 Trial of Major War Criminals, Nuremberg (London, 1946) 85. See Matthew Lippmann, 'Nuremberg Forty-Five Years Later' (1991) 7 *Connecticut Journal of International Law* 1, 39.

[26] The SS (and SD), Gestapo, and the leadership corps of the Nazi party, were declared criminal subject to the significant limitation that for conviction for membership in such organizations, the accused had to have knowledge of the criminal ends of the group. Nuremberg IMT, Judgment and Sentences, reprinted in (1947) 41 *AJIL* 172, 249–52.

[27] 21 Trial of Major War Criminals, Nuremberg (London, 1946) 531–47. It is notable that Nikitchenko's dissent was not published in the standard reference for the judgment in the *AJIL*.

[28] As the judgment accurately stated, the evidence was 'overwhelming, in its volume and its detail'. Nuremberg IMT, Judgment and Sentences, 224.

[29] Despite the possible novelty of the crimes against humanity charge (see Chapter 11) the defence did not seriously challenge the counts, owing to the nature of the conduct they covered, in particular the Holocaust. Even the Nazi's chief legal apologist, Karl Schmitt, considered the charges justified, see Kreß, 'Versailles – Nuremberg – The Hague' (n. 14) 22.

[30] (1929) UKTS 29.

[31] See further Chapter 13; Sellars, *'Crimes Against Peace'* (n. 12) chs. 4–5; and Sheldon Glueck, *War Criminals: Their Prosecution and Punishment* (New York, NY, 1944); *contra* Sheldon Glueck, *The Nuremberg Trial and Aggressive War* (New York, NY, 1946). For the Tribunal's views on superior orders, see Section 16.8.

law at the time.[32] Probably the Tribunal's most famous holding, however, is its firm affirmation of direct liability under international law, which has become a foundational statement in international criminal law:

crimes against international law are committed by men, not abstract entities, and only by punishing individuals who commit such crimes can the provisions of international law be enforced ... individuals have international duties which transcend the national obligations of obedience imposed by the individual state.[33]

The 'principles' of the IMT's Charter and judgment were quickly affirmed by the UN General Assembly in its Resolution 95(1).[34] Although some aspects of the Tribunal's decision were controversial in international law,[35] others have proved highly influential, especially its holding that the 1907 Hague Regulations represented customary international law.[36]

6.3.3   Assessment of the Nuremberg IMT

The Nuremberg IMT is often accused of being an example of 'victor's justice', although it is not always clear precisely what this concept means. This accusation contains a number of linked, but different, allegations. These are that the trial itself was not fair, in particular that the judges were biased against the accused;[37] that the applicable law was designed to guarantee a conviction; and that similar acts were committed by the prosecuting state(s) but were not prosecuted (i.e. a plea of *tu quoque*).[38]

With respect to the first issue, some aspects of the Nuremberg trial were imperfect. There was, for example, a heavy reliance on affidavit evidence,[39] and a considerable disparity in resources between the prosecution and the defence. However, given the standards applicable to trials at the time, the proceedings were viewed, basically, as fair.[40] Even so, a reasonable case can be made that the presence of neutral judges, or a judge from Germany, would have increased the legitimacy of the proceedings.[41] In relation to the critiques of the law, it is true that the law on crimes against humanity and peace was defined by the Allies in London, with the actions of the Nazis in mind,[42] and at least in relation to crimes against peace, the Charter was, in essence, *ex post facto* legislation. It might be

---

[32] Nuremberg IMT, Judgment and Sentences, 217.   [33] *Ibid.* 221.   [34] UN Doc. A/64/Add.1.

[35] In addition to the debate about crimes against peace, considerable controversy surrounds the determination of the Tribunal that conspiracy existed as a mode of liability in international criminal law. It is questionable whether it did at the time. However, it may be that the conduct was criminal under other modes of participation. On modes of participation see Sections 15.2 and 15.5.5.

[36] See e.g. *Legal Consequences of the Construction of a Wall in the Occupied Palestinian Territory* [2004] ICJ Reports 136, para. 89; *Case concerning Armed Activities on the Territory of the Congo* (*Democratic Republic of the Congo* v. *Uganda*), Merits, [2005] ICJ Reports; ICJ General List 116, para. 217. See Michael J. Kelly and Timothy L. H. McCormack, 'Contributions of the Nuremberg Trial to the Subsequent Development of International Law' in David A. Blumenthal and Timothy L. H. McCormack (eds.), *The Legacy of Nuremberg: Civilising Influence or Institutionalized Vengeance?* (Leiden, 2008) 101.

[37] Richard H. Minear, *Victor's Justice: The Tokyo War Crimes Trial* (Princeton, NJ, 1971) 74–124.

[38] See Cryer, *Prosecuting International Crimes* (n. 4) 199–202.   [39] Lippmann, 'Nuremberg Forty-five Years Later' (n. 25) 27.

[40] *Ibid.* 39.

[41] But see Arthur Goodhart, 'Questions and Answers Concerning the Nuremberg Trials' (1947) 1 *International Law Quarterly* 525, 527.

[42] See e.g. M. Cherif Bassiouni, *Crimes Against Humanity in International Criminal Law*, 2nd ed. (The Hague, 1999) 9–10; Payam Akhavan, 'The Perils of Progressive Jurisprudence: The *Nullum Crimen Sine Lege* Principle in International Criminal Law' (2022) 75 *Current Legal Problems* 45, 49–52.

doubted, however, whether the Nazis truly thought that their actions were not criminal according to principles of law recognized by the community of nations, especially after the Moscow Declaration of 1943. If this was the relevant standard at the time, the critiques of the Nuremberg IMT on point become less convincing.

The final aspect of the victor's justice critique, that similar acts by the Allies were not prosecuted, has some purchase, although the Allies had not committed mass crimes of the magnitude of the Holocaust. The defence were not permitted to raise the issue of crimes committed by the Allies, although Kranzbühler cleverly raised the *tu quoque* issue as one of law, by alleging that unrestricted submarine warfare was permitted by customary international law, as the US Chief of the Pacific Navy, Chester Nimitz, had admitted that US practice in that sphere was the same as that charged against the naval defendants.[43] The judges did not agree with that proposition of law, but because of the Allied practices they refrained from assessing the sentences of Dönitz and Raeder by reference to the war crimes charges relating to submarine warfare. The *tu quoque* argument also had an effect on the indictments. Owing to the devastation visited upon Germany by Allied (in particular British) bombing, no charges related to the Blitz over the United Kingdom were brought.[44] Soviet conduct in the Soviet Union, Poland, and, late in the war, Germany made other charges difficult to bring without implicitly inviting *tu quoque* responses.

Some criticisms of the Nuremberg IMT do not relate to allegations of 'victor's justice'. Particular amongst these is that the prosecution, in particular the US section, saw the trial as being primarily one of aggression, rather than of the Holocaust.[45] This is supported by the judgment's statement that aggression was the 'supreme international crime'.[46] However, the Tribunal is primarily remembered now as a trial of atrocities rather than of aggression,[47] and the overall judgment on Nuremberg, and its promised legacy of accountability,[48] tends to be quite favourable.

6.4 TOKYO INTERNATIONAL MILITARY TRIBUNAL

6.4.1 Creation of the Tribunal

The Nuremberg IMT's sibling, the International Military Tribunal for the Far East ('Tokyo IMT') was set up in January 1946 by a proclamation of General Douglas MacArthur.[49] MacArthur's actions were authorized by powers granted to him by the

---

[43] 18 Trial of Major War Criminals, Nuremberg (London, 1948) 26–8.

[44] Chris af Jochnick and Roger Normand, 'The Legitimation of Violence: A Critical History of the Law of War' (1994) 35 *Harvard International Law Journal* 49, 91–2.

[45] Mark Osiel, *Mass Atrocity, Collective Memory and the Law* (New Brunswick, NJ, 1997) 225–6.

[46] Nuremberg IMT, Judgment and Sentences, reprinted in (1947) 41 *AJIL* 172, 186. [47] Osiel, *Mass Atrocity* (n. 45) 225–6.

[48] See M. Cherif Bassiouni, 'The Nuremberg Legacy' in M. Cherif Bassiouni (ed.), *International Criminal Law*, 2nd ed. (New York, 1999) vol. III, 195; David Luban, 'The Legacies of Nuremberg' (1987) 54 *Social Research* 779. However, see also Mark Aarons, 'Justice Betrayed: Post-1945 Responses to Genocide' in David A. Blumenthal and Timothy L. H. McCormack (eds.), *The Legacy of Nuremberg: Civilising Influence or Institutionalized Vengeance?* (Leiden, 2008) 69. The Nuremberg Academy is dedicated to the principles embodied in the Nuremberg IMT: see www.nurembergacademy.org.

[49] Special Proclamation, Establishment of an International Military Tribunal for the Far East, 19 January 1946, TIAS No. 1589, at 3. See generally Neil Boister and Robert Cryer, *The Tokyo International Military Tribunal: A Reappraisal* (Oxford, 2008); Neil Boister and Robert Cryer (eds.), *Documents on the Tokyo International Military Tribunal: Charter, Indictment and*

Allied states as Supreme Commander, Allied Powers, to implement the Potsdam Declaration,[50] Principle 10 of which promised 'stern justice' for war criminals. The declaration had been accepted by Japan in its instrument of surrender. The setting up of the Tokyo IMT on the basis of Principle 10 led to a challenge to the jurisdiction of the Tribunal relating to crimes against peace, a challenge which was rejected on the basis that the majority judgment found that, at the time of the surrender, the Japanese government understood that the term 'war criminals' included those responsible for initiating the war.[51]

6.4.2 The Tribunal and the Trial

The Tribunal was made up of eleven judges, nine from the signatory states to the Japanese surrender (Australia, Canada, China, France, New Zealand, the Netherlands, the United Kingdom, the United States, and the Soviet Union), together with one each from India and the Philippines.[52] This unwieldy bench was overseen by the Australian Judge, Sir William Webb, whose conduct of the trial has been criticized.[53] The United States was entitled to appoint the chief prosecutor, whilst the other countries were only permitted to appoint associate prosecutors.[54] The US choice, Joseph Keenan, was probably unsuited to the task, and his professionalism open to challenge.[55] The defence was undertaken by a number of Japanese and American lawyers, the most well-known of whom were Takayanagi Kenzo, a professor of Anglo-American law from Tokyo, and Kiyoso Ichiro, a politician and lawyer.

The trial began with the submission of the indictment to the Tribunal on 29 April 1946. The indictment, in fifty-five counts, charged the twenty-eight defendants[56] with crimes against peace and attendant conspiracies, war crimes, and murders, the last on the basis of a prosecution theory that all killings (including those of combatants) in an unlawful war were homicide.[57] The trial lasted nearly two and a half years, with the majority judgment being pronounced in November 1948. The judgment found all the accused who remained before the IMT at the time of judgment guilty, although not on all the counts with which they had been charged. It sentenced seven defendants to death, one to twenty years'

Judgments (Oxford, 2008); Yuma Totani, *The Tokyo War Crimes Trial: The Pursuit of Justice in the Wake of World War II* (Cambridge, MA, 2008).
[50] See *Hirota* v. *MacArthur*, 338 US 197 (1948).
[51] Tokyo IMT, reprinted in Boister and Cryer, *Documents on the Tokyo International Military Tribunal* (n. 49) 48, 440–1.
[52] On the participants, see Yuki Tanaka, Tim McCormack, and Gerry Simpson (eds.), *Beyond Victor's Justice: The Tokyo War Crimes Trial Revisited* (Leiden, 2011) Part 3; Kerstin von Lingen, *Transcultural Justice and the Tokyo Tribunal* (Leiden, 2018).
[53] See e.g. R. John Pritchard, 'An Overview of the Historical Importance of the Tokyo War Trial' in Chihiro Hosoya, Yasuaki Onuma, Nisuke Ando, and Richard Minear (eds.), *The Tokyo Trial: An International Symposium* (Tokyo, 1986) 90, 92; Boister and Cryer, *Tokyo: A Reappraisal* (n. 49) ch. 4. For a more sanguine view see David Cohen and Yuma Totani, *The Tokyo War Crimes Tribunal.: Law, History, and Jurisprudence* (Cambridge, 2018).
[54] Tokyo IMT Charter, Art. 8. [55] B. V. A. Röling and Antonio Cassese, *The Tokyo Trial and Beyond* (Cambridge, 1992) 16.
[56] Kenji Dohihara, Koki Hirota, Seishiro Itagaki, Heitaro Kimura, Iwane Matsui, Akira Muto, Hideki Tojo, Sadao Araki, Kingoro Hashimoto, Shunroko Hata, Kiichiro Hiranuma, Naoki Hoshino, Okinori Kaya, Koichi Kido, Kuniaki Koiso, Jiro Minami, Takasumi Oka, Hiroshi Oshima, Kenryo Sato, Shigetaro Shimada, Toshi Shiratori, Teiichi Suzuki, Yoshijiro Umezu, Shigenori Togo, Mamoru Shigemitsu. Yosuke Matsuoka and Osami Nagano died during the trial. Shumei Okawa was declared mentally unfit to stand trial. See Tokyo IMT, reprinted in Boister and Cryer, *Documents on the Tokyo International Military Tribunal* (n. 49) 48, 425. On the selection, see Awaya Kentaro, 'Selecting Defendants at the Tokyo Trial' in Tanaka et al., *Beyond Victor's Justice* (n. 52) 57.
[57] These charges were not decided upon, as they were seen as cumulative to the crimes against peace charges. See Boister and Cryer, *Tokyo: A Reappraisal* (n. 49) ch. 6.

imprisonment, one to seven years' imprisonment, and the rest to incarceration for life. In addition to this, there were three dissenting judgments, one concurring judgment, and one separate opinion.

The majority judgment, as a number of Allied governments had indicated to their judges that they wanted them to do,[58] followed the Nuremberg IMT's opinion on practically all aspects of the law, expressly adopting its reasoning in relation to the binding nature of the Tribunal's Charter, the criminality of aggressive war, and the abolition of the absolute defence of superior orders.[59] Perhaps the only major difference was that, unlike the Nuremberg IMT, which did not find it necessary to deal with command responsibility, the Tokyo IMT discussed that principle of liability in some detail, and applied it to both military and civilian defendants.[60] In relation to the facts, the majority judgment decided that there was an overarching conspiracy to initiate aggressive wars, and impose Japanese authority over Asia. It also, less controversially, determined that war crimes were committed both against Allied prisoners-of-war and civilians, perhaps most notably in the Rape of Nanking in 1937.

William Webb, the President of the Tribunal, gave a separate opinion, in which he gave his own views on the law, in particular that the criminality of aggressive war could be based on natural law.[61] Webb also asserted that, as the Emperor was responsible for initiating such wars, his absence ought to be reflected in the sentences meted out to the defendants.[62] Judge Bernard of France also considered that crimes against peace could be based on natural law.[63] He took a more sophisticated approach to command responsibility than the majority.[64] Nonetheless, he considered the trial to have progressed in such a manner that he was not able to reach a judgment on the responsibility of the defendants.[65]

The two major dissenting judgments were given by Judges Röling and Pal, the judges from the Netherlands and from India, respectively. Judge Röling disagreed with the majority (and with the Nuremberg Tribunal) on the question of crimes against peace, taking the view that there was no individual criminal liability for aggression in international law; he was, however, of the view that occupying powers were entitled to imprison those responsible for initiating wars, as they threatened occupying powers' security.[66] He supported this view by pointing out that the Tribunal had sentenced no one to death for committing a crime against peace alone.[67] While that fact does not prove that the majority saw their sentencing practice in that light, he was right to express doubt about the broad way in which the majority derived a criminal conspiracy from the facts (some of which he contested), and the way they applied command responsibility.[68] He argued that a number of the defendants, most notably Shigemitsu and Hirota, should have been acquitted.[69] He took

[58] Sellars, *'Crimes Against Peace'* (n. 12) 234–41, 249, 876.
[59] Tokyo IMT, reprinted in Boister and Cryer, *Documents on the Tokyo International Military Tribunal* (n. 49) 48, 437–9.
[60] *Ibid.* 48,442–7. [61] Separate Opinion of the President, 6.
[62] *Ibid.* 19–20. On the non-indictment of the Emperor, see Yoriko Otomo, 'The Decision Not to Prosecute the Emperor' in Tanaka et al., *Beyond Victor's Justice* (n. 52) 63.
[63] Dissenting Opinion of the Member from France, 10. [64] *Ibid.* 12–18.
[65] *Ibid.* 22. This, though, was probably on the basis that the Tribunal had not followed French criminal procedural law.
[66] Dissenting Opinion of the Member from the Netherlands, 10–51. [67] *Ibid.* 48–9. [68] *Ibid.* 54–135. [69] *Ibid.* 178–249.

a stern line on war crimes though, and would have imposed death sentences on more of the defendants found guilty of those crimes.[70]

Judge Pal gave the longest and most well-known of the dissenting judgments. He denied that crimes against peace were a part of existing international law and noted that, in the absence of a clear definition, the concept of aggression was open to 'interested interpretation'.[71] Pal also gave an interpretation of the facts completely at variance with that of the majority, largely accepting defence arguments that Japan's actions were ad hoc reactions to provocations by Western powers or explained by fear of Communism in China.[72] He gave a lengthy critique of the fairness of the trial proceedings[73] and made clear that he saw the prosecution as hypocritical, owing to the record of many of the prosecuting states in colonialism, and the use of nuclear weapons against Hiroshima and Nagasaki.[74] As a result, he would have acquitted all the defendants, including of the war crimes charges.[75]

His opinion was criticized in Judge Jaranilla's concurring opinion. Jaranilla, the judge from the Philippines, said that Pal ought to have accepted the Charter's provisions on the law, as he accepted an appointment under the Charter.[76] He also asserted that the trial proceedings were fair, and that the atomic bombings were justified, as they brought an end to the war.[77] Jaranilla's appointment was controversial, as he had been a victim of the Bataan Death march, and he therefore ought not to have sat, on the basis that he may have been biased against the defendants.[78] His view that the sentences imposed were too lenient did little to dispel this suspicion.[79]

6.4.3 Assessment of the Tribunal

The view of the Tokyo IMT traditionally adopted by most international criminal lawyers was summed up by the title of the most well-known book on the trial, Richard Minear's *Victor's Justice*.[80] There is something to be said for such a view. Where the Tokyo IMT agreed with its Nuremberg counterpart on the law,[81] the same critiques are applicable to both, although in relation to both conspiracy and command responsibility the Tokyo IMT went further, and, in the judgment of many, too far. The majority's view of the facts was unsubtle, and the idea of 'an all-inclusive seventeen-year criminal conspiracy involving all the accused strained credulity ... [and] betrayed an underlying inability to grasp the dynamics of Japanese politics or a misplaced determination to force, after the fact, unrelated and fortuitous events into a preconceived thesis'.[82] On the other hand, Judge Pal's contrasting view of many of the facts was similarly unconvincing, as he was unduly credulous of the defence's claims that Japan was acting purely altruistically to liberate

[70] *Ibid.* 178. [71] Dissenting Opinion of the Member from India, 69–153, 227–79. [72] *Ibid.* 349–1014. [73] *Ibid.* 280–348.
[74] *Ibid.* 1231–5. [75] *Ibid.* 1226. [76] Concurring Opinion of the Member from the Philippines, 28–32. [77] *Ibid.* 24–7.
[78] *Motion Suggesting the Disqualification and Personal Bias of the Philippine Justice of the Tribunal*, IMTFE Paper 141 (10 June 1946).
[79] Concurring Opinion of the Member from the Philippines, 32–5. [80] Minear, *Victor's Justice* (n. 37).
[81] Prior to the Tokyo IMT's judgment, the UN General Assembly had, in Resolution 95(I), stated that the principles of the Nuremberg IMT's Statute and Judgment reflected international law.
[82] John Piccigallo, *The Japanese on Trial* (Austin, TX, 1979) 212.

Asia from Western colonialism.[83] In addition, the majority were on stronger ground in relation to the war crimes counts.[84]

In spite of the efforts of some of the judges, there were considerable flaws in the trial process. Also, not only was the *tu quoque* argument given some purchase by the bombing of Hiroshima and Nagasaki, it was also raised, from very different perspectives, by two of the judges (Judges Pal and Jaranilla) in their opinions. Cultural misunderstandings and insensitivities affected the trial, and some of the judges appeared to be biased. Evidence of Unit 731, the Japanese chemical and biological weapons unit which engaged in human vivisection, was kept from the Tribunal, as the United States had promised its members immunity in return for information about their experiments.[85] But simple dismissals of the Tokyo IMT as a show trial are un-nuanced.[86] There was far too much disagreement between the judges for it to have been a show trial.[87] Many of the findings on war crimes were accurate, and many of the heavily criticized delays in the trial were occasioned by genuine difficulties, such as difficulties in translating between Japanese and English.[88]

It is unquestionable, however, that politics entered into the indictment process and the release policies for those imprisoned. The Emperor was not indicted, on the ground that his immunity was considered expedient to ensure Japan's post-war stability, and he was deliberately not mentioned by the prosecution nor (with the exception of one slip) the defence.[89] Japan's so-called 'comfort women' system of military sexual enslavement was not charged.[90] Cold War considerations led the United States (the views of which were largely determinative on this matter) to acquiesce in the release of all those imprisoned by 1955.[91]

In spite of the acceptance of the judgment by the Japanese government in Article 11 of the 1952 Peace Treaty, it has been questioned whether its findings were accepted by all parts of Japanese society. However, the question of memories and views of the Second World War in Japan is a complex and contested one both inside and outside Japan.[92] In the West, the Tribunal has, until recently, been largely ignored,[93] and knowledge of it in Japan is waning. Amongst those in Japan with knowledge of the trial, however, there is less support

[83] Boister and Cryer, *Documents on the Tokyo IMT* (n. 49) lxxx–lxxxi.
[84] Boister and Cryer, *Tokyo: A Reappraisal* (n. 49) 202–4.
[85] Röling and Cassese, *The Tokyo Trial* (n. 55) 48–50. On 'Forgotten Crimes' in the Tokyo IMT, see Tanaka et al., *Beyond Victor's Justice* (n. 52) Parts 5–7.
[86] See e.g. Yasuaki Onuma, 'Beyond Victor's Justice' (1984) 11 *Japan Echo* 63; Fujita Hisaku, 'The Tokyo Trial: Humanity's Justice v. Victors' Justice' in Tanaka et al., *Beyond Victor's Justice* (n. 52) 3; Totani, *The Tokyo War Crimes Trial* (n. 49) provides a useful counterpoint to Minear, *Victor's Justice* (n. 37).
[87] See e.g. Totani, *The Tokyo War Crimes Trial* (n. 49); Boister and Cryer, *Tokyo: A Reappraisal* (n. 49).
[88] Tokyo IMT, reprinted in Boister and Cryer, *Documents on the Tokyo IMT* (n. 49) 48, 429–30.
[89] Herbert P. Bix, *Hirohito and the Making of Modern Japan* (London, 2000) ch. 15.
[90] To redress this exclusion, a coalition of civil society groups, lawyers, academics, and former 'comfort women' held the Women's International War Crimes Tribunal on Japan's Military Sexual Slavery in Tokyo in 2000. The resulting 'judgment' is found at archives.wam-peace.org/wt/en/.
[91] R. John Pritchard, 'The International Military Tribunal for the Far East and the Allied National War Crimes Trials in Asia' in M. Cherif Bassiouni (ed.), *International Criminal Law*, 2nd ed. (New York, 1999) vol. III, 142.
[92] See Ian Buruma, *The Wages of Guilt: Memories of War in Germany and Japan* (New York, 1994); Madaoka Futamura, *War Crimes Tribunals and Transitional Justice: The Tokyo Trial and the Nuremberg Legacy* (London, 2007); Boister and Cryer, *Tokyo: A Reappraisal* (n. 49) ch. 11.
[93] Although there has been an upsurge in interest: see e.g. Sarah Finnin and Tim McCormack, 'Tokyo's Continuing Relevance' in Tanaka et al., *Beyond Victor's Justice* (n. 52) 353.

for Japanese actions in the war,[94] and the Tokyo IMT remains a locus of debate amongst those discussing the question of war responsibility in Japan.[95]

6.5 CONTROL COUNCIL LAW NO. 10 TRIALS AND MILITARY COMMISSIONS IN THE PACIFIC SPHERE

In addition to the Nuremberg IMT, the Allied powers occupying Germany also engaged in a large-scale policy of prosecuting war crimes in their respective occupation zones. These were undertaken under the authority of Control Council Law No. 10, which provided for domestic prosecutions of war crimes, crimes against humanity, and crimes against peace.

Twelve major US trials that took place in Nuremberg after the IMT had concluded its business were known as the 'subsequent proceedings'. These included trials of Nazi doctors and judges, the *Einsatzgruppen*, and members of the German High Command. These trials have had a considerable influence on international criminal law.[96] Proceedings in the British zone of Germany were carried out under the Royal Warrant of 1946.[97] There were also proceedings in the French and Soviet zones of Germany. The trials were guided, to varying degrees, by the findings of the Nuremberg IMT.[98]

In the Pacific sphere, a large number of trials were undertaken by the Allies, including the United Kingdom, the United States, Australia, China, and the Philippines. These were conducted on the basis of various domestic war crimes provisions. In the United Kingdom, this was the Royal Warrant. Even though there were thousands of such proceedings, the trials have only recently been subject to an analogous level of interest in the West to those in the European sphere.[99]

Further Reading

Neil Boister and Robert Cryer, *The Tokyo International Military Tribunal: A Reappraisal* (Oxford, 2008)

Neil Boister and Robert Cryer (eds.), *Documents on the Tokyo International Military Tribunal: Charter, Indictment and Judgments* (Oxford, 2008)

Hans Ehard, 'The Nuremberg Trial Against the Major War Criminals and International Law' (1949) 43 *AJIL* 223

Madaoka Futamura, *War Crimes Tribunals and Transitional Justice: The Tokyo Trial and the Nuremberg Legacy* (London, 2007)

---

[94] 'Poll Shows Ignorance of Tokyo Tribunal', Asahi Shimbun, 5 March 2006.
[95] Futamura, *War Crimes Tribunals and Transitional Justice* (n. 92); Boister and Cryer, *Tokyo: A Reappraisal* (n. 49) ch. 11.
[96] For a comprehensive analysis, see Kevin Jon Heller, *The Nuremberg Military Tribunals and the Origins of International Criminal Law* (Oxford, 2011).
[97] See Anthony P. V. Rogers, 'War Crimes Trials under the Royal Warrant: British Practice 1945–1949' (1990) 39 *ICLQ* 780.
[98] See Adam Basak, 'The Influence of the Nuremberg Judgment on the Practice of the Allied Courts in Germany' (1977–8) 9 *Polish Yearbook of International Law* 161.
[99] Yuma Totani, *Justice in Asia and the Pacific Region, 1945–1952: Allied War Crimes Prosecutions* (Cambridge, 2015); Tim McCormack, Georgina Fitzpatrick and Narrelle Morris (eds.), *Australia's War Crimes Trials, 1945–1951* (Leiden, 2016); Suzannah Linton (ed.), *Hong Kong's War Crimes Trials* (Oxford, 2013); Robert W. Miller, 'War Crimes Trials at Yokohama' (1948–9) 15 *Brooklyn Law Review* 19.

George Ginsburgs and Vladimir Kudriavstsev (eds.), *The Nuremberg Trial and International Law* (Dordrecht, 1990)

Kevin Jon Heller, *The Nuremberg Military Tribunals and the Origins of International Criminal Law* (Oxford, 2011)

Hans Kelsen, 'Will the Judgment in the Nuremberg Trial Constitute a Precedent in International Law?' (1947) 1 *International Law Quarterly* 153

Otto Kranzbühler, 'Nuremberg: Eighteen Years Afterwards' (1965) 14 *De Paul Law Review* 333

Matthew Lippmann, 'Nuremberg Forty-Five Years Later' (1991) 7 *Connecticut Journal of International Law* 1

Guénaël Mettraux, *Perspectives on the Nuremberg Trial* (Oxford, 2008)

Richard H. Minear, *Victor's Justice: The Tokyo War Crimes Trial* (Princeton, NJ, 1971)

Frank Reel, *The Case of General Yamashita* (Chicago, IL, 1949)

B. V. A. Röling and Antonio Cassese, *The Tokyo Trial and Beyond* (Cambridge, 1992)

Georg Schwarzenberger, 'The Judgment of Nuremberg' (1947) 21 *Tulane Law Review* 329

Kirsten Sellars, *'Crimes Against Peace' and International Law* (Cambridge, 2013)

Yuki Tanaka, Tim McCormack and Gerry Simpson (eds.), *Beyond Victor's Justice: The Tokyo War Crimes Trial Revisited* (Leiden, 2011)

Telford Taylor, *The Anatomy of the Nuremberg Trial* (London, 1993)

Yuma Totani, *The Tokyo War Crimes Trial: The Pursuit of Justice in the Wake of World War II* (Cambridge, MA, 2008)

Quincy Wright, 'The Law of the Nuremberg Trial' (1947) 41 *AJIL* 37

7

The Ad Hoc International Criminal Tribunals

7.1 INTRODUCTION

Until the early 1990s, it seemed unlikely that any progeny of the Nuremberg and Tokyo International Military Tribunals (IMTs) would appear soon. However, in response to two conflicts in the 1990s (the Yugoslav wars of dissolution and the Rwandan genocide of 1994), the United Nations revived the idea of international criminal tribunals. This chapter will introduce the resulting International Criminal Tribunals for the former Yugoslavia and Rwanda (ICTY and ICTR), explain their practice, and draw out some of the plaudits and criticisms that attended their operation. Both Tribunals have now essentially ended their major business, having transitioned into a residual phase. This chapter does not, however, attempt to provide a comprehensive analysis of the jurisprudence of the Tribunals, as their output is analysed elsewhere in this book.

7.2 INTERNATIONAL CRIMINAL TRIBUNAL FOR THE FORMER YUGOSLAVIA

7.2.1 Creation of the ICTY

Political developments in what was then the Socialist Federal Republic of Yugoslavia in the 1980s led that country to break up through a number of interlinked armed conflicts starting in 1991.[1] The conflicts were characterized by large-scale violations of international criminal law, including sexual offences and the practice of 'ethnic cleansing'. Pictures of concentration camps in Bosnia, which evoked memories of the Holocaust, caused public outcry and demands that something be done about the situation.

Even before the conflict was formally brought to an end in December 1995, the UN Security Council had taken action in relation to prosecuting those crimes. Resolution 780 created a commission to investigate allegations of international crimes in Yugoslavia.[2] The commission did not obtain significant material or financial state support; so its first chairman, Frits Kalshoven, resigned. Its second chairman, M. Cherif Bassiouni, obtained

---

[1] See e.g. Laura Silber and Alan Litle, *The Death of Yugoslavia* (Harmondsworth, 1996). [2] SC Res. 780 (1992), 6 October 1992.

private financing and engaged in considerable evidence gathering in the former Yugoslavia,[3] which culminated in a 1994 report.[4]

While the commission was still at work, the UN Secretary-General consulted states and recommended that the Security Council create a tribunal by resolution.[5] The possibility of creating the tribunal by treaty was canvassed, but rejected on practical grounds.[6] The report annexed a draft Statute for the Tribunal, modelled in some ways on the Nuremberg IMT's Charter, but also creating a cooperation regime which was to be mandatory in nature and streamlined when compared to normal inter-state cooperation.[7]

The Security Council adopted the draft Statute in Resolution 827.[8] Although, at the time, some states and commentators questioned whether the Security Council had the power to set up such a tribunal,[9] there is no longer controversy over the Council's competence to create criminal tribunals.

Resolution 827 set out the aims of the Security Council in establishing the ICTY; these were that, in the circumstances in Yugoslavia, the Tribunal could 'put an end to such crimes and take effective measures to bring to justice the persons who are responsible for them', and thus 'contribute to the restoration and maintenance of peace'.[10] The Council further asserted that it believed that creating the ICTY would 'contribute to ensuring that such violations are halted and effectively redressed'.[11] Such goals were certainly broad and optimistic and perhaps overstated the extent to which criminal punishment alone can create international peace and security. However, the Council only asserted that the ICTY would *contribute* to, rather than single-handedly create, reconciliation in the former Yugoslavia.

7.2.2 Structure of the ICTY

There were three main organs of the ICTY: the Registry, the Office of the Prosecutor, and Chambers.[12] The Registry was responsible for the administrative management of the Tribunal, including, for example, the victims and witnesses programme, transfer of the accused, their conditions of detention, and public affairs. The Office of the Prosecutor was responsible for investigating alleged crimes, seeking indictments, and bringing

---

[3] See generally M. Cherif Bassiouni, 'The United Nations Commission of Experts Established Pursuant to Security Council Resolution 780' (1994) 88 *AJIL* 784; William A. Schabas, 'The Balkan Investigation' in David M. Crane, Leila N. Sadat, and Michael P. Scharf (eds.), *The Founders* (Cambridge, 2018) 44.

[4] *Final Report of the Commission of Experts Established Pursuant to Security Council Resolution 780 (1992)*, UN Doc. S/1994/674 (27 May 1994).

[5] *Report of the Secretary-General Pursuant to Paragraph 2 in Security Council Resolution 808 (1993)*, UN Doc. S/25704 (3 May 1993) para. 20.

[6] A treaty would take too long to conclude, and it might not achieve the necessary ratifications. See also Michael Matheson and David Scheffer, 'The Creation of the Tribunals' (2016) 110 *AJIL* 173, 178–80 (the article does, avowedly, adopt an approach from members of the then US (Clinton) Administration).

[7] See generally Larry D. Johnson, 'Ten Years Later: Reflections on the Drafting' (2004) 2 *JICJ* 368. See further Chapters 5 and 20.

[8] SC Res. 827 (1993), 25 May 1993. See Matheson and Scheffer, 'The Creation of the Tribunals' (n. 6) 174–6.

[9] S.PV/3217, 20–2. See Alfred P. Rubin, 'An International Criminal Tribunal for the Former Yugoslavia' (1994) 6 *Pace International Law Review* 7. Most of these doubts were laid to rest after *Tadić*, ICTY AC, 2 October 1995.

[10] SC Res. 827 (1993), Preamble.

[11] *Ibid.* See also Michael Scharf, 'The Tools for Enforcing International Criminal Justice in the New Millennium: Lessons from the Yugoslavia Tribunal' (1999) 49 *DePaul Law Review* 925, 928–33.

[12] For an overview of the structure and personnel, see Mohamed Shahabuddeen, *International Criminal Justice at the Yugoslav Tribunal: A Judge's Recollection* (Oxford, 2012) 33–49.

matters to trial. Chambers consisted of judges and law officers. The Trial Chambers were subject to the supervision of the Appeals Chamber, the final authority on matters of law in the Tribunal.[13]

7.2.3 Jurisdiction of the ICTY and Its Relationship to National Courts

The ICTY had jurisdiction over war crimes, crimes against humanity and genocide committed after 1 January 1991 on the territory of the former Yugoslavia.[14] Article 2 granted the Tribunal jurisdiction over grave breaches of the Geneva Conventions (which only apply in international armed conflicts),[15] whilst Article 3 provided the Tribunal with jurisdiction over a non-exhaustive list of violations of the laws or customs of war. The Tribunal decided in 1995 that this provision covered war crimes in both international and non-international armed conflicts,[16] a decision that paved the way for some of the Tribunal's most innovative jurisprudence.[17] The Tribunal had jurisdiction over genocide and crimes against humanity pursuant to Articles 4 and 5 of its Statute, respectively. Aggression was not included in the jurisdiction of the ICTY.[18] The open-ended nature of the temporal jurisdiction of the Tribunal meant that it had jurisdiction over the later conflicts in Kosovo and the Former Yugoslav Republic of Macedonia.[19]

The ICTY had, to a great extent, primacy over national courts.[20] Pursuant to this principle, the Tribunal could require states to defer to it any proceedings they were contemplating or undertaking.[21] Rule 9 of the Rules of Procedure and Evidence set out the situations in which deferral was justified and were very broad, effectively allowing the ICTY to demand transfer of cases at will.[22] As the Tribunal wound up its work, however, it went from taking cases from domestic jurisdictions to referring cases back to them.

7.2.4 Milestones in the Practice of the ICTY

Beginnings and the Tadić *Case*

The ICTY began slowly. A skeleton staff, beset with funding problems, had to create an international criminal court effectively from nothing.[23] When they began, investigations were also hampered by the ongoing armed conflicts in Yugoslavia.[24] The first major

---

[13] The *ratio decidendi* of its decisions bound the Trial Chambers: see *Aleksovski*, ICTY AC, 24 March 2000, para. 112. The Appeals Chamber did not bind itself but only departed from its previous jurisprudence if there were 'cogent reasons in the interests of justice' to do so: *ibid*. para. 107. Trial Chambers did not bind one another: *ibid*. para. 113.
[14] ICTY Statute, Arts. 1 and 8. [15] *Tadić*, ICTY AC, 2 October 1995, paras. 79–85. [16] *Ibid*. paras. 86–93. [17] See Chapter 12.
[18] For some reasons, see Matheson and Scheffer, 'The Creation of the Tribunals' (n. 6) 187.
[19] See SC Res. 1160 (1998); *Milutinović et al*., ICTY AC, 8 June 2004; *In re the Republic of Macedonia*, ICTY TC I, 4 October 2002.
[20] ICTY Statute, Art. 9(1). Göran Sluiter, *International Criminal Adjudication and the Collection of Evidence: Obligations of States* (Antwerp, 2002) 81–8.
[21] E.g. *Karadžić et al*., ICTY TC, 16 May 1995. Compare the relationship between the ICC and national courts: see Section 8.6.
[22] ICTY Rules of Procedure and Evidence (RPE), Rule 9(i)–(iii).
[23] See *First Annual Report of the ICTY*, UN Doc. S/1994/1007 (1994) paras. 34–6, 143–9. For an insider's view, see Richard Goldstone, 'The International Criminal Tribunals for Former Yugoslavia and Rwanda' in David M. Crane, Leila N. Sadat, and Michael P. Scharf (eds.), *The Founders* (Cambridge, 2018) 55.
[24] *Second Annual Report of the ICTY*, UN Doc. S/1995/728 (1995) paras. 4, 194–6.

breakthrough occurred in April 1995, when Germany deferred its own proceedings against Duško Tadić, a low-ranking Bosnian Serb, and transferred him to the ICTY for trial.[25]

Tadić challenged the ICTY's jurisdiction over him, asserting among other things that the Security Council had no authority to set up a criminal court. This led to the classic Interlocutory Appeal decision of October 1995.[26] The Appeals Chamber ruled that the ICTY had the authority to review the legality of its own creation (the *Kompetenz-Kompetenz* decision).[27] The majority in *Tadić* held that the Security Council was entitled to invoke its powers under Chapter VII of the UN Charter, as there was an armed conflict in Yugoslavia at the relevant time.[28] The Chamber also determined that the Council could set up a court because the list of measures that the Council can take under Article 41 is not exhaustive.[29]

Kosovo, Milošević, and NATO

By 1996, the ICTY's judicial workload had increased.[30] Around this time, international forces also began to arrest indictees and transfer them to the tribunal.[31] However, the Federal Republic of Yugoslavia remained uncooperative and Croatia transferred only one defendant in 1997.[32] Owing to the increased violence in Kosovo, the Security Council requested that the Prosecutor examine events there.[33] This led, in May 1999, to the ICTY indicting Slobodan Milošević, then President of the Federal Republic of Yugoslavia,[34] for alleged crimes in Kosovo. The Prosecutor was assisted in this process by considerable evidence made available to her by Western states.[35] Also in 1999, some commentators called upon the Prosecutor to investigate NATO states for alleged war crimes during their air campaign in relation to Kosovo. In response, the Prosecutor set up a committee to carry out a preliminary assessment of the evidence presented and to advise her on whether or not to initiate a full investigation. This action caused consternation in some circles.[36] The committee recommended in June 2000 that no full investigation be undertaken.[37]

---

[25] *Ibid.* paras. 179–84.

[26] *Tadić*, ICTY AC, 2 October 1995. See Sarah M. H. Nouwen and Michael Becker, '*Tadić v Prosecutor* (1995)' in Eirik Bjorge and Cameron Miles (eds.), *Landmark Cases in International Law* (Oxford, 2018) 377.

[27] *Tadić*, ICTY AC, 2 October 1995, paras. 14–25. See generally José E. Alvarez, 'Nuremberg Revisited: The Tadić Case' (1996) 7 *EJIL* 245.

[28] *Tadić*, ICTY AC, 2 October 1995, para. 30. Judge Sidhwa agreed, adding that the appraisal of the evidence leading to the determination was 'based on a proper appraisal of the evidence, and was reasonable and fair and not arbitrary or capricious'. Separate Opinion of Judge Sidhwa, para. 61.

[29] *Tadić*, ICTY AC, 2 October 1995, paras. 34–5. It also made the important holding that war crimes law applies in non-international armed conflict (paras. 79–137, see also Chapter 12).

[30] *Fourth Annual Report of the ICTY*, UN Doc. S/1997/729 (1997) para. 72.

[31] *Ibid.* para. 190. Darryl Robinson, 'Trials, Tribulations and Triumphs: Major Developments in 1997 at the International Criminal Tribunal for Yugoslavia' (1997) 35 *Canadian Yearbook of International Law* 179.

[32] *Fourth Annual Report of the ICTY* (n. 30) para. 183.

[33] SC Res. 1160 (1998); *Fifth Annual Report of the ICTY 1998*, UN Doc. S/1998/737 (1998) para. 118. On the surrounding issues, see Diane Orentlicher, *Some Kind of Justice: The Impact of the ICTY in Former Yugoslavia* (Oxford, 2018) 34–45.

[34] *Milošević et al.*, ICTY Judge, 24 May 1999.

[35] *Sixth Annual Report of the ICTY*, UN Doc. S/1999/846 (1999) paras. 126, 128.

[36] See Rachel Kerr, *The International Criminal Tribunal for Former Yugoslavia: An Exercise in Law, Politics and Diplomacy* (Oxford, 2004) 202–3.

[37] *Final Report to the Prosecutor by the Committee Established to Review the NATO Bombing Campaign Against the Federal Republic of Yugoslavia* (8 June 2000) para. 90; (2000) 39 ILM 1257.

This recommendation was accepted by the Prosecutor and caused considerable controversy.[38]

Completion Strategy and the Process of Closing Down

Around 2000, the judges of the ICTY concluded that their work could take them until at least 2016 to complete.[39] A number of states considered this to be too long, as it meant many more years of significant budget contributions from all UN member states to fund the tribunal. The ICTY suggested to the Security Council that there be a 'completion strategy'.[40] This involved a number of steps, the most important of which was the creation of *ad litem* judges, temporary judges who would sit for one case, in order to hear as many cases as possible in a short period of time.[41] In 2001, the Federal Republic of Yugoslavia, after considerable economic and political pressure, began cooperating with the Tribunal, most notably with the surrender of ex-President Milošević to the ICTY. That year, the ICTY handed down its first conviction for genocide, of General Radislav Krstić, for his role in the Srebrenica massacre.[42]

These breakthroughs were followed by an increased willingness of accused persons to plead guilty,[43] increased cooperation with the Tribunal, and the fact that more indictees began to surrender voluntarily to the ICTY.[44] The ICTY revised Rule 11*bis* of the Rules of Procedure and Evidence to permit it to transfer indictments and later, cases, to domestic courts. To do so it had to take into account, *inter alia*, the gravity of the crime, the role of the accused, and the fair trial guarantees that would be accorded to the accused.[45] This was a significant step in the ICTY's completion strategy, as it allowed the ICTY to reduce its docket in favour of domestic accountability, but it did result in some critique that such transfers (and other steps taken to speed up trials) may not be in accordance with fair trial rights. For example, Judge David Hunt stated:

[t]his Tribunal will not be judged by the number of convictions which it enters, or by the speed with which it concludes the Completion Strategy. The … [decisions] in which the Completion Strategy has been given priority over the rights of the accused will leave a spreading stain on this Tribunal's reputation.[46]

Whether or not this is accepted,[47] it is true that the completion strategy led to a number of procedural innovations, and an increased use of documentary evidence.[48]

---

[38] See, in favour of the decision, Kerr, *The International Criminal Tribunal for Former Yugoslavia* (n. 36) 199–204. (Strongly) against, see Michael Mandel, 'Politics and Human Rights in International Criminal Law: Our Case Against NATO and the Lessons to be Learnt from It' (2001–2) 25 *Fordham International Law Journal* 95. More generally see Paolo Benvenuti, 'The ICTY Prosecutor and the Review of the NATO Bombing Against the Federal Republic of Yugoslavia' (2001) 12 *EJIL* 503; Michael Bothe, 'The Protection of the Civilian Population and NATO Bombing on Yugoslavia: Comments on a Report to the Prosecutor of the ICTY' (2001) 12 *EJIL* 531.

[39] *Seventh Annual Report of the ICTY*, UN Doc. S/2000/777 (2000) para. 336.

[40] See generally Dominic Raab, 'Evaluating the ICTY and its Completion Strategy' (2005) 3 *JICJ* 82.

[41] For the authority, see SC Res. 1329 (2000). [42] *Krstić*, ICTY TC I, 2 August 2001.

[43] *Tenth Annual Report of the ICTY*, UN Doc. S/2003/829 (2003) para. 2. See *Plavšić*, ICTY TC III, 23 November 2003.

[44] *Ibid*. para. 232.

[45] See generally Michael Bohlander, 'Referring an Indictment from the ICTY and ICTR to Another Court: Rule 11*bis* and the Consequences for the Law of Extradition' (2006) 55 *ICLQ* 219. See Chapters 5 and 9.

[46] *Milošević*, ICTY AC, Dissenting Opinion of Judge David Hunt on Admissibility of Evidence in Chief in the Form of Written Statement (Majority Decision Given 30 September 2003), 21 October 2003, paras. 21–2.

[47] See Fausto Pocar, 'Completion or Continuation Strategy?' (2008) 6 *JICJ* 655, 657–8; 'Discussion' (2008) 6 *JICJ* 681, 682–7.

[48] O-Gon Kwon, 'The Challenge of the International Criminal Trial as Seen from the Bench' (2007) 5 *JICJ* 360.

Even as the Security Council looked toward the ICTY's closure, the Council was aware that there were matters, such as supervision of prison sentences, release, the possible trial of fugitives, possible contempt cases, and potential reopening of cases, that will last beyond the lifespan of the ICTY. It therefore decided, in Resolution 1966, to establish a 'Residual Mechanism', now called the International Residual Mechanism for Criminal Tribunals or IRMCT (previously known as the Mechanism for International Criminal Tribunals or MICT), to perform these functions for the ICTY and the ICTR.[49]

The Residual Mechanism is, in essence, a pared-down version of the Tribunals; it 'continue[s] the material, territorial, temporal and personal jurisdiction' of the Tribunals,[50] and, where appropriate, refers cases to national jurisdictions.[51] It also has the express power to punish contempt.[52] Like the ICTY (and ICTR), the Residual Mechanism has an Office of the Prosecutor, Chambers, a Presidency, and Registry.[53] It has now replaced both tribunals. The work of the Residual Mechanism is reviewed on a biannual basis, with a view to reducing its functions and staff over time.[54]

The ICTY charged 161 people over its lifespan, with ninety convictions and nineteen acquittals. Other defendants had their indictments withdrawn, had their cases referred to domestic courts, or died. The death of the most (in)famous of these, Slobodan Milošević in 2006, just before the end of his lengthy and often controversial trial, denied the Tribunal the possibility of completing proceedings against one of the main leaders involved in the Yugoslav wars of dissolution. The Tribunal completed its own proceedings and closed its doors on 31 December 2017, with the final decisions, the *Mladić* trial judgment and *Prlić et al.* appeal judgment, having been delivered in November 2017.[55] All appeals and re-trials after that date were heard by the Residual Mechanism, including in *Šešelj*, *Karadžić*, and *Mladić*. In May 2023, the Appeals Chamber of the Residual Mechanism issued its judgment in the re-trial case of *Stanišić and Simatović*, which represented the conclusion of all proceedings related to core crimes brought before the ICTY.[56] The work of the Residual Mechanism is now focused on protection of victims and witnesses, assistance to national jurisdictions, enforcement of sentences, and investigation and trial of allegations of contempt or false testimony.[57]

---

[49] SC Res. 1966 (2010), 22 December 2010. On the background, see Guido Acquaviva, '"Best Before Date Shown": Residual Mechanisms at the ICTY' in Bert Swart, Alexander Zahar and Göran Sluiter (eds.), *The Legacy of the International Criminal Tribunal for the Former Yugoslavia* (Oxford, 2011) 507–36. The Residual Mechanism has identified its ad hoc functions as being the tracking and prosecution of fugitives, appeals, re-trials, trials for contempt and perjury, and review proceedings. Its continuing functions are victim and witness protection, supervising sentences, assisting national jurisdictions, and archive preservation.

[50] See generally the symposium in (2011) 9 *JICJ* 787 et seq. [51] Residual Mechanism Statute, Art. 6. [52] *Ibid.* Art. 1(4).

[53] *Ibid.* Art. 4. [54] SC Res. 1966 (2010).

[55] As an aside, the final verdict, in the *Prlić et al.* case, was attended by drama, in that one of the defendants, Slobodan Praljak, committed suicide in the courtroom after the judgment was read.

[56] *Stanišić & Simatović*, MICT AC, 31 May 2023; *Assessment and Progress Report of the President of the International Residual Mechanism, Judge Graciela Gatti Santana, for the period from 16 November 2022 to 15 May 2023*, UN Doc. S/2023/357 (2023) para. 6.

[57] Residual Mechanism May 2023 report (n. 56) para. 56.

In its twilight, the ICTY's eye increasingly turned to what it termed its 'legacy',[58] which included ensuring that large amounts of its judicial and other materials were properly archived and made available,[59] creating a compilation of its practices,[60] and undertaking capacity building in domestic jurisdictions.[61] However, in late 2012 and early 2013, controversial acquittals, in the *Gotovina* and *Perišić* cases, led to outrage in some quarters,[62] and disquiet amongst some of the judges. This led one judge to criticize the decisions and the President of the ICTY in a (leaked) letter, which in turn required the disqualification of that judge in the deeply troubled *Šešelj* case.[63]

7.2.5 Appraisal of the ICTY

The ICTY itself has set out a number of its achievements. These are that it has promoted accountability rather than impunity, including with respect to leaders; established the facts of the crimes in the former Yugoslavia; brought justice for victims and given them a voice; developed international law; and strengthened the rule of law.[64] The Tribunal has, to some extent, fulfilled these goals.

It is true that the creation of the ICTY contributed to the trend against impunity, not least as its creation and Statute provided a direct precedent for the ICTR, and a slightly less direct one for the International Criminal Court (ICC).[65] Also, the ICTY showed that international prosecutions were possible outside the situation of a complete defeat of one side in a conflict. Equally, at times the Tribunal struggled to contain the size of trials against high-ranking defendants, and similarly had difficulty containing the disruptive conduct of some of them.[66] The Tribunal took great pains to determine what happened in the former Yugoslavia accurately, and spent considerable time and resources to attempt to bring (retributive) justice to victims, even if its practice was not always perfect by the exacting standards of victims' rights advocates,[67] and the experiences of victims appearing before it were not uniformly positive.[68]

---

[58] The term 'legacy' is not a clear one, nor one that can easily be set by a tribunal, Sara Kendall and Sarah M. H. Nouwen, 'Speaking of Legacy: Towards of Ethos of Modesty at the ICTR' (2016) 110 *AJIL* 212, 214–20.

[59] The preservation and management of the ICTR and ICTY's archives is also an important responsibility for the Residual Mechanism: Residual Mechanism Statute, Art. 27.

[60] ICTY and UNICRI, *ICTY Manual on Developed Practices* (Turin, 2009). [61] *Ibid.* para. 53.

[62] *Gotovina and Markač*, ICTY AC, 16 November 2012; *Perišić*, ICTY AC, 13 February 2013. On the former, see Janine Natalya Clark, 'Courting Controversy: The ICTY's Acquittal of Croatian Generals Gotovina and Markač' (2013) 11 *JICJ* 399.

[63] On the saga, see Richard A. Wilson, *Incitement on Trial: Prosecuting International Speech Crimes* (Cambridge, 2017) ch. 4, especially 107–46. The relevant judge left the ICTY fairly soon after. The President of the ICTY convened a new Trial Chamber which acquitted Šešelj; *Šešelj*, ICTY, TC III, 31 March 2016. That acquittal was later overturned by the Appeals Chamber of the Residual Mechanism; *Šešelj*, MICT AC, 11 April 2018.

[64] See www.icty.org/en/about/tribunal/achievements and *Twenty-fourth and Final Report of the International Tribunal for the Former Yugoslavia*, UN Doc. S/2017/662 (1 August 2017) paras. 20 et seq. For another appraisal, see Marko Milanović, 'The Impact of the ICTY on the Former Yugoslavia: An Anticipatory Postmortem' (2016) 110 *AJIL* 233.

[65] Ralph Zacklin, 'The Failings of Ad Hoc International Tribunals' (2004) 2 *JICJ* 541.

[66] See e.g. Göran Sluiter, 'Compromising the Authority of International Criminal Justice: How Vojislav Šešelj Runs His Trial' (2007) 5 *JICJ* 529; Michael P. Scharf, 'Chaos in the Courtroom: Controlling Disruptive Defendants and Contumacious Counsel in War Crimes Trials' (2006–7) 39 *Case Western Reserve Journal of International Law* 155.

[67] Marie-Bénédict Dembour and Emily Haslam, 'Silencing Hearings? Victim–Witnesses at War Crimes Trials' (2004) 15 *EJIL* 151.

[68] Eric Stover, *The Witnesses* (New York, 2007).

The ICTY has had a significant impact on international law.[69] As has been said elsewhere:

What would ICL [international criminal law] look like without the contribution of the Tribunals? It is most likely that ICL would, by comparison, be greatly impoverished: thinner in details, weaker in scope, and perhaps still in its post-Nuremberg hibernation.[70]

The ICTY was the first international criminal tribunal to enter a genocide conviction in Europe, significantly develop international criminal law's understanding of sexual and gender-based crimes, advance the doctrine of superior responsibility, and break new ground on cooperation with national jurisdictions and authorities.[71]

Although the Tribunal has been accused of being too quick to decide that aspects of the law are customary,[72] most of its decisions were well reasoned, were not criticized by states,[73] and were considered to be in line with the *nullum crimen sine lege* principle.[74] The later judgments of the ICTY were largely less discursive of larger issues of law than earlier decisions such as *Tadić*, as many of the major issues were settled in early cases.[75]

On the downside, the ICTY was accused, with varying degrees of accuracy, of various sins against international law and justice.[76] Some accusations, such as that it was systematically biased towards or against one of the sides in the Yugoslav wars of dissolution, were often, albeit not always, self-regarding, supporting judgments that reinforced people's own perceived collective feelings, and rejecting those that did not.[77] Critiques of politicization are easy to make, but the necessity of obtaining cooperation from states likely led to some necessary diplomatic manoeuvres by the ICTY's prosecutors.[78]

Other critiques have included that the Tribunal was too expensive and bureaucratic,[79] that its trials were characterized by delay,[80] violated the rights of defendants,[81] and were far

---

[69] See e.g. Carsten Stahn, Carmel Agius, Serge Brammertz, and Colleen Rohan (eds.), *Legacies of the International Criminal Tribunal for the Former Yugoslavia: A Multidisciplinary Approach* (Oxford, 2020); Milena Sterio and Michael P. Scharf (eds.), *The Legacy of the Ad Hoc Tribunals in International Criminal Law: Assessing the ICTY's and the ICTR's Most Significant Legal Accomplishments* (Cambridge, 2019); Bert Swart, Alexander Zahar, and Göran Sluiter (eds.), *The Legacy of the International Criminal Tribunal for the Former Yugoslavia* (Oxford, 2011).

[70] Darryl Robinson and Gillian McNeill, 'The Tribunals and the Renaissance of International Criminal Law: Three Themes' (2016) 110 *AJIL* 191, 209.

[71] Milena Sterio, 'The Yugoslavia and Rwanda Tribunals: A Legacy of Human Rights Protection and Contribution to International Criminal Justice' in Milena Sterio and Michael P. Scharf (eds.), *The Legacy of the Ad Hoc Tribunals in International Criminal Law: Assessing the ICTY's and the ICTR's Most Significant Legal Accomplishments* (Cambridge, 2019) 11 at 14–21.

[72] See Guénaël Mettraux, *International Crimes and the Ad Hoc Tribunals* (Oxford, 2005) 13–18.

[73] One exception is *Kupreškić et al.*, ICTY TC II, 14 January 2000, paras. 521–36, and UK Ministry of Defence, *The UK Manual of Military Law* (Oxford, 2004) 421.

[74] See generally Mohamed Shahabuddeen, 'Does the Principle of Legality Stand in the Way of Progressive Development of the Law?' (2004) 2 *JICJ* 1007.

[75] E.g. *Mladić*, ICTY TC I, 22 November 2017. This was the last Trial Chamber decision by the ICTY and, while it is expansive, it did little with regard to large-scale new developments in international criminal law.

[76] On the more general questions about criminal prosecution, see Section 2.4.

[77] See Orentlicher, *Some Kind of Justice* (n. 33); Janine N. Clark, *International Trials and Reconciliation: Assessing the Impact of the International Criminal Tribunal for Former Yugoslavia* (Abingdon, 2014).

[78] Victor Peskin, *International Justice in Rwanda and the Balkans: Virtual Trials and the Struggle for State Cooperation* (Cambridge, 2008); Carla del Ponte, *Madame Prosecutor* (New York, 2009).

[79] Zacklin, 'The Failings of Ad Hoc International Tribunals ' (n. 65) 543–4.

[80] See e.g. Patrick L. Robinson, 'Ensuring Fair and Expeditious Trials at the ICTY' (2000) 11 *EJIL* 569. [81] *Ibid.*

removed from the populations of the former Yugoslavia.[82] More generally, it has been alleged that the Tribunal was created in place of more effective action to prevent crimes in the former Yugoslavia.[83]

All of these critiques have some purchase. The ICTY proved to be expensive. Since its founding in 1993, the ICTY cost over US\$2.7 billion.[84] While international justice is expensive,[85] excessive bureaucracy in the United Nations did not help. Trials took a long time, although some delays were the result of attempts to ensure fair trials for defendants, as the ICTY often considered motions made on their behalf that would not have required any detailed response at the domestic level.

Nonetheless, some of the decisions of the Tribunal were controversial in relation to fair trials. For example, the (one-off) decision of the Trial Chamber in the *Tadić* case to grant witnesses complete anonymity proved very controversial, in particular owing to the false testimony of one such protected witness, Dragan Opacić.[86] On the other hand, there have been clear examples of witness tampering on the part of certain defendants and their representatives.[87]

The ICTY did not give sufficient consideration to the question of the Tribunal's distance from the relevant populations in its early practice. This allowed local actors to distort matters,[88] a point the Tribunal attempted to rectify by setting up various 'outreach' programmes.[89] In defence of the Tribunal, it can be said that the relationship between the media and international justice is not simple, in particular as proceedings are rarely akin to the court dramas many are used to watching and there are other calls on their attention.[90] In addition, the security situation in the former Yugoslavia would not have permitted the ICTY to have sat there.

In relation to the final critique mentioned above, that the ICTY was created in place of more effective action to prevent crimes in the former Yugoslavia, it raises an important issue, although it is likely that the best available option was to create a tribunal. If it had not been created, there would not have been any more effective response to the crimes in the former Yugoslavia forthcoming. Equally, a more general issue, that of selectivity, arises whenever an ad hoc tribunal is set up.[91]

---

[82] Laurel E. Fletcher and Harvey Weinstein, 'A World Unto Itself: The Application of International Criminal Justice in Former Yugoslavia' in Eric Stover and Harvey Weinstein (eds.), *My Neighbor, My Enemy: Justice and Community in the Aftermath of Mass Atrocity* (Cambridge, 2004) 29.

[83] See e.g. David Forsythe, *Human Rights in International Relations* (Cambridge, 2000) 221.

[84] Stuart Ford, 'A Hierarchy of the Goals of International Criminal Courts' (2018) 27 *Minnesota Journal of International Law* 179.

[85] David Wippman, 'The Costs of International Justice' (2006) 100 *AJIL* 861.

[86] *Tadić*, ICTY TC II, 7 May 1997, paras. 553–4. See Section 18.4.

[87] See Robert Cryer, 'Witness Tampering in International Criminal Tribunals' (2014) 27 *LJIL* 191.

[88] Mirko Klarin, 'The Impact of the ICTY Trials on Public Opinion in the Former Yugoslavia' (2009) 7 *JICJ* 89.

[89] David Tolbert, 'The International Criminal Tribunal for the Former Yugoslavia: Unforeseen Successes and Foreseeable Shortcomings' (2002) 26(2) *Fletcher Forum of World Affairs* 7, 13–14; Gabrielle Kirk McDonald, 'Problems, Obstacles and Achievements of the ICTY' (2004) 2 *JICJ* 558, 569–70.

[90] Marlise Simons, 'International Criminal Tribunals and the Media' (2009) 7 *JICJ* 83.

[91] Gerry Simpson, 'War Crimes: A Critical Introduction' in Timothy McCormack and Gerry Simpson (eds.), *The Law of War Crimes: National and International Approaches* (The Hague, 1997) 1, 8.

7.3 INTERNATIONAL CRIMINAL TRIBUNAL FOR RWANDA

7.3.1 Creation of the ICTR

Fears of selectivity fed into the decision to create the ICTR. Given the creation of the ICTY for a European conflict, when genocide clearly occurred in Africa, it was considered necessary and appropriate to create an analogous tribunal for crimes committed there.[92] The Security Council members treated the creation of a tribunal for Rwanda largely as they treated the ICTY, beginning with condemnation, then setting up a commission of experts, and, before it reported, deciding to set up an international tribunal.[93]

Unlike the ICTY Statute, the ICTR Statute was drafted by the members of the Security Council, following closely the model of the ICTY Statute.[94] While Rwanda, then a member of the Council, was initially supportive, it did not succeed in including the death penalty, excluding crimes other than genocide from the court's jurisdiction, or granting the court jurisdiction before 1994, and therefore voted against the creation of the ICTR.[95] This did not affect the legality of the creation of the Tribunal, which found its basis, like the ICTY, in Chapter VII of the UN Charter.[96]

7.3.2 Structure of the ICTR

The structure of the ICTR was very similar to that of the ICTY; it too had an Office of the Prosecutor, a Registry, and Trial Chambers, which had the same functions as their counterparts in The Hague. The two Tribunals shared a joint Appeals Chamber and now a joint IRMCT. Originally, the ICTY and ICTR shared a Prosecutor. However, the job was split in 2003 and a separate Prosecutor for the ICTR was appointed.

7.3.3 Jurisdiction of the ICTR and Its Relationship to National Courts

The ICTR, like the ICTY, had jurisdiction over genocide, crimes against humanity, and war crimes,[97] although the definitions of the last two crimes were different from those in the ICTY.[98] The ICTR's jurisdiction over these international crimes was limited to where they occurred in Rwanda, or were committed by Rwandans in neighbouring states, between 1 January and 31 December 1994.[99] The ICTR had primacy over domestic courts, in the same way as the ICTY.[100] Like the ICTY, it also adopted a Rule 11*bis*, which allowed it to refer cases to domestic jurisdictions.

---

[92] Payam Akhavan, 'The International Criminal Tribunal for Rwanda: The Politics and Pragmatics of Punishment' (1996) 90 *AJIL* 501.
[93] SC Res. 935 (1994), 1 July 1994 (Commission) and 955 (1994), 8 November 1994 (Court).
[94] See generally Matheson and Scheffer, 'The Creation of the Tribunals' (n. 6) 176–7.
[95] UN Doc. S/PV.3453, 2, 10–12. China abstained on the resolution.
[96] The ICTR affirmed the legality of its own creation in *Kanyabashi*, ICTR TC II, 18 June 1997. The decision was, however, terse and amounted to little more than a refusal to investigate the legality of Security Council actions.
[97] ICTR Statute, Arts. 2, 3 and 4.   [98] See Chapters 13 and 11.   [99] ICTR Statute, Art. 1.   [100] *Ibid.* Art. 8(1).

7.3.4 Practice of the ICTR

Troubles at the Start

The ICTR began very slowly.[101] Its seat, in Arusha, Tanzania, was only decided upon in February 1995.[102] Also staffing was a problem, recruitment being difficult and slow.[103] Even so, the first indictment was confirmed in November 1995.[104] Early cooperation from some African states was rapid, and proceedings opened against the first two defendants on 30 May 1996.[105] Rwanda, however, remained rather lukewarm in its relations with the Tribunal.

Although funding for the Tribunal at the time was inadequate,[106] there were also concerns about the extent to which resources, and the Tribunal as a whole, were being managed.[107] A highly critical report of the UN Office of Internal Oversight Services of 6 February 1997 uncovered 'mismanagement in almost all areas of the Tribunal, and frequent violations of United Nations rules and regulations'.[108] As a result of the report, both the Registrar's and the Deputy Prosecutor's resignations were sought, and obtained.[109]

Moving Forward

The ICTR's fortunes took an upturn in May 1998, when Jean Kambanda, the Prime Minister of the government that presided over the genocide, pleaded guilty to genocide. Notwithstanding his guilty plea, which recognized, importantly, that genocide had occurred in Rwanda, he was sentenced to life imprisonment.[110] In spite of continuing technical, logistical, and resourcing problems, the Tribunal moved into a phase of increased trial work, which led the Security Council to increase the number of Trial Chambers in April 1998.[111] The first full trial ended in September 1998, with the conviction of Jean-Paul Akayesu for genocide, in a judgment that not only offered the first express application of the Genocide Convention by an international tribunal, but also affirmed that sexual offences could form the *actus reus* of genocide.[112]

The relationship between the ICTR and Rwanda collapsed in 1999. The reason for this was the decision of the Appeals Chamber that the pre-trial detention of Jean-Bosco Barayagwiza violated his human rights, and so the Tribunal should use its inherent power to decline jurisdiction over him.[113] Rwanda was outraged, and suspended cooperation with the Tribunal which, owing to the vast majority of evidence and witnesses being located in Rwanda, made progress with trials very difficult. The Appeals Chamber quickly revisited its decision on the point and determined that, on the basis of further factual submissions by

[101] For an interesting perspective, from the ex-Rwandan minister of Justice, see Gerald Gahima, *Transitional Justice in Rwanda: Accountability for Atrocity* (London, 2013) ch. 4.
[102] SC Res. 977 (1995), 22 February 1995. [103] *First Annual Report of the ICTR*, UN Doc. S/1996/778 (1996) para. 12.
[104] *Ibid.* para. 31. [105] *Ibid.* para. 39. [106] *Ibid.* para. 77. [107] GA Res. 52/213 C.
[108] *Report of the Secretary-General on the Activities of the Office of Internal Oversight Services*, UN Doc. A/51/789 (6 February 1997).
[109] *Second Annual Report of the ICTR*, UN Doc. S/1997/868 (1997) para. 57.
[110] *Kambanda*, ICTR TC I, 4 September 1998. Kambanda unsuccessfully appealed; *Kambanda*, ICTR AC, 19 October 2000. He subsequently, without legal affect, recanted his guilty plea, see Kendall and Nouwen 'Speaking of Legacy' (n. 58) 222.
[111] SC Res. 1165 (1998), 30 April 1998: *Fourth Annual Report of the ICTR*, UN Doc. S/1999/943 (1999) paras. 5, 126.
[112] *Akayesu*, ICTR TC I, 2 September 1998; see Section 10.3.1. [113] *Barayagwiza*, ICTR AC, 3 November 1999.

the Prosecutor, the Tribunal ought to continue to exercise jurisdiction over him, but he ought to receive a reduction in any sentence he received if he were to be convicted to take into account the pre-trial detention issues.[114] Relations between the ICTR and Rwanda then improved, and many thought that politics, more than law, was involved in the decision.[115]

The position of the ICTR improved in 2001 when, pursuant to Security Council Resolution 1329,[116] *ad litem* judges were appointed to assist in trials. Trial work remained slow, however,[117] and pre-trial detention of suspects remained very long. This problem was exemplified in the *Nyiramasuhuko et al.* case where the suspects had been in detention for thirteen to sixteen years due to delays in the trial.[118] The IRMCT found that the delay was unacceptable, stating that 'the Appeals Chamber is of the view that organisational hurdles and lack of resources cannot reasonably justify the prolongation of proceedings that had already been significantly delayed'.[119] The Chamber reduced the sentences on that basis.

Completion Strategy and the Process of Winding Down

As the ICTR began to think in terms of completion, plans were formulated to pass up to forty cases to national jurisdictions, rather than have them prosecuted by the ICTR.[120] To assist the ICTR in completing its judicial business, the Security Council adopted Resolution 1431 in 2002, expanding the pool of *ad litem* judges.[121]

In August 2003, Security Council Resolution 1503 set out the Security Council's timetable for completion, which was the same as that for the ICTY. This resolution also split the role of the Prosecutor in two, creating separate positions of ICTY and ICTR Prosecutor on the stated basis that the job was too large for one person and thus Rwanda was being overlooked.[122] Cases were transferred to France[123] and to Rwanda.[124]

These transfers meant that the trial work of the ICTR ended in December 2012, when the last trial judgment was issued. The ICTR completed its appellate work in 2015. The cases against three high-ranking fugitives from the ICTR were handed over to the Residual Mechanism for trial, and the Mechanism re-issued arrest warrants for them.[125] Two were later confirmed dead and one declared unfit due to dementia part-way through his trial.[126] The Residual Mechanism also reviewed and confirmed the Appeals Chamber's conviction

[114] *Barayagwiza*, ICTR AC, 31 March 2000. In the event, he was convicted, and sentenced to thirty-five years' imprisonment, unlike his co-defendants, both of whom were sentenced to life. *Nahimana, Barayagwiza and Ngeze*, ICTR TC I, 3 December 2003, paras. 1106–7. His sentence was reduced to thirty-two years on appeal.

[115] William A. Schabas, '*Prosecutor v. Barayagwiza*' (2000) 94 *AJIL* 563, 565. [116] SC Res. 1329 (2000), 5 December 2000.

[117] *Ibid*. paras. 1–6. [118] *Nyiramasuhuko et al.*, MICT AC, 14 December 2015. [119] *Ibid*. para. 376.

[120] *Seventh Annual Report of the ICTR*, UN Doc. S/2002/733 (2002) para. 10.

[121] See *Eighth Annual Report of the ICTR*, UN Doc. S/2003/707 (2003) paras. 7–8; *Tenth Annual Report of the ICTR*, UN Doc. S/2005/534 (2005) para. 5.

[122] SC Res. 1503 (2003), 28 August 2003. For the view that this was related to Prosecutor del Ponte's stated willingness to begin investigating allegations against the Rwandan Patriotic Front, see Luc Reydams, 'The ICTR Ten Years On: Back to the Nuremberg Paradigm?' (2005) 3 *JICJ* 977; and del Ponte, *Madame Prosecutor* (n. 78) ch. 9.

[123] *Bucyibaruta*, ICTR TC, 20 November 2007; *Munyeshyaka*, ICTR TC, 20 November 2007.

[124] *Report on the Completion Strategy of the International Criminal Tribunal for Rwanda (as at 10 May 2013)*, UN Doc. S/2013/310 (2013) Annex II.

[125] These were: Félicien Kabuga, Protais Mpiranya, and Augustin Bizimana.

[126] Bizimana and Mpriranya were declared dead and the cases against them terminated in 2020 and 2022 respectively. The declaration of unfitness occurred in *Kabuga*, MICT AC, 7 August 2023.

in the *Ngirabatware* case.[127] The Residual Mechanism continues to monitor trials referred by the ICTR under Rule 11*bis*, track fugitives, engage in witness protection, and oversee the implementation of sentences.[128]

7.3.5 Appraisal of the ICTR

The Tribunal initially came in for a great deal of criticism,[129] but the picture has, over the years, become rosier than critics would suggest. The ICTR had notable success in obtaining, and trying, high-level suspects, including many of the civilian and military ringleaders of the genocide.[130] The early *Akayesu* decision formed an important authoritative determination that genocide had occurred in Rwanda, a point that some in the mid-1990s denied or tried to minimize, or in fact deny.[131] Indeed, the ICTR took judicial notice of the fact that there was genocide in Rwanda in 1994.[132]

The Tribunal assisted in the development of international criminal law, perhaps most notably by its treatment of sexual and gender-based violence,[133] but also in relation to the responsibility of controllers of mass media for incitement to commit genocide.[134] It is nonetheless true that the quality of the legal reasoning contained in judgments of the ICTR was variable.[135]

Trials at the ICTR took an extremely long time and were repeatedly delayed. This was partially because of the difficulties involved in translation of Kinyarwanda into English and French,[136] and the awkward logistics of having the Tribunal based in Arusha, and the Office of the Prosecutor based in Kigali.[137] Problems relating to repeated changes of defence counsel by the defendants also contributed to the dilatory nature of trials,[138] but the judges too did not always help to move things along speedily.[139] Also, attempts to assist victims, although laudable,[140] were not always effective, and the treatment of victims by the Tribunal did not always live up to aspirations, or, on occasion, basic standards.[141]

---

[127] *Ngirabatware*, MICT AC, 27 September 2019. [128] Residual Mechanism May 2023 report (n. 56) paras. 9, 163.

[129] See e.g. Todd Howland and William Calathes, 'The UN's International Criminal Tribunal: Is It Justice or Jingoism for Rwanda? A Call for Transformation' (1998) 39 *Virginia Journal of International Law* 135. For an early (positive) appraisal, see Djiena Wembou, 'The ICTR: Its Role in the African Context' (1997) 321 *International Review of the Red Cross* 685.

[130] Larissa J. van den Herik, *The Contribution of the Rwanda Tribunal to the Development of International Law* (The Hague, 2005) 263. These include Kambanda and top-ranking military officials such as Théoneste Bagosora: *Bagosora et al.*, ICTR TC I, 18 December 2008; and (on appeal) *Bagosora and Nsengiyumva*, ICTR AC, 14 December 2011.

[131] See Gerard Prunier, *The Rwanda Crisis* (London, 1997) 345.

[132] *Karemera et al.*, ICTR AC, 16 June 2006. Some have been critical of this, however: see Kevin Jon Heller, '*Prosecutor v. Karemera*' (2007) 101 *AJIL* 157.

[133] Valerie Oosterveld, 'The Legacy of the ICTY and ICTR on Sexual and Gender-Based Violence', in Milena Sterio and Michael P. Scharf (eds.), *The Legacy of the Ad Hoc Tribunals in International Criminal Law: Assessing the ICTY's and the ICTR's Most Significant Legal Accomplishments* (Cambridge, 2019).

[134] *Nahimana et al.*, ICTR TC I, 3 December 2003 and ICTR AC, 28 November 2007. But see also Dina Temple-Raston, *Justice on the Grass* (New York, NY, 2005); Wilson, *Incitement on Trial* (n. 63); and Chapters 13 and 15.

[135] See van den Herik, *The Contribution of the Rwanda Tribunal* (n. 130) 261.

[136] About which the Tribunal has been candid: see e.g. *Akayesu*, ICTR TC I, 2 September 1998, para. 145.

[137] Eric Møse, 'The Main Achievements of the ICTR' (2005) 3 *JICJ* 920, 923, 927.

[138] *Seventh Annual Report of the ICTR* (n. 120) para. 14.

[139] Alison des Forges and Timothy Longman, 'Legal Responses to the Genocide in Rwanda' in Eric Stover and Harvey Weinstein (eds.), *My Neighbor, My Enemy: Justice and Community in the Aftermath of Mass Atrocity* (Cambridge, 2004) 53–5.

[140] See Møse, 'The Main Achievements' (n. 137) 937; see also the *Fourth Annual Report of the ICTR* (n. 111) para. 113.

[141] Göran Sluiter, 'The ICTR and the Protection of Witnesses' (2005) 3 *JICJ* 962.

One of the major critiques that has been made of the ICTR is its failure to prosecute alleged offences committed by the Rwandan Patriotic Front after the genocide in 1994. The ICTR undertook some investigations into the Rwandan Patriotic Front,[142] but referred allegations back to Rwanda after investigation and the establishment of a *prima facie* case.[143] The necessity of ensuring Rwandan cooperation for prosecutions of *génocidaires* may have been relevant here, although the Prosecutor said that it was owing to the fact that the allegations were less serious than those against Hutu defendants and because of the completion strategy.[144] The non-prosecution of crimes committed against Hutus creates difficulties for some of the broader legacies the ICTR has claimed for itself.

In spite of its claims to its legacy,[145] it has been suggested that the ICTR was both geographically and metaphorically too distant from the people of Rwanda, who remained for the most part uninformed about and unaffected by the Tribunal.[146] The Tribunal created an outreach programme, which included a visitors' centre in Rwanda, radio broadcasts and the creation of a satellite television station,[147] but whether these proved effective is a matter of controversy.[148] It remains the case that perceptions of the ICTR in the area fall upon political and ethnic lines, as with the ICTY.[149] Another critique is the cost of the ICTR, which was fairly high (although lower than the cost of the ICTY).[150]

Further Reading

The website of the ICTY is still available and contains useful information about the Tribunal and its work: www.icty.org. See also the legacy website of the ICTR: http://unictr.irmct.org/. The website of the IRMCT can be found at www.irmct.org/en.

Useful symposia on the ICTY can be found at (2004) 2 *JICJ* 353 and (2002–3) 37 *New England Law Review* 865. Similarly, on the ICTR, see (1997) 321 *International Review of the Red Cross* 665 and (2005) 3 *JICJ* 801. On both, see (2016) 110 *AJIL* 171. The Residual Mechanism is discussed in the symposium in (2011) 9 *JICJ* 787.

Gideon Boas, *The Milošević Trial: Lessons for the Conduct of Complex International Criminal Proceedings* (Cambridge, 2007)

---

[142] *Report of the ICTR to the Security Council 12 May 2008*, UN Doc. S/2008/322 (2008) para. 45.

[143] Eric Møse, 'The ICTR's Completion Strategy: Challenges and Possible Solutions' (2008) 6 *JICJ* 667, 674.

[144] Peskin, *International Justice* (n. 78) ch. 8; Vanessa Thalman, 'French Justice's Endeavors to Substitute for the ICTR' (2008) 6 *JICJ* 995, 1001–2.

[145] For a critique of such claims see Kendall and Nouwen, 'Speaking of Legacy' (n. 58).

[146] José E. Alvarez, 'Crimes of Hate/Crimes of State, Lessons from Rwanda' (1999) 24 *Yale Journal of International Law* 365, 403–18, 459–62. See also Sigall Horovitz, 'The Impact of the International Criminal Tribunal for Rwanda and the Special Court for Sierra Leone on Impunity in Rwanda and Sierra Leone' in Vincent Nmehielle (ed.), *Africa and International Criminal Justice* (The Hague, 2012) 15.

[147] See generally *Fourth Annual Report of the ICTR* (n. 111) para. 1208; *Sixth Annual Report of the ICTR*, UN Doc. S/2001/ 863 (2001) paras. 135 et seq.; *Ninth Annual Report of the ICTR*, UN Doc. S/2004/601 (2004) para. 55; *Tenth Annual Report of the ICTR* (n. 121) paras. 61–3.

[148] See Timothy Longman et al., 'Connecting Justice to Human Experience: Attitudes Towards Accountability and Reconciliation in Rwanda' in Eric Stover and Harvey Weinstein (eds.), *My Neighbor, My Enemy: Justice and Community in the Aftermath of Mass Atrocity* (Cambridge, 2004) 206.

[149] Kendall and Nouwen, 'Speaking of Legacy' (n. 58) 222–4.

[150] For example, the ICTR's annual budget for 2008–9 was approximately US$270 million, the ICTY's US$342 million.

Janine N. Clark, *International Trials and Reconciliation: Assessing the Impact of the International Criminal Tribunal for Former Yugoslavia* (Abingdon, 2014)

Shane Darcy and Joseph Powderly (eds.), *Judicial Creativity at the International Criminal Tribunal* (Oxford, 2010)

Gerald Gahima, *Transitional Justice in Rwanda: Accountability for Atrocity* (London, 2013) ch. 4

John Hagan, *Justice in the Hague: Prosecuting War Crimes in the Balkans* (Chicago, IL, 2003)

Rachel Kerr, *The International Criminal Tribunal for Former Yugoslavia: An Exercise in Law, Politics and Diplomacy* (Oxford, 2004)

Patryk I Labuda, 'The International Criminal Tribunal for Rwanda and Post-Genocide Justice 25 Years On' (2019) 31 *EJIL* 1113

Virginia Morris and Michael P. Scharf, *An Insider's Guide to the International Criminal Tribunal for Former Yugoslavia* (New York, 1995)

Virginia Morris and Michael P. Scharf, *The International Criminal Tribunal for Rwanda* (New York, 1998)

Diane Orentlicher, *Some Kind of Justice: The ICTY's Impact in Bosnia and Serbia* (Oxford, 2018)

Victor Peskin, *International Justice in Rwanda and the Balkans: Virtual Trials and the Struggle for State Cooperation* (Cambridge, 2008)

William Schabas, *The UN International Criminal Tribunals: The Former Yugoslavia, Rwanda and Sierra Leone* (Cambridge, 2006)

Carsten Stahn, Carmel Agius, Serge Brammertz, and Colleen Rohan (eds.), *Legacies of the International Criminal Tribunal for the Former Yugoslavia: A Multidisciplinary Approach* (Oxford, 2020)

Milena Sterio and Michael P. Scharf (eds.), *The Legacy of the Ad Hoc Tribunals in International Criminal Law: Assessing the ICTY's and the ICTR's Most Significant Legal Accomplishments* (Cambridge, 2019)

Bert Swart, Alexander Zahar, and Göran Sluiter (eds.), *The Legacy of the International Criminal Tribunal for the Former Yugoslavia* (Oxford, 2011)

Larissa J. van den Herik, *The Contribution of the Rwanda Tribunal to the Development of International Law* (The Hague, 2005)

8

The International Criminal Court

8.1 INTRODUCTION

The creation of a permanent international criminal court with potentially global jurisdiction is one of the most important developments in international criminal law. The Statute of the International Criminal Court (ICC) not only establishes a judicial institution to investigate and try international crimes, but sets out an influential statement of international criminal law principles. This chapter describes: the creation of the ICC; its main features (such as its jurisdiction and its rules for selecting cases); opposition and criticisms; and a brief assessment of its work, including its controversial and sometimes disappointing early efforts, and the challenges that the Court confronts.

8.2 CREATION OF THE ICC

In spite of the so-called Nuremberg promise that the trials after the Second World War would set a precedent for others,[1] there was no immediate successor to the Nuremberg and Tokyo Tribunals. A permanent court was proposed during the negotiations on the 1948 Genocide Convention, but the final Convention referred only to the possibility of such a court in the future.[2]

When the UN General Assembly approved the Genocide Convention in 1948, it requested the International Law Commission (ILC) to study the desirability of an international court.[3] A special committee produced a draft statute, but the General Assembly postponed the matter until a draft Code of Offences was complete.[4] Progress on the draft Code stalled during the Cold War. It was a proposal in 1989 by Trinidad and Tobago that put the creation of a permanent international criminal court back on the agenda of the United Nations. The General Assembly asked the ILC to draft a statute for a court, and the Commission responded swiftly, producing a final text in 1994.[5]

---

[1] See Section 6.3.2.
[2] Article VI provides that persons charged with genocide are to be tried by a court in the territory where the act was committed or 'by such international penal tribunal as may have jurisdiction with respect to those Contracting Parties which shall have accepted its jurisdiction'.
[3] GA Res. 260(III)B. [4] GA Res. 898(IX).
[5] *Report of the International Law Commission on the Work of its Forty-Sixth Session*, GAOR 49th Session Supp. No. 10, UN Doc. A/49/10 (1994); included, without the commentary, in M. Cherif Bassiouni, *The Statute of the International Criminal Court: A Documentary History* (New York, 1998) 657.

The ICC negotiations took place in the latter half of the 1990s – a fortunate moment in international relations. Cold War divisions had thawed, the international community had developed several ambitious treaties protecting human security, and the ad hoc Tribunals had demonstrated the feasibility of international criminal justice. Nonetheless, a significant number of states still doubted the wisdom of creating a new court, with some of them likely concerned about possible scrutiny. A 'Like-Minded Group', composed of states supportive of a strong and effective Court, was influential in driving forward the process. After a few years of preparatory negotiations, a diplomatic conference was convened in Rome in the summer of 1998 to negotiate and adopt the ICC Statute.

In the five weeks allocated to the Rome Conference, hundreds of controversies needed to be resolved. The disputes ranged from the highly political – like the role of the Security Council – to the technical – such as rules of criminal procedure acceptable to diverse legal systems. Non-governmental organizations attended in large numbers; although they could not take part directly in the negotiations, they helped to push for an effective Court.

The most difficult issues related to jurisdiction, particularly as to which states would have to consent before the Court could exercise its jurisdiction. In the absence of agreement and with two days left before the end of the Conference, a compromise proposal was advanced, including Article 12, in an attempt to balance the conflicting positions of different delegations.

While the great majority of delegations supported the proposed Statute, a few sought to put their own amendments to a vote. India proposed to include a crime of using weapons of mass destruction and to exclude any role for the Security Council.[6] The United States proposed to require the consent of *both* the state of nationality of the suspect and the territorial state.[7] The US proposal was objectionable to most delegations, because it would mean that a powerful state's nationals could commit crimes on the territory of another state and yet not face scrutiny; such a position failed to recognize other states' jurisdiction over their own territories and their ability to pool that jurisdiction, just as the Nuremberg Tribunal had done. The Statute was adopted by a vote of 120 to seven, with twenty-one abstentions.[8]

Contrary to the normal pattern, in which an ILC draft is prepared and then watered down during negotiations, the states negotiating the ICC Statute created a document that was *more* ambitious than the ILC draft. The ILC draft required the concurring consent of *both* the 'territorial state' (the state where the crimes were committed) and the state with custody of the accused. In contrast, the ICC Statute requires the consent of *either* the territorial state or the state of nationality of the accused. The ILC draft let states select the crimes for which they recognized the Court's jurisdiction;[9] the ICC Statute entails automatic acceptance of the core crimes. The ILC draft precluded the ICC from dealing with a situation on the Security Council's agenda, unless the Council permitted it; the ICC

---

[6] UN Doc. A/CONF.183/C.1/L.94 (1998) and UN Doc. A/CONF.183/C.1/L.95 (1998).
[7] UN Doc. A/CONF.183/C.1/L.70 (1998) and UN Doc. A/CONF.183/C.1/L.90 (1998).
[8] The votes were not officially recorded, but China, Israel, and the United States announced that they had been among those who voted against.
[9] The exception was the crime of genocide, for which acceptance would be automatic.

Statute gives a narrower role to the Council (Section 8.6.2). In the ILC draft, proceedings could be triggered only by a state party or the Security Council; the ICC Statute also permits the Prosecutor to initiate investigations on their own initiative.

The Statute received the requisite sixty ratifications faster than expected and entered into force on 1 July 2002. Thus, the Court was brought formally into existence. The Assembly of States Parties, which oversees the administration of the Court, adopted important subsidiary instruments, including the Elements of Crimes and the Rules of Procedure and Evidence (RPE).

8.3 STRUCTURE AND COMPOSITION OF THE ICC

The Court has eighteen judges, who are divided into Pre-Trial, Trial, and Appeals Chambers. The Registry handles administration, and includes, among other sections, the Victims and Witnesses Unit, the Office of Public Counsel for the Defence, and the Office of Public Counsel for Victims.[10] The Office of the Prosecutor carries out preliminary examinations, investigations, and prosecutions.[11] The Assembly of States Parties (ASP) provides management oversight, sets the budget, adopts subsidiary instruments, and elects the judges and the Prosecutor.[12] The election of judges must take into account representation of the principal legal systems of the world, equitable geographical representation, and a fair representation of female and male judges.[13] The Assembly of States Parties has complex voting rules to achieve these requirements.[14]

8.4 CRIMES WITHIN THE JURISDICTION OF THE ICC

The Court has jurisdiction over 'the most serious crimes of international concern': genocide, crimes against humanity, war crimes, and the crime of aggression (Article 5). The ICC Statute goes into more detail in defining the crimes than the Statutes of the ad hoc Tribunals did; many delegations were wary of judicial creativity and wanted codification in advance.[15] The definitions are even further elaborated upon in the 'Elements of Crimes', a subsidiary instrument developed at the request of the United States. The Elements guide the Court in the interpretation and application of the offences.[16]

The oft-stated aim of the process of definition was to codify existing customary law for the purpose of the new Court. However, in crystallizing and clarifying some provisions which had not been previously expressed as written criminal law, the process helped develop customary law.[17] Some provisions arguably pressed the boundaries of

---

[10] ICC Statute, Art. 43. [11] ICC Statute, Arts. 15, 53, and 54. [12] *Ibid*. Art. 112. [13] *Ibid*. Art. 36(8).
[14] Procedure for the Nomination and Election of Judges, the Prosecutor and Deputy Prosecutors of the International Criminal Court: Amendment to operative paragraph 27 of Resolution ICC-ASP/3/Res.6, ICC-ASP/5/Res.5.
[15] See also ICC Statute, Art. 22(2): definitions are to be 'strictly construed and shall not be extended by analogy'.
[16] *Ibid*. Arts. 9 and 21; see Section 8.5 below.
[17] For discussion of the process, see Leila Sadat, *The International Criminal Court and the Transformation of International Law* (New York, 2002) 12, 261–74; Darryl Robinson, 'Crimes Against Humanity: Reflections on State Sovereignty, Legal Precision and the Dictates of the Public Conscience' in Flavia Lattanzi and William Schabas (eds.), *Essays on the Rome Statute of the International Criminal Court* (Rome, 1999) vol. I, 140–4.

existing law as it stood in 1998,[18] but they have since been recognized as established customary law.[19]

On the other hand, some provisions are arguably not as extensive as customary law allows.[20] Article 10 attempts to address this point by providing that the Statute does not limit or prejudice existing or developing rules of international law 'for purposes other than this Statute'. This mitigates the concern that the Statute will in some way freeze the development of customary international law for other jurisdictions. The Court, though, must apply the provisions in the Statute even if customary law creates wider offences.

The status of the ICC Statute is perhaps best described by an International Criminal Tribunal for the former Yugoslavia (ICTY) Trial Chamber in the *Furundžija* case:

> In many areas the Statute may be regarded as indicative of the legal views, i.e. *opinio juris*, of a great number of States ... [R]esort may be had *cum grano salis* to these provisions to help elucidate customary international law. Depending on the matter at issue, the Rome Statute may be taken to restate, reflect, or clarify customary rules or crystallise them, whereas in some areas it creates new law or modifies existing law. At any event, the Rome Statute by and large may be taken as constituting an authoritative expression of the legal views of a great number of States.[21]

Article 21 sets out the sources ('applicable law') for the Court to apply. First and foremost, the Court applies the Statute itself. In doing so, the Court is assisted by two subsidiary instruments – the Elements of Crimes and the Rules of Procedure and Evidence – as long as those provisions are not found by the Court to be inconsistent with the Statute.[22] Where there is a lacuna in the relevant provisions, the Court may then turn to relevant treaties and rules of international law.[23] Failing that, the Court can turn to 'general principles of law', that is, rules common to the legal systems of the world.[24]

---

[18] E.g. the provision on child soldiers: see Herman von Hebel and Darryl Robinson, 'Crimes Within the Jurisdiction of the Court' in Lee, *The Making of the Rome Statute*, 117–18.

[19] E.g. the Special Court for Sierra Leone decided that recruitment of child soldiers was a crime in customary law (*Norman*, SCSL AC, 31 May 2004, paras. 30–53); but see Justice Robertson's view that, 'until the Rome Treaty itself, the rule against child recruitment was a human rights principle and an obligation upon states, but did not entail individual criminal liability in international law. It did so for the first time when the Treaty was concluded and approved on 17th July 1998' (Dissenting Opinion, para. 38).

[20] E.g. Henckaerts and Doswald-Beck, *ICRC Customary Law*, 586, maintain that several war crimes not mentioned in the ICC Statute forms part of customary international law. In addition, the use of biological or chemical weapons was not criminalized in the ICC Statute, due to a stalemate over nuclear weapons; see Chapter 8.

[21] *Furundžija*, ICTY TC II, 10 December 1998, para. 227, supported in *Tadić*, ICTY AC, 15 July 1999, para. 223. See also *Hadžihasanović et al.*, in which the Appeals Chamber gave weight to the adoption of Article 28 (command responsibility) by the Rome Conference, noting that the fact that 'the Rome Statute embodied a number of compromises among the States parties that drafted and adopted it hardly undermines its significance. The same is true of most major multilateral conventions.' (ICTY AC, 16 July 2003, para. 53).

[22] ICC Statute, Arts. 1 and 9. The Pre-Trial Chamber in the *Al Bashir* arrest warrant case has found that 'the Elements of Crimes and the Rules must be applied unless the competent Chamber finds an irreconcilable contradiction' between these documents and the Statute. *Al Bashir Arrest Warrant*, ICC PTC I, 4 March 2009 (ICC-02/05–01/09–3) paras. 128–32. See also Robert Cryer, 'The Definitions of International Crimes in the Al Bashir Arrest Warrant Decision' (2009) 7 *JICJ* 283; Claus Kreß, 'The Crime of Genocide and Contextual Elements' (2009) 7 *JICJ* 297; and Herman von Hebel, 'The Making of the Elements of Crimes' in Lee, *Elements and Rules*, 7–8.

[23] ICC Statute, Art. 21(1)(b). See also Leena Grover, *Interpreting Crimes in the Rome Statute of the International Criminal Court* (Cambridge, 2014).

[24] ICC Statute, Art. 21(1)(c); *Al Bashir Arrest Warrant*, ICC PTC I, 4 March 2009 (ICC-02/05–01/09–3) para. 44.

8.5 JURISDICTION

8.5.1 Personal and Territorial Jurisdiction

Territorial and Active Nationality Jurisdiction

National systems may exercise 'universal jurisdiction' over serious international crimes, meaning that they can prosecute such crimes regardless of where they were committed.[25] In principle, it would have been legally permissible to bestow that same universal jurisdiction upon the ICC, and many delegations favoured that broader approach. Nonetheless, in order to accommodate the concerns of cautious states about a new judicial institution, the ICC is vested with a narrower jurisdiction. Article 12 gives the Court jurisdiction over crimes (1) committed on the territory of states accepting the Court's jurisdiction or (2) committed by nationals of states accepting the Court's jurisdiction.

Territorial and nationality jurisdiction titles were selected as the bases for ICC jurisdiction because these are the two most firmly established bases for jurisdiction in international law.[26] The selection of these two bases was a compromise between contrasting positions. The most ambitious was a German proposal[27] to give universal jurisdiction to the Court. An alternative was a South Korean proposal[28] to confer jurisdiction on the Court with the acceptance of any one of four states: those with territorial jurisdiction, active nationality jurisdiction, passive nationality jurisdiction, or with custody of the suspect. At the other end of the spectrum, the United States argued that the consent of *both* the territorial and the nationality state ought to be required. The South Korean proposal had a great deal of support, but a compromise text was accepted by the conference and is now reflected in Article 12. It gives a more limited jurisdiction to the Court, but one which was thought to facilitate a broader acceptance of the ICC.[29]

How States Accept Jurisdiction

States can accept the Court's jurisdiction in two ways: by becoming states parties, or by issuing a declaration accepting jurisdiction.

Under the ILC draft Statute, a state could ratify the Statute and then choose the crimes for which it would recognize the Court's jurisdiction (the 'opt-in' model).[30] As it became clear during the negotiations that the list of crimes would include only the 'core crimes', the great majority of delegations came to favour 'automatic jurisdiction', meaning that upon ratification a state signifies its acceptance of jurisdiction for all core crimes.

The Statute thus follows the automatic acceptance model, meaning that a state party accepts jurisdiction over all core crimes. There was, however, an exception to this in Article 124 which allowed a state, upon ratification of the Statute, not to accept the jurisdiction of

---

[25] See Chapter 3. [26] See Chapter 3.
[27] The German proposal was contained in the draft text of the Statute submitted to the conference by the Preparatory Committee (UN Doc. A/CONF.183/13 (Vol. III) (1998)).
[28] UN Doc. A/CONF.183/C.I/L.6 (1998).
[29] For the history of the negotiations, see William Schabas and Giulia Pecorella, 'Article 12' in Triffterer and Ambos, *Commentary*, 808–15; Elizabeth Wilmshurst, 'Jurisdiction of the Court' in Lee, *The Making of the Rome Statute*, 127.
[30] Except in respect to genocide, for which acceptance was automatic.

the ICC over war crimes for a period of seven years. This provision was a concession to states wary of the new Court.[31] Only two states, France and Colombia, took advantage of the opt-out regime; France later withdrew its declaration under Article 124 and Colombia's has expired.[32] In 2016, the ASP agreed to remove Article 124 from the Statute.[33]

Another exception to automatic jurisdiction is the more recently added regime for the crime of aggression, which operates with a more complex 'opt-in' system.[34]

Article 12(3) allows a non-party state to declare that it accepts the jurisdiction of the Court, along with the obligation to cooperate fully. Declarations of acceptance of jurisdiction have been made by the Ivory Coast, Palestine, and Ukraine.

Security Council Referrals

In addition, the Court also has jurisdiction where a situation has been referred to the Court by the Security Council under Chapter VII of the UN Charter.[35] The Security Council, using its powers under the UN Charter to maintain international peace and security, can bestow jurisdiction even over crimes committed on the territory or by the nationals of non-party states. This is the same power that the Council has used to create ad hoc Tribunals, but instead of setting up a new institution from scratch, it refers the situation to the existing facility of the ICC.[36]

8.5.2 Temporal Jurisdiction

The ICC does not have jurisdiction over offences committed before the entry into force of the Statute, which was on 1 July 2002. The ICC was created to deal with crimes prospectively rather than to sift through crimes in history.

Furthermore, if a state becomes a party to the Statute after 1 July 2002, the Court may exercise jurisdiction only with respect to crimes committed after the Statute has entered into force for that state (Article 11). The state may, however, make a declaration under Article 12(3) to fill this temporal gap. For example, the declaration of Cote d'Ivoire was retroactive to 1 July 2002.[37]

8.5.3 Persons Over the Age of Eighteen

The Court's jurisdiction is limited to persons at or over the age of eighteen at the time the alleged offence was committed.[38] Setting the age at eighteen avoided the need for a special

---

[31] For criticism of the French attempt at justification of the provision, see Alain Pellet, 'Entry into Force and Amendment of the Statute' in Cassese et al., *Commentary*, 145, 168–9.

[32] The French withdrawal was with effect from 15 June 2008; Colombia's declaration expired on 1 November 2009.

[33] The process requires ratification by seven-eighths of states parties. See also Andreas Motzfeldt Kravik, 'The Assembly of State Parties to the International Criminal Court Decides to Delete Article 124 of the Rome Statute', *EJIL:Talk!* (12 April 2016).

[34] See Chapter 14.

[35] Under Chapter VII, the Council may take decisions, binding on any or all states, to maintain or restore international peace and security.

[36] As in the situations in Darfur and Libya referred to the Court by SC Res. 1593 (2005) and Res. 1970 (2011), respectively.

[37] For critique of retroactive effect, see Andreas Zimmermann, 'Palestine and the International Criminal Court Quo Vadis?' (2013) 11 *JICJ* 303.

[38] See Otto Triffterer and Roger Clark, 'Article 26' in Ambos, *Commentary*, 1247–55.

regime for young offenders; such cases were considered not to be a good use of the Court's slender resources. This does not exclude national jurisdiction over minors for the commission of international crimes under domestic legislation.

8.6 HOW THE COURT WORKS: AN OVERVIEW

8.6.1 'Trigger Mechanisms': Initiating Proceedings

The ICC has jurisdiction over the territory and nationals of more than 120 states. A procedure is needed to 'trigger' the Court's action in particular situations. Article 13 sets out three 'trigger mechanisms':[39] a referral by a state party; a referral by the Security Council; and the opening of an investigation by the Prosecutor acting on his or her own initiative ('*proprio motu*').

State Party Referrals

Only states which are parties to the Statute may refer situations to the Court.

The early practice of the ICC featured a somewhat unexpected development: states referred to the Court situations of atrocities taking place on their own territories. This has been referred to colloquially as 'self-referral'. Seven referrals to the Court have been made by states parties in relation to situations on their own territories: Uganda, Democratic Republic of the Congo (DRC), Central African Republic (two different situations), Mali, Palestine, and Gabon. The self-referral by Gabon did not lead to the opening of a formal investigation, as the available information did not sufficiently indicate crimes amounting to crimes against humanity.[40]

Many observers understandably expected that referrals would be similar to human rights complaints, in which state would complain about events in another state. In accordance with this assumption, some commentators have doubted whether 'self-referral' is permitted in the Statute.[41] However, the Statute simply says that 'a State Party may refer to the Prosecutor a situation', without any limitations.[42] Furthermore the drafting history shows that referrals by 'interested' states, such as territorial states, were specifically foreseen and indeed even preferred.[43] As the drafting history shows, the actual debate in the negotiations was whether states parties who were *not* 'interested states' should *also* be allowed to make referrals, or whether *only* states with a jurisdictional link to the situation (e.g. territory) would be allowed to make a referral.[44]

---

[39] On referral by states, see Philippe Kirsch and Darryl Robinson, 'Referral by States Parties' in Cassese et al., *Commentary*, 619; on initiation by the Prosecutor, see Silvia Fernández de Gurmendi, 'The Role of the International Prosecutor' in Lee, *The Making of the Rome Statute*, 175; on referral by the Security Council, see Lionel Yee, 'The International Criminal Court and the Security Council: Articles 13(b) and 16' in Lee, *The Making of the Rome Statute*, 143.

[40] See e.g. ICC, 'Preliminary Examination – Gabon' at www.icc-cpi.int/gabon.

[41] See e.g. William Schabas, 'First Prosecutions at the International Criminal Court' (2006) 27 *Human Rights Law Journal* 25, 32.

[42] ICC Statute, Art. 14(1).

[43] See Darryl Robinson, 'The Controversy over Territorial State Referrals and Reflections on ICL Discourse' (2011) 9 *JICJ* 355.

[44] See e.g. UN Doc. A/AC.249/1 (1996) paras. 162–3; UN Doc. A/CONF.183/2/Add.1 (1998) at 36.

On the one hand, a self-referral can be of benefit to the Court; it indicates that an international investigation is welcomed and will be supported by the full cooperation of the state concerned. Accordingly, the Prosecutor has expressed the intention to 'seek where possible to make this support explicit through a referral'.[45] On the other hand, there are risks.[46] A government of a divided country may use a referral to seek the Court's intervention against its own political opponents.[47] The referral by Uganda in 2003 concerned the 'situation concerning the Lord's Resistance Army', but the Prosecutor advised that this would be interpreted as covering crimes 'within the situation of northern Uganda by whomever committed'.[48] Self-referrals may also present the risk that states will overburden the Court with cases they could handle themselves. As argued by the defendant in *Katanga*:

if States are granted an unconditional right not to prosecute, this would seriously jeopardise any encouragement of States to prosecute domestically and would negate this persisting and primary responsibility for States to prosecute international crimes.[49]

The concern about over-burdening the Court can be managed: the Prosecutor is not obliged to initiate an investigation in response to every referral, and may decline to investigate a situation on grounds such as lack of gravity, complementarity, and the interests of justice.

Some states parties have made referrals concerning crimes in other territories. Another interesting development has been for *groups* of states parties to join together in making a referral, as was done for the situations in Venezuela (2018) and in Ukraine (2022). Group referrals help convey a widely shared collective concern about a situation.

Security Council Referrals

While some delegations were opposed to the Security Council having a role in referring situations to the Court, most delegations felt that such a role would be both useful and appropriate. The Security Council created the ad hoc Tribunals, illustrating that individual accountability can be part of the Council's response to threats to international peace and security. When the Council refers situations to the ICC, it is not establishing a new institution as it did with the ICTY and the International Criminal Tribunal for Rwanda (ICTR); the situation is being referred to the ICC as it stands, with all the powers and responsibilities laid down by the Statute. The Council, exercising its powers under the UN Charter, can also impose additional obligations on any UN member state, including the obligation to cooperate with the Court.[50]

---

[45] 'Referrals and Communications', Annex to the *Paper on Some Policy Issues Before the Office of the Prosecutor* (5 September 2003) section D, available at www.legal-tools.org/en/browse/ltfolder/0_32297/.

[46] Claus Kreß, 'Self-Referrals and Waivers of Complementarity: Some Considerations in Law and Policy' (2004) 2 *JICJ* 944; Mahnoush Arsanjani and Michael Reisman, 'The Law-in-Action of the International Criminal Court' (2005) 99 *AJIL* 385, 392.

[47] See also William Burke-White, 'Complementarity in Practice: The International Criminal Court as Part of a System of Multi-Level Global Governance in the Democratic Republic of the Congo' (2005) 18 *LJIL* 557, 567–8.

[48] Letter of the Prosecutor of 17 June 2004 attached to the Presidency Decision to assign the situation in Uganda to Pre-Trial Chamber II. See more generally, Payam Akhavan, 'The Lord's Resistance Army Case: Uganda's Submission of the First State Referral to the International Criminal Court' (2005) 99 *AJIL* 403.

[49] *Katanga and Ngudjolo*, ICC AC, 25 September 2009 (ICC-01/04–01/07–1497) para. 63.

[50] See Chapter 21 on how this affects head of state immunity.

In the Rome negotiations, hopes were not high that the Security Council would refer situations, given that any single permanent member could veto any such referral. Confounding such expectations, the Council has referred two situations to the ICC. The situation in Darfur (Sudan) was referred to the ICC under Resolution 1593 (2005). This was a welcome example of the United States allowing – indeed welcoming – the invocation of the Court's jurisdiction, in spite of its objections to the Court (Section 8.11.1). Similarly, the situation in Libya was referred to the Court by Resolution 1970 (2011), adopted by the Council by consensus. Unfortunately, Security Council support has not been robust. For example, while the Rome Statute anticipates that proceedings arising from Security Council referrals should be funded by the United Nations, the Security Council provided no funding.[51] Furthermore, the Security Council has taken no action to follow up on non-cooperation and failures to carry out arrests.

Initiation by the Prosecutor

The power of the Prosecutor to initiate investigations '*proprio motu*', that is, at the Prosecutor's own initiative, was a major controversy in the Rome Conference. On the one hand, many delegations insisted that the Court should not be entirely dependent on the decisions of external political actors (states parties or the Security Council) to trigger its work. On the other hand, some delegations were concerned that the Prosecutor might institute politically motivated investigations. Article 15 seeks to resolve the different concerns, by allowing the Prosecutor to initiate investigations, but with a 'check and balance' of requiring authorization of the Pre-Trial Chamber.

Under Article 15, anyone may send information about crimes to the Prosecutor. The Prosecutor has received thousands of communications from individuals and organizations who want ICC investigations to be opened in situations around the world. The Prosecutor is obliged to assess such information to decide whether 'there is a reasonable basis to proceed with an investigation'. Most communications relate to issues that are manifestly outside the jurisdiction of the Court, but several have led to preliminary examinations and investigations of situations (Section 8.6.3).

The Prosecutor has sought authorization to initiate investigations *proprio motu* in seven situations: Afghanistan, Burundi, Côte d'Ivoire, Georgia, Kenya, Myanmar/Bangladesh, and the Philippines.

8.6.2 Deferral by the Security Council: Article 16

Article 16 reads as follows:

No investigation or prosecution may be commenced or proceeded with under the Statute for a period of 12 months after the Security Council, in a resolution adopted under Chapter VII of the Charter of the United Nations, has requested the Court to that effect; that request may be renewed by the Council under the same conditions.

---

[51] See Robert Cryer, 'Sudan, Resolution 1593 and International Criminal Justice' (2006) 19 *LJIL* 195.

The ILC draft Statute contained an even wider restriction on the Court: it would have prevented the Court from acting on any matter being considered by the Security Council, unless the Council agreed otherwise. That would have meant that Council members could obstruct ICC investigations simply by adding the situation to the Council's agenda. The negotiators of the ICC Statute saw that as unacceptably subordinating the ICC to the Security Council, and thus they reversed the provision.[52] Instead of requiring a positive Council decision to *allow* the ICC to proceed, Article 16 requires a positive decision to *defer* a proceeding. This avoids the veto problem, because ICC proceedings continue unimpeded unless there is a majority vote that a pause is needed. The Council has to act under Chapter VII of the Charter, which requires a 'threat to the peace, breach of the peace or act of aggression'. Article 16 allows the Council, under its primary responsibility for the maintenance of peace and security, to temporarily set aside the demands of justice when it considers the demands of peace to be overriding. It is an example of the ICC coexisting with the established UN structure.

From time to time, requests have been made to the Council to suspend proceedings, for example, in relation to the situations in northern Uganda and in Kenya, and in relation to the arrest warrant against the President of Sudan. All such requests have been unsuccessful, and the Council has taken no action in relation to them. As will be discussed below, Article 16 was invoked in an unexpected and problematic way in 2002 and 2003, when the Bush Administration sought to exempt armed forces from non-party states (Section 8.11).

8.6.3 Preliminary Examination, Investigation, and Prosecution

Upon receipt of a referral or a communication, the Prosecutor conducts a 'preliminary examination' to determine whether an investigation is warranted. At the preliminary examination stage, the Office of the Prosecutor has relatively limited powers, and thus will start by amassing publicly available information, such as UN reports. If a situation warrants, the collection of information grows more intensive and can include field missions.

Unlike other international tribunals, the ICC has jurisdiction over numerous situations that could warrant investigation. Thus, it must select the situations on which it will focus. The purpose of a preliminary examination is to decide whether an investigation is warranted. Article 53 of the Statute stipulates the three factors that must be considered. The first is *jurisdiction*: whether there are crimes within the subject matter jurisdiction of the Court taking place within the personal, territorial, and temporal jurisdiction of the Court. The second criterion is '*admissibility*', which includes two aspects: 'complementarity' and 'gravity'. The complementarity principle is discussed in Section 8.7: it asks whether national proceedings are being carried out genuinely. The gravity requirement, discussed in Section 8.8, asks whether the crimes are grave enough to warrant action by the Court. The third criterion is the '*interests of justice*', which asks whether there are countervailing reasons not to proceed (Section 8.9).

---

[52] Morten Bergsmo and Dan Zhu, 'Article 16' in Ambos, *Commentary*, 933, 935–6.

Preliminary examinations have been started in many situations, including Afghanistan, Bolivia, Colombia, Gabon, the Gaza Flotilla (registered in Comoros and Greece), Georgia, Guinea, Honduras, Iraq, Korea, Nigeria, Palestine, the Philippines, Ukraine, and Venezuela. Several of these preliminary examinations have ended in a conclusion that the requirements for opening investigations have not been met.[53] Preliminary examinations can be re-opened based on new information. For example, a preliminary examination in Palestine ended because Palestine had not yet been recognized as a 'state'. It was re-opened after the UN General Assembly recognized Palestine as an observer state, and the Prosecutor opened an investigation. A preliminary examination into UK actions in Iraq was closed because the gravity standard was not met, but it was re-opened in 2014 based on new communications with new information. That examination was closed again because of complementarity; despite misgivings about some aspects of UK proceedings, it was not shown that they were not 'genuine' (see Section 8.7.2).

Some preliminary examinations (e.g. Colombia) have lasted for years, leading many observers to suggest that they should have time limits.[54] However, while preliminary examinations should not be unnecessarily dilatory, time limits may contradict Statute duties and goals. One issue that must be monitored in preliminary examination is the progress and quality of national proceedings, which can take considerable time to unfold and meaningfully assess.[55] Prematurely closing a preliminary examination removes scrutiny and its resulting incentives; prematurely opening an investigation creates confusion and wastes resources. Some situations may simmer just below the gravity threshold; it makes sense to monitor such situations as opposed to closing the preliminary examination. Accordingly, an independent expert review of the ICC recommended steps to make preliminary examinations timely, but without imposing time limits.[56]

Once an investigation is opened, the Office of the Prosecutor has a more extensive set of legal powers. Investigations are opened in relation to 'situations', which are generally defined in broad geographic and temporal terms. A 'situation' might involve hundreds or thousands of crimes and numerous responsible persons. The Office of the Prosecutor investigates the crime base in order to select cases against the persons most responsible for the most serious crimes.[57] Once adequate evidence is acquired, the Prosecutor may approach the Pre-Trial Chamber seeking an arrest warrant or a summons to appear. At this point, the Court is dealing with particular 'cases': that is, particular persons in relation to particular crimes. If the Chamber issues the warrant, responsibility falls on states to carry

---

[53] Reports on preliminary examinations are available at www.icc-cpi.int.

[54] ICC ASP, 'Independent Expert Review of the International Criminal Court and the Rome Statute System – Final Report', 30 September 2022 (IER Report), paras. 714–7; Andrew Murdoch, 'UK statement to ICC Assembly of States Parties 17th session' (5 December 2018) www.gov.uk; Anni Pues, 'Towards the "Golden Hour": A Critical Exploration of the Length of Preliminary Examinations' (2017) 15 *JICJ* 440.

[55] See Carsten Stahn, 'Damned If You Do, Damned If You Don't: Challenges and Critiques of Preliminary Examinations at the ICC' (2017) 15 *JICJ* 413. On the longest preliminary examination (the situation in Colombia), see Kai Ambos, *The Colombian Peace Process and the Principle of Complementarity of the International Criminal Court* (Dordrecht, 2010).

[56] IER Report (n. 54) paras. 717–9.

[57] Office of the Prosecutor, *Policy Paper on Case Selection and Prioritization* (15 September 2016), available at www.icc-cpi.int/itemsDocuments/20160915_OTP-Policy_Case-Selection_Eng.pdf.

out the arrest. Once a person is arrested, they are brought to the ICC and the 'prosecution' phase begins. The relevant procedures are discussed in Chapter 17.

8.7 COMPLEMENTARITY

The ICTY and ICTR had 'primacy' over national systems, meaning that they had priority and could require national systems to defer to an international prosecution. By contrast, the ICC is 'complementary' to national systems. The ICC is intended to supplement, not supplant, national jurisdictions. National systems have the first opportunity to prosecute cases; the ICC can take a case only where they fail to do so or are unwilling or unable to carry out proceedings genuinely.[58] Indeed, states are encouraged to carry out proceedings themselves: the preamble to the ICC Statute recognizes that every state has a responsibility to exercise its own criminal jurisdiction over international crimes.[59]

The principle of complementarity is based not only on respect for the primary jurisdiction of states, but also on practical considerations of efficiency and effectiveness, since states will generally have the best access to evidence and witnesses and the resources to carry out proceedings. An international court is only one way to enforce international criminal law and it may not be the best option in every instance.[60]

A case will be inadmissible before the ICC if a national authority is investigating or prosecuting the case or has already done so, unless evidence indicates that the state is nevertheless unwilling or unable to carry out proceedings *genuinely*. There is therefore a two-step test: (1) whether there is or was an investigation or prosecution of the case at the national level; and, if so, (2) whether the state is unwilling or unable genuinely to carry out that investigation or prosecution.[61]

8.7.1 First Step: Are There Proceedings at the National Level?

A case can only be inadmissible under complementarity if it is being investigated or prosecuted (Article 17(1)(1)(a)) or it has been investigated (Article 17(1)(b)) by a state with jurisdiction. Article 17(1)(a) deals with ongoing proceedings: 'the case is being investigated or prosecuted by a State which has jurisdiction over it'. Article 17(1)(b) deals with proceedings that were investigated and closed: 'The case has been investigated by a State which has jurisdiction over it and the State has decided not to prosecute the person concerned'. Article 17(1)(c) deals with completed trials: 'The person concerned has already been tried' for the conduct.

Where no state has taken any action in relation to the case, none of these criteria for inadmissibility is met, and thus the case remains admissible before the ICC. It is only where national authorities are engaged or have been engaged in apparent exercise of their own

---

[58] ICC Statute, Art. 17. [59] *Ibid.* Preamble, para. 6. [60] See Chapters 2 and 4.
[61] *Katanga and Ngudjolo*, ICC AC, 25 September 2009 (ICC-01/04–01/07–1497) paras. 1 and 75–9.

jurisdiction that the Court moves on to assess the genuineness of those proceedings under the second step (the 'unwilling' or 'unable' test, discussed in Section 8.7.2).[62]

Article 17 is very commonly misquoted and over-simplified as a one-step test requiring a finding of either 'unwillingness' or 'inability'; that is, 'a case is only admissible at the ICC where the territorial state is unwilling or unable to prosecute'.[63] That misquotation is so prevalent that when the ICC faithfully applied the clearly stated first step in Article 17 (i.e. that there must be national proceedings), it was decried by many as a judicial invention or gloss.[64] However, where a state has brought no proceedings, none of the explicit requirements of investigations or prosecutions in Article 17 are met, and thus the case is plainly admissible before the ICC.[65]

In *Katanga*, the Appeals Chamber provided a careful explanation of the two steps explicitly stated in Article 17. The Chamber rightly described the common error of and leaping to straight to the second step (the unwilling/unable exception) and ignoring the first step (the proceedings requirement) as 'putting the cart before the horse'.[66] To ignore the proceedings requirement not only ignores the text, but would also have bad effects. It would mean that a state could take no action, leaving a case unaddressed, and yet – given the narrow terms of Articles 17(2) and (3) – the ICC would be precluded from acting as long as the state had not collapsed and was not acting for a purpose of shielding perpetrators (see Section 8.7.2). Article 17 rightly requires actual proceedings in order to pre-empt the ICC under complementarity.

An understandable objection to the proceedings requirement in Article 17 is that it seems too easy for states to shirk their shared responsibility and to offload cases onto the ICC, by simply failing to prosecute. The ICC Statute's preamble recalls a 'duty' of states to exercise criminal jurisdiction. If the duty to exercise criminal jurisdiction reflects the classic customary law duty to prosecute or extradite,[67] then surrender to the ICC satisfies the duty and accomplishes the aim of avoiding impunity. Some observers read the preamble as referring to a duty to prosecute domestically and not to extradite or surrender; on this understanding of the duty, recognizing the case as admissible before the ICC seems to undermine the duty. However, this objection overlooks that the ICC has no legal power to *force* states to carry out domestic prosecutions. The ICC may try to encourage proceedings (as will be discussed in Section 8.7.4), but where the state will not act, it would make little sense for the case to also be inadmissible before the ICC, thereby guaranteeing impunity. Furthermore, the ICC controls its own docket, so the concern about the ICC being unwillingly overburdened can be managed: the ICC can decline to exercise jurisdiction where there are good reasons to do so.[68]

---

[62] *Ibid.* paras. 1 and 74–9.

[63] See e.g. Arsanjani and Reisman, 'The Law-in-Action' (n. 46) 395–7; William Schabas, 'Prosecutorial Discretion v. Judicial Activism' (2008) 6 *JICJ* 731, 757.

[64] Arsanjani and Reisman, 'The Law-in-Action' (n. 46); Schabas, 'Prosecutorial Discretion' (n. 63).

[65] Darryl Robinson, 'The Mysterious Mysteriousness of Complementarity' (2010) 21 *Criminal Law Forum* 67.

[66] *Katanga and Ngudjolo*, ICC AC, 25 September 2009 (ICC-01/04–01/07–1497) para. 78. [67] See Chapter 4.

[68] ICC Statute, Art. 53(1)(c) and (2)(c) (interests of justice).

ICC jurisprudence has clarified the requirement of national proceedings. In the Kenya situation, the Appeals Chamber held that the term 'being investigated' requires that a state actually be taking concrete steps; general assurances of an intent to start investigating are not enough.[69] That decision has been criticized on the grounds that more leeway and time should have been given to Kenya.[70] However, the criticism overlooks that the Office of the Prosecutor spent years trying to encourage domestic action, without success. During a preliminary examination, the Office of the Prosecutor gives latitude and time to states to start investigations, as part of the policy of encouraging domestic action. However, once the ICC initiates an investigation, and advances to the point of issuing arrest warrants, something more than future assurances is needed to forestall the exercise of the Court's concurrent jurisdiction.[71]

Article 17 may be invoked by any 'state'; it is not restricted to states on whose territory the crime occurred. It is enough to render a case inadmissible if any state 'with jurisdiction' undertakes criminal proceedings, whatever the basis for jurisdiction may be. Non-party states can also initiate proceedings and invoke the complementarity principle: as long as some judicial system is dealing with a case genuinely, that will satisfy the complementarity test.

8.7.2 Second Step: Unwillingness or Inability to Carry Out Proceedings Genuinely

Where a state purports to be investigating or prosecuting the case, analysis moves to the second step. The ICC must defer to the national efforts, unless the Prosecutor can show that the state is in reality 'unwilling' or 'unable' to carry out the proceedings *genuinely*. The test is deliberately generous to states, making it fairly difficult for the ICC to proceed where national efforts are underway. The term 'genuinely' was chosen in preference to other terms, such as 'effectively'. Delegations from the global South were concerned that the term 'effectively' was too demanding; they did not want to empower the ICC to take over a case just because the national system was not meeting the highest international standards.[72] Thus, the term 'genuinely' requires considerable deference to states: as long as the national proceedings are not a sham and are carried out with a basic level of quality to be 'genuine', the Court will defer.

In determining whether a state is 'unwilling' to carry out proceedings genuinely, the Court must consider factors such as: (1) a purpose of shielding persons from criminal responsibility; (2) unjustified delay inconsistent with an intent to bring the person concerned to justice; and (3) a lack of independence or impartiality inconsistent with an intent to bring the person concerned to justice.[73]

[69] *Muthaura et al.*, ICC AC, 30 August 2011 (ICC-01/09–02/11–274) paras. 1, 2, 40.
[70] Kevin Heller, 'Radical Complementarity' (2016) 14 *JICJ* 637; Carsten Stahn, 'Admissibility Challenges Before the ICC: From Quasi-Primacy to Qualified Deference?' in Carsten Stahn (ed.), *The Law and Practice of the International Criminal Court* (Oxford, 2015).
[71] *Muthaura et al.*, ICC AC, 30 August 2011 (ICC-01/09–02/11–274) paras. 41 and 44.
[72] John Holmes, 'Complementarity: National Courts versus the ICC' in Cassese et al., *Commentary*, 674.
[73] ICC Statute, Art. 17(2). For differing views as to whether the criteria are or are not exhaustive, see Markus Benzing, 'The Complementarity Regime of the International Criminal Court: International Criminal Justice Between State Sovereignty and the Fight Against Impunity' (2003) 7 *Max Planck Yearbook of United Nations Law* 591, 606; Holmes, 'Complementarity'

The factors to assess 'inability' to carry out genuine proceedings are noted in Article 17(3):

In order to determine inability in a particular case, the Court shall consider whether, due to a total or substantial collapse or unavailability of its national judicial system, the State is unable to obtain the accused or the necessary evidence and testimony or otherwise unable to carry out its proceedings.

Thus, where a state sincerely wishes to carry out proceedings, the ICC cannot lightly intervene. It would not be enough that a state is under-resourced or that its system does not meet the highest standards; the factors require much more serious impediments to a plausible trial, such as a 'collapse' of the national system.

The complementarity test is primarily concerned with national proceedings that are too *lenient* (i.e. a sham trial designed to keep the ICC at bay). An interesting controversy has arisen as to whether cases should be admissible at the ICC where the national proceedings are too *harsh*, that is, where they do not conform to international human rights standards and requirements of due process.[74] Some argue the aim of complementarity includes ensuring that persons are tried in proceedings that respect due process. In support of that view, Article 17 does say that the Court should 'have regard' to the principles of due process recognized by international law. The other view is that the Court is primarily concerned with preventing impunity rather than with monitoring the human rights standards of domestic authorities. Where proceedings are too stringent, that is a matter for human rights bodies.

In the *Al Senussi* case in the Libya situation, the ICC Appeals Chamber took a sound middle path. In general, complementarity is concerned with proceedings which will lead to the suspect evading justice, such as sham proceedings to forestall the ICC. However, in extreme cases, where due process violations are so egregious that the proceedings cannot be regarded as providing any genuine justice, then it could be said that the accused is not in fact being 'brought to justice'.[75]

8.7.3 What Is a 'Case'?

Article 17 asks whether the 'case' is being investigated or prosecuted at the national level. That raises the question: what is a 'case'? How much does the national case have to overlap with the ICC case in order to be the same 'case'? The question is more complex than it would be in a simple domestic case of, for example, a single mugging, where the scope of

---

(n. 72) 675; and Darryl Robinson, 'Serving the Interests of Justice: Amnesties, Truth Commissions and the International Criminal Court' (2003) 14 *EJIL* 481, 500.

[74] See e.g. Enrique Rojo, 'The Role of Fair Trial Considerations in the Complementarity Regime of the International Criminal Court: From "No Peace Without Justice" to "No Peace with Victor's Justice"?' (2005) 18 *LJIL* 829; Benzing, 'The Complementarity Regime of the International Criminal Court' (n. 73) 606–7; Federica Gioia, 'State Sovereignty, Jurisdiction and "Modern" International Law: The Principle of Complementarity in the International Criminal Court' (2006) 19 *LJIL* 1095, 1110–13; Frédéric Mégret and Marika Giles Samson, 'Holding the Line on Complementarity in Libya: The Case for Tolerating Flawed Domestic Trials' (2013) 11 *JICJ* 57; and Kevin Jon Heller, 'The Shadow Side of Complementarity: The Effect of Article 17 of the Rome Statute on National Due Process' (2006) 17 *Criminal Law Forum* 255.

[75] See *Gaddafi and Al-Senussi*, ICC AC 24 July 2014 (ICC-01/11–01/11–565).

the 'case' is fairly clear. The ICC deals with large-scale complex crimes, which can involve different accused facing many different possible charges arising from different possible incidents.

The ICC has held that, for a national proceeding to concern the same 'case', the 'national investigations must cover the same individual and substantially the same conduct as alleged in the proceedings before the Court'.[76] This interpretation is supported by various Statute provisions as well as national and international jurisprudence on *ne bis in idem* or 'double jeopardy'.[77]

The 'same conduct' test has given rise to understandable criticisms and concerns. If it is interpreted too rigidly, it would mean that the state has to put forward an almost identical case, including selecting the same charges and incidents out of a very large crime-base, in order to maintain control. This has been described as the 'mind reader' problem, in that the state would have to anticipate the case constructed by the ICC Prosecutor.[78] An overly rigid application would indeed erode the complementarity principle, making it too easy for the Prosecutor to advance a different 'case' and thus sidestep Article 17.

The Appeals Chamber expressed the test more flexibly in a decision in the Kenya situation, referring to '*substantially*' the same conduct.[79] A Pre-Trial Chamber in the *Gaddafi* case also adopted a more flexible approach; the Chamber did not require that the national proceedings concern the same incidents but rather the same *gravamen* or essence of the crime.[80] While some decisions have referred to the two cases sufficiently 'mirroring' each other, which is probably too demanding,[81] the better and more modest question stated in jurisprudence is whether there is sufficient 'overlap'.[82]

What if a state wishes to pursue the same person but for a *different* case? This scenario is addressed in the cooperation provisions of the Statute (Part 9): the state and the Court shall consult as to the sequencing of their respective cases.[83] The consultation mechanism allows the ICC and the state to consider all relevant factors, including the relative gravity of the cases. The Prosecutor can also drop the ICC case under the 'interests of justice' if a person is already punished for related crimes. An understandable concern about the consultation mechanism is that it does not guarantee appropriate deference by the ICC.[84] However, no state has yet requested such a consultation, so it is premature to suppose that the ICC would not show appropriate comity.

Complementarity must also be assessed when the Prosecutor decides to formally open an investigation. This creates an interpretive puzzle, because complementarity refers to

[76] *Ruto et al.*, ICC AC, 30 August 2011 (ICC-01/09–01/11–307) para. 1.
[77] See ICC Statute, Arts. 17(1)(c), 20(3), 89(4), 90(1), 90(2)(a), 90(7), and see Rod Rastan, 'What is "Substantially the Same Conduct": Unpacking the ICC's "First Limb" Complementarity Jurisprudence' (2017) 15 *JICJ* 1.
[78] Schabas, 'Prosecutorial Discretion' (n. 63); Heller, 'Radical Complementarity' (n. 70).
[79] *Muthaura et al.*, ICC AC, 30 August 2011 (ICC-01/09–02/11–274) para. 76. For further discussion of the 'same' (or substantially the same) conduct, see Rod Rastan, 'Situations and Cases: Defining the Parameters' in Carsten Stahn and Mohamed El Zeidy (eds.), *The International Criminal Court and Complementarity* (Cambridge, 2011) 421–58; Sarah Nouwen, 'Fine-Tuning Complementarity' in Brown, *Research Handbook*, 206–31.
[80] *Gaddafi and Al-Senussi*, ICC PTC I, 31 May 2013 (ICC-01/11–01/11–344) paras. 73–83. See also on this point the Prosecution Response, 22 July 2013 (ICC-01/11–01/11–384) paras. 45 et seq.
[81] *Gaddafi and Al-Senussi*, ICC AC 21 May 2014 (ICC-01/11–01/11 OA) paras. 2 and 73. [82] *Ibid.* para. 72.
[83] ICC Statute, Arts. 89(4), 94(1) and 97. [84] Heller, 'Radical Complementarity' (n. 70).

'the case', but at the outset of an investigation, the Prosecutor will not yet have selected specific 'cases'. Accordingly, admissibility is assessed by looking at the set of likely cases for ICC prosecution, in particular, cases involving the persons most responsible for the most serious crimes.[85] Once the Prosecutor seeks an arrest warrant, he or she has identified a specific 'case', and thus the test can be applied more specifically.

8.7.4 Encouraging National Proceedings

One of the aims of the complementarity regime is to encourage genuine national proceedings. Upon ratification of the ICC Statute, many states have reformed their domestic laws to allow national prosecution for international crimes. When the Prosecutor opens an investigation, he or she must notify affected states; one of the objectives of that rule is to induce national proceedings.

The ICC Office of the Prosecutor has announced, as a policy, a 'positive approach to complementarity'.[86] Rather than competing with states for cases, the Office 'will encourage genuine national proceedings where possible'.[87] There are limits to how far the Prosecutor can go in assisting national efforts: the ICC is not a development agency (as many delegates in the Assembly of States Parties have noted). The Office of the Prosecutor has undertaken some efforts, such as sharing expertise and sharing evidence (foreseen in Article 93(10)). As a result, national proceedings have been encouraged in several situations within ICC jurisdiction, including the Central African Republic, Colombia, the DRC, Guinea, Libya, and Uganda.[88]

The policy of the Office of the Prosecutor also recognizes that there are some scenarios where a state needs help addressing mass crimes, and that it is appropriate to turn to the ICC as a suitable forum. One of the conceptions underlying the ICC is that it can serve as a 'facility available to states'.[89] In such instances, rather than pressing for ineffective national proceedings, the Office of the Prosecutor has engaged in consensual 'burden-sharing' in which the ICC prosecutes the persons most responsible. Many interesting policy questions arise as to when the Office of the Prosecutor should try to encourage national proceedings and when it should offer to share the burden with states.[90]

---

[85] *Situation in the Republic of Kenya*, ICC PTC II, 31 March 2010 (ICC-01/09–19) paras. 50, 182 and 188. See further Chapter 17.

[86] Office of the Prosecutor, *Prosecutorial Strategy 2009–2012* 17; Office of the Prosecutor, Strategic Plan 2023–2025 12–13, available at icc-cpi.int.

[87] Office of the Prosecutor, *Prosecutorial Strategy*, ibid.

[88] Office of the Prosecutor, *Strategic Plan 2016–2018*, 32–35; Office of the Prosecutor, *Strategic Plan 2023–2025*, 12–13; see also William W. Burke-White, 'Proactive Complementarity: The International Criminal Court and National Courts in the Rome System of International Justice' (2008) 49 *Harvard International Law Journal* 53; William Burke-White, 'Complementarity in Practice: The International Criminal Court as Part of a System of Multi-Level Global Governance in the Democratic Republic of the Congo' (2005) 18 *LJIL* 557, 567–8.

[89] See e.g. in the negotiating history of the ICC Statute: UN Doc A/AC.249/1 (1996) at 30.

[90] See Carsten Stahn, 'Taking Complementarity Seriously' in Carsten Stahn and Mohamed El-Zeidy (eds.), *The International Criminal Court and Complementarity: From Theory to Practice* (Cambridge, 2011) and Christoph Burchard, 'Complementarity as Global Governance' in the same volume.

8.8 GRAVITY

The other major ground for inadmissibility is that a case 'is not of sufficient gravity to justify further action by the Court'.[91] Of course, all crimes within the Statute are 'grave', but the Statute contemplates an additional threshold of gravity for the selection of situations and cases.

The gravity requirement was not discussed extensively when Article 17 was negotiated; all the attention went to complementarity. However, the ICC faces far greater demand than was initially anticipated; the number of potential situations and cases of serious crimes far exceeds the Court's resources. Thus, gravity has played a major role in the prioritization of situations and cases.[92]

The Office of the Prosecutor has stated that, in assessing gravity, it considers: (1) the scale of the crimes; (2) the nature of the crimes; (3) the manner of their commission; and (4) their impact.[93] These factors have been cited with approval in jurisprudence.[94] 'Scale' refers to the number of crimes and victims. 'Nature' prioritizes crimes such as killing, sexual violence, and other attacks on personal autonomy. 'Manner' includes systematicity, cruelty, discrimination, abuse of power, and vulnerability of victims. 'Impact' includes suffering, increased vulnerability, and social, economic, and environmental damage.[95]

In the *Ntaganda* case, a Pre-Trial Chamber suggested an unusually stringent definition of gravity, requiring that all crimes be widespread or systematic, that they must cause 'social alarm', and that cases can only involve the most senior leaders. The Appeals Chamber found that none of these tests were required by the Statute.[96] The Office of the Prosecutor does focus on persons most responsible, and thus seniority of officials is a consideration, but this is a matter of case selection policy rather than a mandatory legal threshold.

The situations in which investigations have been opened typically involve hundreds or thousands of the gravest forms of crimes (such as murder or sexual violence). The Prosecutor has declined to open investigations in situations with far more limited criminality. These include the first examination into UK abuses in Iraq (four to twelve victims of wilful killing);[97] a shelling by North Korea;[98] and violence during an Israeli interception of some ships headed to Gaza.[99]

The stated policy of the Office of the Prosecutor is to bring charges against those bearing the *greatest responsibility* for the crimes within the ICC's jurisdiction.[100] This is a widely

---

[91] ICC Statute, Arts. 17(1)(d) and 53(1)(c).

[92] See e.g. Margaret deGuzman, *Shocking the Conscience of Humanity: Gravity and the Legitimacy of International Criminal Law* (Oxford, 2020); Mohamed El-Zeidy, 'The Gravity Threshold under the Statute of the International Criminal Court' (2008) 19 *Criminal Law Forum* 35.

[93] ICC OTP, *Report on Prosecutorial Strategy* (14 September 2006) 5; Office of the Prosecutor, *Policy Paper on Preliminary Examinations* (November 2013) paras. 59–66.

[94] *Situation on the Registered Vessels of the Union of the Comoros, the Hellenic Republic and the Kingdom of Cambodia*, PTC I, 16 July 2015, para. 21.

[95] ICC OTP, *Policy Paper on Preliminary Examinations* (November 2013) paras. 59–66.

[96] *Situation in the DRC*, ICC AC, 13 July 2006 (ICC-01/04–169) paras. 66–82.

[97] Office of the Prosecutor's response to communications received concerning Iraq, 10 February 2006. For criticism, see Schabas, 'Prosecutorial Discretion' (n. 63).

[98] ICC OTP, *Situation in the Republic of Korea, Article 15 Report* (23 June 2014).

[99] *Situation on the Registered ...* , PTC I, 29 November 2017 (ICC-01/13–57). See also Marco Longobardo, 'Everything is Relative, Even Gravity' (2016) 14 *JICJ* 1011.

[100] *Paper on Some Policy Issues Before the Office of the Prosecutor* (September 2003) 7, www.icc-cpi.int.

shared approach among international courts, in view of limited resources. Neither the Office of the Prosecutor nor the Appeals Chamber regards it as a legal limitation on the power of the Court.[101]

8.9 INTERESTS OF JUSTICE

The final factor that must be considered in situation or case selection is whether 'there are nonetheless substantial reasons to conclude that an investigation [or prosecution] would not serve the interests of justice'.[102] This is a more discretionary category, which allows the Prosecutor to take into account considerations such as the age or infirmity of the accused. Under this heading, the Prosecutor may also take into account whether the person's rights have been seriously infringed by a state, or whether the person has already been prosecuted for other related crimes.[103]

Under this heading, the Prosecutor must also consider the 'interests of victims'.[104] Accordingly, in deciding whether to open an investigation, the Office of the Prosecutor solicits views of affected communities. While victims may usually support criminal prosecutions, at times they may prefer other responses.[105]

It is controversial whether and when the Prosecutor might defer to traditional justice mechanisms, especially if they are coupled with amnesties from formal domestic prosecution.[106] Some traditional justice mechanisms arguably might not satisfy the requirements of Article 17 (complementarity), which require 'investigation' and 'prosecution'. Thus, any deference to non-judicial responses to atrocities would likely be considered under the 'interests of justice' test. Views differ on the appropriate posture of the Court, but many commentators favour an inclusive concept of 'justice' that embraces alternative approaches, provided that the mechanisms are not simply a guise to shield perpetrators. A particularly interesting case study is the Special Jurisdiction for Peace that operates in Colombia: a peace agreement was reached, featuring an alternative justice mechanism that requires perpetrators to come forward, tell the truth, and face significant but somewhat reduced alternative sentences.[107]

Possibly even more controversial is whether the Prosecutor should defer when there is evidence that ICC proceedings will prolong violence or trigger a return to violence. On the one hand, crime prevention is one of the Statute's aims, so a Prosecutor could very plausibly take a 'do no harm' approach that avoids aggravating crimes. On the other hand, warlords almost inevitably respond with such threats, and arguably criminal law should not succumb to 'blackmail'. Perhaps seeking to avoid such controversies, the Prosecutor's policy paper asserts that the 'interests of peace' are not a consideration under the 'interests of justice',

---

[101] See Ignaz Stegmiller, 'The Gravity Threshold under the ICC Statute: Gravity Back and Forth in Lubanga and Ntaganda' (2009) 9 *ICLR* 547.

[102] ICC Statute, Art. 53(1)(c) and (2)(c).

[103] Office of the Prosecutor, *Policy Paper on the Interests of Justice* (September 2007).

[104] ICC Statute, Art. 53(1)(c) and (2)(c).

[105] Office of the Prosecutor, *Policy Paper on the Interests of Justice* (September 2007).   [106] See Chapter 22.

[107] See e.g. Nicolás Carrillo-Santarelli, 'An Assessment of the Colombian-FARC "Peace Jurisdiction" Agreement', *EJIL:Talk!* (29 September 2015) www.ejiltalk.org/an-assessment-of-the-colombian-farc-peace-jurisdiction-agreement/.

and instead that issue should be left to the UN Security Council which has the power to defer proceedings for the sake of international peace and security.[108] While the desire to avoid 'political' questions is understandable, scholars have argued that this approach understates the discretion that was granted by Statute drafters.[109]

Even more controversial still is the extent to which *feasibility* may be a consideration under the 'interests of justice'. When the Prosecutor sought authorization to open an investigation in Afghanistan – a situation which included wrongdoing by US forces on Afghan territory – a Pre-Trial Chamber declined to authorize the investigation, *inter alia* on the grounds that cooperation would not be forthcoming and hence that the investigation would not be feasible.[110] The decision was greeted with widespread criticism, because it suggested that powerful states could exempt themselves from scrutiny by being as obstructionist as possible.[111] The decision was overturned by the Appeals Chamber.[112]

8.10 COOPERATION

A national court may rely on local police to arrest suspects for the purpose of trial, and on local detention facilities to imprison them on conviction. The ICC has to rely entirely on the international community for these matters. Part 9 of the Statute requires states parties to cooperate with the Court in providing various forms of assistance, such as the taking of evidence and the tracing of assets. Article 89(1) imposes the all-important obligation to surrender any person found within a state's territory when the Court so requests.

As regards sentences of imprisonment imposed by the Court, there is no obligation on states to provide prison facilities. Instead, under Article 103, states can declare their willingness to accept sentenced persons.[113]

If a state that is obliged to cooperate fails to comply with a proper cooperation request from the Court, the Court may refer the matter to the Assembly of States Parties or, in the case of a referral by the Security Council, to the Council.[114] For example, Pre-Trial Chambers have referred Sudan's lack of cooperation with the Court to the Security Council.[115] To date, the Security Council has taken no action in response to reports by the Court on non-cooperation. The Assembly has no powers of enforcement and relies on

[108] See Article 16, discussed above in Section 8.6.2; and see Office of the Prosecutor, *Policy Paper on the Interests of Justice* (September 2007).
[109] Maria Varaki, 'Revisiting the "Interests of Justice" Policy Paper' (2017) 14 JICJ 455.
[110] *Situation in Afghanistan*, ICC PTC II, 12 April 2019 (ICC-02/17-33).
[111] Dapo Akande and Talita de Souza Dias, 'The ICC Pre-Trial Chamber Decision on the Situation in Afghanistan: A Few Thoughts on the Interests of Justice', *EJIL:Talk!* (18 April 2019), <ejiltalk.org>; Luis Moreno Ocampo, 'Deconstructing the International Criminal Court's Decision on Afghanistan', *Just Security* (24 April 2019), <justsecurity.org.>; Luca Poltronieri Rossetti, 'The Pre-Trial Chamber's Afghanistan Decision: A Step Too Far in the Judicial Review of Prosecutorial Discretion?' (2019) 17 *JICJ* 585; Kevin Jon Heller, 'The Appeals Chamber Got One Aspect of the Afghanistan Decision Very Wrong' (9 March 2020) <opiniojuris.org>; David Luban, 'The "Interests of Justice" at the ICC: A Continuing Mystery' (17 March 2020), <justsecurity.org>; Lloyd Chigowe, 'The ICC and the Situation in Afghanistan: A Critical Examination of the Role of the Pre-Trial Chambers in the Initiation of Investigations *Proprio Motu*' (2022) 35 *LJIL* 699.
[112] *Situation in Afghanistan*, ICC AC, 5 March 2020 (ICC-02/17-138). See further Chapter 17. [113] See Chapter 19.
[114] ICC Statute, Art. 87(7). [115] *Harun and Ali Kushayb*, ICC PTC I, 25 May 2010 (ICC-02/05–01/07–57).

public expressions of concern and informal good offices. In an ongoing review of the ICC's effectiveness, proposals have been made to strengthen responses to non-cooperation.[116]

The Prosecutor has to conduct investigations in situations of ongoing violence or conflict; thus security issues often present considerable challenges for the investigators and witnesses in the field. The possibilities of collecting evidence are often limited. Although the commission of atrocities may be common knowledge, information about incidents and command structures may be very difficult to obtain; local governments may be unwilling or unable to provide significant assistance; humanitarian organizations in the field may be reluctant to assist so as not to put at risk their continued presence; international peacekeeping missions may not have a wide enough mandate or may wish to avoid prejudicing their neutrality; and other governments may not wish to disclose evidence obtained by their intelligence services. Seen against such difficulties as these, the provisions of the Statute for enforcing the Court's requests have been described as 'paltry, at best'.[117]

8.11 OPPOSITION TO THE ICC

At the time its Statute was adopted, the ICC enjoyed strong support from much of the international community. However, some states voiced legal and political objections.[118] One criticism, advanced particularly by the United States, is that the ICC asserts jurisdiction over nationals of a state not a party to the Statute without that state's consent.[119] The US argues that such jurisdiction contradicts international law, since treaties cannot create obligations for non-party states without consent.[120] However, the Statute clearly does not impose any obligations on non-party states. The fact that a foreign court or tribunal may have jurisdiction over a state's *nationals*, on grounds such as territorial jurisdiction, is nothing new. For example, anyone travelling to an EU country becomes subject to EU laws and institutions, even though those were created by treaties to which one's home state is not party. This is a basic application of territorial sovereignty.

While it undoubtedly affects a state's *interests* that the Court may obtain jurisdiction over its nationals, that is not a ground for claiming that the Statute is contrary to international law. International law permits states, acting collectively, to delegate to an international court the jurisdiction which they would be entitled to exercise themselves, as was done for

[116] IER Report (n. 54), paras. 751–6; Olympia Bekou, 'The Independent Expert Review of the ICC: What Next for Cooperation?' (2022) 21 *Washington University Global Studies Law Review* 15; Jeremy Sarkin, 'Reforming the International Criminal Court to Achieve Increased State Cooperation in Investigations and Prosecutions of International Crimes' (2020) 9 *International Human Rights Law Review* 27.
[117] Leila Sadat and Richard Garden, 'The New International Criminal Court: An Uneasy Revolution' (2000) 88 *Georgetown Law Journal* 381, 389. See further Chapter 20 (cooperation) and 21 (immunities).
[118] See generally Dominic McGoldrick, 'Political and Legal Responses to the International Criminal Court' in McGoldrick et al., *The Permanent ICC*, 389.
[119] Under Art. 12. There is an extensive literature on the arguments; see e.g. Eve La Haye, 'The Jurisdiction of the International Criminal Court' (1999) 46 *Netherlands International Law Review* 1; M. Scharf, 'The ICC's Jurisdiction over the Nationals of Non-Party States: A Critique of the US Position' (2001) 64 *Law and Contemporary Problems* 98; Madeline Morris, 'High Crimes and Misconceptions: The ICC and Non Party States' (2000) 64 *Law and Contemporary Problems* 131; Frédéric Mégret, 'Epilogue to an Endless Debate: The International Criminal Court's Third Party Jurisdiction and the Looming Revolution of International Law' (2001) 12 *EJIL* 241; Dapo Akande, 'The Jurisdiction of the International Criminal Court over Nationals of Non-Parties: Legal Basis and Limits' (2003) 1 *JICJ* 618.
[120] Vienna Convention on the Law of Treaties, Art. 34.

example in the Nuremberg Tribunal.[121] Indeed, the US was a leading champion of inter-national tribunals (Nuremberg, Tokyo, ICTY, ICTR, and Special Court for Sierra Leone (SCSL)) and only had a distinct change of heart when confronted with an institution that might apply those same principles of accountability to its own actions.

Other provisions of the Statute have given rise to controversy.[122] Some arguments are based on a general mistrust of the ICC.[123] For example, one criticism is that states with effective legal systems do not have a complete guarantee that the Court will not take over the prosecutions of their nationals, because the Court itself gets to judge whether the national court is 'unable or unwilling' to deal with a case genuinely. On this view, the complementarity principle is not a reliable safeguard, since the ICC might misapply it.

This chapter will focus on the two most vocal sources of opposition to the ICC: the United States and the African Union.[124] Ironically, their concerns are almost diametrically opposed: that the Court is a tool of the weak intended to harass powerful actors, or that it is a tool of the strong to target less powerful actors.

8.11.1 United States

Under the Clinton Administration, the United States signed the ICC Statute on 31 December 2000, the last day that it was possible to do so. The Clinton Administration was not hostile to the goals of international justice, but was preoccupied with the possible chilling effect on US military operations, and the fear of frivolous proceedings against US service members.[125] In response to such concerns, several checks and balances were added to the Statute.

The Bush Administration brought much fiercer opposition to the ICC. In May 2002, the United States made clear its intention not to ratify the Statute, legally freeing it from any obligation not to undermine the object and purpose of the Statute.[126]

The Bush Administration took many steps to prevent the possibility of US nationals being tried by the Court. The American Service-Members' Protection Act prohibits US cooperation with the ICC, provides for the cessation of military and other aid to states parties which do not sign a non-surrender agreement with the United States, and authorizes the use of military force to release persons arrested by the ICC.[127]

---

[121] The Nuremberg judgment decided that that trial was justified on the basis that what states could do alone could be done together: '[T]hey have done together what any one of them might have done singly; for it is not to be doubted that any nation has the right thus to set up special courts to administer law' (Nuremberg IMT, Judgment and Sentences, reprinted in (1947) 41 *AJIL* 172, 216).

[122] See e.g. Michael Lohr and William Lietzau, 'One Road Away from Rome: Concerns Regarding the International Criminal Court' (1999) 9 *US Air Force Journal of Legal Studies* 33.

[123] John Bolton, 'The Risks and Weaknesses of the International Criminal Court from an American Perspective' (2000–1) 41 *Virginia Journal of International Law* 186; David Forsythe, 'The United States and International Criminal Justice' (2002) 24 *Human Rights Quarterly* 974.

[124] For discussion of the opposition of some other states, see Lu Jianping and Wang Zhixiang, 'China's Attitude Towards the ICC' (2005) 3 *JICJ* 608; Bakhtiyar Tuzmukhamedov, 'The ICC and Russian Constitutional Problems' (2005) 3 *JICJ* 621; Usha Ramanathan, 'India and the ICC' (2005) 3 *JICJ* 621; Hirad Abtahi, 'The Islamic Republic of Iran and the ICC' (2005) 3 *JICJ* 635.

[125] David Scheffer, 'A Negotiator's Perspective on the International Criminal Court' (2001) 167 *Military Law Review* 1.

[126] Vienna Convention on the Law of Treaties, Art. 18.

[127] 2002 Supplemental Appropriations Act for Further Recovery from and Response to Terrorist Attacks on the United States, as amended; see Sean Murphy, 'Contemporary Practice of the United States' (2002) 96 *AJIL* 975. Other US legislation, the

The United States also sought to use the Security Council to exempt US nationals from the Court's jurisdiction. The US at first threatened not to participate in peacekeeping missions unless it was granted immunity from the Court. Council members were hesitant to undermine the basic rules of jurisdiction and accountability, and suggested that the US simply withdraw its relatively few forces in those missions. The US then escalated its threat, declaring that it would veto the DRC peacekeeping mission and all subsequent missions, causing chaos in troubled situations around the world.[128] In the end, the highly controversial Security Council Resolution 1422 (2002) was pushed through. That Resolution invoked Article 16 (see Section 8.6.2), requiring the ICC to defer any cases concerning personnel from a contributing state not a party to the Rome Statute over acts or omissions relating to a United Nations operation. The Resolution was renewed for twelve months in 2003.[129] The following year, however, following abuses in Abu Ghraib, there was no longer majority support in the Security Council for such exemptions.

The Bush Administration also approached every country in the world to request a bilateral agreement not to surrender US nationals or officials to the ICC.[130] The United States threatened to withdraw military assistance and economic aid and to apply other sanctions, such as blocking membership in NATO, for countries that refused to sign. These agreements were highly controversial, because they were perceived as putting citizens of one country above the law, and as denying states' jurisdiction over their own territory. Many states refused to sign, and suffered losses of millions of dollars to programmes on matters such as counter-terrorism, drug trafficking, peace processes, wheelchair distribution, and HIV/AIDS education.[131] Over 100 states were convinced to sign such agreements. Eventually, the Bush Administration found that the campaign was counterproductive, as it was undermining programmes of cooperation that also benefited the United States, and other states such as China were stepping in to fill gaps in aid. US Secretary of State Condoleezza Rice observed that blocking aid to countries fighting terrorism is 'shooting ourselves in the foot'.[132]

The United States argued that Article 98(2) of the ICC Statute permitted such agreements. However, Article 98(2) was created to respect Status of Forces Agreements (SOFAs), which allow a state sending troops to another state to retain criminal jurisdiction over its troops for certain kinds of offences. Even with the broadest interpretation, Article 98(2) refers to a 'sending state', which at least requires that the person be 'sent' by the state, whereas the US agreements would protect all US nationals, including tourists.[133]

Foreign Relations Authorization Act (HR 3427), Public Law No. 106–113, §§ 705–706, of 29 November 1999 also bans US funding of the Court.

[128] See e.g. Aly Mokhtar, 'The Fine Art of Arm-Twisting: The US, Resolution 1422 and Security Council Deferral Power under the Rome Statute' (2002) 3 *ICLR* 295; Neha Jain, 'A Separate Law for Peacekeepers: The Clash Between the Security Council and the International Criminal Court' (2005) 16 *EJIL* 239; Carsten Stahn, 'The Ambiguities of Security Council Resolution 1422 (2002)' (2003) 14 *EJIL* 85.

[129] Resolution 1487(2003).   [130] For the text of one example, that of East Timor, see (2003) 97 *AJIL* 201.

[131] On the subject generally, see David Scheffer, 'Article 98(2) of the Rome Statute: America's Original Intent' (2005) 3 *JICJ* 333; Markus Benzing, 'US Bilateral Non-Surrender Agreements and Article 98 of the Statute of the International Criminal Court: An Exercise in the Law of Treaties' (2004) 8 *Max Planck Yearbook of United Nations Law* 182; Harmen van der Wilt, 'Bilateral Agreements Between the US and States Parties to the Rome Statute' (2005) 18 *LJIL* 93.

[132] Mark Mazzetti, 'U.S. Cuts in Africa Aid Said to Hurt War on Terror', *New York Times*, 23 July 2006.

[133] See e.g. EU Council of Ministers, 2459th Session, GAER Doc. 12134/02 (30 September 2002); reprinted in McGoldrick et al., *The Permanent ICC*, 430–1.

Relations thawed during the second term of the Bush Administration and during the Obama Administration. The Bush Administration allowed a Security Council referral to the ICC (Darfur), as did the Obama Administration (Libya). The Obama Administration participated in negotiations and provided modest forms of cooperation.

With the advent of the Trump Administration, the US returned to an overtly hostile approach, including threats against the ICC and its personnel. When the ICC opened an investigation in Afghanistan – a situation which could potentially include torture by US agents on Afghanistan territory – the US took the extraordinary action of imposing personal sanctions on anyone (1) involved in ICC investigations of US personnel; or (2) who 'materially assists' such investigations.[134] Under the order, US Secretary of State Pompeo imposed an asset freeze and travel ban on ICC Prosecutor Fatou Bensouda and staff member Phakiso Mochochoko. Such sanctions are normally reserved for terrorist organizations; the US measures were widely condemned.[135]

Under the Biden Administration, these executive orders were lifted. Furthermore, as the ICC opened an investigation into Ukraine, the US again shifted position to enable cooperation with the investigation.[136] Thus, the US position is highly variable, depending on the party in power and the political interests of the moment.

8.11.2 African Union

A large number of African states are parties to the ICC Statute,[137] and African states pressed to establish a Court and to ensure that crimes on the African continent are no longer neglected. However, relations between the ICC and some African states, and particularly with the African Union (AU) have become tense.

The AU has adopted resolutions urging non-cooperation with the Court. Resolutions of the AU Assembly have criticized the arrest warrant against President Al Bashir, noting 'the unfortunate consequences that the indictment has had on the delicate peace processes underway in the Sudan';[138] asked for the Security Council to request deferral of the proceedings against Al Bashir and the proceedings in the Libyan and Kenyan situations;[139] decided that member states should not cooperate in the execution of the arrest warrant against Al Bashir;[140] and expressed concern at the charges against the President and Deputy President of Kenya and their impact on peace efforts in Kenya.[141]

The most important accusation against the Court is that it applies double standards. At one point, in 2017, ten out of eleven situations were located in Africa, leading many to argue, understandably, that the Court is too focused on crimes in less powerful countries. Other points of contention are the possible impact on peace and security in the region, and

---

[134] US President, Executive Order on Blocking Property Of Certain Persons Associated With The International Criminal Court, 11 June 2020, <trumpwhitehouse.archives.gov>.
[135] Jennifer Hansler, 'US sanctions International Criminal Court officials, *CNN*, 2 September 2020 <cnn.com>.
[136] Natasha Bertrand and Jennifer Hansler, 'Biden to allow US to share evidence of Russian war crimes with International Criminal Court', *CNN*, 27 July 2023 <cnn.com>.
[137] Thirty-three as of April 2024. [138] Assembly/AU/December/3(XIII), 2009.
[139] See Assembly/AU/December/366(XVII), 2011. [140] *Ibid.* [141] Assembly/AU/13(XXI), 2013.

the view that heads of state should not be prosecuted while in office.[142] The AU position is not monolithic: many AU member states oppose the resolutions.

In response to concerns about an anti-African bias, the following counterpoints are often made. First, most of the African situations were taken on at the request of African states themselves, for example through self-referrals requesting the Court to intervene and assist with mass atrocities.[143] Two situations were referred by the Security Council, but one of those, Libya, was at the request of the new authorities. Even amidst the strongest AU backlash against the Court, Gabon, another African state, requested the Court's intervention in 2016.

Second, when one considers the Statute's criteria – jurisdiction, gravity, and complementarity – one sees that many of the gravest admissible situations within the Court's jurisdiction are indeed concentrated in parts of Africa that are currently undergoing instability. Some accuse the ICC of 'double standards' when it does not act in relation to situations outside its jurisdiction, but like all courts of law, the ICC must respect its legal jurisdictional limits.

Third, ICC officials respond that the Court's involvement is in support of African victims, who are being killed and harmed in great numbers.[144] Indeed, the frequent neglect of crimes in the region was the impetus for so many African states to support the creation of the ICC. Current accusations of neocolonialist intervention should be assessed in the context of the previous accusations that *failure* to act was a sign of Western racism, indifference, and double standards.[145]

Whatever the merits of the various arguments, the extreme preponderance of situations located on one continent in early ICC practice is problematic. A global institution should be seen to be acting in a greater diversity of situations, so that international justice is both done and seen to be done across the board.

In 2017, an AU resolution called for mass withdrawal from the ICC (although on closer inspection the document was less about withdrawal and more about reforming the ICC).[146] Three states announced their intention to withdraw in 2017: Burundi, the Gambia, and South Africa. Burundi, which had mass crimes on its territory, withdrew (however, the ICC initiated an investigation prior to the withdrawal date and retains jurisdiction over those crimes).[147] Gambia initiated withdrawal, but the regime was replaced by a new elected leadership, and the withdrawal was withdrawn. South Africa initiated a withdrawal, but it was halted by

---

[142] Christa Gaye Kerr, 'Sovereign Immunity, the AU and the ICC: Legitimacy Undermined' (2020) 41 *Michigan Journal of International Law* 195.

[143] Involvement in the Kenya situation was initiated under the prosecutor's *proprio motu* powers, but was based on government acceptance that the Court would act if local authorities failed to do so.

[144] See e.g. Fatou Bensouda, *The ICC: A Response to African Concerns* (10 October 2012) www.icc-cpi.int.

[145] See e.g. Makau Mutua, 'Never Again: Questioning the Yugoslav and Rwanda Tribunals' (1997) 11 *Temple International and Comparative Law Journal* 167; Kingsley Chiedu Moghalu, 'Image and Reality of War Crimes Justice: External Perceptions of the International Criminal Tribunal for Rwanda' (2002) 26 *Fletcher Forum of World Affairs* 21.

[146] African Union, *Withdrawal Strategy Document* (12 January 2017) www.hrw.org/sites/default/files/supporting_resources/icc_withdrawal_strategy_jan._2017.pdf; Mark Kersten, The African Union's 'ICC Withdrawal Strategy' (6 February 2017) www.justiceinconflict.org; Franziska Boehme, 'Exit, Voice and Loyalty: State Rhetoric about the International Criminal Court' (2018) 22 *International Journal of Human Rights* 420; Kurt Mills, '"Bashir is Dividing Us": Africa and the International Criminal Court' (2012) 34 *Human Rights Quarterly* 404.

[147] ICC Statute, Art. 127(2).

a domestic court decision. The Philippines government, under scrutiny for mass killings, also withdrew.[148] While withdrawals are regrettable for the broader project of international criminal law, it should be recalled that the ICC is the first international criminal law institution that even allows the possibility of withdrawal by the regimes that it monitors.[149]

In 2017, the Assembly of States Parties (ASP) held a session to discuss the AU concerns, and African states raised several important concerns: the over-focus on Africa; the fact that Security Council members can refer situations without joining the Court; immunities of head of states; the need to take better account of adverse consequences of interventions; more support for national prosecutions; and better engagement with governments.[150] Many African states voiced continued support for the Court, and measures have already been undertaken to address some concerns.[151] It is to be hoped that the Court and the ASP will try to better address legitimate concerns raised by the states that have been on the frontline of international justice, and indeed many measures have already been taken.

For instance, more recently, the Court has corrected course and finally begun to act in situations outside of Africa. These include the situations in Georgia, Afghanistan, Palestine, Myanmar/Bangladesh, Philippines, Venezuela, and Ukraine. The resulting docket is much more balanced, both in terms of regions and the power of the actors under scrutiny, although that will, of course, bring its own new challenges.

8.12 APPRAISAL

Assessments of the Court's record to date are mixed, and have grown increasingly negative, although there has been a resurgence of support following some very recent successful cases and steps taken to investigate in the Ukraine situation. The two most prevalent criticisms concern the paucity of concrete results from the Court, and the Court's earlier extensive focus on situations in Africa. Beyond that, a chorus of criticism reflects various contradictory expectations upon the Court.[152]

After twenty-two years of operations, the Court has produced only five convictions for core crimes, as well as several more for offences against the administration of justice (e.g. witness tampering). Several cases ended in acquittals, or were withdrawn due to insufficient evidence following witness intimidation, and in others charges were not confirmed. Acquittals are part of a healthy system of criminal justice, but the low rate of successful prosecutions suggests systemic dysfunctions.[153] As just one example, in the *Bemba* case,

---

[148] Jennifer Tridgell, 'The Departed: Implications of the Philippines' Withdrawal from the ICC', *Opinio Juris* (12 April 2018) <www.opiniojuris.org>.

[149] Darryl Robinson, 'Take the Long View of International Justice', *EJIL:Talk!* (24 October 2016) <www.ejiltalk.org>.

[150] Manisuli Ssenyonjo, 'African States Failed Withdrawal from the Rome Statute of the International Criminal Court: From Withdrawal Notifications to Constructive Engagement' (2017) 17 *ICLR* 749; Darryl Robinson, *Feeling a Way Forward for International Justice – ICC, Africa and the World* (22 November 2016) www.ejiltalk.org.

[151] Resolution on consultations pursuant to Art. 97(c) of the Rome Statute of the International Criminal Court, ICC-ASP/16/Res.3 (14 December 2017), clarifies the 'consultation mechanism' for states wishing to consult on a cooperation request.

[152] One issue of the *JICJ* focuses on such assessments and the many problems facing international criminal justice: (2013) 11(3) *JICJ*.

[153] Douglas Guilfoyle, 'This Is Not Fine: The International Criminal Court Is in Trouble', *EJIL:Talk!* (21 March 2019) www.ejiltalk.org.

a historic conviction for command responsibility over sexual violence, issued by a unanimous Trial Chamber, was overturned in a highly controversial split decision of the Appeals Chamber in 2018, based on a novel approach to appellate review.[154]

Different commentators point to different causes for the low conviction rate. The most common narrative is to ascribe the failures to inadequate investigations by the Office of the Prosecutor.[155] Early investigative practices of the Office of the Prosecutor were too focused on delivering fast results and produced evidence that was too thin. Other practices, such as using intermediaries to reach witnesses, have created problems when those intermediaries were unreliable. However, the narrative about thin cases may be too simplistic when the prosecution presents 77 witnesses and over 700 items of evidence (*Bemba* case), or 82 witnesses and over 4,500 items of evidence (*Gbagbo* case), of quality comparable to the evidence in other successful international prosecutions. Thus, some commentators point to problems arising from idiosyncratic interpretations of law by the judges, including evidentiary expectations and standards of review that are unprecedented in national or international jurisprudence.[156] A third possible cause is inadequate state cooperation and lack of support from the Security Council. Massive witness intimidation has led to the collapse of some cases, and persons have been prosecuted for witness tampering.[157] It seems likely that all of the above considerations have played a role in the delays and problems.

In response to these and other problems, the Assembly of States Parties established a far-reaching Independent Expert Review to prepare recommendations to improve the performance, efficiency, and effectiveness of the Court in 2019. The Panel produced a searching report with 384 recommendations, and the ASP and the organs of the ICC have been engaged in their implementation.[158]

Another set of criticisms concerns the high number of situations of situations in Africa, giving rise to accusations of bias, as discussed in Section 8.11.[159] Indeed, one of the deeper criticisms of the ICC and international criminal law in general is whether and to what extent these institutions are destined to reflect the structural inequality of the world. The ICC has at least rebalanced and diversified its focus, with several investigations outside of Africa, including in Afghanistan, Georgia, Myanmar/Bangladesh, Palestine, the Philippines, Venezuela, and Ukraine.

---

[154] *Prosecutor v Jean-Pierre Bemba Gombo*, ICC AC, ICC-01/05-01/08-xx, 8 June 2018; Leila Sadat, 'Fiddling While Rome Burns? The Appeals Chamber's Curious Decision in Prosecutor v Jean-Pierre Bemba Gombo', *EJIL:Talk!* (12 June 2018) ejiltalk.org; Diane Marie Amann, 'In Bemba and Beyond, Crimes Adjudged to Commit Themselves', *EJIL:Talk!* (13 June 2018) ejiltalk.org; Miles Jackson, 'Commanders' Motivations in Bemba', *EJIL:Talk!* (15 June 2018) ejiltalk.org; Jennifer Trahan, 'Bemba Acquittal Rests on an Erroneous Application of Appellate Review Standard' (25 June 2018), opiniojuris.org; Joseph Powderly and Naimh Hayes, 'The Bemba Appeal: A Fragmented Appeals Chamber Destabilises the Law and Practice of the ICC' (26 June 2018), *Human Rights Doctorate* (blog), humanrightsdoctorate.blogspot.com; Alex Whiting, 'Appeal Judges Turn the ICC on its Head with Bemba Decision' (14 June 2008), justsecurity.org; Susana SáCouto and Patricia Viseur Sellers, 'The Bemba Appeals Chamber Judgment: Impunity for Sexual and Gender-Based Crimes' (2019) 27 *Wm & Mary Bill Rts J* 599.
[155] Maxence Peniguet and Thierry Cruvellier, 'Acquittal of Gbagbo and Blé Goudé: A Hammering for the Prosecutor's Office', *JusticeInfo.Net* (15 January 2019) www.justiceinfo.net.
[156] Sadat, 'Fiddling' (n. 154); Trahan, 'Bemba' (n. 154); Ben Batros, 'The ICC Acquittal of Gbagbo: What Next for Crimes against Humanity?', *Just Security* (18 January 2019) www.justsecurity.org; Paul Bradfield, 'No Case to Answer? Show Me the (Standard of) Proof!', *Opinio Juris* (20 January 2019) www.opiniojuris.org.
[157] See e.g. *Ruto and Sang*, ICC TC V, 5 April 2016; *Bemba et al.*, ICC AC, 8 March 2018. [158] IER Report (n. 54).
[159] See John Dugard, 'Palestine and the International Criminal Court: Institutional Failure or Bias?' (2013) 11 *JICJ* 563.

In addition to good-faith grievances and disagreements, sophisticated and well-resourced misinformation campaigns have creatively and successfully expanded on such themes to undermine perceptions of the Court and to distract from its inquiries into mass atrocities.[160]

Other criticisms reflect the high and often contradictory expectations that have been placed on the Court. ICC investigations are expected to be fast, comprehensive, and inexpensive, even while carried out in uncontrolled territories without extensive external support, and yet also meet the highest procedural and evidentiary standards. ICC investigations are frequently condemned for falling short on any one of these contradictory requirements. As these expectations cannot all be satisfied, a more feasible set of priorities and expectations must be developed. Furthermore, the Court is continuously criticized for intervening too late or too soon, for reaching too high or too low, for being too close to states or too distant, and for being too deferential or too imperious. Each of these criticisms sounds plausible in isolation, but a more measured perspective would notice the outright contradictions and trade-offs in competing goals.[161]

Budget is another perennial issue. International criminal justice is expensive, although not out of line with comparably complex domestic proceedings.[162] The Court has a substantial budget, but it also deals with more situations than all other international tribunals combined. Resource limits are restraining its ability to launch important cases.

On a more positive note, the Court is arguably finding its footing. Important trials concerning Dominic Ongwen (of the Lord's Resistance Army) and Bosco Ntaganda ended with convictions, showing that the Court can carry out investigations and trials in difficult situations, in a gender-competent and gender-sensitive manner. Several other trials are underway. The Court has launched seven situation investigations in regions other than Africa, providing a more representative and varied docket. The investigation in Ukraine appears to have re-invigorated enthusiasm for the Court.[163] Of course, the latest investigations – affecting the interests of influential states such as the United States, Israel, and Russia – bring with them new challenges and criticisms from powerful actors. For example, when the ICC issued an arrest warrant against Vladimir Putin for directing crimes in Ukraine, Russia responded with arrest warrants against ICC judges and the Prosecutor for 'unlawful accusations' and 'unlawful decisions'.[164]

At the moment, the most tangible successes in international criminal law lie in national implementation and prosecution.[165] The Rome Statute system has contributed to an

---

[160] See e.g. 'Kenya's Social Media Election: Attack Ads and Data Mining', *Sunday Times* (17 July 2017); Janet Anderson and Benjamin Duerr, 'In a Storm of Lies and Half-truths: The Role of Media Professionals in Spreading and Combatting Misinformation about the International Criminal Court' (2022) 20 *JICJ* 191; Sara Ochs, 'Fake News & International Criminal Law' (2021) 66 *St. Louis University Public Law Review.*

[161] Darryl Robinson, 'Inescapable Dyads: Why the International Criminal Court Cannot Win' (2015) 28 *LJIL* 323.

[162] Daniel McLaughlin, *International Criminal Tribunals: A Visual Overview* (New York, 2013) 77, www.leitnercenter.org; Stuart Ford, 'What Investigative Resources Does the International Criminal Court Need to Succeed?: A Gravity-Based Approach' (2017) 16 *Washington University Global Studies Law Review* 1.

[163] Milena Sterio, 'The Ukraine Crisis and the Future of International Court and Tribunals' (2023) 55 *Case Western Reserve Journal of International Law* 479.

[164] Leila Sackur, 'Russia issues retaliatory arrest warrant for International Criminal Court prosecutor', *NBC News* (20 May 2023) <nbcnews.com>.

[165] Marieke Wierda, *The Local Impact of the International Criminal Court: From Law to Justice* (Cambridge, 2023); Patrick Labuda, *International Criminal Tribunals and Domestic Accountability: In the Court's Shadow* (Oxford, 2023).

increase in national legislation and judicial capacity. Several countries, in all geographic latitudes, are engaging in prosecutions of international crimes, with assistance and encouragement from the ICC and states parties. The Rome Statute system has contributed to an upsurge in accountability for mass atrocities.

Further Reading

Kai Ambos, *Treatise on International Criminal Law*, 2nd ed. (Oxford, 2021) vol. I

Kai Ambos (ed.), *The Rome Statute of the International Criminal Court: A Commentary*, 4th ed. (Oxford, 2022)

Olympia Bekou and Robert Cryer (eds.), *The International Criminal Court* (Abingdon, 2005)

Antonio Cassese, Paola Gaeta, and John R. W. D. Jones (eds.), *The Rome Statute of the International Criminal Court: A Commentary* (Oxford, 2002)

Charles Jalloh and Ilias Bantekas (eds.), *The International Criminal Court and Africa* (Oxford, 2017)

Mark Kersten, *Justice in Conflict: The Effects of the International Criminal Court's Interventions on Ending Wars and Building Peace* (Oxford, 2016)

Philippe Kirsch and John Holmes, 'The Rome Conference of an International Criminal Court: The Negotiating Process' (1999) 93 *AJIL* 2

Jann Kleffner, *Complementarity in the Rome Statute and National Criminal Jurisdictions* (Oxford, 2008)

Roy Lee (ed.), *The International Criminal Court: The Making of the Rome Statute* (The Hague, 1999)

Sarah Nouwen, *Complementarity in the Line of Fire: The Catalysing Effect of the International Criminal Court in Uganda and Sudan* (Cambridge, 2013)

Steven Roach, *Governance, Order and the International Criminal Court: Between Realpolitik and a Cosmopolitan Court* (Oxford, 2009)

Leila Sadat, *The International Criminal Court and the Transformation of International Law* (New York, NY, 2002)

Philippe Sands (ed.), *From Nuremberg to the Hague: The Future of International Criminal Justice* (Cambridge, 2003) chs. 2 and 4

William Schabas, *The International Criminal Court: A Commentary on the Rome Statute* 2nd ed. (Oxford, 2016)

William Schabas, *An Introduction to the International Criminal Court*, 5th ed. (Cambridge, 2017)

Benjamin Schiff, *Building the International Criminal Court* (Cambridge, 2008)

Carsten Stahn, *The Law and Practice of the International Criminal Court* (Oxford, 2015)

Carsten Stahn and Mohamed El Zeidy (eds.), *The International Criminal Court and Complementarity* (Cambridge, 2011)

9

Other Hybrid and Special Courts

9.1 INTRODUCTION

Following the establishment of modern international criminal tribunals and courts in the 1990s, several other judicial institutions with international elements, variously referred to as 'internationalized', 'hybrid', 'mixed', or 'special', have been set up. The attractiveness of this model is that such courts would be able to overcome the known operational limitations and legitimacy deficits of international criminal jurisdictions, which are expensive and operate away from the state in question for security and logistical reasons. Hybrid tribunals are often embedded in the local justice system. Therefore, they are better placed to address sovereignty concerns and empower the state emerging from conflict or transitional period. They also promote local ownership of the accountability processes, enable a more active involvement by victims and affected communities, and build judicial and prosecutorial capacity in post-conflict societies while delivering credible, yet less costly, justice.[1] A hybrid tribunal may present a viable alternative in situations where the International Criminal Court (ICC) cannot exercise jurisdiction or where a new international court cannot be established due to insufficient support by the international community.

Different models for internationalized courts have been deployed depending on the political circumstances which accompanied their establishment, the relevant legal context, and the preferences of the actors involved. There is not a single agreed definition of mixed or hybrid courts, and various classifications may be proffered.[2] The legal basis for the establishment will serve as the ground for typology of hybrid courts and the organizing principle of this chapter. Accordingly, the following broad classes of internationalized jurisdictions can be distinguished: (1) courts established by an agreement, being either a bilateral agreement between a state and an international organization (such as the United Nations, the European Union, or the African Union) or a multilateral agreement between (regional) states; (2) courts established by an international transitional administration temporarily replacing weak or unavailable domestic institutions; and (3) courts established and administered by a state under national law but with international support.

---

[1] E.g. Laura A. Dickinson, 'The Promise of Hybrid Courts' (2003) 97 *AJIL* 295, 302–7.
[2] E.g. Sarah Williams, *Hybrid and Internationalized Criminal Tribunals: Selected Jurisdictional Issues* (Oxford, 2012) 249–51 (distinguishing between hybrid and internationalized tribunals).

Insofar as each of these hybrid institutions will have a primary and direct legal basis either in international or national law, it could appropriately be labelled as either (domesticated) international or (internationalized) domestic. 'Hybrid court' is not a legal term of art but rather an imperfect descriptive label conveying a distinct combination of international and national elements with respect to composition, applicable law, substantive jurisdiction, and so on. In other words, hybridity is a matter of degree. The proliferation of forms of international participation in domestic accountability mechanisms precludes neat categorization. The existing hybrid models do not exhaust any possible future options, whether in terms of the degree of national control over decision-making, applicable substantive and procedural law, or funding schemes.

The following sections (9.2–9.4) describe the different types of hybrid tribunals and set out the features of various experiments that account for the institutional diversity in this area. The chapter also zeroes in on the arrangements of individual courts in the political and legal context which shaped them. The ICC is typically seen as the centrepiece of the system and a preferred option for international criminal adjudication. However, this overstates the ICC's position, capped by limited temporal jurisdiction, complementarity, and inherent resource constraints. Moreover, even where the ICC has jurisdiction, alternative solutions may still be preferred for legal, practical, or political reasons (Section 9.5). These arguments attest to the continued need for, and relevance of, internationalized courts in the future.

9.2 COURTS ESTABLISHED BY AGREEMENT BETWEEN A STATE AND AN INTERNATIONAL ORGANIZATION OR BETWEEN STATES

The Special Court for Sierra Leone (SCSL) and the Residual SCSL, the Extraordinary Chambers in the Courts of Cambodia (ECCC), and the Special Tribunal for Lebanon (STL) are examples of hybrid courts created by bilateral agreements between the UN and the respective state's government. In the case of the STL, the Security Council brought the provisions of the agreement into effect by a resolution under Chapter VII of the UN Charter, providing the Tribunal with a multilateral treaty basis. The Extraordinary African Chambers (EAC) were established by an agreement between Senegal and the African Union (AU). The ECCC and EAC formed part of the domestic judiciaries while the SCSL and STL were separate entities. All courts have (or had) both international and national officials and adjudicated primarily international crimes in practice. Only the STL dealt with terrorism and related offences under the Lebanese Criminal Code. If established, the Criminal Chamber in the African Court of Justice and Human and People's Rights will exercise jurisdiction over a broader range of international and transnational crimes.

9.2.1 Special Court for Sierra Leone and Residual Special Court

Almost a decade of violent civil war began in 1991 when a rebel group, the Revolutionary United Front (RUF), entered Sierra Leone from neighbouring Liberia, aiming to overthrow the government. The ensuing stages of the conflict featured all forms of gross human rights violations committed by various warring factions including the RUF, Armed Forces Revolutionary Council (AFRC), and the Civil Defence Forces (CDF). But it was particularly characterized by the use of child soldiers and widespread mutilation of civilians by amputation of limbs. The conflict ended in 2000 with the intervention of a British force and a large UN peacekeeping presence.

The SCSL was established by a treaty between Sierra Leone and the UN. A request from the President of Sierra Leone to the Security Council for the creation of a special court to deal with crimes committed in the civil war led to a Council Resolution requesting the Secretary-General to enter into negotiations with Sierra Leone.[3] An agreement between the government and the UN Secretary-General, attaching the Statute of the Court, was concluded on 16 January 2002.[4] Thereafter, Sierra Leone adopted implementing legislation,[5] and the SCSL began work in July 2002.

The UN Secretary-General has described the SCSL as 'a treaty-based *sui generis* court of mixed jurisdiction and composition'.[6] The international judges, who were appointed by the UN Secretary-General, formed a majority; a minority was appointed by the government of Sierra Leone. The UN also appointed the Prosecutor and the Registrar, and Sierra Leone a Deputy Prosecutor.

Unlike the UN ad hoc Tribunals, the SCSL was not a subsidiary organ of the UN Security Council but a separate international institution. That it was nonetheless a stepsister of the Tribunals is attested by the statutory provision directing the SCSL Appeals Chamber to seek guidance in their Appeals Chamber's decisions.[7] As clarified in the Sierra Leonean implementing legislation, the SCSL was not part of the Sierra Leonean legal system. The SCSL Statute provided that the SCSL and national courts of Sierra Leone had concurrent jurisdiction, but the SCSL had primacy.[8] Its judge-adopted Rules of Procedure and Evidence (RPE) were based on those of the International Criminal Tribunal for Rwanda (ICTR) and amended at their own pace to meet the SCSL's needs.[9]

Having established its competence to determine its own jurisdiction, the SCSL dismissed several legality challenges. It found that the Sierra Leonean government and the UN Secretary-General had the powers to agree to establish the Court and that this act was compatible with the Lomé Peace Agreement.[10] With reference to the International Court of Justice (ICJ)'s *DRC* v. *Belgium* judgment, the SCSL established that immunity did not bar

---

[3] SC Res. 1315(2000), 14 August 2000.
[4] Agreement between the United Nations and the Government of Sierra Leone, 16 January 2002, 2178 UNTS 13, and the Statute of the SCSL, both available at the Residual Special Court's website, www.rscsl.org.
[5] Special Court Agreement (2002) Ratification Act, Supplement to Sierra Leone Official Gazette, Vol. 130, No. 2, 7 March 2002 (as amended).
[6] Report by the Secretary-General on the Establishment of a Special Court for Sierra Leone, UN Doc. S/2000/915 (4 October 2000) para. 9 ('Report on SCSL Statute').
[7] SCSL Statute, Art. 20(3).   [8] *Ibid*. Art. 8. On *ne bis in idem*, see *ibid*. Art. 9.
[9] *Ibid*. Art. 14. The SCSL RPE were amended in total fourteen times. One peculiarity, intended to speed up the process, was that jurisdictional challenges were heard by the Appeals Chamber as the first and last instance: SCSL RPE, r. 72.
[10] *Kallon, Norman and Kamara*, SCSL AC, 13 March 2004; *Kallon and Kamara*, SCSL AC, 13 March 2004; *Fofana*, SCSL AC, 25 May 2004 (UN competence); and *Gbao*, SCSL AC, 25 May 2004. See Peace Agreement between the Government of Sierra Leone and the Revolutionary United Front of Sierra Leone (RUF), signed on 7 July 1999 after a meeting in Lomé, Togo ('Lomé Peace Agreement').

prosecution at the SCSL of a head of state (President Taylor of Liberia) because it was an international court.[11] This is controversial, however, as Liberia was not a party to the SCSL Agreement, nor had the head of state immunity been lifted by Liberia or the Security Council.[12] The SCSL also confirmed that the amnesty granted in the Lomé Peace Agreement did not bar prosecution of international crimes at the SCSL.[13] In fact, this was one motive behind seeking an internationalized solution.

The SCSL had jurisdiction over persons 'who bear the greatest responsibility for serious violations of international humanitarian law and Sierra Leonean law' committed in the territory of Sierra Leone since 30 November 1996.[14] The reference to 'greatest responsibility' was intended as guidance for a prosecutorial policy rather than a formal limitation of jurisdiction.[15] The SCSL was meant to target a limited number of perpetrators and to have a short period of operation. Offences by peacekeepers and related personnel were, with some exceptions, left to the jurisdiction of the sending state.[16] One controversial issue was what to do with the many child soldiers who had committed serious crimes during the civil war. The solution adopted in the Statute was to exclude jurisdiction over children under the age of fifteen at the time of the crime and to include special provisions about treatment before and after conviction of juvenile offenders (between fifteen and eighteen years of age).[17]

Owing to the nature of the conflict, the SCSL's subject-matter jurisdiction was confined to crimes against humanity and to war crimes committed in a non-international armed conflict.[18] Yet, the Court decided that the war crimes within its jurisdiction might be prosecuted regardless of the nature of the armed conflict.[19] The Court's jurisdiction also covered some specified crimes under Sierra Leonean law, but they were not prosecuted in practice.[20] The definition of crimes against humanity was inspired by, but not identical to, the definition in the ICTR Statute. The inclusion of recruitment of child soldiers in the list of war crimes in Article 3 was challenged as a breach of the principle of legality, but the Court determined that this crime had a basis in customary international law before November 1996.[21]

The Court indicted a total of thirteen suspects; two indictments were subsequently withdrawn owing to the death of the accused. Three joint trials of nine accused, the members of RUF, AFRC, and CDF, took place, and eight persons were convicted on charges of war crimes and crimes against humanity. On appeal, the convictions and

---

[11] *Taylor*, SCSL AC, 31 May 2004; see further Chapter 21. See also *Case concerning the Arrest Warrant of 11 April 2000 (Democratic Republic of the Congo* v. *Belgium*), ICJ, Judgment of 14 February 2002. For a commentary, see Micaela Frulli, 'The Question of Charles Taylor's Immunity' (2004) 2 *JICJ* 1118.

[12] See Section 21.4.4.

[13] SCSL Statute, Art. 10; *Kallon and Kamara*, SCSL AC, 13 March 2004. Cf. Lomé Peace Agreement, Art. IX. See Chapter 22.

[14] SCSL Statute, Art. 1(1). The date relates to an earlier peace agreement between the government of Sierra Leone and the RUF, signed in Abidjan on 30 November 1996 ('Abidjan Peace Agreement').

[15] UN Secretary-General, Report on SCSL Statute (n. 6) para. 30; *Kallon, Kamara and Kanu*, SCSL AC, 3 March 2008, paras. 272–85.

[16] SCSL Statute, Art. 1(2) and (3).

[17] *Ibid.* Arts. 7, 15(5) and 19(1). As a practical matter, no charges were brought against those under eighteen.

[18] *Ibid.* Arts. 2–4. [19] *Fofana*, SCSL AC, 25 May 2004.

[20] SCSL Statute, Art. 5 (offences related to abuse of girls and wanton destruction of property).

[21] *Norman*, SCSL AC, 31 May 2004; cf. Dissenting Opinion of Justice Robertson (asserting that non-forcible enlistment had first entered international criminal law with the ICC Statute in 1998).

sentences in two of the cases were largely upheld.[22] The third case, against members of the government-associated CDF, proved controversial. The majority found the accused guilty of some of the charges, but one Sierra Leonean judge on the trial bench argued for full acquittals on the basis that the actions of the CDF were primarily dictated by necessity.[23] The relatively lenient sentences imposed were disputed.[24] The Appeals Chamber's majority reversed the judgment with respect to some counts and increased the sentences substantially. Again, a Sierra Leonean member of the Chamber ruled in favour of acquittal and lenient sentences since the CDF fought 'for the restoration of the democratically elected Government'.[25] The Appeals Chamber majority thus honoured the principle that all parties to a conflict are subject to the same rules and liable for the same punishment in case of violations.

The last SCSL defendant was the former President of Liberia, Charles Taylor, who was convicted on eleven counts of crimes against humanity and war crimes by the Trial Chamber and sentenced to fifty years' imprisonment.[26] The trial was held at the premises of the ICC in The Hague, by special arrangement owing to security concerns.[27] While one accused (Johnny Paul Koroma) was rumoured to have died, arrangements have been made for his trial in another jurisdiction if he is alive and captured.[28] Taylor's conviction and sentence were reaffirmed on appeal,[29] and, hence, the SCSL finished all its cases in 2013, the first modern tribunal to complete its mandate.

The SCSL was plagued by budgeting problems throughout its existence, as it was funded entirely through voluntary contributions. Nevertheless, it left behind a substantial legacy, including the clarification of international criminal law principles, first practice with regard to the use of child soldiers and attacks against peacekeepers as a war crime, and forced marriage as 'other inhumane act' of crimes against humanity, and institutional and procedural innovations.[30] Located in Sierra Leone, it was intended to contribute to national peace and stability and to the long-lasting development of the domestic justice system and national institutions through 'legacy projects'.

After the SCSL closed down, it was succeeded by the Residual Special Court for Sierra Leone (RSCSL) which continues its jurisdiction, functions, and powers in accordance with the Agreement between the UN and the Sierra Leonean government.[31] The RSCSL is a small body that supervises the enforcement of sentences and reviews applications for early release, provides witness and victim protection, and maintains SCSL archives. Whilst its primary seat is in Sierra Leone, it has an interim seat in the Netherlands with a sub-office

---

[22] *Brima, Kamara and Kanu*, SCSL TC II, 20 June 2007, and SCSL AC, 22 February 2008; *Sesay, Kallon and Gbao*, SCSL TC I, 2 March 2009, and SCSL AC, 26 October 2009.

[23] *Fofana and Kondewa*, SCSL TC I, 2 August 2007; cf. Separate Concurring and Partially Dissenting Opinion of Hon. Justice Bankole Thompson, para. 100.

[24] *Fofana and Kondewa*, SCSL TC I, 9 October 2007.

[25] *Fofana and Kondewa*, SCSL AC, 28 May 2008; cf. Partially Dissenting Opinion of Hon. Justice George Gelaga King, para. 93.

[26] *Taylor*, SCSL TC II, 18 May 2012 and 30 May 2012.   [27] See SC Res. 1688(2006), 16 June 2006.

[28] Rule 11*bis*, added to the SCSL RPE on 27 May 2008.   [29] *Taylor*, SCSL AC, 26 September 2013.

[30] E.g. Charles Chernor Jalloh (ed.), *The Sierra Leone Special Court and its Legacy: The Impact for Africa and International Criminal Law* (Cambridge, 2013).

[31] Agreement between the United Nations and the Government of Sierra Leone on the Establishment of Residual Special Court for Sierra Leone, 11 August 2010, ratified by Sierra Leone through the Residual Special Court for Sierra Leone (Ratification) Act, 2011. Annexed to the agreement is the Residual SCSL Statute.

in Sierra Leone.[32] It has a President and the Trial and Appeals Chambers, to which international and national judges are assigned from a roster and may be called to serve upon need, and the Prosecutor and Registrar who are appointed by the UN Secretary-General.[33]

9.2.2 Extraordinary Chambers in the Courts of Cambodia

Another approach was followed to deal with the atrocities committed during the Khmer Rouge rule in Cambodia under Pol Pot, which lasted from 1975 to 1979 when the regime was ousted by invading Vietnamese forces. During these years an estimated 1.7 million people died by execution, starvation, and forced labour.

The introduction of the ECCC was the culmination of a long process which began with a request from Cambodia to the UN for assistance in bringing Khmer Rouge officials to justice, followed by a UN expert group report recommending the establishment of an ad hoc Tribunal.[34] Cambodia insisted on a domestic solution, however, and negotiations between the Cambodian government and the UN started in 1999. They broke down in 2002 and the UN Secretary-General withdrew from the process having concluded that the Cambodian court, as then envisaged, would not guarantee the required independence, impartiality, and objectivity. Cambodia wished to retain full control over the institution and found the terms of UN assistance under the proposed UN–Cambodia agreement unacceptable.

Nevertheless, later in 2002, the UN General Assembly requested the Secretary-General to resume negotiations towards establishing the Chambers modelled on Cambodian law.[35] When an agreement between the UN and the Royal Government of Cambodia was finally concluded, it was adopted by the General Assembly in May 2003,[36] and ratified by the Cambodian National Assembly in October 2004.[37] As any international agreement, it is subject to the law of treaties and cannot be circumvented by Cambodian legislation.

Unlike the SCSL, the ECCC formed part of the judicial system of Cambodia and applied municipal law. Its Pre-Trial Chamber (PTC), however, concluded that the ECCC has distinctive features and is an entirely 'independent entity within the Cambodian court structure'.[38] It can be regarded as a domestic court assisted by the UN in accordance with a bilateral agreement.[39] The Chambers had jurisdiction to try 'senior leaders of Democratic Kampuchea and those most responsible for the crimes and serious violations of Cambodian

---

[32] Residual SCSL Statute, Art. 6.
[33] *Ibid.* Arts. 11–15. There are no fewer than sixteen judges on the roster, who are remunerated on a pro-rata basis if called upon by the President to serve. See Art. 11(1).
[34] See e.g. Helen Jarvis, 'Trials and Tribulations: The Long Quest for Justice for the Cambodian Genocide' in Simon M. Meisenberg and Ignaz Stegmiller (eds.), *The Extraordinary Chambers in the Courts of Cambodia: Assessing their Contribution to International Criminal Law* (The Hague, 2016) ch. 2.
[35] GA Res. 57/228A, 18 December 2002.
[36] GA Res. 57/228B, 13 May 2003 (to which the UN–Cambodia Agreement is attached).
[37] UN–Cambodia Agreement, Arts. 2 and 31. The agreement is implemented by Cambodian national legislation (*Kram*) under which the ECCC operate: Law on the Establishment of Extraordinary Chambers in the Courts of Cambodia for the Prosecution of Crimes Committed during the Period of Democratic Kampuchea, NS/RKM/1004/006 (2004).
[38] *Kaing Guek Eav*, ECCC PTC, 3 December 2007, paras. 17–20.
[39] The UN Assistance Mission to Khmer Rouge Trials (UNAKRT) provided technical assistance to the ECCC: see www.unakrt-online.org/.

penal law, international humanitarian law and custom, and international conventions recognised by Cambodia'.[40]

The material jurisdiction covered genocide under the 1948 Genocide Convention, crimes against humanity as defined in the ICC Statute, grave breaches of the Geneva Conventions, and certain other crimes under Cambodian law.[41] War crimes in non-international armed conflicts were not covered because Cambodia was not party to the Additional Protocols before 1980 and there were doubts as to the customary status of these crimes when they were committed.[42] The temporal jurisdiction was retroactive and limited to crimes committed between 17 April 1975 and 6 January 1979. Given the death of Pol Pot in April 1998, the one person probably most responsible never stood trial.

The mixed composition of the Chambers and the prosecution was a matter of dispute during the negotiations with the UN. The Cambodian side insisted on having a majority of national judges in the Pre-Trial, Trial, and Supreme Court Chambers. For balance, a qualified majority is required for any decision: four out of five Pre-Trial and Trial Chamber judges and five out of seven Supreme Court Chamber judges.[43] This is a difficult solution which could result in deadlock and an acquittal even if all the international judges vote for a conviction; for a decision to pass, at least one international judge should cast a vote in favour along with Cambodian judges.

The UN–Cambodia Agreement stipulates that the ECCC's procedures shall be in accordance with Cambodian procedural law.[44] Owing to the civil law origin of the Cambodian criminal procedure, investigative judges were responsible for the investigations. The Office of Co-Investigating Judges was formed by one international and one local judge operating together, with disagreements being resolved by a PTC, again with Cambodian judges in the majority.[45] A similar scheme applied to the two Co-Prosecutors.[46] All the judges and prosecutors were appointed by the Cambodian Supreme Council of Magistracy, although the international officials were nominated by the UN Secretary-General.

Hence, the ECCC was domestic in nature both with respect to the majority of local judges and regarding applicable law. However, a 'super-majority' required for decision-making ensured a degree of international control. In part of applicable procedural law, the agreement stated that the procedure shall be in accordance with Cambodian law, but it also allowed guidance to be sought from 'procedural rules established at the international level' where the Cambodian law was absent, unclear, or deficient in light of international standards.[47] Thus, the ECCC judges adopted Internal Rules (IR) in order to 'consolidate applicable Cambodian procedure for proceedings before the ECCC' and to address gaps and inconsistencies with international fair trial standards.[48] The procedure reflected the

---

[40] UN–Cambodia Agreement, Art. 1. [41] *Ibid.* Art. 9.
[42] Report of the Group of Experts for Cambodia Established Pursuant to General Assembly Resolution 52/135, UN Doc. A/53/850-S/1999/231 (16 March 1999) paras. 72–5.
[43] UN–Cambodia Agreement, Arts. 3(2), 4(1) and 7(2). [44] *Ibid.* Art. 12. [45] *Ibid.* Arts. 5 and 7. See also Internal Rules, r. 72.
[46] *Ibid.* Art. 6 and Internal Rules, r. 71. [47] *Ibid.* Art. 12(1).
[48] ECCC IR, 12 June 2007, Preamble. The IR were amended ten times (Rev. 10, 27 October 2021). Following a defence challenge to the judicial power to promulgate the detailed IR, the ECCC upheld their constitutionality and superiority vis-à-vis Cambodian law: *Nuon Chea*, ECCC PTC, 26 August 2008, paras. 14–15, and 25 February 2009.

civil law scheme based on judicial rather than party-led investigations,[49] and allowed victims to participate and to request moral and collective reparations as civil parties.[50]

The efforts to insulate the ECCC from political pressure by the Cambodian government have not been successful, raising serious issues of prosecutorial and judicial independence and compromising the UN's involvement.[51] Moreover, the ECCC's unique institutional and procedural features tended to undermine its efficient operation. The pronounced division between national and international officials required the complicated and lengthy process of settling disagreements by yet another divided body, the PTC. The combination of full-length judicial investigations as per civil law procedure with largely adversarial trials led to protracted proceedings.[52]

The ECCC's first case was that of Kaing Guek Eav (Duch), the head of the infamous Tuol Sleng prison (S21), who had been detained since 1999. Duch actively cooperated with the ECCC investigation and provided detailed information about the crimes at trial.[53] Ultimately, he was convicted of crimes against humanity, war crimes, and the domestic offences of murder and torture and sentenced to life imprisonment.[54] Case 002 concerned four surviving leaders of the Khmer Rouge charged with genocide, crimes against humanity, and war crimes. As a result of Ieng Sary's death and Ieng Thirith's unfitness to stand trial,[55] only Nuon Chea ('Brother No. 2') and Khieu Samphan remained in the case. Given their frail state of health, the trial had to be conducted in two segments, both resulting in convictions and life sentences.[56]

The Cambodian government did not want the ECCC to take on further cases, referring to their potentially adverse impact on national reconciliation and stability. Although cases 003 and 004 were opened due to the PTC's inability to reach the required 'super-majority',[57] all ECCC organs remained split along national/international lines throughout, creating the perception that the Cambodian officials did not act impartially. The unresolved dispute on whether the defendants were the 'most responsible persons' within the ECCC's personal jurisdiction precluded trials against Meas Muth (003), Ao An (004/02), and Yim Tith (004).[58] The charges against Im Chaem (004/01) were dismissed for the lack of personal jurisdiction after the investigation, and the PTC did not reach a super-majority to overturn that decision.[59]

---

[49] Internal Rules, rr. 55–69. [50] *Ibid.* rr. 23*bis*–23*quinquies*, 80*bis*(4), 90–91, 94, 100, etc.

[51] E.g. Diane Orentlicher, "'Worth the Effort'? Assessing the Khmer Rouge Tribunal" (2020) 18(3) *JICJ* 615–40.

[52] See e.g. Sergey Vasiliev, 'Trial Process at the ECCC: The Rise and Fall of the Inquisitorial Paradigm in International Criminal Law?' in Simon M. Meisenberg and Ignaz Stegmiller (eds.), *The Extraordinary Chambers in the Courts of Cambodia: Assessing their Contribution to International Criminal Law* (The Hague, 2016) ch. 15.

[53] See Thierry Cruvellier, *Master of Confessions: The Making of a Khmer Rouge Torturer* (New York, 2014); Alexander Hinton, *Man or Monster? The Trial of a Khmer Rouge Torturer* (Durham, 2016).

[54] *Kaing Guek Eav*, ECCC TC, 26 July 2010 (sentencing Duch to twenty-five years in prison) and ECCC SCC, 3 February 2012 (amending the sentence to life imprisonment).

[55] Ieng Thirith died on 22 April 2015 and proceedings against her were discontinued.

[56] Case 002/01: *Nuon Chea and Khieu Samphan*, ECCC TC, 7 August 2014 and ECCC SCC, 23 November 2016; Case 002/02: *Nuon Chea and Khieu Samphan*, ECCC TC, 16 November 2018, 2229–32; *Khieu Samphan*, ECCC SCC, 23 December 2022, 825 (affirmed on appeal). Nuon Chea died on 4 August 2019 aged ninety-three.

[57] Cases 003 and 004, ECCC PTC, 18 August 2009.

[58] Case 003 (*Meas Muth*), ECCC PTC, 17 April 2021, 40 and SCC, 17 December 2021, para. 44; Case 004/02 (Ao An), ECCC SCC, 10 August 2020, para. 71; Case 004 (Yim Tith), ECCC SCC, 28 December 2021, para. 32.

[59] *Im Chaem* (Case 004/1), ECCC OCIJ, 10 July 2017 (reasons); *Im Chaem* (Case 004/1), ECCC PTC, 28 June 2018 (reasons).

With the appeal judgment in *Khieu Samphan* (002/02) in December 2022, the ECCC concluded its final case, leaving behind a rich and contested legacy.[60] On the one hand, it has made an important contribution by judicially establishing the truth about the Khmer Rouge crimes and by holding some of its senior functionaries accountable. Its outreach programme has promoted public awareness and dialogue about the past in Cambodia; no less than half a million visitors have attended the ECCC hearings.[61] On the other hand, the ECCC's hybrid model has proved ineffective and should not be replicated in future experiments with international assistance to domestic justice efforts. Besides alleged governmental interference with cases 003 and 004, the Tribunal continuously faced claims of institutionalized corruption and financial shortages, which undermined the integrity of its proceedings and its independence and legitimacy.

9.2.3 Special Tribunal for Lebanon

Upon the killing of Lebanon's former Prime Minister, Rafiq Hariri, in an explosion in Beirut on 14 February 2005, the Security Council established a commission to assist the Lebanese authorities in their investigation of the assassination, including the links to neighbouring Syria.[62] Lebanon requested the creation of an international tribunal, and the Secretary-General was asked by the Security Council to negotiate an agreement with the government of Lebanon on a 'tribunal of an international character'.[63] After negotiations with Lebanon and the members of the Security Council, the Secretary-General presented a draft agreement and a Statute for a tribunal, which were accepted by the Security Council.[64] The government of Lebanon signed the agreement but because of difficulties with ratification of the agreement by Lebanon, it could not come into force in accordance with its terms. At the request of the Lebanese Prime Minister, the Security Council therefore brought its provisions into force by means of a Chapter VII Resolution which stated that, unless said difficulties could be resolved, the provisions of the agreement, including the annexed STL Statute, would come into force on 10 June 2007 – which it did.[65]

Like the SCSL, the STL was a treaty-based institution and not a subsidiary organ of the UN (although the provisions of the agreement were brought into force by a Security Council resolution). It was financed by voluntary contributions from the international community (51 per cent) and by Lebanon (49 per cent).[66] Unlike the ECCC, it did not

---

[60] See contributions to the symposium 'Rethinking the Legacy of the ECCC: Selectivity, Accountability, Ownership' in (2020) 18(3) *JICJ* 599–764.

[61] Public Affairs Outreach Figures 2009–2017 as of 30 September 2017, www.eccc.gov.kh/sites/default/files/Outreach%20states tics%20as%20of%20September%202017.pdf.

[62] See SC Res. 1595(2005), 7 April 2005, establishing the UN International Independent Investigation Commission (UNIIIC). SC Res. 1636(2005), 31 October 2005 and 1644(2005), 15 December 2005 required Syria to cooperate with the UNIIIC.

[63] SC Res. 1664(2006), 29 March 2006.

[64] See the Report of the Secretary-General on the Establishment of a Special Tribunal for Lebanon, UN Doc. S/2006/893 (15 November 2006); and Letter dated 21 November 2006 from the President of the Security Council addressed to the Secretary-General, UN Doc. S/2006/911 (24 November 2006).

[65] SC Res. 1757(2007), 30 May 2007. The five members of the Council who abstained on the vote on the resolution criticized the use of a Chapter VII resolution to bypass national constitutional procedures.

[66] STL Agreement, Art. 5(1).

form part of the domestic court system. It sat in Leidschendam, The Netherlands, and had a majority of international judges, including an international pre-trial judge, an international chief prosecutor assisted by a Lebanese deputy prosecutor, a registry, and a defence office.[67] The STL was established for a specific trial or trials with personal jurisdiction covering those responsible for the attack on Hariri and other connected attacks of a similar nature and gravity committed between 1 October 2004 and 12 December 2005 (or any later date set by the parties to the agreement, subject to the Security Council's consent).[68]

The Tribunal applied Lebanese law, with some modifications such as the inapplicability of the death penalty. Crimes within its jurisdiction are crimes under Lebanese criminal law relating to terrorism and 'offences against life and personal integrity, illicit associations and failure to report crimes and offences'.[69] It had no jurisdiction over international crimes.[70] The Tribunal had primacy over national courts in Lebanon.[71] In adopting the Rules of Procedure and Evidence, the judges were guided by the Lebanese Code of Criminal Procedure and the 'highest standards of international criminal procedure'.[72] The peculiarities of the STL process included the possibility of holding trials *in absentia*,[73] as well as victim participation in the proceedings.[74]

In November 2011, the STL Appeals Chamber, presided over by STL President Judge Cassese, issued a seminal decision at the request of the Pre-Trial Judge on the applicable law concerning terrorism, conspiracy, homicide, perpetration, and cumulative charging.[75] Rather than merely supplementing Lebanese law with international law, the Chamber interpreted the former in the context of 'international obligations undertaken by Lebanon with which, in the absence of very clear language, it is presumed any legislation complies'.[76] On the basis of a liberal (and controversial) interpretation, the appeal judges concluded that there had emerged a crime of terrorism under customary international law and purported to define this crime as it was to be applied by the Tribunal.[77]

In June 2011, an indictment was confirmed and arrest warrants were issued against four accused with links to the powerful political and military organization Hezbollah,[78] which in turn had political repercussions in Lebanon. The arrest warrants were not executed and the Trial Chamber decided to hold the trial *in absentia*, concluding that each of the accused 'has

---

[67] STL Statute, Arts. 7, 8(1), 9(3), 11(3)–(4). [68] *Ibid*. Art. 1. [69] *Ibid*. Art. 2(a).

[70] The inclusion of crimes against humanity was considered but later rejected due to insufficient support within the Security Council; see the Report, UN Doc. S/2006/893, paras. 23–5.

[71] STL Statute, Art. 4.

[72] *Ibid*. Art. 28. The STL RPE were adopted on 20 March 2009 and have been amended 11 times since; latest version (Rev. 11) dated 18 December 2020.

[73] *Ibid*. Art. 22 and STL RPE, rr. 105*bis*–109. [74] STL Statute, Art. 17, and STL RPE, rr. 86–87.

[75] See *Ayyash et al.*, STL AC, 16 February 2011. The involvement by the AC at an early stage of a case exemplified the STL's procedural innovation. Rr. 68(G) and 176*bis* (added on 10 November 2010) allowed the Pre-Trial Judge to refer to the AC any preliminary question on the interpretation of STL legal framework regarding the applicable law if he or she deems this necessary to review the indictment, and the AC to issue a decision on any such question.

[76] *Ibid*. paras. 19–20.

[77] *Ibid*. paras. 102–13. For criticism, see e.g. Kai Ambos, 'Judicial Creativity at the Special Tribunal for Lebanon: Is There a Crime of Terrorism under International Law?' (2011) 24 *LJIL* 655; Ben Saul, 'The Special Tribunal for Lebanon and Terrorism as an International Crime: Reflections on the Judicial Function' in Schabas et al., *Ashgate Research Companion*, 79–100. On terrorism, see Chapter 14.

[78] *Ayyash et al.*, STL PTJ, 28 June 2011. The arrest warrants were issued in separate decisions the same day, and international arrest warrants were issued against each accused on 8 July 2011.

absconded or otherwise cannot be found'.[79] The accused had court-appointed defence counsel. The *Ayyash et al.* trial was conducted between January 2014 and September 2018, resulting in a conviction of Ayyash on all counts and a sentence of life imprisonment, as well as in the acquittals of Merhi, Oneissi, and Sabra.[80] Subsequently, the Appeals Chamber reversed the acquittals of Merhi and Oneissi and sentenced them to life imprisonment as well.[81]

In 2019, the STL made public a second case against Ayyash concerning three attacks connected to the February attack which took place on 1 October 2004, 21 June 2005, and 12 July 2005 (against Marwan Hamadeh, George Hawi, and Elias El-Murr, respectively). But the start of the trial was cancelled following the Registrar's notification of severe funding shortfall making the continuation of the activities beyond 31 July 2021 impossible, leading to a stay of proceedings.[82]

The third category of cases concerned contempt and obstruction of justice involving two individuals and two Lebanese media outlets in connection with disclosure of information about purported confidential witnesses in *Ayyash et al.*[83] The first of these prosecutions led to an acquittal of both the company and the individual (on appeal),[84] and the second ended in convictions and pecuniary sentences.[85] The bases for prosecuting and punishing legal entities for contempt remain contentious, both legally and conceptually. The first conviction of a company before an international court has reinvigorated debates about the possibility of, and the need for, corporate criminal liability in international criminal law. However, the implications of this precedent outside of the STL regime have remained limited.

On 1 July 2022, the STL entered a residual phase and its mandate was extended until the end of 2023 only to ensure its 'orderly closure'.[86] A landmark experiment in international justice, the STL's impact and legacy give rise to mixed assessments. A key question is whether a tribunal with such a narrow mandate, which only conducts *in absentia* proceedings due to inability to arrest the accused, is worth the investment, as best conveyed by the sobriquet of 'the most expensive moot court in history'. The STL was shut down in a forced and abrupt, rather than orderly, manner due to donors' unwillingness to continue financing its (ever-sprawling) judicial operations beyond the main case. This example illustrates that funding schemes based on voluntary contributions compromise the imperatives of judicial independence and proper administration of justice.

---

[79] *Ayyash et al.*, STL TC, 1 February 2012. A later request for reconsideration of the decision was dismissed, which was also upheld on appeal: *Ayyash et al.*, STLTC, 11 July 2012 and STLAC, 1 November 2012.
[80] *Ayyash*, STL TC, 18 August 2020, para. 6904 and 11 December 2020, para. 307.
[81] *Merhi and Oneissi*, STL AC, 10 March 2022, 205; *Merhi and Oneissi*, STL AC, 16 June 2022, 26.
[82] *Ayyash*, STL TC II, 13 July 2021.   [83] STL RPE, r. 60*bis*(A).
[84] *Al Jadeed [Co.] SAL/ New TV SAL [NTV] and Al Khayat*, STL Contempt Judge, 18 September 2015 (finding Al Khayat guilty on one count) and 28 September 2015 (sentencing her to a €20,000 fine) and STL Appeals Panel, 8 March 2016 (reversing Al Khayat's conviction and affirming Al Jadeed's acquittal).
[85] *Akhbar Beirut SAL and Al Amin*, STL Contempt Judge, 15 July 2016 (finding both guilty) and 5 September 2016 (sentencing Al Amin to a €20,000 fine and the company to a €6,000 fine).
[86] *STL Fourteenth Annual Report* (2022–2023) 16.

9.2.4 Extraordinary African Chambers

The presidency of Hissène Habré in Chad between 1982 and 1990 was characterized by serious human rights violations. Since 2000, various attempts were made to bring Habré to justice, including in Senegal where he resided since his ousting in 1990.[87] In 2010, the Court of Justice of the Economic Community of West African States (ECOWAS) ruled that Habré must be tried in accordance with a 'special ad hoc procedure of an international character'.[88] Moreover, the ICJ's judgment in *Questions relating to the Obligation to Prosecute or Extradite* ordered Senegal to prosecute Habré without further delay.[89]

Accordingly, an agreement was concluded between the AU and Senegal to establish the Extraordinary African Chambers (EAC) in the courts of Senegal.[90] The EAC Statute formed an integral part of that agreement.[91] Like the STL, the EAC derived its legal basis from an international agreement but applied domestic law while featuring limited international participation.[92] The Chambers were tasked with the prosecution of those most responsible for genocide, crimes against humanity, war crimes, and torture committed in Chad under Habré's rule between 7 June 1982 and 1 December 1990.[93]

The EAC consisted of one Investigative Chamber, one Indicting Chamber, one Trial Chamber, and one Appeals Chamber, all within existing Senegalese courts and composed mainly of Senegalese judges who were nominated by Senegal and appointed by the Chairperson of the AU Commission; the presiding judges of the Trial and Appeals Chambers were to be nationals of another AU member state.[94] The prosecutors had to be Senegalese and were nominated and appointed in the same way.[95] The funding came primarily from international (voluntary) donors.

A noteworthy procedural feature of the EAC was that victims could participate actively in the process as part of the civil party action and obtain reparations.[96] The award of reparations, in the form of compensation, restitution, and rehabilitation, could be ordered by the EAC directly from the convicted person or through the Trust Fund for Victims that was set up for the benefit of victims and their rightful claimants and funded through voluntary contributions.[97]

The Chambers were inaugurated in February 2013. On 2 July 2013, Habré was charged with crimes against humanity, torture, and war crimes, and ordered to be held in pre-trial detention. His trial commenced on 20 July 2015. The jurisdiction was not restricted to Habré, and the prosecutor requested the indictment of five former officials of Habré's

[87] See Reed Brody, *To Catch a Dictator: The Pursuit and Trial of Hissène Habré* (New York, 2022).
[88] *Hissein Habré v. Republique du Senegal*, Court of Justice of ECOWAS, Judgment of 18 November 2010, para. 61. According to the Court, the principle of non-retroactivity would otherwise be violated.
[89] *Questions relating to the Obligation to Prosecute or Extradite* (*Belgium* v. *Senegal*), ICJ, Judgment of 20 July 2012. See Chapter 4.
[90] Agreement between the Government of the Republic of Senegal and the African Union on the Establishment of Extraordinary African Chambers within the Senegalese Judicial System, 22 August 2012, entered into force on 30 January 2013, (2013) 52 ILM 1024.
[91] Statute of the Extraordinary African Chambers within the Senegalese judicial system for the prosecution of international crimes committed on the territory of the Republic of Chad during the period from 7 June 1982 to 1 December 1990 ('EAC Statute').
[92] Emanuele Cimiotta, 'The First Steps of the Extraordinary African Chambers' (2015) 13(1) *JICJ* 177.
[93] EAC Statute, Arts. 3–8. [94] *Ibid*. Arts. 2 and 11. [95] *Ibid*. Art. 12. [96] *Ibid*. Arts. 14 and 27.
[97] *Ibid*. Art. 28. The EAC reparatory scheme was modelled after that of the ICC: see Chapter 18.

administration, although none of them was in Senegal. Senegal and Chad concluded a special agreement on judicial cooperation.[98] Chad had already in 2002 waived Habré's immunity from prosecution abroad, but the EAC Statute explicitly ruled out immunity and amnesty as bars to prosecution.[99] On 30 May 2016, the EAC Trial Chamber found Habré guilty of crimes against humanity, war crimes, rape, forced slavery, mass summary executions, disappearance of persons, and torture, leading to the imposition of a sentence of life imprisonment.[100] Except for the conviction on the charges of direct rape, which had not featured in the original indictment, the Appeals Chamber upheld the trial judgment and sentence.[101] Once the judgment became final, the Chambers were dissolved according to the Statute.[102]

9.2.5 African Criminal Court: Towards a Regional Jurisdiction

The idea of regionalization of international criminal justice is not new.[103] It is the growing tensions between the International Criminal Court and the AU in connection with the former's initial heavy focus on, and alleged bias against, African leaders and the latter's search for 'African solutions for African problems' that have created a momentum for a regional (African) system of enforcement.[104] Indeed, in other fields such as human rights law, regional adjudication has proven to be efficacious and to strengthen compliance. The same could be hoped for in the field of international criminal law.

In 2014, the African Union adopted the Protocol on Amendments to the Protocol on the Statute of the African Court of Justice and Human Rights ('Malabo Protocol').[105] The African Court of Justice and Human Rights was set up in 2004 by merging the African Court of Human and Peoples' Rights and the AU Court of Justice.[106] The Malabo Protocol adds criminal jurisdiction to the general affairs and human rights jurisdiction of the African Court.[107] This extension would enable the Court to adjudicate a wider range of crimes than any of the previous international and hybrid courts did, including those not mentioned in the ICC Statute.[108]

---

[98] Judicial Cooperation Agreement between the Republic of Chad and the Republic of Senegal for the Prosecution of International Crimes Committed in Chad between 7 June 1982 to 1 December 1990, 3 May 2013.

[99] EAC Statute, Arts. 10(3) and 20. In 2011, Habré was reportedly convicted *in absentia* in Chad and, thus, questions relating to *ne bis in idem* could potentially arise: *ibid*. Art. 19 (see also Art. 18(2) on the transfer of criminal prosecutions, which may apply if the judgment is not final).

[100] *Hissein Habré*, Chambre Africaine Extraordinaire D'Assises, 30 May 2016. See Christopher Sperfeldt, 'The Trial Against Hissène Habré: Networked Justice and Reparations at the Extraordinary African Chambers' (2017) 21(9) *International Journal of Human Rights* 1243.

[101] *Hissein Habré*, Chambre Africaine Extraordinaire D'Assises D'Appel, 27 April 2017. [102] EAC Statute, Art. 37.

[103] William Burke-White, 'Regionalization of International Criminal Justice: A Preliminary Exploration' (2003) 38 *Texas International Law Journal* 729.

[104] Charles Chernor Jalloh, 'Regionalizing International Criminal Law?' (2009) 9 *ICLR* 445.

[105] Protocol on Amendments to the Protocol on the Statute of the African Court of Justice and Human Rights, Malabo, 27 June 2014 ('Malabo Protocol'), and Annex: Statute of the African Court of Justice and Human and Peoples' Rights ('African Court Statute').

[106] Protocol to the African Charter on Human and Peoples' Rights on the Establishment of an African Court on Human and Peoples' Rights, Ouagadougou, Organization of African Unity, 10 June 1998, entered into force on 25 January 2004. Under the Malabo Protocol, the title of the Court would be changed to 'African Court of Justice and Human and Peoples' Rights'.

[107] African Court Statute, Art. 16.

[108] *Ibid*. Art. 28A(1). This list may be expanded to cover additional crimes to reflect international law developments: *ibid*. Art. 28A(2).

Thus, next to the traditional four core crimes (genocide, war crimes, crimes against humanity, and the crime of aggression), the African Court's subject-matter jurisdiction would cover ten transnational offences, such as the crime of unconstitutional change of government, piracy, terrorism, mercenarism, corruption, money laundering, trafficking in persons, trafficking in drugs, trafficking in hazardous wastes, and illicit exploitation of natural resources.[109] A notable element in the African Court's procedure under the Malabo Protocol is the possibility for victims to obtain reparations and compensation, including by a judicial order rendered against a convicted person.[110] Moreover, the Statute recognizes the notion of corporate criminal liability, and the Court's personal jurisdiction extends over legal persons other than states.[111]

Some features of the prospective African Court under the Malabo Protocol have attracted criticism. For example, the Statute provides that: '[n]o charges shall be commenced or continued before the Court against any serving AU Head of State or Government, or anybody acting or entitled to act in such capacity, or other senior state officials based on their functions, during their tenure of office.'[112]

This provision accords immunity not only to sitting heads of state or government and persons acting as such, but also to an unidentified category of officials 'based on their functions'. This grant of immunity is controversial. It could also render potential cases admissible at the ICC, although keeping the latter at bay was an important motive for adopting the regional solution in the first place.

The Malabo Protocol will enter into force thirty days after the deposit of instruments of ratification by fifteen member states. At present, it is uncertain whether and when the African Court will be operational since the Protocol has only fifteen signatures and one ratification. Despite the rhetoric about the need for 'African solutions' and the regional tier in the international criminal justice system, in fact there is currently little appetite for it among AU member states.

9.3 COURTS ESTABLISHED BY INTERNATIONAL ADMINISTRATION

Like with agreement-based courts, the authority of hybrid courts established by international (UN) administrations is rooted in international law. In East Timor (Timor Leste) and Kosovo, the 'special panels' were created as a result of international intervention and installation of a UN transitional authority assisting these territories in achieving stability and strengthening public institutions and the rule of law. The War Crimes Chamber of the Court in Bosnia and Herzegovina was established by the Office of High Representative mandated by the Dayton Peace Agreement, with some involvement by the International Criminal Tribunal for the former Yugoslavia (ICTY).[113]

---

[109] *Ibid*. Arts. 28B–28M. See Gerhard Werle and Mauritz Vormbaum (eds.), *The African Criminal Court: A Commentary on the Malabo Protocol* (The Hague, 2017) chs. 4–8; Charles C. Jalloh et al (eds.), *The African Court of Justice and Human and Peoples' Rights in Context: Development and Challenges* (Cambridge, 2019) ch. 8–22.
[110] African Court Statute, Art. 45.   [111] *Ibid*. Art. 46C.
[112] *Ibid*. Art. 46A*bis*. See further Dire Tladi, 'Article 46A *Bis*: Beyond the Rhetoric' in Jalloh et al., *The African Court of Justice and Human and Peoples' Rights in Context* (n. 109) 850–65.
[113] General Framework Agreement for Peace in Bosnia and Herzegovina, 14 December 1995, (1996) 35 ILM 75.

9.3.1 Special Panels for Serious Crimes in Kosovo and East Timor

Following Security Council Resolutions in 1999, the UN temporarily assumed the sovereign prerogatives of the previous authorities in East Timor and Kosovo (Indonesia as the occupying power and Serbia, respectively). Both territories had suffered violence and gross human rights violations during their struggles for independence. The UN Mission in Kosovo (UNMIK) was empowered to exercise all executive and legislative authority in that territory, including the administration of justice.[114] The UN Transitional Administration in East Timor (UNTAET) had similar powers.[115] Their essentially state-building mandates to establish law and order, and a credible and fair justice system, included powers to repeal and enact laws and to administer courts, develop legal policy, assess the quality of justice, and address allegations of human rights violations.[116]

Both territories experienced the destruction of infrastructure, a shortage of qualified lawyers, a compelling security situation, and a history of ethnic discrimination. But, since the contexts in which the Administrations were set to perform their tasks presented different challenges, the objectives and institutional solutions differed somewhat. In Kosovo, where the ICTY had jurisdiction, the main purpose was to ensure sustainable peace between different ethnic groups in society, guarantee respect for the rule of law, and to address a broader range of crimes. In East Timor, the purpose was to rebuild the judicial system from scratch and to enable the prosecution of international crimes in particular. In both cases, more ambitious proposals were rejected.[117]

Kosovo

The appointment of new domestic judges and prosecutors did not quell discriminatory practices in Kosovo, and international judges and prosecutors were embedded in the ordinary courts.[118] UNMIK also assumed the power to assign an international prosecutor, an international investigative judge, or a court panel with a majority of international judges to a particular case, when this was considered necessary 'to ensure the independence and impartiality of the judiciary or the proper administration of justice'.[119] This arrangement became known as 'Regulation 64 Panels'.

The Regulation 64 Panels initially applied pre-existing domestic law, but later provisional criminal and criminal procedure codes were introduced which also included modern definitions of international crimes.[120] The internationalized Panels conducted a large number of war crimes trials against Kosovar Serbs, and the Supreme Court Panels overturned questionable convictions by lower courts. While the international presence improved the

---

[114] Established by SC Res. 1244(1999), 10 June 1999. [115] Established by SC Res. 1272(1999), 25 October 1999.
[116] See further Hansjörg Strohmeyer, 'Collapse and Reconstruction of a Judicial System: The United Nations Missions in Kosovo and East Timor' (2001) 95 *AJIL* 46.
[117] The Kosovo War and Ethnic Crimes Court (KWECC), proposed by a Technical Advisory Commission (UNMIK Regulation 1999/5 of 7 September 1999), and an international criminal tribunal for East Timor, suggested in *Report of the International Commission of Inquiry on East Timor to the Secretary-General*, UN Doc. A/53/850-S/1999/231 (1999) 153.
[118] UNMIK Regulation 2000/6, 15 February 2000 and Regulation 2000/34, 29 May 2000.
[119] UNMIK Regulation 2000/64 on Assignment of International Judges/Prosecutors and/or Change of Venue, 15 December 2000.
[120] UNMIK Regulation 2003/25 and Regulation 2003/26, 6 July 2003. Subsequently, these provisional codes have been replaced by legislation adopted by the Republic of Kosovo.

appearance of objectivity, the legal quality of the work was criticized and there were problems relating to, for example, detention, defence representation, witness protection, and sentencing.[121]

After Kosovo declared independence in February 2008, some of the UNMIK functions were performed by the European Union Rule of Law Mission in Kosovo (EULEX), headquartered in Prishtinë (Priština).[122] The Regulation 64 Panels were replaced with an arrangement under which EULEX judges and prosecutors operated within the national system.[123] EULEX judges adjudicated cases investigated and prosecuted by the Special Prosecution Office of Kosovo, which dealt with all war crimes and terrorism cases.[124] EULEX prosecutors also had the authority to investigate and prosecute such cases.[125] Since 2018 the EULEX, whose mandate will run until 14 June 2025,[126] has played a residual role, such as monitoring selected cases in the Kosovo system, witness protection, and support for the Kosovo Specialist Chambers and the Specialist Prosecutor's Office.[127]

East Timor

UNTAET began with the creation of a new court system consisting of six district courts and a Court of Appeal, all with jurisdiction in both criminal and civil cases.[128] This was soon followed by the establishment of Special Panels for Serious Crimes (SPSC) in the District Court in Dili (the capital) and in the Court of Appeal, with exclusive jurisdiction over certain serious criminal offences and with a mixed composition of East Timorese and international judges.[129] On each Panel, the international judges were in the majority.[130] UNTAET also established a national prosecution service, which included a Special Crimes Unit for the prosecution of crimes before the SPSC.[131] The Unit was headed by the Deputy Prosecutor for Serious Crimes and staffed by both local and international prosecutors.

The SPSC's subject-matter jurisdiction covered genocide, crimes against humanity, and war crimes, as well as domestic crimes of murder, sexual offences, and torture.[132] Regulation 2000/15 provided for definitions of international crimes and general principles of criminal law and penalties.[133] The SPSC had jurisdiction over crimes in East Timor, or elsewhere if committed against an East Timorese citizen, during a limited time period (1 January–25 October 1999).[134] The Panels applied domestic law, UNTAET Regulations,

---

[121] See e.g. reports by the OSCE Mission in Kosovo, Legal System Monitoring Section, at www.osce.org/mission-in-kosovo.
[122] See further www.eulex-kosovo.eu/.
[123] Law No. 03/L-053 on the Jurisdiction, Case Selection and Case Allocation of EULEX Judges and Prosecutors in Kosovo, 13 March 2008.
[124] Law No. 03/L-052 on the Special Prosecution Office of the Republic of Kosovo, 13 March 2008.
[125] Law No. 03/L-053, Arts. 3.1 and 8.1; Law No. 03/L-052.
[126] Council Decision (CFSP) 2023/1095 of 5 June 2023 amending Joint Action 2008/124/CFSP on the European Union Rule of Law Mission in Kosovo.
[127] Press Release 322/18, *EULEX Kosovo: New Role for the EU Rule of Law Mission* (8 June 2018). On the Kosovo Specialist Chambers, see Section 9.4.3.
[128] UNTAET Regulation 2000/11, 6 March 2000 (as amended by UNTAET Regulation No. 2000/14).
[129] UNTAET Regulation 2000/15, 5 July 2000, s. 1.1–1.2.   [130] *Ibid.* s. 22.
[131] UNTAET Regulation 2000/16, 5 July 2000, ss. 5.1 and 14. A legal aid service, including public defenders, was also created: UNTAET Regulation 2001/24, 5 September 2001.
[132] UNTAET Regulation 2000/15, 5 July 2000, s. 1.3.   [133] *Ibid.* ss. 4–6 (and torture, s. 7) and ss. 10–21.   [134] *Ibid.* s. 2(3).

including the Transitional Rules of Criminal Procedure,[135] and, where appropriate, applicable treaties and recognized principles and norms of international law.[136]

After primarily prosecuting the crimes which were committed during the withdrawal by Indonesian forces from East Timor as ordinary offences, later cases also led to convictions for crimes against humanity. Many of those convictions resulted from admissions of guilt made in the circumstances in which it was not fully clear that the defendants had received proper legal advice enabling them to enter an informed and voluntary plea.[137] Moreover, the quality of legal reasoning in SPSC judgments was not always adequate. The Panels often failed to sufficiently address key legal questions, such as the characterization of the conflict for the purpose of war crimes, the prerequisites for crimes against humanity, and the legal import of duress and superior orders.[138] But in many cases, lack of cooperation hindered prosecution efforts. In spite of a bilateral agreement, Indonesia instead pursued proceedings before a much-criticized ad hoc Tribunal in Jakarta.[139]

After general and presidential elections and East Timor's gaining of independence in May 2002, the UN handed over its authority to the new democratic institutions of East Timor. The UNTAET Regulations continued to apply provisionally and the SPSC to function under the authority of the new East Timorese Constitution. In May 2005 the SPSC suspended operations indefinitely. The international judges and prosecutors departed, and the ordinary courts now handle cases involving international crimes.

9.3.2 War Crimes Chamber in the Court of Bosnia and Herzegovina

During the demise of Yugoslavia, tens of thousands of people died and about a million people were displaced in Bosnia and Herzegovina. With the 1995 Dayton Peace Agreement, two 'entities' were created, the Federation of Bosnia and Herzegovina and Republika Srpska. The Office of the High Representative oversees the civilian aspects of the Dayton Agreement. The Court of Bosnia and Herzegovina has jurisdiction over both entities, and within that court a War Crimes Chamber (WCC) was established as a domestic

---

[135] UNTAET Regulation 2000/30, 25 September 2000, as amended by UNTAET Regulation 2001/25, 14 September 2001 (TRCP).

[136] UNTAET Regulation 2000/15, s. 3. See *Armando Dos Santos*, SPSC Court of Appeal, 15 July 2003 (holding controversially that because the occupation of East Timor by Indonesia was illegal, the law of the former colonial power, Portugal, was to be applied instead).

[137] TRCP, s. 29A. For critical analyses, see e.g. Suzannah Linton, 'Prosecuting Atrocities at the District Court of Dili' (2001) 2 *Melbourne Journal of International Law* 414; Suzannah Linton and Caitlin Reiger, 'The Evolving Jurisprudence and Practice of East Timor's Special Panels for Serious Crimes on Admission of Guilt, Duress and Superior Orders' (2001) 4 *Yearbook of International Humanitarian Law* 1.

[138] See e.g. Claus Kreß, 'The 1999 Crisis in East Timor and the Threshold of the Law on War Crimes' (2002) 13 *Criminal Law Forum* 409; Kai Ambos and Steffen Wirth, 'The Current Law of Crimes Against Humanity: An Analysis of UNTAET Regulation 15/2000' (2002) 13 *Criminal Law Forum* 1; Guy Cumes, 'Murder as a Crime Against Humanity in International Law: Choice of Law and Prosecution of Murder in East Timor' (2003) 11 *European Journal of Crime, Criminal Law and Criminal Justice* 40.

[139] See e.g. Suzannah Linton, 'Unravelling the First Three Trials at Indonesia's Ad Hoc Court for Human Rights Violations in East Timor' (2004) 17 *LJIL* 303. East Timor and Indonesia established a joint Commission of Truth and Friendship to report on violence in 1999: see Commission of Truth and Friendship's Final Report on the 1999 Atrocities in East Timor.

institution with international components, stemming from a joint initiative of the ICTY and the High Representative.[140] The WCC began its work in March 2005.

Being part of the reform of the national justice system by the Office of the High Representative, the Chamber was also an essential element of the ICTY completion strategy. It is a domestic court to which the ICTY referred most cases against lower-level perpetrators under Rule 11*bis*.[141] This rule allowed the referral of an indictment against an accused, regardless of whether they were in the ICTY's custody, to any state which had jurisdiction and which was willing and adequately prepared to accept such a case. In total the ICTY referred six cases concerning ten accused to Bosnia and Herzegovina, all adjudicated by the WCC.[142]

The Chamber operates under national law, including criminal and criminal procedure codes introduced by the High Representative in 2003.[143] The Chamber had international judges at both trial and appeal levels. The Special Department for War Crimes set up within the Prosecutor's Office in 2005 prosecuted cases referred to Bosnia and Herzegovina by the ICTY under Rule 11*bis* as well as the 'category 2 cases' in which the ICTY did not issue an indictment.[144] In 2012, the international prosecutors and judges were phased out altogether.

9.4 COURTS ESTABLISHED BY A STATE WITH INTERNATIONAL SUPPORT

The third category of hybrid courts is constituted by domestic courts initiated and/or assisted by international actors. In Iraq, a special national court, the Iraqi High Tribunal, was originally created by the occupying powers and later taken over by the state itself. The War Crimes Chamber in the Belgrade District Court in Serbia was assisted by the Organization for Security and Co-operation in Europe (OSCE). The Special Criminal Court (SCC) for the Central African Republic (CAR) enjoys international support, but is a domestic court rooted in and applying domestic law. Although the origins of the Kosovo Specialist Chambers (KSC) and Specialist Prosecutor's Office (SPO) are traced back to the exchange of letters between the government of Kosovo and the EU High Representative for Foreign Affairs and Security Policy, they were set up on the basis of an amendment to the Kosovo Constitution and other domestic legislation. All these courts applied or apply national law and were or are staffed by national judges, with the notable exception of the KSC where none of the judges is Kosovan. Yet these courts' specialization in core crimes is what makes them part and parcel of international criminal justice and distinguishes them from special internationally assisted domestic courts dealing with ordinary offences, such

---

[140] Law on the Court of Bosnia and Herzegovina, as last amended on 14 December 2009, Official Gazette of BiH, No. 29/00, 16/02, 24/02, 3/03, 37/03, 42/03, 4/04, 9/04, 35/04, 61/04, 32/07 and 49/09.
[141] On Rule 11*bis* referrals, see further Sections 4.2 and 7.2.4.
[142] See 'Status of Transferred Cases, ICTY', www.icty.org/en/cases/transfer-of-cases/status-of-transferred-cases.
[143] Criminal Code of Bosnia and Herzegovina, Official Gazette No. 37/03, and Criminal Procedure Code of Bosnia and Herzegovina, Official Gazette No. 36/03, both of 24 January 2003 (with amendments).
[144] All of these cases have by now been completed: see Department I, Prosecutor's Office of Bosnia and Herzegovina, www.tuzilastvobih.gov.ba/?opcija=sadrzaj&kat=2&id=4&jezik=e.

as the Lockerbie trial before a Scottish court which sat in the Netherlands to adjudicate the case concerning the 1988 bombing of Pan Am Flight 103.

9.4.1 Iraqi High Tribunal

During Saddam Hussein's authoritarian regime, lasting for over thirty-five years, individuals and ethnic communities were violently suppressed and wars were fought against Iraq's neighbours, Iran and Kuwait. In the wake of Hussein's removal from power by coalition forces, a specialized court for genocide, crimes against humanity, and war crimes was created in Iraq, primarily to deal with crimes of the old regime. The Iraqi Tribunal was a domestic court considering its legal basis and the way it was created. Its international aspects are distinctly different, and limited, compared with the courts previously mentioned.

The court began as the Iraqi Special Tribunal for Crimes Against Humanity, which was established by the Iraqi Interim Governing Council on 10 December 2003, authorized by the body representing the occupying powers, the Coalition Provisional Authority. The Statute was drawn up with considerable international input.[145] Concerns were raised about the legal basis for the Tribunal and its legitimacy.[146] These were put to rest by a new law, adopted by the Iraqi Transitional National Assembly in 2005,[147] which provided a new Statute for the Tribunal, now called the Iraqi High Tribunal (IHT), or Supreme Iraqi Criminal Court.

The Tribunal has jurisdiction over certain crimes committed in Iraq or elsewhere between 17 July 1968 (the Ba'athist *coup d'état*) and 1 May 2003 (the 'end of major combat operations') by Iraqi nationals or residents; members of the coalition are thus excluded, as are juridical persons.[148] The subject-matter jurisdiction covers genocide, crimes against humanity, and war crimes, all defined almost exactly as in the ICC Statute but not previously included in Iraqi law,[149] and some crimes under domestic law relating to abuse of power.[150] Interestingly, one of the domestic crimes, 'the pursuit of policies that may lead to the threat of war or use of the armed forces of Iraq against an Arab country', could apply as an analogue of the crime of aggression, though not in relation to the 2003 intervention in Iraq itself.[151]

The Tribunal has concurrent jurisdiction with, but also primacy over, all other Iraqi courts, except for violations of Iraqi laws listed in Article 14, in relation to which there is no primacy. The IHT may under certain circumstances try someone who has already been tried by another Iraqi court.[152] The judges and prosecutors of the Iraqi High Tribunal are all Iraqi

---

[145] Coalition Provisional Authority Order No. 48 of 10 December 2003 (to which the Iraqi Special Tribunal Statute was attached).

[146] See e.g. Ilias Bantekas, 'The Iraqi Special Tribunal for Crimes Against Humanity' (2004) 54 *ICLQ* 237; and M. Cherif Bassiouni, 'Post-Conflict Justice in Iraq: An Appraisal of the Iraq Special Tribunal' (2005) 38 *Cornell International Law Journal* 327.

[147] Law No. 10 of 2005 on the Iraqi High Tribunal, signed by the Iraqi President on 11 October 2005, Al-Waqa'i Al-Iraqiya [Official Gazette of the Republic of Iraq] issue 4006, 18 October 2005 ('IHT Statute'), available at https://ihl-databases.icrc. org/en/national-practice/law-no-10-2005-establishing-supreme-iraqi-criminal-tribunal.

[148] IHT Statute, Art. 1. [149] *Ibid.* Arts. 1(2) and 11–13. [150] IHT Statute, Art. 14.

[151] See Claus Kreß, 'The Iraqi Special Tribunal and the Crime of Aggression' (2004) 2 *JICJ* 347. See Chapter 13.

[152] IHT Statute, Arts. 29–30.

nationals; the Statute allows the appointment of non-Iraqi judges by a national authority, but only if one of the parties in the case is a state.[153] Nonetheless, international advisers, observers, and defence co-counsel may work in the Tribunal,[154] and many did so, particularly in the early days. Coalition members also provided substantial support with regard to funding, training, security, and personnel. However, the Tribunal's power to impose the death penalty had the consequence that many states and international human rights groups were not willing to support it or cooperate with it.[155]

The first trial before the Tribunal was of Saddam Hussein and a further seven former top-ranking officials (the *Dujail* case). On 5 November 2006, Saddam Hussein was sentenced to death for crimes against humanity, albeit not the most notorious crimes that he had allegedly committed, and was hanged soon thereafter, before the second case (the *Anfal* trial), where he was also named defendant alongside six others, was completed.[156] The *Anfal* case concerned large-scale attacks against the Kurdish population in 1988 and resulted in convictions of Ali Hassan al-Majid (or 'Chemical Ali') and four co-defendants.

The IHT trials have been subjected to international criticism for lack of judicial independence, weak guarantees of fair trial, procedural mismanagement, administrative failures, and a lack of outreach to the Iraqi public.[157] Accordingly, their international legitimacy has been seriously tainted. However understandable the wish to try alleged perpetrators in a national court, the IHT's legacy illustrates well the difficulties a domestic court is bound to face when dealing, without previous experience and sufficient guarantees of independence, with vast and complex international crimes in a post-conflict and highly politicized environment.

9.4.2 War Crimes Departments in Serbia

The War Crimes Departments (WCDs) in the Belgrade District Court and the Supreme Court of Serbia are another example of a specialized court for international crimes created with international assistance, primarily the OSCE, but which is entirely national in nature.[158] The War Crimes Departments (called Chambers at first) and a specialized Office of the War Crimes Prosecutor (OWCP) were both established in 2003. The Chambers' jurisdiction extends to crimes committed anywhere in the former Socialist Federal Republic of Yugoslavia, regardless of the citizenship of the perpetrator or victims.

---

[153] *Ibid.* Arts. 4(3) and 28. [154] *Ibid.* Arts. 7(2)–(3), 8(10), 9(7)–(8) and 18(3).
[155] See e.g. Tom Parker, 'Prosecuting Saddam: The Coalition Provisional Authority and the Evolution of the Iraqi Special Tribunal' (2005) 38 *Cornell International Law Journal* 899.
[156] English translations of the IHT judgments in the *Dujail* case, TC, 5 November 2006, and AC, 26 December 2006, and the subsequent *Anfal* case, TC II, 24 June 2007, and AC, 4 September 2007, are available in the International Crimes Database, https://internationalcrimesdatabase.org/Case/187/Al-Dujail/ and https://internationalcrimesdatabase.org/Case/1233/Al-Anfal/.
[157] See e.g. Miranda Sissons and Ari Bassin, 'Was the Dujail Trial Fair?' (2007) 5 *JICJ* 272; M. Cherif Bassiouni and Michael Hanna, 'Ceding the High Ground: The Iraqi High Criminal Court Statute and the Trial of Saddam Hussein' (2006–7) 39 *Case Western Reserve Journal of International Law* 21; Nehal Bhuta, 'Fatal Errors: The Trial and Appeal Judgments in the Dujail Case' (2008) 6 *JICJ* 39.
[158] Law on Organization and Competence of Government Authorities in War Crimes Proceedings, Official Gazette of the Republic of Serbia No. 67/2003.

The ICTY referred some cases to the Chambers, including crimes in Vukovar (Croatia) and Zvornik (Bosnia and Herzegovina), primarily in cases where no ICTY indictment had been issued. Only one post-indictment referral was made under Rule 11*bis*.[159] As the WCDs continue to handle war crimes cases, Serbia adopted and revised (last time in 2021) a national war crimes prosecution strategy in order to enhance the efficiency of investigations and prosecutions and to remedy any known flaws in practice.[160]

However, critical voices argue that war crimes cases continue to be dogged by unwarranted delays, among others due to disinclination by the OWCP to efficiently initiate and pursue them. Too few new indictments have been brought, in particular for crimes in Kosovo and against high-level perpetrators. The protection of victims and witnesses remains insufficient and public visibility of the war crimes cases too low.[161] The main challenges facing the WCDs and OWCP – funding problems, lack of judicial and prosecutorial independence, and political pressures – are indeed not unique to Serbia.

9.4.3   Kosovo Specialist Chambers and Specialist Prosecutor's Office

For various reasons, the ICTY, UNMIK Panels, and EULEX courts only had partial success in ensuring accountability for the crimes committed during and in the aftermath of the Kosovo conflict (1998–9). This emerged clearly from the 2011 report prepared for the Committee on Legal Affairs and Human Rights of the Council of Europe Parliamentary Assembly ('Marty Report').[162] The Marty Report confirmed the allegations by the former ICTY Prosecutor Del Ponte that the Kosovo Liberation Army (KLA) members committed murder, torture, forced disappearances, and illicit trafficking in human organs. To inquire into these allegations, the EU established a Specialist Investigative Task Force (SITF), which concluded in 2014 that there was sufficient evidence for filing an indictment.

The EU and Kosovo authorities negotiated on the approach to be followed and opted for the creation of a domestic specialist criminal jurisdiction. The Kosovo Assembly amended the Constitution to allow the establishment of the Kosovo Specialist Chambers (KSC) and Specialist Prosecutor's Office (SPO) within the Kosovo justice system, and passed the respective law.[163] The KSC is essentially an (internationalized) domestic court which was set up and operates pursuant to national legislation rather than international law. But it applies a mix of both: the Constitution, the KSC Law and other domestic provisions, as well as norms of customary international law and human rights law, including the European

---

[159] See *Vladimir Kovačević*, ICTY Referral Bench, 17 November 2006. However, on 5 December 2007, the Belgrade District Court found this accused unfit to stand trial.

[160] National Strategy for the Prosecution of War Crimes for the Period 2021–2026, Republic of Serbia, www.drzavnauprava.gov.rs/files/NATIONAL%20STRATEGY%20FOR%20WAR%20CRIMES%20PROSECUTION%201.pdf.

[161] See e.g. Humanitarian Law Center, *Report on War Crimes Trials in Serbia During 2021* (Belgrade, May 2022), www.hlc-rdc.org/wp-content/uploads/2022/05/Godisnji_izvestaj_2022-en.pdf; OSCE Mission to Serbia, *War crimes proceedings in Serbia (2020–2021) Summary of the OSCE Mission to Serbia's monitoring results*, www.osce.org/mission-to-serbia/536145.

[162] Dick Marty, Rapporteur, Committee on Legal Affairs and Human Rights, *Report: Inhuman Treatment of People and Illicit Trafficking in Human Organs in Kosovo*, Doc 12462 (Council of Europe, 7 January 2011).

[163] Art. 162 (The Specialist Chambers and the Specialist Prosecutor's Office), Amendment of the Constitution of the Republic of Kosovo, Amendment No. 24, No. 05-D-139, 3 August 2015; Law No. 05/L-053 on Specialist Chambers and Specialist Prosecutor's Office, 3 August 2015, Kosovo ('KSC Law').

Convention on Human Rights (ECHR) and the International Covenant on Civil and Political Rights (ICCPR).[164]

Like the ECCC or EAC, the KSC forms part of the domestic judicial system; the specialist chambers are attached to all levels of the Kosovo judiciary: the Basic Court of Prishtinë, the Court of Appeal, the Supreme Court, and the Constitutional Court.[165] However, unlike their predecessors, the KSC and SPO are located in The Hague, in accordance with the agreement with the host state.[166] Another notable departure from previous experiments in hybrid justice is that all staff, including judges and prosecutors, are international.

The KSC's jurisdiction covers crimes committed during and in the aftermath of the Kosovo conflict, as detailed in the Marty Report and investigated by the SITF; namely, crimes against humanity and war crimes, as well as a number of serious crimes under Kosovan law.[167] Temporal jurisdiction covers the period between 1 January 1998 and 31 December 2000.[168] The KSC has territorial jurisdiction over crimes commenced or committed in Kosovo, as well as jurisdiction based on active and passive nationality principle, that is, crimes by or against Kosovo/Federal Republic of Yugoslavia (FRY) citizens regardless of location.[169] The KSC has primacy over all other Kosovo courts and may order them to defer to its jurisdiction at any stage.[170]

Structurally, the SPO and the KSC are separate and independent entities.[171] The SPO was established on 1 September 2016 and took over the SITF's mandate and staff. The KSC has two organs: the Chambers (associated with the four levels of the Kosovo judiciary) and the Registry.[172] The judges, including the President and other judges who are placed on the roster, are appointed by the Head of the EULEX.[173] The judges adopt and amend the Rules of Procedure and Evidence (RPE),[174] which must reflect the highest human rights law standards as per the ECHR and ICCPR, draw upon the 2012 Kosovo Criminal Procedure Code, and be consistent with the KSC Law.[175] Following the approval of the revised RPE by the Constitutional Court Specialist Chamber,[176] they entered into force on 5 July 2017.[177]

Since the KSC became fully operational in mid-2017, it has initiated multiple cases, including three regarding core crimes and three regarding offences against the

---

[164] KSC Law, Arts. 3(2) and 12. Legally binding norms of international law have superiority over the laws of Kosovo: see Constitution of Kosovo, Arts. 19(2) and 22.

[165] *Ibid.* KSC Law, Art. 3(1).

[166] *Ibid.* art. 3(6)–(7). See Agreement between the Kingdom of the Netherlands and the Republic of Kosovo concerning the Hosting of the Kosovo Relocated Specialist Judicial Institution in the Netherlands, 15 February 2016.

[167] KSC Law, Arts. 1, 6(2) and 13–16. [168] *Ibid.* Art. 7. [169] *Ibid.* Arts. 8–9. [170] *Ibid.* Art. 10. [171] *Ibid.* Art. 24.

[172] *Ibid.* Art. 25.

[173] *Ibid.* Arts 25–29. The first KSC President was appointed on 14 December 2017. On 7 February 2017, further Judges were appointed.

[174] Except for the Constitutional Court Specialist Chamber Judges, whose role is rather to review the constitutionality of the (amended) RPE. *Ibid.* art. 19(1) and (5).

[175] *Ibid.* Art. 19(2)–(3).

[176] *Referral of the Revised RPE pursuant to Article 19(5) of the Law*, KSC President, 31 May 2017 and Constitutional Court Specialist Chamber, 28 June 2017.

[177] Rules of Procedure and Evidence before the Kosovo Specialist Chambers (adopted on 17 March 2017, revised on 29 May 2017, entered into force on 5 July 2017, as last amended on 29 and 30 April 2020) including Rules of Procedure for the Specialist Chamber of the Constitutional Court (adopted and entered into force on 21 July 2017, as amended on 17 March 2020).

administration of justice.[178] In May 2022, KLA Veterans' Association Chairman Hysni Gucati and Deputy Chairman Nasim Haradinaj were convicted of obstructing official persons' performance of their duties, intimidation during criminal proceedings, and violating the secrecy of the proceedings.[179] In December 2022, the Trial Panel convicted Salih Mustafa, a former commander of the BIA guerilla unit, of war crimes of arbitrary detention, torture, and murder, sentencing him to twenty-six years' imprisonment; he was ordered to compensate harm inflicted upon the victims by his crimes.[180] As was expected, a climate of fear and widespread intimidation of (potential) witnesses against former KLA members have posed a significant challenge for the Chambers.[181] While the KSC's legal framework and institutional structure are sufficiently robust to guarantee its independence from domestic politics and to conduct fair and expeditious proceedings, their effectiveness depends on the cooperation of the Kosovo authorities and the continued support of the EU.

9.4.4 Special Criminal Court in the Central African Republic

Since 2012, a violent conflict has been taking place in the Central African Republic (CAR) between the mostly Muslim Séléka insurgents and the Anti-balaka militia groups composed primarily of Christians. In its aftermath, the CAR transitional government and the UN Multidimensional Integrated Stabilization Mission in the CAR (MINUSCA) agreed that the former would establish a Special Criminal Court (SCC) to deal with the crimes.[182]

Although the origins of the SCC can be traced back to an international law instrument (Memorandum of Understanding), the Court can be categorized as an internationally assisted domestic tribunal set up under domestic law.[183] It is incorporated into the CAR's judicial system at all levels: the Investigative Chamber, Indictment Chamber, Assize Chamber, and the Appeals Chamber. Like most other hybrid jurisdictions, the SCC is composed of both international and national judges (the former being in the majority only in the Appeals Chamber). It applies a combination of international and domestic law, although its substantive jurisdiction is rooted in the latter. The SCC is authorized to refer to substantive and procedural norms established at the international level in limited cases:

---

[178] *Salih Mustafa (KSC-BC-2020-05/KSC-CA-2023-02); Pjetër Shala (KSC-BC-2020-04); Hashim Thaçi, Kadri Veseli, Rexhep Selimi and Jakup Krasniqi (KSC-BC-2020-06); Hysni Gucati and Nasim Haradinaj (KSC-BC-2020-07/KSC-CA-2022-01/ KSC-SC-2023-01). Further suspects were arrested in 2023: Dritan Goxhaj, Ismet Bahtjari, and Sabit Januzi.*

[179] *Gucati and Haradinaj*, KSC TP I, 18 May 2022, paras. 1012–18 (sentencing each to a four-and-a-half years' imprisonment and a fine of €100). On appeal, the appellate panel majority reversed convictions for obstructing official persons in performing official duties by serious threat, and reduced their sentences by three months: *Gucati and Haradinaj*, KSC AC, 2 February 2023, para. 442.

[180] *Mustafa*, KSC TP I, 16 December 2022, 322 and 6 April 2023 (ordering Mustafa to compensate the harm inflicted on the victims for an overall sum of €207,000). In December 2023, the Appeals Panel reduced Mustafa's prison sentence to 22 years.

[181] E.g. *Mustafa*, KSC TP I, 16 December 2022, paras. 50–7.

[182] Memorandum d'Entente entre la Mission Multidimensionnelle intégrée des Nations Unies pour la stabilisation en République centrafricaine et le Gouvernement de la République centrafricaine, 7 August 2014.

[183] Loi organique No. 15–003 portant création, organisation et fonctionnement de la Cour Pénale Spéciale, 22 April 2015, promulgated on 3 June 2015, www.legal-tools.org/doc/fd284b/ ('SCC Law') Art. 1 ('une juridiction pénale nationale'). For discussion, see e.g. Patryk Labuda, 'The Special Criminal Court in the Central African Republic: Failure or Vindication of Complementarity?' (2017) 15(1) *JICJ* 175, 181–2.

when the legislation in force does not deal with a specific issue, when there is an uncertainty concerning the interpretation or application of a national norm, or where there is a question about its compatibility with international norms.[184]

The SCC's jurisdiction covers grave violations of human rights and international humanitarian law which have taken place in the CAR territory since 1 January 2003, as defined by the CAR Penal Code[185] and by international law, in particular genocide, crimes against humanity, and war crimes.[186] The SCC has primacy over any other domestic courts in relation to crimes within its competence. The duration of its mandate is five years since operationalization, and it may be renewed only once.[187]

Based in Bangui, the Court became operational in October 2018. The first trial against the members of the rebel group '3 R' (Adoum Issa Sallet, Ousmane Yahouba, and Tahir Mahamat), concerning war crimes and crimes against humanity committed in May 2019, opened in April 2022. It resulted in convictions and lengthy sentences; the convicts were also ordered to pay reparations to the civil parties.[188] Several dozen other cases have been under preliminary analysis and investigation.[189]

9.5 RELATIONSHIP WITH THE ICC

In the case of many of the courts discussed in this chapter, there is no concurrent jurisdiction and hence no jurisdictional conflict with the ICC. Even where the territorial, personal, and subject-matter jurisdictions overlap, the non-retroactive jurisdiction of the ICC prevents it from dealing with many past crimes. But this is different for some of the internationalized courts. For example, the SCC in CAR will operate alongside the ICC, which has been investigating two situations in that country (*CAR I* since 2002 and *CAR II* since 2012). The same could hold for other courts which may become operational in the future (e.g. the African Court's Criminal Chamber).

Since most of the courts form part of the domestic system, the scheme of Article 17 of the ICC Statute (the complementarity principle) will apply to them, and if the ICC has jurisdiction, it will be only complementary.[190] Thus, in case a hybrid tribunal conducts a genuine investigation and prosecution in a case regarding the same suspect and the same conduct that are of interest to the ICC Prosecutor, such a case would normally be inadmissible at the ICC.[191]

---

[184] SCC Law, Art. 3.
[185] Law No. 10.001 on the Central African Penal Code, 6 January 2010, Arts. 152–4 (genocide, war crimes and crimes against humanity) and 118 (torture).
[186] SCC Law, Art. 3. [187] SCC Law, Art. 70.
[188] *Issa Salet, Yaouba, and Mahamat*, SCC Assises Chamber, 31 October 2022, 80 (sentencing Salet to life imprisonment and the other co-accused to twenty years in jail) and 23 June 2023, 38–41. On appeal, the trial judgment was amended and Salet's sentence reduced to thirty years' imprisonment: *Issa Salet, Yaouba, and Mahamat*, SCC Appeals Chamber, 20 July 2023, 133–6.
[189] Human Rights Watch, 'Central African Republic: First Trial at the Special Criminal Court', 12 April 2022, www.hrw.org/news/2022/04/12/central-african-republic-first-trial-special-criminal-court#whatothercases.
[190] See Chapter 8.
[191] But see SCC Law, Art. 37 (the SCC shall relinquish jurisdiction in favour of the ICC when the ICC Prosecutor is seized of a case falling within their concurrent jurisdiction).

Other specialized domestic courts have also been established, for example, in Uganda,[192] with a varying degree of international involvement and sometimes as a direct response to the complementarity principle. Multilateral regional arrangements for the adjudication of international crimes, such as the proposed African Criminal Court, raise similar issues.[193] While they are not explicitly covered by Article 17 which refers to a state, the ICC might apply the principle of complementarity to such courts by analogy. Local and regional arrangements should be accepted and recognized to the greatest extent possible as long as they entail accountability and satisfy the substance of the principle.

9.6 CONCLUDING REMARKS

The use of hybrid justice arrangements, rather than international courts, does not indicate that there is a hierarchy of atrocities, with one level meriting less effort and expenditure from the international community. Indeed, the crimes prosecuted in such courts are no less grave than those coming before the ICC. The ECCC, for example, had to determine responsibility for the atrocities committed in the 'killing fields', and the brutalities dealt with by the Special Court for Sierra Leone were such that the Court could not recall 'any other conflict in the history of warfare in which innocent civilians were subjected to such savage and inhumane treatment'.[194]

The hybrid courts have their disadvantages compared with tribunals established by a Security Council Resolution under Chapter VII of the UN Charter. The principal difficulty is the lack of the Security Council's backing (even theoretical) in inducing and enforcing cooperation. In order to secure cooperation from other states, the hybrid court or state concerned has to establish voluntary arrangements with relevant states or rely on existing agreements. This has led to difficulties for the Bosnia War Crimes Chamber, SPSC, and the STL.

A problem common to all hybrid jurisdictions is the shortage of financial and other resources, which consist chiefly of voluntary contributions by states, in money, personnel, and equipment. Cost-efficiency is one of the main reasons for opting for the hybrid model instead of an international tribunal. Funding difficulties have a detrimental impact not only on the effectiveness of the tribunal concerned, but also on the rights of the accused to a fair trial. The independence and impartiality of the institution are at stake, as was (unsuccessfully) argued before the SCSL.[195] The funding shortfalls compromise the tribunal's ability to complete its cases and the integrity of the whole enterprise, as exemplified by the STL's tribulations. Reliance on voluntary contributions by states, rather than on UN assessed contributions, has led to a precarious existence for some

[192] The International Crimes Division of Uganda's High Court was set up as an attempt, although unsuccessful, to get LRA leader Joseph Kony to sign a peace agreement in spite of an ICC arrest warrant; see Human Rights Watch, *Justice for Serious Crimes Before National Courts: Uganda's International Crimes Division* (2012), and *Kony et al.*, ICC PTC II, 10 March 2009 (ICC-02/04–01/05–377).
[193] See Section 9.2.5.
[194] *Brima, Kamara, and Kanu*, SCSL TC II, 19 July 2007, paras. 34–5. The AFRC defendants were found responsible 'for some of the most heinous, brutal and atrocious crimes ever recorded in human history'.
[195] *Norman*, SCSL AC, 13 March 2004.

institutions, with court staff having to spend a great deal of time fund-raising. Besides the STL, the SCSL and ECCC came near to having their work suspended for lack of funding at various periods of their existence. A further problem is that courts which are largely domestic are vulnerable to political interference in their national systems where the judiciary and the legal system are not strong. Examples include the ECCC and the Iraqi High Tribunal.

Nevertheless, the hybrid tribunals also present important advantages. The creation and work of these courts could impact positively the relevant domestic legal system, and their criminal process may more easily be adapted to the national context. Unlike the purely international courts, which never hold *in situ* proceedings in practice,[196] most of the hybrid courts sit in the country in question and, with the exception of the SCSL and STL, operate within domestic judicial structures.

Hybrid courts are intended to assist in building local capacity, enhancing respect for the rule of law, and providing independent, impartial, and fair criminal proceedings for past crimes. They may thus contribute towards the restoration of the domestic system and set an example for the future. Their outreach programmes can assist with these goals, and the impact will depend on how dedicated and effective these efforts of engagement with the local communities are. The SCSL and ECCC provide examples of successful outreach.

The hybrid courts' case law also contributes to the development of international criminal law. The SCSL has added significantly to jurisprudence on the war crime of conscripting or enlisting children under the age of fifteen years into the armed forces and on the crime against humanity of forced marriage.[197] Although created to suit a particular situation, each of the hybrid courts adds to the global network of arrangements to combat impunity.

With the recent mushrooming of the hybrid tribunals (EAC, KSC, and SCC in CAR) and several further proposals (concerning, among others, South Sudan, Sri Lanka, the Gambia, and Ukraine) on the table, the phenomenon of hybrid justice is experiencing a renaissance. The ICC's jurisdictional and capacity limitations give good reasons to believe that this trend will continue in the near future. Declaring the demise of hybrid courts as a viable and attractive solution has proven premature. In line with the ICC's complementarity principle, international support for domestic efforts will continue, and so will the interest in regional or sub-regional courts specialized in international crimes. While the appetite for UN-sponsored projects such as the SCSL, ECCC, and STL is on the wane, regional organizations such as the EU, AU, and ECOWAS will likely become increasingly involved in the establishment and operation of hybrid courts and show willingness to assist states to these ends.

---

[196] See ICC Statute, Arts. 3 and 62 (the ICC may sit elsewhere than at its seat in The Hague). ICTY RPE, r. 4 and ICTR RPE, r. 4 also allow those Tribunals to exercise their functions away from the seat, but this did not happen in practice. See Section 20.6.3.
[197] On forced marriage, see e.g. *Brima, Kamara, and Kanu*, SCSL AC, 22 February 2008, para. 195; on the recruitment of child soldiers, see *Norman*, SCSL AC, 31 May 2004.

Further Reading

The following websites are useful:

- Residual Special Court for Sierra Leone: www.rscsl.org
- Extraordinary Chambers in the Courts of Cambodia: www.eccc.gov.kh/en
- Special Tribunal for Lebanon: www.stl-tsl.org
- Bosnia War Crimes Chamber: www.sudbih.gov.ba/?jezik=e
- Serbia Office of the War Crimes Prosecutor: www.tuzilastvorz.org.rs/en/
- Kosovo Specialist Chambers and Specialist Prosecutor's Office: www.scp-ks.org/en

Amal Alamuddin, Nidal Nabil Jurdi, and David Tolbert (eds.), *The Special Tribunal for Lebanon: Law and Practice* (Oxford, 2015)

Kai Ambos and Mohamed Othman (eds.), *New Approaches in International Criminal Justice: Kosovo, East Timor, Sierra Leone and Cambodia* (Freiburg im Breisgau, 2003)

Hervé Ascensio, Elisabeth Lambert-Abdelgawad, and Jean-Marc Sorel (eds.), *Les juridictions pénales internationalisées (Cambodge, Kosovo, Sierra Leone, Timor Leste)* (Paris, 2006)

Charles Chernor Jalloh (ed.), *The Sierra Leone Special Court and its Legacy: The Impact for Africa and International Criminal Law* (Cambridge, 2013)

Charles C. Jalloh, Kamari M. Clarike, and Vincent O. Nmiehelle (eds.), *The African Court of Justice and Human and Peoples' Rights in Context: Development and Challenges* (Cambridge, 2019)

Aaron Fichtelberg, *Hybrid Courts: A Comparative Examination of Their Origins, Structure, Legitimacy and Effectiveness* (New York, 2015)

Nina H. B. Jørgensen, *The Elgar Companion to the Extraordinary Chambers in the Courts of Cambodia* (Cheltenham, 2018)

Simon Meisenberg and Ignaz Stegmiller (eds.), *The Extraordinary Chambers in the Courts of Cambodia: Assessing their Contribution to International Criminal Law* (The Hague, 2016)

Cesare Romano, André Nollkaemper, and Jann Kleffner (eds.), *Internationalized Criminal Courts: Sierra Leone, East Timor, Kosovo, and Cambodia* (Oxford, 2004)

Sharon Weill, Kim Thuy Seelinger, and Kerstin Bree Carlson (eds.), *The President on Trial: Prosecuting Hissène Habré* (Oxford, 2020)

Gerhard Werle and Moritz Vormbaum (eds.), *The African Criminal Court: A Commentary on the Malabo Protocol* (The Hague, 2017)

Sarah Williams, *Hybrid and Internationalized Criminal Tribunals: Selected Jurisdictional Issues* (Oxford, 2012)

Part IV

Substantive Law of International Crimes

10
Genocide

10.1 INTRODUCTION

10.1.1 Overview

Genocide 'is a denial of the right of existence of entire human groups, as homicide is the denial of the right to live of individual human beings'.[1] It is a crime simultaneously directed against individual victims, the group to which they belong, and human diversity. What makes genocide particularly abhorrent is the intention to destroy a group of people. This particular intent, a necessary element of the crime, distinguishes it from all other international crimes. It explains why genocide is regarded as having a particular seriousness, and why it has been referred to as the 'crime of crimes'.[2] The seriousness of the crime is underlined by the fact that its prohibition has attained the status of a *jus cogens* norm[3] and an *erga omnes* obligation.[4]

Even though the term 'genocide' is often colloquially used to refer to large-scale killings, the legal concept of genocide is more narrowly circumscribed to a particular subset of atrocities which are committed with the intent to destroy specific groups.[5] Most of the crimes committed by the Khmer Rouge regime in Cambodia in 1975–9, for example, are atrocities which do not readily fit within the narrow legal definition of genocide, however dreadful the suffering they caused.[6]

Both individuals and states may be held responsible for genocide.[7] In the *Bosnian Genocide* case, Bosnia initiated proceedings in the International Court of Justice (ICJ)

---

[1] GA Res. 96(1) (1946).

[2] *Kambanda*, ICTR TC I, 4 September 1998, para. 16. But note the statement of the International Commission of Inquiry on Darfur: genocide 'is not necessarily the most serious international crime. Depending upon the circumstances, such international offences as crimes against humanity or large scale war crimes may be no less serious and heinous than genocide' (UN Doc. S/2005/60. para. 522).

[3] *Case concerning Armed Activities on the Territory of the Congo (DRC v. Rwanda)* Jurisdiction of the Court and Admissibility of the Application, ICJ, Judgment of 3 February 2006, para. 64.

[4] *Reservations to the Convention on the Prevention and Punishment of the Crime of Genocide*, Advisory Opinion [1951] ICJ Rep. 15, 23.

[5] See generally Mark Drumbl, 'The Crime of Genocide' in Brown, *Research Handbook*, 37–44.

[6] While the larger massacres committed by the Khmer Rouge on political grounds could not be charged as genocide, the ECCC Supreme Court Chamber affirmed the Trial Chamber's conviction of Khieu Samphan of genocide against the Vietnamese ethnic minority: *Khieu Samphan*, ECCC SC, 23 December 2022, para. 1638.

[7] This is referred to as a 'duality of responsibilities' by the ICJ under public international law (for states) and international criminal law (for individuals): *Case concerning the Application of the Convention on the Prevention and Punishment of the Crime of*

alleging breaches of the Genocide Convention[8] by Serbia in attempting to destroy protected groups, in particular the Muslim population. The Court confirmed that the Convention not only imposes a duty on states to prevent and punish genocide but also an obligation to refrain from genocide.[9] This is not to introduce a concept of state crime or state criminal responsibility; the obligation is one of state responsibility under general international law.[10]

The standard definition of genocide is contained in Article II of the Genocide Convention, which is replicated verbatim in the Statutes of the ad hoc Tribunals and of the International Criminal Court (ICC). It is:

any of the following acts committed with the intent to destroy, in whole or in part, a national, ethnical, racial or religious group, as such:

(a) Killing members of the group;
(b) Causing serious bodily or mental harm to members of the group;
(c) Deliberately inflicting on the group conditions of life calculated to bring about its physical destruction in whole or in part;
(d) Imposing measures intended to prevent births within the group;
(e) Forcibly transferring children of the group to another group.

Many aspects of this definition raise difficulties of interpretation, which will be examined in Sections 10.1.4–10.4.

10.1.2 Historical Development

The identification of genocide as an international crime arose as a response to the Holocaust. Massacres with the purpose of exterminating national or ethnic minorities were not a twentieth-century novelty, but the term 'genocide' was not coined until 1944 by Raphaël Lemkin, a Polish-Jewish lawyer.[11] The indictment of the defendants at Nuremberg stated that they had conducted:

deliberate and systematic genocide, viz., the extermination of racial and national groups, against the civilian population of certain occupied territories in order to destroy particular races and classes of people, and national, racial or religious groups, particularly Jews, Poles, and Gypsies.[12]

Genocide (Bosnia and Herzegovina v. Serbia and Montenegro), ICJ, Judgment of 26 February 2007 ('*Bosnian Genocide* case') paras. 163, 173–4.

[8] Convention on the Prevention and Punishment of the Crime of Genocide, adopted by the UN General Assembly on 9 December 1948. See generally Anja Siebert-Fohr, 'State Responsibility for Genocide Under the Genocide Convention' in Paola Gaeta (ed.), *The UN Genocide Convention* (Oxford, 2009) 349.

[9] *Bosnian Genocide* case (n. 7) paras. 162–6. The Court also held that Art. III obliges states to refrain from engaging in conspiracy, incitement, attempt and complicity in genocide (para. 167). For comment, see Claus Kreß, 'The International Court of Justice and the Elements of the Crime of Genocide' (2007) 18 *EJIL* 619; Richard Goldstone and Rebecca Hamilton, '*Bosnia v. Serbia*: Lessons from the Encounter of the International Court of Justice with the International Criminal Tribunal for Former Yugoslavia' (2008) 21 *LJIL* 95. The findings in the case were largely followed in *Application of the Convention on the Prevention and Punishment of the Crime of Genocide (Croatia v. Serbia)*, ICJ, Judgment of 3 February 2015.

[10] *Bosnian Genocide* case (n. 7) para. 170.

[11] Raphaël Lemkin, *Axis Rule in Occupied Europe: Laws of Occupation, Analysis of Government, Proposals for Redress* (Washington, 1944) 79. See generally Philippe Sands, *East West Street* (London, 2017).

[12] *The Trial of German Major War Criminals* (London, 1946), Pt I, 22; Indictment presented to the International Military Tribunal, Cmd 6696, 14. For the development of the concept of genocide in the cases brought under Control Council Law No. 10, see

However, genocide as such was not a crime within the jurisdiction of the Nuremberg Tribunal, and the term was not mentioned in its judgment. As the International Criminal Tribunal for Rwanda (ICTR) said many years later:

> The crimes prosecuted by the Nuremberg Tribunal, namely the holocaust of the Jews or the 'Final Solution', were very much constitutive of genocide, but they could not be defined as such because the crime of genocide was not defined until later.[13]

All of the crimes prosecuted by the Nuremberg Tribunal and its immediate successors were defined as having a connection with war. It was because of this restriction in the definition of crimes against humanity that it was necessary to recognize the crime of genocide as a separate international crime. This was done in General Assembly Resolution 96(1) of 11 December 1946. Two years later, the Genocide Convention was concluded, having been drafted largely by the Sixth Committee of the UN General Assembly; it came into force on 12 January 1951. In the same year, the ICJ declared that the prohibitions contained in the Convention constituted customary international law.[14]

Although Article VI of the Genocide Convention refers to the possibility of an international court being available to try cases of genocide, it was not until the establishment of the ad hoc Tribunals in 1993 and 1994 that this became a reality. The first conviction for genocide by an international court was recorded on 2 September 1998 by the ICTR, of Jean-Paul Akayesu, a Rwandan mayor. Two days after his conviction, Jean Kambanda, the former Prime Minister of Rwanda, was sentenced to life imprisonment after pleading guilty to genocide, conspiracy, incitement, complicity in genocide, as well as crimes against humanity.

10.1.3 Relationship to Crimes Against Humanity

Genocide has obvious similarities to crimes against humanity.[15] As mentioned in Section 10.1.2, the Nuremberg defendants were charged with war crimes and crimes against humanity for what would now be prosecuted as genocide. The Genocide Convention makes clear in Article I that genocide can be committed in times of peace as well as in war and there is no nexus between genocide and armed conflict.[16]

The chief difference between the two categories of crimes is the intent to destroy the whole or part of a group, which is a necessary element of genocide. The interests protected by the law against genocide are narrower than for crimes against humanity. The law against genocide protects the rights of certain groups to survival, and thus human diversity,[17] but the similar crime against humanity – persecution 'against any identifiable group or collectivity on political, racial, national, ethnic, cultural, religious, gender . . . or other grounds that

---

Matthew Lippman, 'The Convention on the Prevention and Punishment of the Crime of Genocide: Fifty Years Later' (1998) 15 *Arizona Journal of International and Comparative Law* 415.

[13] *Kambanda*, ICTR TC I, 4 September 1998, para. 16.

[14] *Reservations to the Convention on the Prevention and Punishment of the Crime of Genocide*, Advisory Opinion [1951] ICJ Rep. 15, 23.

[15] *Kayishema*, ICTR TC II, 21 May 1999, para. 89.   [16] See Section 11.2.1.

[17] 'Those who devise and implement genocide seek to deprive humanity of the manifold richness its nationalities, races, ethnicities and religions provide.' *Krstić*, ICTY AC, 19 April 2004, para. 36.

are universally recognised as impermissible under international law' – protects groups from discrimination rather than elimination. Thus, 'when persecution escalates to the extreme form of willful and deliberate acts designed to destroy a group or part of a group, it can be held that such persecution amounts to genocide'.[18]

10.1.4 Nature of Genocide

Unlike crimes against humanity, the crime of genocide does not explicitly include any objective requirement of scale. The threshold for a crime against humanity is its connection to a widespread or systematic attack directed against a civilian population. In contrast, the gravity of genocide is primarily marked by the subjective *mens rea* (the intent to destroy a national, ethnic, racial, or religious group as such), which in principle is only in the mind of the perpetrator.

However, if the threshold for genocide is only a mental element, without an objective requirement of scale or serious threat, that would raise important questions about the nature of genocide and its status as the 'crime of crimes'. Can it be 'genocide' where an isolated individual acts with a fervent, albeit unrealistic, intent to destroy a group? During the negotiation of the ICC Elements of Crimes, for example, the US delegation pointed out that an isolated hate crime, if committed with the requisite intent, would satisfy the description in the Genocide Convention, and yet it would seem absurd to label a single murder by an isolated individual as a 'genocide'.[19]

The International Criminal Tribunal for the former Yugoslavia (ICTY), in the *Jelisić* case, stated that killings committed by a single perpetrator are enough:

to establish the material element of the crime of genocide and it is *a priori* possible to conceive that the accused harboured the plan to exterminate an entire group without this intent having been supported by any organisation in which other individuals participated.

The Chamber 'did not discount the possibility of a lone individual seeking to destroy a group as such'.[20] Such a view is not supported consistently in the case law, or in academic writing,[21] with some taking the view that the very nature of genocide requires a structural element.[22] Mark Drumbl rightly notes that '[a]rchetypically, genocide is a collective crime',[23] but a collective element is not a legally required element of the crime.[24]

---

[18] *Kupreškić et al.*, ICTY TC II, 14 January 2000, para. 636.
[19] Valerie Oosterveld, 'Context of Genocide' in Roy Lee et al. (eds.), *The International Criminal Court: Elements of Crimes and Rules of Procedure and Evidence* (New York, 2001) 44, 45.
[20] *Jelisić*, ICTY TC, 14 December 1999, para. 100.
[21] Even in *Jelisić*, the Trial Chamber stated, at para. 78: 'the Trial Chamber will have to verify that there was both an intentional attack against a group and an intention on the part of the accused to participate in or carry out this attack'. And see *Kayishema*, ICTR TC II, 21 May 1999, paras. 94, 276. On both sides of the academic debate, see William Schabas, 'The *Jelisić* Case and the *Mens Rea* of the Crime of Genocide' (2001) 14 *LJIL* 125; William Schabas, 'Darfur and the "Odious Scourge": The Commission of Inquiry's Findings on Genocide' (2005) 18 *LJIL* 871; Otto Triffterer, 'Genocide: Its Particular Intent to Destroy in Whole or in Part the Group as Such' (2001) 14 *LJIL* 399; John Quigley, *The Genocide Convention: An International Law Analysis* (Aldershot, 2006) 164–70; Antonio Cassese, 'Is Genocidal Policy a Requirement for the Crime of Genocide?' in Paola Gaeta (ed.), *The UN Genocide Convention* (Oxford, 2009) 128.
[22] Hans Vest, 'A Structure-based Concept of Genocidal Intent' (2007) 5 *JICJ* 781.
[23] Drumbl, 'The Crime of Genocide' (n. 5) 38.
[24] Kai Ambos, *Treatise on International Criminal Law*, Vol. I, *Foundations and General Part*, 2nd ed. (Oxford, 2021) 355–8.

It is ordinarily assumed, therefore, that several protagonists are involved in the crime of genocide.[25] Although it is not a formal element of the crime that there be a genocidal plan,[26] the Tribunals have noted that it would be difficult to commit genocide without one.[27] The only realistic exception may be a case in which others were committing crimes against humanity without genocidal intent, but a single perpetrator had the intent to eliminate a group while committing the same atrocities. In such a situation, the surrounding crimes against humanity would already provide the pattern of mass atrocities, so it might be conceivable for an individual with the necessary intent to carry out acts that could be described as 'genocide'.[28]

Two different ways have been proposed for ensuring that the crime of genocide includes some objective dimension of scale or a threat to a group. The first approach is that taken in the ICC Elements of Crimes, which add a 'contextual element' to the *actus reus*, requiring that the conduct for which the defendant is on trial takes place in the context of 'a manifest pattern of similar conduct' or is of itself able to destroy at least part of the group. This contextual element rules out most situations of isolated crimes by requiring either a broader pattern of crimes or a concrete threat to the group. It is discussed in more detail at Section 10.3.2.

The alternative approach, proposed in the context of the intent requirement, is that there must be an organized and widespread plan to exterminate a group and the perpetrator must act with *knowledge* that the commission of the individual act would, or would be likely to, further the implementation of the plan.[29] This approach, which has not to date been accepted in jurisprudence of international Tribunals, is discussed in Section 10.4.1.

10.2 PROTECTED GROUPS

Not all groups of people are protected by the Genocide Convention.[30] The Convention lists only national, ethnic, racial, and religious groups, and the list is a closed one. During the negotiation of the Convention, attempts were made to include other groups, such as social and political ones, but those proposals failed.[31] Ever since the conclusion of the Convention, there have been criticisms of its narrow focus and proposals have been made to expand it, but these have all been similarly unsuccessful.[32] It has also been

---

[25] *Krstić*, ICTY TC I, 2 August 2001, para. 549. [26] *Jelisić*, ICTY AC, 19 July 2001, para. 48.
[27] *Kayishema*, ICTR TC II, 21 May 1999, para. 94; *Jelisić*, ICTY TC, 14 December 1999, para. 101.
[28] See Valerie Oosterveld and Charles Garraway, 'The Elements of Genocide' in Roy Lee et al. (eds.), *The International Criminal Court: Elements of Crimes and Rules of Procedure and Evidence* (New York, 2001) 41, 47–8.
[29] See John R. W. D. Jones, 'Whose Intent is It Anyway?' in Lal Chand Vohrah et al. (eds.), *Man's Inhumanity to Man: Essays in Honour of Antonio Cassese* (The Hague, 2003) 467.
[30] See generally Lars Berster, 'Article II' in Christian Tams, Lars Berster, and Björn Schiffbauer, *Convention on the Prevention and Punishment of the Crime of Genocide: A Commentary* (Oxford, 2014) 99–115.
[31] UN GAOR, 3rd session, 6th Committee, 664; see William Schabas, *Genocide in International Law*, 2nd ed. (Cambridge, 2009) 153–71.
[32] For attempts made during the ICC negotiations, see *Report of the Ad Hoc Committee on the Establishment of an International Criminal Court*, UN GAOR 50th Sess., Supp. No. 22, A/50/22 (1995) paras. 60–1 and *Report of the Preparatory Committee on the Establishment of an International Criminal Court*, vol. I, UN GAOR, 51st Sess., Supp. No. 22, A/51/22 (1996) paras. 59–60. See generally, David Nersessian, *Genocide and Political Groups* (Oxford, 2010).

suggested that other groups come within the scope of genocide by virtue of customary international law.[33]

Another approach has been to expansively interpret the existing terms so as to include other groups within the definition. For example, the ICTR Trial Chamber in the *Akayesu* case determined on the basis of a (mis)reading of the *travaux préparatoires* that the drafters of the Convention intended to protect any stable and permanent group, rather than the groups specifically mentioned.[34] This approach was followed by the Commission of Inquiry established at the request of the Security Council to investigate violations of international criminal law in Darfur.[35] The Commission stated that this expansive interpretation had 'become part and parcel of international customary law'.[36]

While stability and permanence were certainly used as criteria by some delegates in the Sixth Committee to argue for or against the inclusion of a particular group in the drafting of the Convention, there is no evidence that these criteria were accepted as an open-ended description of protected groups. The enumerated list of groups, rightly or wrongly, was intended to be exhaustive.[37] The view that the Convention list of groups is not exhaustive is not supported by case law other than *Akayesu*, nor by general state practice and *opinio juris*, and cannot be seen as reflective of current law. The ICTY Appeals Chamber[38] and the ICC have adopted this view.[39]

There are national jurisdictions that have adopted wider formulations of the protected groups in their domestic law.[40] At the domestic level, states are entitled to use broader definitions without requiring other states to accept them.[41] It has been rightly said that it is precisely because of the rigours of the definition, and because of its focus on crimes aimed at the eradication of particular groups, that the label of 'genocide' is especially stigmatizing.[42]

10.2.1 National, Ethnic, Racial, and Religious Groups

Given that national, ethnic, racial, and religious groups are the exclusive beneficiaries of the protection of the Genocide Convention, it is unfortunate that there is no internationally recognized definition of any of the terms it uses. It is difficult to attribute a distinct meaning

---

[33] Beth Van Schaack, 'The Crime of Political Genocide: Repairing the Genocide Convention's Blind Spot' (1997) 106 *Yale Law Journal* 2259.

[34] *Akayesu*, ICTR TC I, 2 September 1998, para. 516. For critique see Schabas, *Genocide* (n. 31) 151–3. In support, see Diane Marie Amann, 'International Decisions: *Prosecutor v Akayesu*' (1999) 93 *AJIL* 195.

[35] SC Res. 1564 (2004), 18 September 2004. The Commission ('the Darfur Commission') was established by the UN Secretary-General 'to investigate reports of violations of international humanitarian law and human rights law in Darfur by all parties, to determine also whether or not acts of genocide have occurred, and to identify the perpetrators of such violations with a view to ensuring that those responsible are held accountable'. See generally Drumbl, 'The Crime of Genocide' (n. 5) 43–6.

[36] *Report of the International Commission of Inquiry on Violations of International Humanitarian Law and Human Rights Law in Darfur*, UN Doc.S/2005/60 (2005) para. 501.

[37] Ambos, *Treatise on International Criminal Law* (n. 24) 341, 346. [38] *Krstić*, ICTY AC, 19 April 2004, paras. 6–8.

[39] *Al Bashir*, ICC PTC I, 4 March 2009 (ICC-02/05–01/09–3) paras. 134–7.

[40] For example, see the Spanish *Pinochet* case, noted in (1999) 93 *AJIL* 690, especially 693. More generally see Ambos, *Treatise on International Criminal Law* (n. 24) 347; Fanny Martin, 'The Notion of "Protected Groups" in the Genocide Convention and its Application' in Paola Gaeta (ed.), *The UN Genocide Convention* (Oxford, 2009) 112.

[41] Genocide charges against General Pinochet were not considered in the extradition process in the United Kingdom, on the basis that they relied on an interpretation of genocide broader than that in international law; see David Turns, 'Pinochet's Fallout: Jurisdiction and Immunity for Criminal Violations of International Law' (2000) 20 *Legal Studies* 566, 567–8.

[42] Schabas, *Genocide* (n. 31) 10.

to each group, since they overlap considerably.[43] The ICTR attempted to give each one a meaning. In its judgments, it described a national group as a 'collection of people who are perceived to share a legal bond based on common citizenship, coupled with reciprocity of rights and duties'.[44] It described the 'conventional definition' of racial group as 'based on the hereditary physical traits often identified with a geographical region, irrespective of linguistic, cultural, national or religious factors'.[45] It defined an ethnic group as 'a group whose members share a common language or culture',[46] and 'a religious group includes denomination or mode of worship or a group sharing common beliefs'.[47]

However, defining each term creates challenges. The ICTR Trial Chamber in *Akayesu* ran into difficulties in assessing whether the Tutsi were a protected group in the context of the widespread massacres in Rwanda.[48] Having defined an ethnic group as sharing a common language or culture, the evidence before the Chamber made it clear that this was not the trait that distinguished the Tutsis from the Hutus. The Chamber had to rely on the fact that Rwandans were required to carry identification cards indicating the ethnicity of the bearer as Hutu, Tutsi, or Twa and that the Tutsi constituted a group referred to as 'ethnic' in official classifications. It was only by virtue of its determination that any 'stable and permanent' group was covered by the Convention, and therefore by the ICTR Statute, that the Chamber was able to find that the Tutsi were a protected group.[49] As mentioned above, the decision on this point is not legally defensible. That would not, however, change the outcome in this case, as the Tutsi are considered an ethnic group on the correct interpretation of the Convention, and the ICTR since took judicial notice of that fact.[50]

The better approach, followed by the *Krstić* Trial Chamber, is to recognize that the list is exhaustive but to accept that the four groups were not given distinct and different meanings in the Convention. As the judges said:

The preparatory work of the Convention shows that setting out such a list was designed more to describe a single phenomenon, roughly corresponding to what was recognised, before the Second World War, as 'national minorities', rather than to refer to several distinct prototypes of human groups. To attempt to differentiate each of the named groups on the basis of scientifically objective criteria would thus be inconsistent with the object and purpose of the Convention.[51]

The groups also 'help to define each other, operating much as four corner posts that delimit an area within which a myriad of groups covered by the Convention find protection'.[52] This 'four corners' approach avoids the difficulties of fitting a group such as the Tutsis precisely

---

[43] For a powerful argument in favour of identifying separate meanings, see Claus Kreß, 'The Crime of Genocide under International Law' (2006) 6 *ICLR* 461.
[44] *Akayesu*, ICTR TC I, 2 September 1998, para. 511. [45] *Ibid*. para. 513.
[46] *Ibid*. paras. 512–15 and see *Kayishema*, ICTR, TC II, 21 May 1999, para. 98. [47] *Ibid*.
[48] For critique of the Chamber's reasoning, see Payam Akhavan, 'The Crime of Genocide in the ICTR Jurisprudence' (2005) 3 *JICJ* 989.
[49] *Akayesu*, ICTR TC I, 2 September 1998, para. 702. [50] *Karemera et al.*, ICTR TC III, 11 December 2006.
[51] *Krstić*, ICTY TC I, 2 August 2001, paras. 555–6 (footnotes not included); the Chamber followed the approach in Schabas, *Genocide* (n. 33) 128–32; and see *Rutaganda*, ICTR TC I, 6 December 1999, para. 56. See also Doudou Thiam, Special Rapporteur, *Fourth Report on the Draft Code of Offences Against the Peace and Security of Mankind*, UN Doc. A/CN.4/398 (11 March 1986) para. 56.
[52] Schabas, *Genocide* (n. 31) 129.

into one of the listed categories, but ensures that it comes within the area of protection that was intended by the negotiators, while also respecting the negotiators' intent that the list be a closed one.

10.2.2 Identifying the Group and Its Members

As is clear from the wording of the different parts of the *actus reus* of the offence, the acts must be directed at members of the group. However, determination of the groups and their members is not a simple matter.[53] There are genuine difficulties in deciding if a person is a member of the group. For example, should the group be identified objectively (pointing to factual distinctions) or subjectively (based on perceptions)?[54]

It is by no means clear that groups intended to be protected by the Genocide Convention always have an objective existence in the manner which the drafters thought. Groups are often social constructs, rather than scientific facts. This problem was discussed by the Darfur Commission, owing to the fact that, although the United States had described the crimes committed in Darfur as 'genocide',[55] on close analysis the question of group existence in Darfur was complicated. The Commission found that the Fur, Massalit, and Zaghawa groups did not appear to make up ethnic groups distinct from those to which their attackers belonged. They had the same religion, and the same language, though the 'Africans' spoke their own dialect in addition to Arabic, while the 'Arabs' spoke only Arabic. Years of inter-marriage and coexistence had blurred the distinction between the groups. The sedentary or nomadic character of the groups appeared to constitute one of the main distinctions between them.[56]

The Commission relied upon a partially subjective concept of groups in deciding that the victim groups nevertheless came within the scope of the crime of genocide. Victims and perpetrators had 'come to perceive themselves as either "African" or "Arab"'. A 'self-perception of two distinct groups' had emerged.[57] When the same question came before the ICC Pre-Trial Chamber in the *Al Bashir* case, the majority found that each of the three groups had 'its own language, its own tribal customs and its own traditional links to its lands' and was therefore a distinct ethnic group. The majority did not consider it necessary to explore the subjective or objective approach to the definition of groups.[58] In her dissent, Judge Ušacka argued that the three groups ought to be taken together as, in the Darfurian context, the ethnic faultline was considered to fall along the grounds of 'Arab' and 'African', the latter encompassing all three groups.[59]

A subjective approach has its attractions: that is, the criterion for the identification of members of the group is that a perpetrator considers the victims to be members of a group he

---

[53] See e.g. Berster, 'Article II' (n. 30) 99–115.
[54] In the human rights context, see the decision of the Human Rights Committee in *Lovelace* v. *Canada* (22/47).
[55] House Concurrent Resolution 467, Senate Concurrent Resolution 133, 22 July 2004.
[56] Report, UN Doc. S/2005/60, para. 508. [57] *Ibid.* para. 511.
[58] *Al Bashir*, ICC PTC I, 4 March 2009 (ICC-02/05–01/09–3) para. 137 and note 152. Judge Ušacka adopted the mixed objective/ subjective approach used by the ICTY and ICTR; Partially Dissenting Opinion of Judge Ušacka, para. 23. The decision of the majority was accepted in *Al Bashir*, ICC PTC I, 12 July 2010 (ICC-02/05–01/09–95) para. 9.
[59] *Ibid.* paras. 24–6.

or she is targeting. The most significant factor in a particular case may be that the perpetrators have the specific intent to destroy a group identified by themselves. As was said in the *Bagilishema* case:

A group may not have precisely defined boundaries and there may be occasions when it is difficult to give a definitive answer as to whether or not a victim was a member of a protected group. Moreover, the perpetrators of genocide may characterize the targeted group in ways that do not fully correspond to conceptions of the group shared generally, or by other segments of society. In such a case, the Chamber is of the opinion that, on the evidence, if a victim was perceived by a perpetrator as belonging to a protected group, the victim should be considered by the Chamber as a member of the protected group, for the purposes of genocide.[60]

However, reliance on a purely subjective approach is uncomfortable, as it may be, as with all racism, that perceptions may be based on imagined distinctions rather than objective ones.[61] While the ad hoc Tribunals have in some cases appeared to use an entirely subjective approach,[62] the better view is that the group must have some form of at least perceived reality in the first place; otherwise the Convention could be used to protect fictitious national, ethnic, racial or religious groups.

It now seems settled that the identification of members of the group cannot be solely subjective. To overcome the problems of purely objective and purely subjective approaches, the Tribunals have adopted an approach that blends the two. The approach is sensitive to the fact that the idea of a separate group may not have a basis in objective facts, but can be a set of reified beliefs about difference. Thus, determining whether a group is a protected one should be 'assessed on a case-by-case basis by reference to the objective particulars of a given social or historical context, and by the subjective perceptions of the perpetrators'.[63]

In addition, it is now well established that, notwithstanding some case law to the contrary,[64] a group cannot be defined 'negatively', that is, by identifying persons not sharing the group characteristics of the perpetrators, for example, 'non-Serbs'.[65] It is also the case that where a person has a mixed identity, if he or she is targeted on the basis of membership of the protected group, the person so targeting them may be guilty of genocide. Thus, in the *Ndindabahizi* case, the ICTR accepted that a half-Belgian, half-Rwandan man, who was targeted as a Tutsi in the Rwandan genocide, was, in context, a member of a protected group.[66]

---

[60] *Bagilishema*, ICTR TC I, 7 June 2001, para. 65. [61] See Schabas, 'Darfur and the "Odious Scourge"' (n. 21) 879.
[62] *Kayishema*, ICTR TC II, 21 May 1999, para. 98; *Jelisić*, ICTY TC, 14 December 1999, paras. 69–72.
[63] *Semanza*, ICTR TC III, 15 May 2003, para. 317. For a critique, see Richard Wilson, *Writing History in International Criminal Tribunals* (Cambridge, 2011) ch. 7.
[64] *Jelisić*, ICTY TC, 14 December 1999, paras. 70, 71; and see Judge Shahabuddeen's powerful dissent in *Stakić*, ICTY AC, 22 March 2006, paras. 8–18.
[65] *Stakić*, ICTY TC II, 31 July 2003, para. 512; ICTY AC, 22 March 2006, paras. 19–28. See also *Bosnian Genocide* case (n. 7) paras. 193–4.
[66] *Ndindabahizi*, ICTR TC I, 15 July 2004, paras. 467–9. The conviction was overturned on appeal, on factual rather than legal grounds. *Ndindabahizi*, ICTR AC, 16 January 2007, para. 117.

10.3 MATERIAL ELEMENTS

10.3.1 Prohibited Acts

Not every act committed with the intent to destroy, in whole or in part, a protected group will lead to a conviction for genocide. Only those which are mentioned in Article II of the Convention may form the *actus reus* of genocide. Further, it is important to remember that it is not necessary to show that the relevant act assisted in destroying a protected group: what is needed is that it was committed with the intent to destroy the group. Although all of the underlying crimes are defined by reference to victims in the plural, the ICC Elements of Crimes state that even one victim suffices, if the relevant act is committed with the necessary intent. This does, though, create issues with respect to Article 6(c), which refers to inflicting conditions of life on the 'group'.

Killing

Article II(a) covers the paradigmatic conduct that amounts to genocide: killing members[67] of the group. However, there are certain interpretative problems which needed to be resolved. The English term 'killing' (which the ICC Elements of Crimes state is interchangeable with 'caused death') is neutral as to whether the killing is intentional, or whether reckless (or perhaps even negligent) causing of death suffices. The term used in the French version of the Genocide Convention, '*meurtre*', is more precise as it refers to intentional killing. In *Kayishema*, the ICTR determined that there is virtually no difference between the terms in the English and French versions of the Convention.[68] The act must be intentional but not necessarily premeditated.[69] If there is doubt about the intention to kill, rather than the intention to cause serious harm, it is of course possible to charge the defendant pursuant to Article II(b) of the Convention for the conduct that led to the death.

Causing Serious Bodily or Mental Harm to Members of the Group

Article II(b) of the Convention criminalizes the causing of serious bodily or mental harm to victims. The ICTY has determined that the harm needs to constitute 'a grave and long-term disadvantage to a person's ability to lead a normal and constructive life'.[70] The ICTR in the *Akayesu* case broke new ground in deciding that rape and other acts of sexual violence can constitute genocide; sexual violence was found to be an integral part of the process of destruction in the Rwanda genocide.[71] The ICC Elements follow this approach.[72]

   Owing to its concerns about the possible breadth of the mental harm aspect of genocide, the United States entered an 'understanding' to the Convention upon ratifying, which stated that the term 'means permanent impairment of mental faculties through drugs, torture or similar techniques'. Serious mental harm does mean more than minor or temporary impairment of

---

[67] Note, however, that one killing may suffice.
[68] *Kayishema*, ICTR AC, 1 June 2001, para. 151; for a critique see David Nersessian, 'The Contours of Genocidal Intent: Troubling Jurisprudence from the International Criminal Tribunals' (2002) 37 *Texas International Law Journal* 231.
[69] See e.g. *Stakić*, ICTY TC II, 31 July 2003, para. 515. [70] *Krstić*, ICTY TC, 2 August 2001, para. 513.
[71] *Akayesu*, ICTR TC I, 2 September 1998, para. 731. [72] ICC Elements of Crimes, Art. 6(b), note 3.

mental faculties,[73] but neither mental nor physical harm need be permanent.[74] Obviously, as the term 'serious' is one which involves a value judgement,[75] there will be differing views on what treatment is included. In *Kayishema*, it was held that decisions on what is meant by serious bodily or mental harm should be made on a case-by-case basis.[76]

Deliberately Inflicting on the Group Conditions of Life Calculated to Bring About Its Physical Destruction in Whole or in Part

This category of prohibited acts comprises methods of destruction whereby the perpetrator does not immediately kill the members of the group, but which seek to bring about their physical destruction in the end.[77] The ICC Elements of Crimes interpret the term 'conditions of life' as including but 'not necessarily restricted to, deliberate deprivation of resources indispensable for survival, such as food or medical services, or systematic expulsion from homes'.[78] Unlike the two previous categories, this is not a result-based form of the crime[79] but it requires that the conditions are 'calculated' to achieve the result.[80]

The question of the forced migration of people, commonly known by the ugly term 'ethnic cleansing', has been addressed under this subparagraph of Article II. This practice, when committed by the Serbs to eliminate the Muslim presence in large parts of Bosnia-Herzegovina, was regarded by ad hoc Judge Lauterpacht in the ICJ provisional measures ruling of 13 September 1993 as constituting genocide,[81] though his view was not shared by the majority. As seen above, the ICC Elements give 'systematic expulsion from homes' as one of the illustrations of this category of prohibited act.

Ethnic cleansing does not necessarily constitute genocide.[82] In the *Eichmann* case, the District Court of Jerusalem found that, before 1941, Nazi persecution of the German Jewish population was aimed at persuading them to leave Germany. Only later did the policy develop into one of extermination. Since the court doubted that there was a specific intent to exterminate before 1941, Eichmann was acquitted of genocide for acts before that date.[83]

Eichmann is authority for the proposition that insofar as the objective of a forced migration is 'only' to remove a group or part of it from a territory, it differs from that of genocide. In *Brđanin*, for example, the Trial Chamber found a 'consistent, coherent and criminal strategy of cleansing the Bosnian Krajina' but determined that the crimes had been committed with 'the sole purpose of driving people away'.[84] There was no evidence that they had been

---

[73] *Semanza*, ICTR TC III, 15 May 2003, para. 321.

[74] *Akayesu*, ICTR TC I, 2 September 1998, para. 502. The *Kayishema* Trial Chamber gave perhaps a narrower interpretation as 'harm that seriously injures the health, causes disfigurement or causes any serious injury to the external, internal organs or senses'; *Kayishema*, ICTR TC II, 21 May 1999, para. 109.

[75] See Berster, 'Article II' (n. 30) 118–21.

[76] *Ibid.* para. 110. Examples of mental harm were given in *Blagojević*, ICTY TC I, 17 January 2005, para. 647.

[77] *Akayesu*, ICTR TC I, 2 September 1998, para. 505. See generally Berster, 'Article II' (n. 30) 121–6.

[78] ICC Elements of Crimes, Art. 6(c), note 4.   [79] See e.g. *Stakić*, ICTY TC II, 31 July 2003, para. 517.

[80] As pointed out in Kreß, 'The Crime of Genocide' (n. 43) 481–3, 'calculated' and 'physical destruction' are not simple concepts.

[81] *Application of the Convention on the Prevention and Punishment of the Crime of Genocide (Bosnia and Herzegovina v. Yugoslavia (Serbia and Montenegro))* [1993] ICJ Rep. 325, 431–2. Ethnic cleansing was also considered genocide by the ICTY in the decision confirming the second indictment in *Karadžić and Mladić*; review of the Indictments pursuant to Rule 61 of the Rules of Procedure and Evidence, ICTY TC I, 11 July 1996, para. 94.

[82] Berster, 'Article II' (n. 30) 131–2.

[83] *Attorney-General of Israel v. Eichmann* (1968) 36 ILR 5 (DC). See Schabas, *Genocide* (n. 31) 233–4.

[84] *Brđanin*, ICTY TC II, 1 September 2004, para. 118.

committed with the intent required for genocide.[85] The fact of forced migration alone is not enough for a court to deduce the special intent of destruction of the group.

The matter was usefully summed up by the ICJ in the *Bosnian Genocide* case:

> Neither the intent, as a matter of policy, to render an area 'ethnically homogeneous', nor the operations that may be carried out to implement such policy, can *as such* be designated as genocide: the intent that characterizes genocide is 'to destroy, in whole or in part' a particular group, and deportation or displacement of the members of a group, even if effected by force, is not necessarily equivalent to destruction of that group, nor is such destruction an automatic consequence of the displacement. This is not to say that acts described as 'ethnic cleansing' may never constitute genocide, if they are such as to be characterized as, for example, 'deliberately inflicting on the group conditions of life calculated to bring about its physical destruction in whole or in part', contrary to Article II, paragraph (c), of the Convention . . . the term 'ethnic cleansing' has no legal significance of its own. That said, it is clear that acts of 'ethnic cleansing' may occur in parallel to acts prohibited by Article II of the Convention, and may be significant as indicative of the presence of a specific intent *(dolus specialis)* inspiring those acts.[86]

Imposing Measures Intended to Prevent Births Within the Group

Article II(d) of the Genocide Convention, replicated in, for example, the Rome Statute, was inspired by the Nazis' practice of forced sterilization before and during the Second World War. Other examples of these measures are sexual mutilation, forced birth control, separation of the sexes, prohibition of marriages, and forced abortion.[87] The ICTR, in *Akayesu*, added two other examples: 'rape can be a measure intended to prevent births when the person raped subsequently refuses to procreate' and when a woman of the targeted group is 'deliberately impregnated by a man of another group, with the intent to have her give birth to a child who will consequently not belong to its mother's group'.[88] This provision includes an additional intent requirement, as the measures imposed must have been intended to prevent births within the group.[89]

Forcibly Transferring Children of the Group to Another Group

Forcibly transferring children of one group to another group is a form of genocide which has received little judicial consideration[90] and has been described as a 'conceptual mis-fit' in the list of prohibited acts.[91] Probably the most authoritative interpretative source on the point is to be found in the ICC Elements of Crimes (Article 6(e)), defining children as being those below eighteen and noting that:

---

[85] *Ibid.* para. 989. See also *Stakić*, ICTY TC II, 31 July 2003, paras. 519, 557 and ICTY AC, 22 March 2006, paras. 46–8.
[86] *Bosnian Genocide* case (n. 7) para. 190.
[87] *Akayesu*, ICTR TC I, 2 September 1998, para. 507. As Grey notes, forced abortion 'was expressly considered in the Genocide Convention's drafting history as a measure aimed at preventing births'. She would add deliberately causing a miscarriage to this list: Rosemary Grey, 'A Legal Analysis of Genocide by "Imposing Measures Intended to Prevent Births": Myanmar and Beyond' (2024) 26(3) *Journal of Genocide Research*, DOI: 10.1080/14623528.2023.2252662.
[88] *Akayesu, ibid.* paras. 507–8. [89] *Popović et al.*, ICTY TC II, 10 June 2010, para. 819.
[90] Although see *Akayesu*, ICTR TC I, 2 September 1998, para. 509. The ICJ looked at the issue, rather sceptically, in the *Bosnian Genocide* case (n. 7) para. 362. For general consideration, see Berster, 'Article II' (n. 30) 128–31.
[91] This is because it does not reflect purely physical or biological genocide like the other acts in the list: Grey (n. 87).

[t]he term 'forcibly' is not restricted to physical force, but may include threat of force or coercion, such as that caused by fear of violence, duress, detention, psychological oppression or abuse of power, against such person or persons or another person, or by taking advantage of a coercive environment.

This provision, Article II(e), was included in the Genocide Convention as a compromise for the exclusion of cultural genocide. In 1997, the Australian Human Rights and Equal Opportunities Commission decided that the forcible transfer of Aboriginal children to non-Indigenous institutions and families constituted genocide.[92] The wording of the Commission's findings indicated, however, that it was 'cultural genocide' that it had in mind, since the objective of the transfers was to assimilate the children into non-Aboriginal society. The mainstream view is that cultural genocide is not within the scope of the Convention,[93] nor in customary law,[94] although forcibly transferring children can be close to such a concept. Canada's Truth and Reconciliation Commission subsequently used the term 'cultural genocide' in 2015 to describe government acts between 1867 and 2000 which included forcible removal of Indigenous children from their homes and communities and transfer to residential schools in which the children were prohibited from speaking their language or practicing their culture.[95] However, the 2019 report of Canada's National Inquiry into Missing and Murdered Indigenous Women and Girls simply used the term 'genocide', stating that Canada's treatment of Indigenous peoples satisfies the Genocide Convention definition.[96]

10.3.2 'Contextual Element'

The ICC Elements of Crimes have an additional material element, which was introduced to avoid the problem that isolated hate crimes could fall within the Convention definition, diluting the seriousness of the term 'genocide'.[97] In relation to each prohibited act, the element requires that:

[t]he conduct took place in the context of a manifest pattern of similar conduct directed against that group or was conduct that could itself effect such destruction.[98]

The first branch of this element reflects the more likely situation, where the individual accused is acting within a broader context in which others are also committing acts of genocide (or crimes against humanity) against the targeted group.[99] The adjective

---

[92] Cited in Schabas, *Genocide* (n. 31) 205.   [93] See Section 10.4.1.
[94] *Krstić*, ICTY TC, I, 2 August 2001, para. 580; *Krstić*, ICTY AC, 19 April 2004, para. 25.
[95] The Commission referred to 'cultural genocide' throughout its reports. For a discussion of its relation to forcible transfer of children, see Truth and Reconciliation Commission of Canada, *Canada's Residential Schools: The Legacy, The Final Report of the Truth and Reconciliation Commission of Canada*, Vol. 5 (2015), 10, 125–6.
[96] Chief Commissioner Marion Buller et al., *Reclaiming Power and Place: The Final Report of the National Inquiry into Missing and Murdered Indigenous Women and Girls*, Volume 1a (Ottawa, 2019) 50–4. See also Chief Commissioner Marion Buller et al., *A Legal Analysis of Genocide, Supplementary Report of the National Inquiry into Missing and Murdered Indigenous Women and Girls* (Ottawa, 2019).
[97] See Section 10.1.4.   [98] Oosterveld and Garraway, 'The Elements of Genocide' (n. 28) 41, 44, 45.
[99] Or, if the other perpetrators do not have the genocidal intent, they may be committing crimes against humanity rather than genocide, while still in a 'manifest pattern of similar conduct'.

'manifest', included at the insistence of the United States, means that the pattern must be a clear one and not one of a few isolated crimes occurring over a period of years.[100]

The second branch applies where the conduct in question 'could itself effect such destruction'. Although by far the less likely scenario, this could occur where a group is particularly small or where the accused has access to powerful means of destruction (such as the use of a nuclear or biological weapon) with genocidal intent. In such a case, there is no need for a pattern of similar conduct, since the accused is in a position to pose a real threat to a protected group. The provision would be relevant for prosecutions of ringleaders and instigators. It would also capture those who had the means to destroy a group but for whatever reason managed to cause only a single death or a few deaths, such that there would be no objective 'pattern'.[101]

The contextual element does not entirely exclude the possibility of a 'lone *génocidaire*', since it requires similar conduct, not similar intent;[102] the second clause of the element also envisages a single perpetrator with the means to destroy the group or part of it. The element requires either a pattern of crimes, or a concrete danger to a group, thereby ruling out isolated hate crimes.

The Elements of Crimes are equivocal on the mental element attaching to this element:

Notwithstanding the normal requirement for a mental element provided for in article 30, and recognizing that knowledge of the circumstances will usually be addressed in proving genocidal intent, the appropriate requirement, if any, for a mental element regarding this circumstance will need to be decided by the Court on a case-by-case basis.[103]

The 'contextual element' was based very loosely on two passages in the *Akayesu* trial judgment.[104] The ICTY Trial Chamber in *Krstić* adopted the element although it was not obliged to,[105] but the Appeals Chamber was hostile to the Trial Chamber's view:

The Trial Chamber relied on the definition of genocide in the Elements of Crimes adopted by the ICC. This definition, stated the Trial Chamber, 'indicates clearly that genocide requires that "the conduct took place in the context of a manifest pattern of similar conduct"'. The Trial Chamber's reliance on the definition of genocide given in the ICC's Elements of Crimes is inapposite . . . the requirement that the prohibited conduct be part of a widespread or systematic attack does not appear in the Genocide Convention and was not mandated by customary international law. Because the definition adopted by the Elements of Crimes did not reflect customary law as it existed at the time Krstić committed his crimes, it cannot be used to support the Trial Chamber's conclusion.[106]

In the ICC, on the other hand, a majority in a Pre-Trial Chamber took the view that the contextual provision in the Elements is not inconsistent with the ICC Statute and has therefore applied it.[107] The Chamber took the view that the contextual element was 'fully

[100] Oosterveld and Garraway, 'The Elements of Genocide' (n. 28) 47.
[101] Wiebke Ruckert and Georg Witschel, 'Genocide and Crimes Against Humanity in the Elements of Crimes' in Fischer et al., *International and National Prosecution*, 66.
[102] Oosterveld, 'Context of Genocide' (n. 19) 47–8. [103] Elements of Crimes, 'Introduction', Art. 6, para. 3.
[104] *Akayesu*, ICTR TC I, 2 September 1998, paras. 520 and 523. [105] *Krstić*, ICTY TC I, 2 August 2001, para. 682.
[106] *Krstić*, ICTY AC, 19 April 2004, para. 224.
[107] *Al Bashir*, ICC PTC I, 4 March 2009 (ICC-02/05–01/09–3) paras. 117–33 and *Al Bashir*, ICC PTC I, 12 July 2010 (ICC-02/05–01/09–95) para. 13. But the majority's conclusion (in the first decision) that the contextual element means that 'the relevant

consistent with the traditional consideration of the crime of genocide as the "crime of crimes".[108] Indeed, if genocide is to be seen as a particularly serious crime, it might be argued that 'scale and gravity'[109] must be maintained and the ICC Elements provision offers a formulation which has been accepted and adopted by consensus by the parties to the Rome Statute for the purposes of the ICC.

10.4 MENTAL ELEMENTS

The mental elements of genocide comprise both the requisite intention to commit the underlying prohibited act (such as killing) and the intent special to genocide. It is the special intent 'to destroy in whole or in part [a protected group] as such' that distinguishes genocide from other crimes.[110] But determining the meaning to be attributed to this intent requirement is a matter of some difficulty. There are four aspects to be considered, and they are interconnected. Does every perpetrator have to have a specific intent to destroy or is it sufficient, either for all, or at least for non-leaders, that they have knowledge of a collective plan and foresee that their conduct will further it? What is the meaning of 'destroy' for the purpose of the special intent? What is the 'whole' or 'part' of a group? What is the meaning of 'as such': is motive relevant? These four issues are considered below.

10.4.1 Intent

It is worth emphasizing that, unlike the crime of aggression, genocide is not a crime that may be committed only by those who lead and plan a campaign of destruction. The rank and file may also be *genocidaires*, provided they have the requisite intent.[111] The intention differs from the 'normal' intent in criminal law, as exemplified in Article 30 of the ICC Statute, which is a less stringent requirement than the special intent for genocide. Article 30 is, however, relevant to the underlying acts and to some other forms of liability in relation to genocide.[112]

In time of armed conflict, where the intention is to defeat the opposing side, it may be difficult to assess whether mass killings are committed with a genocidal intent or with the intent of winning the war. The findings of the ICTY in the *Krstić* case and of the Commission of Inquiry on Darfur provide useful illustrations. The defence in *Krstić* argued that the purpose of the killings in Srebrenica was not to destroy the group as such, but to remove a military threat; this was evidenced by the fact that men of military age had been

conduct presents a concrete threat to the existence of the targeted group' imposes a requirement not included in the element; see Separate and Partly Dissenting Opinion of Judge Anita Ušacka, para. 19, note 26. See also Claus Kreß, 'The Crime of Genocide and Contextual Elements: A Comment on the ICC Pre-Trial Chamber's Decision in the *Al Bashir* Case' (2009) 7 *JICJ* 1, and Robert Cryer, 'The Definitions of International Crimes in the *Al Bashir* Arrest Warrant Decision' (2009) 7 *JICJ* 283.

[108] *Al Bashir*, ICC PTC I, 4 March 2009 (ICC-02/05–01/09–3) para. 133.   [109] *Krstić*, ICTY TC I, 2 August 2001, para. 549.
[110] *Kambanda*, ICTR TC I, 4 September 1998, para. 16; *Kayishema*, ICTR TC II, 21 May 1999, para. 91.
[111] *Kayishema*, ICTR AC, 1 June 2001, para. 170.   [112] For other forms of participation in genocide, see Section 15.4.

Genocide

targeted. The Trial Chamber held, however, as affirmed by the Appeals Chamber, that the killings did constitute genocide. As they said:

the Bosnian Serb forces could not have failed to know, by the time they decided to kill all the men, that this selective destruction of the group would have a lasting impact upon the entire group. Their death precluded any effective attempt by the Bosnian Muslims to recapture the territory. Furthermore, the Bosnian Serb forces had to be aware of the catastrophic impact that the disappearance of two or three generations of men would have on the survival of a traditionally patriarchal society ... The Bosnian Serb forces knew by the time they decided to kill all of the military aged men, that the combination of those killings with the forcible transfer of the women, children and elderly would inevitably result in the physical disappearance of the Bosnian Muslim population at Srebrenica. Intent by the Bosnian Serb forces to target the Bosnian Muslims of Srebrenica as a group is further evidenced by their destroying homes of Bosnian Muslims in Srebrenica and Potocari and the principal mosque in Srebrenica soon after the attack. Finally, there is a strong indication of the intent to destroy the group as such in the concealment of the bodies in mass graves, which were later dug up, the bodies mutilated and reburied in other mass graves ... By killing all the military aged men, the Bosnian Serb forces effectively destroyed the community of the Bosnian Muslims in Srebrenica and eliminated all likelihood that it could ever re-establish itself on that territory.[113]

On the other hand, the Appeals Chamber decided that General Krstić himself did not personally have a genocidal intent and hence was not liable as a principal.[114] He was, however, held liable as an accessory to the genocidal attack on Srebrenica.[115]

Proof of Special Intent

Direct evidence of genocidal intent is difficult to find. The ad hoc Tribunals have been prepared to deduce intent from circumstantial evidence, including the actions and words of the perpetrator. In *Seromba*, for example, the defendant, a priest, had approved the decision to destroy a church to kill those inside it, had shown the bulldozer driver the weakest side of the church and directed him to destroy it. The Appeals Chamber found that Seromba 'knew that there were approximately 1,500 Tutsis in the church and that the destruction of the church would necessarily cause their death'.

More questionably, the ICTR Trial Chamber also stated in the *Akayesu* case that intent may be deduced from the behaviour of others, from:

the general context of the perpetration of other culpable acts systematically directed against that same group, whether these acts were committed by the same offender or by others. Other factors, such as the scale of atrocities committed, their general nature, in a region or a country, or furthermore, the fact of deliberately and systematically targeting victims on account of their membership of a particular group, while excluding the members of other groups, can enable the Chamber to infer the genocidal intent of a particular act.[116]

[113] *Krstić*, ICTY TC I, 2 August 2001, paras. 595–7. [114] *Krstić*, ICTY AC, 19 April 2004, para. 134.
[115] *Ibid.*, paras. 135–44. Similarly, the Darfur Commission decided that the policy of attacking, killing and forcibly displacing members of some tribes in Darfur did not show the special intent of genocide, but rather the intent 'to drive the victims from their homes, primarily for purposes of counter-insurgency warfare'; Report, UN Doc. S/2005/60 (2005) para. 518.
[116] *Akayesu*, ICTR TC I, 2 September 1998, para. 523.

This was somewhat tempered by the Appeals Chamber in *Stakić*, which noted that the Trial Chamber in that case 'considered whether the apparent intentions of others ... could provide indirect evidence of the Appellant's own intentions when he agreed with those others to undertake criminal plans'.[117] As the Appeals Chamber also noted, all the evidence (such as the type of attacks, discriminatory animus, the use of derogatory slurs, attacks on religious sites and 'targeting of ... leaders for death or slander')[118] must be taken together when determining intent since, looking at each piece individually rather than cumulatively as the Trial Chamber did, 'obscured the proper inquiry'.[119]

Intention versus Knowledge

Some point to the reality that foot soldiers may be following orders without necessarily having an intent to destroy a whole group, thereby creating a problem of evidence if the intent to destroy the group was measured through each individual foot soldier.[120] In relation to an accused who participated in a genocidal campaign, courts may therefore face the difficult choice between acquittal for lack of evidence of the special intent as normally defined and 'squeezing ambiguous fact patterns into the specific intent paradigm'.[121] Courts may be tempted to ease the requirements of evidence by drawing wide implications from their findings of fact, thus establishing the special intent 'by the evidentiary backdoor'.[122] These difficulties have led commentators to propose alternative formulations of the intent necessary for genocide. In particular, Alexander Greenawalt has suggested:

In cases where a perpetrator is otherwise liable for a genocidal act, the requirement of genocidal intent should be satisfied if the perpetrator acted in furtherance of a campaign targeting members of a protected group and knew that the goal or manifest effect of the campaign was the destruction of the group in whole or in part.[123]

This 'knowledge-based' approach, which is more akin to what is required by Article 30 of the ICC Statute, is to be distinguished from the 'purpose-based' approach used by the ad hoc Tribunals and the ICC in interpreting the crime of genocide. Some commentators argue that the purpose-based approach goes beyond what is envisaged in the Genocide Convention.[124] They distinguish between the collective intent, manifested in an overall genocidal plan or campaign, and the individual intent which, in their view, need involve only knowledge of the plan on the part of the individual perpetrator together with foresight or recklessness as to the occurrence of the planned destruction.[125]

---

[117] *Stakić*, ICTY AC, 22 March 2006, para. 40. [118] *Ibid*. para. 53. [119] *Ibid*. para. 55.
[120] Harmen van der Wilt, 'Complicity in Genocide and International v. Domestic Jurisdiction: Reflections on the *van Anraat* Case' (2006) 4 *JICJ* 241–2.
[121] Alexander Greenawalt, 'Rethinking Genocidal Intent: The Case for a Knowledge-based Interpretation' (1999) 99 *Columbia Law Review* 2265, 2281.
[122] Claus Kreß, 'The Darfur Report and Genocidal Intent' (2005) 3 *JICJ* 565, 572.
[123] Greenawalt, 'Rethinking Genocidal Intent' (n. 121) 2288; and see Alicia Gil Gil, *Derecho penal internacional. Especial consideratión del delito de genocidio* (Madrid, 1999); Kreß, 'The Darfur Report' (n. 122) 577.
[124] Otto Triffterer, 'Genocide, Its Particular Intent to Destroy in Whole or in Part the Group as Such' (2001) 14 *LJIL* 399; Jones, 'Whose Intent?' (n. 29) 478.
[125] See Jones, 'Whose Intent?' (n. 29); Kreß, 'The Darfur Report' (n. 122) 576–7.

If such an approach were adopted, it would recognize the different roles of individuals involved in a collective act of genocide. In *Krstić*, however, the Appeals Chamber, while noting that the intent to destroy must be discernible in the joint participation of the crime itself, held that individual participators must each have the necessary intent.[126] This insistence on the special intent for each individual perpetrator remains the standard required for the crime of genocide by the case law and may be seen as correctly reflecting the need to reserve genocide convictions only for those who have the highest degree of criminal intent. In practice, however, accessorial modes of liability, such as aiding and abetting,[127] can allow conviction of persons as an accessory to genocide if they have knowledge of the genocide.[128] Prosecutors who are not sure of being able to prove the special intent are likely to charge such lesser modes of liability rather than genocide as a principal perpetrator.

10.4.2 'To Destroy'

Genocidal intent is eliminatory. The destruction specified in the Convention is physical or biological, although the means of causing the destruction of the group may be by acts short of causing the death of individuals.[129] Other forms of destruction – for example, the social assimilation of a group into another, or attacks on cultural characteristics which give a group its own identity – do not constitute genocide if they are not related to physical or biological destruction of the group. The *travaux préparatoires* of the Convention indicate that the inclusion of cultural genocide was hotly debated and eventually rejected.[130]

Some national jurisdictions have extended the meaning of genocide to cover other forms of destruction within their own law.[131] However, as the Trial Chamber in *Krstić* (which was quoted approvingly on appeal) put it:

despite recent developments, customary international law limits the definition of genocide to those acts seeking the physical or biological destruction of all or part of the group. An enterprise attacking only the cultural or sociological characteristics of a human group in order to annihilate these elements which give to that group its own identity distinct from the rest of the community would not fall under the definition of genocide.[132]

The Trial Chamber in the later case of *Blagojević* appears to have departed from this in finding that 'the forcible transfer of individuals could lead to the material destruction of the group, since the group ceases to exist as a group, or at least as the group was'. It emphasized 'that its reasoning and conclusion are not an argument for cultural genocide, but rather an attempt to clarify the meaning of physical and biological destruction'.[133] In the *Bosnian Genocide* case, the ICJ confirmed that genocide was limited to physical or biological

---

[126] *Krstić*, ICTY AC, 19 April 2004, para. 549. [127] See Section 15.4.
[128] *Krstić*, ICTY AC, 19 April 2004, paras. 133, 134. See also *Stakić*, ICTY AC, 22 March 2006, para. 47: no genocidal intent existed when the defendant's 'intention was only to displace the Bosnian Muslim population and not to destroy it'.
[129] *Ibid.* para. 95. [130] Summarized in Schabas, *Genocide* (n. 31) 207–14.
[131] See e.g. the decision of the German Federal Constitutional Court, 2 BvR 1290/99, 12 December 2000, para. III(4)(a)(aa).
[132] *Krstić*, ICTY TC I, 2 August 2001, para. 580; *Krstić*, ICTY AC, 19 April 2004, para. 25. 101; *Blagojević and Jokić*, ICTY TC I, 17 January 2005, para. 666.
[133] *Blagojević and Jokić*, ICTY, TC I, 17 January 2005, para. 666.

destruction of a group.[134] If the transfer of members of a group results in the splitting up of the group, that is not genocide unless done with an intent to physically destroy the group. However, acts of ethnic cleansing and attacks on cultural and religious property may be significant evidence towards establishing the intent to destroy.[135]

10.4.3 'In Whole or in Part'

There must be an intent to destroy the protected group in whole or in part. This aspect of the intention[136] has caused considerable controversy. This is because the ambit of the protections granted by the prohibition of genocide is heavily dependent on how broadly or narrowly the relevant group is conceptualized.

The first issue is defining the relevant geographical scope. To take an example from a clear case of genocide – Rwanda – the Hutu *génocidaires* did not appear to want to destroy all Tutsis everywhere in the world, but only in Rwanda.[137] The relevant group could be conceived of as Tutsis everywhere, in which case Rwandan Tutsis were protected only as a 'part' of that group. Or it could be thought that the relevant group was Rwandan Tutsis. According to the ICJ, 'it is widely accepted that genocide may be found to have been committed where the intent is to destroy the group within a geographically limited area'.[138]

A second issue is the meaning of 'part' of a group. The case law of the Tribunals has established that the intention must be to target at least a 'substantial' part of the group,[139] and this has been confirmed by the ICJ, which opined:

the intent must be to destroy at least a substantial part of the particular group. That is demanded by the very nature of the crime of genocide: since the object and purpose of the Convention as a whole is to prevent the intentional destruction of groups, the part targeted must be significant enough to have an impact on the group as a whole.[140]

The findings in *Krstić* illustrate the difficulties of determining both the whole and the substantial part of the group for the purpose of assessing whether the special intent is present. The Trial Chamber determined that the Bosnian Muslims constituted the protected group and 'the Bosnian Muslims of Srebrenica or the Bosnian Muslims of Eastern Bosnia constitute a part of the protected group'.[141] This finding was affirmed by the Appeal Chamber, which also pointed out that, in determining what a 'substantial' part was, the prominence of the targeted individuals within the group as well as the number targeted (in absolute and in relative terms) could also be relevant; hence, both qualitative and quantitative criteria should be considered. 'If a specific part of the group is emblematic of the

---

[134] *Bosnian Genocide* case (n. 7) para. 344; *Croatia* v. *Serbia* (n. 9) para. 136. For critique see Lars Berster, 'The Alleged Non-Existence of Cultural Genocide' (2015) 13 *JICJ* 677.

[135] There have been some suggestions that the *Bosnian Genocide* case, and the later *Croatia* v. *Serbia* case (n. 9) ought to be considered (at least *lex ferenda*) incorrect: Berster, 'The Alleged Non-Existence of Cultural Genocide' (n. 134).

[136] It is worth emphasizing that this part of the offence is a part of the mental element, not the material elements of genocide – it is not necessary to establish whether all or part of a group was actually destroyed to prove genocide.

[137] *Krstić*, ICTY AC, 19 April 2004, para. 13. [138] *Bosnian Genocide* case (n. 7) para. 199.

[139] *Kayishema*, ICTR TC II, 21 May 1999, para. 96; *Bagilishema*, ICTR TC I, 7 June 2001, para. 64; *Semanza*, ICTR TC III, 15 May 2003, para. 316.

[140] *Bosnian Genocide* case (n. 7) para. 198. [141] *Krstić*, ICTY TC I, 2 August 2001, para. 560.

overall group, or is essential to its survival, that may support a finding that the part qualifies as substantial'.[142] In the *Krstić* case, the fate of the Srebrenica Muslims was considered emblematic of that of all Bosnian Muslims.

The decision has been criticized as having set too low a threshold for the scale of genocide.[143] The killings were of 7,000–8,000 men, and it therefore appeared that the people targeted formed part of a group. However, the Chamber also took into account the fact that women and children were transferred from the area, to argue that the 'part' of the group was the Bosnian Muslims of Srebrenica. The prosecution had urged the ICTY to take the view that the Bosnian Muslims of Srebrenica were the relevant whole group.[144] If the Chamber had accepted this, it would have made proving genocide considerably simpler for the prosecution, as the Bosnian Muslim men of military age could have been seen as a substantial part of the group. This would, however, have diluted the concept of genocide considerably.

Another example of the issues that arise with 'in whole or in part' can be seen in the ECCC's consideration of the Khmer Rouge targeting of ethnic Vietnamese. The defendant, Khieu Samphân, argued that the protected group was limited to ethnic Vietnamese living in Cambodia at the relevant time, and argued that he could not be held responsible for acts carried out those who were residents of Vietnam.[145] The Supreme Court Chamber rejected this contention, classifying the 'whole' as all Vietnamese people regardless of residency, and the 'part' was Vietnamese people 'who in fact lived in Cambodia, Vietnamese soldiers, fishermen, refugees, and other civilians who were captured in Cambodia or its territorial waters', thus including a wider range of victims than the defendant's formulation.[146]

10.4.4 'As Such'

There must be an intent to destroy the group, or part of it, 'as such'. During the negotiation of the Convention, there were those who wanted to include *motive* as a necessary element of genocide. Others did not. The compromise which allowed agreement to be reached was to exclude any explicit reference to motive, but to include the words 'as such'.[147] While these words are therefore relied upon by some as evidence of the need for motive,[148] the *travaux préparatoires* disclose that that was not the meaning that all the negotiators attached to the words.

The motive for which a crime is committed, as opposed to the intention with which it is committed, is ordinarily irrelevant to guilt in criminal law. But the discriminatory nature of

---

[142] *Krstić*, ICTY AC, 19 April 2004, para. 12.

[143] William Schabas, 'Was Genocide Committed in Bosnia and Herzegovina? First Judgments of the International Criminal Tribunal for the Former Yugoslavia' (2002) 25 *Fordham International Law Journal* 23, 45–7: 'categorising [the atrocities] as "genocide" seems to distort the definition unreasonably'. See also Katherine Southwick, 'Srebrenica as Genocide? The *Krstić* Decision and the Language of the Unspeakable' (2005) 8 *Yale Human Rights and Development Law Journal* 188, 206–11.

[144] *Krstić*, ICTY TC I, 2 August 2001, para. 545. [145] *Khieu Samphân*, ECCC SC, 23 December 2022, para. 1596.

[146] *Ibid.*, paras. 1597–8. As a result of this formulation, the Supreme Court Chamber upheld Khieu Samphân's conviction for genocide against the Vietnamese: *ibid.* para. 1638.

[147] The negotiations are well summarized in Greenawalt, 'Rethinking Genocidal Intent' (n. 121) 2259, 2274–9; and Schabas, *Genocide* (n. 31) 294–306.

[148] See the discussion in Quigley, *The Genocide Convention* (n. 21) 120–6.

genocide seems to require a motive: the victims are singled out not by reason of their individual identity but *because* of their membership of a national, ethnic, racial, or religious group.[149] It is not surprising, therefore, that decisions by the ad hoc Tribunals have sometimes used the language of motive, referring to the need for the accused to 'seek' or 'aim at' the destruction of the group.[150] While the case law of the Tribunals is sometimes apparently conflicting, they do distinguish between motive and genocidal intent.[151] Personal motivation (such as a wish to profit financially from the genocide) for the perpetrator's participation in the crime is not relevant, but having a discriminatory purpose for the crime is intrinsic to the special intent.[152] Further, in cases where a set of facts and their consequences may have different explanations, a consideration of motive may be relevant in assessing intent, even though it will not itself be decisive.[153]

10.5   OTHER MODES OF PARTICIPATION

The 'other acts' of participation in genocide are listed in Article III of the Convention.[154] Conspiracy, 'direct and public incitement', attempt, and complicity are expressly incorporated in the Statutes of the ad hoc Tribunals. The ICC, on the other hand, relies on the general principles of law in Part 3 of its Statute, which apply to all of the crimes within the jurisdiction of the Court, for these forms of liability. The exception is incitement to genocide, for which specific provision was made in Article 25(3)(e) of the ICC Statute. For the ICC, the omission of conspiracy, due to hesitations of civil law countries, has left a gap, although the Statute's Article 25(3)(d) provision on contribution to a common purpose may largely fill it. Further discussion of these other acts and of command responsibility in relation to genocide may be found in Chapter 15.

Further Reading

Hirad Abtahi and Philippa Webb, *The Genocide Convention: The Travaux Préparatoires* (The Hague, 2008)
Payam Akhavan, *Reducing Genocide to Law* (Cambridge, 2012)
Caroline Fournet, *Genocide and Crimes Against Humanity* (Oxford, 2013)
Paula Gaeta (ed.), *The UN Genocide Convention: A Commentary* (Oxford, 2009)
Alexander Greenawalt, 'Rethinking Genocidal Intent: The Case for a Knowledge-based Interpretation' (1999) 99 *Columbia Law Review* 2259
Nina Jørgensen, 'The Definition of Genocide: Joining the Dots in the Light of Recent Practice' (2001) 1 *ICLR* 285

---

[149] *Niyitegeka*, ICTR AC, 9 July 2004, para. 53; *Musema*, ICTR AC, 16 November 2001, para. 165.
[150] See e.g. *Jelisić*, ICTY AC, 5 July 2001, para. 46; *Rutaganda*, ICTR AC, 26 May 2003, para. 524.
[151] *Krstić*, ICTY TC, 12 August 2001, para. 561; and see *Tadić*, ICTY AC, 15 July 1999, paras. 269, 270.
[152] *Krstić*, ICTY TC I, 2 August 2001, para. 545; *Krstić*, ICTY AC, 19 April 2004, para. 45; *Kayishema and Ruzindana*, ICTR AC, 1 June 2001, para. 161; *Stakić*, ICTY AC, 22 March 2006, para. 45; *Jelisić*, ICTY AC, 5 July 2001, para. 49.
[153] See criticism of the *Krstić* case on the ground that the Trial Chamber did not take any account of motive, in Southwick, 'Srebrenica as Genocide?' (n. 143). See further Paul Behrens, 'Genocide and the Question of Motive' (2012) 10 *JICJ* 501.
[154] See Paola Gaeta (ed.), *The UN Genocide Convention: A Commentary* (Oxford, 2009) Part III.

Claus Kreß, 'The Crime of Genocide under International Law' (2006) 6 *ICLR* 461

Raphael Lemkin, *Axis Rule in Occupied Europe: Laws of Occupation, Analysis of Government, Proposals for Redress* (Washington DC, 1944)

Raphael Lemkin, 'Genocide as a Crime Under International Law' (1947) 41 *AJIL* 145

Guénaël Mettraux, *International Crimes: Law and Practice. Vol. I: Genocide* (Oxford, 2019)

Marco Odello and Piotr Łubiński (eds.), *The Concept of Genocide in International Criminal Law: Developments after Lemkin* (London, 2020)

John Quigley, *The Genocide Convention: An International Law Analysis* (Aldershot, 2006)

William Schabas, *Genocide in International Law*, 2nd ed. (Cambridge, 2009)

Malcolm Shaw, 'Genocide in International Law' in Yoram Dinstein (ed.), *International Law at a Time of Perplexity* (Dordrecht, 1989) 797

Dinah Shelton (ed.), *The Encyclopaedia of Genocide and Crimes Against Humanity* (Farmington Mills, 2005) vols. I–III

Pavel Šturma and Milan Lipovský (eds.), *The Crime of Genocide: Then and Now – Evolution of a Crime* (Leiden, 2022)

Christian Tams, Lars Berster, and Björn Schiffbauer, *Convention on the Prevention and Punishment of the Crime of Genocide* (Oxford, 2014)

11

Crimes against Humanity

11.1 INTRODUCTION

11.1.1 Overview

Crimes against humanity are as old as humanity itself.[1] However, it is only in the last century that the international legal prohibition of crimes against humanity has emerged, and it is only in the last twenty-five years that the precise contours of the crime have been clarified.

Whereas genocide and war crimes have been codified in conventions with widely accepted definitions, crimes against humanity have been defined in slightly different ways in a series of different instruments. The law of crimes against humanity was initially created to fill certain gaps in the law of war crimes, but many parameters were left undefined. With increased application of international criminal law since the mid-1990s, a transnational conversation between national and international jurisprudence has clarified the law of crimes against humanity that we know today.

A crime against humanity involves the commission of certain inhumane acts, such as murder, torture, or rape, in a certain context: they must be part of a widespread or systematic attack directed against a civilian population. It is this context that elevates crimes that might otherwise fall exclusively under national jurisdiction to crimes of concern to the international community as a whole. An individual may be liable for crimes against humanity if they commit one or more inhumane acts within that broader context. It is not required that the individual be a ringleader or architect of the broader campaign.

11.1.2 Historical Development

The most significant early reference to 'crimes against humanity' as a legal concept was a joint declaration by France, Great Britain, and Russia in 1915. Responding to the massacre of Armenians by Turkey, the joint declaration denounced 'crimes against humanity and civilization' and warned of personal accountability.[2] After the First World War, an

---

[1] Jean Graven, 'Les crimes contre l'humanité' (1950) 76 *Hague Recueil* 427, 433.

[2] For more information on these historical developments, see United Nations War Crimes Commission, *History of the United Nations War Crimes Commission and the Development of the Laws of War* (London, 1948); Roger Clark, 'Crimes Against

international war crimes commission recommended the creation of an international tribunal to try not only war crimes but also 'violations of the laws of humanity'.[3] However, the US representatives objected to the references to the 'laws of humanity' on the grounds that these were not yet precise enough for criminal law, and the concept was not pursued at that time.[4]

In the wake of the Second World War, the drafters of the Nuremberg Charter were confronted with the question of how to respond to the Holocaust and the massive crimes committed by the Nazi regime. The classic definition of war crimes did not include crimes committed by a government against its own citizens. The drafters therefore included 'crimes against humanity', defined in Article 6(c) as:

> murder, extermination, enslavement, deportation and other inhumane acts committed against any civilian population, before or during the war, or persecutions on political, racial or religious grounds in execution of or in connection with any crime within the jurisdiction of the Tribunal, whether or not in violation of the law of the country where perpetrated.

Three major features may be noted. First, the reference to 'any' civilian population meant that even crimes committed against fellow citizens were included. This was a major advance given that, at that time, international law generally regulated conduct between states and said little about a government's treatment of its own population.[5] Second, the reference to 'population' was understood to create some requirement of scale, but the precise threshold was specified neither in the Charter nor in the Nuremberg judgment. Third, the requirement of connection to war crimes or the crime of aggression in effect meant that crimes against humanity could occur only with some 'nexus' to armed conflict.[6]

It remains controversial whether the Nuremberg Charter created new law, or whether it recognized an existing crime.[7] In any case, many argued that the principle of non-retroactivity had to give way to the overriding need for accountability for large-scale murder and atrocities recognized as criminal by all nations.[8] Perhaps because of this uncertainty in the status of crimes against humanity, the Nuremberg judgment tended to blur discussion of crimes against humanity and war crimes and provided very little guidance on the particular elements of crimes against humanity.[9]

Humanity' in G. Ginsburgs and V. N. Kudriavstsev (eds.), *The Nuremberg Trial and International Law* (Dordrecht, 1990); Egon Schwelb, 'Crimes Against Humanity' (1946) 23 *British Yearbook of International Law* 178.

[3] The Inter-Allied Commission on the Responsibility on the Authors of the War. See Section 6.1.

[4] War Crimes Commission, *History* (n. 2).   [5] War Crimes Commission, *History* (n. 2) 192–3.

[6] The text as originally adopted contained a semi-colon following the word 'war', which would give rise to the interpretation that the connection requirement applied only to persecution. This was promptly amended by the Berlin Protocol of 6 October 1945, which replaced the semi-colon with a comma, thereby supporting the interpretation that the connection requirement applied to all crimes against humanity. See Clark, 'Crimes Against Humanity' (n. 2) 190–2.

[7] See e.g. M. Cherif Bassiouni, *Crimes Against Humanity: Historical Evolution and Contemporary Application* (Cambridge, 2011).

[8] Hans Kelsen, 'Will the Judgment in the Nuremberg Trial Constitute a Precedent in International Law?' (1947) 1 *International Law Quarterly* 153, especially at 165; see also E. Schwelb, 'Crimes Against Humanity' (1946) 23 *British Yearbook of International Law* 178; and see the treatment of the question in *R v. Finta* [1994] 1 SCR 701; *Polyukhovich* [1991] HCA 32; (1991) 172 CLR 501, 661–2, High Court of Australia; *Eichmann*, 36 ILR 18 (Dist. Ct 1961), aff'd, 36 ILR 277 (Sup. Ct 1962).

[9] Nuremberg International Military Tribunal (IMT), Judgment and Sentences, reprinted in (1947) 41 *AJIL* 172, especially at 248–9.

The Tokyo Charter included a similar definition with some modifications.[10] The Allied Control Council, creating law for occupied Germany, adopted Control Council Law No. 10 with a similar definition. Control Council Law No. 10 added rape, imprisonment, and torture to the list of inhumane acts, and did not require a connection to war crimes or aggression.

The concept of crimes against humanity was promptly endorsed by the UN General Assembly.[11] In the decades that followed, there was only a limited body of national cases,[12] as well as a few treaties and instruments recognizing enforced disappearance and apartheid as crimes against humanity.[13] The International Law Commission (ILC) also developed several definitions as part of its work on a draft code of international crimes.

A major advance occurred when the Security Council created the International Criminal Tribunal for the former Yugoslavia (ICTY) and the International Criminal Tribunal for Rwanda (ICTR) in response to mass crimes in the former Yugoslavia and Rwanda. The Statute of each Tribunal contained a list of acts based on the Control Council Law No. 10 list. The ICTY Statute (Article 5) defined the contextual threshold as 'when committed in armed conflict, whether international or internal in character, and directed against any civilian population'. The Tribunal itself, referring to previous authorities, interpreted this threshold as requiring a 'widespread or systematic attack'.[14] The ICTR Statute (Article 3) defined the context as 'when committed as part of a widespread or systematic attack against any civilian population on national, political, ethnic, racial or religious grounds'. Thus, the definitions are similar, except that the ICTY Statute requires armed conflict and the ICTR Statute requires discriminatory grounds.

The ICC Statute, adopted in 1998, recognizes the same contextual threshold in Article 7: 'when committed as part of a widespread or systematic attack directed against any civilian population'. The ICC Statute rejects both the armed conflict and the discriminatory grounds requirements, as these were not considered to be necessary elements in customary international law. The ICC Statute requires a 'State or organizational policy', which is controversial, as is discussed in Section 11.2.3. The ICC Statute definition contains the same list of acts as previous instruments, and adds forced transfer of population, sexual slavery, enforced prostitution, forced pregnancy, enforced sterilization, sexual violence, gender-based persecution, enforced disappearance, and the crime of apartheid.[15] The ICC Statute

---

[10] Article 5(c) of the Tokyo Charter included the same definition with the omission of racial and religious persecution, on the ground that such crimes had not occurred in that theatre of conflict. The term 'any civilian population' was also deleted, on which basis the prosecution argued that all killing during an aggressive war was murder. Such arguments were rejected at Nuremberg and Tokyo, as they would undermine the distinction between the law governing justification for armed conflict and the law governing conduct during armed conflict. See Chapters 6 and 12.

[11] GA Res. 95(I), UN Doc. A/64/Add.1 (1946).

[12] Including cases in France, the Netherlands, Israel, Canada, and Australia, as discussed at Section 11.2.3. See also Joseph Rikhof, 'Crimes Against Humanity, Customary International Law and the International Tribunals for Bosnia and Rwanda' (1995) 6 *National Journal of Constitutional Law* 231; Matthew Lippman, 'Crimes Against Humanity' (1997) 17 *Boston College Third World Law Journal* 171; Leila Sadat Wexler, 'The Interpretation of the Nuremberg Principles by the French Court of Cassation: From Touvier to Barbie and Back Again' (1994) 32 *Columbia Journal of Transnational Law* 289.

[13] Examples include the Convention on the Non-Applicability of Statutory Limitations to War Crimes and Crimes Against Humanity 1968, the Apartheid Convention 1973, the Inter-American Convention on Enforced Disappearance 1994 and the UN Declaration on Enforced Disappearance 1992.

[14] *Tadić*, ICTY TC II, 7 May 1997, para. 644; *Tadić*, ICTY AC, 15 July 1999, para. 248. [15] See ICC Statute, Art. 7.

includes supplementary definitions in Article 7(2), some of which have been generally welcomed as helpful clarifications, whereas others have been controversial, as will be discussed in Section 11.3.1.

Additional sources on the definition of crimes against humanity may now be found in national and international jurisprudence, the ICC Elements of Crimes, and instruments of other tribunals, such as the Special Court for Sierra Leone (SCSL). Each of these includes a comparable list of acts as well as the now-standard requirement of a widespread or systematic attack directed against any civilian population. In addition, the International Law Commission has produced a draft convention on crimes against humanity, affirming the obligations of states to prevent and punish such crimes; that convention is under discussion at the UN General Assembly.[16] The draft convention adopts the ICC definition of the crime, with minor adjustments.[17]

11.1.3 Relationship to Other Crimes

War crimes and crimes against humanity frequently overlap. For example, a mass killing of civilians during an armed conflict could constitute both types of crimes. There are, however, significant differences. First, unlike war crimes, crimes against humanity may occur even in the absence of armed conflict. Second, crimes against humanity require a context of widespread or systematic commission, whereas war crimes do not; a single isolated incident can constitute a war crime. Third, war crimes law was originally based on reciprocal promises between parties to a conflict, and hence primarily focuses on protecting 'enemy' nationals or persons affiliated with the other party to the conflict. The law of crimes against humanity protects victims regardless of their nationality or affiliation. Fourth, war crimes law regulates conduct even on the battlefield and against military objectives,[18] whereas the law of crimes against humanity concerns actions directed primarily against civilian populations.[19]

Thus, the 'international dimension' of war crimes arises from the armed conflict, and the 'international dimension' of crimes against humanity arises from the attack on a civilian population. Cumulatively, the two bodies of law, working together, penalize atrocities committed during armed conflict or committed on a widespread or systematic basis. Isolated crimes occurring in the absence of armed conflict continue to be governed by national criminal law and human rights law. War crimes law is sometimes useful to interpret some aspects of crimes against humanity, so that the two bodies of law work together.[20]

---

[16] See e.g. Leila Nadya Sadat (ed.), *Forging a Convention on Crimes Against Humanity* (Cambridge, 2011); International Law Commission, Draft Articles on Prevention and Punishment of Crimes Against Humanity, in UN Doc A/74/10 (2019) (<legal.un. org>); Leila Nadya Sadat, 'Little Progress in the Sixth Committee on Crimes Against Humanity' (2022) 54 *Case W. Res. J. Int'l L.* 89.

[17] Margaret deGuzman, 'Defining Crimes Against Humanity: Practicality and Value Balancing' (2020) 6 *African J Intl Crim Justice* 204. The Convention definition removes the definition of 'gender' and adjusts the 'connection' requirement in 'persecution'; see Section 11.3.9.

[18] See Chapter 12. [19] See Section 11.2.4.

[20] Of course, care must be taken when extending humanitarian law concepts outside the context of armed conflicts. See Section 11.2.4; and see Payam Akhavan, 'Reconciling Crimes Against Humanity with the Laws of War' (2008) 6 *JICJ* 21.

Genocide was initially regarded as a particularly odious form of crime against humanity,[21] one committed with the intent to destroy, in whole or in part, a national, ethnical, racial, or religious group as such. However, over time the definitions of the two crimes have evolved and they now pose differing requirements.[22]

11.2 COMMON ELEMENTS (CONTEXTUAL THRESHOLD)

As already noted, the contemporary definition of a crime against humanity entails the commission of a listed inhumane act, in a certain context: the listed act must be committed as part of a 'widespread or systematic attack directed against a civilian population'.

11.2.1 Aspects Not Required

No Nexus to Armed Conflict

The Nuremberg and Tokyo Charters both required a connection to war crimes or to aggression, in effect requiring some nexus to armed conflict.[23] On the other hand, Control Council Law No. 10 did not include such a requirement. Subsequent case law of military tribunals split over whether such a nexus must be read into the definition. For example, the *Flick* and *Weizsäcker* cases imported the requirement from the Nuremberg Charter, whereas the *Ohlendorf* and *Altstötter* decisions concluded that it was unnecessary.[24]

Subsequent international conventions[25] did not require a nexus to armed conflict. The ICTY Statute, adopted in 1993 by the Security Council, restricted crimes against humanity to those committed in armed conflict, but the Security Council promptly reversed this position in 1994, when it adopted the ICTR Statute without such a requirement. Finally, after extensive debates at the 1998 Rome Conference, agreement was reached on a definition of crimes against humanity rejecting any such requirement (Article 7).[26]

Today, it seems well settled that a nexus to armed conflict is not required. The majority of instruments and precedents oppose such a requirement. The limitation in the Nuremberg Charter is generally seen as a jurisdictional limitation only,[27] and the ICTY Statute definition appears to be the anomaly. Indeed, the jurisprudence of the ICTY itself concludes

---

[21] War Crimes Commission, *History* (n. 2) 196–7. [22] See Section 10.1.3.

[23] See e.g. Bassiouni, *Crimes Against Humanity* (n. 7) 136–46.

[24] *United States* v. *Ohlendorf et al.*, 4 TWC 411 (1948); *United States* v. *Altstötter et al.* (the 'Justice Trial'), VI LRTWC I (1947); *United States* v. *Flick*, IX LRTWC 1 (1948); *United States* v. *Weizsäcker* (the 'Ministries Trial'), 14 TWC 1 (1949).

[25] Including the Genocide Convention, the Convention on the Non-Applicability of Statutory Limitations to War Crimes and Crimes Against Humanity 1968, the Apartheid Convention 1973, and the Inter-American Convention on Enforced Disappearance 1994.

[26] Darryl Robinson, 'Defining Crimes Against Humanity at the Rome Conference' (1999) 93 *AJIL* 43.

[27] War Crimes Commission, *History* (n. 2) 192–3; see also Clark, 'Crimes Against Humanity' (n. 2) 196; Diane Orentlicher, 'Settling Accounts: The Duty to Prosecute Human Rights Violations of a Prior Regime' (1991) 100 *Yale Law Journal* 2537, 2588–90.

that the requirement is a deviation from customary law.[28] This view is also supported by national case law, international bodies of experts, and the writings of commentators.[29] No requirement of armed conflict has appeared in subsequent definitions of crimes against humanity.

No Requirement of Discriminatory Animus

Article 3 of the ICTR Statute requires that crimes against humanity be committed on 'national, ethnic, racial or religious grounds'.[30] Such a requirement was supported by a few cases in France, but did not appear in most precedents.[31] ICTY jurisprudence holds that discrimination is not a general requirement for crimes against humanity.[32] The ICC Statute, adopted in 1998, also rejected a discrimination requirement. The ICTR Appeals Chamber has held that the restriction in the ICTR Statute is not customary law and restricts only that Tribunal.[33] Thus, it would appear that discriminatory grounds are not required in customary law, except for the specific crime of persecution, discussed in Section 11.3.9.

11.2.2 Widespread or Systematic

The formula of a 'widespread or systematic attack directed against any civilian population' emerged in the 1990s as the accepted contextual threshold. The emergence of a generally accepted formulation, elaborating upon the laconic Nuremberg definition, has contributed to clarity and consistency in this area of law. Nonetheless, some aspects of the definition of these terms remain to be resolved.

The 'widespread or systematic' test is disjunctive:[34] a prosecutor need only satisfy one or the other threshold. However, in addition to 'widespread or systematic', there must also be an 'attack'. As will be discussed in Section 11.2.3, some authorities indicate that an 'attack directed against a civilian population' necessarily entails at least some modest degree of scale and organization.[35] This would mean that, while the rigorous thresholds of 'widespread' or 'systematic' are disjunctive, the 'attack' requires at least some minimal dimension of each.

---

[28] *Tadić*, ICTY TC II, 7 May 1997, para. 627; *Tadić*, ICTY AC, 15 July 1999, paras. 282–8.
[29] *Eichmann* (1968) 36 ILR 5, 49 (DC); *Barbie* (1988) 78 ILR 124, 136 (Cour de Cassation); ILC Report 1996, UN Doc. A/51/10 (1996) 96; Orentlicher, 'Settling Accounts' (n. 27) 2588–90; Theodor Meron, 'International Criminalization of Internal Atrocities' (1995) 89 *AJIL* 554; Beth van Schaack, 'The Definition of Crimes Against Humanity: Resolving the Incoherence' (1999) 37 *Columbia Journal of Transnational Law* 787. The Extraordinary Chambers in the Courts of Cambodia also concluded that there was no nexus requirement even in the 1970s: *Nuon Chea and Khieu Samphân*, ECCC AC, 23 November 2016, para. 711.
[30] For discussion, see David Scheffer, *All the Missing Souls: A Personal History of the War Crimes Tribunals* (Princeton, NJ, 2012).
[31] Some French cases, including *Barbie*, 78 ILR 124 (Cour de Cassation) and *Touvier*, 100 ILR 338 (Cour d'Appel), suggested that a policy of discrimination is required.
[32] *Tadić*, ICTY TC II, 7 May 1997, para. 652; *Tadić*, ICTY AC, 15 July 1999, paras. 282–305.
[33] *Akayesu*, ICTR AC, 1 June 2001, paras. 461–9.
[34] The French version of the ICTR Statute referred to the requirements conjunctively (*généralisée et systématique*), but this was held to be a simple error: *Akayesu*, ICTR TC I, 2 September 1998, para. 579.
[35] See ICC Statute, Art. 7(2)(a); and see *Haradinaj et al.*, ICTY TC I, 3 April 2008, para. 122.

The term 'widespread' has been defined in various ways, and generally connotes the 'large-scale nature of the attack and the number of victims'.[36] No specific numerical limit has been set. While 'widespread' typically refers to the cumulative effect of numerous inhumane acts, it could also be satisfied by a singular act of exceptional magnitude.[37]

The term 'systematic' has also been defined in various ways. Early decisions set high thresholds: in *Akayesu*, it was defined as (1) thoroughly organized; (2) following a regular pattern; (3) on the basis of a common policy; and (4) involving substantial public or private resources.[38] In *Blaškić*, it was defined by reference to four factors: (1) a plan or objective; (2) large-scale or continuous commission of linked crimes; (3) significant resources; and (4) implication of high-level authorities.[39] The most recent cases seem to be settling on 'the organised nature of the acts of violence and the improbability of their random occurrence'.[40] Consistent with the ordinary meaning of the term, it may be that the hallmark of 'systematic' is a high degree of organization, and that features such as patterns, continuous commission, use of resources, planning, and political objectives are important factors.

11.2.3 Attack

The term 'attack' is not used in the same sense as in the law of war crimes. An 'attack' need not involve the use of armed force; it can encompass mistreatment of the civilian population.[41] It refers to a broader course of conduct, involving prohibited acts, of which the acts of the accused form part.[42]

The ICC Statute defines 'attack' in Article 7(2)(a):

a course of conduct involving the multiple commission of acts referred to in paragraph 1 against any civilian population, pursuant to or in furtherance of a state or organisational policy to commit such attack.

This definition requires that there must be at least some minimal level of scale ('multiple' acts) and some minimal level of collectivity (the 'policy' element). The definition screens out truly isolated crimes ('multiple') and truly unconnected crimes ('policy'). In addition to these two low-threshold requirements for an 'attack', there must also be *either* a high level of scale ('widespread') *or* a high level of collective coordination ('systematic').

---

[36] *Tadić*, ICTY TC II, 7 May 1997, para. 206; *Kunarac et al.*, ICTY TC II, 22 February 2001, para. 428; *Nahimana*, ICTR AC, 28 November 2007, para. 920; *Al Bashir Arrest Warrant*, ICC PTC I, 4 March 2009 (ICC-02/05–01/09–3) para. 81; *Taylor*, SCSL TC, 18 May 2012, para. 511.
[37] *Kordić and Čerkez*, ICTY TC, 26 February 2001, para. 176; *Blaškić*, ICTY TC I, 3 March 2000, para. 206; ILC Draft Code, 94–5.
[38] *Akayesu*, ICTR TC I, 2 September 1998, para. 580.   [39] *Blaškić*, ICTY TC, 3 March 2000, para. 203.
[40] See e.g. *Nahimana et al.*, ICTR AC, 28 November 2007, para. 920; *Karadžić*, ICTY TC, 24 March 2016, para. 477; *Al Bashir Arrest Warrant*, ICC PTC I, 4 March 2009 (ICC-02/05–01/09–3) para. 81; *Taylor*, SCSL TC II, 18 May 2012, para. 511. As will be suggested below, improbability of random occurrence arguably should not only be an aspect of the 'systematic' test, it should already be inherent in the concept of an 'attack'. Otherwise widespread but random crime would constitute a crime against humanity.
[41] ICC Elements of Crimes, 'Crimes Against Humanity Introduction', para. 3; *Kunarac et al.*, ICTY AC, 12 June 2002, para. 86; *Akayesu*, ICTR TC I, 2 September 1998, para. 581; *Taylor*, SCSL TC, 18 May 2012, para. 506.
[42] ICC Statute, Art. 7(2)(a); *Tadić*, ICTY TC II, 7 May 1997, para. 644; *Akayesu*, ICTR TC I, 2 September 1998, para. 205.

The requirement of 'multiple' crimes has not been controversial. Tribunal jurisprudence similarly confirms there must at least be multiple acts or multiple victims in order to warrant the label 'attack directed against a civilian population'.[43] These acts may be all of the same type or of different types.[44] A single event (planting a bomb) can constitute a 'multiple' commission of prohibited acts (for example, murders).[45] Recall that the multiple crimes requirement applies to the *attack*, not the actions of the accused; it suffices that the accused commit a single act within the context of an attack. The requirement of 'multiple acts' is not synonymous with 'widespread': both terms measure scale, but 'multiple' is a low threshold and 'widespread' is higher.

Controversy Concerning the Policy Element

The controversial aspect is the 'policy' element. The deeper question underlying this issue is what links different acts together so that they can be said to constitute an 'attack'. Crime may often be 'widespread' – for example, in a high-crime area or in anarchy following a natural disaster – without amounting to a crime against humanity. The unconnected acts of individuals acting on their own initiative are not sufficient; some thread of connection between acts is needed so that they can collectively be described as an *attack directed against a civilian population*. Some legal authorities make this proposition explicit, by indicating that there must be an underlying governmental or organizational policy that directs, instigates, or encourages the crimes. Other authorities reject such a requirement. It is therefore controversial whether the policy element is a necessary component of crimes against humanity.

Divide in the Authorities

National jurisprudence on crimes against humanity following the Second World War frequently indicated that governmental policy is a requirement.[46] In the 1990s, the very same authorities that established the 'widespread or systematic' test also expressly coupled it with a requirement of policy or of direction, instigation, or encouragement by a state or organization.[47] Early Tribunal cases tended to follow this approach.[48]

At the Rome Conference, there was considerable opposition to a disjunctive 'widespread or systematic' test, on the grounds that 'widespread' on its own would be problematic, since

---

[43] ICC Statute, Art. 7(2)(a); *Kunarac et al.*, ICTY TC II, 22 February 2001, para. 415; *Krnojelac*, ICTY TC II, 15 March 2002, para. 54.

[44] *Kayishema*, ICTR TC II, 21 May 1999, para. 122.

[45] *Kordić*, ICTY TC, 26 February 2001, para. 176; *Blaškić*, ICTY TC I, 3 March 2000, para. 206; ILC Draft Code, 94–5.

[46] Examples include: Justice Trial, VI LRTWC I (1947); *Brandt* (the 'Doctors Trial'), IV LRTWC 91 (1947) (US Military Tribunal); *Barbie*, 78 ILR 124 (Court of Cassation), 6 December 1983 (France); *Menten* (1987) 75 ILR 362–3 (Netherlands); *R* v. *Finta* [1994] 1 SCR 701, 814 (Canada); *Polyukhovich* (1991) 172 CLR 501 (Australia); *Pinochet (No. 3)* [1999] 2 All ER 97 (United Kingdom) (Lord Hope and Lord Millett; but see *contra* Lord Browne-Wilkinson).

[47] Commission of Experts (the Former Yugoslavia), *Final Report of the Commission of Experts Established Pursuant to Security Council Resolution 780(1992)*, UN Doc. S/1994/674 (27 May 1994) 23; Commission of Experts (Rwanda), *Final Report of the Commission of Experts Established Pursuant to Security Council Resolution 935(1994)*, UN Doc. G/SO 214 (9 December 1994) para. 135; ILC, *Report on the Work of its Forty-Eighth Session (ILC Draft Code)*, UN Doc. A/51/10 (1996) 93 and 95–6; and see Gay McDougall, *Final Report on Systematic Rape, Sexual Slavery and Slavery-Like Practices during Armed Conflict*, UN Doc. E/CN.4/ Sub.2/1998/13 (1998).

[48] *Tadić*, ICTY TC II, 7 May 1997, para. 644; *Bagilishema*, ICTR TC I, 7 June 2001, para. 78.

it includes rampant but unconnected crime. It was argued in response that the concept of an 'attack' excluded random crimes, because the crimes have to be connected. The cautious states agreed to the disjunctive 'widespread or systematic' test, provided that the definition of 'attack' included this clarification. Article 7(2)(a) therefore defines 'attack' and includes a policy element, which was based on the ICTY jurisprudence of the time (the *Tadić* decision), the ILC draft Code, and other authorities. 'Policy' was understood as a low threshold which could be inferred from the manner in which the acts occur.[49] Article 7 provided that the policy need not be that of a government and could also be that of an organization, as noted in *Tadić* and other authorities.

Strong concerns were already growing about the policy element, both in Tribunal jurisprudence and in scholarly literature. The major concerns were that it imposed a novel burden, that it would be difficult to prove, and that it contradicted the disjunctive test.[50] Tribunal cases began to split, with some supporting the element, then some declining to take a position, and then some expressing doubt.[51] Finally, in *Kunarac*, the ICTY Appeals Chamber held, rather categorically, that 'nothing in the Statute or in customary international law ... required proof of the existence of a plan or policy to commit these crimes'.[52] Whereas decisions on other issues of customary law have provided an extensive review of precedents, the Appeals Chamber resolved this major controversy with reasoning appearing only in a single footnote. Several scholars have noted that none of the cited authorities actually supports the proposition for which they are cited, and some of them contradict it; furthermore, many contrary authorities were ignored.[53]

Thus, the main indicators of customary law are now divided. On the one hand, the ICC Statute indicates that policy is required. The Statute was adopted by a great number of states purporting to codify existing customary law, and hence it is a strong indicator of customary law. A similar requirement appears in some national jurisprudence and legislation, which is also an indication of customary law.[54] On the other hand, Tribunal jurisprudence, which also purports to reflect customary law, rejects the policy element. Many – perhaps

---

[49] *Tadić*, ICTY TC II, 7 May 1997, paras. 653–5; Robinson, 'Defining Crimes Against Humanity' (n. 26) 50–1; Timothy H. L. McCormack, 'Crimes Against Humanity' in McGoldrick et al., *The Permanent ICC*.

[50] See Margaret McAuliffe deGuzman, 'The Road from Rome: The Developing Law of Crimes Against Humanity' (2000) 22 *Human Rights Quarterly* 335; Phyllis Hwang, 'Defining Crimes Against Humanity in the Rome Statute of the International Criminal Court' (1998) 22 *Fordham International Law Journal* 457. The most thorough argument against the policy element appears in Guénaël Mettraux, 'The Definition of Crimes Against Humanity and the Question of a "Policy" Element' in Leila Nadya Sadat (ed.), *Forging a Convention on Crimes Against Humanity* (Cambridge, 2011).

[51] *Kupreškić et al.*, ICTY TC II, 14 January 2000, paras. 554–5; *Kunarac et al.*, ICTY TC II, 22 February 2001, para. 432; *Kordić and Čerkez*, ICTY TC, 26 February 2001, paras. 181–2; *Krnojelac*, ICTY TC II, 15 March 2002, para. 58.

[52] *Kunarac et al.*, ICTY AC, 12 June 2002, para. 98. The reasoning of the Chamber closely follows Guénaël Mettraux, 'Crimes Against Humanity in the Jurisprudence of the International Criminal Tribunals for the Former Yugoslavia and Rwanda' (2002) 43 *Harvard International Law Journal* 237, 270–82.

[53] For commentary critical of the Chamber's claims about past precedents, see Claus Kreß, 'On the Outer Limits of Crimes Against Humanity: The Concept of Organization Within the Policy Requirement: Some Reflections on the March 2010 ICC Kenya Decision' (2010) 23 *LJIL* 855; William Schabas, 'State Policy as an Element of International Crimes' (2008) 98 *Journal of Criminal Law and Criminology* 953; M. Cherif Bassiouni, 'Revisiting the Architecture of Crimes Against Humanity: Almost a Century in the Making, with Gaps and Ambiguities Remaining – The Need for a Specialized Convention' in Leila Nadya Sadat (ed.), *Forging a Crime Against Humanity* (Cambridge, 2011) 43.

[54] See e.g., Mariano Gaitan, 'The Nexus Element in the Definition of Crimes Against Humanity: An Analysis of Argentine Jurisprudence' (2021) 27 *Southwestern Journal of International Law* 265.

a majority – of scholars, assume the correctness of the *Kunarac* ruling, and thus regard the ICC Statute requirement as the departure from custom.

Much of the controversy over the policy element may result from differing understandings of what the element *means*.[55] Some commentators reject the policy element, but agree that random criminality of individuals does not amount to an 'attack'.[56] To other commentators, that is precisely what the policy element means:[57] if we agree to exclude crimes of individuals acting on their own initiative, then the necessary logical corollary is to require some instigation or encouragement by something *other than* individuals, namely a state or organization. Some scholars argue that this connection to states or organizations reflects the fundamental essence of crimes against humanity: crimes against humanity are 'politics gone cancerous', as the human capacity for organized action is twisted for harmful ends.[58]

Implications for Jurisdictions Rejecting a Policy Element

For those jurisdictions which have rejected the term 'policy', it is essential not to lose sight of the principle that unconnected random acts cannot constitute an 'attack'.[59] Tribunal jurisprudence often asserts that unconnected random acts are excluded, but does not seem to have any legal element that actually performs this function. The requirement of 'widespread' crime does not suffice, because crimes in a region may be rampant yet unconnected. Recent Tribunal jurisprudence mentions the element of 'improbability of random occurrence', but only as part of the definition of 'systematic'.[60] However, the improbability of random occurrence must surely be a requirement for all 'attacks'.[61] In the absence of some such clarification, a literal and mechanistic application of Tribunal definitions would encompass widespread but random crimes of individuals, which would be overbroad.[62]

Although Tribunal jurisprudence overtly rejects a policy element, it quietly re-injects something very similar when it requires that 'identifiable population' was 'targeted' or was a 'primary object', all of which imply some direction or coordination from some source.[63] Furthermore, in *Haradinaj*, a Chamber found that a 'relatively small number of incidents', lacking scale or frequency, and without significant evidence of structure, organization, or targeting, did not amount to an attack directed against a civilian population.[64] This

---

[55] See e.g. Mettraux, 'Crimes Against Humanity' (n. 52) 275, rejecting some authorities as precedent for a policy element because all they meant is to exclude isolated crimes.

[56] Mettraux, 'Crimes Against Humanity' (n. 52) 254, 273, and 275.

[57] See e.g. Yoram Dinstein, 'Crimes Against Humanity after Tadić' (2000) 13 *LJIL* 273, 389; Simon Chesterman, 'An Altogether Different Order: Defining the Elements of Crimes Against Humanity' (2000) *Duke Journal of Comparative and International Law* 283, 316.

[58] See e.g. David Luban, 'A Theory of Crimes Against Humanity' (2004) 29 *Yale Law Journal* 85, 90; see also Kai Ambos and Steffen Wirth, 'The Current Law of Crimes Against Humanity: An Analysis of UNTAET Regulation 15/2000' (2002) 13 *Criminal Law Forum* 1, 26–34; William Schabas, 'State Policy as an Element of International Crimes' (2008) 98 *Journal of Criminal Law and Criminology* 953.

[59] *Kunarac et al.*, ICTY TC II, 22 February 2001, para. 422.

[60] *Kunarac et al.*, ICTY TC II, 22 February 2001, para. 429; *Krnojelac*, ICTY TC II, 15 March 2002, para. 57.

[61] Ambos and Wirth, 'The Current Law' (n. 58) 30–1.

[62] See e.g. David Luban, 'A Theory of Crimes Against Humanity' (2004) 29 *Yale Law Journal* 85; Ambos and Wirth, 'The Current Law' (n. 58) 30–1; Geoffrey Robertson, *Crimes Against Humanity: The Struggle for Global Justice* (London, 1999) 311 and 314.

[63] See e.g. *Kunarac et al.*, ICTY AC, 12 June 2002, paras. 90–2; *Stakić*, ICTY TC, 31 July 2003, para. 627; *Stakić*, ICTY AC, 22 March 2006, para. 247.

[64] *Haradinaj et al.*, ICTY TC I, 3 April 2008.

common-sense finding on the implicit requirements of an 'attack' is strikingly similar to Article 7(2)(a) of the ICC Statute.

Implications for Jurisdictions Requiring a Policy Element

For those jurisdictions that apply a policy element, the element must be interpreted, in accordance with jurisprudence, as a modest threshold that simply excludes random action.[65] The danger with the word 'policy' is that, in many minds, it connotes a bureaucratic measure formally adopted at highest level. However, the precedents high-light three important features in interpreting the legal term of art, 'policy'. First, a policy need not be formally adopted, nor expressly declared, nor stated clearly and precisely.[66] Thus, it must be given its ordinary meaning of 'a course of action adopted as advantageous or expedient',[67] as opposed to its bureaucratic sense of a formal and official strategy. Second, the element may be satisfied by inference from the manner in which the acts occur;[68] it is sufficient to show the improbability of random occurrence. Third, it is not required to show *action* by a state or organization; case law indicates that the requirement is satisfied by 'explicit or implicit approval or endorsement' or that the conduct is 'clearly encouraged' or 'clearly fits within' a general policy.[69] Thus, inaction designed to encourage the crimes would also suffice.[70]

Unfortunately, some early ICC decisions imbued the policy element with new and stringent requirements, unsupported by any legal authority, that would make crimes against humanity difficult to prove, exactly as opponents of the policy element had feared.[71] For example, some early Pre-Trial Chamber decisions equated the policy element with 'systematic', that is, 'thoroughly organized'.[72] Such an interpretation neglects the authorities that the element can be satisfied by active or passive encouragement.[73] It would also create a contradiction within Article 7, by effectively requiring 'systematic' in all cases. The coherence of Article 7 requires that the policy element be a more modest requirement than 'systematic'. Later ICC jurisprudence correctly noted that the policy element is indeed less demanding than 'systematic'.[74]

---

[65] McAuliffe deGuzman, 'The Road from Rome' (n. 50) 374; Darryl Robinson, 'Crimes Against Humanity: A Better Policy on "Policy"' in Stahn, *The Law and Practice of the ICC*.

[66] *Tadić*, ICTY TC II, 7 May 1997, para. 653; *Blaškić*, ICTY TC I, 3 March 2000, paras. 204–5; *Bemba Gombo*, ICC PTC II, 15 June 2009 (ICC-01/05–01/08–424) para. 81; *Katanga and Ngudjolo*, ICC PTC I, 30 September 2008 (ICC-01/04–01/07–717) para. 396 (albeit also requiring, contradictorily, that an attack must be 'thoroughly organized').

[67] *Oxford English Dictionary*, 2nd ed. (Oxford, 1989) vol. XII, 27, provides this as the 'chief living sense'.

[68] *Tadić*, ICTY TC II, 7 May 1997, para. 653; *Blaškić*, ICTY TC I, 3 March 2000, para. 204; *Bemba Gombo*, ICC PTC II, 15 June 2009 (ICC-01/05–01/08–424) para. 81.

[69] *Kupreškić*, ICTY TC II, 14 January 2000, paras. 554–5.

[70] Commission of Experts (the Former Yugoslavia), *Final Report* (n. 47) 23. The ICC Elements of Crimes, note 6, reach this result but in a particularly tortured manner, twice emphasizing a need for action, before acknowledging, in a restrictive manner, the possibility of passive encouragement. The ICC Elements of Crimes also add that inaction alone is not enough to infer a policy; this cannot be interpreted as repudiating the preceding sentence. Rather, it acknowledges that there may be other reasons for inaction (lack of knowledge of crimes, lack of ability), and hence policy should not be inferred without considering alternative explanations.

[71] Leila Sadat, 'Crimes Against Humanity in the Modern Age' (2013) 107 *AJIL* 334.

[72] *Katanga and Ngudjolo*, ICC PTC I, 30 September 2008 (ICC-01/04–01/07–717) para. 396; *Gbagbo*, ICC PTC III, 30 November 2011 (ICC-02/11–01/11–9) para. 37.

[73] *Kupreškić*, ICTY TC II, 14 January 2000, paras. 554–5; ICC Elements of Crimes, note 6; Ambos and Wirth, 'The Current Law' (n. 58) 31–4.

[74] *Katanga*, ICC TC II, 7 March 2014 (ICC-01/04–01/07–3436-tENG), paras 1108–13.

In another example, a majority of the ICC Pre-Trial Chamber examining the charges against Laurent Gbagbo, President of Côte d'Ivoire, requested 'specific information about meetings at which this policy/plan was allegedly adopted, as well as how the existence and content of this policy/plan was communicated or made known to members . . . once it was adopted'.[75] However, prior national and international jurisprudence had consistently held that proof of formal adoption is not required and that a policy may be inferred from the manner in which events occur.[76] National and international cases show that a policy can be inferred from the sheer improbability of the rival hypothesis that the acts were all a coincidence not directed or encouraged by a state or organization.[77]

Fortunately, the same Pre-Trial Chamber later affirmed, when confirming the charges, that there is no requirement that a policy be formally adopted.[78] Subsequent ICC jurisprudence has aligned with existing transnational jurisprudence.[79] For example, the *Katanga* judgment helpfully noted:

As regards proof of the existence of such a policy, it is important to underline that it is relatively rare . . . that a State or organisation seeking to encourage an attack against a civilian population might adopt and disseminate a pre-established design or plan to that effect. In most cases, the existence of such a State or organisational policy can therefore be inferred by discernment of, *inter alia*, repeated actions occurring according to a same sequence, or the existence of preparations or collective mobilisation orchestrated and coordinated by that state or organisation.[80]

State or Organization

Another controversy concerns the interpretation of 'state or organization'. This seemingly technical issue brings to the fore the essence of the crime. The issue arose in ICC proceedings concerning the Kenya situation, which involved over a thousand killings and hundreds of rapes, orchestrated by political parties. The Pre-Trial Chamber split as to whether political parties constitute an 'organization'.[81] The majority took a broad approach, adopting a factor-based test that would include any organization capable of directing mass crimes. Judge Kaul, in dissent, argued that an organization must be 'state-like'.

Some scholars supported the narrower view ('state-like'), as a way to distinguish crimes against humanity from 'ordinary' crimes, such as crimes by terrorist organizations, criminal organizations, slavery rings, and so on.[82] Most of the scholarly literature endorses the broader view, which includes any organization with capacity to do significant harm; on this view, crimes against humanity include any collective effort to inflict massive crimes on

---

[75] *Gbagbo*, ICC PTC I, 3 June 2013 (ICC-02/11–01/11–432) para. 44. See also the stringent approach applied in *Mbarushimana*, ICC PTC I, 16 December 2011 (ICC-01/04–01/10–465) paras. 242–67, declining to find a policy despite documentary evidence, oral testimony and circumstantial evidence.
[76] Robinson, 'Crimes Against Humanity' (n. 65). [77] *Fofana and Kondewa*, SCSL AC, 28 May 2008, para. 307.
[78] *Gbagbo*, ICC PTC, 12 June 2014 (ICC-02/11–01/11–656-Red) paras. 208 and 216.
[79] *Katanga*, ICC TC II, 7 March 2014 (ICC-01/04–01/07–3436-tENG), paras. 1094–113; *Ntaganda*, Judgment, ICC TC VI, 8 July 2019 (ICC-01/04–02/06), paras 673–5; *Ongwen*, ICC TC IX, 4 February 2021 (ICC-02/04–01/15), paras 2674–82.
[80] *Katanga*, ICC TC II, 7 March 2014 (ICC-01/04–01/07–3436-tENG) para. 1109.
[81] *Situation in Kenya*, ICC PTC II, 31 March 2010 (ICC-01/09–19).
[82] Kreß, 'On the Outer Limits' (n. 53); William Schabas, 'Prosecuting Dr Strangelove, Goldfinger, and the Joker at the International Criminal Court: Closing the Loopholes' (2010) 23 *LJIL* 847.

a civilian population.[83] The narrower view espoused by Judge Kaul has not been adopted by any other Chamber, and the broader view is now consistently reflected in the ICC's jurisprudence.[84] It is also compatible with the ordinary meaning of the term 'organization',[85] as well as the purpose of the policy element, which is to exclude random acts of individuals acting on their own initiative.[86]

11.2.4 Any Civilian Population

The seemingly simple word 'any' highlights the central innovation and *raison d'être* of crimes against humanity. The law of crimes against humanity not only protects enemy nationals, it also covers, for example, crimes by a state against its own citizens.[87] The nationality or affiliation of the victim is irrelevant.

The term 'civilian' connotes crimes directed against non-combatants rather than combatants. The term 'population' indicates that 'a larger body of victims is visualised', and that 'single or isolated acts against individuals' fall outside the scope of the concept.[88] The reference to population implies 'crimes of a collective nature', but does not require that the entire population be targeted.[89]

Interesting controversies arise as to whether military personnel (including prisoners-of-war) are protected by the law of crimes against humanity. It is widely accepted that crimes against military personnel, outside of combat situations, can be included if they are part of a broader attack directed at civilians.[90] After all, the population need only be '*predominantly* civilian in nature'; the 'presence of certain non-civilians in their midst does not change the character of the population'.[91] Furthermore, it is not required that each individual victim is civilian.[92]

The controversy arises where an attack is directed entirely or largely against former combatants, such as prisoners-of-war. There are two main views. On the first approach, the term 'civilian' in crimes against humanity is simply 'the antonym of combatant'.[93] This was the view taken in early Tribunal decisions, holding that 'civilian' includes all those no

---

[83] Sadat, 'Crimes Against Humanity' (n. 71); Charles Jalloh, 'What Makes a Crime Against Humanity a Crime Against Humanity?' (2013) 28 *American University International Law Review* 381; Rogier Bartels and Katharine Fortin, 'Law, Justice and a Potential Security Gap: The "Organization" Requirement in International Humanitarian Law and International Criminal Law' (2016) 21 *Journal of Conflict and Security Law* 29; Elissa Bookbinder, 'Crimes Committed Against Civilian Populations by Transnational Criminal Organizations Should be Considered Crimes Against Humanity and Leaders Prosecuted by ICC' (2015–2016) 23 *Willamette J Int'l L and Dis. Res.* 255; Thomas Obel Hansen, 'The Policy Requirement in Crimes Against Humanity: Lessons from and for the Case of Kenya' (2011) 43 *The George Washington International Law Review 1*; Tilman Rodenhäuser, 'Beyond State Crimes: Non-State Entities and Crimes Against Humanity' (2014) 27 *LJIL* 913.

[84] *Bemba Gombo*, ICC PTC II, 15 June 2009 (ICC-01/05–01/08–424) para. 81; *Katanga and Ngudjolo*, ICC PTC I, 30 September 2008 (ICC-01/04–01/07–717) para. 396; *Situation in Côte d'Ivoire*, ICC PTC III, 3 October 2011 (ICC-02/11–14).

[85] Gerhard Werle and Boris Burghardt, 'Do Crimes Against Humanity Require the Participation of a State or a "State-Like" Organization?' (2012) 10 *JICJ* 1151.

[86] As suggested above in this section. [87] War Crimes Commission, *History* (n. 2) 241. [88] *Ibid.* 193.

[89] *Tadić*, ICTY TC II, 7 May 1997, para. 644; *Kunarac et al.*, ICTY TC II, 22 February 2001, para. 425.

[90] *Tolimir*, ICTY AC, 8 April 2015, paras. 141–2.

[91] *Tadić*, ICTY TC II, 7 May 1997, para. 638; see also *Kordić and Čerkez*, ICTY TC III, 26 February 2001, para. 180.

[92] See e.g. *Martić*, ICTY AC, para. 307; *Mrkšić*, ICTY AC, 5 May 2009, paras. 30–3.

[93] Dinstein, 'Crimes Against Humanity after Tadić' (n. 57) 388; *Final Report of the Commission of Experts Established Pursuant to Security Council Resolution 780 (1992)*, UN Doc S/1994/674 Annex (1994) para. 78.

longer taking part in hostilities at the time the crimes were committed, including former combatants who had laid down arms or who had been placed *hors de combat* (wounded or detained).[94] On this first approach, the term 'civilian' serves a functional purpose: it simply exclude military actions against *legitimate military objectives* in accordance with international humanitarian law. Attacks on military targets are more appropriately assessed under the laws of war, a more detailed, special regime governing the killing and wounding of adversary combatants.[95] On this view, 'civilian' encompasses everyone who is not a military objective; thus it includes prisoners-of-war, who are now 'out of the fight' and no longer combatants.

The second approach arose following the *Martić* case, in which the ICTY Appeals Chamber transplanted the definition of 'civilian' from Article 50 of Additional Protocol I. The Article 50 definition of 'civilian' excludes prisoners-of-war and combatants otherwise rendered *hors de combat*.[96] That approach has been widely followed in subsequent Tribunal cases.[97]

However, there are reasons to doubt that the transplant from Additional Protocol I is appropriate. The definition of 'civilian' in Additional Protocol I appears in a detailed treaty regime that also grants protection to prisoners-of-war. By contrast, the term 'civilian' in the crimes against humanity definition arose three decades earlier, and was based on the simpler bifurcation between those taking part in hostilities and those who are not. The Appeals Chamber said that the principle of distinction (the duty to distinguish between lawful targets and civilians) supported its approach,[98] but actually the principle supports the *opposite*: a targeting of prisoners-of-war is equally prohibited under the principle of distinction.

Several commentators have doubted the soundness of this transplant from Additional Protocol I.[99] It has the undesirable effect that mass extermination and torture of prisoners-of-war would not be a crime against humanity. It also contradicts post-Second World War jurisprudence, which addressed crimes against humanity against military personnel.[100] It arbitrarily excludes persons from protection by virtue of their profession, whereas the alternative interpretation has a rational and narrow purpose (to exclude attacks against legitimate military objectives in armed conflict, which are to be assessed instead under humanitarian law). It may be hoped that other jurisdictions will critically examine the Tribunal's reasoning before following the same path.[101]

---

[94] *Akayesu*, ICTR TC, 2 September 1998, para. 582; *Tadić*, ICTY TC II, 7 May 1997, para. 643; *Kordić and Čerkez*, ICTY TC III, 26 February 2001, para. 180; *Blaškić*, ICTY TC, 3 March 2000, para. 214. See also Ambos and Wirth, 'The Current Law' (n. 58) 22–6. Note that a current member of an armed force or organization remains a combatant even in moments when they are not armed or in combat, and thus may be lawfully attacked by an enemy party to the conflict. See e.g. *Blaškić*, ICTY AC, 29 July 2004, para. 114.

[95] See e.g. Ambos and Wirth, 'The Current Law' (n. 58) 22–6.   [96] *Martić*, ICTY AC, 8 October 2008, paras. 296–302.

[97] *Katanga*, ICC TC II, 7 March 2014 (ICC-01/04–01/07–3436-tENG) para. 1102.

[98] *Martić*, ICTY AC, 8 October 2008, note 806.

[99] Gerhard Werle and Florian Jeßberger, *Principles of International Criminal Law*, 3rd ed. (Oxford, 2014) 335; Leila Nadya Sadat, 'Putting Peacetime First: Crimes Against Humanity and the Civilian Population Requirement' (2017) 31 *Emory International Law Review* 197; Ambos and Wirth, 'The Current Law' (n. 58) 25–6 and 85; Rachel Killean, Eithne Dowds, and Amanda Kramer, 'Soldiers as Victims at the ECCC: Exploring the Concept of "Civilian" in Crimes Against Humanity' (2017) *LJIL* 685; Kai Ambos, 'The ECCC's Contribution to Substantive ICL: The Notion of "Civilian Population" in the Context of Crimes Against Humanity' (2020) 18 *JICJ* 689.

[100] Antonio Cassese et al., *Cassese's International Criminal Law*, 3rd ed. (Oxford, 2013) 101–3.

[101] At the SCSL in the *Taylor* case, both the prosecution and the defence agreed that 'civilian' means 'non-combatants', yet the Trial Chamber opted to follow the narrower approach of the ICTY: *Taylor*, SCSL TC, 18 May 2012, paras. 508–10.

The Extraordinary Chambers in the Courts of Cambodia (the ECCC) encountered an intriguing related question: what if there is a murderous purge directed against a government's own army? On the first view (the 'functional' approach), the victims are not legitimate military objectives, because they are not from an adverse party, and hence widespread or systematic killing of them would be a crime against humanity. On the second view (the status-based approach), they would be excluded because they served in a military. This would leave a lacuna, because their extermination would likely not constitute a war crime either, since they are not affiliated with an adverse party.[102] The ECCC Investigating Judges adopted the functional approach (in which 'civilian' is contrasted to combatants who may be lawfully targeted), thus recognizing such violence as a crime against humanity.[103] Unfortunately, the Trial Chamber ultimately took the narrower view that anyone serving in the military could not be a 'civilian' for the purpose of crimes against humanity.[104] In that particular case, attacks on former fighters no longer taking part in hostilities could still be considered as crimes against humanity, because they were part of a broader attack directed at the (predominantly civilian) population of Cambodia.[105]

11.2.5 Link Between the Accused and the Attack

With respect to the individual accused, all that is required is that the accused commits a prohibited act, that the act objectively falls within the broader attack, and that the accused was aware of this broader context.[106]

Only the attack, not the acts of the individual accused, needs to be widespread or systematic.[107] A single act by the accused may be a crime against humanity if it forms part of the attack.[108] The act of the accused may also in itself constitute the entire 'attack', if it is of great magnitude, for example, the use of a biological weapon against a civilian population.[109] Generally, the accused need not be an architect of the attack, need not be involved in the formation of any policy, and need not be affiliated with any state or organization nor even share in the ideological goals of the attack, so long as there is a nexus between the conduct of the defendant and the attack.[110]

---

[102] See e.g. Geneva Convention III, Art. 4.
[103] ECCC Office of the Co-Investigating Judges, 'Notification on the Interpretation of "Attack Against Any Civilian Population" in the Context of Crimes Against Humanity with Regard to a State's or Regime's Own Armed Forces', *Meas Muth*, ECCC OCIJ, 7 February 2017.
[104] *Nuon (Chea) and Khieu (Samphan)*, ECCC Trial Chamber, 16 November 2018 (002/19–09–2007/ECCC/TC E465), paras. 306–12.
[105] *Ibid.* at paras. 317–18.
[106] *Tadić*, ICTY AC, 15 July 1999, para. 271. To determine if an act is 'part of' an attack, one may consider its characteristics, aims, nature or consequence: *Semanza*, ICTR TC, 15 May 2003, para. 326. A crime may be committed several months after, or several kilometres away from, the main attack, and still, if sufficiently connected, be part of the attack: *Krnojelac*, ICTY TC II, 15 March 2002, para. 127.
[107] *Kunarac*, ICTY AC, 12 June 2002, para. 96; *Blaškić*, ICTY AC, 29 July 2004, para. 101.
[108] *Kunarac*, ICTY AC, 12 June 2002, para. 96; *Blaškić*, ICTY AC, 29 July 2004, para. 101.
[109] *Blaškić*, ICTY TC I, 3 March 2000, para. 206.
[110] See the denunciation cases at Section 11.2.6. For a review of domestic law on the 'nexus' requirement, see Gaitan, 'Nexus Element' (n. 54).

Furthermore, the acts of the accused need not be of the same type as other acts committed during the attack. For example, if an organization launches a killing campaign, and a person commits sexual violence in the execution of that campaign, the person is guilty of the crime against humanity of sexual violence.

11.2.6 Awareness of Context

In addition to the requisite mental elements for the particular offences, the accused must also be aware of the 'broader context in which his actions occur', namely, the attack directed against a civilian population.[111] It is the context of a widespread or systematic attack against a civilian population that makes an act a crime against humanity, and hence knowledge of this context is necessary in order to make one culpable for a crime against humanity as opposed to an ordinary crime or a war crime.[112]

Tribunal cases indicate that awareness, wilful blindness, or knowingly taking the risk that one's act is part of an attack will suffice.[113] The ICC Elements of Crimes, following the applicable law, note that the mental element required for 'contextual elements' is modest:[114] for example, it is not required that the perpetrator had detailed knowledge of the attack or its characteristics or of the policy.[115] In most conceivable circumstances, the existence of a widespread or systematic attack would be notorious, and knowledge could not credibly be denied. Thus, knowledge may be inferred from the relevant facts and circumstances.[116]

The perpetrator need not share in the purpose or goals of the overall attack.[117] The mental requirement relates to knowledge of the context, not motive.[118] After the Second World War, several cases dealt with instances where individuals had denounced others to the Nazi regime, for personal opportunistic reasons. Such persons were held liable for crimes against humanity, because even though they acted out of personal motives, their actions were objectively part of the persecutory system, and they acted with knowledge of the system and the likely consequences.[119]

---

[111] *Tadić*, ICTY AC, 15 July 1999, para. 248; *Kupreškić et al.*, ICTY TC II, 14 January 2000, para. 134.

[112] *Tadić*, ICTY TC II, 7 May 1997, para. 656; *Kupreškić et al.*, ICTY TC II, 14 January 2000, para. 138; *Semanza*, ICTR TC, 15 May 2003, para. 332; and see also *R v. Finta* [1994] 1 SCR 701, 819: '[T]he mental element of a crime against humanity must involve an awareness of the facts or circumstances which would bring the acts within the definition of a crime against humanity'.

[113] *Tadić*, ICTY TC II, 7 May 1997, para. 657; *Kunarac et al.*, ICTY AC, 12 June 2002, para. 102; *Blaškić*, ICTY TC I, 3 March 2000, para. 251; *Krnojelac*, ICTY TC II, 15 March 2002, para. 59; *Šainović*, ICTY AC, 23 January 2014, paras. 267–71; see also *R v. Finta* [1994] 1 SCR 701, 819.

[114] See e.g. Maria Kelt and Herman von Hebel, 'General Principles of Criminal Law and the Elements of Crimes' in Lee, *Elements and Rules*, 34–5.

[115] ICC Elements of Crimes, 'Crimes Against Humanity Introduction', para. 2, states that it is not required that the perpetrator 'had knowledge of all characteristics of the attack or the precise details of the plan or policy of the State or organisation'; see also *Blaškić*, ICTY TC I, 3 March 2000, para. 251; *Kunarac et al.*, ICTY AC, 12 June 2002, para. 102; *Taylor*, SCSL TC II, 18 May 2012, paras. 513 and 515; *Bemba Gombo*, ICC PTC II, 15 June 2009 (ICC-01/05–01/08–424) para. 88. Furthermore, given that Article 30 is only a default rule applying 'unless otherwise provided', arguably the ICC can follow applicable law (Article 21), namely the jurisprudence which 'otherwise provides' that awareness of risk is sufficient for contextual elements: Ambos and Wirth, 'The Current Law' (n. 58) 36–42.

[116] ICC Elements of Crimes, 'General Introduction', para. 3.   [117] *Kunarac et al.*, ICTY AC II, 22 February 2001, para. 103.

[118] *Tadić*, ICTY AC, 15 July 1999, paras. 271–2, overturning a suggestion to the contrary by the Trial Chamber.

[119] See the cases discussed in *Tadić*, ICTY AC, 15 July 1999, paras. 255–69.

11.3 PROHIBITED ACTS

11.3.1 List of Prohibited Acts

The foregoing sections discussed the 'contextual elements': the surrounding backdrop of the widespread or systematic attack. We shall now look at the 'prohibited acts': the crimes carried out by perpetrators within that broader context.

The list of prohibited acts has gradually evolved over the decades. The first list, appearing in the Nuremberg Charter, comprised murder, extermination, enslavement, deportation, persecution, and other inhumane acts. Shortly thereafter, Control Council Law No. 10 added rape, imprisonment, and torture. The ICTY and ICTR Statutes follow the same expanded list.

In 1998, the ICC Statute added sexual slavery, enforced prostitution, forced pregnancy, other sexual violence, enforced disappearance, and apartheid. At first glance, this may seem to be an expansion on existing customary law. Recall, however, that the list of prohibited acts in the precedents ended with the residual clause 'or other inhumane acts'. Given that sexual slavery and these other acts are clearly inhumane acts, the additions in Article 7 simply elaborate explicitly what was already contained implicitly in the residual clause.

For each of the following crimes, the normal mental element applies where no specific observations are made to the contrary. Thus, the relevant conduct must be committed intentionally and with knowledge of the relevant circumstances.[120] With respect to legal requirements (for example, 'unlawful') or other normative requirements (for example, 'inhumane', 'severe'), it is not required that the perpetrator personally considered the conduct inhumane or severe; it is sufficient that the perpetrator was aware of the underlying *facts* that satisfy the element.[121]

11.3.2 Murder

The crime of murder is well known to all legal systems and is an archetypal form of crime against humanity. There is general conformity between Tribunal jurisprudence and the ICC Elements of Crimes, that murder refers to unlawfully and intentionally causing the death of a human being.[122]

Tribunal jurisprudence, consistent with many national systems, indicates that the mental element is satisfied if the perpetrator intends to kill, or intends to inflict grievous bodily harm likely to cause death and is reckless as to whether death ensues.[123] It is unclear whether the ICC will be able to adopt the same approach, in light of the different wording of Article 30 (mental element).[124]

---

[120] See e.g. ICC Statute, Art. 30.
[121] See e.g. ICC Statute, Art. 32(2); ICC Elements of Crimes, 'General Introduction', para. 4.
[122] ICC Elements of Crimes, Art. 7(1)(a); *Akayesu*, ICTR TC I, 2 September 1998, para. 589; *Jelisić*, ICTY TC I, 14 December 1999, para. 35; *Kupreškić et al.*, ICTY TC II, 14 January 2000, paras. 560–1.
[123] See e.g. *Čelebići*, ICTY TC II, 16 November 1998, para. 439; *Akayesu*, ICTR TC I, 2 September 1998, para. 589; *Kordić and Čerkez*, ICTY TC, 26 February 2001, para. 236.
[124] Given that Article 30 is only a default rule applying 'unless otherwise provided', it was long thought that applicable law (jurisprudence) could 'otherwise provide', and thus the ICC would be able to follow established jurisprudence confirming different mental elements for specific crimes. See for example, in an earlier edition of the Ambos commentary: Christopher

11.3.3 Extermination

The major question with the crime of extermination has been how to distinguish it from the crime against humanity of murder. Both involve killing, but 'extermination' connotes killing on a large scale. Tribunal jurisprudence and the ICC Elements of Crimes indicate that extermination involves killing by the accused within a context of mass killing.[125]

Thus, the first and major difference between murder and extermination is that extermination requires a surrounding circumstance of mass killing.[126] The perpetrator need not carry out the mass killing personally; a defendant only needs to know of the context of mass killing.[127]

A second difference is that extermination expressly includes indirect means of causing death. This distinction was recognized as early as the 1948 UN War Crimes Commission, which included 'implication in the policy of extermination without any direct connection with actual acts of murder'.[128] Tribunal jurisprudence also includes indirect means of causing death.[129] Article 7(2)(b) of the ICC Statute expressly includes 'inflicting conditions of life . . . calculated to bring about the destruction of part of a population', a phrase adapted from the Genocide Convention.[130]

The accused need not personally be responsible for a substantial number of deaths. A single killing by the accused is sufficient provided that the accused is aware of the necessary context of mass killing.[131] The ICC Elements of Crimes follow the same interpretation.[132]

There are also significant overlaps between extermination and the crime of genocide. The major difference between the two crimes is the requisite special intent for the crime of genocide (the intent to destroy a group as such). Moreover, genocide can only be committed where there is an intent to target one of four types of groups (national, ethnical, racial, or religious).[133]

11.3.4 Enslavement

The accepted definition of enslavement is 'exercising the powers attaching to the right of ownership' over one or more persons. This definition is drawn from the 1926 Slavery Convention and the 1956 Supplementary Slavery Convention, and has been adopted in the ICC Statute (Article 7(2)(c)) and in Tribunal jurisprudence.[134]

Enslavement may take various forms. First, it includes the traditional concept of 'chattel slavery', that is to say the treatment of persons as chattels, as in the slave trade. With respect

---

Hall and Carsten Stahn, 'Article 7' in O. Triffterer and K. Ambos (eds.), *Rome Statute of the International Criminal Court: A Commentary*, 3rd ed. (Beck, 2016), 183–4.

[125] ICC Elements of Crimes, Art. 7(1)(b); *Kayishema and Ruzindana*, ICTR TC II, 21 May 1999, para. 147.

[126] Whereas a crime against humanity of murder can occur on the basis of a single killing, committed in the context of a widespread or systematic attack based on other crimes.

[127] For careful discussion of the crime of extermination, see the ECCC decision in *Nuon Chea and Khieu Samphân*, ECCC AC, 23 November 2016. And see *Stanišić and Župljanin*, ICTY AC, 30 June 2016, paras. 1021–2.

[128] War Crimes Commission, *History* (n. 2) 194.

[129] *Rutaganda*, ICTR TC, 6 December 1999, para. 81; *Kayishema and Ruzindana*, ICTR TC II, 21 May 1999, para. 146.

[130] Genocide Convention 1948, Art. 2(c).

[131] *Stakić*, ICTY AC, 22 March 2006, paras. 260–1; see also *Kayishema and Ruzindana*, ICTR TC II, 21 May 1999, para. 147.

[132] ICC Elements of Crimes, Art. 7(1)(b), Element 1. [133] See Chapter 10.

[134] 1926 Slavery Convention, Art. 1; 1956 Supplementary Slavery Convention; *Kunarac*, ICTY TC II, 22 February 2001, para. 539; *Krnojelac*, ICTY TC II, 15 March 2002, para. 353. See also Jean Allain (ed.), *The Legal Understanding of Slavery* (Oxford, 2012).

to 'chattel slavery', the Slavery Convention includes the capture, acquisition, sale, exchange, transport, or disposal of persons with intent to reduce them to slavery or to sell or exchange them.[135]

Second, as noted in the ICC Elements of Crimes, enslavement also includes 'reducing a person to a servile status' as defined in the 1956 Supplementary Slavery Convention. This includes practices of debt bondage, serfdom, forced marriage, and child exploitation, as defined in that Convention.[136]

Third, the ICC Statute explicitly includes human trafficking (Article 7(2)(c)).[137]

Fourth, forced labour can also constitute enslavement.[138] International instruments prohibit forced or compulsory labour, with various recognized exceptions, such as military and national service, normal civic obligations, hard labour as lawful punishment for crime, and certain forms of labour for prisoners-of-war.[139] In *Krnojelac*, the Appeals Chamber held that severely overcrowded conditions, deplorable sanitation, insufficient food, locked doors, frequent beatings, psychological abuse, and brutal living conditions rendered it impossible for detainees to consent to work and that their labour was indeed forced.[140]

Fifth, other activities may also amount to enslavement. The ICTY Appeals Chamber in the *Kunarac* decision indicated that relevant factors include:

control of someone's movement, control of physical environment, psychological control, measures taken to prevent or deter escape, force, threat of force or coercion, duration, assertion of exclusivity, subjection to cruel treatment and abuse, control of sexuality and forced labour.[141]

A specific form of enslavement, namely, sexual slavery, is discussed in Section 11.3.8.

11.3.5 Deportation or Forcible Transfer

Deportation and forcible transfer of a population are frequently seen examples of crimes against humanity, particularly in contexts of 'ethnic cleansing'. The terms refer to forced displacement of persons by expulsion or other coercive acts from the area in which they are lawfully present, without grounds permitted under international law.[142]

'Deportation' is generally regarded as referring to displacement across a border, whereas 'forcible transfer' is generally regarded as referring to internal displacement.[143] ICTY jurisprudence follows this distinction. In the *Stakić* case, the ICTY Appeals Chamber confirmed that 'deportation' must be across a border, usually a de jure border, or in some

---

[135] 1926 Slavery Convention, Art. 1(2). The ICC Elements of Crimes also list, as examples, such transactions as 'purchasing, selling, lending, or bartering'.

[136] ICC Elements of Crimes, note 11; 1956 Supplementary Slavery Convention, Art. 1.

[137] See also Tom Obokata, 'Trafficking of Human Beings as a Crime Against Humanity' (2005) 54 *ICLQ* 445; Valerie Oosterveld, 'Sexual Slavery and the International Criminal Court: Advancing International Criminal Law' (2003) 25 *Michigan Journal of International Law* 605, 643.; Karen L. Corrie, 'Could the International Criminal Court Strategically Prosecute Modern Day Slavery?' (2016) 14 *JICJ* 285.

[138] ICC Elements of Crimes, note 11.

[139] See e.g. 1949 Geneva Convention III, Arts. 49–57; International Covenant on Civil and Political Rights (ICCPR), Art. 8(3); and the 1930 Forced or Compulsory Labour Convention.

[140] *Krnojelac*, ICTY TC II, 15 March 2002, paras. 193–5.   [141] *Kunarac et al.*, ICTY AC, 12 June 2002, para. 119.

[142] ICC Statute, Art. 7(2)(d); *Stakić*, ICTY AC, 22 March 2006, para. 278; ILC Draft Code, 1996, 100.

[143] ILC Draft Code, 1996, 100.

circumstances a de facto border, but in any event crossing of 'constantly changing front-lines' would not suffice.[144]

The deportation or transfer must be *forced* in order to be a crime against humanity.[145] This does not require actual physical force, but may also include the threat of force, coercion, psychological oppression, or other means of rendering displacement involuntary.[146] Thus, if a group flees of its own genuine volition, for example to escape a conflict zone, that would not be forced displacement.[147] On the other hand, if a group flees to escape deliberate violence and persecution, they would not be exercising a genuine choice.[148]

The forced displacement must also be unlawful under international law. Most or all states carry out legitimate acts of deportation on a frequent basis. Deportation of aliens not lawfully present in the territory is an established practice of states.[149] International humani-tarian law, for example, allows transfers when the security of the population or imperative military reasons so demand. Such transfers must meet certain stringent conditions and humanitarian safeguards.[150]

A striking example of displacement by coercion, currently under investigation by the ICC, is the violence in Myanmar that forced hundreds of thousands of Rohingya to flee to neighbouring Bangladesh.[151]

11.3.6 Imprisonment

Although imprisonment did not appear in the Nuremberg or Tokyo Charters, it was listed in Control Council Law No. 10 and subsequent definitions. The term 'imprisonment' includes detention in prison-like conditions and other serious forms of confinement. Out of an abundance of caution, the ICC Statute added 'or other severe deprivation of physical liberty' to ensure that situations such as house arrest were included.[152]

The imprisonment must be arbitrary to constitute a crime against humanity. After all, there are many contexts in which persons may be lawfully detained, including upon lawful arrest, conviction following lawful trial, lawful deportation or extradition procedures, quarantine and, during armed conflict, assigned residence, internment on security grounds,

---

[144] *Stakić*, ICTY AC, 22 March 2006, para. 300. The Appeals Chamber therefore allowed the appeal from an anomalous Trial Chamber decision which had held that 'deportation' could be internal. For other cases, see *Krstić*, ICTY TC I, 2 August 2001, para. 521; *Krnojelac et al.*, ICTY TC II, 15 March 2002, para. 474; *Kupreškić et al.*, ICTY TC II, 14 January 2000, para. 566; *Đorđević*, ICTY AC, 27 January 2014, limiting the possibility of de facto borders within a state.

[145] ICC Statute, Art. 7(2)(d); *Krstić*, ICTY TC I, 2 August 2001, para. 528; *Krnojelac*, ICTY TC II, 15 March 2002, para. 475.

[146] ICC Elements of Crimes, Art. 7(1)(d); *Stakić*, ICTY AC, 22 March 2006, para. 281; *Krnojelac*, ICTY TC II, 15 March 2002, para. 475; *Kunarac et al.*, ICTY TC II, 22 February 2001, para. 129.

[147] Jean Pictet, *Commentary on Geneva Convention IV* (Geneva, 1960) 279; Akhavan, 'Reconciling Crimes Against Humanity' (n. 20) 34–5.

[148] *Krstić*, ICTY TC I, 2 August 2001, para. 530.

[149] The question whether an individual was 'lawfully' present would probably be assessed under international as well as national law. For example, a government could not circumvent the definition of this crime through an arbitrary legislative act declaring members of a group not lawfully present.

[150] Geneva Convention IV 1949, Art. 49; Additional Protocol I, Art. 87. Vincent Chetail, 'Is There any Blood on My Hands? Deportation as a Crime of International Law' (2016) 29 *LJIL* 917.

[151] *Article 15 Decision Bangladesh/Myanmar*, ICC PTC III, 14 November 2019 (ICC-01/19–27).

[152] Hall and Stahn, 'Article 7' (n. 124) 202.

and internment of prisoners-of-war.[153] Tribunal jurisprudence refers to imprisonment without due process of law.[154] Article 7(1)(e) of the ICC Statute refers to deprivation 'in violation of fundamental rules of international law'.

The requirement that the imprisonment be 'arbitrary' does not mean that a minor procedural defect would expose all involved to international prosecution; significant failings are required. For this reason, the ICC Elements of Crimes refer to the 'gravity of the conduct' being such as to violate fundamental rules of international law.[155] Tribunal jurisprudence states that deprivation will be arbitrary and unlawful 'if no legal basis can be called upon to justify the initial deprivation of liberty'.[156] Even where the initial detention was justified, imprisonment will become arbitrary if the legal basis ceases to apply and the person remains imprisoned.[157]

While caution must always be used when relying on human rights standards in a criminal law context,[158] the three categories suggested by the UN Working Group on Arbitrary Detention seem to capture the forms of this crime admirably: (1) absence of any legal basis for the deprivation of liberty; (2) deprivation of liberty resulting from exercise of specified rights and freedoms (that is to say, political prisoners); and (3) 'when the total or partial non-observance of the international human rights norms relating to the right to a fair trial . . . is of such gravity as to give the deprivation of imprisonment an arbitrary character'.[159]

11.3.7   Torture

The crime of torture appeared in Control Council Law No. 10 and subsequent definitions of crimes against humanity. The prohibition against torture is well established in numerous conventions and instruments.[160] It is well recognized as a norm of customary law and amounts to *jus cogens*.[161]

Much of the definition in the 1984 Convention Against Torture (CAT) is also accepted as the core definition for torture as a crime against humanity or war crime: the intentional infliction of severe pain or suffering, whether physical or mental, upon a person.[162] There are, however, several open questions.

The first question is whether the torturer must be linked to a state. The CAT definition requires that the pain or suffering be 'inflicted by or at the instigation of or with the consent or acquiescence of a public official or other person acting in an official capacity'.[163] In *Kunarac*, the ICTY held that this is not required in international criminal law.[164] Human

---

[153]   Geneva Convention IV 1949, Arts. 5, 42 and 43; Geneva Convention III 1949, Arts. 21–32.
[154]   *Kordić and Čerkez*, ICTY TC III, 26 February 2001, para. 302; *Krnojelac*, ICTY TC II, 15 March 2002, para. 113.
[155]   ICC Elements of Crimes, Art. 7(1)(e), Element 2.   [156]   *Krnojelac*, ICTY TC II, 15 March 2002, para. 114.
[157]   E.g. if the procedural safeguards of Art. 43 of the Geneva Convention IV 1949 for internment of civilians are disregarded: *Kordić and Čerkez*, ICTY TC III, 26 February 2001, para. 286; *Čelebići*, ICTY TC II, 16 November 1998, para. 579.
[158]   See Section 1.4.1.   [159]   *Report of the UN Working Group on Arbitrary Detention*, UN Doc. E/CN.4/1998/44 (1998) para. 8.
[160]   These include the Universal Declaration of Human Rights, the ICCPR, the ECHR, the American Convention on Human Rights (ACHR), the African Charter on Human and Peoples' Rights, the CAT, the Inter-American Convention to Prevent and Punish Torture, and the Geneva Conventions and their Additional Protocols.
[161]   *Čelebići*, ICTY TC II, 16 November 1998, para. 454. For discussion of the crime of torture under the Convention Against Torture, see Section 14.3.
[162]   CAT, Art. 1.   [163]   *Ibid.*   [164]   *Kunarac et al.*, ICTY TC II, 22 February 2001, paras. 387–91.

rights law focuses on the state because it regulates state treatment of human beings. International criminal law holds individuals accountable for crimes, and applies to everyone whether or not affiliated with a state. Similarly, the ICC Statute and the ICC Elements of Crimes do not require a link between the act of torture and a public official.[165] Thus, torture by rebel groups, paramilitaries, and others is included.

The second question is whether torture must be for a specific 'purpose'. The CAT definition requires a purpose such as 'obtaining from him or a third person information or a confession, punishing him for an act he or a third person has committed or is suspected of having committed, or intimidating or coercing him or a third person, or for any reason based on discrimination of any kind'.[166] Many authorities, including the CAT and Tribunal jurisprudence, regard the purpose element as a defining feature of torture.[167] On this approach, the prohibited purpose distinguishes torture from inhuman treatment.

In other authorities, such as the jurisprudence of the European Court of Human Rights (ECtHR), the difference between torture and the lesser violation of 'inhuman treatment' is *severity*: the special stigma of torture requires infliction of 'very serious and cruel suffering'.[168] Article 7 of the ICC Statute followed this approach and did not include a purpose element. (Further adding to the uncertainty, the ICC Elements of Crimes adopted the 'purpose' requirement with respect to the war crime of torture but not with respect to the crime against humanity of torture. The divergent treatment arose from following respective authorities,[169] but it does seem to create an anomaly.)

Third, the ICC Statute, while dropping any requirements of purpose or link to an official, adds a requirement that the victim be in the 'custody or control' of the perpetrator. The requirement should not be onerous since, as a practical matter, torture entails such custody or control. Various explanations have been offered for this addition, including establishing a link of power or control given the deletion of a link to a public official, or excluding the use of force against military objectives during armed conflict.[170]

Tribunal jurisprudence and regional human rights bodies have recognized that rape can constitute a form of torture.[171] Rape causes severe pain and suffering, both physical and psychological. In *Furundžija*, the ICTY convicted the accused of torture for acts during an interrogation, including sexual threats, rapes, and forced nudity, inflicted on the victim for purposes of intimidation, humiliation, and extracting confession.[172]

---

[165] ICC Statute, Art. 7(2)(e); but see Art. 7(2)(a) which appears to require some sort of linkage between a state or organization and the attack as a whole, albeit not the particular crimes of the accused.

[166] ICC Statute, Art. 7(2)(e).

[167] *Akayesu*, ICTR TC I, 2 September 1998, paras. 593–5; *Čelebići*, ICTY TC II, 16 November 1998, para. 459; *Furundžija*, ICTY TC II, 10 December 1998, para. 161; *Krnojelac*, ICTY TC II, 15 March 2002, para. 180.

[168] *Ireland* v. *United Kingdom*, ECtHR, Judgment of 18 January 1978, para. 167; *Selmouni* v. *France*, ECtHR, Judgment of 28 July 1999, para. 105; *Aydin* v. *Turkey*, ECtHR, Judgment of 25 September 1997, para. 82.

[169] Delegates followed Tribunal precedents with respect to war crimes, but they did not do so for crimes against humanity, out of fidelity to the decision taken at the Rome Conference not to require such an element for the crime against humanity of torture. Note 14 to the ICC Elements of Crimes therefore specifies that no purpose element is required.

[170] Darryl Robinson, 'Elements of Crimes Against Humanity' in Lee, *Elements and Rules*, 90; Hall and Stahn, 'Article 7' (n. 124) 253.

[171] *Akayesu*, ICTR TC I, 2 September 1998, para. 597; *Kunarac et al.*, ICTY AC, 12 June 2002, para. 150; *Semanza*, ICTR TC, 15 May 2003, para. 482; *Čelebići*, ICTY TC II, 16 November 1998, para. 495; *Fernando and Raquel Mejia* v. *Peru*, Inter-American Commission on Human Rights, 1 March 1996; *Aydin* v. *Turkey*, ECtHR, Judgment of 25 September 1997, para. 86.

[172] *Furundžija*, ICTY TC II, 10 December 1998, para. 267.

11.3.8 Rape and Other Forms of Sexual Violence

The crime of rape appeared in Control Council Law No. 10 and subsequent instruments, including the ICTY and ICTR Statutes. The 1996 draft Code of Crimes prepared by the ILC proposed that the definition be updated by adding enforced prostitution and other forms of sexual abuse.[173] The ICC Statute took up the idea of modernizing the definition, by including 'rape, sexual slavery, forced pregnancy, enforced sterilisation, or any other form of sexual violence of comparable gravity' (Article 7(1)(g)).[174] The inclusion was seen not as an expansion but rather as an acknowledgment that these acts, which have persisted throughout history, are inhumane acts falling within the definition of crimes against humanity.[175]

The same definitions apply both in crimes against humanity and in war crimes, so the relevant issues for both war crimes and crimes against humanity will be discussed here.

Rape

The crime of rape has two components. The first is a physical invasion of a sexual nature. The second component is, according to some authorities, the presence of coercive circumstances or, according to other authorities, the absence of consent.

The first component, the conduct element, was described in *Akayesu*, the first case defining the crime against humanity of rape. The ICTR Trial Chamber held that rape 'is a form of aggression and . . . cannot be captured in a mechanical description of objects and body parts', which led it to the definition 'a physical invasion of a sexual nature, committed on a person in circumstances which are coercive'.[176] A rift emerged in Tribunal jurisprudence, however, when a subsequent decision of an ICTY Trial Chamber (*Furundžija*) concluded that greater clarity was needed, and defined the physical element (rather mechanically) as: the sexual penetration, however slight, of (1) the vagina or anus of the victim by the penis of the perpetrator or any other object, or (2) the mouth of the victim by the penis of the perpetrator.[177] This definition was subsequently endorsed by the ICTY Appeals Chamber in *Kunarac*.[178]

The ICC Elements of Crimes falls in between the two definitions:

The perpetrator invaded the body of a person by conduct resulting in penetration, however slight, of any part of the body of the victim or of the perpetrator with a sexual organ, or of the anal or genital opening of the victim with any object or any other part of the body.[179]

This definition is closer to the later Tribunal jurisprudence, in that it is comparably specific, yet it is slightly broader and gender-neutral.

---

[173] Report of the International Law Commission on the Work of its Forty-Eighth Session, 1996, GAOR 51st Session, Supp. No. 10 (A/51/10) 102–3.

[174] See e.g. Vienna Declaration, World Conference on Human Rights, UN Doc. A/CONF.157/24 (1993) Part I, para. 28, and Part II, para. 38; Beijing Declaration and Platform for Action, Fourth World Conference on Women, 15 September 1995, UN Doc. A/ CONF.177/20 (1995) and UN Doc. A/CONF.177/20/Add.1 (1995) ch. II, paras. 114–15*bis*.

[175] For a more detailed overview of the advances and difficulties, see Kelly Askin, 'Prosecuting Wartime Rape and Other Gender-Related Crimes under International Law: Extraordinary Advances, Enduring Obstacles' (2003) 21 *Berkeley Journal of International Law* 288.

[176] *Akayesu*, ICTR TC I, 2 September 1998, paras. 597–8. [177] *Furundžija*, ICTY TC II, 10 December 1998, para. 185.

[178] *Kunarac et al.*, ICTY TC II, 22 February 2001, para. 127. [179] ICC Elements of Crimes, Art. 7(1)(g)–1, Element 1.

The second component is less settled; some sources focus on coercive circumstances and some focus on absence of consent. Early Tribunal jurisprudence required coercive circumstances: namely, coercion, force, or threat of force against the victim or a third person.[180] This approach was followed in the ICC Elements of Crimes, albeit significantly expanded:

> The invasion was committed by force, or by threat of force or coercion, such as that caused by fear of violence, duress, detention, psychological oppression or abuse of power, against such person or another person, or by taking advantage of a coercive environment, or the invasion was committed against a person incapable of giving genuine consent.[181]

More recently, Tribunal jurisprudence moved away from cataloguing coercive circumstances and focused on the lack of consent of the victim. In *Kunarac*, an ICTY Trial Chamber analysed various legal systems and concluded that the correct element was lack of consent of the victim, thereby penalizing violations of sexual autonomy.[182] The ICTY Appeals Chamber confirmed this approach and held that force or threat of force may be relevant in providing clear evidence of non-consent, but force is not an element per se of rape.[183]

Strong arguments can be made that the new line of cases better reflects national legal systems and indeed the underlying principle of sexual autonomy.[184] On the other hand, Catharine MacKinnon argues that the 'coercion' approach is preferable to the 'non-consent' approach.[185] She argues that, in circumstances of 'mass sexual coercion', an inquiry into consent is decontextualized and unreal.[186] War crimes and crimes against humanity of sexual violence are almost invariably committed in coercive circumstances where consent or reasonable belief in consent is simply not a credible possibility. Where such circumstances are shown, inquiry into consent should not be necessary.[187]

On either approach, it is desirable to adopt procedural and evidentiary rules to limit how the issue of consent may be raised, in order to prevent harassment of witnesses and spurious lines of questioning (see Section 17.10).

Sexual Slavery

Sexual slavery is a particularly serious form of enslavement.[188] The first element of sexual slavery is identical to enslavement.[189] The additional requirement is that the perpetrator caused the victim to engage in one or more acts of a sexual nature.[190] Particularly egregious examples include the 'comfort stations' maintained by the Japanese in the Second World

---

[180] *Akayesu*, ICTR TC I, 2 September 1998, para. 598; *Furundžija*, ICTY TC II, 10 December 1998, para. 185.
[181] ICC Elements of Crimes, Art. 7(1)(g)–1, Element 2. [182] *Kunarac et al.*, ICTY TC II, 22 February 2001, paras. 440–60.
[183] *Kunarac et al.*, ICTY AC, 12 June 2002, para. 129.
[184] Kristen Boon, 'Rape and Forced Pregnancy under the ICC Statute: Human Dignity, Autonomy and Consent' (2001) 32 *Columbia Human Rights Law Review* 625.
[185] Catharine MacKinnon, 'Defining Rape Internationally: A Comment on *Akayesu*' (2005/6) 44 *Columbia Journal of International Law* 940.
[186] *Ibid.* 950.
[187] The judgment in *Katanga*, ICC TC II, 7 March 2014 (ICC-01/04–01/07–3436-tENG) para. 965 found proof of any one of these coercive circumstances sufficient.
[188] McDougall, *Final Report on Systematic Rape* (n. 47) para. 30. [189] ICC Elements of Crimes, Art. 7(1)(g)–2, Element 1.
[190] ICC Elements of Crimes, Art. 7(1)(g)–2, Element 2.

War and the 'rape camps' in the former Yugoslavia.[191] The examples of enslavement from the Tribunal cases, discussed above,[192] would clearly qualify as sexual slavery.

Sexual slavery includes many acts that in the past would have been categorized as 'enforced prostitution'.[193] The latter concept is problematic in that it obscures the violence involved and mischaracterizes the harm done to the victim. Thus, the term 'sexual slavery' is generally preferred as properly reflecting the nature and seriousness of the crime.[194] The SCSL was the first tribunal to enter convictions for sexual slavery; in doing so the Court has explored overlaps with the concept of 'forced marriage', discussed in Section 11.3.12.[195] The ICC has also convicted individuals for sexual slavery.[196]

Enforced Prostitution

Enforced prostitution is prohibited in Geneva Convention IV, but as an example of an attack upon a woman's honour.[197] The ICC Statute lists it as a crime against humanity and war crime in its own right, removing the outdated linkage to 'honour'.

The ICC Elements of Crimes refer to (1) causing one or more persons to engage in one or more acts of a sexual nature; (2) by force or by threat of force (or under the coercive circumstances, as noted above in the discussion of rape).[198] In addition, pursuant to a US proposal, it is required that (3) 'the perpetrator or another person obtained or expected to obtain pecuniary or other advantage in exchange for or in connection with the acts of a sexual nature'.[199] There were considerable misgivings among some delegations concerning the paucity of precedent for this element. In the end, however, it was adopted in order to create some distinction from sexual slavery and in light of the ordinary meaning of the term 'prostitution'. In the absence of such anticipated advantage, the relevant conduct could still be prosecuted as sexual slavery or sexual violence.

Forced Pregnancy

The inclusion of 'forced pregnancy' was the subject of intense debate in the negotiation of the ICC Statute.[200] It had previously been recognized in international instruments.[201] The inclusion recognized a particular harm inflicted on women, including during the conflicts in the former Yugoslavia, where captors indicated that they tried to impregnate women and hold them until it was too late to obtain an abortion.[202]

[191] *Final Report on Systematic Rape* (n. 188) para. 30. [192] See Section 11.3.4.
[193] *Final Report on Systematic Rape* (n. 188) para. 31.
[194] Oosterveld, 'Sexual Slavery' (n. 137); Kelly D. Askin, 'Women and International Humanitarian Law' in Kelly D. Askin and Dorean M. Koenig (eds.), *Women and International Human Rights Law* (Ardsley, NY, 1998) vol. I, 48; Rhonda Copelon, 'Surfacing Gender: Re-Engraving Crimes Against Women in Humanitarian Law' (1994) 5 *Hastings Law Journal* 243.
[195] *Sesay, Kallon and Gbao* (the 'RUF case'), SCSL TC I, 2 March 2009; *Taylor*, SCSL TC II, 18 May 2012.
[196] *Ongwen*, ICC AC, 15 December 2022, paras. 1685–6; *Ntaganda*, ICC TC VI, 8 July 2019, Disposition.
[197] Geneva Convention IV 1949, Art. 27: 'Women shall be especially protected against any attack on their honour, in particular against rape, enforced prostitution, or any form of indecent assault'.
[198] ICC Elements of Crimes, Art. 7(1)(g)–3, Element 1. [199] ICC Elements of Crimes, Art. 7(1)(g)–3, Element 2.
[200] Cate Steains, 'Gender Issues' in Lee, *The Making of the Rome Statute*, 363–9.
[201] Vienna Declaration, World Conference on Human Rights, UN Doc. A/CONF.157/24 (1993) Part II, para. 38; Beijing Declaration and Platform for Action, Fourth World Conference on Women, 15 September 1995, UN Doc. A/CONF.177/20 (1995) and UN Doc. A/CONF.177/20/Add.1 (1995) ch. II, para. 115.
[202] Commission of Experts (the Former Yugoslavia), *Final Report* (n. 47) paras. 248–50.

Some delegations were concerned that the concept would be used to criminalize national systems that did not provide a right to abortion, which would conflict with their religious convictions and their constitutional provisions. It was agreed that discussion of the right to abortion will continue in a human rights context[203] but was not part of the crimes against humanity debate. Agreement was reached on the following definition: (1) unlawful confinement, (2) of a woman forcibly made pregnant, and (3) with the intent of affecting the ethnic composition of a population or carrying out other grave violations of international law.[204] The reference to grave violations of international law includes, for example, biological experiments. For greater clarity, Article 7(2)(f) states that '[t]his definition shall not in any way be interpreted as affecting national laws relating to pregnancy'. The ICC's first prosecution and conviction for forced pregnancy took place in *Ongwen*.[205]

Enforced Sterilization

The ICC Statute is the first treaty expressly recognizing enforced sterilization as a crime against humanity and war crime. The conduct has, however, been prosecuted before in the context of unlawful medical experiments such as were seen in the Second World War.[206] The ICC Elements of Crimes require that (1) the perpetrator deprived one or more persons of biological reproductive capacity; and (2) that the conduct was neither justified by the medical or hospital treatment of the persons concerned nor carried out with their genuine consent.[207] This definition is not restricted to medical operations, but could also include an intentional use of chemicals for this effect.[208] The concept of 'genuine consent' excludes consent obtained by deception.[209]

Other Sexual Violence

The ICC Statute also includes 'other sexual violence of comparable gravity'. The ICC Elements of Crimes elaborate the following elements: (1) the perpetrator committed an act of a sexual nature against one or more persons *or* caused one or more persons to engage in an act of a sexual nature, (2) by force or threat of force or coercion,[210] and (3) the gravity of the conduct was comparable to the other offences in Article 7(1)(g).[211]

The UN Special Rapporteur on systematic rape, sexual slavery and slavery-like practices observed that sexual violence includes:

any violence, physical or psychological, carried out by sexual means or targeting sexuality. Sexual violence covers both physical and psychological attacks directed at a person's sexual characteristics, such as forcing a person to strip naked in public, mutilating a person's genitals or slicing off a woman's breasts. Sexual violence also characterizes situations in which two victims are forced to perform sexual acts on one another or to harm one another in a sexual manner.[212]

---

[203] On the difference between human rights and crimes against humanity, see Section 1.4.1.   [204] ICC Statute, Art. 7(2)(f).
[205] *Ongwen*, ICC TC IX, 24 February 2021, para. 3062. This was confirmed on appeal.
[206] *Brandt* (the 'Doctors Trial'), IV LRTWC 91.   [207] ICC Elements of Crimes, Art. 7(1)(g)–5, Elements 1 and 2.
[208] Eve La Haye, 'Sexual Violence' in Lee, *Elements and Rules*, 195. The ICC Elements of Crimes exclude 'birth control measures with a non-permanent effect'.
[209] ICC Elements of Crimes, note 55.   [210] With the same list of coercive circumstances discussed above in the context of rape.
[211] ICC Elements of Crimes, Art. 7(1)(g)–6, Elements 1 and 2.
[212] McDougall, *Final Report on Systematic Rape* (n. 47) paras. 21–2.

11.3.9 Persecution

Persecution involves the intentional and severe deprivation of fundamental rights, against an identifiable group or collectivity on prohibited discriminatory grounds.

Discriminatory Grounds

The fundamental feature of persecution is that it be committed on discriminatory grounds. The ICTY and ICTR Statutes refer to persecution on political, racial, or religious grounds. The ICC Statute contains an updated and more inclusive list of prohibited grounds: political, racial, national, ethnic, cultural, religious, or gender.[213] In addition, the ICC list is cautiously open-ended, adding 'other grounds that are universally recognised as impermissible under international law'. The standard of 'universal' means that the threshold required to read in additional grounds is a high one, but a high standard was considered necessary in order to satisfy the principle of legality.

Severe Deprivation of Fundamental Rights

Until recently, the crime of persecution was not well defined, and Tribunal jurisprudence rightly emphasized the need for adequate precision.[214] The test developed in Tribunal jurisprudence requires (1) a gross or blatant denial (2) on discriminatory grounds (3) of a fundamental right, laid down in international customary or treaty law, and (4) reaching the same level of gravity as other crimes against humanity.[215] Although there is some different terminology, this is generally compatible with the ICC definition, which refers to intentional and severe deprivation of fundamental rights on specified discriminatory grounds.

These elements provide the needed precision for criminal law. Nonetheless, the test necessarily remains somewhat open with respect to the particular *acts* that may constitute persecution, as it is impossible to anticipate all future examples. Tribunal jurisprudence has noted that:

Neither international treaty law nor case law provides a comprehensive list of illegal acts encompassed by the charge of persecution, and persecution as such is not known in the world's major criminal justice systems. [Thus] the crime of persecution needs careful and sensitive development in light of the principle of *nullum crimen sine lege*.[216]

[213] On ambiguities and controversies about the ICC Statute definition of 'gender', see e.g. Valerie Oosterveld, 'The ICC Policy Paper on Sexual and Gender-Based Crimes: A Crucial Step for International Criminal Law' (2018) 24 *William & Mary Journal of Women and the Law* 443; and more recently, ICC Office of the Prosecutor, Policy on the Crime of Gender Persecution', December 2022, <icc-cpi.int>.
[214] *Kupreškić et al.*, ICTY TC II, 14 January 2000, para. 618: 'However, this Trial Chamber holds the view that in order for persecution to amount to a crime against humanity it is not enough to define a core assortment of acts and to leave peripheral acts in a state of uncertainty. There must be clearly defined limits on the types of acts which qualify as persecution. Although the realm of human rights is dynamic and expansive, not every denial of a human right may constitute a crime against humanity'.
[215] See e.g. *Kupreškić et al.*, ICTY TC II, 14 January 2000, para. 621.
[216] *Kordić and Čerkez*, ICTY TC, 26 February 2001, para. 694.

Gravity or Severity

Tribunal jurisprudence indicates that persecution requires a gravity comparable to other crimes against humanity;[217] in the ICC definition, this requirement may be subsumed in the requirements of 'severe' deprivation.

Connection to Other Acts?

The ICC Statute contains an additional requirement, that persecution be committed in connection with (1) any crime within the jurisdiction of the Court or (2) any other act listed in Article 7(1). This requirement was included because of the concern of several states that the concept of persecution was too elastic. The fear was that all practices of discrimination, more suitably addressed by human rights bodies, would be labelled as 'persecution', giving rise to international prosecutions. The connection requirement was inserted to ensure at least a context of more typical forms of criminality.

The customary law status of this requirement is open to doubt. Such a requirement is not applied in Tribunal jurisprudence; in *Kupreškić*, an ICTY Trial Chamber found that, 'although the Statute of the ICC may be indicative of the *opinio juris* of many states, Article 7(1)(h) is not consonant with customary international law'.[218] In any event, the requirement should not pose a significant obstacle for legitimate prosecutions of persecution, since it is satisfied by a linkage to even *one* other recognized act (a killing or other inhumane act), which one would expect to find in any situation warranting international prosecution.

Mental Element

In addition to the normal mental element relating to the conduct and the broader context, persecution requires a particular intent to target a person or group on prohibited grounds of discrimination.[219] Tribunal jurisprudence indicates that a particular *intent* to discriminate is required, not simply *knowledge* that one is acting in a discriminatory way.[220]

Relationship to Other Crimes

Persecution and genocide each require a particular discriminatory intent. In the case of genocide, however, the intent is more specific: it must be an intent to destroy a national, ethnical, racial, or religious group as such. Genocide can only be based on the listed acts (see, for example, Article 6 of the ICC Statute); in contrast, the conduct potentially amounting to persecution is broader. Acts amounting to other crimes against humanity can constitute persecution if the additional aggravating element of discriminatory intent is present.

---

[217] See e.g. *Kupreškić et al.*, ICTY TC II, 14 January 2000, paras. 619 and 621; *Kvočka et al.*, ICTY TC I, 2 November 2001, para. 185; *Ruggiu*, ICTR TC, 1 June 2000, para. 21.

[218] *Kupreškić et al.*, ICTY TC II, 14 January 2000, para. 580. Antonio Cassese argues persuasively that the requirement is inconsistent with the elimination of the general nexus requirement in the Nuremberg Charter and therefore is a restriction on customary law: Antonio Cassese, 'Crimes Against Humanity' in Cassese et al., *Commentary*, 376.

[219] ICC Elements of Crimes, Art. 7(1)(h), Element 3; *Kordić and Čerkez*, ICTY TC, 26 February 2001, para. 212.

[220] *Krnojelac*, ICTY TC II, 15 March 2002, para. 435; *Kordić and Čerkez*, ICTY TC, 26 February 2001, para. 212.

Examples of Persecutory Acts

Persecutory acts include the prohibited acts already listed in the definition of crimes against humanity, when committed with discriminatory intent.[221] Examples that have been prosecuted include murder, extermination, imprisonment, deportation, transfer of populations, torture, enslavement, and beatings (inhumane acts).[222] In 2019, the *Ntaganda* case at the ICC entered convictions for persecution based on listed prohibited acts, such as murder and sexual violence, as it was directed against an ethnic group.[223]

In addition, they can include other conduct that severely deprives political, civil, economic, or social rights. Examples include the passing of discriminatory laws, restriction of movement and seclusion in ghettos, the exclusion of members of an ethnic or religious group from aspects of social, political, and economic life, including exclusion from professions, business, educational institutions, public service, and inter-marriage.[224] It also includes overt violence such as burning of homes and terrorization.[225] The ICTR Appeals Chamber has held that, while hate speech alone does not constitute persecution, hate speech and calls to violence that contribute to acts of violence can be of comparable gravity to other crimes and hence constitute acts of persecution.[226]

Attacks on property can constitute persecution. The *Blaškić* decision affirmed that persecution includes 'targeting property, so long as the victimised persons were specially selected on grounds linked to their belonging to a particular community'.[227] Examples include destruction of private dwellings, businesses, symbolic buildings, looting and plunder of businesses and private property, boycott of businesses and shops, and forcing the group out of economic life.[228] Destruction of culturally and religiously significant property can also qualify.[229]

11.3.10 Enforced Disappearance

The ICC Statute expressly includes enforced disappearance as a crime against humanity. Enforced disappearance was exemplified in the 'Night and Fog Decree' issued by the Nazis, to execute people and to provide no information to the families as to their whereabouts or fate.[230] It was also a prevalent feature under military regimes in Latin America in the 1980s and is still practised today in various regimes around the world. Enforced disappearance is expressly recognized as a crime against humanity in various treaties.[231]

---

[221] *Kupreškić et al.*, ICTY TC II, 14 January 2000, paras. 593–607.
[222] *Tadić*, ICTY TC II, 7 May 1997, paras. 704–10; *Kupreškić*, ICTY TC II, 14 January 2000, para. 594.
[223] *Ntaganda*, Judgment, ICC TC VI, 8 July 2019 (ICC-01/04–02/06–2359), paras 987–1024.
[224] *Kupreškić et al., ibid.* paras. 608–15. [225] *Krstić*, ICTY TC I, 2 August 2001, para. 537.
[226] *Nahimana et al.*, ICTR AC, 28 November 2007, paras. 986–8. [227] *Blaškić*, ICTY TC I, 3 March 2000, para. 233.
[228] *Ibid.* paras. 220–33.
[229] *Đorđević*, ICTY AC, 27 January 2014, paras. 560–2. See also Sebastián A. Green Martínez, 'Destruction of Cultural Heritage in Northern Mali: A Crime Against Humanity?' (2015) 13 *JICJ* 1073.
[230] Nuremberg IMT, Judgment and Sentences, reprinted in (1947) 41 *AJIL* 172, 230.
[231] 1992 UN Declaration on the Protection of All Persons from Enforced Disappearance; 1994 Inter-American Convention on the Forced Disappearance of Persons; 2006 International Convention on the Protection of All Persons from Enforced Disappearance, and see specifically paras. 4, 5, and 6 of the Preamble to the respective instruments.

The definition in the ICC Statute is based on the UN Declaration and the Inter-American Convention,[232] and refers to the:

arrest, detention or abduction of persons by, or with the authorisation, support or acquiescence of, a state or political organisation, followed by a refusal to acknowledge that deprivation of freedom or to give information on the fate or whereabouts of those persons, with the intention of removing them from the protection of law for a prolonged period of time.[233]

A welcome development in the negotiation of the ICC Elements of Crimes was the realization that there are various ways in which an *individual* may be liable for this crime. Previous definitions simply described the whole system of enforced disappearance, but it is unlikely that a single individual would be involved in the arrest, detention, or abduction phase, as well as the refusal to acknowledge the deprivation or to provide information. Enforced disappearance typically involves many actors. Therefore, the ICC Elements of Crimes recognize that the crime may be committed (1) by arresting, detaining, or abducting a person, with knowledge that a refusal to acknowledge or give information would be likely to follow in the ordinary course of events, *or* (2) by refusing to acknowledge the deprivation of freedom or to provide information on the fate or whereabouts, with knowledge that such deprivation had occurred.[234] Previous instruments required commission, authorization, support, or acquiescence from the state. The ICC Statute expanded this to refer as well to 'political organizations', consistent with the fundamental proposition that crimes against humanity may be committed by non-state actors.

Enforced disappearance may involve other crimes such as killing, torture, or arbitrary imprisonment. The essence of the crime, however, is that the friends and families of the direct victims do not know whether the persons concerned are alive or dead. It is this uncertainty that is the hallmark of enforced disappearance.

11.3.11 Apartheid

The ICC Statute includes the crime of apartheid as a crime against humanity. Apartheid was recognized as a crime against humanity in instruments such as the 1968 Convention on the Non-Applicability of Statutory Limitations to War Crimes and Crimes Against Humanity and the 1973 Apartheid Convention.[235]

The definition was generalized to refer not only to the situation which had prevailed in South Africa but also any similar situations in the future. Article 7(2)(h) of the ICC Statute defines it as:

inhumane acts of a character similar to those referred to in paragraph 1, committed in the context of an institutionalised racial regime of systematic oppression and domination by one racial group over any other racial group and committed with the intention of maintaining that regime.

[232] UN Declaration, Preamble, para. 3 and Inter-American Convention, Art. 2. [233] ICC Statute, Art. 7(2)(i).
[234] Georg Witschel and Wiebke Rückert, 'Crime Against Humanity of Enforced Disappearance of Persons' in Lee, *Elements and Rules*, 98–103.
[235] Convention on Statutory Limitations, Art. 1(b), quoted in Apartheid Convention, Preamble, para. 5.

The definition of crimes against humanity has always included a residual clause encompassing other inhumane acts of a similar character. Thus, by requiring in the definition of the crime of apartheid that the inhumane acts be 'of a character similar to those referred to in paragraph 1', the drafters ensured that they did not exceed existing law. The ICC Statute simply provides an express recognition of the crime of apartheid where inhumane acts are committed in the context of an institutionalized racial regime of systematic oppression and domination.[236]

11.3.12 Other Inhumane Acts

All definitions of crimes against humanity close with the general residual clause 'or other inhumane acts'. A residual clause remains necessary because:

However much care were taken in establishing all the various forms of infliction, one would never be able to catch up with the imagination of future torturers who wished to satisfy their bestial instincts; and the more specific and complete a list tries to be, the more restrictive it becomes.[237]

Jurists have, however, been sensitive that any such residual clause must be infused with adequate precision to satisfy the criminal law principle of legality.[238] The ICC Statute provides the necessary threshold by requiring that the inhumane acts (1) be of a similar character to other prohibited acts; and (2) cause great suffering or serious injury to body or to mental or physical health.[239] Tribunal jurisprudence provides the threshold by requiring 'similar gravity and seriousness' to other prohibited acts.[240]

The accused must intend to inflict serious bodily or mental harm.[241] It is not required that the accused considered his or her actions 'inhumane', it is sufficient that the accused was aware of the factual circumstances that established the character of the act.[242]

The Tribunal Statutes, unlike the ICC Statute, do not expressly include forced disappearance, sexual violence, forced prostitution and forced transfer of populations in their list of prohibited acts, and hence Tribunal jurisprudence has found that each of these are encompassed in the Tribunal Statutes under 'other inhumane acts'.[243] Other acts that have been characterized as inhumane acts include mutilation, severe bodily harm, beatings, serious physical and mental injury, inhumane or degrading treatment falling short of the definition of torture, imposing inhumane conditions in concentration camps, forced nudity, and forced marriage.[244]

---

[236] For discussion of a first national case on the crime against humanity of apartheid, see Gerhard Kemp and Windell Nortje, 'Prosecuting the Crime against Humanity of Apartheid: The Historic First Indictment in South Africa and the Application of Customary International Law', (2023) 21 *JICJ* 405.

[237] *Blaškić*, ICTY TC, 3 March 2000, para. 237, referring to Jean Pictet, *Commentary on Geneva Convention IV* (Geneva, 1960) 54.

[238] Gillian MacNeil, *Legality Matters: Crimes Against Humanity and the Problems and Promise of the Prohibition on Other Inhumane Acts* (Springer, 2021).

[239] ICC Statute, Art. 7(1)(k).   [240] See e.g. *Kayishema and Ruzindana*, ICTR AC, 1 June 2001, para. 583.

[241] ICC Elements of Crimes, Art. 7(1)(k); *Blaškić*, ICTY TC I, 3 March 2000, para. 243.

[242] ICC Elements of Crimes, Art. 7(1)(k), Element 3; *Čelebići*, ICTY TC II, 16 November 1998, para. 543.

[243] *Kvočka et al.*, ICTY TC I, 2 November 2001, para. 208; *Kupreškić et al.*, ICTY TC II, 14 January 2000, para. 566.

[244] *Akayesu*, ICTR TC I, 2 September 1998, paras. 685–97; *Tadić*, ICTY TC II, 7 May 1997, para. 730; *Blaškić*, ICTY TC I, 3 March 2000, para. 239; *Kvočka et al.*, ICTY TC I, 2 November 2001, para. 209; *Čelebići*, ICTY TC II, 16 November 1998, paras. 554–8.

The SCSL has recognized the phenomenon in which women and girls are abducted and forced to serve as 'bush wives' as an inhumane act. One Trial Chamber and the Appeals Chamber recognized 'forced marriage' as an 'inhumane act', with the Appeals Chamber defining it as 'forced conjugal association with another person resulting in great suffering, or serious physical or mental injury on the part of the victim'.[245] Another Trial Chamber preferred not to use the term 'forced marriage', on the ground that marriage was a misnomer for what happened to the victims, describing it instead as 'conjugal slavery' and holding that the phenomenon is already encompassed within the crime of sexual slavery.[246] Forced marriage has also been recognized at the ICC in the *Ongwen* case.[247] In the *Kenyatta* case at the ICC, a Pre-Trial Chamber held that being forced to watch family members being killed or mutilated is an inhumane act.[248] An intriguing contemporary question is whether toxic pollution – effectively poisoning a population – can constitute an 'inhumane act', giving rise to 'environmental crimes against humanity'.[249]

Further Reading

Kai Ambos and Steffen Wirth, 'The Current Law of Crimes Against Humanity: An Analysis of UNTAET Regulation 15/2000' (2002) 13 *Criminal Law Forum* 1

M. Cherif Bassiouni, *Crimes Against Humanity: Historical Evolution and Contemporary Application* (Cambridge, 2011)

Charles Chernor Jalloh, 'What Makes a Crime Against Humanity a Crime Against Humanity' (2013) 28 *American University International Law Review* 381

Claus Kreß, 'On the Outer Limits of Crimes Against Humanity: The Concept of Organization Within the Policy Requirement: Some Reflections on the March 2010 ICC Kenya Decision' (2010) 23 *LJIL* 855

David Luban, 'A Theory of Crimes Against Humanity' (2004) 29 *Yale Law Journal* 85

Darryl Robinson, 'Crimes Against Humanity: A Better Policy on "Policy"' in Stahn, *The Law and Practice of the ICC*

Leila Sadat, 'Crimes Against Humanity in the Modern Age' (2013) 107 *AJIL* 334

William Schabas, 'State Policy as an Element of International Crimes' (2008) 98 *Journal of Criminal Law and Criminology* 953

---

[245] *Brima, Kamara and Kanu*, SCSL AC, 22 February 2008, para. 195; *Sesay, Kallon and Gbao, SCSL AC*, 26 October 2009, para. 2307; *Sesay, Kallon and Gbao*, SCSL TC I, 2 March 2009, paras. 164–8.

[246] *Taylor*, SCSLTC II, 18 May 2012, paras. 424–8. Valerie Oosterveld, 'Gender and the Charles Taylor Case at the Special Court for Sierra Leone' (2012) 19 *William and Mary Journal of Women and the Law* 7.

[247] *Ongwen*, ICC TC IX, 4 February 2021 (ICC-02/04–01/15), paras 2741–53, confirmed on appeal. For an analysis, see Kathleen Maloney, Melanie O'Brien, and Valerie Oosterveld, 'Forced Marriage as the Crime Against Humanity of 'Other Inhumane Acts' in the International Criminal Court's *Ongwen* Case' (2023) *International Criminal Law Review*, doi.org/10.1163/15718123-bja10157.

[248] *Kenyatta*, ICC PTC II, 23 January 2012 (ICC-01/09–01/11–373) paras. 267–80, 428.

[249] Jessica Durney, 'Crafting a Standard: Environmental Crimes as Crimes Against Humanity Under the International Criminal Court' (2018) 24 *Hastings Environmental Law Journal* 413; Luigi Prosperi and Jacob Terrosi, 'Embracing the 'Human Factor': Is There New Impetus at the ICC for Conceiving and Prioritizing Intentional Environmental Harms as Crimes Against Humanity?' (2017) 15 *JICJ* 509; Caitlin Lambert, 'Environmental Destruction in Ecuador: Crimes Against Humanity Under the Rome Statute?' (2017) 30 *LJIL* 707.

12

War Crimes

12.1 INTRODUCTION

12.1.1 Overview

A war crime is a serious violation of the laws and customs applicable in armed conflict (also known as international humanitarian law, or IHL) which gives rise to individual criminal responsibility under international law. Because the law of war crimes is based on IHL, the present section will explain the relevant underlying principles of IHL. Section 12.2 will review issues common to all war crimes, namely: the existence of armed conflict; the nexus between the conduct and the armed conflict; and the role of the perpetrator and victim. Section 12.3 will survey the specific offences constituting war crimes.

Unlike crimes against humanity, war crimes have no requirement of widespread or systematic commission. A single isolated act can constitute a war crime. For war crimes law, it is the context of armed conflict that justifies international concern.

12.1.2 A Brief History of Humanitarian Law

Laws and customs regulating warfare can be traced back to ancient times. While such norms have varied between civilizations and centuries, and were often shockingly lax by modern standards, it is significant that diverse cultures around the globe have recorded agreements, religious edicts, and military instructions laying out ground rules for military conflict.[1]

Codification and progressive development at the international level was spurred in part by the efforts of one individual. In 1859, Henri Dunant, a businessman from Geneva, witnessed the aftermath of the Battle of Solferino, and was shocked by the horrors of wounded soldiers left to die on the battlefield. He published a poignant and evocative account of the carnage, urging measures to reduce such unnecessary suffering.[2] This appeal

---

[1] See e.g. Leslie Green, *The Contemporary Law of Armed Conflict*, 3rd ed. (Manchester, 2008) 20–53; Mary Ellen O'Connell, 'Historical Development and Legal Basis' in Dieter Fleck (ed.), *Handbook of International Humanitarian Law*, 3rd ed. (Oxford, 2013) 1–41; Marco Sassoli, Antoine A. Bouvier, and Anne Quintin, *How Does Law Protect in War?*, 3rd ed. (Geneva, 2011), ch. 3.
[2] Henri Dunant, *Un Souvenir de Solférino* (Geneva, 1862).

promptly led to the creation of the International Committee of the Red Cross in 1863 and the adoption of the first Geneva Convention.[3]

Since then, many treaties have further developed IHL. The Hague Conventions limit the methods and means of warfare, in order to reduce unnecessary destruction and suffering. The most important of these is the 1907 Hague Regulations, which recognized that 'the right of belligerents to adopt means of injuring the enemy is not unlimited', and laid down many provisions on the methods and means of warfare that are now recognized as customary law.

The Geneva Conventions primarily focus on protecting civilians and others who are not active combatants. The four Geneva Conventions of 1949, adopted in response to the inhumanities of the Second World War, considerably updated previous Geneva Conventions. The 1949 Conventions deal with the sick and wounded in the field ('Geneva Convention I'), the wounded, sick, and shipwrecked at sea ('Geneva Convention II'), prisoners-of-war ('Geneva Convention III'), and civilians ('Geneva Convention IV'). In 1977, these rules were again updated by two Additional Protocols (APs), the first concerning international armed conflicts ('AP I') and the second, non-international (sometimes described as 'internal') armed conflicts ('AP II').

Other significant treaty developments have strengthened the protection of cultural property,[4] the restrictions on certain weapons (such as biological and chemical weapons and anti-personnel mines),[5] and the prohibition on the use of child soldiers.[6]

The provisions of the 1907 Hague Regulations, as well as much of the 1949 Geneva Conventions, have come to be recognized as customary law; hence they apply regardless of whether parties to a conflict have ratified those conventions.[7] Some, but not all, provisions of the Additional Protocols have obtained recognition as customary law.[8]

12.1.3 Key Principles of Humanitarian Law

The resulting principles may be summarized in different ways, but key elements include:

- Non-combatants are to be spared from various forms of harm; this category includes not only civilians but also former combatants, such as prisoners-of-war and fighters rendered *hors de combat* ('out of the fight') because they are wounded, sick, shipwrecked, or have surrendered.

---

[3] 1864 Geneva Convention for the Amelioration of the Condition of the Wounded in Armies in the Field.

[4] 1954 Hague Convention for the Protection of Cultural Property in the Event of an Armed Conflict, 14 May 1954, and two Protocols thereto, the 1954 First Hague Protocol, 24 May 1954, and the 1999 Second Hague Protocol, 29 March 1999.

[5] Convention on the Prohibition of the Development, Production and Stockpiling of Bacteriological (Biological) and Toxin Weapons and on Their Destruction, 10 April 1972; Convention on Prohibitions or Restrictions on the Use of Certain Conventional Weapons Which be Deemed to be Excessively Injurious or to Have Indiscriminate Effects, 10 October 1980; four Protocols thereto including Convention on the Prohibition of the Development, Production, Stockpiling and Use of Chemical Weapons and on Their Destruction, 13 January 1993; Convention on the Prohibition of the Use, Stockpiling, Production and Transfer of Anti-Personnel Mines and on Their Destruction, 18 September 1997.

[6] Optional Protocol to the Convention on the Rights of the Child on the Involvement of Children in Armed Conflict, adopted and opened for signature, ratification and accession by GA Res. A/RES/54/263, 25 May 2000.

[7] Theodor Meron, *Human Rights and Humanitarian Norms as Customary Law* (Oxford, 1999) 41–62.

[8] See e.g. *Hamdan* v. *Rumsfeld*, 126 S Ct 2749 (2006) (regarding Art. 75 of AP I); *Strugar*, ICTY AC, 22 November 2002, para. 9 (regarding Arts. 51 and 52 of AP I); Meron, *Human Rights and Humanitarian Norms* (n. 7) 62–78.

- Combatants must distinguish between military objectives and the civilian population, and attack only military objectives (the principle of distinction).
- In attacking military objectives, combatants must take measures to avoid or minimize collateral civilian damage and refrain from attacks that would cause excessive civilian damage (the principle of proportionality).
- Even when one is attacking military targets, there are limits on the methods and means of war, to reduce unnecessary suffering and to maintain respect for humanitarian principles.

The goal of abolishing armed conflict altogether is left to other legal and political domains.[9] IHL restrains how armed conflict is conducted, when it does break out.

A fundamental principle of IHL is the complete separation of the *jus ad bellum* (the law regulating whether a state may resort to armed conflict) and the *jus in bello* (the law governing conduct within armed conflict). In previous centuries, some scholars had suggested that the party fighting a 'just' war should benefit from more permissive IHL provisions.[10] The problem with this proposition is that both sides usually claim to be fighting with 'just' cause, leading to confusion as to the applicable rules. Moreover, the victims of armed conflict still need protection regardless of the purpose of the conflict. In order to advance the fundamental humanitarian aims of IHL, it is now a clearly established principle that IHL applies equally and uniformly, irrespective of the reasons for the conflict.[11] *Jus ad bellum* considerations have no bearing on the interpretation or application of IHL in a conflict. Hence, one cannot argue that a war was unjustified and therefore that all killings of combatants were war crimes or that all attacks were disproportionate.[12] Conversely, even if forces are fighting in legitimate self-defence of their country, they are still fully accountable for war crimes.[13] The question whether a state's decision to resort to force was legal or illegal is addressed under other law, such as the UN Charter, and now the crime of aggression.[14]

12.1.4 The Challenge of Regulating Warfare

War in many ways seems to be the antithesis of law, leading to the mistaken saying that *silent enim leges inter arma* (law is silent in war). Normal legal and moral rules – including the basic prohibitions on killing and destruction – are to some extent displaced in armed

---

[9] See e.g. Preamble to and Arts. 1 and 2 of the 1907 Hague Regulations: 'Seeing that while seeking means to preserve peace and prevent armed conflicts between nations, it is likewise necessary to bear in mind the case where the appeal to arms has been brought about by events which their care was unable to avert; Animated by the desire to serve, even in this extreme case, the interests of humanity and the ever progressive needs of civilization'.

[10] See e.g. Hugo Grotius, *De Jure Belli ac Pacis* (1625); Peter Haggenmacher, *Grotius et la doctrine de la guerre juste* (Paris, 1983) 597–612.

[11] See e.g. AP I, Preamble, para. 5: 'provisions ... must be fully applied in all circumstances ... without any adverse distinctions based on the nature or origin of the conflict or on the causes espoused by or attributed to the parties to the conflict'; and see Sassoli, Bouvier, and Quintin, *How Does Law Protect in War?* (n. 1) ch. 1, p. 14–20; *United States* v. *List* (the 'Hostages case'), VIII LRTWC 59 (1948); François Bugnion, 'Guerre juste, guerre d'agression et droit international humanitaire' (2002) 84 *Revue International de la Croix-Rouge* 523. See, however, discussion of AP I, Art. 1(4) in Section 12.2.2.

[12] See e.g. Sassoli, Bouvier, and Quintin, *How Does Law Protect in War* (n. 1) ch. 1, p. 19–20; *United States* v. *Altstötter* (the 'Justice Trial'), VI LRTWC 1, 52 (1947).

[13] *Boškoski and Tarčulovski*, ICTY AC, 19 May 2010, para. 51; *Fofana and Kondewa*, SCSL AC, 28 May 2008, paras. 531–4.

[14] See Chapter 13.

conflict, and combatants cannot be punished for lawful acts of war. Nonetheless, the outbreak of armed conflict does not create a legal vacuum. The law that grants permission to engage in violence also imposes limits on that violence. Militaries must be under responsible command and they are legally required to ensure compliance with IHL rules. Of course, *enforcement* of international norms, which can be challenging in the best of circumstances, is all the more difficult in the context of a deadly struggle among armed groups.[15] International criminal justice is one means of deterring violations and educating people that some basic laws still apply in all circumstances.

The tension between military and humanitarian considerations permeates IHL and war crimes law. When appraising war crimes law, it is important to consider the chaotic situations faced in armed conflict and the requirements of military effectiveness. Destruction and death will occur even in lawfully conducted conflict. Mistakes may occur, with tragic consequences, without necessarily amounting to war crimes.

While IHL involves a balancing of military and humanitarian considerations, it is also clear that the *weight* assigned to these considerations has been shifting over the years in a progressive direction. This process has been aptly referred to as 'the humanization of humanitarian law'.[16] Many factors have contributed to this process. International law and the international community have increasingly emphasized protecting human beings as opposed to exclusively focusing on state interests, resulting in the adoption of stricter rules.

In addition, the phenomena of mass media, democratization, and globalization mean that images of civilian suffering are more readily available. Technological advances have raised expectations about the precision of attacks.[17] Those who plan operations know that any incidents causing significant civilian casualties can erode support from domestic populations, coalition partners, and the international community. Anecdotal evidence also suggests that awareness of international criminal justice institutions is inducing greater compliance among military leaders.[18] Of course, trends are not all positive, especially if political norms about protecting human beings erode. Some states fighting non-state actors with little regard for humanitarian law, have sought to deny or restrict the application of IHL, creating new challenges.[19] Other states have sought to curtail avenues to hold soldiers legally accountable for wrongdoing.[20] And some states, like Syria in its internal conflict or Russia in its invasion of Ukraine, are credibly alleged to engage in widespread violations of IHL.[21]

[15] Hersch Lauterpacht, 'The Problem of the Revision of the Law of War' (1952) 29 *British Yearbook of International Law* 360, 382.
[16] Theodor Meron, 'The Humanization of Humanitarian Law' (2000) 94 *AJIL* 239.
[17] Michael N. Schmitt, 'Precision Attack and International Humanitarian Law' (2005) 87 *International Review of the Red Cross* 445.
[18] See Chapter 2.
[19] Toni Pfanner, 'Asymmetric Warfare from the Perspective of Humanitarian Law and Humanitarian Action' (2005) 87 *International Review of the Red Cross* 149; Luisa Vierucci, 'Prisoners of War or Protected Persons Qua Unlawful Combatants? The Judicial Safeguards to which Guantanamo Bay Detainees are Entitled' (2003) 1 *JICJ* 284.
[20] Dan Sabbath, 'Peers vote to halt plans to limit UK soldier's accountability for war crimes', *The Guardian*, 13 April 2021.
[21] UN Human Rights Council, 'Report of the Independent International Commission of Inquiry on Ukraine', 15 March 2023, UN Doc A/HRC/52/62; UN Human Rights Council, 'Report of the Independent International Commission of Inquiry on the Syrian Arab Republic', 7 February 2023, UN Doc. A/HRC/52/69.

12.1.5 Relationship Between War Crimes and IHL

War crimes law criminalizes only a subset of the rules of IHL.[22] The major question is which rules of IHL constitute a criminal offence when violated.

Some treaties, such as the Geneva Conventions, expressly criminalize violations of identified fundamental provisions.[23] War crimes may also be found in customary law, even in the absence of a treaty provision criminalizing the norm. For example, the Nuremberg Tribunal held that key provisions of the 1907 Hague Regulations reflected customary law and that violations amounted to crimes, even though the 1907 Hague Regulations did not expressly criminalize such violations.[24]

The open-ended definitions in the International Criminal Tribunal for the former Yugoslavia (ICTY) and International Criminal Tribunal for Rwanda (ICTR) Statutes empowered judges to identify and apply war crimes arising from customary international law.[25] In the seminal *Tadić* decision on jurisdiction, the ICTY Appeals Chamber gave guidance on how to identify war crimes in customary law. The decision confirmed that not every IHL violation amounts to a war crime.[26] Such a conclusion is clearly correct, since IHL includes a great many technical regulations that would be inappropriate for criminalization.[27] For example, Geneva Convention III requires that prisoners-of-war have a canteen where they may purchase foodstuffs, soap, and tobacco at local market prices, and that they be given a specific monthly advance of pay depending on rank;[28] an unavailability of tobacco would be a breach of IHL, but it is not a war crime.

The Appeals Chamber in *Tadić* set the following requirements for war crimes within the jurisdiction of the ICTY: (1) the violation must infringe a rule of IHL; (2) that rule must be found in customary law or applicable treaty law; (3) the violation must be 'serious', in that the rule protects important values and the breach involves grave consequences for the victim; and (4) the violation must entail individual criminal responsibility.[29]

This test has been applied in subsequent Tribunal cases.[30] The test has been criticized because it hinges largely on the adjective 'serious', without giving concrete guidance.[31] In an article presaging the *Tadić* decision, Theodor Meron (later President of the ICTY) referred to factors such as whether the norm is directed to individuals, whether it is unequivocal in character, the gravity of the act, and the interests of the international community.[32]

---

[22] M. Bothe, 'War Crimes' in Cassese et al., *Commentary*, 387–8. [23] See Section 12.1.6.

[24] Nuremberg IMT, Judgment and Sentences, reprinted in (1947) 41 *AJIL* 172, 218 and 248–9; *United States* v. *von Leeb*, XII LRTWC 1, 61–2 and 86–92.

[25] ICTY Statute, Art. 3; ICTR Statute, Art. 4. [26] *Tadić*, ICTY AC, 2 October 1995, para. 94.

[27] See e.g. Henckaerts and Doswald-Beck, *ICRC Customary Law*, 568; and Hersch Lauterpacht, 'The Law of Nations and the Punishment of War Crimes' (1944) 21 *British Yearbook of International Law* 58, 78–9.

[28] Geneva Convention III, Arts. 28 and 60. [29] *Tadić*, ICTY AC, 2 October 1995, para. 94.

[30] See e.g. *Galić*, ICTY TC, 5 December 2003, paras. 13–32; *Galić*, ICTY AC, 30 November 2006, paras. 86–98, applying the test to find a war crime of committing acts of violence with the primary purpose of spreading terror among the civilian population. See also Chapter 14; and Robert Cryer, '*Prosecutor* v. *Galić* and the War Crime of Terror Bombing' (2005–6) 2 *Israel Defence Forces Law Review* 73.

[31] Georges Abi-Saab, 'The Concept of War Crimes' in Sienho Yee and Wang Tieya (eds.), *International Law and the Post-Cold War World: Essays in Memory of Li Haopei* (London, 2001) 112.

[32] Theodor Meron, 'International Criminalization of Internal Atrocities' (1995) 89 *AJIL* 554, 562.

Since war crimes are serious violations of IHL, it is often necessary to refer to the relevant principles of IHL to interpret international criminal law in this area.[33] This is why the chapeau of Article 8(2)(a) of the International Criminal Court (ICC) Statute refers to the provisions of the relevant Geneva Conventions, and the chapeau (the opening words) of Article 8(2)(b) refers to 'the established framework of international law'. That reference directs interpreters to consider the relevant rules of IHL when interpreting the various provisions.[34]

IHL and war crimes law have similar aims but somewhat different scopes and consequences. IHL is addressed to governments and other parties to a conflict; it sets out the main standards expected in armed conflict, and violations can lead to orders for compensation or other satisfaction. In contrast, war crimes law is addressed to individuals, it is limited to the most serious crimes, and it can result in imprisonment of a person as a war criminal. For these reasons, similar provisions may warrant a more restrictive interpretation in the context of war crimes law, consistent with the narrower focus of war crimes law on the most serious violations, as well as general principles of criminal law. For example, IHL requires that, before any sentencing of protected persons, a party must provide a fair trial affording all indispensable judicial guarantees.[35] A minor breach of even one such right would fall below this standard and violate IHL, requiring an appropriate remedy. But conducting a trial with a single minor error would surely not be a war crime.[36]

12.1.6 The Evolution of War Crimes Law

War crimes law deals with the *criminal responsibility of individuals* for serious violations of IHL. National laws have long provided for prosecution of war crimes.[37] For example, the Lieber Code recognized criminal liability of individuals for violations of its strictures, and similar provisions appear in the military manuals of many countries.[38]

Following some prominent historical examples of war crimes prosecutions,[39] and after abortive efforts to conduct international trials at the end of the First World War,[40] the Nuremberg Charter gave form to the international law of war crimes. Article 6(b) of the Charter included:

War crimes: namely, violations of the laws or customs of war. Such violations shall include, but not be limited to, murder, ill-treatment or deportation to slave labour or for any purpose of civilian population of or in occupied territory, murder or ill-treatment of prisoners-of-war or persons on the seas,

---

[33] Peter Rowe, 'War Crimes' in McGoldrick et al., *The Permanent ICC*, 217–19.
[34] This understanding is now confirmed in ICC Elements of Crimes, 'Introduction to War Crimes', para. 2, and dovetails with ICC Statute, Art. 21(1)(b).
[35] Geneva Conventions, Common Art. 3.
[36] ICC Elements of Crimes, note 59; Diletta Marchesi, 'The War Crime of Sentencing or Execution without Due Process in the Al Hassan Case: The Interpretative Pitfalls Hidden in the Application of the Crime', *Armed Groups and International Law*, 26 July 2023, at www.armedgroups-internationallaw.org.
[37] Timothy L. H. McCormack, 'From Sun Tzu to the Sixth Committee: The Evolution of an International Criminal Law Regime' in Timothy L. H. McCormack and Gerry J. Simpson (eds.), *The Law of War Crimes: National and International Approaches* (The Hague, 1997).
[38] Instructions for the Government Armies of the United States in the Field, General Orders No. 100, 24 April 1863.
[39] See e.g. the 1474 trial of Peter von Hagenbach for crimes during the occupation of Breisach. [40] See Chapters 4 and 6.

killing of hostages, plunder of public or private property, wanton destruction of cities, towns or villages, or devastation not justified by military necessity.

The Nuremberg Tribunal recognized key provisions of the 1907 Hague Regulations as giving rise to individual criminal responsibility under customary law.[41]

The four Geneva Conventions of 1949 included 'grave breach' provisions, which expressly recognize certain violations as *crimes* subject to universal jurisdiction.[42] These provisions are now regarded as customary international law.[43] Additional Protocol I to those Conventions ('AP I'), adopted in 1977, introduced additional 'grave breaches', although not all of these have attained recognition as customary law.[44]

The ICTY Statute definition of war crimes included grave breaches of the Geneva Conventions as well as 'other violations of other laws or customs of war'; the latter offered an open-ended list with five examples.[45] The ICTR Statute included serious violations of Common Article 3 and of Additional Protocol II of 1977 ('AP II'), again featuring an open-ended list.[46]

The ICC Statute, adopted in 1998, contains a longer and more comprehensive list of war crimes than any of the Tribunal Statutes. Unlike previous lists, however, the list in Article 8 is not open-ended; it is exhaustive. Some states, such as the United States, which had been quite content to impose an open-ended list upon others (Nuremberg, ICTY, ICTR), had a notable change of heart when confronted with a permanent court that could potentially apply to their own forces.[47] There may also have been a concern to avoid the initiatives of judge-made law within the ad hoc Tribunals.[48] In any event, despite the seeming double standards, an exhaustive list is certainly more consistent with criminal law principles, particularly the principle *nullum crimen sine lege*.

The ICC Statute contains an extensive list of fifty offences, including grave breaches of the Geneva Conventions, serious violations of Common Article 3, and other serious violations drawn from various sources. Since the goal of the drafters was to reflect customary law rather than to create new law, many provisions from previous instruments were excluded because of a lack of consensus on their customary law status. The ICC list, while lengthy, does not include all war crimes recognized in customary law; an example often cited is the general prohibition on the use of chemical or biological weapons.[49] Article

---

[41] Nuremberg IMT, Judgment and Sentences, reprinted in (1947) 41 *AJIL* 172, 218; *von Leeb*, XII LRTWC 1, 86–92 (1949).

[42] Geneva Convention I, Art. 49; Geneva Convention II, Art. 51; Geneva Convention III, Art. 130; and Geneva Convention IV, Art. 147. See Chapter 3 for a discussion of whether these provisions confer universal jurisdiction strictly so called.

[43] See ICTY Statute, Art. 2; ICC Statute, Art. 8(2)(a); and *Legality of the Threat or Use of Nuclear Weapons*, Advisory Opinion, 8 July 1996 [1996] 1 ICJ Reports 226, paras. 79 and 82.

[44] AP I, Art. 85. But see the study of customary law undertaken under ICRC auspices: Henckaerts and Doswald-Beck, *ICRC Customary Law*. The study is updated periodically, see www.icrc.org/eng/assets/files/other/customary-international-humanitarian-law-i-icrc-eng.pdf.

[45] ICTY Statute, Art. 3. The list included use of poisonous weapons or weapons calculated to cause unnecessary suffering; wanton destruction; attack on undefended places; seizure or destruction of historic monuments, works of art, or institutions dedicated to certain purposes; and plunder.

[46] ICTR Statute, Art. 4. The list included murder; cruel treatment; torture; mutilation; collective punishments; hostage taking; terrorism; and outrages on dignity, which includes rape, enforced prostitution and indecent assault; pillage; and passing sentences without proper trial.

[47] See Robert Cryer, *Prosecuting International Crimes* (Cambridge, 2005) 263–9.

[48] See William Schabas, *Introduction to the International Criminal Court*, 5th ed. (Cambridge, 2017) 83–4.

[49] See Section 12.3.7. Poisonous and asphyxiating gases are however included: Art. 8(2)(b)(xviii).

10 of the ICC Statute emphasizes that the absence of a provision in the ICC Statute list does not affect its status as existing or developing international law.

Other internationalized courts, such as the Sierra Leone Special Court (SCSL) and the Iraq Special Tribunal, have included crimes from the ICC list in their statutes. Article 14 of the Iraq Special Tribunal Statute copied the ICC Statute definitions, providing another instance of state practice confirming those definitions. The SCSL Statute includes violations of Common Article 3 and a short list of other serious violations, reflecting certain crimes from the ICC Statute, namely, attacks directed against civilians, attacks on humanitarian aid workers, and child conscription.[50]

12.1.7 War Crimes in Non-International Armed Conflicts

Traditionally, neither IHL nor war crimes law applied in non-international armed conflicts. Before the advent of human rights law, states were largely allowed to deal with their own citizens as they pleased, in particular in situations of rebellion and insurrection. This was seen as an 'internal affair', in which other states should have no say. States sought to preserve latitude in putting down rebels, and they did not wish to bestow any possible recognition on rebel groups. Exceptionally, states involved in intense internal conflicts occasionally recognized a situation of 'belligerency', in which case IHL was applied to the conflict.[51]

During the negotiation of the four Geneva Conventions of 1949, several delegations pressed for recognition of rules in non-international conflicts; other delegations strongly opposed such a development.[52] After intense discussions, agreement was reached to include in each Convention a single article common to all of the conventions – hence 'Common Article 3' – laying out some very basic norms applicable even in non-international armed conflicts. Even this very modest provision was an achievement.

Regulation of internal armed conflict was expanded significantly in AP II of 1977. Again, the negotiation was difficult, with many states opposing regulation. Agreement was reached on a short list of provisions, expanding upon and developing the rules in Common Article 3, but it was still much shorter than the list applicable to international armed conflict.[53]

Significantly, Common Article 3 and AP II contained no 'grave breaches' provisions, leading many to conclude that violations of those provisions were not criminalized. As of 1990, it was widely accepted that war crimes law did not apply in non-international armed conflict.[54]

---

[50] SCSL Statute, Arts. 3 and 4.
[51] See e.g. Eric David, *Principes de droit des conflits armés*, 2nd ed. (Brussels, 1999) 124–7; Lindsay Moir, *The Law of Internal Armed Conflict* (Cambridge, 2002) 3–21.
[52] ICRC, *Commentary to the First Geneva Convention* (Cambridge, 2016), mn. 375–88.
[53] Howard S. Levie, *The Law of Non-International Armed Conflict* (Dordrecht, 1987) 27–90; Michael Bothe, *New Rules for Victims of Armed Conflict* (The Hague, 1982) 605–8; Yves Sandoz et al., *Commentary on the Additional Protocols of 8 June 1977* (Geneva, 1987) 1336.
[54] '[A]ccording to humanitarian law as it stands today, the notion of war crimes is limited to situations of international armed conflict': ICRC, DDM/JUR442 b (25 March 1993) para. 4 (cited in the Separate Opinion of Judge Li, *Tadić*, ICTY AC, 2 October 1995, para. 7); Denise Plattner, 'The Penal Repression of Violation of International Humanitarian Law' (1990) 30 *International Review of the Red Cross* 409.

By the 1990s, the gap in coverage had become increasingly problematic, and several factors converged to precipitate a necessary legal evolution. First, non-international conflicts had increased in magnitude and duration, causing vastly more civilian deaths than in previous centuries.[55] Second, non-international conflicts had become more prevalent than international conflicts,[56] making change necessary if war crimes law was to have continued relevance for victims of conflict. Third, the increasing interdependence of states meant that internal conflicts had greater consequences for surrounding regions, increasing the urgency of regulating them.[57] Fourth, the increased prioritization of human rights and human security meant that states were more willing to insist on extending protection even in contexts previously considered an 'internal affair'.[58]

The Security Council took the first major step forward when it adopted the ICTR Statute. Because the conflict in Rwanda was internal, the Council was confronted with the question of whether war crimes law applies in non-international conflict. The Council concluded in the affirmative, recognizing serious violations of Common Article 3 and core provisions of AP II as war crimes in the ICTR Statute.

The *Tadić* decision on jurisdiction by the ICTY Appeals Chamber led to a seismic shift in the law.[59] The decision reviewed state practice, resolutions of the League of Nations, General Assembly, Security Council and European Union, International Court of Justice (ICJ) decisions, and military codes of conduct. The Chamber concluded that the traditional stark dichotomy between the rules applicable in international and non-international conflicts was becoming blurred, and that some war crimes provisions were now applicable in internal armed conflicts. The Chamber held that there had not been a wholesale transposition or a complete convergence, but rather that '*only a number of rules* and principles . . . have gradually been extended to apply to internal conflicts'.[60] Moreover, 'this extension has not taken place in the form of a full and mechanical transplant of those rules to internal conflicts; rather, *the general essence* of those rules, and not the detailed regulation they may contain, has become applicable to internal conflicts'.[61] To determine whether a norm also applies in internal armed conflict, one must consider: whether there is clear and unequivocal recognition of the norm; state practice indicating an intention to criminalize the norm; the gravity of the acts; and the interest of the international community in their prohibition.[62]

The *Tadić* decision was seen as groundbreaking at the time,[63] but it was rapidly absorbed by the international community. The approach was followed soon afterward by the ICTR,[64]

[55] UN Development Programme, *Human Development Report 2005* (2005) 153–61.
[56] Human Security Centre, *Human Security Report 2005* (Oxford, 2005) 22–5.
[57] UNDP, *Human Development Report 2005* (n. 55) 157.
[58] *Tadić*, ICTY AC, 2 October 1995, paras. 94–6; see e.g. Theodor Meron, 'International Criminalization of Internal Atrocities' (1995) 89 *AJIL* 554; Darryl Robinson and Herman von Hebel, 'War Crimes in Internal Conflicts: Art. 8 of the ICC Statute' (1999) 2 *Yearbook of International Humanitarian Law* 193.
[59] *Tadić*, ICTY AC, 2 October 1995, para. 126. [60] *Ibid*. (emphasis added). [61] *Ibid*. (emphasis added).
[62] *Ibid*. paras. 128 and 129.
[63] See e.g. Christopher Greenwood, 'International Humanitarian Law and the Tadić Case' (1996) 7 *EJIL* 265; George Aldrich, 'Jurisdiction of the International Criminal Tribunal for the Former Yugoslavia' (1996) 90 *AJIL* 64; Geoffrey Watson, 'The Humanitarian Law of the Yugoslavia War Crimes Tribunal: Jurisdiction in Prosecutor v. Tadić' (1996) 36 *Virginia Journal of International Law* 687.
[64] *Kanyabashi*, ICTR TC II, 18 June 1997, para. 8.

and, more significantly, it received a remarkable level of state acceptance during the negotiation of the ICC Statute.[65] Although a determined minority in Rome strongly opposed the inclusion of war crimes in internal conflicts, a clear majority was equally strongly committed to their inclusion. Opposition gave way to acceptance of Common Article 3 and a limited list of other fundamental provisions in the Statute. Significantly, the approach taken by the Rome Conference largely followed that of *Tadić*, identifying fundamental prohibitions and transposing them to internal conflicts.[66]

In the result, roughly half of the provisions from international conflicts were transplanted to non-international conflicts in the ICC Statute. For other provisions, there was no consensus that they were so fundamental that customary law at that point recognized them to be applicable also in non-international conflicts. While the recognition of half of the provisions was a remarkable achievement in 1998, there is good reason to believe that the list of war crimes in Article 8(2)(e) falls short of the list that the *Tadić* test would permit. For example, the prohibition of starvation as a means of warfare, the use of chemical weapons, attacking civilian objects, and launching disproportionate attacks, are all fundamental provisions with long recognition in the laws and customs of war, and hence merit application in non-international conflicts.[67] As noted in Section 12.1.6, Article 10 affirms that nothing in the ICC Statute limits the development of other international law.

The law continues to move towards increased convergence. A major International Committee of the Red Cross and Red Crescent (ICRC) study of customary law suggested a large degree of convergence in the law for different types of conflicts.[68] In 2010, the Kampala Review Conference amended the ICC Statute to reflect that poisoned weapons, asphyxiating gases, and 'dum-dum' bullets (see Section 12.3.6) are prohibited in internal armed conflict as well as international armed conflict.[69] In 2019, the Assembly of States Parties also added the crime of starvation to the list of war crimes in non-international armed conflict.[70]

Given the ongoing convergence, it would be useful in any future catalogues of war crimes to *consolidate* those provisions that are common to both international and non-international conflicts. The bifurcated structure in the current statutes can create unnecessary complications, because it requires a determination of the character of an armed conflict in order to know which provisions to charge (for example, Article 8(2)(b) or (e)), even where the provisions are similar or identical. Bifurcation sometimes makes it necessary to collect evidence and litigate on complex issues, such as the involvement of third states,[71] to determine the status of the conflict, even though it is irrelevant to the role and liability of the

---

[65] In effect, the theory of partial convergence of the law of international and internal armed conflicts was put to the international community: Claus Kreß, 'War Crimes Committed in Non-International Armed Conflict and the Emerging System of International Criminal Justice' (2001) 30 *Israel Yearbook on Human Rights* 1, 5; Moir, *The Law of Internal Armed Conflict* (n. 51) 160–7.

[66] Robinson and von Hebel, 'War Crimes in Internal Conflicts' (n. 58) 197–200. [67] Kreß, 'War Crimes' (n. 65) 37, 39.

[68] Henckaerts and Doswald-Beck, *ICRC Customary Law.*

[69] Amal Alamuddin and Philippa Webb, 'Expanding Jurisdiction over War Crimes under Article 8 of the ICC Statute' (2010) 8 *JICJ* 1219.

[70] Tom Dannenbaum, 'Siege Starvation: A War Crime of Societal Torture' (2022) 22 *Chicago Journal of International Law* 368.

[71] See Section 12.2.2.

perpetrator and the gravamen of the offence. Indeed, this problem arose already in the first case tried by the ICC, the *Lubanga* case. The Prosecutor characterized the conflict as non-international, the Pre-Trial Chamber recharacterized the conflict as international, and then the Trial Chamber concluded it was a non-international armed conflict after all. The debate was irrelevant to the criminal wrongdoing, yet necessary to determine whether charges should fall under Article 8(2)(b) or (e).[72]

The ICTY has partially sidestepped such problems by relying heavily on Common Article 3 and other provisions applicable in non-international conflicts, on the ground that these more limited provisions apply in all conflicts.[73] In any future catalogue of war crimes, it would be efficient to establish one list of crimes applicable in both types of conflict, plus a short list of those crimes applicable only in international conflict.[74] Such a list would not entail any change in customary law, but would simply be a clearer presentation of the existing legal situation.

12.2 COMMON ISSUES

In this section, we will survey issues that cut across all the specific types of war crime: identifying an armed conflict; classifying the conflict as international or non-international; the nexus between the conduct and the armed conflict; and the status of the perpetrator and the victim.

12.2.1 Armed Conflict

The essential element for any war crime is the nexus with armed conflict. It is the dangerous and volatile situation of armed conflict that warrants international interest and gives rise to international jurisdiction over the crime. Early IHL depended for its application on a formal declaration of a state of war, but this was problematic because parties to conflict could raise formalistic arguments denying a state of war.[75] To avoid this problem, current IHL and war crimes law focus on the objective existence of armed conflict, even if one or both of the parties deny the formal state of war.[76]

The concept of 'armed conflict' includes not only the application of force between armed forces, but also an invasion that meets no resistance,[77] aerial bombing, or an unauthorized border crossing by armed forces.

---

[72] *Lubanga*, ICC PTC I, 29 January 2007 (ICC-01/04–01/06–803) paras. 200–37; *Lubanga*, ICC TC I, 14 March 2012 (ICC-01/04–01/06–2842) paras. 503–67.

[73] *Delalić et al.*, ICTY AC, 20 February 2001, para. 150 (holding that prohibitions from internal armed conflict also apply in international armed conflict since the latter has broader regulation). See also the *Nicaragua* case of the ICJ, holding that Common Art. 3 applies to all forms of conflict: *Case concerning Military and Paramilitary Activities in and Against Nicaragua* (*Nicaragua* v. *USA*), Merits [1986] ICJ Reports 14, para. 218.

[74] As a model, see the German Code of Crimes Against International Law, <www.gesetze-im-internet.de/englisch_vstgb/englisch_vstgb.html> reproduced in Gerhard Werle, *Principles of International Criminal Law* (The Hague, 2005) 428–33.

[75] ICRC, *Commentary to the First Geneva Convention* (n. 52) 32–3.   [76] See e.g. Geneva Conventions, Art. 2.

[77] Geneva Convention I, Art. 2.

The state of armed conflict does not end with each particular ceasefire; rather, it continues until the 'general close of military operations'.[78] The state of armed conflict also continues during occupation, that is to say, when another state takes and holds control over a territory.[79]

IHL classifies armed conflicts into two categories: international and non-international (the latter are sometimes referred to as 'internal' armed conflicts). As noted above (Section 12.1.7), the rules are more extensive in international armed conflicts.

In the case of state-to-state conflict, most authorities indicate that *any* resort to force involving military forces amounts to armed conflict.[80] In the case of non-international conflict, a certain threshold of intensity and organization must be met, in order to distinguish armed conflict from mere internal disturbances and riots, as is discussed in Section 12.2.3.[81]

12.2.2 Distinguishing Between International and Non-International Conflicts

The paradigmatic situation of international armed conflict is the resort to force between the military forces of states. The Geneva Conventions were drafted with this straightforward scenario in mind. However, outside this paradigm, complex issues can arise, for example, with respect to wars of national liberation, UN enforcement operations, foreign intervention through proxy forces, and conflicts with armed groups located in foreign territories.[82]

Invitation

The first and easiest case is where a state is fighting armed groups on its territory, and invites another state to assist. The conflict remains a non-international armed conflict, because the two states are not engaged in hostilities with each other. This outcome is quite uncontroversial.[83]

Wars of National Liberation

According to Article 1(4) of AP I, international armed conflict includes conflicts in which 'peoples are fighting against colonial domination and alien occupation and against

---

[78] Geneva Convention IV, Art. 6. According to Tribunal jurisprudence, the state of armed conflict extends 'until a general conclusion of peace is reached, or in the case of internal armed conflict, until a peaceful settlement is achieved'. *Tadić*, ICTY AC, 2 October 1995, para. 70.

[79] See e.g. 1907 Hague Regulations, Art. 52; Geneva Convention IV, Art. 6; ICC Elements of Crimes, note 34; *Naletilić*, ICTY TC I, 31 March 2003, paras. 214–17.

[80] Tribunal jurisprudence requires 'protracted' violence for internal conflict but not for state-to-state conflict: *Tadić*, ICTY AC, 2 October 1995, para. 70. According to the ICRC commentary on the Geneva Conventions, the concept of armed conflict includes 'any difference arising between two states and leading to the intervention of members of the armed forces': ICRC, *Commentary to the First Geneva Convention* (n. 52) 20; and see the discussion in Claus Kreß, 'The 1999 Crisis in East Timor and the Threshold of the Law of War Crimes' (2002) 13 *Criminal Law Forum* 409, 412–13; Dapo Akande, 'Classification of Armed Conflicts: Relevant Legal Concepts' in Elizabeth Wilmshurst (ed.), *International Law and the Classification of Conflict* (Oxford, 2012) 32, 41.

[81] See Section 12.2.3.

[82] The complexities of these distinctions have further strengthened calls for a single body of IHL applicable in all conflicts: James Stewart, 'Toward a Single Definition of Armed Conflict in International Humanitarian Law: A Critique of Internationalized Armed Conflict' (2003) 85 *International Review of the Red Cross* 313.

[83] *Katanga*, ICC TC II, 7 March 2014 (ICC-01/04–01/07–3436) 1184; Dieter Fleck, 'The Law of Non-International Armed Conflicts' in Dieter Fleck (ed.), *Handbook of International Humanitarian Law*, 3rd ed. (Oxford, 2013) 581, 605.

racist regimes in the exercise of their right of self-determination'. As a matter of treaty law, this definition applies to any prosecutions based on the grave breaches regime of AP I.[84]

It is unclear whether this special rule about fighting for self-determination also applies in the general law of war crimes, which is based on customary law.[85] The scant state practice leaves the provision's customary status unclear. The paradigmatic case of a people resisting foreign colonial domination can be more readily seen as 'international'. On the other hand, a conflict involving local oppressed groups fighting against a discriminatory regime may be a worthy cause but it would seem counter-factual to describe it as 'international'.[86]

Proxy Forces

A seemingly internal conflict may be rendered international where local armed groups are, in reality, acting on behalf of an external state. For example, in the *Tadić* case, to determine whether the grave breaches provision applied, the Chamber had to determine whether the conflict was international, which in turn depended on whether acts of certain forces in Bosnia (the VRS) were attributable to the Federal Republic of Yugoslavia (FRY). The FRY had purported to withdraw its forces (the JNA) from Bosnia, but left behind the VRS, composed of former JNA soldiers of Bosnian origin, with the same officers, the same weapons, the same equipment, the same suppliers, and the same objectives, with funding still coming from the FRY.

The majority of the Trial Chamber referred to the ICJ's decision in the *Nicaragua* case, which had adopted a stringent 'effective control' test to determine whether acts of an armed band could be attributed to a state.[87] The majority in the Trial Chamber found that, while the FRY had the capacity to direct operations, there was no evidence of specific orders or that the FRY had actually directed operations.[88] The decision was criticized in a powerful dissent and in commentary for not reflecting the reality of the situation.[89]

The Appeals Chamber replaced the test of 'effective control' with a more flexible test of 'overall control' over armed groups.[90] Under the 'overall control' test, it is not necessary to produce evidence of specific orders or instructions relating to particular military actions.[91] It is sufficient to establish 'overall control going beyond the mere financing and equipping of such forces and involving also participation in the planning and supervision of military operations'.[92] Accordingly, the Appeals Chamber found that FRY's involvement had

---

[84] AP I, Art. 85. [85] See e.g. discussion in Robin Geiß and Andreas Zimmermann, 'Article 8' in Ambos, *Commentary*, 625–7.

[86] Doubting the customary law status, see Dapo Akande, 'Classification of Armed Conflicts: Relevant Legal Concepts' in Elizabeth Wilmshurst (ed.), *International Law and the Classification of Conflict* (Oxford, 2012) 32, 49. On the fundamental separation between 'just cause' and IHL, see Section 12.1.3.

[87] *Case concerning Military and Paramilitary Activities in and Against Nicaragua* (*Nicaragua* v. *USA*), Merits [1986] ICJ Reports 14, para. 115.

[88] *Tadić*, ICTY TC II, 7 May 1997, paras. 588–607.

[89] See McDonald, Dissent in *Tadić*, ICTY TC II, 7 May 1997; see e.g. Theodor Meron, 'Classification of Armed Conflict in the Former Yugoslavia: *Nicaragua*'s Fallout' (1998) 92 *AJIL* 236.

[90] *Tadić*, ICTY AC, 15 July 1999, para. 137. [91] *Ibid.* para. 145. [92] *Ibid.*

internationalized the conflict. The Appeals Chamber's approach has been adopted by others as the test for determining whether external involvement internationalizes a conflict,[93] but the decision has raised some controversies.[94]

Transnational Conflict

Another contemporary situation that is not well addressed by the Geneva Conventions is where a state engages in conflict with a non-state armed group on the territory of another state.[95] Examples include the conflict between Uganda and armed groups roaming in the Democratic Republic of the Congo (DRC); US attacks on Al Qaeda personnel in Pakistan; and fighting between many states and the ISIL (Da'esh) in Syria. On the one hand, such a conflict does not involve a clash between the forces of two states, and hence does not seem 'international'. On the other hand, the conflict is not entirely within the territory of a single state, and thus it is not purely 'internal' in the classic sense.

Where the armed group is affiliated with the territorial state, or where the intervening state attacks the territorial state's assets and infrastructure, then the conflict is between two states and is international in character. Where the intervening state engages only with the armed group, and the armed group is not affiliated with the territorial state, state practice and jurisprudence favour treating such conflicts as non-international.[96] This may at first sound counter-intuitive, because the action crosses borders and affects the interests of another state. However, it may be the most plausible approach, since there are not hostilities between two states. Furthermore, an armed group cannot necessarily fulfil all of the obligations applicable in international armed conflicts, and thus the laws on non-international armed conflict are likely the most appropriate fit.[97]

12.2.3 Distinguishing Armed Conflict from Riots and Disturbances

The previous section discussed the line between international and non-international armed conflict. There is another threshold, dividing 'armed conflict' from mere riots and disturbances, which are insufficient to activate IHL and the law of war crimes. It is sometimes difficult to determine the point at which civil strife crosses the threshold to amount to armed conflict.

---

[93] The test has been adopted by the ICC: see e.g. *Lubanga*, ICC TC I, 14 March 2012 (ICC-01/04–01/06–2842) para. 540.

[94] In a subsequent case, the ICJ disapproved of the ICTY Appeals Chamber's purported distinguishing of *Nicaragua* and its pronouncements on general international law. The ICJ conceded, without deciding, that 'overall control' may be an appropriate test for determining the character of armed conflict in international criminal law, but it is not an appropriate test for determining the responsibility of states under general international law: *Case concerning the Application of the Convention on the Prevention and Punishment of Genocide (Bosnia and Herzegovina v. Serbia and Montenegro)*, ICJ General List 91, paras. 402–7. See also James Crawford, *State Responsibility: The General Part* (Cambridge, 2013) 145–56.

[95] See generally Claus Kreß, 'Some Reflections on the International Legal Framework Governing Transnational Armed Conflicts' (2010) 15 *Journal of Conflict and Security Law* 245.

[96] *Lubanga*, ICC TC I, 14 March 2012 (ICC-01/04–01/06–2842) para. 541; *Hamdan* v. *Rumsfeld*, 126 S Ct 2749, 2757 (2006); and see the examples in Sivakumaran, *The Law of Non-International Armed Conflict* (Oxford, 2012) 228–32. But see also Dapo Akande, 'Classification of Armed Conflicts: Relevant Legal Concepts' in Elizabeth Wilmshurst (ed.), *International Law and the Classification of Conflict* (Oxford, 2012) 32, 70–9, for authorities that the conflict would be international.

[97] Elizabeth Wilmshurst (ed.), *International Law and the Classification of Conflicts* (Oxford, 2012); Noam Lubell, 'Fragmented Wars: Multi-Territorial Military Operations Against Armed Groups' (2017) 93 *International Legal Studies* 215.

The widely accepted test to distinguish armed conflicts from mere riots or disturbances focuses on two criteria: (1) the *intensity* of the conflict; and (2) the *organization* of the parties. The test was elaborated by the ICTY Appeals Chamber in the *Tadić* case, which stated that 'armed conflict exists whenever there is a resort to armed force between States or *protracted armed violence* between governmental authorities and *organised armed groups* or between such groups within a State'.[98] The test has been adopted by the ICTR, the SCSL, and the ICC, and is widely accepted as the applicable test.[99]

The 'intensity' requirement is that the armed violence be 'protracted' rather than sporadic or isolated. Relevant factors include the seriousness of attacks, their geographic spread and temporal persistence, the mobilization of government forces, the distribution of weapons, and whether the situation has attracted the attention of the UN Security Council.[100]

As for the 'organization of the parties' requirement, courts have looked at various non-exhaustive factors. For example, in the *Haradinaj* case, an ICTY Chamber referred to factors such as: the existence of a command structure; disciplinary mechanisms; headquarters; control of territory; access to weapons; military training; ability to plan and carry out military operations; and ability to speak with one voice and negotiate and conclude agreements such as ceasefire or peace accords.[101] In the *Lubanga* case, an ICC Trial Chamber similarly summarized past jurisprudence as referring to factors such as internal hierarchy, command structure, equipment and weapons, and ability to plan and carry out military operations.[102]

A slightly higher threshold appears in Additional Protocol II. AP II stipulates that it only applies to armed conflicts:

which take place in the territory of a High Contracting Party between its armed forces and dissident armed forces or other organized groups which, under responsible command, exercise such control over a part of its territory as to enable them to carry out sustained and concerted military operations and to implement this protocol.[103]

---

[98] *Tadić*, ICTY AC, 2 October 1995, para. 70 (emphasis added).

[99] See e.g. *Akayesu*, ICTR TC, 12 September 1998, paras. 619–20; *Taylor*, SCSL TC, 18 May 2012, paras. 563–4; *Lubanga*, ICC TC, 14 March 2012 (ICC-01/04–01/06–2842) paras. 534–8. See also Jann Kleffner, 'The Legal Fog of an Illusion: Three Reflections on "Organization" and "Intensity" as Criteria for the Temporal Scope of the Law of Non-International Armed Conflict' (2019) 95 *International Law Studies* 161; Marten Zwanenburg, 'Double Trouble: The 'Cumulative Approach' and the 'Support-Based Approach' in the Relationship Between Non-State Armed Groups' (2021) 22 *Yearbook of International Humanitarian Law* 43; Martha Bradley, '"Protracted Armed Conflict": A Conundrum. Does Article 8(2)(f) of the Rome Statute Require an Organised Armed Group to Meet the Organisational Criteria of Additional Protocol II?' (2019) 32 *South African Journal of Criminal Justice* 291.

[100] *Tadić*, ICTY TC II, 7 May 1997, paras. 562–7; *Akayesu*, ICTR TC, 12 September 1998, paras. 619–20; *Lubanga*, ICC TC I, 14 March 2012 (ICC-01/04–01/06–2842) para. 538. The Inter-American Human Rights Commission appears to have applied a rather lower threshold for the 'protracted' nature of the conflict. An attack by forty-two persons on military barracks, resulting in a military response to retake the barracks, lasting around thirty hours and resulting in the deaths of twenty-nine attackers and several state agents, was found sufficient to constitute an armed conflict: *La Tablada*, IACHR Report No. 55/97, Case No. 11.137, Argentina; OEA/L/V/II.97, Doc. 38, 20 October 1997.

[101] *Haradinaj*, ICTY TC, 3 April 2008, paras. 37–60. Helpful indicators are also listed in *Boškoski and Tarčulovski*, ICTY TC, 10 July 2008, paras. 175–205.

[102] *Lubanga*, ICC TC I, 14 March 2012 (ICC-01/04–01/06–2842) para. 537. For a more thorough review of the jurisprudence, see Sivakumaran, *The Law of Non-International Armed Conflict* (n. 96) 167–80.

[103] AP II, Art. 1(1). Green, *The Contemporary Law* (n. 1) 67, regards the test as 'so high that it would exclude most revolutions and rebellions'.

Among the unique requirements in AP II are that one party must be a state (thus excluding group-versus-group conflict) and that the armed group must have control over territory. While those requirements apply under AP II as a matter of treaty law, they have not been accepted as part of the general customary international law of war crimes. Tribunal jurisprudence and the ICC Statute recognize armed conflict entirely between armed groups.[104] Tribunal jurisprudence and the ICC Statute also reject control of territory as a *requirement*, although it can be an important *indicator* of the intensity of the conflict.[105] Thus, these restrictions do not affect the interpretation of 'armed conflict' in the customary law of war crimes.[106]

12.2.4 Nexus Between Conduct and Conflict

In order to constitute a war crime, conduct must be linked to an armed conflict. For example, the ICC Elements of Crimes require that the conduct be committed 'in the context of and associated with' an armed conflict.[107]

The term 'in the context of' refers to the temporal and geographic context in a broad sense: the conduct occurred during an armed conflict and on a territory in which there is an armed conflict.[108] This requirement is very general, since a state of armed conflict is recognized throughout the territory, beyond the time and place of the hostilities.[109] War crimes can be temporally and geographically remote from the actual fighting.[110]

The phrase 'associated with' refers to the specific nexus between the conduct of the perpetrator and the conflict, and matches the ICTY requirement that the conduct be 'closely related to' the conflict.[111] Not all criminal activity on a territory experiencing armed conflict amounts to a war crime. For example, if a person kills a neighbour purely out of jealousy or because of a private dispute over land, and this happens to occur during an armed conflict, that is not a war crime.[112]

In the *Kunarac* judgment, the ICTY Appeals Chamber provided a helpful elaboration of this test, focusing on whether the existence of conflict played a substantial part in the perpetrator's *ability* to commit a crime, his *decision* to commit it, the *manner* in which it was committed, or the *purpose* for which it was committed.[113] Hence, it is sufficient that the perpetrator acted in furtherance of or under the guise of the armed conflict.[114] In assessing

---

[104] ICC Statute, Art. 8(2)(f); *Tadić*, ICTY AC, 2 October 1995, para. 70.

[105] ICC Statute, Art. 8(2)(f); *Akayesu*, ICTR TC I, 2 September 1998, paras. 619–20. In *Lubanga*, the Pre-Trial Chamber confirmed that territorial control is not a requirement: *Lubanga*, ICC PTC I, 29 January 2007 (ICC-01/04–01/06–803) para. 233.

[106] As discussed in cases such as *Tadić*, ICTY AC, 2 October 1995, para. 70; *Akayesu*, ICTR TC I, 2 September 1998, paras. 619–20; *Lubanga*, ICC PTC I, 29 January 2007 (ICC-01/04–01/06–803) para. 233.

[107] See e.g. ICC Elements of Crimes, Art. 8(2)(a)–I. The test was referenced by the ICTR in *Kayishema*, ICTR TC II, 21 May 1999, para. 187, although the Chamber ultimately declined to articulate a legal test: *Ibid.* para. 188.

[108] Knut Dörmann, Eve La Haye, and Herman von Hebel, 'War Crimes' in Lee, *Elements and Rules*, 120–1.

[109] *Tadić*, ICTY AC, 2 October 1995, para. 70; *Bemba*, ICC TC III, 21 March 2016 (ICC-01/05–01/08–3343) para. 128.

[110] *Kunarac*, ICTY AC, 12 June 2002, para. 57.

[111] *Tadić*, ICTY AC, 2 October 1995, para. 70. While some nexus is needed, the crime need not be committed during combat, nor need it be part of a policy or practice or in the interests of a party to the conflict: *Tadić*, ICTY TC II, 7 May 1997, paras. 572–3.

[112] Knut Dörmann, *Elements of War Crimes under the Rome Statute of the International Criminal Court* (Cambridge, 2003) 19–20.

[113] See *Kunarac*, ICTY AC, 12 June 2002, para. 58. [114] *Ibid.*

these questions, one may take into account, *inter alia*, the following factors: the status of perpetrator (for example, combatant); the status of the victim (for example, non-combatant, combatant of opposing party); whether the act serves a goal of a military campaign; and whether it was committed in the context of the perpetrator's official duties.[115] The ICC has followed the *Kunarac* approach.[116]

12.2.5 Perpetrator

War crimes law does not only govern members of armed forces or groups and their leaders. The fact that a perpetrator is a member of an armed force is a factor in showing the nexus to armed conflict, but it is not a requirement.[117] Civilians can commit war crimes, provided that conduct is linked to the armed conflict.[118]

The perpetrator must have some awareness of the armed conflict. Although early Tribunal jurisprudence did not inquire into knowledge of the conflict,[119] in *Kordić* and subsequent cases, the ICTY Appeals Chamber concluded that the knowledge of the accused of the factual context of armed conflict is indeed required, as the armed conflict is an element of the crime.[120] Similarly, the ICC Elements of Crimes[121] require that the person was 'aware of factual circumstances that established the existence of an armed conflict'.[122] The Elements clarify that the accused need not make the *legal* evaluation that there is an armed conflict, nor need he or she know of the *classification* of the armed conflict.[123] In any event, it is difficult to conceive of situations where a perpetrator's conduct could satisfy the nexus to conflict, if the perpetrator was somehow unaware of the armed conflict going on around him or her.

12.2.6 Victim or Object of the Crime

The definitions of many war crimes contain additional requirements about the victim or object of the crime. For example, for grave breaches of the Geneva Conventions, the crime must affect 'protected persons or objects'.[124] Protected persons include civilians, prisoners-of-war, and combatants who are no longer able to fight because they are sick, wounded, or

---

[115] *Kunarac*, ICTY AC, 12 June 2002, para. 59; *Rutaganda*, ICTR AC, 26 May 2003, para. 569.
[116] *Bemba*, ICC TC III, 21 March 2016 (ICC-01/05–01/08–3343) para. 142; *Ongwen*, ICC TC IX, 4 February 2021 (ICC-02/04–01/15–1762-Red) para. 2689.
[117] *Akayesu*, ICTR AC, 1 June 2001, paras. 444–5.
[118] See e.g. *Essen Lynching Trial*, I LRTWC 88; *Tesch* (the 'Zyklon B case'), I LRTWC 93.
[119] *Tadić*, ICTY TC II, 7 May 1997, para. 572.
[120] *Kordić*, ICTY AC, 17 December 2004, para. 311; *Naletilić*, ICTY AC, 3 May 2006, paras. 116–20. In both cases, the Appeals Chamber required knowledge of 'the *factual* circumstances, e.g. that a foreign state was involved in the armed conflict' (emphasis in original). This test is more onerous than that in the ICC Elements of Crimes, where knowledge of the international character of the conflict is not required: ICC Elements of Crimes, 'Introduction to War Crimes', para. 3.
[121] Dörmann et al., 'War Crimes' (n. 108) 121–3. Some national jurisprudence reaches the same conclusion: see e.g. the Supreme Court of Canada decision of *R* v. *Finta* [1994] 1 SCR 701, 820.
[122] See e.g. ICC Elements of Crimes, Art. 8(2)(a)(i), Element 5.
[123] ICC Elements of Crimes, 'Introduction to War Crimes', para. 3; *Katanga and Ngudjolo*, ICC PTC I, 30 September 2008 (ICC-01/04–01/07–717) para. 387; *Bemba Gombo*, ICC TC III, 21 March 2016 (ICC-01/05–01/08–3343) para. 146.
[124] See e.g. Geneva Convention IV, Art. 147; ICC Statute, Art. 8(2)(a); and ICTY Statute, Art. 2.

shipwrecked.[125] Similarly, Common Article 3 protects 'persons no longer taking active part in hostilities, including members of armed forces who have laid down their arms and those placed *hors de combat* by sickness, wounds, detention, or other cause'. These restrictions are necessary because some acts, such as wilful killing, are not a crime when committed against a combatant. Civilians who directly participate in hostilities may also be targeted for the duration of their participation.[126]

Other war crimes specify a particular victim or object of the crime (for example, civilian population, civilian objects, persons involved in humanitarian assistance, undefended towns, etc.).[127] Some war crimes regulate battlefield conduct, to reduce unnecessary suffering of combatants, and hence even combatants are protected as victims of such crimes.[128]

Because IHL originally developed as a series of reciprocal promises between parties to a conflict, most of IHL regulates conduct towards those affiliated with the 'enemy'.[129] For this reason, many war crimes require that the victim be 'in the hands of'[130] or 'in the power of'[131] an adverse party.[132] Some of the most important protections for civilians arise in Geneva Convention IV, which protects persons 'who find themselves, in case of a conflict or occupation, in the hands of a Party to the conflict or Occupying Power of which they are not nationals'.[133] This provision was drafted bearing in mind a classic state-to-state international armed conflict.

However, recent history has shown that conflicts can be far more complex. The armed conflict in Bosnia was international in character, due to the involvement of neighbouring states, yet it was also predominantly an ethnic conflict. Persons were frequently detained and abused by persons of another ethnic group, yet they were all of the same nationality. Applying the Geneva Conventions literally, the victims would not be entitled to protection, because all concerned held the same passport, even though they were in fact hostile parties.

In the *Tadić* decision, the ICTY Appeals Chamber held that the crucial test is allegiance, and that ethnicity rather than nationality may become the ground of allegiance.[134] Thus, the Chamber chose to look at the substance of the relations rather than formalities.[135]

What about acts committed against members of the accused's own armed group? In the *Ntaganda* case, the ICC considered rape and sexual slavery committed against child

---

[125] See e.g. Geneva Convention I, Arts. 12 and 13; Geneva Convention II, Arts. 12 and 13; Geneva Convention III, Art. 4; and Geneva Convention IV, Art. 4.
[126] *Katanga*, ICC TC II, 7 March 2014 (ICC-01/04–01/07–3436-tENG) para. 789. [127] ICC Statute, Art. 8(2)(b)(i)–(v).
[128] See e.g. *ibid.* Art. 8(2)(b)(vi), (vii), (xi), (xii) and (xvii)–(xx).
[129] There are exceptions; for example, Art. 75 of AP I protects *all* persons in the hands of a party to conflict; and see Section 12.3.8 concerning child soldiers. As the emphasis has shifted to the duty of any party towards victims of conflict, the role of reciprocity is diminishing in IHL, although it is still significant: see René Provost, *International Human Rights and Humanitarian Law* (Cambridge, 2002) 121–238. Sivakumaran, *The Law of Non-International Armed Conflict* (n. 96) 246–9, argues that many IHL provisions protect persons on the 'same side'.
[130] Geneva Convention IV, Art. 4.
[131] See e.g. Geneva Convention III, Art. 4; ICC Elements of Crimes, Art. 8(2)(b)(x)–I, Element 4.
[132] It has been suggested that the requirement of 'in the hands of' or 'in the power of' is also needed to distinguish provisions safeguarding 'protected persons' from provisions regulating methods and means of combat. For example, it might be anticipated that an aerial bombing of a military target will cause a civilian death, but this is not a 'wilful killing' since the civilian is not 'in the hands' of the attacking party. On this view, a comparable requirement should be imported into non-international conflicts: Kreß, 'War Crimes' (n. 65).
[133] Geneva Convention IV, Art. 4. [134] *Tadić*, ICTY AC, 15 July 1999, para. 166. [135] *Ibid.* para. 168.

soldiers in the accused's own army. It was a live question whether 'same-side' violations are war crimes: after all, the Geneva Conventions, with their origin in reciprocity, apply when victims are 'protected persons', namely, civilians or persons *hors de combat* who are in the hands of the adversary. However, as both the Trial and Appeals Chamber noted, while those limits appear in war crimes based on the Geneva Conventions (Article 8(2)(a) and (c) of the ICC Statute), the other crimes drawn from other customary law sources do not contain that limit (Article 8(2)(b) and (e)). The Appeals Chamber reviewed customary international law precedents and found that 'international humanitarian law does not contain a general rule that categorically excludes members of an armed group from protection against crimes committed by members of the same armed group'.[136] Thus, rape and sexual slavery of child soldiers is indeed a war crime. Noting defence concerns about possible overbreadth in including violence within an armed group, the Appeals Chamber emphasized that the conduct must also meet the requirement of a nexus to the armed conflict.[137]

12.2.7 'Jurisdictional' Threshold in the ICC Statute

Article 8(1) of the ICC Statute provides that the ICC 'shall have jurisdiction in respect of war crimes in particular when committed as part of a plan or policy or as part of a large-scale commission of such crimes'. In principle, even a single isolated act can constitute a war crime, so Article 8(1) does not lay down a legal element for a war crime. Article 8(1) is rather an indicator to the ICC as to how it ought to exercise its jurisdiction; namely, to focus its resources not on isolated war crimes but on the most serious situations. The term 'large-scale' is either synonymous with, or less demanding than, the 'widespread' element of crimes against humanity. 'Plan or policy' is less demanding than 'systematic', corresponding instead to the lower threshold in Article 7(2)(a).[138] The words '*in particular*' confirm that this is a *guide* rather than a requirement.[139] Thus, the ICC may still act with respect to isolated war crimes which are of sufficient gravity to warrant action, such as crimes with a particularly grave impact.

12.3 SPECIFIC OFFENCES

12.3.1 Lists of War Crimes in the Statutes of the Tribunals and the ICC

This section examines the specific offences that constitute war crimes. We will start by looking at the lists of war crimes in the relevant instruments.

---

[136] *Ntaganda*, ICC AC, 15 June 2017 (ICC-01/04–02/06–1962) para. 63.
[137] *Ibid.* para. 68. See also Rosemary Grey, 'Sexual Violence Against Child Soldiers: The Limits and Potential of International Criminal Law' (2014) 16 *International Feminist Journal of Politics* 601; Tilman Rodenhäuser, 'Squaring the Circle? Prosecuting Sexual Violence Against Child Soldiers by Their "Own Forces"' (2016) 14 *JICJ* 171; Joanna Nicholson, *Fighting and Victimhood in International Criminal Law* (New York, 2018) ch. 5.
[138] See Chapter 11. The Appeals Chamber in *Situation of the DRC*, ICC AC, 13 July 2006 (ICC-01–04–169) para. 70, also notes that Art. 8(1) does not refer to 'systematic'.
[139] Article 8(1) was discussed by the Appeals Chamber in *Situation of the DRC*, ICC AC, 13 July 2006 (ICC-01–04–169) paras. 70–1, and by the ICC Office of the Prosecutor, Response to Communications Concerning the Situation in Iraq, 10 February 2006, www.icc-cpi.int (under 'Structure of the Court', 'Office of the Prosecutor', 'Communications and Referrals', 'Iraq').

The ICTY Statute lists grave breaches of the Geneva Conventions (Article 2) and other violations of the laws and customs of war, drawing on other customary law sources (Article 3).[140] The ICTR Statute lists only serious violations of common Article 3 and AP I (Article 4). The ICC Statute follows the same approach of listing by source, and is the most elaborate. It features four lists: grave breaches of the Geneva Conventions (Article 8(2)(a)); other serious violations of the laws and customs applicable in international armed conflict (Article 8(2)(b)); serious violations of Common Article 3 (Article 8(2)(c)); and other serious violations of the laws and customs applicable in non-international armed conflict (Article 8 (2)(e)). The 'other serious violations' lists in Article 8(2)(b) and (e) are drawn from various sources that were accepted as customary law, including provisions from the 1907 Hague Regulations, Additional Protocols to the Geneva Conventions, and other sources.

Because of the desire to adhere to customary law, the drafters of the ICC Statute relied on provisions from well-accepted instruments. Even when there was overlap, overlapping provisions were often included to avoid missing any customary crimes. The drafters also declined to consolidate overlapping provisions, as this would have been seen as legislating. As a result of this reliance on various sources, there is considerable duplication. Furthermore, the order of the provisions in Article 8(2)(b) and (e) largely reflects the original instruments and the order of proposals, rather than any thematic groupings. The list has been described as 'unwieldy',[141] a 'hodgepodge',[142] lacking 'a clear and analytically convincing structure',[143] and not readily comprehensible to commanders.[144]

While there are many possible ways to group and order the specific war crimes, this chapter will present them in the following order. We will examine provisions protecting non-combatants (Section 12.3.2) and then two provisions governing military attacks: the principle of distinction (Section 12.3.3) and proportionality (Section 12.3.4). We shall then examine prohibitions relating to property (Section 12.3.5), prohibited weapons (Section 12.3.6), and prohibited methods of warfare (Section 12.3.7). Finally, there are two significant war crimes provisions that do not fall neatly into the above categories, as they protect other interests (Section 12.3.8).

12.3.2 Crimes Against Non-Combatants

Violence and Mistreatment

Probably the most important rules of war crimes law are the prohibitions against mistreatment of non-combatants (including civilians, prisoners-of-war, and wounded or sick former

[140] *Report of the Secretary-General Pursuant to Paragraph 2 of Security Council Resolution 808(1993)*, UN Doc. S/25704 (3 May 1993).
[141] M. Cherif Bassiouni, 'Negotiating the Treaty of Rome on the Establishment of an International Criminal Court' (1999) 32 *Cornell International Law Journal* 462.
[142] Bothe, 'War Crimes' (n. 22) 396.
[143] Kreß, 'War Crimes' (n. 65) 29. See also Cottier and Lippold, 'Article 8' in Ambos, *Commentary*, 355–7.
[144] While recognizing that sticking to traditional text made Art. 8 acceptable, Sunga notes that it would have been desirable to consolidate the provisions and build coherence, rather than following *lex lata* so literally, and that the result makes the list less comprehensible to commanders, thereby hindering compliance among even the most cooperative: Lyal Sunga, 'The Crimes Within the Jurisdiction of the International Criminal Court' (1998) 6(4) *European Journal of Crime, Criminal Law and Criminal Justice* 377, 393–4.

combatants). These prohibitions are derived from the basic principle that non-combatants must be treated humanely. Intentional violations of these provisions make up the majority of war crimes charges in national and international jurisdictions.

The war crime of murdering (or 'wilfully killing')[145] protected persons is well-recognized.[146] Recall that killing of *combatants* is permitted in lawfully conducted operations; furthermore, civilians may also die as a consequence of military actions against military objectives, and such deaths must be assessed using the more specific rules on disproportionate collateral damage.

Torture, inhuman treatment, mutilation, and biological, medical, or scientific experiments are also prohibited in any armed conflict.[147] The elements of torture and inhuman treatment have been discussed in Chapter 11, in relation to crimes against humanity.[148]

Human experimentation is prohibited in different instruments.[149] The prohibitions contain similar elements, of endangering the physical or mental health or integrity of persons, not being justified by medical reasons (the treatment of the person), and not being carried out in the person's interest.[150]

The war crime of 'wilfully causing great suffering or serious injury to body or health' arises from the 'grave breach' provisions of the Geneva Conventions.[151] The crime can include actions that deliberately cause long-lasting and serious harm without amounting to torture.[152] The war crime of 'committing outrages upon personal dignity, in particular humiliating and degrading treatment', is drawn from Common Article 3 and the Additional Protocols,[153] and therefore applies in any armed conflict. The prohibition is broader than the previously mentioned prohibitions, and includes acts aimed at humiliating and ridiculing persons, or forcing them to perform degrading acts.[154] The conduct must meet a certain objective level of seriousness to be considered an outrage upon personal dignity. Indignities against corpses can fall within the prohibition.[155]

The most important development in this area is the recognition that various forms of sexual violence amount to war crimes. Throughout history, international law has largely

---

[145] The ICC Statute, following the precedents, uses the term 'wilful killing' in international armed conflict, and 'murder' in non-international armed conflict. The elements are the same and correspond to those for the crime against humanity of murder, as already discussed in Chapter 11.
[146] ICC Statute, Art. 8(2)(a)(i) and (c)(i); ICTY Statute, Art. 2(a); ICTR Statute, Art. 4(a); Geneva Convention IV, Art. 147; Geneva Conventions, Common Art. 3.
[147] ICC Statute, Art. 8(2)(a)(ii), (b)(x), (c)(i) and (e)(xi); ICTY Statute, Art. 2(b), reflecting the grave breach provisions (e.g. Geneva Convention IV, Art. 147); Geneva Conventions, Common Art. 3; and AP I, Art. 11.
[148] See Chapter 11. However, unlike in crimes against humanity, the ICC Elements of Crimes say that the war crime of torture has a *purpose* requirement: that the perpetrator inflicted pain or suffering 'for such purposes as obtaining information or a confession, punishment, intimidation or coercion or for any reason based on discrimination of any kind'. In the absence of such a purpose, the conduct could still amount to inhuman treatment.
[149] Biological experiments appear in the Geneva Convention grave breach provisions, and medical or scientific experiments appear in AP I.
[150] See e.g. ICC Elements of Crimes, Art. 8(2)(ii)–3 and (b)(x)–2.
[151] See e.g. ICC Statute, Art. 8(2)(a)(iii); ICTY Statute, Art. 2(c); Geneva Convention IV, Art. 147. Under the ICC Statute, the provision applies only in international armed conflict.
[152] *Delalić et al.*, ICTY TC II, 16 November 1998, paras. 508–11; *Akayesu*, ICTR TC I, 2 September 1998, para. 502; *Blaškić*, ICTY TC I, 3 March 2000, para. 156; *Kordić*, ICTY TC, 26 February 2001, para. 245.
[153] Geneva Conventions, Common Art. 3; Geneva Convention IV, Art. 95; AP I, Arts. 75(2)(b) and 85(4)(c); AP II, Art. 4(2)(e); ICC Statute, Art. 8(2)(b)(xxi) and (c)(ii).
[154] *Aleksovski*, ICTY TC, 25 June 1999, para. 56; *Kunarac*, ICTY TC II, 22 February 2001, paras. 501–4.
[155] See e.g. ICC Elements of Crimes, note 49.

done a poor job of dealing with the sexual abuses routinely committed against women.[156] Licence to rape has often been seen by combatants as an expected occurrence after the taking of a city or village, and a means of terrorizing the enemy.[157] Sexual violence has been pervasive in armed conflicts.[158] While IHL has criminalized rape for centuries, this was not always explicit, and it was rarely prosecuted. IHL treaties, negotiated by men, tended to reflect the perspectives and concerns of men, and thus did not explicitly recognize sexual violence as a form of war crime.[159] Article 27 of Geneva Convention IV stipulated that women should be protected against rape, but did not make rape a grave breach. Sexual violence was mentioned again in the Additional Protocols, but not as a crime.[160] Moreover, it was listed as an example of 'outrages upon personal dignity', which treated rape as an attack on 'honour', trivializing the nature of the violation.

The ICTY Statute did not list rape as a war crime (although it was listed as a crime against humanity). This lacuna triggered the efforts to establish that rape could fall within the definition of grave breaches, such as 'torture' or 'inhuman treatment'.[161] It also reinforced the need to establish that rape is a war crime per se.[162] The ICTR Statute was an improvement, in that its war crimes provision expressly included rape, enforced prostitution, and other forms of sexual violence.[163] However, mirroring the language of Additional Protocol II, these were included as 'outrages upon personal dignity'. The ICC Statute took the further step, explicitly recognizing rape, sexual slavery, enforced prostitution, forced pregnancy, enforced sterilization, and other sexual violence as war crimes.[164] For the elements of these offences, see the discussion in Chapter 11.

Further compounding the historical lack of *legal* recognition of crimes of sexual violence, an additional problem was that investigators and prosecutors shied away from investigating bringing charges of sexual violence even when applicable law did recognize the crime. For example, in the Nuremberg proceedings, where there was ample evidence of widespread use of rape as a weapon of war, the French prosecutor simply submitted a dossier and asked forgiveness 'if I avoid citing the atrocious details' – even though many atrocious details were scrutinized thoroughly in relation to other charges.[165] As a result, there were no convictions for sexual violence in the Nuremberg proceedings. The record of the Tokyo Tribunal was somewhat better, as there were war crimes

---

[156] Elizabeth Odio-Benito, 'Sexual Violence as a War Crime' in Pablo Antonio Fernandez-Sánchez (ed.), *The New Challenges of Humanitarian Law in Armed Conflict* (Brill, 2005).

[157] See e.g. Kelly Askin, *War Crimes Against Women: Prosecution in International Tribunals* (Martinus Nijhoff, 1997) 12–42.

[158] See e.g. Susan Brownmiller, *Against Our Will: Men, Women and Rape* (New York, 1975); Christine Chinkin, 'Rape and Sexual Abuse of Women in International Law' (1994) 5 *EJIL* 1.

[159] Some military codes did recognize sexual violence as a punishable war crime; for example, the Lieber Code provided the death penalty for rape.

[160] AP II, Art. 4(2)(e), referring to rape, enforced prostitution and indecent assault; AP I, Art. 75(2)(b), referring to enforced prostitution and indecent assault.

[161] Patricia Viseur Sellers and Kaoru Okuizumi, 'International Prosecution of Sexual Assaults' (1997) 7 *Transnational Legal and Contemporary Problems* 45; see *Akayesu*, ICTR TC I, 2 September 1998, para. 731 (rape and sexual violence can constitute the *actus reus* of other crimes); *Delalić et al.*, ICTY TC II, 16 November 1998, paras. 475–96 (rape can constitute torture where the elements of torture are satisfied).

[162] Theodor Meron, 'Rape as a Crime under International Humanitarian Law' (1993) 87 *AJIL* 424.   [163] ICTR Statute, Art. 4(e).

[164] ICC Statute, Art. 8(2)(b)(xxii).

[165] Gabrielle Kirk McDonald, 'Crimes of Sexual Violence: The Experience of the International Criminal Tribunal' (2000) 39 *Columbia Journal of Transnational Law* 1, 10.

convictions of leaders for rapes and sexual violence, including in relation to the 'Rape of Nanking', in which Japanese soldiers raped approximately 20,000 women and children.[166] The sexual slavery of women as 'comfort women' by the Japanese military was, however, largely overlooked.[167] In response to these experiences, many non-governmental organizations (NGOs), academics, and lawyers have successfully pressed the ICTY and ICTR to ensure that crimes of sexual violence are diligently investigated and prosecuted.[168] These efforts have culminated in rules of procedure sensitive to victims, gender advisers on staff, and several landmark decisions. In the same spirit, the ICC Statute has a number of provisions to ensure the effective investigation and prosecution of such crimes, while preserving the safety, dignity, and privacy of victims and witnesses.[169] Even with such provisions in place, the ICC has often struggled to bring successful sexual and gender-based violence cases; new policies are aimed at improving this track record, and recent convictions or sexual violence in the *Ongwen* and *Ntaganda* cases are promising signs.[170]

Other Legal Interests of Protected Persons

War crimes law also protects other rights of persons. For example, several provisions protect liberty and mobility rights. In international conflicts, the unlawful deportation, transfer or confinement of civilians is a grave breach.[171] In non-international conflicts, there is a more modest prohibition on displacement of the civilian population for reasons unrelated to the conflict.[172] Since IHL permits the transfer and/or confinement of civilians under certain conditions, it is necessary to refer to IHL to determine whether a particular act is unlawful.[173] Taking hostages is also a war crime in either type of armed conflict.[174]

Other provisions protect the legal rights of persons. Punishment of protected persons without a regular trial is a grave breach (international conflict) and a serious violation of Common Article 3 (non-international conflict).[175] In international conflict, it is also a war crime to abolish

---

[166] *Ibid.*

[167] *Ibid.* The crime was mentioned only in the Tokyo International Military Tribunal (IMT), reprinted in Neil Boister and Robert Cryer, *Documents on the Tokyo International Military Tribunal* (Oxford, 2008) 49, 617.

[168] Christine Chinkin, 'Women: The Forgotten Victims of Armed Conflict' in Helen Durham and Timothy L. H. McCormack (eds.), *The Changing Face of Conflict and the Efficacy of International Humanitarian Law* (The Hague, 1999).

[169] ICC Statute, Art. 36(8)(b) (judges with expertise in violence against women and children); Art. 42(6) (advisers on sexual and gender violence and violence against children); Art. 44(2) (staff with such expertise); Art. 54(1)(b) (Prosecutor to respect interests of victims and witnesses and take into account sexual violence, gender violence and violence against children); and Art. 68 (protection of victims and witnesses and participation in proceedings). See e.g. Valerie Oosterveld, 'The Making of a Gender-Sensitive International Criminal Court' (1999) 1 *International Law FORUM du droit international* 38.

[170] Susana SáCouto and Patricia Viseur Sellers, 'The Bemba Appeals Chamber Judgment: Impunity for Sexual and Gender-Based Crimes?' (2019) 27 *William & Mary Bill of Rights Journal* 1; Tania Altunjan, 'The International Criminal Court and Sexual Violence: Between Aspirations and Reality' (2021) 22 *German Law Journal* 878; ICC OTP, 'Policy Paper on Sexual and Gender-Based Crimes', 20 June 2014, www.icc-cpi.int/news/policy-paper-sexual-and-gender-based-crimes-0; *Ongwen*, ICC TC IX, 4 February 2021 (ICC-02/04–01/15–1762-Red) para. 2689.

[171] See ICC Statute, Art. 8(2)(a)(vii); ICTY Statute, Art. 2(g); and Geneva Convention IV, Art. 147. Significantly, this provision appears only in Geneva Convention IV, allowing the conclusion that only civilians may be victims of this offence.

[172] See ICC Statute, Art. 8(2)(e)(viii); AP II, Art. 17(1). [173] See e.g. Geneva Convention IV, Arts. 41–43, 68, 78 and 79–141.

[174] See e.g. ICC Statute, Art. 8(2)(a)(viii) and (c)(iii); Geneva Convention IV, Arts. 34(4) and 147; AP I, Art. 75(2)(c); and AP II, Art. 4(2)(c). See also *United States* v. *Altstötter* (the 'Justice Trial'), VI LRTWC 1; *Blaškić*, ICTY TC I, 3 March 2000, para. 158.

[175] ICC Statute, Art. 8(2)(a)(vi) and (c)(iv); ICTY Statute, Art. 2(f); ICTR Statute, Art. 3(g); Geneva Convention III, Art. 130; Geneva Convention IV, Art. 147; Geneva Conventions, Common Art. 3(1)(d). See *Hamdan* v. *Rumsfeld*, 126 S Ct 2749 (2006), finding that military tribunals established by the US government, allowing the exclusion of the accused from his own trial, did not meet the Common Art. 3 standard.

or suspend the rights and legal actions of nationals of a hostile party.[176] The crime of punishment without regular trial is being considered by the ICC in the *Al Hassan* case.[177]

It is a war crime to compel persons to fight against their own side during international conflicts. There are two overlapping provisions on this matter, one from the Geneva Conventions (it is a grave breach to compel a prisoner-of-war or civilian to serve in the forces of a hostile power),[178] and one from the Hague Conventions (it is a war crime to compel persons to participate in operations of war against their own country).[179] The two provisions overlap but have a different focus; one focuses on *conscription* into forces (fighting against any party) and the other focuses on the forced breach of loyalty in fighting *one's own country* (whether or not as part of military forces).[180]

Slavery and forced labour, while not listed as war crimes in the ICC Statute, have been recognized as war crimes in Tribunal jurisprudence.[181]

12.3.3 Attacks on Prohibited Targets (Principle of Distinction)

The principle of distinction requires belligerents to distinguish between military objectives and the civilian population and objects, and to 'direct their operations only against military objectives'.[182] As explained in Section 12.1.3, this is a cardinal principle of IHL.[183]

The relevant IHL instruments provide guidance on the differences between civilians and military objectives. In cases of doubt whether a person is a civilian, that person shall be considered to be a civilian.[184] With respect to 'civilian population', '[t]he presence within the civilian population of individuals who do not come within the definition of civilians does not deprive the population of its civilian character'.[185] The population must be of a 'predominantly civilian nature'.[186] Civilian objects are 'all objects which are not military objectives'.[187]

Military objectives include combatants, whether on or off duty, as well as objects:

which by their nature, location, purpose or use make an effective contribution to military action and whose total or partial destruction, capture or neutralization, in the circumstances ruling at the time, offers a definite military advantage.[188]

---

[176] ICC Statute, Art. 8(2)(b)(xiv); 1907 Hague Regulations, Art. 23(h).

[177] Diletta Marchesi, 'Criminalizing Acts of Rebel Governance as War Crimes: An Assessment Focused on the War Crime of Sentencing or Execution without Due Process' (2023) 21 *JICJ* 353.

[178] ICC Statute, Art. 8(2)(a)(v); Geneva Convention III, Art. 130; Geneva Convention IV, Art. 147.

[179] ICC Statute, Art. 8(2)(b)(xv); 1907 Hague Regulations, Art. 23(h).

[180] The ICC Elements of Crimes combine both aspects in the elements of Art. 8(2)(a)(v).

[181] *Krnojelac*, ICTY TC II, 15 March 2002, paras. 350–60; *Naletilić*, ICTY TC, 31 March 2003, paras. 250–61. To determine the ambit of these prohibitions, one must consult IHL rules such as Arts. 49–57 of Geneva Convention III on authorized work and working conditions.

[182] AP I, Art. 48; see also AP I, Art. 51 and AP II, Art. 13. For a discussion on the law of targeting, see Michael N. Schmitt, 'Fault Lines in the Law of Attack' in Susan C. Breau and Agnieszka Jachec-Neale (eds.), *Testing the Boundaries of International Humanitarian Law* (London, 2006) 277–92.

[183] *Legality of the Threat or Use of Nuclear Weapons*, Advisory Opinion (n. 43) 257, para. 78. [184] AP I, Art. 50(1).

[185] *Ibid.* Art. 50(3).

[186] *Tadić*, ICTY TC II, 7 May 1997, para. 638; *Blaškić*, ICTY TC, 3 March 2000, para. 214; *Strugar*, ICTY TC II, 31 January 2005, para. 282.

[187] AP I, Art. 50(3); also *Blaškić*, ICTY TC, 3 March 2000, para. 180; *Kordić*, ICTY TC, 26 February 2001, para. 53; *Strugar*, ICTY TC II, 31 January 2005, para. 282.

[188] This definition, found in AP I, Art. 52(2), is widely accepted as reflecting customary law. For further discussion of this two-part test, see e.g. Yoram Dinstein, 'Legitimate Military Objectives under the Current Jus in Bello' (2001) 31 *Israel Yearbook on*

The war crimes of directing attacks against civilians or the civilian population,[189] or against civilian objects,[190] are the most elementary and straightforward expression of the principle of distinction.

The ICC Statute also specifically prohibits attacks on personnel, installations, and vehicles involved in a humanitarian assistance or peacekeeping mission in accordance with the UN Charter.[191] This provision does not go beyond existing customary law, because it only protects those 'entitled to the protection given to civilians', and thus it is simply a specific illustration of the prohibition on attacking civilians.[192]

Two other prohibitions flow from the principle of sparing the civilian population. First, it is prohibited to use the starvation of civilians as a method of war, including wilfully impeding relief supplies.[193] That problem remains tragically relevant today.[194] Second, under Tribunal jurisprudence, it is a war crime to commit acts of violence primarily intended to spread terror among the civilian population.[195] The *Taylor* decision of the SCSL explored the potentially gendered dimension of the latter offence, with the use of sexual violence and sexual slavery as a means of terrorizing a population.[196]

The other 'prohibited target' provisions are specific examples of this prohibition, focusing on certain specially protected objects or interests. These include: attacking or bombarding undefended towns, villages, dwellings, or buildings which are not military objectives;[197] intentionally directing attacks against buildings dedicated to 'religion, education, art, science or charitable purposes, historic monuments, hospitals, and places where the sick and wounded are collected, provided they are not military objectives';[198] and directing attacks against buildings, transport, and personnel using the distinctive emblems of the Geneva Conventions.[199]

Human Rights 1; Sandoz et al., *Commentary on the Additional Protocols* (n. 53) 635–7, notes 2014–18. The definition can still give rise to disagreement as to its application; see e.g. the controversial analysis of attacks on TV stations in the ICTY, *Final Report to the Prosecutor by the Committee Established to Review the NATO Bombing* (13 June 2000), www.icty.org/sid/10052.

[189] ICC Statute, Art. 8(2)(b)(i) and (e)(i); AP I, Art. 51(2); AP II, Art. 13(2). [190] ICC Statute, Art. 8(2)(b)(ii); AP I, Art. 62(1).
[191] ICC Statute, Art. 8(2)(b)(iii) and (e)(iii); see also SCSL Statute, Art. 4(b). The provision was inspired by the 1994 UN Convention on the Safety of UN and Associated Personnel (1999) 2051 UNTS 391.
[192] The restriction to those with civilian status means that peacekeepers engaged in military operations under Chapter VII are not protected. This is a necessary outcome consistent with general principles of IHL; otherwise, for one side of the conflict, killing combatants would be a crime.
[193] ICC Statute, Art. 8(2)(b)(xxv); AP I, Art. 54; see also, on the general duty not to impede relief, Geneva Convention IV, Arts. 10, 23, 59–63 and 108–111 and AP I, Arts. 70–71.
[194] Susan Power, 'Siege Warfare in Syria: Prosecuting the Starvation of Civilians' (2016) 8 *Amsterdam Law Forum* 1; Rogier Bartels, 'Denying Humanitarian Access as an International Crime in Times of Non-International Armed Conflict: The Challenges to Prosecute and Some Proposals for the Future' (2015) 48 *Israel Law Review* 281; Tom Dannenbaum, 'Legal Frameworks for Assessing the Use of Starvation in Ukraine', *Just Security*, 22 April 2022, www.justsecurity.org.
[195] *Galić*, ICTY TC, 5 December 2003, paras. 87–138; *Galić*, ICTY AC, 30 November 2006, paras. 87–104. See AP I, Art. 51(2) and AP II, Art. 13(2): '[a]cts or threats of violence the primary purpose of which is to spread terror among the civilian population are prohibited'; Cryer, 'Prosecutor v. Galić' (n. 30) 73. For further discussion of the crime of terrorism, see Chapter 14.
[196] *Taylor*, SCSL TC II, 18 May 2012, para. 2035; Valerie Oosterveld, 'Gender and the Charles Taylor Case at the Special Court for Sierra Leone' (2012) 19 *William and Mary Journal of Women and the Law* 7; Kristen Keith, 'Deconstructing Terrorism as a War Crime: The Charles Taylor Case' (2013) 11 *JICJ* 813.
[197] ICC Statute, Art. 8(2)(b)(v); ICTY Statute, Art. 3(c); 1907 Hague Regulations, Art. 25; AP I, Art. 59(1).
[198] ICC Statute, Art. 8(2)(b)(ix) and (e)(iv); 1907 Hague Regulations, Arts. 27 and 56; and see the 1954 Hague Convention for the Protection of Cultural Property and the 1999 Second Protocol to the Hague Convention. For analysis, see Roger O'Keefe, 'Protection of Cultural Property under International Criminal Law' (2010) 11 *Melbourne Journal of International Law* 339.
[199] ICC Statute, Art. 8(2)(b)(xxiv) and (e)(ii).

The *Al Mahdi* case at the ICC highlights the protection of historic, religious, and cultural property. Al Mahdi was the head of the 'morality police' in an Al Qaeda-affiliated rebel group in Mali. In 2012, Al Mahdi oversaw the destruction of ten well-known mausoleums in Timbuktu, which were irreplaceable parts of the historic heritage of Mali and which were all World Heritage Sites. At his trial in 2016, Al Mahdi pleaded guilty and apologized for the destruction, and was sentenced to nine years' imprisonment.[200] In 2021, the ICC OTP published a written policy on protection of cultural heritage in its work.[201]

12.3.4 Attacks Inflicting Excessive Civilian Damage

Principle of Proportionality

The companion to the principle of distinction is the principle of proportionality: even where an attack is directed against a military objective, the anticipated incidental civilian damage must not be disproportionate to the anticipated military advantage.[202] This principle is well established as customary law.[203]

No other principle of IHL illustrates so clearly the tension between military and humanitarian considerations. The various prohibitions on mistreatment of civilians are important but they are legally and conceptually straightforward, whereas the prohibition on disproportionate attacks poses problems of interpretation even for – indeed, particularly for – military forces striving to comply fully with IHL. Even with precision weapons and sophisticated intelligence, military strikes often result in significant civilian casualties, injuries, and property damage. As the prohibition on disproportionate attacks brings to the fore many complex and sensitive questions, this chapter will examine it in some detail.

The prohibition is criminalized in Article 85(3)(b) of AP I and in Article 8(2)(b)(iv) of the ICC Statute. Article 8(2)(b)(iv) of the ICC Statute criminalizes:

Intentionally launching an attack in the knowledge that such attack will cause incidental loss of life or injury to civilians or damage to civilian objects or widespread, long-term and severe damage to the natural environment which would be clearly[204] excessive in relation to the concrete and direct overall military advantage anticipated.

The application of this test therefore requires an assessment of:

(a) the anticipated civilian damage or injury;
(b) the anticipated military advantage; and
(c) whether (a) was excessive in relation to (b).

---

[200] *Al Mahdi*, ICC TC VII, 27 September 2016 (ICC-01/12–01/15–171); Mark Ellis, 'The ICC's Role in Combatting the Destruction of Cultural Heritage' (2017) 49 *Case Western Reserve Journal of International Law* 23; Paige Casaly, 'Al Mahdi Before the ICC: Cultural Property and World Heritage in International Criminal Law' (2016) 14 *JICJ* 1199.

[201] ICC OTP, 'Policy on Cultural Heritage', 14 June 2021, www.icc-cpi.int/news/icc-prosecutor-fatou-bensouda-publishes-policy-cultural-heritage-cultural-heritage-repository.

[202] AP I, Art. 51(5)(b).

[203] Henckaerts and Doswald-Beck, *ICRC Customary Law*, 46–50; *Kupreškić*, ICTY TC II, 14 January 2000, paras. 522–6; Schmitt, 'Fault Lines' (n. 182) 292.

[204] The AP I standard is 'excessive' whereas the ICC Statute standard is 'clearly excessive'.

First Side of the Equation: Harm to Civilians, Civilian Objects, and the Environment

The terms 'civilian', 'civilian population', and 'civilian object' are discussed in Section 12.3.3.

Article 8(2)(b)(iv) of the ICC Statute differs from Article 85(3)(b) of AP I in that it also includes damage to the environment in the proportionality assessment. The inclusion of environmental considerations is consistent with other authorities.[205] The terminology is drawn from Article 35(3) of AP I, which prohibits attacks causing 'widespread, long-term and severe damage to the natural environment'.[206] The ICC Statute is more restrictive than Article 35(3) of AP I, since the damage must satisfy not only the 'widespread, long-term and severe' requirement but also the disproportionality test.[207]

Second Side of the Equation: Military Advantage

Military objectives include combatants, whether they are on or off duty, unless they have surrendered, are sick or wounded, or have ceased to take part in hostilities.[208] Objects may also be military objectives, as defined above.[209] Article 8(2)(b)(iv) also requires an assessment of the 'concrete and direct overall military advantage anticipated'.[210] The obvious tension between these modifiers ('concrete and direct' versus 'overall') is addressed in note 36 of the Elements of Crimes:

The expression 'concrete and direct overall military advantage' refers to a military advantage that is foreseeable by the perpetrator at the relevant time. Such advantage may or may not be temporally or geographically related to the object of the attack.[211]

One example of an anticipated advantage that is specific and foreseeable, yet not temporally or geographically linked to the target, could be a feint. For example, in the Second World War, the Allies attacked military targets in the Pas de Calais, but the greater intended contribution was to deceive Germany into believing that the amphibious assault would take place there rather than in Normandy.[212]

Comparing the Two Sides of the Equation: Proportionality Test

It is simple to state the proportionality test, but it is profoundly difficult to assess compliance with it in practice, given that: (1) assessing the anticipated civilian damage is a difficult task, requiring a prediction of consequences based on available information under circumstances of urgency; (2) assessing the anticipated military advantage involves the same

---

[205] *Legality of the Threat or Use of Nuclear Weapons*, Advisory Opinion (n. 43) 226, para. 30; ICTY, *Final Report* (n. 188) para. 15.

[206] On these terms, see ILC, GAOR, 46th Session, Supp. No. 10 (A/46/10) 276; and Dörmann, *Elements of War Crimes* (n. 112) 175. More generally, see Jay E. Austin and Carl E. Bruch, *The Environmental Consequences of War* (Cambridge, 2000); Karen Hulme, *War Torn Environment: Interpreting the Legal Threshold* (Brill, 2004).

[207] Steven Freeland, *Addressing the Intentional Destruction of the Environment During Warfare under the Rome Statute of the International Criminal Court* (Cambridge, 2015).

[208] AP I, Arts. 43, 48 and 51(3).   [209] See Section 12.3.3.

[210] On 'concrete and direct', see Sandoz et al, *Commentary on the Additional Protocols* (n. 53) para. 2209. On 'overall', see statements of understanding of Belgium, Canada, Germany, Italy, the Netherlands, New Zealand, Switzerland, and the United Kingdom, available in Adam Roberts and Richard Guelff (eds.), *Documents of the Laws of War*, 3rd ed. (Oxford, 2000) 499–512.

[211] ICC Elements of Crimes, note 36. The footnote was the subject of intense negotiations.

[212] Dörmann, *Elements of War Crimes* (n. 112) 171.

problems of variables and uncertainties, taking into account the broader military strategy and possible future ramifications of the action; and (3) comparing the two is even more challenging, given that they are entirely unlike properties with no common unit of measurement.[213]

Because of these difficulties, decision-makers should be allowed some 'margin of appreciation' when their decisions are reviewed.[214] During the negotiation of the ICC Statute, many states were concerned about the inclusion of Article 8(2)(b)(iv) on the grounds that the officials and judges of the ICC would not be likely to have military experience and hence would apply an incorrectly onerous standard, and that the Court would be reviewing decisions *ex post facto* with the benefit of hindsight, failing to take into account the 'fog of war' (incomplete information, urgency, confusion, limited time for critical decisions).[215]

To address these concerns, and to provide a 'margin of appreciation', the term 'clearly' was inserted into the Rome Statute, so that the ICC will act only with respect to cases that are 'clearly excessive'.[216] Some see this as an unfortunate restriction on the standard in AP I.[217] Alternatively, it may be seen as an appropriate clarification, given that the Statute deals not with *civil* liability of the parties to a conflict, but rather with individual *criminal* liability.[218] Both the ICRC study on customary law and the ICTY report on NATO bombing concluded that inclusion of the word 'clearly' does not entail a significant new hurdle, since prosecution would be viable only in cases where the proportionality requirement was clearly breached.[219]

Some authorities indicate that proportionality must be assessed from the point of view of a 'reasonable military commander'[220] or 'a reasonably well-informed person in the circumstances of the actual perpetrator, making reasonable use of the information available to him'.[221] However, even such points of reference do not provide measurable ratios of military advantage and civilian damage that would be considered disproportionate.[222] A review of state practice, even among states with traditions of IHL compliance and

---

[213] Bothe, 'War Crimes' (n. 22) 398; see also ICTY, *Final Report* (n. 188) para. 48; W. J. Fenrick, 'Targeting and Proportionality During the NATO Bombing Campaign Against Yugoslavia' (2001) 12 *EJIL* 489, 499; Schmitt, 'Fault Lines' (n. 183) 292–8.

[214] Stefan Oeter, 'Methods and Means of Combat' in Dieter Fleck (ed.), *Handbook of International Humanitarian Law*, 3rd ed. (Oxford, 2013) 205; see also Fenrick, 'Targeting and Proportionality' (n. 213) 499.

[215] The provision has therefore been highlighted as creating undue exposure for commanders working in good faith. See e.g. David Scheffer, 'Statement in the 6th Committee of the General Assembly', 21 October 1998, US Mission to the UN, Press Release No. 179; Cassandra Jeu, 'A Successful Permanent International Criminal Court: Isn't It Pretty to Think So?' (2004) 26 *Houston Journal of International Law* 411.

[216] Herman von Hebel and Darryl Robinson, 'Crimes Within the Jurisdiction of the Court' in Lee, *The Making of the Rome Statute*, 111.

[217] Cryer, *Prosecuting International Crimes* (n. 47) 277–9.   [218] D. Pfirter, 'Article 8(2)(b)(iv)' in Lee, *Elements and Rules*, 148.

[219] Henckaerts and Doswald-Beck, *ICRC Customary Law*, 576–7; ICTY, *Final Report* (n. 188) para. 21; see also Stefan Wehrenberg, 'Article 8' in Ambos, *Commentary*, at 424–8.

[220] ICTY, *Final Report* (n. 188) 13 June 2000, para. 50. See the comments on this standard in Paolo Benvenuti, 'The ICTY Prosecutor and the Review of the NATO Bombing Campaign Against the Federal Republic of Yugoslavia' (2001) 12 *EJIL* 503, 517; and Michael Bothe, 'The Protection of the Civilian Population and NATO Bombing on Yugoslavia: Comments on a Report to the Prosecutor of the ICTY' (2001) 12 *EJIL* 531, 535.

[221] *Galić*, ICTY TC, 5 December 2003, para. 8.

[222] One of the few relevant cases is *Galić*, where shells were fired in the midst of a football tournament. The Trial Chamber noted the presence of some soldiers at the game, but found that an attack on a crowd of approximately 200 people, including numerous children, was excessive in relation to the military advantage anticipated: *Galić*, ICTY TC, 5 December 2003, para. 387.

political incentive to minimize collateral damage, suggests that significant numbers of casualties can be inflicted in pursuit of military advantages without falling foul of the prohibition.

At times, tribunals and investigative bodies are confronted with a pattern of damage (for example, artillery impacts) and must attempt to assess whether war crimes were committed.[223] Because civilian objects may be hit inadvertently even when all appropriate precautions are taken, it can be difficult to assess whether the persons launching the attack: (1) deliberately targeted civilian objects; (2) were indiscriminate between military and civilian objects; (3) targeted military objectives but with excessive foreseeable collateral damage; or (4) targeted military objectives and the damage was proportionate or reasonably unanticipated. In the *Gotovina* decision, the Trial Chamber used, as a factor, whether there were military objectives within 200 metres of artillery impacts, but the Appeals Chamber disagreed with this approach and entered an acquittal.[224] The acquittal was controversial, because the trial decision may not have used the factor as rigidly as the Appeals Chamber suggested.[225] Because of the uncertainty about the standards, this is a difficult war crime to prosecute, but it does at least allow a criminal law response to the most glaringly disproportionate attacks.[226]

Mental Element

The knowledge of the perpetrator at the time of launching the attack is a crucial element of this crime.[227] This is consistent with general principles of criminal law[228] and with state practice.[229]

It is clear that a perpetrator must have awareness of the extent of the anticipated harm and military advantage. Must the perpetrator personally consider that the attack was 'clearly excessive'? Or is it sufficient that what the perpetrator knew about the (military) advantages and (civilian) risks is in fact disproportionate enough to satisfy the 'clearly excessive' standard? The general rule in criminal law is that it is the accused's awareness of *facts* that matters; liability does not hinge on the accused's personal opinions and normative evaluations. Thus, as a matter of basic criminal law, knowledge of facts, which are objectively disproportionate, should suffice. However, note 37 to the ICC Elements of Crimes suggests that this crime requires that the perpetrator personally completes a particular value judgement.[230] While the provisions of the ICC Elements of Crimes should not lightly be

---

[223] See e.g. ICC OTP, *Response to Communications Received concerning Iraq*, 9 February 2006, www.legal-tools.org/doc/ 5b8996; *Situation in Georgia*, ICC PTC I, 13 October 2015, paras. 204–11; ICTY, *Final Report* (n. 188); *Report of the United Nations Fact-Finding Mission on the Gaza Conflict*, UN Doc. A/HRC/12/48 (15 September 2009); *Gotovina*, ICTY AC, 16 November 2012.

[224] *Gotovina*, ICTY AC, 16 November 2012.

[225] Janine N. Clark, 'Courting Controversy: The ICTY's Acquittal of Croatian General Gotovina and Markač' (2013) 11 *JICJ* 399.

[226] See e.g. *Galić*, ICTY TC, 5 December 2003, para. 387; ICTY, *Final Report* (n. 188) para. 21. *Report of the International Commission of Inquiry on Darfur* (25 January 2005) para. 260, observes that the principle of proportionality 'remains a largely subjective standard' but it 'nevertheless plays an important role, first of all it must be applied in good faith, and secondly because its application may involve the prohibition of at least the most glaringly disproportionate injuries to civilians'.

[227] ICC Elements of Crimes, Art. 8(2)(b)(iv), para 3; ICC Elements of Crimes, note 37, second sentence.

[228] ICC Statute, Art. 30 (mental element) and Art. 32 (mistake of fact).

[229] See e.g. declarations by Algeria, Australia, Belgium, Canada, Egypt, Germany, Ireland, the Netherlands, New Zealand, Spain, and the United Kingdom that what is relevant is 'the information available to them at the relevant time'.

[230] ICC Elements of Crimes, note 37.

disregarded, this particular footnote was included at the last minute of the negotiations, without any discussion in the working group. Furthermore, there are grave reasons to doubt its compatibility with general principles of criminal law and hence the ICC Statute.[231] The Elements footnote has been criticized as making the 'perpetrator, in a way, the judge in his own cause'.[232] Commentators have suggested that the provision should be interpreted as expressing the need for a margin of appreciation, but not as insulating reckless or incredible assessments.[233]

12.3.5 War Crimes Against Property

Several war crimes concern property, namely, its destruction, appropriation, seizure, and pillage.[234] The ICC Statute contains provisions from the Geneva Conventions and the 1907 Hague Regulations, which overlap considerably but which were both included for completeness.[235]

In addition, *pillage* of property is also a war crime.[236] Pillage is distinct from appropriation or seizure because it refers to taking for private or personal use[237] as opposed to taking for military purposes.[238] It is more akin to the domestic crime of theft. For pillage, there is no 'balancing' with military necessity, since the property is not taken for military reasons.

12.3.6 Prohibited Means of Warfare (Weapons)

Each of the foregoing provisions was aimed primarily at sparing *non-combatants* and their property as much as possible from the effects of war. War crimes law also contains provisions that regulate the 'methods and means' of conducting hostilities. These provisions are distinct in that *combatants* are also beneficiaries of the protections granted. 'Methods' refers to prohibited tactics (Section 12.3.7) and 'means' refers to prohibited weapons.

There are two rationales for the prohibition on certain weapons. One is to protect civilians: some weapons are *inherently indiscriminate* – that is to say, they cannot be used in a manner distinguishing civilian and military. The other is to protect combatants: some weapons cause superfluous injury or *unnecessary suffering*.[239]

---

[231] Art. 9 of the ICC Statute requires that the ICC Elements of Crimes be consistent with the ICC Statute.

[232] Bothe, 'War Crimes' (n. 22) 400.

[233] D. Pfirter, 'War Crimes' in Lee, *Elements and Rules*, 151; see also Dörmann, *Elements of War Crimes* (n. 112) 165.

[234] See e.g. ICC Statute, Art. 8(2)(a)(iv), (b)(xiii), (b)(xvi), (e)(v), and (e)(xii).

[235] See e.g. *ibid.* Art. 8(2)(a)(iv), based on the Geneva Conventions and Art. 8(2)(b)(xiii), based on 1907 Hague Regulations, Art. 23(g). The ICC Statute includes both provisions, because the Hague Regulation provision is more inclusive and hence more useful, whereas excluding the Geneva Convention provision would have meant an incomplete list of grave breaches.

[236] ICC Statute, Art. 8(2)(b)(xvi) and (e)(v); ICTR Statute, Art. 4(f); ICTY Statute, Art. 3(e) (plunder being synonymous with pillage); 1907 Hague Regulations, Art. 28; Geneva Convention IV, Art. 33.

[237] ICC Elements of Crimes, Art. 8(2)(b)(xvi), Element 2.

[238] *Bemba Gombo*, ICC TC III, 21 March 2016 (ICC-01/05–01/08–3343) para. 124.

[239] Note here the underlying peculiarity of IHL and war crimes law. It is accepted that one may kill combatants, and that combat operations may inflict great suffering on combatants, so the rather modest objective is to reduce *superfluous* injury or *unnecessary* suffering. In regulating weapons, states therefore examine the military efficacy of a particular weapon as well as its consequences to determine if it inflicts *unnecessary* suffering, which can be a rather fine question.

Weapons which have been banned from the battlefield include poison and poisoned weapons;[240] asphyxiating or poisonous gases and analogous liquids, materials, or devices;[241] and 'dum-dum' or 'hollow point' bullets (bullets which expand or flatten easily upon impact).[242] Use of these weapons was recognized as a war crime in the ICC Statute; more recently, at the Kampala Review Conference in 2010, the Statute was amended to recognize these war crimes in non-international armed conflict as well.[243]

Chemical weapons and biological and toxic weapons are equally prohibited under the customary law of war crimes.[244] However, even though the customary law status of these crimes was not disputed at the Rome Conference, these crimes were excluded from the ICC Statute due to a stand-off with respect to nuclear weapons. At the Conference, some delegations, most notably India, insisted on the inclusion of nuclear weapons in the list of prohibited weapons.[245] However, there was no agreement that nuclear weapons were prohibited per se under customary law. Indeed, the International Court of Justice had specifically found that nuclear weapons are not prohibited per se.[246] A large number of delegations then insisted that it was unfair to exclude nuclear weapons – 'the rich man's weapons of mass destruction' – but to include biological and chemical weapons – 'the poor man's weapons of mass destruction'.[247] When no breakthrough could be found for this impasse, the drafters deferred the whole issue: no such weapons were included in Article 8, but a placeholder was inserted, inviting review of the question once the Statute is open for amendment at a future review conference.[248]

While chemical[249] and nuclear weapons are not prohibited per se in the ICC Statute, their use can still constitute a war crime if they are employed in a manner contravening other provisions, such as the prohibition on clearly excessive attacks. Indeed, the ICJ has noted that in most imaginable circumstances, the use of nuclear weapons would be likely to fall foul of one of the existing prohibitions.[250]

---

[240]   ICC Statute, Art. 8(2)(b)(xvii); 1907 Hague Regulations, Art. 23(a).
[241]   ICC Statute, Art. 8(2)(b)(xviii); Geneva Chemical Weapons Protocol, 17 June 1925.
[242]   ICC Statute, Art. 8(2)(b)(xix); Declaration on the Use of Bullets Which Expand or Flatten Easily in the Human Body, 29 July 1899.
[243]   Now ICC Statute, Art. 8(2)(e)(xiii)–(xv).
[244]   See e.g. Henckaerts and Doswald-Beck, *ICRC Customary Law*, 1607–770; Bacteriological and Toxin Weapons Convention 1972; Chemical Weapons Convention 1993.
[245]   Explanation of Vote by Mr Dilip Lahiri, Head of Delegation of India, on the Adoption of the Statute of the International Court, 17 July 1998, United Nations Diplomatic Conference of Plenipotentiaries on the Establishment of an International Criminal Court Rome, 15 June–17 July 1998, Official Records, vol. II, 122.
[246]   *Legality of the Threat or Use of Nuclear Weapons*, Advisory Opinion (n. 43) 226, paras. 52 and 74.
[247]   Michael Cottier and David Krivanek, 'Article 8' in Ambos, *Commentary*, 515–16; von Hebel and Robinson, 'Crimes Within the Jurisdiction' (n. 216) 113–16; for detailed discussion of the history and its implications, see Roger S. Clark, 'The Rome Statute of the International Criminal Court and Weapons of a Nature to Cause Superfluous Injury or Unnecessary Suffering, or Which are Inherently Indiscriminate' in John Carey, William V. Dunlap and P. John Pritchard (eds.), *International Humanitarian Law: Challenges* (Ardsley, NY, 2003).
[248]   ICC Statute, Arts. 8(2)(b)(xx), 121 and 123.
[249]   Some chemical weapons would fall within the definition of Art. 8(2)(b)(xviii) and hence would be prohibited under the ICC Statute.
[250]   *Legality of the Threat or Use of Nuclear Weapons*, Advisory Opinion (n. 43), held that the use of nuclear weapons would be illegal if they were used in contravention of specific rules, such as the principle of proportionality. The ICJ indicated that, in most conceivable circumstances, the use of nuclear weapons would contravene a rule of IHL (para. 95), but it did not rule out the possibility of a legal use (para. 97).

In 2017, amendments to the Rome Statute added microbial or biological agents, blinding laser weapons, and weapons that injure with fragments undetectable by X-ray.[251] Each of these prohibitions is widely accepted as customary law.[252]

Other weapons are frequently mentioned as candidates for a comprehensive prohibition. Anti-personnel mines (APMs) cannot distinguish between combatants and civilians, and remain long after the conflict has ended, causing a great toll of suffering for civilians. APMs are the subject of a widely ratified Convention,[253] and therefore the use of such weapons may be on its way to becoming a war crime under customary law. Before concluding that the use of APMs is a war crime under customary law, one would have to consider the large number of states that have not accepted the norm, and the contrary state practice among major military powers. Similarly, cluster bombs[254] are also becoming prohibited by many states. A convention banning cluster munitions entered into force in 2010 and has been adopted by well over 100 countries.[255] That trend is promising, but it would be early to assert that there is a general customary law prohibition on their use.

12.3.7 Prohibited Methods of Warfare

In addition to the prohibition on certain *means* of warfare (weapons), war crimes law also prohibits certain *methods* of warfare. Such rules are based not only on notions of honour and humanity, but also on preventing deliberate abuse of the rules of IHL to obtain an advantage over the enemy, since this would rapidly undermine compliance with IHL.

It is a war crime to kill or wound a combatant who has surrendered or is otherwise *hors de combat* ('out of the fight'),[256] a prohibition which is drawn from the 1907 Hague Regulations and AP I.[257] Compliance with this norm not only shows respect for IHL and for the humanity of the surrendering combatant, but also helps to encourage surrender rather than fights to the death.

The war crime of 'declaring that no quarter will be given' refers to orders or announcements that no prisoners will be taken or that there will be no survivors.[258] Such orders violate the duty to spare persons who are *hors de combat* or who are civilians. It is a crime whether the declaration is made publicly or as a private order.[259]

---

[251] Resolution on amendments to Article 8 of the Rome Statute of the International Criminal Court, ICC-ASP/16/Res.4., 14 December 2017.

[252] 1972 Convention on the Prohibition of the Development, Production and Stockpiling of Bacteriological (Biological) and Toxin Weapons and on Their Destruction, 1015 UNTS 163; 1980 Protocol on Non-Detectable Fragments, 1342 UNTS 168; 1995 Protocol on Blinding Laser Weapons, 1380 UNTS 370.

[253] 1997 Ottawa Convention on the Prohibition of the Use, Stockpiling, Production and Transfer of Anti-Personnel Mines and on their Destruction, 2056 UNTS 241.

[254] Cluster bombs drop numerous bomblets and hence are valued by the military for attacking soft targets over a certain area (e.g. vehicles). However, because of their area effect, they can cause significant incidental damage. In addition, some bomblets fail to detonate on impact, remaining behind as a continuing hazard to civilians.

[255] Convention on Cluster Munitions, Dublin, 30 May 2008.

[256] ICC Statute, Art. 8(2)(b)(vi), as clarified in the ICC Elements of Crimes.

[257] 1907 Hague Regulations, Art. 23(c); AP I, Arts. 41 and 42.

[258] ICC Statute, Art. 8(2)(b)(xii) and (e)(x); 1907 Hague Regulations, Art. 23(d); see also AP I, Art. 40.

[259] ICC Elements of Crimes, Art. 8(2)(b)(xii); AP I, Art. 40.

The war crime of 'killing or wounding treacherously a combatant adversary' is drawn from the 1907 Hague Regulations.[260] This antiquated language raises the question: what is killing '*treacherously*' during combat, when enemy forces are making all efforts to deceive and kill each other? The answer is found in the concept of 'perfidy', that is to say, 'inviting the confidence of an adversary to lead him to believe that he is entitled to, or obliged to accord protection' under the rules of IHL, with intent to betray that confidence.[261] Thus, it is not deception per se that makes an act perfidious. Deception and ruses are a sound aspect of military strategy and tactics. Ruses, such as the use of camouflage, decoys, mock operations, and misinformation, mislead the adversary but do not invite the confidence of the adversary with respect to the protection of IHL.[262]

Perfidy, however, involves a false promise to bestow protection, or an invitation to accord protection with an intent to betray that confidence. Examples of perfidy include feigning an intent to negotiate under a flag of truce, feigning an intent to surrender, feigning incapacitation by wounds or sickness, feigning civilian or non-combatant status, and feigning protected status by use of signs or emblems of the United Nations or of the Geneva Conventions.[263] Thus, to pretend to surrender in order to attack the enemy off-guard is a war crime, as is promising to take persons prisoner in order to massacre them once they relinquish their weapons. Perfidy not only breaches a code of honour, it also undermines compliance with IHL, since adversaries learn that compliance with IHL will be used against them, undermining efforts to reduce suffering in war.

The war crime of 'making improper use of a flag of truce, of the flag or of the military insignia and uniform of the enemy or of the United Nations, as well as of the distinctive emblems of the Geneva Conventions, resulting in death or serious personal injury' also concerns perfidy.[264] For example, the laws of war require combatants not to attack or disrupt those working under the emblem of the ICRC, so that they can, *inter alia*, help to deliver relief supplies and check on detainees.[265] The protective force of these symbols would be greatly eroded if combatants were to use those symbols to conceal military operations, leading the adversary to distrust such symbols or to respect them at their own peril. For permissible and impermissible uses of such symbols, flags, emblems, and uniforms, one must refer to relevant IHL rules.[266]

Finally, it is a war crime to use 'human shields', that is to say, to utilize 'the presence of a civilian or other protected person to render certain points, areas, or military forces immune from military operations'.[267] The use of human shields is prohibited in the Geneva Conventions, but is not expressly recognized as a 'grave breach' (a crime);

---

[260] ICC Statute, Art. 8(2)(b)(xi) and (e)(ix); 1907 Hague Regulations, Art. 23(b); see also AP I, Art. 37.
[261] ICC Elements of Crimes, Art. 8(2)(b)(xi), Elements 1 and 2; AP I, Art. 37. [262] AP I, Art. 37(2).
[263] 1907 Hague Regulations, Arts. 23(c), (f), 24, 33, 34, 35, 40 and 41; AP I, Arts. 37, 38, 39 and 85(3)(f).
[264] ICC Statute, Art. 8(2)(b)(vii); 1907 Hague Regulations, Art. 23(f), adding also UN insignia in accordance with AP I, Arts. 37 and 38.
[265] See e.g. ICC Statute, Art. 8(2)(b)(iii) and (xxiv).
[266] See e.g. AP I, Art. 39(2): enemy uniforms may not be worn while engaged in attack, but might be used in other circumstances, such as espionage.
[267] ICC Statute, Art. 8(2)(b)(xxiii), drawing from Geneva Convention III, Art. 23(1), Geneva Convention IV, Art. 28 and AP I, Arts. 51(7) and 58.

nonetheless delegates drafting the ICC Statute agreed that it was a serious violation established in customary law. It has been recognized as a war crime in ad hoc Tribunal jurisprudence.[268] The use of human shields abuses the adversary's respect for IHL to frustrate attacks on legitimate targets. The prohibition covers both bringing civilians to the military targets and bringing military targets to civilians.[269] The fact that an adversary is illegally using human shields does not relieve the attacking force from the duty not to launch attacks causing excessive incidental harm.[270]

The ICC Statute recognizes each of the above crimes in international armed conflict, whereas in non-international armed conflict it only recognizes treacherous killing and declaring no quarter.

12.3.8 War Crime Provisions Protecting Other Values

Finally, there are two war crimes provisions that do not originate in classic concerns of reciprocal protection of persons and property affiliated with the 'other side', and may be characterized as protecting interests and values other than those listed above.

Transfer of Population into Occupied Territory

It is a war crime for an occupying power to transfer parts of its own civilian population into the territory it occupies.[271] This provision protects a value distinct from the other 'transfer' crimes, because it is not aimed at protecting enemy civilians who have fallen under a party's power; it refers to transfer of a party's own nationals, and does not require that the transfer be forcible. The purpose of this provision is to ensure respect for the temporary nature of occupation, and to prevent an occupying power from changing the demographic composition of a territory in order to make the occupation permanent.

The inclusion of this provision was controversial during the Rome Conference, with Israel voicing strong opposition.[272] However, the majority of delegations at the conference agreed to its inclusion because the *legal* basis for the provision was well established: the provision was based on Article 85(4)(a) of AP I, which in turn was based on Article 49 of Geneva Convention IV.[273]

---

[268] See e.g. *Blaškić*, ICTY TC I, 3 March 2000, paras. 742–3. [269] AP I, Art. 51(7). [270] *Ibid.* Art. 51(8).

[271] ICC Statute, Art. 8(2)(b)(viii); AP I, Art. 85(4)(a); Geneva Convention IV, Art. 49. The second variation of this war crime, transferring 'all or parts of the population of the occupied territory within or outside this territory', is more akin to the other transfer-related war crimes, since it protects the original population, although this provision is also intended to prevent ethnic cleansing.

[272] Statement by the Head of the Delegation of Israel, Judge Eli Nathan, 17 July 1998, United Nations Diplomatic Conference of Plenipotentiaries on the Establishment of an International Criminal Court Rome, 15 June–17 July 1998, Official Records, vol. II, 122.

[273] The insertion of the words 'directly or indirectly' in the ICC Statute was controversial, with some arguing it was inherent in the definition and others arguing that it expanded the definition. This controversy was put to rest when a footnote was added to the ICC Elements of Crimes, clarifying that the term 'transfer' is to be interpreted in accordance with existing IHL, enabling the ICC Elements of Crimes to be adopted by consensus. ICC Elements of Crimes, note 44; Herman von Hebel, 'War Crimes' in Lee, *Elements and Rules*, 158–62. See also Michael Cottier and Elisabeth Baumgartner, 'Article 8' in Ambos, *Commentary*, 455–70.

Child Soldiers

War crimes law prohibits the use of child soldiers, namely, 'conscripting or enlisting children under the age of fifteen years into armed forces or groups or using them to participate actively in hostilities'.[274]

The proliferation of inexpensive and light weapons, which can be carried and wielded by children, has led to an increase in the use of child soldiers, who are seen as cheap, malleable, and expendable. It is estimated that over 300,000 children are being used as child soldiers in the world today.[275] Child soldiers are often used for the most dangerous missions and for tasks such as detecting land mines.[276] They are frequently subjected to extreme abuse, sexual assault, and sexual slavery. The use of child soldiers has been addressed in cases of the SCSL and was the subject of the *Lubanga* case, the first trial before the ICC.

This provision is not aimed solely at protecting enemy civilians who have fallen under an adverse party's power; its primary purpose is to protect all children.[277]

The recognition of this crime was initially controversial during the negotiations of the ICC Statute, because it had not previously been recognized expressly as a criminalized prohibition. However, agreement was reached to include it in the ICC Statute because it was a well-established prohibition protecting important values (appearing in Article 77(2) of AP I, Article 4(3)(c) of AP II, and Article 38(3) of the Convention on the Rights of the Child) and it was a serious violation warranting criminalization. The crime was also recognized in Article 4(c) of the SCSL Statute. In a split decision, the SCSL held that the provision was already customary international law prior to the adoption of the ICC Statute in 1998; that is to say, that the ICC Statute codified an existing customary norm rather than forming a new one.[278]

In 2000, an Optional Protocol to the Convention on the Rights of the Child was adopted, raising the minimum ages for conscription and for participation in hostilities to eighteen.[279] However, the *criminal* prohibition continues to deal with those who use child soldiers under fifteen years of age, since the new limits are treaty law and have not developed into customary law, let alone customary international criminal law.

The ICC Statute provision recognizes three distinct offences: conscripting, enlisting, and using children to participate actively in hostilities. The term 'conscripting' refers to forcible

---

[274] ICC Statute, Art. 8(2)(e)(vii) and (b)(xxvi); SCSL Statute, Art. 4(c). Article 8(2)(b)(xxvi) contains an additional restriction, so that it applies only to recruitment into 'national' armed forces, which may appear to exclude armed groups. Such a restriction is not found in any other instruments and seems rather inconsonant with general principles of humanitarian law, and there is therefore reason to doubt its applicability for other jurisdictions: ICC Statute, Art. 10.

[275] Anaise Muzima, 'Reimagining the Scope of Children's Legal Protection During Armed Conflicts under International Humanitarian Law and International Criminal Law' (2018) 8 *Western Journal of Legal Studies* 19.

[276] P. W. Singer, *Children at War* (New York, 2005); *Annual Report of the Special Representative of the Secretary-General for Children and Armed Conflict*, UN Doc. A/HRC/37/47 (8 January 2018); *Children and Armed Conflict, Report of the Secretary-General*, UN Doc. A/72/361–S/2017/821 (24 August 2017); Coalition to Stop the Use of Child Soldiers, *Child Soldiers International Annual Report 2016–17*, www.child-soldiers.org/news/annual-report-2016–17.

[277] The prohibition on the use of child soldiers is a norm of both IHL and human rights law: AP II, Art. 4(3)(c); and Convention on the Rights of the Child 1989, Art. 38(3).

[278] *Norman*, SCSL AC, 31 May 2004. See also the Dissent of Judge Robertson.

[279] Optional Protocol to the Convention on the Rights of the Child on the Involvement of Children in Armed Conflict, adopted and opened for signature, ratification and accession by GA Res. A/RES/54/263, 25 May 2000. The age for voluntary recruitment may be set at any age above fifteen, but specified conditions are to be followed.

recruitment, whereas 'enlisting' encompasses 'voluntary' recruitment,[280] to the extent that decisions of children under fifteen, usually living in circumstances of poverty, hardship, and armed conflict, may be described as 'voluntary'. 'Enlisting' includes 'any conduct accepting the child as part of the militia'.[281]

The term 'using children to participate actively in hostilities' obviously includes participation in combat. It also includes more indirect contributions to hostilities, and is somewhat broader than the IHL term of art, 'direct participation in hostilities', which is used to determine when a person loses civilian immunity and can be lawfully targeted.[282] The ICC Appeals Chamber in the *Lubanga* judgment of the ICC noted that the prohibition on active participation includes scouting, spying, sabotage, carrying supplies to the frontline, and the use of children as decoys, couriers, or at military checkpoints.[283] The SCSL prohibits a similar list of activities.[284]

The ICC Elements of Crimes apply a modified mental element for this crime, namely, that the perpetrator 'knew or should have known' that the persons were under the age of fifteen years. The modified standard was adopted in SCSL jurisprudence as well.[285] The first judicial treatment by the ICC interpreted the provision, plausibly, as covering situations where the perpetrator failed to know the age because of a failure to exercise due diligence in the circumstances.[286] Some commentators have expressed concern that 'should have known' is an inappropriate standard in criminal law.[287] However, criminal law routinely imposes duties on individuals, and a failure to carry out the duty can satisfy the requisite elements, including mental elements.[288] In crimes designed to protect children, it is not uncommon to impose a duty to take reasonable steps to ascertain age.[289] It is entirely plausible that parties to a conflict have a positive duty to verify the age of children before recruiting them or using them in hostilities.[290]

Further Reading

Dapo Akande, 'Classification of Armed Conflicts: Relevant Legal Concepts' in Elizabeth Wilmshurst (ed.), *International Law and the Classification of Conflict* (Oxford, 2012) 32

---

[280] *Lubanga*, ICC PTC I, 29 January 2007 (ICC-01/04–01/06–803) paras. 246–7; *Fofana and Kondewa*, SCSL AC, 28 May 2008, para. 140; *Taylor*, SCSL TC, 18 May 2012, paras. 442–3; *Lubanga*, ICC TC I, 14 March 2012 (ICC-01/04–01/06–2842) paras. 607–18.

[281] *Fofana and Kondewa*, SCSL AC, 28 May 2008, para. 144.

[282] *Lubanga*, ICC TC I, 14 March 2012 (ICC-01/04–01/06–2842) para. 627.

[283] *Lubanga*, ICC AC, 1 December 2014, para. 334.

[284] *Taylor*, SCSL TC, 18 May 2012, para. 444; *Brima, Kamara and Kanu*, SCSL TC, 20 June 2007, para. 737.

[285] See e.g. *Taylor*, SCSL TC, 18 May 2012, para. 439. [286] *Ibid.* para. 358.

[287] Bothe, 'War Crimes' (n. 22) 117–18. Some commentators also query whether the Elements can provide for a modified mental element. Article 30 provides a default mental element 'unless otherwise provided'. The question is whether the Elements can so 'provide'. The view endorsed in *Lubanga* (para. 359), and by the Assembly of States Parties (Elements of Crimes, 'General Introduction', para. 2), is that the Elements can 'provide otherwise'; see also Donald Piragoff and Darryl Robinson, 'Article 30' in Ambos, *Commentary*, 1332; Roger Clark, 'The Mental Element in International Criminal Law: The Rome Statute of the International Criminal Court and the Elements of Offences' (2001) 12 *Criminal Law Forum* 291.

[288] See e.g. the principle of command responsibility, which also imposes duties of inquiry and hence a 'should have known' standard: ICC Statute, Art. 28.

[289] As an example, see Canada's Criminal Code, RSC 1985, C-46, s. 150(4), (5) and (6), providing, in the context of sexual assault, that it is no defence that the accused believed that a person was over sixteen unless the accused 'took all reasonable steps to ascertain the age' of the person.

[290] C. H. B. Garraway, 'War Crimes' in Lee, *Elements and Rules*, 207.

Kelly Askin, *War Crimes Against Women: Prosecution in International Tribunals* (Brill, 1997)

Michael Bothe, 'War Crimes' in Cassese et al., *Commentary*, 379–426

Michael Cottier et al., 'Article 8' in Ambos, *Commentary*, 317–685

Knut Dörmann, *Elements of War Crimes under the Rome Statute of the International Criminal Court* (Cambridge, 2003)

Knut Dörmann et al., 'War Crimes' in Lee, *Elements and Rules*, 109–218

Dieter Fleck (ed.), *Handbook of International Humanitarian Law*, 4th ed. (Oxford, 2021)

Leslie Green, *The Contemporary Law of Armed Conflict*, 3rd ed. (Manchester University Press, 2008)

Jean-Marie Henckaerts and Louise Doswald-Beck, *Customary International Humanitarian Law* (Cambridge, 2000)

Howard M. Hense (ed.), *The Law of Armed Conflict: Constraints on the Contemporary Use of Military Force* (Aldershot, 2005)

Claus Kreß, 'War Crimes Committed in Non-International Armed Conflict and the Emerging System of International Criminal Justice' (2001) 30 *Israel Yearbook on Human Rights* 1

Eve La Haye, *War Crimes in Internal Armed Conflicts* (Cambridge, 2008)

Theodor Meron, 'The Humanization of Humanitarian Law' (2000) 94 *AJIL* 239

Lindsay Moir, *The Law of Internal Armed Conflict* (Cambridge, 2002)

Adam Roberts and Richard Guelff, *Documents of the Laws of War*, 3rd ed. (Oxford, 2000)

Anthony Rogers, *Law on the Battlefield*, 3rd ed. (Manchester University Press, 2012)

Marco Sassoli, Antoine A. Bouvier, and Anne Quintin, *How Does Law Protect in War?*, 3rd ed. (ICRC, 2011), www.icrc.org/en/document/how-does-law-protect-war-0

Sandesh Sivakumaran, *The Law of Non-International Armed Conflict* (Oxford, 2012)

13

Aggression

13.1 INTRODUCTION AND HISTORY: CRIMINALIZING AGGRESSION

13.1.1 Overview

The crime of aggression, or 'crime against peace' as it was referred to in the charters of the Nuremberg and Tokyo International Military Tribunals (IMT), is committed by a leader or policy-maker of a state which participates in an act of aggression carried out by the state.[1] The prevention of acts of aggression is one of the primary purposes of the United Nations.

The crime of aggression differs from all other core international crimes in being inextricably linked to an act of aggression by a state against another state. The use of a country's troops against its own population does not come within the crime, nor do attacks on a state by a non-state group. Such operations might involve other crimes within the International Criminal Court's (ICC) jurisdiction, such as crimes against humanity and war crimes, but not the crime of aggression. This criminal prohibition can be said to protect state sovereignty by punishing attacks on states, but also to encroach on sovereignty by going behind the state to make individual leaders directly accountable under international law for planning, preparing, initiating, and executing such attacks.

13.1.2 Historical Development

Leaving aside historical curiosities,[2] the first international trial for the crime of aggression, under the name of 'crimes against peace', was before the Nuremberg IMT following the Second World War.[3] There was an attempt at a trial after the First World War: the 1919 Treaty of Versailles provided for the establishment of a special tribunal to try Kaiser Wilhelm II. The intention was to try him not for 'aggression', but for 'a supreme offence against international morality and the sanctity of treaties',[4] a provision that was explained as having 'not a juridical character as regards its substance, but only in its form. The ex-Emperor is arraigned as

---

[1] The most comprehensive work on the crime of aggression is Claus Kreβ and Stefan Barriga (eds.), *The Crime of Aggression* (Cambridge, 2017) vols. I and II.
[2] E.g. the trial of Conradin von Hohenstaufen in 1268 for what now would be termed waging aggressive war.
[3] See further Section 6.3. [4] 1919 Treaty of Versailles, Art. 227. See Section 6.2.

a matter of high international policy.'[5] The Kaiser, however, took refuge in the Netherlands and was never put on trial.

During the Second World War, the discussions in the United Nations War Crimes Commission and elsewhere, which preceded the drafting of the London Charter setting up the Nuremberg IMT, showed that it was by no means a widely held view that a crime of aggression existed under international law at that time.[6] Nevertheless, agreement was reached on Article 6(a) of the IMT Charter, which defined 'crimes against peace' as the 'planning, preparation, initiation, or waging of a war of aggression, or a war in violation of international treaties, agreements, or assurances, or participation in a common plan or conspiracy for the accomplishment of any of the foregoing'. The equivalent provisions in the Charter of the Tokyo IMT and in Control Council Law No. 10 were very similar.[7]

The Nuremberg IMT had to deal with the objection of the accused that, in its reference to crimes against peace, the Charter created new law and that the Tribunal was applying law *ex post facto*. The Tribunal dismissed this claim by ruling that, ever since the 1928 Kellogg–Briand Pact,[8] the planning and waging of aggressive war as such had been a crime under international law:

In the opinion of the Tribunal, the solemn renunciation of war as an instrument of national policy necessarily involves the proposition that such a war is illegal in international law; and that those who plan and wage such a war, with its inevitable and terrible consequences, are committing a crime in so doing.[9]

This reasoning was followed in the judgment of the Tokyo Tribunal, although Judges Röling, Bernard, and Pal in their dissenting judgments disagreed with it.[10] Indeed, the Kellogg–Briand Pact had not been intended to give rise to individual criminal responsibility.[11]

Whatever the merits of the decisions by the two Tribunals as to the status of the crime after the Second World War, it is widely accepted that there is now a crime of aggression under customary international law.[12] The customary law crime remains as expressed in the

---

[5] *Reply of the Allied and Associated Powers to the Observations of the German Delegation and the Conditions of Peace* (HMSO Misc. No. 4, 1919).

[6] See Ian Brownlie, *International Law and the Use of Force by States* (Oxford, 1963) 159–66.

[7] The Charter of the Tokyo IMT defined crimes against peace as 'the planning, preparation, initiation, or waging of a declared or undeclared war of aggression, or a war in violation of international law, treaties, agreements or assurances'; Control Council Law No. 10, Art. II(a), began: 'Initiation of invasions of other countries and wars of aggression in violation of international laws and treaties, including but not limited to planning . . . ' (as in the London Charter).

[8] General Treaty for the Renunciation of War, 27 August 1928.

[9] Nuremberg IMT, Judgment and Sentences, reprinted in (1947) 41 *AJIL* 172, 218.

[10] Tokyo IMT, reprinted in Neil Boister and Robert Cryer (eds.), *Documents on the Tokyo International Military Tribunal* (Oxford, 2008) 48, 437–9. Judge Röling did, however, agree that the occupiers were entitled to prosecute for the initiation of wars on the basis that the perpetrators threatened their security. See Section 6.4.2.

[11] See further Section 6.3.2. For an overview of the critical responses on this ground immediately following the judgment, see Thomas Weigend, '"In General a Principle of Justice": The Debate on the "Crime against Peace" in the Wake of the Nuremberg Judgement' (2012) 10 *JICJ* 41.

[12] See Brownlie, *International Law and the Use of Force* (n. 6) 185–94; Yoram Dinstein, *War, Aggression and Self-Defence*, 6th ed. (Cambridge, 2018). That was not, however, the universal view in 1950 when the Nuremberg principles were discussed in the Sixth Committee of the GA (GAOR 5th Session, 6th Committee, 231st meeting); and see Christian Tomuschat, 'Crimes Against the Peace and Security of Mankind and the Recalcitrant Third State' (1995) 24 *Israel Yearbook on Human Rights* 41, 53.

law and jurisprudence of the Nuremberg IMT, supplemented by the subsequent proceedings under Control Council Law No. 10 and by the Tokyo IMT.

Following the judgment of the Nuremberg Tribunal, the recently formed United Nations was quick to endorse the law as laid down in the judgment. The General Assembly affirmed 'the principles of international law' recognized by the London Charter and the Nuremberg judgment, and in 1947 directed the new International Law Commission (ILC) to formulate those principles and to prepare a code of offences against the 'peace and security of mankind'.[13] Thereafter, progress stalled. The ILC's draft principles, which described the crime of aggression in the same way as the London Charter, were neither accepted nor rejected by the General Assembly.[14] In 1950, the ILC was requested to elaborate a definition of aggression[15] but did not succeed in reaching agreement, the Special Rapporteur indeed deciding that aggression 'by its very essence, is not susceptible of definition'.[16] Although the ILC included a provision on aggression in its 1954 Draft Code of Offences against the Peace and Security of Mankind, the General Assembly decided that the Code raised problems 'closely related to that of the definition of aggression' and postponed further consideration until the special committee, established by the General Assembly in 1952 to consider the definition of aggression, had reported.[17]

After protracted intergovernmental negotiations, a 'definition of aggression' was finally adopted in 1974 by General Assembly Resolution 3314[18] and recommended to the Security Council for guidance. Resolution 3314 began with a broad definition of state acts of aggression and then listed specific examples.[19] It is clear that the Resolution does not, as such, provide a customary law definition for the individual crime of aggression. Article 5.2 provides:

A war of aggression is a crime against international peace. Aggression gives rise to international responsibility.

This distinguishes *wars* of aggression, participation in which engages individual criminal responsibility, from *acts* of aggression, engaging the responsibility of states.[20] After a revival of its earlier mandate,[21] the ILC adopted a draft Code of Crimes Against the

---

[13] Res. 95(1) of 11 December 1946 and Res. 177(11) of 21 November 1947. [14] See Res. 488(V) of 12 December 1950.

[15] ILC Res. 378B(V), 17 November 1950. See further Ahmed Rifaat, *International Aggression* (Stockholm, 1979).

[16] UN Doc. A/CN.4/44, 69.

[17] GA Res. 897(IX), 4 December 1954. The definition of aggression in the draft code read, in part: 'Any act of aggression, including the employment by the authorities of a State of armed force against another State for any purpose other than national or collective self-defence or in pursuance of a decision or recommendation of a competent organ of the United Nations'; threats were also included.

[18] GA Res. 3314(XXIX), 14 December 1974. The definition is contained in the annex to the Resolution. See Thomias Bruha, 'The General Assembly's Definition of Aggression' in Claus Kreβ and Stefan Barriga (eds.), *The Crime of Aggression* (Cambridge, 2017) 142, 147–65.

[19] See Section 13.2.3.

[20] For the negotiating history on this point, see Bengt Broms, 'The Definition of Aggression' (1977) 154 *Hague Recueil* 299; Benjamin Ferencz, *Defining International Aggression* (New York, 1975) vol. II, 45. The Friendly Relations Declaration contains a similar provision: 'A war of aggression constitutes a crime against the peace, for which there is responsibility under international law'. Declaration on Principles of International Law concerning Friendly Relations and Cooperation Among States in accordance with the Charter of the United Nations (Resolution 2625(XXV) of 24 October 1970), Annex, para. I.

[21] GA Res. 36/106, 10 December 1981, by which the ILC was invited to resume its work on the draft Code of Offences Against the Peace and Security of Mankind.

Peace and Security of Mankind in 1996, which included the crime of aggression but without a definition.[22] The ILC stated in its commentary that individual responsibility for the crime was incurred only if the conduct of the state was 'a sufficiently serious violation of the prohibition' in Article 2(4) of the UN Charter.[23] The Code was not adopted by governments, their attention being absorbed by the negotiations on the crimes within the jurisdiction of the ICC.

International Criminal Court Negotiations

The international negotiations to establish the ICC began on the basis of the draft Statute proposed by the ILC in 1994.[24] This included an undefined crime of aggression, on condition that no complaint of an act of aggression could be brought before the court unless the Security Council had first determined that a state had committed that act.[25] The provision was controversial and, during the negotiations for the establishment of the ICC, opinion was divided on three issues: whether the crime of aggression should be included in the Statute at all; how it should be defined; and how and whether a role for the Security Council should be reflected in the Statute.[26]

Different proposals incorporating the crime of aggression were transmitted to the Rome Conference,[27] but there was again failure to reach agreement on the definition and on the role for the Security Council.[28] The final compromise was reflected in Article 5(1) and (2) of the ICC Statute. Article 5(1)(d) includes the crime of aggression in the jurisdiction of the court, but (the now abolished) Article 5(2) provided that:

The Court shall exercise jurisdiction over the crime of aggression once a provision is adopted in accordance with Articles 121 and 123 defining the crime and setting out the conditions under which the Court shall exercise jurisdiction with respect to this crime. Such a provision shall be consistent with the relevant provisions of the Charter of the United Nations.

Accordingly, the ICC was not able to try any case of aggression until the states parties to the Statute reached agreement on this further provision.

Following subsequent lengthy negotiations,[29] the Review Conference of the ICC Statute, held in Kampala in 2010, adopted by consensus amendments to the Statute which delete

[22] (1996) II(2) *Yearbook of the International Law Commission* 42. See James Crawford, 'The Work of the International Law Commission on Aggression' in Claus Kreß and Stefan Barriga (eds.), *The Crime of Aggression* (Cambridge, 2017) 233.

[23] *Yearbook of the ILC* (n. 22) 42.   [24] See Section 8.2.

[25] See Draft Statute for an International Criminal Court (1994) II(2) *Yearbook of the International Law Commission* 26, at 43, Art. 23(2).

[26] For the early discussions, see *Report of the Ad Hoc Committee on the Establishment of an International Criminal Court*, GAOR 50th Session, Supp. No. 22 (A/50/22), paras. 63–71; *Report of the Preparatory Committee on the Establishment of an International Criminal Court*, vol. I, GAOR 51st Session, Supp. No. 22 (A/51/22).

[27] The proposals can be found in the *Report of the Preparatory Committee on the Establishment of an International Criminal Court*, UN Doc. A/ CONF.183/2, included in the official records of the conference (UN Doc. A/CONF.183/13 (vol. III)) at 14–15.

[28] For a brief description of the negotiations at Rome, see Herman von Hebel and Darryl Robinson, '*Crimes Within the Jurisdiction of the Court*' in Lee, *The International Criminal Court: The Making of the Rome Statute* (Boston, 1999) 79, 81–5.

[29] For a summary of the negotiations in the Preparatory Commission, see Silvia Fernandez de Gurmendi, 'The Working Group on Aggression at the Preparatory Commission for the International Criminal Court' (2002) 25 *Fordham International Law Journal* 589. See also Roger Clark, 'Rethinking Aggression as a Crime and Formulating its Elements: The Final Work-Product of the Preparatory Commission for the International Criminal Court' (2002) 15 *LJIL* 859; Stefan Barriga and Claus Kreß (eds.), *The Travaux Préparatoires of the Crime of Aggression* (Cambridge, 2011). For details of the negotiations in Kampala, see

Article 5(2) from the Statute and set out a definition of the crime of aggression (in the new Article 8*bis*) and arrangements for the Court to exercise jurisdiction over it (in the new Articles 15*bis* and 15*ter*); new Elements for the crime were also adopted.[30] The Kampala amendments were accompanied by seven interpretative 'understandings'.[31] These provided that the Court was not able to exercise its jurisdiction over the crime of aggression until a further decision allowing it to do so was taken by the Assembly of States Parties. Such a decision was not permitted to take place until after 1 January 2017.

Although the draft definition of aggression put before the Review Conference had been negotiated beforehand, the proceedings in Kampala were complex and difficult. The resulting amendments, the means of bringing them into force, and the 'understandings' all provide material for an unusually high degree of disagreement and differences of interpretation.[32] The decision to activate the jurisdiction of the Court over the crime of aggression was taken by the Assembly of States Party to the Rome Statute in December 2017.[33]

13.1.3 Definition in the ICC Statute

The crime of aggression is defined in Article 8*bis* of the Statute as:

the planning, preparation, initiation or execution, by a person in a position effectively to exercise control over or to direct the political or military action of a State, of an act of aggression which, by its character, gravity and scale, constitutes a manifest violation of the Charter of the United Nations.

In turn, 'act of aggression' is defined as:

the use of armed force by a State against the sovereignty, territorial integrity or political independence of another State, or in any other manner inconsistent with the Charter of the United Nations. Any of the following acts, regardless of a declaration of war, shall in accordance with the United Nations General Assembly Resolution 3314(XXIX) of 14 December 1974, qualify as an act of aggression: [the amendment then lists the acts set out in that Resolution].

The definition of aggression thus incorporates all three of the different approaches which had been discussed in the early part of the negotiations. One school of thought had favoured using as a definition the list of acts of aggression in General Assembly Resolution 3314. This met with arguments that the list was illustrative only, thus conflicting with the *nullum crimen* principle[34] if it was used to define the crime, and that the purpose of the Resolution was to assist the Security Council,[35] not to define the crime.

Claus Kreß and Leonie von Holtzendorff, 'The Kampala Compromise on the Crime of Aggression' (2010) 8 *JICJ* 1179, 1201–17; Barriga and Kreß, *The Crime of Aggression* (n. 1).

[30] Annex II to RC/Res.6. A new Art. 25(3*bis*) was also added to ensure that the provision in the Statute on superior responsibility applies only to those leaders who are included in the definition of aggression as perpetrators of the crime.

[31] On these understandings, see Kevin Jon Heller, 'The Uncertain Legal Status of the Aggression Understandings' (2012) 10 *JICJ* 229.

[32] See e.g. Astrid Reisinger Coracini and Pål Wrange, 'The Specificity of *the Crime of Aggression*' in Claus Kreß and Stefan Barriga (eds.), *The Crime of Aggression* (Cambridge, 2017) 307; Leena Grover, 'Interpreting the Crime of Aggression' in *ibid*. 373.

[33] As of September 2023, forty-five states have ratified/acceded to the amendments on the crime of aggression.

[34] See Section 1.5.1. [35] GA Res. 3314(XXIX), 14 December 1974, para. 4.

A second approach to the definition was to specify that participation in *any* unlawful use of force by a state under the UN Charter was criminal. Both of these approaches found their way into the definition. A third category of proposals started from the proposition that only participation in a 'war of aggression' was prohibited by customary international law. To deal with the fact that formally declared wars between states are now uncommon, suggestions were made to define an act of aggression as the unlawful use of force and to add an unlawful purpose such as military occupation or annexation or a 'threshold' of manifest illegality. The definition, as finally agreed, does not have a requirement of purpose but includes a threshold which needs to be crossed before the ICC can try the crime: the act of aggression must be one which 'by its character, gravity and scale, constitutes a manifest violation of the Charter of the United Nations'.

Discussion of the material and mental elements of the crime in Sections 13.2 and 13.3 is based on the definition adopted at Kampala ('the ICC definition') and the elements included in the Elements of Crime document. The case law of the post-Second World War tribunals is also considered, as they have been the only international tribunals to otherwise try the crime – so far.

13.1.4 Relationship to Other Crimes

Aggression provides an *occasion* for the commission of the other crimes. In the view of the Nuremberg Tribunal:

[t]o initiate a war of aggression . . . is not only an international crime; it is the supreme international crime differing only from other war crimes in that it contains within itself the accumulated evil of the whole.[36]

Aggression differs markedly from genocide, crimes against humanity, and war crimes in that, unlike those crimes, it concerns the *jus ad bellum* (the law governing recourse to armed conflict) and therefore raises questions of international law regarding state responsibility for aggressive acts.[37] To understand this crime, it is necessary to understand the rules of international law on these questions; they are discussed briefly in Section 13.2.2.

A further distinction from the other crimes is that, while genocide, crimes against humanity, and war crimes may be committed by members of the armed forces of a state or by those affiliated with a state, aggression can only be committed on behalf of a state and as part of a state plan or policy. Expansion of the crime to acts by non-state entities has not been widely supported.[38] Further, unlike other international crimes, aggression is now

---

[36] Nuremberg IMT, Judgment and Sentences, reprinted in (1947) 41 *AJIL* 172, 186.
[37] See further Claus Kreβ, 'The State Conduct Element of Aggression' in Claus Kreβ and Stefan Barriga (eds.), *The Crime of Aggression* (Cambridge, 2017) 412.
[38] But see Mark Drumbl, 'The Push to Criminalize Aggression: Something Lost Amid the Gains?' (2009) 41 *Case Western Reserve Journal of International Law* 291; David Scheffer, 'The Missing Pieces in Article 8*bis* (Aggression) of the Rome Statute' (2017) 58 *Harvard International Law Journal* 183. The 2006 Protocol on Non-Aggression and Mutual Defence in the Great Lakes Region [of Africa] defines aggression as including acts by non-state actors and requires states to criminalize acts of aggression as so defined.

considered a leadership crime and is only committed by persons in policy-making positions in a state.[39]

13.2 MATERIAL ELEMENTS

The collective act of aggression by a state is the point of reference for the act of the individual perpetrator. Under the ICC definition, the crime is committed (1) by a perpetrator in a leadership position in a state (2) who has participated (3) in an act of aggression by the state (4) which 'by its character, gravity and scale, constitutes a manifest violation of the Charter of the United Nations'. Each of these aspects is described in the following subsections.[40]

13.2.1 Perpetrators

The crime of aggression is a 'leadership crime': it can only be committed by leaders and high-level policy-makers.[41] Thus, the ICC definition and Elements require that a person be 'in a position effectively to exercise control over or to direct the political or military action' of the state which committed the act of aggression. While the reference in the London Charter to the 'waging' of a war of aggression seems to imply that all persons carrying out the state's acts of aggression are individually responsible, from the general down to the foot soldier, that is not how the Charter was interpreted in practice.[42]

The point may be illustrated by *Von Leeb and others* (the 'High Command case'), tried before an American Military Tribunal constituted under Control Council Law No. 10.[43] The fourteen accused were all in positions of high military authority: thirteen generals and one admiral. But they were acquitted of the charge of crimes against peace on the ground that 'the criminality which attaches to the waging of an aggressive war should be confined to those who participate in it at the policy level'.[44] In spite of their senior military positions, the defendants were not at the required policy level and they were not held responsible for implementing the aggressive plans. Accordingly, in countries where military personnel are largely kept out of political decisions on the initiation of force, it is more likely that political superiors would be held responsible for the crime of aggression.

The exact threshold of criminal responsibility is not clear and there was not complete consistency in the findings of the Nuremberg IMT and in the subsequent proceedings.[45] But somewhere 'between the Dictator and Supreme Commander of the military forces of

---

[39] See Section 13.2.1.

[40] And see more generally Carrie McDougall, *The Crime of Aggression under the Rome Statute of the International Criminal Court*, 2nd ed. (Cambridge, 2021) ; Kreß and Barriga, *The Crime of Aggression* (n. 1) chs. 11, 13–15.

[41] Reisinger Coracini and Wrange, 'Specificity' (n. 32) 309–12.

[42] See G. Brand, 'The War Crimes Trials and the Laws of War' (1949) 26 *British Yearbook of International Law* 414, 419. For a useful compilation of relevant sections of the post-Second World War case law, see UN Secretariat, *Historical Review of Developments Relating to Aggression*, PCNICC/2002/WGCA/L.1 (2002).

[43] XII LRTWC 1 (1948).

[44] *Ibid*. 67. One defendant committed suicide and no judgment was given. Eleven of the accused were convicted of war crimes and crimes against humanity.

[45] Brownlie, *International Law and the Use of Force* (n. 6) 205.

the nation and the common soldier is the boundary between the criminal and the excus-able participation in the waging of an aggressive war by an individual engaged in it'.[46]

The relevant levels of policy-making in the post-Second World War tribunals were not necessarily confined to the members of government or the military. Some of the accused in the proceedings subsequent to Nuremberg were industrialists, not part of the government but closely associated with it. In *Krauch and others* (the 'IG Farben case'),[47] the accused were acquitted on the ground that, like Albert Speer, one of the Nuremberg IMT defendants, their efforts 'were in aid of the war effort in the same way that other productive enterprises aid in the waging of war'.[48] Their responsibility was below that of planning and leading. The ICC definition, however, appears to retreat from some earlier case law, in that it excludes persons who are not political leaders but nonetheless have power to shape and influence policy.[49]

The crime of aggression constitutes participation in a collective act by a state against another state. Neither the ICC definition nor customary law extends the crime to acts committed by individual mercenaries not sponsored by a state, nor to other non-state actors, even though the devastation caused by such acts may be comparable to inter-state military action.[50]

13.2.2 Planning, Preparation, Initiation, or Execution

The nexus between the state's act of aggression and the act of the individual leader or other high-level policy-maker is described in the ICC definition as 'planning, preparation, initiation or execution', closely following Article 6 of the Nuremberg IMT Charter which referred to the 'planning, preparation, initiation or waging' of an aggressive war. The Charter also included 'participation in a common plan or conspiracy', but conspiracy is not included in the ICC definition. Still, as interpreted by the Nuremberg IMT, conspiracy differed little from planning and preparation[51] and the charge of conspiracy was in effect superfluous.[52] It is difficult to distinguish planning from preparation in the jurisprudence. Preparation had to be closely linked with planning; preparation for some vague future programme of aggression was not sufficient.[53]

Participation in threats to use military force does not come within the crime of aggres-sion. The collective act must have been completed in order to find criminal responsibility.

---

[46] XII LRTWC 67 (1948). [47] X LRTWC 1 (1948); see also *Krupp and others*, X LRTWC 69 (1948).

[48] Nuremberg IMT, Judgment and Sentences, reprinted in (1947) 41 *AJIL* 172 321.

[49] See Kevin Heller, 'Retreat from Nuremberg: The Leadership Requirement in the Crime of Aggression' (2007) 18 *EJIL* 477.

[50] For a contrary view, see Jeremy Pizzi, 'Profiteers of Misery: Aggression, the Leadership Clause, and Private Military and Security Companies' (2023) 21 *JICJ* 291; Nikola R. Hajdin, 'Responsibility of Private Individuals for Complicity in a War of Aggression' (2022) 116(4) *AJIL* 788. The African Union has, however, adopted an extensive definition of aggression which appears to include acts by non-state actors (African Union Non-Aggression and Common Defence Pact 2005).

[51] Quincy Wright, 'The Law of the Nuremberg Trial' (1947) 41 *AJIL* 38, 68.

[52] See Brownlie, *International Law and the Use of Force* (n. 6) 201. Charges of conspiracy were more important to the Tokyo IMT, which relied on the concept of inchoate conspiracy; its rulings have also been extensively criticized; see the comment and authorities cited in Neil Boister and Robert Cryer, *The Tokyo International Military Tribunal: A Reappraisal* (Oxford, 2008) ch. 8.

[53] Nuremberg IMT, Judgment and Sentences, reprinted in (1947) 41 *AJIL* 172, 222.

For the ICC, this is confirmed in Element 3.[54] The threat of aggression was not included in the Charters of the Nuremberg or Tokyo IMTs, nor in Control Council Law No. 10. The unopposed invasions of Austria and Czechoslovakia, following the successful threat of aggressive force, were treated as evidence of the aggressive conspiracy but were not charged as crimes against peace before the Nuremberg IMT. They were, however, charged in indictments under Control Council Law No. 10 (which included 'invasions' within the jurisdiction of the tribunals constituted under it).[55]

For the ICC, the question will arise as to the applicability of the modes of liability provisions in Article 25 of the Statute. For the crime of aggression, that Article has been amended only in respect of superior responsibility: the new Article 25(*3bis*) provides that the concept applies only to those leaders who are included in the definition of aggression as perpetrators of the crime. But there has been no amendment to the rest of the Article.[56] The Prosecutor will have to show that a policy-level accused planned, prepared, initiated, or executed an act of aggression that was in fact committed, *and* that the accused fulfilled the elements of a mode of liability under Article 25.

As for defences to the crime, the provisions of the ICC Statute for other crimes (in Article 31) will also apply to individuals charged with aggression. In addition, the defences under public international law relating to the state act of aggression will be available to the defendant in arguing that the state concerned did not commit an act of aggression. It would have been preferable had this been made clearer in the Kampala amendments but, as indicated below, it is a necessary inference from their wording.

13.2.3 Act of Aggression

The collective act in which the individual participates is the act of aggression of a state committed against another state. The ICC definition, in paragraph 1, describes this collective act as 'the use of armed force by a State against the sovereignty, territorial integrity or political independence of another State, or in any other manner inconsistent with the Charter of the United Nations'. This wording is similar (though not identical to Article 2(4) of the Charter, thus requiring reference to the rules of international law regarding the unlawful use of force by states. The effect of paragraph 1 is that any unlawful use of force by a state is defined as an 'act of aggression' for the purpose of the ICC definition.

Paragraph 2 gives examples. It lists the acts set out in General Assembly Resolution 3314 (XXIX) of 1974 and provides that any of these acts, 'in accordance with' that Resolution, qualify as an act of aggression for the purpose of the ICC definition. The list of acts includes

---

[54] Element 3 states: 'The act of aggression – the use of armed force by a State against the sovereignty, territorial integrity or political independence of another State, or in any other manner inconsistent with the Charter of the United Nations – was committed.'

[55] E.g. in the case of *United States* v. *Weizsäcker et al.* (the 'Ministries Trial'), the tribunal held: 'The fact that the aggressor was here able to so overawe the invaded countries does not detract in the slightest from the enormity of the aggression, in reality perpetrated. The invader here employed an act of war'. Judgment, 11–13 April 1949, *Trials of War Criminals Before the Nuremberg Military Tribunals* (United States Government Printing Office) vol. XIV, 330.

[56] See Roger S. Clark, 'Individual Conduct', and 'General Principles of Liability' in Claus Kreß and Stefan Barriga (eds.), *The Crime of Aggression* (Cambridge, 2017) 565 and 590, respectively.

invasion, bombardment, and annexation of another state's territory; attack on another state's armed forces; and sending armed groups which commit aggressive acts against another state. The definition indicates that this is a non-exhaustive list.[57]

The incorporation in the ICC definition of a major part of the 1974 General Assembly definition does not lead to an entirely comfortable result. The 1974 definition states that the Council may conclude that, in specific circumstances, a listed act does *not* constitute aggression.[58] Further, the description of each of the acts in the 1974 Resolution as an act of aggression appears to indicate that a listed use of force is aggression even though there may be a justifiable defence under public international law.[59]

These problems can mostly be resolved by sensible application of the provisions of the ICC definition. First, the reference to the list of acts qualifying as aggression 'in accordance with' the 1974 Resolution can be interpreted to mean that any relevant conditions and qualifications in the 1974 definition are incorporated. For example, Article 6 of the 1974 definition,[60] which can be regarded as preserving Charter provisions on the legality of certain acts, can be applied so as to import international law defences to allegations of aggressive acts. Second, it is not the state's act of aggression (whether in the 1974 list or not) which founds individual criminality, but only an act which 'constitutes a manifest violation' of the Charter.

Whether an act of aggression has been committed by a state, a necessary part of the crime of aggression will need to be determined under public international law – the *jus ad bellum*. This area of public international law is briefly explained in the next two subsections.

International Law Regarding the Use of Force by a State[61]

Article 2(4) of the Charter of the United Nations reads as follows:

All Members shall refrain in their international relations from the threat or use of force against the territorial integrity or political independence of any State, or in any other manner inconsistent with the purposes of the United Nations.

The Charter put in place a new structure for international peace and security, requiring the settlement of disputes by peaceful means and introducing a collective system for states to act through the United Nations to suppress aggression and other breaches of international peace. While the collective system has developed in a different direction from that envisaged by the drafters, the prohibition on the use of force remains as set out in Article 2(4). This is the fundamental legal principle governing the use of force and it reflects customary international law.[62]

---

[57] Kreß, 'The State Conduct' (n. 37) 435–51. [58] GA Res. 3314(XXIX), 14 December 197, Arts. 2 and 4.
[59] For other difficulties arising from the transposition of the resolution to the ICC definition, see Claus Kreß, 'The Crime of Aggression Before the First Review of the ICC Statute' (2007) 20 *LJIL* 851, 857.
[60] 'Nothing in this Definition shall be construed as in any way enlarging or diminishing the scope of the Charter, including its provisions concerning cases in which the use of force is lawful.'
[61] This is an extremely brief discussion of this area of public international law. For in-depth analysis, see Brownlie, *International Law and the Use of Force* (n. 6); Dinstein, *War, Aggression* (n. 12); Christine Gray, *International Law and the Use of Force*, 4th ed. (Oxford, 2018) chs. 2, 4, and 6; Christian Henderson, *The Use of Force and International Law* (Oxford, 2018).
[62] *Case concerning Military and Paramilitary Activities In and Against Nicaragua* (*Nicaragua* v. *USA*) [1986] ICJ Reports 14, paras. 188–90.

Although the provision is at the heart of the rules of international law on the use of force, its interpretation and application are not easy. In particular, there are differences of view as to the exceptions to the prohibition. The only exceptions universally accepted are, first, individual or collective self-defence, and, second, force authorized by the Security Council acting under Chapter VII of the Charter. There is controversy over whether there is also an exception for humanitarian intervention.

Self-Defence

The relevant provision of the Charter is Article 51, which provides:

Nothing in the present Charter shall impair the inherent right of individual or collective self-defence if an armed attack occurs against a Member of the United Nations, until the Security Council has taken measures necessary to maintain international peace and security.

The Charter does not elaborate on the conditions for a lawful use of force in self-defence, but international law mandates that self-defence is lawful only if it is *necessary* to use force, and only if that force is *proportionate*, that is, not excessive in relation to the need to avert or respond to the attack.[63] A classic formulation of the applicable rules is that of US Secretary of State Webster in the 1837 *Caroline* incident.[64] In an exchange of correspondence with the British, he stated that, for action to be lawful, there must be a 'necessity of self-defence, instant, overwhelming, leaving no choice of means, and no moment for deliberation' and that the action must not be 'unreasonable or excessive; since the act justified by the necessity of self-defence, must be limited by that necessity, and kept clearly within it'.

Commentators differ as to whether force may be used in anticipatory self-defence, that is to say, against an attack that is threatened and not ongoing. On one view, the right to self-defence applies only once an armed attack has begun.[65] The contrary view, that states have a right to act in order to avert the threat of an imminent attack, is supported not least by the practical argument that it is unrealistic in all cases to await an actual attack; this consideration applies particularly to threats from weapons of mass destruction.[66] The International Court of Justice (ICJ) has left open the issue of the lawfulness of a response to the threat of an imminent armed attack.[67] However, the claim to 'pre-emptive self-defence' to prevent the emergence of a security threat is widely rejected as impermissible under international law.[68] Further controversial questions about the right to self-defence

---

[63] The requirements of necessity and proportionality have been confirmed by the ICJ; see e.g. *Case concerning Armed Activities on the Territory of the Congo* (*Democratic Republic of the Congo* v. *Uganda*) [2005] ICJ Reports 168, para. 147.

[64] The incident concerned the destruction over the Niagara Falls of a steamer thought to be supplying Canadian rebels against the British. See Robert Jennings, 'The Caroline and Macleod Cases' (1938) 32 *AJIL* 86.

[65] See Brownlie, *International Law and the Use of Force* (n. 6) 275–8; Dinstein, *War, Aggression* (n. 12) 201–5 (but giving a wide interpretation of what constitutes the start of the attack justifying self-defence).

[66] See e.g. Derek Bowett, *Self-Defence in International Law* (Manchester, 1958) 184–93; Bruno Simma et al. (eds.), *The Charter of the United Nations: A Commentary*, 3rd ed. (Oxford, 2013) 1423, 1424.

[67] *Case concerning Military and Paramilitary Activities In and Against Nicaragua* (*Nicaragua* v. *USA*) [1986 ICJ Reports 14, para. 194. See also *Case concerning Armed Activities on the Territory of the Congo* (*Democratic Republic of the Congo* v. *Uganda*) [2005] ICJ Reports 168, para. 143.

[68] The claim is made in the 2002 'National Security Strategy of the United States' (2002) 41 ILM 1478; see Christopher Greenwood, 'International Law and the Pre-emptive Use of Force: Afghanistan, Al-Qaida and Iraq' (2003) 4

include whether the 'armed attack' must cross some threshold of intensity before self-defence is justified.[69]

One of the frequent questions of modern times is whether there is a right of self-defence against non-state organizations operating from another state; for example, whether military force may lawfully be used by a threatened state against terrorist groups located in the territory of another state. Commentators differ as to whether force may be used against such groups.[70] Developing state practice may support, but probably does not yet confirm, the view that states have the right of self-defence against terrorist groups in other states where the 'harbouring' states are unable or unwilling to deal with the threat themselves.[71]

Authorization under Chapter VII

The Security Council, acting under Chapter VII of the UN Charter, may authorize the use of force, either by UN peacekeeping or peace-enforcement missions or by coalitions of forces of states. Such authorizations provide an undoubted exception to the prohibition on the use of force set out in Article 2(4).

Humanitarian Intervention

This term is given to military action taken for humanitarian purposes but without Security Council authorization and without the agreement of the state concerned. On its face, such action breaches the prohibition on the use of force set out in Article 2(4), but commentators differ as to whether interventions such as that in 1991 in northern Iraq and in 1999 by NATO in Kosovo are nevertheless lawful. The conservative, and the better, view is that humanitarian intervention is contrary to international law; a few doubtful examples of humanitarian practice cannot constitute a new rule of customary international law. Other commentators state either that there is an emerging norm of customary law which allows the implementation by the international community of the responsibility to protect, or that such intervention is already lawful under existing international law. These views rely on arguments about the interpretation of Article 2(4) and as to the continued existence of

---

San Diego International Law Journal 7; for a contrary view, see Ruth Wedgwood, 'The Fall of Saddam Hussein: Security Council Mandates and Preemptive Self-Defense' (2003) 97 *AJIL* 576, 582–5.

[69] See *Case concerning Military and Paramilitary Activities In and Against Nicaragua (Nicaragua* v. *USA)* [1986] ICJ Reports 14, paras. 191 and 195; and *Oil Platforms (Islamic Republic of Iran* v. *USA)* [2003] ICJ Reports 3, paras. 51, 63–4 and 72; for critique of this point, see Oscar Schachter, 'In Defense of International Rules on the Use of Force' (1986) 53 *University of Chicago Law Review* 113.

[70] For arguments in favour of the right to self-defence in such circumstances, see Christopher Greenwood, 'International Law and the "War on Terrorism"' (2002) 78 *International Affairs* 301; Michael Byers, 'Terrorism, the Use of Force and International Law after 11 September' (2002) 51 *ICLQ* 401; for arguments against, see Antonio Cassese, 'Terrorism is Also Disrupting Some Crucial Legal Categories in International Law' (2001) 12 *EJIL* 993; Eric Myjer and Nigel White, 'The Twin Towers Attack: An Unlimited Right to Self-Defence?' (2002) 7 *Journal of Conflict and Security Law* 5. See also *Legal Consequences of the Construction of a Wall in the Occupied Palestinian Territory*, Advisory Opinion [2004] ICJ Reports 36, para. 139; and *Case concerning Armed Activities on the Territory of the Congo (Democratic Republic of the Congo* v. *Uganda)* [2005] ICJ Reports 168, paras. 146, 147. The majority decisions in both cases have been criticized on this point: see e.g. Separate Opinions, in the former case by Judge Higgins, paras. 33–6, in the latter by Judge Kooijmans, paras. 26–30 and Judge Simma, paras. 7–12. See also Sean Murphy, 'Self-Defence and the Israeli Wall Advisory Opinion: An *Ipse Dixit*' (2005) 99 *AJIL* 62.

[71] For useful overviews of state practice, see Christian Tams, 'The Use of Force Against Terrorists' (2009) 20 *EJIL* 1; and Tom Ruys, *'Armed Attack' and Article 51 of the UN Charter: Evolutions in Customary Law and Practice* (Cambridge, 2010) 419.

a customary law right which has not been displaced by the Charter.[72] Military interventions such as these remain a difficulty in defining the crime of aggression.[73]

13.2.4 'A Manifest Violation of the UN Charter'

As we have seen, the ICC definition as agreed in Kampala effectively encompasses every unlawful use of force by a state within the term 'act of aggression'. But the commission by a state of an act of aggression does not in itself criminalize the participation in that act by the state's leaders. The crime is constituted by participation (in the manner and by the persons discussed above)[74] in an act which 'by its character, gravity and scale, constitutes a manifest violation of the Charter of the United Nations'. The origin of this threshold requires explanation.

The crime of aggression under customary international law is generally regarded as being limited to participation in a 'war of aggression'.[75] Although formally declared war is now uncommon and the term is not employed in the legal regimes of the UN Charter and the Geneva Conventions, it is possible to give the term content even when it has lost its currency in international relations.[76] There were accordingly attempts during the course of the ICC Statute negotiations to include within the definition only such uses of force which could be regarded as equating to a 'war', whether because they were large scale or because of the aggressive aim or intention of the leadership.[77] For example, one of the proposals put forward by Germany in the negotiations referred to the unlawful use of force carried out 'with the object or result of establishing a military occupation of, or annexing' the foreign territory.[78] Those purposes would, however, have excluded acts which might be regarded as properly coming within the criminal category,[79] for example, aggressive wars to extract economic or political advantages of some kind. The ICC definition as finally

---

[72] All of these views are discussed in J. L. Hozgrefe and Robert Keohane (eds.), *Humanitarian Intervention* (Cambridge, 2003); see also Bruno Simma, 'NATO, the UN and the Use of Force: Legal Aspects' (1999) 10 *EJIL* 1; Nico Krisch, 'Unilateral Enforcement of the Collective Will: Kosovo, Iraq, and the Security Council' (1999) 3 *Max Planck Yearbook of United Nations Law* 59; International Development Research Centre, *The Responsibility to Protect: Report of the International Commission on Intervention and State Sovereignty* (Ottawa, 2001).

[73] For the view that humanitarian intervention is included within the definition of aggression, see Kriangsak Kittichaisaree, 'The NATO Military Action and the Potential Impact of the International Criminal Court' (2000) 4 *Singapore Journal of International and Comparative Law* 498, 506, 507.

[74] See Section 3.2.1 and Section 3.2.2.

[75] See e.g. T. Bruha, *Die Definition der Aggression* (Berlin, 1980) 126; Claus Kreß, 'The German Chief Federal Prosecutor's Decision Not to Investigate the Alleged Crime of Preparing Aggression Against Iraq' (2004) 2 *JICJ* 245, 249. See to the contrary Richard Griffiths, 'International Law, the Crime of Aggression and the *Ius ad Bellum*' (2002) 2 *International Criminal Law Review* 301, 303–4; Mary Ellen O'Connell and Mirakmal Niyazmatov, 'What is the Crime of Aggression? Comparing the *Ius ad Bellum* and the ICC Statute' (2012) 10 *JICJ* 189.

[76] See e.g. Dinstein, *War, Aggression* (n. 12) ch. 6.

[77] This is variously described as a special intent required for participants in aggression, or as a material element of the crime: Stefan Glaser, 'Quelques remarques sur la définition de l'aggression en droit international pénal' in S. Hohenleitner et al. (eds.), *Festschrift für Theodor Rittler* (Aalen, 1957) 383; Brownlie, *International Law and the Use of Force* (n. 6) 213; Kreß, 'The German Chief Federal Prosecutor's Decision' (n. 75) 256; Claus Kreß, 'Time for Decision: Some Thoughts on the Immediate Future of the Crime of Aggression: A Reply to Andreas Paulus' (2009) 20 *EJIL* 1129, 1136–42; Antonio Cassese, 'On Some Problematic Aspects of the Crime of Aggression' (2007) 20 *LJIL* 841, 848.

[78] PCNICC/1999/DP.13, 80; Clark, 'Rethinking Aggression as a Crime' (n. 29) 878.

[79] For a critique of the term and the rest of the definition, see Andreas Paulus, 'Second Thoughts on the Crime of Aggression' (2009) 20 *EJIL* 1117, 1119–25.

agreed did not include reference to the purpose of the use of force, nor a special intent (as in genocide).

Instead, the threshold of 'manifest violation' was included. It raises obvious difficulties of interpretation.[80] 'Manifest', according to the *Oxford English Dictionary*, means 'evident to the eye, mind or judgment; obvious'. We may say that even a minor border skirmish may be evident and obvious. However, the reference to gravity and scale appears to exclude even obvious violations of the *jus ad bellum* if they are of insufficient severity.

Two of the 'understandings' which were adopted at Kampala as a means of interpretation of the amendments relate to this threshold. The first states that:

aggression is the most serious and dangerous form of illegal use of force, and that a determination whether an act of aggression has been committed requires consideration of all the circumstances of each particular case, including the gravity of the acts concerned and their consequences, in accordance with the Charter of the United Nations.[81]

The second understanding provides:

the three components of character, gravity and scale must be sufficient to justify a 'manifest' determination. No one component can be significant enough to satisfy the manifest standard by itself.[82]

In spite of the opaque drafting of these understandings, it is apparent from the reading of the definition of the crime itself that there must be a finding with respect to each one of the three elements of character, gravity, and scale, although the meaning of 'character' may be difficult to agree upon.

The reference to 'gravity and scale', and the first understanding set out above, do make it clear that 'manifest violation' does, at the least, include only violations that are manifestly serious in scale and effect. It has also been suggested that the term means 'manifestly unlawful', with the intention of excluding grey areas of public international law on the use of force mentioned above.[83] It should be noted, however, that a proposal by the US delegation at Kampala that there should be a specific exclusion of force used for humanitarian intervention was not accepted by the Conference.[84] That 'manifest violation' refers to both seriousness and manifest illegality would appear to be supported in the *travaux préparatoires*.[85] Additionally, the amended Elements make clear that the violation must be 'manifest' to the Court, not simply to the aggressor or victim states.[86]

---

[80] Kreß, 'The State Conduct' (n. 37) 505–38. [81] RC/Res.6, Annex III, Understanding No. 6. [82] *Ibid*. Understanding No. 7.

[83] See e.g. Kreß, 'The Crime of Aggression Before the First Review' (n. 59); the term 'fully accords with the goal of the Statute's drafters to confine the Court's jurisdiction to atrocious behaviour that indisputably violates general customary international law' (at 859). Although written before the Review Conference, this comment refers to the text as agreed.

[84] Note that the view of Kreß on the reason for non-acceptance of the US proposal for exclusion was that there was not necessarily disagreement on the substance but that 'it would not be appropriate to address key issues of current international security law in the form of understandings drafted not with all due care, but in the haste of the final hours of diplomatic negotiations'. Kreß and von Holtzendorff, 'The Kampala Compromise on the Crime of Aggression' (n. 29) 1205.

[85] E.g. para. 24 of the 2008 Report of the Special Working Group reads as follows: 'Delegations supporting this threshold clause noted that it would appropriately limit the Court's jurisdiction to the most serious acts of aggression under customary international law, thus excluding cases of insufficient gravity and falling within a grey area'.

[86] The 'term "manifest" is an objective qualification'. RC/Res.6, Annex II, Introduction, para. 3.

A great deal, however, is being demanded of the term 'manifest violation'. The law lacks the necessary certainty if state leaders cannot predict in advance whether they will be vulnerable to prosecution or not. This would depend upon the meaning eventually ascribed by the ICC to the term and upon whether the ICC concludes that the state's act is not sufficiently serious, for the violation not to be regarded as 'manifest'.

13.3 MENTAL ELEMENTS

The amendments to the ICC Elements of Crimes adopted at the Kampala Review Conference include two mental elements, Elements 4 and 6. Element 4 requires that the perpetrator is aware of the factual circumstances establishing the inconsistency of the use of armed force by the state with the Charter of the United Nations. Element 6 requires that the perpetrator is aware of the factual circumstances establishing the manifest violation of the Charter. There is no requirement to prove that the perpetrator knew of the illegality or made a legal evaluation of the act's inconsistency with the Charter or of its 'manifest' nature.[87] Provided, therefore, that the perpetrators intended to lead their country into a conflict and knew of the circumstances surrounding the conflict, it is not necessary that they knew that the conflict was unlawful.

The post-Second World War case law indicates that the intent to participate in the aggressive act was present if the perpetrator had knowledge of the collective intent to initiate and wage aggressive war but continued to participate. Two examples from the Nuremberg trial will suffice. Schacht was at some relevant periods President of the Reichsbank and a central figure in Germany's rearmament programme. 'But', said the Tribunal, 'rearmament of itself is not criminal under the Charter. To be a crime against peace under Article 6 of the Charter it must be shown that Schacht carried out this rearmament as part of the Nazi plans to wage aggressive wars.'[88] He was acquitted, since it could not be inferred from the evidence that he knew of the plans for aggressive war. Bormann rose to a position of great power and had great influence over Hitler. But the evidence did not show that he knew of the plans; he did not attend the crucial planning meetings. He was thus acquitted of the crimes against peace charges.[89]

13.4 PROSECUTION OF AGGRESSION IN THE ICC

It is only as a result of the amendments adopted at the Review Conference in Kampala that the ICC will be able to try the crime of aggression. However, the compromise provisions agreed upon at Kampala include two preliminary hurdles. First, the ICC could only exercise jurisdiction over an alleged crime committed more than one year after thirty states have ratified or accepted the amendments.[90] This threshold was met in 2016. Second, the Court may only exercise jurisdiction 'subject to a decision to be taken after 1 January 2017 by the

---

[87] Introduction, paras. 2 and 4. [88] Nuremberg IMT, Judgment and Sentences, reprinted in (1947) 41 *AJIL* 172, 300.
[89] *Ibid.* 329. [90] RC/Res.6, Annex I, Art. 15*bis*, para. 2; Art. 15*ter*, para. 2.

same majority of States Parties as is required for the adoption of an amendment to the Statute'.[91] This was achieved by consensus on 14 December 2017.[92] When this occurred, the states parties agreed to activate the ICC's jurisdiction from 17 July 2018.[93]

13.4.1 Jurisdiction of the ICC

As a result of the provisions of the Statute and of the Kampala amendments, the rules for ICC jurisdiction over the crime of aggression differ from those for other crimes. Recall that for the other three crimes, the general rule in Article 12 is that the Court has jurisdiction if the alleged crime was committed by a national of a state party or on the territory of a state party; there is no possibility for states parties of opting out and jurisdiction can extend to the nationals or territory of non-party states if the conditions of Article 12 are met. However, for aggression, states parties have a choice as to the jurisdiction they wish to accept (although it is not entirely clear how that choice is made, or how wide it is, as discussed later in this section) and there is no jurisdiction over aggression when it is committed by the nationals of a non-party state or committed on the territory of such a state. This is a departure from the general jurisdictional regime of Article 12. There will be jurisdiction without these qualifications if the Security Council refers a situation of aggression to the Court: in that case, there is no need for any state to have accepted the amendments.[94] Of course, the possibility of accepting jurisdiction *ad hoc* under Article 12(3) still applies.[95]

The Kampala amendments have left uncertainties about aspects of the Court's jurisdiction; these uncertainties result from disagreements at the Review Conference about which amendment procedures to use, and the decisions taken to resolve them. The principal difficulty is whether the nationals or territory of a state which does not accept the amendments are subject to the Court's jurisdiction. On the one hand, the amendments provide that a state party may make a declaration that it does not accept the jurisdiction of the Court in respect of acts of aggression it commits (Article 15*bis*(4)). This has to be contrasted with Article 121(5) of the existing Statute, the second sentence of which provides that, for a state party which has not accepted an amendment relating to the crimes subject to the Court's jurisdiction, there will be no jurisdiction when the crime covered by the amendment is committed by that state party's nationals or on its territory.

---

[91] RC/Res.6, Annex I, Art. 15*bis*, para. 3; Art. 15*ter*, para. 3.

[92] ICC/ASP/16/Res 5. On this see Claus Kreß, 'On the Activation of the ICC's Jurisdiction over the Crime of Aggression' (2018) 16 *JICJ* 1; Andreas Zimmermann, 'A Victory for the Rule of Law? Or All's Well that Ends Well' (2018) 16 *JICJ* 119; Stefan Barriga and Niels Blokker, 'Entry into Force and State Consent: Cross-Cutting Issues' in Claus Kreß and Stefan Barriga (eds.), *The Crime of Aggression* (Cambridge, 2017) 621.

[93] ICC/ASP/16/Res 5, para. 1.

[94] RC/Res.6, Annex I, Art. 15 *ter*. See Neils Blokker and Stefan Barriga, 'Conditions for the Exercise of Jurisdiction Based on Security Council Referrals' in Claus Kreß and Stefan Barriga (eds.), *The Crime of Aggression* (Cambridge, 2017) 646, 648–51.

[95] Note that Ukraine is not able to do this, which has led to a number of proposals to create an aggression tribunal to address Russia's full-scale invasion of Ukraine in 2022 and the ongoing armed conflict. There has been much discussion of the merits and demerits of these proposals. See, e.g., Tom Dannenbaum, 'A Special Tribunal for the Crime of Aggression?' (2022) 20(4) *JICJ* 859; Jennifer Trahan, 'The Need for an International Tribunal on the Crime of Aggression Regarding the Situation in Ukraine' (2023) 46 *Fordham International Law Journal* 671.

On their face, these two provisions, Article 15*bis*(4) and Article 121(5), conflict. The former appears to be based on an assumption that there will be jurisdiction, once the amendments have entered into force, unless a state party accepts the amendments and then opts out, with the further oddity that the opt-out seems to extend only to acts of aggression committed by the opting-out state. However, the natural interpretation of Article 121(5) of the existing Statute leaves the nationals and territory of a state party which does not accept the Kampala amendments unaffected by the Court's jurisdiction.[96]

Commentators differ on the explanations for the conflicting provisions and their interpretation.[97] The better view, in accordance with the relatively clear wording of Article 121(5) and its history, would seem to be that the nationals and territory of a state party are not exposed to the Court's jurisdiction over the crime of aggression until the state ratifies or accepts the Kampala amendments.[98] If a state party accepts the amendments, it then has the choice of opting out, under Article 15*bis*, but only in relation to acts of aggression it commits itself.

The contrary view is that states parties will have to accept the amendments and then opt out if they do not want their nationals to be tried for aggression. However, such an interpretation of the Article 121 amendment procedures effectively amends Article 121 itself, a step not possible except through the amendment procedures set out in Article 121(4).[99] Accepting this interpretation would circumvent what had been intended as a safeguard for states which did not want to have new crimes included without their consent, and allows new amendments to be adopted in the future by a two-thirds majority or under whatever procedures the Assembly of States Parties may choose.

Another difficulty relates to states not party. The amendments provide that the Court has no jurisdiction over the crime of aggression with respect to a state that is not a party to the Statute 'when committed by that State's nationals or on its territory'.[100] The result is that the Court cannot try any of those nationals for the crime of aggression nor any aggression committed on their territory by others – unless the Security Council refers the situation to the Court. The removal of states not party to the Statute from the ambit of the Court's aggression jurisdiction, although perhaps politically desirable, involves an amendment to the Statute which should have been done by the slower procedure of Article 121(4). Whether or not this attempt to

---

[96] RC/Res.6, para. 1, provides that the amendments shall enter into force in accordance with Art. 121(5), confirming that the Conference considered that this provision applies even though the amendments went wider than amendments to Art. 5.

[97] For a useful and critical analysis, see Andreas Zimmermann, 'Amending the Amendment Provisions of the Rome Statute' (2012) 10 *JICJ* 209. For a differing account, see Kreß and von Holtzendorff, 'The Kampala Compromise' (n. 29); among other points, the authors describe an interpretative approach by which Art. 121(5) does not preclude ICC jurisdiction over a national of a non-ratifying state party when the alleged aggression was committed within the territory of a state party that *has* ratified or accepted the amendment. This approach relies on Art. 12(2) of the Statute (which allows the Court to exercise its jurisdiction over the nationals of states that are not parties to the Statute whenever their acts are committed on the territory of a state party) and conflicts with the history of the ICC Statute; see e.g. Mauro Politi, 'The ICC and the Crime of Aggression' (2012) 10 *JICJ* 267, 280.

[98] ICC-ASP/16/Res.5, 14 December 2017, para 2: 'Confirms that, in accordance with the Rome Statute, the amendments to the Statute regarding the crime of aggression adopted at the Kampala Review Conference enter into force for those states parties which have accepted the amendments one year after the deposit of their instruments of ratification or acceptance and that in the case of a state referral or *propio motu* investigation the Court shall not exercise its jurisdiction regarding a crime of aggression when committed by a national or on the territory of a state party that has not ratified or accepted these amendments'.

[99] For reference to statements by Japan at the Review Conference and France at the subsequent Assembly of States Parties, expressing disagreement with the procedures used, see Politi, 'The ICC and the Crime of Aggression' (n. 97) 281–2.

[100] RC/Res.6, Annex I, Art. 15*bis*, para. 5.

amend the Statute has been successful may, like the other defects of the amendments, have to be determined by the Court.

13.4.2 The Role of the Security Council

The crime of aggression presupposes that an aggressive act has been committed by a state. When the ILC included aggression in its draft Statute, it considered that it was not appropriate for the ICC to try individuals in the absence of a finding of aggression against the state concerned.[101] To hold an individual responsible for a crime of participation in a state's act condemns the state itself. The ILC proposed that, in view of the Security Council's responsibilities under the UN Charter, the way to resolve the problem was to require that, before the ICC could exercise its jurisdiction, there had to be a prior determination by the Security Council that a state had committed the act of aggression which was the subject of the proceedings.[102] The legal effect of any such determination would be for the ICC itself to decide.

As explained in Section 13.1.2, this provision was not included in the ICC Statute, and Article 5(2) left the question for further negotiations. The requirement in that Article that the conditions for the exercise of the ICC's jurisdiction must be 'consistent with the relevant provisions of the Charter of the United Nations' was interpreted by some as requiring a determination by the Council, prior to ICC prosecution, that the state concerned had committed aggression.[103]

However, those opposing a Security Council filter were in a large majority. The arguments were largely of a political or practical nature. On the one hand, to require the Court to act only after the Council's determination would have given the permanent members of the Council an effective veto over prosecutions relating to themselves and their allies. The Court ought to be allowed to act without Council interference.[104] The Council has, in fact, very rarely made a determination of aggression,[105] and if this inaction continues there would be a risk that the Court would be blocked from ever considering a case of aggression.

On the other hand, if the ICC, in the absence of a Security Council determination, had to decide that an act of aggression had taken place, it might infringe on the responsibilities of the Council with regard to the actions of the state concerned. There could be a risk that investigations undertaken by the ICC for an act of aggression without a prior Council authorization might bring about an escalation of the situation.[106] To avoid the Council

---

[101] James Crawford, 'The ILC's Draft Statute for an International Criminal Tribunal' (1994) 88 *AJIL* 134, 147.

[102] Art. 23(2) of the ILC Draft Statute. See Crawford, 'The ILC's Draft Statute' (n. 101); and James Crawford, 'The ILC Adopts a Statute for an International Criminal Court' (1995) 89 *AJIL* 404, 411.

[103] This was the understanding of the United Kingdom, as indicated in its statement made on the adoption of the Statute on 17 July 1998 (UN Doc. A/CONF.183/13 (vol. II) 124); see also Rolf Fife, 'Criminalizing Individuals for Acts of Aggression Committed by States' in Morten Bergsmo (ed.), *Human Rights and Criminal Justice for the Downtrodden* (Leiden and Boston, 2003) 53, 67.

[104] See e.g. Antonio Cassese, 'The Statute of the International Criminal Court: Some Preliminary Reflections' (1999) 10 *EJIL* 144, 147.

[105] Although in relation to several situations the Council has described certain conduct as acts of aggression: see *Historical Review*, PCNICC/2002/WGCA/L.1, paras. 381–404.

[106] See e.g. Andreas Zimmermann, 'The Creation of a Permanent International Criminal Court' (1998) 2 *Max Planck Yearbook of International Law* 169, 203.

blocking a case through inertia, it was suggested that, if the Council failed to act, the UN General Assembly or the ICJ under its advisory jurisdiction should be able to make a determination of responsibility by a state prior to trial of an individual by the ICC.

At the Review Conference, the question whether there should be a role for a UN organ was one of the most divisive. Agreement on a final text was secured by linking the Security Council role with the jurisdictional reach of the Court over the crime, as discussed in the previous section. The final result, as set out in new Articles 15*bis* and 15*ter*, is that, if the Security Council refers to the ICC a situation of aggression, the ICC will have jurisdiction as for the other crimes in the Statute and there is no need for a Council determination of an act of aggression by a state.

If the situation is referred to the Court by a state party, or if the Prosecutor initiates an investigation *proprio motu*, the Prosecutor must notify the UN Secretary-General and ascertain whether the Security Council has made a determination of an act of aggression by the state concerned. If the Council has done so, the Prosecutor may proceed with the investigation. If no such determination has been made within six months of the notification, the Prosecutor may proceed but must secure authorization for the investigation from the Pre-Trial Division.[107] The Security Council may also ask for a suspension of proceedings under Article 16 in the usual way.

13.4.3 Implications of the Prosecution of Aggression Before the ICC

The outcome of the Kampala Review Conference was greeted with great enthusiasm.[108] More than sixty years after the Nuremberg IMT judgment, the international community had finally reached agreement on the future prosecution of the crime of aggression. Before joining the chorus, it is wise to consider the concerns which have been expressed about the implications of prosecuting the crime.

As we have seen, there is concern about the ambiguity of the definition.[109] Some scholars, while recognizing the problem, point out that the extent of uncertainty is not unique among other international or domestic crimes and that the ICC will have to resolve the outstanding matters[110] while exercising its discretion with great care.[111]

Another concern relates to what might amount, in effect, to the invocation of criminal law to regulate the use of force by states. For some, turning the ICC into a forum for litigating disputes between states risks harm both to the Court and to the maintenance of international peace and security.[112] The determination of whether there has been an act of aggression by a state will be a necessary part of the Court's decision on an individual's criminal responsibility, and such determinations by a criminal court will be likely to have wider repercussions.

---

[107] The amendment (Art. 15*bis*, para. 8) specifies the Division rather than a Pre-Trial Chamber. For comment, see Stefan Barriga and Niels Blokker, 'Conditions for the Exercise of Jurisdiction Based on State Referrals and *Proprio Motu* Investigations' in Claus Kreß and Stefan Barriga (eds.), *The Crime of Aggression* (Cambridge, 2017) 652.

[108] Kreß and von Holtzendorff, 'The Kampala Compromise on the Crime of Aggression' (n. 29) 1180: the amendments were adopted with 'an outburst of collective joy'.

[109] E.g. Michael Glennon, 'The Blank-Prose Crime of Aggression' (2010) 35 *Yale Journal of International Law* 71, written before the adoption of the Kampala amendments but making reference to the definition there adopted.

[110] Martti Koskenniemi, 'A Trap for the Innocent … ?' in Claus Kreß and Stefan Barriga (eds.), *The Crime of Aggression* (Cambridge, 2017) 1359.

[111] Marko Milanovic, 'Aggression and Legality: Custom in Kampala' (2012) 10 *JICJ* 165.

[112] Fife, 'Criminalizing Individuals' (n. 103) 70–3.

Further, the ICC will need to enter into highly political and controversial questions of public international law.[113] The legal principles of the *jus ad bellum* give rise to more controversy than the *jus in bello*, and have dogged the international community for decades.[114] This leads to a related concern that the prosecution of aggression may have 'collateral implications' for public international law outside the context of criminal law. The 'understanding' adopted at Kampala seeks to lessen this possibility:

It is understood that the amendments that address the definition of the act of aggression and the crime of aggression do so for the purpose of this Statute only. The amendments shall, in accordance with article 10 of the Rome Statute, not be interpreted as limiting or prejudicing in any way existing or developing rules of international law for purposes other than this Statute.

However, the future practice of the ICC in choosing to prosecute particular acts may, it has been argued, influence existing views of the justifiability of certain uses of force under the *jus ad bellum*, and the higher threshold given in the definition of the crime of aggression may seem to condone lesser uses of force by a state.[115]

The practical difficulties for the ICC in particular cases are likely to be severe. The constitution and procedures of the ICC are designed for the determination of individual, not state, responsibility.[116] The concept of complementarity, fundamental to the success of the ICC, does not fit well with the crime of aggression.[117] Except where the documents of a defeated state are available to the international community, as with Germany and Japan in the Second World War – when the Tribunals had a glut of the defeated governments' most secret papers[118] – there will be difficulties of access to evidence.

Before the adoption of the Kampala amendments, some commentators expressed doubts about the inclusion of aggression in the ICC Statute at all,[119] and about whether its inclusion would be more than pure symbolism.[120] If one prediction may be safely made, it is that there will not be many prosecutions for aggression before the Court. However, if the existence of ICC jurisdiction acts as a deterrent to even a few war-mongering presidents and prime ministers, it has the potential thereby to save many lives.

---

[113] Theodor Meron, 'Defining Aggression for the International Criminal Court' (2001) 25 *Suffolk Transnational Law Review* 1. See also Erin Creegan, 'Justified Uses of Force and the Crime of Aggression' (2012) 10 *JICJ* 59.

[114] See e.g. Kreß, 'The Crime of Aggression Before the First Review' (n. 59) 851 (international criminal law is 'ill-equipped to decide major controversies about the content of existing legal rules').

[115] The first concern is expressed by Michael Wood and Marko Milanovic (eds.), *The Oxford Handbook on the Use of Force* (Oxford, 2015) 533, 553; the second by O'Connell and Niyazmatov, 'What is the Crime of Aggression?' (n. 75).

[116] One important aspect of the ICC Statute is the attention given to the needs of victims of crimes; for example, they are accorded rights of participation in trials and rights of protection and reparation. Whereas the victims of the other crimes within the jurisdiction of the Court are individuals, the victim of an act of aggression is in reality a state. See James Boeving, 'Aggression, International Law, and the ICC: An Argument for the Withdrawal of Aggression from the Rome Statute' (2005) 43 *Columbia Journal of Transnational Law* 557, 583–8. See also Shane Darcy, 'Accident and Design: Recognizing Victims of Aggression in International Law' (2021) 70 *International & Comparative Law Quarterly* 103.

[117] Indeed, Beth van Schaack, '*Par in Parem Imperium Non Habet*' (2012) 10 *JICJ* 133, argues that the ICC be allowed to exercise de facto primacy over the crime of aggression.

[118] In Japan, however, many of the relevant papers had been burnt.

[119] See e.g. Antonio Cassese, 'The Statute of the ICC: Some Preliminary Reflections' (1999) 10 *EJIL* 144, 146; a suggestion to delete aggression from the Statute was made in Matthias Schuster, 'The Rome Statute of an International Criminal Court and the Crime of Aggression: A Gordian Knot in Search of a Sword' (2003) 14 *Criminal Law Forum* 1.

[120] William Schabas, 'The Unfinished Work of Defining Aggression: How Many Times Must the Cannonballs Fly, Before They are Forever Banned?' in McGoldrick et al., *The Permanent ICC*, 124, 141.

Further Reading

The definition of aggression and the other amendments adopted at Kampala are available on the website of the ICC, www.icc-cpi.int. One issue of the *Journal of International Criminal Justice* (2012) 10 *JICJ*, is devoted entirely to articles on the crime of aggression in light of the Kampala amendments (1–288). There is a further symposium, on the 2017 decision to activate the ICC's jurisdiction over aggression, in (2018) 16 *JICJ* 1–89.

M. Cherif Bassiouni and Benjamin Ferencz, 'The Crime Against Peace' in M. Cherif Bassiouni (ed.), *International Criminal Law*, 2nd ed. (New York, 1999) vol. I, 313

Neil Boister and Robert Cryer, *The Tokyo International Military Tribunal: A Reappraisal* (Oxford, 2008)

Ian Brownlie, *International Law and the Use of Force by States* (Oxford, 1963)

Yoram Dinstein, *War, Aggression and Self-Defence*, 6th ed. (Cambridge, 2018)

Rolf Einar Fife, 'Criminalizing Individuals for Acts of Aggression Committed by States' in Morten Bergsmo (ed.), *Human Rights and Criminal Justice for the Downtrodden* (Leiden and Boston, 2003) 53

Claus Kreß and Stefan Barriga (eds.), *The Crime of Aggression* (Cambridge, 2017) vols. I and II

Carrie McDougall, *The Crime of Aggression under the Rome Statute of the International Criminal Court*, 2nd ed. (Cambridge, 2021).

Leila Nadya Sadat, *Seeking Accountability for the Unlawful Use of Force* (Cambridge, 2018)

Kirsten Sellars, *Crimes Against Peace in International Law* (Cambridge, 2013)

14

Other International Crime: Terrorism, Torture, and Ecocide

14.1 INTRODUCTION

14.1.1 Overview

To focus only on the 'core crimes' and their prosecution would be to ignore a substantial area of criminal law with international implications; there are other crimes of international concern which have a serious impact on people's security and welfare, as well as the security and welfare of communities and countries.[1] These 'other crimes' include 'transnational crimes'[2] such as terrorism, universal jurisdiction crimes such as torture, and emerging crimes such as ecocide. Some of these are also covered by customary international law or are international crimes when committed in certain circumstances (for example, as crimes against humanity).[3]

14.2 TERRORISM

14.2.1 Introduction

The phenomenon of terrorism presents a number of difficulties of legal categorization.[4] One challenge is that international law governing the suppression of terrorism has developed in

---

[1] In Res. 56/120, the UN General Assembly expressed deep concern over 'the impact of transnational organised crime on the political, social and economic stability and development of societies': UN Doc. A/RES/56/120 (2002).

[2] Transnational crimes are crimes which have actual or potential transboundary effects. The line between transnational and international crimes is not always a clear one, see Charles Chernor Jalloh, 'The Distinction Between "International" and "Transnational" Crimes in the African Criminal Court' in Harmen Van der Wilt and Christophe Paulussen (eds.), *Legal Responses to Transnational and International Crimes* (Cheltenham, 2017) 272. It is, however, now in common use. See further Chapter 1. Other examples of transnational crimes are drug trafficking (UN Convention Against Illicit Trafficking in Narcotic Drugs and Psychotropic Substances 1988), piracy (UN Law of the Sea Convention 1982, Arts. 100–105), slavery (1926 Slavery Convention; the UN Supplementary Convention on the Abolition of Slavery, the Slave Trade and Institutions and Practices Similar to Slavery 1956; the UN Convention on the Law of the Sea 1982, Art. 99), apartheid (International Convention on the Suppression and Punishment of the Crime of Apartheid 1973), enforced disappearances (International Convention for the Protection of All Persons from Enforced Disappearance 2006), corruption (UN Convention Against Corruption 2003), cutting undersea cables (Convention on the Protection of Undersea Cables 1884, 24 Stat. 989, Treaty Series 380), and transnational organized crime, including people trafficking, smuggling migrants, and illegal arms trafficking (UN Convention Against Transnational Organized Crime 2000; Protocol to Prevent, Suppress and Punish Trafficking in Persons, Especially Women and Children, supplementing that Convention; Protocol Against the Smuggling of Migrants by Land, Air and Sea, supplementing that Convention; Protocol Against the Illicit Manufacturing of and Trafficking in Firearms, their Parts and Components and Ammunition, supplementing that Convention).

[3] Enforced Disappearances Convention, Preamble, Art. 5. On the overlaps between enforced disappearances in the Convention on Enforced Disappearances and its crime against humanity counterpart, see Irene Girgiou, 'State Involvement in the Perpetration of Enforced Disappearance and the Rome Statute' (2013) 11 *JICJ* 1001.

[4] See generally Neil Boister, *An Introduction to Transnational Criminal Law*, 2nd ed. (Oxford, 2018) ch. 7.

a piecemeal manner, often in reaction to specific events, and therefore did not develop from a commonly accepted foundational core. A second is the problem of defining terrorism. A third challenge is the question of whether 'terrorism' is a useful or necessary legal term.[5] Finally, there is the question of the status of terrorism under international law – is it an international or transnational crime, or both?

The fight against terrorism is now multifaceted[6] and includes measures imposed by the UN Security Council, such as financial sanctions. However, the primary paradigm to address terrorism remains criminal law, particularly domestic criminal law, and terrorist acts constitute criminal offences. At present, terrorist acts can be prosecuted in an international court only if they amount to war crimes, crimes against humanity, or genocide. It is true that one internationalized court, the Special Tribunal for Lebanon, had jurisdiction over terrorist acts (see Chapter 9), but this jurisdiction was expressed in its Statute to be over crimes under Lebanese, not international, law.[7] The transnational and international criminal law aspects of terrorism are discussed further in Sections 14.2.4 and 14.2.5 below.

14.2.2 Development of International Cooperation Against Terrorism

In spite of some historical precursors, which did not materialize,[8] the United Nations only took on the task of defining and prohibiting terrorism when the General Assembly set up a committee on terrorism in 1972, which ultimately failed to reach agreement, despite meeting until 1979. There was disagreement as to whether acts committed by national liberation movements for causes such as decolonization should be excluded from any definition of terrorism. There were also arguments that terrorist activities should not be banned unless the causes of terrorism were understood and resolved.

Global Counter-Terrorism Agreements

The difficulty of securing international agreement on an unqualified and general condemnation of terrorism led to the adoption of a 'thematic' approach to cooperation to prevent and criminalize terrorist acts. International agreements were negotiated on specific areas of terrorist activity, each separately defined. There are eleven of these agreements, each of which was negotiated in reaction to specific kinds of terrorist threats prevalent at the time the agreements were concluded.[9] For example, two of the

---

[5] 'We have cause to regret that a legal concept of "terrorism" was ever inflicted upon us. The term ... serves no operative legal purpose': R. R. Baxter, 'A Sceptical Look at the Concept of Terrorism' (1973/4) 7 *Akron Law Review* 380. 'Terrorism is a term without legal significance ... The term is at once a shorthand to allude to a variety of problems with some common elements and a method of indicating community condemnation for the conduct concerned': Rosalyn Higgins, in discussing early attempts at a definition of terrorism in Rosalyn Higgins and Maurice Flory (eds.), *Terrorism and International Law* (London, 1997) 28.

[6] See John P. Grant, 'Beyond the Montreal Convention' (2004) 36 *Case Western Reserve Journal of International Law* 453, 472.

[7] STL Statute, Art. 2. However, the Special Tribunal for Lebanon, in *Ayyash et al.*, STL AC, 16 February 2011, decided to apply Lebanese law in accordance with what it determined to be international customary law (see Section 14.2.5).

[8] See e.g. League of Nations Doc. C.546(1).M.383(1).1937.V. For an interesting review of its negotiation, see Ben Saul, 'The Legal Response of the League of Nations to Terrorism' (2006) 4 *JICJ* 78.

[9] There are at present thirteen agreements altogether, but two of them, as explained below, do not follow the same model of state cooperation. The eleven agreements are: 1970 Convention for the Suppression of Unlawful Seizure of Aircraft (the 'Hague Convention'); 1971 Convention for the Suppression of Unlawful Acts Against the Safety of Civil Aviation (the 'Montreal Convention') and its 1988 Protocol for the Suppression of Unlawful Acts of Violence at Airports Serving International Civil

earliest conventions, the 1970 Convention for the Suppression of Unlawful Seizure of Aircraft (Hague Convention) and 1971 Convention for the Suppression of Unlawful Acts Against the Safety of Civil Aviation (Montreal Convention), deal with the safety of civil aviation, following a growing number of hijackings of commercial flights and other offences against air travel (such as violent acts endangering the safety of aircraft in flight) at the time.[10] The impetus for the drafting of the 1988 Convention on the Suppression of Unlawful Acts Against the Safety of Maritime Navigation was the hijacking in 1985 of the *Achille Lauro*, an Italian cruise ship, and the accompanying murder of a US citizen of Jewish origin.

The eleven agreements have as their purpose the effective *national* prosecution of specified acts. They commonly include these elements: the obligation to take alleged offenders into custody, the principle *aut dedere aut judicare* (requiring states either to extradite an offender or to consider the case for prosecution),[11] a universal jurisdiction provision requiring states to act when the alleged offender is present on its territory, and obligations on states parties to give assistance in criminal and extradition proceedings.[12] In their provisions on extradition, the three most recent agreements further specify that the offence in question may not be regarded as a political offence for the purpose of extradition or mutual legal assistance.[13]

With the conclusion of the Terrorist Bombing Convention in 1997, most kinds of 'terrorist' conduct had been covered in one or more of these agreements, including aircraft and ship hijacking, violence at commercial airports, using aircraft for criminal purposes, unlawful acts against fixed platforms on continental shelves, attacks against diplomats, hostage-taking, terrorist financing, and nuclear terrorism. A proposal was then introduced to negotiate a 'comprehensive' convention to explicitly address all forms of terrorism, which required a definition of terrorism.[14] The hope of finally agreeing upon a definition of terrorism for the purpose of such a convention had received some impetus from a General

---

Aviation; 1973 Convention on the Prevention and Punishment of Crimes Against Internationally Protected Persons, including Diplomatic Agents; 1979 International Convention Against the Taking of Hostages; 1980 Convention on the Physical Protection of Nuclear Material; the 1988 Convention on the Suppression of Unlawful Acts Against the Safety of Maritime Navigation (the 'SUA Convention') and its 1988 Protocol for the Suppression of Unlawful Acts Against the Safety of Fixed Platforms Located on the Continental Shelf; 1997 International Convention for the Suppression of Terrorist Bombings (the 'Terrorist Bombing Convention'); 1999 International Convention for the Suppression of the Financing of Terrorism (the 'Terrorist Financing Convention'); and 2005 International Convention for the Suppression of Acts of Nuclear Terrorism (the 'Nuclear Terrorism Convention'). Within the list of global terrorism agreements are often included the 1963 Convention on Offences and Certain Other Acts Committed on Board Aircraft (the 'Tokyo Convention') and the 1991 Convention on the Marking of Plastic Explosives for the Purpose of Detection, but these two differ from the others: the objective of the Tokyo Convention is primarily to assign powers and jurisdiction to different states and persons in relation to activities on board aircraft, while the Plastic Explosives Convention provides for the marking of explosives and the prevention of possession and transfer of unmarked explosives. The UN Convention on the Safety of United Nations and Associated Personnel 1994 (annexed to GA Res. 49/59) is sometimes added to the list: although not drafted primarily as an instrument against terrorism, it follows the same model as the terrorism agreements.

[10] See Christopher Joyner and Robert Friedlander, 'International Civil Aviation' in M. Cherif Bassiouni (ed.), *International Criminal Law*, 2nd ed. (New York, 1999) vol. I, 837.
[11] For discussion of *aut dedere aut judicare* obligations, see Chapter 4.
[12] See e.g., Convention for the Suppression of Unlawful Seizure of Aircraft 1970, Arts. 4(2), 6, 7, 8, 10.
[13] Terrorist Bombing Convention 1997, Art. 11; Terrorist Financing Convention 1999, Art. 14; and Nuclear Terrorism Convention 2005, Art. 15. See Chapter 5.
[14] The proposal was made by India in 1996: UN Doc. A/C.6/51/6.

Assembly Resolution of 1994,[15] adopted by consensus, which annexed a Declaration on Terrorism containing the following provision:

Criminal acts intended or calculated to provoke a state of terror in the general public, a group of persons or particular persons for political purposes are in any circumstances unjustifiable, whatever the considerations of a political, philosophical, ideological, racial, ethnic, religious or other nature which may be invoked to justify them.

The Resolution, unlike previous ones, had no preambular reference to acts committed by a national liberation movement; it made quite clear that terrorism was condemned whatever the motivation and by whomever it was committed. Unfortunately, the hope that a similarly unqualified definition could be agreed was not fulfilled. As a result of the lack of agreement on the definition of terrorism, the UN negotiations for a comprehensive convention which began in 1997 have been in deadlock for years.[16] The difficulties of reaching agreement on a definition relate largely to two connected questions: are there causes which justify acts otherwise classed as terrorism, which should therefore be excluded? And should 'state terrorism' be included?

Regional Counter-Terrorism Agreements

There are a number of international counter-terrorism agreements which have been concluded within the forums of regional organizations.[17] Like the global conventions, these agreements are generally focused on methods of international cooperation with the aim of national prosecution. Another regional initiative is the European Union's 2017 Directive on combating terrorism.[18]

Security Council Resolutions

The Security Council has determined that suppression of international terrorism is essential for the maintenance of international peace and security. For example, Resolution 1368 (2001), adopted on 12 September 2001, stated that the terrorist attacks in Washington and New York were, 'like any act of international terrorism ... a threat to international peace and security'. Resolution 1373 (2001), adopted under Chapter VII of the Charter, imposed extensive obligations on states in relation to the suppression of terrorist acts, including the financing of terrorism. The Resolution, which was controversial when adopted,[19] decides,

---

[15] Declaration on Measures to Eliminate International Terrorism (1994), annexed to GA Res. 49/60 of 9 December 1994.

[16] The Ad Hoc Committee established by General Assembly Resolution 51/210 of 17 December 1996 met from 1996–2013 without any resolution of the issue. This was followed by a Working Group created by the UN General Assembly's Sixth Committee. That Working Group also has not come to an agreement, as evidenced in the annual UN General Assembly resolution on the topic: see 'Measures to eliminate international terrorism', UN Doc. A/RES/77/113 (2022).

[17] Arab Convention on the Suppression of Terrorism 1998; Convention of the Organization of the Islamic Conference on Combating International Terrorism 1999; European Convention on the Suppression of Terrorism 1977; Organization of American States Convention to Prevent and Punish Acts of Terrorism Taking the Form of Crimes Against Persons and Related Extortion that are of International Significance 1971; OAU Convention on the Prevention and Combating of Terrorism 1999; South Asian Association for Regional Co-operation, Regional Convention on Suppression of Terrorism 1987; Treaty on Cooperation among the States Members of the Commonwealth of Independent States in Combating Terrorism 1999; European Convention on the Prevention of Terrorism 2005.

[18] Directive (EU) 2017/541 of the European Parliament and of the Council of 15 March 2017 on combatting terrorism and replacing Council Framework Decision 2002/475/JHA and amending Council Decision 2005/671/JHA, OJ L 88.

[19] Res. 1373 (2001) was criticized as Security Council 'legislation' in a field which is the preserve of intergovernmental agreement; for discussion, see Matthew Happold, 'Security Council Resolution 1373 and the Constitution of the United Nations' (2003) 16 *LJIL* 593; Paul Szasz, 'The Security Council Starts Legislating' (2002) 96 *AJIL* 901; Stefan Talmon, 'The Security Council as World Legislature' (2005) 99 *AJIL* 175.

inter alia, that all states must ensure that any person who participates in financing, planning, preparing for, perpetrating, or supporting terrorist acts is brought to justice, and states must establish such acts as serious criminal offences in their law with appropriately serious penalties (paragraph 2(e)). It imposes binding obligations, establishes the Counter-Terrorism Committee to monitor their implementation, and is a significant part of the international counter-terrorism effort.

14.2.3 Definition of Terrorism

As mentioned above, no definition of terrorism has yet been agreed for the purpose of a *global* prohibition of terrorist acts in a legally binding instrument. None of the eleven global conventions defines terrorism except the Terrorist Financing Convention, and that is only for a secondary purpose.[20] Some of the agreements do not even mention the word 'terrorism',[21] which exemplifies the view that it is possible to deal with terrorism without creating specific 'terrorist' offences. There are, however, definitions of a kind. Each of the regional counter-terrorism agreements has a definition of terrorism for the purpose of the agreement; while some merely list the offences covered by the global Conventions with or without other serious offences,[22] others create their own generic definitions.[23] Security Council Resolution 1566 (2004) has a description of terrorism (said not to be a 'definition');[24] it covers only the acts included in the global Conventions, and specifies that they are committed with 'the purpose to provoke a state of terror ... intimidate a population or compel a government or an international organization to do or to abstain from doing any act'.

Leaving aside the early terrorism Conventions, there are generally two or more aspects to the terrorism definitions used by states in national and international instruments: first, the underlying *act*, which is generally a criminal offence in itself; and, second, the *purpose* of coercion of a state or international organization, and/or the purpose of causing alarm among the population. There is sometimes an additional requirement of political or ideological motive and, in relation to international terrorism, a transnational character to the underlying act. While there is particular controversy about the authors of terrorism – whether freedom fighters and state agents are excluded – there is also diverging practice in relation to all other aspects of the definition.[25]

---

[20] Art. 2 of the Convention refers to the offence of financing acts of terrorism, which are defined as acts covered by the terrorism Conventions and 'any other act intended to cause death or serious bodily injury to a civilian, or to any other person not taking an active part in the hostilities in a situation of armed conflict, when the purpose of such act, by its nature or context, is to intimidate a population, or to compel a Government or an international organisation to do or to abstain from doing any act'.

[21] E.g. Organization of American States Convention to Prevent and Punish Acts of Terrorism Taking the Form of Crimes Against Persons and Related Extortion that are of International Significance 1971, Art. 2.

[22] See e.g. the European Convention on the Suppression of Terrorism 1977, Art. 1; European Convention on the Prevention of Terrorism 2005, Art. 1.

[23] See e.g. the Arab Convention on the Suppression of Terrorism 1998, Art. 1(2); 'Any act or threat of violence, whatever its motives or purposes, that occurs in the advancement of an individual or collective criminal agenda and seeking to sow panic among people, causing fear by harming them, or placing their lives, liberty or security in danger, or seeking to cause damage to the environment or to public or private installations or property or to occupying or seizing them, or seeking to jeopardize a national resources.'

[24] See, in particular, the remarks of the representative of Brazil on the adoption of the resolution (UN Doc. S/PV 3053).

[25] See the discussion in Robert Kolb, 'The Exercise of Criminal Jurisdiction over International Terrorists' in Andrea Bianchi (ed.), *Enforcing International Law Norms against Terrorism* (Oxford, 2004) 227. But see Antonio Cassese, 'Terrorism as an

Material Elements

The *actus reus* of the crime of terrorism is the underlying act. With the exception of the Terrorist Financing Convention, the eleven global terrorism agreements require or imply that the underlying act must be an offence in itself.[26] The regional agreements mostly do the same, either by listing the offences covered by the global agreements, or within their own generic definitions. The draft comprehensive convention lists the underlying acts of causing death or serious personal injury, serious damage to property including public transport or the environment, or damage to property or systems which results in major economic loss.[27]

There is divergent practice with regard to which actors can commit terrorism. In spite of the unqualified condemnation of terrorism in the 1994 General Assembly declaration,[28] the Arab, Organization of Islamic Cooperation, and Organization of African Unity (OAU, now African Union) Conventions include an exception for acts committed by peoples struggling against foreign occupation or for national liberation in accordance with the principles of international law.[29]

It is clear that the targeting of civilians, however just the cause of the conflict, is unacceptable. Attempts have therefore been made to solve the problem of definition by specifying that only civilians are the targets of terrorism (as in Article 2(1)(b) of the Terrorist Financing Convention).[30] As a complete solution, this is defective. The standard definition of 'civilian' comes from the *ius in bello*, which is not applicable in peacetime. Also, this solution does not address the question of how to deal with insurgents of various kinds, as either combatants or common criminals[31] – admittedly, this is a very difficult issue.

Linked to the question of national liberation movements is that of 'state terrorism'. The long-standing Western position has been that wrongful acts by states are more appropriately regulated by the ordinary rules of state responsibility rather than under criminal law.[32]

International Crime' in *ibid*. 213, and Antonio Cassese, 'The Multifaceted Criminal Notion of Terrorism in International Law' (2006) 4 *JICJ* 1, for the view that the practice shows a consistent approach and that it is therefore a misconception to allege that there is no generally agreed definition of terrorism; he followed this view when President of the Special Tribunal for Lebanon in finding that there was an international customary law definition of terrorism in *Ayyash et al.*, STL AC, 16 February 2011, para. 85.

[26] See e.g. Art. 2(1) of the Terrorist Bombing Convention 1997 which lists acts committed 'unlawfully and intentionally'. Art. 2 of the Terrorist Financing Convention 1999 prohibits the provision or collection of funds (the underlying act) with the intention that the funds should be used for terrorist acts.

[27] Draft Comprehensive Convention, Art. 2(1) . For a critique of individual elements of the draft Convention's elements, see Alexandra Orlova and James Moore, '"Umbrellas" or "Building Blocks"? Defining International Terrorism and Transnational Organized Crime in International Law' (2005) 27 *Houston Journal of International Law* 267, 271–6.

[28] See Section 14.2.2.

[29] OAU Convention, Art. 3(1); Arab Convention, Preamble, Art. 2(a); OIC Convention, Art. 2. It is not clear whether the reference to international law in these instruments is only to the *ius ad bellum* (as the wording in at least the first two mentioned agreements would indicate) or also to international humanitarian law (as is sometimes claimed): see Mahmoud Hmoud, 'The Organization of the Islamic Conference' in Guiseppe Nesi (ed.), *International Cooperation in Counter-Terrorism* (Aldershot, 2006) 166; see also Michael de Feo, 'The Political Offence Concept in Regional and International Conventions Relating to Terrorism' in *ibid*. 116–19. If the latter is a permissible interpretation of these agreements, those committing terrorist acts would be excluded from the exemption since terrorism is prohibited by international humanitarian law.

[30] The Supreme Court of Canada has stated that this definition 'catches the essence of what the world understands by terrorism' (*Suresh* v. *Canada* [2002] SCC 1, para. 98). See also *Report of the Secretary-General's High-Level Panel on Threats, Challenges and Change*, UN Doc. A/59/565 (2004) para. 164.

[31] See Jan Klabbers, 'Rebel with a Cause? Terrorists and Humanitarian Law' (2003) 14 *EJIL* 299.

[32] See e.g. the statement of the UK representative in the Security Council of 18 January 2002: 'None of these seminal texts [the global terrorism agreements] refer to State terrorism, which is not an international legal concept. We must be careful not to get

This was also the view of the former UN Secretary-General in his report, *In Larger Freedom*.[33] It is similarly reflected in Article 19(2) of the Terrorist Bombing Convention. The opposing point of view that terrorism is prohibited 'by whomever committed',[34] including state actors, has been put forward in the negotiations on the comprehensive convention.[35]

Mental Elements

Terrorism is distinguished from other crimes based on the *purpose* with which the underlying acts are committed. Like genocide, terrorism in its most typical form is a compound offence: it needs both the *mens rea* appropriate to the underlying offence, and a special intent for terrorism itself. There are two kinds of victims of terrorism: both the targets of the underlying offence and the 'real' targets, who are sought to be coerced.

Terrorism agreements differ in their descriptions of the special intent. Spreading terror[36] would seem the most obvious purpose, but it is broad and may be difficult to prove. The draft comprehensive convention uses the same formulation as the Terrorist Financing Convention, specifying a purpose or intention of intimidating a population or persuading a government to act.[37] Some instruments are even wider. The EU Directive includes the 'aim' of 'seriously destabilizing or destroying the fundamental political, constitutional, economic or social structures of a country or an international organization'.[38] The OAU Convention includes the intention to 'create general insurrection in a State'.[39] Most of the eleven terrorism agreements mentioned in Section 14.2.2 avoid specifying the intent or purpose for which the criminal acts must be committed.[40] This approach allowed for the conclusion of these agreements, but it does have the disadvantage that they implicitly include acts committed for merely personal or commercial reasons, and thus miss the unique feature of terrorism.

Intent must be distinguished from motive. While some national definitions include a motive with which the terrorist act is committed,[41] most international formulations,

---

caught up in the rhetoric of political conflict. If States abuse their power, they should be judged against the international conventions and other instruments dealing with . . . humanitarian law', UN Doc. S/PV.4453 (2002), paras. 24–5.

[33] 'It is time to set aside debates on so-called "State terrorism". The use of force by states is already thoroughly regulated under international law', UN Doc. A/59/2005, para. 91.

[34] GA Res. 49/60(1994).

[35] It was also the view of Oscar Schachter, 'The Lawful Use of Force by a State Against Terrorists in Another Country' (1989) 19 *Israel Yearbook on Human Rights* 209, 210.

[36] The definition in the CIS Convention includes terrorizing the population as one of the purposes for which terrorist acts are committed. See also Additional Protocol I, Art. 51(2).

[37] Draft Comprehensive Convention, Art. 2(1). [38] EU Directive on Combating Terrorism, Art. 3(2)(c).

[39] OAU Convention on the Preventing and Combating of Terrorism 1999, Art. 1(3)(a)(iii).

[40] For exceptions, see the Hostages Convention, Art. 1 (since the imposition of conditions of release is an intrinsic part of the offence of hostage-taking); Terrorist Financing Convention, Art 2; Terrorist Bombing Convention, Art. 5; and Nuclear Terrorism Convention, Art. 6.

[41] See e.g. the UK definition set out in the Terrorism Act 2000, s. 1, as amended by the Terrorism Act 2006 and the Counter-Terrorism Act 2008: terrorism means the use or threat of action which involves serious violence against a person or serious danger to property, endangers a person's life, creates a serious risk to public health or safety, or is designed seriously to interfere with or disrupt an electronic system where 'the use or threat is designed to influence the government or an intergovernmental organization or to intimidate the public or a section of the public', and it is made 'for the purpose of advancing a political, religious, racial or ideological cause'.

including the draft comprehensive convention, do not. Motive cannot be a justification of terrorist action, and, if the intention is specified, it is unnecessary to limit the offence further by requiring the action to have a political, religious, or other motive.

14.2.4 Prosecution and Other National Measures

The multilateral conventions, like other suppression conventions, focus on international cooperation and include *aut dedere aut judicare* obligations. The goal is national prosecution, although this can be challenging. National courts may have to grapple with the difficulties of how terrorism is defined, particularly if national law incorporates international law.[42] Another major difficulty arises from the nature of the evidence on which the charges are based, for example, where the evidence is intelligence-based.

Both the UN General Assembly and the Security Council have stressed that, in taking counter-terrorism measures, states should comply with international human rights law.[43] Some of the global terrorism conventions expressly require that terrorist suspects be treated fairly in proceedings against them, and provide that there is no obligation to extradite where a state has substantial grounds to believe that the extradition request has been made for the purpose of punishing on the basis of race, religion, or political opinion.[44] However, for the most part, the agreements leave to national systems the responsibility of protecting the rights of the accused, a responsibility which must be exercised in accordance with international human rights obligations.

14.2.5 Terrorism As an International Crime

There is no international court or tribunal which has jurisdiction over an international crime of terrorism as such.[45] In the negotiation of the ICC Statute, there was some support for including terrorism within the jurisdiction of the ICC, but that view did not prevail. A Resolution adopted at the Rome Conference[46] recommended that a review conference consider crimes of terrorism, but the matter was not taken up at the Kampala Review Conference in 2010. The Netherlands put forward a proposal to give the ICC jurisdiction over terrorism, but this proposal has not been taken further.[47]

A terrorist act may be an international crime within the meaning used in this book if it falls within one of the established categories of international crimes. The organized use of terror in

---

[42] For a discussion of an illustrative case in Italy's Supreme Court of Cassation, see Lucia Aleni, 'Distinguishing Terrorism from Wars of National Liberation in the Light of International Law' (2008) 6 *JICJ* 525.

[43] See e.g. GA Res. 51/210, 17 December 1996, para. 3; SC Res. 1456 (2003), para. 6 of the Annex.

[44] See e.g. Nuclear Terrorism Convention 2005, Arts. 12 and 16.

[45] As we have seen, terrorism did come within the jurisdiction of the Special Tribunal for Lebanon, an internationalized court, but was based on Lebanese domestic law.

[46] Resolution F of the Final Act of the Rome Diplomatic Conference.

[47] See proposal of the Netherlands, Annex 3 to report of the Working Group on Amendments, ICC-ASP/10/32 (2011). This proposal is not currently under active discussion by the Working Group on Amendments of the ICC's Assembly of States Parties: Report of the Working Group on Amendments, ICC-ASP/21/22 (1 December 2022).

the Second World War was considered as both a war crime and a crime against humanity by the Nuremberg Tribunal.[48]

Terrorism As a War Crime

Acts of terrorism are prohibited by international humanitarian law and may constitute war crimes. Article 51(2) of Additional Protocol I provides:

The civilian population as such, as well as individual civilians, shall not be the object of attack. Acts or threats of violence the primary purpose of which is to spread terror among the civilian population are prohibited.[49]

This prohibition and its criminalization are part of customary international law.[50] While acts of terrorism were included specifically in the list of violations of common Article 3 in the Statutes of the International Criminal Tribunal for Rwanda (ICTR) and of the Special Court for Sierra Leone (SCSL),[51] the International Criminal Tribunal for the former Yugoslavia (ICTY) had no such explicit wording in its Statute. However, the ICTY held that it has jurisdiction by virtue of the general wording of Article 3 of its Statute (violation of the laws and customs of war).[52] Terrorism is not within the list of war crimes in Article 8 of the ICC Statute.

In the first case involving terrorism before an international court, the ICTY convicted General Galić on the war crimes charge of 'acts of violence the primary purpose of which is to spread terror among the civilian population', based upon command responsibility for a protracted campaign of shelling and sniping in civilian areas of Sarajevo.[53] Evidence was given that civilians were attacked while attending funerals, while in ambulances and buses, while gardening, and while shopping in markets; the main thoroughfare of Sarajevo became known as 'Sniper Alley'. The Tribunal found that the campaign was intended to terrorize the civilian population; it had no discernible military significance.

The Trial Chamber first had to find that the war crime of terror was a 'violation of the laws and customs of war', criminalized at the time of the commission of the alleged offence. For reasons relating to the perceived need to consider only 'serious' violations of treaty law as war crimes,[54] it specifically left to one side the question of whether it had jurisdiction over acts of violence which did not cause death or injury.[55] The SCSL subsequently found that it is indeed unnecessary to prove actual death or injury in order to constitute this war crime.[56]

In *Galić*, the Appeals Chamber confirmed that actual terrorization of a civilian population is not an element of the crime, it is to be expected that *all* acts of war will result in general fear in the country concerned.[57] As regards the mental element, the Trial Chamber required the prosecution:

[48] Nuremberg IMT, Judgment and Sentences, reprinted in (1947) 41 *AJIL* 172 at e.g. 229, 231, 289, and 319.
[49] Additional Protocol I, Art. 51(2); Geneva Convention IV, Art. 33(1); Additional Protocol II, Arts. 4(2)(d) and 13(2).
[50] *Galić*, ICTY AC, 30 November 2006, paras. 87–98. Judge Shahabuddeen in his Separate Opinion noted that the Appeals Chamber was not suggesting, in this finding, that a comprehensive definition of terror was known to customary international law; only the 'core concept'.
[51] ICTR Statute, Art. 4(d); and SCSL Statute, Art. 3(d). [52] In *Galić*, ICTY TC I, 5 December 2003.
[53] *Ibid*. For lengthy discussion of the war crime of terrorism in a later case, see *D. Milošević*, ICTY AC, 12 November 2009.
[54] See Chapter 12.
[55] Robert Cryer, '*Prosecutor v. Galić* and the War Crime of Terror Bombing' (2005–6) 2 *Israel Defence Force Law Review* 73. *Galić*, ICTY AC, 30 November 2006, para. 100.
[56] *Fofana and Kondewa*, SCSL AC, 28 May 2008, paras. 350–2. [57] *Galić*, ICTY AC, 30 November 2006, para. 104.

to prove not only that the accused accepted the likelihood that terror would result from the illegal acts – or, in other words, that he was aware of the possibility that terror would result – but that that was the result which he specifically intended. The crime of terror is a specific-intent crime.[58]

The spreading of terror does not have to be the only purpose of the acts,[59] but it does have to be the *primary* purpose. This was accepted and reiterated by the SCSL.[60]

In sum, the international case law shows that there are three elements in the war crime of acts of terrorism: (1) acts or threats of violence; (2) the accused wilfully made the civilian population or individual civilians not taking direct part in hostilities the objects of those acts or threats of violence; and (3) the acts or threats were carried out with the specific intent of spreading terror among the civilian population.

Terrorism as a Crime Against Humanity

Terrorist acts are not listed as crimes against humanity in the Statutes of the ad hoc Tribunals or the ICC. It is, however, clear that acts of terror may also fall within one or more of the prohibited acts in the definition of crimes against humanity. In *Galić*, the accused was charged with and convicted of crimes against humanity of murder and inhumane acts on the basis of the same facts as the war crime of terror.[61] Similarly, after 11 September 2001, states and public figures condemned the terrorist acts in New York and Washington as crimes against humanity.[62]

A Customary Law Definition of an International Crime of Terrorism?

The Appeals Chamber of the Special Tribunal for Lebanon has determined that there is a crime of terrorism under customary international law:

a number of treaties, UN resolutions, and the legislative and judicial practice of States evince the formation of a general *opinio juris* in the international community, accompanied by a practice consistent with such *opinio*, to the effect that a customary rule of international law regarding the international crime of terrorism, at least *in time of peace*, has indeed emerged. This customary rule requires the following three key elements: (i) the perpetration of a criminal act (such as murder, kidnapping, hostage-taking, arson, and so on), or threatening such an act; (ii) the intent to spread fear among the population (which would generally entail the creation of public danger) or directly or indirectly coerce a national or international authority to take some action, or to refrain from taking it; (iii) when the act involves a transnational element.[63]

However, there is debate as to the correctness of this conclusion. One commentator is of the view that the Appeals Chamber's 'conclusion has scant empirical grounding in state practice, its reasoning is poorly substantiated, and it ultimately plays fast and loose with custom

---

[58] *Ibid.* [59] *Ibid.* [60] See, e.g., *Fofana and Kondewa*, SCSL AC, 28 May 2008, para. 356.

[61] *Galić*, ICTY TC I, 5 December 2003. See also *Krstić*, ICTY TC I, 2 August 2001, paras. 607, 653.

[62] See, e.g., Colleen Swords, 'At the Department of Foreign Affairs 2001-2' (2002) *Canadian Yearbook of International Law* 469; Antonio Cassese, 'Terrorism is Also Disrupting Some Crucial Legal Categories of International Law' (2001) 12 *EJIL* 99, 994; Frédéric Mégret, 'Justice in Times of Violence' (2003) 14 *EJIL* 327, 332–4.

[63] *Ayyash et al.*, STL AC, 16 February 2011, para. 85. The Tribunal then went on to 'interpret and apply' Lebanese law (which was the only applicable law under its Statute) in accordance with the customary rule as found by the Tribunal, thereby significantly broadening the provisions of Lebanese law.

formation'.[64] This may be a harsh assessment, but there is some support for the conclusion that the Special Tribunal was incorrect.[65] The position of the Special Tribunal for Lebanon has, however, been quoted approvingly in UK courts for the proposition that there is a defined international crime of terrorism.[66] But the idea has, as of yet, remained unpersuasive.

14.3 TORTURE

14.3.1 Introduction

Torture is not an international crime as the term is used in this book[67] since it is not punishable *as such* by any international court or tribunal, but under certain conditions it may constitute genocide, a crime against humanity, or a war crime.[68] It is included here because there is clearly international consensus on the condemnation, suppression, and domestic criminalization of torture. There is an absolute prohibition of torture in international law, both in treaty and customary law.[69] The prohibition applies even in times of national emergencies or wars, and there are no exceptions or justifications.[70] It amounts to *ius cogens*[71] and states incur international responsibility if their officials commit torture.[72] It offends against a fundamental value of the international community, as illustrated in the widely ratified Convention Against Torture and Other Cruel, Inhuman and Degrading Treatment or Punishment of 1984 (widely referred to by its acronym, CAT).[73]

14.3.2 UN Convention Against Torture

The UN Convention Against Torture was concluded to 'make more effective' the already existing prohibition under international law.[74] It requires states parties to criminalize the

---

[64] Ben Saul, 'Legislating from a Radical Hague: The United Nations Special Tribunal for Lebanon Invents an International Crime of Transnational Terrorism' (2011) 24 *LJIL* 677. The case, decided when Antonio Cassese was the President of the Chamber, followed the view expressed in his academic writings, e.g. 'Terrorism as an International Crime' (n. 25); and in 'The Multifaceted Criminal Notion of Terrorism in International Law' (n. 25).

[65] The ruling is criticized by Saul (n. 64) 677, and Kai Ambos, 'Judicial Creativity at the Special Tribunal for Lebanon: Is There a Crime of Terrorism under International Law?' (2011) 24 *LJIL* 655. To the contrary, see Manuel Ventura, 'Terrorism According to the Special Tribunal for Lebanon's Interlocutory Decision on the Applicable Law: A Defining Moment or a Moment of Defining?' (2011) 9 *JICJ* 1021.

[66] *R* v. *Gul*, UK Court of Appeal, 22 February 2012.

[67] In some classifications, torture is an international crime. The House of Lords in *Pinochet (No. 3)* regarded it as such (*R* v. *Bow Street Metropolitan Stipendiary Magistrate, ex parte Pinochet Ugarte (No. 3)* [1999] 2 All ER 97, 198, 249, 260, 288) though their Lordships' remarks are not always easy to follow. In Antonio Cassese et al., *Cassese's International Criminal Law*, 3rd ed. (Oxford, 2013) 132–4, torture is described as an international crime.

[68] See Section 11.3.7 and Section 12.3.2 above. [69] For a list of international instruments prohibiting torture, see Section 11.3.7.

[70] 1984 UN Convention Against Torture, Art. 2(2): 'No exceptional circumstances whatsoever, whether a state of war or a threat of war, internal political instability or other public emergency, may be invoked as a justification for torture'. The classic argument that torture is sometimes justifiable may be found in Alan M. Dershowitz, *Why Terrorism Works: Understanding the Threat, Responding to the Challenge* (New Haven, CT, 2002); for a response to such claims, see Paola Gaeta, 'May Necessity be Available as a Defence Against Torture in the Interrogation of Suspected Terrorists?' (2004) 2 *JICJ* 762.

[71] *Questions relating to the Obligation to Prosecute or Extradite* (*Belgium* v. *Senegal*), ICJ General List 144, 20 July 2012, para. 99. See also the claim of Canada and the Netherlands against Syria under the CAT: Joint Application Instituting Proceedings Concerning a Dispute under the Convention Against Torture and Other Cruel, Inhuman or Degrading Treatment or Punishment (*Canada and Netherlands v. Syria*), filed with the Registry 8 June 2023.

[72] *Furundžija*, ICTY TC II, 10 December 1998, para. 153.

[73] Neil Boister, 'Transnational Criminal Law?' (2003) 14 *EJIL* 953, 967. As of September 2023, the CAT had 173 states parties.

[74] Preamble to the Convention.

offence of torture in their domestic law, including attempts and complicity as well as participation (Article 4).[75] The Committee Against Torture, established by the CAT, has confirmed that states must define torture as a separate offence in their criminal law, but they do not have to reproduce the Convention definition verbatim; they may adopt a wider definition.[76]

Material Elements

As defined in Article 1 of the CAT – and specifically for the purpose of the CAT – the crime has two objective elements. First, it comprises 'any act by which severe pain or suffering, physical or mental', is inflicted on a person; and second, it is committed 'by or at the instigation of or with the consent or acquiescence of a public official or other person acting in an official capacity'.

The first element contains a severity requirement: this 'criterion is significant, for it is this which distinguishes torture from "cruel, inhuman or degrading treatment or punishment", which is also criminalized by Article 16 of the CAT and customary international law.'[77] Others argue that the distinction between these crimes is instead in the *purpose* for which the pain or suffering is inflicted.[78]

The second element (link to a public official) is not present in some other definitions of torture, such as in Article 7(2)(e) of the Rome Statute. The Inter-American Convention to Prevent and Punish Torture 1985 provides an even wider definition as it does not specify a purpose or a level of pain and suffering; indeed, it does not have an element of pain or suffering at all if the act is intended 'to obliterate the personality of the victim or to diminish his physical or mental capacities'.[79] The ICTY has pronounced the CAT's definition as reflecting customary international law, but only for the purpose of state obligations under the CAT, not with respect to the meaning of the crime more generally.[80]

There is no definitive list of conduct amounting to torture.[81] Acts such as physical violence, infliction of intense pain, and bodily mutilation can amount to torture.[82] Sexual violence 'necessarily gives rise to severe pain or suffering, whether physical or mental';[83] 'rape involves the infliction of suffering at a requisite level of severity to place it in the category of torture'.[84] Solitary confinement may be torture,[85] and 'waterboarding' has been widely acknowledged to constitute torture.[86] Torture may also be wholly psychological. The Special Rapporteur on Torture identified these common forms of psychological torture: the deliberate and purposeful

---

[75] See Nigel Rodley and Matt Pollard, 'Criminalisation of Torture: State Obligations under the United Nations Convention Against Torture and Other Cruel, Inhuman and Degrading Treatment or Punishment' (2006) 2 *European Human Rights Law Review* 115 at note 17.

[76] Committee Against Torture, General Comment No. 2, UN Doc. CAT/C/GC/2 (24 January 2008), paras. 8, 9, 11.

[77] Robert Currie and Joseph Rikhof, *International and Transnational Criminal Law*, 3rd ed. (Toronto, 2020) 334.

[78] Manfred Nowak and Elizabeth Arthur, *The United Nations Convention Against Torture* (Oxford, 2008) 69.

[79] See Arts. 1(2), 2 and 3. For the definition and the case law, see Laurence Burgorgue-Larsen and Amaya Ubeda de Torres, *The Inter-American Court of Human Rights: Case Law and Commentary* (Oxford, 2011) 369.

[80] *Kunarac et al.*, ICTY AC, 12 June 2002, paras. 146, 147 (and the other cases there cited); and *Kvočka et al.*, ICTY AC, 28 February 2005, para. 284.

[81] Nigel Rodley and Matt Pollard, *The Treatment of Prisoners under International Law*, 3rd ed. (Oxford, 2009), reviews the authorities at ch. 3 ('What Constitutes Torture and Other Ill-Treatment?'); and see *Delalić et al.*, ICTY TC II, 16 November 1998, paras. 461–9.

[82] Currie and Rikhof (n. 77), 334. [83] *Kunarac et al.*, ICTY AC, 12 June 2002, para. 150.

[84] *Delalić et al.*, ICTY TC II, 16 November 1998, para. 489. [85] *Krnojelac*, ICTY TC II, 15 March 2002, para. 183.

[86] E.g. by US Attorney-General Holder in his confirmation hearing in January 2009.

infliction of fear, phobia, or anxiety; purposeful domination and subjugation inducing a profound sense of helplessness, hopelessness, and total dependency on the torturer; the systematic and deliberate violation of privacy, dignity, and sexual integrity; deliberate sensory manipulation and disorientation; attacking the victim's need for social and emotional rapport, for example through isolation, arbitrary detention, and persecution.[87] There is no absolute threshold level of pain or suffering.[88] Factors such as the age, vulnerability, and state of health of the victim are relevant, but not exclusive factors.[89]

The CAT definition refers to acts but not to omissions. However, omissions can rise to the level of torture – such as the failure to provide a prisoner with food or water – if all of the other elements of intention, purpose, and connection with a public official are present.[90]

Pain or suffering arising only from lawful punishment, or incidental to it, is excluded from the definition of torture.[91] Article 1(2) makes clear that, by excluding various means of punishment from its definition of torture, the CAT does not legitimize any act which would be contrary to some other provision of international law.

The CAT definition of torture is limited to acts committed by 'a public official or other person acting in an official capacity'.[92] That limitation is not included in the definition of torture as a crime against humanity, nor in the requirements for war crimes.[93] Furthermore, there may in any event be duties on the state to prevent and punish torture committed by private actors.[94]

Mental Elements

The pain or suffering must be 'intentionally' inflicted. The CAT also requires that the act is committed against a person with specific intent (Article 1(1)):

for such purposes as obtaining from him or a third person information or a confession, punishing him for an act he or a third person has committed or is suspected of having committed, or intimidating him or a third person, or for any reason based on discrimination of any kind.

This list of requisite purposes is narrow. While it is not exhaustive, the wording demands that other purposes must be of the same kind as those in the list. If the act is committed for essentially private purposes, such as sheer sadism, it would appear not to be covered, although it might be expected that a court interpreting the words would strive to bring any such act within the ambit of the definition.[95] States implementing the CAT in

---

[87] Special Rapporteur on torture and other cruel, inhuman or degrading treatment or punishment, 'Report on psychological torture and ill-treatment', A/HRC/43/49 (20 March 2020), paras. 43–67.

[88] *Kunarac et al.*, ICTY AC, 12 June 2002, para. 149.

[89] See William A. Schabas, *The European Convention on Human Rights: A Commentary* (Oxford, 2015) 169–70.

[90] *Delalić et al.*, ICTY TC II, 16 November 1998, para. 468; J. Hermann Burgers and Hans Danelius, *The United Nations Convention on Torture* (Dordrecht, 1988) 118.

[91] CAT, Art. 1. For the view that there is no meaningful scope of application of this exclusion and that it must therefore simply be ignored, see Manfred Nowak, *The United Nations Convention on Torture: A Commentary* (Oxford, 2008) 84.

[92] The term clearly goes beyond state officials. For discussion of its meaning, see Sandesh Sivakumaran, 'Torture in International Human Rights and International Humanitarian Law: The Actor and the Ad Hoc Tribunals' (2005) 18 *LJIL* 541.

[93] See Section 11.3.7 and Section 12.3.2. [94] See Schabas, *European Convention* (n. 89) 190–4.

[95] Burgers and Danelius maintain that the common element in the list is the existence of a state interest or policy, but that even where the purpose is sadistic there is usually an aspect of punishment or intimidation to bring it within the list: J. Herman Burgers and Hans Danelius, *The United Nations Convention Against Torture: A Handbook on the Convention Against Torture and Other Cruel, Inhuman or Degrading Treatment or Punishment* (Leiden, 1988) 119.

domestic law are not obliged to confine the offence to acts committed only with the listed purposes; the United Kingdom, for example, has not included any requirement of purpose.[96]

14.3.3 Prosecution and Other National Measures

The CAT incorporates the *aut dedere aut judicare* principle (Article 7), requiring states to take a wide jurisdiction to prosecute and, if they do not prosecute, to extradite to anywhere in the world.[97] It is generally recognized that there is universal jurisdiction under customary international law in respect of acts of torture.[98] Article 5(2) of the CAT requires a state party to 'establish its jurisdiction' over acts of torture when the alleged offender is 'present in any territory under its jurisdiction' and the state does not extradite that person. Article 6(2) and Article 7(1), respectively, require a state party, when a person who has allegedly committed an act of torture is found on its territory, to hold a preliminary inquiry into the facts and, if it does not extradite the person, to 'submit the case to its competent authorities for the purpose of prosecution'. The nature and scope of this duty is discussed in Section 4.3.1.

 The Convention imposes other obligations. For example, states may not use information obtained by torture in legal proceedings (Article 15);[99] states must afford effective remedies and adequate reparation to the victims of torture (Article 14); and states may not deport, extradite, or otherwise transfer a person to a country where there are substantial grounds for believing that the person would be in danger of being tortured (Article 3).[100]

14.3.4 Torture As an International Crime

Torture falls within the jurisdiction of the ICC and the International Residual Mechanism for Criminal Tribunals (as it was in the ad hoc Tribunals) only if committed under certain conditions: it is included expressly within the definitions of crimes against humanity and war crimes where all other relevant requirements are met.[101] For war crimes and crimes against humanity, perpetrators are not limited to persons acting in an official capacity. Furthermore, the list of prohibited purposes is extended – indeed, no 'purpose' is required for the prosecution of crimes against humanity before the ICC.

---

[96] See Criminal Justice Act 1988, s. 134.

[97] Some commentators suggest that the Convention requires states to take universal jurisdiction to allow them to prosecute an act of torture, regardless of whether the state where the act was committed, or the state of nationality of the victim or suspect, is a state party or not: Rodley and Pollard, 'Criminalisation of Torture' (n. 75) 131. This approach would conflict with the ordinary principles of treaty interpretation. See generally on universal jurisdiction Section 3.5.

[98] See Section 3.5.1.

[99] See Tobias Thienel, 'The Admissibility of Evidence Obtained by Torture under International Law' (2006) 17 *EJIL* 349.

[100] See also case law on the interpretation of Art. 3 of the European Convention on Human Rights, which makes clear that it is not possible to balance other rights and interests against the protection of a person from being deported to a country where that person will be subjected to torture or ill-treatment (e.g. *Saadi* v. *Italy*, 37201/06, 28 February 2008).

[101] See Arts. 7(1)(f), 8(2)(a)(ii), and 8(2)(c)(i) of the Rome Statute, and Art. 1(1) of the IRMCT Statute, which incorporates Arts. 2(b) and 5(f) ICTY Statute and 3(f) and 4(a) ICTR Statutes. For discussion of torture as a crime against humanity and as a war crime, see Section 11.3.7 and Section 12.3.2.

14.4 ECOCIDE

At present, genocide, crimes against humanity, war crimes, and aggression – as well as terrorism and torture – are 'anthropocentric', meaning that they focus on harms to humans and human society.[102] There is only one crime in the ICC Statute which is 'ecocentric' – that is to say, encompassing harm to the environment as a crime in its own right – namely, the war crime of launching a disproportionate attack with the knowledge that the attack will cause significant destruction to the natural environment (Article 8(2)(b)(iv)). A successful environmental war crime prosecution under that provision would be difficult, as one would have to prove 'widespread, long-term, and severe' environmental damage, in addition to proving disproportionality and all the other complex elements of that crime (see Section 12.3.4).[103] It is also possible that environmental harm could be considered in a crime against humanity case (for example, poisoning the environment and therefore affecting a population might be an 'inhumane act')[104] or a genocide case (where there was an intent to destroy a human group through environmental damage).[105] But the primary focus of these offences is on the harm to humans and human interests; the offences are not designed for prosecuting massive environmental harm as such.

However, egregious environmental wrongdoing can create harms equal to, or dramatically exceeding, the established international crimes – harms transcending national boundaries and jeopardizing the health and well-being of present and future generations of human and non-human animals. The ongoing, multiple, escalating ecological crises have fuelled the impetus to recognize a new serious international crime of 'ecocide'. Such a crime could be a 'transnational' crime, recognized in many national legal systems because of its transboundary significance; it could also someday become a fifth 'core crime', added to the jurisdiction of international courts.[106]

The term 'ecocide' combines 'eco' (*oikos*), for ecosystem (or home), and 'cide', for killing or cutting down. The term was coined by biologist Arthur Galston in the early 1970s, in response to the massive use of Agent Orange in Vietnam. Several scholars have advanced possible definitions for ecocide over the years.[107] The late Polly Higgins, a UK lawyer, was a particularly influential advocate for the proposed new crime.[108] The objective behind

---

[102] Frédéric Mégret, 'The Problem of an International Criminal Law of the Environment' (2011) 36 *Colum J Envtl L* 195.

[103] Mark Drumbl, 'Waging War against the World: The Need to Move from War Crimes to Environmental Crimes' (1998) 22 *Fordham Int'l L J* 122; Jessica Lawrence & Kevin Jon Heller "The First Ecocentric Environmental War Crime: The Limits of Article 8(2)(b)(iv) of the Rome Statute" (2007) 20 *Geo Int'l Envtl L Rev* 72; Matthew Gillett, *Prosecuting Environmental Harm before the International Criminal Court* (Cambridge, 2022).

[104] Luigi Prosperi & Jacop Terrosi, 'Embracing the "Human Factor": Is There New Impetus at the ICC for Conceiving and Prioritizing Intentional Environmental Harms as Crimes Against Humanity? (2017) 15 *JICJ* 509; Jessica Durney, 'Crafting a Standard: Environmental Crimes as Crimes Against Humanity Under the International Criminal Court' (2018) 24 *Hastings Environmental Law Journal* 413; Caitlin Lambert, 'Environmental Destruction in Ecuador: Crimes Against Humanity Under the Rome Statute?' (2017) 30 *LJIL* 707; Darryl Robinson, 'Environmental Crimes Against Humanity' (2 June 2020), *Opinio Juris*, opiniojuris.org.

[105] Tim Lindgren, 'Ecocide, Genocide and the Disregard of Alternative Life-Systems' (2018) 22 *International Journal of Human Rights* 525; Tara Smith, 'Creating a Framework for the Prosecution of Environmental Crimes in International Criminal Law' in William A. Schabas et al. (eds.), *The Ashgate Companion to International Criminal Law: Critical Perspectives* (Abingdon, 2013).

[106] On 'transnational' crimes and 'international crimes', see Section 1.1.

[107] See e.g. Mark Allan Gray, 'The International Crime of Ecocide' (1996) 26 *California Western International Law Journal* (1996) 215.

[108] P. Higgins, *Eradicating Ecocide: Laws and Governance to Stop the Destruction of the Planet*, 2nd ed. (Shepheard-Walwyn, 2016).

creating a crime of ecocide is to increase the stigma, sanction, and robustness of enforce-ment for the most egregious environmental wrongdoing. Such a crime would reframe severe pollution and destruction as the serious harm that it is, rather than as a mere regulatory or administrative matter.[109]

In 2021, an international panel of experts, led by Philippe Sands and Dior Fall Sow, advanced a proposed definition of ecocide.[110] The proposal attracted both support and concerns, and counter-proposals.[111] The idea of a crime of ecocide has taken flight, with many national parliaments working to develop and adopt such a crime; for example, the European Parliament is deliberating about a directive for all EU legal systems to adopt a crime of ecocide.[112] Various expert bodies have produced definitions with intriguing variations on the International Panel of Experts definition.[113]

Defining a crime of ecocide is difficult, because environmental law contains almost no concrete prohibitions addressed to individuals that are suitable for criminalization.[114] Instead, environmental law lays out various principles for sustainably sharing and managing resources. As a result, there are many challenges in trying to develop a legally grounded and viable definition of a crime with the requisite clarity and specifi-city. One issue is how significant the harm must be. Most proposals use some combination of the words 'widespread', 'long-term', and 'severe', either conjunctively or disjunctively,[115] to describe the required level of environmental damage. That formula has been used in various instruments already.[116] A second issue is the mental element: environmental laws often use low fault standards, such as strict liability; however, a serious crime likely requires a higher standard, like intent or recklessness. Some proposals require awareness of a significant likelihood of harm (a standard akin to recklessness or *dolus eventualis*).[117] The current European Parliament draft includes two different levels of fault: 'intentional' or 'negligent' ecocide.[118] A third issue is whether and how to craft a 'wrongfulness' element, so that activity becomes criminal

---

[109] Rob White, 'Climate Change, Ecocide and The Crimes of the Powerful' in Gregg Barak (ed.), *The Routledge International Handbook of the Crimes of the Powerful* (London, 2015).

[110] International Expert Panel for the Legal Definition of Ecocide, *Commentary and Core Text* (2021), ecocidelaw.com/legal-definition-and-commentary-2021.

[111] For two prominent critical commentaries, see Kai Ambos, 'Protecting the Environment through Criminal Law?', EJIL:Talk!, 29 June 2021, www.ejiltalk.org; Kevin Jon Heller, 'Skeptical Thoughts on the Crime of Ecocide – That Isn't', *Opinio Juris*, 23 June 2021, www.opiniojuris.org.

[112] Kate Mackintosh, 'European Parliament Votes Unanimously for Ecocide', 10 April 2023, *Opinio Juris*, www.opiniojuris.org; Darryl Robinson, 'The Ecocide Wave is Already Here: National Momentum and the Value of a Model Law', 23 February 2023, *Just Security*, www.justsecurity.org.

[113] Promise Institute for Human Rights Group of Experts, 'Proposed Definition of Ecocide' (2021), available at ecocidelaw.com; European Law Institute, 'ELI Report on Ecocide' (2023) available at europeanlawinstitute.eu; European Parliament, 'Report on the proposal for a directive of the European Parliament and of the Council on the protection of the environment through criminal law and replacing Directive 2008/99/EC', 28 March 2023, A9-0087/2023, available at europarl.europa.eu.

[114] For surveys of the issues, see Darryl Robinson, 'Ecocide – Puzzles and Possibilities' (2022) 20 *JICJ* 313; Adam Branch and Liana Minkova, 'Ecocide, the Anthropocene, and the International Criminal Court' (2023) 37 *Ethics & International Affairs* 51.

[115] International Expert Panel, 'Commentary' (n. 110), 5 and 8.

[116] Protocol Additional to the Geneva Conventions of 12 August 1949, 8 June 1977, Arts 35(3), 55(1); 1976 Convention on the Prohibition of Military or any Hostile Use of Environmental Modification Techniques ('ENMOD Convention'), 10 December 1976, 1108 UNTS 151; International Law Commission, *Draft Code of Crimes against the Peace and Security of Mankind*, in *ILC Yearbook, Vol II*, Part 2, UN Doc. A/46/10, at Arts. 21 and 26; ICC Statute, Art. 8(2)(b)(iv).

[117] International Expert Panel, 'Commentary' (n. 110), 11. [118] European Parliament, 'Report' (n. 113), 10.

when it violates environmental principles of sustainable development. Not all high-impact activity is wrongful under current environmental law principles, and arguably it is not feasible to immediately ban all such activities (particularly where there are not yet any less-harmful alternatives), without first undergoing significant social, economic, and technological reforms.[119] Thus, none of the major recent proposals seeks to cover *all* activity producing environmental harm; instead, they focus on only the most irresponsible activity that violates principles of sustainable development. To achieve this, proposals refer to conduct that is 'unlawful', 'wanton', or 'fraudulent or corrupt', though each of these terms presents its own challenges.[120] A fourth issue is whether the crime of ecocide should require causation (i.e. that severe environmental damage actually occurs) or whether it can be based on 'endangerment', that is, acting with knowledge that one is likely to cause serious environmental harm.[121] The debates on the crime of ecocide are evolving extremely quickly, and many answers to such questions could well emerge in the near future.

Further Reading

Transnational Crimes

Neil Boister, *An Introduction to Transnational Criminal Law*, 2nd ed. (Oxford, 2018)

Neil Boister and Robert Currie (eds.), *Routledge Handbook on Transnational Criminal Law* (London, 2015)

Robert Currie and Joseph Rikhof, *International and Transnational Criminal Law*, 2nd ed. (Toronto, 2014).

Harmen Van der Wilt and Christophe Paulussen (eds.), *Legal Responses to Transnational and International Crimes* (Cheltenham, 2017)

Terrorism

Andrea Bianchi (ed.), *Enforcing International Law Norms against Terrorism* (Oxford, 2004)

Helen Duffy, *The 'War on Terror' and the Framework of International Law*, 2nd ed. (Cambridge, 2009)

Rosalyn Higgins and Maurice Flory (eds.), *Terrorism and International Law* (London, 1997)

Stella Margariti, *Defining International Terrorism: Between State Sovereignty and Cosmopolitanism* (The Hague, 2017)

Giuseppe Nesi (ed.), *International Cooperation in Counter-Terrorism* (Aldershot, 2006)

---

[119] Robinson, 'Puzzles' (n. 114), 321–4 and 332–8. [120] *Ibid.*, 338–43.
[121] International Expert Panel, 'Commentary' (n. 110), 12.

Eric Rosand, 'Security Council Resolution 1373, the Counter-Terrorism Committee, and the Fight Against Terrorism' (2003) 97 *AJIL* 333

Ben Saul (ed.), *Research Handbook on International Law and Terrorism* (Cheltenham, 2014)

Christian Walter et al. (eds.), *Terrorism as a Challenge for National and International Law: Security versus Liberty?* (Berlin, 2004)

Torture

Ahcene Boulesbaa, *The UN Convention on Torture and the Prospects for Enforcement* (The Hague, 1999)

J. Herman Burgers and Hans Danelius, *The United Nations Convention Against Torture: A Handbook on the Convention Against Torture and Other Cruel, Inhuman or Degrading Treatment or Punishment* (Leiden, 1988)

Manfred Nowak and Elizabeth Arthur, *The United Nations Convention Against Torture* (Oxford, 2008)

Nigel Rodley and Matt Pollard, 'Criminalisation of Torture: State Obligations under the United Nations Convention Against Torture and Other Cruel, Inhuman and Degrading Treatment or Punishment' (2006) 2 *European Human Rights Law Review* 115

Lene Wendland, *A Handbook on State Obligations under the UN Convention Against Torture* (Geneva, 2002)

Ecocide

Darryl Robinson, 'Ecocide – Puzzles and Possibilities' (2022) 20 *JICJ* 313

Adam Branch and Liana Minkova, 'Ecocide, the Anthropocene, and the International Criminal Court' (2023) 37 *Ethics & International Affairs* 51

15

General Principles of Liability

15.1 INTRODUCTION

The substantive definitions of crimes discussed in Chapters 10–13 provide only a part of the picture of criminal liability. The general principles of liability apply across the various different offences and provide for the doctrines by which a person may commit, participate in, or otherwise be found responsible for those crimes. They include forms of liability such as aiding and abetting, which are familiar to all domestic criminal lawyers, as well as principles like command responsibility, which are specific to international criminal law. The various forms of liability not only have different conduct elements, but also different mental elements. Unlike in domestic law – where the traditional image of a criminal is the primary perpetrator, such as the person who pulls the trigger – in international criminal law, the paradigmatic offender is often the person who orders, masterminds, or takes part in a plan at a high level.[1] International crimes tend to occur against a backdrop of collective criminality.[2] As a result, principles of liability play a comparatively large role in international criminal law.[3]

This chapter will discuss the principles of liability from two points of view: the ambit of liability recognized in international law;[4] and the appropriateness of those principles from the point of view of foundational principles of criminal law.[5] Important critiques have been made about compliance with such principles.[6] It must be noted at the outset, though, that the different modes of liability – for example, aiding/abetting, joint perpetration, and

---

[1] Such persons are often referred to as 'those bearing greatest responsibility' for international crimes (see e.g. SCSL Statute, Art. 1) or 'the most senior leaders suspected of being responsible for' international crimes (SC Res. 1534(2004)).

[2] See e.g. Elies van Sliedregt, *Individual Criminal Responsibility in International Criminal Law* (Oxford, 2012) ch. 2; André Nollkaemper and Harmen van der Wilt (eds.), *System Criminality in International Law* (Cambridge, 2009).

[3] See William Schabas, 'Enforcing Individual Criminal Responsibility in International Criminal Law: Prosecuting Accomplices' (2001) 843 *International Review of the Red Cross* 439. Equally, as we shall see, some forms of liability in international criminal law allow people who would traditionally be seen as accomplices to be viewed as principal perpetrators. See also Héctor Olásolo, *The Criminal Responsibility of Senior Political and Military Leaders as Principals to International Crimes* (Oxford, 2009) ch. 1.

[4] As was mentioned in Section 8.4, the ICC Statute ought not to be taken straightforwardly as determinative of customary international criminal law.

[5] See further on this point, Robert Cryer, 'General Principles of Liability in International Criminal Law' in McGoldrick et al., *The Permanent ICC*, 233.

[6] For a variety of views, see George Fletcher, 'The Theory of Criminal Liability and International Criminal Law' (2012) 10 *JICJ* 1029; Darryl Robinson, 'A Cosmopolitan Liberal Account of International Criminal Law' (2013) 26 *LJIL* 127; James Stewart, 'The End of Modes of Liability for International Crimes' (2012) 25 *LJIL* 165; Markus Dubber, 'Common Civility: The Culture of Alegality in International Criminal Law' (2011) 24 *LJIL* 923; Elies van Sliedregt, 'The Curious Case of International Criminal Liability' (2012) 10 *JICJ* 1171; Schachar Eldar, 'Exploring International Criminal Law's Reluctance to Resort to Modalities of Group Responsibility: Five Challenges to International Prosecutions and their Impact on Broader Forms of Responsibility'

common purpose liability – are not watertight compartments, and that there are overlaps between them.[7] Where they overlap, the International Criminal Tribunal for the former Yugoslavia (ICTY) has suggested that 'the Trial Chamber has a discretion to choose which is the most appropriate head of responsibility under which to attach criminal responsibility to the accused'.[8]

15.2 PERPETRATION/COMMISSION

The concept of commission is well established in international criminal law.[9] For example, in the *Jaluit Atoll* case in 1945, three Japanese soldiers were convicted of personally shooting prisoners-of-war.[10] Article 7(1) of the ICTY Statute (Article 6(1) of the International Criminal Tribunal for Rwanda (ICTR) Statute and Article 6(1) of the Special Courts for Sierra Leone (SCSL) Statute are similar) imposes liability, *inter alia*, on any 'person … [who] committed' an international crime. This description is, however, deceptively simple, as it begs the question of precisely who can be considered to have 'committed' a crime. As the ICTY has said, this primarily refers to 'the physical perpetration of a crime by the offender himself, or the culpable omission of an act that was mandated by a rule of criminal law'.[11]

The concept of 'commission' (synonymous with 'perpetration') is not limited to physical commission. Article 25(3)(a) of the International Criminal Court (ICC) Statute criminalizes conduct of a person who '[c]ommits such a crime whether as an individual, jointly with another or through another person, regardless of whether that other person is criminally responsible'.

One issue is whether or not perpetration can occur by omission, that is, by failing to act. In customary law, this is certainly the case, so long as the charge relates to a failure to live up to a duty to act, and the omission has a 'concrete influence' on the crime.[12] Although there is some doubt that perpetration by omission is recognized in the ICC Statute,[13] owing to the fact that a proposed general provision criminalizing omissions was not included in the final Statute,[14] the better view is that liability for omissions was not categorically excluded by

---

(2013) 11 *JICJ* 331. For an attempt to create a comprehensive study postulating the bases for such doctrine, see Kai Ambos, *Treatise on International Criminal Law*, vol. I, *Foundations and General Part*, 2nd ed. (Oxford, 2021).

[7] Mohamed Shahabuddeen, *International Criminal Justice at the Yugoslav Tribunal: A Judge's Recollection* (Oxford, 2012) 216–17.

[8] *Krnojelac*, ICTY TC II, 15 March 2002, para. 173. Trial chambers are not inherently precluded from entering a conviction for a crime on the basis of more than one mode of liability, if this is necessary to reflect the totality of an accused's criminal conduct. *Đorđević*, ICTY AC, 27 January 2014, para. 831. In the ICC, see *Al Mahdi*, ICC TC VIII, 27 September 2016 (ICC-01/12–01/15–171), paras. 60–1

[9] This concept is synonymous with 'perpetration'; the two will be used interchangeably here.

[10] *United States v. Masuda and others* (the 'Jaluit Atoll case'), I LRTWC 71 (1945).

[11] *Tadić*, ICTY AC, 15 July 1999, para. 188. See similarly *Kvočka et al.*, ICTY TC I, 2 November 2001, para. 251.

[12] *Orić*, ICTY AC, 3 July 2008, para. 94. See generally Ambos, *Treatise on International Law* (n. 6) 180–97 (where it is suggested that it is a general principle rather than custom). For a list of positive obligations in humanitarian law, see Yves Sandoz, Christoph Swiniarski and Bruno Zimmermann (eds.), *Commentary on the Additional Protocols of 8 June 1977 to the Geneva Conventions of 8 August 1949* (Geneva, 1987) 1009. One example of a conviction for an omission is *Delalić et al.*, ICTY TC II, 16 November 1998, paras. 1092–6, 1101–5.

[13] Per Saland, 'International Criminal Law Principles' in Lee, *Making of the Rome Statute*, 212.

[14] Kerstin Weltz, *Die Unterlassungshaftung im Völkerstrafrecht* (Freiburg im Breisgau, 2004) 320 et seq.

the drafters.[15] The ICC Elements of Crimes deliberately avoid the term 'acts' in favour of 'conduct', on the ground that the latter term includes acts or omissions.[16]

In the context of Article 25(3)(a), the ICC has identified three forms of perpetration: where the defendant

(1) physically carries out all elements of the offence (direct commission);
(2) has, together with others, control over the offence by reason of the essential tasks assigned to him (joint commission); or
(3) has control over the will of those who carry out the objective elements of the offence (indirect commission, through another person).[17]

The first form is basic perpetration. The second is joint or co-perpetration, the third is indirect perpetration, that is, perpetration by means of using a person – the principal – as a tool who physically commits the crime. Joint and indirect commission will be discussed below. First, however, it is necessary to canvass the form of commission known as 'joint criminal enterprise', as it has been developed by the ICTY, ICTR, and other courts relying on customary law.

15.2.1 Joint Criminal Enterprise[18]

The Charters of the Nuremberg and Tokyo International Military Tribunals (IMTs) both provided that those who participated in a 'common plan or conspiracy to commit any of the foregoing crimes are responsible for all acts performed by any person in execution of such a plan'.[19] The form of liability contained in these provisions, which both Tribunals determined only applied to crimes against peace,[20] is often called conspiracy.[21] The use of 'conspiracy' in this regard is misleading, as it causes confusion between this type of liability and the separate inchoate offence of conspiracy known to some common law systems.[22] Conspiracy as an inchoate offence means the mere agreement to commit crimes can generate liability.[23] In international criminal law, 'conspiracy' only exists in relation to genocide.[24]

Article 7(1) of the ICTY Statute, Article 6(1) of the ICTR Statute, and Article 6(1) of the SCSL Statute do not contain any express provision on this form of liability.[25] Nonetheless, the ICTY has developed a detailed jurisprudence on *committing* crimes by participating in a 'joint criminal enterprise' (or common purpose). The leading judgment on the point is in

---

[15] See also Section 15.3 below.
[16] See e.g. Maria Kelt and Herman von Hebel, 'The Making of the Elements of Crimes' in Lee, *Elements and Rules*, 14.
[17] *Katanga and Ngudjolo*, ICC PTC I, 30 September 2008 (ICC-01/04–01/07–717) para. 488.
[18] For a useful overview, see Elies van Sliedregt, *The Criminal Responsibility of Individuals for Violations of International Humanitarian Law* (The Hague, 2003) 94–110. See also the symposium and anthology in (2007) 5 *JICJ* 67–244.
[19] Nuremberg IMT Charter, Art. 6; Tokyo IMT Charter, Art. 5(c).
[20] Nuremberg IMT, Judgment and Sentences, reprinted in (1947) 41 *AJIL* 172, 221–2; Tokyo IMT, reprinted in Neil Boister and Robert Cryer, *Documents on the Tokyo International Military Tribunal* (Oxford, 2008) 48, 449. Judges Bernard and Jaranilla dissented on this: Dissenting Opinion of the Member from France, at 5–7; Concurring Opinion of the Member from the Philippines, 1–7.
[21] It was also called so by the Tribunals themselves.   [22] *Milutinović et al.*, ICTY AC, 21 May 2003, para. 23.
[23] David Ormerod and Karl Laird, *Smith, Hogan, and Ormerod's Criminal Law*, 16th ed. (Oxford, 2021) 435–59.
[24] 1948 Genocide Convention, Art. 3(d). See William Schabas, *Genocide in International Law*, 2nd ed. (Cambridge, 2008) ch. 6.
[25] See, for discussion, Harmen van der Wilt, 'Joint Criminal Enterprise: Possibilities and Limits' (2007) 5 *JICJ* 91, 102–8.

Tadić. Tadić had been acquitted at trial level of involvement in the killing of five civilians by an armed group of which he was a member, as there was no evidence he was personally involved in the killings. The Appeals Chamber overturned this acquittal and set out its understanding of commission by virtue of participation in a joint criminal enterprise (JCE). The Chamber began by looking at Article 7(1) of the ICTY Statute. It decided that, as the purpose of the Statute was to cover all those responsible for international crimes in the former Yugoslavia, Article 7(1) does not exclude those modes of participating in the commission of crimes which occur where several persons having a common purpose embark on criminal activity that is then carried out either jointly or by some members of this plurality of persons.[26] It supported this finding by pointing to the nature of many international crimes, in particular that they are committed jointly by large numbers of people.[27] Since the *actus reus* and *mens rea* were not set out in the ICTY Statute, the Appeals Chamber looked to customary law, primarily as evidenced in case law.

Actus Reus

Having reviewed post-Second World War proceedings,[28] such as the *Almelo* case[29] and the *Essen Lynching Trial*,[30] the Appeals Chamber in *Tadić* determined that there was a customary basis for JCE liability in three types of cases: (1) 'co-perpetration, where all participants in the common design possess the same criminal intent to commit a crime (and one or more of them actually perpetrate the crime, with intent)' (JCE I); (2) so-called 'concentration camp cases' (JCE II); and (3) where crimes are committed by members of the group, outside its common purpose, but as a foreseeable incident of it (JCE III).[31] It further determined that all three types shared a common *actus reus*, namely, that there was:

(i) a plurality of persons;
(ii) the existence of a common plan, design or purpose which amounts to or involves the commission of a crime provided for in the Statute;
(iii) participation of the accused in the common design involving the perpetration of one of the crimes provided for in the Statute.[32]

The Appeals Chamber in *Tadić* elaborated on these criteria. For example, 'the common plan or purpose may materialise extemporaneously and be inferred from the fact that a plurality of persons acts in unison to put into effect a joint criminal enterprise'.[33] Participation in the common plan or design 'need not involve commission of a specific crime under one of those

---

[26] *Tadić*, ICTY AC, 15 July 1999, paras. 189–90. Another case has, controversially, determined that Art. 7(1) is not exhaustive: *Milutinović et al.*, ICTY AC, 21 May 2003, para. 20. Still, the Appeals Chamber in *Stakić* appeared to frown on new doctrines being introduced into the Tribunal's jurisprudence: *Stakić*, ICTY AC, 22 March 2006, para. 59.
[27] *Tadić*, ICTY AC, 15 July 1999, para. 191.
[28] Not all of which, it must be noted, firmly based their forms of liability in international law.
[29] *Otto Sandrock*, I LRTWC 35 (1945).   [30] *Erich Heyer*, I LRTWC 88 (1945).
[31] *Tadić*, ICTY AC, 15 July 1999, para. 220. See also *Gacumbitsi*, ICTR AC, 7 July 2006, Separate Opinion of Judge Shahabuddeen, para. 40.
[32] *Tadić*, ICTY AC, 15 July 1999, para. 227.   [33] *Ibid.*

provisions ... but may take the form of assistance in, or contribution to, the execution of the common plan or purpose'.[34] It also said that the conduct must be 'in some way ... directed to the furthering of the common plan or purpose'.[35] It may occur by virtue of an omission.[36] Membership in the group per se is not enough to ground liability on this basis.[37] There has to be some form of action by the defendant to contribute to the crimes involved in the implementation of the plan.[38]

There is no requirement that the contribution made by the defendant is a 'necessary or substantial' one,[39] but a later Appeals Chamber decision in the *Brđanin and Talić* case said that it needs to be 'significant'.[40] The Appeals Chamber in that case took the view that the direct perpetrators 'on the ground' do not have to be a part of the enterprise, so long as the crimes can be imputed to one member of the enterprise.[41]

There is sense in the Appeals Chamber's position, in that the usual collective nature of the crimes means that it would be practically impossible to prove the *mens rea* of all of the direct perpetrators when trying high-level participants.[42] In asserting this position, though, the ICTY has opened itself up to criticism on the ground that it is stretching liability beyond the appropriate bounds of culpability.[43] It ought to be borne in mind, however, that a person is only responsible for crimes which relate to the plan or purpose to which they subscribed.[44] If the common plan or purpose fundamentally changes, then this is a new plan or purpose;[45] thus the person would only be liable if they agree to the expansion. The ICTY has stated that, 'it is not necessary to show that the JCE members *explicitly* agreed to the expansion of criminal means; this agreement may materialise extemporaneously and be inferred from circumstantial evidence'.[46]

Mens Rea

Although the conduct element of all of the forms of JCE liability is the same, the distinction between them comes in via the mental element. The Appeals Chamber in *Tadić* remains the standard reference on the point:

the *mens rea* element differs according to the category of common design under consideration. With regard to the first category, what is required is the intent to perpetrate a certain crime (this being the

---

[34] *Ibid.* See also *Krajišnik*, ICTY AC, 17 March 2009, para. 695.
[35] *Tadić*, ICTY AC, 15 July 1999, para. 229, The requirement is not exactly clear, however.
[36] *Prlić et al.*, ICTY AC, 29 November 2017, para. 139; *Karadžić*, ICTY TC, 24 March 2016, para. 566. But see also *Župljanin and Stanišić*, ICTY AC, 30 June 2016, para. 109.
[37] *Milutinović*, ICTY AC, 21 May 2003, para. 26; *Brđanin and Talić*, ICTY TC II, 1 September 2004, para. 263.
[38] *Brđanin and Talić*, ICTY TC II, 1 September 2004, para. 263. [39] *Kvočka et al.*, ICTY AC, 28 February 2005, para. 97.
[40] *Brđanin and Talić*, ICTY AC, 3 April 2007, para. 430. The exact difference between 'substantial' and 'significant' is not entirely clear, but has been repeated; see *Krajišnik*, ICTY AC, 17 March 2009, para. 215, although see *Popović et al.*, ICTY AC, 30 January 2015, para. 1378.
[41] *Brđanin and Talić*, ICTY AC, 3 April 2007, paras. 410–14; but see the Dissenting Opinion of Judge Shahabuddeen, paras. 4–20. Nor does there have to be an agreement with the direct perpetrator for them to commit the crime: *ibid.* paras. 418–19.
[42] In *Krajišnik*, the Appeals Chamber noted that not all members have to be named; reference by group may be enough in some circumstances, but the 'rank and file consist[ing] of local politicians, military and police commanders, paramilitary leaders, and others' was too vague. See *Krajišnik*, ICTY AC, 17 March 2009, para. 156.
[43] E.g. Van der Wilt, 'Joint Criminal Enterprise' (n. 25); Cliff Farhang, 'Point of no Return: Joint Criminal Enterprise in Brđanin' (2010) 23 *LJIL* 137.
[44] *Blagojević and Jokić*, ICTY TC I, 7 January 2005, para. 700.
[45] *Krajišnik*, ICTY TC I, 27 September 2006, para. 1903. See also *ibid.* para. 701, note 2157, although, if the later plan or purpose is broader, he or she may still be liable for those crimes that fall within the narrower aspect agreed to.
[46] *Krajišnik*, ICTY AC, 17 March 2009, para. 163. See also *Ayyash et al.*, STL AC, 16 February 2011, para. 246.

shared intent on the part of all co-perpetrators). With regard to the second category (which is really a variant of the first),[47] personal knowledge of the system of ill-treatment is required (whether proved by express testimony or a matter of reasonable inference from the accused's position of authority), as well as the intent to further this common concerted system of ill-treatment. With regard to the third category, what is required is the *intention* to participate in and further the criminal activity or the criminal purpose of a group and to contribute to the joint criminal enterprise or in any event to the commission of a crime by the group. In addition, responsibility for a crime other than the one agreed upon in the common plan arises only if, under the circumstances of the case, (i) it was *foreseeable* that such a crime might be perpetrated by one or other members of the group, and (ii) the accused *willingly took that risk*.[48]

As ought to be clear, the first category of JCE (JCE I) is close to the concept of joint perpetration: the various participants share the *intention* to commit the crime that occurs. This is possibly slightly diluted in the second type (JCE II), where *knowledge* of the system of ill-treatment suffices rather than the intent to commit the specific crime.[49] The broadest form of liability comes in JCE III, where the *foresight* of a crime is said to be the test. This test was applied in the *Tadić* case where the Appeals Chamber found that Tadić willingly took the risk that ethnic cleansing would lead to killings; the deaths were natural and foreseeable consequences of the common purpose.[50] 'Willingly taking risks' means that negligence does not suffice. It corresponds to the lowest degree of intent: recklessness or *dolus eventualis*.[51]

Nature of Joint Criminal Enterprise Liability

The Appeals Chamber in *Milutinović et al.* determined that JCE liability is a form of 'committing', in the language of Article 7(1) of the ICTY Statute.[52] Even if JCE I and JCE II can be considered a form of primary liability[53] – which is not beyond controversy since it uses the language of *participating* (in crimes committed by others) and hence indicates it is rather secondary or complicity liability – it might be questioned whether JCE III liability could really be seen as a form of 'commission'.[54] After all, it does not require proof of a shared intent but mere foresight, which indicates a role outside the 'inner circle' and hence a lesser form of blameworthiness. However, the ICTY has been consistent that this is the case.[55]

---

[47] But see *Kvočka et al.*, ICTY AC, 28 February 2005, para. 86; Steven Powles, 'Joint Criminal Enterprise: Criminal Liability by Prosecutorial Ingenuity and Judicial Creativity?' (2004) 2 *JICJ* 606, 609–10.

[48] *Tadić*, ICTY AC, 15 July 1999, para. 228 (emphasis in original).

[49] Although in both instances the Appeals Chamber has said the participants must share the physical perpetrator's *mens rea*: *Krnojelac*, ICTY AC, 17 September 2003, para. 83.

[50] *Tadić*, ICTY AC, 15 July 1999, paras. 228, 231–2.

[51] For a useful overview of the difference between negligence, recklessness, and *dolus eventualis* see: Mohamed Badar and Iryna Marchuk, 'A Comparative Study of the Principles Governing Criminal Responsibility in the Major Legal Systems of the World (England, United States, Germany, France, Denmark, Russia, China, and Islamic Legal Tradition)' (2013) 24 *Criminal Law Forum* 1, 31–5.

[52] *Milutinović et al.*, ICTY AC, 21 May 2003, para. 20; *Kvočka et al.*, ICTY AC, 28 February 2005, paras. 79–80.

[53] Aspects of joint criminal enterprise can perhaps appropriately be seen as forms of commission, given the often large-scale perpetration of international crimes; see e.g. Jens Ohlin, 'Three Conceptual Problems with the Doctrine of Joint Criminal Enterprise' (2007) 5 *JICJ* 69, 70, 72–4.

[54] See also *ibid*. 85–8.

[55] See e.g. *Popović et al.*, ICTY AC, 30 January 2015, para. 1672; *Mladić*, ICTY TC I, 22 November 2017, para. 3557.

The nature of joint criminal enterprise liability is important. From the point of view of the principle of fair labelling, grouping all forms of JCE as primary forms of liability lumps together rather different levels of culpability. There is no distinction between those who are in essence joint perpetrators, but with a simple division of labour, from those whose conduct is much closer to aiders and abettors. The Appeals Chamber has admitted that this may be disquieting, but claimed that such matters can be dealt with satisfactorily in sentencing.[56]

Perhaps unsurprisingly, JCE liability has proved very controversial; academics[57] and later judicial decisions have been critical of the ICTY's approach to establishing the law here. The Pre-Trial Chamber of the Extraordinary Chambers in the Courts of Cambodia (ECCC), for example, has determined, through a review of the same materials as the ICTY relied upon, that customary law did not contain a broad principle of joint enterprise liability equivalent to JCE III between 1975 and 1979.[58] The ICTY responded that JCE was 'well established in both customary international law and the jurisprudence of the tribunal',[59] and had repeatedly reaffirmed its earlier holdings.[60]

From the point of view of fairness to the defendant, the vague, 'elastic' nature of the doctrine has led to claims that it is overbroad, thus reliant on prosecutorial discretion rather than law to keep it in check.[61] This is particularly the case where large-scale enterprises are charged.[62] Fears have also been expressed about the extent to which it encourages prosecutors to bring indictments that assert joint enterprises in a very general manner, making preparation difficult for the defence.[63]

Turning to the *mens rea*, a person could be convicted as a principal before the ICTY and ICTR of specific intent crimes such as genocide, even if that person did not have the relevant *mens rea* for that offence, so long as the crimes were a natural and foreseeable consequence of the enterprise he or she was involved in on the basis of JCE.[64] This has led to criticisms of JCE liability, as allowing the prosecution to circumvent the proper *mens rea* requirements for such serious crimes.[65] The principle, however, remained popular with the

---

[56] *Brđanin and Talić*, ICTY AC, 3 April 2007, para. 432.
[57] Robert C. Clarke, 'Return to Borkum Island: Extended Joint Criminal Enterprise Responsibility in the Wake of World War II' (2011) 9 *JICJ* 839; Alison Marston Danner and Jenny S. Martinez, 'Guilty Associations: Joint Criminal Enterprise, Command Responsibility and the Development of International Criminal Law' (2005) 93 *California Law Review* 75, 110–17; Powles, 'Joint Criminal Enterprise' (n. 47) 614–17; Ohlin, 'Three Conceptual Problems' (n. 53) 75–6; Olásolo, *Criminal Responsibility* (n. 3) ch. 2.
[58] *Ieng Sary et al.*, ECCC PTC, 20 May 2010, paras. 75–88. [59] *Prlić et al.*, ICTY AC, 29 November 2017, paras. 51–2.
[60] *Martić*, ICTY AC, 8 October 2008, paras. 80–1; *Krajišnik*, ICTY AC, 17 March 2009, paras. 652–72.
[61] Mark Osiel, 'The Banality of Good: Aligning Incentives Against Mass Atrocity' (2005) 105 *Columbia Law Review* 1751, 1799–1802; Danner and Martinez, 'Guilty Associations' (n. 57) 135–46; Mohamed Elawa Badar, 'Just Convict Everyone! Joint Perpetration from Tadić to Stakić and Back Again' (2006) 6 *ICLR* 302. Equally, see Katrina Gustafson, 'The Requirement of an "Express Agreement" for Joint Criminal Enterprise Liability: A Critique of Brđanin' (2007) 5 *JICJ* 134; Antonio Cassese, 'The Proper Limits of Criminal Liability under the Doctrine of Joint Criminal Enterprise' (2007) 5 *JICJ* 109, 116–23; and *Brđanin and Talić*, ICTY AC, 3 April 2007, paras. 426–32.
[62] E.g. *Brđanin and Talić*, ICTY AC, 3 April 2007, paras. 420–5.
[63] Guénaël Mettraux, *International Crimes and the Ad Hoc Tribunals* (Oxford, 2006) 293; Osiel, 'The Banality of Good' (n. 61) 1803. Although the ICTY did not think this problematic: see *Limaj et al.*, ICTY AC, 27 September 2007, para. 104.
[64] *Karemera et al.*, ICTR AC, 22 October 2004, paras. 30–1. However, this position has been rejected by the Special Tribunal for Lebanon (STL): *Ayyash et al.*, STL AC, 16 February 2011, para. 248.
[65] Mettraux, *International Crimes* (n. 63) 265; Osiel, 'The Banality of Good' (n. 61) 1796. For a defence, see Elies van Sliedregt, 'Joint Criminal Enterprise as a Pathway to Convicting Individuals for Genocide' (2007) 5 *JICJ* 184.

ICTY's prosecutors.[66] It does go some way to describing the joint nature of many international crimes and explaining the culpability of some participants not otherwise easily brought under the ambit of criminality, in spite of their blameworthiness.[67]

JCE's defenders point to the requirement that the accused willingly took the risk of the offence occurring within the scope of the joint enterprise as a significant limitation.[68] In addition, the policy considerations relating to the danger of collective activity and attributing liability in such circumstances means, for them, that JCE is justifiable.[69] Whether these considerations answer the question of whether liability ought to be attributed in such circumstances is debatable.[70] Owing to the fact that JCE III does not fall under the jurisdiction of the ICC,[71] its significance has decreased. It is still relevant for prosecutions under customary international law.

In *Thaçi et al.* before the Kosovo Specialist Chambers (KSC), the defendants were charged with participating in a JCE.[72] Article 16(1) of the KSC Statute is identical to Article 7(1) of the ICTY Statute. The KSC regards JCE III as part of joint enterprise liability, which can be read into 'committing' in Article 16(1) of the KSC Statute.[73]

15.2.2 Co-perpetration

The second type of perpetration noted by the ICC is commonly known as joint or co-perpetration. It performs an analogous function to JCE, although is probably not as broad. Co-perpetration in general:

is originally rooted in the idea that when the sum of the coordinated individual contributions of a plurality of persons results in the realisation of all the objective elements of a crime, any person making a contribution can be held vicariously responsible for the contributions of all the others and, as a result, can be considered as a principal to the whole crime.[74]

At least one Trial Chamber in the ICTY attempted to introduce a form of 'co-perpetratorship'.[75] In the *Stakić* case, the Trial Chamber asserted the existence of such a form of liability, although its support came from doctrine and national analogies, rather than direct sources of international law.[76] The Appeals Chamber in that case determined that

---

[66] See e.g. Nicola Piacente, 'Importance of the Joint Criminal Enterprise Doctrine for ICTY Prosecutorial Policy' (2004) 2 *JICJ* 446.

[67] Mettraux, *International Crimes* (n. 63) 292; Osiel, 'The Banality of Good' (n. 61) 1786–90, but see 1802; Danner and Martinez, 'Guilty Associations' (n. 57) 132–4.

[68] Cassese, 'The Proper Limits of Criminal Liability' (n. 61); Shahabuddeen, *International Criminal Justice* (n. 7) 222–3; Antonio Cassese et al., *Cassese's International Criminal Law*, 3rd ed. (Oxford, 2013) 170.

[69] Shahabuddeen, *International Criminal Justice* (n. 7) 224–6.

[70] For critique, see Wayne Jordash, 'Joint Criminal Enterprise Liability: Result Oriented Justice' in Schabas et al., *Ashgate Research Companion*, 133.

[71] *Katanga*, ICC TC II, 7 March 2014 (ICC-01/04–01/07–3436-tENG) para. 1619.

[72] *Thaçi et al.*, KSC SPO, 27 February 2023, paras. 32–57. The Kosovo Specialist Chambers is a 'hybrid' court: see Chapter 9.

[73] *Thaçi et al.*, KSC P T J, 22 July 2022. See also *Mustafa*, KSC TC, 16 December 2022, para. 734.

[74] *Lubanga*, ICC PTC I, 29 January 2007 (ICC-01/04–01/06–803) para. 326.

[75] Care must be taken when reading judgments on this point, as sometimes such a term is used to mean joint perpetration or the liability of a person participating in a joint criminal enterprise. See, for the former, e.g. *Furundžija*, ICTY TC II, 10 December 1998, para. 252; for the latter, see e.g. *Vasiljević*, ICTY AC, 25 February 2004, para. 102; *Kvočka et al.*, ICTY AC, 28 February 2005, para. 90.

[76] *Stakić*, ICTY TC II, 31 July 2003, para. 440.

'[t]his mode of liability, as defined and applied by the Trial Chamber, does not have support in customary international law or in the settled jurisprudence of this Tribunal'.[77] The Appeals Chamber preferred to see it as being a form of joint criminal enterprise liability.[78] The Trial Chamber itself admitted that it was 'aware that the end result of its definition of co-perpetration approaches that of the aforementioned joint criminal enterprise and even overlaps in part'.[79]

The doctrine of co-perpetration plays a large part in the practice of the ICC.[80] The jurisprudence on direct co-perpetration formed the basis of the ICC's first conviction, in the *Lubanga* case.[81] The basic requirements were identified in the majority decision in the *Lubanga* trial judgment (which was upheld on appeal):

(i) there was an agreement or common plan between the accused and at least one other co-perpetrator that, once implemented, will result in the commission of the relevant crime in the ordinary course of events;

(ii) the accused provided an essential contribution to the common plan that resulted in the commission of the relevant crime;

(iii) the accused meant to … [commit the relevant crime] or he was aware that by implementing the common plan these consequences 'will occur in the ordinary course of events'; [and]

(iv) the accused was aware that he provided an essential contribution to the implementation of the common plan.[82]

Actus Reus

Let us take the requirements in turn. The first requirement of a common plan is analogous to that in JCE liability.[83] Case law has established that the plan need not be express;[84] it may be inferred from later concerted action.[85] After early inconsistency in the jurisprudence of the ICC on whether or not the plan has to be directed to committing a crime,[86] the matter seems to have been settled by the ICC Appeals Chamber in the *Lubanga* case. The Chamber stated that it does not,[87] but that crimes need to be foreseen as a 'virtual certainty' in order for liability to arise.[88]

The majority of judicial views given so far about the conduct of the co-perpetrator require that the contribution must be *essential* to the commission of the objective elements of the crime, meaning that the co-perpetrator could frustrate the commission of the crime by not undertaking their part.[89] The 'essential contribution' requirement

---

[77] *Stakić*, ICTY AC, 22 March 2006, para. 62. See also *Milutinović et al.*, ICTY TC III, 22 March 2006.

[78] *Stakić*, ICTY AC, 22 March 2006, paras. 62–3. [79] *Stakić*, ICTY TC II, 31 July 2003, para. 441.

[80] For a detailed exegesis on point, see Elies van Sliedregt and Lachezar Yanev, 'Co-Perpetration Based on Joint Control over the Crime' in Jérôme de Hemptinne, Robert Roth, and Elies van Sliedregt (eds.), *Modes of Liability in International Criminal Law* (Cambridge, 2019).

[81] *Lubanga*, ICC TC I, 14 March 2012 (ICC-01/04–01/06–2842) para. 994. The decision has not gone uncriticized on point: Steffen Wirth, 'Co-Perpetratorship in the Lubanga Trial Judgment' (2012) 10 *JICJ* 971, 984–5.

[82] *Ibid.* para. 1018; *Lubanga*, ICC AC, 1 December 2014 (ICC-01/04–01/06–3122) para. 473.

[83] Wirth, 'Co-Perpetration' (n. 81) 986; van Sliedregt, *Individual Criminal Responsibility* (n. 2) 100.

[84] *Lubanga*, ICC PTC I, 29 January 2007 (ICC-01/04–01/06–803) para. 348. [85] *Ibid.* para. 345.

[86] Van Sliedregt, *Individual Criminal Responsibility* (n. 2) 100.

[87] *Lubanga*, ICC AC, 1 December 2014 (ICC-01/04–01/06–3122) para. 446. [88] *Ibid.* para. 448.

[89] *Lubanga*, ICC PTC I, 29 January 2007 (ICC-01/04–01/06–803) paras. 347–8.

comes from the alleged basis of co-perpetration being the joint control of the crime[90] and the fact that this is a form of primary liability for the relevant offence.[91] This requirement was largely constructed along the lines of criminal law theory developed in one jurisdiction (Germany), particularly by reference to the work of Claus Roxin.[92] This has been criticized.[93] Nonetheless, the Appeals Chamber has stated that any such reliance is not a direct application of these approaches, but is merely an aid in interpreting the Rome Statute.[94]

The 'essential contribution' requirement has been supported on the basis that co-perpetration is a form of principal liability (perpetration/commission), rather than complicity. According to the requirement's supporters, Article 25(3) creates a hierarchy of forms of participation, with perpetration (in Article 25(3)(a), including co-perpetration) as primary responsibility being more serious than other forms of liability (Article 25(3)(b)–(d)).[95] Hence, the argument goes, it ought to have higher thresholds. Although it is possible to derive such a hierarchy from the structure of the ICC Statute ('hierarchy thesis'),[96] the forms of liability overlap, and there is nothing in the Statute or its *travaux* that indicates that the drafters of the ICC Statute intended such a rigid hierarchy.[97] In *Bemba et al.* the Appeals Chamber rejected the hierarchy thesis and recognized that,

[a] mode of liability describes a certain typical factual situation that is subsumed within the legal elements of the relevant provision, and that the difference between committing a crime and contributing to the crime of others would normally reflect itself in a different degree of participation and/or intent within the meaning of rule 145 (1) (c) of the Rules. This however does not mean that the principal perpetrator of a crime/offence necessarily deserves a higher sentence than the accessory to that crime/offence.[98]

---

[90] For detailed elaboration of this idea, see Héctor Olásolo, *The Responsibility of Senior Political and Military Leaders as Principals to International Crimes* (Oxford, 2009) chs. 4–5.

[91] *Lubanga*, ICC AC, 1 December 2014 (ICC-01/04–01/06–3122) para. 469.

[92] For details, see e.g. Thomas Weigend, 'Perpetration Through an Organization: The Unexpected Career of a German Legal Concept' (2011) 9 *JICJ* 91; van Sliedregt, *Individual Criminal Responsibility* (n. 2) 83–8; Jens Ohlin, 'Co-Perpetration German *Dogmatik* or German Invasion?' in Carsten Stahn (ed.), *The Law and Practice of the International Criminal Court* (Oxford University Press 2015) 517–37.

[93] Separate Opinion of Judge Adrian Fulford in *Lubanga*, ICC TC I, 14 March 2012 (ICC-01/04–01/06–2842) paras. 8–12; Concurring Opinion of Judge Christine Van den Wyngaert in *Ngudjolo*, ICC TC II, 18 December 2012 (ICC-01/04–02/12), paras. 5–6, 50–57; Separate opinion of Judge Howard Morrison on Mr Ntaganda's appeal in *Ntaganda*, ICC AC, 30 March 2021 (ICC-01/04-02/06-2666-Anx2) paras. 3–7; Partly concurring opinion of Judge Chile Eboe-Osuji in *Ntaganda*, ICC AC, 30 March 2021 (ICC-01/04-02/06-2666-Anx5), paras. 36–43; See also Weigend, 'Perpetration Through an Organization' (n. 92) 105–6.

[94] *Lubanga*, ICC AC, 1 December 2014 (ICC-01/04–01/06–3122) paras. 470–1. Roxin actually rejected the 'essentiality' theory as defined by the *Lubanga* majority: for co-perpetratorship, he requires a 'substantial' contribution to the common plan as regarded *ex ante* but he writes that the contribution of a co-perpetrator need not be 'causal' for the offence as a whole. Claus Roxin, *Strafrecht Allgemeiner Teil* (2005), Section 25, marginal note 213. See Elies van Sliedregt and Bettina Weißer, 'The Ntaganda case and individual criminal liability at the ICC: Foreword' (2022) 20 *JICJ* 627 – 35.

[95] *Lubanga*, ICC AC, 1 December 2014 (ICC-01/04–01/06–2842) paras. 467–9.

[96] See *Bemba et al.*, ICC AC, 8 March 2018 (ICC-01/05–01/13–2275-Red) paras. 59–60; Ambos, *Treatise on International Law* (n. 6) 146–8, 152–3.

[97] Separate Opinion of Judge Adrian Fulford in *Lubanga*, ICC TC I, 14 March 2012 (ICC-01/04–01/06–2842) paras. 6–9; Concurring Opinion of Judge Van den Wyngaert in *Ngudjolo*, ICC TC II, 18 December 2012 (ICC-01/04–02/12–3) paras. 12– 15, 66–70. See also van Sliedregt, *Individual Criminal Responsibility* (n. 2) 85–6.

[98] *Bemba et al.*, ICC AC, 8 March 2018 (ICC-01/05–01/13–2275-Red) para. 60.

It is at the level of sentencing, not at the conviction level, that the degree of responsibility is expressed. Still, the 'essential contribution' requirement remains a core element of co-perpetration, as does the idea of 'control' of the crime. The latter means that co-perpetrators coordinate their efforts and both contribute in a meaningful way to the commission of the crime, which is then mutually attributable to them.

For co-perpetration, it is generally accepted that the contribution does not require physical presence at the scene of the crime, nor need it occur at the time of the offence per se.[99]

Mens Rea

Turning to the subjective elements, the Pre-Trial Chamber in *Lubanga* made clear that the co-perpetrators, including the accused, must have the mental element for the relevant crime.[100] This has been supported in other decisions of the ICC,[101] most notably by the Appeals Chamber in *Bemba et al.*[102]

At the pre-trial level in *Lubanga*, it was held to be sufficient if the co-perpetrator realized that the implementation of the plan 'may' lead to the commission of a relevant crime.[103] This would bring the mental element close to the *dolus eventualis* standard of JCE III where defendants are held liable for the consequences (crimes) of a common plan that they foresaw *might* occur and willingly accepted. However, this interpretation was all but explicitly overruled by the Appeals Chamber in the *Bemba et al.* case, which supported the Trial Chamber's view (albeit in a slightly different context) requiring foresight that the crimes 'will' occur, and 'that any lower *mens rea* threshold, such as *dolus eventualis*, recklessness and negligence, [was] insufficient'.[104]

15.2.3 Indirect Perpetration/Perpetration Through Another Person

The third form of perpetration identified in the ICC Statute is perpetration through another. Commission through another person recognizes the concept of 'innocent agency', by which a person commits a crime through an unwitting person, who cannot be considered to have any culpable part in the crime, for example, because they were incapable of understanding the nature of their acts, or because they were an inadvertent participant or were acting under duress. In that situation, the 'innocent agents' have not exercised any form of choice, the concept which underlies criminal responsibility at the most basic level.[105]

---

[99] Concurring Opinion of Judge Van den Wyngaert, *Ngudjolo*, ICC TC II, 18 December 2012 (ICC-01/04–02/12–3) para. 47; Separate Opinion of Judge Adrian Fulford in *Lubanga*, ICC TC I, 14 March 2012 (ICC-01/04–01/06–2842) para. 15; *Lubanga*, ICC PTC I, 29 January 2007 (ICC-01/04–01/06–803) paras. 347–8.

[100] *Lubanga*, ICC PTC I, 29 January 2007 (ICC-01/04–01/06–803) paras. 349–60.

[101] *Bemba et al.*, ICC AC, 8 March 2018 (ICC-01/05–01/13–2275-Red) para. 835; *Bemba*, ICC PTC II, 15 June 2009 (ICC-01/05–01/08–424) para. 351; *Ruto et al.*, ICC PTC II, 23 January 2012 (ICC-01/09–01/11–373) paras. 291–2.

[102] *Bemba et al.*, ICC AC, 8 March 2018 (ICC-01/05–01/13–2275-Red) para. 676.

[103] *Lubanga*, ICC PTC I, 29 January 2007 (ICC-01/04–01/06–803) para. 361.

[104] *Bemba et al.*, ICC AC, 8 March 2018 (ICC-01/05–01/13–2275-Red) para. 835.

[105] See e.g. Andrew Simester et al., *Simester and Sullivan's Criminal Law: Theory and Doctrine*, 8th ed. (Oxford, 2022) 215–17.

Article 25(3)(a) goes further by recognizing the possibility of perpetration through a *guilty* agent . This appears to be close to the concept in German law of the '*Hintermann*' ('background man') perpetrator, where the mastermind of an operation who controls the will of those who directly commit the offence is taken to be a direct perpetrator rather than a secondary party or an accomplice.[106]

The ICC has held that indirect perpetration may also occur through control of an organization.[107] This, based expressly on Roxin's theory of *Organisationsherrschaft*,[108] is the idea that control over an organization can lead to perpetration through that organization. In such circumstances, although the crimes are committed in the first instance by others, they are attributed to the controller of the organization. For liability to accrue this way, the defendant must control (or be in 'functional domination' of) an organization, which must be hierarchically organized, with sufficient subordinates that if the orders are not carried out by one subordinate, another will do so nearly automatically.[109]

In other words, '[t]he leader must use their control over the apparatus to execute crimes, which means that the leader, as the "*Hintermann*" or perpetrator behind the perpetrator, mobilises their authority and power within the organisation to secure compliance with their orders'.[110] In this instance, the person needs to be aware of the nature of their organization and their role within it, and the fact that compliance with their orders would be 'near automatic'.[111] They also need to have the *mens rea* of the underlying crime. This derives from the simple fact that, if they are to be considered the perpetrator through others, they must have the *mens rea* for the offence.

Overall, it may be said that Roxin's theory, although having achieved some measure of acceptance in German courts, has been the subject of considerable criticism in Germany for setting high standards such as 'domination' of an organization, a condition that may not be appropriate to do the normative work Roxin hoped, even domestically.[112] A related critique is that, even if it was appropriate in the domestic context in which it was developed (Nazi criminality), it may not be more generally applicable,[113] in particular in less formal settings such as modern conflicts involving non-state actors and militias.[114]

15.2.4 Indirect Co-perpetration

Co-perpetration has been the subject of further expansion, *inter alia*, through the *Lubanga* and *Katanga and Ngudjolo Chui* cases, by mixing the two types of perpetration described

---

[106] See e.g. Claus Kreß, 'Claus Roxin's Lehre von der Organisationsherrschaft und das Völkerstrafrecht' (2006) *Goltdammers Archiv für Strafrecht* 304. For support in the ICTR, see *Gacumbitsi*, ICTR AC, 7 July 2006, Separate Opinion of Judge Schomburg, paras. 14–23; but see Separate Opinion of Judge Shahabuddeen, paras. 42–52, and Partially Dissenting Opinion of Judge Güney, paras. 2–9.
[107] *Ibid.* paras. 500–10.
[108] See Claus Roxin, 'Crimes as Part of Organized Power Structures' (2011) 9 *JICJ* 193, as adopted in *Katanga and Ngudjolo*, ICC PTC I, 30 September 2008 (ICC-01/04–01/07–717) para. 498.
[109] *Katanga and Ngudjolo*, ICC PTC I, 30 September 2008 (ICC-01/04–01/07–717) paras. 515–17. [110] *Ibid.* para. 514.
[111] *Ibid.* para. 534. [112] Weigend, 'Perpetration Through an Organization' (n. 92) 94–101. [113] *Ibid.* 107.
[114] Stefano Manacorda and Chantal Meloni, 'Indirect Perpetration versus Joint Criminal Enterprise: Concurring Approaches in the Practice of International Criminal Law' (2011) 9 *JICJ* 159, 171.

above.[115] The idea is that a co-perpetrator in an organization can be co-responsible for the crimes committed by those for whom another co-perpetrator is responsible through indirect perpetration.

To take an example, a Foreign Minister may be a participant in a common plan with a Minister of Defence that will lead to the commission of war crimes. The Minister of Defence is in control of the armed forces, but the Foreign Minister is not. On the basis of the common plan, the Foreign Minister could be held responsible by indirect co-perpetration for the offences of the armed forces, as the criminality of the Defence Minister would be attributed to the Foreign Minister, and this would include the Defence Minister's indirect perpetration of the offences by the armed forces. This is said, helpfully, to mix co- and indirect perpetration, and acts in a manner similar to JCE, since the *Brđanin and Talić* case determined that the physical perpetrators did not have to be members of the JCE.[116]

The ICC has set out the requirements of indirect co-perpetration as follows:

(i) the suspect must be part of a common plan or an agreement with one or more persons;

(ii) the suspect and the other co-perpetrator(s) must carry out essential contributions in a coordinated manner which result in the fulfilment of the material elements of the crime;

(iii) the suspect must have control over the organization;

(iv) the organization must consist of an organized and hierarchal apparatus of power;

(v) the execution of the crimes must be secured by almost automatic compliance with the orders issued by the suspect;

(vi) the suspect must satisfy the subjective elements of the crimes;

(vii) the suspect and the other co-perpetrators must be mutually aware and accept that implementing the common plan will result in the fulfilment of the material elements of the crimes; and

(viii) the suspect must be aware of the factual circumstances enabling him to exercise joint control over the commission of the crime through another person(s).[117]

As can be seen, requirements (i) to (vii) are very much an amalgam of the requirements of co-perpetration and indirect perpetration. The customary basis of this type of liability has been rejected on a number of occasions.[118] However, this is not a fatal objection to co-perpetration, as it is said to be a creature of the ICC Statute which, pursuant to Article 21 of the Statute, is the primary source of law for the ICC.[119] A more directed critique has come from Judge Van den Wyngaert, who has said that 'co-perpetration through another *person*' cannot be expanded out to the organizational context on the interpretation of the ICC Statute.[120]

---

[115] See Ambos, *Treatise on International Law* (n. 6) 156–60.

[116] See Jens Ohlin, 'Second Order Linking Principles: Combining Vertical and Horizontal Forms of Liability' (2012) 25 *LJIL* 771.

[117] *Ruto et al.*, ICC PTC II, 23 January 2012 (ICC-01/09–01/11–373) para. 292, relying on *Bemba*, ICC PTC II, 15 June 2009 (ICC-01/05–01/08–424) paras. 350–1; *Katanga and Ngudjolo*, ICC PTC I, 30 September 2008 (ICC-01/04–01/07–717) paras. 500–14, 527–39; *Al Bashir Arrest Warrant*, ICC PTC I, 4 March 2009 (ICC-02/05–01/09–3) paras. 209–13.

[118] E.g. *Stakić*, ICTY AC, 22 March 2006, para. 62; *Ayyash et al.*, STL AC, 16 February 2011, para. 256; Yudan Tan, *The Rome Statute as Evidence of Customary International Law* (Leiden/Boston, 2021) 256–64.

[119] See e.g. *Ruto et al.*, ICC PTC II, 23 January 2012 (ICC-01/09–01/11–373) para. 289.

[120] Concurring Opinion of Judge Van den Wyngaert in *Ngudjolo*, ICC TC II, 18 December 2012 (ICC-01/04–02/12–3) paras. 52–64.

In *Ntaganda*, the majority of the Appeals Chamber upheld this form of liability, with two judges voicing disagreement. According to Judges Morrison and Osuji-Eboe, indirect co-perpetration resulted from an erroneous interpretation of Art. 25(3)(a). Judge Morrison proposed the ICC abandon indirect co-perpetration,

[i]f only because the theory's complexity lends the theory a certain elasticity so that criminal responsibility may be broadly stretched over: (i) groups that are not as tightly organised as the hierarchical power structures envisaged by Roxin; and (ii) figures whose power to control the crimes committed through such groups is dubious.[121]

Judge Ibáñez, in a separate opinion, voiced support, repeating many of the points made in the early ICC case law to justify importation of indirect co-perpetration and the control theory.[122] In her view, the control theory and indirect co-perpetration is the most appropriate way to capture the liability of those who mastermind international crimes.[123]

The future of international criminal law is one of indirect enforcement before domestic courts. The ICC, and its case law, is a point of orientation for domestic legal orders. An awareness of its important role in the legal world and in the rich diversity of national legal orders would not have led to a decision favouring a very complex participation model like the German one.[124] It is preferable to try a combination of the features of different models to create a unique interpretation of Article 25(3) of the ICC Statute. A strong argument for such an approach would be that it actually reflects the way Article 25(3) emerged: as a compromise among the contracting parties of the Statute.[125]

15.3 AIDING AND ABETTING

Liability for aiding and abetting (or 'encouraging') international crimes is not new.[126] A notable example of a prosecution for aiding a war crime was the *Zyklon B* case,[127] in which two German industrialists were convicted of supplying poison gas for use in concentration camp killings. The existence of liability for aiding and abetting is uncontroversial; it is recognized, for example in Article 7(1) of the ICTY Statute, Article 6(1) of the ICTR Statute, and Article 6(1) of the SCSL Statute, which all provide for responsibility of 'a person … who aided and abetted in the planning, preparation or execution' of

[121] *Ntaganda*, ICC AC, 30 March 2021, Separate opinion of Judge Howard Morrison on Mr Ntaganda's appeal (ICC-01/04-02/06-2666-Anx2) para. 17.
[122] *Ntaganda*, ICC AC, 30 March 2021, Separate opinion of Judge Luz Del Carmen Ibáñez Carranza (ICC-01/04-02/06-2666-Anx3) 83–125.
[123] As a Peruvian lawyer she will have been familiar with the control theory. It was at the basis of the conviction of former Peruvian leader Fujimori for crimes against humanity. Corte Suprema de Justicia de la República, Primera Sala Penal Transitoria, Exp. N° 19-2001-09A.V., Judgment, 30 December 2009.
[124] For the complexities of Roxin's theory and its reception in different jurisdictions see the Symposium on the *Ntaganda* case and indirect co-perpetration in 20 (2022) *JICJ*, issue 3.
[125] Elies van Sliedregt, 'Perpetration and Participation in Article 25(3) of the Statute of the International Criminal Court', in Carsten Stahn (ed.), *The Law and Practice of the International Criminal Court* (Oxford, 2015).
[126] For a detailed exegesis on point, see Manuel J. Ventura, 'Aiding and Abetting' in Jérôme de Hemptinne, Robert Roth, and Elies van Sliedregt (eds.), *Modes of Liability in International Criminal Law* (Cambridge, 2019).
[127] *Tesch and others*, I LRTWC 93 (1945).

an international crime. However, there have been, and remain, considerable controversies about its scope.[128]

There are also overlaps between JCE liability and aiding and abetting. [129] There is a difference in terms of blameworthiness. The ICTY said that, where people have participated in a joint criminal enterprise, to convict them 'only as an aider and abettor might understate the degree of their criminal responsibility',[130] and thus 'aiding and abetting is a form of responsibility which generally warrants lower sentences than responsibility as a co-perpetrator'.[131] The view of the ICTY on this topic needs to be understood against the background of regarding JCE as a form of 'commission' whereas aiding and abetting is secondary participation/complicity.[132] The ICC Appeals Chamber has taken the view that commission is, all things being equal, a more serious form of responsibility than secondary participation.[133]

The law on aiding and abetting in the ad hoc Tribunals was explained by the *Tadić* appeal judgment of 1999. This set out the requirements as follows:

The aider and abettor carries out acts specifically directed to assist, encourage or lend moral support to the perpetration of a certain specific crime … and this support has a substantial effect upon the perpetration of the crime … the requisite mental element is knowledge that the acts performed by the aider and abettor assist the commission of a specific crime by the principal.[134]

There are a number of things worth noting about this definition. To begin with, the conduct which aids or abets must have a direct and 'substantial' effect on the commission of the crime. However, this should not be taken as setting a particularly high standard: the ICTY has seen it more as meaning any assistance which is more than *de minimis*.[135] As the SCSL has said:

International Tribunals never required that, as a matter of law, an aider and abettor must provide assistance in a particular manner such as providing assistance to the physical actor that is then used in the commission of the crime.[136]

---

[128] There is also a question as to whether complicity in genocide, criminalized in Art. 3(e) of the Genocide Convention, is different from this form of liability; the Appeals Chamber in *Krstić*, ICTY AC, 19 April 2004, paras. 138–44, hinted that the two differ. Since then the case has been read by the Appeals Chamber as establishing that 'the prohibited act of complicity in genocide, which is included in the Genocide Convention and in Article 2 of the Statute, encompasses aiding and abetting'. *Ntakirutimana and Ntakirutimana*, ICTR AC, 13 December 2004, paras. 371 and 500; however, this leaves the door open for 'other forms of complicity' than aiding and abetting. See further *Blagojević and Jokić*, ICTY TC I, 7 January 2005, para. 679. See Chile Eboe-Osuji, 'Complicity in Genocide" versus "Aiding and Abetting Genocide"' (2005) 3 *JICJ* 56; Payam Akhavan, 'The Crime of Genocide in the ICTR Jurisprudence' (2005) 3 *JICJ* 989; Jesse Ingle, 'Aiding and Abetting by Omission Before the International Criminal Tribunals' (2016) 14 *JICJ* 747.

[129] The similarities and differences are discussed in *Tadić*, ICTY AC, 15 July 1999, para. 229, and *Kvočka et al.*, ICTY AC, 28 February 2005, para. 90; *Bemba et al.*, ICC TC VII, 19 October 2016 (ICC-01/05–01/13–1989-Red) para. 87.

[130] *Tadić*, ICTY AC, 15 July 1999, para. 192.

[131] *Vasiljević*, ICTY AC, 25 February 2004, para. 182; *Orić*, ICTY TC II, 30 June 2006, para. 281. See also *Tadić*, ICTY AC, 15 July 1999, para. 191.

[132] See *Orić*, ICTY TC II, 30 June 2006, para. 282.

[133] *Lubanga*, ICC AC, 1 December 2014 (ICC-01/04–01/06–3122) paras. 467–9. Although, for support, see *Bemba et al.*, ICC TC VII, 19 October 2016 (ICC-01/05–01/13–1989-Red) paras. 85–6.

[134] *Tadić*, ICTY AC, 15 July 1999, para. 229.

[135] See e.g. Kai Ambos, 'Article 25' in Triffterer and Ambos, *Commentary*, 1004.

[136] *Taylor*, SCSL AC, 26 September 2013, para. 371.

It is also the case that the conduct itself need not be intrinsically criminal so long as its factual effect results in the assistance of the criminal act.[137] The Tribunals have accepted, amongst other things,[138] that standing near victims whilst armed to prevent them escaping amounts to aiding,[139] as does providing weapons to a principal,[140] or taking principals to the scene of a crime and pointing at people to be killed.[141] Allowing resources for which a person is responsible to be used for crimes may also suffice.[142] The ICC has explained that the Rome Statute's concept of aiding 'implies practical or material assistance'.[143]

The case law of international tribunals offers guidance on the complexities of causation. According to the Appeals Chamber in *Tadić*, there can be multiple causes that lead to the victim's death: it 'must simply form a link in the chain of causation, it is not necessary that this participation to be a *sine qua non*, or a that the offence would not have occurred but for his participation'.[144] In the *Salih Mustafa* case, the KSC rejected the defence argument that 'substantial contribution' requires a single cause of death. The Appeals Chamber held that:

The acts and conduct of MUSTAFA and other BIA members substantially contributed to the Murder Victim's death by placing him in a situation in which he was unable to escape the military offensive. In other words, the acts and omissions of MUSTAFA and his subordinates had a substantial effect on the Murder Victim being shot, which in turn medically caused his death.[145]

Amongst other things, although presence per se does not amount to encouragement,[146] the presence of a superior at the scene of an offence may suffice for liability for abetting by tacit approval.[147] Indeed, according to both the ad hoc Tribunals and the ICC:

the notion of 'abet' describes the moral or psychological assistance of the accessory to the principal perpetrator, taking the form of encouragement of or even sympathy for the commission of the particular offence. The encouragement or support shown need not be explicit. Under certain circumstances, even the act of being present at the crime scene (or in its vicinity) as a 'silent spectator' can be construed as tacit approval or encouragement of the crime.[148]

Omissions may suffice for aiding or abetting if there is an obligation on the defendant to prevent the crime and the ability to intervene.[149] In *Popović*, the accused failed in his legal duty to protect prisoners, which substantially contributed to their subsequent murder.

[137] *Ibid.* para. 395. [138] For a useful overview of some of the conduct that has been held to aid or abet, see *ibid.* para. 369.
[139] *Vasiljević*, ICTY AC, 25 February 2004, para. 134. Judge Shahabuddeen in that case considered this to suffice for co-perpetratorship through joint criminal enterprise liability: see Partially Dissenting Opinion of Judge Shahabuddeen, para. 40.
[140] *Ntakirutimana and Ntakirutimana*, ICTR AC, 13 December 2004, para. 530. [141] *Ibid.* para. 532.
[142] *Krstić*, ICTY AC, 19 April 2004, para. 137.
[143] *Bemba et al.*, ICC TC VII, 19 October 2016 (ICC-01/05–01/13–1989-Red) para. 88.
[144] *Tadić*, ICTY AC, 15 July 1999, para. 199. On the issue of multiple causes, see James G. Stewart, 'Overdetermined Atrocities' (2012) 10 *JICJ* 1189–218.
[145] *Mustafa*, KSC SPO, 23 June 2023, para. 143. [146] *Orić*, ICTY TC II, 30 June 2006, para. 283.
[147] *Aleksovski*, ICTY AC, 24 March 2000, paras. 36–7; *Brđanin and Talić*, ICTY AC, 3 April 2007, para. 273. Whether or not the obligation has to be imposed by the criminal law is an open question: *Mrkšić and Šljivančanin*, ICTY AC, 5 May 2009, paras. 148–52.
[148] *Bemba et al.*, ICC TC VII, 19 October 2016 (ICC-01/05–01/13–1989-Red) para. 89.
[149] *Orić*, ICTY TC II, 30 June 2006, para. 283; *Milutinović et al.*, ICTY TC III, 26 February 2009, para. 90. See also Ingle, 'Aiding and Abetting by Omission' (n. 128).

Moreover, 'the lending of practical assistance, encouragement, or moral support may occur before, during, or after the crime or underlying offence occurs'.[150]

In *Bemba et al.*, the ICC Appeals Chamber was asked to rule on the question whether there is a minimum threshold for assistance or encouragement under Article 25(3)(c) but it did not do so.[151] The judges held that 'the form of contribution under Article 25(3)(c) of the Statute does not require the meeting of any specific threshold'.[152] It:

> only requires that the assistance in the commission (or attempted commission) of the crime be provided for the purposes of facilitating such commission without indicating whether the conduct must have also had an effect on the commission of the offence.[153]

Although the ICTY Appeals Chamber said in *Tadić* that the conduct needs to be 'specifically directed' towards aiding or abetting the relevant crimes, for a long time this statement played little part in the jurisprudence of the ad hoc Tribunals.[154] It had not been treated as determinative, or even relevant, until the *Perišić* trial judgment, which convicted the defendant partly on the basis of the Chamber's rejection of the specific direction standard.[155] This finding was successfully challenged on appeal. The Appeals Chamber determined that the *Tadić* formula stood, in large part on the basis that later cases did not discuss this purported criterion and were not dealing with remote assistance.[156] In such cases, a majority of the judges in the Appeals Chamber held, against powerful dissents, that it was necessary to show specific direction.[157]

The acquittal of *Perišić* on appeal was criticized on grounds that the requirement is unsupported in other cases and commentary, and national law;[158] seemed to conflate *actus reus* and *mens rea* considerations;[159] and also appeared to create a separate form of aiding and abetting in 'remote' cases, which was 'retrogressive'.[160] It is also thought that it could lead to high-ranking figures providing assistance to rebels and others with impunity.[161]

The SCSL Appeals Chamber in the *Taylor* case, whilst acknowledging that they were not bound by ICTY jurisprudence, rejected the standard in firm terms as a matter of law.[162] In

---

[150] *Milutinović et al.*, ICTY TC III, 26 February 2009, para. 91.

[151] Manuel Ventura, 'Aiding and Abetting and the International Criminal Court's *Bemba et al.* Case: The ICC Trial and Appeals Chamber Consider Article 25(3)(c) of the Rome Statute' (2020) 20 *ICLR* 1138, 1143–52.

[152] *Bemba et al.*, ICC TC VII, 19 October 2016 (ICC-01/05–01/13–1989-Red) para. 93.

[153] *Bemba et al.*, ICC AC, 8 March 2018 (ICC-01/05–01/13–2275-Red) para. 1327.

[154] *Mrkšić and Šljivančanin*, ICTY AC, 5 May 2009, para. 159. A detailed history of those cases that discussed it may be found in *Perišić*, ICTY AC, 28 February 2013, paras. 28–31.

[155] *Perišić*, ICTY TC I, 6 September 2011, para. 126 (with Dissenting Opinion of Judge Moloto).

[156] The assistance in *Perišić* was the provision of arms and other material from Belgrade to Bosnian Serb forces.

[157] *Perišić*, ICTY AC, 28 February 2013, paras. 38–40. See also Partially Dissenting Opinion of Judge Liu, para. 3.

[158] James Stewart, 'Specific Direction is Unprecedented: Results from Two Empirical Studies', www.ejiltalk.org/specific-direction-is-unprecedented-results-from-two-empirical-studies. But see Kai Ambos and Ousman Njikam, 'Charles Taylor's Criminal Responsibility' (2013) 11 *JICJ* 789.

[159] *Perišić*, ICTY AC, 28 February 2013, Separate Opinion of Judge Ramaroson. In their Separate Opinion (paras. 3–4), Judges Meron and Agius almost admit this, saying that, were they to qualify the matter outside precedent, they would do so as a matter of *mens rea*.

[160] James Stewart, 'The ICTY Loses its Way on Complicity', http://opiniojuris.org/2013/04/03/guest-post-the-icty-loses-its-way-on-complicity-part-1.

[161] Partially Dissenting Opinion of Judge Liu, *Perišić*, ICTY AC, 28 February 2013, para. 3. The majority had admitted the issue (para. 72), but they provided no convincing answer to the problem. Judge Harhoff's incautious criticism of the requirement on this basis, though, led to disqualification proceedings against him in another case: see *Šešelj*, ICTY Chamber convened by order of the Vice-President, 28 August 2013.

[162] Judge Avis Fischer was particularly trenchant: *Taylor*, SCSL AC, 26 September 2013, paras. 716–20. Judge Winter agreed.

an extraordinary development in early 2014, a differently constituted Appeals Chamber of the ICTY, in the *Šainović et al.* case,[163] concluded that *Perišić* was 'unequivocally' wrong and that the specific direction requirement was not part of customary law.[164] This followed a detailed review of the post-Second World War jurisprudence and national laws on point, similar to that undertaken in the *Taylor* case.[165]

In spite of the 'specific direction' standard canvassed above, the customary *mens rea* here is knowledge, not purpose.[166] The SCSL has consistently held that this includes 'awareness of the substantial likelihood' of an offence occurring,[167] but it is alone in seeing knowledge this way.

There is the question of how much knowledge about a crime is necessary. For example, does the aider or abettor have to know who or what is going to be attacked or how it will be attacked? The Appeals Chamber in *Tadić* asserted that 'awareness … of the essential elements of the crime committed by the principal would suffice'.[168] When a person knows that more than one crime might be committed, the ICTY has said that:

> it is not necessary that the aider and abettor should know the precise crime that was intended and which in the event was committed. If he is aware that one of a number of crimes will probably be committed, and one of those crimes is in fact committed, he has intended to facilitate the commission of that crime, and is guilty as an aider and abettor.[169]

In ICC case law, the question arose over what constitutes 'effect' (on the crimes) and to what extent proof of awareness on the part of the person who is aided or encouraged is required. In *Bemba et al.*, a contempt case related to the giving of false testimony, the Appeals Chamber held that acts of assistance can have an effect on the crimes even when they are given to an intermediary (who was in touch with the witnesses). The judges held that what ultimately matters is whether 'it can be established, as a factual matter, that this assisted the commission or attempted commission of a crime or offence'.[170] Aside from those specific cases where aiding and abetting concerns (tacit) encouragement or moral support to the principal perpetrator – which *does* require awareness of encouragement/ approval on the part of the principal perpetrator[171] – there is no general requirement of such awareness.[172] Thus, defendant Mangenda's rendering of moral support and encouragement

---

[163] *Šainović et al.*, ICTY AC, 23 January 2014, paras. 1617–50.

[164] *Ibid.* para. 1650. See Leila Sadat, 'Can the ICTY Šainović and Perišić Cases be Reconciled?' (2014) 108 *AJIL* 475; Andrea Carcano, 'Of Fragmentation and Precedents in International Criminal Law' (2016) 14 *JICJ* 771.

[165] The rejection of the requirement of specific direction in *Šainović et al.* was later affirmed by the Appeal Chamber in the *Popović et al.* case and the Trial Chamber's acceptance of the *Perišić* standard formed part of the basis for the Appeals Chamber requiring a re-trial in the *Stanišić and Simatović* case: *Popović et al.*, ICTY AC, 30 January 2015, para. 1758; *Stanišić and Simatović*, ICTY AC, 9 December 2015, paras. 104–8.

[166] *Taylor*, SCSL AC, 26 September 2013, paras. 413–37. [167] *Ibid.* para. 438.

[168] *Tadić*, ICTY AC, 15 July 1999, para. 164. See also *Orić*, ICTY TC II, 30 June 2006, para. 288.

[169] *Furundžija*, ICTY TC II, 10 December 1998, para. 246. Approved in *Blaškić*, ICTY AC, 29 July 2004, para. 50.

[170] *Bemba et al.*, ICC AC, 8 March 2018 (ICC-01/05–01/13–2275-Red), para. 1330.

[171] See Ventura, 'Aiding and Abetting' (n. 126) 1154–5, referring to ICTR and ICTY case law: *Ntagerura et al.*, ICTR, AC, 7 July 2006, para. 374; *Nyiramasuhuko et al.*, AC, 14 December 2015, paras. 2087–2089; *Šainović et al.* ICC AC, 23 January 2014, paras. 1687–9.

[172] Ventura, 'Aiding and Abetting' (n. 126) 1155 with reference to *Bemba et al.*, ICC AC, 8 March 2018 (ICC-01/05–01/13–2275-Red), para. 1330.

to intermediary Kilolo was aiding and abetting under Article 25(3)(c) since it had an effect on the witnesses giving false testimony.

A hugely important aspect of aiding and abetting liability at the ICC is the *mens rea* standard. The definition of aiding and abetting in the ICC Statute is different from that used by the ICTY and ICTR. The ICC Statute provides for responsibility of anyone who

[f]or the purpose of facilitating the commission of such a crime, aids, abets, or otherwise assists in its commission or its attempted commission, including providing the means for its commission.[173]

The purpose standard is a more demanding *mens rea* than the knowledge test of the ad hoc and hybrid tribunals.[174] In *Bemba et al.*, the Trial Chamber provided clarity by holding that the aider and abettor's *mens rea* was twofold requiring (1) a *mens rea* in relation to the crime committed by the principal and (2) a *mens rea* in relation to aider or abettor's act of encouragement or assistance.[175] The judges held that the purpose standard only applies to the aider and abettor's *own conduct*. Article 30 – de default mental element – continues to apply to the *mens rea* in relation to the crime committed by the principal perpetrator(s), that is, knowledge and intent.

15.4 ORDERING, INSTIGATING, SOLICITING, INDUCING, AND INCITING

15.4.1 Ordering

Because many international crimes are committed by a large number of people acting together, it is frequently the case that such crimes are committed at the behest of a superior authority.[176] If defendants in war crimes trials are to be believed, almost every crime is committed pursuant to orders. It has never really been questioned that those ordering international crimes are responsible for them. The reason given by those supporting a defence of superior orders in the early nineteenth century was that liability was more appropriately placed on the person who gave the order than the person who carried it out.[177] Although it is possible to see those giving orders to commit international crimes as perpetrators acting through innocent or guilty agents, the ICC Statute and the Statutes of the ICTY, ICTR, and SCSL all treat it as a separate form of liability.[178] The core aspect of the crime of ordering, as interpreted by the ad hoc Tribunals and the ICC, is that a 'person in a position of authority uses it to convince another to commit an offence'.[179]

---

[173] ICC Statute, Art. 25(3)(c).
[174] Van Sliedregt, *Individual Criminal Responsibility* (n. 2) 128; Miles Jackson, *Complicity in International Law* (Oxford, 2015) 50; Kai Ambos (ed.), *The Rome Statute of the International Criminal Court: A Commentary*, 3rd ed. (Munich, 2016) 1009.
[175] Bemba et al., ICC TC VII, 19 October 2016 (ICC-01/05–01/13– 1989-Red) para. 97.
[176] See generally van Sliedregt, *Individual Criminal Responsibility* (n. 2) 102–9; Manuel Ventura, 'Ordering' in Jérôme de Hemptinne, Robert Roth, and Elies van Sliedregt (eds.), *Modes of Liability in International Criminal Law* (Cambridge, 2019), 284–306.
[177] See e.g. Lassa Oppenheim, *International Law* (London, 1906) vol. II, 264–5.
[178] ICC Statute, Art. 25(3)(b); ICTY Statute, Art. 7(1); ICTR Statute, Art. 6(1); SCSL Statute, Art. 6(1).
[179] *Akayesu*, ICTR TC I, 2 September 1998, para. 483; *Blaškić*, ICTY TC I, 3 March 2000, para. 601; *Bemba et al.*, ICC TC VII, 19 October 2016 (ICC-01/05–01/13–1989-Red) para. 77.

This requires three things: a superior/subordinate relationship; the transmission of an order; and the relevant mental element. In relation to the first of these, it is not necessary that the relationship be a legal one; the point is whether there is, factually, 'some position of authority on the part of the accused that would compel another to commit a crime in following the accused's order'.[180] The transmission of an order can be established by circumstantial evidence.[181] An example of this would be when there are a remarkable number of similar actions over a disparate area in a short time. A court does not need a paper copy or a tape of an order to convict on this basis. A person does not have to be the author of an order to become liable for ordering in international criminal law: passing it down the chain of command can be enough.[182] Similarly, a person who issues an order does not have to pass it directly to the person who commits the crime: it may go through a number of intermediaries' hands first.[183] This form of liability cannot attach to a pure omission,[184] and the order must at least substantially contribute to the commission of the crime.[185]

The mental element of ordering was set out by the ICTY as being 'the awareness of the substantial likelihood that a crime will be committed in the execution of that order … Ordering with such awareness has to be regarded as accepting that crime.'[186] Article 30 of the ICC Statute requires the ordering person to act with direct intent; the order must be issued willingly. Additionally, knowledge of the criminal consequence is required. The issuer of the order must mean to cause the consequence or be aware that it will occur following their orders in the ordinary course of events. More precisely, they must know with virtual certainty that their order will lead to the commission of crimes.[187] This excludes recklessness or *dolus eventualis*.

The ICC, in *Lubanga*, made clear that ordering in Article 25(3)(b) of the Statute is a form of secondary liability; a person is responsible only when the ordered crime 'occurs or is attempted' by the principal perpetrator.[188] The ICTY and ICTR have conceptualized ordering in the same way.[189] Ordering is accessorial/secondary liability and as such different from indirect perpetration in 25(3)(a), which is principal liability. Yet, it is a thin line that runs between Article 25(3)(a) and (3)(b). In fact, it has been argued that, because of the contested and complex theory of indirect co-perpetration, it would be better to use ordering liability instead.[190]

---

[180] *Semanza*, ICTR AC, 20 May 2005, para. 361. See also *Kordić and Čerkez*, ICTY TC III, 26 February 2001, para. 388; and ICTY AC, 17 December 2004, para. 28. In *Gacumbitsi*, ICTR AC, 7 July 2009, para. 182; the Appeals Chamber noted that this is not the same as the requirement in command responsibility of effective control, as it 'requires merely authority to order, a more subjective criterion depends on the circumstances and the perceptions of the listener'.

[181] *Blaškić*, ICTY TC I, 3 March 2000, para. 281.

[182] Nuremberg IMT, Judgment and Sentences, reprinted in (1947) 41 *AJIL* 172, 282; *Kupreškić et al.*, ICTY TC II, 14 January 2000, para. 862.

[183] *Blaškić*, ICTY TC I, 3 March 2000, para. 282. [184] *Galić*, ICTY AC, 30 November 2006, para. 176.

[185] E.g. *Milutinović et al.*, ICTY TC III, 26 February 2009, para. 88. [186] *Blaškić*, ICTY AC, 29 July 2004, para. 42.

[187] *Lubanga*, ICC AC, 1 December 2014, paras. 448–50. [188] *Lubanga*, ICC AC, 1 December 2014, para. 462.

[189] *Blaškić*, ICTY TC I, 3 March 2000, paras. 281–2; *Kordić and Čerkez*, ICTY TC III, 26 February 2001, para. 388; *Akayesu*, ICTR TC I, 2 September 1998, para. 483.

[190] Johannes Block, 'Ordering as an Alternative to Indirect Co-Perpetration: Observation on the Ntaganda Case' (2022) 20 *JICJ* 717–32.

15.4.2 Instigating, Soliciting, Inducing, and Inciting

Instigation, which the ICTY has described as 'prompting',[191] and the ICTR as 'urging or encouraging'[192] another to commit a crime, seems to be largely the same as soliciting or inducing in Article 25(3)(b) of the ICC Statute.[193] The ICC has held that soliciting and inducing crimes are part of instigating crimes 'in the sense that they refer to a form of conduct by which a person exerts psychological influence on another person as a result of which the criminal act is committed'.[194] It has also said that solicitation is at the lower level of this form of responsibility, being where someone 'asks or urges the physical perpetrator to commit the criminal act'.[195] Inducement, on the other hand, represents a stronger method of instigation, that involves 'influence … either by strong reasoning, persuasion or conduct implying the prompting of the commission of the offence'.[196] It is the element of coercion that distinguishes the two. In the more general sense, the Trial Chamber in *Blaškić* made clear that instigation can be express or implied.[197] It must, however, be a causative factor (but need not be the only cause) of the conduct element of the underlying crime.[198]

With regard to the mental element, rather like for ordering, the ICTY has said that:

> a person who instigates another person to commit an act or omission with the awareness of the substantial likelihood that a crime will be committed in the execution of that instigation, has the requisite *mens rea* for establishing responsibility [for] instigating. Instigating with such awareness has to be regarded as accepting that crime.[199]

Some cases have seen the giving of orders which are not carried out as a form of incitement/ instigation.[200]

Direct and public incitement to genocide is specifically criminalized, in essentially the same terms, by Genocide Convention, Article 3(c),[201] ICTY Statute, Article 4(3)(c), ICTR Statute, Article 2(3)(c), and ICC Statute, Article 25(3)(e). Unlike the other crimes of encouragement discussed here, for liability to accrue, it is not necessary to prove that anyone even attempted to commit genocide as incitement to genocide is, like conspiracy, an inchoate crime.[202]

---

[191] *Blaškić*, ICTY TC I, 3 March 2000, para. 280. [192] *Bagilishema*, ICTR AC, 2 July 2002, para. 30.

[193] See e.g. van Sliedregt, *Individual Criminal Responsibility* (n. 2) 108. See also Mettraux, *International Crimes* (n. 63) 281, noting that there is considerable overlap between instigation and abetting.

[194] *Bemba et al.*, ICC TC VII, 19 October 2016 (ICC-01/05–01/13–1989-Red) para. 73. The precise relationship is discussed in *ibid*. paras. 74ff.

[195] *Bemba et al.*, ICC TC VII, 19 October, 2016 (ICC-01/05–01/13–1989-Red) para. 75. [196] *Ibid*. para. 76.

[197] *Bemba et al.*, ICC TC VII, 19 October 2016 (ICC-01/05–01/13–1989-Red) para. 78. See also *Blaškić*, ICTY TC I, 3 March 2000, para. 270.

[198] *Bemba et al.*, ICC TC VII, 19 October 2016 (ICC-01/05–01/13–1989-Red) para. 81; *Gacumbitsi*, ICTR AC, 7 July 2006, para. 129; *Kordić and Čerkez*, ICTY AC, 17 December 2004, para. 27.

[199] *Kordić and Čerkez*, ICTY AC, 17 December 2004, para. 32. See similarly *Orić*, ICTY TC II, 30 June 2006, para. 279, which also asserts that the instigator must accept the intentional commission of the relevant crime. *Quaere* whether this is necessary for crimes for which a lesser mental element is required or consistent with the Appeals Chamber's finding in *Kordić and Čerkez*.

[200] *Meyer* (the 'Abbaye Ardenne' case), IV LRTWC 97, 98 (1945).

[201] 1948 Convention on the Prevention and Punishment of the Crime of Genocide. See generally Richard A. Wilson, *Incitement on Trial: Prosecuting International Speech Crimes* (Cambridge, 2017); Gregory S. Gordon, *Atrocity Speech Law: Foundation, Fragmentation, Fruition* (Oxford, 2017); James E. K. Parker, *Acoustic Jurisprudence: Listening to the Trial of Simon Bikindi* (Oxford, 2015). For critique of a more generally applicable notion of incitement to international crimes, see Wibke K. Timmermann, 'Incitement Speech in the Former Yugoslavia: The Šešelj Trial Chamber Judgment' (2017) 15 *JICJ* 13.

[202] *Nahimana et al.*, ICTR AC, 28 November 2007, para. 678; *Akayesu*, ICTR TC I, 2 September 1998, para. 562; *Mugesera* v. *Canada* [2005] 2 SCR 100, paras. 84–5.

The main case in the ad hoc Tribunals is the ICTR's *Media* case.[203] Drawing, *inter alia*, on the Nuremberg IMT's verdicts on Julius Streicher and Hans Frizsche, the Trial Chamber in that case decided that, in determining liability, the purpose and context of any communication is important.[204] The result was approved by the Appeals Chamber, who also noted that the effect the incitement had on an audience is a relevant factor.[205] On the basis of the earlier *Akayesu* case, the Trial Chamber in the *Media* case determined that the crime required 'a call for criminal action to a number of individuals in a public place or to members of the general public at large by such means as the mass media, for example, radio or television'.[206] So far, determining what is public has not been too difficult, most prosecutions being based on speeches to large groups of people or the mass media.[207] It has been held that:

Incitement is 'public' when conducted through speeches, shouting or threats uttered in public places or at public gatherings, or through the sale or dissemination, offer for sale or display of written material or printed matter in public places or at public gatherings, or through the public display of placards or posters, or through any other means of audiovisual communication.[208]

As the last part of the quote implies, the Internet and e-mail may raise interesting questions regarding the 'public' requirement. Interpreting what is direct is not simple. As the Trial Chamber in *Akayesu* said:

the direct element of incitement should be viewed in the light of its cultural and linguistic content. Indeed, a particular speech may be perceived as 'direct' in one country, and not so in another, depending on the audience. The Chamber further recalls that incitement may be direct, and nonetheless implicit.[209]

The Appeals Chamber has largely agreed, noting that simple 'hate speech' may not be enough; the incitement must be to commit genocide, although that call need not be express, so long as it is direct.[210] Particularly difficult issues of culture, context, and interpretation arise here, especially when prosecutions are occurring outside the *locus delicti*.[211] For a conviction for incitement to genocide, the defendant must personally have genocidal intent; knowledge of the intentions of others alone is not enough.

---

[203] *Nahimana et al.*, ICTR TC I, 3 December 2003. [204] *Ibid*. paras. 1000–10.
[205] *Nahimana et al.*, ICTR AC, 28 November 2007, paras. 698–700.
[206] *Nahimana et al.*, ICTR TC I, 3 December 2003, para. 1011.
[207] In *Kalimanzira*, ICTR AC, 28 October 2010, para. 159, it was decided that supervising a roadblock did not amount to direct public incitement, as it did not involve 'public' speech. However, in *Ngirabatware*, the ICTR Appeals Chamber said that a speech to 150–250 people at a roadblock was public for the purpose of the offence, as it was not only to those who were staffing the roadblock; *Ngirabatware*, MICT AC, 18 December 2014, paras. 52–4.
[208] *Kalimanzira*, ICTR TC III, 22 June 2009, para. 515. More generally on incitement, see Manuel J. Ventura, 'Ordering' in Jérôme de Hemptinne, Robert Roth, and Elies van Sliedregt (eds.), *Modes of Liability in International Criminal Law* (Cambridge, 2019) 284–306.
[209] *Akayesu*, ICTR TC I, 2 September 1998, para. 557; see also *Kalimanzira*, ICTR TC III, 22 June 2009, para. 514.
[210] *Nahimana et al.*, ICTR AC, 28 November 2007, paras. 693, 703. The ICTR held that songs may suffice: *Bikindi*, ICTR TC III, 2 December 2008, para. 389.
[211] See e.g. *Nahimana et al.*, ICTR AC, 28 November 2007, paras. 704–15. See also William Schabas, 'Mugesera v. Minister of Citizenship and Immigration' (1999) 93 *AJIL* 529.

15.5 COMMON PURPOSE LIABILITY[212]

The ICC Statute recognizes common purpose liability in Article 25(3)(d).[213] It provides for accessory liability for someone who:

contributes to the commission or attempted commission of such a crime by a group of persons acting with a common purpose. Such contribution shall be intentional and shall either:

i. Be made with the aim of furthering the criminal activity or criminal purpose of the group, where such activity or purpose involves the commission of a crime within the jurisdiction of the Court; or
ii. Be made in the knowledge of the intention of the group to commit the crime.

From the text of the provision, it is clear that this does not recognize recklessness or *dolus eventualis*,[214] and therefore does not provide for liability on a basis akin to JCE III.[215] That said, it does not seem to require a 'significant' contribution to the plan, requiring only that the participation be 'in any other way' than those identified in Articles 25(3)(a)–(c).[216] ICC Pre-Trial Chamber I held, distinguishing liability under Articles 25(3)(a) and (d), that the contribution made to a group acting with a common purpose need not be 'essential', but merely 'significant'.[217] However, the Appeals Chamber has been coy on this point; it did not express an opinion on the 'contribution threshold'.[218]

Separately, Pre-Trial Chamber I held that the suspect does not need to be a member of the group that acts with the common purpose for liability to arise under this provision.[219] It has further determined that the 'group acting with a common purpose' meant the same as it did in the context of Article 25(3)(a) (that there be a common plan between at least two people), which is discussed above.[220] The Chamber did make clear, though, that Article 25(3)(d) largely covers what is caught under JCE I and II.[221] An important difference between this provision and JCE is that, whereas JCE is considered a form of 'commission', liability, Article 25(3)(d) is a form of complicity/accessorial liability. Because of the rejection of the 'hierarchy thesis' in *Bemba et al.*,[222] this does not make much material difference; one form of liability is not necessarily more blameworthy than the other.

---

[212] For a good overview: Marjolein Cupido, 'Group Acting With A Common Purpose', in De Hemptinne et al., *Modes of Liability in International Criminal Law*, 309–36.
[213] Cassese et al., *Cassese's International Criminal Law* (n. 68) 175, asserting that, rather than Art. 25(3)(d), ICC Statute, Art. 25 (3)(a), by providing for liability for those committing crimes 'jointly with another', 'implicitly permits' JCE liability. But the ICC has not taken this path, and this remains very much a minority view.
[214] *Mbarushimana*, ICC PTC I, 16 December 2011 (ICC-01/04–01/10–465) paras. 288–9.
[215] Jens Ohlin, 'Joint Criminal Confusion' (2009) 2 *New Criminal Law Review* 406, 410–16. See also Ambos, *Treatise on International Law* (n. 6) 122–3.
[216] Van Sliedregt, *Individual Criminal Responsibility* (n. 2) 146. For a detailed analysis, see Kai Ambos, 'The ICC and Common Purpose: What Contribution is Required under Article 25(3)(d)?' in Stahn, *The Law and Practice of the ICC*, 592.
[217] *Mbarushimana*, ICC PTC I, 16 December 2011 (ICC-01/04–01/10–465) paras. 276–84.
[218] *Mbarushimana*, ICC AC, 30 May 2012 (ICC-01/04–01/10– 514) paras. 64–9. *Katanga* did not deal with the matter, although Judge Fernández de Gurmendi rejected such a requirement (para. 15).
[219] *Mbarushimana*, ICC PTC I, 16 December 2011 (ICC-01/04–01/10–465) paras. 273–5. [220] *Ibid.* para. 271.
[221] *Katanga*, ICC TC II, 7 March 2014 (ICC-01/04–01/07–3436-tENG) para. 1619.
[222] *Bemba et al.*, ICC AC, 8 March 2018 (ICC-01/05-01/13 A6 A7 A8 A9) paras. 59–60. See also under Section 5.2.2.

15.6 PLANNING, PREPARATION, ATTEMPT, AND CONSPIRACY

15.6.1 Planning and Preparing

Planning or preparing a war of aggression was criminalized in Article 6(a) of the Charter of the Nuremberg IMT and Article 5(a) of the Charter of the Tokyo IMT. Both also contained a clause that read:

leaders, organisers, instigators and accomplices participating in the formulation of a common plan … to commit any of the foregoing crimes are responsible for all acts performed by any person in execution of such a plan.

Both Tribunals read this as being limited to crimes against peace, however. Such crimes are usually considered at the national level to amount to inchoate (incomplete) crimes that are punishable without proof that the crime itself was completed.

Article 7(1) of the ICTY Statute, as well as ICTR Statute, Article 6(1), and SCSL Statute, Article 6(1), all criminalize those who 'aided and abetted in the planning, preparation or execution' of an international crime. As aiding and abetting is a secondary form of liability, which requires a primary crime to be committed or attempted to attach to, these instruments imply that planning is a primary offence, which in turn implies that planning and preparation are in themselves enough, and do not require that the crimes planned or prepared actually occurred.[223]

For planning,[224] however, the ICTY Appeals Chamber has held differently, stating that '[t]he *actus reus* of "planning" requires that one or more persons design the criminal conduct constituting one or more statutory crimes that are later perpetrated'.[225] A number of Trial Chamber decisions, in particular from the ICTR, have been criticized as misunderstanding the nature of 'planning',[226] but the definition on point is now settled before the Tribunals.[227] Either way, the planning must have a substantial effect on the commission of the crime,[228] although the planning need not necessarily relate to the commission of a particular offence, but can be of an objective that is to be achieved by the commission of crimes.[229] The perpetrator does not have to be the originator of, or one of the prime movers in, the plan. The question is one of substantial contribution.[230] Owing to the activation of the crime of aggression in December 2017 (which took effect on 17 July 2018), there is an opportunity for the ICC to develop the details of this form of liability.[231]

---

[223] For policy reasons in support (on the basis of the severity of international crimes and prevention), see Cassese et al., *International Criminal Law* (n. 68) 204–5.

[224] There is no modern jurisprudence on 'preparing' as a separate crime.

[225] *Kordić and Čerkez*, ICTY AC, 17 December 2004, para. 26.   [226] Mettraux, *International Crimes* (n. 63) 279–80.

[227] *Taylor*, SCSL AC, 26 September 2013, para. 494.   [228] *Kordić and Čerkez*, ICTY AC, 17 December 2004, para. 26.

[229] *Boškoski and Tarčulovski*, ICTY AC, 19 May 2010, paras. 171–2; *Taylor*, SCSL AC, 26 September 2013, para. 493.

[230] *Boškoski and Tarčulovski*, ICTY AC, 19 May 2010, para. 154; *Taylor*, SCSL AC, 26 September 2013, para. 494.

[231] See Chapter 13.

15.6.2 Attempt

The Statutes of all the international criminal tribunals prior to the ICC Statute are silent on attempt liability other than for genocide.[232] The ICTY Prosecutor showed an unwillingness to prosecute attempts to commit international crimes, preferring to conceptualize them under other headings of liability (for example, 'violence to life and person' or 'inhumane acts' rather than attempted murder).[233] However, there is sufficient evidence from the post-Second World War era to show such a form of liability exists in custom.[234]

The ICC Statute expressly criminalizes attempts to commit international crimes in Article 25(3)(f): a person is liable if he or she:

> Attempts to commit such a crime by taking action that commences its execution by means of a substantial step, but the crime does not occur because of circumstances independent of the person's intentions. However, a person who abandons the effort to commit the crime or otherwise prevents the completion of the crime shall not be liable if that person completely and voluntarily gave up the criminal purpose.

The formulation at Rome was a compromise, making it difficult to interpret precisely when a person has 'commence[d] its execution by a substantial step'.[235] As can be seen, the ICC Statute recognizes that, if an attempt is abandoned, or a person prevents the crime, they will not be liable for attempt. However, if they abandon their role in the crime, and it is completed by others, it is possible that liability for aiding and abetting or participating in a joint criminal enterprise might still arise.

15.6.3 Conspiracy

Conspiracy, in the sense of the inchoate crime of agreeing to commit a crime, was applied by the Nuremberg and Tokyo IMTs to crimes against peace, not war crimes or crimes against humanity.[236] The reason for that limitation was that there was considerable disagreement between the judges on whether or not such a principle existed in international law.[237] This also led the Nuremberg IMT to take a narrow view of conspiracy, stating that '[t]he conspiracy must be clearly outlined in its criminal purpose. It must not be too far removed from the time of decision and of action'.[238] The Tokyo IMT, although also limiting its decision to conspiracies to commit crimes against peace, took a very broad interpretation of the concept of conspiracy.[239]

---

[232] ICTY Statute, Art. 4(d); ICTR Statute, Art. 2(d). See generally Ambos, *Treatise on International Law* (n. 6) ch. I.

[233] See *Vasiljević*, ICTY TC I, 29 November 2002. See Antonio Cassese, 'Black Letter Lawyering vs Constructive Interpretation: The Vasiljević Case' (2004) 2 *JICJ* 265, 266–71, *contra* Mettraux, *International Crimes* (n. 63) 293–5.

[234] Cassese, 'Black Letter Lawyering' (n. 233). See also Commentary, XV LRTWC 89 (1949).

[235] Albin Eser, 'Individual Criminal Responsibility', in Antonio Cassese, *The Rome Statute of the International Criminal Court*, 811–13; Ambos, 'Article 25' (n. 135) 488–9.

[236] Nuremberg IMT, Judgment and Sentences, reprinted in (1947) 41 *AJIL* 172, 224.

[237] See Telford Taylor, *The Anatomy of the Nuremberg Trials* (London, 1993) 36, 50.

[238] Nuremberg IMT, Judgment and Sentences, reprinted in (1947) 41 *AJIL* 172, 222. It must also be noted that the Tribunal was dealing with conspiracies which had manifested themselves in later crimes, so was not, strictly speaking, dealing with inchoate conspiracies.

[239] See Section 6.4.3.

Under current international law, conspiracy does not exist as a form of liability for war crimes or crimes against humanity.[240] Conspiracy to commit genocide, however, is a separate offence.[241] It is included in Article 3(b) of the Genocide Convention, and it is clear that the type of conspiracy included is of the inchoate type.[242] The same crime is included in Article 4(3)(b) of the ICTY Statute and Article 2(3)(b) of the ICTR Statute. It is not, however, present in the ICC Statute. According to the ICTR, conspiracy to commit genocide is '[a]n agreement between two or more persons to commit the crime of genocide'.[243] This can be implicit, as well as express.[244] It has also determined, rightly, that:

[w]ith respect to the *mens rea* of the crime of conspiracy to commit genocide … it rests on the concerted intent to commit genocide, that is to destroy, in whole or in part, a national, ethnic, racial or religious group, as such. Thus … the requisite intent for the crime of conspiracy to commit genocide is, *ipso facto*, the intent required for the crime of genocide that is the *dolus specialis* of genocide.[245]

15.7 COMMAND/SUPERIOR RESPONSIBILITY

Command responsibility[246] is an inculpatory doctrine[247] specific to international criminal law, which does not have an equivalent general principle of liability at the domestic level.[248] It is a broad form of liability, which is justified by the privileges, honours, and responsibilities that command entails.[249] Command responsibility as a whole has a lengthy history, going back roughly 2,500 years to the China of Sun Tzu.[250] The responsibility of a commander extends far beyond international criminal liability, and disciplinary or administrative action can be pursued even if there is no criminal liability.[251] Discussion here, however, is specifically on the criminal responsibility of a commander for offences committed by his or her subordinates. An early and clear example of such liability, which is remarkably similar to modern command responsibility, may be found in the French Code instituted by Charles VII of Orléans in 1439, which stated:

The King orders that each captain or lieutenant be held responsible for the abuses, ills and offences committed by members of his company, and that as soon as he receives any complaint concerning any

---

[240] *Hamdan* v. *Rumsfeld*, 126 S Ct 2749, 2777–85 (2006). The Supreme Court in this case was clear that it was discussing conspiracies that are offences on their own, not forms of participation in completed crimes, see *ibid.* 2785, note 40.

[241] Although it does not merge with the offence if the conspiracy leads to genocide: *Gatete*, ICTR AC, 9 October 2012, paras. 260–4 (double convictions have little point).

[242] Schabas, *Genocide* (n. 24) 260; *Kajelijeli*, ICTR TC II, 1 December 2003, para. 788; *Musema*, ICTR TC I, 27 January 2000, para. 187. It is, however, a continuing offence: *Popović et al.*, ICTY TC, 10 June 2010, para. 876.

[243] *Musema*, ICTR TC I, 27 January 2000, para. 189; *Kajelijeli*, ICTR TC II, 1 December 2003, para. 787; *Ntagerura et al.*, ICTR AC, 7 July 2006, para. 92.

[244] *Nahimana et al.*, ICTR AC, 28 January 2007, paras. 896–8.   [245] *Musema*, ICTR TC I, 27 January 2000, para. 192.

[246] See generally Guénaël Mettraux, *The Law of Command Responsibility* (Oxford, 2009); van Sliedregt, *Individual Criminal Responsibility* (n. 2) ch. 8; and Ambos, *Treatise on International Law* (n. 6) 197–232.

[247] The terms 'command responsibility' and 'superior responsibility' are functionally synonymous, although the former is sometimes taken as limited to military personnel, which it need not be.

[248] However, there are some analogues in limited areas of domestic criminal law.

[249] See e.g. *Hadžihasanović et al.*, ICTY AC, 16 July 2003, para. 14. See also Cryer, 'General Principles' (n. 5) 260–1.

[250] See W. Hays Parks, 'Command Responsibility for War Crimes' (1973) 62 *Military Law Review* 1, 1–20.

[251] *Bagilishema*, ICTR AC, 2 July 2002, para. 36.

such misdeed or abuse, he bring the offender to justice so that the said offender be punished in a manner commensurate with his offence, according to these ordinances. If he fails to do so or covers up the misdeed or delays taking action, or if, because of his negligence or otherwise, the offender escapes and thus evades punishment, the captain shall be deemed responsible for the offence as if he had committed it himself and be punished in the same way as the offender would have been.[252]

The foundation of the modern law of command responsibility may be found in the Report of the Commission of Inquiry on the Responsibility of the Authors of the War in 1919, which opined that superiors could be held responsible for crimes of their subordinates where they knew of them but did not intervene.[253] The first major modern case on the principle was the *Yamashita* case.[254] The case has proved controversial and many of its factual findings, and the fairness of the trial, have been subject to considerable critique.[255] The Nuremberg IMT did not deal with command responsibility in this sense in any real way. The Tokyo IMT, however, took a very broad interpretation of the principle, which at times appeared to shade into joint criminal enterprise liability.[256] Command responsibility was included in military manuals after the Second World War,[257] but made its first clear appearance in a treaty in 1977, in Articles 86 and 87 of Additional Protocol I to the Geneva Conventions.

In a provision that is similar to, but not quite the same as, the provisions of Additional Protocol I, Article 7(3)[258] of the ICTY Statute reads:

The fact that [crimes were] committed by a subordinate does not relieve his superior of criminal responsibility if he knew or had reason to know that the subordinate was about to commit such acts or had done so and the superior failed to take the necessary and reasonable measures to prevent such acts or to punish the perpetrators thereof.[259]

Article 28 of the ICC Statute[260] is more detailed, reading:

In addition to other grounds of criminal responsibility under this Statute for crimes within the jurisdiction of the Court:

(a) A military commander or person effectively acting as a military commander shall be criminally responsible for crimes within the jurisdiction of the Court committed by forces under his or her

---

[252] Theodor Meron, *Henry's Laws and Shakespeare's Wars* (Oxford, 1993) 149, note 40.
[253] 'Report of the Commission on the Responsibility of the Authors of the War' (1920) 14 *AJIL* 95, 121.
[254] *United States* v. *Yamashita*, 327 US 1 (1945).
[255] See e.g. M. Cherif Bassiouni, *Crimes Against Humanity in International Criminal Law*, 2nd ed. (The Hague, 1999) 427–31; Anne-Marie Prevost, 'Race and War Crimes: The 1945 War Crimes Trial of General Tomoyuki Yamashita' (1992) 14 *Human Rights Quarterly* 303, 318–19; Richard Lael, *The Yamashita Precedent: War Crimes and Command Responsibility* (Wilmington, DE, 1982); Mettraux, *Law of Command Responsibility* (n. 246) 5 et seq.
[256] Tokyo IMT, reprinted in Boister and Cryer, *Documents on the Tokyo International Military Tribunal* (n. 20) 48, 442–7. This engendered dissents from Judges Bernard (12–18), Röling (Dissenting Opinion of the Member from the Netherlands at 54–61) and Pal (Dissenting Opinion of the Member from India at 1027–225). See Boister and Cryer, *Documents on the Tokyo International Military Tribunal* (n. 20) 205–36.
[257] US Department of the Army Field Manual, *The Law of Land Warfare*, FM 27–10 (1956) (as revised) para. 501. See also the 1958 British Manual, *The Law of War on Land, being Part III of the Manual of Military Law* (London, 1958) para. 631.
[258] This Article was taken as applying both to international and non-international armed conflicts as a matter of customary international law: *Hadžihasanović et al.*, ICTY AC, 16 July 2003, paras. 10–31.
[259] ICTR Statute, Art. 6(1) and SCSL Statute, Art. 6(1), are essentially the same. The latter, post-dating the ICC Statute, may be a rejection of aspects of the ICC Statute's definition of the concept.
[260] See generally William Schabas, *The International Criminal Court: A Commentary on the Rome Statute*, 2nd ed. (Oxford, 2016) 607; Otto Triffterer, 'Article 28' in Triffterer and Ambos, *Commentary*, 1056.

effective command and control, or effective authority and control as the case may be, as a result of his or her failure to exercise control properly over such forces, where:

(i)   That military commander or person either knew or, owing to the circumstances at the time, should have known that the forces were committing or about to commit such crimes; and

(ii) That military commander or person failed to take all necessary and reasonable measures within his or her power to prevent or repress their commission or to submit the matter to the competent authorities for investigation and prosecution.

(b) With respect to superior and subordinate relationships not described in paragraph (a), a superior shall be criminally responsible for crimes within the jurisdiction of the Court committed by subordinates under his or her effective authority and control, as a result of his or her failure to exercise control properly over such subordinates, where:

(i)   The superior either knew, or consciously disregarded information which clearly indicated, that the subordinates were committing or about to commit such crimes;

(ii)   The crimes concerned activities that were within the effective responsibility and control of the superior; and

(iii) The superior failed to take all necessary and reasonable measures within his or her power to prevent or repress their commission or to submit the matter to the competent authorities for investigation and prosecution.

The Trial Chamber in *Čelebići* helpfully elaborated the requirements of command responsibility under customary law:[261] first, a superior/subordinate relationship; second, the 'mental element'; and, third, a failure to take reasonable measures to prevent or punish violations of international criminal law.[262] This trio was adopted by the ad hoc Tribunals and is a helpful list of the requirements.[263] To those, with which the ICC has concurred,[264] the Rome Statute has added another requirement: causation.[265] The elements interact, and understandably were described by one ICC Judge as 'a medley of layers of evidence, or moving parts, that must be reckoned with'.[266]

15.7.1 Superior/Subordinate Relationship

Where there are the clear formal chains of command that characterize modern well-disciplined armies, this criterion may appear simple to apply. However, modern conflicts

---

[261] The taxonomy, though, finds a basis in Judge Röling's Opinion in the Tokyo IMT, 59–61.

[262] *Čelebići* case, ICTY TC II, 16 November 1998, para. 344; *Blaškić*, ICTY TC I, 3 March 2000, para. 294; *Orić*, ICTY TC II, 30 June 2006, para. 294, added that crimes were committed by those other than the superior. This is true, but does not really add to the specifics of the principle of liability. The Chamber added it only as it had been challenged by the defence, *Orić ibid.* para. 295. The Chamber asserted that all forms of participation in ICTY Statute, Art. 7(1) sufficed to fulfil this criterion: paras. 295–306, 328. This is probably correct, as long as it is remembered that the mental element for superior responsibility must still be fulfilled: Gerhard Werle and Florian Jeßberger, *Principles of International Criminal Law*, 4th ed. (Oxford, 2020) 136–7.

[263] See e.g. *Aleksovski*, ICTY TC I*bis*, 25 June 1999, paras. 69–71; *Kayishema and Ruzindana*, ICTR TC II, 21 May 1999, para. 209; *Blaškić*, ICTY TC I, 3 March 2000, para. 294.

[264] *Bemba*, ICC TC VIII, 19 October 2016 (ICC-01/05–01/13–1989-Red) para. 170.

[265] Werle and Jeßberger, *Principles* (n. 262) 136–7.

[266] *Bemba*, ICC AC, 8 June 2018, Opinion of Judge Eboe-Osuji (ICC-01/05–01/08–3636-Anx3) para. 153; see also *Bemba*, ICC AC, 8 June 2018 (ICC-01/05–01/08–3636-Red) para. 167.

are not always fought on this basis and by such forces.[267] Therefore, the standard is that of 'effective control', defined as 'a material ability to prevent or punish criminal conduct'.[268] It is required that 'the accused has to be, by virtue of his position, senior in some sort of formal or informal hierarchy to the perpetrator'.[269] The de jure position of the superior is not determinative of this; it is largely factual ability to prevent and punish that counts.[270] Equally, a de jure position may be evidence of effective control.[271] Issuance of orders may also be good evidence,[272] but, if they are not obeyed, this will count the other way.[273] Other factors which are probative in this regard include the capacity to alter command structures and promote or remove people, and the ability to require people to engage or withdraw from hostilities.[274] Payment of salaries and reliance on logistical support lines of reporting are also relevant.[275] In the end, however, the issue must be decided on a case-by-case basis,[276] and it ought to be noted that even the fact that it is necessary to use force to enforce authority does not automatically mean that a person does not have effective control over subordinates.[277]

It is clear that superior responsibility also attaches to civilian superiors.[278] The standard of control is again 'effective control', 'in the sense that he exercised a degree of control over … [subordinates] which is similar to the degree of control of military commanders'.[279] Also, as Article 28(b)(ii) of the ICC Statute shows, the crimes must fall within the area of responsibility of a civilian commander. The ICTY has on occasion been criticized for taking a narrow approach to effective control, against a background of fluid levels of control and multiple lines of command.[280]

---

[267] For an excellent discussion of aspects of command responsibility in such contexts, see Sandesh Sivakumaran, 'Command Responsibility in Irregular Groups' (2012) 10 *JICJ* 1129.

[268] *Čelebići* case, ICTY AC, 20 February 2001, para. 256; the standard set out there has been repeated consistently, see e.g. *Popović et al.*, ICTY AC, 30 January 2015, para. 1857. See generally Mettraux, *Law of Command Responsibility* (n. 246) ch. 9.

[269] *Halilović*, ICTY AC, 16 October 2007, para. 59; *Bemba*, ICC TC III, 21 March 2016 (ICC-01/05–01/08–3343) para. 184.

[270] *Delalić et al.*, ICTY AC, 20 February 2001, paras. 186–98; *Halilović*, ICTY AC, 16 October 2007, para. 59; *Kajelijeli*, ICTR AC, 23 May 2005, para. 85. See also e.g. *United States v. List et al.* (the 'Hostages case'), VIII LRTWC 89 (1948); Tokyo IMT, reprinted in Boister and Cryer, *Documents on the Tokyo International Military Tribunal* (n. 256) 48, 820.

[271] *Delalić et al.*, ICTY AC, 20 February 2001, para. 197; *Hadžihasanović and Kubura*, ICTY AC, 22 April 2008, para. 21. There is no presumption, however, that de jure positions give rise to effective control: *Orić*, ICTY AC, 3 July 2008, paras. 91–2.

[272] This is the case even where that accused's superior has also ordered the offences: *Nizeyimana*, ICTR TC III, 19 June 2012, para. 1528.

[273] *Blaškić*, ICTY AC, 29 July 2004, paras. 69 and 399. See also *Strugar*, ICTY AC, 17 July 2008, para. 254; *Halilović*, ICTY AC, 16 October 2007, para. 207. As noted by Mettraux, *Law of Command Responsibility* (n. 246) 176–8, the nature and type of order is relevant, as is whether the person signing the order is, in essence, just passing it on for his or her superiors. Orders to the person may be relevant evidence of their material abilities, but this depends on the interpretation of the order: *Halilović*, ICTY AC, 16 October 2007, para. 193.

[274] *Bemba*, ICC TC III, 21 March 2016 (ICC-01/05–01/08–3343) para. 188; these were not challenged on appeal. See also Mettraux, *Law of Command Responsibility* (n. 246) 164–70.

[275] *Perišić*, ICTY TC I, 6 September 2011, para. 1672. For some contextual factors in irregular groups, see *Brima et al.*, SCSL TC II, 20 June 2007, para. 788.

[276] In addition, a failure to initiate investigations, either because there is no ability to do so, or because a person has failed to take the necessary and reasonable steps international criminal law requires: see *Halilović*, ICTY AC, 16 October 2007, paras. 175–80, 182.

[277] *Hadžihasanović and Kubura*, ICTY AC, 22 April 2008, para. 228.

[278] *Bagilishema*, ICTR AC, 2 July 2002, para. 52; *Orić*, ICTY TC II, 30 June 2006, para. 308. This is also provided for expressly in Art. 28(b) of the ICC Statute. See also Tokyo IMT, reprinted in Boister and Cryer, *Documents on the Tokyo International Military Tribunal* (n. 256) 48, 442–7; *United States v. Karl Brandt et al.* (the 'Doctors Trial'), IV LRTWC 91–3 (1947). Some are a little uncomfortable about this, e.g. van Sliedregt, *Individual Criminal Responsibility* (n. 2) 209.

[279] *Bagilishema*, ICTR AC, 2 July 2002, para. 52, overturning the Trial Chamber on point. As the Appeals Chamber noted (*ibid.*), the way authority is exercised may not be the same.

[280] Osiel, 'The Banality of Good' (n. 61) 1774–9. The ICTY has admitted the fluidity of such situations: *Orić*, ICTY TC II, 30 June 2006, paras. 309–10.

The ICTY Appeals Chamber, in its split 3:2 decision in *Hadžihasanović et al.*, determined that for superior responsibility to arise the crimes must be committed whilst the superior had effective control over the offenders.[281] Defendant Kabura had taken up his position as acting commander of the Bosnian Army on 1 April 1993 while the crimes he was charged with had been committed by subordinates before that date. The Appeals Chamber held that, since he had no effective control over subordinates before 1 April, there was no command responsibility even though he failed to punish subordinates for those crimes once he assumed command. The case has particular relevance for failure to punish liability and has generated considerable debate.[282] The dissenting judges in particular were very critical of the majority, and asserted that the decision was wrong in law.[283] In spite of the controversy, the ICTY Appeals Chamber has considered the matter as settled.[284] The ICC Statute, by requiring that offences occur as 'a result of … [a superior's] failure to exercise control properly over such forces' leads to the same result as the majority decision in *Hadžihasanović et al.*[285]

15.7.2 Mental Element

The mental element of command responsibility is one of its most controversial aspects.[286] This is in part because of the broad ambit of this type of liability, which accrues essentially by omission. The discord is not helped by the opaque nature of the finding in the seminal *Yamashita* case, and the fair trial issues that still cast a pall over that proceeding. The fact that the various documents dealing with the matter use different terminology does not help. The ICTY has been at great pains to explain that superior responsibility is not a form of strict liability.[287] The leading authority in the ICTY determined that:

[A superior] may possess the *mens rea* for command responsibility where: (1) he had actual knowledge, established through direct or circumstantial evidence, that his subordinates were committing or about to commit crimes … or (2) where he had in his possession information of a nature, which at the least, would put him on notice of the risk of such offences by indicating the need for additional investigation in order to ascertain whether such crimes were committed or were about to be committed by his subordinates.[288]

---

[281] *Hadžihasanović et al.*, ICTY AC, 16 July 2003, paras. 37–56. For a commentary, see: Barrie Sander, 'Unravelling the Confusion Concerning Successor Superior Responsibility in the ICTY Jurisprudence' (2010) 23 *LJIL* 105–35.

[282] See Mettraux, *International Crimes* (n. 63) 301; *contra* Christopher Greenwood, 'Command Responsibility and the Hadžihasanović Decision' (2004) 2 *JICJ* 598. One ICTY Trial Chamber has seemingly doubted it: *Orić*, ICTY TC II, 30 June 2006, para. 335.

[283] *Hadžihasanović et al.*, ICTY AC, 16 July 2003, Partially Dissenting Opinion of Judge Shahabuddeen, paras. 1–40; Separate and Partially Dissenting Opinion of Judge Hunt, paras. 6–34. Part of the disagreement related to the way in which the nature of superior responsibility is seen: see Section 15.7.5.

[284] *Perišić*, ICTY AC, 28 February 2013, para. 117. [285] *Bemba*, ICC PTC II, 15 June 2009 (ICC-01/05–01/08–424) para. 424.

[286] See generally Mettraux, *Law of Command Responsibility* (n. 246) ch. 10; Ambos, *Treatise on International Law* (n. 6) 220–8.

[287] E.g. *Delalić et al.*, ICTY AC, 20 February 2001, paras. 226 and 239.

[288] *Ibid*. paras. 223 and 241. 'Commission' in this regard includes the various forms of liability: *Blagojević and Jokić*, ICTY AC, 9 May 2007, para. 280; but a finding on the liability of a subordinate on some form of responsibility seems necessary: *Orić*, ICTY AC, 3 July 2008, paras. 47–8; *Thaçi et al.* KSC, 27 February 2023, Lesser Redacted Amended Indictment, para. 55.

It is accepted that actual knowledge can be determined by direct proof, or with reference to circumstantial evidence.[289] Relevant circumstantial evidence for this purpose includes:

the number, type and scope of illegal acts, time during which the illegal acts occurred, number and types of troops and logistics involved, geographical location, whether the occurrence of the acts is widespread, tactical tempo of operations, *modus operandi* of similar illegal acts, officers and staff involved, and location of the commander at the time.[290]

What the superior knew or had reason to know must be related to crimes, and the type of crimes committed.[291] It is not sufficient that a commander is aware of some general form of criminality.[292] Such information can be relevant for proof that the superior had reason to know of offences,[293] although they do not need to know the precise identities of the perpetrators.[294] The Appeals Chamber in *Strugar* held that under the correct legal standard sufficiently alarming information putting a superior on notice of the risk that crimes might subsequently be carried out by his subordinates and justifying further inquiry is sufficient to hold a superior liable under Article 7(3).[295]

The Trial Chamber in the *Blaškić* case, in an opinion which canvassed some jurisprudence not discussed in *Čelebići*, took a broader approach to the 'had reason to know standard' than the latter decision, and came to the conclusion that:

if a commander has exercised due diligence in the fulfilment of his duties yet lacks knowledge that crimes are about to be or have been committed, such lack of knowledge cannot be held against him. However, taking into account his particular position of command and the circumstances prevailing at the time, such ignorance cannot be a defence where the absence of knowledge is the result of negligence in the discharge of his duties: this commander had reason to know within the meaning of the Statute.[296]

Despite considerable academic support,[297] this standard did not prevail in the ad hoc Tribunals,[298] and any talk of negligence has been disavowed by the Appeals Chamber.[299] The *Čelebići* standard of 'knew or had reason to know' (excluding 'should have known')

---

[289] *Blaškić*, ICTY TC I, 3 March 2000, para. 307; *Orić*, ICTY TC II, 30 June 2006, paras. 319–20; *Halilović*, ICTY TC I, 16 November 2005, para. 66.

[290] *Delalić et al.*, ICTY AC, 20 February 2001, para. 238; *Bemba*, ICC TC III, 21 March 2016 (ICC-01/05–01/08–3343) para. 193. See also the list in Mettraux, *Law of Command Responsibility* (n. 246) 214–15.

[291] *Orić*, ICTY TC II, 30 June 2006, paras. 298–303, took a broad approach, asserting that this included complicity and inchoate offences. This has been severely criticized, however: Ambos, *Treatise on International Law* (n. 6) 213–14.

[292] *Krnojelac*, ICTY AC, 17 September 2003, para. 155; *Orić*, ICTY AC, 3 July 2008, paras. 169–74; and Mettraux, *Law of Command Responsibility* (n. 246) 200–2.

[293] *Strugar*, ICTY AC, 7 June 2006, para. 301.

[294] *Blagojević and Jokić*, ICTY AC, 9 May 2007, para. 287. Their existence must be proved, however: *Orić*, ICTY AC, 3 July 2008, para. 35.

[295] *Strugar* ICTY AC, 7 June 2006, para. 304   [296] *Blaškić*, ICTY TC I, 3 March 2000, para. 332.

[297] Monica Feria Tinta, 'Commanders on Trial: The Blaškić Case and the Doctrine of Command Responsibility under International Law' (2000) 47 *Netherlands International Law Review* 293, 314–22; Yoram Dinstein, *The Conduct of Hostilities under the Law of International Armed Conflict* (Cambridge, 2004) 24; Robert Kolb, 'The Jurisprudence of the Yugoslav and Rwandan Criminal Tribunals on their Jurisdiction and on International Crimes' (2000) 69 *British Yearbook of International Law* 259, 301. Support is not universal though: see Bing Bing Jia, 'The Doctrine of Command Responsibility: Current Problems' (2000) 3 *Yearbook of International Humanitarian Law* 131, 155–60.

[298] *Blaškić*, ICTY AC, 29 July 2004, paras. 58–64; *Bagilishema*, ICTR AC, 3 July 2002, para. 35.

[299] *Bagilishema*, ICTR AC, 2 July 2002, paras. 34–5; *Blaškić*, ICTY AC, 29 July 2004, para. 63; *Halilović*, ICTY TC I, 16 November 2005, para. 71.

became the accepted one in the ad hoc Tribunals for both military and civilian superiors.[300]

Article 28 of the ICC Statute sets a different standard for military and non-military superiors, the standard for the former being that the superior 'knew or, owing to the circumstances at the time, should have known that the forces were committing or about to commit such crimes'. For civilians, it is that the civilian superior 'knew, or consciously disregarded information which clearly indicated, that the subordinates were committing or about to commit such crimes'. Commentators have questioned whether this distinction is consistent with customary law,[301] and the ICTR Appeals Chamber has at least implicitly rejected the ICC Statute *mens rea* for civilian superiors.[302]

The ICC has established that the *mens rea* for military commanders in the ICC Statute, 'should have known', is a criminal negligence standard,[303] and that failure to seek out information could lead to liability.[304] In doing so, the Pre-Trial Chamber expressly departed from the standards set elsewhere:

> The Chamber is mindful of the fact that the 'had reason to know' criterion embodied in the statutes of the ICTR, ICTY and SCSL sets a different standard to the 'should have known' standard under article 28(a) of the Statute. However, despite such a difference, which the Chamber does not deem it necessary to address in the present decision, the criteria or indicia developed by the ad hoc tribunals to meet the standard of 'had reason to know' may also be useful when applying the 'should have known' requirement.[305]

It has been argued that a criminal negligence standard is a more principled and predictable standard of liability, appropriate in the special context of military command.[306]

15.7.3 Failure to Take Measures

The final link in the chain of liability under customary law is the failure or refusal to take 'necessary and reasonable measures' to prevent or punish the offences the superior knew or culpably ought to have known of. It is important to emphasize in this regard that liability may accrue to a superior for a failure to prevent or a failure to punish those crimes. The two types of liability are separate.[307] There is no necessity that a person knew or should have known of the offences before they occurred for failure to punish liability to arise. Similarly, if a superior knew or should have known of impending offences before they occurred, it is no defence to a

---

[300] *Bagilishema*, ICTR AC, 2 July 2002, paras. 26–37. The ICTR had, on occasion, applied the ICC Statute standard: *Kayishema and Ruzindana*, ICTR TC II, 21 May 1999, paras. 227–8, and had been criticized for it. See Alexander Zahar, 'Command Responsibility of Civilian Superiors for Genocide' (2001) 14 *LJIL* 591.
[301] See Greg Vetter, 'Command Responsibility of Non-Military Superiors in the International Criminal Court (ICC)' (2000) 25 *Yale Journal of International Law* 89; van Sliedregt, *Individual Criminal Responsibility* (n. 2) 191–2; Robert Cryer, *Prosecuting International Crimes: Selectivity and the International Criminal Law Regime* (Cambridge, 2005) 321–3.
[302] *Bagilishema*, ICTR AC, 2 July 2002, paras. 26–37.
[303] *Bemba*, ICC PTC II, 15 June 2009 (ICC-01/05–01/08–424) para. 429. [304] *Ibid*. paras. 432–3. [305] *Ibid*. para. 434.
[306] Darryl Robinson, 'A Justification of Command Responsibility' (2017) 28 *Criminal Law Forum* 633; Darryl Robinson, *Justice in Extreme Cases. Criminal Law Theory Meets International Criminal Law* (Cambridge University Press, 2020) 206–18.
[307] *Hadžihasanović et al.*, ICTY AC, 16 July 2003, Partial Dissenting Opinion of Judge Shahabuddeen, paras. 35–6. See also *Blaškić*, ICTY AC, 29 July 2004, paras. 78–85; *Halilović*, ICTY TC I, 16 November 2005, para. 94; *Orić*, ICTY TC II, 30 June 2006, paras. 325–6.

charge of failing to take adequate measures to suppress them that he chose to allow them to occur, then punished the perpetrators.[308] As has been said, 'a superior's failure to prevent the commission of the crime by a subordinate, where he had the ability to do so, cannot simply be remedied by subsequently punishing the subordinate for the crime'.[309]

The measures which can be expected were explained by the ICC's Appeals Chamber as requiring:

consideration of what measures were at his or her disposal in the circumstances at the time … However, it is not the case that a commander must take each and every possible measure at his or her disposal. Despite the link between the material ability of a commander to take measures (which is directly connected to his or her level of authority) and what he or she might reasonably have been expected to do, it is not the case that a commander is required to employ every single conceivable measure within his or her arsenal, irrespective of considerations of proportionality and feasibility. Article 28 only requires commanders to do what is necessary and reasonable under the circumstances.[310]

This is consistent with the approach of the ICTY on point.[311]

Thus, the measures that can be expected to be taken depend on the precise nature of the control exercised by the superior. As the ICC Statute states, this can mean acts intended to prevent or punish where that is possible, and/or, where appropriate, submitting the matter to the appropriate prosecutorial organs.[312] What measures may be expected of a superior relates to what power the superior has, and this requires a contextual analysis, as was shown in the *Bemba* case.[313] As the majority in the Appeals Chamber said in that case, 'a commander cannot be blamed for not having done something he or she had no power to do'.[314] The Chamber also noted that efforts must be taken to avoid hindsight bias.[315] In the *Bemba* case, the extent of the measures undertaken by the defendant to investigate, ask for investigations, and counteract international crimes deeply divided the court.[316]

There are certain circumstances in which the possibility that the duty to punish may be fulfilled by the use of disciplinary sanctions rather than criminal prosecutions 'cannot be excluded',[317] but, for international crimes, these will be rare.[318] What can be expected of irregular groups with regard to punishment is a further complicating factor, although not an insuperable one.[319] Precisely what is required in relation to the fulfilment of the duty to

---

[308] *Blaškić*, ICTY TC I, 3 March 2000, para. 336; *Strugar*, ICTY TC II, 31 January 2005, para. 373; *Halilović*, ICTY TC I, 16 November 2005, para. 72. See also *Bemba*, ICC PTC II, 15 June 2009 (ICC-01/05–01/08–424) para. 436.
[309] *Orić*, ICTY TC II, 30 June 2006, para. 326. In addition, to fail to take measures may be considered tacit acceptance of the crime: see *Halilović*, ICTY TC I, 16 November 2005, para. 95.
[310] *Bemba*, ICC AC, 8 June 2018 (ICC-01/05–01/08–3636-Red) para. 169.
[311] *Blaškić*, ICTY AC, 29 July 2004, para. 72. See e.g. Ambos, *Treatise on International Law* (n. 6) 217–20.
[312] See also *Halilović*, ICTY AC, 16 October 2007, para. 182. Formal legal competence to take the necessary measures to prevent or repress the crime is not required: see *Delalić et al.*, ICTY TC II, 16 November 1998, para. 395.
[313] *Bemba*, ICC AC, 8 June 2018 (ICC-01/05–01/08–3636-Red).
[314] *Bemba*, ICC AC, 8 June 2018 (ICC-01/05–01/08–3636-Red) para. 167. [315] *Ibid.* para. 170.
[316] See *Bemba*, ICC AC, 8 June 2018 (ICC-01/05–01/08–3636-Red).
[317] *Hadžihasanović and Kubura*, ICTY AC, 22 April 2008, para. 33.
[318] *Ibid.* paras. 149–55. As this case notes though (*ibid.*), if matters are referred on, it will not always be determinative that those authorities do not take sufficient action.
[319] See Sivakumaran, 'Command Responsibility' (n. 267) 1144–50. See further Sandesh Sivakumaran, 'Courts of Armed Opposition Groups: Fair Trials or Summary Justice?' (2009) 7 *JICJ* 489.

punish was a deeply controversial matter in the *Bemba* case, which only passed by a bare majority, and turned on evidential matters, relating in part to what measures were, and ought to have been taken by the defendant, especially with regard to the requests for investigation that had been undertaken, and the geographical distance between the superior and the forces on the ground.[320]

15.7.4 Causation

The question of causation is an awkward one in relation to superior responsibility. This is, to a large extent, because superior responsibility is a form of liability for omission, to which causation is difficult, but not impossible, to apply.[321] This has caused considerable confusion as failure to prevent and failure to punish liability are entirely separate forms of liability.[322] For the latter form of liability, it is often said that causation logically cannot be a requirement.[323] With respect to the former case, the Trial Chamber in *Čelebići*, with which the Appeals Chamber in *Blaškić* agreed,[324] said that it:

> found no support for the existence of a requirement of proof of causation as a separate element of superior responsibility ... This is not to say that, conceptually, the principle of causality is without application to the doctrine of command responsibility insofar as it relates to the responsibility of superiors for their failure to prevent the crimes of their subordinates. In fact, a recognition of a necessary causal nexus may be considered to be inherent in the requirement of crimes committed by subordinates and the superior's failure to take the measures within his powers to prevent them. In this situation, the superior may be considered to be causally linked to the offences, in that, but for his failure to fulfil his duty to act, the acts of his subordinates would not have been committed.[325]

In the *Orić* case, the Trial Chamber was certain that there was no requirement of causation for either type of superior responsibility, as, 'even with regard to the superior's failure to prevent, a requirement of causation would run counter to the very basis of this type of superior responsibility as criminal liability of omission'.[326] This appears to misunderstand the idea of negative causation, where an omission permits something to occur. Leaving a window open allows the rain in, even if it does not cause a change in the weather. Still, the Appeals Chamber in *Hadžihasanović and Kubura* reaffirmed its view that no causation requirement exists.[327]

The ICC Statute, by imposing the general requirement for liability that the crimes occur *as a result of* a failure to supervise subordinates, excludes liability where there is no form of causation, even in the expanded sense that a failure to prevent may facilitate

---

[320] *Bemba*, ICC AC, 8 June 2018 (ICC-01/05–01/08–3636-Red) paras. 171, 173, 180, 189. See generally Miles Jackson, 'Geographical Remoteness in Bemba', *EJIL Talk*, 30 July 2018, www.ejiltalk.org/geographical-remoteness-in-bemba/#more-16367.

[321] See generally Otto Triffterer, 'Causality, a Separate Element of the Doctrine of Superior Responsibility as Expressed in Article 28 of the Rome Statute?' (2002) 15 *LJIL* 179; Darryl Robinson, 'How Command Responsibility Got So Complicated: A Culpability Contradiction, its Obfuscation and a Simple Solution' (2012) 13 *Melbourne Journal of International Law* 1.

[322] *Bemba*, ICC TC III, 21 March 2016 (ICC-01/05–01/08–3343) para. 201.   [323] *Orić*, ICTY TC II, 30 June 2006, para. 338.

[324] *Blaškić*, ICTY AC, 29 July 2004, paras. 75–7. See also *Halilović*, ICTY TC I, 16 November 2005, para. 77.

[325] *Delalić et al.*, ICTY TC II, 16 November 1998, paras. 398–9.   [326] *Orić*, ICTY TC II, 30 June 2006, para. 338.

[327] *Hadžihasanović and Kubura*, ICTY AC, 22 April 2008, para. 39.

commission.[328] The most recent appellate jurisprudence on causation, in the *Bemba* case, revealed a deep division on the issue, with the plurality opinions deliberately expressing no view on point. As was said by Judges van den Wyngaert and Morrison:

The question of whether superior responsibility requires causation has been a live issue in legal writings for many years, and the present Judgment will unfortunately not give the long-awaited judicial answer, as the judges are divided and could only express themselves in opinions.[329]

The requisite degree of causal contribution remains contentious. The controversy hinges in part on how superior responsibility is conceptualized.[330] If superior responsibility is a mode of liability, that is, a form of complicity/participation in the crime committed by the subordinate, as the ICC Statute and Tribunal jurisprudence suggest, then fundamental principles of justice arguably require that the accused's dereliction at least contributed in some way to crimes, for example by making them easier or more likely.[331]

15.7.5 Nature of Superior Responsibility

The nature of responsibility attributed to a superior under this principle of liability is controversial.[332] Some domestic legislation (including that of the United Kingdom, which follows Article 28 almost *verbatim*) criminalizes superior responsibility as a form of complicity.[333] Others believe,[334] and the Canadian and German legislation imply, that it is a separate offence of omission, on the ground that it would be unfair to hold a person vicariously liable for the serious crimes of another based on a relaxed mental element. In this view, command responsibility is in essence a more serious form of a dereliction of duty charge.[335] There was confusion about the basis of liability in the Secretary-General's report relating to the ICTY Statute, which said that command responsibility is a form of 'imputed responsibility or criminal negligence'.[336]

---

[328] *Bemba*, ICC AC, 8 June 2018; Dissenting Opinion of Judge Sanji Mmasenono Monageng and Judge Piotr Hofmański (ICC-01/ 05–01/08–3636-Anx1-Red) paras. 339–40; Separate Opinion of Judge Van den Wyngaert and Judge Morrison (ICC-01/05–01/ 08–3636-Anx2) paras. 51–6; Concurring Separate Opinion of Judge Eboe-Osuji (ICC-01/05–01/08–3636-Anx3) paras. 166, 185.

[329] Separate Opinion of Judge Van den Wyngaert and Judge Morrison (ICC-01/05–01/08–3636-Anx2) para. 51.

[330] *Bemba*, ICC AC, 8 June 2018, Separate Opinion of Judges van den Wyngaert and Morrison (ICC-01/05–01/08–3636-Anx2) paras. 51–6; *contra* Dissenting Opinion of Judge Sanji Mmasenono Monageng and Judge Piotr Hofmański (ICC-01/05–01/ 08–3636-Anx1-Red) paras. 319–41.

[331] Robinson, 'How Command Responsibility Got So Complicated' (n. 321).

[332] See *Halilović*, ICTY TC I, 16 November 2005, paras. 42–54. See Miles Jackson, 'Command Responsibility', in De Hemptinne et al. (eds.), *Modes of Liability in International Criminal Law* (n. 80) 409–32; Roberta Arnold and Miles Jackson, 'Article 28: Responsibility of Commanders and Other Superiors', in Ambos (ed.), *Rome Statute of the International Criminal Court* (2021) (n. 172) mn. 6–16; Darryl Robinson, 'How Command Responsibility Got So Complicated: A Culpability Contradiction, its Obfuscation and a Simple Solution' (2012) 13 *Melbourne Journal of International Law* 1; Chantal Meloni, 'Command Responsibility: Mode of Liability for the Crimes of Subordinates or Separate Offence of the Superior?' (2007) 5 *JICJ*, 619–637; Elies van Sliedregt, 'Command Responsibility at the ICTY: Three Generations of Case Law and Still Ambiguity' in Bert Swart, Alexander Zahar and Göran Sluiter (eds.), *The Legacy of the International Criminal Tribunal for Former Yugoslavia* (Oxford, 2011) 377; Panagiota Kotzamani, 'Towards a unified approach to superior responsibility in international criminal law: Establishing the links between participation in the crime and the superior responsibility doctrine' (2022) 35 *LJIL* 679–697.

[333] International Criminal Court Act 2001, s. 65.

[334] Kai Ambos, 'Superior Responsibility' in Cassese et al., *Commentary*, 850–5.

[335] On the 'general duty to prevent' on superiors, see *Halilović*, ICTY TC I, 16 November 2005, paras. 81–8.

[336] *Report of the Secretary-General Pursuant to Paragraph 2 of Security Council Resolution 808*, UN Doc. S/25704 (1993) para. 56.

In *Hadžihasanović et al.*, Judge Shahabuddeen challenged the idea that command responsibility is a form of complicity, opining that '[c]ommand responsibility imposes responsibility on a commander for failure to take corrective action in respect of a crime committed by another; it does not make the commander party to the crime committed by that other'.[337] As he accepted, the ambit of superior responsibility is intrinsically linked to its conceptualization.[338] Relying, in part, on Judge Shahabuddeen's opinion, the Trial Chamber in *Halilović* asserted that:

> command responsibility is responsibility for an omission. The commander is responsible for the failure to perform an act required by international law. This omission is culpable because international law imposes an affirmative duty on superiors to prevent and punish crimes committed by their subordinates.[339]

This is consistent with the fact that the ICTY considers that Article 7(1) and (3) provide distinct categories of criminal liability which exclude cumulative convictions for the same count based on the same facts.[340] Such views have also gained support in the Appeals Chamber. In *Krnojelac*, that Chamber, in a rather 'throwaway' line, said '[i]t cannot be overemphasised that, where superior responsibility is concerned, an accused is not charged with the crimes of his subordinates but with his failure to carry out his duty as a superior to exercise control'.[341]

The ICTR Appeals Chamber subsequently attempted to square the circle, providing that, although the culpable conduct in command responsibility is the failure to prevent or punish,[342] 'the seriousness of the superior's conduct in failing to prevent or punish crimes must be measured to some extent by the nature of the crimes to which this relates, i.e. the gravity of the crimes committed by the direct perpetrator(s)'.[343] They further held that:

> The Statute does not accord any 'lesser' form of individual criminal responsibility to superior responsibility. Whilst the Appeals Chamber also recognizes that, in appropriate cases, a conviction under Article 6(3) of the Statute may result in a lesser sentence to that imposed in the context of an Article 6(1) conviction it reiterates its view that, in the circumstances of this case, superior responsibility is not to be seen as less grave than criminal responsibility under Article 6(1) of the Statute. The Appeals Chamber also recalls the well-established principle of gradation in sentencing, which holds that leaders and planners should bear heavier criminal responsibility than those further down the scale.[344]

Under the ICC Statute, command responsibility is treated as a form of liability for the underlying offences. Although some elements of Article 28 of the ICC Statute could be read as creating a dereliction of duty-type offence,[345] it quite clearly imputes the crimes of the

---

[337] *Hadžihasanović et al.*, ICTY AC, 16 July 2003, Partial Dissenting Opinion of Judge Shahabuddeen, para. 33. See also *Orić*, ICTY TC II, 30 June 2006, para. 294.

[338] *Hadžihasanović et al.*, ICTY AC, 16 July 2003, para. 33. [339] *Halilović*, ICTY TC I, 16 November 2005, para. 54.

[340] *Blaškić*, ICTY AC, 29 July 2004, para. 91; but see *Delalić et al.*, ICTY AC, 20 February 2001, paras. 745–6. See section 19.3.3.

[341] *Krnojelac*, ICTY AC, 13 September 2003, para. 171. [342] *Ntabakuze*, ICTR AC, 8 May 2012, para. 282.

[343] *Ibid.* para. 302. The two steps may be traced back to *Hadžihasanović et al.*, ICTY AC, 22 April 2008, para. 318, which, in turn, refers back to the *Čelebići* case: *Delalić et al.*, ICTY AC, 20 February 2001, para. 313.

[344] *Ntabakuze*, ICTR AC, 8 May 2012, para. 303. [345] Ambos, 'Superior Responsibility' (n. 334) 850–5.

subordinates to the superior,[346] which is more consistent with a form of complicity. Where there is a duty to intervene, and knowledge of an offence, it can be more easily seen that there is a complicity base for liability on the basis of traditional aiding/abetting ideas.[347]

Whichever way it is formulated in international criminal law, command responsibility is un-nuanced, covering many different forms of liability under one heading. It moves from deliberate failures to intervene despite a duty to do so, which fall close to traditional complicity ideas, to, in essence, conduct which is close to, if not the same as, negligent dereliction of duty.[348] This is recognized by the German law relating to the subject, which deals separately with failure to know of offences in dereliction of duty, failure to report an offence, and knowing tolerance of an offence when there is a duty and an ability to intervene to prevent it.[349] By running all these concepts together, like joint criminal enterprise, the concept of superior responsibility can be criticized from the point of view of the principle of fair labelling, and on the basis that it 'display[s] a measure of insensitivity to the degree of the actor's own personal culpability'.[350]

15.8 MENTAL ELEMENTS

It is an important principle in criminal law that a person must have some form of culpability for his or her conduct. [351] This is usually shown through his or her state of mind when he or she acted (or failed to act). There are various forms of mental element that apply to international crimes, from intention, through recklessness to (arguably) negligence.[352] Different offences, and different forms of liability require different forms of *mens rea*. Hence, for the most part, they are thus dealt with when dealing with the specific offence or principle of liability.

There is little in the general parts of the Statutes of the ICTY, ICTR, and SCSL that deals with *mens rea*. Thus, it had to be dealt with at the level of case law.[353] Perhaps the broadest statement that has been made was that by the Trial Chamber in *Blaškić* that, in relation to grave breaches, 'the *mens rea* ... includes both guilty intent and recklessness which may be

---

[346] Article 28 provides that the commander 'shall be criminally responsible for crimes within the jurisdiction of the Court committed by forces under his or her effective command and control'. See *Bemba*, ICC PTC II, 15 June 2009 (ICC-01/05-01/08-424) para. 405. It is interesting, as Miles Jackson notes, that, while in *Bemba* the appeal judges agreed that superior responsibility is a mode of liability, they did not agree on the requirement of causation (which determines how one regards command responsibility: as mode of liability or separate offence): Miles Jackson, 'Causation and the Legal Requirement of Command Responsibility after Bemba at the International Criminal Court' (2022) 20 *JICJ*, 437-458.
[347] See the German Code of Crimes Against International Law, s. 4.
[348] See Mirjan Damaška, 'The Shadow Side of Command Responsibility' (2001) 49 *American Journal of Comparative Law* 455, 460–71. See generally the symposium in (2007) 5 *JICJ* 599–682.
[349] German Code of Crimes Against International Law, ss. 13 and 14.
[350] See Damaška, 'The Shadow Side' (n. 348) 456; Chantal Meloni, 'Command Responsibility: Mode of Liability for Subordinates or Separate Offence of the Superior?' (2007) 5 *JICJ* 619; Volker Nerlich, 'Superior Responsibility under Article 28 of the Rome Statute: For Exactly What Is the Superior Held Responsible?' (2007) 5 *JICJ* 665. For a partial solution, see Robinson, 'How Command Responsibility Got So Complicated' (n. 332) 30–5.
[351] For a useful comparative overview of different *mens rea* standards see: Badar and Marchuk, 'A Comparative Study of the Principles Governing Criminal Responsibility in the Major Legal Systems' (n. 51) 1–48.
[352] Or, in analogous, but not identical civil law terms, *dolus directus, dolus indirectus, dolus eventualis* and *culpa*. On the issue generally, see Ambos, *Treatise on International Law* (n. 6) ch. VII. For a very useful comparative and international law approach, see Mohamed Elewa Badar, *The Concept of Mens Rea in International Criminal Law: The Case for a Unified Approach* (Oxford, 2013).
[353] See William Schabas, *The UN International Criminal Tribunals: The Former Yugoslavia, Rwanda and Sierra Leone* (Cambridge, 2006) 292–3.

likened to serious criminal negligence'.[354] This is probably too broad. Criminal negligence is mainly at issue in relation to superior responsibility and is not a generally applicable form of *mens rea*.[355]

The ICTY and ICTR have been surprisingly reticent in setting out the ingredients of intent in the abstract, rather than in the context of specific crimes or modes of liability. Discussions in their case law were sometimes confused by the use of the term 'intent', which often refers to *mens rea* generally.[356] The Appeals Chamber in *Čelebići* asserted that an 'intentional act or omission … is an act which, judged objectively, is deliberate and not accidental',[357] but this is decidedly unclear, as there are considerable differences between that which is 'deliberate' and that which is 'not accidental'. Intention has been used to mean only deliberate acts,[358] but the case law on point is inconclusive, not least because, as the Tribunals have tended to accept that recklessness suffices for many crimes, they have not drawn the boundaries between intention and recklessness clearly.[359]

It has been argued that the default standard for *mens rea* in the ad hoc Tribunals appears to be recklessness.[360] The practice of the SCSL does little to counteract this assertion. Whether or not this is correct, the ICC Statute takes a different track, setting intention as the default mental element to be applied. Article 30 of the ICC Statute reads:

1. Unless otherwise provided, a person shall be criminally responsible and liable for punishment for a crime within the jurisdiction of the Court only if the material elements are committed with intent and knowledge.

2. For the purposes of this article, a person has intent where: (a) In relation to conduct, that person means to engage in the conduct; (b) In relation to a consequence, that person means to cause that consequence or is aware that it will occur in the ordinary course of events.

3. For the purposes of this Article, 'knowledge' means awareness that a circumstance exists or a consequence will occur in the ordinary course of events. 'Know' and 'knowingly' shall be construed accordingly.

One ICC Pre-Trial Chamber has attempted to use the jurisprudence of the ad hoc Tribunals to read *dolus eventualis* into Article 30.[361] This interpretation was rejected by the Appeals Chamber of the ICC in the *Lubanga* case, which interpreted Article 30 as excluding advertent recklessness or *dolus eventualis* as a general mental element.[362]

---

[354] *Blaškić*, ICTY TC I, 3 March 2000, para. 152; see also *Kayishema and Ruzindana*, ICTR TC II, 21 May 1999, para. 146.
[355] The Secretary-General described superior responsibility as 'imputed responsibility or criminal negligence': *Report of the Secretary-General Pursuant to Paragraph 2 of Security Council Resolution 808(1993)*, UN Doc. S/25704 (1993) para. 56. See also section 15.7.2. Some Elements of Crimes (e.g. those to Art. 8(2)(b)(xxvi)) also adopt a 'should have known' standard, which muddies the waters a little. See *Lubanga*, ICC TC I, 14 March 2012 (ICC-01/04–01/06–2842) paras. 1011–12.
[356] *Blaškić*, ICTY TC I, 3 March 2000, para. 474. The confusion probably arises out of the difference between the meaning of 'intention' in civil and common law countries. In civil law countries, it is a synonym for *mens rea*; in common law countries, it is a specific type of *mens rea*.
[357] *Delalić et al.*, ICTY AC, 20 February 2001, para. 426.   [358] *Aleksovski*, ICTY TC I*bis*, 25 June 1999, para. 56.
[359] *Blaškić*, ICTY AC, 29 July 2004, para. 42; although it is clear that neither concept requires motive: see van Sliedregt, *Individual Criminal Responsibility* (n. 2) 48–9.
[360] Werle and Jeßberger, *Principles* (n. 262) 153–4; van Sliedregt, *Individual Criminal Responsibility* (n. 2) 48–50.
[361] *Lubanga*, ICC PTC I, 29 January 2007 (ICC-01/04–01/06–803) paras. 350–5.
[362] *Lubanga*, ICC AC, 1 December 2014 (ICC-01/04–01/06–3122) para. 449.

Article 30 sets the mental element bar high; it requires either direct intent (mean to engage in conduct) or indirect intent (awareness that consequence will occur). The ICC Statute by default adopts a highly culpable form of mental element for all of the offences. This may have a specific effect in relation to the offences for which customary international law and many domestic systems differ as to *mens rea* from the provision in the ICC Statute and the ICC Elements of Crimes. An example is in relation to Article 8(2)(b)(i): attacking civilians arguably requires a higher *mens rea* (intention) than that required by customary international law, for which recklessness suffices.[363]

Article 30 applies in the ICC absent specific provision in its documents.[364] The drafters of the ICC Statute excluded any lesser mental element, unless the Statute (or the Elements of Crimes) expressly provided for one (as in Article 28). This minimized the chance of the ICC going outside its own legal framework to determine, for example, that customary international law set a lower standard than those instruments. It has been suggested that it could,[365] but this seems unlikely.[366] The practice of the ICC to date has been to accept lower *mens rea* standards set out in the Statute or the Elements of Crimes, but not outside these instruments.[367] With regard to the more demanding standard of 'purpose' in Article 25(3)(c), the ICC made clear in *Bemba et al.* that when it comes to the *mens rea* with regard to the underlying crime, committed by the principal perpetrator, Article 30 still applies.

Mindful of the twofold intent of the accessory (viz. firstly, the principal offence and, secondly, the accessory's own conduct), the Chamber clarifies that this elevated subjective standard relates to the accessory's facilitation, not the principal offence.[368]

Further Reading

There are helpful symposia on joint criminal enterprise, command responsibility, co-perpetration, and indirect co-perpetration at (2007) 5 *JICJ* 67–244; (2007) 5 *JICJ* 599–682; (2011) 9 *JICJ* 85–226; and (2022) 20 *JICJ*, respectively.
Kai Ambos, *Treatise on International Criminal Law*, vol. I, *Foundations and General Part* (Oxford, 2013)

[363] See William Fenrick, 'A First Attempt to Adjudicate Conduct of Hostilities Offences: Comments on Aspects of the ICTY Trial Decision in the Prosecutor v. Tihomir Blaškić' (2000) 13 *LJIL* 931, 936–43; See also Marta Bo, 'Autonomous Weapons and the Responsibility Gap in light of the *Mens Rea* of the War Crime of Attacking Civilians in the ICC Statute' 19 (2021) *JICJ* 275–99.

[364] As will be seen, precisely where is not necessarily clear; see also Roger Clark, 'The Mental Element in International Criminal Law: The ICC Statute of the International Criminal Court and the Elements of Offences' (2002) 12 *Criminal Law Forum* 291, 321. On Art. 30's default position, see also ICC Elements of Crimes, General Introduction, para. 2.

[365] Knut Dörmann, 'War Crimes in the Elements of Crimes' in Fischer et al., *International and National Prosecution*, 98; Wirth, 'Co-Perpetration' (n. 81) 990–5.

[366] Maria Kelt and Herman von Hebel, 'General Principles of Criminal Law and Elements of Crimes' in Lee, *Elements and Rules*, 29–30; Ambos, *Treatise on International Law* (n. 6) 291; van Sliedregt, *Individual Criminal Responsibility* (n. 2) 45–50.

[367] E.g. *Lubanga*, ICC PTC I, 29 January 2007 (ICC-01/04–01/06–803) paras. 356–9; *Bemba*, ICC PTC II, 15 June 2009 (ICC-01/05–01/08–424) paras. 136, 353.

[368] *Bemba et al.* Trial Judgment, supra note 16, para. 97.

Roberta Arnold and Miles Jackson, 'Article 28: Responsibility of Commanders and Other Superiors', in Ambos (ed.), *Rome Statute of the International Criminal Court* (Beck, 2021), mn. 6–16

Mohamed Elewa Badar, *The Concept of Mens Rea in International Criminal Law: The Case for a Unified Approach* (Oxford, 2013)

Antonio Cassese (ed.): *The Rome Statute of the International Criminal Court : a commentary.* Vol. 1 (Oxford, 2002),

Robert Cryer, *Prosecuting International Crimes: Selectivity and the International Criminal Law Regime* (Cambridge, 2005) ch. 6

Jérôme de Hemptinne, Robert Roth and Elies van Sliedregt (eds.), *Modes of Liability in International Criminal Law* (Cambridge, 2019)

Neha Jain, *Perpetrators and Accessories in International Criminal Law* (Oxford, 2014)

Guénaël Mettraux, *The Law of Command Responsibility* (Oxford, 2009)

Héctor Olásolo, *The Criminal Responsibility of Senior Political and Military Leaders as Principals to International Crimes* (Oxford, 2009)

Per Saland, 'International Criminal Law Principles' in Lee, *The Making of the Rome Statute*, 189

William Schabas, 'Hate Speech in Rwanda: The Road to Genocide' (2000) 46 *McGill Law Journal* 141

William Schabas, *The UN International Criminal Tribunals: The Former Yugoslavia, Rwanda and Sierra Leone* (Cambridge, 2006) ch. 9

Elies van Sliedregt, *The Criminal Responsibility of Individuals for Violations of International Humanitarian Law* (The Hague, 2003)

Elies van Sliedregt, *Individual Criminal Responsibility in International Law* (Oxford, 2012)

Lachezar Yanev, *Theories of Co-perpetration in International Criminal Law* (Leiden, 2018)

16

Defences/Grounds for Excluding Criminal Responsibility

16.1 INTRODUCTION

Defences, or 'grounds for excluding criminal responsibility',[1] are an oft-forgotten aspect of international criminal law. Jurisprudence from the international criminal tribunals and the ICC on the matter is sparse, and not always satisfactory. There are a number of reasons for this, one of which also explains the relative lack of scholarly attention given to most defences in international criminal law.[2] This is the tendency towards a lack of sympathy for defendants in international criminal proceedings.[3] Other reasons include the fact that in international tribunals, the prosecutor's choice of defendants rarely includes those who have plausible claims of defences recognized by the law. Defences are, however, a fundamental part of criminal law, and reflect important limitations on the proper scope of punishable conduct. It is the purpose of this chapter to set out and critique the law relating to defences, in both treaty-based and customary international law. This chapter is primarily concerned with substantive defences to international crimes. It does not deal with issues such as immunity, youth, *ne bis in idem*, or limitation periods. These are not defences for conduct, but pleas as to the jurisdiction or right of a court to try a person, which are separate matters.

16.1.1 Types of Defences

At the outset, certain terminological and conceptual matters ought to be clarified. In the common law world, it is usual to speak of 'defences' in the omnibus sense, whereas in civil law jurisdictions a firm distinction is drawn between types of defences, in particular between justifications and excuses.[4] 'Justifications', broadly speaking, are pleas that the

---

[1] Although this chapter uses 'defences', it is not to be taken as representing a position on the doctrinal controversies about the choice of terminology.

[2] Superior orders are an exception to this trend; see Section 16.8.

[3] See Barbora Holá and Maja Munivrana, 'There is Something Special about War Criminals:Constructing and Assessing the Rehabilitation of War Criminals at the ICTY/IRMCT and in Croatia' (2021) 21(1) *JICJ* 89–112.

[4] See generally Antonio Cassese, 'Justifications and Excuses in International Criminal Law' in Cassese et al., *Commentary*, 951; Elies van Sliedregt, *Individual Criminal Responsibility in International Law* (Oxford, 2012) 215–17; Kai Ambos, *Treatise on International Criminal Law*, vol. I: *Foundations and General Part* (Oxford, 2021) 304–7. The distinction is not entirely unknown to the common law, however, see A. P. Simester et al., *Simester and Sullivan's Criminal Law: Theory and Doctrine*, 6th ed. (London, 2016) ch. 17.

conduct of the defendant was acceptable, and thus necessarily lawful. It is difficult, for example, to argue that a person acting in self-defence has done anything which the law seeks to prevent. 'Excuses', broadly speaking, do not seek to defend the conduct of the defendant per se, but look to say that, in the particular instance, the *defendant* ought not be blamed for what they did. The boundary between the different types of defences is not especially clear.[5] It is not clear that there was agreement on the justification–excuses distinction at Rome, hence the neutral terminology of the ICC Statute, 'grounds for excluding criminal responsibility' rather than 'defences', 'justifications', or 'excuses'. The distinction remains, nonetheless, useful for understanding the appropriate ambit of some defences.[6]

There is another set of 'defences', however, which also require consideration. These are what can be termed 'failure of proof defences'.[7] These defences are usually denials that a person can be held responsible on the basis that the prosecution has failed to show a fundamental element of the offence. As a result, some national legal systems do not treat these issues as defences. These pleas often relate to the presence or otherwise of *mens rea*. Consent is a notable example in relation to offences to which failure of proof is relevant. Such defences, depending on the circumstances, may also operate across the justification/excuse divide.[8] They are dealt with here, as the ICC Statute impliedly treats them as defences. For instance, what Article 32 of the Statute qualifies as a defence of mistake of fact or law, may feature as a failure of proof (lack of *mens rea*) defence in a given national legal system. A final introductory point is that defences here are those that serve, as the ICC Statute puts it, to 'exclude criminal responsibility'. Other factors, such as inexperience or pressure not amounting to (exculpatory) duress are merely mitigating factors, which go to sentencing rather than responsibility.[9]

16.2 ICC STATUTE AND DEFENCES

Although the ICC Statute is neither a complete, nor an entirely accurate, statement of defences as they exist in international criminal law, it is the first treaty that attempts to deal with defences in any systematic way.[10] Its provisions were the outcome of compromises between a large number of states, some of which came from the common law tradition, and some from their civil law counterparts. While the provisions therefore leave something to be desired from a criminal law point of view, they provide a sensible structure within which to investigate defences in international criminal law. Article 31 sets out a reasonable

---

[5] See George Fletcher, *Rethinking Criminal Law* (New York, 1978) 759 et seq.; Kent Greenawalt, 'The Perplexing Borders of Justification and Excuse' (1984) 84 *Columbia Law Review* 1897.

[6] See e.g. Kai Ambos, 'Other Grounds for Excluding Criminal Responsibility' in Cassese et al., *Commentary*, 1003, 1036–7; Illan Rua Wall, 'Duress, International Criminal Law and Literature' (2006) 4 *JICJ* 724.

[7] Ambos, *Treatise on International Criminal Law* (n. 4) 307–8.

[8] Cassese, 'Justifications and Excuses' (n. 4) 953–4 treats some such defences as excuses, but others (consent) as a justification.

[9] See Section 19.3.2.

[10] See Albin Eser, 'Article 31' in Triffterer and Ambos, *Commentary*, 1125–31. See generally Roger O'Keefe, *International Criminal Law* (Oxford, 2015) ch. 6, and Gerhard Werle and Florian Jeßberger, *Principles of International Criminal Law*, 3rd ed. (Oxford, 2014).

proportion of the defences which are applicable to international crimes, providing for defences of insanity, intoxication, self-defence (including defence of others or, exceptionally, property), duress, and necessity.

Certain points ought to be noted at the outset. First, as Article 31(1) makes clear, it is not intended to be exhaustive. There are other parts of the Statute (in particular Articles 32 and 33, which deal with mistakes of fact and law and the defence of superior orders, respectively) that are also relevant. Second, as the definitions of defences given in the Statute are the outcome of difficult negotiations, Article 31(2) provides that 'the Court shall determine the applicability of the grounds for excluding criminal responsibility provided for in this Statute to the case before it'. The ICC has discretion to determine the factual applicability of a defence before entering into serious discussion of it at trial. In other words, the Court may require an 'air of reality' of a defence to be established before permitting detailed argument and evidence to be tendered.[11]

Article 31(3) of the ICC Statute recognizes that there are defences applicable to international crimes which it does not enumerate. Article 31(3) reads:

At trial, the Court may consider a ground for excluding criminal responsibility other than those referred to in paragraph 1 where such a ground is derived from applicable law as set forth in Article 21.[12]

Pursuant to this Article, a defendant may plead defences before the ICC which have their basis outside the ICC Statute, that is, in other applicable treaties, customary law, and general principles of law.[13] There are a number of such defences, to which we will return. However, because of the hierarchy of sources established in Article 21 (which places the Statute at the apex of authority), any argument that defences contained within Article 31 are narrower than those under customary law are not admissible under this head, although they may have purchase in arguments about the appropriate application of Article 31(2).

16.3 MENTAL INCAPACITY

Mental incapacity[14] is a defence which often, although not always, amounts to a claim of lack of proof. It ought to be distinguished from the procedural plea of unfitness to plead.[15] Article 31(1)(a) of the ICC Statute is the first codification of this defence in international law, and applies when:

---

[11] This is particularly relevant where evidence, such as of consent in sexual offences, is sensitive and examination of witnesses can be distressing. See ICC Rules of Procedure and Evidence (RPE), r. 72.

[12] Other than the ICC Statute, the Elements of Crimes and RPE, Art. 21 provide for the use of applicable treaties, principles and rules of international law (i.e. custom) and 'failing that' general principles of law.

[13] If seeking to do so, the defence must inform the Trial Chamber and the Prosecutor in advance, giving them sufficient time to prepare on point: ICC RPE, r. 80.

[14] See generally Peter Krug, 'The Emerging Mental Incapacity Defense in International Criminal Law: Some Initial Questions of Implementation' (2000) 96 *AJIL* 317; Maartje Krabbe, *Excusable Evil: An Analysis of Complete Defenses in International Criminal Law* (Antwerp, 2014) 11, 32; Isabelle Xavier, 'The Incongruity of the Rome Statute Insanity Defence and International Crime' (2016) 14 *JICJ* 793.

[15] See Eser, 'Article 31' (n. 10) 1125, 1137.

The person suffers from a mental disease or defect that destroys that person's capacity to appreciate the unlawfulness or nature of his or her conduct, or capacity to control his or her conduct to conform to the requirements of law.

Although parts of the provision are quite restrictive, Article 31(1)(a) is a fairly uncontroversial formulation of the defence. It encompasses three situations. The first is the mental incapacity plea, which is when a person is *incapable* of understanding the nature of his or her conduct. The usual example given to explain this situation of an incapability to understand is a person who cuts the victim's throat delusionally thinking that it is a loaf of bread.[16] There is no point convicting such a person, who is in need of treatment rather than imprisonment. The second situation, covered by Article 31(1)(a), is where a person is incapable of appreciating the unlawfulness of his or her conduct. Such a person may well deserve exemption from liability, but this is not quite the same as exemption under the first head. Appreciation of unlawfulness involves a more subtle analysis than the concept that the drafters were probably trying to codify, which is that the person was incapable of understanding the wrongfulness of the conduct ('destroys that person's capacity').

The final concept recognized by Article 31(1)(a) is that of the 'irresistible impulse', where a person understands the nature and wrongfulness of the conduct, but is unable, due to mental illness, to stop from acting as they did.[17] There is no requirement that insanity is permanent. It is sufficient that the person's capacity was destroyed at the time of the impugned conduct. As with the other forms of the defence, such a plea will require expert evidence from both sides.[18]

It is notable that Article 31(1)(a) requires destruction, rather than impairment, of ability. This is a high standard; an all-or-nothing conception of the insanity plea.[19] Diminished responsibility is no defence in the ICC Statute, nor is it in the jurisprudence of the ad hoc Tribunals, which treated any such claim as one of mitigation of sentence.[20] This is similar to the way the issue was treated in the post-Second World War trials in which it was raised,[21] and in the ICC Rules of Procedure and Evidence.[22]

At the ICC, in the *Ongwen* case, counsel raised the defence of mental incapacity. Ongwen, a former child soldier, had been kidnapped at a very young age and forced to join the Lord Resistance Army (LRA). As an LRA commander, he committed multiple war crimes and crimes against humanity, including sexual and gender-based crimes. The

---

[16] This is, of course, also a mistake of fact, but it would be extremely hard to persuade a fact-finder that this belief was honestly held without proof of mental incapacity.

[17] In such an instance, the claim stands on the border of denial of proof (of voluntary action (i.e. *actus reus*)) and excuse.

[18] See Krug, 'The Emerging Mental Incapacity Defense' (n. 14). In the ICTY, the defence bore the burden of proof (on the balance of probabilities) with respect to this defence, see *Delalić et al.*, ICTY AC, 20 February 2001, para. 582.

[19] Lee Hiromoto and Landy F. Sparr, '*Ongwen* and Mental Health Defenses at the International Criminal Court' (2023) 51 *American Academy of Psychiatry Law* 61–71, 61, 67.

[20] See *Delalić et al.*, ICTY AC, 20 February 2001, paras. 580–90; ICTY RPE, r. 67(B)(i)(b). The Trial Chamber in *Vasiljević*, ICTY TC I, 29 November 2002, paras. 282–3, defined diminished responsibility as 'an impairment to his capacity to appreciate the unlawfulness of or the nature of his conduct or to control his conduct so as to conform to the requirements of the law'. In *Jelisić*, ICTY TC, 14 December 1999, para. 125, 'personality disorders … [and] … borderline, narcissistic and anti-social characteristics' were insufficient to diminish responsibility.

[21] *Gerbsch* XIII LRTWC 131, 132, 137 (1948). See also Antonio Cassese et al., *Cassese's International Criminal Law*, 3rd ed. (Oxford, 2013) 225.

[22] ICC RPE, r. 145(2).

defence argued he suffered from a dissociative disorder; in such a state, it was difficult to distinguish right from wrong.[23] The ICC Trial Chamber found Ongwen guilty of most charges. With regard to Ongwen's mental capacity, the judges found that 'Dominic Ongwen did not suffer from a mental disease or defect at the time of the conduct relevant under the charges'.[24] They also rejected the idea of mitigating the sentence.[25] This should be reserved for 'exceptional cases' only.[26] Ongwen was convicted and sentenced to twenty-five years' imprisonment. The conviction and sentence were upheld by the Appeals Chamber.[27]

One unfortunate aspect of Article 31(1)(a) is its failure to provide for a special verdict in the eventuality of a person being acquitted on the basis of mental incapacity. This is important; in domestic systems, a person who is acquitted on the basis of lack of mental capacity is necessarily liable to some other form of order, which provides for psychiatric evaluation and treatment.[28] It is hoped that some arrangements may be found with the mental health authorities in states supportive of the ICC that will provide for those who have been acquitted by the ICC, but are in need of treatment or confinement on the basis of their disorder.[29]

16.4 INTOXICATION

The commission of international crimes by the intoxicated has more of a history than might be thought.[30] In the Second World War, the *Sonderkommandos*, who were forced to work in the concentration camps they were held in, were frequently given intoxicants. Many of the participants in Rwanda's genocide were intoxicated.[31] Child soldiers are often given drugs or alcohol to loosen their inhibitions and increase their ferocity.[32] After the Second World War, at least one case accepted the existence of a partial defence of intoxication, although it was rejected on the facts.[33]

Although it might be queried if those most responsible for international crimes, who are likely to be the defendants before the ICC, will have much resort to the defence,[34] intoxication is dealt with in Article 31(1)(b) of the ICC Statute, which provides for the exclusion of responsibility when:

---

[23] *Ongwen*, ICC TC IX, 12 March 2020 (ICC-02/04-01/15-T-258-ENG) 72–3.

[24] *Ongwen*, ICC TC IX, 4 February 2021 (ICC-02/04-01/15-1762-Red) para. 2580.

[25] Ongwen also raised the defence of duress. This will be discussed in Section 16.6 below.

[26] *Ongwen*, ICC IX, 6 May 2021 (ICC-02/04-01/15-1819-Red) para. 103.

[27] *Ongwen*, ICC AC, 15 December 2022 (ICC-02/04-01/15-2023). In her partly dissenting opinion, Judge Ibáñez Carranza explored the issue of the relevance of the childhood experience of Dominic Ongwen to the mitigation of his sentence. *Ongwen*, Partly Dissenting Opinion of Judge Luz del Carmen Ibáñez Carranza, 15 December 2022 (ICC-02/04-01/15-2023-Anx1) paras. 87–153.

[28] In the United Kingdom, see e.g. the Criminal Procedure (Insanity and Unfitness to Plead) Act 1991.

[29] See William Schabas, *The International Criminal Court: A Commentary on the Rome Statute*, 2nd ed. (Oxford, 2016) 640–1. See also ICC Regulations of the Court, reg. 103(6), which allows for a detained person to be sent to a specialized psychiatric unit.

[30] On the defence generally, see Krabbe, *Excusable Evil* (n. 14) ch. 6.

[31] William Schabas, *Genocide in International Law* (Cambridge, 2008) 398.

[32] Matthew Happold, *Child Soldiers in International Law* (Manchester, 2004) 16–17; Mark Drumbl, *Reimagining Child Soldiers in International Law and Policy* (Oxford, 2012) 80.

[33] *Chusaburo* III LRTWC 76, 78.

[34] Ambos, 'Other Grounds' (n. 6) 1031; Schabas, *The International Criminal Court* (n. 29) 641–3 (considering that the provision 'borders on the absurd').

The person is in a state of intoxication that destroys that person's capacity to appreciate the unlawfulness or nature of his or her conduct, or capacity to control his or her conduct to conform to the requirements of law, unless the person has become voluntarily intoxicated under such circumstances that the person knew, or disregarded the risk, that, as a result of the intoxication, he or she was likely to engage in conduct constituting a crime within the jurisdiction of the Court.

The nature of the plea is that the mental element is not formed due to the intoxication; thus, it is a plea of failure of proof. However, debate on the defence in Rome was awkward, as some delegations were opposed to its inclusion at all, considering intoxication as an aggravating factor rather than a possible defence.[35] As a result of this, the scope of the defence in Article 31(1)(b) is narrow.

16.4.1 Voluntary and Involuntary Intoxication

The primary focus of the text of the Article is involuntary intoxication, that is to say when a person unwittingly becomes intoxicated owing to inadvertent consumption of drugs or alcohol. Voluntary intoxication is only a defence when a person did not realize that he or she might engage in conduct prohibited by the Statute whilst intoxicated, and was not at fault by disregarding such a risk.[36] This, in essence, is a recklessness test.[37] Taking drink or drugs to gain 'Dutch courage' will not provide the basis for a defence under this provision as the person will know of at least the risk (and almost inevitably more) that he or she will commit the offence whilst under the influence.[38] Even so, some have questioned whether customary law allows for any defence of voluntary intoxication,[39] and the International Criminal Tribunal for the former Yugoslavia (ICTY) has said that even involuntary intoxication only 'could be' a mitigating circumstance, and that voluntary intoxication is often an aggravating factor.[40]

16.4.2 Destruction of Capacity

The intoxication must have destroyed the person's capacity to understand the nature or unlawfulness of the conduct, or ability to conform to the law's dictates. Impairment, even of a substantial nature, is insufficient to exclude a person's liability.[41]

It is not clear precisely how specific the risk of conduct has to be to exclude the defence. 'Conduct constituting a crime within the jurisdiction of the court' could be broad, simply

---

[35] Ambos, 'Other Grounds' (n. 6) 1029–30. Most (although not all) domestic systems provide for some form of defence of involuntary intoxication, but some states refuse to accept voluntary intoxication as a defence, on policy grounds. The ICTY said that 'in contexts where violence is the norm and weapons are carried, intentionally consuming drugs or alcohol constitutes an aggravating rather than a mitigating factor': *Kvočka et al.*, ICTY TC I, 2 November 2001, para. 706, and ICTY AC, 28 February 2005, paras. 707–8.
[36] Where someone is at fault in failing to realize, his or her liability is said to rest on this prior fault.
[37] Van Sliedregt, *Individual Criminal Responsibility* (n. 4) 229.
[38] Eser, 'Article 31' (n. 10) 877; Ambos, *Treatise on International Law* (n. 4) 329.
[39] Werle and Jeßberger, *Principles of International Criminal Law* (n. 10) 255–6; Ambos, *Treatise on International Law* (n. 4) 330.
[40] *Kvočka et al.*, ICTY TC I, 2 February 2001, para 706, see van Sliedregt, *Individual Criminal Responsibility* (n. 4) 233.
[41] See Elies van Sliedregt, *The Criminal Responsibility of Individuals for Violations of International Humanitarian Law* (The Hague, 2003) 249.

meaning any physical act or omission prohibited in the Statute, for example, killing, engaging in inhumane treatment, or inflicting serious injury. Or it could be interpreted more narrowly, meaning that the person must have known or disregarded the risk that he or she would engage in the specific conduct for which he or she is being prosecuted.

Also, there is ambiguity about whether the reference to 'conduct' includes the relevant circumstantial elements (for example, that there was an armed conflict, there was a widespread or systematic attack on the civilian population, or a manifest pattern of similar events), although given the phrasing of Article 30 of the ICC Statute, they would appear to be included.[42] Still, it is difficult to see the ICC acquitting someone on such a basis.

16.4.3 A Complete Defence

In common law systems such as the United Kingdom, intoxication is only a defence to certain crimes (known, rather unfortunately in the context of international crimes, as crimes of 'specific intent').[43] Pleas that *mens rea* is not established owing to voluntary intoxication are not admissible in crimes of 'basic intent', which tend to be less serious versions of crimes of 'specific intent' (for example, murder is a crime of specific intent, manslaughter is one of basic intent). The result of a plea of intoxication is thus usually a conviction for a less serious offence.[44] The ICC Statute does not adopt such a position. The intoxication defence is a complete defence.

16.5 SELF-DEFENCE, DEFENCE OF OTHERS, AND OF PROPERTY[45]

It has never been questioned that people have the right to defend themselves. Indeed, (non-mistaken) self-defence is often considered a paradigmatic justification of conduct.[46] It was raised as a defence in post-Second World War case law.[47] The ICTY Trial Chamber in *Kordić and Čerkez* accepted that customary law recognized self-defence.[48] Article 31(1)(c) provides for an acquittal when:

[t]he person acts reasonably to defend himself or herself or another person or, in the case of war crimes, property which is essential for the survival of the person or another person or property which is essential for accomplishing a military mission, against an imminent and unlawful use of force in a manner proportionate to the degree of danger to the person or the other person or property protected. The fact that the person was involved in a defensive operation conducted by forces shall not in itself constitute a ground for excluding criminal responsibility under this subparagraph.

---

[42] Eser, 'Article 31' (n. 10) 878 (who considers contextual elements to be included).
[43] See generally, David Ormerod, *Smith and Hogan's Criminal Law*, 13th ed. (Oxford, 2011) 314–21. The term could cause confusion owing to its use in international criminal law, in particular when referring to the intention required for genocide.
[44] In civil law systems, there is often a crime of committing an offence whilst intoxicated; see e.g. German Criminal Code, s. 323a.
[45] See generally, van Sliedregt, *The Criminal Responsibility of Individuals* (n. 4) 254–67; Werle and Jeßberger, *Principles of International Criminal Law* (n. 10) 236–9; Krabbe, *Excusable Evil* (n. 14) ch. 3.
[46] See e.g. George Fletcher, *The Grammar of Criminal Law* (Oxford, 2007) vol. I, 23–7, 50–1.
[47] See *Tessmann (Willi)* XV LRTWC 177 (1947). [48] *Kordić and Čerkez*, ICTY TC III, 26 February 2001, paras. 448–52.

16.5.1 Imminent, Unlawful Use of Force

The criminal defence of self-defence should not be confused with self-defence by states under Article 51 of the United Nations Charter.[49] In addition, this defence is not available in relation to any threat. It is limited to action in response to 'an imminent and unlawful use of force'.[50] What is imminent is a matter of appreciation, although Article 31(1)(c) does make clear that a person must not wait for someone else to strike the first blow.[51] 'Unlawful' means that there is no right of self-defence against a lawful attack.[52] At the domestic level, defence against the insane or highly intoxicated is acceptable, and there seems to be no reason to doubt that the same would apply here. The distinction between justifications and excuses is of some assistance here. Justified actors are not acting unlawfully, whereas those who are merely excused (the insane and the very intoxicated being two examples) are acting unlawfully, and thus can be defended against. Some suggest that the 'force' can be psychological, as well as physical,[53] but this is not universally accepted.[54]

The expansion of the defence, with respect to war crimes, to protect 'mission essential property'[55] was controversial in the negotiations at Rome. According to Cassese, 'this extension is manifestly outside the *lex lata* and may generate quite a few misgivings'.[56] Given that many states have limited rights to use force to protect, for example, nuclear installations, and UN Rules of Engagement often provide for defence of mission essential property, this criticism may be a little harsh.[57] On the other hand, Belgium considered this provision contrary to *jus cogens* and therefore issued a declaration at the time of its ratification.[58] This defence (in particular the reference to 'mission essential property') does have links to military necessity, and ought to be limited by that.[59] Nonetheless, some fear that aspects of this provision are open to abuse have some foundation.[60] As the Article clarifies, however, the simple fact that a state is acting in self-defence is not enough in itself to invoke this provision. There does not appear to be any acceptance in this provision of mistaken self-defence; when a person reasonably (but wrongly) believes that there is such an attack.[61]

---

[49] *Martić*, ICTY AC, 8 October 2008, para. 268. See also Eser, 'Article 31' (n. 10) 1144–6.
[50] *Kordić and Čerkez*, ICTY TC III, 26 February 2001, para. 451.
[51] Eser, 'Article 31' (n. 10) 1146 defines imminent as 'immediately antecedent, presently exercised or still enduring'.
[52] This ought to exclude, for example, attacks on military property which are lawful under international humanitarian law (IHL). This would obviate the criticism that the defence may delegitimize attacks that are lawful under IHL, thus altering IHL through the back door; for such a critique see Cassese et al., *International Criminal Law* (n. 21) 213.
[53] Ambos, *Treatise on International Criminal Law* (n. 4) 339. [54] *Ibid.*; Eser, 'Article 31' (n. 10) 1146.
[55] Property essential to the survival of a person may be different here, as parasitic on protection of the person's life. Ambos, *Treatise on International Criminal Law* (n. 4) 340.
[56] Antonio Cassese, 'The Rome Statute of the International Criminal Court: Some Preliminary Reflections' (1999) 10 *EJIL* 144, 154–5.
[57] It might be questioned if a civilian stealing a truck full of small arms ought to be protected in this situation, although in that situation it is quite possible the person would be considered (or reasonably believed) to be taking an active part in hostilities, thus forfeiting their protection.
[58] Although incorrect as a matter of law (see Schabas, *The International Criminal Court* (n. 29) 489), this is state practice, accompanied by *opinio juris*, thus relevant for the determination of customary law, as well as interpretation of the ICC Statute.
[59] Nobuo Hayashi, 'Requirements of Military Necessity in International Humanitarian Law and International Criminal Law' (2010) 28 *Boston University International Law Journal* 39, 134–8.
[60] See Ambos, 'Other Grounds' (n. 6) 1033.
[61] Eser, 'Article 31' (n. 10) 1146, and see Section 16.7.1 on mistake of fact. See *contra* Cassese et al., *International Criminal Law* (n. 21) 212.

16.5.2 Reasonable and Proportionate Response

Not every reaction to an attack is acceptable. For a response to be defended on the basis of Article 31(1)(c), it must be reasonable to resort to force, and the level of force must be 'proportionate to the degree of danger' faced.[62] Proportionality is not a test which can be set down with scientific precision in advance. However, in applying the test, 'such considerations as the nature of the weapon in the hands of the accused, the question whether the assailant had any weapon, and so forth, have to be considered'.[63] 'Eagle-eye' hindsight is to be avoided when appraising proportionality, as a person does not have the luxury of time to weigh things very carefully when there is an imminent or ongoing attack. Article 31(1)(c) does not create a duty to retreat[64] or any specific rules on what the response must be, other than setting down the test of proportionality to the level of danger. This test is to be applied by the court; the defendant's view of their actions is not determinative. The ICTY has provided some brief comments on the defence, rejecting it in relation to a charge of killing civilians, on the basis that it considered 'the perpetrators' conduct, even if an immediate illegitimate attack could be assumed, to be disproportionate, where other ways of thwarting any possible danger instead of firing lethal shots were available'.[65] This implies that lethal force should be a last resort, but in cases where the defence is raised much will depend on the facts and what could be considered proportionate in the specific context. The defence is further limited by the language of Article 31(3)(c) (the person 'acts ... to defend'), which implies that the person must intend to act in defence.[66]

16.6 DURESS AND NECESSITY

Situations in which international crimes are committed tend to be ones in which there is group activity, and therefore some level of coercion of an offender by colleagues can often be expected.[67] In such situations, painful choices sometimes have to be made. Article 31(1)(d), the first codification at the international level of duress, provides for a defence when:

[t]he conduct which is alleged to constitute a crime within the jurisdiction of the Court has been caused by duress resulting from a threat of imminent death or of continuing or imminent serious bodily harm against that person or another person, and the person acts necessarily and reasonably to avoid this threat, provided that the person does not intend to cause a greater harm than the one sought to be avoided. Such a threat may either be:

 (i) Made by other persons; or
 (ii) Constituted by other circumstances beyond that person's control.

The duress provision in the ICC Statute is a mixture of two types of duress: duress as a choice of evils and duress as compulsion.[68] They are, however, markedly different: duress

---

[62] See van Sliedregt, *Individual Criminal Responsibility* (n. 4) 236–8. [63] *Tessmann (Willi)* XV LRTWC 177 (1947).
[64] *Tessmann (ibid.)* could be read as requiring this. [65] *Gotovina*, ICTY TC I, 15 April 2011, para. 1730.
[66] See also Werle and Jeßberger, *Principles of International Criminal Law* (n. 10) 238; but see Ambos, *Treatise on International Criminal Law* (n. 4) 342 for the view that knowledge suffices.
[67] Such colleagues may, of course, become liable themselves for offences they encouraged, assisted, or participated in.
[68] Article 31 has been criticized for rolling the two defences together, not least as duress is an excuse, and most examples of necessity are justifications: see Eser, 'Article 31' (n. 10) 1149–50.

as compulsion *excuses* the defendant (the conduct is still unlawful). Duress as necessity *justifies* the conduct; it is a choice-of-evils defence where the defendant made the right choice – acting necessarily and reasonably – to avoid a greater threat.[69]

Although this was the first *codification* of duress, it was the Nuremberg International Military Tribunal that laid down the first test for duress, while discussing the defence of superior orders.[70] There is considerable jurisprudence on duress and necessity in other post-Second World War cases,[71] such as *Krupp*,[72] *Flick*,[73] *Krauch*,[74] and *von Leeb*.[75] Much of this jurisprudence was canvassed in the ICTY in one of its few fully reasoned decisions on defences, *Prosecutor* v. *Erdemović*.[76] Dražen Erdemović who, with a gun against his head, was forced to execute civilians, could not rely on the duress as a complete defence. The majority of the Appeals Chamber held that duress does not apply to cases involving the killing of innocent civilians.[77] There were strong dissents from two of the judges.[78] In the *Erdemović* case, the duress plea, whilst it did not exonerate the defendant, led to a lower sentence.

16.6.1 Imminent Threat Beyond the Control of the Accused

The first requirement is that there is a threat of 'imminent death or of continuing or imminent serious bodily harm'. Apart from being imminent, the threat must be external and serious. Thus, it is clear that blackmail or other threats not involving imminent serious violence will not suffice. The requirements of proportionality ('not causing greater harm') and of acting necessarily and reasonably are applied less strictly for duress as compulsion than in cases concerning duress as a choice of evils.[79] This can be explained by the fact that a person who acts under compulsion-duress suffers from an abnormal mental state. If duress functions as an excuse – that is, the will is overborne by threats – it should not be an impediment to invoking it for any wrongful act, including murder. The threats may be against the accused or others; there is no requirement that there be any particular relationship between the accused and the people threatened. The threat must be real, however, and not simply believed to exist by the defendant.[80]

---

[69] Van Sliedregt, *Individual Criminal Responsibility* (n. 4) 242.
[70] See Yoram Dinstein, *The Defence of 'Obedience to Superior Orders' in International Criminal Law* (The Hague, 1965) 147–56. For superior orders, see Section 16.8.
[71] See Commentary, XV LRTWC 170–5 (1949). [72] X LRTWC 69, 156 (1948) [73] IX LRTWC 1, 19 (1947).
[74] X LRTWC 1, 54, 57 (1948). [75] XII LRTWC 1, 144, 149 (1948). [76] *Erdemović*, ICTY AC, 7 October 1997.
[77] *Ibid*. Separate and Dissenting Opinion of Judge Li, paras. 1–12; Joint Separate Opinion of Judges McDonald and Vohrah, paras. 32–89.
[78] *Ibid*. Separate and Dissenting Opinion of Judge Stephen, paras. 23–67; Separate and Dissenting Opinion of Judge Cassese, paras. 11–51. For critical comments, see e.g. Peter Rowe, 'Duress as a Defence to War Crimes After Erdemović: A Laboratory for a Permanent Court?' (1998) 1 *YIHL* 210; David Turns, 'The International Criminal Tribunal for the Former Yugoslavia: The *Erdemović* Case' (1998) 47 *ICLQ* 461; Claus Kreß, 'Zur Methode der Rechtsfindung im Allgemeinen Teil des Völkerstrafrechts. Die Bewertung von Tötungen im Nötigungsnotstand durch die Rechtsmittelkammer des Internationalen Straftribunals für das ehemalige Jugoslawien im Fall Erdemović' (1999) 111 *Zeitschrift für die gesamte Strafrechtswissenschaft* 597; Robert Cryer, 'One Appeal, Four Opinions, Two Philosophies and a Remittal' (1998) 2 *Journal of Armed Conflict Law* 193; Aaron Fichtelberg, 'Liberal Values In International Criminal Law: A Critique of *Erdemović*' (2008) 6 *JICJ* 3. For a rare example of support of the majority, see Yoram Dinstein, 'Defences' in McDonald and Goldman, *Substantive and Procedural Aspects*, 367, 376.
[79] Van Sliedregt, *Individual Criminal Responsibility* (n. 4) section 9.7.2.
[80] The *Krupp* case may have seen things differently, *Krupp*, X LRTWC 69, 148 (1948). See also Commentary, XV LRTWC 174 (1948).

As recognized by Article 31(1)(d)(ii), the threat must be outside the control of the defendant. The use of the term 'other' in that part of the Article implies that this condition also applies to duress in (i). This would probably exclude the situation where a person had 'courted' the threats by others, such as in the instance where a person had joined a group notorious for its criminality. This condition was considered a part of customary law by Judges Cassese and Stephen in *Erdemović*,[81] and is consistent with national practice.[82]

16.6.2 Necessary and Reasonable Actions

As with self-defence, pressure, be it from another or by virtue of circumstance, does not suffice to defend any reaction. The pressure must constitute a serious threat and reactions of the person seeking to use the defence must be both necessary and reasonable in the circumstances to avoid the threat. Domestic courts, in judging if and when a person can rely on a ground excluding criminal responsibility, are often confronted with the question as to whether 'a reasonable person' in the defendant's circumstances would have perceived the (accused's) conduct as necessary. The concept of 'reasonableness' plays a central role in allowing defences such as self-defence, intoxication, and duress.[83]

The question that arises is what can be expected of soldiers who have undergone military training and are expected to put themselves in harm's way to protect others.[84] In such circumstances, the test is perhaps best formulated as what would be considered necessary and reasonable by a service-member of the experience and rank of the defendant.

16.6.3 Causation

It is an express requirement that the threats *caused* the impugned conduct. If a person would have acted as they did anyway, they will not be able to take advantage of this defence. Article 31(1)(d) is silent on whether the threats have to be the sole cause of the defendant's conduct, or whether they only need to be one of a number of causes. This also means, though, that there is nothing in the Article that would require the ICC to take the view that the relevant threat needs to be the sole cause of the conduct. The issue has yet to arise before the ICC.

---

[81] *Erdemović*, ICTY AC, 7 October 1997, Separate and Dissenting Opinion of Judge Cassese, para. 16; Separate and Dissenting Opinion of Judge Stephen, para. 68.
[82] Werle and Jeßberger, *Principles of International Criminal Law* (n. 10) 243–4.
[83] The reasonable person standard is an 'objective' standard, in that it ignores the defendant's subjective or actual mental state. It is rooted in the law's search for generally accepted standards of conduct applicable to all individuals. However, numerous attempts have been made by (national) Courts to 'individualise' the standard by taking into account a defendant's personal characteristics when determining the objective reasonableness of having acted in self-defence. See Kevin Jon Heller, 'Beyond the Reasonable Man? A Sympathetic but Critical Assessment of the Use of Subjective Standards of Reasonableness in Self-Defense and Provocation Cases' (1998) 26 *AJIL* 5.
[84] See e.g. the comments in *R v. Dudley and Stevens* (1884–85) LR 14 QBD 273, 287; Werle and Jeßberger, *Principles of International Criminal Law* (n. 10) 209.

16.7 MISTAKE OF FACT AND LAW

Mistakes of fact and law[85] are issues which tend to be dealt with differently by civil and common law systems. Civil law jurisdictions tend to be more generous with regard to mistakes of law, allowing for defences where there are reasonable mistakes relating to various aspects of crimes or defences.[86] Although there might be a trend away from this, in common law systems mistakes generally only provide an excuse when they serve to undermine *mens rea*, making the plea one of failure of proof.[87] Article 32 of the ICC Statute appears to adopt the (perhaps over-strict)[88] common law approach, providing that:

1. A mistake of fact shall be a ground for excluding criminal responsibility only if it negates the mental element required by the crime.
2. A mistake of law as to whether a particular type of conduct is a crime within the jurisdiction of the Court shall not be a ground for excluding criminal responsibility. A mistake of law may, however, be a ground for excluding criminal responsibility if it negates the mental element required by such a crime, or as provided for in article 33.

16.7.1 Mistake of Fact

Article 32(1) is unequivocal. A mistake of fact is only relevant to liability if it serves to show that the defendant did not have the *mens rea*.[89] For example, if a person bombed a civilian bunker believing it was a military command centre, there would not be liability on the basis of this provision. Interestingly, Article 32(1) does not contain any express requirement that the mistake be a reasonable one.[90] One practical limitation, however, is that the less reasonable a belief is, the less likely it is that a claim that a person honestly held that belief will be accepted. Questions may arise about the situation where a person is at fault in making the mistake, such as if he or she was drunk or reckless when he or she decided what he or she believed.

From its terms, it seems that mistakes of fact which, if they were true, would provide the basis of a defence, do not fall under Article 32, as they do not relate to *mens rea*.[91] Earlier cases allowed such mistakes to negate responsibility.[92] Beyond this, certain provisions of

---

[85] See generally Albin Eser, 'Mental Elements: Mistake of Fact and Mistake of Law' in Cassese et al., *Commentary*, 889 and 934–46; van Sliedregt, *Individual Criminal Responsibility* (n. 4) ch. 10; Ambos, *Treatise on International Criminal Law* (n. 4) 368–76; Otto Triffterer and Jens David Ohlin, 'Article 32' in Triffterer and Ambos, *Commentary*, 1161. Also, there is a 'grey zone' in which it is difficult to separate off mistakes of fact and law: see Thomas Weigend, 'The Harmonization of General Principles of Criminal Law: The Statutes and Jurisprudence of the ICTY, ICTR and the ICC: An Overview' (2004) 19 *Nouvelles Etudes Pénales* 319, 333.

[86] See Fletcher, *Rethinking Criminal Law* (n. 5) 683–91.

[87] In relation to mistakes of law, these are relevant, for example, in relation to the requirement of dishonesty in theft.

[88] Ambos, *Treatise on International Criminal Law* (n. 4) 375–6.

[89] As such, a good case can be made that it adds little, if anything, to Article 30's requirements on *mens rea*, Werle and Jeßberger, *Principles of International Criminal Law* (n. 10) 246.

[90] Cassese et al., *International Criminal Law* (n. 21) 222 appears to consider that any mistake must be reasonable to found a defence under Art. 32(1).

[91] Eser, 'Mental Elements' (n. 85) 945 argues that Art. 32(1) ought to apply by analogy to mistakes relating to justifications (as opposed to excuses), but the terms of Art. 32(1) do not provide particularly fertile soil for such arguments. See also Werle and Jeßberger, *Principles of International Criminal Law* (n. 10) 211; Ambos, *Treatise on International Criminal Law* (n. 4) 374–5.

[92] See e.g. *United States v. List*, VIII LRTWC 1, 69.

the Elements of Crimes[93] (and the Statute itself, in Article 28, on command responsibility) exclude mistakes of fact where the person should have known of the relevant facts.[94]

16.7.2 Mistake of Law

Like mistakes of fact, mistakes of law, with one exception (which, as we shall see, occurs with respect to superior orders), must negate *mens rea*. This defence does not include mistakes (or ignorance) about whether conduct is criminalized by the ICC Statute,[95] or whether a defence exists in law.[96] Nor does it deal with errors about the ambit of defences. The only acceptable mistake in Article 32(2) is where an element of a crime requires a legal evaluation, and the mistake relates to this, for example, where a person takes property under a mistaken belief that he or she is its owner, or may lawfully take it.[97] The crime of aggression could raise difficult issues in this regard, but the definition of the crime requires that there be a manifest violation of the UN Charter. This reference to the UN Charter, on the face of it, is a legal one where making a mistake would be susceptible to negating the required *mens rea*.[98] Yet the Elements of Crime are clear: 'there is no requirement to prove that the perpetrator has made a legal evaluation as to the "manifest" nature of the violation of the Charter of the United Nations'.[99] Moreover, it requires proof that the defendant was 'aware of the *factual* circumstances that established such a manifest violation of the Charter of the United Nations'[100] and 'of the *factual* circumstances that established that such a use of armed force was inconsistent with the Charter of the United Nations'.[101] So, even if 'an honest and reasonable belief that a use of force was not unlawful would be irrelevant to the satisfaction of [the] *mens rea* [of] aggression'.[102] There is room for the mistake of law defence in the ICC Statute with regard to certain war crimes and crimes against humanity[103] but overall the approach is restrictive. This does not mean that national proceedings cannot take a more generous approach, especially in those systems where mistake of law can be a defence beyond the negation of *mens rea*.[104]

---

[93] See e.g. Elements of Crimes, Art. 8(2)(b)(xxvi).

[94] Although the distinction ought to have relevance when it comes to describing the relevant conduct of the accused and determining the sentence of any convicted person.

[95] See Thomas Weigend, 'Intent, Mistake of Law and Co-Perpetration in the *Lubanga* Decision on Confirmation of Charges' (2008) 6 *JICJ* 471, 474–6.

[96] See Neil Boister, 'Reflections on the Relationship Between the Duty to Educate in Humanitarian Law and the Absence of a Defence of Mistakes of Law in the Rome Statute' in Richard Burchill, Nigel White, and Justin Morris (eds.), *International Conflict and Security Law* (Cambridge, 2005) 32, 38–43.

[97] For a broad view of what this would cover, see Kevin Jon Heller, 'Mistake of Legal Element, the Common Law, and Article 32 of the Rome Statute' (2008) 6 *JICJ* 419. For critique of Heller's view, see van Sliedregt, *Individual Criminal Responsibility* (n. 4) 283–5 and Annemieke Van Verseveld, *Mistake of Law: Excusing Perpetrators of International Crimes* (The Hague, 2012) 89.

[98] Antonio Coco, *The Defence of Mistake of Law in International Criminal Law. A Study on Ignorance and Blame* (Oxford, 2022) 189.

[99] ICC Elements of Crimes, Art 8*bis*, Introduction, para 4.   [100] ICC Elements of Crimes, Art 8*bis*, para 4.

[101] ICC Elements of Crimes, Art 8*bis*, Elements, para 6, emphases added.

[102] Carrie McDougall, *The Crime of Aggression under the Rome Statute of the International Criminal Court* (Cambridge, 2012) 197. As Coco argues: 'the version of mistake of law adopted by the ICC Statute is clearly the 'denial of *mens rea*' one, due to a precise drafting choice taken in Rome. As such, the concept of mistake of law as an excuse is alien to the ICC Statute, and only creative interpretations of its provisions or actual amendments could introduce it'. Coco, *The Defence of Mistake* (n. 98) 190.

[103] Coco, *The Defence of Mistake of Law* (n. 98) 171–89, 191.   [104] *Ibid.*, 191.

16.8 SUPERIOR ORDERS

The defence of superior orders has a lengthy history,[105] and reflects the tension between the importance of international law and of military discipline.[106] Originally, the tendency was to accept that orders amounted to a defence for those who carried them out, and thus that liability accrued to the person who ordered the offence, rather than the one who carried that order out (*respondeat superior*).[107] This was not the uniformly accepted position, though; even by the late nineteenth century there was significant evidence that the *respondeat superior* principle, where superior orders was a complete defence, had been replaced by the rule that orders only protected a subordinate if they were not manifestly unlawful.[108] Such a position crystallized after the First World War, if not before.[109] The position seemed to change, however, with Article 8 of the Nuremberg IMT Statute, which read: 'the fact that the defendant acted pursuant to an order of his government or of a superior shall not free him from responsibility, but may be considered in mitigation of punishment if the Tribunal determines that justice so requires'.[110] The Nuremberg IMT explained that provision as follows:

> The provisions of this article are in conformity with the law of all nations. That a soldier was ordered to kill or torture in violation of the international law of war has never been recognised as a defence to such acts of brutality, though, as the Charter here provides, the order may be urged in mitigation of punishment.[111]

After this, and UN General Assembly Resolution 95(I),[112] which affirmed the Nuremberg Charter and Judgment, it might be thought that international law no longer permitted superior orders as a defence. However, case law and practice on the point from the period up to the creation of the ICTY was more equivocal.[113] The Genocide Convention, and the Geneva Conventions, for example, contain no provision on superior orders, although the Torture Convention excludes reliance on them.[114] Article 7(4) of the ICTY Statute (and Article 6(4) of the International Criminal Tribunal for Rwanda (ICTR) Statute) essentially repeat Article 8 of the Nuremberg IMT Statute. The ICC Statute, on the other hand, takes a different approach, largely returning to the 'manifest illegality' test.[115] The ICC Statute

---

[105] See e.g. Dinstein, *The Defence of 'Obedience to Superior Orders'* (n. 70) 93–103, van Sliedregt, *Individual Criminal Responsibility* (n. 4) 287–92.

[106] See e.g. Martha Minow, 'Living Up to Rules: Holding Soldiers Responsible for Abusive Conduct and the Dilemma of the Superior Orders Defence' (2007) 52 *McGill Law Journal* 1.

[107] Lassa Oppenheim, *International Law* (London, 1906) vol. II, 264–5.

[108] William Winthrop, *Military Law and Precedents* (Washington, 1896) 446–7.

[109] See e.g. *Llandovery Castle* (1922) 16 *AJIL* 708.

[110] Charter of the International Military Tribunal, annex to the London Agreement on the Prosecution and Punishment of the Major War Criminals of the European Axis Powers 82 UNTS 279, Art. 8. Tokyo IMT Charter, Art. 6, is largely the same: see Special Proclamation: Establishment of an International Military Tribunal for the Far East, 19 January 1946, TIAS no. 1589.

[111] 'Nuremberg IMT: Judgment' (1947) 41 *AJIL* 172, 221.   [112] GA Res. 95(I), UN Doc. A/64/Add.1 (1946).

[113] Paula Gaeta, 'The Defence of Superior Orders: The Statute of the International Criminal Court versus Customary International Law' (1999) 10 *EJIL* 172; *contra* Charles Garraway, 'Superior Orders and the International Criminal Court: Justice Delivered or Justice Denied?' (1999) 836 *International Review of the Red Cross* 785.

[114] Torture Convention 1984, Art. 2.

[115] Special Court for Sierra Leone (SCSL) Statute, Art. 6(4) notably returns to the Nuremberg/Tokyo/ICTY/ICTR standard, as do the Statutes of other (varyingly authoritative) internationalized tribunals such as the Special Tribunal for Lebanon (STL) and Extraordinary Chambers in the Courts of Cambodia (ECCC), see Cassese et al., *International Criminal Law* (n. 21) 229.

has been criticized for this, although such critiques rely on the (controversial) assertion that the Nuremberg IMT Charter reflects customary law.[116] Also, it must be remembered that the person giving the order will be responsible for his or her part in the crime whether or not the defence applies. Against this backdrop, Article 33 adopt a narrow view of the applicability of superior orders as a defence:

1. The fact that a crime within the jurisdiction of the Court has been committed pursuant to an order of a government or of a superior, whether military or civilian, shall not relieve that person of criminal responsibility unless:

    (a) That person was under a legal obligation to obey orders of the government or the superior in question;

    (b) The person did not know that the order was unlawful; and

    (c) The order was not manifestly unlawful.

2. For the purposes of this article, orders to commit genocide or crimes against humanity are manifestly unlawful.

As can be seen, Article 33 provides that superior orders are not a defence unless the three cumulative conditions are fulfilled.[117] However, where the conditions of defence under Article 33 are not fulfilled, there is the possibility of mitigation for those who acted under orders.[118]

16.8.1 Obligation to Obey

For the defence to apply, the person obeying the order must be under a legal obligation to obey orders in domestic law. This will be the case for soldiers in all countries, but civilians may be in a different position in different states. The reference in Article 33(1)(a) to 'orders' is deliberate. In some states, the obligation is only to obey lawful orders,[119] and it was necessary to generalize the reference to 'orders'. Otherwise, in those states, at any time the defence could apply, there would be no obligation to obey the particular order. There have been suggestions that a superior/subordinate relationship is required.[120] This is only correct insofar as it could be an aspect of the requirement that there must be a legal obligation on the person to obey orders. This requirement creates an interesting question about the status of orders from rebel authorities and commanders. Owing to the requirement that there be a legal obligation to obey orders, it appears that such orders cannot form the basis of a defence of obedience.[121] Furthermore, it has been asserted that if a person mistakenly

---

[116] Cassese et al., *International Criminal Law* (n. 21) 228; Gaeta, 'The Defence of Superior Orders' (n. 113). It might be noted that the International Law Commission (ILC) adopted the position in 1996 that the Nuremberg provision was the relevant standard, see the Draft Code of Crimes Against the Peace and Security of Mankind 1996, Art. 5.

[117] Werle and Jeßberger, *Principles of International Criminal Law* (n. 10) 251–3. The order must also have a causal link to the commission of the offence: van Sliedregt, *Individual Criminal Responsibility* (n. 4) 324.

[118] Werle and Jeßberger, *Principles of International Criminal Law* (n. 10) 253.

[119] In the United Kingdom, Armed Forces Act 2006, s.12(1).

[120] Andreas Zimmermann, 'Superior Orders' in Cassese et al., *Commentary*, 957, 968.

[121] *Ibid.* 969; and see van Sliedregt, *Individual Criminal Responsibility* (n. 4) 323–4. Ambos is less certain of this: Ambos, *Treatise on International Criminal Law* (n. 4) 381.

believes himself or herself to be under an obligation to obey an order, a defence of mistake of law may be pleaded.[122] However, according to Article 32, mistakes of law only exculpate if they negate *mens rea* (or as provided in Article 33), and, since such a mistake would not do so, this would not apply here.

16.8.2 Knowledge of Unlawfulness

The nature of the defence in the ICC Statute is, as implied by Article 32(2), an expanded form of a mistake of law defence.[123] Therefore, if a person knows that an order is unlawful, he or she cannot use that order as a defence. This undermines one asserted explanation of the defence, namely, that a subordinate is placed in a dilemma with respect to an unlawful order: obey and run the risk of criminal liability for an international crime, or disobey and face liability for a military offence of disobedience.[124] For a person to be placed in such a situation, they would have to know that the order is unlawful, and so would be prohibited from relying on superior orders by Article 33.

16.8.3 Manifest Illegality

Ignorance of the unlawfulness of the order is not enough to exempt a subordinate from liability. That ignorance must, in essence, be forgivable. Put another way, the subordinate must not be at fault in not knowing that the order was unlawful. The manifest illegality test now exists to help evaluate if a defendant was culpably ignorant of the illegality of the order.[125] If an order is manifestly illegal, there is no defence that can be based on it, irrespective of whether or not the subordinate knew it was unlawful. It must be remembered, though, that 'no sailor and no soldier can carry with him a library of international law, or have immediate access to a professor in that subject'.[126] Some cases have attempted to provide a definition of manifest illegality. The *Eichmann* case, for example, stated that:

[t]he distinguishing mark of a 'manifestly unlawful order' should fly like a black flag above the order given … [n]ot formal unlawfulness, hidden or half-hidden, nor unlawfulness discernible only to the eyes of legal experts, but a flagrant and manifest breach of the law.[127]

The *High Command* case, however, framed the test as whether the order was 'criminal on its face'.[128] The *Finta* case in Canada said an order could not be relied upon if it was 'so outrageous as to be manifestly unlawful'.[129] It might be questioned, however, if any of these formulations provide a clear standard. The question remains (analogously to the test

---

[122] See Otto Triffterer and Stephanie Bock, 'Article 33' in Triffterer and Ambos, *Commentary*, 1182, 1194.
[123] But not a plea of failure of proof. See Claus Kreß, 'War Crimes Committed in Non-International Armed Conflicts and the Emerging System of International Criminal Justice' (2000) 30 *Israel Yearbook on Human Rights* 103, 150.
[124] Where the obligation to obey orders is not limited to lawful orders.
[125] Earlier cases sometimes used the test to determine if, in fact, the person knew the order was unlawful; see Dinstein, *The Defence of 'Obedience to Superior Orders'* (n. 70) 26–37.
[126] *Peleus* (1945) 13 ILR 248, 249. [127] *Attorney-General of Israel* v. *Eichmann* (1961) 36 ILR 277.
[128] *Von Leeb*, XII LRTWC 1, 74 (1948). [129] *R* v. *Finta* (1989) 104 ILR 285, 322.

of reasonableness in duress): manifest to whom?[130] A different standard may be expected, for example, of fully trained army lawyers or high-ranking officials from that of young, low-ranking soldiers who are on their first tour of duty. The role of culture, propaganda and 'common knowledge' may also be relevant to the extent to which unlawfulness is manifest.[131] Integrating such considerations into the manifest illegality test, even if it relates to conduct in a context of collective and systemic evildoing,[132] will still bar resort to the superior orders defence. The Canadian *War Crimes and Crimes Against Humanity Act* attempts to deal with this difficulty by providing that:

An accused cannot base their defence . . . [of superior orders] . . . on a belief that an order was lawful if the belief was based on information about a civilian population or an identifiable group of persons that encouraged, was likely to encourage or attempted to justify the commission of inhumane acts or omissions against the population or group.[133]

16.8.4 Genocide and Crimes Against Humanity

Article 33(2) was intended to ensure that superior orders could be pleaded in cases involving war crimes (or, possibly, the crime of aggression) but not genocide or crimes against humanity. The wording, however, is unfortunate, as it focuses on 'orders to commit genocide or crimes against humanity' rather than focusing on the perpetrator's *mens rea*.[134] It also, illegitimately, assumes that every example of a war crime will necessarily be less serious than every example of a crime against humanity, and (perhaps more legitimately) every example of genocide.[135]

The amendments to the ICC Statute relating to the crime of aggression do not exclude the general principles of liability in the Statute and the possibility of superior orders being a defence cannot entirely be excluded. The conditions for liability for aggression, in particular that the defendant be at a 'policy' level and that the violation of the UN Charter be 'manifest', render it very unlikely that such a defence would succeed,[136] even though the concepts of manifest illegality and manifest violation of the UN Charter in Article 33(1)(c) and Article 8*bis*(1) were not specifically drafted with each other in mind.

---

[130] For a discussion of one state's relevant cases, see Ziv Bohrer, 'Clear and Obvious? A Critical Examination of the Superior Orders Defense in Israeli Case Law' (2005–2006) 2 *Israel Defence Force Law Review* 197. See also Larry May, *Crimes Against Humanity: A Normative Account* (Cambridge, 2005) 185–7.

[131] See e.g. Mark Osiel, *Mass Atrocity, Ordinary Evil and Hannah Arendt: Criminal Consciousness in Argentina's Dirty War* (New Haven, CT, 2001).

[132] Arne J. Vetlesen, *Evil and Human Agency, Understanding Collective Evildoing* (Cambridge, 2005) ch. 5. Specifically with regard to low-level perpetrators: Alette Smeulers, 'Why Serious International Crimes Might Not Seem 'Manifestly Unlawful' to Low-Level Perpetrators' (2019) 17 *JICJ* 105-123; Emmanuel Sarpung Owusu, 'Guilty of Having Been Obedient: A Fresh Dissection of the Superior Orders Controversy' (2021) 12 *Journal of International Humanitarian Legal Studies* 279–313.

[133] 2000, c. 24, s. 14(3).

[134] See further Robert Cryer, 'Superior Orders in the International Criminal Court' in Richard Burchill, Nigel White, and Justin Morris (eds.), *International Conflict and Security Law* (Cambridge, 2005) 49, 63–7.

[135] Zimmermann, 'Superior Orders' (n. 120) 972. See also German Code of Crimes Against International Law, s. 3, which applies the manifest illegality principle to all crimes.

[136] McDougall, *Crime of Aggression* (n. 102) 198.

16.8.5 Relationship of Superior Orders to Other Defences

The existence of superior orders may also give rise to other defences, in particular mistake of fact and duress. If an order contains a factual assertion, such as 'bomb the enemy arms cache at particular coordinates', and it turns out that the building at those coordinates is a hospital, the order forms the factual underpinning for a defence of mistake of fact, rather than superior orders, as the factual basis asserted in the order would undermine *mens rea*. Duress may be relevant because, as Judge Cassese stated in *Erdemović*:

> Superior orders may be issued without being accompanied by any threats to life or limb. In these circumstances, if the superior order is manifestly illegal under international law, the subordinate is under a duty to refuse to obey the order. If, following such a refusal, the order is reiterated under a threat to life or limb, then the defence of duress may be raised, and superior orders lose any legal relevance.[137]

The way in which Article 33 of the Rome Statute is framed renders the defence in the ICC an expanded form of a mistake of law defence. It is expanded as it does not require the mistake of legality to undermine *mens rea*.[138]

16.9 OTHER DEFENCES

There are other defences that may apply in international criminal law which are not directly enumerated in the ICC Statute.[139] The three main defences falling under this head are consent and, more controversially, reprisals, and military necessity.[140] The new amendments to the ICC Statute on the crime of aggression do not include any new defences to the crime. A justification by a state for a use of force, such as self-defence under Article 51 of the UN Charter, will be pleaded by the defendant not as a separate defence to a charge of the crime of aggression, but as a failure to prove an essential element of the crime.[141]

16.9.1 Consent

Certain offences, in particular sexual offences, are subject to 'defences' of consent.[142] Indeed, the absence of consent is a definitional aspect of some international crimes. However, as many situations in which international crimes occur are inherently coercive, especially when people are confined, the reality of any consent must be carefully

---

[137] *Erdemović*, ICTY AC, 7 October 1997, Separate and Dissenting Opinion of Judge Cassese, para. 15. Although orders lose their legal relevance, they retain an evidential one.

[138] Cryer, 'Superior Orders' (n. 134) 58–60.

[139] See e.g. Werle and Jeßberger, *Principles of International Criminal Law* (n. 10) 258–61.

[140] *Tu quoque*, a plea that others (in particular, prosecuting states) have committed similar offences, is not a defence in law: *Kupreškić et al.*, ICTY TC II, 14 January 2000, paras. 515–20; *Kunarac*, ICTY AC, 12 June 2002, para. 87; although, admittedly, it can affect the legitimacy of proceedings. See e.g. Robert Cryer, *Prosecuting International Crimes: Selectivity and the International Criminal Law Regime* (Cambridge, 2005) ch. 4.

[141] See Chapter 13.

[142] See e.g. William Schabas, *The UN International Criminal Tribunals* (Cambridge, 2006) 341–3. Outside this context, Art. 52 of Geneva Convention III also only allows certain forms of work to be undertaken by PoWs if they consent.

investigated,[143] and assumptions about autonomy that are the norm in domestic law are not necessarily applicable in international criminal law.[144]

The ICTY was sceptical of claims of consent in the circumstances that surround international crimes, in particular with respect to sexual offences.[145] In the *Kunarac* case, for example, the Appeals Chamber said that 'the circumstances giving rise to the present appeal and that prevail in most cases charged as either war crimes or crimes against humanity will be almost universally coercive. That is to say, true consent will not be possible.'[146] The ICTR held that the prosecution must prove that consent was not present.[147] However, owing to the nature of international crimes, it added that 'the Trial Chamber is free to infer non-consent from the background circumstances, such as an ongoing genocide or the detention of the victim' rather than the specific relationship between the defendant and the victim.[148] Similarly, rather than proving that the accused did not know of the lack of consent, it suffices that 'the accused was aware, or had reason to be aware, of the coercive circumstances that undermined the possibility of genuine consent'.[149]

In relation to sexual offences, the ICC Elements of Crimes vitiates any purported consent where certain offences are committed:

by force, or by threat of force or coercion, such as that caused by fear of violence, duress, detention, psychological oppression or abuse of power, against such person or another person, or by taking advantage of a coercive environment, or the invasion was committed against a person incapable of giving genuine consent.[150]

In the *Bemba* case, the Trial Chamber held that the Prosecution does not need to prove the victim's lack of consent.[151] In cases where a person is incapable of giving consent, the Prosecution will only have to prove that the victim's capacity to give genuine consent was affected by natural, induced, or age-related incapacity.[152]

Owing to the sensitivity of evidence relating to consent, the ICC Rules of Procedure and Evidence set up a special regime for when and how the court is to hear it.[153] This is a careful balance of the facts that almost inevitably surround international crimes, and the (remote)

---

[143] *Naletilić and Martinović*, ICTY TC I, 31 March 2003, para. 519 saw the test as being of 'true' or 'real' consent. In *Kunarac et al.*, ICTY AC, 12 June 2002, paras. 132–3, the Chamber notes that in the circumstances of the victim's detention, 'the circumstances . . . were so coercive as to negate any possibility of consent', although it appeared (*ibid.* para. 131) to consider that consent was not an element of the offence. In most cases relating to international crimes, it is difficult to think of situations in which consent would be a genuine issue. See Wolfgang Schomburg and Ines Peterson, 'Genuine Consent to Sexual Violence Under International Criminal Law' (2007) 101 *AJIL* 121, 128–31. More generally, see Noëlle Quénivet, *Sexual Offences in Armed Conflict and International Law* (The Hague, 2005).

[144] Schomburg and Peterson, 'Genuine Consent' (n. 143) 125 et seq.

[145] *Ibid.* See also Catherine MacKinnon, 'The ICTR's Legacy on Sexual Violence' (2008) 14 *New England Journal of International and Comparative Law* 101.

[146] *Kunarac et al.*, ICTY AC, 12 June 2002, para. 130. [147] *Gacumbitsi*, ICTR AC, 7 July 2006, para. 153. [148] *Ibid.* para. 155.

[149] *Ibid.* para. 157; see also Schomburg and Peterson, 'Genuine Consent' (n. 143) 137–8. In relation to the crime of forced marriage which is not, according to the SCSL, inherently a sexual offence, consent was an issue which was, in the circumstances, necessarily excluded: *Prosecutor v. Brima Kamara and Kanu*, SCSL AC, 22 February 2008, paras. 187–203.

[150] Elements of Crimes, Art. 8(2)(b)(xxii–1), this includes, 'natural, induced or age-related incapacity'. Other elements also note that 'genuine consent' can be vitiated through deception, see e.g. Elements of Crimes, Art. 8(2)(b)(xxii–5).

[151] *Bemba*, ICC TC III, 21 March 2016 (ICC-01/05–01/08–3343) para. 105.

[152] *Bemba*, ICC TC III, 21 March 2016 (ICC-01/05–01/08–3343), para. 106 with a reference to Elements of Crime, footnotes 16 and 64.

[153] ICC RPE, rr. 70–2. See also ICTY and ICTR RPE, r. 96.

possibility that a defendant might genuinely believe in the existence of consent. Outside this context, the ICC has rejected the defence of consent with respect to the charge of enlisting and conscripting child soldiers. The judges held: 'enlisting is a "voluntary" act, whilst conscripting is forcible recruitment. In other words, the child's consent is not a valid defence'.[154]

16.9.2 Reprisals

Reprisals are responses to violations of humanitarian law that would themselves otherwise amount to violations of that law.[155] They are a crude and often dangerous form of law enforcement, but remain lawful in limited situations, and subject to a number of stringent requirements. The ICTY summed up those restrictions as being:

(a) the principle whereby they must be a last resort in attempts to impose compliance by the adversary with legal standards (which entails, amongst other things, that they may be exercised only after a prior warning has been given which has failed to bring about the discontinuance of the adversary's crimes); (b) the obligation to take special precautions before implementing them (they may be taken only after a decision to this effect has been made at the highest political or military level; in other words they may not be decided by local commanders); (c) the principle of proportionality (which entails not only that the reprisals must not be excessive compared to the precedent unlawful act of warfare, but also that they must stop as soon as that unlawful act has been discontinued); and (d) 'elementary considerations of humanity'.[156]

There are prohibitions on reprisals against the wounded, sick and shipwrecked, prisoners of war, interned civilians, and those in occupied territories,[157] which are considered customary.[158] The prohibitions on reprisals against other civilians and against cultural property, laid down in Articles 51.6 and 53(c) of Additional Protocol I, are of a more dubious customary status.[159] The ICTY, in the *Kupreškić et al.* case, asserted that they were customary; however, this conclusion has been the subject of significant academic critique,[160] and the UK Military Manual expressly disavows this conclusion.[161] Another ICTY Trial Chamber, in the *Martić* case, did not follow the *Kupreškić* decision on point, and was implicitly upheld on point by the Appeals Chamber, which appraised the relevant actions with reference to the criteria applicable to lawful reprisals rather than relying upon a blanket customary ban on reprisals.[162]

---

[154] *Lubanga*, ICC PTC I, 29 January 2007 (ICC-01/04–01/06–803) para. 247.
[155] As such, there is no evidence that reprisals could be a defence to crimes against humanity or genocide.
[156] *Kupreškić et al.*, ICTY TC II, 14 January 2000, para. 535.
[157] Geneva Convention I, Art. 46; Geneva Convention II, Art. 47; Geneva Convention III, Art. 13; Geneva Convention IV, Art. 33.
[158] Henckaerts and Doswald-Beck, *ICRC Customary Law*, 519–20.
[159] *Kupreškić et al.*, ICTY TC II, 14 January 2000, paras. 527–35.
[160] Christopher Greenwood, 'Belligerent Reprisals in the Jurisprudence of the International Criminal Tribunal for the Former Yugoslavia' in Fischer et al., *International and National Prosecution*, 359. See also Kreß, 'War Crimes' (n. 123) 153 et seq.
[161] Ministry of Defence, *Manual of the Law of Armed Conflict* (Oxford, 2004) 421.
[162] *Martić*, ICTY TC I, 12 July 2007, paras. 464–8, and ICTY AC, 8 October 2008, paras. 263–7.

Throughout history, armed conflicts have caused serious harm to the natural environment. Article 55(2) of Additional Protocol I stipulates that 'attacks against the natural environment by way of reprisals is prohibited'. Despite this unequivocal prohibition and the documentation of eco-centric harm in Syria's civil war and in the Ukraine conflict, it has not been carried through to the criminalization of this conduct.[163]

16.9.3 Military Necessity[164]

Military necessity is no longer, if it ever was, a general defence. As was said in the *Hostages* case, '[m]ilitary necessity or expediency do not justify a violation of positive rules ... [which are] ... superior to military necessities of the most urgent nature except where the regulations themselves specifically provide to the contrary'.[165] Thus, military necessity is only a defence where rules expressly incorporate it as, for example, ICC Statute, Article 8(2)(a)(iv) and (perhaps) Article 31(1)(c) do. It is difficult to define in the abstract what is or is not a matter of military necessity, but two things are reasonably clear: neither mere expediency[166] nor political necessity[167] is sufficient.[168]

Further Reading

Kai Ambos, *Treatise on International Criminal Law*, vol. I, *Foundations and General Part*, 2nd ed. (Oxford, 2021) ch. 8

Antonio Cassese, *International Criminal Law*, 2nd ed. (Oxford, 2008) chs. 12–13

Roger Clark, 'The Mental Element in International Criminal Law: The Rome Statute of the International Criminal Court and the Elements of Offences' (2002) 12 *Criminal Law Forum* 291

Antonio Coco, *The Defence of Mistake of Law in International Criminal Law. A Study on Ignorance and Blame* (Oxford, 2022)

Robert Cryer, *Prosecuting International Crimes: Selectivity and the International Criminal Law Regime* (Cambridge, 2005) ch. 6

Yoram Dinstein, 'Defences' in McDonald and Goldman, *Substantive and Procedural Aspects*, vol. I, 367

Albin Eser, 'Article 31' in Triffterer and Ambos, *Commentary*, 1125

Leslie Green, *Superior Orders in National and International Law* (Leyden, 1976)

Frits Kalshoven, *Belligerent Reprisals* (Leyden, 1976)

Maartje Krabbe, *Excusable Evil: An Analysis of Complete Defenses in International Criminal Law* (Antwerp, 2014)

---

[163] There is no grave breaches or war crimes provision explicitly outlawing reprisals against the natural environment. For proposals to fill this lacuna, see Matthew Gillett, 'Criminalizing Reprisals against the Natural Environment' (2023) 87 *International Review of the Red Cross* 1–34.

[164] See further van Sliedregt, *Individual Criminal Responsibility* (n.4) 295–8; Hayashi, 'Requirement of Military Necessity' (n. 59).

[165] *List*, VIII LRTWC 66–9. [166] Geoffrey Best, *Humanity in Warfare* (London, 1983) 64. [167] Commentary, XV LRTWC 176.

[168] For a useful, very detailed, discussion of the case law on point, see Hayashi, 'Requirement of Military Necessity' (n. 59).

Matthew Lippman, 'Conundrums of Armed Conflict: Criminal Defences to Violations of the Humanitarian Law of War' (1996) 15 *Dickinson Journal of International Law* 1

Larry May, *Crimes Against Humanity: A Normative Account* (Cambridge, 2005) ch. 10

Larry May, *War Crimes and Just War* (Cambridge, 2007) ch. 13

Mark Osiel, *Obeying Orders: Atrocities, Military Discipline and the Law of War* (New Brunswick, 1999)

William Schabas, *The UN International Criminal Tribunals* (Cambridge, 2006)

Otto Triffterer and Stephanie Bock, 'Article 33' in Triffterer, *Observers' Notes*, 1182

Elies van Sliedregt, *Individual Responsibility in International Criminal Law* (Oxford, 2012) Part 3

Annemieke Van Verseveld, *Mistake of Law: Excusing Perpetrators of International Crimes* (The Hague, 2012)

Part V

International Criminal Procedure and Sentencing

17

International Criminal Procedure

17.1 GENERAL ISSUES

Every international or hybrid criminal tribunal, from Nuremberg onwards, has needed to develop its own procedural system based on the often limited legal framework and inconclusive past experiments. Each such system incorporated elements from the major domestic traditions of common law and civil law which were combined in unique ways. As a result, from its relatively recent state of inexistence or underdevelopment, international criminal procedure has matured into a sophisticated branch of law and an autonomous subdiscipline.[1]

The procedural schemes of international criminal jurisdictions are methodically compared and their advantages and weaknesses are widely debated. They influence each other and domestic law and practice. The increased prominence of procedure in discourses about international criminal justice is justified: whether the accused will be convicted or walk free often revolves around procedural questions.[2] The quality of procedural law and its application in practice are key to the courts' success in fulfilling their primary mandates as criminal justice institutions. Their demonstrated ability to meet the applicable standards of fairness is a cornerstone of their credibility and long-term legitimacy.

This chapter provides an overview of the main themes of international criminal procedure.[3] The discussion primarily focuses on the International Criminal Court (ICC). While the International Criminal Tribunal for the former Yugoslavia (ICTY) and the International Criminal Tribunal for Rwanda (ICTR) have now closed down, and the Residual Mechanism (MICT) will also wind down eventually, their procedures are referenced for comparison.[4]

---

[1] Editors' Introduction in Sluiter et al., *International Criminal Procedure*, 1–7; Sergey Vasiliev, 'General Rules and Principles of International Criminal Procedure: Definition, Nature and Identification' in Sluiter and Vasiliev, *International Criminal Procedure*, ch. 1. Cf. Georg Schwarzenberger, 'Province of International Judicial Law' (1983) 1 *Notre Dame International Law Journal* 21.

[2] E.g. *Bemba*, ICC AC, 8 June 2018 (ICC-01/05–01/08–3636-Red) paras. 116–18, 196–200 (acquitting Bemba by majority, among others, because the acts he was convicted of fell outside the 'facts and circumstances described in the charges'). See Section 17.7.2.

[3] For comprehensive and comparative studies, see Boas, *Practitioner Library III*; Sluiter et al., *International Criminal Procedure*; Kai Ambos, *Treatise on International Criminal Law*, vol. III: *International Criminal Procedure* (Oxford, 2016); Christoph Safferling, *International Criminal Procedure* (Oxford, 2012).

[4] See Chapter 9.

17.1.1 Legal Traditions

International criminal procedure has been shaped by the approaches originating in the two major legal traditions: common law (Anglo-American) and civil law (Continental, or Romano-Germanic). The common law model is often characterized as 'accusatorial' (or 'adversarial') and the civil law model as 'inquisitorial'. These labels are imperfect and stand for historical models or 'ideal types' rather than real and contemporary systems. Under a classic 'inquisitorial' approach, one official both prosecutes and adjudicates the case. This is unthinkable in most modern systems, all of which are 'accusatorial' because the two functions are kept separate.[5] No domestic system embodies a pure model, and there are considerable differences between countries that historically belong to the same tradition. Moreover, some systems, for example in Scandinavia, are harder to place within either of the models, as they combine the elements of both for historical reasons. In spite of these terminological shortcomings, the shorthands 'adversarial' and 'inquisitorial' will be used in this chapter for the sake of convenience alongside the common law and civil law labels.

Both systems aim at establishing the truth and guaranteeing fairness but adhere to incommensurate understandings of these notions, leading to different arrangements. A fundamental difference is the role of parties and judges. Under the adversarial model, the investigations and evidentiary presentations at trial are driven by the parties, each striving to impress on adjudicators its version of events. The prosecution and the defence gather evidence in support of their respective cases and present it in court. At trial, lay jurors decide on the facts of the case and determine the verdict while the professional judge oversees the proceedings. She is confined to the modest role of a passive referee whose role is to secure fairness and the equality of arms. A more active approach by the judge would upset the balance by derailing case presentations and swaying the jury. Stricter rules on the admissibility of evidence are meant to protect the jurors from prejudicial information and to preserve fairness. If the process has been fair and the equality of arms has been preserved, the strongest case will prevail and the 'procedural truth' will emerge from the 'adversarial duel'.

By contrast, under the inquisitorial model, investigations and trials are judge-led. The role of the parties is limited to assisting the court in establishing the 'material', or 'object-ive', truth. An official bound by the duty of objectivity – an investigative judge or a prosecutor – takes charge of, or closely supervises, the inquiry. She instructs the police and looks after the defence interests. A case file (dossier) is assembled and the truth of its content is then probed at trial. There is only one case ('case of the truth'), which is controlled by the court, to which parties may contribute by proposing new evidence and by participating in the examination of evidence at trial. The trial court, composed of professional judges deciding both on the verdict and the sentence, possibly joined by lay jurors, has full access to the dossier. This enables the judges to take the lead in the examination of evidence and any new material proposed by the parties. The objective of

---

[5] Kai Ambos, 'International Criminal Procedure: "Adversarial", "Inquisitorial" or Mixed?' (2003) 3 *ICLR* 1.

ascertaining the material truth, bolstered by the professional adjudicators' control over decision-making, entails more relaxed admissibility rules.

In developing international criminal procedures, their architects typically started from the system most familiar to them, to then consider solutions offered by another system that could prove useful in meeting the needs of the tribunal. The adversarial model may appear attractive given the great importance it attaches to the fair trial guarantees for the accused. But insofar as the parties are expected to conduct their own investigations and procure evidence for their cases, this model may be less suitable where the ability to do so depends upon state cooperation.[6] The focus on objective truth-finding in inquisitorial systems also appears better attuned to the perceived need for impartial judicial inquiry and the aim of creating an accurate historical record, rightly or wrongly attributed to international criminal tribunals.[7] Moreover, the judge-driven process, which is not based on a rigid division into two cases, leaves room for active victim participation.[8]

Naturally, the drafters of the Rules of Procedure and Evidence (RPE) have endeavoured to combine in them the best of both worlds. Whilst international criminal practitioners naturally favour their own domestic systems, such 'procedural narcissism' has over time given way to a more pragmatic approach whereby the advantages of different systems could be recruited in the construction of a fair and effective international criminal procedure by fusing their elements into a hybrid framework.[9] However, this exercise is fraught with risks and complications. Plucking and amalgamating elements from different legal traditions, which have developed for centuries and grown to be part of internally coherent procedural schemes, can lead to sub-par solutions falling short of the standards and guarantees adopted in any given domestic system.[10] International criminal tribunals are procedural laboratories in which hybridized and innovative solutions have been grafted and tested, with mixed results.[11]

17.1.2 International Models

Historically, the regulation of international criminal proceedings has evolved in several ways. First, the level of detail and sophistication of procedural law increased considerably from early to later tribunals. The early statutes said very little about procedures, leaving the adoption and amendment of the RPE to the judiciary. In the modern tribunals, the judges

---

[6] See Chapter 20. See Michael Bohlander, 'Paradise Postponed? For a Judge-Led Generic Model of International Criminal Procedure and an End to "Draft-as-You-Go"' (2014) 45 *Netherlands Yearbook of International Law* 331 (arguing that judge-led procedure is more suitable due to its efficiency). Cf. Sergey Vasiliev, 'Trial Process at the ECCC: The Rise and Fall of the Inquisitorial Paradigm in International Criminal Law?' in Simon Meisenberg and Ignaz Stegmiller (eds.), *The Extraordinary Chambers in the Courts of Cambodia: Assessing their Contribution to International Criminal Law* (The Hague, 2016) 389.

[7] See Chapter 2.   [8] See Chapter 18.

[9] See *Erdemović*, ICTY AC, 7 October 1997, Judge Cassese's Dissenting Opinion, paras. 1–6.

[10] Mirjan Damaška, 'Epistemology and Legal Regulation of Proof' (2003) 2 *Law, Probability and Risk* 117, 121 ('In their natural habitat, each set of practices is part of a larger procedural whole, with its own internal coherence ... Creating a successful mixture is not like shopping in a boutique of detachable procedural forms, in which one is free to purchase some and reject others').

[11] Megan Fairlie, 'The Marriage of Common and Continental Law at the ICTY and Its Progeny, Due Process Deficit' (2004) 4 *ICLR* 243; Rupert Skilbeck, 'Frankenstein's Monster: Creating a New International Criminal Procedure' (2010) 8(2) *JICJ* 451.

took their legislative function to heart and developed comprehensive codes of criminal procedure akin to those found in domestic systems. With the ICC, states did, however, not cede the bulk of procedural law-making to the judges and instead regulated procedures with a painstaking degree of detail in the Statute and the RPE.

Second, international criminal procedures have been in flux in comparative law terms. The preferred balance between common law and civil law, and the character of the resulting hybrid systems, has not been the same at all times, even within each tribunal's regime. The historical and modern tribunals had a strong common law imprimatur, although over time the ICTY and ICTR adopted more civil law elements. At the ICC, the civil law influence has been strong from the outset.

The Nuremberg and Tokyo Charters contained only basic provisions on procedure.[12] The judges also developed Rules of Procedure which were not very detailed.[13] In practice, solutions had to be improvised to manage the trials and dispense with procedural motions. The procedures, in particular at the International Military Tribunal for the Far East, reflected a strong Anglo-American influence. But there were also deviations from the common law model, notably the relaxed rules on the admissibility of evidence and trial by a panel of judges instead of a jury.[14] As a result of the Soviet and French participation in the drafting of the Nuremberg International Military Tribunal (IMT)'s Charter, it reflected a greater civil law influence. The IMT allowed trials *in absentia* and gave the defendants a right to make statements at a preliminary hearing and at trial.[15] When assessed by the standards of the day, preceding the advent of modern human rights, the Nuremberg and Tokyo criminal procedures were essentially fair.[16] Today, these tribunals would hardly stand the test of fairness. The protections were minimal and did not include a right to remain silent or to appeal against a conviction.[17]

The ICTY and ICTR Statutes, adopted by UN Security Council Resolutions, included only a few basic procedural provisions and left the procedure to be fleshed out by the judges. In doing so, judges could use little guidance other than the human rights standards, general principles of law, and the Nuremberg and Tokyo precedents.[18] As early ICTY decisions explained, the procedures were a 'unique amalgam of common and civil law features'.[19] In fact, except for the liberal admissibility rules and further civil-law-inspired reforms passed to enhance judicial control and expedite the tribunal's work,[20] procedures for the investigation and trial remained mainly adversarial. The RPE were amended multiple times, with this flexibility and dynamism at times affecting legal

---

[12] Nuremberg Charter, Arts. 16 (fair trial), 17–25 (powers and trial procedure), and 26–29 (judgment and sentence); Tokyo Charter, Arts. 9–10 (fair trial), 11–15 (powers and trial procedures), and 16–17 (judgment and sentence).

[13] Nuremberg Charter, Art. 13; Tokyo Charter, Art. 7. The Nuremberg Rules, adopted on 29 October 1945, and the Tokyo Rules of Procedure and Evidence (RPE), promulgated on 25 April 1946.

[14] Nuremberg Charter, Arts. 2 and 19; Tokyo Charter, Arts. 2 and 13(a). [15] Nuremberg Charter, Arts. 12, 16(b) and 24(j).

[16] See Chapter 6.

[17] The defendants could only request a reduction of sentences. Nuremberg Charter, Arts. 26 and 29, and Tokyo Charter, Art. 17.

[18] *First Annual Report of the ICTY*, UN Doc. A/49/342-S/1994/1007 (29 August 1994) para. 54. On the use of general principles of law as a source, see Vasiliev, 'General Rules and Principles' (n. 1) 74–6.

[19] *Tadić*, ICTY TC II, 5 August 1996, para. 14. Similarly, *Delalić et al.*, ICTY TC II, 1 May 1997, para. 15.

[20] See Section 17.8.2. See further Máximo Langer, 'The Rise of Managerial Judging in International Criminal Law' (2005) 53 *American Journal of Comparative Law* 835; Daryl Mundis, 'From "Common Law" Towards "Civil Law": The Evolution of the ICTY Rules of Procedure and Evidence' (2001) 14 *LJIL* 367.

certainty.[21] The MICT RPE, also adopted and amended by the judges, draw upon the Tribunals' Rules.[22] The Residual Mechanism conducts trials and appeals, but may not open new cases except with respect to contempt of court and perjury.[23]

During the negotiations on the ICC Statute and Rules, states made an unprecedented effort to devise and adopt procedural solutions satisfactory to the proponents of the two major legal traditions and suited to the Court's objectives and anticipated needs.[24] The ICC's legislation embodies a unique consensus on the criminal procedure and painstakingly avoids terminology specific to any domestic system, reflecting the drafting approach of 'constructive ambiguity'.[25] Although the coherence of some elements of the ICC process can be questioned, it bridges the two traditions in a creative and, on many issues, rather promising manner, while also drawing inspiration from international human rights and soft law standards. This is demonstrated, among others, by the addition of a Pre-Trial Chamber, admission of guilt procedure, and provisions related to victim participation and reparations.

The ICC judges' procedural law-making role is quite limited. They may only provisionally amend the RPE, subject to states parties' approval,[26] and adopt the Regulations of the Court necessary for its routine functioning (and for filling any remaining gaps).[27] The ICC procedural law therefore presents a multi-layered and hierarchically structured system. The Statute, RPE, and the Regulations together establish an enclosed, nearly exhaustive regime.[28] Although a great degree of uniformity in practice could be expected, many issues were left to the discretion of the Chambers, resulting in case-by-case variation. Albeit at a slower pace than at the ad hoc Tribunals, the ICC procedure has been evolving in the context of the 'Lessons Learnt' process within the Court and the ICC Assembly of States Parties (ASP)'s Study Group of Governance (established in 2010), which have served as a framework for the structured dialogue on, and preparation of, amendment proposals.[29]

Produced by a creative fusion of elements derived from different systems and further legislative innovations, the ICTY, ICTR, and ICC procedural systems are considered unique (*sui generis*) or hybrid, rather than distinctly civil law or common law.[30] While a

---

[21]   ICTY RPE were amended fifty times (1994–2015) and ICTR RPE twenty-three times (1995–2015). See Göran Sluiter, 'Procedural Lawmaking at the International Criminal Tribunals' in Shany Darcy and Joseph Powderly (eds.), *Judicial Creativity at the International Criminal Tribunals* (Oxford, 2010) ch. 13.

[22]   MICT Statute, Art. 13. The Rules have been amended seven times since adoption in 2012: MICT RPE (Rev.7, 9 December 2020).

[23]   MICT Statute, Art. 1.

[24]   On the ICC negotiations, see Silvia Fernández de Gurmendi, 'International Criminal Law Procedures: The Process of Negotiations' in Lee, *The Making of the Rome Statute*, 217–27; Silvia Fernández de Gurmendi and Håkan Friman, 'The Rules of Procedure and Evidence of the International Criminal Court' (2000) 3 *Yearbook of International Humanitarian Law* 289.

[25]   Claus Kress, 'The Procedural Law of the International Criminal Court in Outline: Anatomy of a Unique Compromise' (2003) 1 *JICJ* 603–17.

[26]   ICC Statute, Art. 51(3). The first provisional amendment of the RPE (Rule 165) was made on 10 February 2016.

[27]   ICC Statute, Art. 52.

[28]   See *ibid.* Art. 21(1). The ICC is reluctant to turn to national procedural practices for guidance. See e.g. *Lubanga*, ICC AC, 14 December 2006 (ICC-01/04–01/06–772) paras. 28–35 ('abuse of process' doctrine); *Lubanga*, ICC PTC I, 8 November 2006 (ICC-01/04–01/06–679) paras. 35–42, and ICC TC I, 30 November 2007 (ICC-01/04–01/06–1049) para. 41 ('witness proofing').

[29]   Silvia Fernández de Gurmendi, 'Enhancing the Court's Efficiency: From the Drafting of the Procedural Provisions by States to their Revision by Judges' (2018) 16(2) *JICJ* 341; Hirad Abtahi and Shehzad Charania, 'Expediting the ICC Criminal Process: Striking the Right Balance Between the ICC and States Parties' (2018) 18(3) *ICLR* 383.

[30]   Patrick Robinson, 'Ensuring Fair and Expeditious Trials at the International Criminal Tribunal for the Former Yugoslavia' (2000) 11 *EJIL* 569, 574 ('neither common law accusatorial nor civil law inquisitorial, nor even an amalgam of both; it is *sui generis*'); Ambos, 'International Criminal Procedure' (n. 5) 34–5; Mark Findlay, 'Synthesis in Trial Proceedings? The Experience of International Criminal Tribunals' (2001) 50 *ICLQ* 26.

new entirely coherent tradition has not necessarily emerged, the divide has been bridged in one way or another. The procedural models and practice of international criminal jurisdictions serve as a source of guidance and inspiration for the hybrid courts and domestic systems which are increasingly prosecuting and trying core crimes. However, international criminal procedure was not devised for automatic adoption at the domestic level. It was framed against the specific circumstances of international courts and thus does not in every respect represent 'best practice' for states.

17.2 ACTORS

17.2.1 Judges

The role of the judges at the ICTY and ICTR generally corresponded to that under the adversarial model. They played a limited role in the parties' investigations, mostly in relation to orders for state cooperation, and remained relatively passive (by the civil law standards) during trials. The judges could also order parties to present additional evidence and summon a witness on their own initiative, hinting at a more active involvement in fact-finding.[31] In practice, however, this power was used very sparingly.

Over time, the ICTY judges gave themselves a stronger role in the management of pre-trial proceedings to expedite case docket and tackle delays in case preparation and disclosure attributable to the parties.[32] The Trial Chambers exercised tighter control over the length of the parties' cases, and pre-trial judges were introduced to press forward with trial preparation.[33] Although these reforms were sometimes characterized as 'inquisitorial', it is more accurate to describe them as enacting a 'managerial judging system'.[34] The judges acted merely as case managers rather than fact-finders in the pre-trial stage while the parties remained in charge of investigations and presentation of evidence.

The ICC Statute envisages a more active role for the Pre-Trial Chamber (PTC) judges as early as prior to and during investigations.[35] While reflecting a stronger civil law influence, the role of this Chamber falls short of that of an investigative judge in the 'inquisitorial' system. The PTC does not conduct investigations itself but only ensures human rights supervision and facilitates investigations by the parties, including by assisting them in obtaining state cooperation.[36] Early judicial involvement helps ensure the rights of the suspect and the protection of other interests, including those of victims and states.[37] The appropriate balance between the PTC's authority and the prosecutorial prerogatives in respect of investigation had to be found, and the ICC practice has exposed palpable tensions in that regard.

The role of the judges in the pre-trial (case) and trial proceedings at the ICC is delineated but not regulated exhaustively in the Statute and the RPE. The PTC judges' principal

---

[31] ICTY and ICTR RPE, r. 98. [32] ICTY RPE, rr. 65*bis*, 73*bis*, 73*ter*; no such rules were formally adopted by the ICTR.
[33] ICTY RPE, r. 65*ter*. [34] See Langer, 'The Rise of Managerial Judging' (n. 20). [35] ICC Statute, Arts. 15 and 53–58.
[36] Olivier Fourmy, 'Powers of the Pre-Trial Chambers' in Cassese et al., *Commentary*, 1207–30; Göran Sluiter, 'Human Rights Protection in the Pre-Trial Phase' in Stahn and Sluiter, *Emerging Practice*, ch. 24.
[37] ICC Statute, Art. 57(3).

function in the pre-trial stage is the issuance of the arrest warrant or summons to appear, which marks the start of the case focused on a specific individual.[38] Moreover, the PTC confirms charges, thereby committing the person for trial and fixing the scope of the case for that stage.[39] The organization of trial is not regulated in detail in the ICC legal instruments and each Trial Chamber holds a discretionary power to define, in consultation with the parties, the trial procedures to be followed in a case.[40]

17.2.2 Prosecutor

The prosecutor is a key actor and a true motor driving behind international criminal proceedings, in which they represent the interests of the (international) community. The prosecutor takes charge of the selection of situations and/or cases, conduct of an investigation, choice of prosecutorial targets, prosecution of cases, presentation of evidence at trial, bringing appeals, and so on. The onus to prove the guilt of the accused at trial, as well as the burden of meeting the applicable evidentiary thresholds at previous stages, rests squarely with the prosecutor.[41] The ICC Prosecutor's role as the 'officer of justice' goes further than that at the Tribunals. It also encompasses the duty of objective truth-seeking, that is, the obligation to investigate both inculpatory and exculpatory circumstances equally, even though this duty does not necessarily extend to the trial phase.[42]

The prosecutor enjoys a high degree of institutional independence and procedural autonomy, subject to varying degrees of judicial supervision in different jurisdictions. If one considers the confirmation of indictment/charges procedures and the possibility of modifying a legal characterization of facts,[43] such supervision appears greater in the ICC than in the other tribunals. Indeed, the scope of judicial control over prosecutorial discretion has been a recurrent controversy at the ICC. But, on the other hand, the expansion of case-management competence of ICTY judges, including their power to invite or even *direct* the prosecutor to reduce the number of counts charged,[44] would tilt the assessment the other way. Beyond their procedural role, prosecutors to a large extent shape the docket and legacy of the courts and serve as the public face of international criminal justice. However, such representative functions should be performed professionally and impartially, in conformity with their status as officers of the court.

17.2.3 Defence

The Statutes and RPE provide for the fundamental rights of those suspected or accused of a crime. Among the rights of the suspect (charged person) are the rights to remain silent, to

---

[38] *Ibid.* Art. 58. [39] *Ibid.* Art. 61. [40] *Ibid.* Art. 64(2), (3)(a) and (8)(b); ICC RPE, r. 140.
[41] See e.g. ICC Statute, Arts. 61(5) and 66(2).
[42] *Ibid.* Art. 54(1)(a). See Sergey Vasiliev, 'Trial' in Luc Reydams, Jan Wouters and Cedric Ryngaert (eds.), *International Prosecutors* (Oxford, 2012) ch. 13.
[43] ICTY RPE, Art. 19(1), and ICTY RPE r. 47; cf. ICC Statute, Art. 61 and ICC Regulations of the Court, reg. 55.
[44] ICTY RPE, r. 73*bis*(D)–(E).

legal assistance during questioning, and to interpretation and translations.[45] Once the judge or the PTC (ICC) confirms the charges, the person's status is changed to that of the accused. The accused has more extensive rights than the suspect, which reflects international human rights standards.[46]

The adequate protection of the rights of suspects and accused in international criminal proceedings, and hence preserving their fairness and integrity, is inconceivable without a strong and professional defence. The assistance by a defence counsel is a cornerstone right which has been consistently upheld by international criminal jurisdictions. Specific qualifications are required of counsel, with nuances among the courts.[47] The Registry is responsible for the vetting of qualifications, assistance to counsel, and administration of the legal aid system, while Chambers exercise supervision.[48] Although most defendants are represented by counsel, some prefer to represent themselves. The risks of ineffective defence and obstructive behaviour during trials raise the question of whether legal assistance can be imposed against the will of the accused.

Mandatory representation is accepted in civil law systems but not in common law.[49] The ICTY Appeals Chamber upheld a right to self-representation even in cases of abuse by the accused, arguing that the right may be limited only to the minimum extent necessary to ensure reasonably expeditious proceedings.[50] Different tools to ensure a more effective legal representation have been employed: *amici curiae* (friends of the court) to assist the judges,[51] 'stand-by counsel',[52] and 'privileged associates'.[53] But the right to self-representation is not absolute, and counsel has sometimes been imposed.[54]

The ICC Statute also recognizes the right to legal representation of the person's own choosing, and if necessary free of cost.[55] The Registrar maintains a list of counsel, but the defendant may also choose a counsel not on the list, provided that the counsel meets the required qualifications and is willing to be included in the list.[56] In addition, the ICC has a system of public defence (ad hoc) counsel to assist in the early stages of an investigation, among others for the purpose of unique investigative opportunities.[57] Such counsel may be appointed from the list or from the independent Office of Public Counsel for the Defence.

---

[45] ICTY Statute, Art. 18(3); ICTR Statute, Art. 17(3); MICT Statute, Art. 16(3); ICTY and ICTR RPE, r. 42; MICT RPE, r. 40; and ICC Statute, Art. 55(2).
[46] ICTY Statute, Art. 21; ICTR Statute, Art. 20; MICT Statute, Art. 19; and ICC Statute, Art. 67. At the ICC, these rights are applicable, in principle, from the first appearance: ICC RPE, r. 121(1).
[47] ICTY and ICTR RPE, r. 44; MICT RPE, r. 42; ICC RPE, r. 22; and ICC Regulations of the Court, regs. 67–68.
[48] ICTY and ICTR RPE, r. 45; MICT RPE, r. 43.
[49] See Mirjan Damaška, 'Assignment of Counsel and Perceptions of Fairness' (2005) 3 *JICJ* 3.
[50] *Milošević*, ICTY AC, 1 November 2004, paras. 17–18. See also *Šešelj*, ICTY AC, 8 December 2006 (affording primacy to the right to self-representation).
[51] *Milošević*, ICTY TC III, 30 August 2001.
[52] *Šešelj*, ICTY TC II, 9 May 2003; *Karadžić*, ICTY TC III, 15 April 2010 and 21 June 2012.
[53] *Šešelj*, ICTY TC III, 10 February 2010 (by entering into a confidentiality agreement with the Registry, two persons could access confidential information, the courtroom, and the accused, on a privileged basis).
[54] *Milošević*, ICTY AC, 1 November 2004; *Šešelj*, ICTY TC I, 21 August 2006; and *Karadžić*, ICTY TC III, 5 November 2009; *Norman et al.*, SCSL TC I, 8 June 2004, paras. 8 and 27. See ICTY RPE, r. 45*ter*; ICC Statute, Art. 67(1)(d) and ICC Regulations, reg. 76(1).
[55] ICC Statute, Arts. 55(2) and 67(1)(d). See *Updated Report of the Court on the Progress of the Development of Proposals for Adjustments to the Legal Aid Remuneration System as of 2019*, ICC-ASP/16/32 (8 November 2017).
[56] ICC RPE, r. 22; ICC Regulations of the Court, regs. 69–76.
[57] ICC Statute, Art. 56, and ICC Regulations of the Court, reg. 77. See e.g. *Situation in the DRC*, ICC PTC I, 26 April 2005 (ICC-01/04–21).

17.2.4 Victims and Witnesses

Victims are afforded a substantially stronger role at the ICC than before other international tribunals. This role includes an independent right to participate and be represented in the proceedings and the right to claim reparations, over and above their traditional role as witnesses that is familiar from the ad hoc Tribunals.[58]

The term 'witness' is not defined in the Rules, but there is a distinction between 'expert witnesses'[59] and other witnesses.[60] As a corollary of the adversarial approach at the ICTY and ICTR, the parties had the primary responsibility for their cases and could call (prosecution or defence) witnesses. Witnesses called by the court, typically after the defence case, were referred to as 'chamber witnesses'.[61] Similar provisions apply at the ICC.[62] In practice, all ICC trials so far have been divided into prosecution and defence cases, with most witnesses having been called by the parties and some by judges or by legal representatives of the victims. Several decisions emphasized, however, that witnesses are not attributable to either party but instead are 'witnesses of the Court'.[63] The Trial Chambers have frequently exercised their power to call (expert) witnesses in practice.

A witness giving testimony under solemn declaration (a neutral term for 'oath') is obliged to speak the truth and risks being held criminally liable for false testimony.[64] A protection against self-incrimination is provided for, although the witness may be compelled to answer incriminating questions under an assurance that the information will not be used for prosecution against him or her.[65] Witness privileges may apply, notably the lawyer–client privilege.[66] Other privileges, such as those of (former) staff members of certain organizations (International Committee of the Red Cross and Red Crescent (ICRC) and the Tribunals) or members of certain professions (war correspondents), were recognized in the Tribunals' jurisprudence.[67] Privileges also apply for confidential (national security) information.[68] Witnesses and participating victims at the ICC are granted various protective measures, which may trigger issues regarding the rights of the accused.[69]

---

[58] See Chapter 18.
[59] ICTY and ICTR RPE, r. 94*bis*; MICT RPE, r. 116; and ICC RPE, r. 140(3). See also ICC RPE, rr. 91 and 191 and ICC Regulations of the Court, reg. 44.
[60] See Yvonne McDermott, 'Regular Witness Testimony' and Suzannah Linton, 'Testimony of Expert Witnesses, Journalists, ICRC, and UN Staff' in Sluiter et al., *International Criminal Procedure*, 859–938.
[61] ICTY and ICTR RPE, r. 98; MICT RPE, r. 120. E.g. *Milošević*, ICTY TC III, 18 February 2004; *Krajišnik*, ICTY TC I, 24 April 2006. Cf. *Jelisić*, ICTY TC I, 11 December 1998 (all witnesses are 'witnesses of justice', and not of either of the parties, once they have made the solemn declaration).
[62] ICC Statute, Arts. 64(6)(b) and 69(3); ICC RPE, rr. 76 and 79. But cf. ICC Statute, Arts. 64(6)(b) and 93(1)(e). On the ICC's power to compel witnesses' attendance, see Section 20.2.3.
[63] *Lubanga*, ICC PTC I, 8 November 2006 (ICC-01/04–01/06–679) para. 26, and ICC TC I, 30 November 2007 (ICC-01/04–01/06–1049) para. 34; *Muthaura et al.*, ICC PTC II, 4 April 2011 (ICC-01/09–02/11–38) para. 10.
[64] ICTY and ICTR RPE, rr. 90–91; MICT RPE, rr. 106 and 108; ICC Statute, Arts. 69(1) and 70 and ICC RPE, r. 66.
[65] ICTY and ICTR RPE, r. 90(E); MICT RPE, r. 106(E); and ICC RPE, rr. 65, 74–75 (also covering incrimination of family members).
[66] ICTY and ICTR RPE, r. 97; MICT RPE, r. 119 (lawyer–client).
[67] *Simić et al.*, ICTY TC III, 27 July 1999 (ICRC); *Delalić et al.*, ICTY TC II, 8 July 1997 (Tribunal staff); *Brđanin and Talić*, ICTY AC, 11 December 2002, reversing ICTY TC II, 7 June 2002 (war correspondents); *Brima et al.*, SCSL TC II, 16 September 2005, reversed in SCSL AC, 26 May 2006 (on human rights workers). See also ICC RPE, r. 73 (on ICRC privilege and special provisions).
[68] ICTY and ICTR RPE, r. 70; MICT RPE, r. 76; ICC Statute, Art. 72. See also *Milošević*, ICTY AC, 23 October 2002 and ICTY TC III, 30 October 2003.
[69] See Chapter 18.

17.2.5 States and International Organizations

Courts and tribunals inevitably render decisions affecting state interests, for example, decisions regarding the exercise of jurisdiction or state cooperation. On such issues, states may intervene in the proceedings. In the ICTY, states 'directly affected' by a decision could request a review, and this right was exercised with respect to, *inter alia*, an order to a state to provide documents,[70] an order to NATO (and the Stabilisation Force (SFOR)) to provide reports and documents,[71] a request for arrest and surrender,[72] and disclosure of confidential information.[73] But a general right to intervene or file statements of interest in the proceedings was not recognized.[74]

At the ICC, states are given greater scope for intervention owing to the 'trigger mechanisms' and the principle of complementarity.[75] A referring state (or the Security Council) may request a review of the Prosecutor's decision not to investigate or to prosecute.[76] States that would normally exercise jurisdiction over the crimes may request deferral of jurisdiction and challenge the admissibility of the case.[77] The Security Council also has the power to require the temporary deferral of an investigation or prosecution.[78] Moreover, certain decisions may be appealed by an affected state,[79] and states may also seek a ruling on the legality of a request for cooperation and partake in the proceedings regarding a failure to cooperate.[80]

Additionally, states and organizations (and individuals) may be allowed to make *amicus curiae* submissions on legal or other issues.[81] The ICC has used this mechanism for granting states leave (or for inviting them) to file submissions in proceedings to which they are not a party.[82]

17.3 RIGHTS

17.3.1 Standards

The UN Secretary-General's report on the ICTY Statute underlined, as axiomatic, that internationally recognized human rights standards regarding the rights of the accused must be fully respected at all stages of the proceedings.[83] Compliance with human rights is a

---

[70] *Blaškić*, ICTY AC, 29 October 1997 (Croatia against a *subpoena duces tecum*); *Kordić and Čerkez*, ICTY AC, 26 March 1999.
[71] *Simić et al.*, ICTY AC, 27 March 2001.
[72] *Bobetko*, ICTY AC, 29 November 2002. Cf. *Gotovina et al.*, ICTY AC, 17 January 2008 (Croatia's request for a review of the decision to deny provisional release was rejected).
[73] *Milošević*, ICTY AC, 23 October 2002.
[74] *Gotovina and Markač*, ICTY AC, 8 February 2012, paras. 14–17. For a critical comment, see Mirjan Damaška, 'Unacknowledged Presences in International Criminal Justice' (2012) 10(5) *JICJ* 1239.
[75] ICC Statute, Arts. 18–19. See further Chapter 8. [76] ICC Statute, Art. 53(3). [77] *Ibid*. Arts. 18(2) and 19(2). [78] *Ibid*. Art. 16.
[79] *Ibid*. Art. 82(1)(d) and (2). [80] *Ibid*. Art. 87(7); ICC Regulations of the Court, regs. 108–109.
[81] ICTY and ICTR RPE, r. 74; MICT RPE, r. 83; ICC RPE, r. 103.
[82] E.g. *Gbagbo*, ICC AC, 12 December 2012 (ICC-02/11–01/11–321) paras. 39–43 and PTC I, 14 March 2013 (ICC-02/11–01/11–418) (observations on the defendant's admissibility challenge); *Ruto and Sang*, ICC TC V(A), 24 April 2013 (ICC-01/09–01/11–700) and 3 July 2013 (ICC-01/09–01/11–798) (allegations of non-cooperation); *Request under Regulation 46(3) of the Regulations of the Court*, ICC PTC I, 21 June 2018 (ICC-RoC46(3)-01/18–28) (requesting Myanmar's submissions regarding the Prosecutor's request for jurisdictional ruling).
[83] *Report of the Secretary-General Pursuant to Paragraph 2 of Security Council Resolution 808(1993)*, UN Doc. S/25704 (3 May 1993) para. 106.

matter of credibility and legitimacy of international criminal justice and is also important
for securing cooperation from states.

International courts are not parties to international human rights instruments, and the
interpretations of the respective standards by human rights courts and treaty monitoring
bodies are not binding on the tribunals. But such external case law may have 'persuasive
authority' or reflect customary international law.[84] Moreover, the underlying human rights
principles, such as those in Article 14 of the International Covenant on Civil and Political
Rights (ICCPR), are incorporated into the Tribunals' Statutes and RPE. Therefore, the
Tribunals frequently referred to international human rights treaties and case law in their
decisions.[85] At times, they also departed from the standards developed for domestic
proceedings, invoking their own unique structure, subject-matter jurisdiction, or operational circumstances; in turn, this led to criticisms.[86]

Over and above elaborate provisions on the rights of the accused and other participants,
the ICC Statute requires that interpretation and application of all law (including the Statute
itself) 'must be consistent with internationally recognized human rights'.[87] Although
irresolvable conflicts are exceptionally rare, on one occasion the Court set aside a statutory
provision (Article 93(7)) because its application in accordance with Article 21(3) was not
possible in the circumstances.[88] The Court routinely refers to human rights law when
defining or clarifying procedural concepts or legal tests.[89]

In the past the Court was criticized for its reluctance to assess the fairness of national law
and practice, for instance, in the context of arrest and surrender and admissibility
determinations.[90] The threshold for passing a negative judgement on domestic proceedings
is set very high because it is not the role of the ICC as a complementary court to pronounce

---

[84] *Barayagwiza*, ICTR AC, 3 November 1999, para. 40 (the European Convention on Human Rights (ECHR) and the American Convention on Human Rights (ACHR) and related jurisprudence are persuasive authority as evidence of international custom); *Kajelijeli*, ICTR AC, 23 May 2005, para. 209 (ICCPR reflects customary international law); *Delalić et al.*, ICTY TC II, 28 April 1997, para. 27 (European Court of Human Rights (ECtHR) and UN Human Rights Committee (HRC) decisions 'authoritative and applicable'). Cf. *Tadić*, ICTY TC II, 10 August 1995, paras. 17–30 (limited value of human rights interpretations by other judicial bodies).
[85] Antonio Cassese, 'The Influence of the European Court of Human Rights on International Criminal Tribunals: Some Methodological Remarks' in Morten Bergsmo (ed.), *Human Rights and Criminal Justice for the Downtrodden: Essays in Honour of Asbjørn Eide* (Leiden, 2003) 19–52; Triestino Mariniello and Paolo Lobba (eds.), *Judicial Dialogue on Human Rights: The Practice of International Criminal Tribunals* (Leiden, 2017).
[86] E.g. *Kunarac et al.*, ICTY TC II, 22 February 2001, para. 470. See Gabrielle McIntyre, 'Defining Human Rights in the Arena of International Humanitarian Law: Human Rights in the Jurisprudence of the ICTY' in Gideon Boas and William Schabas (eds.), *International Criminal Law Developments in the Case Law of the ICTY* (Dordrecht, 2003) 193–238; Mirjan Damaška, 'Should National and International Justice Be Subjected to the Same Evaluative Framework?' in Sluiter et al., *International Criminal Procedure*, 1418–22.
[87] ICC Statute, Art. 21(3). On the meaning of Art. 21(3), see Alain Pellet, 'Applicable Law' in Cassese et al., *Commentary*, 1080–1; Lorenzo Gradoni, 'The Human Rights Dimension of International Criminal Procedure' in Sluiter et al., *International Criminal Procedure*, 74–95; Rebecca Young, '"Internationally Recognized Human Rights" Before the International Criminal Court' (2011) 60 *ICLQ* 189.
[88] *Katanga and Ngudjolo*, ICC TC II, 9 June 2011 (ICC-01/04–01/07–3003). See Section 20.2.3.
[89] E.g. *Situation in the DRC*, ICC PTC I, 17 January 2006 (ICC-01/04–101) paras. 52–3 ('proceedings'); *Al Bashir*, ICC AC, 3 February 2010 (ICC-02/05–01/09–73) para. 31 ('reasonable grounds to believe'); *Gaddafi and Al-Senussi*, ICC AC, 12 June 2012 (ICC-01/11–01/11–175) paras. 26–8 (presumption of innocence).
[90] Göran Sluiter, 'Human Rights Protection in the ICC Pre-Trial Phase' (n. 36) 459–75. See e.g. *Gbagbo*, ICC PTC I, 15 August 2012 (ICC-02/11–01/11–212) para. 112 (where the Court was not involved in the detention, no determination of a rights violation during detention can be made); *Gaddafi and Al-Senussi*, ICC AC, 24 July 2014 (ICC-01/11–01/11–565) paras. 3 and 230 (a case may be admissible where rights violations at the national level are so egregious that they are 'inconsistent with an intent to bring that person to justice'). Cf. *Lubanga*, ICC PTC I, 29 January 2007 (ICC-01/04–01/06–803–275) paras. 62–90 (conducting a thorough analysis of national seizure measures when assessing admissibility of evidence).

on human rights compliance of national jurisdictions.[91] However, this restrictive reading of the ICC's mandate is open to debate.

17.3.2 Independence and Impartiality

Human rights treaties provide for an institutional guarantee of an independent and impartial tribunal or court established by law as a key aspect of the right to a fair trial. Independence requires an institutional and functional separation from the executive and legislative powers, as well as from the parties.[92]

A separate but related problem for international criminal jurisdictions is their dependence on cooperation by states and others.[93] This dilemma became evident in the *Barayagwiza* case, after the Rwandan government suspended cooperation with the ICTR, following which the Tribunal could not obtain the attendance of witnesses.[94] Non-cooperation has also contributed to the collapse of certain cases at the ICC.[95] But a court's dependence on cooperation does not mean it lacks independence, which rather goes to the integrity and autonomy of judicial decision-making. Somewhat differently, the detention of the MICT Judge Akay in his state of nationality (Turkey), followed by his non-reappointment by the Secretary-General, demonstrates that states sometimes undermine the judicial independence of the Tribunals, while 'parent' international organizations do not stand up for their judges, as they should.[96] Politicized attacks on the courts and coercive measures taken against their officials by states also pose a grave threat to judicial and prosecutorial independence.[97]

The Tribunals considered and invariably dismissed challenges to the legality of their creation, holding that they had been established in accordance with the rule of law and thus satisfied the requirements.[98] The fact that they were created by the Security Council raised questions about their institutional independence.[99] However, domestic courts are also subject to executive and legislative powers as regards budgets and appointments, and this alone does not rule out their independence. Importantly, as the Tribunals' parent body, the Council did not seek to exert influence on specific cases.

The guarantee of an impartial and independent court has a personal dimension: judges, too, must be independent and impartial.[100] Should they show actual bias or appearance of such, that is, when a reasonable and properly informed observer might reasonably

---

[91] See further Chapter 8. [92] E.g. *Ringeisen* v. *Austria*, ECtHR, 16 July 1971, para. 95. [93] See Chapter 20.

[94] *Barayagwiza*, ICTR AC, 3 November 1999 and 31 March 2000, Separate Opinions of Judges Vohrah and Nieto-Navia.

[95] *Kenyatta*, ICC TC V(B), 3 December 2014 (ICC-01/09–02/11–982) paras. 74–9; Statement of the Prosecutor of the International Criminal Court, Fatou Bensouda, on the withdrawal of charges against Mr. Uhuru Muigai Kenyatta, 5 December 2014.

[96] *Ngirabatware*, MICT AC, 31 March 2017; Statement of the President on the Non-reappointment of Judge Akay, MICT, 3 July 2018.

[97] E.g. Press release, 'The Presidency of the Assembly of States Parties stands firmly by the International Criminal Court, its elected officials, and its personnel', ICC-ASP-20230520-PR1721, 23 May 2023.

[98] E.g. *Tadić*, ICTY AC, 2 October 1995; *Kanyabashi*, ICTR TC II, 18 June 1997, paras. 37–50.

[99] José Alvarez, 'Nuremberg Revisited: The Tadić Case' (1996) 7 *EJIL* 245, 253–4; Jessica Almqvist, 'A Human Rights Appraisal of the Limits to Judicial Independence for International Criminal Justice' (2015) 28(1) *LJIL* 91.

[100] ICTY Statute, Art. 13; ICTR Statute, Art. 12; MICT Statute, Art. 9. See also ICTY and ICTR RPE, rr. 14–15 and MICT RPE, rr. 17–18.

apprehend bias, they become liable for disqualification.[101] Although there were many such requests at the Tribunals, they succeeded only in a few cases.[102] There is a strong presumption of impartiality that is not easy to rebut.

The Statute of the ICC, which was established by treaty as an independent international organization, also provides for the guarantees of independence and impartiality of the judges and the Prosecutor (and deputy prosecutors), as well as the right of the accused to a 'fair hearing conducted impartially'.[103] The non-renewable term in office of the judges and prosecutors is one way of ensuring independence and impartiality. A judge or the Prosecutor may be disqualified when 'the circumstances would lead a reasonable observer, properly informed, to reasonably apprehend bias'.[104] This may relate to a personal interest in the outcome, prior involvement in the case, service with a government during judicial tenure, or public airing of a prejudicing opinion.[105]

17.3.3 Presumption of Innocence

Another fundamental human rights principle is that the accused shall be presumed innocent until proven guilty beyond reasonable doubt according to law.[106] Unlike the Tribunals' Statutes, which speak of an 'accused', the ICC Statute extends this presumption to 'everyone', thus making it applicable also during investigation.[107] The ICC Trial Chamber relied upon this principle to excuse one accused, the Deputy President of Kenya, from continuous presence at trial contrary to an explicit statutory provision.[108] Not only the judges but also the prosecution staff have the duty to respect the presumption of innocence, although the content of that duty varies, especially for in-court statements.[109]

One corollary of the presumption of innocence is the right to remain silent and not be compelled to incriminate oneself or confess guilt, which applies throughout.[110] Silence may

---

[101] ICTY and ICTR RPE, r. 15(B); MICT RPE, r. 18(B). See *Furundžija*, ICTY AC, 21 July 2000, paras. 177–91; *Rutaganda*, ICTR AC, 26 May 2003, paras. 39–49.

[102] *Karemera et al.*, ICTR AC, 28 September 2004 and 22 October 2004, paras. 62–8; *Šešelj*, ICTY Chamber, 28 August 2013.

[103] ICC Statute, Arts. 36 (qualifications and election of judges), 40 (independence of judges), 41 (excusing and disqualification of judges), 42(5)–(8) (independence, impartiality and disqualification of the Prosecutor), 45 (solemn undertaking) and 67(1) (fair trial rights). See also ICC RPE, rr. 5–6 and 33–35.

[104] ICC Statute, Arts. 41(2) and 42(7)–(8) and ICC RPE, rr. 33–34. See *Banda and Jerbo*, ICC Plenary of Judges, 5 June 2012 (ICC-02/05–03/09–344-Anx) para. 11; *Lubanga*, ICC Plenary of Judges, 3 August 2015 (ICC-01/04–01/06–3154-AnxI); *Gaddafi and Al-Senussi*, ICC AC, 12 June 2012 (ICC-01/11–01/11–175) paras. 31–4 (the Prosecutor not disqualified yet criticized for inappropriate statements). See further Hirad Abtahi, Odo Ogwuma, and Rebecca Young, 'The Composition of Judicial Benches, Disqualification and Excusal of Judges at the International Criminal Court' (2013) 11 *JICJ* 379.

[105] ICC Statute, Art. 42(7) and ICC RPE, r. 34(1); *Lubanga*, ICC Plenary of Judges, 11 June 2013 (ICC-01/04–01/06–3040); *Gaddafi and Al-Senussi*, ICC AC, 12 June 2012 (ICC-01/11–01/11–175); *Ntaganda*, ICC Presidency, 20 June 2019 (ICC-01/04–02/06–2355), Annex I (re: Judge Ozaki). See also *Sesay et al.*, SCSL AC, 13 March 2004; *Furundžija*, ICTY AC, 21 July 2000, paras. 169–215; *Norman et al.*, SCSL AC, 28 May 2004.

[106] ICTY Statute, Art. 21(3); ICTR Statute, Art. 20(3); MICT Statute, Art. 19(3); ICC Statute, Art. 66(1).

[107] ICC Statute, Art. 66(1) (although Art. 66(1) is contained in Part 6, 'The Trial'). See *Bemba*, ICC PTC II, 14 August 2009 (ICC-01/05–01/08–475) para. 37; *Mbarushimana*, ICC PTC I, 31 January 2011 (ICC-01/04–01/10–51) para. 8.

[108] *Ruto and Sang*, ICC TC V(A), 18 June 2013 (ICC-01/09–01/11–777) para. 48; cf. ICC Statute, Art. 63(1) ('[t]he accused shall be present during the trial'). Although the decision was reversed on appeal (*Ruto and Sang*, ICC AC, 18 June 2013 (ICC-01/09–01/11–1066)), Ruto was subsequently excused based on the freshly-adopted Rule 134*quater* (ICC-ASP/12/Res.7). See *Ruto and Sang*, ICC TC V(A), 18 February 2014 (ICC-01/09–01/11–1186).

[109] *Gaddafi and Al-Senussi*, ICC AC, 12 June 2012 (ICC-01/11–01/11–175) paras. 25–8.

[110] ICTY and ICTR RPE, r. 42(A)(iii); MICT RPE, r. 40(A)(iii); ICC Statute, Art. 55(1)(a) and (2)(b).

not be used as evidence to prove guilt or interpreted as an admission of guilt.[111] An accused refusing to express an opinion as to his or her guilt or innocence shall be considered as not having admitted any guilt.[112]

Another effect of the presumption is that the prosecution must prove the defendant's guilt beyond reasonable doubt, and in case of doubt the accused must be found not guilty (*in dubio pro reo*).[113] Any defences at the Tribunals needed to be established by the accused 'on the balance of probabilities'.[114] But the ICC Statute also envisages the right for the accused 'not to have imposed on him or her any reversal of the burden of proof or any onus of rebuttal'.[115] This provision raises the issue of whether the defence is expected to prove the existence of grounds for excluding criminal responsibility under Article 31. In *Ongwen*, the ICC Appeals Chamber clarified that the defence must present evidence to substantiate its allegations. Yet, this evidentiary burden does not shift the onus of proving the guilt of the accused from the prosecution, as it still must establish the elements of the crimes, including the mental elements, and the mode of liability beyond reasonable doubt.[116]

17.3.4 Public, Fair, and Expeditious Proceedings

The principle of a public hearing allows a public scrutiny of the judicial proceedings and thus a protection against unfairness and arbitrary action by the courts. The Statutes provide for public hearings and delivery of the judgment in public.[117] However, the Tribunals also allowed closed sessions for reasons of public order or morality, safety, security, or non-disclosure of the identity of a protected victim or witness, and the protection of the interests of justice.[118] The ICC Statute provides for two exceptions: protection of the accused, victims, and witnesses; and protection of confidential or sensitive evidence.[119] In all international criminal jurisdictions, protective measures are applied extensively.

While the right to a fair trial as spelled out in the Statutes pertains first and foremost to the accused, fairness as the mandatory attribute of the proceedings benefits all participants including the prosecution.[120] In the ICC, where victims and states also have certain procedural rights, the concept of 'fairness' is more multi-layered.[121] It necessitates finding

[111] ICC Statute, Arts. 55(2) and 67(1)(g). See e.g. *Brđanin*, ICTY TC II, 1 September 2004, para. 24.
[112] ICTY and ICTR RPE, r. 62; and MICT RPE, r. 64; ICC Statute, Art. 64(8)(a).
[113] ICTY and ICTR RPE, r. 87(A); MICT RPE, r. 104(A); ICC Statute, Art. 66.
[114] *Delalić et al.*, ICTY AC, 20 February 2001, para. 603.
[115] ICC Statute, Arts. 66(2)–(3) and 67(1)(i). Cf. ICTY Statute, Art. 21; ICTR Statute, Art. 20; and MICT Statute, Art. 19, which simply refer to the accused being proven guilty 'according to the provisions of the present Statute'.
[116] *Ongwen*, ICC AC, 15 December 2022 (ICC-02/04-01/15-2022-Red) para. 340.
[117] ICTY Statute, Arts. 21(2) and 23(2); ICTR Statute, Arts. 20(2) and 22(2); ICC Statute, Arts. 64(7), 67(1) and 74(5). See also ICTY RPE, rr. 78 and 98*ter*; ICTR RPE, r. 78; MICT RPE, rr. 92 and 122.
[118] ICTY and ICTR RPE, r. 79; and MICT RPE, r. 93. See ICCPR, Art. 14(1) and ECHR, Art. 6(1).
[119] ICC Statute, Arts. 64(7) and 68(1). See also Art. 72(5)(d) (national security information) and ICC RPE, r. 72 (relevance or admissibility of evidence in cases of sexual violence) and rr. 87–88 (protective and special measures).
[120] E.g. *Karemera et al.*, ICTR TC III, 7 December 2004, para. 26; *Milutinović et al.*, ICTY TC III, 30 August 2006, para. 10; and *Situation in Uganda*, ICC PTC II, 19 December 2007, para. 27. See further Vasiliev, 'Trial' (n. 42) 735–8; Yvonne McDermott, 'Rights in Reverse: A Critical Analysis of Fair Trial Rights under International Criminal Law' in Schabas et al., *Ashgate Research Companion*, 165–80.
[121] See Sergey Vasiliev, 'Procedural Fairness in the International Criminal Court' in Arman Sarvarian, Filippo Fontanelli, Rudy Baker, and Vassilis Tzevelekos (eds.), *Procedural Fairness in International Courts and Tribunals* (London, 2015) 361–79.

an equilibrium between the rights of all participants, subject to the prioritization of the rights of the accused, as is made clear in the statutory provisions on victim participation and protective measures.

A fundamental element of a fair trial is the principle of equality of arms, requiring that each party must be given a reasonable opportunity to prepare and present its case under conditions which do not put it at a substantial disadvantage vis-à-vis the opponent.[122] The Tribunals adopted a less demanding interpretation of this principle than domestic courts, owing to the difficulties encountered by the parties in tracing and gaining access to evidence.[123] The accused must have adequate time and facilities to prepare the defence, but this does not mean parity of (financial or human) resources between the parties.[124] The ICC takes a similar legal stance, and the emphasis is rather placed on the adequacy or sufficiency of resources made available to the parties.[125]

Moreover, the accused has the right to prompt and detailed information about the charges, to disclosure of, and access to, the prosecutor's evidence, to defence counsel, to examine witnesses against him or her, and to call witnesses under equal conditions.[126] The right to call witnesses places a positive duty upon the Tribunal to assist the accused with summonses, safe conducts, and other measures necessary for obtaining the testimony.[127]

Each Statute recognizes the right of the accused to be tried without 'undue delay'.[128] The ICTY and ICTR were criticized for excessively long proceedings, which in some extreme cases ran for more than a decade.[129] Although comparisons with historical IMTs are not very telling, the Nuremberg trial lasted some ten months and covered all of the Second World War in the Western theatre. Numerous challenges were launched by the accused claiming violations of this right by the Tribunals, but to no avail.[130] Proponents of different legal traditions tend to attribute delays to different causes. Common law commentators blame the flexible regime for the admissibility of evidence, while civil law observers refer to dilatory tactics of parties to adversarial proceedings and argue for a more active judicial role in the investigation and, based on a 'dossier', at trial.[131] The managerial reforms implemented by the ICTY and, to a more limited extent, ICTR to achieve more expeditious proceedings (some of which were replicated in ICC practice) did not have the expected effect.[132]

---

[122] See further Masha Fedorova, *The Principle of Equality of Arms in International Criminal Proceedings* (Antwerp, 2012).

[123] E.g. *Tadić*, ICTY AC, 15 July 1999, paras. 44 and 52.

[124] E.g. *Kayishema and Ruzindana*, ICTR AC, 1 June 2001, paras. 67–9; *Kordić and Čerkez*, ICTY AC, 17 December 2004, paras. 175–6 and ICTY AC, 11 September 2001, paras. 5–9.

[125] E.g. *Lubanga*, ICC TC I, 14 December 2007 (ICC-01/04–01/06–1091) para. 19 ('absolute equality of arms' is impossible to create); *Kony et al.*, ICC PTC II, 19 August 2005 (ICC-02/04–01/05–20) para. 30.

[126] ICTY Statute, Art. 21(4); ICTR Statute, Art. 20(4); MICT Statute, Art. 19(4); ICC Statute, Art. 67(1).

[127] *Tadić*, ICTY TC II, 26 June 1996; *Kupreškić et al.*, ICTY TC II, 6 October 1998.

[128] ICTY Statute, Art. 21; ICTR Statute, Art. 20; MICT Statute, Art. 19; ICC Statute, Art. 67. See also ICCPR, Art. 14(3).

[129] The period between the arrest and surrender and trial judgment (i.e. excluding appeals) was twelve years in the ICTR's *Government II (Bizimungu et al.)* case and thirteen years in the ICTY's *Šešelj* case.

[130] See e.g. *Bizimungu et al.*, ICTR TC II, 30 September 2011, paras. 66–79 (cf. Partially Dissenting Opinion of Judge Emile Francis Short, paras. 3–7).

[131] See e.g. Peter Murphy, 'No Free Lunch, No Free Proof: The Indiscriminate Admission of Evidence Is a Serious Flaw in International Criminal Trials' (2010) 8 *JICJ* 539; Stéphane Bourgon, 'Procedural Problems Hindering Expeditious and Fair Justice' (2004) 2 *JICJ* 526; Jérôme de Hemptinne, 'The Creation of Investigating Chambers at the International Criminal Court' (2007) 5 *JICJ* 402.

[132] See Máximo Langer and Joseph Doherty, 'Managerial Judging Goes International, but Its Promise Remains Unfulfilled: An Empirical Assessment of the ICTY Reforms' (2011) 36 *Yale Journal of International Law* 241.

International investigations and prosecutions are complex, factually, legally, and politically, and therefore often more time-consuming than domestic ones. Effective case management is indispensable but it can only do so much to reduce the length of the proceedings.

17.4 JURISDICTION AND ADMISSIBILITY PROCEDURES

The Tribunals had jurisdiction over a single 'situation' (encompassing multiple 'cases'), and their jurisdiction and admissibility procedures were rather basic. Challenges to their jurisdiction, of which there have been many in practice, were dealt with as preliminary motions and carried a right of interlocutory appeal.[133]

By contrast, the ICC's jurisdiction extends over multiple situations, and its exercise is subject to the complementarity principle. Accordingly, the ICC has detailed rules for assessing and challenging jurisdiction and admissibility.[134] The Prosecutor and the Chambers must make relevant assessments at various stages, including opening an investigation or seeking an arrest warrant. States with jurisdiction over the crimes may request deferral by the ICC at the outset of an investigation (Article 18) and bring challenges to jurisdiction or admissibility (Article 19). The admissibility test is always case-specific and, therefore, the ICC must examine admissibility in the early stages (before any particular case is selected) more generally in relation to 'potential cases'.[135]

Jurisdiction or the admissibility of a case may be challenged at any time prior to the commencement of the trial, and exceptionally thereafter.[136] This right is afforded to: (1) the accused or a person for whom a warrant of arrest or a summons to appear has been issued; (2) any state with concurrent jurisdiction over the crimes and where investigation or prosecution has been commenced; and (3) any state from which acceptance of jurisdiction is required.[137] To ensure that the scheme is more manageable, states must make their challenge at the earliest opportunity and a person or a state may make a challenge only once.[138]

The admissibility of a case must be determined on the basis of the facts as they exist at the time of the proceedings concerning the challenge.[139] A state or a person challenging the admissibility of a case bears the burden of proving that the case is inadmissible, based on the evidence with 'a sufficient degree of specificity and probative value'.[140] The state must be able to demonstrate that it is taking 'concrete and progressive steps' toward ascertaining the person's responsibility'.[141]

---

[133] ICTY and ICTR RPE, r. 72; MICT RPE, r. 79. [134] See Chapter 8. [135] See Section 8.6.7.
[136] ICC Statute, Art. 19(4); see also *ibid.* Arts. 17(1)(c) and 20(3) and ICC RPE, rr. 58–60. On the meaning of 'prior to or at the commencement of the trial', see *Katanga and Ngudjolo*, ICC PTC II, 16 June 2009 (ICC-01/04–01/07–1213) paras. 29–50.
[137] ICC Statute, Art. 19(2). [138] *Ibid.* Art. 19(4)–(5).
[139] *Katanga and Ngudjolo*, ICC AC, 25 September 2009 (ICC-01/04–01/07–1497) para. 56.
[140] *Ruto et al.*, ICC AC, 30 August 2011 (ICC-01/09–01/11–307) paras. 2, 62; *Muthaura et al.*, ICC AC, 30 August 2011 (ICC-01/09–02/11–274) paras. 2, 61; *Gaddafi*, ICC PTC I, 5 April 2019 (ICC-01/11-01/11-662) paras. 32–3.
[141] *Gaddafi and Al-Senussi*, ICC PTC I, 31 May 2013 (ICC-01/11–01/11–344) paras. 54–5.

17.5 INVESTIGATION

17.5.1 Initiation

The ICTY and ICTR had clear jurisdictional mandates as to crimes, persons, territory, and timeframe, set out in their respective Statutes.[142] Within these parameters, the Prosecutors were competent to initiate investigations.[143] No judicial permission was required, nor was there an obligation to investigate all crimes within the Tribunals' jurisdiction.

Unlike the Tribunals, the ICC has preliminary procedures to select and prioritize situations for investigation from among many within its jurisdiction. There are three 'trigger mechanisms' that allow the Court to actively exercise its jurisdiction and thus can lead to an investigation: a state party can refer a situation; the Security Council can refer a situation; or the Prosecutor can request permission to open an investigation *proprio motu* (on their own motion).[144]

Under any of these trigger mechanisms, the Prosecutor must be satisfied that there is a 'reasonable basis to proceed' with an investigation. They must consider three factors: (1) jurisdiction; (2) admissibility (the complementarity principle and the requirement of 'sufficient gravity'); and (3) the 'interests of justice'.[145] This process of information gathering and analysis is called a 'preliminary examination'.[146] At this stage, the Prosecutor has limited powers; they collect information to determine whether an investigation is warranted.

Where a situation is referred by a state party or the Security Council, a positive decision by the Prosecutor to open an investigation is sufficient. By contrast, where the Prosecutor wishes to initiate an investigation *proprio motu*, they need approval from the PTC which is to satisfy itself that there is a reasonable basis to proceed with an investigation and that (potential) cases arising from it fall within the Court's jurisdiction.[147] In the first five situations in which the Prosecutor initiated investigations *proprio motu*, the PTC applied the same three-pronged legal test as the Prosecutor.[148] However, the practice changed substantially after the Appeals Chamber ruled in the *Situation in Afghanistan* that a PTC decision under Article 15(4) should not include determinations on admissibility and the interests of justice.[149]

When the Prosecutor declines to open an investigation following a state party or Security Council referral, the referring party may request the Chamber to review that decision and

---

[142] See Chapter 7.
[143] No new investigations could be opened after 2004 as a result of the Completion Strategy: see Section 7.2.4.
[144] ICC Statute, Art. 13. [145] *Ibid.* Art. 53(1) and ICC RPE, r. 48.
[146] ICC OTP, *Policy Paper on Preliminary Examinations* (November 2013).
[147] ICC Statute, Art. 15(4); ICC Regulations, reg. 49. See further Section 8.3.6.
[148] ICC Statute, Art. 53(1)(a)–(c). *Situation in Kenya*, ICC PTC II, 31 March 2010 (ICC-01/09–19); *Situation in Côte d'Ivoire*, ICC PTC III, 3 October 2011 (ICC-02/11–14 240); *Situation in Georgia*, ICC PTC I, 27 January 2016 (ICC-01/15-12); *Situation in Burundi*, ICC PTC III, 9 November 2017 (ICC-01/17-9-Red); *Situation in Bangladesh/Myanmar*, ICC PTC III, 14 November 2019 (ICC-01/19-27).
[149] *Situation in Afghanistan*, ICC AC, 5 March 2020 (ICC-02/17-138) paras. 24–467 (holding that Art. 53(1) applies only in case of state party or the Security Council referrals). See e.g. *Situation in the Philippines*, ICC PTC I, 15 September 2021 (ICC-01/21-12). For a criticism, see Lloyd T. Chigowe, 'The ICC and the Situation in Afghanistan: A Critical Examination of the Role of the Pre-Trial Chambers in the Initiation of Investigations *Proprio Motu*' (2022) 35 *LJIL* 699 (the AC inappropriately limited the scope of PTC review of prosecutorial decisions to initiate an investigation).

invite the Prosecutor to reconsider it.[150] In case the Prosecutor decides not to investigate solely on the 'interests of justice' ground, the Chamber may request the Prosecutor to reconsider on its own initiative.[151] In the former case, the Chamber requests are not binding and the Prosecutor may still decline to initiate an investigation upon reconsideration. This is what happened in the now-closed *Situation on Registered Vessels of the Union of the Comoros etc.*[152] But where the Prosecutor's decision not to proceed is based on the 'interests of justice', it only becomes effective if confirmed by the Chamber. A system of checks and balances between the Prosecutor and the judiciary is built into the ICC Statute, and in case of referrals judicial supervision is stronger with respect to prosecutorial decisions not to proceed based on the discretionary ground of the 'interests of the justice'.

The selection of situations and cases has always been a highly contentious matter because of the amount of discretion held by the Prosecutor. A 'situation' typically includes a large number of crimes, incidents, and potential defendants. Within a given 'situation', an investigation will yield a limited set of more specific 'cases' which may be selected for prosecution in accordance with the relevant criteria. The Prosecutor will accord priority to cases involving: (1) the gravest crimes; (2) those most responsible; and (3) the main types of victimization, including a focus on sexual and gender-based crimes and crimes against children.[153] In assessing gravity, the prosecutor looks at the scale, nature, and manner of commission, and the impact of the crimes.[154] The gravity of possible future cases within a situation will be part of the 'situational gravity' assessment when prioritizing among several situations competing for the prosecutor's attention.

17.5.2 Conduct

At both the ad hoc Tribunals and the ICC, the Prosecutor is in charge of the criminal investigation and has the authority to take necessary measures.[155] The ICC Pre-Trial Chamber also exercises important functions in that context, albeit not as an investigating body. This concerns the protection of victims and witnesses, preservation of evidence, protection of persons who have been arrested or appeared in response to a summons (including in cases of unique investigative opportunity), and protection of national security information.[156]

The prosecutors at the Tribunals were not obliged to actively search for exculpatory evidence but only to disclose it if it came into their possession. By contrast, the ICC Prosecutor has a statutory duty of objectivity, that is, the obligation to 'investigate

---

[150] ICC Statute, Art. 53(3)(a).   [151] *Ibid.* Art. 53(3)(b).
[152] *Situation on Registered Vessels of the Union of the Comoros* . . ., ICC PTC I, 16 July 2015 (ICC-01/13–34) (requesting the Prosecutor to reconsider decision not to proceed). The Prosecutor reconsidered and affirmed her decision: ICC OTP, 20 November 2017 (ICC-01/13–57) and Article 53(1) Report, 6 November 2014 (ICC-01/13–6-AnxA).
[153] ICC OTP Regulations, reg. 34; ICC OTP, *Policy Paper on Case Selection and Prioritisation* (15 September 2016) paras. 35–46; ICC OTP, *Policy on the Crime of Gender Persecution*, 7 December 2022, para. 82 (investigative and prosecutorial focus on 'most responsible'); ICC OTP, *Strategic Plan 2023–2025* (13 June 2023) para. 59 and 61–2.
[154] ICC Regulations of the OTP, reg. 29(2). See also ICC OTP, *Policy Paper on Preliminary Examinations* (November 2013) paras. 61–6; *Policy on the Crime of Gender Persecution* (n. 153) para. 67 ('multiple forms of persecution, the multi-faceted character of the . . . acts, and the resulting suffering, harm and other impacts').
[155] ICTY and ICTR RPE, r. 39(ii); MICT RPE, r. 36(B); ICC Statute, Art. 54(1)(b).   [156] ICC Statute, Arts. 56 and 57(3).

incriminating and exonerating circumstances equally'.[157] Compliance with this duty posed problems in the earlier cases as the potentially exculpatory evidence was not methodically searched for and collected.[158]

Each investigation is conducted by a multidisciplinary team of lawyers, investigators, analysts, psychologists, international cooperation advisers, forensic experts, and country specialists.[159] Investigative measures include questioning individuals (suspects, victims, witnesses, and experts), collecting written and other material, exhuming mass graves, and other forensic measures. The suspect's rights to remain silent, to obtain legal assistance, and to interpretation must be observed at questioning; serious breaches might affect the use of statements at trial.[160] A key task, shared by the prosecution and the Chambers, is to provide for the protection of victims and witnesses.[161]

Without an international police force to carry out the investigative measures and enforce court orders, the investigation depends to a large extent upon the cooperation of states and other entities such as peacekeeping forces.[162] The Prosecutor is entitled to seek cooperation in the investigation.[163] A Chamber may also issue necessary orders and warrants; any orders to states for the production of documents must be sufficiently specific.[164] The defence may thus seek cooperation from a state and, in the ICC, an order directed to the Prosecutor regarding specific investigative measures.[165] The ICC Prosecutor's power to conduct on-site investigations is very limited and encompasses non-coercive measures only.[166] But if the state has collapsed, the ICC Pre-Trial Chamber may authorize the Prosecutor 'to take specific investigative steps within the territory of a State without having secured the cooperation of that State', which is not explicitly restricted to non-coercive measures.[167]

International criminal investigations are challenging, given restricted access to evidence, lack of cooperation by states and other actors, ongoing security concerns, cultural and linguistic barriers, and different views on best practices in multinational and multidisciplinary teams.[168] The mixed success regarding confirmation of charges and prosecutions during the first two decades of the Court's existence led to intense criticism of the ICC Prosecutor's approach to investigations. Judges thoroughly criticized the prosecution's investigative practices and case strategies, noting repeatedly its failure to verify the credibility and reliability of the evidence and bring strong cases to trial.[169] These

[157] ICC Statute, Art. 54(1)(a).
[158] See e.g. Caroline Buisman, 'The Prosecutor's Obligation to Investigate Incriminating and Exonerating Circumstances Equally: Illusion or Reality?' (2014) 27(1) *LJIL* 205.
[159] On the 'unified teams' concept, see Proposed Programme Budget for 2022, ICC-ASP/20/10 (16 August 2021) paras. 239–45.
[160] ICTY Statute, Art. 18(3); ICTR Statute, Art. 17(3); MICT Statute, Art. 16(3); ICTY and ICTR RPE, r. 42; MICT RPE, rr. 40–41; ICC Statute, Art. 55. See e.g. *Halilović*, ICTY AC, 19 August 2005; *Delalić et al.*, ICTY TC II, 2 September 1997, para. 55.
[161] See Chapter 18.   [162] See Chapter 20.
[163] ICTY Statute, Art. 18(2); ICTR Statute, Art. 17(2); MICT Statute, Art. 16(2); ICC Statute, Art. 54(3)(c).
[164] ICTY RPE, rr. 54 and 54*bis*; MICT RPE, rr. 55–56; ICC Statute, Art. 57(3) and ICC RPE, r. 105. See e.g. *Blaškić*, ICTY AC, 29 October 1997, para. 32.
[165] ICC Statute, Art. 57(3)(b); e.g. *Banda and Jerbo*, ICC TC IV, 1 July 2011 (ICC-02/05–03/09–169) para. 31.
[166] ICC Statute, Art. 99(4). Cf. ICTY Statute, Art. 18(2); ICTR Statute, Art. 17(2); MICT Statute, Art. 16(3). See further Section 20.6.3.
[167] ICC Statute, Arts. 54(2) and 57(3)(d) and ICC RPE, r. 115.
[168] Hiroto Fujiwara and Stephan Parmentier, 'Investigations' in Reydams et al. *International Prosecutors* (n. 42) 573–5.
[169] E.g. *Lubanga*, ICC TC I, 14 March 2012 (ICC-01/04–01/06–284) paras. 124–68 and 896; *Ngudjolo*, ICC TC II, 18 December 2012 (ICC-01/04–02/12–3) paras. 115–23; *Kenyatta*, ICC TC V(B), 3 December 2014 (ICC-01/09–02/11–981) paras. 47–52; Opinion of Judge Cuno Tarfusser, *Gbagbo and Blé Goudé*, ICC TC I, 16 July 2019 (ICC-02/11-01/15-1263-AnxA) paras. 89–95 and Reasons of Judge Geoffrey Henderson (ICC-02/11-01/15-1263-AnxB-Red), *ibid.* paras. 66–91, 2038–41.

discontents brought about a substantial revision of the Prosecutor's policies and practices.[170] Thus, heavy reliance upon intermediaries without adequate supervision, revealed as a serious problem in the first cases,[171] was addressed by developing guidelines, a code of conduct, and a model contract for intermediaries. Moreover, the initial approach of small-scale and target-driven investigations, resulting in overly narrow charges, gave way to the strategy oriented at open-ended, in-depth investigations in a smaller number of situations. The prosecution also strove to bring more manageable cases, prioritized considering their relative gravity and prospect of success, as a way to deliver results in a courtroom and ensure a higher conviction rate.[172]

17.6 COERCIVE MEASURES

In any criminal investigations and proceedings, it must be possible to resort to coercive measures, such as arrest, search of premises, seizure of documents, etc. For such measures, the prosecutor will have to resort to the cooperation of states or other entities such as international military or police forces. While the Tribunals' prosecutors were entitled, under certain conditions, to undertake coercive measures directly on a state's territory,[173] the ICC Prosecutor's powers are limited to non-coercive measures and, other than in a failed state scenario, they have to go through national authorities.[174] Evidence obtained in contravention of the Statute or internationally recognized human rights may be declared inadmissible, which applies also to items seized by national authorities or international peacekeepers.[175]

17.6.1 Arrest and Detention

At the Tribunals, arrest warrants were issued by a judge following confirmation of the indictment in whole or in part, the applicable standard being a *'prima facie* case'.[176] Persons were generally detained upon being transferred to the Tribunal.[177] But in accordance with human rights law, there was also a possibility for the accused to request provisional release.[178] The Trial Chamber could order it if satisfied that the accused would appear for trial and, if released, would pose no danger to any victim, witness, or other persons. The initial requirement of 'extraordinary circumstances' as a precondition for release was deleted because, in human rights law, detention must be the exception rather than the rule.

---

[170] E.g. Full Statement of the Prosecutor, Fatou Bensouda, on external expert review and lessons drawn from the Kenya situation, 26 November 2019.
[171] *Lubanga*, ICC TC I, 7 March 2011 (ICC-01/04–01/07–2690-Red) and 14 March 2012 (ICC-01/04–01/06–284) paras. 482, 484; *Katanga*, ICC TC II, 7 July 2011 (ICC-01/04–01/07–3064) paras. 42–9.
[172] *Independent Expert Review of the International Criminal Court and the Rome Statute System; Final Report*, 30 September 2020 ('IER Report') para. 743 *et seq.*; ICC OTP, *Strategic Plan 2023–2025* (n. 159) paras. 22–4.
[173] E.g. *Kordić and Čerkez*, ICTY TC III, 25 June 1999 (the investigation, resulting in the seizure of certain material, 'was perfectly within the Prosecutor's powers as provided for in the Statute'); *Blaškić*, ICTY AC, 29 October 1997, para. 55. See Section 20.6.3.
[174] ICC Statute, Art. 57(3)(d).
[175] *Ibid.* Art. 69(7). See also *Lubanga*, ICC PTC I, 29 January 2007 (ICC-01/04–01/06–803) paras. 62–94.
[176] ICTY and ICTR RPE, rr. 47(H)(i) and 54; MICT RPE, rr. 48(H)(i) and 57.
[177] ICTY and ICTR RPE, r. 64; MICT RPE, r. 67.
[178] ICTY and ICTR RPE, r. 65; MICT RPE, r. 68. See ICCPR, Art. 9(3); ECHR, Art. 5(1); ACHPR, Art. 6; ACHR, Art. 7(1).

At the ICC, the PTC issues arrest warrants and, if the person is surrendered, decides on interim release.[179] Unlike at the Tribunals, the Chamber is required to review its rulings on interim release or detention periodically on its own motion (at least every 120 days) and may do so at any time on the request of a party.[180] Upon confirmation of charges, the Trial Chamber takes over the function of reviewing detention; such reviews do not occur automatically after the start of the trial.[181]

For the arrest warrant to be issued, there must be 'reasonable grounds to believe' that the person has committed a crime and, additionally, the risk that the suspect will abscond, obstruct or endanger the investigation or court proceedings, or continue to commit related crimes.[182] The same prerequisites must be assessed when the ICC decides on interim release and, if any criterion is not met, the person is to be released, with or without conditions.[183] The ICC also has the option to issue a 'summons to appear' instead of an arrest warrant, when this is considered sufficient to ensure the person's appearance.[184]

17.6.2 Remedying Violations

The Tribunals' Statutes had no explicit provision for challenges to the legality of deprivation of liberty, comparable to the common law remedy of *habeas corpus*.[185] Nonetheless, the ICTR Appeals Chamber held in *Barayagwiza* that a detained individual must have recourse to a court to challenge the lawfulness of detention.[186]

When the violation of the accused's rights is considered 'serious and egregious', the Tribunals had a discretionary power to stay the proceedings temporarily or dismiss the case with reference to the 'abuse of process' doctrine.[187] This is an exceptional measure, however, and less drastic remedies would normally be employed, such as a reduction of an imposed sentence or, if acquitted, compensation.[188]

The same power and obligation to decline to exercise jurisdiction exists at the ICC.[189] A permanent stay is an exceptional remedy, to be applied when it is 'impossible to piece together the constituent elements of a fair trial'.[190] A conditional stay may be imposed if

---

[179] ICC Statute, Arts. 58(5), 91 (arrest and surrender) and 92 (provisional arrest). [180] *Ibid.* Art. 60(3) and ICC RPE, r. 118(2).
[181] E.g. *Bemba*, ICC TC III, 1 April 2010 (ICC-01/05–01/08–743) para. 25. Chambers Practice Manual, 7th edition (2023) para. 85.
[182] ICC Statute, Art. 58(1). On the evidentiary standard, see *Al Bashir*, ICC AC, 3 February 2010 (ICC-02/05–01/09–73) paras. 31–9; *Gbagbo*, ICC PTC I, 30 November 2011 (ICC-02/11–01/11–9) para. 27.
[183] ICC Statute, Art. 60(2) and ICC RPE, r. 118 (and r. 119 on conditional release).
[184] ICC Statute, Art. 58(7) and ICC RPE, r. 119. See *Abu Garda*, ICC PTC I, 7 May 2009 (ICC-02/05–02/09–15); cf. *Harun and Al Kushayb*, ICC PTC I, 27 April 2007 (ICC-02/05–01/07–1) paras. 115–24 (summonses found insufficient).
[185] The writ of *habeas corpus* is a judicial remedy in common law jurisdictions originating from Magna Carta and allowing to challenge executive committals.
[186] *Barayagwiza*, ICTR AC, 3 November 1999, para. 88. See also Universal Declaration of Human Rights, Art. 8; ICCPR, Art. 9 (4); ECHR, Art. 5(4); ACHR, Art. 7(6) and ACHPR, Art. 7(1)(a).
[187] *Barayagwiza*, ICTR AC, 3 November 1999, para. 74; *Dragan Nikolić*, ICTY TC II, 9 October 2002, para. 114, and ICTY AC, 5 June 2003, paras. 28–30; *Nahimana et al.*, ICTR AC, 4 August 2004; *Karadžić*, ICTY TC III, 8 July 2009, paras. 80–8.
[188] E.g. *Kajelijeli*, ICTR AC, 23 May 2005, paras. 206, 254–5, 320; *Rwamakuba*, ICTR TC III, 31 January 2007; and *Gatete*, ICTR AC, 9 October 2012, para. 286.
[189] *Lubanga*, ICC AC, 14 December 2006 (ICC-01/04–01/06–772) paras. 24–39; *Lubanga*, ICC TC I, 13 June 2008 (ICC-01/04–01/06–1401) paras. 90–1.
[190] *Lubanga*, ICC AC, 8 October 2010 (ICC-01/04–01/06–2582) para. 55; *Lubanga*, ICC AC, 21 October 2008 (ICC-01/04–01/06–1486) and TC 7 March 2011 (ICC-01/04–01/07–2690-Red); *Mbarushimana*, ICC PTC I, 1 July 2011 (ICC-01/04–01/10–264) 7–8 ('gross violations').

the unfairness can be cured, for example when disclosure of exculpatory evidence was prevented by the provider of the material, pending the adoption of adequate remedial measures.[191] In addition, the Statute guarantees anyone who has been the victim of unlawful arrest or detention an enforceable right to compensation.[192] A reduction in sentence is also a possible remedy.[193] In exceptional circumstances where 'a grave and manifest miscarriage of justice' has been established, a person released from detention following a final acquittal or termination of the proceedings may be awarded compensation.[194]

Can the legality of domestic coercive measures be reviewed and, if so, which legal standard should be applied? The Tribunals reviewed domestic actions when the possible violation could be attributed to them.[195] In *Kajelijeli*, however, the ICTR held it was not competent to pronounce itself on the responsibility of the state for any violations, only on faults attributable to the Tribunal.[196]

Some fugitives came within the ICTY jurisdiction through irregular rendition practices such as luring and abduction.[197] The Appeals Chamber concluded in *Nikolić* that sovereign and individual rights must be weighed against the interest of bringing those accused of 'universally condemned offences' to justice (the 'Eichmann exception').[198] A minor intrusion, particularly when the violated state is in default of its cooperation obligations and/or has not complained, was not sufficient to decline jurisdiction.

The ICC Statute provides that the legality of the arrest process in the custodial state is primarily a matter for domestic courts, which, however, may not consider the legality of the ICC warrant.[199] The Court's role is not to review the correctness of domestic decisions, but instead 'to see that the process envisaged by [national] law was duly followed and that the rights of the arrestee were properly respected'.[200] The Court will only divest itself of jurisdiction if fundamental rights violations have resulted from 'concerted action' between the Prosecutor and national authorities or third parties.

17.7 PROSECUTION

17.7.1 Decision to Prosecute

It is the prosecutor's prerogative to decide whether and whom to indict, but the prosecution of the case is subject to judicial review. The charges or indictment must be confirmed by a judge or a chamber to progress to a pre-trial stage.

---

[191] E.g. *Lubanga*, ICC TC I, 13 June 2008 (ICC-01/04–01/06–1401), and ICC AC, 21 October 2008 (ICC-01/04–01/06–1486) paras. 80–3.
[192] ICC Statute, Art. 85(1). [193] *Lubanga*, ICC TC, 10 July 2012 (ICC-01/ 04–01/06–2901) paras. 89–90.
[194] ICC Statute, Art. 85(3). See *Bemba*, ICC PTC II, 18 May 2020 (ICC-01/05-01/08-3694) (refusing compensation).
[195] *Barayagwiza*, ICTR AC, 3 November 1999; *Kajelijeli*, ICTR AC, 23 May 2005; *Delalić et al.*, ICTY TC II, 2 September 1997, confirmed in ICTY AC, 20 February 2001, paras. 528–64.
[196] *Kajelijeli*, ICTR AC, 23 May 2005, paras. 219–21, 252.
[197] E.g. *Dokmanović*, ICTY TC II, 22 October 1997. See also *Simić et al.*, ICTY TC III, 18 October 2000 (Stevan Todorović was abducted from Serbia by unknown individuals and delivered to SFOR, with whom the prosecutor had a confidential cooperation agreement. Todorović then entered into a plea agreement).
[198] *Dragan Nikolić*, ICTY AC, 5 June 2003, paras. 24–7. On the *Eichmann* case, see Chapter 3 and Section 5.4.7.
[199] ICC Statute, Art. 59(2)(c) and (4). [200] *Lubanga*, ICC AC, 14 December 2006 (ICC-01/04–01/06–772) paras. 41–2.

At the ICTY and ICTR, the decision whether to prosecute was a matter of broad discretion. The required standard for prosecuting was a '*prima facie* case'.[201] There was no obligation to prosecute all possible cases.[202] The prosecutorial focus was on those bearing the greatest responsibility, and internal 'selection criteria' guided the work. In light of the demands of the Completion Strategy, this focus was further narrowed down to 'most senior leaders suspected of being most responsible'.[203] There were only very limited grounds to challenge the exercise of discretion: for example, discriminatory or otherwise unlawful or improper motives.[204]

For the case to be prosecuted at the ICC, there must be a 'sufficient basis for prosecution', which involves the consideration of the following three factors: sufficient basis to seek an arrest warrant or a summons; admissibility; and the interests of justice.[205] A decision not to prosecute is subject to judicial review by the Pre-Trial Chamber under the same terms as a decision not to commence an investigation.[206] Within the universe of cases meeting the criteria for prosecution, the ICC Prosecutor employs a case selection policy of focusing on the persons most responsible for the crimes.[207] This does not mean exclusively targeting most senior leaders but may also entail prosecuting lower-level perpetrators, whose conduct is 'particularly grave or notorious', not least in order to build cases upwards.[208]

17.7.2 Indictment and Charges

Upon investigation, the Prosecutor prepares a charging instrument, referred to as 'indictment' in the Tribunals and 'document containing the charges' (DCC) at the ICC. This instrument delineates the prosecution case and ultimately defines the scope of the trial.[209]

Framing an indictment or charges is a complex exercise. International indictments often cover multiple alleged perpetrators and criminal incidents taking place in different geographic locations over long periods of time.[210] It is almost inevitable that such indictments are less specific on the facts underlying the charges than is the norm in civil law jurisdictions. But an adequate degree of specificity is critical to upholding the rights of the accused to a fair hearing, to be informed promptly and in detail of the nature and cause of the charges, and to have adequate time and facilities for the preparation of the defence.[211]

Over time, after numerous challenges to the form of indictments, a relatively consistent practice has evolved at the Tribunals.[212] The indictment must include the 'material facts'

[201] ICTY Statute, Art. 18(4); ICTR Statute, Art. 17(4); MICT Statute, Art. 16(4).
[202] *Sikirica et al.*, ICTY TC, 5 May 1998 (an otherwise valid indictment withdrawn due to a new prosecutorial strategy).
[203] UNSC Res. 1503(2003), 28 August 2003 and 1534(2004), 26 March 2004, para. 5.
[204] *Delalić et al.*, ICTY AC, 20 February 2001, paras. 596–618. [205] ICC Statute, Art. 53(2). [206] *Ibid.* Art. 53(3)(b).
[207] See n. 153. [208] ICC OTP, *Policy Paper on Case Selection and Prioritisation* (15 September 2016) paras. 42–3.
[209] ICTY Statute, Art. 18(4); ICTR Statute, Art. 17(4); MICT Statute, Art. 16(4); ICTY and ICTR RPE, r. 47(C) and MICT RPE, r. 48(C); ICC Statute, Art. 61(3)(a).
[210] See Elinor Fry, 'International Crimes and Case Demarcation: What Are We Trying to Prove?' (2015) 27(2) *Florida Journal of International Law* 163.
[211] ICTY Statute, Art. 21(2) and (4)(a)–(b); ICTR Statute, Art. 20(2) and (4)(a)–(b); MICT Statute, Art. 19(2) and (4)(a)–(b); ICC Statute, Art. 67(1) (a)–(b).
[212] For a survey of case law, see *Blaškić*, ICTY, AC, 29 July 2004, paras. 207–21; *Ntakirutimana*, ICTR AC, 13 December 2004, paras. 21–9, 469–77. See also Håkan Friman et al., 'Charges' in Sluiter et al., *International Criminal Procedure*, 384–97.

underpinning the charges, with enough detail to allow the preparation of the defence. What constitutes a material fact, however, depends on the formulation of the legal charge and the elements of the offences; and the required specificity, in terms of dates, locations, identity of the victims, and other details, will depend mainly on the nature of the alleged criminal conduct. While some defects in the indictment could be cured through amendment and giving the defence additional time to prepare, fundamental flaws could result in the Trial Chamber disregarding the charge or a reversal of conviction on appeal.[213]

At the ICC, the accused must be provided with a 'detailed description of the charges' before the confirmation hearing.[214] With the experience of the Tribunals in mind, the ICC Regulations are more detailed concerning the content of the DCC.[215] At the ICC, the Pre-Trial Chamber and not the Prosecutor has the final say on the framing of the charges. By confirming the charges, the Pre-Trial Chamber fixes the 'facts and circumstances' encompassed within the charges that can subsequently be tried, thus binding the Trial Chamber.[216] Crucially, a conviction may not be based on 'facts and circumstances' *not* described in the charges.[217]

As in a domestic context, indictments may be amended or withdrawn by the Prosecutor.[218] Amendments and clarifications were common at the ICTY and ICTR, and the required judicial approval was normally granted; the main issue being whether the amendment would cause unfair prejudice to the accused or result in delays.[219] An entirely new charge required a new confirmation and support by evidence.

After confirmation, the ICC Prosecutor may amend the charges only with the permission of the Pre-Trial Chamber. Additional or more serious charges require a new confirmation procedure.[220] A withdrawal of charges after confirmation and before the trial commences is not contemplated in the Statute or RPE. But it was accepted by a Trial Chamber when the prosecution no longer had a reasonable prospect of securing evidence for a conviction and the accused did not object.[221] After the trial commences, the charges may be withdrawn with leave of the Trial Chamber.[222]

Another question of great practical relevance is what should happen if the legal label chosen by the Prosecutor to characterize the conduct in the indictment is found not to be suitable, and if the facts established at trial rather indicate that the accused should be convicted under a different legal provision. Must the court acquit the accused on a legal technicality? To prevent this, the Tribunals followed a common law approach of allowing multiple counts to be stated in the indictment from which the court could choose the most

---

[213] E.g. *Krnojelac*, ICTY AC, 17 September 2003, paras. 138–42; *Muhimana*, ICTR AC, 21 May 2007, paras. 217–18, 224–6 (cf. the Dissenting Opinion by Judge Schomburg).
[214] ICC Statute, Art. 61(3); ICC RPE, r. 121(3).
[215] ICC Regulations, reg. 52. See e.g. *Bemba*, ICC PTC II, 15 June 2009 (ICC-01/05–01/08–424) paras. 65–70.
[216] ICC Statute, Arts. 61(7) and (9) and 74(2). See *Lubanga*, ICC TC I, 13 December 2007 (ICC-01/04–01/06–1084) paras. 39–43.
[217] *Bemba*, ICC AC, 8 June 2018 (ICC-01/05–01/08–3636-Red) paras. 105–16.
[218] ICTY RPE, ICTR RPE and MICT RPE, rr. 50–51; ICC Statute, Art. 61 (4). See Friman et al., 'Charges' (n. 212) 415–23.
[219] E.g. *Naletilić and Martinović*, ICTY TC I, 14 February 2001; *Kovačević*, ICTY AC, 2 July 1998; *Karemera et al.*, ICTR AC, 19 December 2003.
[220] ICC Statute, Art. 61(4) and (9). See *Kenyatta*, ICC PTC II, 21 March 2013 (ICC-01/09–02/11–700-Corr) (amendment granted); cf. *Ruto and Sang*, ICC PTC II, 16 August 2013 (ICC-01/09–01/11–859) (belated amendment rejected).
[221] *Muthaura and Kenyatta*, ICC TC V, 18 March 2013 (ICC-01/09–02/11–696) para. 11.   [222] ICC Statute, Art. 61(9).

suitable legal characterization. By contrast, the ICC adheres to the civil law approach, in that it recognizes the principle of *iura novit curia* ('court knows the law'), whereby the judges may modify the legal characterization of the facts subject to relevant guarantees.

Regulation 55 of the ICC Regulations of the Court allows a Trial Chamber to determine that the facts and circumstances pleaded should be characterized as a different crime or a different form of liability than that charged and notify the participants that the legal label may be subject to change.[223] Any such legal recharacterization may not exceed 'facts and circumstances' described in the charges and is subject to safeguards affording the accused adequate time and facilities to prepare, adjust their defence strategy, and, if necessary, re-examine previous witnesses or call new evidence.[224] The ICC Chambers have made use of the power to issue a notice on the possible change of the mode liability in some cases.[225] The practice with respect to Regulation 55 proved particularly problematic, and arguably prejudicial to the accused, in the *Katanga* case, among others, due to the lateness of the notification which was made during deliberations.[226]

17.8 PRE-TRIAL PROCESS

17.8.1 First Appearance and Confirmation of Charges

In conformity with human rights law, the suspect makes the initial appearance before the judge promptly upon arrival at the Tribunal or Court.[227] The Chamber checks that the person has been served with the indictment (Tribunals) or arrest warrant (ICC) and that his or her rights have been respected. At the Tribunals, the accused was formally charged and allowed to enter a plea to the charges at the initial (or further) appearance. In case of a plea of not guilty, a date for trial was set, while a guilty plea, if accepted by the Chamber, led directly to a sentencing hearing.[228] At the ICC, the purpose of the first appearance, apart from the assurance of rights, is to set a date for the confirmation of charges.[229]

For the person to be formally committed for trial, the indictment or charges must be judicially reviewed, which ensures that they concern crimes within jurisdiction and that prosecution is warranted by the supporting evidence. Judicial review of the indictment at the Tribunals took place *prior to* the arrest and surrender of the person in a simple and *ex parte* (prosecution-only) process.[230] The evidentiary threshold for confirmation ('*prima*

---

[223] ICC Regulations of the Court, reg. 55(1)–(2).

[224] *Ibid.* reg. 55(3). E.g. *Lubanga*, ICC AC, 8 December 2009 (ICC-01/04–01/06–2205).

[225] E.g. *Al Hassan*, ICC TC X, 25 June 2021 (ICC-01/12-01/18-1211-Red); *Ali Kushayb*, ICC TC I, 18 March 2022 (ICC-02/05-01/20-634). See further Håkan Friman, 'Trial Procedures, with a Particular Focus on the Relationship Between the Proceedings of the Pre-Trial and Trial Chambers' in Stahn, *The Law and Practice of the ICC*, 916–19.

[226] *Katanga and Ngudjolo*, ICC TC II, 21 November 2012 (ICC-01/04–01/07–3319) (Judge van den Wyngaert dissenting) and ICC AC, 27 March 2013 (ICC-01/04–01/07–3363) (Judge Tarfusser dissenting); *Katanga*, ICC TC II, 7 March 2014 (ICC-01/04–01/07–3436-tENG) (Judge Christine Van den Wyngaert dissenting, ICC-01/04–01/07–3436-AnxI, 11 March 2014). See Melanie Klinkner, 'Is All Fair in Love and War Crimes Trials? Regulation 55 and the *Katanga* Case' (2015) 15 *ICLR* 396; Kevin Jon Heller, '"A Stick to Hit the Accused With": The Legal Recharacterization of Facts under Regulation 55' in Stahn, *The Law and Practice of the ICC*, 981–1006.

[227] ICTY and ICTR RPE, r. 62; MICT RPE, r. 64; ICC Statute, Art. 60(1) and ICC RPE, r. 121. See ICCPR, Art. 9(3); ECHR, Art. 5(3); ACHR, Art. 7(5).

[228] See Section 17.10. [229] See also Chambers Practice Manual (n. 181) paras. 10–14.

[230] ICTY Statute, Art. 19; ICTR Statute, Art. 18; MICT Statute, Art. 18.

facie case') was low: a credible case which, if not contradicted by the defence, would be a sufficient basis to convict the accused on the charge.[231]

By contrast, the ICC has a much more elaborate confirmation procedure, with a robust process for the disclosure of evidence and an adversarial and public hearing held *after* the person's first appearance.[232] The person is entitled to challenge the Prosecutor's evidence and to present his or her own evidence.[233] The Chamber is to assess each charge and either confirm or dismiss it, or it may request the Prosecutor to consider providing further evidence or amending a charge.[234] The Prosecutor must support the charges with 'sufficient evidence to establish substantial grounds to believe that the person committed the crime charged', at this stage normally documentary or summary evidence.[235] The 'substantial grounds' threshold is higher than the '*prima facie*' standard.[236]

The nature and strength of evidence required by the confirmation standard, and the exact procedural purpose of the confirmation, are contentious.[237] The major concern has been that the confirmation process easily turns into a 'trial before the trial' unless the Pre-Trial Chamber exercises restraint and refrains from prejudging matters best reserved for the judges at trial. In practice, confirmation procedures have been long, with hearings lasting days, witnesses being examined, and lengthy and detailed decisions being issued; they also contributed little to expediting trials. At the same time, confirmations have served a useful screening purpose. The charges were rejected in several cases, thereby blocking weak cases from progressing further. The question remains how to preserve this advantage while keeping confirmations manageable and precluding 'mini-trials', and the approaches across Pre-Trial Chambers have varied significantly.[238]

17.8.2 Preparation for Trial

An average international trial lasts for several years and involves examination of dozens of witnesses. Such a complex and large-scale operation is easily derailed. A thorough preparation by the judges and parties is therefore a *sine qua non* for the smooth running of the trial proceedings.

As part of preparation, the Chamber should attend to a range of preliminary issues which would cause delays if not resolved before trial, including jurisdictional challenges, evidentiary matters (in particular the disclosure of evidence), and protective measures for witnesses.[239] It must also decide on joinder or severance of trials against multiple accused.[240] Joint trials may promote judicial economy, avoid duplication of evidence and repeated witness appearances, and ensure the consistency of verdicts, but a related concern is the possible prejudice to the accused as a result of a lengthier process and any conflict of interests.

---

[231] E.g. *Milošević*, ICTY Judge, 22 November 2001, paras. 11–15. [232] ICC Statute, Art. 61(1). [233] *Ibid.* Art. 61(6).
[234] *Ibid.* Art. 61(7). [235] *Ibid.* Art. 61(5). [236] *Mbarushimana*, ICC AC, 30 May 2012 (ICC-01/04–01/10–514) para. 43.
[237] E.g. *Gbagbo*, ICC PTC I, 3 June 2013 (ICC-02/11–01/11–432) para. 25 ('strongest possible case based on a largely completed investigation') and 12 June 2014 (ICC-02/11–01/11–656-Red), Dissenting Opinion of Judge Van den Wyngaert, para. 4: 'realistic chance of supporting a conviction beyond reasonable doubt'. Triestino Mariniello, 'Questioning the Standard of Proof: The Purpose of the ICC Confirmation of Charges Procedure' (2015) 13 *JICJ* 579.
[238] IER Report (n. 172) paras. 483–9. [239] ICTY and ICTR RPE, rr. 54, 72–73; MICT RPE, rr. 55, 70, 79–80.
[240] ICTY RPE, rr. 48, 49 and 82; ICTR RPE, rr. 48, 48*bis*, 49 and 82; MICT RPE, rr. 49 and 97.

At the ICC, preparatory activities also involve the Trial Chamber issuing directions for the conduct of trial, organizing victim participation and representation, deciding on victim applications, and determining any case admissibility challenges. The ICC Statute and RPE do not regulate the conduct of trial proceedings in detail. Before each trial, the Trial Chamber (or a designated single judge)[241] determines the trial scheme, in consultation with the parties.[242] Judges issue directions on how the process will be structured and evidence submitted and examined, which are subject to further rulings at trial.[243]

A controversial issue, on which the main legal traditions offer cardinally different approaches, is whether the parties may substantively prepare witnesses by going through their statements shortly before testimony ('witness proofing'), as opposed to merely acquainting witnesses with the trial process ('witness familiarization'). Witness preparation was routinely allowed in the ICTY and ICTR.[244] The ICC prohibited it in the first cases, referring to 'helpful spontaneity' of unprepared witnesses.[245] Subsequently, several Trial Chambers authorized witness preparation, although practice has not been uniform.[246]

In the interest of efficiency, all courts have employed case-management tools allowing judges to exercise control over trial preparation, such as pre-trial (or pre-appeal) judges,[247] status conferences,[248] and pre-trial and pre-defence conferences.[249] Some of these practices have now been consolidated by the judges in their Manual.[250] Judges may restrict the number of witnesses at trial and the time available to the respective party for presenting evidence at trial. At the ICC, setting up a framework for the conduct of each trial and coordination of preparatory activities are time-consuming activities.[251] But this is time well-invested if it ultimately allows the trial to run its course uninterrupted.

17.8.3 Disclosure of Evidence

Providing timely and full access to incriminating evidence is a fundamental feature of a fair trial, allowing the accused to prepare their defence. In civil law systems, all the incriminating and exonerating material collected during the investigation is contained in a case file

---

[241] ICC RPE, r. 132*bis* (adopted by Res. ICC-ASP/11/Res.2, 21 November 2012).
[242] ICC Statute, Arts. 64(3)(a) and 8(b); ICC RPE, r. 140(1); ICC Regulations of the Court, reg. 54.
[243] See e.g. *Ongwen*, ICC TC IX, 13 July 2016 (ICC-02/04–01/15–497); *Ntaganda*, ICC TC VI, 2 June 2015 (ICC-01/04–02/06–619), 30 January 2017 (ICC-01/04–02/06–1757), 11 May 2017 (ICC-01/04–02/06–1900); *Al Mahdi*, ICC TC VIII, 22 July 2016 (ICC-01/12–01/15–136); *Al Hassan*, ICC TC X, 6 May 2020 (ICC-01/12-01/18-789-AnxA); *Ali Kushayb*, TC I, 4 October 2021 (ICC-02/05-01/20-478) and 15 December 2022 (ICC-02/05-01/20-836).
[244] E.g. *Limaj et al.*, ICTY TC III, 10 December 2004; *Milutinović et al.*, ICTY TC III, 12 December 2006; *Karemera et al.*, ICTR AC, 11 May 2007, para. 7.
[245] *Lubanga*, ICC PTC I, 8 November 2006 (ICC-01/04–01/06–679), ICC TC I, 30 November 2007 (ICC-01/04–01/06–1049), and ICC TC I, 23 May 2008 (ICC-01/04–01/06–1351); *Bemba*, ICC TC III, 18 November 2010, ICC-01/05–01/08–1016 (Judge Ozaki dissenting, 24 November 2010, ICC-01/05–01/08–1039).
[246] *Ruto and Sang*, ICC TC V, 2 January 2013 (ICC-01/09–01/11–524); *Muthaura and Kenyata*, ICC TC V, 2 January 2013 (ICC-01/09–02/11–588); *Ntaganda*, ICC TC VI, 16 June 2015 (ICC-01/04–02/06–652). Cf. *Bemba et al.*, ICC TC VII, 15 September 2015; *Gbagbo and Blé Goudé*, ICC TC I, 2 December 2015 (ICC-02/11–01/15–355); *Al Mahdi*, ICC TC VIII, 22 July 2016 (ICC-01/12–01/15–136) para. 5.
[247] ICTY RPE, rr. 65*ter* and 107; MICT RPE, rr. 70 and 135; ICC RPE, r. 132*bis*.
[248] ICTY and ICTR RPE, r. 65*bis*; MICT RPE, r. 69; ICC RPE, r. 132; and ICC Regulations, reg. 54.
[249] ICTY and ICTR RPE, rr. 73*bis* and 73*ter*; MICT RPE, rr. 81–82; ICC Regulations, reg. 54.
[250] Chambers Practice Manual (n. 181) paras. 76–83.
[251] In the ICC's first, narrowly framed, case, the Trial Chamber had held fifty-four status conferences and delivered 275 written and 347 oral decisions: *Lubanga*, ICC TC I, 14 March 2012 (ICC-01/04–01/06–2842) paras. 10–11.

which is available to the accused. But in common law, the prosecution has extensive disclosure obligations which also cover material that is favourable to the accused. Defence disclosure is much more restricted and is often postponed until the Prosecutor has presented evidence at trial. Defendants have the right to remain silent and not to cooperate in their own conviction. Another issue is the extent to which the evidence should be disclosed by the parties to the court before the trial. Such disclosure allows the judges to prepare for and control the trial more actively but it should not be such as to taint the court's impartiality (or give rise to such perception).

At the Tribunals, the Prosecutor had extensive and continuous obligations concerning pre-trial disclosure.[252] The obligation to disclose also extended to exculpatory and other relevant material in the custody of the Prosecutor.[253] However, certain material was exempt from disclosure,[254] and the Trial Chamber could allow non-disclosure of specific information. Defence disclosure was also required with respect to alibi or any special defences (such as diminished or lack of mental responsibility) before the commencement of the defence case.[255] However, failure by the defence to disclose did not prevent it from raising a defence or presenting evidence supporting it.

At the ICC, separate disclosure takes place for the confirmation process and for the trial. The Chambers play a significant role in coordinating the process and issue extensive instructions. They are empowered to order disclosure, as long as documents and information have not been previously disclosed and do not fall within the exceptions.[256] The Statute places an important obligation upon the Prosecutor to disclose evidence that is exculpatory, mitigating, or which may affect the credibility of prosecution evidence.[257] The contrasting statutory obligations to disclose exculpatory material and to protect confidential information were put to the test in *Lubanga*, leading to a stay of the trial at one point.[258] Ultimately, the Prosecutor secured the permission of the information-providers to submit the undisclosed material to the Trial Chamber for an *ex parte* review.[259] The same issue arose in *Banda and Jerbo*, where the Trial Chamber considered appropriate counter-balancing measures following refusal of disclosure by one provider.[260] Late and incomplete disclosure of evidence to the defence has been a recurring problem at the ICC and subject only to half-hearted response from the judges.[261]

17.9 EVIDENTIARY RULES

Many 'adversarial' systems, particularly those with jury trials, have strict and technical rules regarding the admission and exclusion of evidence meant to protect lay fact-finders

---

[252] ICTY and ICTR RPE, rr. 66, 92*bis* and 94*bis*; MICT RPE, rr. 71, 110 and 116.

[253] ICTY and ICTR RPE, r. 68 and MICT RPE, r. 73. [254] ICTY and ICTR RPE, r. 70 and MICT RPE, r. 76.

[255] ICTY and ICTR RPE, r. 67 and MICT RPE, r. 72. Regarding the timing of the defence disclosure, see also ICTY RPE, r. 65*ter* and MICT RPE, r. 70.

[256] ICC Statute, Arts. 61(3) and 64(3)(c). For exceptions, see ICC RPE, rr. 81–82. [257] ICC Statute, Art. 67(2).

[258] ICC Statute, Arts. 67(2) and 54(3)(e). *Lubanga*, ICC TC I, 13 June 2008 (ICC-01/04–01/06–1401) and ICC AC, 21 October 2008 (ICC-01/04–01/06–1486). See Section 20.6.2.

[259] *Lubanga*, ICC AC, 21 October 2008 (ICC-01/04–01/06–1486) para. 48, and TC I, 23 January 2009. See also ICC RPE, r. 83.

[260] *Banda and Jerbo*, ICC TC IV, 23 November 2011 (ICC-02/05–03/09–259), 26 October 2012 (ICC-02/05–03/09–407-Red) and 21 June 2013 (ICC-02/05–03/09–442-Red2).

[261] E.g. ICC RPE r. 121(8). See IER Report (n. 179) paras. 476–82.

from unreliable or improper evidence. But 'inquisitorial' systems follow the principle of 'free evaluation' and adopt a flexible approach towards admission, because there, professional judges (along with lay assessors) weigh the totality of the evidence and provide their findings in a reasoned opinion.

In international criminal trials, an appropriately high evidentiary standard is warranted as these courts have to 'shoulder the heavy burden of establishing incredible facts by means of credible evidence'.[262] The evidentiary approach at the Tribunals was flexible and unhindered by technical rules from the outset, in a marked deviation from the common law systems.[263] Where professional judges try both fact and law, there is no need to protect jurors from irrelevant prejudicial material. The same is true for the ICC. The complex factual situations, large amounts of evidence, and difficulties in obtaining it warrant greater flexibility, but this also raises issues of fairness and efficiency of the proceedings.[264] The amount of evidence can be reduced if the parties agree on alleged facts and thus limit the contested issues, but such agreements on core matters of the case are very rare.[265]

The Tribunals were not bound by national rules of evidence.[266] Each Tribunal had the discretion to 'admit any relevant evidence which it deem[ed] to have probative value' and to exclude evidence 'if its probative value [wa]s substantially outweighed by the need to ensure a fair trial'.[267] In addition, evidence obtained by methods casting 'substantial doubt on its reliability' or if its admission would seriously damage the integrity of the proceedings, was subject to mandatory exclusion.[268] Relevance denotes the pertinence of evidence to an allegation or issue in the trial, while probative value means its ability to prove or disprove an alleged fact. Reliability depends on circumstances such as the origin, content, corroboration, truthfulness, voluntariness, and trustworthiness of the evidence.[269]

Over time, the ICTY practice, and then the RPE, evolved from a preference for oral testimony towards a more ready acceptance of written evidence and transcripts of evidence in lieu of oral evidence, where it went to the proof of matters other than acts and conduct of the accused as charged in the indictment.[270] The main purpose was to expedite the trial process while affording the accused the opportunity to cross-examine the relevant witness if her evidence could be relied upon to reach a conviction on the charges. Controversial at the

---

[262] *Kupreškić et al.*, ICTY TC II, 14 January 2000, para. 758 and ICTY AC, 23 October 2001, paras. 34–40 (on domestic principles).
[263] *First Annual Report of the ICTY* (n. 18), para. 72.
[264] See Patricia Wald, 'To Establish Incredible Events by Credible Evidence: The Use of Affidavit Testimony in Yugoslavia War Crimes Tribunal Proceedings' (2001) 42 *Harvard International Law Review* 535; Murphy, 'No Free Lunch, No Free Proof' (n. 131).
[265] ICC RPE, r. 69. See e.g. *Banda and Jerbo*, ICC TC IV, 28 September 2011 (ICC-02/05–03/09–227).
[266] ICTY and ICTR RPE, r. 89(A); MICT RPE, r. 105(A). See also ICC Statute, Art. 69(8) and ICC RPE, r. 63(5).
[267] ICTY RPE, r. 89(C)–(D) and MICT RPE, r. 105(C)–(D). Cf. the ICTR RPE which only set out the first part on admission: r. 89(C).
[268] ICTY and ICTR RPE, r. 95; MICT RPE, r. 117. The ICTY seldom applied this rule, but the ICTR did so more often, albeit concluding that not all unlawfully obtained evidence must automatically be excluded. See *Karemera et al.*, ICTR TC III, 2 November 2007 and 25 January 2008; cf. *Halilović*, ICTY AC, 16 October 2007, paras. 28–41, Separate Opinions of Judges Meron and Schomburg.
[269] E.g. *Tadić*, ICTY TC II, 5 August 1996, paras. 15–19; and *Musema*, ICTR TC I, 27 January 2000, paras. 38–42.
[270] ICTY RPE, rr. 92*bis* and 92*ter*; MICT RPE, r. 110. ICTR introduced no such rules.

time, this approach came to be embraced as necessary given the efficiency gains it delivered in lengthy and complex international trials.[271]

The ICC's framework for the admission of evidence is substantially similar. The Trial Chambers have the power to rule on the admissibility or relevance of evidence upon the application of a party or on its own motion and may assess freely all evidence submitted to it in assessing relevance and admissibility.[272] In this assessment, the ICC judges are guided by considerations of probative value and any prejudice the evidence may cause to 'a fair trial or to a fair evaluation of the testimony of a witness'.[273] Evidence must be excluded if obtained by means of a violation of the Statute or of the internationally recognized human rights which casts substantial doubt on reliability, or if the admission would undermine the integrity of the process.[274]

In practice, the ICC has proceeded on the presumption in favour of admission. It has been generous in admitting large volumes of documentary and circumstantial evidence, such as UN and NGO reports, by means of so-called 'bar table motions', that is, directly and without introduction through a witness. The Trial Chambers typically consider the relevance and probative value as part of the 'holistic assessment' of all evidence submitted at trial and defer the determination of admissibility of individual items of proof until deliberations.[275] This approach has been endorsed on appeal, but it has strong opponents, both within and outside the Court.[276]

At the ICC, no legal requirement of corroboration of evidence can be imposed, particularly for crimes of sexual violence.[277] With regard to such crimes, the issue of consent requires special attention. In coercive circumstances, a claim of sexual consent cannot be credible.[278] Consent can be inferred neither from silence or lack of resistance, nor from words or conduct of a victim incapable of giving genuine consent.[279] The special exclusionary rules are meant to protect the victims of such crimes from spurious lines of questioning.

17.10 GUILTY PLEA AND ADMISSION OF GUILT

Common law and civil law systems take different approaches when the accused confesses to the crimes charged. A common law 'guilty plea' is a formal admission of responsibility by the accused which, if accepted by the court, automatically leads to a conviction.

---

[271] *Milošević*, ICTY TC III, 21 March 2002 and ICTY AC, 30 September 2003. See Steven Kay, 'The Move from Oral Evidence to Written Evidence' (2004) 2 *JICJ* 495; Boas, *Practitioner Library III*, 352–7; Iain Bonomy, 'Making War Crimes Trials Work: Balancing Fairness and Expedition' in Gideon Boas, William Schabas and Michael Scharf (eds.), *International Criminal Justice: Legitimacy and Coherence* (Cheltenham, 2012) 44, 57.
[272] ICC Statute, Art. 64(9)(a); ICC RPE, r. 63(2). [273] ICC Statute, Art. 69(4). [274] *Ibid.* Art. 69(7).
[275] See *Lubanga*, ICC TC I, 14 March 2012 (ICC-01/04–01/06–2842) paras. 93–118 and ICC AC, 1 December 2014 (ICC-01/04–01/06–3121) para. 22; *Ngudjolo*, ICC TC II, 18 December 2012 (ICC-01/04–02/12–3) paras. 33–72; *Bemba*, ICC TC III, 21 March 2016 (ICC-01/05–01/08–3343) para. 218.
[276] *Bemba et al.*, ICC AC, 8 March 2018 (ICC-01/05–01/13–2276-Red) paras. 572–600 (upholding the holistic approach, see para. 598; Judge Henderson dissenting, ICC-01/05–01/13–2275-Anx). See also Separate Opinion of Judge Christine Van den Wyngaert and Judge Howard Morrison, *Bemba*, ICC AC, 8 June 2018 (ICC-01/05–01/08–3636-Anx2) paras. 14–18.
[277] ICC RPE, r. 63(4).
[278] See e.g. *Kunarac et al.*, ICTY AC, 12 June 2002, paras. 127–9, 131. See also *Ntaganda*, ICC TC VI, 8 July 2019 (ICC-01/04–02/06-2359) paras. 934–5.
[279] ICC RPE, r. 70.

By contrast, civil law systems generally treat confession – the defendant's acknowledgement of incriminating facts – as one piece of evidence which in itself does not relieve the court from its independent duty to establish the truth.

The Tribunals followed the common law approach under which a 'guilty plea' was to be formally reviewed by the Chamber and, if the relevant requirements were met, a finding of guilt was to be entered, after which the case progressed directly to sentencing.[280] The test was whether the guilty plea was voluntary, informed, and unequivocal, and whether there was a sufficient factual basis for the crime and the participation of the accused in it.[281] The later ICTY practice evinced a more thorough examination of the statements of the agreed facts and their consistency with the admitted crimes.[282]

Negotiations and agreements between the parties regarding guilty pleas and sentencing recommendations the prosecution could make, are referred to as 'plea bargaining'. Plea bargaining has long existed in common law jurisdictions, and analogous procedures have increasingly become accepted in civil law jurisdictions.[283] Negotiated justice is a widely debated matter in domestic systems: while proponents highlight the judicial economy of plea bargaining, opponents focus on inequality before the law and the risk of materially incorrect verdicts.

The idea of a prosecutor negotiating a settlement regarding offences as grave as international crimes may appear objectionable and inconsistent with the goal of fighting impunity. Thus, the Tribunals initially did not have a provision on plea bargaining.[284] But the benefits of this practice in the cases before the Tribunals – efficiency, truth discovery, and sparing witnesses from reliving traumatic experiences – soon became clear. Plea bargaining did occur in practice, and a rule was adopted to formalize it, stating that agreements between the parties were not binding on the Chambers.[285] The Chambers' departure from the sentencing recommendations as per the plea agreements ultimately had a discouraging effect on the defendants. No new agreements were concluded in the later years of the Tribunals' existence.[286]

The ICC Statute refrains from using the common-law term 'guilty plea' and instead adopts a more neutral 'admission of guilt'. It is a hybrid procedure, in that it leans more towards the civil-law view that a confession is merely one piece of evidence; yet it also allows simplified proceedings in case of an admission.[287] The assessment of the admission of guilt by the Trial Chamber includes a stronger focus on the submitted facts and any evidence.[288] An important difference from the Tribunals is that the ICC Trial Chamber

---

[280] ICTY RPE, rr. 62*bis* and 62*ter*; ICTR RPE, rr. 62 and 62*bis*; MICT RPE, rr. 64–65. Cf. ICTY Statute, Art. 20(3), ICTR Statute, Art. 19(3) and MICT Statute, Art. 18(3), directing that, regardless of the plea, there be a 'trial'.
[281] See *Erdemović*, ICTY AC, 7 October 1997, paras. 17–21, and the Dissenting Opinion of Judge Cassese.
[282] See e.g. *Babić*, ICTY AC, 18 July 2005, paras. 8–10; and *Deronjić*, ICTY AC, 20 July 2005, paras. 12–19. Cf. *Jelisić*, ICTY AC, 5 July 2001, para. 87 (unless cogent reasons indicate otherwise, the sentence should be based on the agreed facts).
[283] See Jenia Iontcheva Turner and Thomas Weigend, 'Negotiated Justice' in Sluiter et al., *International Criminal Procedure*, 1400–5.
[284] *First Annual Report of the ICTY* (n. 18), para. 74. [285] ICTY RPE, r. 62*ter*(B); ICTR RPE, r. 62*bis*(B).
[286] Twenty defendants pleaded guilty at the ICTY (the last guilty plea by Zelenović in 2007); and nine at the ICTR (the last one by Bagaragaza in 2009). See Nancy Combs, *Guilty Pleas in International Criminal Law: Constructing a Restorative Justice Approach* (Stanford, CA, 2007).
[287] ICC Statute, Art. 65 and ICC RPE, r. 139. [288] ICC Statute, Art. 65(1).

holds a broader discretion in deciding upon the consequences of a valid admission. In case it finds that the admission satisfies the formal requirements, it may convict the accused; but it may also, in the interests of justice and in particular in the interests of victims, opt for a more complete presentation of the facts and request the Prosecutor to present additional evidence, or order a trial under the ordinary procedures.[289]

Despite the fact that the issue of plea bargaining was highly controversial during the negotiations, the Statute leaves scope for agreements between parties, stating that no agreement regarding the admission of guilt or modification of charges or penalties would be binding on the Court.[290] In *Al Mahdi*, the first case disposed of by an admission of guilt, the Trial Chamber imposed the penalty of nine years' imprisonment – the lowest threshold of the range the parties had agreed that the Prosecutor would recommend.[291] However, it is not evident from the Chamber's reasoning whether this recommendation played any role in the calculation of the sentence. In 2020 the ICC Prosecutor adopted policy guidelines setting factors to be considered before concluding and framing admission of guilt agreements.[292]

17.11 TRIAL STAGE

The trial is the central stage of international criminal proceedings, both in terms of its length and procedural functions. This is when the parties formally submit evidence to the court and plead on the merits of their cases, enabling judges to determine the guilt or innocence of the defendant and, if appropriate, the penalty. In accordance with the principle of a fair and public hearing, all evidence on which the Trial Chamber's decision is based should be presented and examined during trial, that is, it must form part of the trial record.[293]

While the trials must in principle be public, closed sessions are allowed for specified reasons: public order and morality, safety, and security of a victim or witness, protection of confidential or sensitive information, or the protection of the interests of justice.[294] The Trial Chambers have broad powers to manage the proceedings before them and maintain order in the course of the hearing.[295] Disruptive persons, including the accused, may be removed from the courtroom.[296] But unlike the Nuremberg IMT, neither the Tribunals nor the ICC may proceed with the trial in the absence of the accused (*in absentia*).[297]

The trial covers hearings reserved for the opening statements, presentation of evidence, and closing arguments, upon which the court adjourns for deliberations and, in due course,

---

[289] *Ibid.* Art. 65(2) and (4). See e.g. *Al Mahdi*, ICC TC VIII, 27 September 2016 (ICC-01/12–01/15–171) para. 7 (the prosecution presented the testimony of three witnesses).
[290] ICC Statute, Art. 65(2). See Turner and Weigend, 'Negotiated Justice' (n. 283) 1389–92.
[291] *Al Mahdi*, ICC TC VIII, 27 September 2016 (ICC-01/12–01/15–171) paras. 106–9, and ICC OTP and Defence, 18 February 2016 (ICC-01/12–01/15–78-Anx1-Red2) para. 19(a).
[292] ICC OTP, Guidelines for Agreements Regarding Admission of Guilt (October 2020) paras. 17–27.
[293] See ICC Statute, Arts. 64(10) and 74(2).
[294] ICTY and ICTR RPE, rr. 78–79; MICT RPE, rr. 92–93; ICC Statute, Arts. 63 and 64(7).
[295] E.g. ICC Statute, Art. 64(9)(b). [296] ICTY and ICTR RPE, r. 80; MICT RPE, r. 94; ICC Statute, Arts. 63(2) and 71(1).
[297] ICTY Statute, Art. 21(4)(d); ICTR Statute, Art. 20(4)(d); MICT Statute, Art. 19(4)(d) and ICC Statute, Art. 63. Cf. ICC RPE, r. 134*quater* (excusal from presence due to extraordinary public duties). See William Schabas, '*In Absentia* Proceedings before International Criminal Courts' in Sluiter and Vasiliev, *International Criminal Procedure*, 335–80.

delivers the judgment on the merits.[298] At the ICC, after the judgment establishing the guilt ('Article 74 decision'), separate hearings may be held devoted to the determination of sentence and reparations.[299]

In the ICTY and ICTR, trials followed the two-case model, with the prosecution making submissions and presenting evidence first and defence following thereafter. The bifurcation into the prosecution and defence cases has also been the practice in all of the cases at the ICC so far. One nuance in the ICC trial scheme, however, is the additional step, or a 'third case': evidence submitted by participating victims.[300] The ICC's approach to sequencing trials was not inevitable given the presiding judge's broad powers to give directions for the conduct of the proceedings.[301] This considerable discretion could result in different approaches being taken in different cases, although this has not resulted (and is unlikely to result) in largely judge-led trials.[302] There has also been a degree of harmonization of practice across Trial Chambers, although fragmentation persists on some issues.[303]

Before the Tribunals, the presentation of evidence at trial followed an 'adversarial' sequence: prosecution evidence, defence evidence, prosecution evidence in rebuttal, defence evidence in rejoinder, evidence ordered by the Chamber, and evidence regarding sentencing.[304] For every witness, examination-in-chief, cross-examination, and re-examination were to be allowed, and the judge might ask questions at any stage.[305] The Chamber was to exercise control over the mode and order of interrogating witnesses, with a view to efficiency, and the cross-examination was limited in scope.[306] The relevant ICC rule is more open-ended and refrains from using common-law terminology. It leaves room for a different approach to witness examination, including less of a distinction between prosecution and defence witnesses, and a possibility of the examination starting with a free statement and questions by the judges, not the parties.[307]

At the Tribunals, the accused could request, and the Chamber could enter on its own motion, a judgment of acquittal after the presentation of the prosecution case, a so-called 'mid-trial acquittal'.[308] The rationale behind this common-law-inspired procedure is that where the accused has 'no case to answer' because the prosecution evidence is so insufficient that no reasonable tribunal could convict on that basis, there is no point in continuing with the presentation of the defence evidence.[309] This procedure is not expressly provided in the ICC legal framework, but it has been permitted in some trials and disallowed in others with reference to case-specific circumstances.[310] The Appeals

[298] ICTY RPE, rr. 84–87; ICTR RPE, rr. 84–88; MICT RPE, rr. 100–104; ICC Statute, Art. 64(8) and ICC RPE, rr. 140–142.
[299] See Chapters 18–19. [300] See Section 18.5.4. [301] ICC Statute, Art. 64(8)(b) and ICC RPE, r 140. See Section 17.8.2.
[302] Megan A. Fairlie, 'The Unlikely Prospect of Non-adversarial Trials at the International Criminal Court' (2018) 16(2) *JICJ* 295.
[303] See e.g. Section 17.8.2 (on witness preparation). [304] ICTY and ICTR RPE, r. 85 and MICT RPE, r. 102.
[305] The cross-examination is a cornerstone of the common law trials, which Wigmore famously called 'the greatest legal engine ever invented for the discovery of truth'. See John H. Wigmore, *A Treatise on the Anglo-American System of Evidence at Trials in Common Law*, 3rd ed. (Boston, 1940) 29, s. 1367.
[306] ICTY and ICTR RPE, r. 90(F) and (H) and MICT RPE, r. 106(F) and (H). [307] ICC RPE, r. 140(2).
[308] ICTY and ICTR RPE, r. 98*bis* and MICT RPE, r. 121.
[309] E.g. *Delalić et al.*, ICTY AC, 20 February 2001, para. 434 ('evidence (if accepted) upon which a reasonable tribunal of fact *could* be satisfied beyond reasonable doubt of the guilt of the accused on the particular charge in question').
[310] ICC Statute, Art. 64(6)(f). Allowing 'no case to answer' procedure: *Ruto and Sang*, ICC TC V(A), 3 June 2014 (ICC-01/09–01/11–1134); *Gbagbo and Blé Goudé*, ICC TC I, 4 June 2018 (ICC-02/11–01/15–1174). Cf. *Ntaganda*, ICC TC VI, 1 June 2017 (ICC-01/04–02/06– 1931); *Ongwen*, ICC TC IX, 18 July 2018 (ICC-02/04–01/15–1309).

Chamber articulated the standard of proof at this stage as sufficiency in law to sustain a conviction on one or more of the charges.[311]

The judgment must contain reasons, which allows a subsequent review of the legal and factual findings.[312] As majority decisions are permitted, both majority and minority opinions are to be included. While the ICC Statute clearly strives towards unanimity,[313] in practice many of the decisions, both interlocutory and on the merits, have featured separate opinions. If exercised with restraint, as a measure of last resort,[314] the prerogative of writing individually serves useful purposes in judicial decision-making. The importance of this form of judicial expression is that it allows a judge to make public her principled disagreement with the majority. Although dissenting opinions can be highly critical of the majority's reasoning, they may nevertheless strengthen the credibility of the judicial institution, provided that they are written in the spirit of collegiality and using respectful language.[315] Such opinions may be relied upon by the parties in preparing their appeals and considered by future Chambers and legislators, thereby contributing to the progressive development of the law. Majority and minority judges should continue seeking consensus and allow each other the opportunity to provide feedback on and amend their respective drafts. To enable appeals, separate or dissenting opinions ought to be issued simultaneously with the judgment, which has not always been done in practice.[316]

17.12 APPEALS AND REVIEW

17.12.1 Appeal Against Judgment and Sentence

The Nuremberg and Tokyo IMTs did not provide for appeals, but today anyone convicted of a crime is entitled to a review of the conviction and sentence by a higher court.[317] The right of appeal is provided in all international criminal jurisdictions. More in line with civil law systems, this includes prosecution appeals against acquittals. On appeal, the Appeals Chamber may affirm, reverse, or revise the appealed decision.[318] Alternatively, it may set aside the judgment and order a new trial before a different Trial Chamber.[319] Detailed procedures are set out for each court.[320]

At the Tribunals, appeals against trial judgments or sentencing judgments were of a corrective nature, and not new trials (trials *de novo*).[321] The process was limited to

---

[311] *Gbagbo and Blé Goudé*, ICC AC, 31 March 2021 (ICC-02/11-01/15-1400) para. 301.
[312] ICTY Statute, Art. 23 and ICTY RPE, r. 98*ter*; ICTR Statute, Art. 22 and ICTR RPE, r. 88; MICT Statute, Art. 21 and MICT RPE, r. 122; ICC Statute, Art. 74 and ICC RPE, r. 144. Cf. ICC Statute, Art. 83(4).
[313] ICC Statute, Art. 74(5). [314] Chambers Practice Manual (n. 181) para. 104. [315] *Ibid.* para. 106 [316] *Ibid.* paras. 110–6.
[317] E.g. ICCPR, Art. 14(5); Protocol no. 7 to the ECHR, Art. 2; ACHR, Art. 8(2)(h); African Charter on Human and Peoples' Rights (ACHPR), Art. 7(1)(a).
[318] ICTY Statute, Art. 25(2); ICTR Statute, Art. 24(2); MICT Statute, Art. 23(2); and ICC Statute, Art. 81(2).
[319] ICTY RPE, r. 117(C); ICTR RPE, r. 118(C); MICT RPE, r. 144(C); ICC Statute, Art. 81(2).
[320] ICTY RPE, rr. 107–118; ICTR RPE, rr. 107–119; MICT RPE, rr. 131–145; ICC RPE, rr. 149–158 and ICC Regulations, regs. 57–65.
[321] ICTY Statute, Art. 25; ICTR Statute, Art. 24; and MICT Statute, Art. 23. See e.g. *Kupreškić et al.*, ICTY AC, 23 October 2001, paras. 22 and 408.

correcting errors of law invalidating the decision[322] and errors of fact resulting in a 'miscarriage of justice'. The threshold for intervening in factual determinations was high and required that the Trial Chamber's conclusion be one 'which no reasonable trier of fact could have reached'.[323] The burden of proof on appeals was not absolute regarding points of law, but the party must at least identify the alleged error, present arguments, and explain how the error invalidated the decision.[324]

As to sentencing, the Tribunals took the view that the Appeals Chamber should not revise the sentence unless the Trial Chamber committed a 'discernible error' in exercising its discretion or failed to follow applicable law.[325]

The ICC Statute lists the following grounds of appeal: procedural error, error of fact, and error of law, and, as an additional ground in case of conviction, 'any other ground that affects the fairness or reliability of the proceedings or decision'.[326] Regarding sentences, the main ground of appeal is a disproportion between the crime and the sentence.[327] A reversal, amendment, or remittal to a new trial before a Trial Chamber requires that the 'proceedings were unfair in a way that affected the reliability of the decision or sentence' or that 'the decision or sentence ... was materially affected by error of fact or law or procedural error', which further qualifies the standard of review.[328] The Appeals Chamber is not restricted by the appeals either on the sentence or on the conviction, and may on its own motion raise the questions to set aside a conviction or reduce a sentence.[329]

The interpretation of the standard of review with regard to errors of law has been fairly uniform in the ICC practice and accorded with the Tribunals' interpretations. On such matters, the Appeals Chamber does not defer to the Trial Chamber's interpretation but arrives at its own conclusions, intervening only if the error materially affected the decision.[330] A greater margin of deference is normally due to the factual findings of the trial judges because they hear witnesses and examine evidence first-hand. Their findings would not be disturbed other than in cases of a 'clear error', that is where a conclusion could not have reasonably been reached from the evidence before the trial court.[331] Controversially, this standard was further clarified (or adjusted) in the *Bemba* appeal to allow the appeal judges to interfere with the trial court's findings 'whenever the failure to interfere may occasion a miscarriage of justice'.[332] While such review falls short of a *de novo* assessment of evidence, it does imply a more substantive and intrusive approach to assessing the Trial Chamber's reasoning on the

[322] See e.g. *Erdemović*, ICTY AC, 7 October 1997 (invalid guilty plea); *Tadić*, ICTY AC, 10 September 1999 (re-sentencing after reversal of acquittal); *Muvunyi*, ICTR AC, 29 August 2008 (insufficient reasoning in the judgment).
[323] E.g. *Tadić*, ICTY AC, 15 July 1999, para. 64; and *Akayesu*, ICTR AC, 1 June 2001, para. 178; *Furundžija*, ICTY AC, 21 July 2000, para. 37.
[324] E.g. *Krnojelac*, ICTY AC, 17 September 2003, para. 10; and *Ntakirutimana*, ICTR AC, 13 December 2004, para. 7.
[325] E.g. *Tadić*, ICTY AC, 26 January 2000, para. 22; and *Musema*, ICTR AC, 16 November 2001, para. 395.
[326] ICC Statute, Art. 81(1).   [327] *Ibid.* Arts. 81(2) and 83(3).   [328] *Ibid.* Art. 83(2).   [329] *Ibid.* Art. 81(2).
[330] *Bemba*, ICC AC, 8 June 2018 (ICC-01/05–01/08–3636-Red) para. 36; *Lubanga*, ICC AC, 1 December 2014 (ICC-01/04–01/06–3121-Red) paras. 18–19; *Ngudjolo*, ICC AC, 7 April 2015 (ICC-01/04–02/12–271-Corr) para. 20.
[331] *Lubanga*, ICC AC, 1 December 2014 (ICC-01/04–01/06–3121-Red) paras. 21 and 27. On reasonableness, see *Ntaganda*, ICC AC, 30 March 2021 (ICC-01/04-02/06-2666-Red) paras. 39–43.
[332] *Bemba*, ICC AC, 8 June 2018 (ICC-01/05–01/08–3636-Red) para. 40 (stating that the Rome Statute does not provide for the notion of appellate deference).

evidence before it, considering the quality of that evidence, against the beyond reasonable doubt standard.[333]

17.12.2 Interlocutory Appeals

Appeals against any rulings other than the judgment on the merits (guilt or innocence, sentence, and reparations) are called interlocutory appeals. Their purpose is to ensure the timely disposition of, and obtain clarity on, matters that should be resolved without waiting until the appellate review of the decision on the merits. Albeit not provided for in the Statutes, interlocutory appeals were soon accepted in the ICTY and ICTR practice and subsequently in the RPE.[334]

Such appeals are also allowed at the ICC.[335] But, since interlocutory appeals are in themselves time- and resource-consuming, only certain decisions are subject to such review. Decisions on jurisdiction and admissibility are always open to appeal, and so are decisions concerning provisional release and certain measures ordered by the Pre-Trial Chamber during the investigation. All other decisions require leave to appeal by the Chamber issuing the challenged decision.[336] To obtain leave, the party must show that the decision 'involves an issue that would significantly affect the fair and expeditious conduct of the proceedings or the outcome of the trial' and for which 'an immediate resolution by the Appeals Chamber may materially advance the proceedings'.[337]

17.12.3 Review and Revision

The Statutes of the Tribunals and the ICC make provision for review proceedings, an exceptional remedy against miscarriage of justice.[338] While the Tribunals allowed either party to seek review, thus allowing the Prosecutor to apply for review of an acquittal,[339] revision at the ICC applies only to a conviction or sentence.[340]

Review is possible when the following cumulative requirements are met: there is (1) a 'new fact'; (2) that fact was not known to the applicant at the time of the original proceedings; (3) the failure to discover the new fact was not due to the applicant's lack of due diligence; and (4) the new fact could have been a decisive factor in reaching the original decision.[341] Revision at the ICC requires important 'new evidence', unavailable during the trial for reasons not attributable to the moving party. In addition, the ICC Statute allows

---

[333] *Ibid.* paras. 42, 44–6.
[334] *Tadić*, ICTY AC, 2 October 1995, paras. 4–6; ICTY and ICTR RPE, rr. 72–73. See also MICT RPE, r. 132.
[335] ICC Statute, Art. 82 and ICC RPE, rr. 154–158.
[336] *Situation in Uganda*, ICC AC, 13 July 2006 (ICC-02/04–01/05–92) (no extraordinary review available).
[337] ICTY and ICTR RPE, rr. 72(B)(ii) and 73(B); MICT RPE, rr. 79(B)(ii) and 80(B); ICC Statute, Art. 82(1)(d).
[338] ICTY Statute, Art. 26; ICTR Statute, Art. 25; MICT Statute, Art. 24; and ICC Statute, Art. 84.
[339] The Prosecutor may seek review within one year after the final judgment; for the convicted person there is no time limit: ICTY RPE, r. 119; ICTR RPE, r. 120; and MICT RPE, r. 146.
[340] ICC Statute, Art. 84(1).
[341] *Barayagwiza*, ICTR AC, 31 March 2000, para. 41; *Delalić et al.*, ICTY AC, 25 April 2002, para. 8.

revision when decisive evidence at trial turns out to be false, forged, or falsified, or in case of serious misconduct or breach of duty by a participating judge.

17.13 OFFENCES AGAINST THE ADMINISTRATION OF JUSTICE

All international criminal jurisdictions have provisions on prosecution and punishment of offences directed against the administration of justice. Since the ICTY and ICTR Statutes are silent on the matter, the suppression of such offences was considered an inherent power derived from the judicial function of the Tribunals.[342] However, judicial criminalization raised questions with respect to the principle of legality.

Therefore, for the Residual Mechanism and the ICC, this power is explicitly laid down in the Statutes.[343] While the list of qualifying acts in the provisions of the ICTY, ICTR, and the Residual Mechanism is not exhaustive, the list of offences for the ICC is. Another important difference is that prosecution and punishment of these offences is a shared responsibility between the ICC and the states parties.[344] The penalties for offences against the administration of justice include a prison sentence (up to seven years at the ICTY and MICT and up to five at the ICTR), a fine, or a combination of the two; misconduct at the ICC may lead to a fine and other measures.[345]

The ICC has punished five individuals for witness interference in the *Bemba II* case.[346] Arrest warrants in two further cases in the *Situation in Kenya* remain to be executed. The Court should make greater use of Article 70 in the future considering that reportedly witness interference is pervasive in the cases before it.[347]

17.14 CONCLUDING REMARKS

A comprehensive presentation and critical assessment of the procedural law and practice of the international criminal jurisdictions is beyond the scope of this chapter, and indeed this book. Qualitative assessments of international criminal procedure are bound to be coloured by one's own domestic legal background or the procedural tradition one is most familiar with. It is high time to abandon the preoccupation with the common law versus civil law divide in international criminal procedure because international procedural systems should be viewed in their own right. This, it is hoped, would facilitate a clearer application of principles developed in the international context instead of through the lens of one's own domestic legal experience.[348] Given the multiplicity of jurisdictional forums and procedural pluralism, there is a need for a more robust theory and methodology of international criminal procedure.[349]

---

[342] ICTY and ICTR RPE, r. 77. See also e.g. *Tadić*, ICTY AC, 31 January 2000, para. 13.
[343] MICT Statute, Art. 1(4); MICT RPE, r. 90; ICC Statute, Arts. 70 and 71; and ICC RPE, rr. 162–172.
[344] ICC Statute, Art. 70(4). Cf. ICTY and ICTR RPE, r. 77(C); MICT RPE, r. 90(C).
[345] The ICC may also order forfeiture: ICC RPE, r. 166(2).
[346] *Bemba et al.*, ICC TC VII, 19 October 2016 (ICC-01/05–01/13–1989-Red) and ICC AC, 8 March 2018 (ICC-01/05–01/13–2275-Red).
[347] See Section 18.4.   [348] Boas, *Practitioner Library III*, 14–17.
[349] Sluiter et al., *International Criminal Procedure*, 3–7; Christoph Safferling, *International Criminal Procedure* (Oxford, 2012) ch. 3.

One common yardstick to serve as the foundation for such a theory is found in international human rights standards and principles. But their content is subject to different interpretations and the approaches towards implementation vary. Moreover, unique circumstances and challenges specific to international criminal jurisdictions, for example, concerning international cooperation, must also be considered when interpreting and applying human rights standards in that context.[350] It may be unreasonable to impose on international tribunals the exact same parameters of procedural fairness as those applied to domestic systems.

The ICTY and ICTR, beginning with limited guidance, have shown that international criminal proceedings can be conducted in accordance with the highest standards of procedural justice, in particular the rights of the accused. However, the length of their proceedings was the principal target of criticism. The response to that critique was a shift from an adversarial party-driven procedural model to a more active role of the judges in managing the pre-trial and trial process. While this development was generally welcomed and can be deemed an epitome of procedural creativity of judge-legislators, the actual success of the managerial judging reforms has been questioned, as those reforms may have instead lengthened the process.

For the ICC, on the other hand, some 'inquisitorial' features and a stronger role for victims were present from the outset; a novel set-up to which neither the Tribunals nor most domestic analogies provide real guidance. To some these procedures are a major advancement in terms of fairness compared to previous experiments; others would object that the ICC proceedings are highly inefficient and rather confusing. Over two decades into the ICC's existence, the proper distribution of roles and powers between the Pre-Trial, Trial, and the Appeals Chamber, as well as between the judges and the prosecution, remains not fully settled. Numerous other criticisms continue to be raised in respect of the Prosecutor's investigative practices, the overblown confirmation process, the unsatisfactory victim reparation process, and other matters.

The most common line of critique in relation to international criminal proceedings is that they are far too slow and unacceptably long, in particular when the suspect or accused is deprived of his or her liberty. It is often argued that the success of international criminal jurisdictions depends upon a more expeditious process. But it is important to acknowledge that their cases are legally and factually complex which, together with special challenges to investigations and prosecutions, must be factored into expectations towards the process. Investigating too quickly and narrowly, as a means for expediency, is at odds with the expectations as to their quality and depth and some of the broader goals of international criminal justice.

Consultations on the reforms necessary for the streamlined procedural operation of the ICC have been ongoing in the ASP's Study Group on Governance, receiving a new impulse from the critical 2020 Report of Independent Experts. In the meantime, ICC judges have

---

[350] See Krit Zeegers, *International Criminal Tribunals and Human Rights Law: Adherence and Contextualization* (The Hague, 2016).

used their power to provisionally amend the RPE very sparingly. Instead, they have continued experimenting with different procedural approaches, searching for common ground and workable solutions, and consolidating best practices in their dynamic and authoritative Chambers Practice Manual. Any future procedural reforms at the ICC will be gradual and piecemeal, being pursued by both the states and the Court. An ongoing constructive dialogue between them is key to the success of this undertaking. It is also important that all actors view international criminal procedure as a system on its own, rather than through the lens of common law or civil law preferences. The grand divide, however, has not disappeared and continues to overshadow practitioners' approach to interpreting and applying procedural norms at the ICC and elsewhere.

Further Reading

Kai Ambos, *Treatise on International Criminal Law*, vol. III: *International Criminal Procedure* (Oxford, 2016)

Boas, *Practitioner Library III*

Cassese et al., *Commentary*, chs. 28–38

John Jackson and Sarah Summers, *The Internationalization of Criminal Evidence: Beyond Common Law and Civil Law Traditions* (Cambridge, 2012)

Karim Khan, Caroline Buisman, and Christopher Gosnell (eds.), *Principles of Evidence in International Criminal Justice* (Oxford, 2010)

Karim Khan, Rodney Dixon, and Sir Adrian Fulford (eds.), *Archbold International Criminal Courts: Practice, Procedure and Evidence*, 4th ed. (London, 2013)

Lee, *Elements and Rules*

Christoph Safferling, *International Criminal Procedure* (Oxford, 2012)

Sluiter and Vasiliev, *International Criminal Procedure*

Sluiter et al., *International Criminal Procedure*

Salvatore Zappalà, *Human Rights in International Criminal Proceedings* (Oxford, 2003)

Krit Zeegers, *International Criminal Tribunals and Human Rights Law: Adherence and Contextualization* (The Hague, 2016)

18

Victims in International Criminal Justice

18.1 INTRODUCTION

Traditionally, the accused is at the centre of the criminal process as the actor who is afforded fair trial rights. The opposing party is the public prosecutor representing the interests of society. But where does that leave the victim who also has a legitimate interest in the case? Domestic systems address this issue in different ways.[1]

An adversarial process, where two opposing parties present their respective cases, leaves little room for a strong and independent participatory role of the victim. The victim may report an offence, testify at trial, and make sentencing submissions but does not become a full-fledged third party. In inquisitorial systems, judges play a primary role in ascertaining the truth and there is no bifurcation into two partisan cases. This design leaves a greater scope for victims to participate in their own right.[2]

Domestic systems also vary with respect to the victim's right to obtain compensation from the perpetrator of the crime. In common law systems, this is typically a claim to be pursued in a separate civil process. In civil law countries, particularly based on the French legal tradition, such claims are handled as part of civil party action within the criminal proceedings (*partie civile*). In addition, certain criminal sanctions are of a compensatory nature, for example, orders for restitution of property.

Internationally, there has been an increasing focus on the role of victims in criminal justice. Opinions differ on how to meet the interests of victims to participate and to obtain protection and remedies in that context. Retributive and utilitarian thinking places the accused at the forefront, while restorative justice theories put the victims at the centre.[3] The adoption of the Victims Declaration by the UN General Assembly in 1985 prodded many countries to make their criminal justice systems more victim-friendly.[4] Improving victim services and communication at relevant stages upholds the dignity of victims and prevents 'secondary victimization' by insensitive law-enforcement. The 'Van Boven/

---

[1] Mikaela Heikkilä, *International Criminal Tribunals and Victims of Crimes* (Åbo, 2004) 43–56; Sergey Vasiliev, 'Article 68(3) and Personal Interests of Victims in the Emerging Practice of the ICC' in Stahn and Sluiter, *Emerging Practice*, 679–86.
[2] On the domestic procedural models, see Section 17.1.1.
[3] Heikkilä, *International Criminal Tribunals* (n. 1) 23–42; Alessandra Cupini, *The Participation of Victims in International Criminal Proceedings: An Expressivist Justice Model* (Abingdon, 2022) ch. 3.
[4] Declaration of Basic Principles for Victims of Crime and Abuse of Power, GA Res. 40/34 (29 November 1985) ('1985 UN Victims Declaration').

Bassiouni Principles', adopted in 2005, affirmed victims' right to a remedy and to reparation for gross violations of international human rights and international humanitarian law.[5]

18.2 VICTIMS AND INTERNATIONAL CRIMINAL JUSTICE

One objective behind the creation of international criminal jurisdictions was to provide redress to the victims of atrocities. Victims only played a very limited role as prosecution witnesses at the Nuremberg trial.[6] Similarly, the International Criminal Tribunal for the former Yugoslavia (ICTY) and the International Criminal Tribunal for Rwanda (ICTR) procedures were adversarial in nature, and victims' only function was to give evidence. Their right to obtain protection and support from the Tribunal was related to that function. Even with respect to restitution of property, victims were not parties to the proceedings.[7] This marginalization was criticized as unsatisfactory in light of the Tribunals' mandate to bring justice to the victims.[8]

By contrast, the International Criminal Court (ICC) legal framework contains extensive provisions on victim participation, legal representation, and reparations. This ambitious regime was far from evident and proved highly controversial during the negotiations.[9] Many have hailed the inclusion of victims in the ICC proceedings as a major advance.[10] It has been described as representing a much-needed move away from the purely retributive justice paradigm.[11] At the same time, critics warned that it is a potentially harmful experiment in a still fragile system.[12] Another oft-heard criticism is that victim participation risks upsetting the delicate balance between the parties. It might have a negative impact on the rights of the accused.[13] Yet others suggest that the ICC approach is still insufficient. The selectivity in international prosecutions is at odds with an increased recognition of the right of all victims to a remedy and to reparations in international human rights law.[14]

The ICC should enable meaningful and effective victim participation as the Statute requires, but its inability to provide full redress should be honestly acknowledged to avoid raising false hopes.[15] The underlying ambition to provide justice to individual victims

---

[5] Basic Principles and Guidelines on the Right to a Remedy and Reparations for Victims of Gross Violations of International Human Rights Law and Serious Violations of International Humanitarian Law, GA Res. 2005/35 (16 December 2005) ('Van Boven/Bassioni Principles').

[6] Sam Garkawe, 'The Role and Rights of Victims at the Nuremberg International Military Tribunal' in Herbert Reginbogin and Christoph Safferling (eds.), *The Nuremberg Trials: International Criminal Law since 1945* (Munich, 2006) 86–94.

[7] ICTY and ICTR RPE, r. 105 and MICT RPE, r. 129 (the motion by the Prosecutor or the Trial Chamber's *proprio motu* action is needed).

[8] Claude Jorda and Jérôme de Hemptinne, 'Status and Role of the Victim' in Cassese et al., *Commentary*, 1387–98.

[9] Christopher Muttukumaru, 'Reparations to Victims' in Lee, *The Making of the Rome Statute*, 262–70; Gilbert Bitti and Håkan Friman, 'Participation of Victims in the Proceedings' in Lee, *Elements and Rules*, 456–74.

[10] See e.g. Theo van Boven, 'Victims' Rights and Interests in the International Criminal Court' in Doria et al., *Legal Regime*, 895–906.

[11] Silvia Fernández de Gurmendi and Håkan Friman, 'The Rules of Procedure and Evidence of the International Criminal Court' (2001) 3 *Yearbook of International Humanitarian Law* 289, 312.

[12] See e.g. Alexander Zahar and Göran Sluiter, *International Criminal Law: A Critical Introduction* (Oxford, 2007) 75–6.

[13] E.g. Salvatore Zappalà, 'The Rights of Victims v. the Rights of the Accused' (2010) 8 *JICJ* 137.

[14] Cécile Aptel, 'Prosecutorial Discretion at the ICC and Victims' Right to Remedy' (2012) 10 *JICJ* 1357. Cf. Conor McCarthy, 'Victim Redress and International Criminal Justice' (2012) 10 *JICJ* 351.

[15] Emily Haslam, 'Victim Participation at the International Criminal Court: A Triumph of Hope over Experience?' in McGoldrick et al., *The Permanent ICC*, 319.

and the related discourse about the ICC being the 'court for the victims' is bound to generate unrealistic expectations. The ICC should not be seen as the main forum for redress – states must take on this burden.[16] The Court adopted a strategy in relation to victims in 2009 and revised it in 2012.[17] Besides being now more than one decade old, this strategy falls short of spelling out exactly how the goal of giving effect to victims' rights is to be achieved, and its implementation in practice has not been fully consistent.[18]

Giving victims procedural standing, and allowing them rights beyond protection and general support when testifying, is now a mainstream approach in international criminal justice. Except for the Special Court for Sierra Leone (SCSL), which was based on the ad hoc Tribunals' procedural model, most internationalized courts now recognize the victims' participatory and reparatory rights.[19] In the Extraordinary Chambers in the Courts of Cambodia (ECCC), victims participated as civil parties and could claim moral and collective reparations.[20] The Statute of the Special Tribunal for Lebanon (STL) also allowed for victim participation, but civil claims were to be placed before national courts.[21] Before the Extraordinary African Chambers (EAC) in Senegal, victims participated and obtained reparations as civil parties.[22] In these jurisdictions, the victim scheme draws upon the domestic (French-influenced) arrangements. In the Kosovo Specialist Chambers (KSC), victims may participate in the proceedings (without prejudice to their potential witness role), be represented, and obtain reparations from the convict.[23]

18.3 DEFINITION OF VICTIMS

The question of who formally qualifies as a 'victim' is important because the number of eligible victims, and hence the pressures and resource demands on the criminal justice system, depend on whether a broader or a more restrictive definition is adopted. The ICTY and ICTR definition exemplifies a broad interpretation, which is understandable in the absence of victims' participatory rights from their regime.[24] The ICC Rules include a general definition influenced by the 1985 UN Victims Declaration and intended for all purposes (protection, participation, and reparations).[25] Victims are 'natural persons who

---

[16] See Luke Moffett, *Justice for Victims Before the International Criminal Court* (Abingdon, 2014).

[17] *Court Revised Strategy in Relation to Victims*, ICC-ASP/11/38 (5 November 2012). See also International Criminal Court Strategic Plan 2023–2025, paras. 37–9.

[18] See Gaelle Carayon and Jonathan O'Donohue, 'The International Criminal Court's Strategies in Relation to Victims' (2017) 15 *JICJ* 567, 570–1. Res. ICC-ASP/21/Res.2, Strengthening the International Criminal Court and the Assembly of States Parties (9 December 2022) para. 117 (requesting the Court to initiate consultations on an updated strategy).

[19] See Chapter 9.

[20] ECCC Internal Rules, rr. 23*bis*–23*quinquies*, 80*bis*(4), 90–91, 94, 100. See Rachel Killean, *Victims, Atrocity and International Criminal Justice: Lessons from Cambodia* (Abingdon, 2018); Maria Elander, *Figuring Victims in International Criminal Justice: The Case of the Khmer Rouge Tribunal* (Abingdon, 2018).

[21] STL Statute, Arts. 17 and 25. See further Jérôme de Hemptinne, 'Challenges Raised by Victims' Participation in the Proceedings of the Special Tribunal for Lebanon' (2010) 8 *JICJ* 165; Howard Morrison and Emma Pountney, 'Victim Participation at the Special Tribunal for Lebanon' in Amal Alamuddin, Nidal Nabil Jurdi and David Tolbert (eds.), *The Special Tribunal for Lebanon: Law and Practice* (Oxford, 2014) ch. 9.

[22] EAC Statute, Arts. 14 and 27–28. See Section 9.2.4.   [23] KSC Law, Art. 22.

[24] ICTY and ICTR RPE, r. 2(A) ('A person against whom a crime over which the Tribunal has jurisdiction has allegedly been committed.'); MICT RPE, r. 2(A).

[25] 1985 UN Victims Declaration (n. 4). Silvia Fernández de Gurmendi, 'Definition of Victims and General Principle' in Lee, *Elements and Rules*, 427–34.

have suffered harm as a result of the commission of any crime within the jurisdiction of the Court' and 'organizations or institutions that have sustained direct harm to any of their property ... dedicated to religion, education, art or science or charitable purposes, and to their historic monuments, hospitals and other places and objects for humanitarian purposes'.[26]

A victim is someone who has suffered 'harm'. 'Harm' to natural persons (which may include deceased persons)[27] denotes hurt, injury, and damage.[28] This covers material, physical, and psychological or emotional harm, but only so long as it is suffered personally by the victim ('personal harm'). A mere impersonal or collective harm on account of impairment of rights does not qualify one for participation.[29] 'Indirect victims', such as family members of someone killed or of a child soldier, are covered by the definition.[30] The harm must relate to a crime within the jurisdiction of the Court and arise from the crimes being investigated or prosecuted.[31] Harm to organizations, however, should be 'direct' and relate to certain property.[32] The determination of what evidence is sufficient is done on a case-by-case basis.[33]

Other international and hybrid courts' definitions of 'victim' benefit from the ICC jurisprudence and are more specific on the issue of harm. For instance, the STL definition covers natural persons who have suffered 'physical, material, or mental harm as a direct result of an attack' within STL jurisdiction.[34] In turn, the KSC definition limits victims to natural persons who have *personally* suffered harm (including physical, mental, or material), as a *direct* result of a crime within the KSC jurisdiction.[35]

18.4 PROTECTION OF VICTIMS AND WITNESSES

Protection is a difficult and demanding task for any criminal jurisdiction, and particularly so for an international tribunal. Witnesses are sometimes threatened and even murdered.[36] Pervasive witness interference has been a major challenge at the ICC.[37]

---

[26] ICC RPE, r. 85.
[27] Practice has varied on whether applications can be made on behalf of deceased persons: *Situation in Darfur*, ICC PTC I, 14 December 2007 (ICC-02/05–111-Corr) para. 36 (excluding deceased persons from the notion of victim); and *Bemba*, ICC PTC III, 12 December 2008 (ICC-01/05–01/08–320) para. 40 (including deceased persons); *Yekatom and Ngaïssona*, ICC PTC II, 5 March 2019 (ICC-01/14-01/18-141) para. 36.
[28] *Lubanga*, ICC TC I, 18 January 2008 (ICC-01/04–01/06–1119) para. 92 (cf. Judge Blattmann's dissent, paras. 4–5), and ICC AC, 11 July 2008 (ICC-01/04–01/06–1432) paras. 31–2.
[29] *Lubanga*, ICC AC, 11 July 2008 (ICC-01/04–01/06–1432) paras. 31–2, 35 and 37.
[30] *Ibid.* para. 32 (cf. Judge Pikis' dissent, para. 3); *Lubanga*, ICC TC I, 18 January 2008 (ICC-01/04–01/06–1119) para. 91, and 8 April 2009 (ICC-01/04–01/06–1813).
[31] See Section 18.5.2.
[32] This covers, for example, schools and hospitals. See *Situation in the DRC*, ICC PTC I, 18 August 2011 (ICC-01/04–597) paras. 10, 30–4.
[33] *Kony et al.*, ICC AC, 23 February 2009 (ICC-02/04–179) para. 38. [34] STL RPE, r. 2(A). [35] KSC Law, Art. 22(1).
[36] Two witnesses who testified in the *Akayesu* and *Ruzindana* trials were killed: *Second Annual Report of the ICTR*, A/52/582-S/1997/868 (13 November 1997) para. 51. In 2014, someone who had been considered as a witness until suspicions arose about his involvement in witness corruption was found dead: Statement of the Office of the Prosecutor regarding the Reported Abduction and Murder of Mr. Meshak Yebei (9 January 2015); 'ICC deeply concerned with reported death of Mr Meshack Yebei; stands ready to assist Kenyan investigations' (6 January 2015). On 16 July 2022, Christopher Koech, a witness scheduled to testify at the ICC in the Article 70 case against Paul Gicheru, died under unclear circumstances in Kakamega, Kenya, and Gicheru himself passed away three months later in Kenya while on interim release from the ICC; both cases raised suspicions of poisoning.
[37] Open Society Justice Initiative, *Witness Interference in Cases before the International Criminal Court* (November 2016) 5.

The tribunals are greatly reliant upon live evidence, but international witnesses are particularly vulnerable given the substantial likelihood of their exposure and becoming targets of reprisals. The ICC often conducts investigations during conflicts, which exacerbates risks. These factors have necessitated the development of thorough victim and witness protection regimes.[38] International courts have a more limited range of possible protective measures than national authorities. They do not have their own police forces and depend upon states and peacekeepers to offer the more robust protective measures.[39] However, the domestic authorities are not always invested in ensuring the safety of the ICC's (potential) witnesses and may be a source of threat rather than protection.[40]

Witness protection was primarily a responsibility of the Chambers at the ad hoc Tribunals. At the ICC, it is distributed among different organs.[41] Special units for victim and witness issues, including protective measures and security arrangements, operate within the Registries of international tribunals and courts.[42] In order to avoid 'secondary victimization', these units also provide support measures in some way similar to social welfare services.[43]

The protection may be motivated by security or privacy reasons or because of a generally volatile security situation in a country. The victims' age, gender, health, and the nature of the crime, particularly sexual and gender-based violence, are factors adding to their vulnerability and prompting enhanced measures.[44] The circumstances in which the courts operate are such that witnesses and victims are often very anxious and may refuse to collaborate unless various protective measures are taken. Since coercing a person to give evidence is seldom a realistic option, protective measures have been abundantly used.[45]

In court, measures are often taken to prevent disclosure to the public (screening, voice or image distortion, use of pseudonyms, and a ban on photography). Postponed disclosure, closed sessions, and testimony by video-link may also be employed. Out-of-court protective measures are possible only to a limited extent. Some witness protection programmes, in particular relocation, must be used sparingly and modalities less burdensome for witnesses and their families are preferred.[46] Relocation is a measure of last resort for cases of serious security threats. It may necessitate the cooperation of a state other than where the witness resides. Ad hoc requests for cooperation are time-consuming and, as far as urgent relocation is concerned, have a low implementation rate. Therefore,

---

[38] ICTY Statute, Arts. 20(1) and 22; ICTR Statute, Arts. 19(1) and 21; ICTY RPE and ICTR RPE, rr. 39(ii), 69, 75 and 79; ICC Statute, Arts. 54(1)(b) and (3)(f), 57(3)(c), 64(6)(e) and 68(1)e; ICC RPE, rr. 87–88.

[39] See Chapter 20.

[40] E.g. *Situation in Burundi*, ICC PTC III, 9 November 2017 (ICC-01/17–9-Red) para. 13; Statement of the Prosecutor of the International Criminal Court, Fatou Bensouda, on the Withdrawal of Charges Against Mr. Uhuru Muigai Kenyatta (5 December 2014).

[41] Markus Eikel, 'External Support and Internal Coordination: The ICC and the Protection of Witnesses' in Stahn, *The Law and Practice of the ICC*, 1106 (shared responsibility caused uncertainties in early practice).

[42] ICTY RPE and ICTR RPE, r. 34; ICC Statute, Arts. 43(6) and 68(4) and ICC RPE, rr. 16–19.

[43] ICC RPE, r. 17(2)(a). See also Eric Stover, *The Witnesses: War Crimes and the Promise of Justice in The Hague* (Philadelphia, PA, 2007) 79–91.

[44] ICC Statute, Art. 68(1). [45] See Section 20.2.3.

[46] Guido Acquaviva and Mikaela Heikkilä, 'Witnesses: Protection and Testimony' in Sluiter et al., *International Criminal Procedure*, 826 ('an extreme form of protection').

the Tribunals and the ICC have concluded special (confidential) agreements with states to enable this protective measure.[47]

Precautionary measures present a cheaper, and possibly more effective, alternative to *ex post facto* responses to any identified threat. One option is to develop investigative practices whereby contacts with vulnerable witnesses and victims are avoided as much as possible. However, resulting practices, such as heavy reliance on intermediaries and limited on-site investigations by ICC investigators, have been widely criticized because they affect the quality of the prosecution case.[48]

Family members and even potential witnesses may also be afforded protection.[49] The ICC Appeals Chamber has extended protective measures to 'persons at risk on account of the activities of the Court'. This allows non-disclosure of identification information of 'innocent third parties' and Court staff.[50]

Protection programmes must be equally available to both parties and be employed in a neutral fashion. The responsibility for these matters, including relocation, is therefore placed upon special units within the Registry. The ICC Appeals Chamber rejected the Prosecutor's attempt to 'preventively relocate' witnesses unilaterally and concluded that the relevant Chamber was the final arbiter in case of disagreement between the Prosecutor and the Registry.[51] Nonetheless, the process of accepting witnesses into the ICC Protection Programme is cumbersome, and it has caused disclosure complications and delays in the past.[52]

Given the impact of protective measures on fair trial principles, a careful balancing of interests is required.[53] However, judicial rulings have not always justified such measures well.[54] Protection from public identification deviates from the principle of a public trial. Even more problematic are measures withholding the witness's identity from the accused, as they may compromise rights to adequate time and facilities for the preparation of the defence and to examine prosecution witnesses. Particularly controversial is the use of anonymous witnesses, that is, witnesses whose identity is not known to the accused. An early ICTY decision allowed this practice, influenced by the Tribunal's impotence concerning physical protection,[55] but it was sharply criticized, particularly by proponents of the adversarial approach.[56] This practice was never repeated, not least because one of the anonymous witnesses in that case was shown to have fabricated his testimony. The ICC Statute and

---

[47] *Report of the Court on Cooperation*, ICC-ASP/21/24 (20 October 2022) para. 46 (the Registry has concluded twenty-five witness relocation agreements but they are not always implemented).

[48] Caroline Buisman, 'Delegating Investigations: Lessons to be Learned from the Lubanga Judgment' (2013) 11 *Northwestern Journal of International Human Rights* 30; Christian de Vos, 'Investigating from Afar: The ICC's Evidence Problem' (2013) 26(4) *LJIL* 1009.

[49] See e.g. *Ngirabatware*, ICTR TC II, 6 May 2009.

[50] *Katanga*, ICC AC, 13 May 2008 (ICC-01/04–01/07–475) paras. 109–10 (Judge Pikis dissenting).

[51] *Katanga*, ICC AC, 26 November 2008 (ICC-01/04–01/07–776) (but the Prosecutor may take 'temporary emergency measures'; para. 103).

[52] *Katanga and Ngudjolo*, ICC PTC I, 25 April 2008 (ICC-01/04–01/07–428) paras. 61–2.

[53] ICTY Statute, Art. 22; ICC Statute, Art. 64(2).

[54] Göran Sluiter, 'The ICTR and the Protection of Witnesses' (2005) 3 *JICJ* 962; Acquaviva and Heikkilä, 'Witnesses' (n. 46) 823–6. Similar criticisms have been raised against the ICTY and ICC, albeit to a lesser extent.

[55] *Tadić*, ICTY TC II, 10 August 1995 (Judge Stephen dissenting).

[56] E.g. Monroe Leigh, 'The Yugoslav Tribunal: Anonymity is Inconsistent with Due Process' (1996) 90 *AJIL* 235 and (1997) 99 *AJIL* 80; Christine Chinkin, 'Due Process and Witness Anonymity' (1997) 99 *AJIL* 75. See also Michael Kurth, 'Anonymous Witnesses Before the International Criminal Court: Due Process in Dire Straits' in Stahn and Sluiter, *Emerging Practice*, 622–3.

Rules do not squarely address this issue since no consensus could be reached during negotiations.[57] The identity of witnesses may be withheld from disclosure to the defence, but different interpretations are possible as to whether witnesses may remain anonymous at trial.[58] The better view is that the identity may be withheld only 'prior to the commencement of the trial', for example, during the confirmation process.[59]

The ICC Trial Chambers have not allowed participants with a dual status (victim-witnesses) to remain anonymous vis-à-vis the defence.[60] Victims who appear before the Chamber in person to present their views and concerns (rather than to give evidence under oath) assume a more active role. This requires them to relinquish their anonymity (unless there are exceptional circumstances).[61] However, the victims who are not also witnesses may have their identities protected from the parties because their anonymity does not undermine a fair trial.[62]

The objective of protecting (potential) witnesses is also served by preventing and sanctioning witness interference. Following the example of the ICTY, the ICC Rules of Procedure and Evidence (RPE) were amended in 2013 to allow, in limited circumstances and subject to relevant guarantees, the admission of prior recorded testimony of persons who have subsequently died or been subjected to interference.[63] In an effort to tackle witness interference, several Article 70 cases have been brought, with varying success. One (*Bemba et al.*) has been completed and resulted in convictions.[64] The two Article 70 arrest warrants in the Kenya situation remain outstanding in respect of two suspects (Bett and Barasa).[65] The case against Paul Gicheru progressed to the judgment phase but was terminated in October 2022 after his passing while on interim release.[66]

18.5 VICTIM PARTICIPATION AT THE ICC

The ICC Statute and RPE provide for several regimes of victim participation, each with its application procedures, notification and admission requirements, procedural rights, and participatory modalities.[67] Victims may initiate proceedings regarding protective measures

---

[57] Helen Brady, 'Protective and Special Measures for Victims and Witnesses' in Lee, *Elements and Rules*, 450–3.
[58] On non-disclosure, see e.g. *Lubanga*, ICC AC, 11 July 2008 (ICC-01/04–01/06–1432). See also Claus Kreß, 'Witnesses in Proceedings before the International Criminal Court: An Analysis in the Light of Comparative Criminal Procedure' in Fischer et al., *International and National Prosecution*, 309, 364–82 (ICC judges were left with a policy choice).
[59] ICC Statute, Art. 68(5) and ICC RPE, r. 81(4). See e.g. *Lubanga*, ICC AC, 13 October 2006 (ICC-01/04–01/06–568) paras. 34–9.
[60] *Katanga and Ngudjolo*, ICC TC II, 3 December 2009 (ICC-01/04–01/07–1665-Corr) para. 22, and 22 January 2010 (ICC-01/04–01/07–1788) paras. 92–3; *Bemba*, ICC TC III, 22 February 2012 (ICC-01/05–01/08–2138) para. 23; *Ongwen*, ICC TC IX, 17 June 2016 (ICC-02/04–01/15–471) para. 13 and 6 March 2018 (ICC-02/04–01/15–1199-Red) note 26.
[61] *Ongwen*, ICC TC IX, 17 June 2016 (ICC-02/04–01/15–471) para. 14; *Banda*, ICC TC IV, 20 March 2014 (ICC-02/05–03/09–545) para. 19.
[62] *Lubanga*, ICC TC I, 18 January 2008 (ICC-01/04–01/06–1119) paras. 130–1; *Ongwen*, ICC TC IX, 17 June 2016 (ICC-02/04–01/15–471) para. 11; *Katanga and Ngudjolo*, ICC TC II, 22 January 2011 (ICC-01/04–04/07–1788) paras. 92–3.
[63] ICC RPE, r. 68(2)(c)–(d). See ICTY RPE, rr. 92*quater* (unavailable persons) and 92*quinquies* (persons subjected to interference).
[64] ICC Statute, Art. 70(1)(c). See *Bemba et al.*, ICC TC VII, 19 October 2016 (ICC-01/05–01/13–1989-Red) and AC, 8 March 2018 (ICC-01/05–01/13–2275-Red).
[65] *Barasa*, ICC PTC II, 2 August 2013 (ICC-01/09–01/13–1-Red2); *Gicheru and Bett*, ICC PTC II, 10 March 2015 (ICC-01/09–01/15–1-Red).
[66] *Gicheru*, ICC TC III, 14 October 2022 (ICC-01/09-01/20-337).
[67] The following participatory regimes can be identified: (1) Part II regime (ICC Statute, Arts. 15(3) and 19(3); ICC RPE, rr. 50 and 59); (2) general regime (ICC Statute, Art. 68(3); ICC RPE, rr. 89–93; and ICC Regulations of the Court, reg. 86); (3) reparations regime (ICC Statute, Arts. 75(3) and 82(4)); and (4) Rule 93 regime (ICC RPE, r. 93, last sentence).

and reparations and, with regard to the latter, they may appeal decisions, being therefore *parties* to those proceedings. In all other proceedings, they are instead 'participants' with more limited and conditional rights.[68]

Victim participation under the general regime of Article 68(3) is a right with explicit caveats. Namely, it must be shown that personal interests are affected, that the procedural stage is appropriate for participation, and that the rights of the accused and a fair trial will not be compromised.[69] This legal test is copied almost *verbatim* from the UN Victims Declaration.[70] The exercise of this right – where, when, and how – is to be firmly controlled by the Chamber. The judges have the challenging task of giving effect to victims' rights while ensuring that a 'second prosecution' is avoided. It has also been imperative to find practical solutions in light of the large number of eligible victims. For example, 5,229 victims were granted the right to participate in the *Bemba* trial and 4,107 participants were admitted in the *Ongwen* trial.

The ICC jurisprudence in this area has been steadily developing, contributing to the gradual clarification of the contours of the participatory regime. Procedural and practical issues such as the system to apply for participation, arrangements for legal representation, and determination of participation modalities have occupied considerable time and resources on the part of all involved. Critical questions have been raised about the sustainability of the regime, given the significant number of victims seeking to be admitted to participate in the proceedings.[71] Given the ASP's concern with continued backlogs related to the handling of victim applications, the Court conducted a review of the victim admission scheme.[72] The challenging task of streamlining it and devising workable solutions fell to the judiciary and the Registry, leading over time to more consolidated practice. The gist of those solutions has been to vest the Registry with the bulk of tasks relating to the processing of the applications, while the Chambers retain supervisory and decision-making responsibilities, and to make victim representation and participation collective to the extent possible.

18.5.1 Purposes of Participation

The purposes behind victim participation are not made explicit in the ICC Statute and had to be clarified by the Court when construing the requirement of 'personal interests' in Article 68(3). Those considerations should inform whether, when, and how participation ought to take place and shape the content of victims' rights accordingly. At the same time, they must be realistic and consistent with the rights of the defence and the overall procedural system.

---

[68] *Situation in the DRC*, ICC AC, 19 December 2008 (ICC-01/04–556) paras. 50 and 55.
[69] On this regime, see Vasiliev, 'Article 68(3)' (n. 1) 639–48; Tatiana Bachvarova, *The Standing of Victims in the Procedural Design of the International Criminal Court* (Leiden, 2017) ch. 3.
[70] Vasiliev, 'Article 68(3)' (n. 1) 651–3.
[71] E.g. Christine Van den Wyngaert, 'Victims Before International Criminal Courts: Some Views and Concerns of an ICC Trial Judge' (2011) 44 *Case Western Reserve Journal of International Law* 475; Sergey Vasiliev, 'Victim Participation Revisited: What the ICC is Learning about Itself' in Stahn, *The Law and Practice of the ICC*, 1138–46.
[72] *Report of the Court on the Review of the System for Victims to Apply to Participate in Proceedings*, ICC-ASP/11/22 (5 November 2012).

The Court's victim strategy contains a detailed list of victims' rights in various parts of the proceedings.[73] It is questionable, however, whether the ICC regime is underpinned by a coherent and comprehensive view of the purposes of victim participation.

One obvious purpose would be to contribute to the prosecution and punishment, if appropriate, and to help ensure that the truth is exposed.[74] The other objectives are to provide reparations and other forms of satisfaction and to give victims a voice; victims must be treated with dignity and respect to avoid secondary victimization. Participation could also contribute to making the offender more conscious of the injuries and suffering inflicted on others.

Broader restorative and reconciliatory aims are sometimes attached to victim participation.[75] It can be argued that participatory rights should not be linked exclusively to an interest in seeking a conviction and a harsh penalty. Not all victims are necessarily in favour of prosecutions, and reparations at the ICC are not conditioned upon prior participation. Moreover, the presentation of 'views and concerns' is clearly distinct from the submission of evidence, which may indicate the existence of goals beyond enabling conviction. However, the expression of 'views and concerns' remains subject to the conditions set out in Article 68(3). The interpretation of those conditions in practice has generally been aligned with pragmatic considerations such as ensuring fair and expeditious proceedings and establishing the guilt or innocence of the accused and thus informed by a narrower view of the goals of a criminal trial.

18.5.2 Conditions for Participation

Article 68(3) provides for victim participation as a qualified right. The Chambers *shall* permit victims to express their views and concerns subject to the following conditions: (1) victim applicants formally qualify as 'victims'; (2) their 'personal interests' are affected; (3) their participation is 'appropriate' at the relevant stage; and (4) the manner of participation is not prejudicial to or inconsistent with the rights of the accused and a fair and impartial trial. Hence, the Chambers hold considerable discretion in deciding when and how victims may exercise their participatory rights.

The Chambers determine first whether an individual applicant satisfies the Rule 85 requirements and may be granted the status of victim in a situation or a case. This status comes with procedural rights and modalities which vary by stage and activity. Most rights are realized through a Legal Representative of Victims (LRV). Once granted, the victim status applies throughout the proceedings unless the Chamber modifies a previous ruling.[76] 'Case victim' status is inextricably linked to the charges: the harm that

---

[73] *Report of the Court on the Revised Strategy in Relation to Victims: Past, Present and Future*, ICC-ASP/11/40, 8–13 (5 November 2012).

[74] *Katanga and Ngudjolo*, ICC PTC I, 13 May 2008 (ICC-01/04–01/07–474) paras. 31–44; Summary of Trial Chamber II's Judgment of 7 March 2014, pursuant to Art. 74 of the Statute in the case of The Prosecutor v. Germain Katanga, para. 9 (noting the victims' 'meaningful contribution to establishing the truth in relation to certain aspects of the case').

[75] Hans-Peter Kaul, 'Victims' Rights and Peace' in Thorsten Bonacker and Christoph Safferling (eds.), *Victims of International Crimes: An Interdisciplinary Discourse* (The Hague, 2013) 223–9. Cf. Vasiliev, 'Victim Participation Revisited' (n. 71) (practice demonstrates that participation rather promotes the purposes of a victim-friendly, yet essentially retributive, court).

[76] ICC RPE, r. 89(1); ICC Regulations of the Court, reg. 86(8).

a victim claims to have suffered must be caused by the events encompassed within the charges.[77] As the case progresses from confirmation to trial, if some of the charges have not been confirmed, participants who no longer satisfy the Rule 85 requirements cannot continue participating in the case while others continue in the process without re-admission.[78] Subsequently, the Chamber is to define the participatory modalities. A more direct participation (presenting views and concerns in person, giving testimony, submission of other evidence) requires a separate application and determination by the Chamber.

The admission under Article 68(3) and Rule 89 encompasses the collection, translation, redaction, and judicial vetting of applications. Victims should apply in writing to the Registrar; the application forms are gathered, and their completeness is verified, by the Victim Participation and Reparation Section staff with assistance by local intermediaries. In *Ali Kushayb*, a single judge authorized the use of an entirely electronic application form to facilitate the collection of multiple offline applications in areas with limited internet connectivity.[79] The Registry then transmits applications to the Chamber, implements any redactions, and forwards (some of) the applications to the parties for observations (their right to reply not being absolute), after which the Chamber determines the applicants' eligibility.[80] Considering the large number of applications and the complexity of this protocol, the admission process has been the main bottleneck and a primary focus of streamlining efforts.[81]

The Chambers have tried different solutions, including the better division of tasks between the judges and the Registry and simplifying the application process. In the *Kenya* cases, the Trial Chamber ventured a pragmatic 'differentiated approach'.[82] For victims who wished to participate through a common legal representative, the formal application process culminating in a judicial determination of status was replaced with a simple registration in a database maintained by the Registry. Victims only needed to apply under Rule 89 if they intended to appear directly before the judges in person or via video-link (but few of them were expected to do so).[83] Due to its inconsistency with Rule 89, this simplified scheme was not subsequently used. In other cases, judges still vetted all applications, but the Registry took on a more prominent role by conducting an eligibility assessment, grouping the applications, and recommending a specific course of action to the judges.[84] The workload on the Chambers and the Registry staff was also reduced by

---

[77] *Lubanga*, ICC AC, 11 July 2008 (ICC-01/04–01/06–1432) paras. 2 and 62–4, reversing ICC TC I, 18 January 2008 (ICC-01/04–01/06–1119) paras. 93–5.
[78] *Chambers Practice Manual*, 7th edition (2023) para. 97(ii). See *Gbagbo*, ICC TC I, 6 March 2015 (ICC-02/11–01/11–800) para. 41; *Katanga*, ICC TC II, 26 February 2009 (ICC-01/04–01/07–933) paras. 8–15.
[79] *Ali Kushayb*, ICC PTC II, 4 November 2020 (ICC-02/05-01/20-198), paras. 10–4 (the signature field is replaced with a solemn undertaking text field in the electronic form to remove the need for intermediaries to travel with printing and scanning equipment and external sources of electricity).
[80] ICC RPE, r. 89(1) and (2).
[81] Van den Wyngaert, 'Victims Before International Criminal Courts' (n. 74); Vasiliev, 'Victim Participation Revisited' (n. 71) 1147–52.
[82] *Ruto and Sang*, ICC TC V, 3 October 2012 (ICC-01/09–01/11–460) paras. 24–5; *Muthaura and Kenyatta*, ICC TC V, 3 October 2012 (ICC-01/09–02/11–498) paras. 23–4.
[83] *Ruto and Sang*, ICC TC V, 3 October 2012 (ICC-01/09–01/11–460) paras. 48–58. See also *Muthaura and Kenyatta*, ICC TC V, 3 October 2012 (ICC-01/09–02/11–498).
[84] E.g. *Ongwen*, ICC PTC II, 27 November 2015 (ICC-02/04–01/15–350); *Ntaganda*, ICC TC VI, 6 February 2015 (ICC-01/04–02/06–449).

adopting a (partly) collective approach,[85] and by using a simplified one-page application form, which has become the preferred approach.[86]

Ultimately, the case-by-case judicial experimentation has led to the development of a uniform scheme for admission of victim participants generally applicable at all procedural stages, as set out in the Chambers Practice Manual.[87] Chambers are not bound by this default scheme but may adopt it (or depart from it in some respects) in the exercise of their wide discretion, considering the number of victims' applications.[88] Under this so-called 'A-B-C Approach', the Registry is to classify victim applicants into three categories: (A) applicants who clearly qualify as victims; (B) applicants who clearly do not qualify as victims; and (C) applicants for whom the Registry is unable to make a clear determination. Judges receive all applications on a rolling basis and may always decide to authorize or reject applicants in Groups A and B, but barring clear and material errors by the Registry they would validate its assessment when deciding on the applications.[89] Only Group C applications, redacted as appropriate, are transmitted to the parties and LRVs for observations and would require individual vetting by the Chamber. This scheme offers the advantages of higher efficiency and speed while saving judicial resources.[90]

The evidentiary standard for admission is *prima facie* – an appropriately low threshold at a stage when the detailed analysis of credibility and reliability of the applications would be premature.[91] The applications are assessed 'on the merits of their intrinsic coherence' and in light of all information available.[92] The applicants are generally not required to corroborate their statements with evidence, except for the proof of identity.[93] Given that establishing identity may present special challenges in (post-)conflict settings, the Chambers have been flexible in interpreting inconsistencies in the applicants' favour. The judges have also accepted a variety of documents, for example, school or church records, hospital and voting registration cards, letters from local authorities, and declarations signed by two witnesses able to prove their identity.

Similarly, the required causal link between the crime and the harm allegedly suffered by the victim may be difficult to establish at the admission stage. This warrants a relaxed evidentiary

---

[85] The applicants could submit a group application (based on a commonality of the crimes and harm suffered), possibly accompanied by brief individual declarations: see e.g. *Gbagbo*, ICC PTC III, 6 February 2012 (ICC-02/11–01/11–33), 5 April 2012 (ICC-02/11–01/11–86) and 4 June 2012 (ICC-02/11–01/11–138). See also *Situation in Uganda*, ICC PTC II, 9 March 2012 (ICC-02/04–191) para. 22.

[86] *Ntaganda*, ICC PTC II, 28 May 2013 (ICC-01/04–02/06–67) paras. 21–5; *Ongwen*, ICC PTC II, 4 March 2015 (ICC-02/04–01/15–205) paras. 14–22; *Gbagbo*, ICC TC I, 6 March 2015 (ICC-02/11–01/11–800) para. 50; *Ntaganda*, ICC TC VI, 6 February 2015 (ICC-01/04–02/06–449) paras. 22–6.

[87] *Chambers Practice Manual* (n. 78) paras. 96–7.

[88] E.g. *Yekatom and Ngaïssona*, ICC PTC II, 5 March 2019 (ICC-01/14-01/18-141) para. 41; *Al Hassan*, ICC TC X, 12 March 2020 (ICC-01/12-01/18-661) para. 21.

[89] *Chambers Practice Manual* (n. 78) para. 96. See e.g. *Ali Kushayb*, ICC PTC II, 20 May 2021 (ICC-02/05-01/20-398) paras. 29–32.

[90] For a positive assessment, see *Independent Expert Review of the International Criminal Court and the Rome Statute System*, Final Report, 30 September 2020 ('IER Report') para. 849.

[91] *Katanga and Ngudjolo*, ICC PTC I, 2 April 2008 (ICC-01/04–01/07–357) 8–9; *Gbagbo*, ICC PTC III, 4 June 2012 (ICC-02/11–01/11–138) paras. 21, 23, 27 and 31; *Ntaganda*, ICC TC VI, 6 February 2015 (ICC-01/04–02/06–449) para. 30; *Ali Kushayb*, ICC PTC II, 20 May 2021 (ICC-02/05-01/20-398) para. 41.

[92] *Katanga and Ngudjolo*, ICC PTC I, 2 April 2008 (ICC-01/04–01/07–357) 8–9; *Bemba*, ICC PTC III, 12 December 2008 (ICC-01/05–01/08–320) para. 31; *Gbagbo*, ICC PTC III, 4 June 2012 (ICC-02/11–01/11–138) para. 21.

[93] See e.g. *Kony et al.*, ICC AC, 23 February 2009 (ICC-02/04–01/05–371) paras. 35–8; *Ongwen*, ICC PTC II, 27 November 2015 (ICC-02/04–01/15–350).

standard and a preliminary, non-prejudicial determination. But this also means that such
a determination may have to be reversed later on. In several cases, some victims' status was
withdrawn after they had given unreliable evidence.[94]

The notion of 'personal interests' is decisive because it reflects the rationale behind
participation, although it is not clear what specific interests are covered by it.[95] Such
interests may vary by victim and shift in the course of the process. During the 'situation'
phase, the victims' interests are considered as quite general and consist in having crimes
investigated and the perpetrator(s) charged, apprehended, and prosecuted.[96] 'Personal
interests' cannot be confined to reparations because victims need not have participated
previously to obtain them.[97] Nor can they impinge upon the Prosecutor's authority with
regard to investigations, such as by victims exerting pressure on them to investigate
a situation or to prosecute a case.[98] Victims may be heard on issues pertaining to the
Prosecutor's prerogatives only when allowed by the Statute, for example in the context of
judicial authorization of *proprio motu* investigations and review of decisions not to
investigate or prosecute.[99] However, they have no role in triggering such a review or in
otherwise challenging or compelling prosecutorial action.

The participation of victims must also be 'appropriate' at the respective stage of the
proceedings. The ICC Rules contain scattered references to different moments at which general
participation is appropriate.[100] Often the issue has been assessed with respect to the manner of
participation.[101] This goes to the fourth condition under Article 68(3) – the rights of the accused
and fairness – which presupposes a delicate balancing act. A number of defence rights might be
affected by victim participation, not least the right to be tried without undue delay. Victims are
more likely to support the prosecution than the defence, which poses challenges to the equality
of arms and the placement of the onus on the Prosecutor.[102] Tensions also lurk in the
combination of the victim and witness capacities. Although the two roles are incompatible in
some domestic systems, dual status is routinely allowed at the ICC.[103]

18.5.3 Legal Representation

At the ad hoc Tribunals, the Prosecutors typically positioned themselves as the representatives of victims' interests. However, this is far from self-evident. The interests of the

[94] *Lubanga*, ICC TC I, 14 March 2012 (ICC-01/04–01/06–2842) paras. 484, 1363 (withdrawing the status of three victims);
Katanga, ICC TC II, 7 July 2011 (ICC-01/04–01/07–3064) paras. 42–9 (revoking two victims' status given the LRV's doubts
about the veracity of their accounts).
[95] For discussion, see Vasiliev, 'Article 68(3)' (n. 1); Bachvarova, *The Standing of Victims* (n. 69) 121–7.
[96] *Situation in the DRC*, ICC PTC I, 17 January 2006 (ICC-01/04–101-tEN-Corr) paras. 63–4 and 72. See also *Bemba*, ICC PTC
III, 12 December 2008 (ICC-01/05–01/08–320) para. 90 (victims' and prosecution's interests do not always coincide).
[97] *Lubanga*, ICC TC I, 18 January 2008 (ICC-01/04–01/06–1119) para. 98. Cf. *Lubanga*, ICC AC, 16 May 2008 (ICC-01/04–
01/06–1335) paras. 42–6 (protection and reparations as examples of personal interests).
[98] *Lubanga*, ICC AC, 19 December 2008 (ICC-01/04–556) paras. 52–3. See ICC Statute, Art. 42.
[99] ICC Statute, Art. 15(3) and ICC RPE, r. 50; ICC Statute, Art. 53(3) and ICC RPE, rr. 92(2), 107(5) and 59(1)(a). See *Situation
on the Registered Vessels . . .*, ICC PTC I, 24 April 2015 (ICC-01/13–18).
[100] ICC RPE, rr. 89(1) ('opening and closing statements'); 91(1)(a) (witness questioning, i.e. at confirmation and/or trial); 92(2)
(Art. 53 proceedings); 92(3) ('hearing to confirm charges').
[101] *Lubanga*, ICC PTC I, 17 January 2006 (ICC-01/04–101-tEN-Corr) paras. 56–60. For an elaboration of 'appropriateness', see
Judge Blattmann's Separate and Dissenting Opinion in *Lubanga*, ICC TC I, 18 January 2008 (ICC-01/04–01/06–1119).
[102] ICC Statute, Art. 66(2). [103] E.g. *Lubanga*, ICC TC I, 5 June 2008 (ICC-01/04–01/06–1379).

prosecution and the victims often diverge in relation to case strategy, selection of incidents for inclusion within charges, and the approach to guilty pleas.

Legal representation is a right of participating victims at the ICC. Article 68(3) makes an explicit reference to LRVs and Rule 90 defines the scope and parameters of that right. An LRV is guaranteed more extensive participation than an unrepresented victim, which may incentivize victims to be represented. For instance, modalities such as the attendance of hearings or questioning witnesses, experts, and the accused are not available without a legal representative.[104]

LRVs and victims are supported in various ways by the Office of Public Counsel for Victims (OPCV), such as by providing legal research assistance or by appearing before the Chambers on specific issues.[105] The OPCV operates as an independent office within the Registry and falls within its remit only for administrative purposes. The Chambers may also appoint OPCV counsel as LRVs when the interests of justice so require, including as counsel for unrepresented victims.[106] Some Chambers have preferred representation by OPCV counsel over external counsel, and the OPCV's role in representing victims has grown over the years. This has been controversial since such appointments may come in tension with the victims' right to choose their representatives.

A related issue concerns the power of the Chamber to impose *common* legal representation. The starting point is that victims shall be free to choose an LRV but this freedom is not unlimited.[107] If multiple victims are participating (which is normally the case), the Chamber may, for the sake of efficiency, request victims to choose a common legal representative (CLR).[108] The victims' views and the need to respect local traditions and to assist specific groups of victims must be taken into account.[109] If the victims are unable to choose a CLR, the judges may request the Registrar to do so while taking all reasonable measures to ensure representation of the distinct interests and to avoid conflicts of interests.[110] OPCV lawyers have often been assigned to serve as CLRs under Rule 90(3).[111]

CLRs may be necessary, and thus be imposed by the Court, to make the trial more manageable and avoid having multiple victim lawyers participate in the process.[112] Various Chambers have indicated that victims' common views might best be expressed by a CLR, and so far all participating victims have been represented collectively. Conflicting interests of individual victims motivate separate representation, but efficiency militates in favour of restricting the number of LRVs in a case.[113] The practice has varied, with a clear tendency towards a more collective approach. While in *Lubanga*, 129 victims were represented by seven LRVs, in *Katanga and Ngudjolo* 366 victims were divided into two groups, each represented by a lawyer. Towards the end of the *Bemba* trial, 5,229 victims were represented by only one OPCV lawyer and one external LRV.[114] Two OPCV lawyers represented 2,149 victims in the *Ntaganda* trial. The 4,107 victims participating in the *Ongwen* case were divided into two groups, each represented by an LRV team, one of which was led by

---

[104] ICC RPE, r. 91(3)(a). [105] ICC Regulations of the Court, reg. 81(1). [106] *Ibid.* reg. 80. [107] ICC RPE, r. 90(1).
[108] *Ibid.* r. 90(2). [109] ICC Regulations of the Court, reg. 79(2). [110] ICC RPE, r. 90(3)–(4).
[111] ICC RPE, r. 90(3) and ICC Regulations of the Court, reg. 80. See e.g. *Ongwen*, ICC PTC II, 27 November 2015 (ICC-02/04–01/15–350) para. 21; *Gbagbo*, ICC PTC III, 4 June 2012 (ICC-02/11–01/11–138) paras. 42–5.
[112] ICC RPE, r. 91(2). [113] ICC RPE, r. 90(4). [114] *Bemba*, ICC TC III, 21 March 2016 (ICC-01/05–01/08–3343) para. 23.

two external counsel chosen by the victims, and the other by an OPCV lawyer and (external) field counsel.

Given the difficulties in representing groups of such size, questions have been raised as to whether this can be a meaningful, rather than merely symbolic, representation.[115] A collective approach ensures a more manageable process but affects the victims' autonomy as subjects, rather than mere objects, of the proceedings.

18.5.4 Participation in Different Procedural Stages

At the ICC, victim participation is not confined to any particular stage of the process; the manner of participation depends on the participatory regime and procedural stage. The Court has reiterated consistently that the participation should be 'effective and meaningful' as opposed to 'purely symbolic'.[116] However, what this means remains unclear, with forms of participation being largely a matter of judicial discretion.

Like in a domestic context, victims may provide the Prosecutor with information about the crimes, but this is not a formal report of a crime (*notitia criminis*) which automatically triggers an investigation. Instead, such information may contribute to the Prosecutor seeking authorization to commence an investigation under Article 15 and feed into the Pre-Trial Chamber's decision on this matter. As part of the authorization process, victims can make 'representations' to the Chamber ('Part II regime').[117] Likewise, victims may submit 'observations' in the jurisdiction and admissibility proceedings relating to situations or cases, and there have been multiple instances of such participation.[118] Further, victims may participate in a review of the Prosecutor's decision not to investigate or prosecute ('general regime'), although they are not competent to initiate it.[119] Victims have also been allowed to present their 'views and concerns' pursuant to Article 68(3) in the proceedings concerning the Prosecutor's request to be authorized to resume an investigation despite a state's request for deferral.[120]

Once there is a 'case', that is, when a warrant of arrest or summons to appear is issued, many assessments become more straightforward, such as showing the link between the harm and the relevant crimes. Arrest proceedings, confirmation hearings, and the trial are

---

[115] Emily Haslam and Rod Edmunds, 'Whose Number is it Anyway?: Common Legal Representation, Consultations and the "Statistical Victim"' (2017) 15 *JICJ* 931. See also Sara Kendall and Sarah Nouwen, 'Representational Practices at the International Criminal Court: The Gap Between Juridified and Abstract Victimhood' (2014) 76 *Law and Contemporary Problems* 235.

[116] E.g. *Lubanga*, ICC TC I, 18 January 2008 (ICC-01/04–01/06–1119) para. 85, and ICC AC, 11 July 2008 (ICC-01/04–01/06–1432) para. 97.

[117] ICC Statute, Art. 15(3) and ICC RPE, r. 50. See e.g. *Situation in Côte d'Ivoire*, ICC PTC III, 6 July 2011 (ICC-02/11–6) and 3 October 2011 (ICC-02/11–14); *Situation in Georgia*, ICC PTC I, 27 January 2016 (ICC-01/15–12) para. 2; *Situation in Afghanistan*, ICC PTC II, 12 April 2019 (ICC-02/17-33) para. 27.

[118] ICC Statute, Art. 19(3). See e.g. *Situation in Palestine*, ICC PTC I, 5 February 2021 (ICC-01/18-143) paras. 37–48; *Gbagbo*, ICC PTC III, 15 June 2012 (ICC-02/11–01/11–153); *Al Senussi*, ICC PTC I, 11 October 2013 (ICC-01/11–01/11–466-Red); *Ruto et al.*, ICC PTC II, 4 April 2011 (ICC-01/09–01/11–31); *Katanga and Ngudjolo*, ICC TC II, 16 June 2009 (ICC-01/04–01/07–1213).

[119] ICC Statute, Art. 53(3) and ICC RPE, r. 92(2).

[120] ICC Statute, Art. 18(2). See e.g. *Situation in Afghanistan*, ICC PTC II, 8 November 2021 (ICC-02/17-171).

instances where victims' personal interests are at stake and participation takes place in accordance with Article 68(3) and the Chamber's directions.

Article 68(3) expressly refers to participation in 'the proceedings'. The early case law allowed general participation in the investigative stage.[121] However, the Appeals Chamber soon ruled that the conduct of the investigation is the Prosecutor's prerogative and victim participation at that stage must be confined to judicial proceedings ('a judicial cause pending before a Chamber').[122] Thus, instead of allowing participation generally during the investigation, the available forms of participation during particular activities at that stage should be addressed.[123] Modes of participation such as 'to be heard' and 'to file documents', were regarded as too unspecific and not meaningful. However, more far-reaching modalities, such as requesting specific proceedings or requesting the Prosecutor to provide information on 'the status of the investigation',[124] are incompatible with the Statute and the appellate jurisprudence.

Moreover, the Pre-Trial Chamber limited the scope of participation under Article 68(3) by narrowing down the notion of 'proceedings' to 'criminal proceedings'. It ruled that the victims in the *Al Bashir* case did not have the right to participate in the proceedings regarding South Africa's non-compliance because that case involved 'international cooperation and judicial assistance' which 'fundamentally differ[s] from the criminal proceedings before the court'.[125] However, there is no basis for this restrictive interpretation in the legal framework or previous jurisprudence.[126]

The ICC legal framework provides limited guidance on what forms of participation are available at different stages. More active modalities (attending hearings, making oral interventions, questioning of witnesses, experts, and accused, making opening and closing statements, etc.) are expressly foreseen for LRVs.[127] The Chambers have worked out a more ambitious scheme in practice. From the first trial onwards, participating victims have also been permitted to tender evidence pertaining to guilt or innocence, as well as to challenge the admissibility of such evidence.[128] This form of participation is fundamentally different from expressing 'views and concerns' (which are not equated to evidence).[129]

---

[121] *Situation in the DRC*, ICC PTC I, 17 January 2006 (ICC-01/04–101-tEN-Corr) paras. 28–54.

[122] *Situation in the DRC*, ICC AC, 19 December 2008 (ICC-01/04–556) paras. 36–54 and *Situation in Darfur*, ICC AC, 2 February 2009 (ICC-02/05–177).

[123] *Situation in the DRC*, ICC PTC I, 11 April 2011 (ICC-01/04–593) paras. 9–13; *Situation in Libya*, ICC PTC I, 24 January 2012 (ICC-01/11–18).

[124] *Lubanga*, ICC PTC I, 17 January 2006 (ICC-01/04-101-tEN-Corr) para. 75; *Situation in the DRC*, ICC PTC I, 26 September 2007 (ICC-01/04–399).

[125] *Al Bashir Arrest Warrant*, ICC PTC II, 9 March 2017 (ICC-02/05–01/09–286) paras. 5–7.

[126] Victims were permitted to participate in the Art. 87(7) proceedings before: *Kenyatta*, ICC AC, 24 April 2015 (ICC-01/09–02/11–1015).

[127] ICC RPE, rr. 91–93. See e.g. *Katanga and Ngudjolo*, ICC PTC I, 13 May 2008 (ICC-01/04–01/07–474) paras. 127–45; *Bemba*, ICC PTC III, 12 December 2008 (ICC-01/05–01/08–320) paras. 101–10; *Gbagbo*, ICC PTC III, 4 June 2012 (ICC-02/11–01/11–138) paras. 46–60; *Ruto et al.*, ICC PTC II, 23 September 2011 (ICC-01/09–01/11–340); *Ruto and Sang*, ICC TC V, 3 October 2012 (ICC-01/09–01/11–460) paras. 63–77.

[128] See e.g. *Lubanga*, ICC TC I, 18 January 2008 (ICC-01/04–01/06–1119) paras. 108–9, 119–22, upheld by the Appeals Chamber majority: ICC AC, 11 July 2008 (ICC-01/04–01/06–1432) para. 93 (Judges Pikis and Kirsch recording strong dissents); *Katanga and Ngudjolo*, ICC PTC I, 13 May 2008 (ICC-01/04–01/07–474) paras. 30–44, 101–3, and ICC AC, 16 July 2009.

[129] For analysis and criticism, see Håkan Friman, 'The International Criminal Court and Participation of Victims: A Third Party to the Proceedings' (2009) 22 *LJIL* 485, 492–8; Vasiliev, 'Victim Participation Revisited' (n. 71) 1168–76.

The Chambers justified it with reference to their power to request the submission of all evidence necessary for the determination of truth.[130]

Victims are also entitled to appeal orders on reparations, although it is questionable whether they may appeal decisions regarding protective measures.[131] In other appeals, the general provision of Article 68(3) applies and participation is allowed if 'personal interests' are affected by the matter under appeal. Thus, a right of participation was granted in appeals against interim release decisions.[132] However, the Appeals Chamber ruled inadmissible the victims' appeal against a decision rejecting the authorization of an investigation because they do not qualify as 'parties' in the appeal proceedings regarding Article 15(4) decisions.[133]

18.6 REPARATIONS TO VICTIMS

The ICTY and ICTR did not provide for reparations to victims. The relevant rule on compensation referred to domestic proceedings and stated that the judgment of the Tribunal 'shall be final and binding as to the criminal responsibility of the convicted person for such injury'.[134] Successive ICTY Presidents noted the lack of compensation to victims as a major shortcoming and proposed to establish a claims commission, to no avail.[135]

The ICC has the power to order reparations directly to, or in respect of, victims, including restitution, compensation, and rehabilitation.[136] This prerogative was a contentious matter during the drafting of the Rome Statute.[137] The drafters left it to the judges to establish the principles and to determine the scope and extent of any damage, loss, or injury. In doing so, judges may draw inspiration from the Van Boven/Bassiouni Principles,[138] human rights case law, international mass-claims processes, and domestic compensation schemes. Orders for reparations have been issued in four cases and become final following appeals.[139] In one case (*Ongwen*), appellate reparations proceedings are currently ongoing. Although no general principles have been formally established to apply across cases, in its first reparations judgment in *Lubanga* the Appeals Chamber laid the groundwork for such Court-wide principles, to be elaborated and refined in the later jurisprudence.

---

[130] ICC Statute, Art. 69(3).
[131] ICC Statute, Art. 82(4). See *ibid.* Art. 82(1), which limits the right to appeal against 'other decisions' to 'either party' (i.e. the prosecution and the defence); the ICC Statute and the RPE do not provide for the victims' right to appeal decisions regarding protective measures.
[132] See *Lubanga*, ICC AC, 13 February 2007 (ICC-01/04–01/06–824); *Bemba*, ICC AC, 3 September 2009 (ICC-01/05–01/08–500).
[133] For the reasoning, see *Situation in Afghanistan*, ICC AC, 4 March 2020 (ICC-02/17-137) paras. 12–23. Cf. Dissenting Opinion of Judge Luz del Carmen Ibáñez Carranza, 10 March 2020 (ICC-02/17-137-Anx-Corr).
[134] ICTY and ICTR RPE, Rr 106; see also MICT RPE, r. 130.
[135] See e.g. ICTY press release, 'The judges of the ICTY acknowledge the right of victims of crimes committed in the former Yugoslavia to seek compensation', JL/P.I.S./528-e, 14 September 2000; Address of Judge Patrick Robinson, ICTY President, to the United Nations General Assembly, 8 October 2009.
[136] ICC Statute, Art. 75; ICC RPE, rr. 94–99.   [137] See e.g. Muttukumaru, 'Reparations to Victims' (n. 9) 262–70.
[138] Van Boven/Bassioni Principles (n. 5).
[139] *Lubanga*, ICC AC, 3 March 2015 (ICC-01/04–01/06–3129) and ICC TC, 7 August 2012 (ICC-01/04–01/06–2904); *Katanga*, ICC AC, 8 March 2018 (ICC-01/04–01/07–3778-Red) and ICC TC II, 24 March 2017 (ICC-01/04–01/07–3728); *Al Mahdi*, ICC AC, 8 March 2018 (ICC-01/12–01/15–259-Red2) and ICC TC VIII, 17 August 2017 (ICC-01/12–01/15–236); *Ntaganda*, ICC TC VI, 8 March 2021 (ICC-01/04-02/06-2659); ICC AC, 12 September 2022 (ICC-01/04-02/06-2782); and ICC TC II, 14 July 2023 (ICC-01/04-02/06-2858-Red).

While there was an early debate on whether ICC reparations are of a civil nature or rather a penal sanction,[140] they can be deemed a *sui generis* restorative measure to the benefit of the victims. Both individual and collective awards are foreseen and the Trust Fund for Victims (TFV), which is not an organ of the Court but a separate entity established within the Rome Statute system, is the main conduit for the payment of the awards.[141] The TFV also has a general assistance mandate under which it may provide support for physical or psychological rehabilitation or material support for the benefit of victims or their families. However, such support must not be inconsistent with the judicial activities of the Court and is thus subject to the relevant Chamber's approval.[142] The TFV collects court-ordered fines and forfeitures as well as voluntary contributions from states and private donors; the operational costs are paid for by the ICC's budget. In order to secure future reparations, the Court may request states to freeze assets, which it has done regularly when issuing arrest warrants.[143]

In its judgment on reparations in *Lubanga*, the Appeals Chamber established that a reparation order must: (1) be directed against the convicted person; (2) establish and inform him of his liability with respect to the reparations awarded in the order; (3) specify the type of reparations ordered (collective, individual or both); (4) define the harm caused to direct and indirect victims as a result of the crimes for which the person was convicted, as well as identify the modalities of reparations that the Trial Chamber regards as appropriate; and (5) identify the victims eligible to benefit from the awards for reparations or set out the criteria of eligibility based on the link between the harm suffered by the victims and the crimes for which the person was convicted.[144]

Crucially, convicted persons have a duty to repair harm and must be held personally liable for reparations towards the victims. Indigence does not shift the convicted person's liability to the TFV. The latter may advance the payment but the convicted person remains liable and must refund it when possible.[145] Reparations are grounded in the individual criminal responsibility of the convicted person and hence are an extension of penal sanction rather than a form of civil damages. In the subsequent cases, the principles formulated by the Appeals Chamber in *Lubanga* were held to be applicable, *mutatis mutandis*, despite the different nature of the crimes at hand.[146] Yet, the ICC's fourth reparations order (*Ntaganda*) – issued controversially even before the conviction became final – adapted the *Lubanga* principles in notable respects.[147] Among others, the Trial Chamber held that in

---

[140] Birte Timm, 'The Legal Position of Victims in the Rules of Procedure and Evidence' in Fischer et al., *International and National Prosecution*, 306–8.

[141] ICC Statute, Arts. 75(2) and 79 and ICC RPE, rr. 98 and 221. The TFV has a board of directors and is governed by Regulations of the Trust Fund for Victims, ICC-ASP/4/Res.3 (3 December 2005). See further www.trustfundforvictims.org.

[142] TFV Regulations (ICC-ASP/4/Res.3), reg. 50. See *Situation in Uganda*, ICC PTC II, 19 March 2008 (ICC-02/04–126) (approval of proposed activities in Uganda).

[143] ICC Statute, Art. 57(3)(e). See further Section 20.6.4.

[144] *Lubanga*, ICC AC, 3 March 2015 (ICC-01/04–01/06–3129) para. 1. See Carsten Stahn, 'Reparative Justice after the Lubanga Appeal Judgment New Prospects for Expressivism and Participatory Justice or "Juridified Victimhood" by Other Means?' (2015) 13 *JICJ* 801.

[145] *Ibid*. paras. 102–5.

[146] *Katanga*, ICC TC II, 24 March 2017 (ICC-01/04–01/07–3728) paras. 30–31; *Al Mahdi*, ICC TC VIII, 17 August 2017 (ICC-01/12–01/15–236) para. 26.

[147] The *Ntaganda* order was partially reversed and the matter remanded to Trial Chamber II: *Ntaganda*, ICC AC, 12 September 2022 (ICC-01/04-02/06-2782).

determining the amount of the convict's liability, the extent of the harm and the costs to repair it must be the primary consideration, rendering modes of liability, gravity of the crimes, or mitigating factors irrelevant in departure from previous case law.[148] With respect to the criteria for identifying *direct* victims eligible for reparations, the Chamber added children born out of rape and sexual slavery, while other children of the women and girls who became victimized by such crimes could qualify as indirect victims suffering a transgenerational trauma.[149]

With the initial framework for reparations in place, the Chambers, in coordination with the TFV, have been working out finer details of the reparatory regime and the implementation schemes in individual cases. These tasks have posed significant challenges, being a truly uncharted territory for the ICC. One such area, riddled with disagreements between the judges and the TFV, is making assessments of the convicted person's monetary liability for individual and collective reparations.

In an additional order in *Lubanga*, the Trial Chamber set the total amount of reparations at US$10,000,000.[150] The *Katanga* reparation order envisaged the payment to each of the 297 victims of an individual symbolic award of US$250.[151] Al Mahdi's liability for the harm he caused to the community of Timbuktu by participating in the destruction of mausoleums was fixed at €2.7 million, to be paid in individual and collective reparations. The Chamber also awarded the symbolic €1 reparation to be paid to the Malian state and to UNESCO.[152] Ntaganda's monetary liability, set initially at the unprecedented amount of US$30,000,000, was eventually raised to US$31,300,000.[153]

Besides the issue of insufficiency of available funds, the expeditious and orderly implementation of reparations has emerged as a major challenge. In some cases, significant delays attributable to the TFV prodded closer judicial scrutiny while independent experts flagged governance and management issues within its Secretariat and the lack of a fundraising strategy.[154]

18.7 AN ASSESSMENT

The focus on victims is far greater at the ICC than it was at the ICTY and ICTR, and this trend has continued in subsequent internationalized courts. The fundamental controversy is whether the involvement of victims in international criminal proceedings is worthwhile, or whether it detracts from the 'core mandate' of prosecuting international crimes. This goes back to the question of the objectives of international criminal justice.[155] Apart from the normative influence of restorative justice ideals reflected in victims' rights, their involvement is believed to boost the legitimacy of international criminal justice institutions, but

---

[148] *Ntaganda*, ICC TC VI, 8 March 2021 (ICC-01/04-02/06-2659) para. 98. [149] *Ibid.* paras. 122 and 182.
[150] *Lubanga*, ICC TC II, 21 December 2017 (ICC-01/04–01/06–3379-Red-Corr).
[151] *Katanga*, ICC TC II, 24 March 2017 (ICC-01/04–01/07–3728) para. 300.
[152] *Al Mahdi*, ICC TC VIII, 17 August 2017 (ICC-01/12–01/15–236) paras. 106–7 and 134.
[153] *Ntaganda*, ICC TC II, 14 July 2023 (ICC-01/04-02/06-2858-Red) paras. 358–60.
[154] *Al Mahdi*, ICC TC VIII, 12 July 2018 (ICC-01/12–01/15–273-Red) paras. 9–22. See also IER Report (n. 90) paras. 890 and 942.
[155] See Chapter 2.

only if the participation and reparation schemes and related expectations are properly managed. Balancing vis-à-vis the rights of the accused is imperative, not least because a fair trial is quintessential to legitimacy.

Some domestic systems (e.g. in the Nordic countries) combine far-reaching victims' rights with an adversarial process and could serve the ICC as a source of inspiration. However, the ICC victim participation scheme is not only a novelty in international criminal tribunals but also *sui generis* in comparative law terms. The ICC's legal framework leaves key choices to the judges. Making the participatory scheme work is a daunting task, which has resulted in a quagmire of judicial decisions. The large numbers of victims, novel character of procedures, and resource constraints pose particular challenges. The Chambers have pursued the goal of ensuring that victim participation is 'meaningful' rather than merely symbolic, occasionally taking it too far. The practice has raised serious questions concerning the proper role of victims, the rights of the accused, and trial efficiency. At the same time, the limited extent to which individual victims, and not only more lawyers, get involved in the judicial process can be problematic. Is there a point in spending enormous resources on legal representatives instead of funding more direct forms of assistance to victims? It is difficult to backtrack from a laid course, but in order to find a workable system the Court needed to test different solutions. The time for experiments has, however, run out.

The ICC reparations regime is an unprecedented and often praised restorative justice element in international criminal law. Its contours became clearer as several cases reached the reparations stage and seminal appellate and trial case law emerged, although the system is still developing. The ICC reparation mandate is not intended to prejudice any other existing international or domestic reparations options,[156] nor can it be seen as a master solution. The resources available for reparations remain very limited and clearly insufficient to satisfy the needs of all victims in the cases and situations the Court is dealing with. The Court must by all means avoid raising unrealistic expectations.

For the ICC, the policy choice of a victim-oriented approach was made when its Statute was adopted. It is up to the Court to implement that approach in the best possible way. Victim participation, reparations, and protection are closely linked to each other and form part of the broader procedural framework. Measures to provide protection, to make participation more efficient, and to safeguard the fair trial rights of the accused may limit the victims' involvement. A delicate balancing of different interests is required, and there is some room for the ICC to further refine its practices.

Considering the difficulties in the implementation, combined with the ICC's other shortcomings, it is easy to dismiss the victim-centred approach as well intended but bound to fail and argue that it should be abandoned. However, providing redress to victims of atrocities and giving voice to the voiceless is a noble and valid goal. There are good arguments why it should be pursued within international criminal justice. But this ambition requires better comprehension of victims' needs and concerns and effective advocacy by

---

[156] ICC Statute, Art. 75(6).

repeat players and insiders of the institutions. The Court has been taking its victim justice mandate and related challenges seriously and has to some extent succeeded in making its victim inclusion scheme as meaningful as possible. Much work lies ahead and contestation around the best ways to give effect to the ICC's victim mandate is bound to continue.

Further Reading

Tatiana Bachvarova, *The Standing of Victims in the Procedural Design of the International Criminal Court* (Leiden, 2017)

Thorsten Bonacker and Christoph Safferling (eds.), *Victims of International Crimes: An Interdisciplinary Discourse* (The Hague, 2013)

Alessandra Cuppini, *The Participation of Victims in International Criminal Proceedings: An Expressivist Justice Model* (Abingdon, 2022)

Carla Ferstman and Mariana Goetz (eds.), *Reparations for Victims of Genocide, War Crimes and Crimes Against Humanity* (Leiden, 2020)

Rachel Killean, *Victims, Atrocity and International Criminal Justice: Lessons from Cambodia* (Abingdon, 2018)

Luke Moffett, *Justice for Victims Before the International Criminal Court* (Abingdon, 2014)

Kinga Tibori-Szabó and Megan Hirst (eds.), *Victim Participation in International Criminal Justice: A Practitioner's Guide* (The Hague, 2017)

19

Punishment and Sentencing

19.1 INTERNATIONAL PENAL REGIME

International treaties which provide for individual criminal responsibility for certain violations of their provisions, do not regulate applicable penalties or sentencing in any detail. The Genocide Convention and the 1949 Geneva Conventions merely stipulate that penalties shall be 'effective' and the Torture Convention provides that the penalties shall be 'appropriate' and take into account the grave nature of the offence.[1] Customary international law is not easy to ascertain beyond general sentencing principles because states hold different views on what penalties may be appropriate. International provisions on penalties and sentencing leave states with wide leeway to legislate on appropriate sentences. This has generated concerns as to whether the international penal regime fully complies with the principle of legality of punishment (*nulla poena sine lege*), which requires some advance clarity about penalties.[2]

The Nuremberg and Tokyo International Military Tribunals (IMTs) had the power to impose 'death or such other punishment as shall be determined ... to be just'.[3] At Nuremberg, twelve of the accused were sentenced to death, three to life imprisonment, and four to fixed-term prison sentences. The Tokyo trial produced seven death sentences, sixteen sentences of life imprisonment, and two of fixed-term imprisonment. The penalties were considered rooted in customary international law, although that view remains contested.[4] IMTs paid little attention to sentencing considerations in their judgments, except for the brief mention of mitigating factors.[5]

The development of international human rights standards after World War II, and the growing rejection of capital punishment in particular, had implications for the penal

---

[1] 1948 Genocide Convention, Art. V; Geneva Convention I, Art. 49; Geneva Convention II, Art. 50; Geneva Convention III, Art. 129; Geneva Convention IV, Art. 146; 1984 Torture Convention, Art. 4(2).

[2] Silvia D'Ascoli, *Sentencing in International Criminal Law: The Approach of the Two Ad Hoc Tribunals and Future Perspectives for the International Criminal Court* (Oxford, 2011) 291; Damien Scalia, *Du principe de légalité des peines en droit international pénal* (Brussels, 2011).

[3] Nuremberg Charter, Art. 27 and Tokyo Charter, Art. 16. In addition, the Nuremberg Tribunal could deprive the convicted person of stolen property: Nuremberg Charter, Art. 28.

[4] William Schabas, 'War Crimes, Crimes Against Humanity, and the Death Penalty' (1997) 60 *Albany Law Review* 733, 735.

[5] See e.g. Judgment in *Trial of the Major War Criminals before the International Military Tribunal* (Nuremberg, 1947) 306, 315, 333 and 336 (regarding Funk, Dönitz, Speer, and Von Neurath); Majority Judgment in Neil Boister and Robert Cryer (eds.), *Documents on the Tokyo International Military Tribunal: Charter, Indictment and Judgments* (Oxford, 2010) 619 (regarding Shigemitsu).

regimes of the International Criminal Tribunal for the former Yugoslavia (ICTY) and the International Criminal Tribunal for Rwanda (ICTR). State practice has ranged from extensive use of capital punishment to its complete abolition. This divide is also reflected in international human rights treaties. The International Covenant on Civil and Political Rights (ICCPR) and European Convention on Human Rights (ECHR) restrict, but do not prohibit, the death penalty, while protocols to those treaties provide for prohibitions that states may set aside in times of war.[6] However, Protocol No. 13 to the ECHR prohibits capital punishment in all circumstances.[7] States parties are therefore treaty-bound to abolish the death penalty, and a customary international law norm to that effect may be emerging.[8] Although a universally accepted absolute prohibition of the death penalty does not exist today, the international penal regime has come to embody a more progressive position.

The principal penalty for the core crimes at the UN ad hoc Tribunals was imprisonment for life or a defined period.[9] The Tribunals also had the power to order the return of property and proceeds of crime to their rightful owners but this additional penalty was never applied.[10] For contempt of court or false testimony under solemn declaration, fines could also be imposed as an alternative or in addition to a fixed term of imprisonment.[11] The Statutes of the Tribunals provided that in determining the sentence the judges shall have recourse to the general practice regarding prison sentences in the courts of the former Yugoslavia and Rwanda, respectively. In practice, this did not entail an obligation to conform to national practice, only to take it into account and explain any departure from it.[12] Domestic sentencing practices could not be applied automatically due to differences relating to the nature, scope, and scale of the core crimes.

The issue of applicable penalties was controversial in the International Criminal Court (ICC) negotiations.[13] Some states insisted on the inclusion of the death penalty as a prerequisite for the Court's credibility and its deterrent function. But many others could not accept this position in light of their treaty commitments and for policy reasons. Likewise, some states objected to life imprisonment for human rights and constitutional reasons. The compromise was to establish the penalty of imprisonment for a fixed term not exceeding thirty years or, when justified by the extreme gravity of the crime and the individual circumstances of the convicted person, life imprisonment.[14] Another aspect of

---

[6] ICCPR, Art. 6(2) and ECHR, Art. 2(2); Second Optional Protocol to the ICCPR, 15 December 1989, Art. 2 (allowing for reservations); and Protocol No. 6 to the ECHR, 28 April 1983, Art. 2.

[7] Protocol No. 13 to the ECHR, 3 May 2002. See also *Öcalan v. Turkey*, ECtHR, 12 May 2005, paras. 150–75; *Al-Saldoon and Mufdhi* v. *United Kingdom*, ECtHR, 2 March 2010, paras. 115–43.

[8] William Schabas, *The Abolition of the Death Penalty in International Law*, 3rd ed. (Cambridge, 2002) 19. Arguably, abolitionist states must not facilitate the death penalty elsewhere: Bharat Malkani, 'The Obligation to Refrain from Assisting the Use of the Death Penalty' (2013) 62 *ICLQ* 523.

[9] ICTY Statute, Art. 24; ICTR Statute, Art. 23; and MICT Statute, Art. 22. See also ICTY and ICTR RPE, r. 101 and MICT RPE, r. 125.

[10] ICTY Statute, Art. 24(3); ICTR Statute, Art. 23(3); and MICT Statute, Art. 22(4).

[11] See ICTY and ICTR RPE, r. 77(G) and 91(G) (fines not exceeding €100,000 and US$10,000, respectively); MICT Statute, Art. 22(1) and MICT RPE, rr. 90(G) and 108(G) (fines not exceeding €50,000).

[12] See e.g. *Kunarac et al.*, ICTY TC II, 22 February 2001, para. 829; *Krstić*, ICTY AC, 19 April 2004, para. 260; and *Semanza*, ICTR AC, 20 May 2005, para. 377.

[13] See Rolf Einar Fife, 'Penalties' in Lee, *The Making of the Rome Statute*, 319–43.

[14] ICC Statute, Art. 77(1); ICC RPE, r. 145(3) ('the existence of one or more aggravating circumstances').

the compromise was the provision assuring that the regulation of penalties in the ICC Statute would not affect the imposition by states of penalties allowed in their national law, even if different from those applicable at the ICC.[15] This is a step away from the idea of a uniform system with harmonized penalties for international crimes.[16]

The ICC may also impose fines and order forfeiture of proceeds, property, and assets derived directly or indirectly from the relevant crime.[17] The forfeited money or other property may be transferred to the Trust Fund for Victims (TFV) and the payment of awards for reparations may be ordered.[18] Offences against the administration of justice at the ICC may be punished by a maximum five-year sentence, a fine, or both.[19] In the *Bemba II* (Article 70) case, the Appeals Chamber rejected as inconsistent with the *nulla poena* principle an 'inherent power' of a Trial Chamber to pronounce a conditionally suspended sentence or to conditionally suspend the execution of an imposed custodial sentence.[20]

The ICC legal framework reflects the effort to ensure stricter compliance with the *nulla poena* principle because it offers more detailed guidance for the determination of sentence.[21] In particular, the ICC Rules of Procedure and Evidence (RPE) specifies mitigating and aggravating circumstances and provides a non-exhaustive list of additional factors to be taken into account besides the circumstances both of the convict and of the crime.[22]

19.2 PURPOSES OF PUNISHMENT

The purposes of punishment have been the subject of a long-standing debate in international criminal law. Classical penal objectives in domestic systems are retribution, general and special deterrence, public protection (incapacitation), rehabilitation, and social integration of the offender. The relevance and achievability of the objectives of punishment in general, and in international criminal justice in particular, are contentious issues. Some consider that retribution ('just desert') is the appropriate philosophical justification for international punishment, although ensuring proportionate sentences matching the gravity of the core crimes poses special challenges.[23] Others emphasize the utilitarian justification of deterrence – special (vis-à-vis the convict) and general (vis-à-vis other potential offenders) – as the principal rationale for punishment. However, deterrence is also not without difficulties, particularly so in the context of international criminal law. International punishment is not

---

[15] ICC Statute, Art. 80.
[16] M. Cherif Bassiouni, *Introduction to International Criminal Law* (New York, NY, 2002) 682; cf. Nancy Amoury Combs, 'Seeking Inconsistency: Advancing Pluralism in International Criminal Sentencing' (2016) 41 *Yale Journal of International Law* 1.
[17] ICC Statute, Art. 77(2). [18] *Ibid.* Arts. 75(2) and 79(2). See Section 18.5. [19] *Ibid.* Art. 70(3).
[20] *Bemba et al.*, ICC AC, 8 March 2018 (ICC-01/05–01/13–2276) paras. 73–80.
[21] ICC Statute, Art. 78(1) and ICC RPE, r. 145. *Lubanga*, ICC AC, 1 December 2014 (ICC-01/04–01/06–3122) para. 32 ('comprehensive scheme for the determination and imposition of a sentence').
[22] ICC RPE, r. 145(1)(c) and (2).
[23] See e.g. Bassiouni, *Introduction to International Criminal Law* (n. 16) 681; Alexander Greenawalt, 'International Criminal Law for Retributivists' (2014) 35(4) *University of Pennsylvania Journal of International Law* 969; Jens Ohlin, 'Proportional Sentences at the ICTY' in Bert Swart, Alexander Zahar, and Göran Sluiter (eds.), *The Legacy of the International Criminal Tribunal for the Former Yugoslavia* (Oxford, 2011) ch. 11. See Section 2.2.1.

inevitable, especially for powerful suspects, and the empirical evidence that the existence of international tribunals – or the penalties they mete out – actually deter core crimes is mixed at best.[24] In turn, aims such as rehabilitation and social reintegration may be too unrealistic for the tribunals to pursue because the range of penalties is limited and the enforcement is outsourced to states.[25]

In the absence of consensus regarding the objectives of punishment, the tribunals typically refer to domestic penal theories, the extraordinary nature and gravity of core crimes, and broader goals of international criminal justice.[26] The ICTY, ICTR, and ICC emphasize retribution and general deterrence as primary purposes of punishment having equal importance.[27] Yet, the ICTY Appeals Chamber also held that deterrence should not be given 'undue prominence' in sentencing.[28] Retribution should be seen as 'just desert' and not as fulfilling the desire for vengeance.[29]

Other penal objectives have also featured in the case law: rehabilitation,[30] protection of society, stigmatization and public reprobation,[31] restoration of peace, and reconciliation.[32] The objective of rehabilitation has not played a predominant role in sentencing due to the serious nature of the crimes,[33] but in limited cases, it came into play when weighing individual mitigating circumstances[34] and in early-release decisions.[35] Overall, the inventories of sentencing objectives have varied by case.

---

[24] Natalie Hodgson, 'Exploring the International Criminal Court's Deterrent Potential: A Case Study of Australian Politics' (2021) 19 *JICJ* 913; Frank Neubacher, 'Criminology of International Crimes' in Florian Jeßberger and Julia Geneuss (eds.), *Why Punish Perpetrators of Mass Atrocities? Theoretical and Practical Perspectives on Punishment in International Criminal Law* (Cambridge, 2019) 32. See Section 2.2.2.

[25] Mark Drumbl, 'International Punishment from "Other" Perspectives' in Róisín Mulgrew and Denis Abels (eds.), *Research Handbook on International Penal System* (Cheltenham, 2016) ch. 16; Barbora Holá, Joris van Wijk, and Jessica Kelder, 'Effectiveness of International Criminal Tribunals: Empirical Assessment of Rehabilitation as Sentencing Goal' in Nobuo Hayashi and Cecilia Bailliet (eds.), *Legitimacy of International Criminal Tribunals* (Cambridge, 2017) ch. 14.

[26] E.g. Preamble to the ICC Statute, paras. 4–5; *Lubanga*, ICC TC I, 10 July 2012 (ICC-01/04–01/06–2901) para. 16.

[27] See e.g. *Delalić et al.*, ICTY AC, 20 February 2001, para. 806; *Serushago*, ICTR TC I, 15 February 1999, para. 20; *Katanga*, ICC TC II, 23 May 2014 (ICC-01/04–01/07–3484) para. 37; *Bemba*, ICC TC III, 21 June 2016 (ICC-01/05–01/08–3399) para. 10; *Al Mahdi*, ICC TC VIII, 27 September 2016 (ICC-01/12– 01/15–171) para. 66; *Ntaganda*, ICC TC VI, 7 November 2019 (ICC-01/04–02/06–2442) paras. 9–10; *Ongwen*, ICC TC IX, 6 May 2021 (ICC-02/04–01/15–1819-Red) paras. 60 and 389.

[28] See e.g. *Tadić*, ICTY AC, 26 January 2000, para. 48; *Aleksovski*, ICTY AC, 24 March 2000, para. 185; *Mrkšić and Šljivančanin*, ICTY AC, 5 May 2009, para. 415.

[29] *Kordić and Čerkez*, ICTY AC, 17 December 2004, para. 1075; *Ongwen*, ICC TC IX, 6 May 2021 (ICC-02/04–01/15–1819-Red) para. 389. See also Section 2.2.1.

[30] *Delalić et al.*, ICTY AC, 20 February 2001, para. 806; cf. *Kunarac et al.*, ICTY TC II, 22 February 2001, para. 844 (questioning rehabilitation as a sentencing purpose); *Ongwen*, ICC TC IX, 6 May 2021 (ICC-02/04–01/15–1819-Red) para. 60. See Section 2.2.4.

[31] *Ntakirutimana*, ICTR TC I, 21 February 2003, paras. 881–2; cf. *Kunarac et al.*, ICTY TC, 22 February 2001, para. 843 (protection of society not very relevant). See Section 2.2.5.

[32] *Kamuhanda*, ICTR TC II, 22 January 2004, paras. 753–4, and ICTR AC, 19 September 2005, para. 351; *Momir Nikolić*, ICTY TC I, 2 December 2003, para. 93. See also *Katanga*, ICC TC II, 23 May 2014 (ICC-01/04–01/07–3484) para. 38; *Bemba*, ICC TC III, 21 June 2016 (ICC-01/05–01/08–3399) para. 11; *Al Mahdi*, ICC TC VIII, 27 September 2016 (ICC-01/12–01/15–171) para. 67.

[33] *Delalić et al.*, ICTY AC, 20 February 2001, para. 806 ('a relevant factor … not one which should be given undue weight'); *Krajišnik*, ICTY AC, 17 March 2009, para. 806; *Popović et al.*, ICTY TC II, 10 June 2010, para. 2130; *Katanga*, ICC TC II, 23 May 2014 (ICC-01/04–01/07–3484) para. 38; *Bemba*, ICC TC III, 21 June 2016 (ICC-01/05–01/08–3399) para. 11; *Al Mahdi*, ICC TC VIII, 27 September 2016 (ICC-01/12–01/15–171) para. 67; *Ongwen*, ICC TC IX, 6 May 2021 (ICC-02/04–01/15–1819-Red) para. 60 ('to a lesser extent').

[34] E.g. *Erdemović*, ICTY TC I, 29 November 1996, para. 111 (considering the 'corrigible personality' as a mitigating factor); *Katanga*, ICC TC II, 23 May 2014 (ICC-01/04–01/07–3484) paras. 38 and 144; *Al Mahdi*, ICC TC VIII, 27 September 2016 (ICC-01/12–01/15–171) para. 97.

[35] Barbora Holá, Jessica Kelder, and Joris van Wijk, 'Rehabilitation and Early Release of Perpetrators of International Crimes: A Case Study of the ICTY and ICTR' (2014) 14 *ICLR* 1177–203.

The lack of certainty on the relative weight of the punishment goals and their impact on sentence calculations gives rise to perceptions of an inconsistent approach. Moreover, their relationship with the broader aims of international criminal justice is difficult to discern from the sentencing jurisprudence.[36] For instance, the pragmatic rationales behind plea bargaining in the Tribunals and sentencing rebates depart from the idea of punishment based on the gravity of the crime (retribution) and could weaken its deterrent function.[37] Another criticism is that the sentences rendered by international tribunals may appear too lenient when compared with domestic practice for ordinary crimes such as murder.[38] Disparities in sentencing for core crimes between international and domestic courts also raise concerns about systemic coherence.[39] This may be problematic considering that international courts often adjudicate cases of senior military and political leaders believed to be most responsible whilst the latter deal with mid- and lower-level perpetrators.

19.3 SENTENCING PRACTICE

19.3.1 General Approach

Judges hold a broad discretion in sentencing which is an aspect of their obligation to individualize a penalty to fit the individual circumstances of the convicted person and the gravity of the crime.[40] No sentencing tariffs or scales for the different crimes are provided either in the statutes or the case law. The ICTY Appeals Chamber repeatedly declined to set down a definitive list of sentencing guidelines.[41] While emphasizing the principle of consistency in sentencing, it found a comparison with the sentences imposed in other cases to be of limited assistance, unless the previous decisions related to the same offence and the circumstances were substantially similar.[42] The courts have regularly drawn support from each other's rulings with regard to the goals of punishment and the interpretation of sentencing principles and factors.[43] Occasionally, they have also paid attention to each other's sentencing practice on more specific issues. For example, the ICC Trial

---

[36] E.g. *Brđanin*, ICTY TC II, 1 September 2004, para. 1092 ('rehabilitation, social defence and restoration . . . are important for achieving the goals of this Tribunal'). See further Sergey Vasiliev, 'Punishment Rationales in International Criminal Jurisprudence: Two Readings of a Non-Question' in Florian Jeßberger and Julia Geneuss (eds.), *Why Punish Perpetrators of Mass Atrocities? Theoretical and Practical Perspectives on Punishment in International Criminal Law* (Cambridge, 2019) ch. 4.

[37] Ralph Henham and Mark Drumbl, 'Plea Bargaining at the International Criminal Tribunal for the Former Yugoslavia' (2005) 16 *Criminal Law Forum* 56.

[38] Mark Harmon and Fergal Gaynor, 'Ordinary Sentences for Extraordinary Crimes' (2007) 5 *JICJ* 683; Jens Ohlin, 'Towards a Unique Theory of International Criminal Sentencing' in Sluiter and Vasiliev, *International Criminal Procedure*, ch. 10.

[39] Barbora Holá and Hollie Nyseth Brehm, 'Punishing Genocide: A Comparative Empirical Analysis of Sentencing Laws and Practices at the International Criminal Tribunal for Rwanda (ICTR), Rwandan Domestic Courts, and Gacaca Courts' (2016) 10(3) *Genocide Studies and Prevention: An International Journal* 59.

[40] ICTY Statute, Art. 24(2); ICTR Statute, Art. 23(2) and ICTY and ICTR RPE, r. 101; MICT Statute, Art. 22(3) and MICT RPE, r. 125; ICC Statute, Art. 78(1).

[41] See e.g. *Furundžija*, ICTY AC, 21 July 2000, para. 238; *Delalić et al.*, ICTY AC, 20 February 2001, para. 715; and *Krstić*, ICTY AC, 19 April 2004, para. 242.

[42] See e.g. *Delalić et al.*, ICTY AC, 20 February 2001, paras. 719–20, 756–9; *Kamuhanda*, ICTR AC, 19 September 2005, paras. 361–2; *Momir Nikolić*, ICTY AC, 8 March 2006, paras. 38–54; *Strugar*, ICTY AC, 17 July 2008, paras. 336 and 348; *Ntabakuze*, ICTR AC, 8 May 2012, paras. 297–300.

[43] See e.g. *Bemba*, ICC TC III, 21 June 2016 (ICC-01/05–01/08–3399) para. 17 (referring to the ICTY and ICTR case law on the principle of gradation in sentencing and greater degree of responsibility of superiors); *Ntaganda*, ICC TC VI, 7 November 2019 (ICC-01/04–02/06–2442) para. 15; *Ongwen*, ICC TC IX, 6 May 2021 (ICC-02/04–01/15–1819-Red) para. 103.

Chamber in *Lubanga* took into account the practice of the Special Court for Sierra Leone (SCSL) regarding the same type of offences.[44]

The aggregate sentence should reflect the totality of the criminal conduct and the overall culpability of the offender.[45] The gravity of the offence, including the form and degree of participation in the crimes, is the principal consideration in sentencing.[46] The Tribunals and the ICC have not recognized any abstract hierarchy of crimes, although genocide has generally been regarded as more serious than crimes against humanity and war crimes.[47] The jurisprudence is not fully consistent on whether crimes against humanity and war crimes are equally grave,[48] as some chambers have held that the former must carry a higher penalty.[49] According to the ICC Trial Chamber in *Ntaganda*, not all core crimes are of equivalent gravity: crimes against property are generally less grave than crimes against persons.[50] Yet, the broad acceptance of cumulative convictions reduces the practical importance of the debate about the hierarchy of crimes.[51]

The jurisprudence is not uniform on how the form of responsibility impacts the sentence. Both ad hoc Tribunals established that aiding and abetting generally warrants lower sentences than co-perpetration.[52] However, the SCSL Appeals Chamber rejected this conclusion as unsupported in customary international law.[53] Further, the ICTY and ICTR rejected the argument that superior responsibility as such should be seen as less grave and attract a lesser sentence than other forms of individual criminal responsibility; rather, those in positions of authority should generally bear greater responsibility.[54] Earlier ICC jurisprudence suggested that Article 25(3) of the ICC Statute establishes a hierarchy of modes of liability in descending order from (a) to (d).[55] This view proved controversial and was overwhelmingly rejected.[56] The ICC also rejected any hierarchy of forms of principal

---

[44] *Lubanga*, ICC TC I, 10 July 2012 (ICC-01/04–01/06–2901) paras. 12–15.

[45] *Martić*, ICTY AC, 8 October 2008, para. 350; *Ntabakuze*, ICTR AC, 8 May 2012, para. 267; *Ntaganda*, ICC TC VI, 7 November 2019 (ICC-01/04–02/06–2442) para. 11.

[46] ICTY Statute, Art. 24(2); ICTR Statute, Art. 23(2); MICT Statute, Art. 22(3); and ICC Statute, Art. 78(1). See also *Delalić et al.*, ICTY AC, 20 February 2001, paras. 731 and 741; *Blaškić*, ICTY AC, 29 July 2004, para. 683; *Šešelj*, MICT AC, 11 April 2018, para. 179; *Katanga*, ICC TC II, 23 May 2014 (ICC-01/04–01/07–3484) paras. 39–40; *Ntaganda*, ICC TC VI, 7 November 2019 (ICC-01/04–02/06–2442) para. 14.

[47] *Kambanda*, ICTR TC I, 4 September 1998, paras. 16 and 42; *Krstić*, ICTY TC I, 2 August 2001, para. 700, and ICTY AC, 19 April 2004, paras. 36–7 and 275. Cf. *Serushago*, ICTR TC I, 5 February 1999, paras. 13–14 (considering genocide and crimes against humanity to be of an equally grave nature).

[48] *Tadić*, ICTY AC, 26 January 2000, para. 69; *Kayishema and Ruzindana*, ICTR AC, 1 June 2001, para. 367.

[49] *Tadić*, ICTY TC II, 14 July 1997, para. 73; *Erdemović*, ICTY AC, 7 October 1997 (majority) paras. 20–6; and *Kambanda*, ICTR TC I, 4 September 1998, para. 4.

[50] *Ntaganda*, ICC TC VI, 7 November 2019 (ICC-01/04–02/06–2442) para. 14.

[51] Cumulative convictions may be entered under different statutory provisions for the same conduct where each of them has a materially distinct element not contained within the other. See *Delalić et al.*, ICTY AC, 20 February 2001, paras. 412–13; *Musema*, ICTR AC, 16 November 2001, paras. 358–70; *Kordić and Čerkez*, ICTY AC, 17 December 2004, para. 1033.

[52] *Vasiljević*, ICTY AC, 25 February 2004, para. 182; *Kajelijeli*, ICTR TC II, 1 December 2003, para. 963.

[53] *Taylor*, SCSL AC, 26 September 2013, paras. 666–70 and at 305 (affirming the fifty-year sentence); cf. *Sesay et al.*, SCSL TC I, 8 April 2009, para. 20; *Taylor*, SCSL TC II, 26 April 2012, para. 94, and 30 May 2013, para. 21 (all following the ICTY and ICTR practice).

[54] *Ntabakuze*, ICTR AC, 8 May 2012, para. 303; *Dragomir Milošević*, ICTY AC, 12 November 2009, para. 334.

[55] *Lubanga*, ICC PTC I, 29 January 2007 (ICC-01/04–01/06–803) paras. 330–5 and ICC TC I, 14 March 2012 (ICC-01/04–01/06–2842) paras. 996–9; and *Katanga and Ngudjolo*, ICC PTC I, 30 September 2008 (ICC-01/04–01/07–717) paras. 506–8. See further Chapter 15.

[56] *Katanga*, ICC TC II, 23 May 2014 (ICC-01/04–01/07–3484) para. 61; *Katanga*, ICC TC II, 7 March 2014 (ICC-01/04–01/07–3436) paras. 1386–7; *Bemba et al.*, ICC AC, 8 March 2018 (ICC-01/05–01/13–2276) paras. 59–62. See also Separate Opinion of Judge Adrian Fulford in *Lubanga*, ICC TC I, 14 March 2012 (ICC-01/04–01/06–2842) paras. 8–9, and Concurring Opinion

perpetration in Article 25(3)(a) of the Statute for sentencing purposes.[57] Nor has superior responsibility been regarded as lower or higher in terms of gravity than any mode of liability in Article 25(3).[58] The punishment always depends on the facts of the case and gravity must be assessed *in concreto*.

The sentencing practice of the ICTY and ICTR has been criticized for being unpredictable and inconsistent, both within the same Tribunal and between them.[59] Some authors have also deemed their sentences to be too lenient.[60] The final sentences imposed by the ICTY and ICTR span a broad range, from three years' imprisonment to life imprisonment. Life sentences were meted out in ICTR cases regarding genocide and, more rarely, by the ICTY for genocide and/or crimes against humanity.[61]

Empirical studies conclude, however, that the sentencing of the Tribunals is fairly logical and consistent and follows certain patterns, despite the opacity of their rulings. Thus, high-ranked perpetrators in influential positions receive longer sentences; more extensive criminal activities are punished more severely than isolated single acts; genocide is punished most harshly, while crimes against humanity generate longer sentences than war crimes; and aiders and abettors are punished less severely than those who participate more directly in the atrocities.[62] At the ICC, the sentences rendered by the Trial Chambers following the five core crime convictions thus far, have ranged from nine years (*Al Mahdi*) to thirty years (*Ntaganda*).

19.3.2 Aggravating and Mitigating Circumstances

The ICTY and ICTR judges are required to consider any aggravating and mitigating circumstances in passing sentences, but neither their Statutes nor the RPE define those factors in detail.[63] The ICC RPE provides a non-exhaustive list of mitigating and aggravating circumstances inspired by the Tribunals' case law.[64] In the ad hoc Tribunals and the ICC, the Prosecutor must establish any aggravating circumstances beyond reasonable

---

of Judge Van den Wyngaert in *Ngudjolo*, ICC TC II, 18 December 2012, paras. 22–30. Cf. *Lubanga*, ICC AC, 1 December 2014 (ICC-01/04–01/06–3121-Red) para. 462 (principals are more blameworthy than accomplices).

[57] *Ntaganda*, ICC TC VI, 7 November 2019 (ICC-01/04–02/06–2442) para. 16.

[58] *Bemba*, ICC TC III, 21 June 2016 (ICC-01/05–01/08–3399) para. 16.

[59] E.g. John R.W.D. Jones and Steven Powles, *International Criminal Practice*, 3rd ed. (Oxford, 2003) 778–80; cf. Frederik Harhoff, 'Sense and Sensibility in Sentencing: Taking Stock of International Criminal Punishment' in Ola Engdahl and Pål Wrange (eds.), *Law at War: The Law as It Was and the Law as It Should Be* (Leiden, 2008) 121, 134–7.

[60] E.g. Harmon and Gaynor, 'Ordinary Sentences for Extraordinary Crimes' (n. 38); Sam Szoke-Burke, 'Avoiding Belittlement of Human Suffering: A Retributivist Critique of ICTR Sentencing Practices' (2012) 10 *JICJ* 561.

[61] See e.g. *Akayesu*, ICTR AC, 1 June 2001; *Stakić*, ICTY TC II, 31 July 2003 (life imprisonment replaced on appeal by a fixed term sentence of forty years: ICTY AC, 22 March 2006; *Galić*, ICTY AC, 30 November 2006, paras. 455–6 (a twenty-year sentence increased after appeal to life imprisonment); *Lukić and Lukić*, ICTY TC III, 20 July 2009 and ICTY AC, 4 December 2012; and *Tolimir*, ICTY TC II, 12 December 2012.

[62] Barbora Holá, Alette Smeulers, and Catrien Bijleveld, 'Is ICTY Sentencing Predictable? An Empirical Analysis of ICTY Sentencing Practice' (2009) 22 *LJIL* 79; and Barbora Holá, Alette Smeulers, and Catrien Bijleveld, 'Consistency of International Sentencing: ICTY and ICTR Case Study' (2012) 9 *European Journal of Criminology* 539; Joseph Doherty and Richard Steinberg, 'Punishment and Policy in International Criminal Sentencing: An Empirical Study' (2016) 110 *AJIL* 48.

[63] ICTY and ICTR RPE, r. 101; MICT RPE, r. 125. See e.g. *Musema*, ICTR AC, 16 November 2001, para. 395.

[64] ICC RPE, r. 145(2).

doubt.[65] The defendant is required to prove mitigating circumstances on a lower ('balance of probabilities') standard.[66]

The aggravating factors identified in the ICTY and ICTR jurisprudence include, among others, the scale of the crimes; the length of time during which they continued; the age, number, and suffering of the victims; the nature of the perpetrator's involvement; premeditation and discriminatory intent; abuse of power; and position as a superior.[67] While a high position should not automatically aggravate, and a low rank or subordinate function should not automatically mitigate, the sentence,[68] the abuse of a superior position may well be an aggravating factor.[69] A high level of authority, or the status of being known and respected, such as a priest, may be considered as an aggravating circumstance (where it is not an element of the mode of liability).[70] Similarly, the ICC RPE lists as aggravating factors: relevant prior convictions; abuse of power or official capacity; particularly defenceless victims; multiple victims; particular cruelty; and discrimination.[71] Only circumstances directly related to the offence of which the defendant was convicted or to that person him- or herself may be considered aggravating.[72] But a factor may not be treated as aggravating if it has been taken into account as an aspect of gravity as an element of the actual crime or mode of liability. 'Double-counting' is prohibited.[73]

The *Ntaganda* Trial Chamber took into account that murders had been committed against particularly defenceless victims and with particular cruelty and that victims had been raped repeatedly and were of young age.[74] The *Ongwen* trial judges did not count abuse of power or official capacity in aggravation because there was no 'special lawful relationship' between the defendant and his victims which he would have abused as an LRA commander.[75]

The only mitigating circumstance specified in the ICTY, ICTR, and Residual Mechanism (MICT) RPE is substantial cooperation with the Prosecutor before or after conviction.[76]

---

[65] E.g. *Delalić et al.*, ICTY AC, 20 February 2001, para. 763; *Kajelijeli*, ICTR AC, 23 May 2005, para. 294; *Lubanga*, ICC TC I, 10 July 2012 (ICC-01/04–01/06–2901) paras. 32–3; *Katanga*, ICC TC II, 23 May 2014 (ICC-01/04–01/07–3484) para. 34; *Bemba*, ICC TC, 21 June 2016 (ICC-01/05–01/08–3399) para. 18; *Ongwen*, ICC TC IX, 6 May 2021 (ICC-02/04–01/15–1819-Red) para. 53.

[66] The circumstance must be 'more probable than not': *Delalić et al.*, ICTY AC, 20 February 2001, para. 590; *Kajelijeli*, ICTR AC, 23 May 2005, para. 294; *Lubanga*, ICC TC I, 10 July 2012 (ICC-01/04–01/06–2901) para. 34; *Bemba*, ICC TC, 21 June 2016 (ICC-01/05–01/08–3399) para. 19; *Ntaganda*, ICC TC VI, 7 November 2019 (ICC-01/04–02/06–2442) para. 24.

[67] See e.g. *Blaškić*, ICTY AC, 29 July 2004, para. 686 (with further references).

[68] See e.g. *Delalić et al.*, ICTY AC, 20 February 2001, para. 847; *Krstić*, ICTY TC I, 2 August 2001, para. 709.

[69] See e.g. *Kayishema and Ruzindana*, ICTR AC, 1 June 2001, paras. 358–9; *Stakić*, ICTY AC, 22 March 2006, para. 411.

[70] See e.g. *Rugambarara*, ICTR TC II, 16 November 2007, para. 26; *Seromba*, ICTR AC, 12 March 2008, para. 230.

[71] ICC RPE, r. 145(2).

[72] *Stakić*, ICTY TC II, 31 July 2003, para. 911; *Simba*, ICTR AC, 27 November 2007, para. 82; *Ntaganda*, ICC TC VI, 7 November 2019 (ICC-01/04–02/06–2442) para. 18; cf. *Delalić et al.*, ICTY AC, 20 February 2001, paras. 780–9 (also conduct at trial, indicating a lack of remorse, was considered an aggravating factor).

[73] *Blaškić*, ICTY AC, 29 July 2004, para. 693; *Deronjić*, ICTY AC, 20 July 2005, paras. 106–7; *Momir Nikolić*, ICTY AC, 8 March 2006, paras. 57–67; *Simba*, ICTR AC, 27 November 2007, para. 320; *Ntaganda*, ICC TC VI, 7 November 2019 (ICC-01/04–02/06–2442) para. 20; *Ongwen*, ICC TC IX, 6 May 2021 (ICC-02/04–01/15–1819-Red) para. 53; *Ntaganda*, ICC AC, 30 March 2021 (ICC-01/04–02/06–2667-Red) para. 123.

[74] *Ntaganda*, ICC AC, 30 March 2021 (ICC-01/04–02/06–2667-Red) paras. 78–84, 121–7.

[75] *Ongwen*, ICC TC IX, 6 May 2021 (ICC-02/04–01/15–1819-Red) para. 134.

[76] ICTY and ICTR RPE, r. 101(B)(ii) and MICT RPE, r. 125(B)(ii). See e.g. *Jokić*, ICTY TC I, 18 March 2004, paras. 93–6, and ICTY AC, 30 August 2005, paras. 87–9; and *Zelenović*, ICTY AC, 31 October 2007, para. 24 (the cooperation need not be substantial for mitigation).

Cooperation with the Court is also a mitigating factor at the ICC.[77] A related issue is to what extent a guilty plea should be a mitigating factor.[78] Usually, such pleas are linked to an agreement between the accused and the prosecution, which may include non-binding recommendations to the court as to the sentence. Sentencing discounts can encourage guilty pleas, which is important for reasons of judicial economy or in order to spare victims from having to testify. While guilty pleas have generally been considered in mitigation, the Chambers have avoided declaring a guaranteed discount and have instead adopted an individualized approach to the mitigating effect of a guilty plea.[79] In some cases, the Tribunals found that the aggravating circumstances outweighed the mitigating effect of a guilty plea,[80] and departed from the sentencing recommendations.[81]

Other mitigating factors have included: an expression of remorse; voluntary surrender; assistance to detainees or victims; and personal circumstances, such as good character with no prior convictions, age, comportment in detention, family circumstances, and, in exceptional cases, poor health.[82] Hence, many mitigating circumstances relate to conduct subsequent to the crime, and this was the case when the Tribunal attached significant weight to the contributions of the accused to peace.[83] Factors directly related to the crime in question are also of importance, such as indirect or limited participation[84] and circumstances falling short of constituting grounds for excluding criminal liability (duress and diminished mental responsibility).[85] In the *CDF* case, the SCSL Appeals Chamber dismissed the positive political motive of supporting the democratically elected regime as a ground to mete out shorter prison terms, holding that allowing a 'just cause' to mitigate the sentence would contravene the sentencing purpose of affirmative prevention and lead to a conflation of *ius ad bellum* and *ius in bello*.[86] The ICTR also established that the sentence may be reduced as a remedy for violations of the convicted person's procedural rights.[87] As with aggravating circumstances, 'double-counting' mitigating factors is not permitted.[88]

At the ICC, the RPE expressly mentions mitigating factors such as substantially diminished mental capacity or duress (when these fall short of constituting grounds for excluding criminal responsibility), as well as the convicted person's conduct after the crime, including any efforts to compensate the victims and cooperation with the Court.[89] Such circumstances neither must directly relate to the crimes of which the person was convicted nor need be

---

[77] ICC RPE, r. 145(2)(a)(ii). See also *Lubanga*, ICC TC I, 10 July 2012 (ICC-01/04–01/06–2901) paras. 90–1; *Katanga*, ICC TC II, 23 May 2014 (ICC-01/04–01/07–3484) paras. 32, 127–8; *Al Mahdi*, ICC TC VIII, 27 September 2016 (ICC-01/12–01/15–171) paras. 97, 101–2.

[78] See further Section 17.10.

[79] See Pascale Chifflet and Gideon Boas, 'Sentencing Coherence in International Criminal Law: The Cases of Biljana Plavšić and Miroslav Bralo' (2012) 23 *Criminal Law Forum* 135.

[80] See e.g. *Kambanda*, ICTR TC I, 4 September 1998, paras. 60–2, and ICTR AC, 19 October 2000, paras. 125–6.

[81] See e.g. *Dragan Nikolić*, ICTY TC II, 18 December 2003, and ICTY AC, 4 February 2005 (a sentence of twenty-three years imposed when the recommendation was fifteen years; reduced to twenty years on appeal).

[82] See e.g. *Blaškić*, ICTY AC, 29 July 2004, para. 696 (with further references).

[83] See e.g. *Krajišnik and Plavšić*, ICTY TC III, 27 February 2003, paras. 85–94; *Babić*, ICTY AC, 18 July 2005, paras. 55–9.

[84] See e.g. *Babić*, ICTY AC, 18 July 2005, paras. 39–40.   [85] *Blaškić*, ICTY AC, 29 July 2004, para. 696.

[86] *Fofana and Kondewa*, SCSL TC I, 9 October 2007, paras. 80 and 86, and SCSL AC, 28 May 2008, paras. 533–4 (concurring with *Kordić and Čerkez*, ICTY AC, 17 December 2004, para. 1082). The Sierra Leonean judges of both Chambers dissented and voted to acquit on the same ground. See Section 12.1.3.

[87] E.g. *Semanza*, ICTR AC, 31 May 2000, at 34 and 20 May 2005, paras. 323–9, 389; *Kajelijeli*, ICTR AC, 23 May 2005, paras. 320–4.

[88] See e.g. *Limaj et al.*, ICTY AC, 27 September 2007, para. 143.   [89] ICC RPE, r. 145(2)(a).

limited by the scope of the confirmed charges.[90] In its sentencing practice, the ICC has accorded substantial weight to admissions of guilt and expressions of compassion and sincere remorse.[91] The judges have also accorded limited weight, in line with their broad discretion on this matter,[92] to the convicted person's personal circumstances (age and family situation),[93] palpable and genuine efforts to promote peace and reconciliation,[94] initial reluctance to commit the crime, and the employment of less destructive means of executing the crime.[95] In the landmark *Ongwen* case, the personal history of the defendant – who was abducted into the Lord's Resistance Army at the age of nine, brutalized and traumatized by his upbringing as a child soldier, and rose through its ranks to become a commander – was held to warrant mitigation. By contrast, the Trial Chamber refused to take into account his alleged substantially diminished mental capacity and duress as mitigating factors.[96] This was endorsed by the majority of the Appeals Chamber.[97] In her dissenting opinion, Judge Ibáñez Carranza, however, made clear that she would have reversed the sentence, taking into account Ongwen's childhood experience.[98]

19.3.3 Cumulative or Joint Sentences

The ICTY and ICTR allowed cumulative charges and convictions based on the same underlying conduct. This practice must not prejudice the convicted person, which raises the question of how cumulative convictions may impact sentencing. The jurisprudence of both Tribunals establishes that a Chamber has discretion to impose sentences which are global, concurrent, or consecutive.[99] This was subsequently codified in the RPE.[100] Regardless of method, the final or aggregated sentence should reflect the totality of the culpable conduct in a just and appropriate way.

The ICC Statute provides that a separate sentence is to be pronounced for each crime, together with a joint sentence specifying the total period of imprisonment.[101] The joint sentence must not be less than the highest individual sentence or exceed the maximum sentence according to the Statute. In *Ntaganda*, the Trial Chamber imposed the joint

---

[90] *Ntaganda*, ICC TC VI, 7 November 2019 (ICC-01/04–02/06–2442) para. 24.

[91] *Al Mahdi*, ICC TC VIII, 27 September 2016 (ICC-01/12–01/15–171) para. 100; cf. *Katanga*, ICC TC II, 23 May 2014 (ICC-01/ 04–01/07–3484) paras. 117–21; *Ntaganda*, ICC TC VI, 7 November 2019 (ICC-01/04–02/06–2442) para. 239.

[92] *Ntaganda*, ICC AC, 30 March 2021 (ICC-01/04–02/06–2667-Red) paras. 5 and 174 (individual circumstances will not as a matter of routine be considered in mitigation).

[93] *Katanga*, ICC TC II, 23 May 2014 (ICC-01/04–01/07–3484) para. 88; cf. *Al Mahdi*, ICC TC VIII, 27 September 2016 (ICC-01/12–01/15–171) para. 96 (not considering age, economic background, or expertise in religious matters to be of relevance); *Ntaganda*, ICC TC VI, 7 November 2019 (ICC-01/04–02/06–2442) paras. 208, 210, 244.

[94] *Katanga*, ICC TC II, 23 May 2014, paras. 91 and 144; cf. *Ntaganda*, ICC TC VI, 7 November 2019 (ICC-01/04–02/06–2442) para. 224 (considering Ntaganda's genuine and concrete contribution to peace and reconciliation, or demobilization and disarmament, not established on a balance of probabilities).

[95] *Al Mahdi*, ICC TC VIII, 27 September 2016 (ICC-01/12–01/15–171) para. 89 (Al Mahdi recommended not to use a bulldozer in order not to damage the graves next to the mausoleums that were being destroyed).

[96] *Ongwen*, ICC TC IX, 6 May 2021 (ICC-02/04–01/15–1819-Red) paras. 77–78, 100, 105, 111, 388–97 (handing down a joint sentence of twenty-five years' imprisonment as opposed to life imprisonment).

[97] *Ongwen*, ICC AC, 15 December 2022 (ICC-02/04–01/15–2023).

[98] *Ibid.*, Partly Dissenting Opinion of Judge Luz del Carmen Ibáñez Carranza (ICC-02/04–01/15–2023-Anx1) paras. 87–153.

[99] *Delalić et al.*, ICTY AC, 20 February 2001, para. 429; *Kambanda*, ICTR AC, 19 October 2000, paras. 102–12 (interpreting r. 101 of the respective RPE).

[100] ICTY and ICTR RPE, r. 87(C); MICT RPE, r. 104(C).   [101] ICC Statute, Art. 78(3).

sentence of thirty years' imprisonment – the statutorily mandated maximum definite term – which was also the highest individual sentence imposed for the crime against humanity of persecution. The judges considered this penalty to fully reflect Ntaganda's convictions for multiple other crimes and his overall culpability and turned down victims' requests to elevate the total sentence to life imprisonment.[102]

19.4 SENTENCING PROCEDURES

When the presentation of evidence and submissions relevant to sentencing, as well as judicial deliberations on sentencing matters, are to take place, depends on the structure of the trial as a unified or bifurcated process.[103] Under the bifurcated model, sentencing arguments and evidence can be submitted at a separate hearing when the person is convicted, and the guilt or innocence and the sentence are determined separately. Under the unified model, evidence and submissions on sentence can be presented along with evidence relevant to the determination of guilt or innocence, and one judgment containing both the verdict and the sentence is issued. A unified trial makes it more difficult for the defendant to make effective submissions regarding the appropriate sentence: prior to conviction the defence would normally contest guilt rather than advocate reduction of a potential sentence.

The Nuremberg and Tokyo Tribunals adopted the unified model.[104] Initially, the ICTY Trial Chambers addressed sentencing separately and subsequent to conviction.[105] However, in July 1998 the ICTY RPE were amended to allow for guilt and sentence to be determined in a single judgment also in cases other than guilty pleas.[106] This became the practice in both Tribunals.

The ICC Statute does not rule out unified trials in cases where guilt is contested.[107] The Trial Chamber is directed, in determining the sentence to be imposed, to take into account the sentencing-related evidence presented and submissions made during the trial.[108] But the Statute requires a further hearing on sentencing if either party requests it or if the Chamber so decides on its own motion.[109] In *Lubanga*, the ICC Trial Chamber indicated early on that it would hold a sentencing hearing in case of conviction but allowed evidence relating to sentence during the trial for reasons of efficiency and economy.[110] Separate sentencing hearings have been conducted in all subsequent contested trials. In the event of an accepted

---

[102] *Ntaganda*, ICC TC VI, 7 November 2019 (ICC-01/04–02/06–2442) paras. 248–51.
[103] Guido Acquaviva, 'Single and Bifurcated Trials' in Sluiter et al., *International Criminal Procedure*, 534.
[104] At Nuremberg, sentences were pronounced in a separate session after the oral delivery of verdicts; convicts were unable to address sentencing matters separately. On Tokyo, see Neil Boister and Robert Cryer, *The Tokyo International Military Tribunal: A Reappraisal* (Oxford, 2008) 250 (critical of this procedure).
[105] See *Tadić*, ICTY TC II, 14 July 1997.
[106] ICTY RPE, rr. 87(C) and 100; cf. ICTY RPE, rr. 87 and 100 (IT/32/Rev. 12, 12 November 1997). See also ICTR RPE, rr. 87(C) and 100, and MICT RPE, r. 104(C).
[107] ICC Statute, Art. 76(2); see also *Ongwen*, ICC AC, 15 December 2022 (ICC-02/04–01/15–2023) paras. 1 and 56 (not unreasonable for trial judges to proceed considering the possibility of joint proceedings).
[108] ICC Statute, Art. 76(1); see also *ibid*. Art 76(2) ('before completion of the trial'). [109] *Ibid*. Art. 76(2) and ICC RPE, r. 143.
[110] *Lubanga*, ICC TC I, 29 January 2008 (ICC-01/04–01/06–1140) para. 32; 18 March 2010 (ICC-01/04–01/06–2360) para. 38; and 10 July 2012 (ICC-01/04–01/06–2901) paras. 29–30. See also *Bemba*, ICC TC III, 19 November 2010 (ICC-01/05–01/08–1023) para. 13.

guilty plea at the Tribunals or admission of guilt at the ICC, the case moves to a sentencing hearing.[111] In *Al Mahdi*, the defendant admitted guilt, and the ICC Trial Chamber decided, with the agreement of the parties, that judgment and sentence would be rendered simultaneously following the trial hearing.[112]

A sentence may be appealed both at the Tribunals and at the ICC,[113] and an appeal against a conviction or acquittal may also lead to a revision of sentence. Due to the corrective nature of the ICTY and ICTR appeals proceedings, the test is whether the Trial Chamber has committed a 'discernible error' in the exercise of its sentencing discretion, something that the appellant must demonstrate.[114] If a conviction is modified or acquittal reversed on appeal, however, the Appeals Chamber will either refer the matter back to the Trial Chamber for sentencing[115] or itself impose a new sentence.[116] At the ICTY and ICTR, time-limited sentences were occasionally replaced by life imprisonment.[117] The sentences entered or increased by the Appeals Chamber are controversial because no further appeal is possible, which some judges deemed inconsistent with the right to appeal.[118] A different test for amending the penalty on appeal applies at the ICC: whether 'the sentence is disproportionate to the crime'.[119] In the *Bemba II* case, the Appeals Chamber reversed the sentences and remanded this matter to the Trial Chamber for a new determination.[120]

19.5 PARDON, EARLY RELEASE, AND REVIEW OF SENTENCE

The prisoner may be eligible for pardon, commutation of the sentence, or early release in the state where the sentence is served (see Section 19.6), but the Tribunals retained control over the sentence and the final say on the matter.[121] The Tribunals applied the same rules to prisoners who were not transferred to a state but remained in their detention centres in The Hague or Arusha. Upon receiving a notice from the enforcing state or a direct petition by the convicted person, the President, together with other judges, considered the gravity of the crimes, the prisoner's demonstration of rehabilitation, any substantial cooperation with the Prosecutor, and personal circumstances. The functions of the ICTY and ICTR with respect to pardon and commutation of sentences have been performed by the Residual Mechanism

---

[111] ICTY RPE, rr. 62*bis* and 100; ICTR RPE, rr. 62(B) and 100; MICT RPE, rr. 65 and 124. See ICC Statute, Arts. 65 and 76(2) (the phrase '[e]xcept where article 65 applies' means that, in case of an accepted admission, sentencing is not conducted under Article 76; there is no further sentencing hearing but only one 'trial hearing' prior to the combined judgment and sentence). *Al Mahdi*, ICC TC VIII, 22 July 2016 (ICC-01/12–01/15–136) para. 7.
[112] *Al Mahdi*, ICC TC VIII, 27 September 2016 (ICC-01/12–01/15–171) para. 5. [113] See Section 17.2.1.
[114] *Delalić et al.*, ICTY AC, 20 February 2001, para. 725; *Semanza*, ICTR AC, 20 May 2005, para. 374.
[115] *Tadić*, ICTY AC, 15 July 1999, para. 27.
[116] *Blaškić*, ICTY AC, 29 July 2004, para. 726; *Ntabakuze*, ICTR AC, 8 May 2012, paras. 313–16.
[117] *Gacumbitsi*, ICTR AC, 7 July 2006, para. 206; *Galić*, ICTY AC, 30 November 2006, paras. 454–5.
[118] Referring to ICCPR, Art. 14(5), see Dissenting Opinions of Judge Pocar in *Rutaganda*, ICTR AC, 26 May 2003, paras. 1–4; *Semanza*, ICTY AC, 20 May 2005, paras. 1–4; *Galić*, ICTY AC, 30 November 2006, paras. 3–4.
[119] ICC Statute, Arts. 81(2) and 83(2) and (3). See *Lubanga*, ICC AC, 1 December 2014 (ICC-01/04–01/06–3122) paras. 39 and 44; *Bemba et al.*, ICC AC, 8 March 2018 (ICC-01/05–01/13–2276) paras. 21–5; *Ntaganda*, ICC AC, 30 March 2021 (ICC-01/04–02/06–2667-Red) paras. 19–32.
[120] *Bemba et al.*, ICC AC, 8 March 2018 (ICC-01/05–01/13–2276) paras. 359–62.
[121] ICTY Statute, Art. 28 and ICTY RPE, rr. 123–125; ICTR Statute, Art. 27, and ICTR RPE, rr. 124–126. See ICTY, Practice Direction on the Procedure for the Determination of Applications for Pardon, Commutation of Sentence and Early Release of Persons Convicted by the International Tribunal (IT/146, 7 April 1999).

since 1 July 2012 and 1 July 2013, respectively.[122] The Residual Mechanism adheres to the ICTY practice of early release upon the completion of two-thirds of the sentence. An increasing number of ICTY and ICTR convicted persons have been subject to early release in recent years.[123] This practice has attracted criticism as being inconsistent with the goals of punishment and of international criminal law. Sentences are commuted almost automatically after serving two-thirds and the assessment of the convicted person's rehabilitation is rather limited, if not *pro forma*.

As part of the compromise reached at the Rome Conference regarding applicable penalties, the ICC Statute makes provision for an automatic review of sentences, which is analogous to an early release or a pardon.[124] The review must take place when two-thirds of the sentence has been served, or twenty-five years of life imprisonment, and a decision not to reduce the sentence must be reviewed at regular intervals.[125] The grounds for the reduction of sentence relate to post-conviction cooperation or change of circumstances. The ICC appellate panel reduced Katanga's twelve-year sentence considering his cooperative attitude, dissociation from the crimes, his prospect of resocialization and resettlement, and changed family circumstances.[126] Likewise, Al Mahdi's nine-year sentence was reduced by two years considering his early and continuing willingness to cooperate with the ICC as well as his resocialization and resettlement prospects.[127]

19.6 ENFORCEMENT

International criminal tribunals do not have their own prison system or autonomous means to execute non-custodial sentences. Instead, they have to rely on states willing to provide cooperation for the enforcement of punishments.[128] This is a voluntary undertaking by states and may have conditions attached, for example, regarding the nationality of the prisoner, or acceptance of only a limited number of prisoners, or a right to reject any individual prisoner. There is little appetite among states to move away from the voluntary scheme of enforcement of sentences towards a compulsory system because it could require them to commit substantial resources and to accept some notorious international prisoners in politically unfavourable circumstances.[129]

---

[122] MICT Statute, Art. 26 and MICT RPE, rr. 149–51. MICT, Practice Direction on the Procedure for the Determination of Applications for Pardon, Commutation of Sentence and Early Release of Persons Convicted by the ICTR, the ICTY, or the Mechanism (MICT/3/Rev.1, 24 May 2018).

[123] E.g. *Bisengimana*, MICT President, 11 December 2012, paras. 17 and 20; and *Serushago*, MICT President, 13 December 2012, paras. 16–18; *Petković*, MICT President, 16 December 2021, paras. 77–9. Cf. *Bagaragaza*, ICTR President, 24 October 2011 (early release after three-quarters of the sentence had been served); *Popović*, MICT President, 30 January 2023 (no compelling or exceptional circumstances to justify granting early release prior to reaching his two-thirds eligibility threshold).

[124] ICC Statute, Art. 110 and ICC RPE, rr. 223–4.

[125] Every three years unless it is decided to do so at a shorter interval. ICC Statute, Art. 110(5) and ICC RPE, r. 224(3). See e.g. *Lubanga*, ICC Panel of AC judges, 22 September 2015 (ICC-01/04–01/06–3173) (deciding to review Lubanga's sentence in two years); *Lubanga*, ICC Panel of AC judges, 3 November 2017 (ICC-01/04–01/06–3375) (declining to reduce the sentence).

[126] *Katanga*, ICC Panel of AC judges, 13 November 2015 (ICC-01/04–01/07–3615) para. 111 (reducing the twelve-year sentence by three years and eight months).

[127] *Al Mahdi*, ICC Panel of AC judges, 25 November 2021 (ICC-01/12–01/15–434-Red3) paras. 75 and 77.

[128] ICTY Statute, Art. 27; ICTR Statute, Art. 26; ICC Statute, Art. 103. See Róisín Mulgrew, *Towards the Development of the International Penal System* (Cambridge, 2013) 33–102.

[129] See *ibid*. 33–5.

The supervision of ICTY and ICTR sentence enforcement was taken over by the Residual Mechanism.[130] While the ICTY convicts serve their sentences in a number of European states, the ICTR prisoners were transferred to Benin, Mali, Senegal, as well as Italy and Sweden. The SCSL transferred all convicted persons, except Charles Taylor, to Rwanda under an agreement of 18 March 2009.[131] The ICC has concluded thirteen enforcement agreements with states thus far.[132]

The enforcing state may not modify the length of the sentence or release the convicted person without the approval of the Tribunal or Court.[133] The legal frameworks and enforcement agreements provide for notifications and consultations on matters which could affect the terms or extent of the imprisonment.[134] Disapproval of an impending domestic measure may cause a transfer of the enforcement to another state.[135]

Conditions of imprisonment are in accordance with domestic law, but subject to the Tribunal or Court's supervision.[136] The ICC Statute additionally requires compliance with 'widely accepted international treaty standards governing treatment of prisoners' and no better or worse treatment than other prisoners convicted of similar offences.[137] There is therefore a division of responsibility between the supervising international jurisdiction and the enforcing state concerning the welfare of the prisoner and the length of the sentence to be served.[138]

The ICC Statute also provides for the obligatory enforcement of fines, forfeiture orders, and reparation orders by national authorities at the request of the Court.[139] Here, too, the state of enforcement must not modify the fines or orders. Enforcement by national authorities is also foreseen concerning restitution of property or the proceeds thereof to victims at the ICTY and ICTR.[140]

Further Reading

Penalties and Sentencing

Nadia Bernaz, 'Sentencing and Penalties' in Schabas and Bernaz, *Routledge Handbook*, 289–303

Silvia D'Ascoli, *Sentencing in International Criminal Law: The Approach of the Two Ad Hoc Tribunals and Future Perspectives for the International Criminal Court* (Oxford, 2011)

---

[130] SC Res. 1966(2010), 22 December 2010; MICT Statute, Art. 25 and MICT RPE, rr. 127–128.
[131] *Taylor*, RSCSL Judge, 21 May 2015.
[132] These countries are: Argentina, Austria, Belgium, Colombia, Denmark, Finland, Georgia, Mali, Norway, Serbia, Slovenia, Sweden, and the United Kingdom.
[133] ICTY Statute, Art. 28; ICTR Statute, Art. 27; MICT Statute, Art. 26 and ICC Statute, Arts. 105(1) and 110(1).
[134] ICC Statute, Art. 103(2); MICT RPE, r. 149. [135] See ICC Statute, Art. 104 and ICC RPE, rr. 209–10.
[136] ICTY Statute, Art. 27; ICTR Statute, Art. 26; MICT Statute, Art. 25; and ICC Statute, Art. 106. On internal and external oversight, see Mulgrew, *Toward the Development of the International Penal System* (n. 128) 131–43.
[137] ICC Statute, Art. 106(2). A similar requirement is included in the enforcement agreements.
[138] See Mulgrew, *Toward the Development of the International Penal System* (n. 128) 45–84.
[139] ICC Statute, Arts. 75(5) and 109. See also ICC RPE, rr. 212 and 217–222 and ICC Regulations of the Court, reg. 116.
[140] ICTY and ICTR RPE, r. 105 and MICT RPE, r. 129.

Mark Drumbl, *Atrocity, Punishment and International Law* (Cambridge, 2007)

Rolf Einar Fife, 'Penalties' in Lee, *The Making of the Rome Statute*, 319–43

Rolf Einar Fife, 'Penalties' in Lee, *Elements and Rules*, 555–73

Florian Jeßberger and Julia Geneuss (eds.), *Why Punish Perpetrators of Mass Atrocities? Theoretical and Practical Perspectives on Punishment in International Criminal Law* (Cambridge, 2019)

Jens Ohlin, 'Towards a Unique Theory of International Criminal Sentencing' in Sluiter and Vasiliev, *International Criminal Procedure*, ch. 10

William A. Schabas, 'Penalties' in Cassese et al., *Commentary*, 1497–534

William A. Schabas, *The UN International Criminal Tribunals: The Former Yugoslavia, Rwanda and Sierra Leone* (Cambridge, 2006) ch. 14

Immi Tallgren, 'The Sensibility and Sense of International Criminal Law' (2002) 13(3) *EJIL* 561

Enforcement of Penalties

Denis Abels, *Prisoners of the International Community* (The Hague, 2012) ch. 7

Hirad Abtahi and Steven Arrigg Koh, 'The Emerging Enforcement Practice of the International Criminal Court' (2012) 45 *Cornell International Law Journal* 1

Claus Kreß and Göran Sluiter, 'Enforcement' in Cassese et al., *Commentary*, chs. 43–5

Róisín Mulgrew, *Towards the Development of the International Penal System* (Cambridge, 2013)

Róisín Mulgrew and Denis Abels (eds.), *Research Handbook on International Penal System* (Cheltenham, 2016)

Part VI

Relationship between National and International Systems

20

State Cooperation with the International Courts and Tribunals

20.1 NATURE OF THE COOPERATION REGIMES

State cooperation with the Tribunals and the International Criminal Court (ICC) departs in many important ways from state-to-state cooperation in criminal matters.[1] State obligations vis-à-vis the international criminal jurisdictions are more far-reaching. The rationale behind the more stringent cooperation regimes is that these jurisdictions are created by the international community to investigate and prosecute the most serious crimes of international concern.

Elevated cooperation duties towards international tribunals always have a treaty basis and therefore are rooted in consent. By their legal nature, their statutes are either multilateral treaties consented to by states (ICC), or enactments of the UN Security Council binding on UN member states under Chapter VII of the UN Charter (International Criminal Tribunal for the former Yugoslavia (ICTY), International Criminal Tribunal for Rwanda (ICTR), and the International Residual Mechanism for Criminal Tribunals (MICT), or Tribunals).[2] The Tribunals and Security Council referrals of situations to the ICC form part of international efforts to preserve or restore international peace and security, necessitating a stricter cooperation regime.[3] In addition, it is assumed, rightly or wrongly, that traditional restrictions on cooperation need not apply since the international jurisdictions act in accordance with the highest standards of criminal procedure and due process. By contrast, the hybrid and special courts are typically set up by agreements between the relevant state and the United Nations, legislative acts of domestic or transitional administration authorities or by another method not generating obligations for third states.[4] Such courts are integrated into domestic judicial systems to varying degrees and can only demand cooperation and assistance from the state for which they were created.

The successful operation of international criminal jurisdictions to a large extent depends upon the willingness and ability of states to provide cooperation. These courts cannot themselves execute their decisions, such as an arrest warrant, on the territory of a state.

---

[1] See Chapter 5. [2] UN Charter, Arts. 25 and 41.
[3] ICTY Statute, Art. 29; ICTR Statute, Art. 28; MICT Statute, Art. 28; ICC Statute, Part 9.
[4] The legal regimes of the (Residual) Special Court for Sierra Leone (SCSL), Special Tribunal for Lebanon (STL) and the Kosovo Specialist Chambers (KSC) did not create obligations for third states, absent a separate agreement. See SCSL Agreement, Art. 17; STL Statute, Art. 15; and KSC Law, Art. 55. See further Chapter 9.

Unlike the case of the Nuremberg and Tokyo International Military Tribunals (IMTs), which were established and operated by the occupying powers, modern-day international courts do not have direct access to a police force. As the ICTY Appeals Chamber concluded in its landmark decision in *Blaškić*, enforcement powers must be expressly provided and cannot be regarded as inherent in an international criminal tribunal.[5] Cooperation is at the heart of effective international criminal proceedings. Cassese famously referred to the ICTY as 'a giant without arms and legs [which] needs artificial limbs to walk and work ... [a]nd these artificial limbs are state authorities'; thus, '[i]f the cooperation of states is not forthcoming, the ICTY cannot fulfil its functions'.[6] This dependence on state cooperation, which the Tribunals are unable to ensure themselves, has led to many difficulties in practice.[7]

The *Blaškić* decision found that interstate and state–tribunal cooperation regimes represent different models: the former is 'horizontal' and the latter 'vertical' in nature.[8] This characterization is now commonly used. The distinction conveys the stricter obligations owed by states to the international jurisdictions, non-reciprocity, and the right of the requesting party (the Court or Tribunal) to interpret and determine the duties of cooperation.[9] The general duty to cooperate with the Tribunals is binding on all UN member states and backed by the Security Council's Chapter VII powers.[10] It contains no qualifications or exceptions: a truly vertical scheme.[11] The same applies to the MICT whose cooperation regime is also extended to contempt and perjury offences and covers assistance to national authorities.[12]

The state-negotiated ICC scheme also contains a duty to cooperate but it is in some respects closer to interstate cooperation. In particular, the ICC regime is based on requests instead of orders, certain grounds for postponement or refusal exist, and the scope for conducting on-site investigations and compelling individuals to give evidence is very limited. The weaknesses of the ICC cooperation regime, sometimes referred to as a middle ground between a vertical and a horizontal model, have often been criticized.[13] Moreover, the available means of enforcing the states' duty to cooperate with the ICC, such as referral of any cooperation failures to the Assembly of States Parties (ASP) or to the

---

[5] *Blaškić*, ICTY AC, 29 October 1997, para. 25.

[6] Antonio Cassese, 'On Current Trends Towards Criminal Prosecution and Punishment of Breaches of International Humanitarian Law' (1998) 9 *EJIL* 2 13.

[7] See e.g. Mark Harmon and Fergal Gaynor, 'Prosecuting Massive Crimes with Primitive Tools: Three Difficulties Encountered by Prosecutors in International Criminal Proceedings' (2004) 2 *JICJ* 403; and Yolanda Gamarra and Alejandra Vicente, 'United Nations Member States' Obligations Towards the ICTY: Arresting and Transferring Lukić, Gotovina and Zelenović' (2008) 8 *ICLR* 627.

[8] *Blaškić*, ICTY AC, 29 October 1997, paras. 47 and 54.

[9] See Göran Sluiter, *International Criminal Adjudication and the Collection of Evidence: Obligations of States* (Antwerp, 2002) 82–8.

[10] SC Res. 827(1993) para. 4 and 955(1994) para. 2 ('Decides that all States shall cooperate fully with the International Tribunal and its organs in accordance with the present resolution and the Statute of the International Tribunal ... including the obligation of States to comply with requests for assistance or orders issued by a Trial Chamber'). See also SC Res. 1966(2010) para. 9.

[11] Sluiter, *International Criminal Adjudication* (n. 9) 147–50. [12] MICT Statute, Arts. 4 and 28(2)–(3).

[13] See e.g. Bert Swart, 'General Problems' in Cassese et al., *Commentary*, 1589–605; Hans-Peter Kaul and Claus Kreß, 'Jurisdiction and Cooperation in the Statute of the International Criminal Court: Principles and Compromises' (1999) 2 *Yearbook of International Humanitarian Law* 143, 158–61; Göran Sluiter, '"I Beg You, Please Come Testify": The Problematic Absence of Subpoena Powers at the ICC' (2009) 12 *New Criminal Law Review* 590.

Security Council, are utterly insufficient.[14] Inadequate state cooperation and the lack of effective enforcement of underlying obligations pose major challenges for the ICC in terms of securing the arrest and surrender of suspects and obtaining evidence.

20.2 OBLIGATION TO COOPERATE

20.2.1 States

The Tribunals were subsidiary organs of the Security Council with powers given by the Security Council to make decisions that are binding on sovereign states.[15] As noted, the duty to cooperate is explicitly laid down in the Statutes. The principle that a treaty cannot impose obligations on states without their consent (*pacta tertiis nec nocent nec prosunt*)[16] confines this duty to UN member states and other states that have accepted cooperation obligations. The Dayton Peace Agreement imposed on the signatories, states of the former Yugoslavia and the Bosnian Serb entity, obligations supplementary to the ICTY Statute. In addition, the ICTY decided that self-proclaimed and non-recognized entities that exercise governmental functions must cooperate.[17]

The Statutes provide a non-exhaustive list of measures with which states are obliged to assist the Tribunals. Traditional grounds for refusal of interstate cooperation are not permitted.[18] But there are nonetheless limitations to the duty; for example, it does not cover relocation of acquitted persons.[19] Nor does it cover the enforcement of sentences, for which separate agreements have been concluded.[20] The Tribunals decided on the scope of the duty in the particular case and could issue binding orders to states and to individuals 'as may be necessary for the purposes of an investigation or for the preparations or conduct of the trial'.[21] The assistance would normally be provided in accordance with national law; the Tribunals sometimes made clear that states have discretion as to how they are to meet a specific request.[22]

The ICC is an intergovernmental organization with international legal personality and powers to request cooperation from the states parties.[23] The Statute explicitly requires these states to 'cooperate fully with the Court' and to ensure that national law allows all specified forms of cooperation.[24] States parties must make any legislative changes necessary to enable them to cooperate fully.

---

[14] See Göran Sluiter, 'Enforcing Cooperation: Did the Drafters Approach It the Wrong Way?' (2018) 16 *JICJ* 382–402.
[15] UN Charter, Art. 29. See *Blaškić*, ICTY TC II, 18 July 1997, paras. 18–23.
[16] 1969 Vienna Convention on the Law of Treaties, Art. 34.
[17] E.g. *Karadžić and Mladić*, ICTY TC I, 11 July 1996, para. 98 (finding that the Bosnian Serb administration, or 'Republika Srpska', is bound to cooperate with the ICTY). See also ICTY RPE, r. 2(A) defining a 'State'.
[18] See further Chapter 5. [19] *Ntagerura*, ICTY AC, 18 November 2008, para. 14.
[20] The ICTY concluded twenty-one such agreements, including five ad hoc agreements with Germany regarding specific accused, and the eight ICTR agreements. These apply to the MICT *mutatis mutandis*, unless superseded by more recent agreements concluded by the MICT with respective states; e.g. agreements with Benin (12 May 2017) and Mali (30 June 2016).
[21] ICTY and ICTR RPE, r. 54 and MICT RPE, r. 55. See Section 20.2.3.
[22] See for example *Gotovina et al.*, ICTY TC I, 16 September 2008.
[23] ICC Statute, Art. 4 and Part 9, in particular Art. 87(1)(a). [24] *Ibid.* Arts. 86 and 88.

The duty to 'cooperate fully' should serve as a general interpretive principle for the specific obligations set out in the Statute.[25] The ICC cannot demand cooperation beyond what the Statute requires. There is a catch-all provision at the end of the list of measures for assistance other than arrest and surrender, allowing the Court to request and obtain other assistance not prohibited by the law of the requested state.[26] Furthermore, since obligations under Part 9 of the ICC Statute are merely a 'lowest common denominator',[27] states may also provide additional cooperation voluntarily.[28] Some grounds for refusal are explicitly laid down in the Statute; in light of the negotiating history, these should be considered as exhaustive.[29] Additional obligations to cooperate may be contained in other agreements, including those concluded by the Court with individual states to enhance cooperation.[30]

The duty to cooperate with the ICC (and Part 9 of the Statute) is triggered when an investigation is formally commenced.[31] It thereafter covers subsequent proceedings. Certain obligations apply after the final verdict, for example, the temporary transfer of a prisoner to the Court for testimony.[32]

20.2.2 Conflicting Obligations

Another important aspect of the different regimes is the relationship between the state's cooperation duties towards the Tribunal or Court and other international obligations. Since the duties vis-à-vis the Tribunals draw their legal force from the UN Charter, these will normally prevail over the member state's obligations under other international agreements.[33] This issue does not arise with respect to hybrid courts and states not party to the agreements establishing them.

The situation is more complex regarding the ICC. If the Security Council imposes cooperation obligations when referring a situation to the Court under Chapter VII of the UN Charter, the equivalent primacy over other international obligations should apply.[34] This is how the ICC has interpreted the cooperation provisions in Security Council Resolution 1593 concerning the *Situation in Darfur, Sudan*.[35] Otherwise, the obligations vis-à-vis the ICC do not have a general primacy.

---

[25] Claus Kreß, 'Penalties, Enforcement and Cooperation in the International Criminal Court' (1998) 6 *European Journal of Crime, Criminal Law and Criminal Justice* 442, 450.

[26] ICC Statute, Art. 93(1)(l). [27] Claus Kreß and Kimberly Prost, 'Preliminary Remarks' in Ambos, *Commentary*, 2450.

[28] States not party to the Statute may also provide cooperation on an ad hoc basis: ICC Statute, Art. 87(5).

[29] ICC Statute, Arts. 72(6)–(7) and 73 (last sentence). See Phakiso Mochochoko, 'International Cooperation and Judicial Assistance' in Lee, *The Making of the Rome Statute*, 310–14.

[30] See ICC Statute, Art. 54(3)(d) and ICC Regulations of the Court, reg. 107.

[31] See Informal Expert Paper, *Fact-Finding and Investigative Functions of the Office of the Prosecutor, Including International Cooperation* (2003) paras. 22–9, www.legal-tools.org/doc/ba368d/pdf/.

[32] ICC RPE, r. 193. [33] UN Charter, Art. 103.

[34] See e.g. Dan Sarooshi, 'The Peace and Justice Paradox: The International Criminal Court and the UN Security Council' in McGoldrick et al., *The Permanent ICC*, 95, 104.

[35] SC Res. 1593(2005), 31 March 2005; *Al Bashir*, ICC PTC I, 4 March 2009 (ICC-02/05–01/09–3) paras. 244–7; *Al Bashir*, ICC PTC II, 11 December 2017 (ICC-02/05–01/09–309) paras. 37–40; *Al Bashir*, ICC PTC II, 6 July 2017 (ICC-02/05–01/09–302) paras. 85–8; see also *Al Bashir*, ICC AC, 6 May 2019 (ICC-02/05–01/09–397) para. 144. See Robert Cryer, 'Sudan, Resolution 1593, and International Criminal Justice' (2006) 19 *LJIL* 195; Dapo Akande, 'The Effect of the Security Council Resolutions and Domestic Proceedings on State Obligations to Cooperate with the ICC' (2012) 10 *JICJ* 299; cf. Asad Kiyani, 'Al-Bashir and the ICC: The Problem of Head of State Immunity' (2013) 12(3) *Chinese Journal of International Law* 467. See further Chapter 21.

Two types of conflicts between the obligations of states are addressed in the ICC Statute: competing requests for cooperation and immunities. On competing requests, the Statute sets out a complex system of factors to determine which request prevails.[36] On possible conflicts with existing immunities, Article 98 addresses state immunity, diplomatic immunity, and similar obstacles (for example, exclusive jurisdiction in status of forces agreements or conditioned re-extradition in extradition agreements). The practice regarding Article 98 has turned out to be highly controversial, as demonstrated by the litigation around the failure by a number of states parties to execute the ICC arrest warrants against the then President of Sudan, Omar Al Bashir, when they had an opportunity to do so.[37] Article 98 provides that where an obligation to respect immunity does exist, '[t]he Court may not proceed with a request' unless a waiver of immunity or consent for surrender has been obtained. Hence, the requested state may raise the issue of conflicting obligations before the Court,[38] but the putative conflict of obligations is not a ground for refusal if the Court still insists on the request.[39] Moreover, it is the Court itself that has the authority to settle any dispute concerning its judicial functions.[40] The greatest controversies arise when it is unclear whether the visiting official still has immunities precluding his or her arrest on behalf of the ICC.[41] If the requested state continues to refuse cooperation, however, the issue may be subject to adjudication by the Court in non-compliance proceedings.[42]

20.2.3 Individuals

The Tribunals have on occasion issued binding orders to individuals to appear and give evidence. These orders are called 'subpoenas' (*subpoena ad testificandum*) since non-compliance may result in liability for contempt. Lacking explicit support in the Statutes, the practice has been based on 'inherent powers'.[43] Jurisprudence, and subsequently also the Rules of Procedure and Evidence (RPE), clarified that a Chamber may issue such orders.[44] The orders, as well as any sanctions, must be enforced by national authorities. According to the ICTY Appeals Chamber in *Blaškić*, states have a duty, when requested, to arrest, compel a person to surrender evidence or bring a witness to the Tribunal to testify.[45] These are far-reaching obligations that depart from the general practice among states, which does not recognize a duty to testify across national borders.[46] In practice, however, only

---

[36] ICC Statute, Arts. 90 and 93(9). [37] See Sections 8.11.1, 21.5.2, and 21.5.4. [38] ICC RPE, r. 195.
[39] *Al Bashir*, ICC PTC II, 11 December 2017 (ICC-02/05–01/09–309) para. 41; *Al Bashir*, ICC AC, 6 May 2019 (ICC-02/05–01/09–397) paras. 129–32.
[40] ICC Statute, Art. 119(1). [41] See Chapter 21. [42] ICC Statute, Art. 87(7) and ICC Regulations, reg. 109.
[43] *Blaškić*, ICTY AC, 29 October 1997, paras. 47 and 55. See Anne-Laure Chaumette, 'The ICTY's Power to Subpoena Individuals, to Issue Binding Orders to International Organisations and to Subpoena their Agents' (2004) 4 *ICLR* 357. MICT Statute, Art. 1(4)(a) empowers the Mechanism to hold a person in contempt but the Statute does not explicitly authorize subpoenas.
[44] ICTY and ICTR RPE, r. 54 and MICT RPE, r. 56. See e.g. *Mrkšić et al.*, ICTY AC, 30 July 2003; *Krstić*, ICTY AC, 1 July 2003.
[45] *Blaškić*, ICTY AC, 29 October 1997, para. 27.
[46] A special scheme exists among the Nordic countries, however, but it does not include effective sanctions in case of non-compliance by the witness. Likewise, a witness invoking the right to refuse to make a deposition under the law of the requesting or requested state party to the Ljubljana–The Hague Convention, or failing to comply with a summons to appear (even if it contains obligations), cannot be subjected to any penalties (or measures of constraint) in those states for that reason: MLA Convention, Arts. 24(1) and 35(4). See Section 5.3.2.

a few states have introduced legislation providing for the forcible transfer of witnesses to the Tribunals, and the Tribunals have framed their requests for state assistance in cautious terms.[47]

In keeping with the traditional 'act of state' doctrine, the Tribunals may not address binding orders to specific state officials for cooperation in their official capacity; such orders must instead be made to the state.[48] The orders may, however, be addressed to officials when acting in their 'private capacity', but still the Tribunal will normally proceed via national authorities and only exceptionally address itself directly to the individual.[49] Subsequently, the 'state official' exception was restricted to apply 'only in relation to the production of documents in their custody in their official capacity', which means that the officials could still be compelled to give evidence of what they saw or heard in the course of exercising official functions.[50] The ICTY and ICTR dismissed claims of immunity, inter alia, regarding the then British Prime Minister Blair and German Chancellor Schröder, and issued a subpoena to the Rwandan Defence Minister.[51] Members of international peace-keeping or peace-enforcing forces with a UN mandate are also compellable.[52] The ICTY Appeals Chamber set aside a subpoena to compel the testimony of a war correspondent (Randal of *The Washington Post*) concerning his reporting on the conflict in the former Yugoslavia.[53] Given a significant public interest in the work of war reporters and the negative impact their compelled testimony would have on their ability to obtain information, war correspondents may only be subpoenaed if their evidence is of direct and important value to the case and cannot reasonably be obtained from another source.[54]

The ICC Statute gives conflicting messages as to whether the Court may compel an individual to cooperate, the suspect or accused being excluded.[55] The cooperation obligations of Part 9 do not extend to private individuals. That said, the Trial Chamber is authorized to 'require the attendance and testimony of witnesses … by obtaining, if necessary, the assistance of States as provided in this Statute', although the RPE restrict the 'compellability of witnesses' to those who actually appear before the Court.[56] Read together with the provision that states are required to 'facilitat[e] the voluntary appearance' of witnesses and experts,[57] the ICC has the power to order a witness to appear before the Court but cannot demand that a state deliver a witness who does not comply.

While the Court might still request non-voluntary crossborder transfer of a witness under the catch-all provision, this can arguably violate the 'existing fundamental legal principle of

---

[47] See e.g. Law on Cooperation with the International Tribunal in respect of the Former Yugoslavia (Germany), 10 April 1995, para. 4(2); Act on the Jurisdiction of the International Tribunal for the Prosecution of Persons Responsible for Crimes Committed in the Territory of the Former Yugoslavia and on Legal Assistance to the International Tribunal (Finland), 5 January 1994, s. 6. See also Sluiter, *International Criminal Adjudication* (n. 9) 253–68.

[48] *Blaškić*, ICTY AC, 29 October 1997, paras. 39–44. [49] *Ibid.* paras. 46–51 and 53–6.

[50] *Krstić*, ICTY AC, 1 July 2003, paras. 24, 26–8.

[51] *Milošević*, ICTY TC III, 9 December 2005; and *Bagosora et al.*, ICTR TC I, 11 September 2006. Cf. the SCSL, which avoided the issue of immunity when refusing to subpoena the President of Sierra Leone: *Norman et al.*, SCSL AC, 11 September 2006, paras. 40–4 (but Judge Robertson, dissenting, addressed the issue). For further discussion of immunities, see Chapter 21.

[52] See e.g. *Simić et al.*, ICTY TC I, 18 October 2000, paras. 62–3; and *Bagosora et al.*, ICTR TC III, 14 July 2006.

[53] *Brđanin and Talić*, ICTY AC, 11 December 2002, para. 50. [54] *Ibid.* paras. 38, 44 and 50.

[55] On the binding effect of the ICC Statute, as a treaty, on individuals, see Marko Milanović, 'Is the Rome Statute Binding on Individuals? (And Why We Should Care)' (2011) 9 *JICJ* 25.

[56] ICC Statute, Art. 64(6)(b) and ICC RPE, r. 65. [57] ICC Statute, Art. 93(1)(e).

general application' in the requested state lacking an explicit authorization in national law.[58] The lack of power to bring witnesses before the Court has been regarded as a serious weakness in the ICC cooperation regime.[59] The ICC has overcome this difficulty in practice by interpreting Articles 64(6)(b) and 93(1)(b) as giving the Trial Chamber the power to compel witnesses, as well as to request a state party to compel witnesses, to testify whenever the Court sits in the territory of that state party or by video-link.[60]

As in ordinary interstate regimes, the Tribunal or Court, instead of issuing a subpoena, may order the temporary transfer of a witness who is already detained in a state.[61] If a subpoena fails to secure the appearance of the witness, for example, because of a medical condition, compelled testimony by video-link can be an alternative.[62]

However, a subpoena power does not guarantee success. In *Haradinaj et al.*, a subpoenaed key witness refused to appear and the Trial Chamber refused the Prosecutor's request for more time to secure his testimony, leading the Appeals Chamber to order a retrial.[63] In the ICC, another difficulty occurred when defence witnesses who were transferred from detention in their home state requested asylum in the Netherlands.[64] The ICC is obliged to return the temporarily transferred detainee to the state once the purposes of the transfer have been fulfilled.[65] But, on the other hand, the Chamber found itself unable to do so consistently with Article 21(3), as that would have deprived the witnesses of their right to apply for asylum and lead to a breach of the non-refoulement principle.[66] It was not within the Chamber's competence to consider the asylum request and the resolution of this matter was in the hands of the Netherlands as the host state.[67] The witness remains in the Court's detention during the asylum process but it could not rule on applications for release as this was a matter for the transferring state.[68] Complications of this kind might discourage states from cooperating with the Court and further hamper its ability to obtain live evidence. Possible solutions are increased reliance upon testimony by video-link or pre-recorded testimony.

---

[58] ICC Statute, Art. 93(1)(l) and (3).

[59] See also Claus Kreß and Kimberly Prost, 'Article 93' in Ambos, *Commentary*, 2543; Göran Sluiter, '"I Beg You, Please Come Testify"' (n. 13).

[60] *Ruto and Sang*, ICC AC, 9 October 2014 (ICC-01/09–01/11–1598) paras. 113 and 132–3; *Ruto and Sang*, ICC TC V(A), 17 April 2014 (ICC-01/09–01/11–1274-Corr2) para. 193 (referencing also Art. 93(1)(d) and (l)).

[61] ICTY RPE and ICTR RPE, r. 90*bis*; MICT RPE, r. 107; and ICC Statute, Art. 93(1)(f) and (7). See e.g. *Karemera et al.*, ICTR TC III, 9 April 2009.

[62] See e.g. *Haradinaj et al.*, ICTY TC I, 14 September 2007. See also ICC Statute, Art. 69(2).

[63] *Haradinaj et al.*, ICTY AC, 19 October 2009, paras. 41–50. See also *Kabashi*, ICTY TC I, 16 September 2011, para. 18 (finding the witness guilty of contempt and sentencing him to two months' imprisonment).

[64] For a critical discussion of ICC practice, see Krit Zeegers, *International Criminal Tribunals and Human Rights Law: Adherence and Contextualization* (The Hague, 2016) 84–90.

[65] ICC Statute, Art. 93(7). [66] *Katanga and Ngudjolo*, ICC TC II, 9 June 2011, para. 73.

[67] See *Lubanga*, ICC TC I, 5 August 2011; *Katanga and Ngudjolo*, ICC TC II, 9 June 2011, paras. 74 and 85.

[68] *Lubanga*, ICC TC I, 15 August 2011 (ICC-01/04–01/06–2766), 25 October 2011 (ICC-01/04–01/06–2785-Conf) and 15 December 2011 (ICC-01/04–01/06–2835); *Djokaba Lambi Longa* v. *The Netherlands*, ECtHR, 9 October 2012. See also *Katanga and Ngudjolo*, ICC TC II, 1 March 2012 (ICC-01/04–01/07–3254) para. 18, and 1 October 2013 (ICC-01/04–01/07–3405) paras. 28 and 35. Ultimately, the Appeals Chamber ordered the return of the detained witnesses to the DRC to be arranged with the Dutch authorities: *Ngudjolo*, ICC AC, 20 January 2014 (ICC-01/04–02/12–158) and 21 May 2014 (ICC-01/04–02/12–179).

20.3 STATES NOT PARTY, INTERNATIONAL ORGANIZATIONS, AND OTHER ENTITIES

In practice, cooperation with states not party has not been much of an issue for the Tribunals owing to the practically universal membership of the United Nations. Switzerland, a non-member at the time of the ad hoc Tribunals' creation, declared that it would cooperate voluntarily. For various reasons, newly independent states emerging after the break-up of Yugoslavia did not contest the applicability of the duty to cooperate on the grounds that they were not UN members. All but one of these states were UN member states when the ICTY Statute was adopted; and Serbia and Montenegro considered itself the successor state to Yugoslavia, although it was not recognized as such by the UN.

The explicit duty to cooperate set out in the ICC Statute is confined to states parties. However, the Court may invite states not party to cooperate in accordance with separate arrangements.[69] Furthermore, states which accept the jurisdiction of the ICC by an Article 12(3) declaration must also cooperate with the Court 'without any delay or exception in accordance with Part 9' of the ICC Statute.[70] Finally, the Security Council may, when referring a situation to the ICC, require that UN member states cooperate with the Court, whether those states are parties to the ICC Statute or not. This was done with respect to Sudan (Darfur) and Libya when the situations in those countries were referred to the ICC Prosecutor.[71] States not party may also choose to cooperate. Past examples include when the United States and Rwanda assisted in the voluntary surrender of the fugitive Bosco Ntaganda to the ICC in March 2013, and when the US forces in the Central African Republic assisted in transferring Dominic Ongwen to the Court in January 2015.

The cooperation of entities other than states has proved indispensable in practice. For example, international forces have carried out most of the arrests for the ICTY. Such action was controversial and there was initial resistance to authorizing, let alone requiring, the NATO Implementation Force in Bosnia and Herzegovina (IFOR) to arrest indicted war criminals.[72] Nonetheless, such authorization was given, but only under restrictive conditions, and it took some time before the first arrest was made.[73] Contributing to this increased willingness to assist was a practice of 'sealed indictments' which reduced the risks to troops effecting the arrests.[74] The ICTY held that its Statute allowed arrests by bodies other than states (such as IFOR or the NATO Stabilisation Force (SFOR)) but did not obligate them to execute the arrest warrants, which is anomalous considering that states did have a duty to cooperate. Arrest warrants were sometimes issued directly to non-state entities instead of

---

[69] ICC Statute, Art. 87(5).

[70] *Ibid.* Art. 12(3); ICC RPE, r. 44(2) ('the provisions of Part 9, and any rules thereunder concerning States Parties, shall apply').

[71] SC Res. 1593(2005), 31 March 2005 and SC Res. 1970(2011), 26 February 2011. See also *Gaddafi and Al-Senussi*, ICC PTC I, 28 August 2013 (ICC-01/11–01/11–420) paras. 13–15 (Mauritania, which was not a party to the Statute, had no duty to cooperate with the ICC).

[72] See Richard Holbrooke, *To End a War*, 2nd ed. (New York, 1998) 221–2.

[73] Dagmar Stroh, 'State Cooperation with the International Criminal Tribunals for the Former Yugoslavia and for Rwanda' (2001) 5 *Max Planck Yearbook of the United Nations Law* 249, 281.

[74] See Gary Jonathan Bass, *Stay the Hand of Vengeance: The Politics of War Crimes Tribunals* (Princeton, NJ, 2000) 265–7.

states, and they were also requested to assist in other ways, for example, with exhumations.[75]

Due mainly to US opposition, the mandate of the UN peacekeeping forces in the Democratic Republic of the Congo (MONUC) initially did not refer to the ICC. More robust assistance in arresting war criminals was only to be provided to the DRC authorities and courts. But later MONUC was given an explicit mandate to cooperate with international efforts to bring perpetrators to justice.[76] In practice, MONUC had provided assistance to the Court for a long time, including in the arrest of suspects. Some of the newer Resolutions explicitly mandate peacekeeping missions to cooperate with the ICC[77] and call upon states to continue their close cooperation with the Court.[78] Resolutions on the UN Stabilization Mission in the Central African Republic (MINUSCA) contain standard references to the ICC, emphasizing the need to ensure accountability for crimes within its jurisdiction, although without addressing cooperation.[79]

Intergovernmental organizations have an international legal personality, separate from that of the constituent states. Regardless of this, the ICTY, by using a 'purposive interpretation' of Article 29 of the Statute, found itself competent to issue binding orders to such organizations. In *Simić et al.*, such an order was issued not only to the participating states of the Stabilization Force (SFOR) but also to SFOR, as a collective state enterprise, and its responsible authority, the North Atlantic Council.[80] Binding orders have also been directed to other entities.[81] The ICC, on the other hand, applies the same scheme to intergovernmental organizations as to states not party, and cooperation thus depends on a voluntary commitment.[82] For example, a cooperation agreement has been concluded with the European Union.[83] A special relationship exists between the ICC and the United Nations and matters having an impact on cooperation are addressed in a Relationship Agreement.[84] A separate agreement was concluded concerning MONUC.[85] The ICC may also seek cooperation from intergovernmental organizations without a prior agreement.[86]

---

[75] See *Dokmanović*, ICTY TC II, 22 October 1997, para. 3 (arrest warrant issued to the United Nations Transitional Administration for Eastern Slavonia, Baranja, and Western Sirmium); *Haradinaj et al.*, ICTY TC II, 19 October 2006 (UNMIK).

[76] Cf. SC Res. 1565(2004), 1 October 2004 and 1856(2008), 22 December 2008.

[77] SC Res. 2098(2013), 28 March 2013 (DRC; MONUSCO), which also welcomed an instance of successful state cooperation with the ICC. See also SC Res. 2100(2013), 25 April 2013 (Mali, MINUSMA).

[78] *Ibid*. See also SC Res. 2095(2013), 14 March 2013 (Libya) and SC Res. 2101(2013), 25 April 2013 (Côte d'Ivoire).

[79] E.g. SC Res. 2659(2022), 14 November 2022, para. 22; SC Res. 2552(2020), 12 November 2020, para. 20. See also *Report on the Activities of the International Criminal Court*, ICC-ASP/16/9 (2 November 2017) para. 17 (acknowledging support of MINUSCA).

[80] *Simić et al.*, ICTY TC III, 18 October 2000, paras. 46–9, 58. SFOR was different from regular UN peacekeeping forces since it consisted of different state-led forces remaining under the control of their respective governments.

[81] See e.g. *Kordić*, ICTY TC III, 4 August 2000 (the European Community Monitoring Mission); and *Haradinaj et al.*, ICTY AC, 10 March 2006 (UNMIK); cf. *Kovačević*, ICTY TC II, 23 June 1998 (refusal to issue an order to the Organization for Security and Co-operation in Europe (OSCE)). See also Chaumette, 'The ICTY's Power to Subpoena' (n. 43) 413–17.

[82] ICC Statute, Art. 87(6).

[83] Agreement between the International Criminal Court and the European Union on Cooperation and Assistance of 10 April 2006 (ICC-PRES/01–01–06).

[84] ICC Statute, Art. 2 and the Negotiated Relationship Agreement between the International Criminal Court and the United Nations of 4 October 2004 (ICC-ASP/3/Res.1).

[85] Memorandum of Understanding between the United Nations and the ICC Concerning Co-operation between MONUC and the ICC, 8 November 2005.

[86] *Banda and Jerbo*, ICC TC IV, 1 July 2011 (ICC-02/05–03/09–170) and 21 December 2011 (ICC-02/05–03/09–268-Red) (cooperation request to the African Union).

The International Committee of the Red Cross and Red Crescent (ICRC) has been granted special treatment, motivated by the special status drawn from its mandate under the Geneva Conventions.[87] In *Simić et al.*, the ICTY found that, in order to discharge its mandate, the ICRC has a right under customary international law not to disclose information relating to its activities.[88] The ICC RPE followed suit with an absolute privilege provision.[89] The ICRC may thus prevent disclosure of information and testimony by present and past ICRC officials or employees before the Court.

20.4 AUTHORITY TO SEEK COOPERATION AND RIGHTS OF PARTIES

As in interstate cooperation, there is a certain inequality between the powers of the prosecution and the defence to seek cooperation, and this is a source of criticism.[90] While the Prosecutor has powers to seek cooperation independently, including provisional arrest and seizure of evidence in urgent cases,[91] the defence is directed to go through a judge.[92] Some states even require such court orders to provide assistance in accordance with national law.[93] Where the state refused to implement an order to produce documents requested by the defence, ICTR Trial Chambers ordered the prosecution to obtain the documents instead.[94] Difficulties in obtaining cooperation, and thus in preparing its case, may cause the defence to seek a stay of the proceedings with reference to a violation of fair trial rights.[95] The Prosecutor may also turn to the relevant Chamber for the grant of necessary warrants or orders, for example, concerning documentary evidence that a state has not produced.[96] The dependence on state cooperation may negatively affect the prosecution as well depending on the circumstances of the case. In the *Situation in Kenya*, the ICC Prosecutor was unable to secure cooperation of the government in obtaining evidence, which ultimately contributed to the withdrawal of charges against Kenyatta.[97]

Another issue is to what extent fair trial rights and other procedural standards must be respected by national authorities when acting on behalf of the Tribunal or Court and what remedies are available when such rights or standards are violated.[98] Importantly, the ICC

---

[87] See Els Debuf, 'Tools to Do the job: The ICRC's Legal Status, Privileges and Immunities' (2016) 97 (897/898) *International Review of the Red Cross* 319.

[88] *Simić et al.*, ICTY TC III, 27 July 1999, paras. 72–4. [89] ICC RPE, r. 73(4).

[90] See e.g. Gabrielle McIntyre, 'Equality of Arms: Defining Human Rights in the Jurisprudence of the International Criminal Tribunal for the Former Yugoslavia' (2003) 16 *LJIL* 269.

[91] ICTY and ICTR RPE, rr. 39–40; MICT RPE, rr. 36–37; and ICC Statute, Art. 54(3)(c)–(d).

[92] ICTY and ICTR RPE, R. 54; MICT RPE, r. 55; ICC Statute, Art. 57(3)(b) and ICC RPE, r. 116.

[93] See e.g. *Setako*, ICTR TC I, 31 March 2009, para. 4; *Katanga and Ngudjolo*, ICC PTC II, 25 August 2008. Cf. *Banda and Jerbo*, ICC PTC I, 17 November 2010 (ICC-02/05–03/09–102) (a cooperation request to Sudan concerning defence investigation on-site was not considered 'necessary' in the pre-confirmation phase).

[94] ICTR RPE, r. 98 (additional evidence); see e.g. *Bagilishema*, ICTR TC I, 8 June 2000, paras. 18–19.

[95] E.g. *Banda and Jerbo*, ICC TC IV, 26 October 2012 (ICC-02/05–03/09–410).

[96] ICTY and ICTR RPE, r. 54; MICT RPE, r. 55; ICC Statute, Art. 57(3)(a). See e.g. *Gotovina et al.*, ICTY TC I, 16 September 2008; cf. *Gotovina et al.*, ICTY TC I, 26 July 2010, paras. 29 and 135 (an order required the Chamber's assessment whether it was sufficiently certain that the requested document was created, if it still existed, and if its whereabouts were ascertainable).

[97] *Kenyatta*, ICC TC V(B), 3 December 2014 (ICC-01/09–02/11–982) paras. 74–9; *Kenyatta*, ICC TC V(B), 3 December 2014 (ICC-01/09–02/11–981) paras. 47–57; and *Kenyatta*, ICC OTP, 5 December 2015 (ICC-01/09–02/11–983).

[98] See further Section 17.6.2.

Statute lays down procedural rights relating to the questioning of a suspect which are explicitly applicable when this is being done by national authorities.[99]

20.5 ARREST AND SURRENDER

The duty to assist with arrest and surrender is explicitly mentioned in the Statutes of the Tribunals and further reinforced in the respective RPE.[100] The arrests were normally executed pursuant to a warrant issued by a Tribunal judge, but in urgent cases the Prosecutor could request provisional arrest to be followed up by a judge-made order for surrender.[101] In case of a failure to execute the arrest warrant within a reasonable time, the Prosecutor could be ordered to report on the measures taken and to submit the indictment along with all the supporting evidence in open court, following which the Trial Chamber was to issue an international arrest warrant to all states and could freeze the assets of the accused.[102]

Although the legal framework does not allow grounds for refusal, states have sometimes refused to execute orders for arrest and surrender on grounds of national law. For example, a US court refused to extradite an accused to the ICTR claiming that there was no extradition treaty, as required by national law.[103] The Federal Republic of Yugoslavia initially refused to transfer indictees to the ICTY on the basis of a constitutional prohibition against extradition of nationals.[104] Moreover, some domestic implementation laws contain double-criminality requirements.[105] However, such traditional grounds for refusing extradition are not compatible with the Tribunal cooperation regime.[106]

The fact remains that the national law of many states, in particular civil law jurisdictions, prohibits 'extradition' of nationals. These strongly held exceptions were advanced in the ICC negotiations and some creative solutions and compromises were required in order to create a regime free from such a ground for refusal. One such solution was to distinguish between 'surrender' (to the Court) and 'extradition' (to a state), and thereby avoid a potential application of ordinary extradition principles and related national requirements.[107] Another element was to satisfy the evidentiary requirements that apply to extradition in many common law jurisdictions. While the judicial authorities of the requested state may not examine the legality of the warrant itself or rule on a *habeas corpus* challenge, the ICC Statute indirectly acknowledges that the state, as part of its surrender procedures, may test evidence and that the Court must support its request with documents,

---

[99] ICC Statute, Art. 55(2).
[100] ICTY RPE, Art. 29(2)(d); ICTY RPE, rr. 56–9; MICT Statute, Art. 28(2)(d); MICT RPE, rr. 57–61.
[101] ICTY RPE and ICTR RPE, rr. 40 and 40*bis*.
[102] ICTY and ICTR RPE, r. 61(D); MICT RPE, r. 63(D). E.g. *Milošević*, ICTY Judge, 24 May 1999, paras. 26–9.
[103] See Göran Sluiter, 'To Cooperate or Not to Cooperate? The Case of the Failed Transfer of Ntakirutimana to the Rwanda Tribunal' (1998) 11 *LJIL* 383; and Mary Coombs, 'International Decisions: In Re Surrender of Ntakirutimana' (2000) 94 *AJIL* 171.
[104] *Fourth Annual Report of the ICTY*, UN Doc. A/52/375-S/1997/729 (18 September 1997) para. 189. [105] See Section 5.3.2.
[106] ICTY and ICTR RPE, r. 58; MICT RPE, r. 60.
[107] ICC Statute, Art. 102. See Michael Plachta, '"Surrender" in the Context of the International Criminal Court and the European Union' (2004) 19 *Nouvelles études pénales* 465. See Section 20.7.

statements or information to meet the requirements.[108] The Statute requires that national requirements for surrender should not be more burdensome than those applicable to interstate extradition. Other issues were resolved by allowing postponements or consultations.[109] By virtue of these detailed provisions, the Statute arguably satisfies any national requirement that there must be an extradition treaty before a person may be transferred.

At the ICC, the Pre-Trial Chamber issues, upon the Prosecutor's application, an arrest warrant. While national authorities enforce the warrant by applying national procedural law, the Statute sets forth minimum requirements concerning the national arrest proceedings and prescribes a division of competences, consultations regarding provisional release, and the speedy execution of the request.[110] In practice, most decisions to issue arrest warrants have included an assessment of the alleged crimes, jurisdiction and admissibility, and Article 58(1) requirements.[111] Arrest warrants have regularly been combined with, or followed by, a request for identification, tracing, and seizing or freezing of assets and property belonging to the suspect.[112]

Although it may appear unnecessary given the narrow subject-matter jurisdiction, the Statute includes a rule of speciality, according to which the Court may not proceed against the person surrendered for any conduct other than that which served as the basis for surrender, unless a waiver is obtained from the surrendering state.[113] In contrast with extradition, subsequent changes to the legal qualification of the conduct by the ICC do not require the state's waiver. Nor is the consent of the person surrendered necessary. When raised in *Mbarushimana*, the Pre-Trial Chamber allowed wide room for inclusion of new crimes in the subsequent charging document without violating the principle.[114] By contrast, the Tribunals rejected the speciality rule by noting that their Statutes do not allow states to refuse surrender on any ground.[115]

A notable omission in the cooperation regimes relates to accepting and guaranteeing the return of a suspect or accused who is granted interim release by the Tribunal or Court. The ICC Appeals Chamber in *Bemba* concluded that the identification of a state that is willing and able to accept the person is a precondition for conditional release and thus that the release depends upon state cooperation.[116] However, states have no obligation to provide such cooperation. To resolve this, the ICC has entered into separate agreements with states

[108] ICC Statute, Art. 91(2) and (4); see Kaul and Kreß, 'Jurisdiction and Cooperation' (n. 13) 165–6.
[109] ICC Statute, Arts. 89(2) (*ne bis in idem* challenge), 89(4) (domestic proceeding concerning other crimes), and 95 (general provision on postponement).
[110] ICC Statute, Arts. 89(1), 58, and 59.
[111] See e.g. *Al-Werfalli*, ICC PTC I, 4 July 2018 (ICC-01/11–01/17–13); *Nouradine Adam*, ICC PTC II, 28 July 2022 (ICC-01/14–41-Red2).
[112] ICC Statute, Art. 57(3)(e); *Lubanga*, ICC PTC I, 24 February 2006 (ICC-01/04–01/06–1-Corr-Red) paras. 130–41; *Lubanga*, ICC PTC I, 31 March 2006 (ICC-01/04–01/06–62). In *Bemba*, a bank account was seized and frozen in Portugal (as per *Bemba*, ICC PTC III, 27 May 2008 (ICC-01/05–01/08–8)), but, since most of the money seemed to have disappeared, the Court requested the national authorities to investigate the matter: see *Bemba*, ICC PTC III, 17 November 2008 (ICC-01/05–01/08–254).
[113] ICC Statute, Art. 101. [114] *Mbarushimana*, ICC PTC I, 16 December 2011 (ICC-01/04–01/10–465-Red) paras. 86–92.
[115] *Kovačević*, ICTY AC, 2 July 1998, para. 37.
[116] See *Bemba*, ICC AC, 2 December 2009 (ICC-01/05–01/08–631-Red) paras. 106–7; cf. *Bemba*, ICC PTC II, 14 August 2009 (ICC-01/05–01/08–475).

on interim release, although so far only two states have been willing to conclude such agreements.[117] Ad hoc arrangements in individual cases may provide a more realistic approach.[118]

In practice, the Office of the Prosecutor (OTP) takes various measures to trace persons who are subject to arrest warrants. The ICC Prosecutor is 'invited' to transmit the collected information to the Chamber and the Registry, but only 'as far as his confidentiality obligations allow'.[119] The ICC Office of the Prosecutor has full access to all Interpol databases. For a long time, it had no special 'tracking unit', like the one which existed at the ICTY. In 2018 the Office set up the Suspects at Large Tracking Team charged with collecting information on the (potential) travel of persons subject to arrest warrants. This team works in cooperation with an inter-organ working group on arrest strategies established jointly by the OTP and the Registry in March 2016.[120]

20.6 OTHER FORMS OF LEGAL ASSISTANCE

The cooperation obligations under the ICTY and ICTR Statutes were not restricted to specified forms of cooperation. It was up to the Tribunal to decide what was required for the case at hand. Some general principles were established in practice. For example, a request for an order to produce documents had to be relatively specific, explain why the documents were relevant for trial, not be unduly onerous, and allow sufficient time for compliance.[121] Normally, the applicant must approach the state for assistance before seeking a court order for the production of documents.[122]

Article 93 of the ICC Statute, on the other hand, sets out various forms of assistance that are to be provided and measures other than those listed are available under the 'catch-all' provision of Article 93(1)(l). Thus, the Court will make a request for assistance and the requested state should thereafter perform the investigative acts or other measures on behalf of the Court.

20.6.1 Grounds for Refusal

No grounds for refusal are provided with respect to cooperation with the Tribunals. Apart from the national security exception,[123] only one ground for refusal for 'other forms' of

---

[117] Framework Agreement between the Argentine Republic and the International Criminal Court on Interim Release, ICC-PRES/25–01–18, 28 February 2018; Agreement between the Kingdom of Belgium and the International Criminal Court on Interim Release, 10 April 2014.

[118] E.g. *Gicheru*, ICC PTC A, 29 January 2021. The ICC terminated the Article 70 proceedings against Paul Gicheru, accused of witness tampering, following his passing under suspicious circumstances on 26 September 2022 while on interim release in Kenya.

[119] E.g. *Mbarushimana*, ICC PTC I, 28 September 2010 (ICC-01/04–01/10–1).

[120] *Independent Expert Review of the International Criminal Court and the Rome Statute System; Final Report*, 30 September 2020 ('IER Report') paras. 767–74.

[121] ICTY RPE, r. 54*bis*; and *Blaškić*, ICTY AC, 29 October 1997, para. 32. See also MICT RPE, r. 56.

[122] *Karadžić*, ICTY TC III, 19 May 2010, para. 16. Cf. *Gatete*, ICTR TC III, 23 November 2009, para. 26 (applying ICTR RPE, r. 98).

[123] See Section 20.6.2.

assistance was retained in the ICC regime: if the requested measure is prohibited on the basis of 'an existing fundamental legal principle of general application' in the requested state.[124] A strict interpretation should apply and the principle must be of a constitutional character.[125] All other grounds for declining assistance that normally apply in interstate cooperation,[126] such as a double-criminality requirement, are disallowed. Nevertheless, the requested state may seek consultation, modification, or postponement of the cooperation, and thus cause disruption and delays, on a number of additional grounds, such as a competing request, an ongoing domestic case, lack of information, or immunity.[127]

20.6.2 National Security Objections

Orders or requests directed to states or individuals may give rise to national security concerns. The question then arises whether the national law of a state should constitute an obstacle to cooperation with the Tribunal or Court. Clearly, a national security exception can jeopardize efficient cooperation and even the rights of the accused (if the information is potentially exculpatory in nature). At the same time, national security is also a legitimate concern. It is unrealistic to believe that a state will readily reveal state secrets or otherwise sensitive information, or even admit to their existence. Hence, both the ICTY RPE and the ICC Statute contain compromise solutions in order to protect national security interests.

The Appeals Chamber in *Blaškić* rejected Croatia's claim that it is for the state to determine its national security needs and that such needs may serve as a ground for refusal. The Chamber decided that a right to refuse by reference to *ordre public*, which is a general cooperation principle, would not be 'fully in keeping with the Statute'.[128] But, since national security concerns deserve to be acknowledged, the Chamber devised a number of mechanisms to protect sensitive information in the Tribunal proceedings.[129] These were later codified in the RPE.[130] They apply also when the information is provided in the form of testimony.[131] For information provided by international organizations, their relationship to member states and others comes into play. For example, the ICTY has ruled that NATO is not required to divulge intelligence information provided to it by states and other entities without the provider's consent.[132]

The ICC Statute allows a state to deny cooperation on national security grounds.[133] Notably, Article 72 several times refers to the 'opinion of the state' as a sufficient motive for advancing claims based on national security interests. The concepts of national security interests and information are not defined anywhere in the Statute and hence the state itself

---

[124] ICC Statute, Art. 93(3); on national security, see Art. 93(4).
[125] See Kreß, 'Penalties, Enforcement and Cooperation' (n. 25) 456–7. [126] See further Chapter 5.
[127] ICC Statute, Arts. 90, 94–8. [128] *Blaškić*, ICTY AC, 29 October 1997, paras. 61–6. [129] *Ibid.* paras. 67–9.
[130] ICTY RPE, rr. 54*bis* and 70. See André Klip, 'Confidentiality Restrictions' (2012) 10 *JICJ* 645.
[131] *Milošević*, ICTY AC, 23 October 2002.
[132] *Milutinović et al.*, ICTY AC, 15 May 2006, paras. 16 and 19–20, reversing the opposite conclusion reached by the Trial Chamber: *Milutinović et al.*, ICTY TC III, 17 November 2005.
[133] ICC Statute, Arts. 72, 73 and 93(4)–(6). See further Donald Piragoff, 'Protection of National Security Information' in Lee, *The Making of the Rome Statute*, 270–94.

determines when such interests are affected.[134] However, it must comply with detailed procedures inspired by the *Blaškić* scheme. Ultimately, it is the Chamber that will make a final determination on the relevance and necessity of the material, as well as on whether a state has complied with its duty to cooperate.[135] If not, the Court may refer the matter to the ASP or the Security Council.[136] Apart from this, the Chamber may make inferences at trial as to the existence or otherwise of a certain fact.[137]

Sensitive information may also be transmitted to the Court on the condition that it be used solely for the purpose of generating new evidence and, thus, not be subject to disclosure without the consent of the provider.[138] This may cause difficulties with respect to the rights of the accused, in particular the right to disclosure of potentially exculpatory evidence.[139] A telling example is the *Lubanga* case where the conflict between the provider's confidentiality obligation and the accused's right to disclosure of exculpatory material at one point led the Trial Chamber to stay the proceedings and order the release of the accused.[140] The prosecution was found to have entered into confidentiality agreements and accepted large amounts of material from the United Nations routinely and without duly appreciating its relevance in future cases.[141] The matter was finally resolved after arrangements were made to allow the Trial Chamber to review the material, so the judges could make an assessment in accordance with Article 67(2) of the ICC Statute. The Appeals Chamber subsequently held that the confidentiality agreement must be respected and hence that other counterbalancing measures must be considered if the provider does not agree to disclosure.[142] The Tribunals adopted a very different approach, as the exculpatory disclosure rules were explicitly made subject to confidentiality provisions vis-à-vis the information provider.[143]

20.6.3 On-Site Investigations and Trials

On-site investigations provide direct access to sites, victims, and witnesses and are often crucial for effective criminal investigations. Potential witnesses may be reluctant to speak in the presence of national authorities, and the questioning may have to be conducted by international investigators alone to be meaningful. Their presence on site also offers an assurance that the investigative measures are taken in accordance with international standards.

In the Tribunals, the Prosecutor's power to conduct on-site investigations was expressly laid down in the Statutes.[144] The Prosecutor could seek assistance from state authorities, but the consent of the state was not required, including for coercive measures such as search and

---

[134] Rod Rastan, 'Article 72' in Ambos, *Commentary*, 2135. [135] ICC Statute, Art. 72(7)(a).
[136] *Ibid.* Arts. 72(7)(a)(ii) and 87(7). [137] *Ibid.* Art. 72(7)(a)(iii). [138] *Ibid.* Arts. 54(3)(e) and 93(8). [139] *Ibid.* Art. 67(2).
[140] *Lubanga*, ICC TC I, 13 June 2008 (ICC-01/04–01/06–1401) (staying the proceedings) and 3 September 2008 (ICC-01/04–01/06–1467) (refusing to lift the stay), ICC AC, 21 October 2008 (ICC-01/04–01/06–1486) (confirming the stay), and ICC TC I, 18 November 2008 (ICC-01/04–01/06-T-98-ENG) (lifting the stay).
[141] *Lubanga*, ICC TC I, 13 June 2008 (ICC-01/04–01/06–1401) para. 72.
[142] *Lubanga*, ICC AC, 21 October 2008 (ICC-01/04–01/06–1486) paras. 3, 43–55.
[143] ICTY RPE, r. 68(iv); ICTR RPE, r. 68(D); MICT RPE, r. 73(D).
[144] ICTY Statute, Art. 18(2) and ICTR Statute, Art. 17(2). See also MICT Statute, Art. 16(2).

seizure.[145] In practice, however, state permission or other involvement was often sought. Moreover, some domestic implementation laws authorized the Prosecutor to act independently on national territory but even then this required special permission.[146]

The ICC Statute contains provisions empowering the ICC Prosecutor to undertake certain measures on the territory of a state party without making a request for assistance by state authorities.[147] But, being controversial, this power is normally confined to non-compulsory measures, for example, taking witness statements on a voluntary basis, and may require consultations and consideration of the state's reasonable conditions and concerns. Exceptionally, the Pre-Trial Chamber may also authorize specific on-site measures to be taken without securing cooperation in the case of a 'failed state' which is clearly unable to execute a request, which arguably includes coercive measures.[148]

Considering the importance of on-site investigations, the scope under the ICC Statute to conduct them is rather narrow. This reflects the horizontal approach to cooperation whereby the ICC is seen as a separate entity, not an extension of the national jurisdiction, and the Court's activities on the state's territory as an intrusion on its sovereignty. In principle, the Prosecutor is not precluded from making a request for assistance in the form of an on-site investigation which goes further than what is explicitly set out in the Statute.[149] However, in practice, the Prosecutor has been cautious with respect to on-site investigations out of concerns for the safety and security of those assisting the Court and the investigators. This has also led to extensive use of intermediaries for contacts with witnesses and victims, a practice that was roundly criticized in the *Lubanga* trial judgment.[150] Defence teams have sometimes been more active in investigating on site than the prosecution, which affected the quality of the prosecution's evidence.[151]

While the ICTY and ICTR conducted their trials in The Hague and Arusha, respectively, the ICC may decide, in the interests of justice, to hear cases in a state other than the Netherlands.[152] This may be seen as desirable as a form of outreach, allowing the Court to bring justice closer to the affected communities. According to the amended Rule 100, the Chamber may recommend holding proceedings *in situ*, taking into account the view of the parties and victims as well as the Registry's assessment. But the decision to do so must be made by the Presidency having consulted with the relevant state and the Chamber.[153] Although several Chambers have considered holding confirmation and trial hearings,

---

[145] See e.g. *Kordić and Čerkez*, ICTY TC III, 25 June 1999.
[146] See e.g. Law on Cooperation (Germany), s. 4(4); Act on the Jurisdiction of the International Tribunal (Finland), s. 7; Federal Order on Cooperation with the International Tribunals for the Prosecution of Serious Violations of International Humanitarian Law of 21 December 1995 (Switzerland), art. 22; Bill relating to the Incorporation into Norwegian Law of the UN Security Council Resolution on the Establishment of an International Criminal Tribunal for the Former Yugoslavia, Law 1994–06.24 38 JD/31–1–1995 (Norway), art. 3.
[147] ICC Statute, Art. 99(4).   [148] *Ibid*. Art. 57(3)(d) and ICC RPE, r. 115.
[149] See Informal Expert Paper, *Fact-Finding and Investigative Functions* (n. 31) para. 57.
[150] *Lubanga*, ICC TC I, 14 March 2012 (ICC-01/04–01/06–2842) para. 482.
[151] Caroline Buisman, 'Delegating Investigations: Lessons to Be Learned from the Lubanga Judgment' (2013) 11 *Northwestern Journal of International Human Rights* 30; Christian de Vos, 'Investigating from Afar: The ICC's Evidence Problem' (2013) 26(4) *LJIL* 1009. See also IER Report (n. 120) 743 (noting criticisms relating to OTP analysts and investigators' 'the apparent lack of situation country knowledge . . ., and the lack of OTP field presence during investigations').
[152] ICC Statute, Arts. 3 and 62(1) and ICC RPE, r. 100.
[153] R. 100 was amended in 2013 (Resolution ICC-ASP/12/Res. 7, para. 1) in order to clarify the procedure and transfer the decision-making power from the plenary of judges to the Presidency.

wholly or partly, in the countries concerned, the *in situ* proceedings have not yet material-ized due to security risks, resource constraints, and anticipated logistical difficulties.[154] Insofar as such conditions are likely to persist in the future, the prospect of the ICC conducting on-site proceedings remains limited, especially considering that less costly and more risk-averse options of using live-streaming and video-link conferencing tech-nologies are available.

20.6.4 Assistance Regarding Coercive Measures

It is controversial whether the ICC may, or should, issue a warrant in connection with a request to national authorities for assistance involving coercive measures. The basic principle is that the request must be executed in accordance with national procedures in the requested state, while procedures prescribed in the request must also be followed.[155] Normally, national law will require a domestic judicial warrant for coercive measures or a judicial review, and this should be sufficient but there could be instances where there is no such judicial supervision. Some therefore have argued that all coercive measures taken on behalf of a Tribunal or Court ought to be subject to a warrant issued by that Tribunal or Court, or, in urgent cases, a subsequent review of the measure.[156]

In Tribunal practice, judge-made warrants for coercive measures other than arrest have sometimes been issued when the measures were to be taken without the assistance of national authorities,[157] including ordering the state to permit the measures to be taken.[158] However, no general requirement of international judicial warrants or review in case of state cooperation has been adopted in written law or in practice. Indeed, an *ex ante* judicial authorization may be time-consuming and an *ex post* review could be sensitive insofar as it would involve an assessment of national law and investigative practice in light of inter-national human rights standards. Instead, the principal way for the Tribunal or Court to perform judicial supervision is to conduct an *ex post facto* assessment with respect to an alleged abuse of process or motions to exclude evidence.

Accordingly, the ICC has so far issued requests, and not warrants, to states concerning coercive measures such as identification, tracing, seizure, and freezing of property for the purpose of eventual forfeiture.[159]

---

[154] E.g. in *Ruto and Sang*, ICC TC V(A), 3 June 2013 (ICC-01/09–01/11–763), the Chamber recommended to the Presidency to allow the trial to be held in Kenya, but on 15 July 2013 the plenary decided (pursuant to the earlier version of r. 100) that the trial should be conducted in The Hague. The defence challenge was unsuccessful: *Ruto and Sang*, ICC Presidency, 6 September 2013 (ICC-01/09–01/11–911). In *Lubanga*, ICC TC I, 8 May 2008 (Annex 2, dated 24 April 2008, para. 105), the idea of an *in situ* trial was considered but rejected. In *Ongwen*, the Pre-Trial Chamber recommended holding a confirmation hearing in Uganda but this was denied: *Ongwen*, ICC Presidency, 28 October 2015 (ICC-02/04–01/15–330); the Trial Chamber decided not to recommend holding the opening of the trial *in situ*: *Ongwen*, ICC TC IX, 18 July 2016 (ICC-02/04–01/15–499) para. 3.

[155] ICC Statute, Art. 99(1).

[156] See Sluiter, *International Criminal Adjudication* (n. 9) 125–8. See also Karel de Meester, 'Coercive Measures, Privacy Rights and Judicial Supervision in International Criminal Investigations: In Need of Further Regulation?' in Sluiter and Vasiliev, *International Criminal Procedure*, 273–309.

[157] See e.g. *Kordić and Čerkez*, ICTY TC III, 25 June 1999; and *Naletilić and Martinović*, ICTY TC I, 14 November 2001.

[158] See e.g. *Karadžić*, ICTY TC (Duty Judge), 11 September 2003.

[159] ICC Statute, Art. 93(1)(k). See e.g. *Bemba*, ICC PTC III, 27 May 2008 (ICC-01/05-01/08-8).

20.7 DOMESTIC IMPLEMENTATION

When international law creates obligations for states, it is not permissible to raise the objection that national law, constitutional or otherwise, prevents the honouring of the obligations.[160] States must make sure that national law allows them to comply with their international obligations, either by direct application of international rules or by implementing legislation. This is required with respect to both the Tribunals and the ICC.[161] Accordingly, a request cannot be refused with reference to the absence of procedures under national law, which also corresponds with the principle that requests be executed in accordance with domestic procedures. However, national law governing procedures should not inhibit the cooperation required. Cooperation with the ICC must also be provided in the manner specified in the request, unless this is specifically prohibited by national law.[162] In practice, however, not all states have introduced implementing legislation or concluded that the cooperation rules have a direct effect in the domestic system. Such legislation, where it exists, provides a basis, *inter alia*, for arrest and surrender, assistance concerning evidence and witnesses, and enforcement of penalties but the scope of cooperation and the means for providing assistance vary. States often fall back on extradition practices and principles in the context of cooperation with the Tribunals.[163] The lack of domestic legislation may create serious problems in practice. Reliance on the ordinary law on extradition and mutual legal assistance to other states may not be sufficient for the purposes of cooperation with the Tribunals while special legislation could speed up the process considerably.[164] With respect to the ICC, various efforts are being made to encourage and assist states to enact implementing legislation.[165]

States have often provided substantive assistance without domestic legislation on cooperation. Even though more than half of states parties still lack ICC cooperation implementing legislation, cooperation has been generally forthcoming.[166] However, the lack of cooperation in relation to some situations, particularly Darfur and Libya, and non-implementation of the Court's warrants for the arrest and surrender in notorious cases like *Al Bashir*, remains a major concern as it undermines the ability of the Court to carry out its mandate.[167] Special agreements have been concluded with states which enhance cooperation in areas such as witness relocation, (interim) release of persons, and enforcement of sentences, but they do not replace the obligation to enact implementing legislation.[168]

---

[160] Vienna Convention on the Law of Treaties, Art. 27. See also *Blaškić*, ICTY TC II, 18 July 1997, para. 84.

[161] SC Res. 827(1993) and 955(1994); and ICC Statute, Art. 88.

[162] See Rod Rastan, 'Testing Co-operation: The International Criminal Court and National Authorities' (2008) 21 *LJIL* 431, 434–5.

[163] For criticism, see Cassese, 'On Current Trends' (n. 6) 13–14.

[164] On the Spanish process to surrender Gotovina to the ICTY (three days after his arrest), see Gamarra and Vicente, 'UN Member States' Obligations' (n. 7) 648–9.

[165] For a collection of such legislation, see www.legal-tools.org and https://demo.hrlc.net/en/. See also *International Criminal Law Guidelines: Implementing the Rome Statute of the International Criminal Court*, Case Matrix Network (CILRAP, September 2017), www.legal-tools.org/doc/e05157/pdf/.

[166] *Report of the Court on Cooperation*, ICC-ASP/20/25 (29 October 2021) para. 47.

[167] *Report of the Court on Cooperation*, ICC-ASP/16/16, para. 40 (fifteen suspects remain at large); *Report of the Bureau on Noncooperation*, ICC-ASP/16/36 (4 December 2017).

[168] See also Section 20.2.1.

The ICC Statute is a complex instrument and domestic implementation is a challenging task. Apart from legal and technical issues, the cooperation obligations have triggered questions concerning national constitutional compatibility.[169] Common problems relate to extradition of nationals and constitutional immunities, in relation to the obligation to arrest and surrender suspects to the ICC. Other areas of controversy are the powers to conduct on-site investigations, life imprisonment, national amnesties, and pardons. Importantly, the states cannot avoid such problems by making reservations to their obligations of cooperation because this is not allowed under the Statute.[170] Constitutional amendments are often difficult politically, if possible at all, and require lengthy and complicated reforms. A few states, such as France, Germany, and Mexico, amended their Constitutions before ratifying the ICC Statute, but most states instead chose to interpret it as compatible with the Constitution.

20.8 NON-COMPLIANCE AND ENFORCEMENT

The ICTY and ICTR Statutes did not address the issue of non-compliance with the duty of cooperation. In *Blaškić*, the Appeals Chamber found that an international tribunal must have powers to make all judicial determinations that are necessary for the exercise of its primary jurisdiction, including making a finding of non-compliance and reporting this to the Security Council.[171] But the Tribunal may not recommend or suggest how the Security Council could or should address the matter.

Similarly, the ICC may make a finding of non-compliance with a request for cooperation and refer the matter to the ASP or, when the Security Council has referred the situation, to the Security Council.[172] For a failure to comply with a cooperation request to be referred, it must have been contrary to the Statute and prevented the Court from exercising its functions and powers. The Chamber has the discretion not to refer the matter even if it has reached such a finding.[173] A breach by a state not party of a legally binding cooperation agreement or arrangement may also be reported.[174]

Having the power to make findings of non-cooperation is important for the credibility of international judicial institutions, but the exercise of that power and its potential implications are highly sensitive matters. Measures such as public condemnation and even collective economic sanctions could be contemplated, but other considerations, such as the need to maintain support for the international jurisdiction, may prevail.[175] Moreover, a finding of non-cooperation could close the door to even partial cooperation and inhibit positive developments in that respect.

---

[169] See Helen Duffy, 'Overview of Constitutional Issues and Recent State Practice' in Claus Kreß, Bruce Broomhall, Flavia Lattanzi and Valeria Santori (eds.), *The Rome Statute and Domestic Legal Orders* (Baden-Baden, 2005) vol. II, 498–514; Darryl Robinson, 'The Rome Statute and its Impact on National Law' in Cassese et al., *Commentary*, 1849–60; and the Venice Commission, *Second Report on Constitutional Issues Raised by the Ratification of the Rome Statute of the International Court*, 76th Plenary Session, Venice, 17–18 October 2008.
[170] See ICC Statute, Art. 120. [171] *Blaškić*, ICTY AC, 29 October 1997, paras. 33–7. [172] ICC Statute, Art. 87(7).
[173] See e.g. *Al Bashir*, ICC PTC II, 6 July 2017 (ICC-02/05-01/09-302) paras. 138–40. [174] *Ibid.* Art. 87(5)(b).
[175] See Bruce Broomhall, *International Justice and the International Criminal Court: Between Sovereignty and the Rule of Law* (Oxford, 2003) 156–7.

In practice, the Security Council has failed to respond effectively to reports of non-compliance by the ICTY. The willingness of regional states to cooperate varied over time, but more recent changes of government improved cooperation. Collective action by states, such as threats to withhold financial aid and making accession to international organizations (such as the EU) subject to full cooperation with the Tribunal, have proved relatively effective.[176] As a result, the ICTY obtained custody over all of the high-level accused and no arrest warrants remained unenforced.[177] The ICTR also experienced instances of non-cooperation by the government of Rwanda.[178] The relationship between the ICTR and the government of Rwanda was troubled at times, with the latter at one point suspending cooperation when the ICTR ordered the release of an accused.[179] As of 2023, three of the ICTR fugitives remain at large and they will be tried in Rwanda if and when apprehended.[180]

The ICC has also experienced non-cooperation and has had to report over a dozen of such instances to the Security Council and the ASP pursuant to Article 87(7).[181] Most of the referrals have concerned failures to execute arrest warrants and/or comply with surrender requests of the Court in the situations referred by the Security Council (Darfur and Libya).[182] The non-enforcement of cooperation obligations remains the real weak spot of the system. The ASP has limited (and toothless) means at its disposal to induce, let alone compel, cooperation and is unable to sanction non-compliance by states parties.[183] Its faint-hearted responses to the Court's non-cooperation reports have had little, if any, effect on recalcitrant members. States parties have also not resorted to dispute settlement to solve differences regarding the interpretation and application of the Statute.[184] In turn, the Security Council is often paralyzed by politics and has an unimpressive track record of providing the Court with the necessary support in the two situations the Council has brought before it. In relation to Sudan, the Security Council has repeatedly failed to act upon reports of non-compliance, leading the Prosecutor at one point to hibernate the investigative activities and shift resources to other cases.[185] The Council's occasional (and only)

---

[176] Gabrielle Kirk McDonald, 'Problems, Obstacles and Achievements of the ICTY' (2004) 2 *JICJ* 558, 562–7.

[177] Slobodan Milošević was surrendered to the ICTY in 2001, Radovan Karadžić in 2008, and Ratko Mladić and Goran Hadžić in 2011.

[178] Erik Møse, 'Main Achievements of the ICTR' (2005) 3 *JICJ* 920, 939–40.

[179] The decision in *Barayagwiza*, ICTR AC, 3 November 1999, was subsequently reversed: ICTR AC, 31 March 2000. See Sections 17.3.2 and 17.7.3.

[180] See 'Searching for the Fugitives, MICT', www.unmict.org/en/cases/searching-fugitives.

[181] See Section 8.10 and 'Non-cooperation', https://asp.icc-cpi.int/non-cooperation. As of September 2023, there have been fifteen Art. 87(7) referrals to the Security Council and/or ASP in the *Situation in Darfur*, one in the *Situation in Kenya* and one in the *Situation in Libya*.

[182] See e.g. *Al Bashir*, ICC PTC II, 11 July 2016 (ICC-02/05–01/09–267) and *S. Gaddafi*, ICC PTC II, 10 December 2014 (ICC-01/11–01/11–577); concerning a failure to consult with the Court and to compel production of material, see *Kenyatta*, ICC TC V(B), 19 September 2016 (ICC-01/09–02/11–1037).

[183] The ASP has adopted procedures for dealing with cases of non-compliance as well as a 'toolkit on cooperation': Assembly Procedures relating to Non-cooperation, ICC-ASP/10/Res.5 (21 December 2011); Toolkit for the Implementation of the Informal Dimension of the Assembly Procedures relating to Non-cooperation, ICC-ASP/16/36/Add.1 (9 November 2016).

[184] ICC Statute, Art. 119(2).

[185] Statement to the United Nations Security Council on the Situation in Darfur, pursuant to SC Res. 1593(2005), 12 December 2014, para. 4. See also Strengthening the International Criminal Court and the Assembly of States Parties, Resolution ICC-ASP/21/Res.2, 9 December 2022, para. 32.

response so far in the form of a presidential statement urging the government of Sudan and others to cooperate fully with the Court, is a far cry from meaningful action.[186]

20.9 COOPERATION AND COMPLEMENTARITY

Numerous cooperation provisions in the ICC Statute reflect the principle of complementarity.[187] The regulation of competing requests, *ne bis in idem* challenges,[188] and simultaneous proceedings in the requested state concerning other crimes,[189] aims to encourage national proceedings. A decision by the Court on admissibility is decisive on whether the Court will go ahead with its investigation or prosecution. A complementarity challenge by a state results in suspension of the investigation by the Prosecutor, although authority to take certain measures may be sought from the Chamber. The state's duty to cooperate remains in effect until the Court orders otherwise, as does an arrest warrant.[190] In line with this, a *ne bis in idem* challenge before a national court may cause the requested state to postpone surrender pending an admissibility decision by the ICC, but the execution of the arrest warrant may not be postponed.[191]

The Statute also provides for some limited assistance that the ICC may grant a state, which is a logical corollary of the complementarity principle.[192] Moreover, the ICC may transfer the suspect or accused to a state that has made a successful admissibility challenge, but only with the approval of the originally surrendering state.[193] Cooperation among states is truly important for the prosecution of crimes where there is more than one state willing and able to exercise jurisdiction, including universal jurisdiction. While the Statute does not address this, its provisions on consultations could possibly be used to reach agreements on sequencing between international and national proceedings and hence to resolve complementarity conflicts.[194]

20.10 CONCLUDING REMARKS

The heavy dependence of international criminal jurisdictions upon cooperation by states and other actors tends to confirm Cassese's metaphorical description of these courts as 'giant[s] without arms and legs'. The distinction between 'horizontal' and 'vertical' cooperation schemes captures a fundamental difference in approach: the 'vertical' model attributes greater powers to the international jurisdiction and imposes greater duties on the states. The scheme of the Tribunals is more 'vertical' than that of the ICC, and the latter is

---

[186] E.g. UNSC Presidential Statement, 16 June 2008, S/PRST/2008/21. [187] See Chapter 8. [188] ICC Statute, Art. 89(2).
[189] *Ibid*. Arts. 89(4) and 94.
[190] *Ibid*. Arts. 19(7)–(9) and 58(4). See also *Gaddafi and Al-Senussi*, ICC PTC I, 4 April 2012 (ICC-01/11–01/11–100), 1 June 2012 (ICC-01/ 11–01/11–163) and 14 June 2013 (ICC-01/11–01/11–354).
[191] ICC Statute, Art. 89(2).
[192] *Ibid*. Art. 93(10). See also MICT Statute, Art. 28(3) and MICT RPE, rr. 87–88, providing for assistance to national authorities in the former Yugoslavia and Rwanda.
[193] ICC RPE, r 185. [194] Carsten Stahn, 'Libya, the International Criminal Court and Complementarity' (2012) 10 *JICJ* 325.

weaker on issues such as arrest by peacekeeping forces, on-site investigations, and powers to bring witnesses before the Court.

Although the distinction between the two models helps in understanding the principles, it does little to explain why cooperation is actually extended or not. Both models provide for indirect rather than direct enforcement. Compliance with the cooperation obligations and the degree and timeliness of assistance provided depend, not so much on the model and formal powers of courts, as on the commitment and will of relevant actors to cooperate with the international justice enterprise, as well as the capacity to induce such will by using political and economic leverage.[195] In view of the difficulties of conducting investigations and trials, and the absence of real sanctions, neither system can be effective unless states are truly willing and able to cooperate. A breach of international obligations may come with a price, but the alternative price for complying may be higher and more direct (for example, in domestic public opinion). The cooperation with a tribunal is contingent on this cost-benefit determination by the requested state or body.

Both the Tribunals and the ICC have been faced with instances of non-compliance or a bare minimum of cooperation. Over time, the Tribunals, backed by the Security Council, powerful states, and regional organizations in a position to exert pressure on the relevant countries, became rather successful in obtaining cooperation.[196] The ICC, however, operates in an even more complex environment. It generally does not have the same strong backing from powerful states as the Tribunals enjoyed. It deals with situations where conflicts are still ongoing, which complicates all forms of cooperation. When the territorial state has not sought the Court's intervention and the investigation has been triggered by a Security Council referral or the Prosecutor's *proprio motu* power, constructive assistance has been even less forthcoming, as demonstrated by the Sudan, Libya, and Kenya situations. The ICC's need for cooperation is greatest when the state most concerned is unwilling or unable to take appropriate action itself – hence the complementarity paradox.[197] Although the ASP has repeatedly emphasized the importance of timely and effective cooperation of states, the available means to ensure that the cooperation duties are complied with are limited and ineffective. This limits the effectiveness of the Rome Statute system.

In practice, international criminal jurisdictions are often cautious not to rush to depict states as uncooperative. They have no real influence over, and should not expect much visible action from, the international political bodies that could induce cooperation or impose sanctions. Instead, strong political support and more informal forms of pressure tend to be more important and effective. For example, the entrenched position of the

---

[195] See e.g. Marco Bocchese, 'Of Crimes and Crowns: When State Leaders Confront International Justice' (2023) 21(3) *JICJ* 487 (explaining variations in state cooperation with the ICC by state/regime leaders' attitudes).
[196] See e.g. Victor Peskin, *International Justice in Rwanda and the Balkans: Virtual Trials and the Struggle for State Cooperation* (Cambridge, 2008) 237.
[197] Paolo Benvenuti, 'Complementarity of the International Criminal Court to National Jurisdictions' in Flavia Lattanzi and William A. Schabas (eds.), *Essays on the Rome Statute of the International Criminal Court* (Ripa Fagnano Alto, 1999) 50; Olympia Bekou and Robert Cryer, 'The International Criminal Court and Universal Jurisdiction: A Close Encounter?' (2007) 56(1) *ICLQ* 49, 63.

African Union dissuading its member states from cooperating with the ICC concerning the arrest warrants against Al Bashir presented a significant challenge.[198]

The ICC cooperation regime may be strengthened and fine-tuned over time, but it is unrealistic to expect that the indirect model for enforcement will ever be replaced. It is likely to remain the weakest link of the Rome Statute system affecting the Court's effectiveness and credibility. Apart from the appearance of impotence in cases of non-compliance, the Court's awareness of real-life constraints can cause selectivity with respect to situations and cases picked for investigation and prosecution, so that the big powers and persons associated with sitting governments are not targeted lacking the prospects of state cooperation. This ultimately would undermine the ICC's credibility.

Further Reading

Olympia Bekou and Daley Birkett (eds.), *Cooperation and the International Criminal Court: Perspectives from Theory and Practice* (Leiden, 2016)

Cassese et al., *Commentary*, chs. 39–42

Yolanda Gamarra and Alejandra Vicente, 'United Nations Member States' Obligations Towards the ICTY: Arresting and Transferring Lukić, Gotovina and Zelenović' (2008) 8 *International Criminal Law Review* 627

Thomas Henquet, 'Mandatory Compliance Powers vis-à-vis States by the Ad Hoc Tribunals and the International Criminal Court: A Comparative Analysis' (1999) 12 *LJIL* 969

Claus Kreß, Bruce Broomhall, Flavia Lattanzi and Valeria Santori (eds.), *The Rome Statute and Domestic Legal Orders* (Baden-Baden, 2005) vol. II

Claus Kreß and Kimberly Prost, 'Part 9' in Ambos, *Commentary*, 2452–699

Roy S. Lee (ed.), *States' Responses to Issues Arising from the ICC Statute: Constitutional, Sovereignty, Judicial Cooperation and Criminal Law* (New York, 2005)

Valerie Oosterveld, Mike Perry, and John McManus, 'The Cooperation of States with the International Criminal Court' (2002) 25 *Fordham International Law Journal* 767

Rod Rastan, 'Testing Co-operation: The International Criminal Court and National Authorities' (2008) 21 *LJIL* 431

Rod Rastan, 'Article 72' in Ambos, *Commentary*, 2127–73

Herwig Roggeman and Petar Šarčević (eds.), *National Security and International Criminal Justice* (The Hague, 2002)

Göran Sluiter, *International Criminal Adjudication and the Collection of Evidence: Obligations of States* (Antwerp, 2002)

Patricia M. Wald, 'Apprehending War Criminals: Does International Cooperation Work?' (2012) 27 *American University International Law Review* 229

---

[198] E.g. Decision by the 13th Ordinary Session of the AU Assembly, 3 July 2009, Doc. Assembly/AU/13(XIII), and subsequent decisions. See Section 8.11.2.

21

Immunities

21.1 INTRODUCTION

21.1.1 Overview

The international law of immunities has ancient roots, extending back not hundreds, but thousands, of years.[1] In order to maintain channels of communication and thereby prevent and resolve conflicts, societies needed to have confidence that their envoys would have safe passage, particularly in times when emotions and distrust were at their highest. Accordingly, international law developed to provide for inviolability of a foreign state's representatives and immunities from the exercise of jurisdiction.

While immunities are valuable in preventing interference with representatives, and thereby maintaining the conduct of international relations, they can also frustrate prosecutions for very serious crimes. In recent decades, as concern for human beings has taken a bigger role in international relations, states have taken more ambitious steps to prosecute international criminals. This emboldened state practice has brought to the fore many questions about the boundaries between accountability and immunity.

It would be an oversimplification to assume that international criminal law simply overrides immunities. Commentators have at times assumed that no immunity of any kind may be raised in response to allegations of genocide, crimes against humanity, or war crimes.[2] Such a view overlooks the different types of immunities, and is contradicted by the great bulk of state practice and jurisprudence.[3] Even the landmark precedents that narrowed immunities also explicitly affirmed that some immunities still apply even with regard to allegations of serious international crimes.[4]

A recurring but flawed argument against immunity is that the prohibitions of international crimes are *jus cogens* – that is, peremptory norms that override contrary rules – and therefore any immunities must give way to the 'higher value' of ensuring prosecution.[5] Such arguments have been considered and rejected in an extensive line of cases in various

---

[1] Linda S. Frey and Marsha L. Frey, *The History of Diplomatic Immunity* (Columbus, OH, 1999); J. Craig Barker, *The Abuse of Diplomatic Privileges and Immunities: A Necessary Evil?* (Aldershot, 1996) 14–31; Montell Ogdon, *Juridical Bases of Diplomatic Immunity* (Washington, DC, 1936) 8–20; Grant V. McLanahan, *Diplomatic Immunity* (New York, 1989) 18–25.

[2] See e.g. Andrea Bianchi, 'Immunity versus Human Rights: The Pinochet Case' (1999) 10 *EJIL* 237; Amnesty International, *Universal Jurisdiction: The Duty of States to Enact and Implement Legislation* (AI Index IOR 53/2001, September 2001) ch. 14.

[3] See Sections 21.3 and 21.4. [4] See Sections 21.2 and 21.5. [5] See e.g. Bianchi, 'Immunity versus Human Rights' (n. 2) 265.

countries, as well as at the European Court of Human Rights (ECtHR) and the International Court of Justice (ICJ).[6] As was observed by the House of Lords in the *Jones* case,[7] the argument depends on a false conflict: *jus cogens* prohibits *committing* the crimes, but it does not mean that all international laws regarding prosecution cease to apply. A state respecting the immunity of another state is not committing a crime and hence is not in conflict with the *jus cogens* prohibition.[8] This understanding was reaffirmed by the ICJ in the *Germany v. Italy* case. Italian courts had declared that they could set aside the immunities of Germany, and Germany brought the question before the ICJ. The ICJ held that the Italian courts were wrong in international law and had themselves broken international law by failing to respect Germany's state immunity.[9]

As was explained by the ICJ in another case, the *Arrest Warrant* case (discussed below), the objective that serious crimes must be punished

> does not *ipso facto* mean that immunities are unavailable whenever impunity would be the outcome ... [I]mmunities serve other purposes which have their own intrinsic value and ... international law seeks the accommodation of this value with the fight against impunity, and not the triumph of one norm over the other. A State may exercise the criminal jurisdiction which it has under international law, but in doing so it is subject to other legal obligations.[10]

Thus, a more sophisticated approach is needed in order to understand this area of law. It will be necessary to distinguish between 'functional' immunity and 'personal' immunity, and to understand the purpose underlying those two types of immunity.

The jurisprudence on international criminal law and immunities has been described as perplexing and contradictory.[11] However, if one keeps in mind the underlying purposes of functional and personal immunity, one will discern a fairly consistent and coherent set of rules. It is nonetheless a complex area with many controversies.

This chapter will strive to introduce the intricacies in as clear a manner as possible. The topic of this chapter is the immunities of individuals in relation to *criminal prosecution* for international crimes, and not state immunity from *civil proceedings*. Under the latter type of immunity, a state (and its assets) may not be subjected to civil proceedings in foreign courts, unless it chooses to submit to such courts. This immunity from civil proceedings is subject to many exceptions; for example, a state is not immune in relation to its commercial activities. There have been many proposals for a 'human rights' or 'international crime'

---

[6] See e.g. *Al-Adsani* v. *United Kingdom*, ECtHR, 21 November 2001; *Tachiona* v. *Mugabe*, 169 F Supp 2d 259 (SDNY, 2001); *Jones* v. *Kingdom of Saudi Arabia* [2006] UKHL 26; [2006] 2 WLR 1424, considering and rejecting arguments based on *jus cogens*, as well as the ICJ *Arrest Warrant* decision, discussed in Section 21.4.2.

[7] *Jones* v. *Kingdom of Saudi Arabia* [2006] UKHL 26; [2006] 2 WLR 1424, paras. 24–8 and 43–63.

[8] Hazel Fox and Philippa Webb, *The Law of State Immunity*, 3rd ed. (Oxford, 2013) 40–1; Lee Caplan, 'State Immunity, Human Rights and *Jus Cogens*: A Critique of the Normative Hierarchy Theory' (2003) 97 *AJIL* 741; Andrea Gattini, 'War Crimes and State Immunity in the *Ferrini* Decision' (2005) 3 *JICJ* 224. But see Lorna McGregor, 'Torture and State Immunity: Deflecting Impunity, Distorting Sovereignty' (2007) 18 *EJIL* 903 (noting that formalistic arguments should not obscure the fact that upholding immunity can lead to impunity).

[9] *Jurisdictional Immunities of the State (Germany* v. *Italy: Greece Intervening)*, ICJ General List 143, 2 March 2012.

[10] Joint Separate Opinion of Judges Higgins, Kooijmans and Buergenthal, para. 79, in the *Arrest Warrant* judgment, discussed in Section 21.4.2.

[11] Rosanne van Alebeek, 'The *Pinochet* Case: International Human Rights Law on Trial' (2001) 71 *British Yearbook of International Law* 29, 47; J. Craig Barker, 'The Future of Former Head of State Immunity after *Ex Parte Pinochet*' (1999) 48 *ICLQ* 937, 938.

exception to state immunity, but such proposals have been met with little success so far.[12] The law governing immunity of officials from criminal prosecution, which is the focus of this chapter, involves different considerations and different tests.[13]

21.1.2 Functional and Personal Immunity

With respect to immunity from prosecution, there is a crucial distinction between 'functional immunity' (also known as immunity *ratione materiae*) and 'personal immunity' (also known as immunity *ratione personae*). The first protects state functions (i.e. official acts) and the second protects the physical person of certain high-ranking officials while they are representing their country.

Functional immunity protects *conduct* carried out on behalf of a state. It flows from a principle of sovereign equality, that a state's policies and actions cannot be judged without some form of consent by that state. If State A could bring criminal proceedings against the individual officials who carried out official functions of State B, then State A would be doing indirectly what it cannot do directly, namely, acting as the arbiter of the conduct of another state. Functional immunity attaches to all persons who carry out state functions. It is permanent and endures for such acts even after that person leaves office. Functional immunity does not provide complete protection of the person; it only covers conduct that was an *official act* of a state. Thus, criminal activity carried out in a *private* capacity remains subject to prosecution. As will be discussed in Section 21.2, an exception to functional immunity has emerged whereby international crimes may also be prosecuted.

Personal immunity is not limited to any particular conduct; it provides complete immunity of the *person* of certain office-holders while they carry out important representative functions. Personal immunity is granted only to a comparatively small set of people, such as heads of state, heads of government, and foreign ministers, as well as diplomats accredited to a host country. Personal immunity is temporary, in that it lasts only for as long as the person is serving in that representative role. There is no exception based on the seriousness of the alleged crime, or whether the acts were private or official, because the rationale is unconnected to the nature of the charge. The rationale was stated in 1740 by Wicquefort:

if Princes had the Liberty of Proceeding against the Embassador who negotiates with them on any Account, or under any Colour whatsoever, the Person of the Embassador would never be in Safety; because those who should have a Mind to make away with Him would never want a Pretext.[14]

---

[12] *Princz* v. *Federal Republic of Germany*, 26 F 3d 1166 (DC Cir. 1994); *Al-Adsani* v. *Government of Kuwait* (1996) 107 ILR 536, CA; *Al-Adsani* v. *United Kingdom*, ECtHR, 21 November 2001; *Tachiona* v. *Mugabe*, 169 F Supp 2d 259 (SDNY, 2001); *Jones* v. *Kingdom of Saudi Arabia* [2006] UKHL 26; [2006] 2 WLR 1424; *Kazemi Estate* v. *Iran* [2014] 3 SCR 176 (Supreme Court of Canada), but see the anomalous Greek case concerning the Distomo massacre, discussed in Ilias Bantekas, 'Prefecture of Voiotia v. Federal Republic of Germany' (1998) 92 *AJIL* 765, which was doubted in subsequent Greek cases and rejected by the German Supreme Court in *Distomo Massacre* (2003) 42 ILM 1030. In *Jurisdictional Immunities of the State* (*Germany* v. *Italy: Greece Intervening*), ICJ General List 143, 2 March 2012, the ICJ rejected arguments for a human rights exception, a *jus cogens* exception, and a 'last resort' exception.
[13] Philippa Webb, 'How Far Does the Systemic Approach to Immunities Take Us?' (2018) 112 *AJIL Unbound* 16.
[14] A. van Wicquefort, *The Embassador and his Functions*, 2nd ed. (London, 1740) 251 (translated into English by John Digby), quoted in Ogdon, *Juridical Bases* (n. 1) 128–9.

To sum up, personal immunity renders a person inviolable, regardless of the nature of the charges, but it only attaches to a limited set of official roles, and it endures only while the person fulfils that official representative position. Conversely, functional immunity protects only conduct carried out in the course of the individual's duties, but does not drop away when a person's role comes to an end, since it protects the conduct, not the person. For both types of immunity, the purpose is not to benefit the individual,[15] but to protect official acts (functional immunity) or to facilitate international relations (personal immunity). It is the state which is the real beneficiary of the immunity, and it is the state which may waive it, irrespective of the wishes of the person claiming the immunity.

The existence of immunity does not mean that there is a lack of substantive legal responsibility, but rather that a foreign state is procedurally prevented from exercising jurisdiction over the alleged offender. Immunities may be waived by the state concerned to allow the foreign state to pursue criminal proceedings.

21.1.3 Examples of Immunities

The most well-developed and well-defined area of immunities is that of diplomatic immunities. Centuries of state practice with diplomatic relations have produced considerable precision as to the rules. The law is now codified in the Vienna Convention on Diplomatic Relations. While serving in a host country, diplomatic agents enjoy *personal* immunity: they are immune from criminal jurisdiction, their person is inviolable, and they may not be arrested or detained.[16] After their term of service in the host country has ended, diplomats continue to enjoy *functional* immunity for acts in the exercise of their functions.[17]

If the diplomat commits a serious crime, the options available to the host state are to request a waiver of immunity from the sending state or to declare the diplomat *persona non grata*.[18] After the diplomat's term is over, the diplomat enjoys only functional immunity, and thus the host authorities may prosecute the diplomat for any crimes committed in a non-official capacity, if they can acquire custody of him or her. Other members of a diplomatic mission enjoy lesser degrees of immunity,[19] as do consular officials.[20]

The contours of head of state immunity are less well defined. There is no codifying convention and state practice on point is limited. The lack of state practice is probably in part a reflection of the immunity and in part due to the reluctance of states to interfere with foreign heads of state.[21] It is widely accepted, however, that heads of state enjoy at least the same immunities as ambassadors: while in office they have absolute personal immunity,[22] and afterwards they have functional immunity for official acts carried out while in office.[23]

---

[15] Vienna Convention on Diplomatic Relations 1961, Preamble, paras. 2–4. [16] *Ibid.* Arts. 29 and 31. [17] *Ibid.* Art. 39(1).
[18] *Ibid.* Arts. 9 and 32. [19] *Ibid.* Art. 37(3). [20] Vienna Convention on Consular Relations 1963.
[21] In one exception, French authorities issued a witness summons to the head of State of Djibouti, a matter brought to the ICJ by Djibouti in *Certain Questions of Mutual Assistance in Criminal Matters (Djibouti v. France)*, 4 June 2008. The Court held that, as the summons was only an invitation, there was no violation by France of its obligations to Djibouti.
[22] Charles Lewis, *State and Diplomatic Immunity*, 3rd ed. (London, 1999) 125; *R v. Bow Street Metropolitan Stipendiary Magistrate, ex parte Pinochet Ugarte (No. 3)* [1999] 2 All ER 97, HL, at 111, 119–20, 152, 168–9, 179 and 181.
[23] Lord Gore Booth (ed.), *Satow's Guide to Diplomatic Practice*, 5th ed. (London, 1979) 9.

While head of state immunity is long established, the position of heads of government and other ministers has not always been as clear.[24] In the *Arrest Warrant* case *(Democratic Republic of the Congo* v. *Belgium)*, the ICJ upheld personal immunity for ministers of foreign affairs, analogous to that of heads of state.[25] This conclusion is understandable, since those officials have an important representative role on the international arena. Similar principles apply to heads of government, such as prime ministers, as their representative function is more sensitive than a minister of foreign affairs and, in many systems, the head of state.[26]

In addition, state representatives travelling to participate in meetings of international organizations enjoy immunities provided in the relevant treaties, which typically include personal immunity.[27] Furthermore, when a state hosts a major summit or meeting outside the context of an international organization (such as a G8 or African Union summit), it is typical practice to extend immunity to visiting delegates. The Convention on Special Missions (1969) sought to provide a general regime for visits of officials to another state on state business.[28] That convention has not been widely ratified,[29] but there is some state practice regarding it as customary international law.[30]

Certain officials of international organizations, such as the United Nations or the International Criminal Court, enjoy immunities as provided in specific conventions.[31] In general, personal immunity is granted sparingly and reserved for the highest officials. Most officials receive only functional immunity even while on official missions.[32]

21.1.4 Underlying Rationales and Values

Historically, various rationales have been put forward in support of immunities. Some of these were legal fictions, such as 'extra-territoriality' (the fiction that the premises of the mission represented an extension of the sending state's territory), 'personal representation' (that the ambassador is equivalent to his or her head of state), or 'personification' (that the head of state personifies the state).[33] Respect for the 'dignity' of the head of state or the sending state has also been a major consideration,[34] as has political expediency – the desire to avoid controversy with other states.[35] However, in recent decades, the law has been

---

[24] Arthur Watts, 'The Legal Position in International Law of Heads of State, Heads of Government and Foreign Ministers' (1995) 247 *Recueil des Cours: Collected Courses of the Hague Academy of International Law* 97.

[25] See Section 21.4.2. [26] Watts, 'The Legal Position' (n. 24) 97–113.

[27] See e.g. in the context of the UN, the Convention on the Privileges and Immunities of the United Nations 1946, 1 UNTS 15.

[28] Convention on Special Missions 1969, Art. 1(a).

[29] The immunities are analogous to those in the Vienna Convention on Diplomatic Relations – see Convention on Special Missions 1969, Arts. 29 and 31.

[30] See Dapo Akande and Sangeeta Shah, 'Immunities of State Officials, International Crimes, and Foreign Domestic Courts' (2011) 21 *EJIL* 815 and Andrew Sanger 'Identification of Special Mission Immunity and The Reception of Customary International Law into English Law (2019) 78 *Cambridge Law Journal* 1; see also *Khurts Bat* v. *Investigating Judge of the German Federal Court* [2011] EWHC 2029 (Admin).

[31] See e.g. Convention on the Privileges and Immunities of the United Nations 1946; Agreement on Privileges and Immunities of the International Criminal Court 2002.

[32] See e.g. Convention on the Privileges and Immunities of the United Nations 1946, Art. V, ss. 18–19, granting full diplomatic immunities to the Secretary-General and Assistant Secretary-Generals and functional immunity to other staff.

[33] See Ogdon, *Juridical Bases* (n. 1) 63–165. [34] See *Schooner Exchange* v. *M'Fadden*, 11 US 116, 137 (1812).

[35] See e.g. *Tachiona* v. *Mugabe*, 169 F Supp 2d 259, 290–1 (SDNY, 2001).

significantly demystified, and immunities are now supported only by more concrete rationales.[36]

With respect to functional immunity, the remaining rationale is the principle that one state may not sit in judgment on another state (also known as *par in parem non habet iudicium*), because doing so would undermine sovereign equality. This is why international law insists that disputes between states may only be brought to appropriate forums with the agreement of states. If a state could prosecute foreign officials for acts of another state, it would indirectly be passing judgment on another state, and could even use prosecutions to force changes in policies of the other state. As is discussed in Section 21.2, however, an exception has emerged for serious international crimes.[37]

The rationale for personal immunity is its value in facilitating international relations. The ICJ has described the inviolability of diplomatic envoys as the most fundamental prerequisite for the conduct of relations between states.[38] The institution of diplomacy is 'an instrument essential for effective co-operation in the international community, and for enabling states, irrespective of their differing constitutional and social systems, to achieve mutual understanding and to resolve their differences by peaceful means'.[39] The existing system of diplomatic relations has made possible global summits, the creation of international organizations, and the development of treaties and a more rules-based international order. It has enabled diplomats to work in antagonistic states to protect nationals and to avert or end conflicts. It also enables UN human rights rapporteurs and international prosecutors to carry out their work in states that might welcome pretexts to frustrate their investigations.[40]

Unfortunately, immunities can also have many perverse effects, shielding persons responsible for spectacular abuses and crimes. This has often led to public outcry. With the increased prioritization of human rights and the rule of law, immunities have rightly come under scrutiny and pressure.

Two main methods have been employed to rebalance the goals served by immunities with the goal of ending impunity. Both methods were foreshadowed by the Nuremberg Charter. The first method was to declare that functional immunity, which protects state conduct from scrutiny, does not extend to international crimes (see Section 21.2). That solution is not transposable to personal immunity, because such immunity is not based on any authorization of the act, but rather aims to preclude any pretext to interfere with high representatives (see Section 21.3). However, Nuremberg serves as a precedent on how to deal with personal immunity: the creation of international criminal tribunals authorized to set aside even personal immunity. We shall look below at different ways that personal immunity may be relinquished before international courts, as well as the more controversial claim that immunities are simply inapplicable before international courts (see Section 21.4).

---

[36] See e.g. Watts, 'The Legal Position' (n. 24) 35–6. [37] See Section 21.2.
[38] *United States Diplomatic and Consular Staff in Iran (United States v. Iran)* (Merits) [1980] ICJ Reports 3, para. 91. [39] *Ibid.*
[40] See e.g. *Difference relating to Immunity from Legal Process of a Special Rapporteur of the Commission on Human Rights,* Advisory Opinion [1999] ICJ Reports 100.

21.2 FUNCTIONAL IMMUNITY AND ITS LIMITS

Traditionally, national governments and courts were so cautious and deferential in dealing with foreign officials that controversial efforts at prosecution simply did not arise. Since the 1990s, this has changed.[41] Considerable authority indicates that functional immunity does not extend to serious international crimes; however, the existence and parameters of this exception are still debated.

21.2.1 The *Pinochet* Precedent

In 1998, Senator Augusto Pinochet, former head of state of Chile, was visiting the United Kingdom when Spain issued a request for his extradition for, *inter alia*, torture. Pinochet was arrested by British authorities. He applied to have the warrants quashed on the ground that he was entitled to immunity as a former head of state.

The case went up to the House of Lords, where it was heard,[42] and then for procedural reasons, reheard.[43] In the final House of Lords decision, six out of seven judges confirmed that the immunity of a former head of state did not prevent his extradition on charges of torture.[44] Each of the judges in the final decision issued a separate opinion, and the reasoning within each opinion was not always clear. As a result, it is difficult to identify a clear *ratio decidendi*. Commentators tend to emphasize different passages and offer different interpretations, and thereby arrive at different views as to the basis of the decision.

The most cautious interpretation, restricted to the terms of the 1984 Torture Convention, is that, where *official involvement* is a necessary element of a crime, there cannot be immunity by reason of official involvement; otherwise the crime would be vacated of content. As noted by Lord Millett:

International law cannot be supposed to have established a crime ... and at the same time to have provided an immunity which is co-extensive with the obligation it seeks to impose.[45]

A broader reading is that the ruling is about international core crimes in general; such crimes may be official acts, but they are not a type of official conduct that attracts functional immunity.[46] Functional immunity protects certain conduct, but it would be contradictory

---

[41] Michael Byers, 'The Law and Politics of the Pinochet Case' (2000) 10 *Duke Journal of Comparative and International Law* 415.

[42] At the first House of Lords hearing, three out of five judges were persuaded that the immunity of a former head of state did not cover such serious international crimes. The essence of the decision was that the commission of certain serious international crimes is condemned by all states as illegal and therefore cannot also be protected by international law as an 'official function'. *R v. Bow Street Metropolitan Stipendiary Magistrate, ex parte Pinochet Ugarte (No. 1)* [1998] 4 All ER 897, HL.

[43] A rehearing was necessitated by the possible appearance of bias of one of the judges in the first hearing, who had some (fairly slender) affiliations with Amnesty International, one of the intervenors. *R v. Bow Street Metropolitan Stipendiary Magistrate, ex parte Pinochet Ugarte (No. 2)* [1999] 1 All ER 577, HL.

[44] *R v. Bow Street Metropolitan Stipendiary Magistrate, ex parte Pinochet Ugarte (No. 3)* [1999] 2 All ER 97, HL.

[45] *Pinochet (No. 3)* (n. 44), 179. Support for this reading can be found in the opinions of Lords Browne-Wilkinson, Saville and Phillips. *Ibid.* 114–15 (Browne-Wilkinson), 169 (Saville), and 190 (Phillips).

[46] See e.g. Christine Chinkin, '*Regina v. Bow Street Stipendiary Magistrate, Ex Parte Pinochet Ugarte (No. 3)*' (1999) 93 *AJIL* 703; Steffen Wirth, 'Immunities, Related Problems, and Article 98 of the Rome Statute' (2001) 12 *Criminal Law Forum* 429; Claus Kreß, 'War Crimes Committed in Non-International Armed Conflict and the Emerging System of International Criminal Justice' (2000) 30 *Israel Yearbook on Human Rights* 103, 158–9.

for international law both to protect conduct and at the same time condemn it and require its prosecution.[47] As Lord Phillips noted, 'no immunity *ratione materiae* could exist for ... a crime contrary to international law'.[48]

The *scope* of the rule depends on which approach is adopted. On the narrowest reading, the scope would be limited to torture and other crimes specifically requiring official participation as an element of the crime.[49] On the broader reading, the rule would potentially cover all serious international crimes. Some judges indicated that a single act of torture would not suffice to override functional immunity, and that it would have to constitute a crime against humanity, that is to say, 'widespread or systematic torture as an instrument of State policy'.[50]

The basis of the *Pinochet* decision and its implications remain shrouded in uncertainty. For the purposes of UK law, the decision has been interpreted narrowly in a subsequent House of Lords case as being confined to the wording of the Torture Convention, which defines the crime by reference to official status and thus removes the immunity by necessary implication.[51] However, for the purposes of international law, the decision is often placed within a line of authorities limiting the availability of functional immunity for core crimes.

21.2.2 Other Authorities: No Functional Immunity for Core Crimes?

A considerable body of international cases, national cases, state practice, and academic commentary support the view that functional immunity does not preclude prosecution for serious international crimes, which is consistent with the broader reading of *Pinochet*.

Authorities Indicating No Functional Immunities for Core Crimes

As the Nuremberg judgment observed:

The principle of international law which, under certain circumstances, protects the representative of a State cannot be applied to acts which are condemned as criminal by international law. The authors of these acts cannot shelter themselves behind their official position in order to be freed from punishment ... individuals have duties which transcend the national obligations of obedience imposed by the individual State. He who violates the laws of war cannot obtain immunity while acting in pursuance of the authority of the State, if the State in authorizing action moves outside its competence under international law.[52]

---

[47] Note that such reasoning would not apply to personal immunity, because personal immunity does not protect *conduct*, it protects persons in particular high representative *roles* from interference on any grounds.

[48] *Pinochet (No. 3)* (n. 44), 190. Similarly, Lords Browne-Wilkinson and Hutton hold that these acts 'could not rank *for immunity purposes* as performance of an official function' (emphasis added). Lord Hope holds that: 'the obligations which were recognized by customary law in the case of such serious international crimes ... are so strong as to override any objection ... on the ground of immunity *ratione materiae*'. Lord Millett cites with approval the *Eichmann* case as authority that official authority is no bar to the exercise of jurisdiction for certain international crimes. *Pinochet (No. 3)* (n. 44) 114 (Browne-Wilkinson), 152 (Hope), 166 (Hutton) and 176–7 (Millett).

[49] Colin Warbrick et al., 'The Pinochet Cases in the United Kingdom' (1999) 2 *Yearbook of International Humanitarian Law* 91, 113–14.

[50] *Pinochet (No. 3)* (n. 44) 144–5 and 150–1 (Hope); see also 177 (Millett) and 188 (Phillips). At least one judge felt that a single act of torture would suffice (presumably with respect to States Parties to the Torture Convention): *ibid.* 166 (Lord Hutton).

[51] See *Jones* v. *Kingdom of Saudi Arabia* [2006] UKHL 26; [2006] 2 WLR 1124, paras. 19 and 79–81.

[52] Nuremberg International Military Tribunal (IMT), Judgment and Sentences, reprinted in (1947) 41 *AJIL* 172, 221.

The legal underpinnings of this proposition are compelling. First, functional immunity protects state conduct from scrutiny, but it would be incongruous for international law to protect the very conduct which it criminalizes and for which it imposes duties to prosecute. Second, the state cannot complain that its sovereignty is being restricted or that a policy is being imposed on it, when the prohibited conduct is generally recognized as an international crime. Third, state agents are normally able to pass responsibility for dubious activities to the state that authorized them, but in the case of serious international crimes, 'individuals have international duties which transcend the national obligations of obedience',[53] and hence they are rightly held to account.

The proposition was endorsed by the International Law Commission (ILC) and the General Assembly as Principle III of the 'Nuremberg Principles'.[54] The ILC reconfirmed the principle in its Draft Code of Crimes.[55]

The same principle has been applied in national cases. In *Eichmann*, the Israeli Supreme Court rejected a plea by Eichmann that he was carrying out official activities. The Court held that there is no immunity for official acts:

when the matter pertains to acts prohibited by the law of nations, especially when they are international crimes of the class of 'crimes against humanity' (in the wide sense) … such acts … are completely outside the 'sovereign' jurisdiction of the State that ordered or ratified their commission, and therefore those who participated in such acts must personally account for them and cannot shelter behind the official character of their task or mission.[56]

In *Bouterse*, the Amsterdam Court of Appeal held that serious international crimes do not attract functional immunity.[57] In addition, a Belgian court in the *Sharon* case, Spanish authorities requesting extradition of Pinochet, and a Spanish court in the *Castro* case, all indicated that there was no functional immunity for serious international crimes, as did a committee of jurists appointed by the African Union recommending prosecution of Hissène Habré, former head of state of Chad.[58]

The proposition has also been supported by international criminal tribunals. For example, in *Blaškić*, the International Criminal Tribunal for the former Yugoslavia (ICTY) recognized functional immunity as a 'well-established rule of customary

---

[53] Trial of the Major War Criminals before the International Military Tribunal, vol. I, Nuremberg 1947, 223.

[54] Affirmation of the Principles of International Law recognized by the Charter of the Nuremberg Tribunal, Resolution 95(I) of the United Nations General Assembly, 11 December 1946; Principles of the Nuremberg Tribunal, Report of the International Law Commission Covering its Second Session, 5 June–29 July 1950, Doc. A/1316, 11–14 and commentaries in (1950) II *Yearbook of the International Law Commission* 374–8.

[55] See e.g. draft Code of Crimes Against the Peace and Security of Mankind (1996) II *Yearbook of the International Law Commission*, Part Two, Art. 7. See also Institut de Droit International, Resolution on the Immunity from Jurisdiction of the State and of Persons Who Act on Behalf of the State in case of International Crimes (2009), which also concluded that there is no functional immunity for core crimes.

[56] *Attorney-General of Israel* v. *Eichmann* (1968) 36 ILR 277, 308–10. The discussion was in the context of 'Act of State', but, as noted by Lord Millett in *Pinochet (No. 3)* (n. 44) 176, the principles are the same.

[57] *Bouterse* (2000) 51 Nederlandse Jurisprudentie 302. An appeal was granted by the Supreme Court on other, jurisdictional, grounds.

[58] See *Immunity of State Officials from Criminal Jurisdiction*, Memorandum by the Secretariat, UN Doc. A/CN.4/596 (31 March 2008) paras. 180–90; Antonio Cassese, 'The Belgian Court of Cassation v. The International Court of Justice: The Sharon and Others Case' (2003) 1 *JICJ* 437, 443–50. On the prosecution of Habré before the Extraordinary African Chambers in Senegal, see Chapter 9.

international law', with the exception that those responsible for 'war crimes, crimes against humanity and genocide . . . cannot invoke immunity from national or international jurisdiction even if they perpetrated such crimes while acting in their official capacity'.[59] Many former officials have been tried for core crimes. The proposition is also supported in much of the literature.[60]

An Open Question?

While these authorities support an 'international crimes' exception to functional immunity, there is also room for doubt and disagreement. Most importantly, the ICJ failed to mention such an exception in the *Democratic Republic of the Congo* v. *Belgium* case (discussed in Section 21.3). It has been argued that there is not sufficient state practice and not sufficient political will to support such an exception.[61] Recently, while clarifying immunity from foreign criminal jurisdiction, the ILC concluded that functional immunity does not insulate core crimes, but the proposition drew scepticism from some members and had to go to a vote, which passed twenty-one to eight.[62] In 2021, the German Federal Court of Justice took note of the controversy in the ILC, but concluded that state practice remains clear that functional immunity does not protect such crimes.[63] There are also questions about the scope of the exception. As noted above, some judgments in the *Pinochet* case indicated that isolated acts of torture would not suffice, but a crime against humanity of torture would. An Italian case, *Lozano*, also suggested that the exception may not include isolated war crimes. The case dealt with a US serviceman in Iraq who opened fire on a car speeding towards a checkpoint, killing an Italian agent and wounding another officer and a reporter.[64] The court found that Lozano's conduct was not a war crime, given the car's rapid approach to the checkpoint.[65] The court affirmed a general exception that functional immunity does not prevail against international crimes,[66] but suggested some thresholds for war crimes, such as that they must be 'odious or inhuman' or involve scale or planning.[67] The ILC's draft

---

[59] *Blaškić*, ICTY AC, 29 October 1997, para. 41. See also *Furundžija*, ICTY TC II, 10 December 1998, para. 140.

[60] See e.g. *Princeton Principles on Universal Jurisdiction* (Princeton University, 2001) 48–50; Paola Gaeta, 'Official Capacity and Immunities' in Cassese et al., *Commentary*, 981; Cassese, 'When May Senior State Officials be Tried for International Crimes? Some Comments on the *Congo v. Belgium* Case' (2002) 13 *EJIL* 853; Steffen Wirth, 'Immunity for Core Crimes? The ICJ's Judgment in the Congo v. Belgium Case' (2002) 13 *EJIL* 877; Hugh King, 'Immunities and Bilateral Agreements: Issues Arising from Articles 27 and 98 of the Rome Statute' (2006) *New Zealand Journal of Public and International Law* 269; Watts, 'The Legal Position' (n. 24) 4; Akande and Shah, 'Immunities of State Officials' (n. 30) 839–46. But see Ingrid Wuerth, '*Pinochet's* Legacy Reassessed' (2012) 106 *AJIL* 731.

[61] O'Keefe, 'Symposium on the Immunity of State Officials: An "International Crime" Exception to the Immunity of State Officials from Foreign Criminal Jurisdiction: Not Currently, Not Likely' (2015) 109 *AJIL Unbound* 167.

[62] International Law Commission, *Immunity of State Officials from Foreign Criminal Jurisdiction*, UN Doc. A/72/10 (2017) paras. 71–4; Chimène I. Keitner, 'Horizontal Enforcement and the ILC's Proposed Draft Articles on the Immunity of State Officials from Foreign Criminal Jurisdiction' (2015) 109 *AJIL Unbound* 161; Dire Tladi, 'The International Law Commission's Recent Work on Exceptions to Immunity: Charting the Course for a Brave New World in International Law?' (2019) 32 *Leiden Journal of International Law* 179.

[63] The decision only addressed low-ranking subordinates. See Claus Kress, 'On Functional Immunity of Foreign Officials and Crimes under International Law' *Just Security*, 31 March 2021, www.justsecurity.org; Peter Frank and Christoph Barthe, 'Immunity of Foreign State Officials Before National Courts' (2021) 19 *JICJ* 700; Aziz Epik, 'No Functional Immunity for Crimes under International Law before Foreign Domestic Courts' (2022) 19 *JICJ* 1263.

[64] Antonio Cassese, 'The Italian Court of Cassation Misapprehends the Notion of War Crimes' (2008) 6 *JICJ* 1077.

[65] *Ibid*. 1084. [66] *Ibid*. 1082.

[67] *Ibid*. 1085–8. Such a requirement would not be entirely unprecedented; several passages in *Pinochet* arguably required 'widespread or systematic' crimes. See Section 21.2.

work on immunity from foreign criminal jurisdiction includes genocide, crimes against humanity, and war crimes as exceptions to functional immunity.[68]

21.3 PERSONAL IMMUNITY: NO EXCEPTION BASED ON THE CRIMES ALLEGED

21.3.1 State Practice and Jurisprudence

While inroads have been made into *functional* immunity, state practice and jurisprudence have consistently upheld *personal* immunity, regardless of the nature of the charges. For example, even in the *Pinochet* decision, all of the Law Lords agreed that, if Pinochet were still a serving head of state, he could not be arrested. A serving head of state has personal immunity, and '[t]he nature of the charge is irrelevant; his immunity is personal and absolute'.[69] 'He is not liable to be arrested or detained on any ground whatever.'[70]

To understand the divergent treatment of functional and personal immunity, one must recall their purposes. Functional immunity relates to the conduct and its authorization by a state, whereas personal immunity flows from a completely different rationale, unconnected with the alleged conduct. Its purpose is to preclude any pretext for interference with a state representative, in order to allow international relations between potentially distrustful states. Thus, personal immunity cannot be set aside without the consent of the relevant state.

The possibility of creating exceptions to personal immunity has been considered but rejected over the years, even in situations where the desire to prosecute was strong, including cases of espionage, murder,[71] and plots against monarchs.[72] In each case, the conclusion reached was that the benefits of upholding the existing system of diplomatic immunities outweighed the disadvantages.[73]

Judicial decisions have confirmed that there is no exception to personal immunity. In 1946, a Canadian case held that a foreign diplomat could not be arrested or detained even after threatening the security of the state, because, '[i]f the diplomat violates the law of nations, it does not follow that the other state has the right to do likewise'.[74]

This view has been upheld in cases concerning serious international crimes. In March 2001, the French Cour de Cassation held in the *Qaddafi* case that a serving head of state is immune from prosecution in national courts in relation to serious acts of terrorism.[75] The Spanish Audiencia Nacional reached a similar conclusion with respect

---

[68] ILC Report (n. 62) 177. [69] *Pinochet (No. 3)* (n. 44) 179 (Millett). [70] *Ibid.* 171 (Millett).

[71] The 1984 murder of British police officer Yvonne Fletcher by a shot fired from the Libyan embassy in London, United Kingdom provoked a massive outcry and a parliamentary review of diplomatic immunities. The review concluded, however, that attempts to renegotiate the Vienna Convention would create more problems than they would solve. See Barker, *The Abuse of Diplomatic Privileges* (n. 1) 135–52.

[72] In 1571 and in 1584, when ambassadors in England were detected in plots against the Crown, some urged that foreign ambassadors should lose their immunity for treason and high crimes. In the end, these arguments did not prevail and the diplomats were expelled. Other countries followed similar practices. See Ogdon, *Juridical Bases* (n. 1) 56–9.

[73] In the United States, proposals for legislation to remove diplomatic immunity for drunk driving and violent crimes have been rejected, on the grounds that complete immunity is essential for diplomatic relations, as otherwise other states could bring false charges and detain diplomats. See Barker, *The Abuse of Diplomatic Privileges* (n. 1) 232.

[74] *Rose* v. *R* (1947) 3 DLR 618, 645. [75] *Qadaffi* (2001) 125 ILR 456.

to allegations of international crimes by Fidel Castro,[76] and the same result was reached in a UK court in a case against President Mugabe.[77] State practice has adhered to the same line. For example, when lobbied by non-governmental organizations (NGOs) to arrest the serving Israeli ambassador, Carmi Gillon, on allegations that he was previously responsible for torture, Denmark refused on the basis of its obligation to respect diplomatic immunity.[78]

21.3.2 The *Arrest Warrant* decision

In April 2000, a Belgian judge issued an international arrest warrant against Abdulaye Yerodia Ndombasi, who was at the time serving as the Minister for Foreign Affairs for the DRC. The DRC brought a suit before the ICJ, arguing that Belgium had failed to recognize the immunity of a serving minister of foreign affairs. The ICJ held, by thirteen votes to three, that Belgium had breached its international legal duties to the DRC 'in that they failed to respect the immunity from criminal jurisdiction and the inviolability which the incumbent Minister for Foreign Affairs of the Democratic Republic of the Congo enjoyed under international law'.[79] The personal immunity enjoyed by a foreign minister cannot be set aside by a national court by charging him or her with war crimes or crimes against humanity.[80] The ICJ examined the non-immunity provisions of the Nuremberg Charter, and the Statutes of the ICTY, International Criminal Tribunal for Rwanda (ICTR), and International Criminal Court (ICC), and found that these did not suggest any exception in customary international law in regard to national courts.[81]

The judgment emphasized that personal immunity does not mean permanent *impunity* for serious crimes. For example, persons may be tried in their home courts; they may be prosecuted if the state waives the immunity; they may be prosecuted once they cease to hold office; and they may be prosecuted before international criminal courts where such courts have jurisdiction.[82]

Which Ministers Enjoy Personal Immunity?

The ICJ recognized immunity for heads of state, heads of government, and ministers of foreign affairs, and left a door open for other ministers.[83] To date, jurisprudence has been cautious in extending personal immunity to other ministers. In the *Mofaz* case, a UK court held that ministers of defence also receive personal immunity, but expressed doubt that ministers of culture, sport, or education would qualify.[84] Other cases indicate that neither Solicitors-General nor ministers of state qualify, nor do leaders of provinces and sub-states.[85] The ILC in its Draft Articles on immunity has suggested that personal immunity

---

[76] *Castro* (1999) 32 ILM 596.
[77] Reproduced in Colin Warbrick, 'Immunity and International Crimes in English Law' (2004) 53 *ICLQ* 769.
[78] Jacques Hartmann, 'The Gillon Affair' (2005) 45 *ICLQ* 745.
[79] *Case concerning the Arrest Warrant of 11 April 2000 (Democratic Republic of the Congo v. Belgium)*, Judgment, 14 February 2002 [2002] ICJ Reports 32, para. 75.
[80] *Ibid.* paras. 56–8. [81] *Ibid.* para. 58. [82] *Ibid.* para. 61.
[83] Dapo Akande, 'International Law Immunities and the International Criminal Court' (2003) 98 *AJIL* 407, 412.
[84] *Application for Arrest Warrant Against General Shaul Mofaz*, reproduced (2004) 53 *ICLQ* 769.
[85] *Immunity of State Officials* (n. 58) paras. 132–6.

is indeed restricted to the 'troika' of heads of state, heads of government, and foreign ministers.[86]

Are Personal Immunities Established for Private Visits?

The *Arrest Warrant* judgment indicated that personal immunity must be recognized even on private visits.[87] There are reasons to doubt this. The comments were *obiter dicta* and a majority of judges dissented from or distanced themselves from this particular finding.[88] The sparse previous authorities refer to such immunities on an *official* visit.[89] Where the host state has not invited the official or consented to the visit, the rationale of an 'implied undertaking' to bestow full immunity does not exist.[90] Moreover, the rationale given by the ICJ, that exposure to proceedings 'could deter the Minister from travelling internationally *when required to do so for the purposes of the performance of his or her official functions*',[91] is manifestly inapplicable to holiday travel. On the other hand, at least some states have suggested that personal immunity should persist during private travel.[92]

21.4 PERSONAL IMMUNITY: INROADS IN INTERNATIONAL COURTS

As the foregoing section showed, authorities have consistently rejected any exception to personal immunity in domestic courts based on the nature of the charges. This raises the unsettling prospect of an accountability gap with respect to such persons while they are in office.

Fortunately, states have devised a way to reduce this accountability gap: to create international tribunals and to empower them to supersede even their personal immunities. In the case of the Nuremberg and Tokyo Tribunals, both Japan and Germany had surrendered. Hence, the Allies could legislate away immunity. In the case of the ad hoc Tribunals, immunities are overridden by virtue of the paramount UN Charter obligation to comply with Chapter VII decisions of the Security Council. In the case of the ICC, states parties relinquish their immunities by treaty. These avenues for relinquishing immunity will be discussed in this section. Particular attention will be given to complexities that arise in Security Council referrals to the ICC, including the controversies around the ICC's arrest warrant against Omar Al Bashir, while he was President of Sudan.

---

[86] ILC Report (n. 62) 175. [87] *Arrest Warrant* (n. 84) para. 55.

[88] Seven out of thirteen judges dissented from or expressed doubts about this finding. See Darryl Robinson, 'The Impact of the Human Rights Accountability Movement on the International Law of Immunities' (2002) 40 *Canadian Yearbook of International Law* 151, 188–9. See also Watts, 'The Legal Position' (n. 24) 72–4; Salvatore Zappalà, 'Do Heads of State in Office Enjoy Immunity from Jurisdiction for International Crimes? The Ghaddafi Case before the French Cour de Cassation' (2001) 12 *EJIL* 595, 606; David Koller, 'Immunities of Foreign Ministers: Paragraph 61 of the Yerodia Judgment as It Pertains to the Security Council and the International Criminal Court' (2004) 20 *American University International Law Review* 15–16; *Immunity of State Officials* (n. 58) para. 128.

[89] Convention on Special Missions 1969, Art. 21; *US Restatement (Third) of Foreign Relations Law*, s. 464, note 14.

[90] On the idea of implied undertaking, see Robert Y. Jennings and Arthur Watts (eds.), *Oppenheim's International Law*, 9th ed. (London, 1992) 1034. In the *Arrest Warrant* case (n. 84) para. 68, even Belgium recognized that 'immunity from enforcement must, in our view, be accorded to all State representatives welcomed as such onto the territory of Belgium (on "official visits") . . . such welcome includes an undertaking by the host State and its various components to refrain from taking any coercive measures against its guest and the invitation cannot become a pretext for ensnaring the individual concerned in what would then have to be labelled a trap'.

[91] *Arrest Warrant* (n. 84) para. 55 (emphasis added). [92] UN Doc. A/CN.4/661 (4 April 2013).

The prosecution of heads of state before international courts is a relatively new frontier in practice. Given the novelty of this development, it is not surprising that numerous controversies have arisen. Indeed, the African Union (AU) has suggested that serving heads of state should be exempt from prosecution,[93] and an AU protocol for an African regional criminal court specifically exempts serving heads of state.[94] Kenya has suggested an amendment to the Rome Statute to this effect;[95] the proposal has not received significant support.

On the one hand, there are strong reasons not to go so far as exempting heads of state. International criminal law aims to hold accountable the persons most responsible for the most serious crimes, and particularly to be sure that those at the highest level do not escape justice. Creating an exemption would create a further incentive for persons abusing their power to cling to that power. On the other hand, there are legitimate concerns and questions about timing of interventions and their impact on governance and stability.[96]

The following sections will focus on *legal* issues in securing relinquishment by states of personal immunities. The two main routes are through Security Council decisions under its paramount power under the UN Charter, or through ratification of the ICC Statute. The most complex and controversial issues arise where there is a Security Council referral to the ICC; it is disputed whether this removes immunities of those states ordered to cooperate. This issue has been hotly contested since the ICC's arrest warrant against Omar Al Bashir, President of Sudan. Section 21.4.4 will examine an alternative theory, raised in the *Taylor* case and adopted in the *Al Bashir* case, that all immunities are simply inapplicable before international courts.

21.4.1 Security Council Decisions and the International Tribunals

One way to remove personal immunity is through a Chapter VII Security Council decision, because all states have consented, under the UN Charter, to comply with Chapter VII decisions. The UN Charter grants the Security Council a broad discretion to determine what measures are appropriate to maintain or restore international peace and security (Articles 41 and 42). All UN member states are obliged to carry out such measures (Articles 25 and 48),[97] and the obligation is paramount even over other treaty commitments.[98]

When creating the ad hoc Tribunals, the Security Council incorporated the principle that the official position of a defendant is no bar before the tribunals,[99] and ordered all states to

---

[93] African Union, Ext/Assembly/AU/Decision 1 (October 2013) para. 10.
[94] Malabo Protocol on Amendments to the Protocol on the Statute of the African Court of Justice and Human Rights, 27 June 2014, article 46A *bis*. See Charles C. Jalloh, Kamari M. Clarke, and Vincent O. Nmehielle (eds.), *The African Court of Justice and Human and Peoples' Rights in Context: Development and Challenges* (Cambridge, 2019); see also Chapter 9.
[95] Kenya Proposal of Amendments, UN Doc. C.N.1026.2013.TREATIES-XVIII.10 (14 March 2014).
[96] Charles Chernor Jalloh, 'Reflections on the Indictment of Sitting Heads of State and Government and Its Consequences for Peace and Stability and Reconciliation in Africa' (2014) 7 *African Journal of Legal Studies* 43.
[97] For further discussion on the power of the Security Council to create Tribunals, see Chapter 7.
[98] See UN Charter, Arts. 25, 41, 49 and especially Art. 103: 'In the event of a conflict between the obligations of the Members of the United Nations under the present Charter and their obligations under any other international agreement, their obligations under the present Charter shall prevail'.
[99] ICTY Statute, Art. 7(2); ICTR Statute, Art. 6(2).

cooperate fully with requests from the Tribunals, including requests for surrender. No exception was created for surrender requests relating to persons otherwise enjoying immunities. Thus, a UN member state receiving a request for surrender is obliged to comply with that request, even if the request conflicts with a duty to respect immunities. By the same token, the state otherwise enjoying the immunities is estopped from raising those immunities as a shield, by virtue of its obligations under the UN Charter.[100] This technique, of ordering cooperation with an instrument that removes immunities, is generally accepted as having removed personal immunities.[101]

Both ad hoc Tribunals carried out proceedings with respect to high governmental officials. In 1998, the ICTR convicted former Prime Minister Jean Kambanda, sentencing him to life imprisonment for genocide and crimes against humanity.[102] In 1999, the ICTY issued the first indictment against a serving head of state, Slobodan Milošević.[103] Although Milošević died of a heart attack before the completion of his trial,[104] his indictment, arrest, and trial remain a valuable precedent on the authority of a Security Council tribunal over heads of state.

21.4.2 Relinquishment Directly to the ICC

The ICC Statute offers another solution to the problem of personal immunity. In the present stage of development of international relations, states are apparently unwilling to allow all other states to set aside their personal immunities; however, a great many states have been willing to create an impartial international court with jurisdiction over serious international crimes, to invest it with safeguards against abuse, and to relinquish even their personal immunities to that court.

States can relinquish their immunities vis-à-vis the ICC by ratifying the ICC Statute. States parties to the ICC Statute are obliged to cooperate with the ICC in accordance with the terms of the Statute, without reservation.[105] Article 27(2) specifies that '[i]mmunities or special personal rules which may attach to the official capacity of a person . . . shall not bar the Court from exercising its jurisdiction'.[106] Thus, states parties accept that any immunities their officials may enjoy under international law will not bar prosecution before the ICC. This provision has required many states to amend domestic legislation and even their constitutions in order to ratify the ICC Statute.[107]

[100] Koller, 'Immunities of Foreign Ministers' (n. 88) 35–6; Gaeta, 'Official Capacity' (n. 60) 989.
[101] See e.g. Rosanne van Alebeek, *The Immunities of States and their Officials in International Criminal Law and International Human Rights Law* (Oxford, 2008) 221; Joanne Foakes, *The Position of Heads of State and Senior Officials in International Law* (Oxford, 2013) 198–9.
[102] *Kambanda*, ICTR TC I, 4 September 1998.
[103] *Milošević*, ICTY Indictment (Judge Hunt), 24 May 1999; *Milošević*, ICTY TC III, 8 November 2001, paras. 26–53.
[104] See Chapter 7.
[105] ICC Statute, Art. 86 (obligation to cooperate), Art. 89 (surrender of persons to the court), and Art. 120 (no reservations). See Chapter 20.
[106] *Ibid.* Art. 27(1): 'official capacity as a Head of State or Government, a member of a Government or parliament, an elected representative or a government official shall in no case exempt a person from criminal responsibility under this Statute'.
[107] See e.g. Claus Kreß and Flavia Lattanzi (eds.), *The Rome Statute and Domestic Legal Orders* (Rome, 2000) vol. I; Darryl Robinson, 'The Rome Statute and its Impact on National Laws' in Cassese et al., *Commentary*, 1849.

In addition, states may also undertake the obligation to cooperate fully by making a unilateral declaration (see, for example, ICC Statute, Articles 12(3) and 87(5)). This obligation entails the same set of cooperation obligations undertaken by states parties.[108] Furthermore, as will be explored in Section 21.4.3, an order of the Security Council can have the same effect.

The ICC Statute contains two provisions that seem to be in tension: Article 27 (removing immunity) and Article 98(1) of the Statute (respecting immunity of 'third states'). Article 98(1) provides that the ICC will not proceed with requests for surrender:

> which would require the requested State to act inconsistently with its obligations under international law with respect to the State or diplomatic immunity of a person or property of a third State, unless the Court can first obtain the cooperation of that third State for the waiver of the immunity.[109]

At first glance, these articles appear contradictory; one seems to reject immunities and the other seems to uphold immunities.[110] However, the provisions apply at different stages. Article 98(1) deals with a specific situation where a state party (or other state obliged to cooperate) is requested to surrender a person, but that person is protected by immunities bestowed by a third state (i.e. a state other than the recipient of the request). In such a case, the requested state would be placed in a position of conflicting obligations: either to breach a duty to carry out an ICC request or to breach a duty to respect immunities of a state not bound to cooperate with the ICC.

The combination of Articles 27 and 98(1) therefore appears to create a regime wherein states parties agree to relinquish all immunities in relation to ICC requests concerning their own officials, while still respecting the existing immunities of states that are not bound to cooperate with the ICC. It is worth recalling that only personal immunities are pertinent here, because functional immunity does not protect conduct which amounts to a core crime.[111]

We can consider three scenarios, in which a state obliged to cooperate with the ICC might be asked to surrender: (1) its own official; (2) an official of another state party; or (3) an official of a non-party state. In the first scenario, concerning the state's own official, Article 98(1) does not apply, since it refers to obligations to a 'third State'. The state is obliged to cooperate without reservation (Article 86).

The second scenario is where the official has personal immunity bestowed by *another* state party. The dominant view is that it would not be necessary for the requested state first to obtain the waiver of the other state party.[112] This is the 'horizontal effect' of Article

---

[108] The obligation undertaken by states parties is also 'to cooperate fully' (Art. 86). Numerous provisions of the Statute articulate the extent of that obligation.

[109] Similarly, Art. 98(2) of the ICC Statute respects obligations under international agreements pursuant to which the consent of a sending state is required to surrender a person of that state to the court. The controversy over the interpretation of Art. 98(2) is discussed in Chapter 8. See generally Claus Kress and Kimberly Prost, 'Article 98' in Triffterer and Ambos, *Commentary*, 2585, 2665–71.

[110] Gaeta, 'Official Capacity' (n. 60) 992–6. [111] See Sections 21.2 and 21.3.

[112] The relationship between Arts. 27 and 98 was discussed in informal meetings at the ICC Preparatory Commission, on the basis of an informal paper by Canada and the United Kingdom, with the conclusion being reached that, '[h]aving regard to the terms of the Statute, the Court shall not be required to obtain a waiver of immunity with respect to the surrender by one State Party of a head of State or government, or diplomat, of another State Party'. See Bruce Broomhall, *International Justice and the*

27(2): indeed, the purpose of Article 27(2) is to remove barriers of immunities to the exercise of jurisdiction by the ICC.[113] There are different interpretive routes by which this conclusion is reached.[114] The most convincing view is that there are no conflicting 'obligations under international law' owed to states parties, because they have relinquished immunities when they accepted the cooperation obligations to the ICC (including Articles 88 and 27).[115] This same analysis applies where the third state has voluntarily taken on those obligations through a unilateral declaration (Articles 12(3) and 87(5)).

The third scenario concerns an official enjoying personal immunity bestowed by a state not bound to cooperate with the ICC. Under the traditional approach, such a state has not relinquished its immunities in favour of the ICC regime, so personal immunity persists. Article 98(1) requires respect for any immunities existing under international law. That respect is appropriate, because the ICC is a treaty creation; it cannot unilaterally strip the rights of states that have not accepted it. (However, see Section 21.5 for the idea of an 'international courts' exception.)

If Article 98(1) is read at face value, as respecting those immunities that still legally apply, this does not mean permanent impunity. First, prosecution is possible if the non-party state agrees to waive the immunity. Second, once the official is no longer serving in a capacity that entails personal immunity, he or she will only have functional immunity, and hence be liable to prosecution for core crimes (Section 21.2). Third, even officials of non-party states would lose their immunities if the Security Council under Chapter VII removes them, as will be discussed in Section 21.4.3.

21.4.3 Security Council Referrals and the ICC

The most intense controversies concern the interplay of Security Council decisions and the ICC Statute. Namely, when the Security Council refers a situation and orders the relevant state to 'cooperate fully', does that produce the same immunity-stripping effect as it did in all previous examples (e.g. where a state ratifies the ICC Statute or where the Security Council orders states to cooperate fully with a tribunal)? This question provoked controversy in the Darfur, Sudan situation. The Security Council referred the situation to the Court under Chapter VII, and ordered Sudan to 'cooperate fully'. In March 2009, a Pre-Trial Chamber of the ICC issued an arrest warrant against Omar Al Bashir, who was then President of Sudan.[116] President Al Bashir then travelled to various countries, which declined to arrest him, leading to proceedings at the ICC examining whether those states had breached their obligations under the Rome Statute.

International Criminal Court: Between Sovereignty and the Rule of Law (Oxford, 2003) 144. ICC jurisprudence also confirms this approach: see e.g. *Al Bashir*, ICC PTC I, 13 December 2011 (ICC-02/05–01/09–140) para. 18.

[113] *Al Bashir*, ICC PTC II, 6 July 2017 (ICC-02/05–01/09–302) paras. 76–83.

[114] Some interpret 'third State' in Art. 98(1) as referring only to non-states parties. However, this view overlooks that the Statute consistently uses the term 'State not party to this Statute' to describe non-states parties, and that 'third State' is routinely used in cooperation treaties to refer to a state other than the requesting and requested states.

[115] See Broomhall, *International Justice* (n.112) 144–5; Wirth, 'Immunities, Related Problems' (n. 46) 456–7; Gaeta, 'Official Capacity' (n. 60) 993–5.

[116] *Al Bashir Arrest Warrant*, ICC PTC I, 4 March 2009 (ICC-02/05–01/09–03).

There are many points of disagreement on the correct legal approach, with different views on the law of personal immunities, the powers of the Security Council, and the interpretation of the Rome Statute. There are plausible arguments and legitimate concerns on all sides. This chapter will attempt only a general introduction to this unfolding debate.

Pre-Trial Chambers have examined these questions when they issued findings of non-compliance against states that have hosted President Al-Bashir without arresting him. The Chambers of the ICC have all reached the same conclusion – that President Al-Bashir was not immune from arrest and surrender to the ICC – but they have given slightly different analyses, adding to the confusion.[117] First, in decisions concerning failures to arrest by Malawi and Chad, a Pre-Trial Chamber adopted the '*Taylor* theory', discussed in Section 21.4.4: that personal immunity does not apply at all before 'international' courts.[118]

Other Pre-Trial Chambers, adjudicating on failures to arrest Al-Bashir by the DRC, South Africa, and Jordan, held that the Security Council order to 'cooperate fully' imposed the general cooperation obligation on Sudan, which includes the immunity-stripping effect of Article 27(2).[119] Accordingly, by virtue of the obligation imposed by the Security Council, Sudan no longer has immunities opposable to arrest and surrender proceedings carried out on behalf of the ICC.

There is an incredible variety of possible legal views on Security Council referrals and immunity. We suggest that the 'relinquishment' theory – including that the obligation to 'cooperate fully' includes a loss of immunity – does the best job of reconciling the law of immunities, the powers of the Security Council, and the provisions of the Rome Statute.[120] As will be explained below, the ICC Appeals Chamber eventually adopted both this theory and a more controversial theory that there are no immunities before an 'international court' (Section 21.4.4). Some jurists find both theories unconvincing, and thus opine that heads of state of non-party states retain their immunity. Thus, there are many disputes about the correct analysis; this chapter will introduce some of the main controversies.[121]

As explained above in relation to Security Council tribunals, a Chapter VII resolution provides the necessary legal authority to remove immunity, since states have already accepted a paramount obligation to comply with such decisions. It is suggested here that

---

[117] Manuel Ventura, 'Prosecutor v Al-Bashir' (2017) 111 *AJIL* 1007.

[118] *Al Bashir Arrest Warrant*, ICC PTC I, 12 December 2011 (ICC-02/05–01/09–139) (the 'Malawi Decision'); *Al Bashir Arrest Warrant*, ICC PTC I, 13 December 2011 (ICC-02/05–01/09–140) (the 'Chad Decision').

[119] *Al Bashir*, ICC PTC II, 6 July 2017 (ICC-02/05–01/09–302) ('the South Africa decision'); *Al Bashir*, ICC PTC II, 11 December 2017 (ICC-02/05–01/09–309) ('the Jordan decision'). In *Al Bashir*, ICC PTC II, 9 April 2014 (ICC-02/05–01/09–195) ('the DRC decision'), the PTC expressed the argument rather more laconically, stating that the Security Council had 'implicitly waived' immunities. This is probably best understood as an under-explained version of the same argument (that the obligation to cooperate fully includes loss of immunity) rather than as an additional legal theory.

[120] Manuel Ventura, 'Prosecutor v Al-Bashir' (2017) 111(4) *AJIL* 1007, 1011. See also 'Amicus Curiae Observations of Professors Robinson, Cryer, deGuzman, Lafontaine, Oosterveld, and Stahn', ICC Amicus Curiae, 17 June 2018 (ICC-02/05–01/09–362).

[121] For literature on the early ICC PTC decisions on immunity, see e.g. Dapo Akande, 'The Legal Nature of Security Council Referrals to the ICC and its Impact on Al Bashir's Immunities' (2009) 7 *JICJ* 333; Erika de Wet, 'Referrals to the International Criminal Court Under Chapter VII of the United Nations Charter and the Immunity of Foreign State Officials' (2018) 112 *AJIL Unbound* 33; Paola Gaeta, 'Does President Al Bashir Enjoy Immunity from Arrest?' (2009) 7 *JICJ* 315; Claus Kreß, 'The International Criminal Court and Immunities under International Law for States Not Party to the Court's Statute' in Morten Bergsmo and Ling Yan (eds.), *State Sovereignty and International Criminal Law*, FICHL Publication Series No. 15 (Beijing, 2012); Dire Tladi, 'The ICC Decisions on Chad and Malawi: On Cooperation, Immunities, and Article 98' (2013) 11 *JICJ* 199.

(1) where the Security Council orders a state to 'cooperate fully' with a court, and (2) the court's statute provides that it does not defer to the immunities of states that are obliged to cooperate, this has been sufficient to override immunities. By requiring a state to cooperate fully, the Security Council creates the same situation as was described in Section 21.4.1: the Security Council has subjected the state to a regime which overrides its immunities.[122]

One common objection is that the mere fact that a situation was triggered by a Security Council referral does not alter the legal positions of states.[123] The assertion is correct, but it misunderstands the basis for the obligation. The obligation does not arise from the mere fact of the referral; it arises rises from the decision of the Security Council, acting under Chapter VII, to oblige the state to 'cooperate fully'.[124] Under the UN Charter, UN member states are obliged to comply with Chapter VII decisions.

Another objection is that the ICC Statute cannot create obligations for non-parties, because it is only a treaty. However, the ICC Statute is not being applied *qua* treaty to a non-party. The *source* of the obligation is the UN Charter and the Chapter VII resolution ordering full cooperation. The Security Council frequently orders states to cooperate with various institutions as a measure to restore peace and security. The *content* of the obligation is delineated by the ICC Statute, because the Security Council has incorporated it by reference.

A related objection is that the Security Council cannot 'transform' a state into a party to a treaty. Again, the objection is correct, but it misperceives the situation. A state ordered to cooperate fully is not transformed into a party, but it does have a set of obligations imposed on it, under Chapter VII of the UN Charter, that are analogous to those of ICC states parties. The Security Council can impose obligations on member states which may be parallel to those found in a treaty.[125] Moreover, a state ordered to cooperate fully takes on only the cooperation-related obligations and only in relation to the specified situation; it does not take on other obligations such as payment of assessed contributions to the Court's budget.

The most plausible objection is that the obligation to 'cooperate fully' is not sufficiently explicit to entail a loss of personal immunity.[126] A few counter-arguments can be made here. First, the obligation to cooperate must include not only Part 9 of the ICC Statute, but also many other important articles throughout the Statute.[127] Second, 'cooperate fully' was the exact term used in the resolutions creating the ICTY and ICTR, and the formula has hitherto been considered perfectly sufficient to remove immunities.[128] In the context of the ICC, the most obvious interpretation of 'cooperate fully' is that a state must cooperate, in

---

[122] Marko Milanovic, 'ICC Prosecutor Charges the President of Sudan with Genocide, Crimes Against Humanity and War Crimes in Darfur', 12 *ASIL Insights*, 28 July 2008, www.asil.org/insights.cfm.

[123] Gaeta, 'Does President Al Bashir' (n. 121) 322–5; Tladi, 'The ICC Decisions on Chad and Malawi' (n. 121) 211.

[124] Akande, 'The Legal Nature of Security Council Referrals' (n. 121) 341–2.

[125] See e.g. SC Res. 1373(2001). The Council can also impose obligations on member states overriding any that arise from a treaty; see e.g. *Case concerning Questions of Interpretation and Application of the 1971 Montreal Convention Arising from the Aerial Incident at Lockerbie (Libya v. United States)*, Provisional Measures, ICJ, 14 April 1992, para. 42.

[126] In this vein, it could be argued the Council decision imposes only Part 9 of the ICC Statute on a state, but not Art. 27, and hence immunities are not relinquished.

[127] As an incomplete list, see ICC Statute, Arts. 3(3), 4(3), 4(4), 18(5), 19(8), 19(11), 27(2), 48, 54(2), 56, 57(3), 59, 64(6), 75(5), and 109.

[128] SC Res. 827 (1993), para. 4, and SC Res. 935(1994), para. 2, both of which have been read in conjunction with the relevant Statute provisions denying immunities.

accordance with the terms of the Statute, to the same extent as a state party.[129] If 'cooperate fully' means cooperation *less* than that required of a state party, then the obligation would be 'cooperate less than fully'.[130]

In 2018, Jordan appealed the question to the ICC Appeals Chamber. The Appeals Chamber decision conforms with the foregoing arguments that the general cooperation obligation, imposed by the Security Council, includes the immunity-stripping effect of Article 27.[131] The Appeals Chamber also embraced the theory that immunities simply do not apply before international courts (Section 21.4.4).

21.4.4 The *Taylor* Theory: Is Personal Immunity Irrelevant Before International Courts?

The foregoing sections proceeded on the basis that personal immunity can only be set aside with the consent of the affected state: either through waiver, through ratification of the ICC Statute, or through ratification of the UN Charter and the paramount obligation to comply with Chapter VII resolutions. An alternative theory is that personal immunities are simply not opposable at all to international courts. This latter theory has the advantage of simplicity: it facilitates international prosecution, it avoids the need to find any form of consent, and it vastly simplifies the Article 98 analysis, because it recognizes immunity for no one. However, the theory also has difficulties, as will be discussed here.

'International Courts' Theory

In June 2003, the Special Court for Sierra Leone (SCSL) issued a warrant for the arrest of Charles Taylor, who at the time was the President of Liberia. Lawyers for Charles Taylor made an application to declare the warrant null and void, on the grounds that he was a serving head of state, enjoying absolute immunity. They conceded that personal immunity could be set aside by the Security Council under Chapter VII, but the SCSL was not supported by any Chapter VII resolutions.

In May 2004, the SCSL held that the SCSL was an 'international court' and as such not barred from prosecuting serving heads of state.[132] The SCSL relied on a passage in the ICJ *Arrest Warrant* decision which made reference to the possibility of prosecution before international courts. The SCSL interpreted that passage as meaning that personal immunities are simply inapplicable before any tribunal that can be characterized as 'international'. Even though the Security Council imposed no Chapter VII obligations upon states to cooperate with the SCSL, the SCSL held that it was created by an agreement between the United Nations and Sierra Leone, and therefore it was an 'international' court.[133]

---

[129] Akande, 'The Legal Nature of Security Council Referrals' (n. 121) 342.
[130] On the potential vagaries of 'cooperate fully', see Göran Sluiter, 'Obtaining Cooperation from Sudan: Where Is the Law?' (2008) 6 *JICJ* 871.
[131] *Al Bashir*, ICC AC, 6 May 2019 (ICC-02/05–01/09–397). [132] *Taylor*, SCSL AC, 31 May 2004, paras. 51–3.
[133] *Ibid.* paras. 34–42.

The same approach was adopted in 2011 by an ICC Pre-Trial Chamber (the 'Malawi decision'). That decision concerned the failure of Malawi, an ICC state party, to execute the arrest warrant against President Al Bashir while he was visiting Malawi.[134] A similar decision was issued against Chad.[135] The Pre-Trial Chamber noted the many cases in which international courts had prosecuted heads of state, and held that a 'critical mass' of states parties to the ICC had been reached, so that customary international law immunities no longer apply before it.[136] The Chamber held that 'when cooperating with this Court and therefore acting on its behalf, states parties are instruments for the enforcement of the *jus puniendi* of the international community'.[137]

The *outcome* of each of these decisions – that is, that immunities were not an obstacle in those cases – can be defended on the more traditional legal grounds discussed in Sections 21.2 and 21.4.3. For the SCSL, Taylor was no longer a head of state at the time of the decision, having stepped down in August 2003, and hence no longer enjoyed personal immunity (Section 21.2). For the Malawi decision, the Chapter VII resolution by the Security Council imposed on Sudan the general cooperation obligation, including loss of immunity (Section 21.4.3).

The most important recent development – the endorsement of the *Taylor* theory by the ICC Appeals Chamber in 2019 – will be discussed later in this section, after first outlining the main reactions to the reasoning in *Taylor*.

Grounds for Scepticism about the 'International Court' Theory

The legal theory advanced in *Taylor* was accepted by some[138] and doubted by many.[139] The reasoning in the Malawi decision was also met with significant scepticism from legal experts.[140] The African Union criticized the decision for changing customary international law, rendering Article 98 redundant, and failing to engage with the effect of a Security Council Resolution on immunities.[141] The following are some of the main reasons that have been advanced for doubting the 'international courts' theory.

First, the *Taylor* decision places inordinate weight on one *obiter dictum* passage in the ICJ's *Arrest Warrant* decision. The ICJ, in explaining that immunity did not necessarily lead to impunity, noted that 'an incumbent . . . Minister for Foreign Affairs may be subject to criminal proceedings before certain international courts, where they have jurisdiction'.[142] The *Taylor* decision interprets this passage as announcing a rule that, as long as a court is 'international', it can disregard personal immunity. A perhaps more

---

[134] Malawi Decision (n. 118). [135] Chad Decision (n. 118). [136] *Ibid.* para. 42. [137] *Ibid.* para. 46.
[138] Gaeta, 'Does President Al Bashir' (n. 121); *Immunity of State Officials* (n. 62) para. 87.
[139] Zsuzsanna Deen-Racsmány, '*Prosecutor v. Taylor*: The Status of the Special Court for Sierra Leone and its Implications for Immunity' (2005) 18 *LJIL* 299; Micaela Frulli, 'The Question of Charles Taylor's Immunity' (2004) 2 *JICJ* 1118; Koller, 'Immunities of Foreign Ministers' (n. 88) 30–41; King, 'Immunities and Bilateral Agreements' (n. 60); van Alebeek, *The Immunities of States* (n. 101) 242 and 275–80; Erika de Wet, 'The Implications of President Al-Bashir's Visit to South Africa for International and Domestic Law' (2015) 13 *JICJ* 1049, 1056–7; Akande, 'The Legal Nature of Security Council Referrals' (n. 121) 339.
[140] However, see the thoughtful defence by Claus Kreß, 'The International Criminal Court and Immunities under International Law for States Not Party to the Court's Statute' in Morten Bergsmo and Ling Yan (eds.), *State Sovereignty and International Criminal Law*, FICHL Publication Series No. 15 (Beijing, 2012) 223–65.
[141] AU Press Release of 9 January 2012, quoted in Kreß, *ibid.* [142] *Arrest Warrant* (n. 84) para. 61.

plausible reading is that the ICJ was simply addressing concerns that its ruling would allow impunity for leaders, and thus was listing possible avenues of recourse. In other words, the ICJ was simply observing that there are international courts with the power to supersede personal immunities in accordance with known principles of law (for example, relinquishment through treaty or Chapter VII powers).

Second, the SCSL argued that personal immunity is rooted in the 'principle that one sovereign state does not adjudicate on the conduct of another state', which 'has no relevance to international criminal tribunals which are not organs of a State but derive their mandate from the international community'.[143] However, that is not the rationale for personal immunity. The principle *par in parem non habet iudicium* is the basis for functional immunity, not personal immunity. Personal immunity exists to protect international relations by precluding any basis to interfere with high representatives without the consent of their sending state.

Third, it is too simplistic to sidestep immunity by asserting that a tribunal is not a state. An international tribunal is a creation of states. If neither the United Kingdom nor Canada has the power to ignore the personal immunity of a third state without consent, then the two together cannot create an international court and bestow upon it a power that they do not possess. The problem remains whether it is two states, or twenty, or sixty: they cannot bestow a power that they do not possess.[144]

The *Taylor* theory emphasizes that international courts are in a 'vertical relationship' with states, ranking hierarchically *above* states and hence not subject to the same limitations.[145] However, international courts only acquire that vertical relationship (the ability to issue orders to states) insofar as states grant them that position, by treaty or other means such as Chapter VII.[146] In general, claiming that one is acting 'on behalf of the international community' does not expand one's powers.

The *Taylor* judgment also emphasized that international courts have limited jurisdiction and safeguards against abuse, and that their collective judgment reduces the potential destabilizing effects of unilateral action.[147] These may be good *policy* arguments for trusting international tribunals, but it does not explain the *legal* basis for setting aside a right of a non-party state. As one commentator has noted, not only does this purported exception 'violate the principle of *pacta tertiis*, but it also ignores the fact that fairness [of the tribunal] has nothing to do with the creation of immunities'.[148] The safeguards may help explain why states are willing to ratify the Statute and relinquish their immunities, but they do not in themselves directly override immunities.

Finally, in the ICC Malawi and Chad decisions, the Chamber pointed to a practice of international tribunals prosecuting heads of state; however, in each of those prior cases, the

---

[143] *Taylor* (n. 132) para. 51. [144] *Nemo dat quod non habet.* [145] Gaeta, 'Does President Al Bashir' (n. 121) 320–2.

[146] Note that this is a very different question from jurisdiction. To acquire jurisdiction over the nationals of a state does not require the consent of the state. See Chapter 8. There are many possible bases on which jurisdiction may be acquired; we deal here with the separate question of obtaining authority to set aside immunities.

[147] See e.g. *Taylor* (n. 132) para. 51; similar possibilities are suggested in Ryszard Piotrowicz, 'Immunities of Foreign Ministers and their Exposure to Universal Jurisdiction' (2002) 76 *Austin Law Journal* 290, 293.

[148] Koller, 'Immunities of Foreign Ministers' (n. 88) 32.

state concerned had directly or indirectly relinquished immunity (see Section 21.4.3). Accordingly, legal commentators have noted that under existing international law, 'it is not the international nature of the court as such but the waiver by the parties (and the Security Council's Chapter VII powers . . .) that accounts for the irrelevance of immunities before it'.[149] The Chamber argued that 120 states have ratified the Statute and thereby renounced their immunities, but that does not prove that all other states have therefore also lost their immunities. The Pre-Trial Chamber decisions were also criticized for essentially disregarding Article 98 of the Statute.[150]

The ICC Al Bashir Decision

In 2018, the issues of immunities before the ICC was brought to the ICC Appeals Chamber by Jordan. A Pre-Trial Chamber had declared that Jordan had breached its obligations by failing to arrest Omar Al-Bashir, while he was the President of Sudan.[151] The Appeals Chamber held that the Security Council resolution requiring Sudan to 'cooperate fully' did indeed impose the full package of cooperation obligations, including the relinquishment of all immunities under Article 27. The Appeals Chamber's analysis conforms to the analysis offered above (Section 21.4.3).[152]

To the surprise of almost all observers, the Appeals Chamber elected to advance an additional basis for its conclusion: it revived the theory in the *Malawi* decision and the *Taylor* decision that there are no immunities before 'international courts'.

The reaction of academics and jurists was largely sceptical and critical of the quality of the reasoning,[153] although some scholars were supportive.[154] The decision was criticized as 'eccentric' and 'convoluted' and for belabouring points of 'limited relevance' at great length, while failing to acknowledge or engage with the many prominent difficulties and concerns with the *Taylor* theory.[155] Many criticisms were, therefore, the same as had been

---

[149] Deen-Racsmány, 'Prosecutor v. Taylor' (n. 139) 318; see also King, 'Immunities and Bilateral Agreements' (n. 60).

[150] Tladi, 'The ICC Decisions on Chad and Malawi' (n. 121).   [151] *Al Bashir*, ICC AC, 6 May 2019 (ICC-02/05–01/09–397).

[152] See also 'Amicus Curiae Observations of Professors Robinson, Cryer, deGuzman, Lafontaine, Oosterveld, and Stahn', ICC *Amicus Curiae*, 17 June 2018 (ICC-02/05–01/09–362).

[153] Dapo Akande, 'ICC Appeals Chamber Holds that Heads of State Have No Immunity Under Customary International Law Before International Tribunals' (EJIL: Talk!, 6 May 2019), www.ejiltalk.org; Dov Jacobs, 'You Have Just Entered Narnia: ICC Appeals Chamber Adopts the Worst Possible Solution on Immunities in the Bashir Case' (Spreading the Jam, 6 May 2019), dovjacobs.com; Asad Kiyani, 'Elisions and Omissions: Questioning the ICC's Latest Bashir Immunity Ruling' (Just Security, 8 May 2019), www.justsecurity.org; Douglas Guilfoyle, 'Is the International Criminal Court Broken?' (2019) 20 *Melbourne Journal of International Law* 401; Sarah M. H. Nouwen, 'Return to Sender: Let the International Court of Justice Justify or Qualify International-Criminal-Court Exceptionalism Regarding Personal Immunities' (2019) 78 *Cambridge Law Journal* 596; Linda Mushoriwa, 'Immunity before the International Criminal Court: Has the Appeals Chamber Decision in the Jordan Appeal Brought Finality?' (2020) 33 *South African Journal of Criminal Justice* 402; Rita Guerreiro Teixeira and Hannes Verheyden, 'Immunities of State Officials and the "Fundamentally Different Nature" of International Courts: the Appeals Chamber Decision in the Jordan Referral re Al Bashir' (2021) 18 *Brazilian Journal of International Law* 98; Luisa Giannini and Roberto Vilchez Yamato, 'Contesting Immunities in the International Criminal Court: An Analysis of the Rulings of the Pre-Trial Chambers and the Appeals Chamber in Al Bashir Case and Its Outcomes' (2021) 18 *Brazilian Journal of International Law* 171; Kevin Jon Heller, 'Options for Prosecuting Russian Aggression Against Ukraine: A Critical Analysis' (2022) *Journal of Genocide Research* (2022); Rosanne van Alebeek, Larissa van den Herik, and Cedric Ryngaert, 'Prosecuting Russian Officials for the Crime of Aggression: What About Immunities?' (2023) 4 *European Convention on Human Rights Law Review* 115, at 121–8.

[154] Claus Kreß, 'Preliminary Observations on the ICC Appeals Chamber's Judgment of 6 May 2019 in the Jordan Referral re Al-Bashir Appeal' (2019) 8 *Torkal Opsahl Occasional Paper Series*; Leila Nadya Sadat, 'Why the ICC's Judgment in the al-Bashir Case Wasn't So Surprising' (Just Security, 12 July 2019), www.justsecurity.org.

[155] Jacobs, 'You Have Just Entered Narnia' (n. 153); Kiyani, 'Elisions and Omissions' (n. 153); Guilfoyle, 'Is the ICC Broken?' (n. 153); Giannini, 'Contesting' (n. 153)

advanced against the *Taylor* reasoning: that it builds a legal edifice on one *obiter* comment in the ICJ's *Arrest Warrant* decision that the comment cannot bear;[156] that it simply ignores contrary state practice;[157] that it misidentifies the rationale for personal immunity and thus fails to engage with the actual issues;[158] that states cannot delegate a power to disregard the rights of a third state when they do not themselves have such a power;[159] and that claiming that one is acting on behalf of the 'international community' does not expand one's powers.[160] Commentators also noted the irony of declaring that 'the law does not readily condone to be done through the back door something it forbids to be done through the front door',[161] and then allowing any two states to create an 'international tribunal' and thereby bypass immunities of non-consenting states.[162]

In a rather novel and controversial argument, the ICC Appeals Chamber proposed to flip the 'burden' of proving a rule: rather than showing that an 'international court' exception to immunity had emerged, the Chamber argued that the burden was on Jordan to provide state practice specifically affirming that international courts are bound by any such rule in the first place. This 'burden shift' argument was widely criticized as an unpersuasive technique to side-step basic rules.[163] By default, the basic constraints of customary law must be respected by all subjects of international law. Naturally, most pronouncements on immunity speak of 'states', since it is almost always states that carry out legal proceedings. Thus, the demand for state practice explicitly confirming that each general rule applies to *international courts specifically* is almost impossible to meet, and would let international courts (and other international organizations) evade almost all general rules. The more convincing and principled stance is that commendably taken by Claus Kreß, a leading proponent of the 'international courts exception': it is for those who argue for an exception to show the practice and *opinio juris* supporting it.[164]

Several observations can also be made *in favour* of the proposed rule. First, customary law is continuously evolving and new customary rules can emerge. Thus, regardless of concerns about whether the reasoning in *Taylor* and *Al Bashir* decisions provided accurate descriptions of how previously existing principles worked, nonetheless the decisions in themselves are still important pieces of state practice and *opinio juris* in their own right. For example, the *Tadić* decision may have been creative when it said war crimes law extends to non-international armed conflict, but it was embraced by states and *became true*, as subsequent practice aligned with it (see Section 12.1.7).

---

[156] Nouwen, 'Return to Sender' (n. 153); Heller, 'Options' (n. 153).
[157] Mushoriwa, 'Immunity' (n. 153); Heller, 'Options' (n. 153); Jacobs, 'You Have Just Entered Narnia' (n. 153); Alebeek et al., 'Prosecuting' (n. 153); Kiyani, 'Elisions and Omissions' (n. 153).
[158] Alebeek et al., 'Prosecuting' (n. 153).
[159] Nouwen, 'Return to Sender' (n. 153); Heller, 'Options' (n. 153); Alebeek et al., 'Prosecuting' (n. 153); Guilfoyle, 'Is the ICC Broken?' (n. 153).
[160] Jacobs, 'You Have Just Entered Narnia' (n. 153). [161] *Al Bashir*, ICC AC, 6 May 2019 (ICC-02/05–01/09–397) para. 127.
[162] Jacobs, 'You Have Just Entered Narnia' (n. 153).
[163] Nouwen, 'Return to Sender' (n. 153); Heller, 'Options' (n. 153); Mushoriwa, 'Immunity' (n. 153); Alebeek et al., 'Prosecuting' (n. 153).
[164] Kreß, 'Preliminary Observations' (n. 154).

Second, the main objections to the 'international courts' theory are all rooted in the agreed positivist logic of the 'Westphalian' model of international law: that states are the fundamental unit of international law, that international law is created by sovereign states, that they are bound by consent, and so on. On this model, states cannot delegate a power to disregard rights of a third state, if they do not have that power themselves. However, perhaps the international courts theory is best understood with a fundamentally different model – a 'cosmopolitan' model – which recognizes that law is created by human beings, and that states are merely one vehicle of governance.[165] On such a model, it is easier to conceive of certain international courts as reflections of the *jus puniendi* (the right to punish) of the international community as a whole, and thus vested with powers autonomous from those delegated by states.[166] The most compelling argument for an 'international court' exception has been advanced by Claus Kreß, who would limit the exception to courts created through negotiations open to all states, with membership open to all states, and a 'genuine universal orientation', as a safeguard against abuse.[167]

Third, the 'international courts' exception has some attractions in policy. It is a much simpler rule than the 'relinquishment' theory, which entails many labyrinthine steps in the case of Security Council referrals (as may be seen in Section 21.4.3). In contrast, the 'international courts' exception is simpler and easy to explain to the public. In addition, for those who prioritize eliminating impunity over other considerations, the rule certainly facilitates prosecutions, and does so without depending on Security Council authorization.[168] Furthermore, if the underlying aim of personal immunity is to prevent frivolous or vexatious interference with high representative officials, it may strike an attractive balance to create an exception for internationally representative courts with checks and balances against abuse and fulfilling all human rights standards, as this would at least help insulate decisions from particular national politics.[169]

Fourth, subsequent practice may arguably be aligning with an 'international court' exception. The 2022 ICC arrest warrant against Russian President Putin cannot be explained under the relinquishment theory (given that Russia is a non-party and there is no Security Council referral), and thus is a piece of practice supporting the 'international court' theory. Subsequent discussions about a possible tribunal to examine the crime of aggression have deliberated about the parameters of the 'international court' exception, thus potentially giving it additional currency.[170] Thus, a simpler customary rule may be emerging; time will tell.

[165] David Held, *Democracy and the Global Order: From the Modern State to Cosmopolitan Governance* (Stanford University Press, 1995); Jürgen Habermas, 'Kant's Idea of Perpetual Peace, with the Benefit of Two Hundred Years' Hindsight', in J. Bohman and M. Lutz-Bachmann (eds.), *Perpetual Peace: Essays on Kant's Cosmopolitan Ideal* (MIT Press, 1997).
[166] Kreß, 'Preliminary Observation' (n. 154). [167] Kreß, *ibid.*, and see Alebeek et al., 'Prosecuting' (n. 153).
[168] Sadat, 'ICC's Judgment' (n. 154). [169] Kreß, 'Preliminary Observation' (n. 154).
[170] Rebecca J. Hamilton, 'Ukraine's Push to Prosecute Aggression: Implications for Immunity Ratione Personae & the Crime of Aggression' (2022) 55 *Case Western Reserve Journal of International Law* 1; Astrid Reisinger Coracini and Jennifer Trahan 'Tribunal to Prosecute the Crime of Aggression Committed Against Ukraine (Part VI): On the Non-Applicability of Personal Immunities' (2022) *Just Security Series* 1.

21.5 CONCLUSION

As may be seen, the interplay of accountability and immunity is complex and controversial. However, as long as one recalls the purpose of functional and personal immunity, an underlying coherence in the law can be found. Functional immunity is more easily dealt with, because many authorities indicate that the immunity does not extend to serious international crimes. Personal immunity has proved more resilient, allowing no exception based on the nature of the crimes alleged. States have, however, relinquished personal immunity to some international jurisdictions; for example, by ratifying the ICC Statute or by virtue of their obligations to the Security Council under Chapter VII of the UN Charter. In addition, there is building support for the view is that personal immunity is never opposable to an international court; this view has been adopted by both the SCSL and the ICC.

Further Reading

Dapo Akande, 'International Law Immunities and the International Criminal Court' (2004) 98 *AJIL* 407

Dapo Akande, 'The Legal Nature of Security Council Referrals to the ICC and its Impact on Al Bashir's Immunities' (2009) 7 *JICJ* 332

Antonio Cassese, 'When May Senior State Officials be Tried for International Crimes? Some Comments on the *Congo v. Belgium* Case' (2002) 13 *EJIL* 853

Erika de Wet, 'The Implications of President Al-Bashir's Visit to South Africa for International and Domestic Law' (2015) 13 *JICJ* 1049

Erika de Wet, 'Referrals to the International Criminal Court Under Chapter VII of the United Nations Charter and the Immunity of Foreign State Officials' (2018) 112 *AJIL Unbound* 33

Zsuzsanna Deen-Racsmány, '*Prosecutor v. Taylor*: The Status of the Special Court for Sierra Leone and its Implications for Immunity' (2005) 18 *LJIL* 299

Joanne Foakes, *The Position of Heads of State and Senior Officials in International Law* (Oxford, 2013)

Micaela Frulli, 'The Question of Charles Taylor's Immunity' (2004) 2 *JICJ* 1118

Paola Gaeta, 'Does President Al Bashir Enjoy Immunity from Arrest?' (2009) 7 *JICJ* 315

David Koller, 'Immunities of Foreign Ministers: Paragraph 61 of the Yerodia Judgment as It Pertains to the Security Council and the International Criminal Court' (2004) 20 *American University International Law Review* 7

Claus Kreß, 'Preliminary Observations on the ICC Appeals Chamber's Judgment of 6 May 2019 in the Jordan Referral re Al-Bashir Appeal' (2019) 8 *Torkel Opsahl Occasional Paper Series*.

Rosanne Van Alebeek, *The Immunities of States and Their Officials in International Criminal Law and International Human Rights Law* (Oxford, 2008) ch. 5

Steffen Wirth, 'Immunities, Related Problems, and Article 98 of the Rome Statute' (2001) 12 *Criminal Law Forum* 429

Steffen Wirth, 'Immunity for Core Crimes? The ICJ's Judgment in the *Congo v. Belgium* Case' (2002) 13 *EJIL* 877

22

Alternatives and Complements to Criminal Prosecution

22.1 INTRODUCTION

There has been something of a swing away from the 'politics of impunity' towards an 'age of accountability', or 'justice cascade' in international law.[1] While accountability is often considered to flow from criminal prosecutions of core crimes – genocide, crimes against humanity, war crimes, and aggression – as was seen in Chapter 2, '[c]riminal prosecution . . . does some things rather well, other things only passably well, and makes an utter hash of still others'.[2] Thus, it is unsurprising that other models have been suggested for dealing with international crimes, on the basis that they fulfil at least some of the purposes of trials, while also addressing other accountability goals that criminal trials are not well-equipped to fulfil. Not all of these other models are mutually exclusive,[3] and indeed there is some debate on the 'sequencing' of responses to international crimes, where different responses are adopted over time for different situations, depending on their feasibility.[4] This chapter will provide an overview of the responses (amnesties, truth and reconciliation commissions, lustration, reparations and civil claims, and local justice mechanisms), alongside some of their positive and negative features.[5]

None of the mechanisms discussed in this chapter are in and of themselves perfect. Each has 'incompleteness and inescapable inadequacy' as a response to international crimes.[6] Just because other mechanisms perform certain roles in a fashion that prosecutions cannot,

---

[1] See e.g. Address of the UN Secretary-General, Ban Ki-moon, to the Review Conference of the International Criminal Court, 'The Age of Accountability', 31 May 2010; Leila Sadat, *The International Criminal Court and the Transformation of International Law: Justice for the New Millennium* (New York, 2002) ch. 3; Katherine Sikkink, *The Justice Cascade: How Human Rights Prosecutions are Changing World Politics* (New York, 2011); *Case concerning the Arrest Warrant of 11 April 2000 (Democratic Republic of the Congo v. Belgium)* [2002] ICJ Reports 3, 14 February 2002, Separate Opinion of Judges Higgins, Kooijmans, and Buergenthal, para. 51; *Case concerning Questions relating to the Obligation to Extradite or Prosecute (Belgium v. Senegal)*, Request for the Indication of Provisional Measures Order of 29 May 2009, ICJ General List 144, Dissenting Opinion of Judge Cançado Trindade, paras. 30–45.

[2] Mark Osiel, 'Ever Again: Legal Remembrance of Administrative Massacre' (1995) 144 *University of Pennsylvania Law Review* 463, 700.

[3] Obviously, amnesties and prosecutions are inconsistent, although amnesties do not have to cover all people or all offences.

[4] Laurel Fletcher, Harvey Weinstein, with Jaimie Rowen, 'Context, Timing and the Dynamics of Transitional Justice: A Historical Perspective' (2009) 31 *Human Rights Quarterly* 163; Juan Mendez, 'Foreword' in Francesca Lessa and Leigh Payne (eds.), *Amnesty in the Age of Human Rights Accountability* (Cambridge, 2012).

[5] See further e.g. W. Michael Reisman, 'Institutions and Practices for Restoring and Maintaining Public Order' (1995) 6 *Duke Journal of International and Comparative Law* 175; Martha Minow, *Between Vengeance and Forgiveness* (Boston, 1998); Ruti Teitel, *Transitional Justice* (New York, 2002).

[6] Minow, *Between Vengeance* (n. 5) 5. See also Katherine Francke, 'Gendered Subjects of Transitional Justice' (2006) *Columbia Journal of Gender and Law* 813: 'Transitional justice will always be both incomplete and messy' (*ibid.* 813).

does not mean that they are necessarily the most appropriate response to international crimes in any particular situation. Each context is unique; there cannot be a 'one size fits all' approach to what ought to be done.[7] Care must therefore be taken when transposing 'lessons' directly from one context to another.

In appraising the way in which international crimes are addressed, it must be remembered that, when decisions are being made about what to do about international crimes, practical limits, such as funding, political support, and the available infrastructure, are important.[8] This is particularly the case for transitional societies or those emerging from conflicts. As was said in relation to the South African post-apartheid transition:

the Constitution seeks to … facilitate the transition to a new democratic order, committed to 'reconciliation between the people of South Africa and the reconstruction of society'. The question is how this can be done effectively with the limitations of our resources and the legacy of the past … The families of those whose fundamental human rights were invaded by torture and abuse are not the only victims who have endured 'untold suffering and injustice' in consequence of the crass inhumanity of apartheid which so many have had to endure for so long. Generations of children born and yet to be born will suffer the consequences of poverty, of malnutrition, of homelessness, of illiteracy and disempowerment generated and sustained by the institutions of apartheid and its manifest effects on life and living for so many. The country has neither the resources nor the skills to reverse fully these massive wrongs. Those negotiators of the Constitution and leaders of the nation who were required to address themselves to these agonising problems must have been compelled to make hard choices. They could have chosen to direct that the limited resources of the state be spent by giving preference to the formidable delictual claims of those who had suffered from acts of murder, torture or assault perpetrated by servants of the state, diverting to that extent, desperately needed funds in the crucial areas of education, housing and primary health care … They were entitled to permit the claims of … school children and the poor and the homeless to be preferred.[9]

These are important points. Equally, however, it must be noted that the language of necessity, appropriateness, or feasibility is open to abuse,[10] potentially ignoring the broader aspects of international crimes. One of the reasons which may justify a separate regime of international criminal accountability is that crimes which are thought to affect all of humanity need to be dealt with sensitively as to both the national and international effects of such crimes. The international community of states has, at least at the level of rhetoric, affirmed the unacceptability of impunity for such crimes.[11] It must also be remembered that transitional societies are not the only societies that need to deal with issues relating to

---

[7] See Mark Drumbl, *Atrocity, Punishment and International Law* (Cambridge, 2007).

[8] See *Secretary-General's Report on the Rule of Law and Transitional Justice in Post-Conflict Societies*, UN Doc. S/2004/616 (23 August 2004) para. 3; Jon Elster, *Closing the Books: Transitional Justice in Historical Perspective* (Cambridge, 2004) ch. 7; Stanley Cohen, 'State Crimes of Previous Regimes: Knowledge, Accountability and the Policing of the Past' (1995) 20 *Law and Social Inquiry* 7, 8.

[9] *Azanian People's Organization (AZAPO) and others* v. *President of the Republic of South Africa* (1996) 4 SA 562 (CC), paras. 42–5.

[10] Susan Dwyer, 'Reconciliation for Realists' (1999) 13 *Ethics and International Affairs* 81.

[11] See e.g. SC Res. 1012, 28 August 1995; 1545, 21 May 2004; 1556, 11 June 2004; and 1564, 18 September 2004; and GA Res. 60/147; *Report of the Independent Expert to Update the Set of Principles to Combat Impunity*, UN Doc. E/CN.4/2005/102 (18 February 2005); see generally Frank Haldemann and Thomas Unger, with Valentina Cadelo (eds.), *The United Nations Principles to Combat Impunity: A Commentary* (Oxford, 2018).

international criminal law. Many stable, democratic states also have nationals, including state officials, who have committed international crimes.

22.2 AMNESTIES

Probably the most well-known, and controversial, alternative to prosecutions are amnesties.[12] An amnesty has been helpfully defined by Mark Freeman as:

an extraordinary legal measure whose primary function is to remove the prospect and consequences of criminal liability for designated individuals or classes of persons in respect of designated types of offences irrespective of whether the persons concerned have been tried for such offences in a court of law.[13]

Amnesties come in all shapes and sizes, and not all are express.[14] They can, for example, block civil claims. Amnesties have a lengthy history in international law. The Treaty of Westphalia, which was considered by many to usher in the modern era in international law and order, contained an amnesty.[15] More recently, amnesties were frequently employed in Latin America during and after the military dictatorships there, often as the price paid for the leaders of those dictatorships to hand over power to civilian governments.[16] Probably the most famous amnesty process is the South African one, although the Colombia peace process, discussed in Section 22.3, is also notable in this regard.[17]

As mentioned above, there are various types of amnesties, which range from those granted by regimes to themselves, such as that in Chile, to those which are voted upon by the population. The latter are usually thought, with some justification, to have greater legitimacy than the former. However, it must also be said that the consent of the population in such instances is often coerced, as the alternative is the continuation in power of an abusive regime or of armed conflict.[18] A further distinction must be made between 'blanket' amnesties, which prevent legal proceedings against all persons without distinction, and those, such as the South African amnesty legislation, which required certain conduct (often full confession of crimes) and/or certain motivations for the crimes (usually political ones) before an amnesty was granted.[19] Amnesties remain a frequent, and controversial, feature of conflict settlement.[20]

---

[12] For detailed studies, see Louise Mallinder, *Amnesty, Human Rights and Political Transitions: Bridging the Peace and Justice Divide* (Oxford, 2008); Mark Freeman, *Necessary Evils: Amnesties and the Search for Justice* (Cambridge, 2009).

[13] Freeman, *Necessary Evils* (n. 12) 13.

[14] *Ibid.*, 13–14. Furthermore, they can be factual, rather than legal, as where exile is offered, as was the case, for a time, for the former President of Liberia, Charles Taylor, in Nigeria. For critique, see Michael Scharf, 'From the eXile Files: An Essay on Trading Justice for Peace' (2006) 63 *Washington and Lee Law Review* 339.

[15] Scott Veitch, 'The Legal Politics of Amnesty' in Emilios Christodoulidis and Scott Veitch (eds.), *Lethe's Law: Justice, Law and Ethics in Reconciliation* (Oxford, 2001) 33.

[16] For discussion, see Elster, *Closing the Books* (n. 8) 62 et seq.

[17] Which has generated a huge literature; see e.g. Charles Villa-Vincencio and Erik Doxtader, *The Provocations of Amnesty* (Cape Town, 2003). On Colombia, see Kai Ambos, *The Colombian Peace Process and the Principle of Complementarity of the International Criminal Court* (Berlin, 2010).

[18] Mark Osiel, *Mass Atrocity, Collective Memory and the Law* (New Brunswick, NJ, 1997) 138.

[19] See e.g. Veitch, 'The Legal Politics of Amnesty' (n. 15) 37–8.

[20] See Mallinder, *Amnesty* (n. 12). The reasons for their frequency are a matter of some controversy: see e.g. Katherine Sikkink, 'The Age of Accountability: The Global Rise of Individual Accountability' in Francesca Lessa and Leigh Payne (eds.), *Amnesty*

22.2.1 International Law and Amnesties

There are a number of claims that amnesties for international crimes are always unlawful.[21] One claim is that amnesties are contrary to the duty to prosecute international crimes. The question of whether or not there is a duty to prosecute all international crimes was canvassed in Chapter 4. In brief, leaving aside treaty-based obligations to prosecute international crimes, it is difficult to prove a duty to prosecute every instance of an international crime on the basis of customary law, human rights obligations, or the *jus cogens* prohibitions that are encapsulated in parts of international criminal law.[22] A related issue is whether there is an exception to any existing duty to prosecute when an amnesty is thought necessary to re-establish peace.[23] Human rights bodies have not been very sympathetic to such claims, and are taking measures to require, and oversee, prosecutions.[24] The UN Human Rights Committee has said that amnesties for state officials for torture are 'generally incompatible' with obligations to investigate, prosecute and prevent human rights violations, although the word 'generally' introduces some doubt into the matter.[25] The International Criminal Tribunal for the former Yugoslavia (ICTY) went further, asserting that the *jus cogens* prohibition on torture also delegitimizes any amnesty for torture.[26] This was also part of the decision of the European Court of Human Rights (ECtHR) in *Ouid Dah*, where the Court agreed that amnesties for torture are generally incompatible with the international prohibition of that crime.[27] The African Commission on Human and Peoples' Rights determined that a Zimbabwean 'clemency order' which prevented prosecution of various serious human rights violations violated the African Charter on Human and Peoples' Rights (ACHPR).[28] The Inter-American Human Rights Court and Commission have been the most strident in declaring amnesties unlawful.[29] The most well-known case in this regard was *Barrios Altos*.[30] In this case, the Inter-American

---

in the Age of Human Rights Accountability (Cambridge, 2012) 19, 20–1; Louise Mallinder, 'Amnesties' Challenge to the Global Accountability Norm? Interpreting Regional and International Trends in Amnesty Enactment' in Francesca Lessa and Leigh Payne (eds.), *Amnesty in the Age of Human Rights Accountability* (Cambridge, 2012) 69.

[21] Diane Orentlicher, 'Settling Accounts: The Duty to Prosecute Human Rights Violations of a Former Regime' (1991) 100 *Yale Law Journal* 2537.

[22] See further Section 4.3.

[23] See e.g. Anja Siebert-Fohr, *Prosecuting Serious Human Rights Violations* (Oxford, 2009) 37 et seq.; and, on the state responsibility aspects of the question, Freeman, *Necessary Evils* (n. 13) 65–8.

[24] See Alexandra Huneeus, 'International Criminal Law by Other Means: The Quasi-Criminal Jurisdiction of the Human Rights Courts' (2013) 107 *AJIL* 1.

[25] General Comment 20, *Compilation of General Comments and General Recommendations Adopted by Human Rights Treaty Bodies*, UN Doc. HRI\GEN\I\Rev.1 (1994) 30.

[26] *Furundžija*, ICTY TC II, 10 December 1998, para. 155. See also *Karadžić*, ICTY TC, 17 December 2008; and Benjamin Brockman-Hawe, 'Decision on the Accused's Second Motion for Inspection and Disclosure: Immunity Issue' (2009) 58 *ICLQ* 726, 730–2. For critique of the ICTY here, see Mark Freeman and Max Pensky, 'The Amnesty Controversy in International Law' in Francesca Lessa and Leigh Payne (eds.), *Amnesty in the Age of Human Rights Accountability* (Cambridge, 2012) 42, 59–60.

[27] *Ould Dah v. France*, ECtHR, 17 March 2009, 17.

[28] *Zimbabwe Human Rights NGO Forum v. Zimbabwe* (2006) AHRLR 128. Other examples include *Degli and others v. Togo* (2000) AHRLR 317.

[29] See e.g. Inter-American Commission on Human Rights, *El Salvador Report, State's Responsibility for 1983 Las Hajas Massacre*, Report No. 26/92 (24 September 1992) para. 169. See generally Siebert-Fohr, *Prosecuting* (n. 23) ch. 3.

[30] *Barrios Altos (Chumbipuma Aguirre et al. v. Peru)*, Inter-American Court of Human Rights, 14 March 2001. See also *Gomes Lund et al. v. Brazil*, Inter-American Court of Human Rights, 24 November 2010; *La Cantuta v. Peru*, Inter-American Court of Human Rights, 29 November 2006.

Court of Human Rights expressly said that the amnesty granted to state agents by the Peruvian government was invalid, and that

This Court considers that all amnesty provisions, provisions on prescription and the establishment of measures designed to eliminate responsibility are inadmissible, because they are intended to prevent the investigation and punishment of those responsible for serious human rights violations such as torture, extrajudicial, summary or arbitrary execution and forced disappearance, all of them prohibited because they violate non-derogable rights recognized by international human rights law.[31]

This is a strong statement, and the case has been interpreted by some as ending the possibility of any amnesties.[32] This may overstate what is probably the most assertive of all the international courts' decisions on point. The case ought also to be read against the backdrop of the nature of the (self) amnesties that were granted, the fact that they were not aimed at reconciliation, related to developed states, and did not involve mass participation in international crimes.[33]

At first sight, one international treaty provision, Article 6(5) of Additional Protocol II relating to Non-international Armed Conflict, appears to argue in favour of amnesties. It reads as follows:

At the end of hostilities, the authorities in power shall endeavour to grant the broadest possible amnesty to persons who have participated in the armed conflict, or those deprived of their liberty for reasons related to the armed conflict, whether they are interned or detained.

However, in its rules of customary international humanitarian law, the International Committee of the Red Cross indicates that Article 6(5) was not intended to cover international crimes.[34]

Claims that amnesties are always contrary to international law are therefore probably in advance of the current law, although UN policy is now formally against amnesties for international crimes.[35] The current position on amnesties in international law was summed up by the Special Court for Sierra Leone (SCSL) in the *Kallon and Kamara* decision:

that there is a crystallising international norm that a government cannot grant amnesty for serious violations of crimes under international law is amply supported by materials placed before the Court [but the view] that it has crystallised may not be entirely correct . . . it is accepted that such a norm is developing under international law.[36]

---

[31] *Barrios Altos, ibid.* para. 41.

[32] Lisa LaPlante, 'Outlawing Amnesty: The Return of Criminal Justice to Transitional Justice Schemes' (2008–9) 48 *Virginia Journal of International Law* 915.

[33] Siebert-Fohr, *Prosecuting* (n. 23) 109; Robert Cryer, 'Accountability in Post-Conflict Societies: A Matter of Judgment, Practice or Principle?' in Nigel White and Dirk Klaasen (eds.), *The United Nations and Human Rights Protection in Post-Conflict Situations* (Manchester, 2005) 267, 269–70; Freeman, *Necessary Evils* (n. 13) 48–50.

[34] International Committee of the Red Cross, *Customary International Humanitarian Law Database*, Rule 159, ihl-databases.icrc.org/en/customary-ihl.

[35] UN practice since the late 1990s (but not before) has been to say that amnesties are not acceptable: see *Report of the Secretary-General on the Establishment of a Special Court for Sierra Leone*, UN Doc. S/2000/915 (4 October 2000) para. 24. For discussion and critique, see Freeman, *Necessary Evils* (n. 13) 88–108.

[36] *Kallon and Kamara*, SCSL AC, 13 March 2004, para. 82.

Similarly, a Trial Chamber of the Extraordinary Chambers in the Courts of Cambodia (ECCC) has said, 'an emerging consensus prohibits amnesties in relation to serious international crimes, based on a duty to investigate and prosecute these crimes and to punish their perpetrators'.[37] A complete prohibition may not yet have completely emerged, but the scope for lawful amnesties has narrowed.[38]

22.2.2 ICC and Amnesties

The Preamble to the International Criminal Court (ICC) Statute affirms 'that the most serious crimes of concern to the international community as a whole must not go unpunished',[39] and that states parties are 'determined to put an end to impunity for the perpetrators of such crimes'; it recalled 'that it is the duty of every state to exercise its criminal jurisdiction over those responsible for international crimes'.[40] Although these provisions do not create legal obligations, a failure to do anything about crimes committed by nationals of, or on the territory of, states parties to the ICC Statute could lead to the ICC exercising its powers to prosecute offenders itself.[41]

A domestic amnesty binds neither the ICC nor its Prosecutor. The Office of the Prosecutor has indicated concern with amnesties from the beginning, originally in the Uganda situation.[42] The Office of the Prosecutor subsequently criticized the possibility of amnesties in Libya,[43] and made clear in the Colombia situation that the Office 'would view with concern any measures that appear designed to shield or hinder the establishment of criminal responsibility of individuals for crimes within the jurisdiction of the Court'.[44]

Although the Prosecutor may decide to take account of amnesties, the Office of the Prosecutor has taken the view that the 'interests of justice' requires the ICC to prosecute international crimes rather than refraining from doing so on political grounds.[45] In taking that view, the Office of the Prosecutor stated that the drafters of the ICC Statute clearly chose prosecution as the appropriate response to international crimes.[46] Hence, when the Prosecutor is dealing with a matter, '[t]he issue is no longer about whether we agree or disagree with the pursuit of justice in moral or practical terms: it is the law', and non-prosecution is a 'last resort'.[47]

---

[37] *Ieng Sary*, ECCC TC, 3 November 2011, para. 53.
[38] Although see Christine Bell, *On the Law of Peace: Peace Agreements and the Lex Pacificatoria* (Oxford, 2008) 240–1; Freeman, *Necessary Evils* (n. 13) *passim*.
[39] See generally Mallinder, *Amnesty* (n. 12) 279–91; Freeman, *Necessary Evils* (n. 13) 73–88; William A. Schabas, 'Principle 20' in Haldemann and Unger, *The United Nations Principles to Combat Impunity* (n. 11) 219. For the view that the ICC Statute implies or creates a duty to prosecute, see Payam Akhavan, 'Whither National Courts? The Rome Statute's Missing Half, Towards an Express and Enforceable Obligation for the Domestic Repression of International Crimes' (2010) 8 *JICJ* 1045.
[40] ICC Statute, Preamble, paras. 4–6. [41] See Section 8.6.5.
[42] See Section 8.12; and William W. Burke-White and Scott Kaplan, 'Shaping the Contours of Domestic Justice: The International Criminal Court and an Admissibility Challenge in the Uganda Situation' in Stahn and Sluiter, *Emerging Practice*, 79.
[43] Statement of the Prosecutor of the International Criminal Court to the Security Council, UN Doc. S.PV/ 6855 (7 November 2012) 3.
[44] *Situation in Colombia, Interim Report* (November 2012) para. 205.
[45] See e.g. Darryl Robinson, 'Serving the Interests of Justice: Amnesties, Truth Commissions and the International Criminal Court' (2003) 14 *EJIL* 481; Michael P. Scharf, 'The Amnesty Exception to the Jurisdiction of the International Criminal Court' (1999) 32 *Cornell International Law Journal* 507.
[46] ICC Office of the Prosecutor, *Policy Paper on the Interests of Justice* (September 2007) 3–4. [47] *Ibid*. 4, 8–9.

The Office of the Prosecutor has taken the position that the 'interests of justice' are not the same as the interests of peace, and its mandate does not cover the latter. Those considerations are, to the Office of the Prosecutor, the domain of the political organs of the United Nations, in particular the Security Council, which has the power to defer (for renewable one-year periods) investigations and prosecutions under Article 16 of the ICC Statute.[48] Whether this is the best means of ensuring that the ICC is seen as apolitical is perhaps an open question.[49] The issue arose in the Colombia situation, with the Office of the Prosecutor monitoring the peace process from 2004–21 and ultimately deciding that the combination of proceedings before the ordinary courts, the Justice and Peace Law Tribunals, and the Special Jurisdiction for Peace relieved any concerns about amnesties.[50]

22.2.3 Domestic Jurisdictions and Amnesties

Domestic amnesties do not bind states other than the granting state; legislation in one state does not alter the jurisdiction of another.[51] It was, in part, for this reason that the Special Court for Sierra Leone declared that it was not unlawful for the United Nations to ignore the amnesty contained in the 1999 Lomé Peace Accord when creating the Special Court for Sierra Leone:

Where jurisdiction is universal, a State cannot deprive another of its jurisdiction to prosecute the offender by the grant of amnesty. It is for this reason unrealistic to regard as universally effective the grant of an amnesty by a State in regard to grave international crimes in which universal jurisdiction exists. A State cannot bring into oblivion and forgetfulness a crime, such as a crime against international law, which other States are entitled to keep alive and remember.[52]

The Court took the view that it was not an abuse of process for the Court to ignore the amnesty, given its perilous status under international law and the fact that the Court was not part of the Sierra Leonean justice system.[53]

The extent to which amnesties granted within a jurisdiction preclude action by municipal courts in that same jurisdiction depends, *inter alia*, on the status of international law in the domestic legal order, and the consistency or otherwise of the amnesty with international law.[54] It is undeniable that judges in some countries are increasingly unlikely to accept

---

[48] See Section 8.9.

[49] See e.g. Jens David Ohlin, 'Peace, Security and Prosecutorial Discretion' in Stahn and Sluiter, *Emerging Practice*, 185; Steven Roach, *Politicizing the International Criminal Court: The Convergence of Politics, Ethics and Law* (New York, 2006). It bears remembering that, as Martti Koskenniemi has said, institutions enact, rather than replace politics: Martti Koskenniemi, *The Gentle Civilizer of Nations: The Rise and Fall of International Law 1870–1960* (Cambridge, 2002) 177. The Prosecutor's point will, however, that the politics have been, and are still to be, determined by others, not by the ICC.

[50] To mark the closing of the preliminary examination and decision not to proceed further, the Prosecutor concluded a Cooperation Agreement with the Government of Colombia. It 'reinforces and further defines the mutual roles the Office and the Government will undertake to ensure that the significant progress achieved by domestic prosecutorial and judicial entities, and in particular by the Special Jurisdiction for Peace, is sustained and strengthened': ICC Office of the Prosecutor, Press Release (28 Oct. 2021).

[51] In *Ould Dah v. France*, ECtHR, 17 March 2009, the European Court of Human Rights decided that a Mauritanian amnesty for torture occurring in Mauritania did not prevent France from prosecuting torture there; see Section 22.2.1.

[52] *Kallon and Kamara*, SCSL AC, 13 March 2004, para. 67.

[53] *Ibid*. And see José Doria, 'The Work of the Special Court for Sierra Leone through its Jurisprudence' in Doria et al., *Legal Regime*, 229, 243. See also Chapter 9.

[54] Mallinder, *Amnesty* (n. 12) 204. For a detailed survey of court decisions on point, see *ibid*., ch. 4.

amnesties. For example, there are a number of examples of domestic courts, after many years of accepting amnesties, coming around to the view that they are unconstitutional or otherwise inapplicable. For example, in 2005 the Argentine Supreme Court declared the amnesties relating to the 'Dirty War' in the 1970s and 1980s to be unconstitutional.[55] In this case, although the Congress had already repealed the amnesty, the Supreme Court, relying on international law, made clear that the amnesty was also unlawful. In other examples, courts have restrictively interpreted amnesties. For example, in Chile, the Supreme Court has determined that neither amnesties nor statutes of limitation apply to offences involving disappearances, since they are 'continuing' offences, and therefore not susceptible to being amnestied.[56]

The ECCC has determined that state practice:

demonstrates at a minimum a retroactive right for third States, internationalised and domestic courts to evaluate amnesties and to set them aside or limit their scope should they be deemed incompatible with international norms.[57]

This may go a little far. Third states and internationalized courts (which are not grounded solely in the domestic legal order) are simply not bound by other states' domestic amnesties, rather than having a right to set them aside or interpret them. Also, many (although not all) domestic courts in the country of the crime have overturned or limited amnesties on the basis of their constitutional provisions, rather than international law directly, but the result is often the same. Still, it bears remembering that the majority of domestic decisions on point have upheld amnesties early after their passage, only later becoming willing to challenge or limit them.[58]

22.2.4 Appraisal of Amnesties

Amnesties are controversial both in law and policy.[59] Those who speak in their favour often claim that it is necessary to have amnesties to bring to an end conflicts, and that to insist on anything more is to condemn others to death or other serious human rights violations, as combatants and others will refuse to relinquish their weapons or power without promises of non-prosecution.[60] Others see the grant of amnesties as giving in to blackmail,[61] and fostering a culture of impunity which encourages the future commission of international crimes.[62]

It has also been said that amnesties do not lead to peace (captured in the phrase 'no peace without justice'), and that 'warlords and political leaders capable of committing human

---

[55] *Simón*, Decision of 14 June 2005, Case No. 17.768. See Christine Bakker, 'A Full Stop to Amnesty in Argentina' (2005) 3 *JICJ* 1106.
[56] *Sepúlveda*, 17 November 2004. See Fannie Lafontaine, 'No Amnesty or Statute of Limitation for Enforced Disappearances: The *Sandoval* Case Before the Supreme Court of Chile' (2005) 3 *JICJ* 469. For an example of a narrow reading from an internationalized tribunal, see *Ieng Sary*, ECCC PTC, 17 October 2008, para. 61.
[57] *Ieng Sary*, ECCC TC, 3 November 2011, para. 53. [58] Mallinder, *Amnesty* (n. 12) 206.
[59] See e.g. Freeman, *Necessary Evils* (n. 13) 17–32.
[60] Anonymous, 'Human Rights in Peace Negotiations' (1996) 18 *Human Rights Quarterly* 249.
[61] Mallinder, *Amnesty* (n. 12) 1–2.
[62] See Anja Sibert-Fohr, *Prosecuting Serious Human Rights Violations* (Oxford, 2009) 281–2.

rights atrocities are not deterred by amnesties obtained, but emboldened'.[63] Granting amnesties, therefore, is considered by many to undermine the deterrent function of international criminal law,[64] and to represent an ugly political compromise. Sometimes this compromise is also seen as one between elites who bargain away the rights of victims with little regard for them.[65] In part, this has led to calls for 'transitional justice from below', where the calls of those outside political elites are given greater respect,[66] although it is accepted that this can also be exclusionary.[67]

Even if the time for 'blanket' amnesties is over, there are other forms of amnesty, such as the South African amnesty, that are accompanied by processes that may render them more acceptable. Conditional amnesties that require truth telling, apply to the less responsible, or are democratically legitimated in the state that passes them, are more likely to be acceptable than those that do not.[68]

Some argue that amnesties can promote reconciliation (however, this argument often comes from perpetrators, rather than victims).[69] Reconciliation is not a simple notion.[70] For example, it is often assumed that reconciliation is a social process, whereas it is at least as much an individual one, between victim and perpetrator.[71] Also, it must be acknowledged that reconciliation, and its partner, forgiveness, often draw upon religious notions, which are not necessarily universalizable.[72] Indeed, some question the philosophical appropriateness of forgiveness at all, or at least in all circumstances.[73] What is certain is that reconciliation cannot be forced upon people, and some victims will not wish to be reconciled with their persecutors, in particular in the absence of remorse.[74] Equally, there is no doubt that forgiveness has accompanied amnesties in certain circumstances.[75]

---

[63] Leila Nadya Sadat, 'The Effect of Amnesties Before Domestic and International Tribunals: Morality, Law and Politics' in Edel Hughes, William Schabas, and Ramesh Thakur (eds.), *Atrocities and International Accountability: Beyond Transitional Justice* (Tokyo, 2007) 225, 227.

[64] See Mallinder, *Amnesty* (n. 12) 17.

[65] Richard A. Wilson, *The Politics of Truth and Reconciliation in South Africa: Legitimizing the Post-Apartheid State* (Cambridge, 2001); Richard Burchill, 'From East Timor to Timor-Leste: A Demonstration of the Limits of International Law in the Pursuit of Justice' in Doria et al., *Legal Regime*, 255, 288–9. Desmond Tutu's response is that the delegations which negotiated the amnesty in South Africa included victims, who were entitled to speak on behalf of all the victims: Desmond Tutu, *No Future Without Forgiveness* (London, 1999) 52–4.

[66] See Kieran McEvoy and Lorna McGregor (eds.), *Transitional Justice from Below: Grassroots Activism and the Struggle for Change* (Oxford, 2008).

[67] Kieran McEvoy and Lorna McGregor, 'Transitional Justice from Below: An Agenda for Research, Policy and Praxis' in Kieran McEvoy and Lorna McGregor (eds.), *Transitional Justice from Below: Grassroots Activism and the Struggle for Change* (Oxford, 2008) 9–10.

[68] See Mallinder, *Amnesty* (n. 12) chs. 2–4 and 10; John Dugard, 'Dealing with the Crimes of a Past Regime: Is Amnesty Still an Option?' (1999) 12 *LJIL* 1001.

[69] Stanley Cohen, *States of Denial: Knowing About Atrocities and Suffering* (Cambridge, 2001) 238–9.

[70] See e.g. Laura Olson, 'Provoking the Dragon on the Patio: Matters of Transitional Justice: Penal Repression vs Amnesties' (2006) 88 *International Review of the Red Cross* 275, 277; Martha Nussbaum, *Anger and Forgiveness: Resentment, Generosity and Forgiveness* (New York, 2016).

[71] Arne J. Vetlesen, *Evil and Human Agency: Understanding Collective Evildoing* (Cambridge, 2005) 272–81.

[72] Thomas Brudholm, 'On the Advocacy of Forgiveness after Mass Atrocities' in Thomas Brudholm and Thomas Cushman (eds.), *The Religious in Responses to Mass Atrocity* (Cambridge, 2009) 124. For a more sanguine view, see Daniel Philpott, 'When Faith Meets History: The Influence of Religion on Transitional Justice' in *ibid.* 174.

[73] See the discussion in Brudholm and Cushman, *The Religious in Responses* (n. 72); and Charles Griswold, *Forgiveness: A Philosophical Investigation* (Cambridge, 2007).

[74] Antje du Bois-Pedain, *Transitional Amnesty in South Africa* (Cambridge, 2007) 232–43, 286–93; Brudholm and Cushman, *The Religious in Responses* (n. 72) 132–5; Olson, 'Provoking the Dragon' (n. 70) 277.

[75] For examples in South Africa, see Tutu, *No Future* (n. 65) 80. See e.g. Mallinder, *Amnesty* (n. 12) 4, 81. E.g. see *ibid.* 243.

Alongside forgiveness, there is also the possibility of forgetfulness, in particular, of victims. After all, the term 'amnesty', as is often pointed out, shares a common Latin root, *amnestia*, with forgetfulness – amnesia.[76] With this comes the risk of increased denial or relativization of international crimes.[77] Not all amnesty processes provide for revelations about what has been done, and, as such, can lead to a deliberate refusal to acknowledge the suffering of victims, or the extent of wrongdoing.[78] This strategy is not necessarily effective, in particular where, as in South America, long-standing victims' rights advocates have kept the suffering of the victims visible, and, as time has gone on, amnesties and the like have been repealed.[79]

Still, international law has not yet developed so far as to prohibit all amnesties in all situations. In spite of the fact that the language of forgiving and forgetting comes easier to the mouths of perpetrators than victims, there have been political defences of amnesties as being necessary measures in post-conflict situations, at least with respect to lower-ranking offenders, and where resources outstrip the possibility of prosecuting any more than a small number of defendants.[80] As a result, amnesties and the criticisms of them are likely to continue to be a feature of responses to international crimes for the foreseeable future.

22.3 TRUTH COMMISSIONS

In part because of the possibility that amnesties will lead to forgetfulness or denial, one of the activities which often accompanies them is the setting up of a truth commission.[81] A truth commission has been defined as a body that:

(1) is focused on the past, rather than ongoing, events; (2) investigates a pattern of events that took place over a period of time; (3) engages directly and broadly with the affected population, gathering information on their experiences;(4) is a temporary body, with the aim of concluding with a final report; and (5) is officially authorised by the state under review.[82]

They may be better than prosecutions at achieving certain aims,[83] and they have been set up as an alternative to prosecutions, especially where the clandestine nature of many of the offences means that they are difficult, if not impossible, to prove to the relevant criminal

---

[76] See e.g. Mallinder, *Amnesty* (n. 12) 4. [77] E.g. see *ibid*. 243. [78] Cohen, *States of Denial* (n. 69) 222, 243.

[79] LaPlante, 'Outlawing Amnesty' (n. 32) 950–6. On an African analogue, in relation to Hissène Habré, see *Case concerning Questions relating to the Obligation to Extradite or Prosecute (Belgium v. Senegal)*, Request for the Indication of Provisional Measures Order of 29 May 2009, ICJ General List 144, Dissenting Opinion of Judge Cançado Trindade, paras. 30–45.

[80] LaPlante, 'Outlawing Amnesty' (n. 32) 923.

[81] Albie Sachs, *The Strange Alchemy of Life and Law* (Oxford, 2009) 84. On truth commissions, see generally Priscilla Hayner, *Unspeakable Truths: Confronting State Terror and Atrocity*, 2nd ed. (London, 2011); Onur Bakiner, *Truth Commissions; Memory, Power, and Legitimacy* (Philadelphia, PA, 2016); Minow, *Between Vengeance* (n. 5) ch. 4; Haldemann and Unger, *The United Nations Principles* (n. 11) Part II.B.

[82] Hayner, *Unspeakable Truths* (n. 81) 11–12. Mark Freeman, *Truth Commissions and Procedural Fairness* (Cambridge, 2006) 18, defines them as 'an ad hoc, autonomous, and victim centred commission of inquiry set up in and authorised by a state for the primary purposes of (1) investigating and reporting on the principal causes and consequences of broad and relatively recent patterns of severe violence or repression that occurred in the state during determinate periods of abusive rule or conflict, and (2) making recommendations for their redress and future prevention'.

[83] See generally Alison Bisset, *Truth Commissions and Criminal Courts* (Cambridge, 2012) ch. 1; Pablo de Grieff, *Report of the Special Rapporteur on the Promotion of Truth, Justice, Reparation and Guarantees of Non-Recurrence*, A/HRC/24/42 (28 August 2013).

standard. They are also a means of attempting to get beyond the 'closing of ranks' that can make prosecution of offences by those in close-knit groups, such as particular regiments or teams, very difficult.

The idea behind many truth commissions is that people will be more willing to speak of their conduct if they are not to be prosecuted for it. This can be important, for example, when people have 'disappeared' and relatives of the victims are caught in limbo, not knowing the fate of their family members. Truth commissions can also enable more victims to tell their story than is possible in a court. Some commissions, such as the Guatemalan Commission, had the authority to make recommendations for reforms, although they were not always taken up.[84] This is indicative of a broader issue; truth commissions are usually only given a mandate to recommend action, and they are not normally given any authority to oversee or ensure its implementation.[85]

The terms of reference setting up a commission will define the timeframe and sometimes the kinds of conduct to be investigated. Their mandates and terms of reference are usually the outcome of negotiations between the relevant parties,[86] and can reflect their relative power. One of the main purposes of truth commissions is to acknowledge the harm that was done to the victims, by writing an official report setting out the violations of their rights. This is thought not only to counter later denials,[87] but also to provide a form of healing for victims,[88] and provide the basis for societal reconciliation. The South African Truth and Reconciliation report named names, whilst the Argentine Commission did not have the authority to do so.[89] When names are named, it is more important to have some form of procedural protection for those giving evidence or admitting crimes.[90] For example, some truth commissions that identified perpetrators gave them advance notice that they had been named and a chance to respond.[91]

There are other possible limits on the reports they issue. The South African report, for example, only had the mandate to deal with political violence. It could not, therefore, deal with issues such as land dispossessions, forcible transfers and other aspects of apartheid.[92] As a result, it could only tell part of the story. Indeed, it could not deal with the use and abuse of the legal and political system in creating and maintaining the apartheid system. In contrast, the Liberian Truth and Reconciliation Commission, although intended to focus primarily on the post-1979 history of that country's conflict, also looked into issues such as corruption, misgovernment, and the role of other states.[93] The general trend is towards broader mandates,[94] which, whilst welcome at some levels, can stretch the limited resources of commissions.

The quality of a commission's report depends in part on the quality of the information available to the commission. It can be difficult to persuade perpetrators to come forward to testify about their role in repressions, or victims to speak about sexual offences committed

---

[84] Hayner, *Unspeakable Truths* (n. 81) ch. 10.
[85] *Report of the Special Rapporteur on the Promotion of Truth* (n. 83) paras. 44, 71–9.
[86] On the various aspects of mandates of truth commissions, see *Report of the Special Rapporteur on the Promotion of Truth* (n. 83) paras. 32–52; Alison Bisset, 'Principle 8' in Haldemann and Unger, *The United National Principles* (n. 11) 116.
[87] Cohen, *States of Denial* (n. 69) ch. 10.　[88] Minow, *Between Vengeance* (n. 5) 66–74.
[89] Hayner, *Unspeakable Truths* (n. 81) ch. 8.　[90] See Freeman, *Truth Commissions* (n. 13).　[91] *Ibid.* ch. 7.　[92] *Ibid.* 73–4.
[93] Truth and Reconciliation Commission of Liberia, *Final Report* (2009) vol. II, ch. 6, 261, 243–51.
[94] *Report of the Special Rapporteur on the Promotion of Truth* (n. 83) paras. 35. 40.

against them in a context that may lead to social stigmatization or ostracization.[95] The confessions of perpetrators can also be framed in a manner which amounts, in fact, to a form of denial.[96] This was, in part, avoided in South Africa by making amnesty applications contingent on attending the Commission and telling the full story. There were some prosecutions for those who refused to testify, or who did not completely disclose their actions.[97] Even so, some important witnesses, such as ex-President Botha, refused to testify before the Commission.

The evidence-taking engaged in by a commission often requires people to incriminate themselves and, in this way, truth commissions sometimes stand in place of prosecutions. This does not, however, have to be the case.[98] For example, the Truth and Reconciliation Commission in Sierra Leone took place at the same time as the Special Court for Sierra Leone.[99] Relations between the two were strained, however, and the Commission was critical of the Special Court in its report, in particular of the fact that the Special Court was not willing to allow Sam Hinga Norman, being tried before that court, to testify before the Commission in the manner it preferred.[100] This is indicative of the difficult problems that relate to the extent to which testimony and other forms of evidence provided to commissions can be used later on in criminal prosecutions, at home, abroad, and before international criminal tribunals, although the latter two will not be bound directly by any promise of confidentiality or non-use granted by the territorial state.[101]

There are questions about the extent to which the reports of truth commissions can reflect any form of 'objective truth', if such a concept exists, and whether they can lead to an agreed history between old enemies.[102] Given the orientation of truth commissions towards victims, they tend not to have the rules of procedure and evidence that are considered necessary in courts to ensure reliability and verification of testimony.[103] Whilst this is understandable and correct, it may impact upon the truth that the report seeks to set out.[104]

It has also been questioned whether truth telling does lead to reconciliation,[105] or an ability to move beyond the past.[106] Similarly, it has been doubted whether truth and reconciliation are congruent goals.[107] Most, though, accept that truth has a role to play in

---

[95] Hayner, *Unspeakable Truths* (n. 81) 77–8. Alison Bisset, 'Principle 10' in Haldemann and Unger, *The United National Principles* (n. 11) 129.

[96] Cohen, *States of Denial* (n. 69) ch. 4. Although see Bisset, 'Principle 10' (n. 95) 123.

[97] Sachs, *The Strange Alchemy* (n. 81) 78.

[98] See generally Bisset, *Truth Commissions* (n. 83); Lyal S. Sunga, 'Ten Principles for Reconciling Truth Commissions and Criminal Proceedings' in Doria et al., *The Legal Regime of the ICC: Essays in Honour of Prof. I.P. Blishchenko* (Netherlands, 2009).

[99] See William Schabas, 'Internationalized Courts and Their Relationship with Alternative Accountability Mechanisms: The Case of Sierra Leone' in Cesare Romano et al. (eds.), *Internationalized Criminal Courts* (Oxford, 2004) 157.

[100] *Witness to Truth: Report of the Truth and Reconciliation Commission for Sierra Leone* (Accra, 2004) vol. 3b, ch. 6; *Norman*, SCSL AC, 28 November 2003.

[101] See generally Bisset, *Truth Commissions* (n. 83) chs. 3–5.

[102] Tutu, *No Future* (n. 65) 33; François du Bois, 'Nothing but the Truth: The South African Alternative to Corrective Justice in Transitions to Democracy' in Emilios Christodoulidis and Scott Veitch (eds.), *Lethe's Law: Justice, Law and Ethics in Reconciliation* (Oxford, 2001) 91; Haldemann and Unger, *United Nations Principles* (n. 11) 59–94.

[103] See Freeman, *Truth Commissions* (n. 13).

[104] Anne Orford, 'Commissioning the Truth' (2006) 15 *Columbia Journal of Gender and Law* 851, 859–60.

[105] Hayner, *Unspeakable Truths* (n. 81) 155–61.

[106] It is possible that the idea that truth allows people to move on is at least in part a religious notion: see e.g. John 8:23: 'And ye shall know the truth, and the truth shall make you free'. It is notable that the South African Truth and Reconciliation Commission often began its hearings with prayers (Sachs, *The Strange Alchemy* (n. 81) 75). See also Minow, *Between Vengeance* (n. 5) 55.

[107] Hayner, *Unspeakable Truths* (n. 81) 182–3.

reconciliation, although few would say that truth alone can achieve such a goal.[108] Much again can depend on what is reported on; commissions which exclude the roles of bystanders and of those who benefited from the system that committed such crimes have been criticized on the basis that they cannot provide for reconciliation, as they exclude a large part of society from their gaze.[109]

Sometimes, as occurred in South Africa, as part of the attempt to promote reconciliation and help provide victims with some form of healing, victims are given the opportunity to attend the hearings and discuss the revelations made by the perpetrators. Some scholars are of the view that truth commissions are particularly well suited to provide healing for victims.[110] Much depends on the attitude of perpetrators, and whether their engagement is full or essentially grudging and formal. Albie Sachs writes of the South African Truth and Reconciliation hearings that:

instead of coming forward and speaking from the heart and crying and being open, most of the perpetrators came in neatly pressed suits, expressing tight body language, with their lawyers next to them, and read prepared statements as though they were in a court of law. Their admissions were important but tended to be limited to a factual acknowledgement of unlawful conduct coupled with a rehearsed apology, rather than encompassing an emotional and convincing acknowledgement of wrongdoing.[111]

Others have used truth and reconciliation hearings as political platforms.[112] The extent to which victims are assisted by the process depends on individual reactions, and these are not easily extrapolated into general statements about victims as a whole. Some victims in South Africa issued a court challenge to the Truth and Reconciliation Commission and the amnesty process, although it was rejected by the South African Constitutional Court.[113]

Truth commissions, as has been said, are both high risk and 'inherently political enterprises'.[114] They are set up for reasons that are both good and bad. They may well be created in some circumstances to ensure that victims are given acknowledgment of their suffering, or as a means of attempting to prevent the recurrence of the crimes.[115] In others, though, 'a cynical government may hope that a truth commission will help exhaust public interest in greater measures of political and legal accountability'.[116] Such critiques have been made in relation to the recommendation of the East Timor Truth and Reconciliation Commission that there be no further prosecutions.[117] There are also well- and poorly designed commissions,[118] and 'a poorly executed truth commission may be worse than no truth commission at all'.[119]

[108] See e.g. Minow, *Between Vengeance* (n. 5) 79–83.
[109] Rama Maini, 'Does Power Trump Morality? Reconciliation or Transitional Justice?' in Edel Hughes, William Schabas, and Ramesh Thakur (eds.), *Atrocities and International Accountability: Beyond Transitional Justice* (Tokyo, 2007) 27, 36.
[110] Minow, *Between Vengeance* (n. 5) 61–79.
[111] Sachs, *The Strange Alchemy* (n. 81) 86–7. A similar problem was noted by the Truth and Reconciliation Commission of Liberia, *Final Report* (2009) vol. II, v.
[112] Minow, *Between Vengeance* (n. 5) 83.
[113] See *Azanian People's Organization (AZAPO) and others v. President of the Republic of South Africa* (1996) 4 SA 562 (CC).
[114] Freeman, *Truth Commissions* (n. 13) 37. [115] *Ibid*. 38. [116] *Ibid*. 37. [117] Burchill, 'From East Timor' (n. 65) 289.
[118] For some of the factors that are relevant in this regard, see *Report of the Special Rapporteur on the Promotion of Truth* (n. 83) paras. 53–70.
[119] Maini, 'Does Power Trump Morality?' (n. 109) 34. The *Secretary-General's Report on the Rule of Law and Transitional Justice* (n. 8) para. 51, takes the view that truth commissions are best formed through consultative processes on mandates and

An interesting alternative approach can be found in Colombia. It emerged as part of a peace agreement between the governmental and FARC rebel forces, ending fifty years of conflict. The 2016 peace agreement created a truth commission, the Special Jurisdiction for Peace, to try crimes against humanity and war crimes committed during the conflict, and an agency to find the remains of those disappeared during the conflict. The truth commission issued its final report in June 2022, and a committee was established to monitor, for seven years, implementation of its recommendations. The Special Jurisdiction is undertaking significant prosecutions, including of former senior FARC commanders, for hostage-taking, extrajudicial executions, and gender-based crimes. Perpetrators who fully cooperate with the Special Jurisdiction and confess to their crimes are subject to alternative punishments, including restrictions on liberty for up to eight years.[120] Ordinary criminal sanctions apply to perpetrators of serious crimes who do not confess or offer false confessions. The ICC Prosecutor has concluded that the Colombian post-conflict justice processes satisfy the complementarity principle and closed his office's preliminary examination of Colombia.[121]

22.4 LUSTRATION

One way of dealing with large-scale administrative complicity in international crimes is lustration: the purging of public servants who are thought to be responsible for international crimes.[122] This was a frequently used mechanism in Eastern Europe after the collapse of Communism there in the late 1980s. There are elements of this approach to international crimes in the removal of members of the Ba'ath party from the Iraqi public service and judiciary. Lustration may be seen as a means of removing corrupt or inefficient staff, but the main purpose is often a form of punishment. Although it can deal in some ways with large-scale complicity, the fact that it is a form of punishment (or is intended to be) is problematic, because it involves serious consequences for people, but is almost always done on a mass basis, without individual hearings to determine what precise responsibility a lustrated person bears. In many totalitarian societies, party membership is necessary for a career in the civil service, and many join essentially as an administrative convenience, and are not personally involved in wrongdoing. As a result, it is questionable whether lustration is consistent with human rights law, in particular the right to a 'competent, independent and impartial' public hearing when a person's rights and obligations are being adjudicated.[123]

---

commissioner selection and that, to be successful, they must enjoy real independence and have credible commissioner criteria and processes, strong public information and communication strategies, be gender and victim-sensitive and provide for reparations. They also need international support. On the funding of such institutions see Howard Varney, 'Principle 11' in Haldemann and Unger, *The United National Principles* (n. 11) 136; on publication, see Catherine Harwood and Carsten Stahn, 'Principle 13' in *ibid*. 152.

[120] For a detailed description of the processes, see Anna Myriam Roccatello and Gabriel Rojas, *A Mixed Approach to International Crimes The Retributive and Restorative Justice Procedures of Colombia's Special Jurisdiction for Peace* (New York, 2020).

[121] See n. 50.

[122] See generally Teitel, *Transitional Justice* (n. 5), ch. 5; Stanley Cohen, 'State Crimes of Previous Regimes: Knowledge, Accountability and the Policing of the Past' (1995) 20 *Law and Social Inquiry* 7.

[123] International Covenant on Civil and Political Rights (ICCPR), Art. 14; *Casanovas v. France*, HRC, 19 July 1994.

Punishment is only appropriate following criminal proceedings.[124] Notwithstanding this, the Liberian Truth and Reconciliation Commission recommended that people whom it had found responsible for grave crimes ought to be barred from public office.[125] The United Nations has undertaken vetting proceedings, for example in Kosovo; however, these are designed as individuated processes, where individuals are identified who have engaged in wrongdoing and are given opportunities to answer allegations against them. This is to ensure that the processes are compatible with international human rights law standards.[126]

22.5 REPARATIONS AND CIVIL CLAIMS

International crimes, where attributable to states, have been the subject of reparations. Germany, for example, has paid over US$60 billion to victims in reparations for the Holocaust. Reparations have also been given to some of those who were the victims of the Argentine junta in the 1970s and 1980s.[127] There is a right to an effective remedy for violations of human rights, which may involve some form of financial recompense.[128] The levels of such reparations are often controversial, however, and many societies in which international crimes are committed do not have large funds to finance reparations programmes. Even so, the symbolic function of reparations can be important.[129]

There may also be the possibility of bringing private civil actions against those responsible for international crimes, either in the state where the activity occurred, or in a third state.[130] The United States is perhaps the most well-known of those third states, owing to its Alien Tort Claims Act and the *Filartiga* jurisprudence on it, which permit non-US nationals to bring tort actions against certain violators of international law.[131] However, recent developments in case law on the Act have limited the extraterritorial reach of such claims considerably.[132] In other countries, such claims may be excluded through lack of jurisdiction or because of immunities attaching to state officials. Civil claims may mean a great deal to victims, as the continued attempts by 'comfort women' to obtain compensation from Japan show.[133] The problem with such claims, even where they succeed, is that it is difficult to enforce the judgments.[134] Evidence gathering is also difficult, and bringing such claims can be expensive. In the absence of a legal aid programme, or lawyers willing to work *pro bono*, such actions can be beyond the means of victims. Also, financial measures may not bring the same satisfaction to victims as would the criminal prosecution and punishment of the offenders.

---

[124] Joel Feinberg, *Doing and Deserving* (1970) 95–118, reprinted in Antony Duff and David Garland (eds.), *A Reader on Punishment* (Oxford, 1994) 71.
[125] Truth and Reconciliation Commission of Liberia, *Final Report* (2009) vol. II, 269–70.
[126] *Secretary-General's Report on the Rule of Law and Transitional Justice* (n. 8) paras. 52–3.
[127] See Hayner, *Unspeakable Truths* (n. 81) ch. II; Teitel, *Transitional Justice* (n. 5) ch. 4. [128] ICCPR, Art. 2(3).
[129] Minow, *Between Vengeance* (n. 5) 100, 102–5.
[130] Although amnesties may limit the possibility of civil actions in the *locus delicti*.
[131] *Filartiga* v. *Peña-Irala*, 630 F 2d 876 (1980); *Sosa* v. *Alvarez-Machain*, 542 US 692 (2004).
[132] *Kiobel* v. *Royal Dutch Petroleum*, 135 S Ct 1659 (2013); *John Doe I, et al. v. Nestlé*, 593 S Ct – (2021). See generally 'Symposium' (2014) 12 *JICJ* 539–614; 'Agora: Reflections on *Kiobel*' (2013) 107 *AJIL* 829.
[133] Seunghyun Nam, 'Court Decisions in the Republic of Korea on Japan's Accountability for Sexual Slavery of the Comfort Women' (2022) 20 *JICJ* 459.
[134] Which may be disappointing for victims expecting to obtain anything other than moral satisfaction from the proceedings.

Finally, the International Criminal Court provides for the possibility of reparations administered by the Trust Fund for Victims, as discussed in Section 18.6.

22.6 LOCAL JUSTICE MECHANISMS

In part because of the increasing acceptance of cultural diversity and legal plurality in relation to the implementation of international criminal law,[135] there has been an increase in interest in local justice mechanisms. Local justice has been said to have 'three key attributes, (1) it focuses on groups rather than individuals, (2) it seeks compromise and community "harmony", and (3) it emphasizes restitution over other forms of punishment'.[136] The practices of local justice are likely too varied to be defined easily in such a way, as they run the gamut of responses from the *gacaca* trials in Rwanda, which are in essence a form of semi-formal court proceeding,[137] to the ceremonial reintegration ceremony *mato oput* in northern Uganda which includes the drinking of a bitter root-based drink. It is possible to see the South African Truth and Reconciliation Commission as being, in part, inspired by local justice ideas, in particular the concept of humaneness and community known in South Africa as *ubuntu*. The Commission has frequently been defended on this basis.[138]

Local justice mechanisms are supported by many, on the basis that they 'may have greater legitimacy and capacity than devastated formal systems, and they promise local ownership, access and efficiency'.[139] In addition, some take the view that such local justice mechanisms can provide a more comprehensive and individuated response to conflicts.[140] Support for local justice mechanisms is often linked to calls for the ICC to show respect for their activities, to avoid culturally insensitivity.[141] The ICC Prosecutor's policy paper on the interests of justice has recognized a role for local justice mechanisms.[142] However, care must be taken not to accept uncritically, 'romanticize'[143] or 'sentimentalize'[144] local justice mechanisms, which, in spite of their positive aspects, can, in fact, also be government-led, questionable on human rights grounds, or reproduce local hierarchies and patriarchies rather than respond to the needs of all.[145] Some may also not be appropriate for

---

[135] See Section 2.4.

[136] Lars Waldorf, 'Mass Justice for Mass Atrocity: Rethinking Local Justice as Transitional Justice' (2006) 79 *Temple Law Review* 1, 9.

[137] See Phil Clark, *The Gacaca Courts, Post-Genocide Justice and Reconciliation in Rwanda: Justice Without Lawyers* (Cambridge, 2010); Paul Bornkamm, *Rwanda's Gacaca Courts: Between Retribution and Reparation* (Oxford, 2012); Gerald Gahima, *Transitional Justice in Rwanda* (London, 2013) ch. 6.

[138] See e.g. Minow, *Between Vengeance* (n. 5) 51. [139] Waldorf, 'Mass Justice' (n. 136) 4.

[140] Lorna McGregor, 'International Law as a Tiered Process: Transitional Justice at the Local, National and International Level' in Kieran McEvoy and Lorna McGregor (eds.), *Transitional Justice from Below: Grassroots Activism and the Struggle for Change* (Oxford, 2008) 47, 61.

[141] Drumbl, *Atrocity* (n. 7) ch. 5 and 187–94; Kamar Maxine Clarke, *Fictions of Justice: The International Criminal Court and the Challenge of Legal Pluralism in Sub-Saharan Africa* (Cambridge, 2009) is a forceful assertion of such a view.

[142] See ICC Office of the Prosecutor, *Policy Paper on the Interests of Justice* (2007) 8, www.icc-cpi.int.

[143] See Padraig McAuliffe, 'Romanticization versus Integration? Indigenous Justice in Rule of Law Reconstruction and Transitional Justice Discourse' (2013) 5 *Göttingen Journal of International Law* 41.

[144] Drumbl, *Atrocity* (n. 7) 148.

[145] McGregor, 'International Law' (n. 140) 61–3; Mark Drumbl, 'Collective Violence and Individual Punishment: The Criminality of Mass Atrocity' (2005) 99 *Northwestern University Law Review* 539, 549; Tim Allen, *Trial Justice: The International Criminal Court and the Lord's Resistance Army* (London, 2007) ch. 6; McAuliffe, 'Romanticization' (n. 143).

international crimes, as they were not developed for such serious offences, or their procedures cannot be invoked, for example, when the victims (or perpetrators) are dead or unknown.[146] At the same time, 'in exploring the relationship between indigenous processes and formal justice mechanisms, the debate should not regress to a stark neo-colonialist versus cultural relativism stand-off ... [and] in considering options for transitional justice, the choice between local and international approaches should not be viewed as exclusive'.[147]

Further Reading

Omer Bakiner, *Truth Commissions Memory, Power and Legitimacy* (Oxford, 2016)

M. Cherif Bassiouni (ed.), *Post-Conflict Justice* (Ardsley, NY, 2002)

Christine Bell, *On the Law of Peace: Peace Agreements and the Lex Pacificatoria* (Oxford, 2008) ch. 12

Alison Bisset, *Truth Commissions and Criminal Courts* (Cambridge, 2012)

Phil Clark, *The Gacaca Courts, Post-Genocide Justice and Reconciliation in Rwanda: Justice Without Lawyers* (Cambridge, 2010)

Stanley Cohen, *States of Denial* (Cambridge, 2001)

David Dyzenhaus, *Judging Judges, Judging Ourselves: Truth, Reconciliation and the Apartheid Legal Order* (Oxford, 1998)

Mark Freeman, *Necessary Evils: Amnesties and the Search for Justice* (Cambridge, 2009)

Frank Haldemann and Thomas Unger, with Valentina Cadelo (eds.), *The United Nations Principles to Combat Impunity* (Oxford, 2018)

Renée Jeffery, *Negotiating Peace: Amnesties, Justice and Human Rights* (Cambridge, 2021)

Neil Kritz, *Transitional Justice: How Emerging Democracies Reckon with Former Regimes* (Washington DC, 1995)

Louise Mallinder, *Amnesty, Human Rights and Political Transitions: Bridging the Peace and Justice Divide* (Oxford, 2008)

Laura Olsen, 'Measures Complementing Prosecution' (2002) 84 *International Review of the Red Cross* 173

Steven Ratner, 'New Democracies, Old Atrocities: An Inquiry in International Law' (1999) 87 *Georgetown Law Journal* 707

Naomi Roht-Arriaza, 'State Responsibility to Investigate and Prosecute Grave Human Rights Violations in International Law' (1990) 78 *California Law Review* 449

William A. Schabas, 'National Amnesties, Truth Commissions and International Criminal Tribunals' in Brown, *Research Handbook*, 373

Elin Skaar, Eric Wiebelhaus-Brahm, and Jemima García-Godos, *Exploring Truth Commission Recommendations in a Comparative Perspective: Beyond Words, Vol. 1* (Cambridge, 2022)

[146] Lino Owor Ogora, *Moving Forward: Traditional Justice and Victim Participation in Northern Uganda* (Wynberg, 2009) 9–10.
[147] McGregor, 'International Law' (n. 140) 72.

Index